Social
PSYCHOLOGY

Eighth Edition

STEPHEN FRANZOI

DEBRA L. OSWALD

Social **PSYCHOLOGY**

Eighth Edition

Publisher and Director of Business Development: Richard Schofield

Production and Fulfillment Manager: Janai Escobedo

Permissions Coordinator: Jade Elk

Graphic Designer/Typesetter: Rhonda Minnema

Managing Editor: Anne Serbulea

Copyeditor: Regina Roths

Proofreader: Teresa Daly

Ancillary Coordinator: Tiffany Ballard

Photo Credits: Front cover image by Franzoi, *Critical Thinking* image and *Self/Social Connection Exercise* image from Shutterstock

Some ancillaries, including electronic and print components, may not be available to customers outside the United States.

LAB BOOK[Plus] ISBN: 978-1-5178-1002-3

TEXTBOOK[Plus] (Loose-Leaf Bundle) ISBN: 978-1-5178-0772-6

eBook[Plus] ISBN: 978-1-5178-0771-9

Loose-Leaf ISBN: 978-1-5178-0769-6

Soft Cover ISBN: 978-1-5178-0770-2

Dedications

To the women in my life: Cheryl, Amelia, and Lillian;

to my parents, Lou and Joyce,

and to my brother and sister, Randy and Susie—

together, and singly, they influence the essential elements of my life.

—*Steve*

To Doug, Evan, Millicent, and William:

for their love, support, and enthusiasm.

—*Deb*

Brief Table of Contents

Chapter 5
Attitudes and Persuasion   148

Chapter 6

Stereotyping, Prejudice, and Discrimination 198

Chapter **7**

Social Influence   252

Chapter **10**

Intimate Relationships   390

Chapter **11**

Aggression 438

Chapter 12
Prosocial Behavior: Helping Others   484

Preface

For the past seven editions this textbook has been a one-author affair but now I am welcoming Dr. Debra Oswald onto this project. Deb and I have worked together on various research projects for a number of years and have also had offices side-by-side within our department for about the same length of time. Two years ago, Deb asked me when I was going to begin work on the new edition, and my reply was, "When you agree to be my co-author!" Luckily, with a little bit of central-route and peripheral-route persuasion (see Chapter 5), she agreed to collaborate again and now here we are with our new eighth edition. It's been a joy working together and I think you will also enjoy our final product.

Steve Franzoi

It was never my plan to co-author a textbook. However, I believe that it is generally a good idea to accept an invitation to work on an interesting project with a valued colleague. It has been my pleasure to work on the eighth edition of this textbook. As an undergraduate psychology major, I became "hooked" on psychology during my first social psychology course and my goal is to similarly engage students with this edition. In this revision, I integrated the newest "cutting-edge research" that would also be of interest and value to undergraduate psychology students. I believe this final edition will resonate with students as they learn about social psychology and how it applies to their own life.

Deb Oswald

So what about this new eighth edition?

One of the most important lessons we have learned as teachers is that you should always have a good story to tell. Fortunately, social psychology is a dynamic science consisting of many fascinating stories. These "scientific stories" form the basis of this text, and our goal as instructors and textbook authors is to emphasize the process of research in social psychology: to engage students in an exploration of how what we know about social psychology has evolved, to put students in the mind-set of the social psychologists who have left their mark on the field. Together, we explore the stories behind these classic and contemporary studies.

As textbook authors, we both also understand that the text, too, must have its own story—one that resonates with students and instructors alike and helps tie all of the various theories and concepts together. In this eighth edition, we continue to emphasize a central theme—one that has worked well for the past editions—that we believe is essential to how we think about social psychology, and that will encourage students to think about their own stories as they explore the concepts in this course.

The Self: An Integrated Theme

Social psychology is sometimes described as a scientific discipline consisting of loosely connected research topics with no "grand theory" to connect everything. Although we have no single theory that neatly packages social psychology for our students, we end the analysis of the topic areas in each chapter with a discussion of how these particular theories and studies "fit" into our overall understanding of social behavior. Throughout the text we emphasize a core concept in social psychology: the self. Social psychology is the study of how the individual, as a self, interacts with the social world. As selves we become active agents in our social world, not only defining reality but also anticipating the future and often changing our behavior to be in line with the anticipated reality. This essential fact of social living has always been at the heart of this book, and it reflects the orientation of social psychology in the 21st century.

To that end, the theme of the self is reflected in this text through the following:

- In Chapter 1, a section titled "The self is shaped by—and shapes—the social environment" introduces this central theme.

- The central theme of the self is integrated through the discussion of key concepts, including the following examples: Chapter 3's extensive examination of various self-related theories; Chapter 4's discussion of how self-esteem influences the hindsight bias and how it is impacted by a person's explanatory style; Chapter 5's look at the role of the self in attitude formation and persuasion; Chapter 6's analysis of self-esteem and prejudice, as well as reducing prejudice through self-regulation; Chapter 7's discussion of compliance and self-consistency; Chapter 8's coverage of reduced self-awareness and deindividuation; Chapter 9's research on gender differences in body esteem; Chapter 10's analysis of the self-inclusionary process of intimacy; Chapter 11's look at the self-regulation of aggressive thoughts; and Chapter 12's research on how giving and receiving help can affect self-esteem.

- Beginning with Chapter 3's analysis of the self, each chapter concludes with a "Big Picture" summary. These summaries discuss how we, as self-reflective creatures, can use the social psychological knowledge covered in the chapter to understand and actively shape our social world.

Emphasizing Social Psychology's Research Basis

Often we hear from instructors that students enter the course assuming that social psychology is "just plain common sense." It's a common goal among most social psychology instructors to emphasize that social psychology is research based and relies heavily on the experimental method.

With this common goal in mind, we emphasize research methods throughout the book in the following ways:

- Chapter 1, discusses the current replication controversy both in social psychology and other sciences, providing historical context for students to later more fully understand the self-correcting nature of science as a discipline of inquiry.

- Chapter 2, "Conducting Research in Social Psychology," expands on the introductory chapter's discussion of social psychology as a scientific discipline and the distinction between the scientific process and everyday thinking. This chapter first explores the process of conducting research, then discusses diverse scientific methods and research strategies, emerging new scientific methodologies and measuring instruments, replication, meta-analysis, and ethical issues.

- Each chapter contains newly published research on social behavior and in-depth descriptions and critiques of selected studies.

- "Applications" sections at the end of Chapters 3–12 demonstrate how the theories and research in a particular area of social psychology can be applied to real-world settings and to your life.

- Throughout all of the chapters in this edition, we have carefully integrated research that represents the "best research practices" for scientifically valid conclusions. This includes reporting meta-analyses and effect sizes when available, reviewing studies that provide methodological and conceptual replications for key theories, and integrating both laboratory and field studies.

- Throughout this edition we have sought to include the newest research, while also streamlining the overall content so that the text was shorter and more "user-friendly." This new edition includes over 435 new references, with the vast majority coming from publications in the last 5 years.

Text Organization Chapter by Chapter

Revising a textbook is like renovating a building. The goal is to retain those designs and features that are essential in maintaining the integrity and attractiveness of the original product, while enhancing and updating the contents so that it will continue to serve a useful function. Just as successful architects base their renovations on the feedback of those who actually live in the buildings being restored, we have substantially based our "renovations" of this eighth edition on the opinions expressed by professors and students who used the seventh edition. For those of you who "inhabited" previous editions, we think you will find many familiar features among the new additions. The primary goal of this updating process was to make the eighth edition of Social Psychology an even better structure for teaching and learning.

The eighth edition offers the following familiar features:

- Critical thinking questions encourage students to examine their own social surroundings while they simultaneously digest social psychological theories and research. These questions often invite students to guess a study's hypotheses or results, or to provide an alternative interpretation of findings. The questions, many of which are new, are either inserted in the captions of figures, tables, and photos, or are displayed in prominent critical thinking sidebars. Answers to the former can be found in the chapter, while the end-of-book appendix offers possible answers to the latter.

- Coverage of diversity and cultural analysis is fully integrated in each chapter, rather than treated as a separate boxed insert or separate chapter. As in previous editions, we seek to foster a sense of inclusion for all readers. For example, in the discussion of social behavior in a cross-cultural context, the particular aspect of culture highlighted is individualism versus collectivism. Why? Throughout much of the history of American social psychology, the concept of individualism has been an influential, yet unexamined, force directing our analysis of social life. Today that is no longer the case. As the study of social psychology has become a cross-cultural endeavor, some of the basic assumptions about the relationship between the individual and the group have been questioned. This text discusses how people from individualist and collectivist cultures respond to similar social situations, helping students to understand the richness and flexibility of social life.

- The evolutionary perspective illuminates how a universal pattern of social behavior might have developed. One of the benefits of cross-cultural research is that it allows us to not only identify those aspects of social behavior that vary from one culture to the next but also to identify social behaviors that are not culturally constrained. When a universal social behavior is identified, discussion turns to how this pattern of behavior may have evolved. Throughout the text we examine how evolutionary forces might have left us with certain behavioral capacities, while also recognizing that current social and environmental forces encourage or discourage the actual development and use of these capacities.

- Social neuroscience uses the latest cutting-edge technology to study the relationship between neural processes of the brain and social processes. This "window into the brain" provides another layer of knowledge in our understanding of social interaction.

- More than 20 Self/Social Connection Exercises contain self-report questionnaires currently being used by researchers. The results of studies employing them are also part of the text material. In these exercises, students are encouraged to consider how this text material relates to their own lives. Thus, as students learn about various social psychological theories and relevant research findings, they also learn something about themselves.

- Bulleted end-of-section summaries provide a concise presentation to better facilitate students' studying. The bulleted summaries in the seventh edition were well received and have been retained in the new edition.

Chapter-by-Chapter Changes

Chapter 1: Introducing Social Psychology

- New chapter-opening story
- Updated coverage of the history of social psychology
- Expanded coverage of cultural trends related to increased self-focus
- Further elaboration regarding the distinction between sex and gender

Chapter 2: Conducting Research in Social Psychology

- New chapter-opening story to highlight recent scientific events
- Increased coverage of current best practices regarding data analysis
- New studies to illustrate various research methods
- To address the current replication crisis, a completely revamped section on standards and procedures to bolster scientific conclusions

Chapter 3: The Self

- Streamlined coverage of self-awareness and self-consciousness theory and research
- New findings that call into question certain aspects of self-regulation theory
- Expanded coverage of self-presentation strategies
- Streamlined coverage of self-enhancement theory and research

Chapter 4: Social Cognition and Person Perception

- New chapter-opening story to highlight current social events
- New research findings regarding schemas and heuristics
- New research on nonconscious mimicry
- New research on implicit personality theories

Chapter 5: Attitudes and Persuasion

- New replication research on the facial feedback hypothesis
- New research on credibility and persuasion

Chapter 6: Stereotyping, Prejudice, and Discrimination

- Updated chapter-opening story to highlight current social events
- Extended discussion of whether stereotypes are accurate and harmful
- Updated discussion of modern racism theories
- New section on the health consequences of stigmatization for targets
- Streamlined discussion of the role of personality traits in prejudice
- New discussion of the role of allies as agents of positive social change

Chapter 7: Social Influence

- New chapter-opening story to highlight current social events
- New research on the automatic activation of conformity
- Revised section on factors impacting conformity
- Revised section on intense social influence and compliance
- Revised Applications section on how the internet influences voting behavior

Chapter 8: Group Behavior

- New chapter-opening story to highlight current social events
- New section on gossiping's impact on groups
- New coverage and research on authoritarian leadership

Chapter 9: Interpersonal Attraction

- New research findings on body esteem
- Streamlined discussion of attractiveness standards
- Updated research on loneliness
- Updated discussion of social skills training programs

Chapter 10: Intimate Relationships

- Revised discussion on the psychology of intimacy
- Revised discussion of attachment
- New research on gender and friendships and cross-sex friendships
- Updated research on online dating and its impact on romantic relationships
- New research on how expressing gratitude benefits romantic relationships

Chapter 11: Aggression

- Streamlined section on hostile aggression
- Revised section on the media and violence
- New research and discussion on sexual violence
- Expanded coverage of cyberbullying

Chapter 12: Prosocial Behavior: Helping Others

- Updated research on the social norms related to helping
- Updated research on helping similar others

Supplements and Resources

Instructor Supplements

A complete teaching package is available for instructors who adopt this book. This package includes an **online lab**, *Instructor's Manual*, **exam bank, PowerPoint® slides, LMS integration**, and **LMS exam bank files**.

Online Lab	BVT's online lab is available for this textbook on two different platforms—BVT*Lab* (at www.BVTLab.com), and LAB BOOK™ (at www.BVTLabBook.com). These are described in more detail in the corresponding sections below. Both platforms allow instructors to set up graded homework, quizzes, and exams.
Instructor's Manual	The *Instructor's Manual* helps first-time instructors develop the course, while also offering seasoned instructors a new perspective on the materials. Each section of the Instructor's Manual coincides with a chapter in the textbook. The user-friendly format begins by providing a chapter summary, learning objectives, and detailed outlines for each chapter. Then, the manual presents lecture discussions, key terms, and class activities. Lastly, additional resources—books, articles, websites—are listed to help instructors review the materials covered in each chapter.
Exam Bank	An extensive exam bank is available to instructors in both hard-copy and electronic form. Each chapter has approximately 50 multiple-choice, 15 true/false, 15 short-answer, and 5 essay questions ranked by difficulty and style. Each question is referenced to the appropriate section of the text to make test creation quick and easy.
PowerPoint Slides	A set of PowerPoint slides with about 40 slides per chapter, including a chapter overview, learning objectives, slides covering all key topics, key figures and charts, and summary and conclusion slides.
LMS Integration	BVT offers basic integration with Learning Management Systems (LMSs), providing single-sign-on links (often called LTI links) from Blackboard, Canvas, Moodle (or any other LMS) directly into BVT*Lab*, eBook^Plus, or the LAB BOOK platform. Gradebooks from BVT*Lab* and the LAB BOOK can be imported into most LMSs.
LMS Exam Bank Files	Exam banks are available as Blackboard files, QTI files (for Canvas), and Respondus files (for other LMSs) so they can easily be imported into a wide variety of course management systems.

Student Resources

Student resources are available for this textbook at both the BVT*Lab* platform and the LAB BOOK platform, as described below. These resources are geared toward students needing additional assistance, as well as those seeking complete mastery of the content. The following resources are available:

Practice Questions	Students can work through hundreds of practice questions online. Questions are multiple choice or true/false in format and are graded instantly for immediate feedback.
Flashcards	BVT*Lab* includes sets of flashcards that reinforce the key terms and concepts from each chapter.
PowerPoint Slides	For a study recap, students can view all of the instructor PowerPoint slides online.
Additional LAB BOOK Resources	On the LAB BOOK platform, comprehension questions are sprinkled throughout each chapter of the eBook, and detailed section summaries are included in the lab. Study tools, such as text highlighting and margin notes, are also available. These resources are not available in BVT*Lab*.

BVT*Lab*

BVT*Lab* is an affordable online lab for instructors and their students. It includes an online classroom with grade book and class forum, a homework grading system, extensive test banks for quizzes and exams, and a host of student study resources.

Course Setup	BVT*Lab* has an easy-to-use, intuitive interface that allows instructors to quickly set up their courses and grade books and to replicate them from section to section and semester to semester.
Grade Book	Using an assigned passcode, students register into their section's grade book, which automatically grades and records all homework, quizzes, and tests.
Class Forum	Instructors can post discussion threads to a class forum and then monitor and moderate student replies.
Student Resources	All student resources for this textbook are available in digital form within BVT*Lab*. Even if a class is not taught in the lab, students who have purchased lab access can still use the student resources in the lab.
eBook	BVT*Lab* includes both a webBook™ and a downloadable eBook (on the VitalSource® platform). For some product bundles, BVT's LAB BOOK can also be accessed from within BVT*Lab*, offering enhanced eBook features and study tools for students, as described below.

LAB BOOK

LAB BOOK is a web-based eBook platform with an integrated lab providing comprehension tools and interactive student resources. Instructors can build homework and quizzes right into the eBook. LAB BOOK is either included with eBOOK^Plus or offered as a standalone product.

Course Setup	LAB BOOK uses the BVT*Lab* interface to allow instructors to set up their courses and grade books and to replicate them from section to section and semester to semester.
Grade Book	Using an assigned passcode, students register into their section's grade book, which automatically grades and records all homework, quizzes, and tests.
Advanced eBook	LAB BOOK is a mobile-friendly, web-based eBook platform designed for PCs, Macs, tablets, and smartphones. LAB BOOK allows highlighting, margin notes, and a host of other study tools.
Student Resources	All student resources for this textbook are available in the LAB BOOK, as described in the Student Resources section above.

Customization

BVT's Custom Publishing Division can help you modify this book's content to satisfy your specific instructional needs. The following are examples of customization:

- Rearrangement of chapters to follow the order of your syllabus
- Deletion of chapters not covered in your course
- Addition of paragraphs, sections, or chapters you or your colleagues have written for this course
- Editing of the existing content, down to the word level
- Customization of the accompanying student resources and online lab
- Addition of handouts, lecture notes, syllabus, and so forth
- Incorporation of student worksheets into the textbook

All of these customizations will be professionally typeset to produce a seamless textbook of the highest quality, with an updated table of contents and index to reflect the customized content.

Acknowledgments

Many people have provided invaluable assistance and understanding while we were revising this text. We first want to thank our families, not only for supporting our writing efforts, but also providing us with wonderful examples of social psychological principles that we used throughout the text.

We also wish to thank the students in our social psychology courses at Marquette University, who are the first to be exposed to our new stories of the social psychological enterprise. In addition, we thank those students using our book at other colleges and universities who wrote us letters and emails concerning their reactions to what they read. The encouragement, enthusiasm, and criticism from all these students have made revising the book much easier.

Our appreciation also goes to our many colleagues in social psychology who graciously provided us with reprints and preprints of recent scientific articles describing advances in our understanding of social behavior. Their responses greatly aided us in preparing the eighth edition of Social Psychology that includes exciting new research and theoretical developments.

Finally, we would like to thank Richard Schofield, Director of Business Development at BVT, for all his logistical support throughout this revision process. Equally important was the work of our editor, Regina Roths, who regularly went far beyond the normal duties of an editor in suggesting ways to improve this current revision, while also gently correcting our snafus; she made the copy-editing process fun and informative. We were also extremely fortunate to work with Production and Fulfillment Manager Janai Escobedo, Managing Editor Anne Serbulea, Graphic Designer/Typesetter Rhonda Minnema, Permissions Coordinator Jade Elk, and Proofreader Teresa Daly. Finally, we want to thank Tiffany Ballard for her work on the ancillary coordination in this edition.

A Special Note to Instructors and Students

Whenever we teach a course in psychology, we learn a lot from our students and fellow instructors about how to make the course better. We would like to have a similar opportunity to learn from you how we can improve this textbook. Your feedback about what you like or do not like about the book is important to us. To make it easy for you to provide this feedback, our school address and email addresses are listed below. We will personally respond to all comments and questions.

Professor Stephen L. Franzoi
Department of Psychology
Marquette University
P.O. Box 1881
Milwaukee, WI 53201-1881
Email: Stephen.Franzoi@marquette.edu

Professor Debra L. Oswald
Department of Psychology
Marquette University
P.O. Box 1881
Milwaukee, WI 53201-1881
Email: Debra.Oswald@marquette.edu

About the Authors

Stephen L. Franzoi is Professor Emeritus in the Psychology Department at Marquette University in Milwaukee, Wisconsin. He received his BS in both psychology and sociology from Western Michigan University, his PhD in psychology from the University of California at Davis, and was a postdoctoral fellow in the Self Program at Indiana University. Professor Franzoi taught both undergraduate and graduate courses in social psychology and in 2013 was honored with the Marquette University Teaching Excellence Award. During his career, he has served as assistant editor of Social Psychology Quarterly and associate editor of Social Problems, and his own research has been published in a number of places, including *Journal of Personality and Social Psychology, Personality and Social Psychology Bulletin, Psychology of Women Quarterly, American Sociological Review, Journal of Research in Personality, Sex Roles,* and *Journal of Personality.* Dr. Franzoi's primary research investigates the impact of gender on body esteem, and he has discussed his work in such media outlets as the *New York Times, USA Today,* National Public Radio, and the *Oprah Winfrey Show.* In his spare time, Dr. Franzoi enjoys relaxing and traveling with his family, bicycling, and making and writing about wine for the Wisconsin Vintners Association.

Debra L. Oswald is a professor in the Psychology Department at Marquette University in Milwaukee, Wisconsin. She received her BA in psychology at the College of Saint Scholastica in Duluth, Minnesota, her PhD in social psychology at Saint Louis University, and completed a postdoctoral fellowship in quantitative psychology at the University of Illinois. Professor Oswald enjoys teaching undergraduate courses in social psychology, psychology of gender roles, and psychology of prejudice. She has also taught honors topic classes such as "Thinking Critically about Psychology in the Media," and the "Psychology of Memoirs" as well as undergraduate and graduate courses in statistical methods. Dr. Oswald strongly supports Kurt Lewin's notion that "there is nothing so practical as a good theory" and through her research she seeks to better understand a variety of socially important topics by applying social psychology theories. Topics she has studied include friendships, sexual coercion, stereotypes and discrimination based on gender, sexual orientation, ethnicity, and religious identity. These papers have been published in journals such as *Sex Roles, Psychology of Women Quarterly, Journal of Applied Social Psychology, Journal of Social and Personal Relationships,* and *Journal of Interpersonal Violence.* Her current research focuses on understanding women's experiences as the target of sexism. In her spare time, Dr. Oswald enjoys spending time with her spouse, Doug, and their three children (Evan, Millicent, and William). They can be found hiking, fishing, and canoeing in the many beautiful Wisconsin State Parks and visiting the local zoo and museums.

Chapter 1

Introducing Social Psychology

FOCUS QUESTIONS

1. What do social psychologists study?
2. How old is the discipline of social psychology?
3. Why was World War II so important in the development of social psychology in the United States?
4. What are the most important organizing concepts and perspectives in social psychology?

CHAPTER OUTLINE

Introduction

1.1 **What Is Social Psychology?**

    1.1a   Social Psychologists Study How We Are Influenced by Others.

    1.1b   Social Psychology Is More Than Common Sense.

    1.1c   Social Psychologists Study How Social Reality Is Created (and Recreated).

    1.1d   Social Psychology Is Studied in Both Psychology and Sociology.

    1.1e   Social Psychology Is a Fairly Young Science.

1.2 **Organizing Concepts and Perspectives in Social Psychology**

    1.2a   The Self Is Shaped by—and Shapes— the Social Environment.

    1.2b   Our Social Thinking Can Be Automatic or Deliberate.

    1.2c   Culture Shapes Social Behavior.

Self/Social Connection Exercise 1.1:
To What Degree Do You Value Individualist and Collectivist Strivings?

    1.2d   Evolution Shapes Universal Patterns of Social Behavior.

    1.2e   Brain Activity Affects and Is Affected by Social Behavior.

    1.2f   Positive Psychology Is an Emerging Perspective in Social Psychology.

Key Terms

Websites

Introduction

Welcome to the wonderful world of social psychology! As the authors of this textbook, we are excited to introduce you to a scientific discipline that we both have worked in for many years. The two of us have been colleagues in the same psychology department for the past 2 decades. We first met one another at a social psychology conference co-hosted by Deb's graduate program while she was working on her PhD at St. Louis University and Steve was a professor at Marquette University. Deb claims that she saw Steve step on the dance floor during one of the conference's evening festivities, but Steve thinks this is unlikely given his checkered past in trying to coordinate body movements with music (see Chapter 10 for the full story). What both Deb and Steve most remember from their conversation at that long-ago conference was their mutual enthusiasm for both research and teaching. Deb also recalls that while Steve was talking enthusiastically about his work at Marquette, teaching social psychology, and conducting research with graduate and undergraduate students, she thought to herself, "That's the kind of job I would like to have someday!"

There's an old folk saying that proclaims, "If wishes were fishes, we'd all cast nets." Well, several years after Deb and Steve's first meeting, Deb cast her net and reeled in that fish by applying for and accepting a social psychology faculty position at Marquette University. Since then, we have collaborated on research that combined our interests in body esteem and sexism, taught similar courses, and even conducted informal social psychology experiments on our colleagues to amuse ourselves during faculty meetings (see Chapter 4, section 4.3a, on *nonconscious mimicry*). Our newest collaboration is about the story of social psychology, so let's begin.

1.1   What Is Social Psychology?

The reason we love social psychology is that it attempts to understand the social dynamics of everyday living. Here, perhaps more than in any other area of psychology, answers are sought to questions that we have all pondered at different times in our lives. Thus you, the new student of social psychology, will likely feel a natural affinity to this subject matter because it directly addresses aspects of your daily experience in the social world. Because human beings learn best through storytelling, in this text, the two of us will tell you many stories that bring to life the scientific study of our social world. Along the way we will also tell you stories about ourselves and about others that illustrate the concepts and theories in the field. Hopefully, in doing so, we will bring an occasional smile to your face.

1.1a   Social Psychologists Study How We Are Influenced by Others.

Gordon Allport (1897–1967), one of the influential figures in social psychology, provided a definition of the field that captures its essence. He stated that **social psychology** is a discipline that uses scientific methods in "an attempt to understand and explain how the thoughts, feelings, and behavior of individuals are influenced by the actual, imagined, or implied presence of others" (Allport, 1985, p. 3).

To better understand this definition, let us consider a few examples. First, how might the actual presence of others influence someone's thoughts, feelings, and behavior? Consider the response that basketball players have to the actions of the opposing team's fans as they prepare to shoot a free throw. Fans from the opposing team often try to rattle players by making loud noises and gesturing wildly in the hope of diverting their attention from the task at hand. Another example of how the presence of others can influence the individual occurs when a member of a group discovers that she holds a different opinion from others on some important issue. Faced with the raised eyebrows and hushed comments, she may abandon her dissent and join the majority.

social psychology

The scientific discipline that attempts to understand and explain how the thoughts, feelings, and behavior of individuals are influenced by the actual, imagined, or implied presence of others

The imagined presence of others might also influence thoughts, feelings, and behavior. Think about past incidents when you were considering doing something that ran counter to your parents' wishes. Although they may not have been present, did their imagined presence influence your behavior? Imaginal figures can guide our actions by shaping our interpretation of events just as surely as figures who are physically present (Honeycutt, 2003; Shaw, 2003). In stressful situations, imagining the presence of others can lower your anxiety and provide you with an emotional security blanket (Andersen & Glassman, 1996; McGowan, 2002). This is why Deb's son Evan (age 8) and daughter Millie (age 5) insist on placing a family photo in their backpacks on the first day of school so they can look at it whenever they feel homesick.

Finally, how can the implied presence of others influence an individual? Have you ever had the experience of driving on the freeway, going well beyond the speed limit, only to pass a sign with a little helicopter painted on it with the words "We're watching you" printed below? Did the implied presence of a police helicopter circling overhead influence your thoughts and feelings, as well as your pressure on the gas pedal? Similarly, fresh footprints on a deserted, snowy path imply that others may be nearby, which might set in motion a series of thoughts: Who might this person be? Should I continue on my way or turn around, just to be safe?

Social psychology is the science of how human beings are influenced by one another during everyday social interaction. Can you think of any social interactions that social psychologists wouldn't study?

Based on this discussion, you should better understand the kinds of topics we will analyze in this book. Although social psychology was once a relatively small field of scholars talking primarily to each other, there are now many opportunities for social psychologists to collaborate with the other sciences. Today, social psychology draws on the insights of sociology, anthropology, neurology, political science, economics, and biology to gain a better understanding of how the individual fits into the larger social system. Capitalizing on this movement toward an "integrative science," in this text we will periodically analyze how sociologists, neuroscientists, anthropologists, ethologists, and biologists explain various aspects of social behavior.

1.1b Social Psychology Is More Than Common Sense.

Occasionally when we meet new people and tell them that we are paid a salary to study how people interact with one another, a few brave souls will press the point and ask, "Isn't social psychology just warmed-over common sense?" One reason people think social psychology simply rephrases what we already know is that its subject matter is so personal and familiar: We all informally think about our own thoughts, feelings, and actions, as well as those of others. Why would such naturally gained knowledge be any different from what social psychologists achieve through scientific observations? In many ways, this is true. For example, consider the following findings from social psychology that confirm what many of us already know:

- Attending to people's faces leads to the greatest success in detecting their lies. (Chapter 4)
- People who are paid a great deal of money to perform a boring task enjoy it more than those who are paid very little. (Chapter 5)
- Men express more hostile attitudes toward women than women do toward men. (Chapter 6)

- People think that physically attractive individuals are less intelligent than those who are physically unattractive. (Chapter 9)

- Playing violent video games or engaging in contact sports allows people to "blow off steam," making them less likely to behave aggressively in other areas of their lives. (Chapter 11)

- Accident victims are most likely to be helped when there are many bystanders nearby. (Chapter 12)

All these findings make sense, and you can probably think of examples from your own life that confirm them in your own mind. However, the problem is that we lied: Social psychological research actually informs us that all these statements are generally false—and the exact opposite is true. Of course, social psychology often confirms many commonsense notions about social behavior, but you will find many instances in this text where the scientific findings challenge your current social beliefs. You will also discover that by learning about the theories and research findings in social psychology, you will have a greater ability to make intelligent life choices. In this case, knowledge really is power.

> "Not everyone's life is what they make it. Some people's life is what other people make it."
>
> —Alice Walker, American author, born 1944

1.1c   Social Psychologists Study How Social Reality Is Created (and Recreated).

Do you realize that you play a vital role in creating your own social world? If you'd like to personally experience your power to actively shape your social reality, spend a few hours interacting with others while consciously smiling (making sure it's not a noticeably forced smile) and then spend another few hours wearing a frown or a scowl. I'm betting that the reactions of those around you—and your own mood—will be appreciably altered by these two different facial expressions (Frank et al., 1993).

> "Imaginations which people have of one another are the solid facts of society."
>
> —Charles Horton Cooley, American sociologist, 1864–1929

The simple fact is that your social reality is not fixed and unchanging, but rather it is malleable and in a constant state of flux. In 1948, sociologist Robert Merton (1910–2003) introduced the concept of the **self-fulfilling prophecy** to describe how others' expectations about a person, group, or situation can actually lead to the fulfillment of those expectations. As Merton described it:

> The self-fulfilling prophecy is, in the beginning, a *false* definition of the situation evoking a new behavior, which makes the originally false conception come *true*. The specious validity of the self-fulfilling prophecy perpetuates a reign of error. For the prophet will cite the actual course of events as proof that he was right from the very beginning. (Merton, 1948, p. 195)

The self-fulfilling prophecy involves a three-step process (refer to Figure 1.1). First, the perceiver (the "prophet") forms an impression of the target person. Second, the perceiver acts toward the target person in a manner consistent with this first impression. In response, the target person's behavior changes to correspond to the perceiver's actions (Diekmann et al., 2003; Madon et al., 2013). The more interactions the target has with the perceiver, and the more this three-step process is repeated, the more likely it is that the target will internalize the perceiver's expectations into his or her own self-concept. Research indicates that behavioral changes brought about by self-fulfilling prophecies can be remarkably long-lasting (Smith, A. E., et al., 1999).

The most famous empirical demonstration of the self-fulfilling prophecy was a study conducted by Robert Rosenthal and Lenore Jacobson (1968) in a South San Francisco elementary school. In this study, the researchers first gave IQ tests to children and then

self-fulfilling prophecy
The process by which someone's expectations about a person or group lead to the fulfillment of those expectations

FIGURE 1.1   The Development of a Self-Fulfilling Prophecy

Self-fulfilling prophecies involve three steps. In step 1, the perceiver forms expectations about the target. In step 2, the perceiver behaves in a manner consistent with those expectations. In step 3, the target responds to the perceiver's actions in a manner that unwittingly confirms the perceiver's initial beliefs. What personal qualities in a perceiver and in a target would make a self-fulfilling prophecy more or less likely?

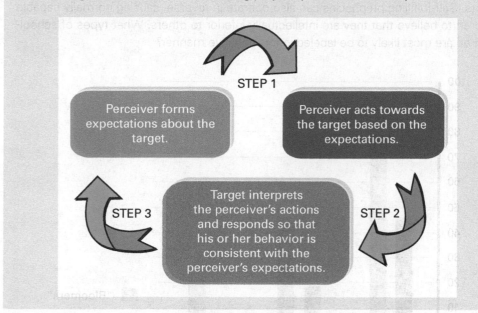

met with their teachers to share the results. At these information sessions, teachers were told that the tests identified certain students in their classroom as "potential late bloomers" who should experience substantial IQ gains during the remaining school year. In reality, this information was false. The children identified as potential late bloomers had been randomly selected by the researchers and did not differ from their classmates. Although the potential late bloomer label was fabricated for these children (approximately 20% of the class), Rosenthal and Jacobson hypothesized that the teachers' subsequent expectations would be sufficient to enhance the academic performance of these students. Eight months later, when the students were again tested, this hypothesis was confirmed. The potential late bloomers not only exhibited improved schoolwork but also showed gains in their IQ scores that were not found among the nonlabeled students (see Figure 1.2).

Follow-up studies indicated that teachers treat differently students who are positively labeled in this manner (Jussim et al., 2009). First, teachers create a warmer *socioemotional climate* for these students than for those who are perceived less positively. Second, they provide these gifted students with more *feedback* on their academic performance than they do their average students. Third, they *challenge* these positively labeled students with more difficult material than the rest of the class. Finally, they provide these students with *greater opportunity* to respond to presented material in class. These positively labeled students are likely to assume the teacher especially likes them and has good judgment or that the teacher is a likable person. Whichever attribution is made, it is likely that the positively labeled students will work harder and begin thinking about themselves as high achievers. Through this behavioral and self-concept change, the prophecy is fulfilled.

"If three people say you are an ass, put on a bridle."

—Spanish proverb

FIGURE 1.2   Improvement in Schoolchildren's IQ Scores Due to the Self-Fulfilling Prophecy

First- and second-grade students identified as potential late bloomers showed a significant improvement in their IQ test scores during the course of the school year. These findings suggest that teachers' expectations about students, regardless of the validity of those findings, can profoundly shape those students' subsequent academic achievements. Self-fulfilling prophecies can also operate in reverse, causing normally capable children to believe that they are intellectually inferior to others. What types of schoolchildren are most likely to be labeled in this negative manner?

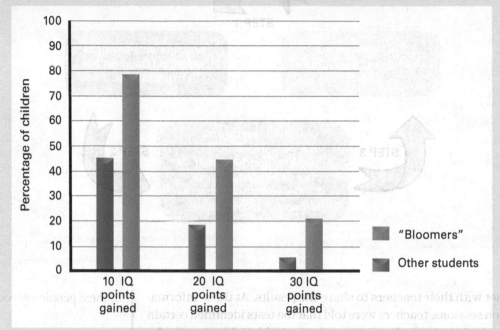

Data source: From *Pygmalion in the Classroom: Teacher Expectation and Pupils' Intellectual Development*, by R. Rosenthal and L. Jacobson, 1968, New York, NY: Holt, Rinehart and Winston. Copyright 1968 by Holt, Rinehart and Winston, Inc.

Unfortunately, not all self-fulfilling prophecies are positive. Teachers and fellow students often treat children who are negatively labeled "troubled" or "disruptive" in a way that reinforces the negative label so that it is more likely to be internalized (Rosenthal, 2003). To better understand this sort of negative self-concept change, Monica Harris and her colleagues (1992) studied the impact of *negative expectancies* on children's social interactions. In the research, 68 pairs of unacquainted boys in third through sixth grade played together on two different tasks. The researchers designated one of the boys in the pairing as the *perceiver* and the other as the *target*. Half of the target boys had been previously diagnosed as being hyperactive, and the rest of the participants—the remaining targets and all the perceivers—had no history of behavioral problems. Prior to playing together, some perceivers were told (independently of their partner's actual behavior) that their partner had a special problem and may give them a hard time: He disrupted class a lot, talked when he shouldn't, didn't sit in his chair, and often acted silly. In contrast, other perceivers were not given this information. One of the activities the two boys mutually engaged in was an unstructured, cooperative task in which they planned and built a design with plastic blocks; the other task was more structured and competitive—separately coloring a dinosaur as quickly as possible, using the same set of crayons. The boys' behavior on both tasks was videotaped and later rated by judges on a number of dimensions, such as friendliness, giving commands, and offering plans or suggestions. The boys also reported their own feelings and reactions to the tasks.

How do you think these different expectations shaped social reality? Consistent with the self-fulfilling prophecy, the target boys with partners who believed they had a behavioral problem enjoyed the tasks less, rated their own performances as poorer, and took less credit for success than did boys with partners who were not expecting such problems. Likewise, boys who held negative expectancies about their partners enjoyed the tasks less, worked less hard on them, talked less, liked their partners less, and were less friendly to them than did perceivers who were not provided with negative expectancies. These findings indicate that when people have negative expectations about others, they are more likely to treat those individuals in a negative manner; targets of such negative treatment

When a student is labeled as "troubled," teachers and peers often treat him/her negatively. This reinforces the "troubled" label and may cause the student to act out more often, fulfilling the prophecy.

react in kind, thus confirming the initial negative expectations. For half of the boys in this study, the negative expectations were groundless; however, this did not alter the outcome of the interaction. Unfortunately, this form of self-fulfilling prophecy is all too common, and over time it leads to negative self-beliefs and low self-esteem. Additional research indicates that these educationally based self-fulfilling prophecies have a stronger impact on elementary school students from lower-income families than on students from more affluent homes (Sorhagen, 2013). This latter finding points to the possibility that teachers' underestimation of poor children's academic abilities may be one factor that contributes to the persistent and worrisome gap in achievement between children from different socioeconomic backgrounds.

How might these findings apply to your own life? Think of instances in your life when the negative expectations of others may have created undesirable self-fulfilling prophecies. If you can identify someone whom you've viewed and treated in a negative fashion, try a little exercise to reverse this process. The next time you interact with that person, put aside your negative expectations and instead treat him as if he were your friend. Based on the research we have reviewed here, by redefining that person in your own eyes, you may create a new definition of social reality in his as well. People you thought were unfriendly, and even hostile, may respond to your redefinition by acting warm and friendly. If you are successful in redefining a particular social reality, you will have fulfilled one of my own prophecies about the readers of this text—namely, that those who learn about social psychological principles will use this knowledge to improve the quality of their social relationships.

To encourage you to apply social psychological knowledge to your daily life, included in this text are opportunities to learn how specific topics relate to you. Each of these *Connection* exercises consists of a self-report questionnaire or technique used by social psychologists in studying a particular area of social behavior. By completing and scoring each measure for yourself, you will gain insight into how this topic relates to your own life. By personally applying social psychological knowledge in this manner, you are not only much more likely to absorb the content of this text (and thereby perform better in this course), but you are also more likely to apply this knowledge outside the classroom.

Do you think that a judge's beliefs about the guilt or innocence of a defendant in a criminal trial could create a self-fulfilling prophecy among the jury, even if the judge does not voice her opinions?

"Self-knowledge is best learned, not by contemplation, but action."

—Johann Wolfgang von Goethe, German author, 1749–1832

1.1d Social Psychology Is Studied in Both Psychology and Sociology.

You might be surprised to learn that there actually are two scientific disciplines known as social psychology, one in psychology and the other in sociology, with the larger of the two being the psychological branch. Both disciplines study social behavior, but they do so from different perspectives (Fiske & Molm, 2010; Gergen, 2012).

The central focus of *psychological social psychology* tends to be individuals and how they respond to social stimuli. Variations in behavior are believed to stem from people's interpretations of social stimuli and differences in their personalities and temperaments. Even when psychological social psychologists study group dynamics, they generally emphasize the processes that occur at the individual level. This text reflects the psychological perspective of social psychology.

In contrast, *sociological social psychology* downplays the importance of individual differences and the effects of immediate social stimuli on behavior. Instead, the focus is on larger group or societal variables—such as people's socioeconomic status, their social roles, and cultural norms. The role these larger group variables play in determining social behavior is of more interest to this discipline than to its psychological "cousin." Therefore, sociological social psychologists are more interested in providing explanations for such societal problems as poverty, crime, and deviance.

Although there have been calls to merge the two branches into a single field—and even a joint psychology–sociology doctoral program at the University of Michigan from 1946 to 1967—their different orientations make it doubtful that this will transpire in the foreseeable future. In the meantime, the two disciplines will continue to provide important, yet differing perspectives on social behavior.

1.1e Social Psychology Is a Fairly Young Science.

As a scientific discipline, social psychology is only 150 years old, with most of the growth occurring during the past 70 years. By most standards, social psychology is a relatively young science (Franzoi, 2007; Morawski & Bayer, 2013).

German psychologist Wilhelm Wundt, founder of psychology, provided some of the earliest scholarly work that inspired the development of social psychology.

("Wundt research group, circa 1880," public domain via Wikimedia)

Dawning of a Scientific Discipline: 1862–1894

German psychologist Wilhelm Wundt (1832–1920), who is widely regarded as the founder of psychology, had a hand in the early development of social psychology. Early in Wundt's career (1862), he predicted that there would be two branches of psychology: physiological psychology and social or folk psychology (*Völkerpsychologie*). In dividing psychology into two branches, his reasoning was that the type of individual psychology studied in the laboratory by physiological psychologists could not account for the more complex cognitive processes required for social interaction. Although social behavior involves distinct individuals, Wundt argued that the product of this social interaction is more than the sum of the individuals' mental activities. Because of this distinction, Wundt asserted that, while physiological psychology was part of the natural sciences and aligned with biology, social psychology was a "social science," with its parent discipline being philosophy. He further argued that, while physiological psychologists should conduct experiments in studying their phenomena, social psychologists should employ nonexperimental methods because such an approach best captures the complexity of social interaction.

Although Wundt's 10 volumes on social psychology influenced scholars in Europe, his work remained largely unknown to American social scientists because it was not translated into English. These young American scientists were also much more interested in being identified with the natural sciences than with continuing an alliance with philosophy, further hindering Wundt's ability to shape their ideas. Although Wundt's notion that social psychology was a social science was compatible with the nineteenth-century conception of psychology as the "science of the mind" and was embraced by a number of European scholars, it was incompatible with the new behaviorist perspective in the United States that emerged during the early years of the twentieth century.

Underlying behaviorism was a philosophy known as *logical positivism*, which contended that knowledge should be expressed in terms that could be verified empirically or through direct observation. This new "science of behavior" had little use for Wundt's conception of social psychology and its reliance on nonexperimental methodology. An emerging American brand of social psychology defined itself in terms of behaviorist principles, using the experiment as its chosen research method. This was especially true for psychological social psychology in America, which would become the intellectual core of the discipline and which developed outside the influence of Wundt's writings. In contrast, Wundt's writings indirectly affected American sociological social psychology because one of its founders, George Herbert Mead (1863–1931), paid serious attention to the German scholar's work. Today, Mead's symbolic interactionist perspective remains an active area of theory and research in American sociology.

Early Years: 1895–1935

Norman Triplett (1861–1931), an American psychologist at Indiana University, is credited with conducting the first social psychology experiment in 1895. In order to investigate how a person's performance of a task changes when other people are present, Triplett asked children to quickly wind line on a fishing reel, either alone or in the presence of other children performing the same task. As predicted, the children wound the line faster when in the presence of other children. Published in 1897, this study formally introduced the experimental method into the social sciences. Eleven years later, in 1908, English psychologist William McDougall (1871–1938) and American sociologist Edward Ross (1866–1951) separately published the first two textbooks in social psychology. Consistent with contemporary psychological social psychology, McDougall's text identified the individual as the principal unit of analysis; Ross's text, true to contemporary sociological social psychology, instead highlighted groups and the structure of society.

Despite the inauguration of this new subfield within psychology and sociology, social psychology still lacked a distinct identity. How was it different from the other subdisciplines? What were its methods of inquiry? In 1924, a third social psychology text, published by Floyd Allport (older brother of Gordon Allport), went a long way in answering these questions for psychological social psychology. Reading his words today, you can see the emerging perspective of psychological social psychology:

In 1924, Floyd Allport (1890–1978) published Social Psychology, *a book that demonstrates how carefully conducted research can provide valuable insights into a wide range of social behaviors.*

> I believe that only within the individual can we find the behavior mechanisms and consciousness which are fundamental in the interactions between individuals. ... There is no psychology of groups which is not essentially and entirely a psychology of individuals. ... Psychology in all its branches is a science of the individual. (Allport, 1924, p. 4)

Allport's conception of social psychology was proposed 11 years after John Watson (1878–1958) had ushered in the behaviorist era in American psychology. Allport's brand of social psychology emphasized how the person responds to stimuli in the social environment, with the group merely being one of many such stimuli. Allport shaped the identity of American social psychology by emphasizing the experimental method in studying such topics as conformity, nonverbal communication, and social facilitation. His call for the pursuit of social psychological knowledge through carefully controlled experimental procedures contrasted with the more philosophical approach that both Ross and McDougall had taken 16 years earlier.

Overseas, German social psychology was being shaped by *Gestalt* psychology, which emphasized that the mind actively organizes stimuli into meaningful wholes. Gestalt social psychologists contended that the social environment is made up not only of individuals but also of relations between individuals, and these relationships have important psychological implications. Thus, Gestalt social psychologists promoted an understanding of groups as real social entities, which directly led to the tradition of group processes and group dynamics that still exists today. These two independently developing schools of thought within psychological social psychology—one in America and the other in Germany—would soon be thrust together due to events on the world scene.

Coming of Age: 1936–1969

During the first three decades of the twentieth century, Allport's conception of social psychology emphasized basic research, with little consideration given to addressing social problems. However, by the mid-1930s, the discipline was poised for further growth and expansion. The events that had the greatest impact on social psychology at this critical juncture in its history were the Great Depression in the United States and the social and political upheavals in Europe generated by the First and Second World Wars.

Following the stock market crash of 1929, many young psychologists were unable to find or hold jobs. Experiencing firsthand the impact of societal forces, many of them adopted the liberal ideals of Franklin Roosevelt's "New Dealers"—or even the more radical left-wing political views of the Socialist and Communist parties. In 1936 these social scientists formed an organization dedicated to scientifically studying important social issues and supporting progressive social action. This organization, the Society for the Psychological Study of Social Issues (SPSSI), contained many social psychologists who were interested in applying their theories and political activism to real-world problems. One of the important contributions the SPSSI made to social psychology was, and continues to be, the infusion of ethics and values into the discussion of social life.

At the same time, the rise of fascism in Germany, Spain, and Italy created a strong anti-intellectual and anti-Semitic atmosphere in many of Europe's universities. To escape this persecution, many of Europe's leading social scientists—such as Fritz Heider, Gustav Ichheiser, Kurt Lewin, and Theodor Adorno—immigrated to America. When the United States entered the war, many social psychologists (both American and European) applied their knowledge of human behavior to wartime programs, including the selection of officers for the Office of Strategic Services (the forerunner of the Central Intelligence Agency) and the undermining of enemy morale (de Miguel et al., 2011; Hoffman, 1992). The constructive work resulting from this collaboration demonstrated the practical applications of social psychology.

During this time of global strife, one of the most influential social psychologists was Kurt Lewin (1890–1947), a Jewish refugee from Nazi Germany. Lewin was instrumental in founding the SPSSI and served as its president in 1941. He firmly believed that social psychology did not have to choose between being a pure science or an applied science. His oft-repeated maxim, "No research without action, and no action without research," continues to influence social psychologists interested in applying their knowledge to current social problems (Ash, 1992). By the time of his death at the age of 57, Lewin had provided social psychology with many of its defining characteristics and had trained many of the young American scholars who would become the leaders of contemporary social psychology (Pettigrew, 2010).

With the end of the war, prospects were bright for social psychology in North America. Based on their heightened scientific stature, social psychologists established new research facilities, secured government grants, and, most important, trained graduate students. Yet while social psychology was flourishing in America, the devastating effects of the world war seriously hampered the discipline overseas—especially in Germany. In this postwar period, the United States emerged as a world power, and just as it exported its material goods to other countries, it also exported its social psychology. Beyond the influence exerted by the liberal leanings of its members, this brand of social psychology also reflected the political ideology of American society and the social problems encountered within its boundaries (Farr, 1996). With its infusion of European intellectuals and the recently trained young American social psychologists, the maturing science of social psychology expanded its theoretical and research base. To understand how a civilized society like Germany could fall under the influence of a ruthless dictator like Adolf Hitler, Theodor Adorno (1903–1969) and his colleagues studied the *authoritarian personality*—analyzing how personality factors emerging during childhood shape later adult obedience and intolerance of minorities. Some years later, Stanley Milgram (1933–1984) extended this line of research in his now-famous obedience experiments, which examined the situational factors that make people more likely to obey destructive authority figures. Social psychologists also focused their attention on the influence of the group on the individual (Asch, 1956) and on the power of persuasive communication (Hovland et al., 1949). The most direct impact that social psychological research had on American society in the 1950s was in the 1954 U.S. Supreme Court decision to end the practice of racially segregated education. The Court's ruling was partly based on research conducted by Kenneth Clark (1914–2005) and Mamie Phipps Clark (1917–1983) indicating that segregation negatively affected the self-concepts of black children. In that same year, Gordon Allport provided a theoretical outline for how desegregation might reduce racial prejudice: the contact hypothesis. Another significant line of research and theorizing during the 1950s was Leon Festinger's (1910–1989) theory of cognitive dissonance (Festinger, 1957), which asserted that people's thoughts and actions were motivated by a desire to maintain cognitive consistency. The simplicity of the theory and its often-surprising findings generated interest and enthusiasm both inside and outside of social psychology for many years.

The 1960s were a time of social turmoil in the United States, with the country caught in the grip of political assassinations, urban violence, social protests, and the Vietnam War. People were searching for constructive ways to change society for the better. Following this lead, social psychologists devoted more research to such topics as aggression, helping, attraction, and love. As the federal government expanded its attempts to cure societal ills with the guidance of social scientists, the number of social psychologists rose dramatically. Among these new social scientists were an increasing number of women and, to a lesser degree, minority members. Whole new lines of inquiry into social behavior commenced, with an increasing interest in the interaction between social situations and personality factors.

("Kenneth B. Clark and Mamie Phipps Clark," circa 1960, by Ken Heyman, courtesy of Library of Congress, ID 96501919)

Kenneth and Mamie Phipps Clark conducted groundbreaking research on the self-concepts of black children. In 1971, Kenneth Clark became the first African American to be elected president of the American Psychological Association.

Becoming a More Inclusive and Self-Critical Science: 1970 to the Present

The explosion of research in the 1960s played a part in another explosion of sorts in the area of research ethics because a few controversial studies appeared to put participants at risk for psychological harm. The most controversial of these studies was the previously mentioned obedience experiments conducted by Milgram, in which volunteers were ordered to deliver seemingly painful electric shocks to another person as part of a "learning experiment." In reality, no shocks were ever delivered—the victim was a confederate and only pretended to be in pain—but the stress experienced by the participants was indeed real. Although this study and others of its kind asked important questions about social behavior, serious concerns were raised about whether the significance of the research justified exposing participants to potentially harmful psychological consequences. Spurred by the debate surrounding these issues, in 1974 the US government developed regulations requiring all institutions seeking federal funding to establish institutional review boards that would ensure the health and safety of human participants.

While concerns were being raised about the ethical treatment of human research participants, social psychologists were simultaneously questioning the validity of their scientific methods and asking themselves whether their discipline was a relevant and useful science to begin with. When social psychology first emerged from World War II and embarked on its rapid expansion, expectations were high that social psychologists could work hand in hand with various organizations to solve many social problems. By the 1970s, with these problems still unsolved, a "crisis of confidence" emerged (Elms, 1975). This disappointment and criticism of social psychology was followed by accusations from women and minorities that past research and theory reflected the biases of a white, male-dominated view of reality, and many began to reassess the field's basic premises. Out of this crisis emerged a more vital and inclusive field of social psychology—one using better social measuring instruments and having more diversity within its membership. Beyond the borders of the United States, European and Latin American social psychological associations were founded by the end of the 1970s, followed in 1995 by the Asian Association of Social Psychology. This overseas social psychology placed more emphasis on intergroup and societal variables than did its American cousin. By the mid-1980s the growing influence of social psychology around the world was well on its way in reshaping the discipline, as scholars in many countries actively exchanged ideas and collaborated on multinational studies. One of the principal questions generated by this exchange of information was: Which aspects of human behavior are *culture specific* (i.e., due to conditions existing within a particular culture), and which ones are due to our shared *evolutionary* heritage? Although social psychology's "professional center of gravity" still resides in the United States, social psychology in other world regions offers the entire field opportunities to escape what some consider the limitations of this "gravitational pull" and to perceive new worlds of social reality (Ross et al., 2010). This multicultural perspective will continue to guide research in the coming years.

Contemporary social psychologists have also continued the legacy of Kurt Lewin and SPSSI by applying their knowledge to the wide array of phenomena that make up everyday life—such as law, health, education, politics, sports, and business. Although SPSSI initially focused primarily on US social issues and governmental policies, as its international membership has grown, global social problems have become a larger part of its work. Whether it is informing members of the U.S. Congress or delegates at the United Nations about relevant scientific findings, members of SPSSI are providing valuable information to guide policy decisions around the world. In commenting on the goals of a social psychology graduate program, past SPSSI president Morton Deutsch captures what many social psychologists still see as its ideal: "I wanted to create tough-minded but tenderhearted students. Science is very important. But science without a heart can be destructive. And a heart without a mind is not very valuable." This interest in applying the principles and findings of social psychology is a natural outgrowth of the search for understanding.

Regarding the tough-minded aspect of social psychology, some have argued that, every few decades, the discipline seems to experience a crisis of its own doing (Pettigrew, 2018). Currently, the crisis with which social psychology is grappling involves a revisiting of a question asked during the first crisis of the 1970s, namely, is social psychology truly a useful science? The form in which this "usefulness" question is currently being framed was prompted by reports that the findings from some social psychological studies were actually false positives, meaning that the researchers had found statistically significant evidence for something that was later found not to be real. For example, in 2015, Brian Nosek and his colleagues reported that 100 research groups around the world had each tried to reproduce the findings from 100 previously published psychological studies using the same scientific methods but were able to do so in only 40% of the studies. Of course, just because a study does not replicate the findings from a previous study does not mean that those previous findings are false. Many other factors might explain why the findings weren't reproduced. It also should be noted that the issue of potential false positives is not unique to social psychology. It is a concern within all scientific disciplines, especially the medical and health sciences where false positives are especially likely to negatively impact people's lives. To address this current crisis within social psychology, many researchers are now systematically attempting to reproduce the findings of past studies (see Chapter 2). In 2013, Nosek and Jeffrey Spies established the Center for Open Science with the goal of increasing the openness, integrity, and reproducibility of scientific research. While the center was initially focused on increasing confidence in the findings conducted within social psychology and psychology in general, the center has recently begun a second reproducibility project for cancer biology research.

In concluding this brief history, if the life of a science is similar to a person's life, then contemporary social psychology is best thought of as a "young adult" among the social sciences; compared to the more established sciences, social psychology is "barely dry behind the ears." Yet it is a discipline where new and innovative ideas are unusually welcome and where new theoretical approaches and scientific methods (often from other scientific disciplines) are regularly incorporated. Social psychologists are justifiably self-critical about their scientific discipline, but they are also justifiably proud that it continues to live up to its promise as an important contributor to understanding our complex social world. Some social psychology milestones are listed in the timeline at the end of this chapter. Let us now examine some of the organizing concepts and perspectives in this discipline.

Section Summary

- Social psychology uses scientific methods to study how the thoughts, feelings, and behaviors of individuals are influenced by the actual, imagined, or implied presence of others.

- Social reality is changeable, with people's expectations about a person, group, or situation often leading to the fulfillment of those expectations.

- Social psychology has both psychological and sociological branches.

- Although social psychology has a distinct American imprint, its focus is becoming increasingly international.

1.2 Organizing Concepts and Perspectives in Social Psychology

If you surveyed social psychologists, you would discover that there is no agreement on a single theoretical perspective that unifies the field. Despite the fact that social psychology has no grand theory that explains all aspects of social behavior, there are some important organizing concepts and perspectives.

1.2a The Self Is Shaped by—and Shapes— the Social Environment.

Throughout most of the past century, the behaviorist perspective in psychology—with its focus on studying only observable actions—prevented the concept of the self from becoming a focus of research in social psychology. During that time, most social psychologists explained people's behavior simply by examining the social cues in the situation, without considering how each person's life experiences and self-evaluations might also shape their responses. Fortunately, some social psychologists argued against such a narrow focus. For example, Gordon Allport's 1943 presidential address to the American Psychological Association presented the following appeal:

> One of the oddest events in the history of modern psychology is the manner in which the self became sidetracked and lost to view. I say it is odd, because the existence of one's self is the one fact of which every mortal person— every psychologist included—is perfectly convinced. An onlooker might say, "Psychologists are funny fellows. They have before them, at the heart of their science, a fact of perfect certainty, and yet they pay no attention to it. Why don't they begin with their own ego, or with our egos—with something we all know about? If they did so we might understand them better. And what is more, they might understand us better." (Allport, 1943, p. 451)

Despite Allport's call to action, it wasn't until the early 1970s that an increasing number of social psychologists (led by their empirical studies and a growing interest in human cognition) backed into a focus on the self (Greenwald & Ronis, 1978). Today in contemporary social psychology, the self and self-related concepts are important explanatory tools of the discipline. But first we must ask: What is the self?

The **self** is both a simple and a complex concept. It is not something located inside your head—it is you, a social being with the ability to engage in symbolic communication and self-awareness. The reason we use *social being* to define the self is because selves do not develop in isolation, but do so only within a social context. Likewise, the reason the cognitive processes of *symbol usage* and *self-awareness* are so important in this definition is that both are essential for us to engage in planned, coordinated activities in which we can regulate our behavior and anticipate the actions of others (Bandura, 2005; Heatherton, 2011). For example, suppose Jack has been working long hours at the office and, as a result, has ignored his wife and children. One day, it dawns on Jack that if he continues in this pattern of "all work and no play," he will be not only dull but also divorced and depressed. Based on this anticipation, he revises his work schedule to enjoy the company of his family. In other words, Jack consciously changes his behavior to avoid what he perceives to be a host of unpleasant future consequences. This ability to analyze surroundings, our possible future realities, and ourselves allows us to actively create and recreate our social world and ourselves.

Self-awareness and symbol usage—and thus, the self—may have evolved in our ancestors as a means to better deal with an increasingly complex social environment (Oda, 2001). For instance, self-awareness not only provided our ancestors with knowledge

self
A symbol-using social being who can reflect on his or her own behavior

about their own behavior, but they could also use this inner experience to anticipate how rivals might behave in the future—perhaps in war or in social bargaining—thus giving them an advantage in these activities. Similarly, the development of language allowed our ancestors to not only better coordinate group activities but also use this symbolic communication to discuss things not physically present, such as a herd of antelope or a band of hostile warriors (Shaffer, 2005). These two defining features of the self became the means by which our ancestors developed an adaptive advantage in their environment, thus increasing their chances of surviving and reproducing.

> "The Self is the honey of all beings, and all beings are the honey of this Self."
>
> —The Upanishads, sacred texts of Hinduism, 800–500 BCE

Selfhood also allowed our ancestors to ponder their existence and mortality: Why are we here? What happens when we die? The artwork and elaborate burial sites created by our ancestors during the Upper Paleolithic period (40,000 years ago) provide compelling evidence that the modern human mind—the self—was emerging during that time (Rossano, 2003). M. Brewster Smith (2002) was one of the social psychologists who contended that this new search for ultimate meaning led to the development of myth, ritual, and religion, which affirmed for each social group its value as "The People." As you will discover throughout this text, this kind of group search for meaning and value profoundly shapes social interactions.

Beyond seeking meaning and value in group life, our ancestors also used self-awareness to size up and understand themselves. The way we think of ourselves (our *self-concept*) influences our social behavior and how we respond to social events. This influence is often dramatically illustrated in situations in which our own performance results in either success or failure. In such situations, many people tend to take credit for positive behaviors or outcomes—but blame negative behaviors or outcomes on external causes (Campbell & Sedikides, 1999; McCall & Nattrass, 2001). For example, when students receive a good grade on an exam, they are likely to attribute it to their intelligence, their strong work ethic, or a combination of the two. However, if they receive a poor grade on the exam, they tend to believe their failure is due to an unreasonable professor or pure bad luck. This tendency to take credit for positive outcomes but deny responsibility for negative outcomes is known as the **self-serving bias**.

How might a self-serving explanation for a personal setback benefit a person's self-confidence and future success?

The most agreed-upon explanation for the self-serving bias is that it allows us to enhance and protect our self-worth. If we feel personally responsible for successes or positive events in our lives but do not feel blameworthy for failures or other negative events, our self-worth is likely to be bolstered. This self-enhancement explanation emphasizes the role of motivation in our self-serving biases. Although the self-serving bias may provide us with a less-than-accurate view of ourselves, it may be "functionally efficient" because it often boosts our self-confidence (Williams et al., 2012). Explaining any current successes as being caused by enduring personality characteristics creates a personal expectation of future success in related tasks, increasing the likelihood that we will attempt new challenges (Taylor & Brown, 1988). Similarly, attributing repeated failures to bad luck or unfortunate situations may well serve to maintain an optimistic belief in the possibility of future success, resulting in our not giving up. Wilmar Schaufeli (1988), for instance, has found that unemployed workers seeking reemployment have more success if they exhibit the self-serving bias in their job search (that is, if they convince themselves that not being hired for a particular job is due to external factors and not to internal ones such as incompetence).

self-serving bias
The tendency to take credit for positive outcomes but deny responsibility for negative outcomes in our lives

Although there appear to be tangible benefits to explaining away negative events, the self-serving bias can create problems if it leads us to repeatedly overlook our own shortcomings in situations where a more realistic appraisal would generate useful corrective steps (Kruger & Dunning, 1999; Robins & Beer, 2001). Further, in group settings, the tendency to take credit for success and deny blame for failure can quickly lead to conflict and dissension among members. For example, the more the members of groups overestimate their individual contributions to group accomplishments, the less they will want to work with each other in the future (Banaji et al., 2003; Caruso et al., 2004).

> "General laws and individual differences are merely two aspects of one problem; they are mutually dependent on each other and the study of the one cannot proceed without the study of the other."
>
> —Kurt Lewin, German-born social psychologist, 1890–1947

As you can see, the self plays an important role in how we think and behave as social creatures. Social psychology's emphasis on the self represents an affirmation of Kurt Lewin's belief that both person and situational factors influence social behavior. Lewin's perspective, later dubbed **interactionism** (Pettigrew & Cherry, 2012), combines personality psychology (which stresses differences among people) with traditional social psychology (which stresses differences among situations). In keeping with Lewin's legacy, throughout this text we will examine how these two factors contribute to the social interaction equation, and we will use the self as the primary "person" variable. The previously mentioned *Self/Social Connection* exercises will further reinforce the idea that social behavior is best understood as resulting from the interaction of a person with situational factors.

1.2b Our Social Thinking Can Be Automatic or Deliberate.

Throughout the history of social psychology there has been a running debate concerning the nature of human behavior. One perspective was that people are moved to act by their needs, desires, and emotions (also known as their *affect*). Social psychologists subscribing to this "hot" approach argued that heated, impulsive action that fulfills desires is more influential than cool, calculated planning of behavior (Zajonc, 1984). The alternative viewpoint was that people's actions are principally influenced by the rational analysis of choices facing them in particular situations. Followers of this "cold" approach asserted that how people think ultimately determines what they want and how they feel (Lazarus, 1984).

In the 1950s and 1960s, the hot perspective was most influential, but by the 1980s the cold perspective dominated the thinking within social psychology. One reason for this shift was the advent of the computer age, which resulted in people's everyday lives being saturated with the terminology and thinking of this new "technoscience." Reflecting this new view of reality, many social psychologists borrowed concepts from cognitive psychology and developed theories of **social cognition** that provided numerous insights into how we interpret, analyze, remember, and use information about our social world (Rendell et al., 2011). These theories often describe people methodically processing information in a fixed sequence, or *serially* working on only one stream of data at a time—like a computer. The sequential computer model of thinking is useful in explaining many aspects of human cognition, especially how we execute certain mental operations or follow certain rules of logic when making some decisions. For instance, if a normally sociable person acts irritable just before taking his midterms, you may logically consider the available information and conclude that his irritability is caused by situational factors.

Despite its usefulness, the computer model is less helpful in explaining other ways of thinking because the human brain is more complex than any existing computer and performs many mental operations simultaneously, "in parallel" (Gabrieli, 1999). For example, why might a former soldier experience a panic attack while at a fireworks

interactionism

An important perspective in social psychology that emphasizes the combined effects of both the person and the situation on human behavior

social cognition

The ways in which we interpret, analyze, remember, and use information about our social world display? In this situation, a more useful model of cognition might conceive of memory as a weblike network of connections among thousands of interacting "processing units"—all active at once. For the former soldier, memories of war and loud explosions are stored in a neural network; activating one part of the network simultaneously activates the rest of the network.

Many social psychologists embraced the social cognitive perspective, but others argued that it dehumanizes social psychology to think of motives and affect as merely the end products of a central processing system. In response to such criticism, cognitively oriented social psychologists established a more balanced view of human nature by blending the traditional hot and cold perspectives into what some termed the *warm look* (Sorrentino, 2003).

Reflecting this warm perspective, most contemporary social cognitive theories discuss how people use multiple cognitive strategies based on their current goals, motives, and needs (Dunning, 1999; Strack & Deutsch, 2012). In such discussions, theorists typically propose **dual-process theories** of social cognition, meaning that our social thinking and behavior are determined by two different ways of understanding and responding to social stimuli (Kliemann et al., 2013; Petty, 2004). One mode of information processing—the legacy of the cold perspective—is based on effortful, reflective thinking, in which no action is taken until its potential consequences are properly weighed and evaluated. The alternative mode of processing information—the legacy of the hot perspective—is based on minimal cognitive effort, in which behavior is often impulsively and automatically activated by emotions, habits, or biological drives. Which of the two avenues of information processing people take at any given time is the subject of ongoing research that we will examine throughout this text. The essential assumption to keep in mind regarding dual-process theories is that many aspects of human behavior result from automatic processes that may occur spontaneously and outside our conscious awareness (Moors & De Houwer, 2006).

Some dual-process theories still rely on the computer model of serial information processing, which assumes that people can engage in only one form of thinking at a time. According to this perspective, in human cognition there often is a conflict between an initial, automatic evaluation and a more deliberate, rational assessment. The only way you can resolve this conflict is by engaging in either effortful thinking or relatively effortless thinking. You can switch back and forth between the two forms of thinking, but you cannot do both simultaneously. In contrast to this sequential "either/or" way of describing human thought, other dual-process theories rely on the neural network model of parallel information processing and describe two mental systems that operate simultaneously, or parallel to one another.

Social scientists who assume parallel-processing systems often make a distinction between *explicit cognition* and *implicit cognition*. **Explicit cognition** involves deliberate judgments or decisions of which we are consciously aware. Although this type of cognition is intentional, it can sometimes be relatively effortless when the task is easy. However, a good deal of explicit thinking consumes considerable cognitive resources. The upside is that it is flexible and can deal with new problems. Trying to understand the definition of explicit cognition is literally an example of said thought process. In contrast, **implicit cognition** involves judgments or decisions that are under the control of automatically activated evaluations occurring without our awareness. This type of thinking is unintentional, it uses few cognitive resources, and it operates quickly—however it is inflexible and often cannot deal with new problems. The unintentional and automatic qualities of implicit cognition are demonstrated by the fact that you cannot stop yourself from reading the words on this page when you see them. Your reading skills are automatically and effortlessly activated.

dual-process theories
Theories of social cognition that describe two basic ways of thinking about social stimuli: one involving automatic, effortless thinking and the other involving more deliberate, effortful thinking

explicit cognition
Deliberate judgments or decisions of which we are consciously aware

implicit cognition
Judgments or decisions that are under the control of automatically activated evaluations occurring without our awareness

How might implicit cognition affect social interaction? Feeling uneasy and irritable around a new acquaintance because she unconsciously reminds you of a disagreeable person from your past is an example of how unconscious, automatically activated evaluations can shape your social judgments. For many years, social psychologists primarily studied and discussed the conscious decision-making that shapes social interaction, but currently there is a great deal of interest in how thinking "below the radar" of conscious awareness can influence social judgments and behavior. Throughout the text, we will discuss how both explicit and implicit cognitive processes shape our social world.

> "In fact, I cannot totally grasp all that I am. Thus, the mind is not large enough to contain itself; but where can that part of it be which it does not contain?"
>
> —St. Augustine, Christian theologian, CE 354–430

1.2c   Culture Shapes Social Behavior.

To what extent do you agree with the following statements?

   I think I am a unique person.

   I enjoy being the center of attention.

   I should be able to live my life any way I want to.

   If I could make the laws, the world would be a better place.

Over the past 30 years, surveys of 16,000 American college students indicate that if you were born after 1980, you are more likely to agree with these statements than if you were born before that year. Why might this be so?

   The answer is cultural experience. In trying to understand how people interpret and respond to social reality, we must remember that people view the world through cultural lenses. By **culture**, we mean the total lifestyle of a people, including all the ideas, symbols, preferences, and material objects that they share. This cultural experience shapes people's view of reality and of themselves and, thus, significantly influences their social behavior (Sieck et al., 2011).

The Social World of American Young Adults

Most of you reading these words are either members of "Generation Y" ("millennials" born between 1981 and 2000) or "Generation Z" ("Boomlets" born after 2001). Your cultural upbringing is very different from that of your parents. You grew up with personal computers, the internet, and cell phones. For many of you, your childhood was chronicled by your parents' video cameras, and it is quite possible that you were treated like a "shining star" and told, "You can be anything you want to be." How has your upbringing shaped your views of yourself and the world around you?

   Using 40 years of data from an annual national survey of American adults, researchers have found that more than two-thirds of millennials see their generation as unique and distinct (Pew Research Center, 2007; Twenge et al., 2015). Illustrating this generational self-view, today many young adults publicly proclaim their individuality by posting personal profiles on social networking sites such as Facebook (Toma & Hancock, 2013). Young adults' desire for individual expression is also demonstrated by the fact that about half of them either have a tattoo, a body piercing, or have dyed their hair a nontraditional color. Indeed, an analysis of 766,513 American books published between 1960 and 2008 found a significant increase in self-focused pronouns over the past half century (Twenge et al., 2013). This cultural shift to heightened literary self-focus is further evidence of the increased valuing of individuality among Americans.

   The value young adults place on their own individuality also extends to accepting differences in others. The two youngest American generations are the most tolerant of

culture
The total lifestyle of a people, including all the ideas, symbols, preferences, and material objects that they share

any generation in stating that homosexuality and interracial dating should be accepted and not discouraged (Twenge et al., 2015). Although more socially tolerant than previous generations, most young adults believe that their generation is more interested in focusing on themselves than in helping others. When asked to identify important life goals of those in their age group, the annual national survey found that most young adults named fortune and fame. About 80% stated that "getting rich" is either the most important or second most important life goal for their peers, with half stating that "becoming famous" is also highly valued. In contrast, less than one-third of young adults identified "helping people who need help" as an important goal of their generation.

Millennials' and Boomlets' desire for self-expression has led many of them to get tattoos or body piercings.
(Shutterstock)

If there is some truth to young Americans' perception of their generation, you might be wondering how your generation became so self-focused in comparison to your parents' generation. Actually, this generational difference is simply a matter of degree. Americans are generally a self-focused people; America's youth are simply the best current example of the particular way in which our culture shapes people's thoughts, feelings, and actions.

The Cultural Belief Systems of Individualism and Collectivism.

Our understanding of these survey findings and social behavior in general relies on two cultural belief systems concerning how individuals relate to their group—namely, individualism and collectivism (David et al., 2014). **Individualism** is a preference for a loosely knit social framework in which individuals are supposed to take care of themselves and their immediate families only. This belief system asserts that society is a collection of unique individuals who pursue their own goals and interests and strive to be relatively free from the influence of others.

As a philosophy of life, traces of individualism can be seen in early Greek and Roman writings and in the values and ideas of the medieval Anglo-Saxon poets of England (Harbus, 2002). However, individualism did not make a significant appearance on the world stage until the sixteenth century, when people became more geographically mobile and, thus, more regularly interacted with radically different cultures. Exposed to different social norms and practices, people began entertaining the possibility of having goals separate from those of their group (Kashima & Foddy, 2002). In the arts, characters in novels and plays were increasingly portrayed as having individual emotional states and as experiencing conflict between their true selves and the social roles assigned to them by their family and community. During the late 1800s and early 1900s—the age of industrialization and urbanization in Western societies—social roles became increasingly complex and compartmentalized. It became common practice to "find" or "create" one's own personal identity rather than being given an identity by one's group. This belief also holds true today in our contemporary society. Self-discipline, self-sufficiency, personal accountability, and autonomy are now highly valued characteristics in a person (Kâğitçibaşi, 1994; Oishi et al., 2007).

Many observers of American culture contend that the history of voluntary settlement in the frontier greatly contributed to the development of individualism in the United States (de Tocqueville, 1969; Turner, 1920). Examples of this individualist orientation can be seen throughout US history. In the 1700s, Thomas Jefferson's penning of the Declaration

individualism
A philosophy of life stressing the priority of individual needs over group needs, a preference for loosely knit social relationships, and a desire to be relatively autonomous of others' influence

of Independence was essentially a bold assertion that individual rights were more important than group rights. In the 1800s, poet/philosopher Ralph Waldo Emerson believed that individualism was the route that—if truly traveled—would result in a spontaneous social order of self-determined, self-reliant, and fully developed citizens. In contemporary America, one can see the influence of individualism in everyday activities. For example, beyond the previously mentioned increased use of self-focused words in American books over the past half century, an analysis of popular American songs finds many more self-focused words compared to other-focused words in the lyrics—significantly more than even a generation ago (DeWall et al., 2011). Similarly, American parents' tendency over the past quarter century to increasingly give their children unusual names reflects the individualist desire to "stand out" from others and be unique (Twenge et al., 2016).

"The union is only perfect when all the individuals are isolated."

—Ralph Waldo Emerson, US philosopher/poet, 1803–1882

In contrast to individualism, there is an alternative perspective known as **collectivism**, which represents a preference for a tightly knit social framework in which individuals can expect relatives or other members of their social group to look after them in exchange for unquestioning loyalty. This cultural belief system asserts that people become human only when they are integrated into a group—not isolated from it. Whereas individualists give priority to personal goals, collectivists often make no distinctions between personal and group goals. When they do make such distinctions, collectivists subordinate their personal goals to the collective good (Grossmann & Na, 2014; Oyserman et al., 2002). Due to the greater importance given to group aspirations over individual desires, collectivist cultures tend to value similarity and conformity, rather than uniqueness and independence. (See Chapter 7 for a more detailed discussion.)

"Human beings draw close to one another by their common nature, but habits and customs keep them apart."

—Confucius, Chinese sage, 551–479 BCE

How do different perspectives on the relationship between the individual and the group influence thought and behavior? Consider a modern, industrialized society with a collectivist orientation: Japan. The Japanese, like other people living in collectivist societies, view group inclusion and allegiance as primary goals in life. Indeed, in Japan the expression for individualist—*kojin-shugi*—refers to a socially undesirable characteristic, suggesting selfishness rather than personal responsibility (Ishii-Kuntz, 1989). Those who defy the group's wishes, often considered heroes in an individualist culture, bring shame upon themselves, their families, and their ancestors in Japan. In North American society, to stand above the crowd and be recognized as unique and special is highly valued. In Japan, such attention detracts from the group. These different perspectives are illustrated in contrasting proverbs or mottos. In North America, "The squeaky wheel gets the grease" and "Do your own thing" are commonly heard phrases, while the Japanese credo is "The nail that sticks up shall be hammered down."

It may surprise you to know that approximately 70% of the world's population lives in cultures with a collectivist orientation (Singelis et al., 1995). Indeed, the collectivist perspective is much older than is the individualist orientation. For most of human history, the group—not the individual—was the basic unit of society. Whether you were born into a clan or a tribe, you would generally live in one geographic region your entire life and would, upon maturing, assume the same social role as your parents. You did not have to "search" for your identity; your group gave it to you. Many social scientists contend that collectivism is the older of the two philosophies because it focuses on the type of thinking and behavior that affords the most protection for people who live in threatening environments, where survival needs are extremely salient (Inglehart & Oyserman, 2004). This is exactly the type of environment that has historically confronted all human groups until fairly recently. In contrast, individualism is a much more recent philosophy of life because it develops among people who inhabit relatively safe environments, where their survival is less dependent on maintaining strong group ties. This liberation from

collectivism

A philosophy of life stressing the priority of group needs over individual needs, a preference for tightly knit social relationships, and a willingness to submit to the influence of one's group immediate physical threats reduces the importance of survival-focused values and gives higher priority to freedom of choice (Imada & Yussen, 2012).

Table 1.1 lists some of the differences between these two cultural ideologies. The majority of cross-cultural researchers currently consider individualism and collectivism to be two ends of a continuum, with the United States, Canada, Australia, and Western European societies located more toward the individualist end and Asian, African, and Latin and South American cultures situated near the collectivist end. Within all cultures, individualist tendencies tend to be stronger in large urban or remote frontier settings (where people are less dependent on group ties), while collectivist tendencies are more pronounced in small regional cities and rural settings (where social relationships are more interdependent) (Conway et al., 2014; Kitayama et al., 2006).

TABLE 1.1 Differences Between Collectivist and Individualist Cultures	
Collectivist	**Individualist**
Identity is based in the social system and given by one's group.	Identity is based in the individual and achieved by one's own striving.
People are socialized to be emotionally dependent on organizations and institutions.	People are socialized to be emotionally independent of organizations and institutions.
Personal and group goals are generally consistent, and when inconsistent, group goals get priority.	Personal and group goals are often inconsistent, and when inconsistent, personal goals get priority.
People explain others' social behavior as being more determined by social norms and roles than by personal attitudes.	People explain others' social behavior as being more determined by personal attitudes than by social norms and roles.
Emphasis is on belonging to organizations, and memberships is the ideal.	Emphasis is on individual initiative and achievement, and leadership is the ideal.
Trust is placed in group decisions.	Trust is placed in individual decisions.

Which perspective is better? Your answer depends on what values you have internalized. As previously mentioned, although individualism and collectivism are seen by many theorists as two ends of a continuum, this doesn't mean that individualist tendencies do not influence people living in collectivist cultures or that collectivist yearnings do not shape individualists (Göregenli, 1997). Indeed, social scientists commonly think of these differing ideologies as reflecting two seemingly universal and common human needs: the need for autonomy and the need for communion (Hornsey & Jetten, 2004; Schwartz, 2003). Thus, although all humans have a need for both autonomy and communion, individualist cultures place greater value on autonomy, while collectivist cultures place greater value on communion. One of the goals of social psychology is to understand how the past experiences and present conditions of others influence their interpretation of social reality; therefore these two contrasting cultural perspectives will regularly figure into our chapter discussions. Spend a few minutes completing *Self/Social Connection Exercise 1.1* to better understand the relative importance of these two cultural orientations in your own life.

"The American cultural ideal of the self-made man, of everyone standing on his own feet, is as tragic a picture as the initiative-destroying dependence on a benevolent despot. We all need each other. This type of interdependence is the greatest challenge to the maturity of individual and group functioning."

—Kurt Lewin, German-born social psychologist, 1890–1947

Self/Social Connection Exercise 1.1

To What Degree Do You Value Individualist and Collectivist Strivings?

Individualist–Collectivist Values Hierarchy

Directions

Listed below are 12 values. Please rank them in their order of importance to you, with "1" being the "most important" and "12" being the "least important."

Pleasure (Gratification of Desires)

Honor of Parents and Elders (Showing Respect)

Creativity (Uniqueness, Imagination)

Social Order (Stability of Society)

A Varied Life (Filled with Challenge, Novelty, and Change)

National Security (Protection of My Nation from Enemies)

Being Daring (Seeking Adventure, Risk)

Self-discipline (Self-restraint, Resistance to Temptation)

Freedom (Freedom of Action and Thought)

Politeness (Courtesy, Good Manners)

Independence (Self-reliance, Choice of Own Goals)

Obedience (Fulfilling Duties, Meeting Obligations)

Directions for Scoring

The individualist and collectivist values are listed in alternating order, with the first (Pleasure) being an individualist value and the second (Honor of Parents and Elders) being a collectivist value. People from individualist cultures, such as the United States, Canada, England, or Australia, tend to have more individualist values than collectivist values in the upper half of their values hierarchy. This order tends to be reversed for those from collectivist cultures, such as Mexico, Japan, Korea, or China. Which of the two cultural belief systems is predominant in your own values hierarchy? If you know people from another culture, how do they rank these values?

A few additional points bear mentioning regarding these two cultural orientations. As already suggested, individualism and collectivism are not permanent, unchanging characteristics of given societies. Individualism is closely linked with socioeconomic development (Welzel et al., 2003). When collectivist cultures become industrialized and experience economic development, they often also develop some of the thinking associated with individualism (Hamamura, 2012). This is at least partly due to the fact that the increased prosperity brought on by economic development minimizes the types of concerns for survival that prompt people to strongly identify with—and unquestioningly submit to—their social group (Oyserman et al., 2002). When economic conditions shift in this manner, many collectivists begin developing an interest in individual, freedom-focused rights and privileges.

Economic conditions around the world are slowly improving, but does this mean that the world is also becoming more individualist as a whole? To answer this question, Henri Santos and his coworkers (2017) examined 51 years of data on individualist practices and values across 78 countries. Their findings indicate that individualist tendencies are substantially increasing in about three-fourths of the countries, with socioeconomic development being the leading cause for that increase. However, one notable exception to this pattern is China, the world's most populous country (with 1.42 billion people), which experienced a decrease in individualist values among its citizens as its economic growth increased.

1.2d Evolution Shapes Universal Patterns of Social Behavior.

One of the added benefits of cross-cultural research is that it not only allows us to identify those aspects of social behavior that vary from one culture to the next but also allows us to identify social behaviors that are common to all cultures. When a universal social behavior is identified, discussion naturally turns to how this pattern of behavior may have evolved. **Evolutionary psychology** may provide useful insights here (Gangestad, 2012).

The evolutionary perspective is partly based on the writings of biologist Charles Darwin (1809–1882), who theorized that genetic changes in the population of a species occur over many generations due to the interaction of environmental and biological variables. **Genes** are the biochemical units of inheritance for all living organisms, and the human species has about 30,000 different genes. According to Darwin (1859, 1871), all living organisms struggle for survival, and within each species, a great deal of competition and genetic variation occurs between individuals. Those members of a species with genetic traits best adapted for survival in their present environment will produce more offspring, and, as a result, their numbers will increase in the population. As the environment changes, however, other members within the species possessing traits better suited to the new conditions will flourish—a process called **natural selection**. In this way, the environment selects which genes of a species will be passed on to future generations. As this process of natural selection continues, and as the features best suited for survival change, the result is **evolution**, a term that refers to the gradual genetic changes that occur in a species over generations. *Reproduction* is central to the natural selection process, and the essence of natural selection is that the characteristics of some individuals allow them to produce more offspring than others.

An example of social behavior from another species that may be the product of natural selection is water splashing by male gorillas. Males regularly create massive water plumes by leaping into pools or by slapping the water with their powerful hands. Why is it that female gorillas do not engage in this behavior nearly to the same degree, and what precipitates male splashing? Evolutionary theorists hypothesized that male gorillas engage in water splashing to intimidate other males and keep them away from their females. To test this hypothesis, researchers observed the splashing displays of lowland gorillas in the Congo over a 3-year period (Parnell & Buchanan-Smith, 2001). They found that more than 70% of the splashing was carried out by dominant males in the presence of males not from their social group, with more than half the displays occurring when no females were present. These findings suggested to the researchers that

(National Telefilm Associates / Public domain, via Wikimedia)

Individualist and collectivist strivings can and do coexist within a person and are often depicted in popular movies. In the 1946 classic Christmas movie, It's a Wonderful Life, *Jimmy Stewart's character, George Bailey, is continually faced with life decisions that pit his own personal desires against his feelings of community obligation. This movie has a clear collectivist message: The self is affirmed by fulfilling the needs of the group. Why do you think this movie's message is so warmly received in North America's individualist culture? Do all societies need their share of George Baileys in order to thrive and prosper?*

"An individual has not started living until he can rise above the narrow confines of his individualistic concerns to the broader concerns of all humanity."
—Martin Luther King Jr., US civil rights leader, 1929–1968

evolutionary psychology
An approach to psychology based on the principle of natural selection

genes
The biochemical units of inheritance for all living organisms

natural selection
The process by which organisms with inherited traits best suited to the environment reproduce more successfully than less well-adapted organisms over a number of generations, which leads to evolutionary changes

evolution
The genetic changes that occur in a species over generations due to natural selection

the splashing was being directed at strange males who might challenge the dominant male's control of his group. They speculated that over the course of gorilla evolution, males who engaged in intimidating behavior like water splashing were more successful in preventing strange males from stealing females from their group than those who did not water splash. Thus, acting tough by literally making a big splash when other males were present resulted in greater reproductive success, and that is why this social behavior persists in the male gorilla population today.

Social psychologists who adopt the evolutionary approach apply a similar type of logic to understanding humans. Many social behaviors extensively studied by social psychologists—such as aggression, helping, interpersonal attraction, romantic love, and stereotyping—are thought to be shaped by inherited traits (Gangestad, 2012). If this is true, then attempts to understand human social behavior should consider how these inherited traits might have given our ancestors a reproductive advantage in their environment, thus maximizing their ability to survive and reproduce.

> "It may metaphorically be said that natural selection is daily and hourly scrutinizing . . . the slightest variations; rejecting those that are bad, preserving and adding up all that are good. . . . We see nothing of these slow changes in progress, . . . we see only that the forms of life are now different from what they formerly were."
>
> —From Darwin (1859)

There are two important points to keep in mind when considering the process of evolution. First, individual organisms don't evolve—populations evolve. The role that individuals play in evolution consists of interacting with the environment, so that their genes can be screened by natural selection. Thus, individuals contribute to a change in their species' population by their own successes or failures in reproducing. Over many generations, the accumulated effects of literally thousands or even millions of individuals' reproductive successes and failures lead to the evolution of the species. The second point to remember is that evolution does not necessarily result in species being transformed into more complex forms of life. Instead, the key feature of the evolutionary process is the degree to which an organism's inborn genetic traits help it adapt to its current environment. Thus, just as a trait that was once highly adaptive can become maladaptive if the environmental conditions change, the reverse is also true: a maladaptive trait can become extremely adaptive.

Use Caution in Applying Evolutionary Principles to Human Social Behavior.

Despite the importance of adding the evolutionary perspective to our explanation of social behavior, many social scientists are cautious about applying these principles to contemporary human behavior (Scher & Rauscher, 2003). The grounds for such caution rest on the fact that when biologists study an animal, they tend to examine it in terms of how it has adapted to its environment so that it can reproduce and pass on its genes. However, when a species changes environments—or when its environment changes— an unavoidable period of time exists in which its biological makeup is not in tune with its surroundings. All species are probably slightly "behind" their environment, but this is especially so for human beings. We are the youngest primate species on earth; our brains and bodies are biologically no different than they were 150,000 years ago, when our ancestors lived on the Pleistocene plains of East Africa. How we behave today in the modern world of city congestion and space-age technology may bear some relation to the roles for which our brains and bodies were originally selected, but the connection is probably weaker than we might think and needs to be interpreted with a great deal of care. In this text, we will approach evolutionary explanations with this sort of justifiable caution—that is, acknowledging that ancient evolutionary forces may have left us with capacities (such as the capacity to behave helpfully), while still recognizing that current social and environmental forces encourage or discourage the actual development and use of those capacities (Tomasello, 2011).

What Is the Difference Between Sex and Gender?

Throughout this text, when comparisons are made between women's and men's decision-making and social behavior, contrasting interpretations regarding any group-based differences will be offered from both the evolutionary and the sociocultural perspectives. In these analyses, it is important to understand the difference between the terms *sex* and *gender* (Lippa, 2005). **Sex** refers to the biological status of being female or male as assigned at birth, while **gender** refers to the meanings that societies and individuals attach to being female and male. Put simply, sex is a matter of genetic construction that categorizes a person as "female" or "male," and gender is a matter of cultural construction that characterizes a person by femininity or masculinity. Sex is something we are, whereas gender is something we do with the help and encouragement of others.

People are often confused by the distinction between sex and gender because the two concepts are generally thought of as going together—that is, female = feminine, and male = masculine. Yet behaviors or interests considered masculine in one culture may be defined as feminine in others. For instance, in certain North African societies, decorating and beautifying the face and body is a sign of masculinity—not femininity. Similarly, within cultures, beliefs about gender transform over time. For instance, in contemporary North American culture, it is now acceptable—even encouraged—for girls to participate in sports that were previously designated only for boys. Among adults, women are now much more actively involved in careers outside the household (a previously masculine domain), and men are more involved in childcare (a feminine domain). Gender is not fixed—it is constantly changing and being redefined. Further, for some people, a person's sex and identification with a specific gender do not conform to traditional cultural norms, and the person may be gender nonconforming. Indeed, many individuals do not neatly fit into the binary distinction of male or female, but rather, reflect a diversity of gendered characteristics. In the case where someone's sex (as assigned at birth based on biological markers) does not meet their self-identified gender, we acknowledge the person as *transgender*.

Because sex is biologically based and gender is culturally based, when research finds that men and women behave differently, we often ask whether this difference is due to sex (biology) or to gender (culture). This is not an idle question. If someone labels the behavior in question a sex difference, the implication is that the cause of the difference is rooted in human biology rather than in social or cultural factors. In contrast, when people talk about gender differences, the implication is that these differences do not stem from biology, but rather, that they develop in the course of socialization as boys and girls learn about appropriate gender-based attitudes, roles, and behaviors (Rudman & Glick, 2008).

Men and women differ biologically in a number of ways. The most basic sex difference is that males carry the chromosomal pattern XY, and females carry the pattern XX. This important difference at the chromosomal level produces differences in female and male anatomy and physical appearance. For instance, a newborn male has a penis and testicles, while a newborn female has a vagina and ovaries. At puberty, a male develops a prominent Adam's apple, while a female's breasts enlarge. Although the changes associated with puberty occur well after birth, no one would seriously argue that boys have been taught how to grow an Adam's apple or that girls learn how to grow breasts. These particular differences are due to biological factors—that is, they are a sex difference and are not due to cultural experience.

However, for approximately 1% to 2% of the population, this typical biological setup does not align (Fausto-Sterling, 2000). These people have disorders of sex development (DSDs), and are known as "intersex." In these cases, the person's chromosomes, hormones, and internal and external reproductive organs do not develop prenatally

sex
The biological status of being female or male

gender
The meanings that societies and individuals attach to being female and male

in the typical manner. For example, someone might have an XY (male) chromosomal pattern but, because of an insensitivity to androgen (male) sex hormones, they develop female-appearing external genitalia and typically identify as female (this is known as *Androgen Insensitivity Syndrome*).

Beyond these identifiable biological differences in chromosome patterns and anatomy, it is extremely difficult—if not impossible—to presently conclude that differences in the way women and men think, feel, and act are clearly due to either sex or gender (Wood & Eagly, 2010). Social psychologists with a biological or evolutionary orientation emphasize biological factors in explaining such differences, whereas those with a sociocultural orientation weigh in with cultural explanations. And, as already mentioned, when discussing genetics—even in those instances when genes influence behavioral differences between two groups, such as men and women—these biologically based differences can be greatly increased or decreased due to social forces.

How great are the differences between women and men in their psychological functioning? This is an issue that will be addressed throughout this text. As a preliminary answer, we can tell you that research conducted over the past 20 years indicates there are many more similarities than differences (Hyde, 2005). Across a wide variety of cognitive skills, psychological motives, and social behaviors, men and women do not differ from one another. Thus, despite cultural stereotypes to the contrary, women and men are remarkably alike in much of their psychological functioning. Reflecting these scientific findings, in this text we do not use the misleading term opposite sex when comparing one sex with the other but instead use the more appropriate term other sex.

1.2e Brain Activity Affects and Is Affected by Social Behavior.

Beyond the organizing principles currently shaping theory and research, social psychologists are constantly exploring new connections with other disciplines—both within and outside the social and behavioral sciences. Like the evolutionary perspective, one new connection that comes from the field of biology is the subfield of **social neuroscience**, which studies the relationship between neural processes in the brain and social processes (J. Cacioppo & S. Cacioppo, 2013; Smith-Lovin & Winkielman, 2010). This analysis emphasizes not only how the brain influences social interaction but also how social interaction can influence the brain.

The increased collaboration between social psychology and neuroscience is largely due to the development of more accurate measures of physiological changes, especially those involving *brain-imaging techniques* that provide pictures—or scans—of this body organ. These techniques generate "maps" of the brains of living people by examining their electrical activity, structure, blood flow, and chemistry. For example, *functional magnetic resonance imaging* (fMRI) measures the brain's metabolic activity in different regions, revealing which parts of the brain are most active in such social tasks as talking or listening to others, watching social interactions, and thinking about oneself. Researchers using fMRI technology have found that when love-struck research participants look at photos of their romantic partners, specific brain regions (like the *caudate nucleus*) that play key roles in motivation and reward—including feelings of elation and passion—exhibit heightened activation (Fisher, 2004).

Similarly, neuroscientists have discovered areas in the **frontal lobe** of the **cerebral cortex** that are of particular importance in understanding self-related processes (Heatherton, 2011). As depicted in Figure 1.3, the cerebral cortex is the wrinkled-looking outer layer of brain tissue that coordinates and integrates all other brain areas into a fully functioning unit. About 90% of our cerebral cortex is of relatively recent evolution, and the frontal lobe is its largest region. The frontal lobe is involved in the coordination

social neuroscience
The study of the relationship between neural processes of the brain and social processes

frontal lobe
The region of the cerebral cortex situated just behind the forehead that is involved in the coordination of movement and higher mental processes, such as planning, social skills, and abstract thinking; the area of the brain that is the originator of self-processes

cerebral cortex
The wrinkled-looking outer layer of the brain that coordinates and integrates all other brain areas into a fully functioning unit; the brain's "thinking" center, much larger in humans than in other animals

of movement and higher mental processes, such as planning, social skills, and abstract thinking. Recent brain-imaging studies indicate that a region in the frontal lobe of the cerebral cortex, called the *anterior cingulate cortex*, is especially active when people are self-aware (Vanhaudenhuyse et al., 2011). The anterior cingulate cortex contains a special type of brain cells or neurons, called *spindle neurons*, which are much larger than other neurons in the brain. These spindle neurons collect waves of neural signals from one region of the brain and send them on to other regions. It appears that the anterior cingulate cortex with its spindle neurons acts as an executive attention system, facilitating self-awareness (Apps & Tsakiris, 2013). Humans are one of only a few species of animals that possess spindle neurons. Additional research indicates that when people are trying to exert self-control over their own thinking and behavior, the anterior cingulate cortex is also actively working in concert with areas in the prefrontal lobe regions (like the *dorsolateral prefrontal cortex* and *orbitofrontal cortex*).

FIGURE 1.3   Brain Regions in the Frontal Lobe Associated with Self Processes

The primary neural source for self-awareness is the frontal lobe of the cerebral cortex, which is the wrinkled-looking front outer layer of the brain. The frontal lobe is involved in the coordination of movement and higher mental processes, such as planning, social skills, and abstract thinking. A region in the frontal lobe, the anterior cingulate cortex, is especially active when people are self-aware.

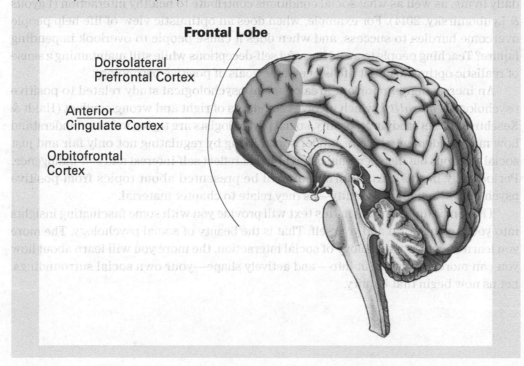

A natural question for you to ask at this point in the discussion of social neuroscience is why such knowledge is important in gaining insight into social interaction (Halpern, 2017). The importance of social neuroscience for social psychology is not that research in this area will reveal the location in the brain of the self, romantic love, or any other topic in social psychology. Instead, its potential power is that it might help social psychologists understand which cognitive processes and motivational states play a role in specific social behaviors. That sort of knowledge is vitally important because the topics in social psychology are often very complex, with competing theories trying to adequately explain the complexity. If social neuroscience's "window into the brain" can identify what type of neural activity is associated with specific types of social thinking and behavior, it will be that much easier to rule out competing explanations. In this way, the neuroscientific perspective provides another layer of knowledge in our understanding of social interaction.

In this text, we discuss some of the findings in this new area of research. For example, when discussing self-awareness and self-regulation (Chapter 3), we examine how the anterior cingulate cortex facilitates the monitoring and controlling of intentional behavior and focused problem solving. Similarly, when discussing attitude formation and change (Chapter 5), we analyze how one brain region engages in an immediate primitive "good-bad" emotional assessment that may be followed by higher-order processing conducted in the brain's cerebral cortex.

1.2f Positive Psychology Is an Emerging Perspective in Social Psychology.

Another psychological perspective that has become increasingly influential within social psychology and the larger discipline of psychology is **positive psychology**, which studies ways to enrich human experience and maximize human functioning (Peterson et al., 2013; Seligman, 2011). Social psychologists who identify themselves as proponents of positive psychology are currently studying what makes people happy and optimistic in their daily living, as well as what social conditions contribute to healthy interaction (Layous & Lyubomirsky, 2014). For example, when does an optimistic view of life help people overcome hurdles to success, and when does it cause people to overlook impending failure? Teaching people to avoid harmful self-deceptions while still maintaining a sense of realistic optimism about life is one of the goals of positive psychology.

An increasingly important area of social psychological study related to positive psychology is *morality*, which involves standards of right and wrong conduct (Haidt & Kesebir, 2010). In studying morality, social psychologists are trying to better understand how moral judgments help or hinder social living by regulating not only fair and just social relations but also personal behaviors that reflect self-interest and self-indulgence. Periodically in this text, information will be presented about topics from positive psychology—including morality—as they relate to chapter material.

The remaining chapters in this text will provide you with some fascinating insights into your social world and yourself. That is the beauty of social psychology. The more you learn about the psychology of social interaction, the more you will learn about how you can more effectively fit into—and actively shape—your own social surroundings. Let us now begin that inquiry.

positive psychology
An approach to psychology that studies ways to enrich human experience and maximize human functioning

Some Milestones in the Field of Social Psychology

1862–1894: **Dawning of a Scientific Discipline**

1862: German psychologist Wilhelm Wundt proposes that psychology establish human or social sciences (*Geistesissenschaften*) to study the higher mental processes involving language, social practices and customs, religion, and art.

("Wundt research group," circa 1880," public domain via Wikimedia)

1895–1935: **The Early Years**

1897: Norman Triplett publishes the first scientific study of social behavior, on a topic that was later called *social facilitation*.

1900: Wundt publishes the first volume of what would become a classic 10-volume set of *Völkerpsychologie* (folk or social psychology), which analyzes a wide variety of social thought and behavior.

1908: Psychologist William McDougall and sociologist Edward Ross separately publish social psychology textbooks.

1920: Willy Hellpach founds the first institute for social psychology in Germany. Adolf Hitler's rise to power leads to the institute's demise in 1933.

(Shutterstock)

1924: Floyd Allport publishes the third social psychology text, clearly identifying the focus for the psychological branch of the discipline and covering many topics that are still studied today.

1925: Emory Bogardus develops the social distance scale to measure attitudes toward ethnic groups. Soon after Louis Thurstone (1928) and Rensis Likert (1932) further advance attitude scale development.

1934: George Herbert Mead's book *Mind, Self, and Society* is published, stressing the interaction between the self and others.

("Adolf Hitler, cropped, restored," circa 1937, from the German Federal Archives under a CC by SA 3.0 Germany license via Wikimedia)

1936–1969: **Coming of Age**

1936: The Society for the Psychological Study of Social Issues is founded. Muzafir Sherif publishes *The Psychology of Social Norms*, describing research on norm formation.

1939: John Dollard and his colleagues introduce the frustration-aggression hypothesis.

1941–1945: Social psychologists are recruited by the US government for the war effort.

1949: Carl Hovland and his colleagues publish their first experiments on attitude change and persuasion.

1950: Theodor Adorno and his colleagues publish *The Authoritarian Personality*, which examines how extreme prejudice can be shaped by personality conflicts in childhood.

1951: Solomon Asch demonstrates conformity to false majority judgments.

1954: Gordon Allport publishes *The Nature of Prejudice*, which provides the framework for much of the future research on prejudice. Social psychologists provide key testimony in the U.S. Supreme Court desegregation case, *Brown v. Board of Education*.

1957: Leon Festinger publishes *A Theory of Cognitive Dissonance*, emphasizing the need for consistency between cognition and behavior.

1958: Fritz Heider publishes *The Psychology of Interpersonal Relations*, laying the groundwork for attribution theory.

1963: Stanley Milgram publishes his obedience research, demonstrating under what conditions people are likely to obey destructive authority figures.

1965: The Society of Experimental Social Psychology is founded. Edward Jones and Keith Davis publish their ideas on social perception, stimulating attribution, and social cognition research.

(State Library and Archives of Florida, circa 1963, via Wikimedia)

1966: The European Association of Experimental Social Psychology is founded. Elaine (Walster) Hatfield and her colleagues publish the first studies of romantic attraction.

1968: John Darley and Bibb Latané present the bystander intervention model, explaining why people often do not help in emergencies.

(continues)

Some Milestones in the Field of Social Psychology *(continued)*

1970–Present: Becoming a More Inclusive and Self-Critical Science

1972:   *Attribution: Perceiving the Causes of Behavior*, written by six influential attribution theorists, is published. Robert Wicklund and Shelley Duval publish *Objective Self-Awareness Theory*, describing how self-awareness influences cognition and behavior.

(Floyd Allport: Courtesy Floyd Henry Allport Papers, University Archives, Special Collections Research Center Syracuse University Libraries. Reprinted with permission.)

1974:   The Society for Personality and Social Psychology is founded. Sandra Bem develops the Bem Sex Role Inventory and Janet Spence and Robert Helmreich develop the Personal Attributes Questionnaire, both of which measure gender roles.

1981:   Alice Eagly and her colleagues begin conducting meta-analyses of gender comparisons in social behavior, reopening the debate on gender differences.

1984:   Susan Fiske and Shelley Taylor publish *Social Cognition*, summarizing theory and research on the social cognitive perspective in social psychology.

1986:   Richard Petty and John Cacioppo publish *Communication and Persuasion: Central and Peripheral Routes*, describing a dual-process model of persuasion.

1989:   Jennifer Crocker and Brenda Major publish their *Psychological Review* article on "Social Stigma and Self-Esteem," examining how people respond to being the targets of discrimination. Susan Fiske provides key testimony in the U.S. Supreme Court gender discrimination case, *Price Waterhouse v. Hopkins*.

("Egyptian waving flag on Qasr al Nil," by Sherif9282, available under a CC by SA 3.0 license via Wikimedia)

1991:   Hazel Markus and Shinobu Kitayama publish their *Psychological Review* article titled "Culture and the self: Implications for cognition, emotion, and motivation."

1995:   Claude Steele and Joshua Aronson publish "Stereotype Threat and the Intellectual Test Performance of African Americans" in the *Journal of Personality and Social Psychology*, presenting their research on how negative stereotypes can shape intellectual identity and performance.

1996:   David Buss and Neil Malamuth publish *Sex, Power, Conflict*, an edited text offering evolutionary and feminist perspectives on sex and gender interactions. A growing number of social psychologists attempt to integrate these previously divergent perspectives.

1998:   In his annual Presidential Address to the American Psychological Association, Martin Seligman calls for the scientific study of positive human functioning and flourishing. Seligman, Christopher Peterson, and Barbara Fredrickson are considered the founders of this new psychological perspective, which came to be called *positive psychology*.

2008:   Gregory Herek and Letitia Anne Peplau provide key testimony in the California State Supreme Court's ruling that barring same-sex marriage violates the state's Constitution.

2010:   An increasing number of social psychologists begin expressing concerns that some previous social psychological findings were actually *false positives*, which triggers what has been called the *replication crisis* in social psychology.

(Because the passage of time ultimately determines what events significantly shape a field, we will wait a few years before adding any more milestones to this list.)

Section Summary

- The self is a central and organizing concept in social psychology.

- Interactionism studies the combined effects of both the situation and the person on human behavior.

- Many contemporary social cognitive theories attempt to reconcile the "hot" and the "cold" perspectives of human nature into a more inclusive "warm look."

- Social psychologists have become more attentive to cultural influences on social behavior.

- The cultural variables of individualism and collectivism are particularly helpful in understanding cultural differences.

- Evolutionary theory is increasingly used to explain social behavior.

- In explaining any male–female differences in social behavior, the evolutionary perspective emphasizes biological factors, and the sociocultural perspective emphasizes cultural factors.

- Integrating ideas from neuroscience into social psychology is becoming more a part of social psychological research and theory.

- Understanding how life can be enriched is one goal of positive psychology, an emerging perspective in social psychology.

■ KEY TERMS

■ WEBSITES

Accessed through https://www.bvtlab.com/sop8

Websites for this chapter include the largest social psychology organization and internet database in the world, as well as national survey results for young American adults and information on the evolutionary perspective.

Social Psychology Network
This is the largest social psychology database on the internet, with more than 5,000 links to psychology-related resources.

Society for Personality and Social Psychology Home Page
This is the website for the largest organization of social and personality psychologists in the world. This organization was founded in 1974.

Pew Research Center
This is the website for the national survey results of the 2007 report "How Young People View Their Lives, Future, and Politics: A Portrait of Generation Next."

Evolutionary Psychology for the Common Person
This website provides an introduction to evolutionary psychology and provides links to other related web resources.

Chapter 2

Conducting Research in Social Psychology

FOCUS QUESTIONS

1. What is the difference between basic research and applied research?

2. What is the purpose of institutional review boards on university campuses where research is conducted using human participants?

3. What does it mean when someone says, "Correlation does not mean causation"?

4. Is it possible to design a study to have strong internal and external validity?

5. What is the value of replicating research?

CHAPTER OUTLINE

Introduction

It's common to see news stories covering social psychological research, because the topics that social psychologists investigate are interesting to everyone, not just other psychologists. Consider these research findings that gained wide media attention over the past decade: Being reminded of Saint Nicholas (aka, Santa Claus) increases sharing in children. Messy environments trigger stereotyping and discrimination by people. Upon marrying, women who change their names are perceived as less competent and are offered lower salaries than women who do not change their names.

Doesn't this research sound fascinating? It certainly grabbed the attention of social psychologists and the general public because it seemed to offer surprising insights into human behavior. Unfortunately, all of the above research is based on the falsified and fabricated data of one social psychologist named Diederik Stapel (Levelt Committee et al., 2012). At the time, Stapel was a highly regarded university professor who was publishing his research in top-tier scientific journals. His fraud was exposed only after three of his doctoral students became suspicious and alerted others about their concerns (Stroebe et al., 2012). A subsequent official review (Levelt Committee et al., 2012) found that, for over a decade, Stapel had published his research and secured valuable grant money and media attention by either fabricating (making up) or manipulating his data to achieve the results he desired. A shocking number of his articles (more than 50) were retracted (removed) from publication for being fraudulent around the time that he was investigated, and some retractions came later (Retraction Watch, 2015). Not surprisingly, as a result of the uncovered research fraud, Stapel was fired from his university position and he voluntarily relinquished his doctorate.

The Stapel scandal came at the height of the replication crisis discussed in Chapter 1 and highlighted the concerns about the integrity of published, peer-reviewed research. Fortunately, social psychology does not involve clinical trials so there was no harm inflicted on patients in treatment, which has periodically occurred with fraudulent or unethical studies in the medical and health fields. However, Stapel's case did highlight the need for the discipline to reevaluate its research methods and publication process. Of course, research fraud is not unique to social psychology, and thankfully, it is infrequent. Across scientific disciplines it is estimated that some type of misconduct occurs in 1.5% of research studies, with the majority of the misconduct involving falsified or fabricated data (Stroebe et al., 2012). Psychology is not especially prone to research fraud; indeed, a review suggests that such misconduct is more likely to occur in the biomedical fields (Stroebe et al., 2012). Yet despite its infrequency, given the media attention and public fascination with social psychological findings, these fraud cases grab our attention and add to criticisms of the field.

One of the takeaway lessons of the Stapel case is that both social psychologists and students of social psychology need to be actively engaged in critically analyzing the research that is presented to them. Recall, it was Stapel's own students who first raised concerns about his previously published studies, which demonstrates the important role that bystanders can play when they notice that something is amiss in their surroundings (see Chapter 12, section 12.2, regarding the topic of bystander intervention). In the final Stapel investigation report (2012), it was noted that there had been ample warning signs about his research, such as identical data across studies, odd statistical impossibilities or errors, findings that too perfectly confirmed hypotheses, and incomplete reporting of research methods. To guard against future fraud and properly identify weaknesses in all research studies that we encounter, we must inform ourselves about research methodology and teach ourselves to be critical thinkers.

Scientific discovery is essentially a form of human problem-solving. The type of problem-solving that occurs in scientific enterprises is highly valued because it enhances our ability to understand, predict, and control the forces that shape our physical and social world. With that thought in mind, in this chapter we will review the most common scientific methods that social psychologists use in their research, as well as how the research process is enhanced by replication, meta-analysis, and improved statistical procedures.

2.1   The Goals and Process of Research

The **scientific method** consists of a set of procedures used to gather, analyze, and interpret information in a way that reduces error and leads to dependable generalizations. This method has been practiced in some form across various disciplines for at least 1,000 years. In comparison to other sciences, social psychology is very young, with just a little over a century of experience using scientific methods. Yet social psychology shares with its sister sciences the same underlying goals in conducting research, and it follows the same basic process in executing the scientific method.

2.1a   Two Research Goals Focus on Acquiring and Applying Knowledge.

Social psychologists conduct both basic and applied research. The goal of **basic research** is simply to increase knowledge about social behavior; in other words, knowledge for knowledge's sake (Fiske, 2004). No attempt is made to solve a specific social or psychological problem. In contrast, **applied research** is designed to increase the understanding of—and solutions to—real-world problems by using current social psychological knowledge (Barton et al., 2009).

Although many social psychologists label themselves as either basic or applied researchers, the efforts of one group often influence those of the other. As in other sciences, the knowledge gained through the work of basic researchers provides applied researchers with a better understanding of how to solve specific social problems. Likewise, when applied researchers cannot solve problems by employing basic research findings, such failure often suggests to basic researchers that they need to refine their theories to better reflect how the social world operates.

One important ethical question surrounding applied research is whether there should be any limits on the use of social psychological knowledge. For example, as you will see in Chapters 5 and 7, basic research has taught us a great deal about the conditions under which people become susceptible to persuasion and influence. Social influence theories could be utilized to help the tobacco industry persuade consumers to purchase their products, which are known to cause serious, long-term health problems. These same theories could also be used to design television, radio, and magazine ads to convince people *not* to use tobacco products. Although most of us would have few qualms about social psychological theory being used to prevent people from consuming products known to cause serious health problems, there would be grave reservations expressed about using these theories to encourage such consumption.

These very concerns have stirred considerable debate about the proper role that social psychologists should play in applying their knowledge in the world (Unger, 2011). One point of view is that the discoveries of any science should be used for the purposes any interested parties consider important. In such endeavors, scientists should be neutral truth-seekers and should not be concerned about how their discoveries are utilized. Followers of this *value-free* perspective believe that social psychologists who use the facts of their science to influence social policy decisions undermine the scientific basis of the discipline (Hammond, 2004). A second point of view, first proposed by Kurt Lewin in the 1940s, is that social science and social action should not be separated. Contemporary followers of this *value-laden* perspective believe that merely studying society and its problems without a commitment to changing society for the better is irresponsible (Álvarez, 2001).

A commonly accepted belief within the philosophy of science is that no science is untouched by the values and politics of the culture in which it is practiced (Harris, 1999). In social psychology, the things studied matter a great deal to people—including those

scientific method
A set of procedures used to gather, analyze, and interpret information in a way that reduces error and leads to dependable generalizations

basic research
Research designed to increase knowledge about social behavior

applied research
Research designed to increase the understanding of—and solutions to—real-world problems by using current social psychological knowledge

who do the investigating. Social psychologists are human beings, and their own values often determine what sort of research and applications they are most interested in undertaking; their values can also influence the theories they develop to explain the social facts (Redding, 2001). Sometimes social psychological theories based on different value orientations will clash, but that does not mean science grinds to a halt. Instead, scientific inquiry persists, studies are conducted and published, and new social facts are discovered. By relying upon the scientific method, social psychology will continue to contribute to our understanding of human behavior, and many of those within the discipline will also use this knowledge to make changes in their personal social worlds.

Our discussion in each chapter of this text will begin with an analysis of the findings of basic research—for as Kurt Lewin (1951) argued, it is essential to have a good understanding of psychological processes *before* trying to solve difficult social problems. Yet, in keeping with Lewin's maxim of "No research without action, and no action without research," throughout the text we will also examine how basic research is applied to important social problems. In addition, each chapter (beginning with Chapter 3) will conclude with an application section in which you can learn how the content of that chapter sheds light on a specific social or personal issue.

2.1b   The Research Process Involves a Series of Steps.

For social psychologists to effectively study social behavior—be it basic or applied research—they must carefully plan and execute their research projects (Sansone et al., 2004). This entire process of scientific inquiry unfolds in six basic steps, which are summarized in Table 2.1.

TABLE 2.1   Steps in the Process of Social Psychological Research
Step 1: Select a topic and review past research.   Ideas come from a variety of sources, including existing theories, past research, current social events, and personal experiences. Social psychologists must also become knowledgeable about past research findings in their area of interest and keep abreast of recently published studies and those reported at scientific meetings.
Step 2: Develop a theory, generate hypotheses, and select a scientific method.   Once the research literature has been digested, a theory must be developed that can be empirically tested using hypotheses that logically flow from the theory. A scientific method must also be selected that allows the hypotheses to be tested in a way that minimizes error and leads to dependable generalizations. Research can be conducted in the laboratory or in the field, and the social psychologist can employ observational, correlational, or experimental methodology.
Step 3: Obtain approval to conduct the study.   Prior to conducting research, all proposed studies must be submitted to institutional review boards (IRBs) for approval. IRBs follow guidelines based on the risk/benefit ratio, which weighs the potential risks to those participating in a study against the benefits that the study may have for advancing knowledge about humanity.
Step 4: Collect the data.   Social psychologists use both qualitative and quantitative data. The three basic techniques of data collection are self-reports, direct observations, and archival information.
Step 5: Analyze the data and reevaluate the theory.   Data can be analyzed using either descriptive or inferential statistics, with the latter mathematical analysis being the more valuable because it allows researchers to generalize their findings to the population of interest. If the results from these analyses do not support the study's hypotheses, the theory from which the hypotheses were derived needs to be reconsidered and perhaps revised.
Step 6: Report the results.   Just because a social psychologist conducts a study does not mean it will be published and make its way into the social psychological literature. In most cases, a scientific journal will not publish a submitted article if there are problems with the hypotheses or methods or flaws in the data analysis. In addition, articles are often rejected for publication because reviewers decide the research isn't very important. Due to these factors, the top journals in social psychology (*Journal of Personality and Social Psychology, Personality and Social Psychology Bulletin*) regularly publish less than 10% of the submitted research articles.

Step 1: Select a Topic and Review Past Research.

Research ideas do not develop in a vacuum. In selecting a topic to study, inspiration can come from someone else's research, from an incident in the daily news, or from some personal experience in the researcher's own life. It is not a coincidence that the research topics chosen by American social psychologists have the greatest meaning to Americans. Social psychologists generally investigate topics that have relevance to their own lives and culture.

Once a topic has been chosen, the researcher must search the scientific literature to determine whether prior investigations of the topic exist. The findings from these previous studies generally shape the course of the current investigation.

Step 2: Develop a Theory, Generate Hypotheses, and Select a Scientific Method.

Prior to conducting research, what precautions do you think social psychologists should take to ensure that the people who participate in their research will not be harmed? Should social psychologists be allowed to study people without their consent?

As previously implied, the basic motivation underlying research is the desire to answer questions. The questions of interest usually revolve around whether some phenomenon can be explained by a particular principle or theory. A **theory** is an organized system of ideas that seeks to explain how two or more events are related. Put simply, a theory provides a particular picture of reality concerning some phenomenon. What makes a good theory depends on a number of factors, some of which are listed in Table 2.2 (Higgins, 2004).

> "There is nothing so practical as a good theory."
> —Kurt Lewin, German-born social psychologist, 1890–1947

TABLE 2.2	What Makes a Good Theory?
Predictive Accuracy: Can it reliably predict behavior?	
Internal Coherence: Are there any logical inconsistencies between any of the theoretical ideas?	
Economy: Does it only contain what is necessary to explain the phenomenon in question?	
Fertile: Does it generate research, and can it be used to explain a wide variety of social behavior?	

The most important factor to the working scientist is the *predictive accuracy* of the theory: Can it reliably predict behavior? A second necessary factor is *internal coherence*; there should not be any logical inconsistencies or unexplained coincidences among any of the theoretical ideas. A third characteristic of a good theory is that it should be *economical*, meaning that it contains only the principles or concepts necessary to explain the phenomenon in question and no more. Finally, a fourth and very important quality in a good theory is whether it is fertile—the ability to fire the imagination of other scientists so that the ideas in the theory are tested and extended to a wide variety of social behavior.

The way that scientists determine the predictive accuracy of a theory is by formulating hypotheses. A **hypothesis** is an educated guess or prediction about the nature of things based upon a theory—it is a logical implication of the theory. The researcher asks, "If the theory is true, what observations should we expect to make in our investigation?" For example, as we noted in Chapter 1, positive psychology is an emerging perspective in psychology. One fascinating area of research asks the question, "What makes people happy?" (which is a nice change from asking why people are unhappy!) (Myers & Diener, 2018). One theoretical perspective is that engaging in activities that people find meaningful and engaging will promote happiness (Csikszentmihalyi, 1997; Diehl et

theory
An organized system of ideas that seeks to explain why two or more events are related

hypothesis
An educated guess or prediction about the nature of things based upon a theory

(Shutterstock)

What factors can lead to personal happiness?

al., 2016). Based on this theory, we could hypothesize that after engaging in a meaningful activity, such as church attendance or a hobby, people should report increased happiness.

After developing a theory and then formulating hypotheses consistent with that theory, researchers must next select a scientific method that allows the hypotheses to be tested in a way that minimizes error and leads to dependable generalizations. The three primary scientific methods used by social psychologists are *observational, correlational,* and *experimental.* Whereas observational research involves describing behavior, correlational and experimental methods involve studying the relationships among variables. Of the three, experimentation is much more widely used by social psychologists in psychology; observational studies are more often conducted by sociological social psychologists; and correlational methods enjoy roughly equal popularity in both disciplines. We will discuss these three methods in the next section of the chapter.

In all scientific methods, social psychologists seek to determine the nature of the relationship between two or more factors, called **variables** because they are things that can be measured and that are capable of changing. When scientists describe their variables, they do so using *operational definitions*. An **operational definition** is a very clear description of how a variable in a study has been measured. For example, one method of assessing a person's happiness is to simply ask people if they are "very happy, pretty happy, or not too happy" (Myers & Diener, 2018). Others might operationally define happiness by counting the number of positive words a person uses to describe how they are feeling. These concrete definitions help other social psychologists know exactly what was measured and allows them to repeat the study if desired.

Step 3: Obtain Approval to Conduct the Study.

Although careful attention to a study's methodology is essential in any scientific investigation, even more important is the safety and psychological security of the research participants (Moyer, 2013; Nagy, 2011). In the 1960s and 1970s, the issue of research ethics was uppermost in the minds of social psychologists because of a few controversial studies that appeared to put participants at risk for psychological harm (Milgram, 1963; Zimbardo, 1972). The most controversial of these studies were Stanley Milgram's obedience experiments, in which volunteers agreed to act as teachers in a learning experiment that in actuality was a study of obedience. During the course of the experiment, the "teachers" were ordered to deliver seemingly painful electrical shocks to a person merely because he was not performing well on a memory task. Even when the victim screamed in agony and demanded to be released, the experimenter insisted that the teacher continue delivering the shocks. In reality, no shocks were ever delivered—the victim only pretended to be in pain—but the stress experienced by the participants in their role as teacher/torturer was indeed real. Despite the fact that this study and others of its kind asked important questions about social behavior that remain relevant today, serious concerns were raised by some social scientists about whether the significance of the research topics justified exposing participants to potentially harmful psychological consequences (Baumrind, 1964; Savin, 1973).

Although unlikely, the psychological harm that could occur in such studies can take many forms. For example, to conduct his obedience studies, Milgram had to use

variables
Factors in scientific research that can be measured and that are capable of changing (varying)

operational definition
A very clear description of how a variable in a study has been measured

deception—a methodological technique in which the researcher misinforms participants about the true nature of what they are experiencing in a study. Deception is used to increase the likelihood that participants' responses are as close as possible to the responses of people in real-world settings—where the topic of study naturally occurs.

There are two main forms of deception in research. One form of deception involves not fully disclosing the true nature of the study until it is over. For example, participants in Milgram's study were told they were involved in a learning experiment but later discovered that the study was actually investigating obedience. If Milgram's participants had been fully informed about the study's purpose, this knowledge very likely would have caused them to act differently. A second form of deception involves exposing participants to a trained member of the research team, called a **confederate**, who follows a script designed to give participants a particular impression about what is going on. In the obedience study, the person who was supposedly receiving the electrical shocks was the confederate. By their nature, confederates misinform participants about the true nature of what they are experiencing.

If you were a member of your college's institutional review board and a research proposal similar to the Milgram obedience study was submitted for approval, what questions would you ask to determine its risk/benefit ratio? Based on your assessment, would you approve the study?

Researchers should use deception cautiously because it can lead participants to lose trust in social scientists if the participants believe the researcher abused them in the course of the investigation. Beyond the possible loss of trust, placing participants in situations where they are encouraged (sometimes through coercion) to engage in antisocial activities may induce feelings of guilt, shame, or inferiority. Although this type of reaction is possible, little empirical evidence indicates that this is typically the case. In Milgram's (1963) obedience research, for example, only 1.3% of those who participated reported any negative feelings about their experiences, and 84% were glad to have participated.

Other studies employing deception have found that the majority of participants are not bothered by subterfuge (Epley & Huff, 1998). Yet even though the incidence of negative consequences to research participation appears to be quite low, social psychologists must be sensitive to the effects such studies can have on individuals' views of themselves and on the discipline of social psychology. Ignoring these potentially negative effects may lead to a "participant beware" atmosphere surrounding social psychological research; such a development would be harmful to all concerned (Elms, 1994).

Spurred by the debate surrounding these issues, in 1974, the US government developed regulations requiring all institutions seeking federal funding to establish **institutional review boards (IRBs)** for research involving human participants (there are also comparable IRBs for studies using nonhuman subjects). These reviewing bodies—which are composed of scientists, medical professionals, clergy, and other community members—make sure that the welfare of human participants is protected (Hantke, 2013; Wolf, 2010). The American Psychological Association subsequently released detailed guidelines on the conduct of research with human participants, focusing on the *risk/benefit ratio*, which weighs the potential risks to those participating in a study against the benefits that the study may have for advancing knowledge about humanity. In assessing proposed studies, priority is always given to the welfare of the participants over any potential benefits of the research.

In addition to assessing risks and benefits, the guidelines for conducting research with human participants also urge scientists to do the following (Pope, 2013; Williams-Jones et al., 2013):

1. Provide adequate information about the research to potential participants, so they can freely decide whether they want to take part. This procedure is known as **informed consent**.

deception
A methodological technique in which the researcher misinforms participants about the true nature of what they are experiencing in a study

confederate
A trained member of the research team who follows a script designed to give participants a particular impression about what is going on

institutional review boards (IRBs)
A panel of scientists and nonscientists who ensure the protection and welfare of research participants by formally reviewing researchers' methodologies and procedures prior to data collection

informed consent
A procedure by which people freely choose to participate in a study only after they are told about the activities they will perform

2. Be truthful whenever possible. Deception should be used only when absolutely necessary and when adequate debriefing is provided.

3. Allow participants the *right to decline* to be a part of the study or to discontinue their participation at any point without this decision resulting in any negative consequences (for example, not receiving full payment for their participation).

4. *Protect participants* from both physical and psychological harm.

5. Ensure that any information provided by individual participants is kept *confidential.*

6. After the study, explain all aspects of the research, attempt to answer all questions, and resolve any negative feelings participants may have. Make sure they realize that their participation contributes to better scientific understanding. **Debriefing** individuals after they complete their participation is very important.

7. Provide participants with information on the results of the research if they request it.

As it now stands, participating in social psychological research is a very low-risk activity, despite the fact that deception is often incorporated into research designs. When treated with respect and dignity, individuals generally come away from the research experience feeling enriched—even if they were initially deceived about its true nature (Christensen, 1988).

Step 4: Collect the Data.

Once the IRB has granted approval, it is time to collect data from your sample. A **sample** is a relatively small group of people who are selected to participate in a given study. The people who are selected to participate in the study come from a **population**, which consists of all the members of an identifiable group from which a sample is drawn. For example, in an investigation of happiness, Hal Hershfield and his coworkers (2016) conducted two studies: the first study consisted of 1,301 people who completed a questionnaire online and in the second study 535 people completed the same questionnaire on paper at an East Coast train station. In both studies participants were asked if they would like to have more time or more money. The researchers found that the participants in both studies who stated they would like more time were happier than participants who stated they would like more money, and this finding was consistent even when controlling for participants' objective amounts of money and time. This suggests that money might not be a strong driver of personal happiness. Keep in mind that while the online participants and the East Coast traveler participants comprised the study's *samples*, the *population* that the researchers sought to generalize their results to was adults in the US. The more similar a sample is to a population, the greater confidence researchers have in generalizing their findings. That is, we might wonder if the findings of East Coast travelers (who perhaps are feeling rushed for time) are consistent with the broader population of people. The fact that the two samples (travelers and an online group of individuals) had similar findings increases our confidence that the conclusions are not unique to one group. However, as we will mention later in this chapter, ideally we would prefer to have a sample that is entirely representative of the population (US adults).

Regarding the data collected from your sample of participants, there are two broad categories: *qualitative* and *quantitative.* Qualitative data exists in a nonnumeric form. For example, Hershfield and his colleagues (2016) asked participants in a third study to explain why they chose money or time. This narrative explanation is qualitative data. In contrast, quantitative data is numerical. A scientist collecting this type of data, might have people report their level of happiness on a numerical scale in which "1" indicates

debriefing
A procedure at the conclusion of a research session in which participants are given full information about the nature and hypotheses of the study

sample
A group of people who are selected to participate in a research study

population
All the members of an identifiable group from which a sample is drawn

"very unhappy" and "5" indicates "very happy." As this example suggests, researchers often collect both qualitative and quantitative data in the same study.

Besides data categories, there are three basic techniques for data collection in social psychology: (1) *self-reports*, (2) *direct observations*, and (3) *archival information*. Collecting data using self-reports allows researchers to measure important subjective states, such as people's perceptions, emotions, or attitudes. *Self/Social Connection Exercise 2.1* provides an example of a commonly used self-report scale in social psychology. The disadvantage of self-report data, however, is that it relies on people accurately describing these internal states—something they are not always willing or able to do (Mathie & Wakeling, 2011). Because of this drawback, many researchers prefer to directly observe people's behavior, recording its quantity and direction of change over time.

Self/Social Connection Exercise 2.1

How Is Self-Esteem Measured Using a Self-Report?

The Rosenberg Self-Esteem Scale (Rosenberg, 1965) is the most widely used self-reporting measure of self-esteem, and it has been translated into many different languages.

Instructions

Read each item below and then indicate the degree to which you agree or disagree using the following response scale:

1 strongly disagree   **3** agree
2 disagree   **4** strongly agree

1. On the whole, I am satisfied with myself.
2. At times I think I am no good at all.*
3. I feel that I have a number of good qualities.
4. I am able to do things as well as most other people.
5. I feel I do not have much to be proud of.*
6. I certainly feel useless at times.*
7. I feel that I'm a person of worth, at least on an equal plane with others.
8. I wish I could have more respect for myself.*
9. All in all, I am inclined to feel that I am a failure.*
10. I take a positive attitude toward myself.

Directions for Scoring

Half of the self-esteem items are reverse-scored; that is, for these items a lower rating actually indicates a higher level of self-esteem. Before summing all 10 items to find out your total self-esteem score, recode those with an asterisk ("*") so that 1 = 4, 2 = 3, 3 = 2, and 4 = 1. Your total self-esteem score can range from 10 to 40, with a higher score indicating a higher level of self-esteem. Scores greater than 25 indicate generally positive attitudes toward the self; those below 25 indicate generally negative self-attitudes.

This technique is widely employed in observational and experimental studies. Finally, researchers sometimes examine existing documents, or archives, to gather information. These accumulated records come from a wide variety of sources (for example, census information, court records, newspaper articles, social media pages, or Twitter) and can provide researchers with a great deal of valuable information (Murphy, 2017; Simonton, 1998). These three ways of collecting information are not always mutually exclusive. For example, the personal memoirs of historical figures represent both self-report and archived data.

Step 5: Analyze the Data and Reevaluate the Theory.

Once the data have been collected, the first part of the fifth step is to conduct data analysis, which usually requires extensive knowledge of statistical procedures and computer software packages. The two basic kinds of statistics are descriptive and inferential. *Descriptive statistics* merely summarize and describe the behavior or characteristics of a particular sample of participants in a study, whereas *inferential statistics* move beyond mere description to make generalizations about the larger population from which the sample was drawn. Inferential statistics are used to estimate the likelihood that a difference found in the people studied would also be found if everyone in the population participated in the study. Social psychologists generally accept a difference as *statistically significant* if the likelihood of it having occurred by mere chance is less than 1 in 20—that is, a probability of less than 5% (McGrath, 2011). Because one of the main objectives of social psychological research is to generalize research findings to the population of interest, inferential statistics are the more valued type of statistic in the discipline.

In addition, current best practices of data analysis recommend that researchers report not only a test of statistical significance, but also report the **effect size** of the phenomenon in question. An effect size is a quantitative measure of the magnitude of the difference between two groups. For example, if a researcher finds that there is a statistically significant difference between two groups, then we know that the difference between the means of the two groups is larger than what you would expect due to chance. However, it doesn't tell us *how much* of a difference there is between the two groups. One common measure of effect size is *Cohen's d*, which indicates the standardized distance between two groups. If Cohen's d is between 0 and .10, this indicates that there really is no meaningful difference between the groups, even if their means have a statistically significant difference. In contrast, a Cohen's d between .11 and .35 reflects a small difference, a Cohen's d between .36 and .65 reflects a moderate difference, and a Cohen's d above .65+ indicates a large difference between the groups.

In the previously discussed research of happiness (Hershfield et al., 2016), we learned that people who would rather have more time than money are significantly happier than people who pick money over time. More importantly, the Cohen d effect size was .37 (study 2), which suggests that the difference in happiness between the two groups was moderate. Effect sizes have become increasingly important in estimating the actual impact that variables under study are likely to have in real-world settings.

"Science has to be understood in its broadest sense, as a method for comprehending all observable reality, and not merely as an instrument for acquiring specialized knowledge."

—Alexis Carrel, French-American surgeon and Nobel Prize winner for medicine, 1873–1944

After data analysis determines whether the hypotheses successfully predicted the outcome of the study, researchers next reevaluate the theory. Were the research hypotheses supported by the data, which thereby supports the validity of the theory? If the data do not support the study's hypotheses, or if only some of the hypotheses are supported, the theory probably needs revising.

effect size
A quantitative measure of the magnitude of the difference between two groups.

Step 6: Report the Results.

As in any scholarly pursuit, for advancements to be made, researchers must share their knowledge with others in the field. This is accomplished by publishing articles in scientific journals, making presentations at professional meetings, or personally informing other researchers. Through such sharing, researchers build upon and refine one another's work, and our understanding of social behavior is enriched.

This final step in the research process is a very important one for the advancement of the discipline. However, others do not uncritically accept these findings. At scientific conventions, where research is often first reported, all steps in the research process are scrutinized, and the study's strengths and weaknesses are illuminated.

When a written report of the study is later submitted to a scientific journal, it is reviewed to determine whether it should be published. So throughout this process of scientific inquiry, there are numerous checks and balances that ultimately determine whether a research project will make its way into the discipline's body of knowledge. As we saw with the Stapel case, sometimes this process fails to catch fraudulent or problematic research. Fortunately, one outcome of that scandal is that an increasing number of scientific journals now require researchers to provide their raw data to external reviewers when submitting their articles for publication, and an increasing number of researchers are voluntarily sharing their data with other researchers once their studies are published (Lindsay, 2017). This heightened vigilance serves to strengthen the scientific discipline of social psychology and the confidence we and the public have for published findings. Indeed, a review of social psychological studies found that the most recently published articles used more robust scientific procedures and practices than articles published a decade ago (Motyl et al., 2017). Our next section will examine those procedures and practices.

Imagine that you are the leader of a team of researchers studying social psychological topics at a university. Under your tutelage, students are learning about the research process while working on your team. Besides instructing them on the proper scientific methods, statistical procedures, and ethical standards to adopt when conducting research, what advice would you give them concerning how they should approach scientific problems in their work?

Section Summary

- Social psychologists conduct both basic and applied research.
- The research process unfolds in sequential steps involving theory building and theory testing.

2.2 Common Scientific Methods

Social psychologists can choose from among a variety of scientific methods. The three most prominent research approaches used in social psychology are observational, correlational, and experimental designs.

"Observation, not old age, brings wisdom."
—Publilius Syrus, ca. 42 BCE

2.2a Description Is the Goal of Observational Research.

In order to understand behavior—so that it can be predicted, controlled, or explained—a scientist must first describe it accurately. **Observational research** is a scientific method involving systematic qualitative and/or quantitative descriptions of behavior. In collecting the data, the scientific observer tries not to manipulate (that is, change)

observational research
A scientific method involving systematic qualitative and/or quantitative descriptions of behavior

the behavior under study—and instead simply records it. Description is the primary goal here. Three common observational methods employed by social psychologists are naturalistic observation, participant observation, and archival research.

Naturalistic Observation

Naturalistic observation is a descriptive method that investigates behavior in its natural environment (Mehl & Conner, 2012). Observation and the recording of behavior sometimes occur over a prolonged period. Settings for such social psychological research could include sporting events, where interactions between opposing fans might be recorded, or neighborhood shopping malls, where the courtship behavior of adolescents might be documented. In studying childhood aggression or social rejection in playgroups, researchers might carefully document students' activities on school playgrounds during recess periods. In such naturalistic settings, observers usually remain as unobtrusive as possible, so that their presence does not influence the behavior under study. In some studies, researchers are not present at all during data collection—hidden video cameras record the events. Later, researchers analyze the behaviors being investigated (Pomerantz et al., 2004). Besides employing naturalistic observation as a primary scientific method, researchers often use it during the initial stages of a project to generate ideas and to gather descriptive data.

One example of a naturalistic observation study was Robert Levine and Ara Norenzayan's (1999) analysis of the pace of everyday life in 31 cultures. Some of the data they collected were measurements of people's average walking speed on city sidewalks, postal clerks' speed in responding to simple requests, and the accuracy of clocks in public settings. Notice that these measurements simply involved the researchers observing how people behaved in their natural surroundings. Their findings indicated that the pace of life was faster in colder and more economically productive cultures (such as Switzerland and Japan) than in those that were hotter and less economically energetic (such as Mexico and Indonesia). Based on these observations, the researchers suggested that the difficulty of working in hot temperatures might explain the slower-paced life in certain cultures around the world.

Robert Levine and Ara Norenzayan analyzed the pace of everyday life of 31 cultures. They collected data on many different things, including the measurement of peoples' walking speed on the sidewalk.

Participant Observation

Another observational method is **participant observation**. Here, as in naturalistic observation, a researcher records behavior as it occurs in its natural environment—but as the name suggests, in participant observation, the researcher does so as a participant in the group being studied (Calzada et al., 2013; Rutherford et al., 2011). One of the chief benefits of this research strategy is that it allows investigators to get closer to what they are studying than any other method.

A classic example of participant observation research in social psychology was Leon Festinger's study of a Chicago-based doomsday cult in the 1950s (Festinger et al., 1956). The leader of the cult, Mrs. Keech, claimed she was in contact with aliens from outer space who had told her the world was going to end on a specific date: December 21. She told reporters that the only survivors of this catastrophe would be members of her group. When Festinger and his coworkers learned of Mrs. Keech, they became interested

naturalistic observation
A descriptive scientific method that investigates behavior in its natural environment

participant observation
A descriptive scientific method where a group is studied from within by a researcher who records behavior as it occurs in its usual natural environment

in documenting how the cult members would react when the doomsday passed with the world still intact. Acting quickly, these researchers infiltrated the cult as participant observers and described the interactions of the members and their leader. This descriptive study was one of the first tests of Festinger's (1957) *cognitive dissonance theory* (see Chapter 5, section 5.3a). The rich narrative accounts emerging from this participant observation research proved invaluable in demonstrating how some of the basic principles of cognitive dissonance operate in a specific—albeit unusual—situation.

Listed below are four advantages of both naturalistic and participant observation research:

1. They allow researchers the opportunity to watch behavior in its "wholeness," providing the full context in which to understand it.
2. They provide researchers the opportunity to record rare events that may never occur in a controlled laboratory environment.
3. They allow researchers the opportunity to systematically record events that were previously seen only by nonscientists.
4. They allow researchers to observe events that would be too risky, dangerous, or unethical to create in the laboratory.

Despite the numerous benefits of using naturalistic and participant observation methods, some problems also bear mentioning. First, due to the absence of control that researchers have in such studies, conclusions must be drawn cautiously. For example, if you observe that shoppers are more likely to donate money after walking out of a store rather than when walking in, do you know for certain what is causing this difference in behavior? Perhaps shoppers have more spare change after making purchases, or perhaps something in the store puts them in a giving mood. Because observational research does not manipulate events to determine their effect on outcomes, researchers must be careful when concluding how events are related to one another.

A second problem is **observer bias**, which occurs when scientists' preconceived ideas about what they are studying affect the nature of their observations. For instance, if you are investigating physical aggression or social exclusion and believe ahead of time that men are more physically aggressive than women—and/or that women are more likely than men to shun others—then you might be more likely to perceive ambiguous actions in terms of gender stereotypes. Such biasing can be minimized if the behaviors observed are carefully defined and more than one observer is trained in identifying them. If these trained observers, working independently, exhibit a high level of agreement in identifying the behaviors, then you have high *interobserver reliability*. With modern technology, researchers often videotape events for later reliability checks.

> "Every journey into the past is complicated by delusions, false memories, false namings of real events."
>
> —Adrienne Rich, US poet, 1929–2012

A third potential problem faced by naturalistic and participant observation researchers is that the researchers' presence can significantly alter the behavior of those being studied and thus taint the data. For example, in studying children's aggressive or exclusionary behavior in a playground setting, the presence of researchers may alter the children's actions. Seeing an older person nearby may cause a few children not to fight or exclude one another from play activities because they fear being punished. The danger of researchers altering participants' behavior due to their presence is especially troublesome in participant observation research, because the researchers are often actively involved in the observed events (Palmer & Thompson, 2010). Although observational researchers assume that, after a period of time, those who are being observed will become accustomed to the researchers' presence, it is difficult to evaluate to what degree this actually occurs.

observer bias
Occurs when preconceived ideas held by the researcher affect the nature of the observations made

Finally, one last problem posed by these observational methods is that, more than any other scientific method, they pose the most ethical problems involving invasion of others' privacy. This is especially true in the minority of studies in which informal consent is not feasible.

Archival Research

The third observational method that we will discuss is **archival research**, which examines already-existing records pertaining to an individual, group, or culture. Examples of archival material include diaries, music lyrics, television programs, census information, novels, newspapers, blogs, and Twitter comments. Archival research is often employed as one component in a larger research effort that includes other scientific methods. For example, in studying friendship networks in high school, a researcher might use information found on social media to evaluate students' physical attractiveness, number of friends, and involvement in school activities. This archival information might be combined with self-reports from students and teachers (collected using a survey), which are then analyzed together.

Archival research looks at existing records pertaining to an individual, group, or culture.

Social scientists regularly use the archival method to examine cultural beliefs and norms, such as how the media (TV programs, movies, magazines, social media) portrays social interactions. For example, Kelly Dillon and Elizabeth Jones (2019) examined whether contestants on competition-based reality television shows accurately reflect the population of the United States. They reviewed 635 contestants from 28 reality TV shows between the years 2000 and 2013. For each show, they recorded the participants' ethnicity, age, gender, and order of elimination from the show. The researchers found that, in their sample of shows, gender was accurately represented—that is, the proportion of men and women on the reality TV shows was approximately the same as in the US population. For ethnicity, whites were overrepresented (the proportion of white contestants was higher than the proportion of whites in the US population). However, Hispanics and multiethnic individuals were underrepresented (fewer than you would expect based on the US population) and African Americans were accurately represented. Furthermore, younger adults (age 18-44) were overrepresented, but middle aged and older adults were underrepresented compared with the US population. Interestingly, gender, age, and ethnicity were not related to when a contestant was eliminated from the show. Based on these findings, the researchers suggested that reality TV shows do not necessarily reflect the reality of the US population.

Dillon and Jones's (2019) archival study of reality TV shows involved analyzing the demographic characteristics of contestants using *content analysis*, a technique in which two or more people (called judges)—working independently—count images, words, sentences, ideas, or whatever other category of information is of interest. As with all scientific inquiry, it is important to clearly define the research variables before beginning a content analysis. It is also important that the judges are carefully trained so that they consistently follow the same guidelines when coding information. If each category of information is clearly defined and if the judges are adequately trained, *interjudge reliability*—which means the same thing as interobserver reliability—should be sufficiently high to ensure that the observations are not the result of observer bias.

archival research
A descriptive scientific method in which already-existing records are examined

2.2b Correlational Research Involves Assessing the Relationship Between Variables.

Besides describing behavior, social psychologists are also interested in learning whether two or more variables are related and, if so, how strongly. When changes in one variable relate to changes in another variable, we say that they *correlate*. **Correlational research** assesses the nature of the relationship between two or more variables that are not controlled by the researcher. For example, in studying the relationship between adults' happiness and money, researchers using the correlational method do not try to influence the participants' financial wealth. Instead, they merely gather information on the amount of money the participants have (perhaps by collecting information on annual income) and self-reported happiness, and then determine how these two variables correlate.

Surveys

Studying the relationships among variables is often accomplished by asking people carefully constructed questions in **surveys**, which are structured sets of questions or statements given to a group of people to measure their attitudes, beliefs, values, or behavioral tendencies (Schuman, 2002). The four major survey techniques are *face-to-face*, *written*, *phone*, and *computer*. The face-to-face format provides highly detailed information and allows researchers the best opportunity to clarify any unclear questions. However, it is costly and there is always the possibility that people's responses might be influenced by the interviewer's presence. Written, phone, and computer surveys eliminate such interviewer bias and are much less expensive. Although obtaining information using surveys is generally relatively easy, the main disadvantage in all four techniques is that they rely on self-report data.

For many years social psychologists have realized that research participants are often unwilling or unable to accurately assess their thoughts and feelings using standard self-report measures. **Social desirability bias** occurs when people respond to survey questions by trying to portray themselves in a favorable light rather than responding in an accurate and truthful manner. Over the years, researchers have discovered that people exaggerate their tendency to engage in such socially desirable behaviors as attending religious services and voting, while underreporting their socially undesirable actions, such as taking illegal drugs or evading taxes (Krosnick, 1999). On the more positive side, it is heartening to know that even when survey participants desire to "look good" in the researchers' eyes, they are also often concerned with the accuracy of their responses (Holtgraves, 2004).

Sometimes this inaccuracy is caused by people being unwilling to admit that they have socially undesirable thoughts and feelings—such as negative stereotypes and racist attitudes. At other times, inaccurate self-reporting can result from being honestly unaware of the unconscious thoughts and feelings that shape one's conscious perceptions and actions. As a means of overcoming such self-report problems, social psychologists have developed computer programs that are designed to tap into participants' unconscious thoughts and feelings. One common implicit or unconscious measure is the **Implicit Association Test (IAT)** (Greenwald et al., 1998) that is designed to measure the strength of automatic associations between different concepts in memory. For example, an implicit or unconscious race bias toward African Americans might be measured by first comparing how quickly participants can press computer keys to categorize pleasant words (such as *gentle* and *kind*) as "good" when these words appear on a computer screen next to black faces rather than white faces. Next, this task is reversed, with participants quickly categorizing unpleasant words (such as *rough* and

correlational research
Research designed to examine the nature of the relationship between two or more naturally occurring variables

surveys
Structured sets of questions or statements given to a group of people to measure their attitudes, beliefs, values, or behavioral tendencies

social desirability bias
A type of response bias in surveys in which people respond to a question by trying to portray themselves in a favorable light rather than responding in an accurate and truthful manner

Implicit Association Test (IAT)
A technique for measuring implicit attitudes and beliefs based on the idea that people will give faster responses to presented concepts that are more strongly associated in memory

mean) as "bad" while these words are presented next to either black or white faces. If participants take longer to categorize pleasant words as "good" when they are paired with black rather than white faces, while also taking longer to categorize unpleasant words as "bad" when they are paired with white rather than black faces, this indicates an implicit race bias. A number of studies suggest that the IAT is a better predictor of some forms of behavior, such as discrimination, than traditional self-report methods and that it is less vulnerable to faking; yet some studies question whether the implicit attitudes measured by the IAT are truly unconscious (Hahn et al., 2014). Currently, the IAT is being used in research all over the world, and we will discuss many of these studies in various chapters in this text.

One of the most important considerations in conducting surveys and other methods is getting responses from people who represent the population as a whole. This *representative sample* is often obtained through **random selection**, which is a procedure in which everyone in the population has an equal chance of being selected for the sample. As long as a sample is selected randomly, you are reasonably assured that the data will represent the overall population.

Today, major polling organizations are typically very careful in securing representative samples in order to avoid errors in generalizing their findings to the population. However, many surveys found in popular magazines or on the internet—asking for your opinions on various personal and social issues—have limited generalizability. Why? Because the results are based only on those people who read the magazine or go to the website and are sufficiently motivated to send in their opinions. The results of such nonrepresentative surveys may not provide an accurate portrayal of societal opinions.

Many social psychologists are also employing the internet as an avenue to collect data (Hine, 2013). One of the biggest advantages in using the internet is that researchers can recruit participants from all over the world and then gather data from them using online surveys. Websites are specifically designed so that researchers can post their studies and collect data, with participants receiving small payments. Advantages of the internet as a data collection site are that studies can be run without the presence of a researcher, without the need for large laboratories, or expensive equipment, and without limitations on the times of day in which the data are collected. These advantages can yield huge data sets.

Web-based studies are not without limitations, however (Heiervang & Goodman, 2011). Although the internet samples may be more diverse than using a convenience sample of college students (who are participating in the study for course credit!), in the US, internet users are more likely than the general population to be white, young, and have children. Thus, obtaining a representative sample is one of the primary concerns with internet studies. Another concern is that, because people often are paid very little money for participating in online studies, they might respond carelessly in order to quickly complete the researchers' assigned tasks. One way that researchers attempt to identify such careless responding is by carefully examining their data to ensure that participants' responses are not simply random (Buhrmester et al., 2018; Wood et al., 2017). Despite these disadvantages, research suggests that online samples typically consist of diverse participants (if not representative samples) who provide reasonably reliable and valid responses (Buhrmester et al., 2011; Peer et al., 2017). Given the advantages of internet-based research, we should expect this procedure for data collection to become more widely used by social psychologists in the future.

The internet has also greatly facilitated the ability of social psychologists to conduct cross-cultural research. However, when conducting cross-cultural surveys, researchers must be mindful of how cultural values can shape people's responses to the rating scales used for survey items. For example, Ayse Uskul and her coworkers (2013) found that survey respondents in China, Turkey, and the US, when asked to rate their own or someone else's success in life, often responded differently to survey items based on

random selection
A procedure for selecting a sample of people to study in which everyone in the population has an equal chance of being chosen

whether the rating scale ranged from "failure to success" or simply indicated "varying degrees of success" with no mention of failure. This different wording was important because China's culture highly values modesty, while Turkish culture highly values honor, and the US is a culture of positivity. Because American respondents were sensitive to the possibility of negativity, they evaluated all targets more positively than did respondents from the other two cultures when the rating scale was a continuum from "failure to success" but not when it was worded in terms of "varying degrees of success." Because of the Chinese respondents' sensitivity to modesty, in both the "failure to success" and the "varying degrees of success" rating conditions, their responses shied away from implying success for themselves, but they were not hesitant in recognizing the success of strangers. Finally, for the honor-sensitive Turkish respondents, when the rating scale ranged from "failure to success," they rated both themselves and their parents more positively than they did strangers—but not when the rating scale was worded in terms of "varying degrees of success." These findings highlight how the wording of cross-cultural surveys must take into account different cultural meanings.

The Correlation Coefficient

Regardless of how information on the relationships among variables is obtained, the primary benefit of conducting correlational research is *prediction*. This method allows researchers to predict a change in one variable by knowing the value of another variable. More specifically, it provides information on the *direction* and *strength* of the relationship between variables. The direction of the relationship between variable A and variable B tells *how* they are related (positively or negatively). The strength of the relationship can be thought of as the degree of accuracy with which you can predict the value of one variable by knowing the value of the other variable. The direction and strength of the relationship between two variables are described by the statistical measure known as the **correlation coefficient** (r). This correlation coefficient can range from –1.00 to +1.00. One can easily visualize a correlation by plotting the two variables on a scattergraph, as is illustrated in Figure 2.1. A correlation close to 0.00 would have dots scattered all around the graph, while a correlation near +1.00 would have dots lining up on an imaginary straight line running between the X and Y axes of the graph. The farther the dots on the graph fall from the imaginary straight line, the lower the correlation.

Returning to the example of happiness, many have wondered if money is associated with happiness (Myers & Diener, 2018). A positive correlation, and one that is near +1.00, would suggest that as people's income (money) increases, so does their happiness. In contrast, a negative correlation, and one that is near –1.00 would suggest that as income increases, happiness decreases. A correlation at or very near zero indicates the absence of a *linear relationship* between these two variables. This zero correlation may mean one of two things: (1) the amount of money one has is not associated with reported happiness, or (2) there is a *curvilinear relationship* between money and happiness.

Research suggests that the actual correlation between money and happiness may be curvilinear (Jebb et al., 2018). In a worldwide sample of 1.7 million people, researchers found that money is positively associated with happiness until an income of about $95,000, and then happiness levels off (no additional money increases happiness). However, the relationship between money and happiness becomes negative around $250,000, suggesting that additional wealth beyond that income point is associated with decreased happiness!

Regarding the strength of any relationship between two social variables, researchers seldom find a perfect or near perfect ($r = -1.00$ or $r = +1.00$) correlation. Certainly, many variables contribute to happiness besides financial wealth. What else might contribute to your sense of happiness? Your personality traits, physical health, the region or country where you live, and your gender and religious beliefs are all likely to be associated with your happiness. Furthermore, even if we could identify all relevant variables influencing

correlation coefficient
A statistical measure of the direction and strength of the linear relationship between two variables, which can range from –1.00 to +1.00

happiness, because of the nature of our subject—humans with self-reflective abilities and minds of their own—we would still be unable to perfectly predict people's feelings.

FIGURE 2.1   Plotting the Relationship Between Variable X and Variable Y on a Graph

Each point represents a pairing of variable X with variable Y for each participant in the study. In the curvilinear relationship graph, the zero correlation is hiding a meaningful relationship, where both high and low levels of X are associated with high levels of Y, but moderate levels of X are associated with low levels of Y. What sort of social variables might have a curvilinear relationship?

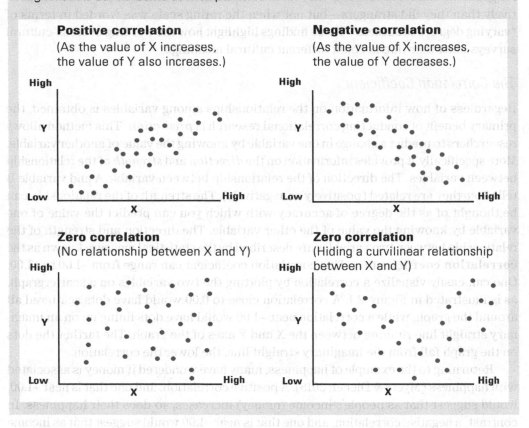

Positive correlation
(As the value of X increases, the value of Y also increases.)

Negative correlation
(As the value of X increases, the value of Y decreases.)

Zero correlation
(No relationship between X and Y)

Zero correlation
(Hiding a curvilinear relationship between X and Y)

The major disadvantage of the correlational method is that it cannot definitively determine the *cause* of the relationship between two variables. That is, beyond knowing the strength and direction of a relationship, it is extremely valuable to know which variable caused a change in the other. Does having money make someone happy, or does being happy result in a person making more money? This methodological disadvantage can result in the *reverse-causality problem*, which occurs whenever either of the two variables correlated with each other could just as plausibly be the cause or the effect.

Sometimes, when you have a significant correlation between two variables, there is only one possible causal direction. For example, a number of studies have found a strong correlation between being the victim of physical abuse as a child and being the perpetrator of family violence as an adult (Straus et al., 1980; Widom, 1989). Because a past event cannot be caused by a future event, researchers conducting these studies can be more confident in asserting that the physical abuse suffered in childhood was a likely cause of the victimization of others in adulthood.

A second problem resulting from the inability to confidently determine causality is that it is possible that a third, unspecified variable causes differences in both variables under study. This is known as the *third-variable problem*. In trying to understand the negative association between happiness and wealth that occurred for high earners, which is generally opposite of what most people expect, the researchers suggest that these high-earning individuals might be experiencing high demands, stress, and limited time to engage in activities that they previously enjoyed (Jebb et al., 2018). Can you think of other possible variables that might also explain the relationship between income and happiness?

2.2c Experimental Research Can Determine Cause-Effect Relationships.

Because correlational studies cannot definitively tell us why variables are related to one another, social psychologists use the **experimental method** to examine cause-effect relationships (Hoyle, 2005). In an experiment, the scientist manipulates one variable by exposing research participants to it at contrasting levels (for example, high, medium, low, no exposure) and then observes what effect this manipulation has on the other variable that has not been manipulated.

The variable that is manipulated is called the **independent variable**, and it is the one the experimenter is testing as the possible cause of any changes that might occur in the other variable. The **dependent variable** is the response measure of an experiment that is *dependent* on the participant's response to the experimenter's manipulation (the independent variable). Once the participants in the study have been exposed to the independent variable, their behavior is carefully monitored to determine whether it varies in the predicted fashion with different levels of the independent variable. If it does, the experimenter can tentatively conclude that the independent variable is the cause of the changes in the dependent variable.

Let's return to the question of happiness. One common finding is that people who engage in experiences that they find meaningful and engaging report more happiness (Csikszentmihalyi, 1997). Kristin Diehl and her colleagues (2016) were interested in whether people who took photographs experienced an increased enjoyment of the activity they documented. This is certainly a timely question given the numerous photos people take throughout their day and post on their social media accounts. To explore this issue, the researchers rented a tour bus that visited the same sites in Philadelphia frequented by other tour buses. On half of the tours, participants were given a camera with instructions to take photos, while on the other tours, participants were not given a camera so they had no opportunity to take any photos. The *independent variable* was whether or not they were able to take photographs. All participants had their personal belongings stored on the bottom level of the bus while they rode on the top level of the bus, ensuring that no one was able to take photos with their cell phones. After completing the tour, participants were asked to rate how much they enjoyed their experience on a scale of 1 (not at all) to 15 (extremely). This enjoyment measure was the *dependent variable* and it was expected to vary, depending on the photo condition to which the participants were assigned. As hypothesized, those who took photographs

experimental method
Research designed to test cause-effect relationships between variables

independent variable
The experimental variable that the researcher manipulates

dependent variable
The experimental variable that is measured because it is believed to depend on the manipulated changes in the independent variable

Taking photographs of an event is associated with an increase in enjoyment.

(Shutterstock)

during the tour reported enjoying it more than those who did not have the opportunity to do so. One conclusion to draw from this experiment is that visually documenting an event increases a person's enjoyment of that event.

Field Experiments

The study just described is a special type of experiment called a *field experiment*, which is similar to the more common *laboratory experiment*, except that it is run in a natural setting (Reis & Gosling, 2010). Because of this more natural atmosphere, participants tend to be less suspicious of what they are experiencing than in laboratory studies; thus, their responses tend to be more spontaneous. This greater realism increases the study's **external validity**, which is the extent to which its findings can be generalized to people beyond those in the study itself (Wilson et al., 2010). Field studies are also advantageous in that they are more likely to have diverse participants and focus on behaviors (rather than self-reported attitudes), which can increase the robustness of the findings (Maner, 2016).

Unfortunately, one drawback to field experiments is that researchers have less control over what is happening to each participant during the study because they are in a setting where many variables are uncontrollable. For example, in the previous example of photo taking on a tour bus, perhaps on one of the tours participants joked a lot and everyone had an especially good time together, while on other tours participants sat quietly without interacting. Or perhaps on other tours, some participants did not pay much attention. Another drawback to field experiments is that experimenters have less control over precisely manipulating and measuring the variables of interest. For example, even when assigned to take photos, some people might take many while others take very few. These problems of control decrease the study's **internal validity**, which is the extent to which cause-and-effect conclusions can be validly made (Edlund et al., 2014). There is often a trade-off between internal and external validity, meaning that if you strengthen one, you tend to weaken the other.

Laboratory Experiments

Most social psychology experiments, by far, are conducted in laboratories. Laboratory studies allow for a high degree of control and have stronger internal validity. For example, in their third study, Diehl and her colleagues (2016) instructed participants to watch a bus tour on a computer while in their research lab. Thus, participants were alone, with no distractions from other people or things in the environment, and the researchers knew exactly what participants observed on the tour because they all were shown the same video. In this study, half of the participants were instructed to take photos while watching the tour using a button they could click with their mouse, while the other participants did not have this option. As they found in the field study, participants who took photos reported enjoying the tour more than those who did not take photos. Furthermore, the researchers instructed participants to report their enjoyment of the tour on multiple occasions, first immediately following watching the video, then again 30 minutes later after completing two unrelated tasks, and then finally one week later. Results indicated that reported enjoyment of the video bus tour decreased over time for those who did not take photos but not for those who did. This finding—in which the combined effect of two independent variables (time duration and photo-taking) is different than when either is alone—is known as an **interaction effect**.

As previously mentioned, the main advantage of a lab experiment like Diehl and her colleagues (2016) study is that variables can be well

external validity
The extent to which a study's findings can be generalized to people beyond those in the study itself

internal validity
The extent to which cause-and-effect conclusions can validly be made in a study

interaction effect
An experimental result that occurs when two independent variables in combination have a different effect on the dependent variable than when either is alone

What are some similarities and some differences between "random assignment" and "random selection"?

controlled, thus increasing internal validity. An important component of this control is that participants can be randomly assigned to the different levels of the independent variable. In **random assignment**, the experimenter, by some random procedure, decides which participants are exposed to which level of the independent variable. Due to this random assignment, the experimenter can be reasonably confident that there are no preexisting average differences between the participants who are in the different experimental conditions. Often in a field study, groupings of participants already exist. In such cases, the researcher must collect additional data to determine if any preexisting differences between the groups might account for different variations of the dependent variable. If such assurances can be obtained or if preexisting conditions can be controlled when the data are analyzed, then the inability to utilize random assignment is less of a threat to the study's internal validity.

Unfortunately, because of the researcher's desire to control as much of the experimental situation as possible in order to properly determine causality, an air of artificiality may exist in the lab. In the Diehl et al. (2016) laboratory study, for instance, the online tour was relatively short and watching a video is not the same as actually being on a live tour. The high degree of control that a researcher can obtain in laboratory experiments often has a price: the danger of artificiality. In contrast, the realism in a field experiment is accompanied by less control over variables that may markedly influence participants' thoughts and actions.

Some social psychologists believe they have found a possible remedy to the dilemma of choosing between greater control and greater realism in experiments. They recommend using *virtual environment technology*, in which they create a virtual research environment using a computer. Once this simulated reality is created, participants wearing virtual reality equipment are "immersed" in the setting. A commonly used piece of virtual reality equipment is a head-mounted or binocular-style device that allows an individual to view three-dimensional images and "walk" through the virtual environment. Despite the fact that this type of simulated environment is completely controlled by the experimenter it has a very "real-world" feel to it, similar to that of a field experiment.

(Getty Images)

Research suggests that participants behave relatively naturally in virtual environment settings (Peck et al., 2013; Sivunen & Hakonen, 2011). Virtual environment technology is currently being used to study such topics as conformity, eyewitness testimony, and violent video games. As this technology advances, psychologists hope to involve senses beyond sight and hearing and to improve the ways people can interact with the virtual creations they encounter. This technology is not meant to replace traditional field and laboratory studies but to provide another research vehicle that social psychologists can use in their work.

Researchers are turning to virtual reality for some of their experiments. The military also uses virtual reality in its training.

One last point about the necessity of laboratory studies. Some types of data collection can only take place in the context of a laboratory study. Social psychologists are increasingly becoming interested in neurological activity that occurs during social interactions. This subfield of social psychology—social neuroscience—requires that participants' neurological activity is measured. New technologies have permitted us to peer deep into the living brain, providing researchers with a unique opportunity to understand how social thinking and behavior are associated with neural activity. The most commonly used brain-imaging technique is the *functional magnetic resonance imaging (fMRI)*.

random assignment
Placement of research participants into experimental conditions in a manner that guarantees that all have an equal chance of being exposed to each level of the independent variable

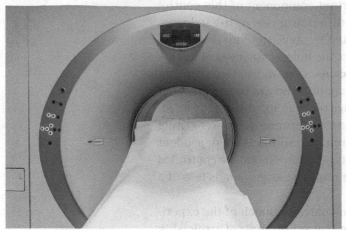

One of the most commonly used brain-scanning techniques is the fMRI.

The fMRI has several advantages over older imaging technology. It can produce a picture of neural activity averaged over seconds, not minutes (Thompson, 2011). Like a standard MRI, fMRI uses magnetism to measure fluctuations in naturally occurring blood oxygen levels—not fluctuations in ingested radioactive glucose. The images produced by fMRI scans are very sharp, and thus they can be used to identify much smaller brain structures than older imaging technology.

Neurological imaging techniques have been increasingly applied to social psychological topics, allowing researchers to explore the neurological underpinnings of experiences such as stereotyping, anger, aggression, love, cooperation, and more. This includes over 20 years of studying the neurological correlates of happiness. A common technique in studying this topic is to induce a happy mood in participants by having them recall a vivid, happy, autobiographical memory. Reviewing seven fMRI studies, Angelo Suardi and his colleagues (2016) concluded that, during recall of happy autobiographical memories, there is neural activation in three areas of the brain: the anterior cingulate cortex, prefrontal cortex, and insula. These areas of the brain are also responsible for pleasure reactions and cognitive processing, which suggests that recalling happy events requires both types of neural processing.

Brain imaging techniques are becoming so good at detecting the ebb and flow of neural activity that it is not far-fetched to predict that this technology will one day be able to literally "read" people's minds, determining such things as their degree of racial prejudice or their truthfulness when answering specific questions (Cacioppo et al., 2004). For example, research by Tatia Lee and her colleagues (2002) indicates that certain areas of the brain are more active when people lie. These researchers are now trying to determine whether this knowledge can be used to produce an effective lie detector that would outperform the conventional polygraph machine.

Such possibilities raise ethical concerns among many scientists and are becoming an important topic of discussion in the new field of *neuroethics*. "If you were to ask me what the ethical hot potato of this coming century is," remarked Arthur Caplan, director of the University of Pennsylvania's Center for Bioethics, "I'd say it's new knowledge of the brain, its structure, and function" (Goldberg, 2003).

Section Summary

- *Observational research* involves systematic qualitative and/or quantitative descriptions of behavior.
  Primary disadvantage: It cannot determine how variables are related to one another.
  Primary disadvantage: It cannot determine how variables are related to one another.
- *Correlational research* provides information on the direction and strength of the relationship between variables.
  Primary advantage: It enables prediction.
  Primary disadvantage: It cannot establish causality.

- *Experimental research* manipulates one or more variables to determine what effect this has on nonmanipulated variables.

    Primary advantage: It can determine causality.

    Primary disadvantage: The high levels of control can make generalization difficult.

- The internet allows researchers to conduct low-cost studies with many participants from around the world and to test them remotely.

- Implicit measures determine the strength of automatic associations in memory.

- Brain-imaging techniques provide researchers with measures of participants' neural activity while they engage in various tasks.

2.3 Standards and Procedures That Bolster Scientific Conclusions

At this point, we hope you recognize that each of the different research methods has both strengths and weaknesses. However, if a number of studies, using different methodologies, have converging results, then we have stronger evidence to support our conclusions. In the example of photo taking and happiness, the researchers conducted a total of nine studies using both field and laboratory methods and found similar results across the studies (Diehl et al., 2016). This convergence of findings across different research methodologies is called *methodological triangulation* and allows us to feel more certain about our conclusions than if we relied on only one type of scientific method. In this section, we will discuss the role of replication and meta-analysis in building a robust body of knowledge.

2.3a Replication and Meta-Analysis Are Essential in Building a Scientifically Based Body of Knowledge

The findings from a single study are far less convincing than the findings from a series of related studies that lead to the same findings. This is also why researchers are so interested in **replication**, which involves repeating a study's scientific procedures using different participants in an attempt to duplicate the findings (Asendorpf et al., 2013). When studies are replicated using different samples, we can feel more secure about the accuracy of the results. Replications can be *direct replications*, in which researchers attempt to exactly repeat what was done in a previous study, using identical materials and procedures but with a new sample. Replications can also be *conceptual replications*, meaning that instead of repeating the exact same study in exactly the same way, we test the previous study's underlying hypotheses using different methods (Crandall & Sherman, 2016). Direct replications are best at increasing confidence in the previous study's findings, whereas conceptual replications help to assess the generalizability of the previous findings. Both types of replications are important for testing and confirming a theory.

As previously discussed in Chapter 1, the replication crisis in social psychology caused social psychologists to seriously consider how to deal with contradictory findings from one study to the next. If, for example, seven studies find that boys are more aggressive than girls and three studies find no differences, what conclusions should be drawn? In the past, researchers used the "majority rules" approach to resolve such controversies. That is, they merely counted up the number of studies that found or did

replication
Repeating a study's scientific procedures using different participants in an attempt to duplicate the findings

not find a particular effect and then concluded that the effect existed if it occurred in the majority of studies. Today, when dealing with contradictory findings from replication studies, researchers use a technique—called meta-analysis—that utilizes more sophisticated comparison procedures. **Meta-analysis** is the use of statistical techniques to summarize results from similar studies on a specific topic to estimate the overall size of the effect (Card & Casper, 2013). The term *meta-analysis* means "analysis of analyses."

When conducting a meta-analysis, the first step is to gather all the research that has been conducted on the topic under scrutiny. This includes unpublished research, because scientific journals are more likely to publish studies with results that support research hypotheses than they are to publish studies that have nonsignificant findings. This sort of publication bias is often referred to as the *file-drawer effect* because the unpublished results are figuratively tucked away in researchers' file cabinets and largely forgotten.

The second step in meta-analysis is to compute the effect size (recall our discussion of Cohen's d) for each study. These effect sizes are then combined (weighted by sample size) into an overall effect size that gives an assessment of the magnitude of the effect across all studies. For example, if one study finds a large effect and another sample finds a small effect, the overall meta-analysis effect size will be moderate in magnitude. In the research on photo taking, the meta-analysis of those studies found an overall effect size of .41, suggesting a moderate difference in enjoyment of the activity between the photo taking and no photo taking conditions (Diehl et al., 2016). This suggests that taking photographs of activities moderately contributes to people's enjoyment of those activities. (This is great news for Deb who just took over 300 photos during a recent week-long family vacation!) Throughout this text, you will see how meta-analysis helps us better understand social psychological findings.

2.3b   The Scientific Method Is Self-Correcting.

Truth in science is never final. Scientific theories are explanations of how things in the world are related to one another and how they operate. Theories are logically constructed and reconfigured from careful observations and testable hypotheses. You can have such overwhelming data supporting your theory that you have very strong confidence that it accurately explains the phenomena in question. Yet, at the core of the scientific journey of discovery is the assumption that any theory can be modified or completely discarded tomorrow if new evidence calls into question its validity. In other words, all theories in science are fundamentally tentative. Thus, if you seek to understand the human mind using the scientific method, it is a mistake to believe that any theory can achieve a "final truth."

An example of why theories should always be considered tentative (i.e., explanations subject to disconfirmation and alteration) involves research on *implicit egotism*, which is a nonconscious attraction to people and things that we associate with ourselves. For example, laboratory studies have found reliable evidence that people evaluate the letters contained within their name more favorably than they do other letters in the alphabet (Nuttin, 1985; Hoorens & Nuttin, 1993). So, for instance, Wendy is more likely to express positive attitudes toward the letters W, E, N, D, and Y than other letters. Laboratory studies also find that people express more liking of products with brand names resembling their own names (Brendl et al., 2005). Over the past decade, a number of social psychologists attempted to generalize these laboratory findings on implicit egotism to explain how it might influence important life decisions. They proposed that because people form positive associations with the sight and sound of their own names, they are more likely to choose spouses, places to live, places to work, and occupations with names similar to their own (Pelham et al., 2002). In a series of provocative studies, these researchers found evidence supporting this *name-letter effect* (e.g., Anseel & Duyck,

meta-analysis
The use of statistical techniques to summarize results from similar studies on a specific topic to estimate the reliability and overall size of the effect

2008; Pelham et al., 2005). Their studies suggested, for instance, that there are more Andrews married to someone named Andrea, there are more Smiths living in Smithville, there are more Freds at Ford Motor Company, and there are more lawyers named Laura than you would expect by chance. These findings were very intriguing because they suggested that who you pick as a life companion, where you choose to live, and what occupation you pursue may be partly influenced by the letters in your name!

As you might guess, this theory and the accompanying research findings created considerable interest among social psychologists, generated a good deal of media coverage, and were widely reported in many social psychology textbooks. However, a recent series of studies conducted by Uri Simonsohn challenges the name-letter effect, stating that the findings supporting this theory are likely due to the researchers failing to control certain factors in their analyses. For example,

Although research in the past 15 years suggested that we are more likely to marry someone who has a name similar to our own, recent studies challenge these findings and call into question the validity of the theory upon which the original research is based.

when Simonsohn (2011a) examined the finding that a higher-than-expected number of workers and their employers share the same initials in their names, his preliminary analyses confirmed the original study's findings (Anseel & Duyck, 2008): More than two-and-a-half times as many people as would be expected worked for a company that shared their initials. However, more in-depth analysis revealed that this significant effect was caused by those cases in the data where the first three letters of a person's last name and the name of their employer matched up, while the effect disappeared altogether for cases where only the first initials matched. The pattern of these results strongly suggested to Simonsohn that the reason past research found an association between workers' and employers' initials was simply because many people work for companies that they started themselves or that were started by their family members. Similarly, Simonsohn (2011b) found evidence that one factor explaining why people tend to marry someone with a similar-sounding name is because certain names, such as Andrew and Andrea or Susan and Stephen, were popular baby names during the same decade, and thus, similar-name marital pairings were statistically more likely when these children reached adulthood. Simonsohn's research and his reinterpretation of previous findings does not mean that implicit egotism is not a real psychological phenomenon, but it does call into question the theory that people base crucial life decisions on an unconscious attraction to a letter. It is still possible that we are attracted to things that have names with the same initials as our own names, but this attraction is likely so small that it only influences decisions in a laboratory setting or decisions in the real world that do not matter much to us, perhaps such as buying soda X over soda Y.

The lesson here is that one of the key strengths of the scientific method is that it is self-correcting. When results from scientific studies do not support stated hypotheses, the researchers who conduct these studies are often understandably disappointed because the findings undermine their confidence in the theories from which their hypotheses were generated. However, many researchers also realize that great discoveries often follow such disappointment. In this regard, social psychologist William McGuire (1999) asserts that the task of science is "not the dull and easy job of showing that a fixed hypothesis is right or wrong in a given context.... Science has the more exciting task of discovering in what senses the hypotheses and its theoretical explanations are true and in what senses false" (p. 407). From this perspective, failure to find support for a research hypothesis provides the opportunity for future discovery (McGuire, 2004). Figure 2.2 illustrates the cyclical nature of the relationship between a theory and a testable hypothesis.

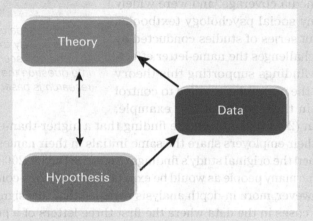

FIGURE 2.2   The Cyclical Nature of the Theory-Hypothesis Relationship

Data from a study provides evidence to support or disconfirm the hypothesis. If the hypothesis is supported, the validity of the theory is also supported, generating new hypotheses to test in future research. If the hypothesis is not supported, the validity of the theory is questioned, prompting researchers to revise the theory to reflect the insights gained from their investigation. This revised theory is then used to develop new hypotheses that are then tested in another round of research.

2.3c The Study of Actual Behavior Is Declining in Social Psychology.

Although emerging technologies such as fMRI, implicit measures, and online data collection provide new avenues by which scientists can study the social behavior of everyday life, some social psychologists are concerned that these technologies are part of a larger trend within the discipline to study social behavior through a cognitive lens that seldom measures actual behavior (Patterson et al., 2011). For example, content analysis of scientific studies published over the past 5 decades in two of the top social psychology journals, *Journal of Personality and Social Psychology* and *Personality and Social Psychology Bulletin,* found that studies with either the independent or dependent variables being actual behavioral measures dropped from about 75% in the 1970s to about 20% during the past 2 decades (Baumeister et al., 2007b; Patterson, 2008). In a review of a sample of articles published in 2016 in the premier journal in social psychology, only 6% studied behaviors (Doliński, 2018). Instead of studying how people behave by directly observing their actions in various social settings, researchers are more likely to either ask people how they think they behave in those settings or measure people's cognitions after showing them stimuli that are often present in those social settings. While self-reports and cognitive reactions can be extremely useful in understanding the psychology of social behavior, most social psychologists would agree that these measurement techniques should not completely replace the actual measurement of behavior. Further, while brain-imaging technology can provide further insight into the complexity of social behavior, it is most likely to do so when studies involve research participants who are immersed in genuine social interactions rather than those who are simply responding to stimuli while laying inside an fMRI scanner in a laboratory (Rilling, 2011).

The need for conducting research that examines behaviors in realistic environments has been noted by social psychologists. Some have called for a renewed focus on research that uses "older" scientific methods, such as observational studies, field studies, and archival data analysis—methods that were common in the past but are currently less frequently used (Cheung et al., 2017). Newer research methodologies are also addressing this decrease in studying behavior. For example, social psychologists have begun to utilize smartphones for data collection (Harari et al., 2016). Smartphones can be used to track a number of behaviors ranging from location (using GPS trackers), social network size, and interactions based on texting and phone call frequency and duration. With applications on the phone, researchers can also instruct participants to easily track and report a variety of behaviors, including sleep. Other researchers (Jackson, et al., 2017) have employed in vivo behavioral tracking, in which researchers use cameras to track participants' movements as they interact with others in a controlled, but realistic setting. This method can gather a wealth of behavioral data and has been used successfully to study group formation and cooperation.

The take-away message of this chapter is that there is no one best scientific method or data collection technique for all research settings. In each investigation, social psychologists must decide not only how to best measure their variables of interest but also what scientific method provides the best opportunity of meeting the study's goals. Given the ability of the observational method to capture the richness of social behavior as it happens, many social psychologists believe that this approach is best suited for *theory building* (Fine & Elsbach, 2000). In contrast, because the experimental method can determine the cause of events, it is generally considered the method best suited for *theory testing*. Finally, confirming a study by replicating with large, diverse samples allows for essential confirmation of the findings and meta-analyses to determine the magnitude of effects (Fiske, 2016). The best overall strategy in developing theories of social behavior that are valid and useful is to take a *multimethod* approach—employing different methods to study the same topic and thereby capitalizing on each method's strengths and controlling for their weaknesses.

Section Summary

- A multimethod approach capitalizes on each method's strengths while controlling for its weaknesses.

- Replication is playing an increasingly important role in establishing the robustness of social psychological research.

- Meta-analysis is a statistical technique to determine whether specific variables have important effects across many studies.

- Scientific theories cannot be proven, and it is a mistake to believe that they can achieve a "final truth."

- Actual behavior is less often measured in social psychology studies today than it was in past decades.

KEY TERMS

■ WEBSITES

Accessed through http://www.bvtlab.com/sop8

Websites for this chapter include those for the main scientific journals in both psychological and sociological social psychology, information on recent theory and research, and a web page containing social psychological studies currently being conducted on the web—many of which you can participate in.

Journal of Personality and Social Psychology Website

Check out the website for the main scientific journal in psychological social psychology. Here you will find current abstracts of journal articles. The journal publishes theoretical and empirical papers on attitudes and social cognition, interpersonal relations and group processes, and personality processes and individual differences.

Social Psychology Quarterly Website

Explore the website for the main scientific journal in sociological social psychology, where you will find information on current journal articles. The journal publishes theoretical and empirical papers on the link between the individual and society.

Society for the Psychological Study of Social Issues

This is the website of the Society for the Psychological Study of Social Issues (SPSSI), an organization of more than 3,000 psychology and other related scientists. The site contains links to SPSSI publications, news about policy, a newsletter, conference information, teaching materials, and more.

Social Psychology Network

Information on this site is devoted to research and teaching to advance the field of social psychology. It contains links to social psychology experts, research groups, and graduate programs around the world. Its resources also include links to social psychology journals, teaching resources, learning programs, blogs and podcasts, a career center, and more.

Society for Personality and Social Psychology

A website devoted to personality and social psychology. The site includes links to the organization's publications and helps connect members to educational events, networking, science funding, and mentoring opportunities.

International Association for Cross-Cultural Psychology

This is the website for an organization devoted to facilitating communication among persons interested in a diverse range of issues involving the intersection of culture and psychology.

Wesleyan's Social Psychology Network

This website contains social psychological studies that are currently being conducted on the internet, many of which you can participate in.

The Self

FOCUS QUESTIONS

1. What is self-awareness, how does it develop, and is it unique to humans?

2. How do conceptions of the self differ in individualist and collectivist cultures?

3. When presenting themselves to others in everyday life, what are some common strategies that people use?

4. What is the "dark side" of high self-esteem?

CHAPTER OUTLINE

Introduction

R olihlahla was born in 1918 into the Madiba clan in a tiny country village in South Africa's Umtata district. Growing up, this young lad initially defined himself in relation to his extended family and clan and his skills at stick fighting with his friends. Yet when his father suddenly died, 9-year-old Rolihlahla was taken far away by his mother to become a ward of the chief of the Thembu people at the Great Place in Mqhekezweni. Later, in describing this event, Rolihlahla stated that he felt like a sapling pulled root and branch from the earth and flung into the center of a stream whose strong current he could not resist; his sense of self underwent a dramatic transformation. Whereas before he was a naive child living a very simple life, Rolihlahla was now confronted by great wealth, power, and educational opportunities. He began hearing the elders' stories of his ancestors' bravery during the wars of resistance against the invaders who had stolen his tribe's lands. He dreamed of becoming part of the freedom struggle of his people, and this dream reshaped his identity.

Fast-forward 35 years to 1962. Rolihlahla had become a licensed attorney and was much better known by the new name given to him by his first schoolteacher (shortly after his father died those many years before)— Nelson Mandela. Although Nelson still defined himself in terms of his family and clan, he also defined himself as being a freedom fighter for the African National Congress and for all people who cherished freedom and equality in his country and around the world. He now sat in a jail cell, awaiting trial, charged by the white apartheid South African government with leaving the country illegally and inciting workers to strike in protest of racial inequality and discrimination.

On the first day of his trial, Nelson noticed that the state's prosecuting attorneys—many of whom he had become acquainted with during his legal career—were uneasy seeing him before them as a criminal defendant. Nelson realized that their discomfort was not simply because he was a colleague brought low but also because he was an ordinary man being punished for his beliefs. These white attorneys were sympathetic. In that moment, Nelson realized he could redefine his social reality in this courtroom, throughout his country, and even around the world by becoming a living symbol of justice. By becoming the representative of the great ideals of freedom, fairness, and democracy in a society that dishonored those virtues, Nelson Mandela realized that he could carry on the fight for his people's freedom within the enemy's fortress. Through sizing up his current situation and reflecting upon its implications (in relation to his own sense of self), Rolihlahla/Nelson once again dramatically reshaped his identity and, in so doing, eventually reshaped the national identity of an entire country.

Although Nelson Mandela was a rare and special person who transformed both himself and much of the world around him, we fellow humans share with him this ability to define and redefine our social reality—and therefore ourselves. What gives us this ability to create an identity for ourselves? How do others help define us? Are some of us more introspective than others, and if so, how does that impact our thinking and behavior? Why do success and failure mean so much to us in certain areas of our lives but not in others? For an answer to these and other questions, we must examine a central concept in social psychology: the self (Swann & Bosson, 2010).

(Leonard Zhukovsky/ Shutterstock)

"It always seems impossible until it's done"
-Nelson Mandela

Nelson Mandela's life illustrates how a person's sense of self is often shaped by others' influence and social circumstances and how that person's sense of self can then shape the identity and social reality of others.

3.1   The Self as Both Active Agent and Object of Attention

As defined in Chapter 1, the **self** is a symbol-using social being who can reflect on his or her own behavior. In studying the self, social psychologists typically make a distinction between the self as subject of awareness and the self as object of awareness.

3.1a   James and Mead Shaped Contemporary Self Theories.

Two of the most influential early contributors to our understanding of the self were psychologist William James (1890) and sociologist George Herbert Mead (1934). Both James and Mead described the self as having two separate aspects: the self as subject of awareness (the *I*) and the self as object of awareness (the *me*). The "I" is the aspect of your self that is actively perceiving, thinking, and behaving in your world, while the "me" is the aspect of your self that the "I" is sometimes perceiving and thinking about. In other words, as a self, *I* am conscious of many things in my world, and sometimes I focus my conscious-ness on myself (*me*). Contemporary social psychologists refer to the "me" as **self-concept**, which is the sum total of a person's thoughts and feelings that define the self as an object (Crocker & Canevello, 2012). Knowing yourself, or at least believing that you know yourself, is critically important in having a purpose and meaning in life (Schlegel et al., 2011). Self-concept also consists of numerous evaluations of the self as being good, bad, or mediocre. This evaluative aspect of self-concept is called **self-esteem**. As you will discover in this chapter, seeking self-knowledge and seeking self-esteem are often important motivating forces in daily living.

(Public domain via Wikimedia)

William James, 1842–1910

> "A self is not something static, tied up in a pretty parcel and handed to the child, finished and complete. A self is always becoming."
>
> —Madeleine L'Engle, US author, 1918–2007

According to James, things become part of your self-concept through your emotional identification with them. Thus, your parents, siblings, friends, and lovers are most likely very impor-tant components of your self-concept. Indeed, your clothes, your iPhone, your major area of study in college, and perhaps even your fuzzy little teddy bear could be elements in your "me." In this regard, your self-concept includes not just that which is inside your body but also anything that symbolizes and affirms who and what you are (Lewandowski et al., 2006). During his many years in prison, Nelson Mandela vividly understood how self-concept involves emotional identification, because he experienced firsthand how prison life robs a person's identity by stripping away emotional attachments; over a 21-year span Mandela was never allowed to even touch his wife's hand, much less embrace her.

> "Nothing is greater than one's self."
>
> —Walt Whitman, US poet, 1819–1892

James's idea that the self in the form of the "me" can extend beyond your physical body is important because it challenges the belief that we are separate, encapsulated egos. His notion of the self-identification process also highlights the ever-changing nature of the self. That is, because who and what you identify with often changes over time, the way you define yourself is not stable; rather it is constantly changing. Your self of today is different, even if only subtly, from your self of yesterday.

Finally, James also believed that the things with which we emotionally identify serve as the basis for judging our self-esteem. He stated that our self-esteem is a measure of our successes in the areas of our lives with which we emotionally identify relative to our aspirations in those areas (Scalas et al., 2013). Thus, if Afnan emotionally identi-fies herself as a budding pianist, her self-esteem will be significantly determined by her successes in piano activities and not in how she performs in activities with which she does not emotionally identify (for example, soccer, sewing, or carpentry).

self
A symbol-using social being who can reflect on his or her own behavior

self-concept
The sum total of a person's thoughts and feelings that define the self as an object

self-esteem
A person's evaluation of his or her self-concept

George Herbert Mead, 1863–1931

(Public domain via Wikimedia)

While James described how emotional identification shapes self-concept, Mead described how the self develops in infancy and how people, as selves, actively shape their social reality. He asserted that a human infant is not born a self but rather that a self *emerges* through social interaction. According to Mead (1925), the self develops as children acquire language and start taking the role of other people in their play activities. An example of role taking would be a child adopting the perspective of "Daddy" and reprimanding himself for disobeying a family rule. Through the symbolic interaction of language and role taking, children develop beliefs about themselves that are largely a reflection of how they believe others perceive them. By internalizing the beliefs and expectations commonly held by the larger society—what Mead called the *generalized other*—the person becomes a fully mature self.

According to Mead, in everyday symbolic interaction, people must continually take account of each other's ongoing acts and reorganize or adjust their own intentions in terms of others' intentions. In effectively understanding others' intentions, Mead stated that people must engage in role taking (also known as *perspective taking*), which is imaginatively assuming the point of view of others and observing their own behavior (the "me") from this other perspective. He believed that it is through such symbolic interaction that humans cease to merely respond to their social environment and instead become "co-actors" in creating—and recreating—their social reality.

Both James's and Mead's theories have profoundly influenced social psychology, with James's writings reflecting the affective or "hot" perspective on the nature of human behavior and Mead's writings reflecting the cognitive or "cold" approach (see Chapter 1, section 1.2b). Their initial ideas on how we define ourselves and how we consciously strive to become what we desire involve two essential human characteristics: *self-awareness* and *self-regulation*. Let us now examine how contemporary social psychologists study the interplay between these two complementary psychological processes.

3.1b   Self-Awareness Is Reflective Thinking.

Stop for a moment and think about your current mood. If you followed our suggestion, you just engaged in **self-awareness**, which is a psychological state in which you focus attention on yourself (Langfur, 2013; Lewis, 2011). Another way to describe self-awareness is that it is a temporary state of mind where you psychologically "step outside yourself" and examine your thoughts, feelings, motives, behavior, or appearance. This "stepping outside one's self" is what Mead considered necessary for the self to develop; children adopt the perspective (or role) of others to examine their own behavior. To have a self-concept, you must be able to engage in self-awareness. As discussed in Chapter 1 (Figure 1.3), a region in the frontal lobe of the cerebral cortex called the *anterior cingulate cortex* is especially active when people are self-aware. The anterior cingulate cortex contains *spindle neurons*, which are a special type of neuron that collect waves of neural information from one region of the brain and send it on to other regions. The anterior cingulate cortex with its spindle neurons acts as an executive attention system, facilitating self-awareness and other intelligent behavior.

Self-Awareness Development

self-awareness

A psychological state in which one takes oneself as an object of attention

You might be surprised to learn that we are not born with self-awareness but rather that we develop it. Psychologists discovered this fact by placing a spot of rouge on babies' noses and then placing them in front of a mirror (Lewis & Brooks, 1978). They reasoned that in order for the infants to recognize the mirror image as their own, they must have an internalized identity that permits them to recognize an external representation of themselves. Infants between ages 9 and 12 months treated their mirror image as if it were another child, showing no interest in the unusual rouge spot; they were not able to take themselves as an object of awareness. Yet those around 18 months of age exhibited self-recognition—and thus, self-awareness ability—by staring in the mirror and touching the mysterious spot on their noses. Recognizing the image in the mirror as their own, they realized that they looked different. Based on such studies, it appears that self-awareness develops at about 18 months of age (Zmyj et al., 2013), which is the same age that Mead stated that the self develops.

Babies around 18 months of age start to exhibit self-recognition.

Perhaps not coincidentally, the development of self-awareness occurs at the same time as children's brains are experiencing a rapid growth of spindle neurons—which are not present at birth—in the frontal lobe of the cerebral cortex (Allman & Hasenstaub, 1999). The only other animals known to have spindle neurons are the great apes, our closest genetic relatives, and certain species of whales and dolphins (Hayashi, 2006; Hof & Van der Gucht, 2007). Not surprisingly, additional research suggests that these species also possess self-awareness (Boysen & Himes, 1999; Morell, 2013). Does this mean that these self-aware animals also possess self-concepts? Contrary to previous scientific beliefs that self-concept development was unique to humans, recent studies suggest that chimpanzees have a sense of self roughly comparable to a human child of 4 years (Hirata et al., 2017).

Disengaging Self-Awareness

Of course, we are not always self-aware. Selfhood is most apparent when we have the luxury of time for contemplation. When we need to focus on difficult tasks requiring quick decisions, neuroimaging studies indicate that self-awareness temporarily disappears as our brains divert cognitive resources toward the task at hand. In one such study, Ilan Goldberg and his colleagues (2006) conducted functional magnetic resonance imaging (fMRI) scans of participants' brains as they identified animals depicted in pictures and also reported their emotional responses. Pictures were either presented slowly or quickly. When pictures were shown slowly, heightened neural activity was observed in the anterior cingulate cortex, but not when pictures were shown quickly. In contrast, speed of picture presentation did not change the amount of neural activity in brain regions that process and make sense of sensory information. In other words, when circumstances require the brain to divert most of its cognitive resources to carry out a difficult task, neural activity in the anterior cingulate cortex is inhibited, which "switches off" self-awareness.

"Self-awareness is, then, one of the most fundamental, possibly the most fundamental, characteristic of the human species. . . . Self-awareness has, however, brought in its train somber companions—fear, anxiety, and death-awareness. . . . A being who knows that he will die arose from ancestors who did not know."

—Theodosius Dobzhansky, Russian-born geneticist, 1900–1975

Disengaging self-awareness in this manner makes sense from an evolutionary perspective (Vince, 2006). When encountering sudden danger, such as stumbling upon a deadly predator, it is not helpful to spend critical seconds wondering how you feel about the situation. Instead, quick action is much more likely to ensure your safety and survival. However, one additional consequence of the fluctuating nature of self-awareness is that, while it may be an adaptive response, disengaging self-awareness may also result in less humane or moral responses (Vincent et al., 2013). That is, in situations requiring quick and difficult choices, we are less likely to consider our personal values or societal standards before responding. As you will see in other chapters, disengaging self-awareness when responding quickly to social events can have profound consequences for our likelihood of acting contrary to our personal values (Chapters 5 and 8), stereotyping and discriminating against others (Chapter 6), flaunting social norms (Chapter 7), lashing out in anger (Chapter 11), and helping those in need (Chapter 12).

Private and Public Self-Awareness

Social scientists have long debated whether personal or social standards are more important in determining people's behavior. Some theorists have assumed that people are motivated primarily by a desire to meet personal goals and are responsive largely to their own attitudes and feelings (Maslow, 1970; Rogers, 1947). Others have argued that we are largely a reflected image of our social group, and that, before acting, we consider how others will judge us (Cooley, 1902; Mead, 1934). Self-awareness research indicates that whether behavior is influenced more by personal or social standards is partially determined by whether self-awareness is focused on private or public self-aspects (Silvia & O'Brien, 2004).

Private self-awareness is the temporary state of being in which you are aware of hidden, private aspects of the self, such as your personal attitudes, beliefs, and current mood. Feeling sad or content, seeing your face in a small mirror, or feeling the hunger pangs of your stomach will likely cause you to become privately self-aware. Two effects of private self-awareness are that you become more aware of the discrepancy between your behavior and your personal standards, and you are more likely to behave in-line with those standards (Froming et al., 1998; Goukens et al., 2009). Private self-awareness also makes you more aware of and responsive to your current moods (Lyubomirsky et al., 1998; Scheier & Carver, 1977). Thus, if you are happy and become privately self-aware, your happiness is intensified. Likewise, if you are angered, private self-awareness causes more anger.

> "There are three things extremely hard: steel, a diamond, and to know one's self."
>
> —Benjamin Franklin, US statesman and scientist, 1706–1790

In contrast to private self-awareness, *public self-awareness* is the temporary state of being in which you are aware of public self-aspects, such as your physical appearance and the way you talk and behave in public settings. Being watched by others, having your picture taken, or seeing yourself in a full-length mirror could induce public self-awareness (Buss, 1980; Green & Sedikides, 1999). One effect of public self-awareness is *greater adherence to social standards of behavior*, meaning a heightened degree of conformity (Duval & Wicklund, 1972). This increased conformity when publicly self-aware is often preceded by concerns about being negatively evaluated by others (Culos-Reed et al., 2002; Mesagno et al., 2009).

As adults, we all have the ability to engage in either private or public self-awareness. However, when some stimulus induces self-awareness, that focus is only temporary. Researchers have also determined that some people spend more time self-reflecting than others. This habitual tendency to engage in self-awareness is known as **self-consciousness**—a personality trait. Just as there are two types of self-awareness, there are also two types of self-consciousness. *Private self-consciousness* is the tendency to be aware of the private aspects of the self, while *public self-consciousness* is the tendency to be aware of publicly displayed self-aspects. These traits are two distinct tendencies; therefore, a person could be very attentive to both sides of the self, attentive to one but inattentive to another, or relatively inattentive to both. Before reading further, spend a few minutes completing the items in *Self/Social Connection Exercise 3.1* to learn more about your own levels of private and public self-consciousness.

self-consciousness
The habitual tendency to engage in self-awareness

Self/Social Connection Exercise 3.1

What Are Your Levels of Private and Public Self-Consciousness?

Self-awareness researchers contend that your levels of private and public self-consciousness predict the degree to which your thinking and behavior are shaped by your "private self" or your "public self." Private and public self-consciousness are measured by items on the Self-Consciousness Scale (SCS: Fenigstein et al., 1975). To take the SCS, read each item below, and then indicate how well each statement describes you using the following scale:

0   extremely uncharacteristic (not at all like me)

1   uncharacteristic (somewhat unlike me)

2   neither characteristic nor uncharacteristic

3   characteristic (somewhat like me)

4   extremely characteristic (very much like me)

1. I'm always trying to figure myself out.
2. I'm concerned about my style of doing things.
3. Generally, I'm not very aware of myself.*
4. I reflect about myself a lot.
5. I'm concerned about the way I present myself.
6. I'm often the subject of my own fantasies.
7. I never scrutinize myself.*
8. I'm self-conscious about the way I look.
9. I'm generally attentive to my inner feelings.
10. I usually worry about making a good impression.
11. I'm constantly examining my motives.
12. One of the last things I do before I leave my house is look in the mirror.
13. I sometimes have the feeling that I'm off somewhere watching myself.
14. I'm concerned about what other people think of me.
15. I'm alert to changes in my mood.
16. I'm usually aware of my appearance.
17. I'm aware of the way my mind works when I work through a problem.

Directions for Scoring

Several of the SCS items are reverse-scored; that is, for these items, a lower rating actually indicates a higher level of self-consciousness. Before summing the items, recode those with an asterisk (*) so that 0 = 4, 1 = 3, 3 = 1, and 4 = 0.

Private self-consciousness: To calculate your private self-consciousness score, add up your responses to the following items: 1, 3*, 4, 6, 7*, 9, 11, 13, 15, and 17.

Public self-consciousness: To calculate your public self-consciousness score, add up your responses to the following items: 2, 5, 8, 10, 12, 14, and 16.

When Fenigstein, Scheier, and Buss developed the SCS, the mean score for college students on private self-consciousness was about 26, whereas the average score of public self-consciousness was about 19. The higher

(continues)

(Self/Social Connection Exercise 3.1 *continued*)

your score is above one of these values, the more of this type of self-consciousness you probably possess. The lower your score is below one of these values, the less of this type of self-consciousness you probably possess. In reading the research findings regarding private and public self-consciousness, consider how your own thinking and behavior might be shaped by the degree to which you are habitually aware of your "private self" and your "public self." Does it provide insight into the degree to which you:

(a) are interested in understanding what "makes you tick"? ⟶ private self-consciousness effect

(b) follow your own personal standards in daily decisions? ⟶ private self-consciousness effect

(c) "stew in your own juices" when someone irritates you? ⟶ private self-consciousness effect

(d) pay a lot of attention to how you look? ⟶ public self-consciousness effect

(e) feel pressure to conform to others' opinions and expectations? ⟶ public self-consciousness effect

(f) feel anxious when the public spotlight is cast your way? ⟶ public self-consciousness effect

Reprinted with permission from "Public and Private Self-Consciousness: Assessment and Theory," by A. Fenigstein, M. F. Scheier and A. H. Bliss, 1975, *Journal of Consulting and Clinical Psychology, 43*(4), pp. 522–527.

Many private self-awareness effects are the same whether they result from the psychological state of private self-awareness or the personality trait of private self-consciousness (Kemmelmeier, 2001; Scheier & Carver, 1980). Individuals high in private self-consciousness are more aware of and behave more in-line with their personal standards, and react more strongly to their current moods, than do their less self-conscious counterparts. Because they are more attentive to their personal attitudes, values, and motives, people with high private self-consciousness tend to have self-concepts that are more complex than do those low in private self-consciousness (Davies, 1994). However, habitual attention to private self-aspects can contribute to depression and chronic unhappiness (Ingram, 1990; Trapnell & Campbell, 1999). Why might this be so? One possibility is that greater attention to private self-aspects intensifies current emotions. When people's experiences fall short of their expectations, prolonging private self-awareness heightens their disappointment. Thus, the *trait* of private self-consciousness or the *state* of private self-awareness might encourage destructive self-critical analysis (Silvia & O'Brien, 2004; Ward et al., 2003). A number of studies suggest that reducing self-awareness by engaging in distracting activities that shift attention away from the self—such as watching television—can improve well-being among depressed individuals (Moskalenko & Heine, 2003; Nix et al., 1995). Taking all these studies into account, it appears that attending to our private selves has both benefits and drawbacks. The insights gained from this research can perhaps help you gauge how your own life might benefit from—or be harmed by—the amount of attention you devote to your private self.

(Shutterstock)

How does our thinking and social behavior change due to us being aware of our private versus public selves?

What about public self-consciousness? As with situationally-induced public self-awareness, persons high in public self-consciousness are more concerned about how others judge them. As a result, they are more conforming to group norms (Chang et al., 2001) and are more likely to withdraw from embarrassing situations (Froming et al., 1990) than are those low in this trait. For example, among college students, individuals with high public self-consciousness have a tendency to conform that results in them consuming more alcohol than individuals who are low in this trait when they believe that drinking is prevalent among their peers (Crawford & Novak, 2013). This tendency to comply with external standards also impacts physical appearance. Individuals with high public self-consciousness are more concerned about their physical appearance and are more likely to judge others based on their looks (Ryckman et al., 1991).

How do these two traits of private and public self-consciousness collectively influence a person's behavior in public settings? As you might expect, people high in private self-consciousness and low in public self-consciousness are the ones most likely to act according to their true attitudes. On the other hand, people high in public self-consciousness—regardless of their level of private self-consciousness—are much less likely to publicly act according to their true attitudes (Scheier, 1980). Therefore, even when people have an accurate understanding of their own attitudes as a result of their habitual private self-focus, being simultaneously high in public self-consciousness can lead to behavior that runs counter to those attitudes.

> "Know thyself? If I knew myself, I'd run away."
>
> —Johann Wolfgang von Goethe, German intellectual, writer, and composer, 1749–1832

Culture and Self-Awareness

Virtually all of the self-awareness research discussed thus far was conducted in the United States—an individualist culture. However, as stated in Chapter 1, most of the world's population resides in collectivist cultures. Is there any evidence that people in individualist and collectivist cultures differ in their self-awareness tendencies? Perhaps. A number of studies have documented how collectivist-oriented East Asians attend more to the perspectives of others than do individualist-oriented Westerners— meaning those from East Asia are more likely than people from Western cultures to habitually view themselves through the eyes of other people (Cohen et al., 2007). Viewing yourself from the perspective of others is another way of saying that you are engaging in self-awareness.

> "The one self-knowledge worth having is to know one's own mind."
>
> —F. H. Bradley, English philosopher, 1846–1924

As already noted, seeing your face in a small mirror induces private self-awareness, which results in you being more aware of the discrepancy between your behavior and your personal standards. Based on these past research findings, Steven Heine and his colleagues (2008) asked college students at a Japanese university and an American university to rate how much a series of 20 positive statements, such as "I am extremely considerate," described them. Next the participants rated how much they wished each of these same statements described them. The discrepancy between these "actual versus ideal" judgments measured how much the participants thought that they fell short of their ideal selves. Half of the participants completed this task while sitting in front of a small mirror, while half did not.

> "He who knows others is clever; He who knows himself has discernment."
>
> —Lao-Tzu, Chinese philosopher and founder of Taoism, sixth century BCE

As depicted in Figure 3.1, the American college students displayed a significantly bigger discrepancy between their actual and ideal selves when completing the task in front of a mirror; another way to describe these findings is to say that the American participants were more self-critical when they were situationally induced into private self-awareness. In contrast, the Japanese students' actual versus ideal judgments were unaffected by whether a mirror was present; the researchers noticed a fair amount of actual versus ideal self discrepancies in both the mirror and nonmirror conditions. Heine and his colleagues argued that these results provide evidence that the Japanese tendency to be self-critical is at least partly caused by them being chronically self-aware; they act as if they have mirrors in their heads. These results suggest that people from East Asian cultures are possibly more self-reflective than Americans.

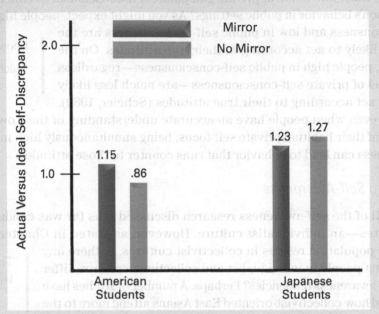

FIGURE 3.1   Effects of a Mirror on American and Japanese College Students' Self-Assessments

American college students who judged their actual versus ideal selves in front of a mirror displayed more discrepancies than American college students who made these same judgments in a room without a mirror. The presence of a mirror had no impact on the self-assessments of Japanese college students.

Data from "Mirrors in the Head: Cultural Variation in Objective Self-Awareness," by S. J. Heine et al., 2008, *Personality and Social Psychology Bulletin, 34*(7), pp. 879–887.

3.1c   Self-Regulation Is the Self's Most Important Function.

In the early 1970s, Walter Mischel and his colleagues tested the ability of children aged 4 to 6 to delay gratification. This came to be known as the Marshmallow Test (Mischel et al., 1972). In this study, children were individually led into a room, empty of distractions, where a marshmallow was placed on a table by a chair. The children were told they could eat the treat now or they could wait for 15 minutes without giving in to temptation, in which case they would be rewarded with a second treat. The children were then left in the room alone. While some of the children immediately ate the marshmallow, others attempted to fight their urge by covering their eyes or turning away so that they couldn't see the treat. Some children kicked the desk, tugged on their pigtails, or flapped their arms to distract themselves. A few even stroked the marshmallow as if it were a tiny stuffed animal! The researchers found that one-third of the children deferred gratification long enough to get the second marshmallow, with age being a major determinant of deferred gratification.

What was really interesting about this study was what Mischel discovered in later follow-up studies with these same children. As teenagers, the children who were previously more successful in delaying gratification were now more academically successful in high school (Shoda et al., 1990). Furthermore, 40 years later, a brain-imaging study of some of these same participants—who were now middle-aged—found more neural activity among the high delayers, compared to the low delayers, in brain regions governing **self-regulation** (Casey et al., 2011), which is the ability to control and direct one's own actions. A recent conceptual replication (Watts et al., 2018) of the Marshmallow Test using a more economically and ethnically diverse sample of children—Mischel's sample consisted largely of white middle-class children with college-educated mothers—found less impressive results in the children's later academic achievement based on their initial ability to delay gratification, but the study's overall findings still suggest that early childhood ability to delay gratification does indeed impact academic success. Not surprisingly, what influences children's ability to not only delay gratification but to also value such self-control are the actions of those around them. Children are more likely to delay gratification and value it after witnessing others in their

Research suggests that children's ability to delay gratification early in life predicts their later academic success. What cognitive process governs the ability to delay gratification?

own social group delay gratification and also observing impulsive behavior—the opposite of delayed gratification—among individuals in groups of which they are not associated (Doebel & Munakata, 2018). In other words, exercising self-control is not just having the personal ability to do so; it is also shaped by the social context. Are others exercising self-control or not, and who are those others?

How is this process of self-regulation related to self-awareness? Simply put, you must be self-aware to self-regulate (Rudasill, 2011). Indeed, self-regulation involves activation of the same brain region—the anterior cingulate cortex—involved in self-awareness, as well as activation of areas in the prefrontal lobe (refer to Figure 1.3 in Chapter 1) associated with selecting and initiating actions (the *dorsolateral prefrontal cortex*) and planning and coordinating behavior designed to achieve goals (the *orbitofrontal cortex*). Brain-imaging studies find significant activation of these brain regions when people are performing difficult tasks requiring considerable cognitive effort and attention but not during simple memory recall tasks (Amodio et al., 2004). Case studies of people with brain damage in these areas find that while they have intact intelligence and comprehension, they have great difficulty maintaining interest and focusing on tasks (Damasio & Anderson, 2003).

As already noted, one of the important functions of self-regulation is that it provides us with the capacity to forgo the immediate gratification of small rewards to later attain larger rewards (Duckworth et al., 2013). Anyone who has ever turned down a party invitation to study for an exam understands this particular benefit of the self-regulatory process. People who learn how to delay gratification early in childhood are better adjusted later in life—academically and socially—than are low self-regulators (de Ridder et al., 2012). However, not all self-regulation is beneficial. Brain-imaging research suggests that obsessive-compulsive disorder, which is characterized by unhealthy levels of self-regulation, typically involves abnormal functioning of the anterior cingulate cortex (McGuire et al., 2013).

In most instances, negative emotions hinder the type of self-regulation necessary for achieving longer-term goals (Tice et al., 2001). When people become upset, they tend to give in to their immediate impulses to make themselves feel better. For example, if you are trying to stop smoking, you are more likely to grab for a cigarette after having an argument with someone. This "weakness" on your part amounts to giving short-term emotion regulation priority over your longer-term self-regulatory goal of being smoke-free.

self-regulation
The ways in which people control and direct their own actions

Although a high capacity for self-regulation appears to improve your chances for success in life, over the past 2 decades there has been a body of research suggesting that self-regulating on one task often makes it harder to immediately self-regulate on unrelated tasks (Baumeister & Alquist, 2009). For example, Mark Muraven and his colleagues (1998) instructed some research participants to exercise self-control by suppressing their emotional reactions to an upsetting movie on environmental disasters. In contrast, other participants were either given no emotional control instructions or were told to increase their emotional responses by "really getting into the film." In this study, self-regulation was measured by determining how long participants would persist at a difficult physical task—namely, squeezing a hand grip as long as possible. Such squeezing requires self-control to resist giving up and releasing the grip. Participants squeezed the grip both before (*pretest*) and after (*posttest*) watching the movie, and the difference between the pre- and posttest was the dependent measure of self-regulation depletion. Consistent with the hypothesis that self-regulation strength is weakened following the exercise of self-control, those who were told to control their emotions while watching the upsetting film exhibited self-regulation depletion, as measured by the hand-grip test. No such depletion was found in the other participants. Because complex tasks require greater self-regulation than simple tasks, these findings suggested that prior self-regulation is most likely to harm people's subsequent activities when these later activities require higher-order cognitive processing (Wheeler et al., 2008).

In explaining such results, Roy Baumeister and his coworkers (1994) proposed that controlling or regulating our behavior is best understood in terms of the following principles from a *strength model of self-regulation*, which is also referred to as the *resource depletion effect*:

1. At any given time, we have only a limited amount of energy available to self-regulate.

2. Each exercise of self-regulation depletes this limited resource for a period of time.

3. Right after exercising self-regulation in one activity, we will find it harder to regulate our behavior in an unrelated activity.

According to this theory, if Tameeka is cramming for final exams and forces herself to study instead of going to a party (self-regulation success), she should be less able to control her anger later that evening (self-regulation failure) when her freeloading roommate eats the dessert that Tameeka was saving for a late-night snack. Consistent with the model, numerous studies have found that exertion of self-control causes a subsequent decline in self-control performance on other tasks—especially when people feel pressured to engage in the first act of self-control (Segerstrom & Nes, 2007). Thus, Tameeka is more likely to lose her temper if she is studying primarily due to external pressures rather than a genuine interest in the course material.

According to the strength model of self-regulation, when would a parent or a spouse be most likely to engage in domestic violence due to losing control of their emotions?

"It is not enough to understand what we ought to be, unless we know what we are; and we do not understand what we are, unless we know what we ought to be."

—T. S. Eliot, American poet, 1888–1965

"Put your hand on a hot stove for a minute, and it seems like an hour. Sit with a pretty girl for an hour, and it seems like a minute. That's relativity."

—Albert Einstein, German-born physicist, 1879–1955

Over the years, hundreds of published studies have supported the strength model of self-regulation (e.g., Baumeister & Vohs, 2016; Tice, 2007). Yet recently, a series of conceptual replications and meta-analytic studies (Carter et al., 2015; Hagger et al., 2016; Hagger et al., 2010; Sripada et al., 2014; Vadillo et al., 2016) have failed to find evidence that exercising self-control on one task depletes available self-regulation resources, which is the central principal of this theory. Given these recent findings, there is a great deal of current debate among scholars regarding the viability of this theory and whether it needs to be revised or wholly abandoned. At this point in time, the best that can be stated with certainty is that although self-regulatory failure appears to be a real psychological phenomenon, the exact way in which such failure occurs is still the subject of ongoing research (Evans et al., 2016; Hagger et al., 2017; Uziel, 2018).

Section Summary

- Both William James and George Herbert Mead identified the self as having two separate aspects: the self as subject of awareness (the "I") and the self as object of awareness (the "me," or self-concept).

- Self-concept is our theory of our personal behavior, abilities, and social relationship constructed with the help of others.

- Self-awareness is necessary for self-concept development.

- The anterior cingulate cortex, located in the frontal lobe of the cerebral cortex, is especially important in self-awareness.

- Humans develop self-awareness at around 18 months of age.

- The great apes and a few other species appear to have self-awareness ability.

- Private self-awareness is a temporary state of being in which we are aware of hidden, private self-aspects. The effects include affect intensification, knowledge clarification, and adherence to personal standards.

- Public self-awareness is a temporary state of being in which we are aware of observable, public self-aspects. The effects are social uneasiness, temporary self-esteem loss, and adherence to social standards.

- The tendencies to habitually engage in either private or public self-awareness are known as the personality traits of private self-consciousness and public self-consciousness, respectively.

- Self-regulation comprises the ways in which we control and direct our actions.

3.2 The Self as a Social Construction

Thus far, we have learned that self-awareness allows us to analyze our thoughts and feelings, and to anticipate how others might respond to us interpersonally. Through self-awareness, we develop a self-concept, which helps us regulate our behavior and adapt to our surroundings (Higgins, 1996). Many years ago, sociologist Charles Horton Cooley (1902) coined the phrase "looking-glass self" to describe the process by which our self-concepts are the *reflective appraisals* of others. Of course, these reflective appraisals represent how we *think* others perceive us—not necessarily how others *actually* perceive us. What are some of the social forces that shape self-beliefs?

> "What you think of yourself is much more important than what others think of you."
>
> —Seneca, Roman playwright, 4 BCE–CE 65

> "Who in the world am I? Ah, that's the great puzzle!"
>
> —Lewis Carroll, British author, 1832–1898, *Alice in Wonderland*

Self/Social Connection Exercise 3.2

Who Are You?

In 1954 sociologists Manford Kuhn and Thomas McPartland devised the Twenty Statements Test (TST) to measure self-concept. Spend a few minutes describing yourself by answering the question "Who am I?" when completing the following 20 "I am…" statements. Respond as if you were giving the answers to yourself, not to someone else.

1. I am _____.
2. I am _____.
3. I am _____.
4. I am _____.
5. I am _____.
6. I am _____.
7. I am _____.
8. I am _____.
9. I am _____.
10. I am _____.

11. I am _____.
12. I am _____.
13. I am _____.
14. I am _____.
15. I am _____.
16. I am _____.
17. I am _____.
18. I am _____.
19. I am _____.
20. I am _____.

Directions for Scoring

Examine your TST responses and code each into one of the following four categories (see Hartley, 1970):

Physical self-description—identify yourself in terms of physical qualities that do not imply social interaction ("I am a male"; "I am a brunette"; "I am overweight")

Social self-description—identify yourself in terms of social roles, institutional memberships, or other socially defined statuses ("I am a student"; "I am a daughter"; "I am a Jew")

Attributive self-description—identify yourself in terms of psychological or physiological states or traits ("I am intelligent"; "I am assertive"; "I am tired")

Global self-description—identify yourself so comprehensively or vaguely that it does not distinguish you from any other person ("I am a human being"; "I am alive"; "I am me").

Which category occurs most frequently for you? Using this classification scheme, Louis Zurcher (1977) found that while American college students in the 1950s and early 1960s tended to describe themselves in terms of social roles, college students in the 1970s identified themselves in terms of psychological attributes. This self-concept trend has continued (Trafimow et al., 1991) and coincides with a rise in individualist attitudes among Americans (Roberts & Helson, 1997). Do your own responses fit this pattern?

Adapted from *Manual for the Twenty Statements Problem*, by W. S. Hartley, 1970, Kansas City, MO: Department of Research, Greater Kansas City Mental Health Foundation. Used with permission by Resource Development Institute (formerly Greater Kansas City Mental Health Foundation).

3.2a Cultural Beliefs About Self-Group Relationships Shape Self-Concept.

In Chapter 1, we examined how the cultural experiences of young adults born between 1966 and the 2000s shaped their views of reality and of themselves. To explore how your cultural upbringing influences your self-beliefs, spend a few minutes completing *Self/Social Connection Exercise 3.2*. You will not only discover something about the psychology of self-development, you may also learn something fascinating about yourself.

Individualist-Collectivist Comparisons

When social psychologists examine how people describe themselves using the Twenty Statements Test (TST), they find interesting cross-cultural differences (Cross & Gore, 2002; Markus & Kitayama, 1991). In general, American, Canadian, and European self-concepts are composed of predominantly attributive self-descriptions, indicating that these individualist cultures foster the development of an **independent self** for their members. Young American adults (see Chapter 1, section 1.2c on The Social World of American Young Adults) most clearly embody the independent self. In contrast, people from collectivist cultures such as China, Mexico, Japan, India, and Kenya have more social self-descriptions, indicating the fostering of an **interdependent self** (Kanagawa et al., 2001; Ma & Schoeneman, 1997). Within the United States, European Americans, African Americans, and Latino Americans tend to have highly independent selves—despite the latter two ethnic groups having collectivist heritages (Oyserman et al., 2002). Latino Americans with interdependent selves are much more likely to be recent immigrants to the country than those with independent selves (Castro, 2003).

This differing view of the individual due to a culture's collectivist or individualist orientation begins to influence children from birth, so that their thinking becomes habitual and automatic (Kashima, 2009; Kitayama et al., 2009). Collectivist and individualist beliefs and values are then reinforced in daily living. They not only shape the structure of self-concept, they also determine beliefs about how self-development should proceed (Hashimoto, 2011). Within collectivist societies, child-rearing practices emphasize conformity, cooperation, dependence, and knowing one's proper place; within more individualist societies, independence, self-reliance, and personal success are stressed. In a series of studies, Qi Wang (2006) documented this difference in child-rearing when mothers from the United States and China shared memories with their 3-year-old children in a semistructured interview setting. When discussing past events with their children, American mothers' conversations made their child the focus of attention, often referring to the child's likes and dislikes. In contrast, Chinese mothers' conversations frequently referred to social norms and group expectations.

One consequence of these differing socialization practices is that in an individualist society, people develop a belief in their own uniqueness and diversity (Miller, 1988). This sense of individuality is nurtured and fostered within the educational system, and its manifestation is considered a sign of maturity (Pratt, 1991). On the other hand, in a collectivist society, uniqueness and individual differences are often seen as impediments to proper self-growth (Kim & Choi, 1994). Instead, the self becomes most meaningful and complete when it is closely identified with—not independent of—the group. Heejun Kim and Hazel Markus (1999) provided a simple demonstration of how these two cultural belief systems influence people's judgments when they asked Americans and East Asians to choose one of five pens like those depicted in Figure 3.2. They found that 77% of the Americans, but only 31% of the East Asians, chose the pen with the uncommon color. These results suggest cultural differences in uniqueness versus conformity needs. Figure 3.3 outlines how cultural differences regarding individualism/collectivism influence the structure of self-concept.

independent self
A way of conceiving of the self in terms of unique, personal attributes, as a being that is separate and autonomous from the group

interdependent self
A way of conceiving of the self in terms of social roles, as a being that is embedded in and dependent on the group

FIGURE 3.2   Which Pen Would You Choose?

When asked to choose one pen from an array of pens like those shown here, 77% of Americans, but only 31% of East Asians, chose the pen with the uncommon color (Kim & Markus, 1999). How does this finding relate to individualist and collectivist beliefs?

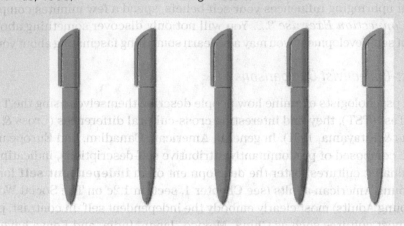

FIGURE 3.3   How Is the Self Construed in Individualist and Collectivist Cultures?

Individualist cultures foster the development of the independent self, while collectivist cultures foster the development of the interdependent self. How might these two different views of the self lead to misunderstandings—and even personal conflicts—when people from individualist and collectivist cultures interact with one another?

Individualist Culture

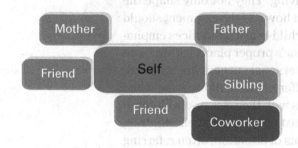

The self should be independent of the group.

Self-concept is primarily defined by internal attributes.

People are socialized to be unique, to validate their internal attributes, to promote their own goals, and to "speak their minds."

Self-esteem is based on the ability to engage in self-expression and the ability to validate internal attributes.

Collectivist Culture

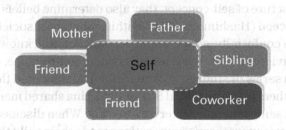

The self should be dependent on the group.

Self-concept is primarily defined by social roles and relationships.

People are socialized to belong, to occupy their proper place, to engage in appropriate behavior, and to "read others' minds."

Self-esteem is based on one's ability to adjust to the group, restrain his or her own desires, and maintain social harmony.

As you see, conceiving of the self as either independent or interdependent has important implications for how we think, feel, and interact in our social world. The ideas and activities of a culture promote a way of life that provides a constant reminder to its members of what type of self is valued. This cultural influence on thinking can literally be observed in the brain scans of people when they are asked to judge themselves and others on various personality traits. Previous research identifies a certain region in the brain's frontal lobes—the medial prefrontal cortex—as being particularly active when people think about their self-concepts. Knowing this, Ying Zhu and her coworkers (2007) asked Chinese and Western European participants to judge the applicability of different traits to themselves, to their mothers, and to another person not emotionally close to them. As expected, the medial prefrontal cortex became highly activated when both Chinese and Western European participants judged themselves but not when they judged the person not emotionally close to them. Interestingly, the medial prefrontal cortex was again highly activated for the Chinese participants when thinking about their mothers, but this was not true for the Western European participants. These findings suggest that, for people from the collectivist country of China, the same region of the brain represents both the self and mother, which is neurologically consistent with their interdependent selves. In contrast, for people from the individualist US, the self is represented in its own unique brain area—even distinct from dear old Mom—which is neurologically consistent with their independent selves (Han, 2013; Han & Northoff, 2009).

Does this mean that the dominant mode of thinking for individualists and collectivists will always be compatible with their respective independent versus interdependent self-concepts (Wu & Keysar, 2007)? The answer is decidedly no. Within these cultures, there will be times when people enter settings that trigger the alternative sense of self. For example, people who live in an individualist culture may watch the movie *It's a Wonderful Life* (see Chapter 1, at the end of section 1.2c) and be reminded how their own lives are deeply intertwined with their family, friends, and community. This setting triggers a spontaneous interdependent self, increasing the likelihood that people will at least temporarily set aside selfish interests, act cooperatively, and attend to others' needs (Gardner et al., 1999). In other words, cultures do not create people with rigidly independent or interdependent selves. Situational factors can trigger spontaneous self-concepts in people that run counter to the independent or interdependent self fostered by their culture (Kühnen et al., 2001; Kühnen & Oyserman, 2002). You might recall that in Chapter 1, at the end of section 1.2c, we discussed a recent study that found that individualist tendencies are substantially increasing in many collectivist countries around the world, primarily spurred on by socioeconomic development (Santos et al., 2017). In essence, as members of these collectivist cultures become wealthier, they may increasingly find themselves in social settings where satisfying personal needs over community needs triggers a more spontaneous independent self. That, over time, strengthens individualist values while weakening collectivist values.

What About Biculturalists?

Although cultures can be characterized as being more oriented toward individualism or collectivism, not everyone living within a particular culture will have the same individualist–collectivist leanings; individuals differ in the degree to which they identify with individualist and collectivist beliefs and values (David et al., 2014). For example, if you are a Native American, Mexican American, Indian American, or Asian American, your cultural heritage may encourage you to seek collectivist goals (Gaines, 1995). The same is true of Jews and Arabs who live in Israel, where a Western individualist ideological system often conflicts with traditional Arab and Jewish collectivist beliefs and values. Numerous studies indicate that individuals with such a *bicultural* background view themselves and the world through both individualist and collectivist lenses, which can cause internal conflict as they attempt to reconcile individualist strivings with collectivist yearnings (Hong et al., 2001; Rattan, 2011; Sussman, 2000).

"I have a very valuable parrot," declared the pet store owner. "It speaks both Spanish and English! If you pull the left leg, he speaks English, and if you pull the right leg, he speaks Spanish." "What happens if you pull both legs at once?" asked the customer. "Will he speak TexMex?" "Noooo," answered the parrot. "I will fall on my ass."

—Mexican American folk tale, adapted from West (1988)

How is this conflict best resolved? Based on studies of Pueblo, Navajo, Latino, Iranian American, Indian American, and Asian American/Canadian children and adults, neither abandoning one's ancestral collectivist culture nor isolating oneself from the dominant individualist culture is good for mental health and social inclusion (Rutland et al., 2012). Instead, successful biculturalism entails retaining ancestral values and practices while incorporating new values and practices from the dominant culture (see section 3.2c). This acknowledgment and acceptance that the two cultural identities are not fully compatible or overlapping results in a self-concept that is both more inclusive and more complex (Benet-Martínez et al., 2006). People who possess dual cultural identities engage in **cultural frame switching**, in which they move between the two different cultural belief systems in response to situational cues and demands (Mok & Morris, 2012; Sui et al., 2007). One Native American woman explained how she successfully attained her PhD while still maintaining her strong tribal ties:

> My family and I talked about the "I" and the "we," all the pressure there was when I was going to school to be this "I," to climb the old ladder, claw your way up to success.... I'm part of a "we" and I've never lost sight of that.... Because of the "we," this community and my family, I can do all of this. (Stratham & Rhoades, 2001, p. 275)

cultural frame switching
The process by which biculturalists switch between different culturally appropriate behaviors depending on the context

By accessing their two different cultural belief systems, biculturalists can engage in culturally appropriate behaviors depending on the social context (Pouliasi & Verkuyten, 2007). Among families who have recently emigrated to a new culture, children and younger adults within the family tend to have an easier time than older adults in successfully engaging in cultural frame switching (Cheung et al., 2011). In other words, people are better able to identify with a new culture if their exposure to it occurs when they are relatively young. This was certainly true for Nelson Mandela. Leaving his collectivist village at 9 years of age and subsequently being exposed to Western-style education with strong individualist values was undoubtedly an important reason that he was later able to adeptly navigate the sometimes conflicting demands of his tribal roots and the industrialized South African society. This melding of the collectivist and individualist orientations not only benefits the health of biculturalists but can also provide long-term benefits to society by infusing it with individuals who deeply understand the value of both autonomy and social obligation (Chiu & Hong, 2005). Nowhere is this better exemplified than in the contributions that Nelson Mandela made to South Africa and to the larger world.

"I have been influenced in my thinking by both West and East."

—Nelson Mandela, South African freedom fighter and president, 1918–2013

If you were to tell someone to "just be yourself," what would that mean to them depending on whether they were from an individualist or a collectivist culture?

3.2b Gender Beliefs Shape Self-Concept.

Gender beliefs and expectations can also have a profound impact on how we define ourselves. For example, one evening as Steve and his family ate dinner, his daughter Amelia, who was 3 years old at the time, surveyed the table and then looked at her father and announced, "Daddy? I'm a girl, and Mommy's a girl, and Lillian's a girl, but you're not a girl. You're a boy." Then, glancing at their dog, Yocker, who was sleeping on the floor near Steve's feet, she added, "and Yocker's a boy too." Ignoring the possibility that his daughter had recognized some characteristics other than sex that had led her to categorize her father with the family dog (perhaps a tendency to stare off into space or to pant at the sight of food), Steve complimented Amelia on her ability to distinguish males from females.

This "Amelia story" describes an identification process that all children experience at approximately this age: **gender identity**—the identification of oneself as a male or a female. Knowing that "I am a girl" or "I am a boy" is one of the core building blocks in a child's developing self-theory (Denny & Pittman, 2007). When children develop gender identity, they strive to act in ways consistent with this identity (Maccoby, 1990). What Amelia demonstrated at the dinner table was a desire to act in-line with her emerging gender identity and her understanding of gender issues.

One important gender distinction that girls and boys often learn in North American culture involves the degree to which they should define themselves in terms of close relationships (Cross & Gore, 2004). Numerous studies indicate that girls are more likely than boys to be raised to think, act, and define themselves in ways that emphasize their emotional connectedness to other people (Gore & Cross, 2006; Maccoby, 1998). Susan Cross contends that this difference in gender socialization results in girls developing cooperative relationships with others and valuing intimate friendships, while boys are more likely to develop more competitive, and less nurturing, social relationships (Cross et al., 2011; Cross & Madson, 1997). According to Cross, these gender differences persist into adulthood, fostering the construction of a *relational* self-concept among women and an *independent* self-concept among men. Individuals who construct a relational self-concept place high value on having warm, close relationships; those who construct an independent self-concept express less interest in cultivating emotional relationships (Cross & Gore, 2002; Cross & Morris, 2003). In Chapter 10 (section 10.3b), we will examine more closely how these differences in gender socialization shape the nature and quality of friendships and romantic relationships.

To what degree are these gender differences in self-concept similar to the cross-cultural differences we previously reviewed? That is, are women's self-concepts in the US similar to the self-concepts of people from collectivist cultures? Actually, it appears that the similarities are more superficial than substantive. A five-culture study by Yoshihisa Kashima and his colleagues (1995) indicates that American and Australian women's self-concepts are not like Asian women's self-concepts. Instead, these researchers found that while individualist-collectivist cultural differences are captured mostly by the extent to which people see themselves as acting as independent agents in relation to the group, gender differences are best summarized by the extent to which people regard themselves as *emotionally related* to other individuals. This suggests that gender socialization has much more to do with encouraging girls to pay attention to the emotional "pulse" of their social relationships (while discouraging boys from doing so) than it has to do with encouraging boys to be independent of the group and girls to be dependent on the group. In other words,

Once girls and boys develop gender identities, they try to behave in ways that are consistent with their identities. What role do others play in shaping our gender beliefs?

(Shutterstock)

gender identity
The identification of oneself as a male or a female

"A race of people is like an individual man—until it uses its own talent, takes pride in its own history, expresses its own culture, affirms its own selfhood, it can never fulfill itself."

—Malcolm X, US Muslim and black nationalist, 1925–1965

individualist-collectivist socialization has decidedly different effects on the nature of self-concept from male-female socialization.

3.2c   Social Identities Establish "What" and "Where" We Are as Social Beings.

Cultural identities and relational self-concepts both involve including others into our self-concepts. Similarly, following the terrorist attacks of September 11, 2001, millions of Americans experienced a renewed sense of national unity and patriotism—most clearly expressed by the sharp increase in the displaying of the American flag (Skitka, 2006). In explaining this process of group identification, contemporary social psychologists have taken William James's notion of the social "me" and developed it into the concept of **social identities**. Social identities are those aspects of our self-concepts that are based on our group memberships (Hogg & Abrams, 1998). They establish *what* and *where* we are in social terms (Ellemers et al., 2002).

One of the consequences of group identification is an internalization of the group's view of social reality. Social identities provide members with a shared set of values, beliefs, and goals relating to themselves and their social world. As George Herbert Mead might describe it, to have a social identity is to internalize the group within the individual, which in turn serves to regulate and coordinate the attitudes and behavior of the separate group members. One recent study (Steffens et al., 2016) also suggests that people who have many social identities exhibit more creative thinking than do those with few social identities, possibly due to the former individuals having a greater diversity of opinions and experience, thus allowing them to think more flexibly.

Yet, if social identities are a representation of the group within the mind of the individual, what happens when we live in a society where our group is devalued by the larger culture? Don't we run the risk of falling victim to a negative self-fulfilling prophecy? This is the dilemma faced by members of social groups that have been subjected to prejudice, discrimination, and negative stereotypes (Crocker et al., 1994). Sometimes the negativity is subtle, perhaps unintentional, such as regularly being mistaken for a foreigner in one's own country—which is a common occurrence among Americans of Asian, Muslim, and Hispanic descent (Huynh et al., 2011). One way that ethnic minority groups have coped with intolerance and nonacceptance is by rediscovering their own ethnic heritage and actively rejecting the negative stereotypes in the larger culture (Joseph & Hunter, 2011). **Ethnic identity**, which is a type of social identity, is an individual's sense of personal identification with a particular ethnic group (Yip, 2005).

In describing ethnic identity formation, most theories propose an age-related progression from the unawareness of ethnic membership to the habitual use of an ethnic category to describe the self (Castro, 2003). For example, Jean Phinney (1991) has proposed a three-stage model (see Table 3.1). In Stage 1, the *unexamined ethnic identity* stage, individuals often have not personally examined ethnic identity issues and may have incorporated negative stereotypes from the dominant culture into their own self-concepts, resulting in feelings of inadequacy (Clark & Clark, 1939; Phinney & Kohatsu, 1997). Some people in Stage 1 may have been exposed to positive ethnic attitudes from others but have simply not incorporated those attitudes into their self-concepts.

(Shutterstock)

Ethnic identity is an individual's sense of personal identification with a particular ethnic group.

social identities
Aspects of a person's self-concept based on his or her group memberships

ethnic identity
An individual's sense of personal identification with a particular ethnic group

TABLE 3.1	Stages in Ethnic Identity Formation
Stage 1	*Unexamined ethnic identity*—Lack of exploration of ethnicity, due to lack of interest or due to having merely adopted other people's opinions of ethnicity
Stage 2	*Ethnic identity search*—Involvement in exploring and seeking to understand the meaning of ethnicity for oneself, often sparked by some incident that focused attention on one's minority status in the dominant culture
Stage 3	*Achieved ethnic identity*—Clear and confident sense of one's own ethnicity; ability to identify and internalize those aspects of the dominant culture that are acceptable and stand against those that are oppressive

In Stage 2, *ethnic identity search*, people have an experience that temporarily dislodges their old worldview, making them receptive to exploring their own ethnicity. In many cases, the catalyst for this exploration is a personal experience with prejudice (Sanders Thompson, 1991). This stage often entails an intense period of searching, in which people passionately consume ethnic literature and participate in cultural events. During Stage 2, some individuals may also develop an *oppositional identity* in which they actively reject values of the dominant culture. While in this oppositional stance, anything associated with the dominant group is typically devalued, whereas anything associated with one's own ethnic group is declared superior and highly valued (Carter, 2003; Cross, 1991).

If your ethnic heritage is relevant to who you think you are, you are experiencing which stage in Phinney's model? Is this model an accurate portrayal of your own ethnic identity development?

The third stage and culmination of this process is a deeper understanding of, and appreciation for, one's ethnicity—what Phinney labels *achieved ethnic identity*. Confidence and security in a newfound ethnic identity allow people to feel ethnic pride along with a new understanding of their own place within the dominant culture. They are able to internalize those aspects of the dominant culture that are acceptable (for example, financial security, independence, pursuit of academics) and stand against those that are oppressive (for example, racism and sexism).

"Born into the skin of yellow women we are born into the armor of warriors."

—Kitty Tsui, Chinese American poet, born 1952

A number of studies support Phinney's view of the mental health benefits of ethnic identity development, among them being high self-esteem and having a stable self-concept (Bailey & Bradbury-Bailey, 2010; Phinney et al., 1997). These findings suggest that when our commitment to, and attitudes toward, our ethnic group are strongly positive, they can serve as buffers to the negative stereotypes in the larger society (Brannon et al., 2015). This process of social identity development in oppressed ethnic groups has parallels in other social groups that have historically been discriminated against, such as women, lesbians and gay men, and the disabled. Although such positive social identities can short-circuit the negative effects that prejudice can inflict on self-esteem, they are not always effective (Major et al., 2007). In Chapter 6 we will examine in greater detail some of these negative effects (see section 6.2e).

Section Summary

- The interdependent self identifies with societal institutions and is more common in collectivist cultures.

- The independent self identifies with personal attributes and is more common in individualist cultures.

- Gender identity is our identification with being female or male.

- In North American culture, women have a greater sense of relational interdependence than men, and this difference is reflected in how women and men define themselves.

- Social identities situate us within clearly defined groups.

- Ethnic identities insulate us from the negative effects of derogatory stereotypes.

3.3 Presenting the Self to Others

When we interact with others, we often try to manage their impressions of us by carefully constructing and monitoring our presented selves (Schlenker & Wowra, 2003). Indeed, sociologist Erving Goffman (1959) suggests that social interaction is like a theatrical performance, with the interactants being the actors on stage playing prescribed roles. While "on stage," people act out "lines" and attempt to maintain competent and appropriately presented selves. In observing this performance, the audience generally accepts the presented selves at face value and treats them accordingly. The acceptance may not be genuine, but Goffman asserts that people have learned to keep their private opinions to themselves, unless the performers prove wholly incompetent. To do otherwise would disrupt the smooth flow of social interaction. Let us examine in more detail these everyday performances.

3.3a Self-Presentations Are Either Consciously or Automatically Constructed.

The process of constructing and presenting the self in order to shape other people's impressions and achieve ulterior goals is known as **strategic self-presentation** (Jones & Pittman, 1982; Nezlek & Leary, 2002). Such impression management can be stressful and is associated with increases in heart rate and blood pressure (Heffner et al., 2002). It can also require considerable self-regulation (see section 3.1c); and, as self-presentation demands increase, people sometimes lose control of their performances (van den Bos et al., 2011). For example, you could go into a job interview intending to convey intelligence and social skill, only to spill coffee all over yourself. Perhaps you can relate to the following account of a woman's ill-fated attempt to impress the parents of her fiancé (Knapp et al., 1986):

> I was invited to my fiancé's home for a special dinner. It was the first time I had met everyone and I was trying to impress them. As we sat down to eat, his father turned to me and said, "I hope you'll say grace." I was so unsettled by this request that I immediately bowed my head and said, "Now I lay me down to sleep...." (p. 40)

strategic self-presentation

Conscious and deliberate efforts to shape other people's impressions in order to gain power, influence, sympathy, or approval

Making social blunders and not being able to project an appropriate presented self often cause embarrassment (Sabini et al., 2001). College students report being embarrassed at least once a week, while younger teenagers become embarrassed even more often (Miller, 1995). Embarrassment is accompanied by an activation of the sympathetic nervous system, which is that part of our nervous system that prepares us to deal with threatening situations. The blushing, sweating, and heart pounding we experience during embarrassing incidents are our body's way of harnessing its energy to respond to the perceived threat (Gerlach et al., 2003). The good news about embarrassment is that onlookers generally judge us less harshly for our social gaffes than we think they do (Savitsky et al., 2001). Further, embarrassing situations are often unpleasant for onlookers as well—and thus they typically help us recover our self-presentations (Marcus et al., 1996). Because friends and loved ones are part of our self-concepts, we can also experience embarrassment when their self-presentations are discredited (Thornton, 2003).

The more skilled we become in particular self-presentations, the more likely it is that they will be automatically activated and guided without conscious monitoring (Tyler, 2012). Such automatic self-presentations are efficient because they conserve cognitive resources that can then be devoted to other tasks. This idea that self-presentation involves both automatic and deliberate cognitive processes reflects the *dual-process* approach to social cognition first introduced in Chapter 1 (see section 1.2b). According to this perspective, human beings employ two broad cognitive strategies in interacting with their social world—one involving effortless thinking and the other involving effortful thinking.

Although we are most aware of employing strategic self-presentations when interacting with strangers or casual acquaintances, these self-presentations also play important roles in our intimate relationships. *Evaluation concerns* and *cognitive effort* are two common differences between the self-presentations we construct in nonintimate and intimate relationships. When socializing with friends and loved ones, we are typically less anxious about how we are being evaluated and more skilled with the self-presentations we commonly employ. As a result, our intimate self-presentations are likely activated and guided with less conscious monitoring than when we are with strangers and casual acquaintances (Gosnell et al., 2011; Schlenker & Wowra, 2003). In other words, they are operating below our level of awareness (implicit cognition), much like a computer program runs in the background without any obvious visual detection on the screen to remind us that it is active. Because these self-presentations are being activated and monitored nonconsciously, we think of them as "more genuine" than those that are more deliberately executed. However, we will consciously attend to and regulate our self-presentations on those occasions when our friends and family "get the wrong impression" of us.

One extremely popular avenue by which people consciously present themselves to others is on online social networking sites such as Facebook, Twitter, and Instagram. One important difference between the manner in which online and offline selves are presented is in the degree of control people have over their self-presentations; people have much greater control in consciously constructing and presenting themselves online compared to normal everyday self-presentations (Schack, 2010). Because of the high degree of control that people have over their online-presented selves, is there any evidence that people exercise this control to construct overly idealized versions of themselves for their profiles?

Are the self-presentations that people post on their Facebook profiles an accurate representation of their actual selves, or are they more likely reflections of their idealized selves?

(Chinnapong / Shutterstock)

Content analysis of social networking sites suggests that at least some people engage in shameless embellishment of their personalities when they create a public self to present to others (Manago et al., 2008). Yet other research suggests that the ability of "friends" to post comments about people's profiles may cause most online self-presenters to monitor and control the construction of unrealistically idealized public selves. One such study investigated profiles on the most popular social networking sites in the United States (Facebook) and Germany (StudiVZ, SchuelerVZ). Mitja Back and his colleagues (2010) obtained the online social network profiles of research participants; then they asked participants to describe their ideal selves and had four friends of each participant describe each participant's actual self. Comparison of their online profiles with their ideal self-descriptions and their friends' descriptions of their actual selves found little evidence that participants presented themselves in an idealized manner online. The findings from these separate studies suggest that while some people may present themselves in an idealized manner in their online profiles, most people construct fairly accurate self-presentations, perhaps partly due to the fact that they realize that their friends will likely provide them with corrective feedback if they stray too far from their actual selves. Additional research indicates that, when presenting themselves to others, people feel more powerful when they believe they are behaving authentically versus inauthentically (Gan et al., 2018), which confirms the following pearls of wisdom contained within William Shakespeare's play *Hamlet*: "This above all; to thine own self be true. And it must follow, as the night the day. Thou canst not then be false to any man (Hamlet Act 1, scene 3, 78–82)."

Do you think that people raised in collectivist cultures might sometimes have different self-presentation concerns than those raised in individualist cultures?

3.3b   Self-Presentation Strategies Differ in Their Goals.

The process of self-presentation often conjures up images of social gamesmanship and deception, but there is nothing necessarily unsavory about strategic self-presentations— we all employ them and we can do so in an authentic manner. When John Nezlek and his coworkers (2007) studied college students' self-presentations, they found that being socially accepted is a powerful motive. While trying to manage others' impressions, students were more concerned about appearing friendly, likable, and honest than about appearing competent and intelligent. Additional research finds that when people engage in these positive self-presentations, they tend to feel happy afterward—often happier than they anticipated they would be prior to the interaction (Dunn et al., 2007). What self-presentation strategies are associated with this valued acceptance and heightened mood?

"The world's a stage, and most of us are desperately unrehearsed."

—Seán O'Casey, Irish playwright, 1880–1964

The most commonly employed self-presentation strategy to gain acceptance is *ingratiation*, in which others' impressions are shaped through flattery (Varma et al., 2006). Because flattery increases recipients' self-esteem, and hence their liking for the flatterer, Edward Jones (1990) calls ingratiation the most fundamental of all strategies—"a pinch or two of ingratiation helps to leaven the other self-presentation strategies as well." As a testament to the power of ingratiation, one study found that business managers who regularly used this self-presentation strategy received the greatest salary increases and the most promotions over a 5-year period (Orpen, 1996). Similarly, a field experiment found that waitresses who complimented customers on their dinner selections received significantly larger tips than servers who did not give compliments (Seiter, 2007). Despite such potential rewards, ingratiation requires social skill, and it is a double-edged sword (Treadway et al., 2007). A meta-analysis of 69 ingratiation studies found that while the recipient of ingratiation is positively affected by the flattery, bystanders who observe the ingratiating self-presentation are more likely to question the motives of the flatterer (Gordon, 1996). These findings suggest that such disparaging terms as *brownnoser* and *apple polisher* are more likely to be used by observers of ingratiation than by recipients.

Another strategy that is often used to gain acceptance is *modesty*. Being modest means underrepresenting your positive traits, contributions, or accomplishments. Modesty can be extremely effective in increasing your likability, and it preserves high levels of perceived competence and honesty (Draelants & Darchy-Koechlin, 2011). Modesty is considered a more feminine response following achievement (Miller et al., 1992). Thus, it is not surprising that women are not only more likely than men to employ it but that they also are more successful in using it (Wosinska et al., 1996). Despite the generally favorable response to modesty, you should use it only when others are aware of your successes and can recognize that an underrepresentation is taking place (Miller & Schlenker, 1985). For example, modesty would not be an effective strategy for a talented student to employ when trying to secure strong letters of recommendation from professors who are unaware of his or her many accomplishments.

In situations where competency is highly valued, people often rely upon *self-promotion*, in which they strive to convey positive information about themselves either through their behavior or by telling others about their positive assets and accomplishments. People who use *self-promotion* want to be respected for their intelligence and competence, and thus this strategy is commonly employed during work-related interactions (Ellis et al., 2002; Stevens & Kristof, 1995). In contrast to modesty, self-promotion is considered to be a more masculine response following achievement, and thus it is not surprising that men are more likely than women to employ self-promotion (Miller et al., 1992). Self-promotion is also a more acceptable self-presentation strategy in individualist cultures than in collectivist cultures, where modest self-presentations are favored (Chen & Jing, 2012). Although often effective in conveying a positive social image, self-promotion does not always result in desirable consequences. This is because in addition to evaluating competence, perceivers also judge such interpersonal dimensions as likability and humility. Therefore, while self-promoters may be seen as competent, they also may be judged as less likable because they are perceived as braggarts (Godfrey et al., 1986; Inman et al., 2004). To counter this social danger, astute self-promoters often acknowledge certain minor flaws or shortcomings along with their many competencies, or enlist others to extol their virtues (Baumeister & Jones, 1978; Pfeffer et al., 2006).

President Donald Trump is much-publicized for his self-praise, which occurs so frequently and is so extravagant that he is widely perceived as a braggart. What self-presentation strategy is he employing and what positive attribution is he seeking?

A self-presentation strategy that tries to thread the needle between self-promotion and modesty is *humblebragging*, where people engage in self-promotion but mask their bragging by complaining about and/or displaying humility about their accomplishments. An example of humblebragging is the following comment from a graduating college student: "I don't know how I was offered two great jobs before so many of my smarter classmates! And now I have to go to work right away with no time for fun!" In employing this strategy, people are seeking to be perceived as both competent and likable, similar goals as those who employ modesty. Unfortunately for those who use it, humblebragging is one of the least effective strategies in achieving self-presentation goals. Research indicates that those who engage in this strategy are viewed as less likable and less competent, because using the strategy makes the humblebragger seem insincere, even more so than a straight-forward self-promoter or a simple complainer (Sezer et al., 2018).

Another strategy that has much in common with self-promotion is *exemplification*, which is a self-presentation designed to elicit perceptions of integrity and moral worthiness while at the same time arousing guilt and emulation in others (Leary, 1996). Exemplifiers often come across as being absorbed by devotion to some cause while also suffering for the welfare of others. Workers who encourage fellow employees to go home while they sacrifice personal time for the "good of the company," religious leaders who profess to "walk with the Lord," and politicians who tell their constituents that they will be a "moral beacon" in government all exemplify this form of strategic self-presentation. Nelson Mandela exhibited this self-presentation strategy in his struggle against apartheid in South Africa. During his 1963 sabotage trial, Mandela gave his famous "Speech from the Dock," which provides an excellent example of successful exemplification. Consider the following excerpt:

> During my lifetime I have dedicated myself to this struggle of the African people. I have fought against white domination, and I have fought against black domination. I have cherished the ideal of a democratic and free society in which all persons live together in harmony and with equal opportunities. It is an ideal which I hope to live for and to achieve. But if needs be, it is an ideal for which I am prepared to die. (Mandela, 1994, p. 368)

The danger of taking on the saint-like role is that, unlike Nelson Mandela, many people cannot live up to such high standards and run the risk of being perceived as hypocritical if their actions deviate from this moral high ground (Stone et al., 1997). Exemplifiers also run the risk of being socially shunned because some people experience guilt and shame while in their presence, due to being reminded of their own shortcomings. Although there are dangers in using this strategy, skillful execution does bring benefits. Leaders who embody exemplification in their presented selves foster strong loyalty and group cohesion among their followers (Rozell & Gundersen, 2003).

Consider the different self-presentation strategies you used today. Under what circumstances, and with whom, did you employ them? Which ones achieved the desired effect? Was there one strategy that you frequently employed? If you didn't use any, why was this the case?

When people want to coerce others into doing something, they might use *intimidation*, a self-presentation tactic that involves arousing fear and gaining power by convincing others that you are powerful and/or dangerous (Christopher et al., 2005). This self-presentation strategy is the hallmark of schoolyard bullies and is also employed by athletes in such aggressive sports as football, hockey, and boxing (Jeffrey et al., 2001). Drivers who tailgate you on the highway are using this strategy to get what they want—a speedy, unencumbered path (Bassett et al., 2002). Parents also use intimidation in its subtler form. A frown, combined with a lowered tone of voice and a pointed index finger, is often sufficient in securing compliance from a child.

"Nobody is better on humility than me."

—Donald Trump, 45th US president (b. 1946)

When people seek to elicit help or sympathy from others based on a sense of social obligation, they rely on *supplication*, a strategy where they advertise their weaknesses or their dependence on others (K. J. Harris et al., 2007). For example, a homeless person asking passersby for spare change relies on a societal norm of empathy for those who are less fortunate (Dordick, 1997). A less extreme example is a student who repeatedly seeks help in completing class assignments, professing an inability to understand the material. This technique—while effective in many circumstances—is loaded with psychological land mines. One danger is that people tend to "blame the victim" (Lerner, 1980), often believing that his/her suffering is self-inflicted. Another danger is that even though supplicators often receive help and support, they are privately judged as poorly functioning individuals (Powers & Zuroff, 1988). Not surprisingly, the final toll of advertising one's incompetence is often a loss of self-esteem (Osborne, 2002).

Perhaps the most interesting of all self-presentation strategies is **self-handicapping**, a strategy in which a person creates obstacles to his or her own performance either to provide an excuse for failure or to enhance success (Maddison & Prapavessis, 2007). For example, the night before an important exam, Barry may go to a party instead of studying. By choosing to socialize, he is greatly decreasing his likelihood of success on the exam. An observer of Barry's actions might conclude that his decision not to study was self-defeating. However, someone versed in social psychological theory might suggest that his actions serve a second purpose: to protect his self-esteem. Putting barriers in the way of your success not only provides you with an excuse for failure, it also enhances your self-esteem if success is secured despite the handicap. Thus, creating obstacles to success can not only *protect* self-esteem, it can also *enhance* it. These are the two primary motives underlying self-handicapping. People are more likely to use this strategy when they are being evaluated on skills or attributes central to their self-concepts rather than on unimportant characteristics (Ferrari & Tice, 2000).

Of the two motives underlying self-handicapping, which is dominant? A series of studies by Diane Tice (1991) indicates that it depends on a person's level of self-esteem. She found evidence that individuals with high self-esteem handicap themselves to enhance their success, and they are largely unconcerned about protecting themselves against failure. In contrast, low self-esteem persons self-handicap to protect themselves from the negative implications of failure. Thus, the desire to further enhance self-esteem appears to motivate high self-esteem people to self-handicap, but it is the desire to protect self-esteem that appears to motivate those low in self-esteem. Table 3.2 summarizes the self-presentation strategies discussed in this section.

self-handicapping
Undertaking actions that sabotage one's performance and enhance the opportunity to excuse the anticipated failure

"It is not whether you really cry. It's whether the audience thinks you are crying."
—Ingrid Bergman, Swedish actress, 1915–1982

TABLE 3.2	Common Self-Presentation Strategies			
	Attributions Sought	**Negative Attributions Risked**	**Emotions Aroused**	**Typical Actions**
Ingratiation	Likable	Brownnoser	Affection	Complimenting, doing favors
Modesty	Likable and competent	Nonassertive	Affection and respect	Understating achievements
Self-promotion	Competent	Conceited	Respect	Making claims about performance
Humblebragging	Likable and competent	Insincere	Sympathy and respect	Bragging, combined with humility and/or complaining
Exemplification	Worthy	Hypocrite	Guilt	Employing self-denial
Intimidation	Dangerous	Blowhard	Fear	Threatening
Supplication	Helpless	Stigmatized	Nurturance	Being self-deprecating
Self-handicapping	Competent	Incompetent	Respect	Creating obstacles

Section Summary

- Self-presentations manage the impression we make on others.

- Self-presentations involve both automatic and deliberate thinking, with well-learned self-presentations often operating on "autopilot."

- Common strategic self-presentations include ingratiation, modesty, self-promotion, humblebragging, exemplification, intimidation, supplication, and self-handicapping.

3.4   Evaluating the Self

As previously noted, *self-esteem* is your evaluation of your self-concept, and both developmental and social psychological research indicates that self-esteem is rooted in interpersonal experiences, with positive social experiences bolstering feelings of self-worth (Cameron & Granger, 2019. Mark Leary and his colleagues (1995) assert that during the course of human evolution, self-esteem emerged as an internal "meter" (a *sociometer*) of our sense of group inclusion. That is, individuals were much more likely to survive and reproduce when firmly embedded within a social group rather than when forced to survive on their own (Leary, 2005). Consistent with the *sociometer model* of self-esteem, when people behave in ways that decrease the likelihood they will be rejected—or when others socially embrace them—their self-esteem increases (Stinson et al., 2010).

3.4a   The Tendency to Self-Enhance Bolsters Self-Esteem and Promotes Health.

While positive social experiences tend to strengthen self-esteem, another key psychological factor influencing feelings of self-worth is the tendency of people to perceive themselves positively even when their social experiences might not warrant such perceptions. For example, most people regard themselves more positively than they regard their peers (Moore & Small, 2007). Longitudinal research suggests that this *better-than-average effect*—combined with the *self-serving bias* effect (see Chapter 1, section 1.2a) of taking credit for positive outcomes but denying responsibility for negative outcomes—offers people protection against social stress and has long-term health benefits (Zuckerman & O'Loughlin, 2006). Both of these personal biases are driven by the *self-enhancement motive*, which is the desire to interpret situations so as to attain positive self-esteem. A recent meta-analytic study covering more than four decades of research and including almost 300 studies totaling more than 120,000 participants found that, regardless of whether people live in individualist or collectivist cultures, the tendency to self-enhance is positively related to happiness and overall mental health (Dufner et al., 2019). Further, there is strong evidence that individuals who tend to self-enhance have an advantage when meeting people for the first time (Anderson et al., 2012; Dufner et al., 2019). In such situations, it appears that self-enhancers' strategic self-presentations are more effective in creating desirable impressions with strangers than are those of individuals who tend not to self-enhance.

Although the self-enhancement motive is found worldwide, collectivist cultures tend to have lower levels of self-esteem than individualist cultures (Schmitt & Allik, 2005), which may be partly due to the fact that people from collectivist cultures are socialized to be more self-critical than people from individualist cultures (Falk et al.,

2009). Underlying this self-critical tendency among collectivists is a greater desire for self-improvement compared to individualists (Heine & Raineri, 2009).

Given that self-enhancement is found in cultures around the world and that this motive has a positive impact on self-esteem, it is not surprising that a multinational study of self-esteem indicates that the majority of people who are identified as having low self-esteem do not see themselves as worthless, incompetent losers (Schmitt & Allik, 2005). Instead, they are people who evaluate themselves *neutrally*—rather than either very positively or very negatively. In most cases, it is only in comparison to the very positive evaluations of people with high self-esteem that these individuals can be described as having "low" self-esteem. The good news here is that most of us do not have very negative self-views; instead, we judge our personalities rather positively (Twenge & Campbell, 2008). Yet what about those individuals who do not self-enhance, and instead, hold themselves in low regard? What are the consequences?

A wealth of research indicates that individuals with low self-esteem are generally more unhappy and depressed, more needful of social acceptance, less willing to take risks to benefit themselves, more likely to encounter academic and financial problems, less likely to have successful careers, and less likely to be physically healthy than are high self-esteem individuals (Orth & Robins, 2013; Orth et al., 2012). There is also evidence that those who differ in self-esteem also differ in their emotional reactions to positive and negative daily events. When experiencing positive emotions following some desirable outcome, high self-esteem individuals tend to savor their feelings, while low self-esteem individuals tend to dampen these emotions and may even become anxious (Wood et al., 2005). In contrast, while negative events generally dampen people's daily moods regardless of their levels of self-esteem, low self-esteem people are more adversely affected because they are much more likely than others to dwell upon these events rather than seeking solutions to them (Kuster et al., 2012; Richter & Ridout, 2011). One reason for this lack of motivation to engage in self-regulation that might improve their circumstances is that low self-esteem people are simply more accustomed to negative moods, and hence they accept them more readily than do high self-esteem individuals.

3.4b There Is a Dark Side to High Self-Esteem.

Thus far we have discussed research that generally extols the virtues of high self-esteem. However, are there instances where high self-esteem is problematic? Based on Heine and Hamamura's (2007) cross-cultural comparisons of self-enhancement tendencies, it appears that individualist cultures are much more likely than collectivist cultures to believe that high self-esteem is essential for mental health and life satisfaction (Spencer-Rodgers et al., 2004; Twenge & Campbell, 2001). Perhaps due to this cultural belief, American social psychologists were rather slow in studying the possible negative effects of wanting to feel good about ourselves (Crocker & Park, 2004). Fortunately, this trend was reversed and several studies found evidence that there can be a hidden cost to trying to achieve or maintain high self-esteem: Certain individuals with superficially high self-esteem react with aggression when someone challenges their favorable self-assessments (Bushman & Baumeister, 2002; Campbell et al., 2004). The source of this aggressive response appears to be a defensive reaction to avoid having to make any downward revision of self-esteem.

People with unstable high self-esteem become angry and hostile when their self-worth is challenged.

(Shutterstock)

Michael Kernis (2003) asserts that it is the stability of high self-esteem that determines whether threats to self-esteem lead to aggression. People with unstable high self-esteem lack confidence in their self-worth and thus often become angry and hostile when their self-esteem is challenged (Kernis & Lakey, 2010; Kernis et al., 2000). Additional research indicates that unstable high self-esteem is associated with *narcissism*, a personality trait characterized by insecurity and the need for constant reassurance (Thomaes & Bushman, 2011). In contrast, *stable* high self-esteem individuals may not enjoy being criticized, but they can control their emotions and are no more aggressive in such circumstances than are low self-esteem people (Taylor et al., 2003).

Underlying the unstable high self-esteem of narcissists are two conflicting types of self-esteem. Their **explicit self-esteem**, their conscious and deliberate self-evaluation, is quite high, but their **implicit self-esteem**, their unintentional and perhaps unconscious self-evaluation, is conflicted and quite low in certain areas (Laws & Rivera, 2012). Explicit self-esteem is what people report when they are asked directly how they feel about themselves on self-report measures. How do we measure implicit self-esteem?

Implicit self-esteem is typically assessed using Implicit Association Test (IAT) measures, which are discussed in Chapter 2 (section 2.2b). One version of this test measures the automatic associations between a person's self-concept and positive and negative affect (DeHart et al., 2013). In one measurement stage, participants categorize pleasant words and self-related words on the same computer key and unpleasant and other-related words on another computer key (self + pleasant; other + unpleasant). In a later stage, the tasks are reversed, and participants categorize unpleasant words and self-related words on one key and other-related words and pleasant words on another computer key (self + unpleasant; other + pleasant). An overall IAT score is computed by taking the difference between the average response times to the two test stages. The assumption is that participants with high implicit self-esteem have many positive associations and few negative associations with the self. As a result, the self + pleasant task will be very easy for them, and they will have fast response times, but the self + unpleasant task will be more difficult, and they will have slower response times. In contrast, it is assumed that participants with low implicit self-esteem have many negative associations and few positive associations with the self. Therefore, they will have faster response times for self + unpleasant associations than for self + pleasant associations. If you would like to take an implicit self-esteem test, check out the website at the end of the chapter.

In a series of studies, Christian Jordan and his coworkers (2003) found support for the hypothesis that unstable high self-esteem individuals have two conflicting types of self-esteem, one consciously positive and the other unconsciously negative. Their results indicate that among individuals with high explicit self-esteem, those with relatively low implicit self-esteem have feelings of self-worth that depend more on others' social approval, their physical appearance, and how well they perform on competitive tasks. Further, after failing at a task, these individuals are likely to quit, while high explicit/high implicit self-esteem individuals often persist in the face of failure. Finally, and of particular interest, the researchers found that while high explicit/low implicit self-esteem individuals

explicit self-esteem
A person's conscious and deliberate evaluation of his or her self-concept

implicit self-esteem
A person's unintentional, and perhaps unconscious, evaluation of his or her self-concept

People with low implicit self-esteem don't like themselves, but typically they are not consciously aware of this negative self-regard. If you were a therapist, how might you use classical conditioning techniques to unconsciously increase a person's low implicit self-esteem?

"One must not be a name-dropper, as Her Majesty remarked to me at luncheon yesterday."

—Norman St. John-Stevas, member of British Parliament, 1929–2012

"We have the paradox of a man shamed to death because he is only the second pugilist or the second oarsman in the world. . . . Yonder puny fellow, however, whom everyone can beat, suffers no chagrin, for he has long ago abandoned the attempt to 'carry that line.'"

—William James, American psychologist and philosopher, 1842–1910 score very high on narcissism, high explicit self-esteem people who also have high implicit self-esteem score very low on narcissism (see Figure 3.4).

FIGURE 3.4   Narcissism as a Function of Implicit Self-Esteem and Explicit Self-Esteem

Jordan and his colleagues (2003) found that explicit self-esteem interacts with implicit self-esteem to create either high or low levels of narcissism. People who are high in explicit self-esteem but low in implicit self-esteem show the highest levels of narcissism. In contrast, those high in both explicit and implicit self-esteem show levels of narcissism no higher than people who are low in both implicit and explicit self-esteem. Why might this unstable form of self-esteem (high explicit/low implicit) be more prevalent in individualist cultures than in collectivist cultures?

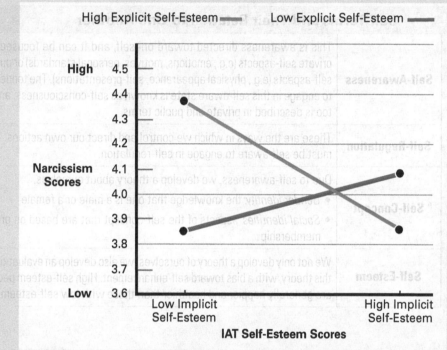

Data source: "'I Love Me...I Love Me Not': Implicit Self-esteem, Explicit Self-esteem, and Defensiveness," by C. H. Jordan et al., 2003, *Motivated Social Perception: The Ontario Symposium, 9*, pp. 117–145.

In viewing this research from a cultural perspective, it may be that the emphasis in individualist cultures on feeling good about oneself has resulted in some people consciously fabricating a high sense of self-worth that is inconsistent with their life experiences. The result is that they have two conflicting types of self-esteem, with the consciously positive form requiring constant bolstering and defense in order for it to survive. When others do not comply with this need and, instead, threaten their self-esteem through social criticism, these unstable high self-esteem people are likely to respond by engaging in antisocial self-enhancement strategies. This is the dark side of high self-esteem.

Section Summary

- Self-enhancement is a motive found in cultures throughout the world and it bolsters self-esteem and promotes health.

- Collectivist cultures tend to have lower levels of self-esteem than individualist cultures.

- Unstable high self-esteem persons become angry and hostile when their self-worth is challenged.

- In Table 3.3, review how the self terms are related to one another.

TABLE 3.3	Self Terms and Their Relation to One Another	
The "I"	Self-Awareness	This is awareness directed toward oneself, and it can be focused on private self-aspects (e.g., emotions, motives, personal standards) or public self-aspects (e.g., physical appearance, self-presentations). The tendency to engage in this self-aware state is known as self-consciousness, and it too is described in private and public terms.
	Self-Regulation	These are the ways in which we control and direct our own actions. You must be self-aware to engage in self-regulation.
The "Me"	Self-Concept	Due to self-awareness, we develop a theory about ourselves. • *Gender identity:* the knowledge that one is a male or a female • *Social identities:* aspects of the self-concept that are based on group membership
	Self-Esteem	We not only develop a theory of ourselves, we also develop an evaluation of this theory, with a bias toward self-enhancement. High self-esteem people are generally happier and healthier than those with low self-esteem.

Applications

Do You Engage in Binge Drinking or Eating to Escape from Yourself?

As you have learned from reading this chapter, we all have the ability to engage in self-awareness. When we experience failure or a significant personal loss, we generally spend some time afterward in focused self-awareness as a means to better understand what happened. Although this self-focus can be quite helpful, most of us soon disengage from intense introspection and return to our normal states of awareness. However, what happens when our failure or loss is very great, such that we can find no ready solution? In such instances, we may become depressed, which increases self-focus, which increases depression, and so forth (Pyszczynski & Greenberg, 1992). Thus, intense self-awareness can be thought of as both resulting from depression as well as contributing to it.

Unfortunately, one way depressed individuals sometimes try to break out of this negative self-aware state is by engaging in self-destructive behaviors that have the side benefit of temporarily reducing self-awareness, thereby temporarily reducing depression (Neighbors et al., 2004). Binge eating and drinking are two activities that can be motivated by a desire to escape from self-awareness. They are also two of the most serious social problems faced by college students today.

Regarding alcohol abuse, Jay Hull (1981) found evidence not only that alcohol reduces self-awareness but also that individuals high in private self-consciousness are more likely to use it to deal with negative information about themselves. In one study, undergraduate participants were given intelligence-related tests and were then randomly given either success or failure feedback (Hull & Young, 1983). Immediately following this feedback, they participated in a seemingly unrelated wine-tasting study. Although the amount of wine consumed by those low in private self-consciousness was not influenced by their previous success or failure, those high in private self-consciousness drank more wine after receiving failure feedback than after success feedback. In effect, consuming alcohol following failure temporarily caused the high private self-conscious individuals to act like low private self-conscious individuals—their degree of self-awareness was reduced, and they were then not as attentive to their failure. Similar results have been found in adolescent alcohol abuse. Following academic failure, high private self-conscious students drink more than low self-conscious students (Hull et al., 1986). These studies suggest that some people—especially high private self-conscious individuals—may use alcohol as a "psychological crutch" to avoid the chronic attention to their own private thoughts and feelings that amplifies emotional pain.

While alcohol seems to reduce self-awareness by physically interfering with cognitive functioning, other techniques can accomplish the same result by simply focusing attention narrowly on concrete, unemotional stimuli. By paying attention to simple, here-and-now movements and sensations, a person can divert attention away from troubling self-aspects (Steele & Josephs, 1990). This shift from self-awareness to "other-awareness" effectively allows the person to avoid the type of self-reflective activities that evoke unpleasant emotion. *Binge eating*, which involves episodes of huge amounts of food consumption, may serve this function for some people. Indeed, difficulties regulating emotion have been found to be a significant triggering mechanism for binge eating (Abramson et al., 2006; Whiteside et al., 2007). By redirecting attentional focus from the self to the simple acts of chewing, tasting, and swallowing, binge eaters may temporarily find relief from depression (Heatherton & Baumeister, 1991). As one binger expressed it, "Eating can help me bury my emotions when I don't want to feel them" (Smith et al., 1989).

(continues)

(**Applications**, *continued*)

Ironically, although some people may engage in binge behavior to escape negative self-awareness, self-regulation theory contends that they must actually consciously engage in self-awareness if they desire to gain control over their self-destructive actions. The following four suggestions, derived from self-regulation theory, indicate how binge drinkers and eaters can work to change their behavior by employing self-reflective thought and a special kind of behavioral intention.

1. *Focus your awareness beyond the immediate situation.* An important mechanism in effective self-regulation of negative behavior is keeping attention focused beyond the immediate situation to more distant, long-range goals (Baumeister & Heatherton, 1996). This sort of situational transcendence is clearly an important factor in effective food or alcohol management because it requires you to forgo the temporary relief of bingeing so that you can achieve your long-term goal of learning to eat and drink responsibly. By focusing on your long-range goal, the more-immediate goal of bingeing on cheesecake or beer becomes cognitively reframed: it becomes an obstacle to your long-term goal rather than an appealing treat.

2. *Pay attention to cues that trigger undesirable behavior.* Certain stimuli in your social environment can serve as signals that you may be "sliding" down a path that leads to your undesirable behavior. The sooner you identify signals of impending undesirable behavior, the better chance you have of controlling your impulse to engage in that behavior (Wegner, 1994). Thus, if you know that arguments with family members have triggered binge behavior in the past, pay attention to your feelings when conversing with these people and try to defuse arguments before they get out of hand.

3. *Recognize when your resolve is weak.* If the strength model of self-regulation (see section 3.1c) is correct, at any given time you have only a limited amount of energy available to self-regulate. Therefore, be aware that you may find it hardest to keep yourself from bingeing with food or alcohol right after exercising a great deal of control in some other unrelated activity.

4. When you realize that your past self-control has been weak, a number of studies indicate that it can be effective to *establish an implementation intention that steers you away from the problematic behavior* (Sheeran, 2002; Schoenmakers et al., 2007). Implementation intentions are statements you make to yourself that, as soon as a particular situation occurs, will automatically initiate goal-directed behavior. For example, if you wanted to avoid engaging in binge drinking at a party, you might make the following implementation intention beforehand: "As soon as people start drinking shots of liquor, I will switch to drinking soda." It appears that forming implementation intentions can cognitively bypass the need for normal self-control, especially when your motivation to self-regulate is low (Brandstätter et al., 2001; Webb & Sheeran, 2003). In effect, by specifying ahead of time when and how you will act, this strategy passes control of behavior to anticipated environmental cues.

THE BIG PICTURE

As stated previously, the self is not something "inside" you. Rather, it is you—a social being with the ability to communicate with others, analyze your past actions, regulate your present behavior, and anticipate the actions of others. In other words, being a self allows you to actively create and recreate your social world.

Your culture and the groups to which you belong significantly shape your self-concept. Further, your social behavior is influenced by what aspect of your self-concept is most salient in a given situation. When you are attentive to your private self-aspects, you behave more in-line with personal standards, while public standards exert greater influence when you are aware of your public self-aspects.

As social beings, we try to maintain competent and appropriate presented selves, and we often consciously try to manipulate people's impressions of us, because doing so successfully brings social rewards and increases self-esteem. There certainly are benefits to high self-esteem, and the need to self-enhance is found in cultures around the world. However, the valuing of self-esteem is sometimes so strong that people with uncertain high self-regard react aggressively when others challenge it. Throughout the remaining chapters, you will see how interpretations of social events are filtered through self-beliefs and self-desires.

▋ KEY TERMS

WEBSITES

Accessed through https://www.bvtlab.com/sop8

Websites for this chapter focus on the self, including cross-cultural research, an international society devoted to the study of the self, and information on the history of the self-concept in the social sciences.

Society for Cross-Cultural Psychology

This is the website for an organization pursuing cross-cultural research from a multidisciplinary perspective.

International Society for Self and Identity

This is the website of an association that promotes scientific study of the human self. Members represent different academic and professional disciplines interested in cognition, emotion, and behavior related to the self.

American Psychological Association

The website for the American Psychological Association contains a web page that discusses the possibility that high self-esteem narcissists tend to be aggressive when criticized.

Project Implicit

The website provides you with the opportunity to assess your conscious and unconscious preferences for over 90 topics, including self-esteem. At the same time, you will be assisting psychological research.

Chapter 4

Social Cognition and Person Perception

FOCUS QUESTIONS

1. How can our schemas unconsciously influence our thinking and behavior?

2. In what ways are heuristics an illustration of human beings' capacity for "useful thinking" versus "stupid thinking"?

3. How might our belief about the stability of personality traits, such as intelligence, relate to our own academic achievement?

4. Why do people from individualist cultures tend to explain others' actions as being caused by their personalities more so than by the situation?

CHAPTER OUTLINE

Introduction

Applications: How do you explain negative events in your life?

> **Preview** . . . People differ in how they make sense of uncontrollable negative life events. How do these differences affect people's health and happiness?

Self/Social Connection Exercise 4.2:
> Do You Have a Pessimistic or an Optimistic Explanatory Style?

The Big Picture

Key Terms

Websites

Introduction

O n September 16, 2018, Dr. Christine Blasey Ford, a professor of psychology at Palo Alto University and a research psychologist at the Stanford University School of Medicine, publicly claimed that the nominee to the United States Supreme Court, Federal Judge Brett Kavanaugh, had sexually assaulted her in 1982, in what she described as an attempted rape, while they were both high school students attending a drinking party. Later that month, seated before the Senate Judiciary Committee and under the sharp focus of the national media, she painted a vivid portrait for the American public of what it is like to be victimized by sexual assault.

> "I was pushed onto the bed, and Brett got on top of me. He began running his hands over my body and grinding into me. I yelled, hoping that someone downstairs might hear me, and I tried to get away from him, but his weight was heavy. Brett groped me and tried to take off my clothes. He had a hard time, because he was very inebriated, and because I was wearing a one-piece bathing suit underneath my clothing. I believed he was going to rape me. I tried to yell for help. When I did, Brett put his hand over my mouth to stop me from yelling. This is what terrified me the most, and has had the most lasting impact on my life. It was hard for me to breathe, and I thought that Brett was accidentally going to kill me."

(United States Senate Committee on the Judiciary, Sept. 2018, via Wikimedia)

Dr. Christine Blasey Ford

(Office of the Vice President, July 2018, via Wikimedia)

On September 27, 2018, both Dr. Ford and Judge Kavanaugh testified before the Senate Judiciary Committee regarding her sexual assault allegation against him. What information did people rely on in judging the truthfulness of their sharply contrasting accounts of this event?

In explaining why she did not report this attempted rape to the police or even to her parents, Ford stated that she was too afraid and ashamed, and that she had tried to convince herself that because Kavanaugh had not succeeded in raping her, she should pretend it didn't happen. When asked by a senator how certain she was that her assailant was Kavanaugh, Ford replied, "100 percent."

Following Professor Ford's testimony, Judge Kavanaugh returned to the committee and angrily denied that he had sexually assaulted Dr. Ford or anyone else, and also attacked the motives underlying the accusations, sometimes openly mocking Democratic senators who questioned him.

> "This whole two-week effort has been a calculated and orchestrated political hit, fueled with apparent pent-up anger about President Trump and the 2016 election, fear that has been unfairly stoked about my judicial record, revenge on behalf of the Clintons and millions of dollars in money from outside left-wing opposition groups. . . . I'm here today to tell the truth. I've never sexually assaulted anyone. Not in high school, not in college, not ever. Sexual assault is horrific. . . . I'm not questioning that Dr. Ford may

have been sexually assaulted by some person in some place at some time. But I have never done this to her or to anyone. That's not who I am, it is not who I was."

As people sat in front of their television sets and watched the drama unfold, they searched for clues to properly define this murky social reality. Prior to these hearings, both Ford and Kavanaugh were known for their truthfulness and integrity, yet now the question that everybody asked was, "Whom do you believe, the professor or the judge?" Following their testimony, the members of the Republican-dominated Senate Judiciary Committee first endorsed Kavanaugh for the Supreme Court, but then recommended that the FBI investigate Ford's sexual assault allegations. In response, President Donald Trump reluctantly ordered the FBI to conduct a very limited one-week investigation, with specific instructions not to interview either Ford or Kavanaugh. When the FBI concluded its investigation and reported that its findings were inconclusive, Kavanaugh was quickly confirmed by a majority vote of the Republican-controlled Senate. He now sits on the Supreme Court and Ford remains a faculty member and research psychologist at her respective universities.

This event, although unusual because of the people involved (two highly respected professionals) and the gravity of the situation (a Supreme Court judge who will undoubtedly be faced with important cases related to sexual assault), is actually similar to events we face on a daily basis, and it illustrates several important aspects of **social cognition**, which is the way we interpret, analyze, remember, and use information about our social world. As discussed in Chapter 1 (section 1.2b), we interpret events and make sense of them using two types of thinking: automatic and relatively effortless thinking, and deliberate and relatively effortful thinking. In this chapter, we will examine how people use this dual-process thinking to organize their knowledge about the social world, form impressions of others, and make sense of people's actions. Let us begin by examining some of the basic principles of social thought.

> **social cognition**
> The ways in which we interpret, analyze, remember, and use information about our social world

4.1 How Does Automatic Thinking Help Us Make Sense of Social Information?

As the Supreme Court confirmation story illustrates, life is often complicated and difficult to understand. Faced with such complexity and thrust into the world as both actors and observers, we rely on two different ways of thinking (Kruglanski & Orehek, 2007). As previously defined in Chapter 1 (section 1.2b), *explicit cognition* involves deliberate judgments or decisions of which we are consciously aware, and *implicit cognition* involves judgments or decisions that are under the control of automatically activated evaluations that occur without our awareness. Being unintentional and consuming few cognitive resources, implicit cognition operates quickly, while explicit cognition is generally a slower process. As you will see, the fast and automatic operation of implicit cognition sets the stage for all social judgments.

4.1a We Are Categorizing Creatures.

A mental grouping of objects, ideas, or events that share common properties is called a *category*. For example, *insect* is a category of animals that have three body divisions (head, thorax, abdomen), six legs, an external skeleton, and a rapid reproductive cycle. Categories are the building blocks of cognition (Markman, 1999; Woll, 2002). Like the heart that pumps life-giving blood throughout the body or the lungs that replenish this blood with oxygen, the scientific consensus is that humans could not survive without automatically categorizing things. Imagine, for example, how lost and bewildered you would be if you attended a college class without an appreciation of some key categories such as professor, student, lecture, chair, or notes.

This automatic tendency to perceive and understand the world in categorical terms is an implicit cognitive process that greatly expands our ability to deal with the huge amount of information constantly presented to us (Dijksterhuis, 2010). Categorization allows us to generalize from one experience to another, making it possible to assign meaning to novel stimuli. Thus, if someone tells you to meet at the student union by the magnolia tree, you probably know what to look for, even if you have never seen a magnolia tree. By understanding the general properties of the category *tree*, you will probably seek out an object that is tall, with branches and leaves. By relating new stimuli to familiar categories, you are much more efficient in understanding and making decisions in your environment.

We also naturally form categories about people based upon their common attributes. This process is called **social categorization** (Pattyn et al., 2013). Starting as young children, we categorize people based on readily apparent physical features, such as gender, ethnicity, and age (Shutts et al., 2010). Even infants as young as 9 months old categorize faces by ethnicity (Anzures et al., 2010). Because categorizing others by physical features is done so frequently, it becomes habitual and automatic—occurring without conscious thought or effort. In fact, such categorization is so automatic that it is probably impossible to inhibit it. Under normal circumstances, can you meet someone and not notice whether the person is male or female? Wouldn't it seem strange not to remember whether the person was young or old?

Exactly how do we mentally group things, including people, into categories? Consider classifying someone based on race. How would you classify someone who has a combination of Caucasian and Afrocentric facial features? Do all Africans or all Caucasians have the same skin color? Research suggests that categorizing has less to do with the features that define *all* members of a category and has more to do with the features that characterize the *typical* member (McGarty, 2004). The most representative member of a category is known as a **prototype**: a mental model that stands for or symbolizes the category (Zimmerman & Sieverding, 2011). Because a prototype is the member that best represents that category for you, other members of that category will vary in how closely they match the prototype. Thus, although patrol officers and undercover officers both fit into our category of police officer, for most of us, patrol officers are more "cop-like." Not surprisingly, we can categorize prototypical members more quickly than those who match the prototype less closely (Olson et al., 2004). Failing to correctly categorize people because they do not resemble the prototype often leads to errors in decision-making. This is why female doctors are more often mistaken for nurses than are male doctors, while male nurses are more likely than female nurses to be miscategorized as doctors. In both cases, the mistaken judgments are due to our culturally derived prototypes for these two professions.

(Shutterstock)

If you encountered this person on campus, would you assume that he was (a) a student, (b) a professor, or (c) a service worker? The social category you place him in will likely be based on how closely he matches your prototypes for these three social roles.

Generally, the more experience we have with a particular category, the more accurate we are in noticing similarities and differences between members of that category. Thus, a bird-watcher will more quickly and accurately identify different types of birds than will someone with limited bird-watching experience. The fact that it is more difficult to notice subtle differences between members of a category with which you have limited exposure helps explain why you may think that members of another ethnic group have faces that "all look the same" to you. While this *other-race effect* is embarrassing during everyday interaction, the consequences can be life changing and extremely negative in cases of eyewitness misidentification (Michel et al., 2009).

social categorization

The process of forming categories of people based on their common attributes

prototype

The most representative member of a category

4.1b Schemas Affect What Information We Notice and Later Remember.

Implicit cognition allows us to group objects, ideas, or events into categories and also to develop theories about those categories. The theories we have about categories are called schemas. A **schema** is an organized structure of knowledge about a stimulus that is built up from experience and that contains causal relations; it is a theory about how the social world operates (Kunda, 1999). The stimulus could be a person, an object, a social group, a social role, or a common event. A student who observes her psychology professor conducting research will have a schema for the professor role and a schema for the research process. Without these schemas, the student would have great difficulty making sense of the professor and her actions. However, with these schemas, the student can not only understand what is happening in the situation but can also go beyond the presented information and anticipate the next set of events that might occur in this setting. Because they provide a theory about the category of interest, schemas also hasten the processing of information and, hence, decision-making. An expert in an area has a well-developed schema and thus can be especially efficient in making related decisions.

We also have schemas about ourselves (*self-schemas*), which are the personal attributes that we identify with. These self-schemas are the ingredients of our self-concepts (see Chapter 3).

One important self-schema is our **gender schema**, which is the cognitive structure for processing information based on perceived female or male qualities. People with well-developed gender schemas habitually organize things in their minds according to gender categories. When information is filtered through a gender schema, social perceptions and judgments typically adhere to cultural standards. For example, if George and Laura have strong gender schemas, they may perceive such things as dogs, football, sports cars, math, and assertiveness as "guy-like"; such things as cats, shopping, hybrid cars, the fine arts, and empathy would then be labeled "girl-like." When people do not conform to our gender schemas, there is often a backlash of negative attitudes. For example, transgender individuals who are physically androgynous in appearance (displaying physical traits that are not easily identified as male or female) are evaluated more negatively than those who display sex-typical characteristics (Stern & Rule, 2018).

For George and Laura, their gender schemas also help them organize and make sense of their lives. If Laura's gender schema causes her to perceive science ability as a male quality—regardless of any inborn potential—Laura is less likely to identify skill in science as an important personal quality (Carli et al., 2016; Miller et al., 2018). Due to this disidentification, she is unlikely to spend time developing her math skills and she is less likely to choose careers that emphasize science. In contrast, perceiving this same "scientist = male" association, George may develop positive attitudes toward science and be more likely to pursue a science-oriented occupation. This is just one example of how schemas can shape our own self-perceptions.

We also have schemas about common events. A **script** describes how a series of events is likely to occur in a well-known situation (Woll, 2002). The script is used as a guide for behavior and problem-solving in the situation. We have numerous scripts, including those for attending class, eating dinner at a restaurant, asking someone out on a date, and even breaking off a romantic relationship. Learning scripts is an important part of the socialization process, and children as young as 3 years of age have well-developed preconceptions about familiar routine events in their lives, such as having lunch at the day care center or getting ready for bed at night (Nelson, 1986). Scripts often help us clear up ambiguities in social situations. For example, if you go over to someone's house for dinner and are later asked to "spend the night," your interpretation of this question will be shaped by the script that you have in mind. If a platonic friend asks this question,

schema
An organized structure of knowledge about a stimulus that is built up from experience and that contains causal relations; a theory about how the social world operates

gender schema
A cognitive structure for processing information based on perceived female or male qualities

script
A schema that describes how a series of events is likely to occur in a well-known situation and which is used as a guide for behavior and problem-solving

(Shutterstock)

We use different scripts for different occasions in our lives. What happens when you misinterpret another person's intentions in a script?

you are likely following a different script than if the questioner is a much-desired romantic partner. Embarrassment is likely if your host has a very different script in mind from your own.

As you can see, once schemas are formed, they can have a profound effect on our social thinking and behavior. Schemas often determine what information in our surroundings we pay attention to and how quickly we process it, what information we form memories about, and what information we later recall when making decisions. In general, we tend to have better memories of past events and people when this information was originally processed through well-formed schemas (Hirt, 1990), but using a schema can also cause us to screen out or "misremember" information that is inconsistent with it. As an example, imagine seeing someone assisting a handicapped person across the street. While watching this situation unfold, you would typically assume that the person is empathetic and helpful. However, what if this individual is a white supremacist? Because empathy and helpfulness are inconsistent with most people's white supremacist schemas, research indicates that in this situation you are much less likely to make the typical spontaneous social judgment of helpfulness (Wigboldus et al., 2003). Instead, you may automatically dismiss this behavioral information as not useful in making inferences about the white supremacist's personality; however, you may also engage in more effortful, non-schema-based thinking and consider what situational factors may be causing him to behave this way (perhaps this is a ploy to rob the handicapped person).

Sometimes, information is so sharply inconsistent with an existing schema that we take great notice of it and store—or *encode*—it into a new, separate schema (Stangor & McMillan, 1992). With our white supremacist, imagine that you learn that he volunteers at a homeless shelter and an AIDS center, and that he strongly believes in social justice and civil rights for all groups. This information may be so inconsistent with your white supremacist schema that you spend time thinking about how he could have become a white supremacist in the first place. This effortful thinking may result in you forming a new schema for "socially progressive white supremacist," while still retaining your more general white supremacist schema.

Schemas also play an important role in what we remember. However, unlike photographs that freeze exact images of past events, our memories are often sketchy reconstructions of the past. Linda Carli (1999) conducted an experiment demonstrating this effect—she asked college students to read a story about a woman named Barbara and a man named Jack who had been dating awhile before going to a ski lodge for the weekend. In one condition of the experiment, Jack proposed marriage to Barbara at the end of the story, whereas in the other condition, the story ended with Jack raping Barbara in their lodge room. Two weeks after reading the Jack-Barbara stories, participants read several details about the two characters and were asked whether this information had appeared in the original story. As depicted in Figure 4.1, Carli found that, in both conditions, participants tended to falsely remember details that were consistent with their original schema for the Barbara and Jack event. Those in the *proposal* condition were likely to falsely remember that "Jack wanted Barbara to meet his parents" and "Jack gave Barbara a dozen roses." Similarly, participants in the *rape* condition were likely to falsely remember that "Jack was unpopular with women" and "Jack liked to drink."

FIGURE 4.1   Schemas and Misremembering the Past

Linda Carli (1999) found that participants who read a story about a man raping his girlfriend were more likely to falsely remember details that were consistent with their rape schema, while those who read a story about a man proposing to his girlfriend were more likely to falsely remember details that were consistent with their proposal schema. What implications does this research have for the validity of witnesses' testimony in criminal trials?

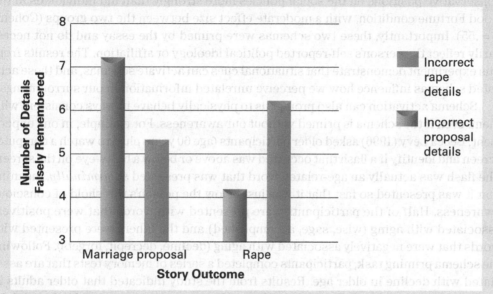

Data source: "Cognitive Reconstruction, Hindsight, and Reactions to Victims and Perpetrators," by L. Carli, 1999, *Personality and Social Psychology Bulletin, 25*(8), pp. 966–979.

4.1c   Schemas Can Be Situationally or Chronically Activated.

Schemas help us make sense out of our world, but what activates a schema from memory? The process by which recent exposure to certain stimuli or events increases the accessibility of certain memories, categories, or schemas is known as **priming**. More than a century ago, psychologist William James described priming as the "wakening of associations." As an example of this memory process, answer the following two questions as quickly as possible: How do you pronounce the word spelled p-o-k-e, and what do you call the white of an egg? If you answered "yolk" to the second question, you've demonstrated priming. Priming is a good example of automatic thinking because it occurs spontaneously and unconsciously (Custers & Aarts, 2007).

In one priming experiment, Christopher Bryan and his colleagues (2009) primed participants' success schemas to determine whether doing so would influence their subsequent support for various social policies. They argued that there are two schemas commonly used to explain a person's success in life. A *Good Fortune* schema explains people's success by focusing on their social advantages and the help they received from others. In contrast, a *Personal Merit* schema explains success by focusing on effort and wise decisions. Most Americans, to some extent, give credence to both explanations of success, but the two schemas appear to differentiate political conservatives and liberals. The Good Fortune schema underlies liberal ideology whereas the Personal Merit schema underlies conservative ideology.

priming

The process by which recent exposure to certain stimuli or events increases the accessibility of certain memories, categories, or schemas

In this experiment, college students were first instructed to write an essay about how they got into their highly selective university (Bryan et al., 2009). Half of the participants were asked to write about their "hard work, self-discipline, and wise decisions" (Personal Merit condition) and the others wrote about the role of "chance, opportunity, and help from others" (Good Fortune condition) (p. 891). After writing the essay, participants completed a questionnaire indicating their support for social policies that are generally divided by political ideologies, such as prisons, unemployment benefits, health care, and taxes. Results indicated that participants in the Personal Merit condition supported the conservative positions on the social policies more strongly than did individuals in the Good Fortune condition, with a moderate effect size between the two groups (Cohen's d = .55). Importantly, these two schemas were primed by the essay and do not necessarily reflect the person's self-reported political ideology or affiliation. The results from this experiment demonstrate that situational cues can activate schemas, and these activated schemas influence how we perceive unrelated information in our surroundings.

Schema activation can also prompt us to physically behave in ways consistent with them, even if the schema is primed without our awareness. For example, in one experiment, Becca Levy (1996) asked older participants (age 60 years plus) to watch a computer screen and identify if a flash that occurred was above or below a bull's-eye on the screen. The flash was actually an age-related word that was presented *subliminally*, meaning that it was presented so fast that it was just below the person's threshold of conscious awareness. Half of the participants were presented with words that were positively associated with aging (wise, sage, accomplished) and the others were presented with words that were negatively associated with aging (decline, decrepit, forgets). Following the schema priming task, participants completed a series of memory tests that are associated with decline in older age. Results from the study indicated that older adults in the positive aging schema condition performed better on the memory tasks than did the adults in the negative aging schema condition. In a second study, Levy tested younger adults using the same experimental procedures. However, they did not show the same differences in memory performance between the positive and negative aging prime conditions. Together, these findings not only suggest that schemas about aging must be self-relevant in order to impact a person's subsequent memory, but they also suggest that such priming can have practical, real-life implications. Memory and physical decline is a real concern for older adults and Levy's (1996) work suggests that subliminal priming of positive aging stereotypes might be an effective intervention for older adults.

In a follow-up study, Levy and her colleagues (2014) investigated the effectiveness of a 4-week intervention in a sample of 100 adults aged 61 to 99. Participants were exposed to either a positive subliminal aging prime or a neutral condition once a week for a total of 4 weeks. Participants also completed measures that assessed their belief in age stereotypes, their self-perception of aging, and physical functioning (strength, gait, balance). Results indicated that after the 4-week intervention, participants in the positive implicit aging condition had more positive age-related stereotypes, had more positive self-perceptions of aging, and had improved physical function. A meta-analysis of 137 studies examining age stereotype priming effects confirmed that positive age priming improves behavioral performance, and that negative age priming impairs performance, compared to the neutral condition (Meisner, 2012). Importantly, the harmful impact of negative aging stereotype is about

(Getty Images)

Positive, age-related stereotypes can contribute to improved physical functioning in older adults.

three times stronger than the impact of the positive aging stereotype prime. The lesson to be learned here is that people who interact with older adults should be cautious not to prime negative aging stereotypes through their comments or actions.

Besides being situationally activated, schemas are often chronically accessible due to past experiences. For example, imagine observing a parent yelling at a child in a public setting. If you suffered from physical abuse growing up, you may habitually perceive such emotionally ambiguous scenes as signs of impending violence. However, if you grew up in a household where family members regularly expressed themselves in a raucous but loving manner, you may expect such situations to end with hugs and smiles. The Applications section at the end of the chapter discusses how people with optimistic versus pessimistic outlooks on life habitually respond in different ways to similar life events. Their contrasting interpretations of positive and negative outcomes can be understood in terms of them having markedly different schemas chronically accessible.

4.1d   Heuristics Are Time-saving Mental Shortcuts.

Here is a question for you: Which two of these four cities—Atlanta, Los Angeles, New York, and St. Louis—have the highest crime rates? In arriving at your answer, you could have conducted a rather time-intensive internet search. However, given our dual-process thinking capabilities, you probably simply relied upon images that came to mind from a host of popular TV shows and picked New York and Los Angeles, which are actually less crime-ridden than Atlanta and St. Louis. This example illustrates the fact that we often employ various mental strategies that require minimal effort. **Heuristics** are time-saving mental shortcuts that reduce complex judgments to simple rules (Tversky & Kahneman, 1974).

In dual-process thinking, heuristics require very little thought; people merely take the shortcut and make the judgment. The downside of using heuristics, however, is that they aren't always accurate. To be useful, heuristics must satisfy two requirements: they must allow us to make quick social judgments, and they must be reasonably accurate. Unfortunately, satisfying the first requirement often works against judgment accuracy (Higgins, 2000). You can make a quick judgment by ignoring a great deal of potentially relevant information in your environment, but what cost does this have for the accuracy of your judgment? And keep in mind that the second requirement of heuristics involves "reasonable" accuracy, not "high" accuracy. With that in mind, let us consider some commonly used mental shortcuts that social psychologists have identified and studied over the years.

The Representativeness Heuristic

During Deb's first few years as a professor, people often mistook her for a student. Why was this so? Well, she did not fit their image of what a university professor should look like. That judgment was an example of the **representativeness heuristic**, which is the tendency to judge the category membership of things based on how closely they match the prototype of that category (Kahneman & Tversky, 1973). Because she was a young woman (inconsistent with the prototypical male professor with a beard and tweed jacket), people guessed that she was a student.

The representativeness heuristic helps people quickly decide in what categories to place others. It is essentially stereotyping operating in reverse. That is, when we stereotype someone, we first place them in a particular social category and then infer that they possess the personal attributes associated with people in that category. When we rely on the representativeness heuristic, we merely reverse this cognitive process: Because a person possesses attributes we associate with a particular social category,

heuristics
Time-saving mental shortcuts that reduce complex judgments to simple rules

representativeness heuristic
The tendency to judge the category membership of things based on how closely they match the "typical" or "average" member of that category

(Shutterstock)

Due to the representativeness heuristic, you are unlikely to recognize this person as a college student because he probably does not match your student prototype.

If the representativeness heuristic is stereotyping operating in reverse, does that mean that stereotyping is also a heuristic?

we infer that he/she must be a member of that category. The old saying "If it looks like a duck and if it quacks like a duck, then it probably is a duck" is an example of the representativeness heuristic. Although this cognitive shortcut is a rapid method of identifying people, it does not consider other important qualifying information. The most important information relates to *base rates*—the frequency with which some event or pattern occurs in the general population.

The tendency to overlook base-rate information was demonstrated in a classic study by Tversky and Kahneman (1973). Research participants were told that an imaginary person named Jack had been selected from a group of 100 men. Some were told that 30 of the men were engineers (a base rate for engineers of 30%), and others were told that 70 were engineers (a base rate of 70%). Half the participants were given no other information, but the other half were given either a description of Jack that fit the common stereotype of engineers (for example, practical, likes to work with numbers) or one that did not. They were then asked to guess the probability that Jack was an engineer. Results indicated that when participants received only information related to base rates, they were more likely to guess that Jack was an engineer when the base rate was 70% than when it was 30%. However, when they received information about Jack's personality and behavior, they tended to ignore the base-rate information and, instead, focus on whether Jack fit their image of an engineer. The tendency to ignore or underuse useful base-rate information and to overuse personal descriptors of the individual being judged has been called the *base-rate fallacy*.

The Availability Heuristic

Steve's friend was planning to purchase a new car, and Steve asked her if she was considering a particular make and model that had received excellent reliability ratings in *Consumer Reports*. Her reply was no, because she had just spoken to someone who had that type of car and was not satisfied with its reliability. In nixing this car from her list, the friend was basing her judgment on the content of this fresh memory. The **availability heuristic** is the tendency to judge the frequency or probability of an event in terms of how easy it is to think of examples of that event (Tversky & Kahneman, 1973). Thus, in estimating the likelihood of car problems with this particular model, Steve's friend relied on the easy accessibility in her memory of this one person's negative experiences. If the information she accessed from memory had been reasonably representative of the actual reliability of these cars, relying on the availability heuristic would have resulted in an accurate assessment. Unfortunately, this was not the case here.

In the use of the availability heuristic, the most important factor for people is not the content of their memory but the *ease* with which this *content* comes to mind (Higgins, 2000). For example, Norbert Schwarz and his colleagues (1991) found that participants who were asked to recall 12 examples of their own assertive behaviors (a difficult cognitive task) subsequently rated themselves as less assertive than participants who were asked to recall only six examples (an easy cognitive task). Thus, individuals would conclude that they must not be assertive if it is difficult to recall personal examples of assertive behavior in their past.

availability heuristic

The tendency to judge the frequency or probability of an event in terms of how easy it is to think of examples of that event

The availability heuristic provides insight into a number of faulty social judgments, including peoples' responses to risks. Highly visible events that have a low probability of occurring (such as terrorism or a mass shooting) can result in people overresponding to the risk. In contrast, people will under-respond, and fail to take proper precautions, for low visibility but high probability events (such as biking or automobile accidents). Cass Sunstein and Richard Zeckhauser (2011) experimentally tested this process by comparing four groups of participants who were told that the chance of getting cancer with the current level of arsenic (a known carcinogen) in the public drinking water was either 1 in 1,000,000 or 1 in 100,000. Furthermore, half of the participants were given a vivid and highly emotional description of cancer (gruesome, painful, etc.), while the others were not. All were then asked the maximum amount of money they were willing to pay to lower the arsenic levels in their drinking water. Results indicated that participants were willing to pay more money to reduce the arsenic level when their risk of getting cancer was relatively high (1/100,000) versus being lower (1/1,000,000), but only if they *did not* receive the vivid description of cancer ahead of time. Participants who first read the vivid description of cancer were willing to pay the same substantial amount of money to reduce the arsenic risk, regardless of their actual risk level. These findings suggest that people are much more likely to try to avoid a health risk when it is presented to them in a vivid and frightening manner, even when the actual probability of the event occurring is very small.

Why is it that people tend to estimate that air travel is more dangerous after reading about a recent aircraft disaster? Upon what heuristic are they basing their estimate?

Despite these examples of social judgment errors, availability is a fairly valid cue for the judgment of frequency because frequent events are more likely than infrequent events to be stored in memory and later recalled. If a doctor is seeing patients during the height of the flu season, the fact that he can easily bring the flu virus to mind will influence how many patients he diagnoses with this ailment. A busy doctor may quickly diagnose ailments as normal influenza and make correct judgments 99.9% of the time; but with "the flu" on his mind, he is also more likely to misdiagnose a far more serious ailment as simple influenza (Weber et al., 1993).

The Anchoring and Adjustment Heuristic

Do you think the population of Cincinnati, Ohio, is more than 100,000? Yes is the correct answer. Now estimate Cincinnati's actual population, and then check the margin of this section for the correct answer. If, instead of asking whether Cincinnati's population is *more than 100,000*, I had asked whether it is *less than 1 million*, your answer probably would have been higher. The reason this effect often happens is because our quantitative judgments are often biased toward an initial anchor point—in our example, this was the 100,000 figure. Later, when making our estimate, we use this anchor as our starting point and, thus, usually insufficiently adjust toward the correct answer. This mental bias is known as the **anchoring and adjustment heuristic** (Epley & Gilovich, 2001; Tversky & Kahneman, 1974).

Jetter and Walker (2017) examined the implications of the anchoring effect for contestants on the TV show *Jeopardy*. In this trivia game, three participants compete to correctly answer questions to earn money. Contestants select questions, of varying dollar amounts, and earn the money if they answer it correctly. In each round, there are three hidden questions, known as *Daily Doubles*, and the contestant who unknowingly

anchoring and adjustment heuristic
A tendency to be biased toward the starting value or anchor in making quantitative judgments

selects that question can wager any amount of money. Importantly, the contestant places the wager after having already selected the question at a specific dollar value. This provides an interesting real-life situation for examining the anchoring effect. Does the initial dollar value of the question influence how much money contestants wager? If anchoring occurs, then the wagers should be lower if the initial dollar value is low and increase with the initial question value. However, rationally, the initial dollar amount should not be a factor in determining the size of the wager because the question difficulty is not associated with the initial question's dollar value.

Consistent with the anchoring effect, an analysis of 12,596 daily clues on *Jeopardy* indicated that as the initial clue value increased, so did the waged amount. In practical terms, for every increase in $100 dollars of the clue value, the wager increased by $29. This increase occurred even when controlling for other variables, such as the category of question (sports, government, etc.) and the contestant's gender. Based on these findings, can you think of situations in your own life where the amount of money you are willing to pay for something changes depending on an initial anchoring value?

During the Kavanaugh confirmation hearings, Donald Trump Jr. stated that he was more concerned about his son being falsely accused of sexual assault than of his daughters being assaulted. Similar sentiments were expressed by other high-profile men, including President Trump. Statistically, women have a 20% chance of being sexually assaulted (National Sexual Violence Resource Center, 2014). In contrast, it's been estimated that men have somewhere between a 0.6% and a 3.2% chance of being falsely accused of committing a sexual assault (Lisak et al., 2010). What cognitive heuristic might be contributing to this heightened concern about men's false accusations? Why do you think people were relying on this heuristic?

Why do arbitrary numbers influence us? In making a judgment, when we are given a number or value as a starting point, we appear to selectively recall information from memory that is consistent with this anchor (Mussweiler & Strack, 2000). For example, if you inherit a painting, you might look at the local antique store and estimate your painting to be valued similarly to one you see there. Furthermore, after starting with the modest price of the antique store painting as the anchor value, you are likely to remember instances when other people sold antiques at a similar modest price. However, if your painting's anchor is the high price from the *Antiques Roadshow*, you are likely to recall from memory stories of people discovering they had inherited masterpieces worth millions. In a very real sense, the anchor becomes a situational cue that triggers relevant memories, just as priming people with words can activate relevant schemas. In both instances, people's automatic, effortless thinking has an effect on the way they make judgments. Fortunately, people who are trained to be aware of this bias and to engage in effortful thinking about the lack of association between the anchor and subsequent decisions are less likely to show the anchoring bias in subsequent decisions (Adame, 2016).

Is Heuristic Thinking "Stupid" Thinking?

Examining the research on heuristics may lead you to conclude that we are irrational decision-makers, with distortions and errors being the most common end products of social thinking. The reality is that although basing decisions on heuristics may lead to errors and may be motivated by lazy thinking, relying on them can be adaptive in conditions where we do not have the luxury of systematically analyzing all our options (Haselton & Nettle, 2006; Lieder et al., 2018). From an evolutionary perspective, human beings can be thought of as having evolved a large number of mental strategies to adapt to their surroundings. In this regard, heuristics and other effortless thinking have been very helpful to us because they yield reasonably accurate and adaptive results under most environmental conditions (Figueredo et al., 2004). For example, reacting quickly in an emergency based only on the information that is most accessible from memory (the availability heuristic) may often be the difference between life and death. Sure, heuristics can lead to sloppy decision-making, but their time-saving quality may sometimes be a literal lifesaver.

Common experience and social psychologists' best-reasoned analysis suggest that we do not always rely on heuristics. Often, we systematically analyze a situation using a variety of information. Research has identified the following conditions that are most likely to lead to the use of heuristics rather than more careful decision-making (Hertwig & Hoffrage, 2013):

1. We simply do not have *time* to engage in systematic analysis.
2. We are *overloaded with information* so that it is impossible to process all that is meaningful and relevant.
3. We consider the issues in question to be *not very important*.
4. We have *little other knowledge* or information to use in making a decision.
5. Something about the situation calls to mind a given heuristic, making it *cognitively available* (priming).
6. We are in a *positive mood*, signaling to us that everything is fine and no effortful thinking is necessary.

Section Summary

- Social categorization entails classifying people into groups based on common attributes.
- Schemas are organized knowledge structures that:
  provide theories about how the social world operates,
  hasten information processing and decision-making, and
  influence what information is remembered and later recalled.
- Priming makes memories, categories, and schemas more accessible.
- Heuristics allow quick judgments with minimal cognitive effort but can cause biased and inaccurate judgments.
  The representativeness heuristic involves judging the category membership of things based on how closely they match the prototype for that category.
  The availability heuristic involves judging the probability of an event in terms of how easy it is to think of examples of it.
  The anchoring and adjustment heuristic involves being biased toward the starting value or anchor in making quantitative judgments.

4.2 How Does Deliberate Thinking Help Us Make Sense of Past Events?

In Chapters 1 and 3, we discussed how imagining future events can help us construct effective self-presentations and how imagining our future self can motivate current behavior. Yet what about past events? How do we employ effortful thinking to make sense of past events?

4.2a   The Hindsight Bias Is Fueled by Our Desire for Sensemaking.

When recalling past events, we often believe that we "knew all along" how things would turn out. After learning that your friend's lover has been unfaithful, you might think, "I could see this coming for some time." Or after your favorite sports team defeats its archrival for the first time in years, you exclaim, "All week long, I could tell that my team would win!" In such instances, this after-the-fact overestimation of our ability to have foreseen the outcome is known as the **hindsight bias** (Arkes, 2013; Hawkins & Hastie, 1990).

Cross-cultural studies indicate that the hindsight bias occurs throughout the world (Pohl et al., 2002). This bias develops by age 3 and is more pronounced among preschoolers and elderly adults due to enhanced memory problems at these ages (Bernstein et al., 2011). A meta-analytic review found that this bias is moderately strong (d = .39 overall), and interventions to reduce this bias, to date, have not been effective (Guilbault et al., 2004).

(Shutterstock)

Based on research on the hindsight bias, why might factory workers who lose their jobs be less likely to claim that they anticipated job troubles than workers who were not laid off?

The most commonly accepted explanation for the hindsight bias is that it is fueled by our desire for accuracy, and we are most likely to rewrite our memory of a past event when the outcome is initially surprising. When thinking about a past event that had a surprising outcome, we appear to selectively recall information in constructing a plausible story that is consistent with the now-known outcome (Müller & Stahlberg, 2007). This "rewriting" of how events occurred allows us to insert the missing causal connections so that the story makes sense given the outcome (Roese & Vohs, 2012). Claiming hindsight reassures us that we understand—and can anticipate—events in our world.

Hindsight biasing can and does occur right after an event's outcome is known, but it tends to gain strength over time, as we increasingly forget our earlier beliefs about what we thought would happen (Bryant & Guilbault, 2002). However, not all unexpected events produce the hindsight bias. It does not occur for events that are so unusual that you simply cannot think of any good reasons for why they would occur (Pezzo, 2003). For instance, few people showed much hindsight bias for the September 11, 2001, terrorist attacks or the 2000 Bush-Gore election results. These events were so unexpected that people could not easily reconstruct their memory of the prior events in a way that would allow them to think that they foresaw the final outcomes.

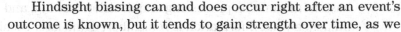

"I just knew I should have picked door number two."

—Let's Make a Deal TV-show contestant

The hindsight bias can also be used to protect self-esteem and reduce disappointment (Roese & Vohs, 2012). For example, Orit Tykocinski (2001) proposed that people may minimize the likelihood of a positive outcome in order to make any negative outcome easier to accept and less damaging to self-esteem. In one study, he examined Israeli students' voting intentions and their perceived probability that their preferred candidate would win. Participants completed a survey both before and after the election. Results indicate that, prior to the election, those who intended to vote for the two major candidates did not differ in their reported probability that their chosen candidate would win. However, after the election, those who had voted for the losing candidate reported that they had previously thought their candidate had a significantly lower chance of winning compared to the winning candidate. This suggests that those who voted for the losing candidate shifted their ratings of the probability of success downward after the election to make the outcome easier to accept: "My candidate never had a chance anyway."

hindsight bias

The tendency, once an event has occurred, to overestimate our ability to have foreseen the outcome

4.2b   Counterfactual Thinking Often Follows Negative and Unexpected Events.

Our social judgments and current moods are also affected by the ease with which we can imagine alternative versions of past events. For example, when watching Olympic competitions, have you noticed that bronze medalists often look much happier than silver medalists? Why would third-place finishers be happier than the athletes who outperformed them? Quite simply because, while the bronze medalists are imagining how they could have finished without a medal, the silver medalists are contemplating how they just missed out on winning a gold medal (McGraw et al., 2005).

In a study of this type of "What if…?" thinking, Neal Roese and his colleagues (1999) asked people to imagine the following day at the ski slopes:

> Hector loves to ski but is cautious and never goes down the expert slope. Yesterday, however, he tried it and broke his leg. Martina also loves to ski and frequently goes down the expert slope. Yesterday she broke her leg going down this slope.

The researchers found that the majority of respondents believed that Hector would feel the greatest regret following his injury; most respondents also expressed greater sympathy toward him than toward Martina. The reason for these different judgments is that we engage in **counterfactual thinking**, which is the tendency to evaluate events by imagining alternative versions or outcomes (Lindberg et al., 2013). We are most likely to engage in counterfactual thinking following negative and unexpected events, and the thoughts that are generated usually deal with how the negative outcome might have been prevented. Counterfactual thinking is also more likely to occur for events that we have some degree of ability to control (Roese et al., 2017). Regarding Hector and Martina, it is easier for us to imagine that Hector would have been uninjured if he had not deviated from his normal cautious skiing style than it is to imagine this altered outcome for Martina, given her tendency to take greater risks on the slopes. Because it is easier to undo Hector's broken leg through counterfactual thinking ("If only he had stuck to his usual routine…"), we are more likely to feel sympathy for him. When our skiers engage in this same "What if…?" thinking, Hector will experience greater regret over his injury than Martina for the same reason.

> "Oh God! That it were possible,
> To undo things done, to call back yesterday!
> That Time could turn up his swift sandy glass,
> To untell the days, and to redeem these hours."
>
> —Thomas Heywood, English dramatist, 1574–1641

Why might a neuroscientist argue that the hindsight bias is triggered by some of the same neurological activity that creates the story lines of dreams?

Why do we engage in counterfactual thinking? One function served by these thoughts is that they can help us feel better following a negative outcome (Roese, 1997). Following a traffic accident in which your car is damaged, you may think, "At least I didn't get hurt." By imagining an even worse outcome, your accident seems less negative by contrast (Sanna et al., 2001). Besides helping us emotionally cope in the present, a second function of counterfactual thinking is that it can better prepare us for the future. By considering alternatives to past actions, we can better understand our mistakes and thereby improve our chances for future success (Smallman, 2013). For example, after doing poorly on an exam you may imagine alternative study strategies that you could have used—such as memorizing key terms or working through the study guide. If you implement these new strategies in preparing for your next exam, you may improve your grade.

> "I know we won silver, but it really just feels like we lost gold."
>
> —Margaretha Sigfridsson, Swedish curling captain, after her team lost to Canada in the 2014 Winter Olympics women's gold-medal match

counterfactual thinking
The tendency to evaluate events by imagining alternative versions or outcomes to what actually happened

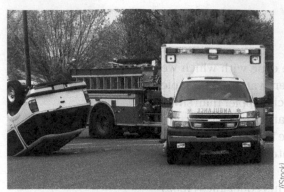

When we engage in counterfactual thinking, we are constantly asking, "What if...?" For example, after a car accident, we may think, "What if I had only gone down a different street?"

Summarizing these two functions, then, we can say that imagining alternative versions or outcomes to what actually happened may not only help us emotionally cope with negative events but may also help us to achieve success in the future. Unfortunately, as discussed in Chapter 3 (section 3.1c), sustaining a negative affect is often necessary to motivate behavioral change. When counterfactual thinking is used to emotionally cope with a negative event, our improved mood can reduce our motivation to take corrective steps to avoid similar negative events in the future (McMullen & Markman, 2000).

Another important function of counterfactual thinking is that it can help us make sense of our lives. Because counterfactual thinking is the pondering of "what might have been," this cognitive process often plays a crucial role in the creation of meaning across the life span (Heintzelman et al., 2013; Hershfield et al., 2013). That is, one way that we make sense of our lives is by identifying "defining moments" that created for us new beginnings and unforeseen twists of fate. Imagining alternative outcomes in those defining moments gives us a sense of who we now are. Such imagining can strengthen our most cherished relationships and our most deeply felt values, but it can also undermine those relationships and values if our defining moments are filled with regrets.

Such regrets are most likely to occur following traumatic life events, when the reality is already the worst-case scenario. For instance, Christopher Davis and his coworkers (1995) interviewed people who had lost a spouse or a child in an accident. The more those people imagined how the tragedy could have been averted by mentally undoing events preceding it, the more distress and guilt they felt. This tendency to engage in counterfactual thinking following traumatic life events also helps to explain why crime victims often blame themselves for their victimization (Davis et al., 1996). In trying to understand how their plight could have been avoided, victims tend to focus on trivial aspects of their own behavior rather than on the causally more significant behavior of the perpetrator. If they can imagine some plausible way in which they *could* have prevented the crime, they may come to believe that they *should* have prevented it. Although crime victims who engage in such counterfactual thinking may not blame themselves for being the cause of their injuries, they may blame themselves for not avoiding the situation that was the cause (Mandel, 2003). Recent studies suggest that psychological therapies that challenge such harmful counterfactual thinking can help people effectively deal with these life tragedies (Petrocelli et al., 2011).

Section Summary

- The hindsight bias involves overestimating our ability to have foreseen the outcome of an event.
- Counterfactual thinking involves evaluating events by imagining alternative versions or outcomes.

4.3 How Do We Form Impressions of Others?

When viewers were watching Ford and Kavanaugh testify before the Senate Judiciary Committee, they were trying to gather information as a means of answering a variety of questions they had about these two individuals. Do they appear defensive or forthcoming when answering questions? Does it seem like they are hiding something from their past? Are they telling the truth? What does their testimony reveal about their personality and temperament? The process by which we try to detect other people's temporary states (such as their emotions, intentions, and desires) and their enduring dispositions (such as their beliefs, traits, and abilities) is known as **person perception** (Gilbert, 1998). This aspect of social cognition is often not a single, instantaneous event but rather comprises a number of ongoing processes. It is also dynamic, involving both explicit and implicit cognition, with judgments being continually updated in response to new information (Freeman & Ambady, 2011). It is analogous to building a "working model" of a person and then using this as a guideline in our actions toward him or her. Person perception is also integrative, meaning that each bit of information about a person is interpreted within the context of all the other information we have about her or him. As you will discover, however, not all bits of information are created equal.

4.3a The Nonverbal Behaviors of Others Shape Our Impressions of Them.

The first phase in person perception is forming first impressions of others, a judgment process that occurs spontaneously and, in some instances, is concluded within the first 100 milliseconds of an interaction (Zebrowitz, 2017). First impressions are often based on **nonverbal communication**, which is the sending and receiving of information using gestures, expressions, vocal cues, and body movements rather than words. Whether a person smiles when greeted by another, how they dress, whether a person's walk is "bouncy" or "purposeful," or whether one's gestures are expansive or constricted can provide important information in developing a working model of those we meet on a daily basis. When forming impressions of others, we rely on static cues, such as facial features and clothing, as well as dynamic cues, such as facial expressions and body movements. Returning to our chapter-opening story, when watching the Senate Judiciary hearings, many viewers reported noticing not only what both Ford and Kavanaugh said, but how they said it. For example, when recounting the alleged sexual assault, Ford sometimes breathed rapidly and her voice occasionally shook, yet she remained composed. In contrast, Kavanaugh openly displayed anger and contempt, and he repeatedly sniffed throughout his testimony and fiddled with his shirt cuffs. Like Ford, his voice shook when he discussed how the accusations had affected his family, and at one point he even broke down in tears. How might these personal displays have played a role in shaping viewers' impressions?

Facial Expressions and Person Perception

More than 2,000 years ago, the Roman orator, Marcus Cicero wrote that the "face is the image of the soul," and today social scientists recognize that the face is a critical stimulus used by people to make judgments about others' personalities, including their cognitive and emotional tendencies (Over & Cook, 2018; Zebrowitz, 2017). For example, people with higher facial width-to-height ratios (wider faces) tend to be perceived by others as being more aggressive, dominant, and threatening than people with lower facial ratios (Geniole, 2015), and as having relatively simple emotional and cognitive abilities (Deska et al., 2018). Other facial features, such as lower eyebrows, are associated with perceptions

person perception
The process by which we try to detect other people's temporary states and enduring dispositions (also called social perception)

nonverbal communication
Communicating feelings and intentions without words

of the person being angry. In contrast, "baby-faced" features, such as large eyes and a round face, are associated with perceptions that the person is warm but low in competence (Zebrowitz, 2017). Importantly, these are perceptions about people's personalities that are based solely on facial features. In the 1800s, Charles Darwin (1872) proposed that *facial expressions* play an important role in human communication, and further, that certain emotional expressions are inborn and understood throughout the world. Studies conducted during the past 30 years generally support Darwin's assertions: There is substantial cross-cultural agreement in both the experience and expression of emotions, although certain emotions are easier to distinguish than others (Ekman, 1994; Elfenbein & Ambady, 2002; Izard, 1994). For example, people from all cultures can easily tell the difference between happiness and anger, but it is harder for them to distinguish adoration from desire. The upshot of these findings is that most researchers have concluded that certain emotions are more basic, or *primary*, than others. Primary emotions are similar to primary colors in perception. By combining primary emotions and altering their intensity, just as we do for primary colors, the full variety of other emotions can be derived. Most classification lists include the following seven primary emotions: *anger,*

disgust, fear, happiness, surprise, sadness, and *contempt* (although some dispute that contempt is a primary emotion). These primary emotions are also the ones people around the world can accurately "read" by examining facial expressions.

Facial expressions signaling specific emotions tend to be brief, lasting between 1 and 5 seconds; and they are hard to produce voluntarily (Keltner & Lerner, 2010). There is a noticeable difference, for example, between a genuine smile of pleasure and a forced smile (although most people still cannot reliably tell the difference). When a smile is genuine, the eyes crease up and the end of the eyebrows dip slightly.

Happiness is a primary emotion easily recognized in people's facial expressions.

When Darwin proposed that certain emotional expressions are universally understood, it was within the context of introducing evolutionary theory to the sciences. He believed that this ability to recognize emotion from the observation of facial expressions was genetically programmed into our species and had survival value for us. Being able to accurately read the facial expressions of others allows us not only to better predict their behavioral intentions ("Do they mean to harm me?") but also to understand how others are interpreting the world ("Why are they afraid? Are we all in danger in this situation?"). This "survival value" hypothesis would predict that we do not attend equally to all facial expressions, but rather we exhibit the most sensitivity to those that would give us the best chances of survival. In other words, we should be most attentive to facial expressions that signal potential danger.

> "Your face, my thane, is as a book where men may read strange matters."
>
> —William Shakespeare, English poet and playwright, 1564–1616, from *Macbeth*, Act 1, Scene 5

Research supports the survival value hypothesis. For instance, a number of studies have shown people pictures of crowds of faces to determine what facial expressions were most recognizable in such a clustered setting. People spot threat-related faces (anger first, fear second) faster and more accurately than non-threat-related faces, even when the non-threat-related faces depicted negative emotions such as sadness (Hansen & Hansen 1988; Öhman et al., 2001). The threat-related faces appeared to "pop out of the crowd," while the non-threat-related faces were often overlooked. Apparently, threat-related facial expressions function as general danger cues, evoking anxiety and preparing people for self-protective action. Furthermore, people are able to accurately detect if a person is conveying threatening facial features from a photograph after seeing the photo for a mere 36 milliseconds (Bar et al., 2006). However, they are not able to accurately detect other traits, such as intelligence, that quickly. Interestingly, people's current psychological needs can sensitize them to specific facial expressions. In one study, when induced with a fear of social rejection and loneliness, participants were quicker to notice faces in a crowd with friendly, welcoming expressions (DeWall et al., 2009). While this evolutionary explanation is frequently used to understand the automatic perceptions of emotional expressions, some recent studies also suggest that trait inferences from faces can be learned over time as people begin to associate certain expressions (such as a scowl) with anger (Over & Cook, 2018). Together, existing research suggests that people might have both a predisposition to identifying threats, as well as an ability to refine this skill with experience.

Body, Movements, and Nonconscious Mimicry

Besides facial cues, the body as a whole can convey a wealth of information (Keating, 2006). When forming an impression of others, the way they adorn their bodies (tattoos, jewelry, makeup, hairstyle) is often used to make inferences about their personalities. For example, women who dress in nonconventional or "provocative" ways are perceived as less intelligent and competent than women who dress more conservatively (Gurung et al., 2018a and 2018b). Likewise, the presence of tattoos increases people's negative ratings of others, although women with tattoos are rated as stronger and more independent than women without tattoos (Broussard & Harton, 2018).

Body movements also convey information about the person. For example, people who walk with a good deal of hip sway, knee bending, loose jointedness, and body bounce are perceived to be younger and more powerful than those who walk with less pronounced gaits (Montepare & Zebrowitz-McArthur, 1988). Numerous studies indicate that observers often infer other people's underlying emotional states by reading their body movements during social interaction. Body movements that are fast, energetic, and spatially expansive signal to observers that the person displaying these movements is angry or elated, rather than sad or bored (Macrae & Quadflieg, 2010).

Laura Naumann and her colleagues (2009) investigated people's ability to accurately judge a target's personality based on photographs of them. The personalities of the targets were assessed by them completing a series of personality profiles and having this personality assessment verified by three of their friends. Research participants who did not know the targets were then shown their photographs and asked to make judgments about their personalities. Results indicated that people's accuracy in rating the targets' personalities was significantly influenced by what type of photographs they were shown. When shown photographs of targets displaying neutral facial expressions and body postures, observers were somewhat accurate in judging their degree of extraversion, but no better than chance in judging any other personality traits. However, when shown photographs where the targets displayed spontaneous facial expressions and body postures, observers' accuracy increased in judging targets' extraversion, openness, likability, and self-esteem. These findings suggest that our ability to accurately perceive other people's personalities improves when we observe their spontaneous facial expressions and body cues rather than those that lack emotional content and individual character. What specific nonverbal cues did observers tend to rely on in making their personality judgments? Additional analyses indicated that observers tended to rate targets as extraverted when they were smiling and had energetic body postures. Targets who were rated as agreeable were more likely to be smiling and have a relaxed stance, while targets who were rated high in conscientiousness dressed neatly. Targets who were rated as high in openness to experiences had distinctive styles of dress. In contrast, targets who were rated as lonely had less energetic stances and appeared tense, unhealthy, messy, and unstylish. Overall, these findings suggest that observers rely on facial expressions, clothing styles, and body postures when assessing others' personalities, and these nonverbal cues do result in some degree of perceptual accuracy. However, although the correlations between observers'

"You know about a person who deeply interests you more than you can be told. A look, a gesture, an act, which to everybody else is insignificant tells you more about that one than words can."

—Henry David Thoreau, philosopher, author, naturalist, 1817–1862

and targets' personality profile ratings were better than chance guesses (r's ranging from .19 to .34), they were only moderately accurate.

Together, this research suggests that body features, body movements, in addition to facial gestures, convey a wide variety of information to others that may well have a significant impact on our perceptions of them. Yet, although there are commonly shared meanings of many physical gestures, it is also true that people from different cultures often assign different meanings to the same physical movements. *Self/Social Connection Exercise 4.1* provides a brief sketch of how certain nonverbal cues are interpreted differently around the world and a suggestion for a nonverbal exercise to try yourself.

Self/Social Connection Exercise 4.1

What Are a Few Cultural Differences in Nonverbal Behavior?

Although a number of facial gestures and body movements appear to convey universal meaning, here are some nonverbal behaviors that are more culture specific. To avoid misunderstandings when traveling overseas or when hosting an international visitor, North Americans should duly note that everyday gestures and accepted interaction patterns in this culture are not universally shared.

Eye contact: Most North Americans and Arabs are taught to look others directly in the eye when conversing. Avoiding eye contact is considered to be a sign of shyness, disinterest, or weakness. In Japan, Nigeria, Puerto Rico, Thailand, and Korea, however, people are taught to avert the eyes and avoid direct eye contact. There, engaging in eye contact is considered intimidating, disrespectful, or perhaps a signal of sexual interest.

Nodding the head: When North Americans nod their heads up and down this means "yes," while shaking their heads from side to side means "no." The opposite meaning holds true in some areas of India and Africa. In Korea, shaking the head means "I don't know."

Shaking hands: North Americans are taught to shake hands as a friendly sign of greeting. A firm, solid grip is thought to convey confidence and good character. Japanese prefer greeting one another by bowing, Southeast Asians press their own palms together in a praying motion, and when Middle Easterners and many Asians shake hands, they prefer a gentle grip, because a firm grip suggests aggressiveness.

Touching: North Americans and people in Asian cultures are generally not very touch oriented, and hugging is almost never done among casual acquaintances, especially among men. In contrast, Latin Americans, Mediterranean cultures, and those in the Middle East often embrace and hold hands as a sign of friendship.

Personal space: North Americans and northern Europeans generally maintain a distance of about 30 inches during normal social interaction. Asians tend to stand farther apart, and Latin Americans, Middle Easterners, and southern Europeans stand very close, often brushing up against one another. In those cultures where space relationships are small, moving away is interpreted as a sign of unfriendliness.

Spend some time breaking each of the above nonverbal social norms for your culture. For example, if you are a North American, when conversing with others, avoid eye contact, reverse your head nodding when voicing agreement and disagreement, press your palms together when greeting others, purposefully touch people, and invade their personal space. What sort of reactions does your norm breaking elicit from your social targets? Ask these individuals whether they noticed your norm breaking and inquire about their cognitive and emotional reactions.

Beyond interpreting the meaning of specific nonverbal gestures, our perception of others is also shaped by **nonconscious mimicry**, which is the tendency to adopt the behaviors, postures, or mannerisms of interaction partners without conscious awareness or intention (Chartrand & Lakin, 2013). What are some examples of nonconscious mimicry? When conversing with others, we tend to mimic their speech tendencies and accents, we laugh and yawn when they do, and we adopt their body postures and gestures (Yoon & Tennie, 2010). Mimicking others' facial expressions appears to be so inborn that 1-month-old infants have been shown to smile, stick out their tongues, and open their mouths when they see someone else doing the same (Meltzoff & Moore, 1989).

Evidence that mimicry is often nonconscious and unintentional comes from a number of studies (van Baaren et al., 2003), including a classic experiment by Tanya Chartrand and John Bargh (1999) where participants interacted with two unknown confederates. For half the participants, the first confederate rubbed her face and the second confederate shook her foot throughout their interaction. For the other participants, the confederates reversed roles. Results revealed that participants mimicked the gestures of the confederates—they rubbed their face more when they were with the face-rubber than the foot-shaker, and they shook their foot more when they were with the foot-shaker than the face-rubber. When the experiment was over and participants were asked about the gestures of the confederates and about their own gestures, they did not report noticing either.

Insight into the biological basis for nonconscious mimicry comes from PET scans and EEG recordings of people's brains while they observe another person performing an action: Similar neural circuits are firing in the observers' brains as are firing in the brains of those who are carrying out the action (Iacoboni, 2007). These specialized neural circuits located in the premotor cortex are called *mirror neurons* (Gallese et al., 2007). The firing of these mirror neurons probably does not directly cause imitative behavior, but they may serve as the basis of imitation learning, which is closely associated with mimicry.

(Franzoi)

Mimicking other's gestures in their presence appears to be spontaneous and nonconscious, and is important in establishing and maintaining emotional ties with them.

How does mimicking affect the person perception process? In a follow-up experiment to their face-rubbing/foot-shaking study, Chartrand and Bargh (1999) found evidence that mimicry increases liking for the imitator. The researchers instructed confederates to subtly imitate the mannerisms of people they were interacting with in a "get acquainted" session (for example, rubbing their face or tapping their foot when their partner did so). Their findings indicated that people whose gestures had been mimicked liked the confederates more than those who had not been mimicked. Mimicry appears to play a role in establishing relationships. People tend to imitate people who they like, and that imitating leads to increased liking from that person (Kämpf et al., 2018). As people interact with one another and establish rapport, they exhibit an increase in mimicking each other's gestures (van Baaren et al., 2006). Men are also more likely to mimic an attractive woman's behaviors if they are romantically attracted to her (Farley, 2014). Furthermore, mimicry can promote prosocial behavior. People are more likely to mimic an individual to whom they feel gratitude for past help, presumably as a way to strengthen that relationship (Jia et al., 2015). The targets of mimickers also become more prosocial to others in the immediate vicinity (van Baaren et al., 2004). Together, these studies suggest that mimicry serves an important function in the establishment and maintenance of social relationships.

nonconscious mimicry
The tendency to adopt the behaviors, postures, or mannerisms of interaction partners without conscious awareness or intention

Not everyone engages in nonconscious behavioral mimicry in all situations. People are less likely to engage in behavioral mimicry when they have been induced to feel pride, possibly because when feeling pride, they are likely self-focused rather than attentive to others (Dickens & DeSteno, 2014). When feeling pride, people might also be concerned about maintaining their power and status, and therefore, are less likely to mimic others who are perceived to be of lower status. Supporting this argument, Claire Ashton-James and Ana Levordashka (2013) found that people who are high in narcissism (a personality trait associated with a heightened desire to be admired by others) engaged in nonconscious behavioral mimicry when interacting with a higher social status person, but not when interacting with someone of lower social status. Interestingly, the people who were high in narcissism reported liking the low- and high-status individuals equally, which suggests that their mimicry was not driven by their positive feelings toward others but instead for their heightened desire to form a positive emotional bond with high-status individuals.

Why do we have this fascinating tendency to mimic? What function does it serve? The reviewed studies suggest that behavioral mimicry supports affiliation goals and prosocial motives, as well as a desire to maintain status and social position. As previously discussed in Chapter 1 (section 1.2d), throughout human evolution, individual survival and success at reproduction depended on our ancestors having successful social interactions. Due to the process of natural selection, behaviors that fostered group cohesion eventually became widespread throughout the human population (Caporael, 2001). Over time, many of these behaviors became automatically activated without awareness. A number of social scientists believe that nonconscious mimicry is an example of this form of automatically activated behavior that creates affiliation and rapport among people, and thereby fosters safety in groups (Chartrand et al., 2005; de Waal, 2002).

4.3b Culture and Gender Influence the Expression of Nonverbal Cues.

Given the important role that emotions play in human interactions, it makes abundant sense that cultures would develop social rules for when and how different emotions are expressed (Mesquita & Frijda, 1992). For example, the cultural belief systems of individualism and collectivism have shaped norms related to acting in ways that might threaten group harmony. That is, collectivists are much more likely than individualists to monitor their behavior so that it does not disrupt the smooth functioning of the group. Regarding emotions, people from collectivist cultures are much more uncomfortable about publicly expressing negative emotions than are people from individualist cultures (McDuff et al., 2017).

How you express your emotions may also be associated with your gender and the resulting social roles that you learned (Brody, 1999). A **social role** is a cluster of socially defined expectations that individuals in a given situation are expected to fulfill. According to Alice Eagly's (1987, 1996) **social role theory**, the different social roles occupied by women and men lead to differences in the perception of their behavior. In other words, because men and women typically operate in different domains within most societies—for example, women in the home and men in the world of paid employment—they engage in different patterns of behavior to properly play their roles. Social role theorists contend that women and men do not differ in their ability to experience an array of emotions, but they do differ in monitoring which emotions they publicly express (Fischer & LaFrance, 2015).

A key factor underlying these gender norms is the exercise of social power and dominance within society. For women, the most acceptable emotional style to publicly display is *extravagant expressiveness*, which is an open style of experiencing and

social role
A cluster of socially defined expectations that individuals in a given situation are expected to fulfill

social role theory
The theory that virtually all of the documented behavioral differences between males and females can be accounted for in terms of cultural stereotypes about gender and the resulting social roles that are taught to the young

communicating emotion associated with nurturing and intimate relationships (Shields, 2002, 2007). For men, the most acceptable emotional style is *manly emotion*, which telegraphs intense emotion under control. The underlying message of manly emotion is that the person is independent and powerful: "I can control my emotion (and thereby, my *self*), and I can harness it to control the situation." In contrast, the underlying message of extravagant expressiveness involves nurturance and service: "My emotion (and thereby, my *self*) is at your service, and I am not seeking power." Kavanaugh's angry and even mocking testimony before the Senate Judiciary Committee was an example of manly emotion, whereas Ford's more vulnerable emotional testimony was more in keeping with extravagant expressiveness.

Gender expectations are also played out via men's and women's nonverbal expressions. In a meta-analysis of about 110,000 participants in 162 studies, Marianne LaFrance and her colleagues (2003) found that women and adolescent girls smile more than men and adolescent boys. However, these gender differences vary depending on the situation. Women smile more than men when they are aware others are watching, but this gender difference is much smaller when there are no observers. Similar results have been found for crying, with women reporting that they cry more in public than do men, but this gender difference disappears for reports of crying alone (Fischer & LaFrance, 2015). Furthermore, in very emotional situations (such as the death of a loved one) men and women report similar frequency of crying, but in more ambiguous situations (such as interpersonal conflict) women report that they cry more than men do. Additional research finds that not only are women more likely to express fear and sadness than are men, they are also less likely to nonverbally express anger, and they are also better than men at masking disappointment with a positive expression (Davis, 1995; McDuff et al., 2017). In

Women tend to smile more than men do when in the presence of other people.

(Getty Images)

thinking about your own upbringing, are your skills at constructing emotions consistent with these gender socialization patterns?

Beyond the gender differences in using specific nonverbal cues, meta-analytic studies indicate that females are significantly more adept than males in *decoding* nonverbal communication. For example, in a review of 75 studies testing the ability of men and women to decode nonverbal behavior, Judith Hall (1978) found that 68% of the investigations reported superior female performance. Later meta-analyses found that this gender difference is greatest for decoding facial expressions, next largest for body cues, and smallest for correctly interpreting voice tone (Hall, 1984). The studies further suggest that this gender difference is not isolated in adult samples but can also be found in adolescents and children. Women are effective at detecting even subtle differences in nonverbal expressions. For example, a recent study found that women were better than men at differentiating a genuine smile from a forced, nonauthentic smile (Spies & Sevincer, 2018). Although these gender differences vary in size from study to study, females appear to be consistently better than males at decoding nonverbal cues (Brody & Hall, 1993).

How might an evolutionary theorist explain the gender differences in decoding nonverbal communication? That is, from an evolutionary perspective, why would it be more beneficial for females than males to have good nonverbal skills?

As with emotional expression, social psychologists principally explain these gender differences in reading nonverbal cues by examining the different social roles played by females and males. Because the social roles played by women tend to have lower status relative to male roles, women have had to learn to be accommodating and polite (Mast & Hall, 2004). This explanation is consistent with research indicating that regardless of gender, those who have less powerful social roles smile more (Fischer & LaFrance, 2015) and are more sensitive to the feelings of their superiors than vice versa (Hecht & LaFrance, 1998).

4.3c   Most of Us Are Poor Deception Detectors.

In considering once again the Senate Judiciary testimony of Ford and Kavanaugh, while it is possible that both witnesses believed they were being truthful in recounting the incident from their high school days, it is more likely that one of them was lying. One sobering fact about daily living is that people are not only capable of being deceptive in their self-presentations, but also that we as social perceivers often unquestioningly accept their lies. As discussed in Chapter 3 (section 3.3), sociologist Erving Goffman (1959) asserted that we generally accept the presented selves of others at face value because to do otherwise would disrupt the smooth flow of social interaction. In this respect, the dynamics of social interaction actually work against easy detection of lies and deceit. Yet how common is lying in everyday life, and how gullible are we to others' deceptions?

Research informs us that, while we are not born liars, by about 4 or 5 years of age we have the ability to effectively tell strategic lies—and this ability increases in sophistication as we mature (Evans et al., 2011; Heyman et al., 2013). During an average week, we lie to about one-third of those with whom we interact, and we also often lie during job interviews (Griffith et al., 2007; Weiss & Feldman, 2006). On average we tell about 10 lies per week, with the greatest lying committed by those of us who are more extroverted and manipulative, who are feeling socially powerful, or who are concerned about creating favorable self-presentations (Kashy & DePaulo, 1996; Yap et al., 2013). Although lying is a fact of life, it is a risky and often costly self-presentation strategy. We dislike those who frequently deceive us and tend to reciprocate with lies of our own (Tyler et al., 2006).

Given that others may try to conceal their true feelings and intentions from us, how do we—as person perceivers—respond to the possibility of such subterfuge? Goffman (1959) contended that when we judge other people's self-presentations, we pay attention to two different types of social stimuli, which he called *expressions*. First, there are expressions that people freely "give" to others in what is typically thought of as their traditional communication patterns. These *given expressions* consist of the words and gestures that people are consciously trying to transmit to others. Besides these strategic gestures, there are also expressions that people "give off," which are mostly nonverbal in nature. *Expressions given off*, also known as *nonverbal leakage*, cover a wide range of behavior unintentionally transmitted and of which people are much less aware. Your lack of gusto when chewing a host's poorly prepared meal, accompanied by the tortured look on your face, are examples of expressions given off. Likewise, from the Senate hearings, Judge Kavanaugh's fidgeting with his shirt cuffs and his incessant sniffing were expressions that he was unintentionally giving off. But what do they reveal, if anything?

Of the two types of expressions, those unintentionally "given off" by self-presenters are better indicators of possible deception than those that are consciously "given" (Ekman & O'Sullivan, 1991). Unfortunately, in those situations where detecting lies is most important to us, we tend to give more weight to messages that people consciously convey to us. James Forrest and Robert Feldman (2000) found that when people were highly involved in a discussion topic, they paid more attention to speakers' words and thus were more easily deceived than less involved people (who attended more to nonverbal behavior).

Although attending to nonverbal behavior can improve our ability to detect lies in others' self-presentations, not all nonverbal cues are equally instructive. One mistake we often make is placing too much importance on the face to reveal deception. We tend to believe that others do not smile when they lie, when in fact smiling is a common device used by deceivers to hide their true feelings (Ekman et al., 1988). We also tend to believe that liars fidget and won't look us in the eye; however, both of these cues are only weakly related to deception (Hartwig & Bond, 2011). In fact, experienced deceivers engage in deliberate eye contact to convince us they are being truthful (Mann et al., 2013). We are also often fooled by the *structure* of people's faces, falsely assuming that baby-faced individuals (with large eyes and symmetrical facial features) and physically attractive persons are more honest than those with mature-looking and less attractive faces (Zebrowitz & Montepare, 1992; Zebrowitz et al., 1996).

It is sometimes possible to detect deception by attending to certain changes in people's speech patterns—what is known as *paralanguage*—and by analyzing the quality of their stories (see Table 4.1). Several studies indicate that when people lie, they give shorter answers, their stories make less sense, their voices sound tense, and their pitch rises slightly (DePaulo et al., 2003; Hauch et al., 2015). Liars' speech is also slower and filled with many pauses ("ahs" and "ums") and other sentence hesitations. Experts believe that the reduced complexity, logic, and fluidity of liars' stories—combined with the heightened voice tension—reflect the additional cognitive burden caused by their attempt to deceive. Liars also tend to use fewer first-person singular pronouns (*I*, *me*, *my*) and sound less involved in their storytelling, which is thought to reflect their attempt to dissociate themselves from the lie (Hauch et al., 2015; Newman et al., 2003). Finally, liars also use negative-emotion words at a higher rate than truth tellers, which may be caused by their feelings of guilt (which triggers negative emotions) (Hauch et al., 2015; Newman et al., 2003; Vrij, 2000). However, use of profanity is positively related to honesty (Feldman et al., 2017). These cues to deception are more likely to be revealed when people are lying about something very important rather than about more trivial matters (DePaulo & Morris, 2004). To some extent, people have an intuitive understanding that these language cues reflect deception and are more likely to judge a person as deceptive if their stories are illogical, improbable, and have few details (Hartwig & Bond, 2011).

TABLE 4.1   What Are Some Possible Verbal Symptoms of Lying?

Symptoms	Likely Causes
Shorter answers to questions Stories make less sense Slower speech filled with pauses and other sentence hesitations	The cognitive burden of concealing the truth interfering with the generation of smooth conversation
Slight rise in voice pitch and vocal tension	Activation of the sympathetic nervous system
Less use of first-person singular pronouns Sound less involved in what they are saying	Psychological attempt to dissociate oneself from the lie
More use of negative-emotion words	Feelings of guilt that trigger negative emotions

However, despite such cues, meta-analysis of more than 200 experiments finds that people are just slightly better than chance—54%—at distinguishing truths from lies, and accuracy drops even further when people are even mildly mentally fatigued (Bond & DePaulo, 2006; Reinhard et al., 2013). This is also the accuracy level of those who make these judgments for a living—such as judges, police officers, CIA polygraphers, and customs inspectors. Indeed, the best of the professional deception detectors (Secret Service agents) are successful only about 70% of the time (Ekman & O'Sullivan, 1991).

People are particularly bad at detecting deception from strangers (Anderson et al., 1999). One important reason for this low level of accuracy among the unacquainted is that people often individually behave in distinctive ways when lying. However, when interacting with strangers, we have no knowledge of their distinctive "lying signals." Fortunately, we do appear to gain insight into people's telltale lying signals the longer we know them. In a longitudinal study of friendship development, researchers found that friends become more accurate in detecting each other's deception as their relationship progresses, improving from 56% accuracy early in the friendship to 66% accuracy after 5 months (Morris et al., 2016). The key ingredient in increasing your ability to detect deception is having relevant information. The more relevant information you have about people who might be deceiving you, and the more relevant information you have about the social context in which the possible deception occurs, the greater your ability to identify lies from truths (Blair et al., 2010; Levine, et al., 2010).

Taken as a whole, the research suggests that deceivers often succeed in duping us regardless of our sex, race, cultural background, socioeconomic status, or educational level, and they are most successful when we do not know them well and the issue is important to us (Geary & DePaulo, 2007). However, it is also true that liars are most likely to reveal deception cues when the issue is important to them. Perhaps the primary reason we so often fail to detect deception is that, by and large, we tend to believe that others are basically honest (Zuckerman et al., 1981). Yet one thing that works to our advantage when dealing with habitual liars is that while we may not detect their deception the first few times, we are more likely to do so as we observe them over time and become more familiar with their self-presentation strategies (Yamagishi et al., 2003).

4.3d We Develop Implicit Personality Theories Based on Central Traits.

The initial phase of person perception often involves little cognitive effort and is based on easily recognizable physical characteristics—such as sex, age, and race—and nonverbal actions presented by the target persons (Park, 1986). If the individuals are of no interest or the interaction is very brief, we will not bother to analyze them further and may judge them based on cultural stereotypes. However, if we are motivated to learn more about these people as individuals, our thinking becomes more deliberate and effortful, resulting in our impressions becoming more abstract and less tied to superficial physical qualities (Van Overwalle et al., 1999). Because personality traits are commonly used in forming impressions (Fiske & Cox, 1979), one of the first questions asked by social psychologists was how traits are combined to form a meaningful picture of a person.

In the 1940s, Solomon Asch worked within the German tradition of *Gestalt psychology*, which studied how the mind actively organizes stimuli into a coherent whole—or *gestalt*. In person perception, Asch hypothesized that our overall impression of others is not simply determined by adding up all their personality traits. Instead, certain traits exert greater influence than do others on people's overall impressions.

(Shutterstock)

Why is it that a person who is described as intelligent, skillful, industrious, determined, practical, and cautious will be perceived much more favorably when they are also described as warm rather than cold, but not when they are described as polite rather than blunt?

In testing this hypothesis, Asch (1946) asked participants to examine a list of discrete traits that belonged to a particular person and then form an impression based on this information. For some participants, the following traits were presented: intelligent, skillful, industrious, warm, determined, practical, and cautious. For other participants, the trait *warm* was replaced with the trait *cold*, but otherwise everything else was identical. Those who had been told that the hypothetical person was warm rated him as significantly more generous, humorous, sociable, and popular than those who had been told that he was cold. In contrast to the effect of switching these two central traits, when Asch switched the traits *polite* and *blunt* in a similar list, the resulting impressions differed very little from one another. Asch concluded that warmth and competence are **central traits** in person perception. The less important traits Asch called *peripheral traits*. Asch's ground-breaking study has been replicated with a large, online sample (Nauts et al., 2014) and in real-life settings (Judd et al., 2005; Kelley, 1950).

More recently, researchers have suggested that morality is a third central trait that also influences impression formation (Goodwin, 2015). Furthermore, the importance of specific traits varies depending on the social context in which we make evaluations (Singh & Teoh, 2000). For example, the traits *intelligent* and *humorous* generally have equal value in forming impressions of people. But *intelligent* would carry more weight for a psychology department's graduate school admissions committee evaluating applicants, while *humorous* would have more of an impact on the owner of a comedy nightclub looking for a new act.

As social thinkers, how do we decide whether other people's actions are primarily caused by their attitudes and personalities versus the circumstances in which they find themselves?

Inspired by Asch's ideas about central traits, social cognitive theorists proposed that people develop **implicit personality theories**. Implicit personality theories are a schema we use to organize and make sense of which personality traits and behaviors go together (Bruner & Taguiri, 1954; Norenzayan et al., 2002). Like many other schemas, implicit personality theories are shaped by both personal experiences and cultural beliefs, and they are often passed from generation to generation (Chiu et al., 2000; Haimovitz & Dweck, 2016).

In analyzing how people develop implicit personality theories, Carol Dweck proposed that people vary in the degree to which they view personality as fixed or malleable (Dweck et al., 1995). Those who endorse a *growth mindset* believe that personality traits, such as intelligence, can be changed and developed over time. In contrast, those who endorse a *fixed mindset* believe that personality and intelligence are unchangeable. People who hold the fixed mindset, compared to a growth mindset, are more likely to rely on stereotypes when forming impressions of individuals from marginalized groups and are also more likely to believe that personality traits are biologically predetermined (Hong et al., 2004; Levy et al., 1998). Similarly, when someone with a fixed mindset observes a person engaging in a negative behavior, they assume the person has negative characteristics and deserves to be punished. However, people with growth mindsets are more likely to consider multiple factors for the behavior and respond to the person in a way that might change the undesirable behavior, such as talking to the person (Dweck et al., 1995).

These two implicit personality mindsets can also influence how people view their own life experiences. For example, David Yeager and his colleagues (2014) found that during the transition to high school, students who had a growth mindset were better able to deal with being socially excluded than those students with a fixed mindset. Furthermore, students with the fixed mindset, compared to those with a growth mindset, reported greater stress, poorer health, and lower grades during their freshman year in high school. For students, these two mindsets appear to influence academic achievement, such that students with growth mindsets have slightly better academic achievement than those with fixed mindsets (Sisk et al., 2018). Fortunately, experimental research testing interventions suggests that training students to have a growth mindset about intelligence can promote academic achievement. Both high school students and first-year college students who initially held a fixed mindset showed improved academic performance after they participated in brief interventions informing them that intelligence is not fixed, but rather, is malleable (Broda et al., 2018; Yeager et al., 2014). Such growth

central traits
Traits that exert a disproportionate influence on people's overall impressions, causing them to assume the presence of other traits

implicit personality theories
A type of schema people use to organize and make sense of which personality traits and behaviors go together

mindset training appears to be especially beneficial for students who are at high risk for academic failure or who are from low socioeconomic status groups (Paunesku et al., 2015; Sisk et al., 2018).

What is your own implicit personality theory about intelligence? How might this mindset influence your academic-related behaviors, such as studying, asking professors for help, and coping with setbacks in challenging courses?

4.3e   We Often Seek Information to Confirm Our First Impressions.

Our tendency to view others in a way that is internally consistent causes us to also selectively seek information about them. For example, based on the questions that were asked by senators who sat on the Senate Judiciary Committee hearings, it was clear that the vast majority of Republican senators wanted to believe Kavanaugh, while the vast majority of Democrat senators wanted to believe Ford. Without variation, senators asked questions designed to confirm their already held beliefs about the two witnesses. This tendency to seek information that supports our beliefs while ignoring disconfirming information is known as the **confirmation bias** (Hart et al., 2009).

In one experiment testing the confirmation bias during first encounters, Mark Snyder and William Swann (1978) asked research participants to find out whether the person with whom they were about to interact was an introvert or an extrovert, depending on the experimental condition. Consistent with the confirmation bias, the questions that participants asked their interaction partners were biased in the direction of the original question. For instance, if they had been asked to find out whether the person was an introvert, they asked questions such as, "What do you dislike about loud parties?" or "In what situations do you wish you could be more outgoing?" However, in the extrovert condition, they asked questions such as, "How do you liven things up at a party?" or "What kinds of situations help you to meet new people?" Because most people can recall both introverted and extroverted incidents from their past, the interaction partners' answers provided confirmatory evidence for either personality trait. Experiments like this indicate that one barrier to accurate social judgments can be our tendency to search for information that will confirm our beliefs more energetically than we pursue information that might refute them (Edwards & Smith, 1996).

> "For a man always believes more readily that which he prefers."
>
> —Francis Bacon, English Renaissance author, 1561–1626

> "When you look for the bad in mankind expecting to find it, you surely will."
>
> —Abraham Lincoln, 16th US president, 1809–1865

We are more likely to engage in the confirmation bias when the situation we are analyzing is one in which we are personally invested and the possible solution is agreeable to us rather than threatening (Dawson et al., 2002). Faced with an agreeable possible solution we are motivated to confirm it and ask ourselves, "*Can* I believe this?" In such situations, our standards of judgment are rather permissive, paving the way for the confirmation bias. On the other hand, when the possible solution is threatening or disagreeable, we adopt a more stringent standard of judgment and instead ask, "*Must* I believe this?" This latter question prompts more critical analysis, increasing the likelihood that any flaws or limitations in the available evidence will be discovered (Ditto et al., 1998). Such confirmation seeking not only leads to mistakes about individuals but also perpetuates incorrect stereotypes about social groups (Yzerbyt et al., 1996).

confirmation bias
The tendency to seek information that supports our beliefs while ignoring disconfirming information

Section Summary

- First impressions are often based on nonverbal behavior.

- We reliably identify seven primary emotions: anger, disgust, fear, happiness, surprise, sadness, and contempt.

- Nonconscious mimicry is automatically activated, and it fosters affiliation and rapport.

- Women and men differ in expressing and detecting emotional states.

- Detecting deception in others is very difficult, but there are some useful cues.

- Central traits exert more influence in personality impressions than peripheral traits.

- Implicit personality theories influence how we view others and ourselves.

- Confirmation bias occurs when we seek information that verifies our beliefs.

4.4 How Do We Construct Causal Explanations for Events?

A few years ago, after a snowstorm, Steve arrived home from work and noticed that his garbage had not been collected. When he phoned the company, an exasperated woman replied to his query by sarcastically stating, "Well sir, with all the snow we had yesterday, I would have thought people wouldn't have been stupid enough to put out their garbage today." Now, despite the public perception of psychologists as detached observers, constantly analyzing other people's behavior and motivation, this psychologist's response was not quite so analytical. Later, however, Steve wondered what caused her to act so rudely. Was she an insensitive person, or was it just a bad day for her?

About a year later, his garbage was not picked up again and he had to contact this woman a second time. Now there was no snowstorm. As he dialed, he wondered if he was about to be chastised again for yet another mental failing. To his relief, she was very cordial and apologetic. Based on this second conversation, he concluded that her previous behavior was most likely not due to some stable personality trait such as rudeness but rather to the situational stress she experienced on that snowy winter day. How did he arrive at this judgment, and how do people in general assign causal explanations for events?

4.4a We Rely Upon Particular Information When Explaining People's Actions.

Everybody has a general theory of human behavior—what Fritz Heider (1958) called a *naive psychology*—and we use it to search for explanations to social events. In searching for understanding, we focus not only on people's personalities but also consider the situational context. Our desire to understand and explain social events is strongest when the events are the actions of other people and are unexpected, unusual, or distressing (Kanazawa, 1992). The process by which we use such information to make inferences about the causes of behavior or events is called **attribution** (Heider, 1958; Ichheiser, 1934, 1943).

attribution

The process by which people use information to make inferences about the causes of behavior or events

In seeking attributions, Heider believed people are motivated by two primary needs: the need to form a logical view of the world and the need to gain control of the environment. Being able to predict how people are going to behave goes a long way in satisfying both of these needs. If we can adequately explain and predict the actions of others, we will be much more likely to view the world as logical and controllable than if we have no clue as to their intentions and dispositions. In satisfying these two needs, Heider asserted that we try to act like *naive scientists*, carefully testing our hypotheses about the behavior of others.

Locus of Causality

In making causal attributions, by far the most important judgment concerns the *locus of causality* (Jones & Davis, 1965). According to Heider, people broadly attribute a given action either to internal states or external factors. An **internal attribution** (also called *person attribution*) consists of any explanation that locates the cause as being internal to the person, such as personality traits, moods, attitudes, abilities, or effort. An **external attribution** (also called *situation attribution*) consists of any explanation that locates the cause as being external to the person under scrutiny, such as the actions of others, the nature of the situation, or luck. In the "garbage" example, Steve ultimately made an external attribution about the woman's actions, explaining her rudeness as being due to job-related stress brought on by adverse weather. For Heider and other attribution theorists, whether Steve's explanation is correct or not is not the issue. Their task is not to determine the *true* cause of events but rather to explain how people *perceive* the causes.

Stability of Causality

Besides making internal or external distinctions, people also attempt to determine whether causes are *stable*. Stable causes are permanent and lasting, while unstable causes are temporary and fluctuating. This stable/unstable dimension is independent of the direction of causality. Some causes, called *dispositional*, are both internal and stable ("She insulted me because she is rude"). Other causes are considered to be internal but unstable ("She insulted me because she has a cold"). Likewise, some causes are seen as external and stable ("She insulted me because I, the external factor, rub people the wrong way"), while others are perceived as external and unstable ("She insulted me because the weather conditions that day made her job very difficult").

4.4b The Covariation Model Explains Attributions Based on Three Types of Information.

One foundational theory that specifically attempts to explain attributions based on observing people over time, across situations, and in comparison to others' actions is Harold Kelley's (1967) **covariation model**. According to Kelley, when making attributions, people use the *covariation principle*, meaning they assume that for something to be the cause of a particular behavior, it must be present when the behavior occurs and absent when it does not occur. In other words, the presumed cause and observed effect must "covary." If your boyfriend or girlfriend becomes cold and irritable only when you spend extended time with others, that is high covariation. If he or she is only occasionally cold and irritable when you spend extended time with others, that is low covariation. In attempting to assign a cause to the cold and irritable behavior, you would observe its covariation with as many potential causes as possible and attribute the effect to the cause with which it has the greatest covariance.

internal attribution

An attribution that locates the cause of an event in factors internal to the person, such as personality traits, moods, attitudes, abilities, or effort

external attribution

An attribution that locates the cause of an event in factors external to the person, such as luck, other people, or the situation

covariation model

An attribution theory that describes how we make judgments about people's actions by observing them over time (consistency information), across situations (distinctiveness information), and in comparison to others' actions (consensus information)

In describing the locus of causality, Kelley elaborated on the internal/external dimension by further distinguishing external attributions in terms of the *entity* and *circumstances.* The *entity* is the object toward which the actor's behavior is directed and can be another person or a thing. *Circumstances* are simply the conditions in which actions or events occur.

In assessing covariation, Kelley stated that people rely on three kinds of information. *Consensus* information deals with the extent to which others react the same way to some stimulus or entity as the person whose actions we are attempting to explain. *Consistency* information concerns the extent to which the person reacts to this stimulus or entity in the same way on other occasions. Finally, *distinctiveness* information refers to the extent to which the person reacts the same way to other, different stimuli or entities. Kelley's theory predicts that people are most likely to attribute another person's behavior to internal and stable (dispositional) causes when consensus and distinctiveness are low but consistency is high. On the other hand, circumstance attributions are most likely when consensus and consistency are low and distinctiveness is high. When all three kinds of information are high, people are likely to make entity attributions.

As a way to further explain this theory, the following example might be helpful. Over the years, both of us have had the experience of having a student fall asleep in class while we are lecturing. Naturally, we wonder why. Did the student have a bad night's sleep (circumstance attribution)? Is this a lazy and unmotivated student (internal attribution)? Are we that boring (entity attribution)? In Table 4.2, we've outlined how Kelley's theory might predict specific attributions about this behavior. The covariation model predicts that we would seek an attribution by gathering consensus, consistency, and distinctiveness information. For consensus, we would look at the behavior of our other students: Is everybody on the verge of dozing off in our class? For consistency, we would consider this student's past classroom behavior: How attentive (or at least awake) has the student appeared in previous class sessions? For distinctiveness, we would gather information about the student's behavior in other professors' classes: Does the student fall asleep only in my class?

TABLE 4.2	Why Did the Student Fall Asleep in My Class?			
		Available Information		
Condition	**Consensus**	**Consistency**	**Distinctiveness**	**Attribution**
1	Low—No other students fall asleep in my class	High—The student has fallen asleep in previous classes of mine	Low—The student falls asleep in other professors' classes	Internal: The student is lazy
2	High—Many students fall asleep in my class	High—The student has fallen asleep in previous classes of mine	High—The student doesn't fall asleep in other professors' classes	Entity: I'm a boring professor
3	Low—No other students fall asleep in my class	Low—The student hasn't fallen asleep in previous classes of mine	High—The student doesn't fall asleep in other professor's classes	Circumstance: The student didn't sleep well last night

For an internal attribution to be made (Condition 1: The student is lazy), there must be evidence for low consensus and distinctiveness and high consistency. This attribution would be likely if none of the other students nod off, the student falls asleep in other professors' classes, and the student has fallen asleep in some of my previous classes as well. For an entity attribution to be made (Condition 2: I'm a boring professor), there must be evidence of high consensus, distinctiveness, and consistency. This attribution is likely if many students fall asleep in my class, and this particular student doesn't fall asleep in other professors' classes, even though the student consistently dozes off in mine. A circumstance attribution would likely be made if consensus and consistency are low but distinctiveness is high (Condition 3). So if no one else is dozing off and the student hasn't fallen asleep in previous classes of mine, or in other professors' classes, some unusual circumstance must have caused this behavior. Perhaps the student didn't get enough sleep last night.

How accurate is the covariation model in explaining the attribution process? Empirical studies generally support its basic assumptions (Chen et al., 1988; Windschitl & Wells, 1997). However, when making dispositional attributions about an actor's actions, we appear to primarily focus on information that can be obtained by attending to the actor (Was his or her behavior distinctive or consistent?). In contrast, our external attributions are more influenced by consensus information.

4.4c   There Are Biases in the Attribution Process.

Attributional theories have advanced our understanding of how we make inferences about the causes of behavior. However, these theories typically assume that the attribution process is highly rational. If people do follow logical principles in assigning causality to events, this cognitive process—likened by some to a computer program—has a few interesting and all-too-illogical human "bugs."

In Chapter 1, we discussed the *self-serving bias*, which involves assigning an internal locus of causality for our positive outcomes and an external locus for our negative outcomes. A desire to enhance or protect self-esteem is the most agreed-upon explanation for this particular attributional bias. Given our discussion in Chapter 3 concerning the high value placed on self-esteem in individualist cultures, it should not be surprising to learn that individualists are more likely to exhibit the self-serving bias than collectivists (Boven et al., 2003; Heine & Lehman, 1999).

The Fundamental Attribution Error

As discussed in Chapter 1, behavior is generally caused by an interaction between an individual's internal characteristics and external factors. However, when explaining other people's actions, we tend to locate the cause in their dispositional characteristics rather than in situational factors. Lee Ross (1977) named this tendency to overestimate the impact of dispositional causes and underestimate the impact of situational causes on other people's behavior the **fundamental attribution error**.

In one classic study to investigate this cognitive bias, Ross and his colleagues (Ross et al., 1977) devised a simulated TV quiz game in which students were randomly assigned to serve in the role of "quizmaster" or "contestant." The quizmasters were told to think up 10 challenging but fair questions, and the contestants were told to answer as many as possible. Under such conditions, the quizmasters were able to devise some rather tough questions; on average, the contestants answered only 4 of the 10 questions correctly. Despite the fact that the quizmaster role gave students playing that part a decided advantage, the contestants failed to discount or take this external factor into account in assigning a causal explanation for the quiz show's results. As you can see in Figure 4.2, contestants saw the quizmasters as far more knowledgeable than themselves. Observers who watched the game, but who were not directly involved in the outcome, also rated the quizmasters as more knowledgeable than the contestants.

fundamental attribution error
The tendency to overestimate the impact of dispositional causes and underestimate the impact of situational causes on other people's behavior

FIGURE 4.2 Fundamental Attribution Error and the TV Quiz Game

Even though students playing the role of quizmaster held a decided advantage over contestants, the contestants failed to discount or take this external factor into account in assigning a causal explanation for the quiz show's results. Like the observers, the contestants judged the quizmasters as more knowledgeable than themselves. What might explain this fundamental attribution error?

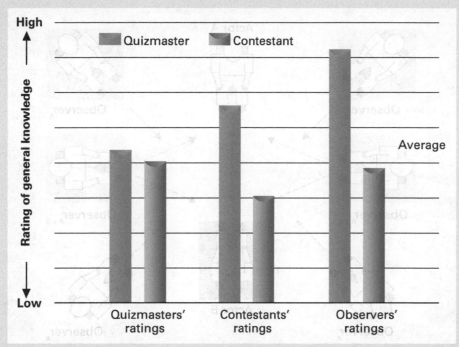

Data source: "Social Roles, Social Control and Biases in Social-Perception Process," by L. Ross et al., 1977, *Journal of Personality and Social Psychology, 35*(7), pp. 485–494.

Why do we engage in this sort of systematic bias? One possibility is that we prefer making dispositional attributions because locating the cause of people's behavior in their attitudes and personalities gives us greater confidence that we can accurately predict their future behavior. Thus, our desire for predictability may make us more susceptible to the fundamental attribution error. A second possibility has to do with what is most noticeable to us as social perceivers. When we observe a person in a social setting, what is often most *perceptually salient* is that particular person: his or her dynamic movements, distinctive voice, and overall physical presence. In comparison, the relatively static situational forces that may actually cause those behaviors are often less salient and therefore less likely to be factored into the attribution equation.

Shelley Taylor and Susan Fiske (1975) tested this hypothesis by varying the seating arrangements of six people who observed two actors engaging in a carefully staged, 5-minute conversation. In each session, observers were seated so they faced actor A, actor B, or both. This seating arrangement is illustrated in Figure 4.3. Following the conversation, the observers were asked questions about the two actors to determine whom they thought had the most impact on the conversation. Results indicated that whichever actor the observers faced was the one they judged as the more dominant member of the dyad. Further research has confirmed perceptual salience as a contributing factor to the fundamental attribution error (Krull & Dill, 1996; Lassiter et al., 2002).

FIGURE 4.3   Perceptual Salience and the Fundamental Attribution Error

This is the seating arrangement for the two actors and six observers in the perceptual salience study. Taylor and Fiske (1975) found that observers rated the actor they could see most clearly as being the dominant contributor to the conversation. How do these findings help explain the fundamental attribution error?

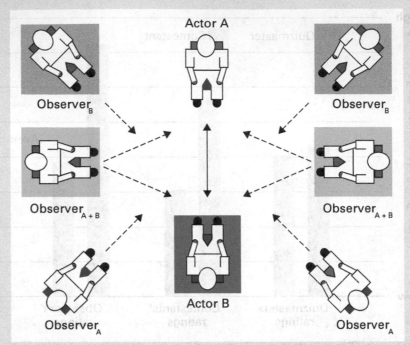

Adapted from "Point of View and Perceptions of Causality," by S. E. Taylor and S. T. Fiske, 1975, *Journal of Personality and Social Psychology, 32*(3), pp. 439–445.

For many years, social psychologists believed that people throughout the world exhibited the fundamental attribution error equally. Yet as more research was conducted in non-Western cultures, it became clear that this particular attribution error was less common in collectivist than individualist cultures. For example, Joan Miller (1984) found that South Asian Indians made more situational attributions when explaining people's everyday behavior, whereas North Americans were much more likely to make dispositional attributions. Faced with such findings, social psychologists began wondering *why* culture affects the fundamental attribution error. Is it because collectivists are less attentive than individualists to how attitudes and personality traits (dispositions) can shape behavior? Or is it due to individualists being less attentive than collectivists to how situational forces can influence behavior?

Subsequent research found that collectivists are just as likely as individualists to take into account people's dispositions when explaining their behavior (Choi et al., 1999; Miyamoto & Kitayama, 2002). Where they differ is in their awareness of the situation's power or the social context (Owe et al., 2013). Collectivists are more attentive to how situational factors may influence people's behavior, and that is apparently why they are less susceptible to the fundamental attribution error. A compelling illustration of this cultural difference is a study conducted by Ara Norenzayan and Richard Nisbett (2000) in which American and Japanese college students were shown an animated underwater scene featuring small fish, frogs, and snails, along with plants, rocks, coral, and some larger, faster-moving focal fish—the stars of the show (see Figure 4.4). After this viewing, participants were asked to recall what they had seen. Both American and Japanese participants equally recalled details of the focal fish, but the Japanese recalled 60% more background features than did the Americans, and the Japanese reported more relationships (e.g., "the frog beside the coral" or "the small fish near the plant").

FIGURE 4.4   Cultural Differences in Attentional Focus

When shown an underwater scene similar to this scene, Americans and Japanese equally recalled the focal fish, but the Japanese recalled 60% more background features. How do these results relate to the fact that the fundamental attribution error is more pronounced in individualist cultures than in collectivist cultures?

(iStock)

It appears that this cultural difference is rooted in different views of the self (Chua et al., 2005). As stated in Chapter 3, individualists view the self as internally driven and relatively uninfluenced by situational forces (the independent self). In contrast, collectivists view the self as dependent on the group and strongly influenced by social obligations (the interdependent self). The interdependent self fosters a greater appreciation of how personal and situational factors interact in shaping behavior, which is essentially how social psychology understands social behavior. Based on these findings, some social psychologists suggest that the type of naive psychology that members of collectivist cultures naturally develop leads to more accurate attributions than are typically made in individualist cultures (Lieberman et al., 2005).

However, as you recall from our discussion in Chapter 3 (section 3.2a), cultures do not create people with rigidly independent or interdependent selves. Situational factors can trigger spontaneous self-concepts in people that run counter to the independent self or interdependent self fostered by their culture (Kühnen & Oyserman, 2002). When this occurs in people whose typical self-views are independent, their situationally induced interdependent self will likely foster a greater awareness of how the interaction of dispositional and situational factors influences others' behaviors. Likewise, when collectivists' thoughts are temporarily shifted to an independent self-view, their social judgments are more likely to suffer from the fundamental attribution error (Hong et al., 2000, 2003).

Whether perceptual salience, individualism, or a combination of these and other factors explain the fundamental attribution error, this particular bias can have significant social consequences. Attributing the behavior of others to internal factors allows social perceivers to block actors' attempts to deny responsibility for negative events with which they are associated (Inman et al., 1993). For example, the tendency to disregard situational forces in explaining the plight of victims within our society (rape victims, street people, disadvantaged minorities, etc.) can result in less sympathy because we hold these people responsible for their condition due to "bad" dispositions (Grubb & Turner, 2012; Sperry & Siegel, 2013).

Actor-Observer Effect

When explaining the actions of others, we are likely to give more weight to internal (dispositional) factors, but when explaining our own behavior, we tend to give more weight to external (or situational) factors. This tendency to attribute our own behavior to external causes, but that of others to internal factors, is known as the **actor-observer effect** (Jones & Nisbett, 1972; Karasawa, 1995). For example, if Charisse is talking with an attractive male stranger and her boyfriend, Singh, sees them from a distance, they may well arrive at different explanations for this social interaction. Although Charisse may attribute it to an external factor (the stranger was asking for directions), Singh may assign an internal cause (Charisse is infatuated with this guy).

Why does the actor-observer effect occur? As with the fundamental attribution error, a likely possibility is perceptual salience. While engaged in a particular activity, the actor's attention is typically turned outward toward the situation, but the observer's attention is likely focused on the actor. Thus, what is salient for the actor (the situation) and what is salient for the observer (the actor) differs due to their perspectives in viewing the event.

The actor-observer effect appears to operate most often when people are explaining recent events in their lives. When explaining events that took place long ago or when predicting events that will occur in the distant future, actors generally make dispositional attributions just like observers (Pronin & Ross, 2006). In such circumstances, situational factors are less salient and even less available in memory or the imagination than is the "self as actor." In other words, people generally adopt an observer perspective rather than an actor perspective when explaining distant events in their lives. Furthermore, this effect is strongest when understanding negative events, such as failures, rather than when understanding positive events such as success (Malle, 2006). This suggests that the actor-observer effect might actually be a type of self-serving bias. That is, we seek to understand our successes and failures in a way that makes us feel good about ourselves; failures are due to the circumstance, but successes are due to internal dispositions.

actor-observer effect
The tendency for people to attribute their own behavior to external causes but that of others to internal factors

dual-process models of attribution
Theories of attribution that propose that people initially engage in a relatively automatic and simple attributional assessment but then later consciously correct this attribution with more deliberate and effortful thinking

4.4d Making Attributions Involves Both Automatic and Deliberate Thinking.

Although the covariation model and other attribution theories provide insights into how we make sense of our social world, they conceive of human beings as *naive scientists* who are highly rational and logical information processors, heavily relying on explicit cognition. In essence, these theories reflect the classic "cold" perspective in social psychology (see Chapter 1, section 1.2b). Many social psychologists now contend that **dual-process models of attribution**, involving both explicit cognition and implicit cognition, best explain the attribution process. The dual-process model reflects the "warm look" of social cognition in social psychology (again, section 1.2b).

According to this dual-process model, automatic and simple attributional assessments typically occur first and are then sometimes followed by more deliberate and effortful analysis (Newman, 2001). Adjustments of initial judgments are most likely to occur among people who doubt their ability to understand the reasons for others' actions (Weary et al., 2006). Furthermore, people from individualist cultures are more likely to make spontaneous trait inferences than are people from collectivist cultures (Shimizu et al., 2017). Regardless of culture, the initial step in the social judgment process involves spontaneous and relatively effortless thinking (Van Hiel et al., 2008), while the second step involves a deliberate and often more effortful adjustment of the first judgment.

As an example of how this process works, let's return to the "garbage lady" incident in which she responded to Steve's phone inquiry about tardy garbage pickup by stating, "Well sir, with all the snow we had yesterday, I would have thought people wouldn't have been stupid enough to put out their garbage today." What explains her behavior? As depicted in Figure 4.5, in the first stage of Steve's attributional thinking he would spontaneously categorize the garbage lady's behavior ("Whoa! That sounds like an insult directed at me!"). In the second stage, he would make an initial dispositional inference ("I think she is a rude person!"). While the first and second stages in this process are automatic and relatively effortless, the third stage is much more deliberate and requires a good deal of cognitive effort. In the third stage, Steve began to consider possible situational factors that might explain the garbage lady's response: "Maybe the weather stressed her out." "Maybe my tone of voice sounded accusatory and this irritated her." "Maybe this is the 50th call she received today, and she's fed up." When we are distracted, too busy, or unmotivated, we may not engage in this second judgmental process because correcting the initial, spontaneous dispositional characterization of other people's behavior is cognitively demanding. In individualist cultures, when we don't engage in deliberate attributional inference, our explanations of other people's actions are likely to fall prey to the fundamental attribution error (Uleman, 1999). However, the tendency to commit this error is greatly reduced when we take the time to engage in more effortful thinking (Deutsch et al., 2006).

FIGURE 4.5   A Dual-Process Model of Attribution

Many contemporary attribution theorists contend that when trying to explain others' behaviors, people from individualist cultures often automatically focus on dispositional factors initially and then later consciously correct this attribution to better account for situational factors. How does this attribution process proceed for people in collectivist cultures?

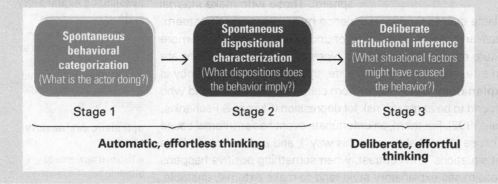

Spontaneous behavioral categorization (What is the actor doing?) → Spontaneous dispositional characterization (What dispositions does the behavior imply?) → Deliberate attributional inference (What situational factors might have caused the behavior?)

Stage 1   Stage 2   Stage 3

Automatic, effortless thinking   Deliberate, effortful thinking

---

Section Summary

- Locus of causality (internal or external) is the most important judgment in making attributions.
- The covariation model describes how we explain behavior by using information about consistency, distinctiveness, and consensus.
- The attribution process is characterized by cognitive biases that cause judgmental errors.
  The fundamental attribution error is the tendency to make internal versus external attributions and is more common in individualist cultures than in collectivist cultures.
  The actor-observer effect is the tendency to make external attributions for our own behavior but internal attributions for others.
- The attribution process involves both automatic and deliberate thinking; more deliberate and effortful thinking may correct for some of our attributional biases.

Applications

How Do You Explain Negative Events in Your Life?

According to Lyn Abramson and her colleagues (1978), people differ in their attributional style, which can affect how they respond to uncontrollable life events. Reactions to uncontrollable events are determined by three types of attributions: *internal versus external*, *stable versus unstable*, and *global versus specific* (that is, whether the event extends to many spheres of life or is confined to one sphere). Those who make *internal* attributions for uncontrollable events tend to experience more negative self-esteem. Individuals who make *stable* and *global* attributions for uncontrollable events are more likely to feel helpless in future events. When all three types of negative attributions are habitually used to explain stressful events in one's life, this attributional tendency is called the **pessimistic explanatory style**; people from cultures around the world who fit this pattern have been found to be at greater risk for depression (Clyman & Pachankis, 2014; Nolen-Hoeksma et al., 1992). For them, an unfortunate event has an internal cause ("It's my fault"), a stable cause ("It will always be this way"), and a global cause ("It's this way in many different situations"). In contrast, when something positive happens to them, people with a pessimistic explanatory style tend to make external, unstable, and specific attributions.

An attributional style that contrasts sharply to the pessimistic style is the **optimistic explanatory style**. Optimists tend to explain negative events in terms of an external

pessimistic explanatory style
A habitual tendency to attribute negative events to internal, stable, and global causes, and positive events to external, unstable, and specific causes

optimistic explanatory style
A habitual tendency to attribute negative events to external, unstable, and specific causes, and positive events to internal, stable, and global causes

cause ("It's someone else's fault"), an unstable cause ("It won't happen again"), and a specific cause ("It's just in this one area"). On the other hand, when faced with positive events, optimists explain them by making internal, stable, and global attributions (Forgeard & Seligman, 2012; Seligman, 1991). Do you think you tend to have an optimistic or a pessimistic explanatory style regarding good and bad events? Spend a few minutes answering the questions in *Self/Social Connection Exercise 4.2.*

Self/Social Connection Exercise 4.2

Do You Have a Pessimistic or an Optimistic Explanatory Style?

To gain insight into how you tend to explain life events, imagine yourself in the two situations described below. Recognizing that events often have many causes, if these situations happened to you, what do you think would be the primary cause of each? Answer questions *a* to *c* about each situation by circling a number from 1 to 5 for each question.

Situation 1

While eating at a restaurant, your dinner companion appears bored.

a. Is this outcome caused by you, by the other person, or by the circumstances?
    Completely caused by other people or circumstances   1 2 3 4 5   *Completely caused by me*

b. Will this cause be present in the future?
    Will never be present again   1 2 3 4 5   *Will always be present*

c. Is this cause unique to this situation, or does it also affect other areas of your life?
    Affects just this situation   1 2 3 4 5   *Affects all situations in my life*

Situation 2

You receive an award for a university or community project.

a. Is this outcome caused by you, by the other people, or by the circumstances?
    Completely caused by other people or circumstances   1 2 3 4 5   *Completely caused by me*

b. Will this cause be present in the future?
    Will never be present again   1 2 3 4 5   *Will always be present*

c. Is this cause unique to this situation, or does it also affect other areas of your life?
    Affects just this situation   1 2 3 4 5   *Affects all situations in my life*

Scoring

For the negative outcome (Situation 1), high scores (4, 5) on questions a to c describe an internal, stable, and global attribution (pessimistic explanatory style). Low scores (1, 2) on these same questions describe an external, unstable, and specific attribution (optimistic explanatory style). For the positive outcome (Situation 2), high scores on questions a to c again describe an internal, stable, and global attribution, but now this indicates an optimistic explanatory style. Low scores indicate a pessimistic explanatory style.

Adapted from "The Attributional Style Questionnaire (ASQ)," by C. Peterson et al., 1982, *Cognitive Therapy and Research, 6*(3), pp. 287–299.

(continues)

(**Applications**, *continued*)

Christopher Peterson and Martin Seligman conducted a series of studies to better understand the relationship between explanatory style and illness. In one of their first studies, the researchers measured college students' attributional style and asked them to list all illnesses they had experienced during the previous month (Peterson & Seligman, 1987). Students also completed this illness measure one year after the initial testing. Results indicated that even after controlling for the number of illnesses reported at the first session, students with an optimistic explanatory style reported fewer illnesses and fewer visits to a physician for diagnosis or treatment of an illness than did those with a pessimistic style.

"The optimist sees the rose and not its thorns; the pessimist stares at the thorns, oblivious to the rose."

—Kahlil Gibran, Lebanese-American poet, 1883–1931

In an archival investigation, the researchers used the responses that 99 male college graduates gave in 1946 to an open-ended questionnaire about their wartime experiences to classify them in terms of their degree of pessimistic explanatory style (Peterson et al., 1988). Although style did not predict health in young adulthood—when nearly all the men were healthy—there was a link between explanatory style and illness by age 45, when health became more variable. After this age, the men who had a pessimistic explanatory style in their youth tended to have more health problems than those who had a more optimistic outlook.

In a second archival study, Peterson and Seligman (1987) investigated the deceased members of the Baseball Hall of Fame who had played between 1900 and 1950. First, they searched the sports pages of old newspapers for the explanations these players gave of their successful and unsuccessful performances. Next, they had independent judges rate these quotes for internality, stability, and globality. Finally, they recorded the age at which each baseball player had died. Results indicated that players who made internal, stable, and global explanations for bad events died at a younger age; those who explained positive events as being due to external, unstable, and specific factors also died at a younger age.

Regarding deaths by disease, additional research indicates that optimists may have better immune systems than pessimists, making them less susceptible to diseases. For example, one study found that optimists have higher numbers of helper T-cells that mediate immune reactions to infection than pessimists (Segerstrom et al., 1998). Combined with the previous results from the college sample and the first archival study, these findings suggest that pessimists may be more stress-prone than optimists (Bennett & Elliott, 2005). A central feature in this susceptibility to stress appears to be the beliefs that people develop about why both positive and negative events occur in their lives.

Does an optimistic explanatory style increase the lifespan of people over that of a pessimistic explanatory style? Archival research of the deceased members of the Baseball Hall of Fame by Peterson and Seligman (1987) suggest this may be the case.

Fortunately, people with a pessimistic explanatory style can be taught to change their self-attributions through cognitive therapy (Meevissen et al., 2011). Typically, this therapy involves keeping a diary of daily successes and failures, and identifying how you contributed to your successes and how external factors caused your failures. Essentially, it trains people to do what most of us do naturally: engage in the self-serving bias (see Chapter 1, section 1.2a) and imagine better possible selves. In one such intervention program among children in mainland China, David Yu and Martin Seligman (2002) found that children with a pessimistic explanatory style who were placed in an "optimistic child" intervention program showed significantly fewer depressive symptoms 6 months later compared with children in the control group. Because people in collectivist cultures are less likely to engage in the self-serving bias than are individualists, it is possible that these "optimistic" intervention programs might be particularly effective in such cultures. However, it is also possible that intervention programs to increase optimistic explanatory style may be short-lived in cultures where the overall approach to the self does not encourage the sort of self-esteem enhancement associated with self-optimism. The lesson to be learned from this research on explanatory style is one of the basic truths of social psychology: Those around you will shape your interpretation of events, and your subsequent social thinking will profoundly influence your emotions and actions.

THE BIG PICTURE

Whether it is in first impressions, attributions, or how we generally try to make sense of our social world, problems can arise at many points in the social judgment process. Adding to this complexity is the fact that sometimes our judgments are under the control of automatically activated evaluations that occur without our awareness. Because of these and other considerations, rational models are often inadequate in reliably describing the social-judgment process. Sometimes judgments must be made very quickly and do not allow for careful observation and logical analysis. At other times, information in our social world is so unreliable, biased, and incomplete that a rational analysis is not possible. In such situations, we typically rely on heuristics and other mental shortcuts as a means to judge our world.

You may be wondering how we survive in a complex and ever-changing world, given that we are predisposed to make such a wide variety of errors. One thing to keep in mind is that our social world is much more flexible and dynamic than the static and artificial laboratory conditions that often characterize social psychological research (Schliemann et al., 1997). In a laboratory study, once a research participant makes a judgmental error, it becomes a data point—frozen in time. However, in the course of everyday life people are constantly revising their social assessments due to feedback from the environment. As a result of this flexibility, many of the social judgment errors committed in the "real world" are corrected through normal interaction with others (Fiske & Haslam, 1996). For example you may meet someone and, based on that limited encounter, form a certain impression. Another person, upon hearing of that impression, may provide new meaningful information that redefines your initial impression. This evolution of social reality is ongoing and can be extremely forgiving of individual judgmental errors, so that you can arrive at "efficient definitions" of others that can be used in the social world.

A second thing to keep in mind is how social cognitive theorists conceive of us as social thinkers. What motivates us in a given situation often determines whether we make careful and rational decisions or quick and sloppy ones. Unlike computers, we have an investment in our self-beliefs and our beliefs about others (Ames, 2004). This psychological fact makes motivational biases likely in social thinking. Through such biases, we can often justify our self-concepts and our worldviews, making it possible for us to more confidently engage in social interaction and meet daily challenges.

Anthony Greenwald (1980), in an analysis of how the self figures into the social cognition equation, makes this very point. He argues that cognitive biases serve very useful and self-protective functions. Likening the self to a totalitarian government, Greenwald states that both are designed to manage (and distort) information so as to maintain a stable and efficiently functioning system. The distortion of reality is functional for both the self and the dictatorship. If this biasing did not occur, the system—either self or governmental—would likely collapse.

In the final analysis, our social judgments should not be expected to be any more accurate or efficient than our self-judgments. When we are faced with contradictory information, our inclination is to distort or explain away the contradictions. These distortions may well have functional value—allowing us to maintain a set of beliefs and perceptions about the world that have proven useful and efficient in making everyday decisions. Just as there are individual differences in the accuracy of self-assessments, there are variations in people's ability to judge their social surroundings. In the final analysis, perhaps a key factor in increasing accuracy both about the self and about others is *curiosity* (Hartung & Renner, 2011). When analyzing the complex and changing nature of both the self and the surrounding social world, being both eager for new information and willing to learn from others will greatly increase your likelihood of making smart personal and social judgments.

KEY TERMS

WEBSITES

Accessed through https://www.bvtlab.com/sop8

Websites for this chapter focus on social cognition and person perception topics, including social categorization, stereotyping, counterfactual thinking, nonverbal communication, and the history of attribution theory.

Association for Psychological Science

This web page maintained by the Association for Psychological Science contains new social cognition articles in such areas as judgment and decision-making, social categorization, stereotyping, and person memory.

Nonverbal Communication Web Page

Dane Archer's web page will introduce you to the topic of nonverbal communication and give you a chance to try to guess the meaning of some real nonverbal communication.

Facial Analysis Website

Is that smile real or fake?
This website examines research at the Massachusetts Institute of Technology regarding how to detect a real from a fake smile.

Chapter **5**

Attitudes and Persuasion

▮ FOCUS QUESTIONS

1. Can you have an unconscious attitude toward something that is opposite of your conscious attitude?
2. Can you form an attitude toward something without forming any beliefs about it?
3. Does an attitude cause you to behave in a way consistent with that attitude, or does behaving a certain way cause you to form an attitude consistent with that behavior?
4. What impact do emotions and humor have on the ability to persuade others to change their attitudes?

▮ CHAPTER OUTLINE

Applications: Are mass media campaigns effective in changing risky health behaviors?

Preview . . . Advertisers and public health officials have spent much time and money on public health campaigns to promote healthy behaviors (quit smoking, stop texting and driving, etc.) but does research suggest these campaigns are effective at changing behaviors?

The Big Picture

Key Terms

Websites

Introduction

Alcohol is a key ingredient at most college parties. It is also the key contributing factor to an array of anti-social behaviors on college campuses, including fights, vandalism, rape, and drunk-driving accidents (NIAAA, 2019). In a national survey of drinking, 17% of US adults reported binge drinking, defined as having four or more drinks on one occasion for women and more than five drinks for men (Kanny et al., 2018). Binge drinking was highest among young adults, with 25% report binge drinking. Surveys from college campuses indicate even higher levels of binge drinking, with about half of all college students indicating they have at some point consumed five or more drinks during a 2-hour period (Wechsler et al., 2002). Every year more than 1,519 college students die from alcohol-related causes and approximately 696,000 students are assaulted by other students who have been drinking (NIAAA, 2019). In addition, one in four students report negative academic consequences as the result of their drinking.

(Getty Images)

Binge drinking is a serious problem on college campuses. What might influence students' attitudes toward excess alcohol consumption?

Imagine for a minute that you are a college administrator trying to figure out how to deal with the problem of excess alcohol consumption on your campus. Further imagine that within the past year you have had the heartbreaking task of informing a mother and a father that their son had died of alcohol poisoning; you also regularly work with campus security and local law enforcement officials in dealing with incidents involving physical and sexual assault in which alcohol was a contributing factor. Do you think you would try to persuade students to change their own attitudes toward alcohol and excess drinking? If so, would you promote "Just Say No" or "Think Before You Drink" ad campaigns to convince students to drink less? Could social psychological theory and research help you develop an effective program to lower students' health and safety risks involving alcohol? This chapter will address these and other questions by examining the social psychological dynamics of attitude formation and change, and the factors that promote and hinder persuasion.

5.1   The Nature of Attitudes

In 1935, in the *Handbook of Social Psychology*, Gordon Allport declared that attitude was social psychology's most indispensable concept:

> Without guiding attitudes the individual is confused and baffled. Some kind of preparation is essential before he can make a satisfactory observation, pass suitable judgment, or make any but the most primitive reflex type of response. Attitudes determine for each individual what he will see and hear, what he will think and what he will do. To borrow a phrase from William James, they "engender meaning upon the world"; they draw lines about and segregate an otherwise chaotic environment; they are our methods for finding our way about in an ambiguous universe. (Allport, 1935, p. 806)

The principal reason the attitude concept has been so popular in social psychology is that attitudes are thought to influence behavior (Friedkin, 2010). Any concept that is believed to have such power is bound to come under serious scrutiny by those who desire to unlock the mysteries of human functioning. Social psychologists are not alone in recognizing the importance of attitudes as a key to behavioral change. Most people believe that if they can influence people's attitudes, their behavior will follow.

5.1a   Attitudes Are Positive or Negative Evaluations of Objects.

Attitudes were initially conceptualized in terms of three distinct components: cognitive, affective, and behavioral (Breckler, 1984). According to this *tricomponent* view, attitudes are made up of our beliefs about an object, our feelings about the object, and our behavior toward the object. Although this definition is appealing because it so neatly carves up the attitude concept into three distinct categories, research indicates that not all three of these components need be in place for an attitude to exist (Huskinson & Haddock, 2004). For example, you could develop a positive attitude toward a product you see on television without developing any beliefs about it or ever engaging in any behavior relevant to the product. Nowadays, social psychologists use a basic unidimensional, or *single-component*, definition in which *evaluation* is central. Here, **attitude** is simply defined as a positive or negative evaluation of an object (Maio et al., 2013). "Objects" include people, things, events, and issues. When people use such words as *like*, *dislike*, *love*, *hate*, *good*, and *bad*, they are usually describing their attitudes. The movement away from the tricomponent attitude definition does not mean that social psychologists no longer consider beliefs, feelings, and behavior important in explaining attitudes. Instead, as illustrated in Figure 5.1, these three sources of evaluative judgment—beliefs, feelings, and past behavior—are thought of as determining attitudes singly or in combination.

Throughout our lives, we form many attitudes; however, these attitudes vary in their strength and importance. An attitude is strong to the extent that it is *accessible*, or easily comes to mind when you encounter the object being evaluated (Fazio, 2007). Likewise, attitudes that are based on emotions, especially positive emotions, tend to be stronger and more accessible from memory (Rocklage & Fazio, 2018). Some of our attitudes play an important role in developing our self-concept (Zunick et al., 2017). The more extreme and positive your attitude toward something, the more likely it is to define your sense of self. For example, you might have strong attitudes about politics, your hometown sport teams, and brands that you prefer, and these attitudes form a core part of your self-concept. Furthermore, our attitudes are stronger to the extent that they are based on our moral beliefs (Luttrell et al., 2016). Morally based attitudes are more predictive of our intention to engage in behaviors and are less likely to change when presented with opposing information than are attitudes that are not based on moral beliefs.

attitude
A positive or negative evaluation of an object

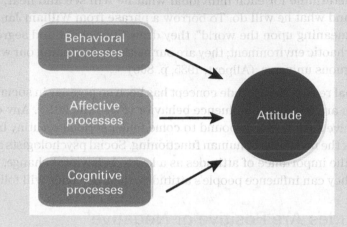

FIGURE 5.1   Three Different Types of Attitude Antecedents

The assumption that attitudes are formed through affective or emotional experiences is reflected in classical conditioning principles and the mere exposure hypothesis. The idea that evaluations are based on behavioral responses is reflected in operant conditioning principles, self-perception theory, and the facial feedback effect. Finally, the claim that attitudes derive from cognitive learning is seen in a host of theories, including the theory of planned behavior and cognitive dissonance theory.

As attitude holders, we are automatic evaluators (Ferguson, 2007; Hering et al., 2013). Brain-imaging studies suggest that when encountering people, things, and events, the *amygdala* in the brain's limbic system engages in an immediate primitive "good–bad" emotional assessment; this may be followed by higher-order processing in the cerebral cortex (Banaji & Heiphetz, 2010). Greater amygdala activity occurs for initial negative assessments than for those that are positive, with much of this evaluative processing being unconscious. The importance of the amygdala in making such "good–bad" assessments is so great that damage to this brain area severely limits the ability to acquire classically conditioned preferences (see section 5.2b). Once the amygdala makes this automatic evaluation, it is the job of the cerebral cortex to analyze and interpret this initial assessment into the subjective experience of various emotions, which often—but not always—leads to consciously held positive or negative attitudes (Stanley et al., 2008).

5.1b Implicit Attitudes May Underlie Explicit Attitudes.

The fact that not all automatic evaluations lead to consciously held attitudes makes implicit cognitive processing even more important because it means that some of our attitudes are unconscious. As discussed in Chapter 4 (see section 4.1), *implicit cognition* involves judgments or decisions that occur automatically without our awareness. An **implicit attitude** is an evaluation that is activated automatically from memory, often without the person's awareness that she or he even possesses it (Di Conza et al., 2010). Liking a certain brand of sneakers because you unconsciously associate them with your favorite sports star is an example of an implicit attitude. Implicit attitudes are simple gut-level evaluations, and whether they will be positive or negative depends on whether the associations activated in memory are pleasant or unpleasant. In contrast, an **explicit attitude** is consciously held, and it is a much more thoughtful and deliberate evaluation. If you consider once again the tricomponent view of attitudes, implicit attitudes are simply produced by the affective component, but explicit attitudes are typically a joint product of affective, cognitive, and behavioral components.

implicit attitude

An attitude that is activated automatically from memory, often without the person's awareness that she or he possesses it

explicit attitude

A consciously held attitude

In Chapter 2 we discussed the most common means of measuring attitudes. Self-reports are used to directly measure explicit attitudes. In contrast, determining a person's implicit attitudes requires less direct methods, with one of the most popular techniques employed by researchers being the Implicit Association Test (IAT), which was described in Chapter 2 (see section 2.2b). Recall that in assessing implicit attitudes, the IAT measures differences in how quickly we have memory associations between target categories (for example, *dog* or *cat*) and evaluative categories (such as *like* or *dislike*). If a person repeatedly responds to one of these pairings (for example, *dog* and *like*) faster than to the other pairing (for example, *dog* and *dislike*), this is interpreted as indicating that the person has a stronger tendency to automatically associate the category dog with positive evaluations.

The idea that you can have two attitudes toward someone or something—one explicit and the other implicit—raises an intriguing question. What happens when a person's explicit and implicit attitudes conflict? For example, you might explicitly report having a negative attitude toward smoking because you learned about its harmful effects, but if you have loved ones who smoke you may implicitly view smoking positively because you associate the habit with those you love. This simultaneous possession of contradictory implicit and explicit attitudes toward the same object is known as **dual attitudes** (Wilson et al., 2000).

Research suggests that people often hold dual attitudes toward issues that are socially sensitive, such as people's attitudes toward pornography, racial and ethnic groups, or their friends' romantic partners (Neumann et al., 2005; Yoo et al., 2010).

5.1c Reference Groups Shape Attitudes.

Think about the social groups to which you belong. When you talk about socially charged topics (for example, politics and religion), how often do you disagree with your friends and family? Do you find yourself largely associating with people who hold similar opinions or do the people in your social groups have opposing opinions that are frequently discussed? If you are like many people, you tend to associate with people who have similar views and you are hesitant to discuss opinions with those with whom you disagree (Frimer et al., 2017). If you do frequently find yourself surrounded by people with differing views, do you find that your own attitudes start to align with this social group?

As inherently social creatures with a strong need to feel included in social groups, one basic social fact is that the groups to which we belong or with which we identify often determine our attitudes. A **reference group** is a group to which people orient themselves, using its standards to judge themselves and the world. An important defining characteristic of a reference group is that people have an *emotional attachment* to it and refer to it for guidance—even if they are not actual members. Reference groups can be large and inclusive, such as an entire nation or religion; but they can also be much smaller, such as one's family or friends.

One of the first and best studies investigating reference group influence on attitudes was the research of Theodore Newcomb in the 1930s, documenting college students' shift in political beliefs during college (Newcomb, 1943). Newcomb wanted to test his hypothesis that people's attitudes are influenced by changes in their reference groups.

dual attitudes
The simultaneous possession of contradictory implicit and explicit attitudes toward the same object

reference group
A group to which people orient themselves, using its standards to judge themselves and the world

(Blulz60 / Shutterstock)

Reference groups, forged during young adulthood, can significantly influence people's attitudes, beliefs, and actions decades later, even when they are no longer immersed within those groups.

To accomplish this task, Newcomb tested the social and political attitudes of the arriving first-year students (who were young women from upper-class conservative families) at Bennington College, and he remeasured their attitudes each year until they graduated.

Newcomb found that, with each passing semester, the students' social and political attitudes became increasingly liberal. Newcomb believed that this attitude change was due to the students' disengagement from their conservative hometown reference group and their integration into a new, more liberal reference group at Bennington. Those students who maintained their conservative political perspective throughout their college years were those who spent their vacations with their parents and frequently traveled home on weekends and therefore did not blend into the Bennington culture.

In two separate follow-up studies of the Bennington College women, Newcomb and his colleagues (1967) demonstrated the importance of reference groups in maintaining attitudes even when the person is no longer immersed within the group. The first follow-up interviews were conducted in the 1960s, 25 years after the original study. These Bennington alumnae were now in their 40s and 50s and were in the top 1% of the population in socioeconomic status. Comparing them with non-Bennington-educated women of comparable wealth, age, religion, and geographic region, Newcomb found that the Bennington women's political attitudes and behavior were much more liberal. In addition, the Bennington women's selection of spouses and friends was partly based on their liberal political preferences. In the 1980s, these Bennington women—now in their 60s and 70s—were contacted again and they still consistently preferred the more liberal candidates in each presidential election (Alwin et al., 1991). In fact, their social and political attitudes were more intensely liberal than most women of their generation (Cohen & Alwin, 1993).

Other studies testing different social groups have replicated Newcomb's overall findings (Marwell et al., 1987; Verkuyten & Yildiz, 2007). For example, college students who enroll in a course covering the psychology of prejudice report lower levels of racism, sexism, and homophobia than students who do not enroll in such courses (Pettijohn & Walzer, 2008). Similarly, African American college students' drinking attitudes are less accepting of binge drinking than the attitudes of white college students—largely due to the differing social norms of their reference groups (Martin et al., 2013).

Together, these findings illustrate the important role that reference groups play in shaping and maintaining social and political attitudes, and in the role that these attitudes play in shaping the life course of those who hold them (Arendt, 2010; Carey et al., 2006). To a substantial degree, your attitudes are shaped by those with whom you affiliate. When you select a college to attend or a group to join, you may also be inadvertently choosing a new social and political perspective. Sometimes, these newly adopted political and social attitudes become the "little surprises" young adults spring upon their parents around the dinner table during semester breaks and summer holidays. If you have had such conversations with your parents, or believe you will in the not-too-distant future, you can now describe the social psychological dynamics of your political transformation as well. Pleasant dining!

Section Summary

- Attitudes are positive or negative evaluations of objects.
- Attitudes are determined by a number of factors, including past behavior, emotions, and cognitions.
- Explicit attitudes are consciously held.

- Implicit attitudes are activated automatically outside of conscious awareness and may conflict with explicit attitudes.

- Reference groups shape and maintain our attitudes, and our life choices.

5.2 How Does Automatic Thinking Shape Attitudes and Behavior?

In this section, we examine theories that explain how attitudes often develop through relatively effortless thinking. Some of these theories are largely feeling or *affect-based* explanations (*mere exposure* and *classical conditioning*), while others involve more behavioral sources (*operant conditioning*).

5.2a Mere Exposure Can Lead to Positive Attitudes.

One day while walking on campus, Steve noticed a young man walking toward him. As he drew closer Steve noticed that his mood had brightened upon seeing the young man. Why was Steve happy to see this perfect stranger? His mind was in overdrive trying to understand this spontaneous positive response. Then Steve realized that he saw this same young man many mornings in the glass booth in the campus parking garage and so he saw him every morning. Steve knew absolutely nothing about this young man, yet he liked him! But why?

Steve's positive attitude is best explained by a theory Robert Zajonc (pronounced like "science") first developed in 1968. Zajonc proposed that simply exposing people repeatedly to a particular object (such as a person in a booth) causes them to develop a more positive attitude toward the object. This phenomenon, which he called the **mere exposure effect**, does not require any action toward the object, nor does it require the development of any beliefs about the object.

Zajonc (1968) conducted several experiments in which increased exposure resulted in greater liking for previously neutral objects. In a classic study, college students were told that they were participating in an experiment on how people learn a foreign language. They were then shown 10 Chinese-like characters for 2 seconds at a time, with instructions to pay close attention as they appeared on the screen. Two of the characters were presented only once, two others twice, two others 5 times, two others 10 times, and a final two were presented 25 times. Besides these 10 characters, Zajonc had two others that the participants did not see at all. Once the exposure trials were completed, participants were told that the characters were Chinese adjectives and they were now going to guess their meaning. The experimenter hastened to add that he realized it would be virtually impossible for them to guess the exact adjective; therefore, they should merely indicate whether each character meant something good or bad in Chinese. Participants then rated the characters—including the two they had not seen—using a 7-point good–bad scale. The results (shown in Figure 5.2) indicated that the more often a character was repeated, the more favorable participants estimated its meaning to be.

Did you know that the widely admired visual symbol of Paris, France—the Eiffel Tower—was initially condemned by many of France's intellectuals and artists when it was completed in 1889 to commemorate the French Revolution's centennial? These critics described it as "useless and monstrous" and a "hateful column of bolted sheet metal." How might mere exposure explain the favorable attitudes most people now hold toward this familiar landmark?

(Shutterstock)

mere exposure effect
The tendency to develop more positive feelings toward objects and individuals the more we are exposed to them

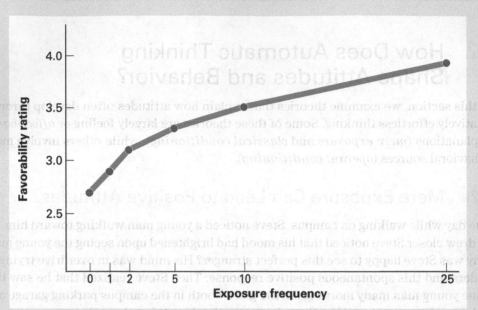

FIGURE 5.2 **Frequency of Exposure and Liking**

Research participants' attitudes toward Chinese-like characters became more positive as the frequency of their exposure to these stimuli increased. Can you think of how the mere exposure effect has influenced your own attitudes?

Source: Data from "Attitudinal Effects of Mere Exposure," by R. B. Zajonc, 1968, *Journal of Personality and Social Psychology Monograph Supplement, 9* (2, part 2), pp. 1–27. Copyright 1968 by the American Psychological Association.

A meta-analysis of 118 studies indicates that the mere exposure effect is robust and that the strongest increase in liking occurs early in the repeated exposures (Montoya et al., 2017). This effect is strongest with children, suggesting one reason why advertising is so effective with younger people. The mere exposure effect is important for our understanding of attitudes in that it illustrates how affect can become associated with an object, independent of any knowledge about that object (Dêchene et al., 2009; Murphy, 2001). These feeling-based attitudes develop outside the realm of rational thoughts and represent a very basic and powerful form of evaluation (Petty et al., 2001). In addition, many attitudes developed by mere exposure are implicit attitudes—that is, they come into existence without the attitude holders' awareness and are automatically activated from memory (Hansen & Wanke, 2009; Kawakami & Yoshida, 2010). The unconscious nature of this process explains Steve's surprise at noticing his positive feelings toward the garage attendant. Before seeing him on campus that day, Steve was unaware that he had formed an implicit positive attitude toward the young man due to the repeated exposures. Research further suggests that even when attitudes formed by mere exposure are consciously held, attitude holders are often still unaware of *why* they hold these attitudes. In Steve's encounter, he had to engage in some effortful thinking before piecing together the "why" underlying his attitude.

Why does repeated exposure lead to positive attitudes? One possibility is that the mere exposure effect has its roots in an evolutionarily adaptive tendency to be attracted to those things that are familiar because they are unlikely to pose a danger to our safety and health. That is, we may have evolved to view unfamiliar objects or situations with caution, hesitation, and even fear (Bornstein, 1989). Such caution in the presence of the unfamiliar enhances our biological fitness because we are better prepared for danger. Only through repeated exposure to that which is unfamiliar does our caution and hesitation subside—the unfamiliar and potentially dangerous become familiar and safe, thus our positive feelings increase. The downside of the mere exposure effect is that it predisposes us to be wary of the unfamiliar, which may explain why people often have an automatic, cautious—and even fearful—response when meeting someone different from them, which can then trigger prejudice and discrimination (see Chapter 6, section 6.2a).

5.2b Attitudes Can Form Through Classical Conditioning.

Now let's consider another life situation. Andrew and Coretta are two young siblings who have developed extremely negative attitudes toward Muslims and Jews despite having no direct contact with anybody from these religions. How did they develop these hostile attitudes? Their hatred may have developed from listening to their parents and other adults use negatively evaluated words such as *greedy, dangerous, dishonest,* and *dirty* in referring to Muslims and Jews. Through such **classical conditioning**, a previously neutral attitude object (the conditioned stimulus) can come to evoke an attitude response (the conditioned response) simply by being paired with some other object (the unconditioned stimulus) that naturally evokes the attitude response (the unconditioned response).

Arthur and Carolyn Staats were two of the first researchers to investigate the classical conditioning of attitudes. In one experiment (Staats & Staats, 1958), they asked participants to remember words paired with various nationality names, such as "German–table," "French–with," "Dutch–gift," and "Swedish–failure." For one group of participants, the target nationality "Dutch" was always followed by a word with a positive meaning, and the target nationality "Swedish" was always paired with negative words. This evaluative pairing was reversed for a second group of participants: "Dutch" was paired with negative words, and "Swedish" was followed by positive words. At the end of the experiment, participants rated how they actually felt about the various nationality groups using a 7-point pleasant–unpleasant scale. As Figure 5.3 shows, the group that heard favorable word pairings with "Dutch" and negative pairings with "Swedish" had more positive attitudes toward the Dutch and less positive attitudes toward the Swedes. These ratings were reversed for the group that had opposite word pairings. Although the attitude shifts were not extreme (participants did not leave the lab hating one nationality and loving the other), the fact that these mild emotional stimuli produced significant attitude shifts caused attitude researchers to sit up and take notice. Classical conditioning could play a role in establishing some of the emotional components of attitudes and prejudice (Conger et al., 2012).

Having reviewed research on the conditioning of attitudes, let's return to our children, Andrew and Coretta. How might they have acquired negative attitudes toward Muslims and Jews by simply hearing their parents use a number of negative adjectives (dirty, dishonest, dangerous, greedy) in referring to these groups? As we have seen, the novel religious labels (like Muslims or Jews) were initially neutral stimuli to the children because they had not previously been associated with either positive or negative adjectives. However, once the negative adjectives were introduced, repeated pairings of the religious labels with these negative adjectives caused Andrew and Coretta to acquire negative attitudes toward these people. They may never have met a Muslim or a Jew, but this attitude conditioning played a significant role in their aversion and hostility nonetheless.

classical conditioning
Learning through association, when a neutral stimulus (conditioned stimulus) is paired with a stimulus (unconditioned stimulus) that naturally produces an emotional response

FIGURE 5.3   Classical Conditioning of Attitudes Toward Different Nationalities

Research by Staats and Staats (1958) demonstrated that classical conditioning could play a role in establishing some of the emotional components of attitudes and prejudice. Participants who heard favorable word pairings with "Dutch" and negative pairings with "Swedish" subsequently had more positive attitudes toward the Dutch and less positive attitudes toward the Swedes. Those individuals who had opposite word pairings had more favorable attitudes toward the Swedes. Can you think of instances in your own life in which certain attitudes toward other social groups have been similarly classically conditioned?

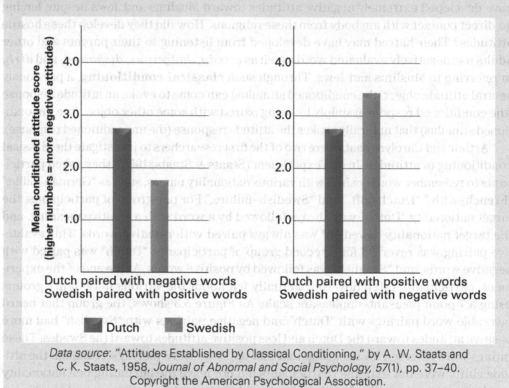

Data source: "Attitudes Established by Classical Conditioning," by A. W. Staats and C. K. Staats, 1958, *Journal of Abnormal and Social Psychology, 57*(1), pp. 37–40. Copyright the American Psychological Association.

Additional studies indicate that classical conditioning of attitudes can occur below the level of conscious awareness, a process known as **subliminal conditioning**. In one such study, Jon Krosnick and his coworkers (1992) showed college students slide photos of a stranger going about her daily activities. These slides were preceded by very brief (13/1,000 of a second) subliminal presentations of photos known to induce either positive emotions (for example, a bridal couple, people laughing, kittens) or negative emotions (for example, a skull, a werewolf, open-heart surgery). These pleasant and unpleasant photos were presented so quickly that the students did not consciously perceive them. However, despite not consciously perceiving these photos, they did affect the students' later attitudes toward the stranger. Those exposed to the positive photos reported more positive attitudes toward this unknown person than did those exposed to the negative photos. These findings and other studies suggest that attitudes can be formed through subliminal conditioning (Veltkamp et al., 2011).

subliminal conditioning

Classical conditioning that occurs in the absence of conscious awareness of the stimuli involved

5.2c Reinforcement and Punishment Can Shape Attitudes.

Because classical conditioning and mere exposure influence emotions, they contribute most directly to shaping the affective component of attitudes (Petty et al., 2001). Yet one of the most powerful ways in which the *behavioral* component can shape attitudes is through **operant conditioning**, a form of learning extensively studied by such behavioral psychologists as Edward Thorndike (1911) and B. F. Skinner (1938). According to operant conditioning principles, when an action toward an object is rewarded or reinforced, it will probably be repeated in the future. On the other hand, if behavior is not rewarded or is punished, similar future actions are less likely. Learning theorists who study attitudes contend that accompanying this increase or decrease of behavior will be an attitude consistent with the behavior. For example, if a child's parents and teachers praise her for doing well in math, she may redouble her efforts and develop a positive attitude toward mathematics in general. However, if her academic accomplishments go unrewarded, her interest in math may diminish and eventually extinguish. She might even develop a negative attitude toward the subject matter.

Although attitudes can develop by being directly rewarded and punished when interacting with the attitude object, they can also develop through the indirect means of *observational learning* (Bandura, 1986). In such instances, attitudes are shaped after observing other people being reinforced or punished when interacting with the attitude object (Chen et al., 2011). Thus you might develop a dislike for rock climbing after a friend is injured during her first attempt to learn this sport. Although your friend's newly formed dislike for rock climbing is due to operant conditioning, your negative attitude is a result of observational learning. In forming attitudes through observational learning, the people whom we observe and imitate are called *role models*, because they teach us how to play social roles. People in our reference groups (see section 5.1c) are often role models for us. Observing these role models helps us as children learn how to behave in our families and in the larger culture, and it also helps us as adults learn the attitudes and skills necessary for career success (Buunk & van der Laan, 2002; Rogoff et al., 2003).

Observational learning can also foster positive attitudes toward unhealthy behaviors, such as binge drinking and smoking. In a recent longitudinal study of the drinking habits of parents and their young adult children, researchers found that after controlling for peer influences and the personalities of both parents and children, parental binge drinking significantly predicted young adult children's binge drinking at age 28—strongly suggesting a pattern of alcohol role modeling (Pedersen & von Soest, 2013). Regarding smoking, survey studies indicate that adolescents who had never smoked were much more likely to later take up the habit if they had watched many Hollywood movies packed with smoking scenes (Dalton et al., 2003). Experimental studies find that as exposure to such movies increases, attitudes toward smoking and smokers become more favorable (Gibson & Maurer, 2000). Teens who identify with movie stars who smoke on screen are those most likely to start smoking (Tickle et al., 2006). Cognitively, what appears to be happening is that observing actors smoking creates implicit associations in memory of smoking with desirability. In turn, these implicit associations later influence personal smoking attitudes and intentions (Dal Cin et al., 2007).

5.2d Nonverbal Behavior Can Shape Attitudes.

Would it surprise you to learn that facing the sun on a bright clear day can trigger aggressive feelings in you? The involuntary frowning that occurs when facing the sun involves the same pattern of facial muscle activation as the expression of anger (Marzoli et al., 2013). This finding is just one example of how attitude researchers have discovered

operant conditioning
A type of learning in which behavior is strengthened if followed by reinforcement and weakened if followed by punishment

that our emotions—and thus our attitudes—can be manipulated by changing our facial expressions, body posture, or other motor responses.

In an innovative experiment, German psychologist Fritz Strack and his colleagues (1988) asked college students to hold a pen in their mouths while they were shown a series of amusing cartoons. Participants in the *lips condition* were instructed to hold the pen tightly with their lips, while those in the *teeth condition* were told to hold the pen with their front teeth (see photographs below). In a control condition, participants were told to hold the pen in their nondominant hand. After reading the cartoons, all students rated how funny the cartoons were, using a 10-point scale. Results indicated that participants who held the pen between their teeth found the cartoons to be the most amusing, followed by those who held it in their hand. Students who held the pen in their lips gave the cartoons the lowest ratings of amusement. Why do you think this was the case?

You can tell by looking at the photographs that holding a pen with the teeth causes a person to smile, while holding it with the lips prevents smiling. Could the participants have inferred their attitudes toward the cartoons based on their facial muscle movements? This possibility is referred to as the **facial feedback effect**, or the tendency of facial expressions to trigger corresponding emotions (Dimberg & Söderkvist, 2011; Lanzetta et al., 1976).

Recent research has debated whether this classic facial feedback finding is replicable. A replication by 17 research labs (Wagenmakers et al., 2016) failed to reproduce the same findings as the original study. However, Strack (2016) noted an important difference between the replication study and original study. Specifically, in the replication study the researchers used a video camera to record participants. This addition of the video camera, although done to allow for an objective recording of the participants, may have unintentionally induced self-awareness in the participants. Self-awareness can influence how people respond to their environment. So, in a third test of the facial feedback effect, Tom Noah and his colleagues (2018) directly tested if the camera influenced the results. When there was no camera, they replicated the original facial feedback effect. People found the comic more amusing if they were holding the pencil between their teeth rather than in their lips. However, the effect did not occur when a video camera was present. This suggests that the camera induced self-awareness, which eliminated the effect of facial feedback on humor ratings. This trajectory of the research on the facial feedback

facial feedback effect
The tendency of facial expressions to trigger corresponding emotions

(Franzoi)

The facial feedback effect is the tendency of changes in facial expression to trigger corresponding changes in emotion. Given this effect, what contrasting emotions might be elicited by holding a pen between one's teeth versus between one's lips?

effect highlights that research replications, even when initially thought of as failures, can help to build the theory and further our understanding of the phenomena of interest.

Besides facial expressions, other expressive behaviors also influence feelings. For instance, have you ever watched passersby and guessed their emotional states based on their body postures? Numerous studies find that in both human and nonhuman primates, expansive open postures reflect high power, while contractive closed postures reflect low power (Darwin, 1872; Park et al., 2013). Not only do these postures reflect power or the lack of power, they also produce feelings of power or powerlessness. For example, Sabine Stepper and Fritz Strack (1993) had participants take a test and then learn about their results while either sitting upright at a normal-height table or sitting slumped over at a short-legged table. Those who sat upright felt prouder after succeeding than those who were slumped over. Another study found that when people were instructed to sit upright and push out their chests, they felt more confident with the ideas they wrote than when they were told to sit in a manner that caused them to be hunched over with their eyes downcast (Briñol et al., 2009). Other research has found that when people nod their head up and down while listening to a taped editorial they later expressed more positive attitudes toward it than those who were instructed to shake their head from side to side (Wells & Petty, 1980).

> "Without doubt, it is a delightful harmony when doing and saying go together."
>
> —Michel de Montaigne, French philosopher, 1533–1592

Because participants in all these studies did not perceive a connection between their motor responses and their attitudes, this suggests that these findings cannot be explained by self-perception. Instead, what may best explain these effects is classical conditioning, where movements such as an upright posture and head nodding have become associated with and facilitate the generation of favorable thoughts; the reverse is true for a slumped posture and head shaking (Förster & Strack, 1996). One takeaway message from this research is that performing actions associated with happiness causes us not only to feel happier but also to perceive other objects in our environment more favorably. Similarly, performing actions associated with sadness causes us to feel sadder and to perceive our world less favorably. So smile and be happy!

Is there any wisdom in parents admonishing their children to straighten their posture and avoid slouching? How might the manner in which parents try to correct slouching destroy these possible benefits?

Section Summary

- Some attitudes form through simple emotional mechanisms.

- In the mere exposure effect, we develop more positive feelings toward objects the more frequently we are exposed to them.

- In classical conditioning, an attitude forms when a previously neutral attitude object (the conditioned stimulus) evokes an attitude response (the conditioned response) by being paired with some other object (the unconditioned stimulus) that naturally evokes the attitude response (the unconditioned response).

- Some attitudes form through performing behaviors.

- In operant conditioning and observational learning, we develop attitudes consistent with reinforced and punished behavior.

- Attitudes can be influenced by our facial expressions, body posture, or other motor responses.

5.3   How Does Deliberate Thinking Shape Attitudes and Behavior?

Although attitudes sometimes develop automatically and with little cognitive effort, they can also be created and maintained through a conscious and deliberate thinking process. One of the most influential approaches in social psychology—especially in the study of explicit attitudes—has been the notion that people are motivated to keep their own explicit cognitions (beliefs, attitudes, self-perceptions) organized in a consistent and tension-free manner. This principle of **cognitive consistency** was first introduced to social psychology by Fritz Heider (1946) and has its roots in 19th-century existentialist writings (Proulx, 2013) and the early 20th-century Gestalt belief that human beings not only expect and prefer their perceptions to be coherent and harmonious but are also motivated to make them so (Koffka, 1935; Köhler, 1929). How might this desire for consistency influence both people's attitudes and their behavior?

5.3a   Self-Justification Can Shape Attitudes.

Over 50 years ago, Leon Festinger (1957) developed the most influential consistency theory of attitudes. His *cognitive dissonance theory* proposed that although we may appear logical in our thinking and behavior, we often engage in seemingly irrational behavior to maintain cognitive consistency. It also describes and predicts how we spend much of our time *rationalizing* our behavior rather than actually engaging in rational action.

Insufficient Justification and Dissonance

Imagine that you volunteer to participate in an experiment and, upon arriving at the lab, are asked to perform two 30-minute tasks. The first task consists of emptying and refilling a tray with spools, and the second consists of repeatedly turning 48 wooden pegs on a board. As you work on these tasks, you silently curse their monotony. Finally, when your hour of boredom ends, the experimenter tells you that the real purpose of the study was to determine if a person's performance is influenced by whether he is told beforehand that it will be "very enjoyable" and "fun" or is told nothing.

Then he tells you that his assistant has not shown up and will not be able to help him with the next participant who will be in the "favorable information condition." The experimenter then asks if you would tell the participant that you had just completed the task (a true statement) and that you found it to be extremely enjoyable (a lie). He offers you some form of reimbursement if you agree. You agree to become the assistant and tell your lie to the waiting participant. When the participant completes the tasks and departs, the experimenter sends you to an office where an interviewer asks you how fun and interesting you actually found the tasks to be. Do you think your attitude toward these tasks would be influenced by whether the experimenter had promised you $1 versus $20 to tell your lie? If yes, which sum of money would lead to the greatest attitude shift?

This is the scenario of a classic cognitive dissonance experiment conducted by Festinger and J. Merrill Carlsmith (1959). As depicted in Figure 5.4, participants who told others (who were actually confederates) that the task was "very enjoyable" and "fun" for a reward of $1 came to believe that it was enjoyable to a far greater degree than did those who said so for $20. These $1 liars also expressed greater enthusiasm for the task than a control group that was not asked to lie. Do these findings surprise you? They certainly surprised a lot of attitude researchers, because they contradicted reinforcement theories, which had predicted that participants who were paid more to lie would exhibit greater attitude change than those who were paid less. Although these findings

cognitive consistency

The tendency to seek consistency in one's cognitions

seemed surprising to many, they are consistent with cognitive dissonance theory. The theory states that if you simultaneously hold two cognitions that are inconsistent ("This was a boring task" and "I told someone it was very enjoyable"), you will experience a feeling of discomfort known as **cognitive dissonance**. Festinger believed that people are naturally motivated to reduce or eliminate the dissonance. How is this cognitive dissonance eliminated or reduced? Table 5.1 lists some ways to reduce dissonance.

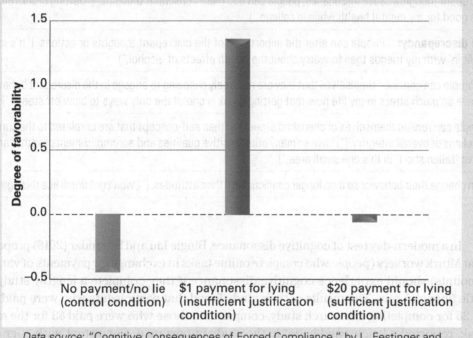

FIGURE 5.4   Insufficient Justification Induces Dissonance and Motivates Attitude Change

Festinger and Carlsmith (1959) predicted that participants who were given insufficient monetary justification for lying (the $1 liars) would experience greater cognitive dissonance and would, therefore, express more liking for the dull task than those who received sufficient monetary justification (the $20 liars). Why would insufficient justification create greater dissonance?

Data source: "Cognitive Consequences of Forced Compliance," by L. Festinger and J. M. Carlsmith, 1959, *Journal of Abnormal and Social Psychology, 58*(2), pp. 203–211.

In the Festinger and Carlsmith study, only two dissonance-reducing outlets were available to the liars: (1) they could add a third cognition to make their attitude–behavior inconsistency less inconsistent, or (2) they could change their attitude about the task. The reason the "$1 participants" showed more attitude change toward the boring task than the "$20 participants" was that the former experienced a greater *amount* of cognitive dissonance. Festinger and Carlsmith reasoned that the $20 participants would not need to change their attitudes because they could justify their actions. They could reduce their dissonance by adding a third cognition that makes the original cognition less inconsistent: Their high payment was *sufficient justification* for their counterattitudinal behavior. The $20 participants had a reasonable justification for lying. The same could not be said for the $1 participants. They were given only $1 for their lie. This amount of payment provided *insufficient justification*

"Inconsistencies of opinion, arising from changes of circumstances, are often justifiable."

—Daniel Webster, American statesman, 1782–1852

cognitive dissonance

A feeling of discomfort caused by performing an action that is inconsistent with one's attitudes for their counterattitudinal behavior. According to Festinger, when people engage in a counterattitudinal behavior without receiving a sufficient reward, they will experience cognitive dissonance. Faced with this dissonance, the $1 group strove to reduce the negative drive state. They could not deny that they lied, so instead they changed their attitude about the task: It was not so boring after all.

TABLE 5.1 Ways to Reduce Cognitive Dissonance
There are a number of ways to reduce dissonance. For example, consider college students who have decided to quit consuming alcohol in excessive amounts but then resume binge drinking. How might they reduce the dissonance aroused by the discrepancy between their attitude ("I don't like binge drinking") and their behavior ("I'm drinking excessively again")?
Common Strategies
Changing attitudes: People can simply change their attitudes to make them consistent with discrepant attitudes or prior behaviors. ("I don't really need to quit. I like getting drunk with my friends.")
Adding cognitions: If two discrepant thoughts cause dissonance, people can add more consonant thoughts. ("Getting drunk relaxes me and makes me happy, which is good for my mental health while in college.")
Altering the importance of the discrepancy: People can alter the importance of the discrepant thoughts or actions. ("It's more important to stay relaxed and to 'fit in' with my friends than to worry about the health effects of alcohol.")
Reducing perceived choice: People can convince themselves that they are not freely choosing to engage in the discrepant behavior. ("I have no choice but to drink. I have so much stress in my life now that getting drunk is one of the only ways to blow off steam.")
Making self-affirmations: People can remind themselves of cherished aspects of their self-concept that are unrelated to the current dissonance, thus restoring their feelings of overall integrity. ("I have so many other positive qualities and accomplishments in other areas of my life, so it's all right that I have 'fallen short' in this one small area.")
Changing behavior: People can change their behavior so it no longer conflicts with their attitudes. ("I won't get drunk like this again.")

In a modern-day test of cognitive dissonance, Bingie Liu and S. Sundar (2018) proposed that Mturk workers (people who complete online tasks in exchange for payments of varying amounts) should experience cognitive dissonance if they complete a lengthy study for little financial gain. The results of their study found that participants who were paid just $0.25 for completing a research study, compared to those who were paid $3 for the same task, reported a heightened belief in the study importance. Consistent with cognitive dissonance, when paid an insufficient amount of money to justify their effort, the study participants justified their effort by inflating their perceived value of the research study. This notion of insufficient justification is so important in understanding how cognitive dissonance operates that it bears reviewing. As Festinger stated, if the reasons for engaging in counterattitudinal behavior are strong (for example, "I was paid $20 to lie"), little or no dissonance will be generated. However, if these reasons are weak ("I was paid only $1 to lie"), then people are confronted with the dissonance-producing thought that they had no strong or clear basis for acting inconsistently with their attitudes. In other words, cognitive dissonance theory demonstrates that the weaker the reasons for acting inconsistently with one's attitudes, the *greater* the pressures to change the attitudes in question.

Freedom of Choice and Dissonance

Another factor that can create cognitive dissonance is freely choosing to engage in a counterattitudinal behavior. For example, let's suppose young Jack tells his grade-school friends that he hates girls, but later they see him sitting next to Betty Lou on the bus. If the bus driver forced Jack to sit next to Betty Lou, he can legitimately explain his close proximity to her as being beyond his control. According to dissonance theory, due to Jack's lack of choice, he is unlikely to feel responsible for his actions; therefore, he will not experience cognitive dissonance. However, if no one forced Jack to sit next to Betty Lou, then his behavior would be seen as freely chosen; therefore, he should experience discomfort due to his dissonant thoughts ("I hate girls, but I sat next to a girl").

Darwyn Linder and his colleagues (1967) conducted an experiment that demonstrated the role that choice plays in dissonance arousal. College students were asked to write essays in favor of a law barring controversial individuals from speaking on campus. This law was actually being discussed in the state legislature, and almost all students opposed its passage. Students were offered either $0.50 or $2.50 for their essays. In the "free-choice" condition, the experimenter stressed the students' freedom to refuse to write the essay, while in the "no-choice" condition, no mention was made about the students' right to refuse. Instead, the experimenter acted as if by volunteering to participate in the study, the students had committed themselves to its requirements.

As predicted by cognitive dissonance theory, when students' free choice was stressed, the group that was paid $0.50 changed their attitude toward the law so that it was more in-line with the essay content, but the attitudes of the group paid $2.50 did not shift. In the "no-choice" condition, the exact opposite effects occurred: The larger amount of money produced greater attitude change (see Figure 5.5). The attitude change in the "no-choice" condition does not conform to dissonance theory but instead follows the principles of operant conditioning (in which external incentives shape attitudes). Thus, to experience dissonance, people must feel that they *freely chose* to behave in a counterattitudinal manner.

FIGURE 5.5   Perceived Choice, Incentive, and Attitude Change

Linder and his colleagues (1967) manipulated participants' freedom of choice and incentive. Consistent with cognitive dissonance theory, in the "free-choice" condition, low-incentive students expressed greater attitude change than high-incentive students; the exact opposite effect occurred in the "no-choice" condition. What do these results tell you about the role that perceived freedom of choice plays in attitude change?

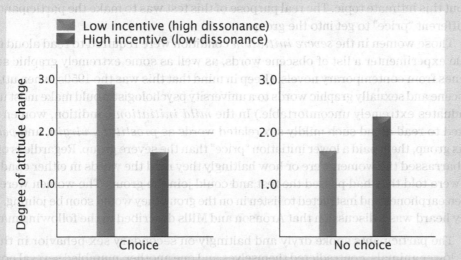

Data source: "Decision Freedom as a Determinant of the Role of Incentive Magnitude in Attitude Change," by D. E. Linder et al., 1967, *Journal of Personality and Social Psychology, 6*(3), pp. 245–254, Copyright 1967 by the American Psychological Association.

Justification of Effort and Dissonance

Although we have seen that using negative incentives—in the form of mild threats—can induce cognitive dissonance, which in turn results in less liking for the attitude object, negative incentives can also lead to *increased liking*. Recall the discussion in Chapter 2 of Leon Festinger's study of doomsday cult members (Festinger et al., 1956). Here, people had given up their worldly possessions and had left loved ones to await the arrival of space aliens. As the evidence mounted that their leader's prophecy was false, many of the cult members increased their psychological commitment to the cult. Were they insane? Not according to cognitive dissonance theory.

After suffering through another losing season and spending considerable money on game tickets and team jerseys, how might cognitive dissonance theory explain many sports fans' steadfast loyalty to their team?

(Olga Bogatyrenko / Shutterstock)

What about romantic decisions? Have you ever tried to convince yourself that a long-standing romantic relationship was "good for you" or worthwhile simply because you had invested a good deal of time and effort into it? Dissonance theorists argue that when people have a bad experience with some group or relationship they have freely chosen to participate in, there is a natural tendency for them to try to transform the bad experience into a good one to reduce cognitive dissonance. In addition, the greater the sacrifice or hardship associated with the choice, the greater the level of dissonance people experience (Cooper et al., 2005).

To better understand the actions of those who incur large costs in questionable ventures, let's look at a classic experiment carried out by Elliot Aronson and Judson Mills (1959) on the effects of the *severity of initiation* on liking for a group. Participants were college women who volunteered to take part in discussions of the psychology of sex. It was their false understanding that these discussions would be analyzed to better understand group dynamics. Prior to being admitted into the discussion group, each woman (except those in the control condition) was told that she would have to take an "Embarrassment Test" to assure the researchers that she could talk frankly and freely about this intimate topic. The real purpose of this test was to make the participants pay a different "price" to get into the group.

Those women in the *severe initiation* condition were required to read aloud to the male experimenter a list of obscene words, as well as some extremely graphic sexual scenes from contemporary novels. (Keep in mind that this was the 1950s, when uttering obscene and sexually graphic words to a university psychologist would make most undergraduates extremely uncomfortable.) In the *mild initiation* condition, women were asked to read aloud such mildly sex-related words as *prostitute, virgin,* and *petting.* This group, then, paid a lower initiation "price" than the severe group. Regardless of how embarrassed the women were or how haltingly they read the words in either condition, all were told they had passed the test and could join the group. The women were then given earphones and instructed to listen in on the group they would soon be joining. What they heard was a discussion that Aronson and Mills described in the following manner:

> The participants spoke dryly and haltingly on secondary sex behavior in the lower animals, contradicted themselves and one another, mumbled several non sequiturs, started sentences that they never finished, hemmed, hawed, and in general conducted one of the most worthless and uninteresting discussions imaginable. (Aronson & Mills, 1959, p. 179)

After listening to this discussion, the women were asked to rate both the discussion and the group members on such evaluative scales as "dull–interesting" and "intelligent–unintelligent." According to dissonance theory, the women in the severe initiation group should have experienced a pair of dissonant thoughts: "I willingly went through a very embarrassing initiation in order to join this sex discussion group"; "These group discussions are dull and worthless." To reduce cognitive dissonance, these women had to alter one of these thoughts. Because they could not deny that they willingly paid a high price to join the group, the only thought they could reasonably alter was their group evaluation. In contrast, the women in the "mild" and "no initiation" groups had invested little—if anything—to join, and thus should not have experienced much dissonance. Consistent with this reasoning, the severe initiation group gave significantly more positive evaluations of the discussion than those who were in either the mild initiation or the control groups (see Figure 5.6).

"That which costs little is less valued."

—Miguel de Cervantes, Spanish writer, 1547–1616

FIGURE 5.6 Cognitive Dissonance and the Effects of Initiations

Participants' attitudes toward the quality of the discussion in the Aronson and Mills (1959) experiment were significantly influenced by the "price" they had to pay to join the group. Based on cognitive dissonance theory, why did those women in the severe initiation condition express greater liking for the quality of the discussion?

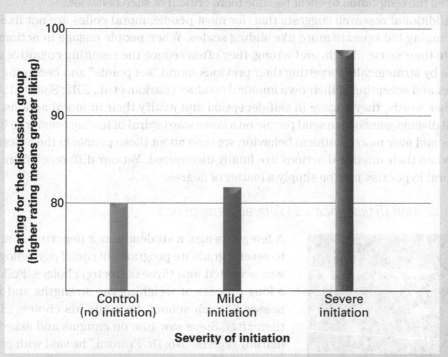

Data source: "The Effect of Severity of Initiation on Liking for a Group," by E. Aronson and J. Mills, 1959, *The Journal of Abnormal and Social Psychology*, 59(2), pp. 177–181.

Replications of this experiment have demonstrated that the effect is strong: The more you pay for something, the more you like it (Axsom, 1989; Gerard & Mathewson, 1966). Is it any wonder that many of the members of Festinger's doomsday cult increased their allegiance when those outside the group were calling it a fraud and a sham? Agreeing with this judgment would have called into question all that they had suffered. Faced with such a choice, they justified to themselves not only the actions of their group but their own actions as well.

"Those who have free seats at a play hiss first."

—Chinese proverb

Immoral Behavior and Dissonance

One area of life where cognitive dissonance often plays a decisive role is in moral reasoning. People care about being moral and behaving ethically (Aquino & Reed, 2002). Despite our motivation to act morally, everyday experience informs us that we are sometimes capable of behaving counter to our own values and moral standards if to do so benefits us in some way. For example, have you ever cheated on a test despite believing that cheating is wrong? Have you ever stolen something despite believing that stealing is wrong? Have you ever lied to a friend despite believing that lying is wrong? If you have engaged in such counterattitudinal actions—which is highly likely—did you revise your self-concept accordingly and think of yourself as a cheater, a thief, and a liar? Probably not. Most likely, you justified your questionable actions in some way. *Moral hypocrisy* is the motivation to appear moral while avoiding the cost of being moral.

In a study examining how students' attitudes toward cheating are affected by their own act of cheating, Judson Mills (1958) first measured sixth graders' attitudes toward cheating and then had them take an exam in which those who scored the highest would win prizes. The exam was designed so that it was almost impossible for students to perform well without cheating. Mills also created the illusion that any cheating could not be detected. Not surprisingly, some of the students cheated. The following day students' attitudes toward cheating were remeasured. Consistent with cognitive dissonance theory, the students who had cheated now expressed more lenient attitudes toward cheating, while those who had resisted the temptation to cheat became more critical of such behavior.

Additional research suggests that, for most people, moral codes are not fixed and unchanging but operate more like sliding scales. When people engage in actions that violate their sense of right and wrong, they often reduce the resulting cognitive dissonance by strategically forgetting their previous moral "set points" and becoming more lenient and accepting of their own immoral conduct (Barkan et al., 2012; Shu et al., 2011). In other words, they engage in self-deception and justify their immoral actions. Such moral disengagement can send people on a downward spiral of having ever more lenient ethics and ever more unethical behavior; we read about these people in the news every day when their unethical actions are finally discovered. Yet our difference from them in moral hypocrisy may be simply a matter of degree.

Postdecision Dissonance and Altered Perceptions

In one study, immediately after placing a bet on a horse race, gamblers were more certain of winning than were gamblers who were still waiting to make their bet. How are these findings an example of postdecision dissonance reduction?

A few years ago, a student in our department applied to several graduate programs in social psychology and was accepted into three of his top choices. Following a long process of weighing the strengths and weaknesses of each school, he made his choice. Shortly thereafter, Steve saw him on campus and asked if he had any regrets. "No, Dr. Franzoi," he said with genuine sincerity. "Since making my decision, I'm even more certain I made the right choice." Then, being the bright student that he was, he smiled and said, "Now I really understand the concept of postdecision dissonance."

What this aspiring social psychologist meant by this statement was that making a decision often arouses cognitive dissonance. As Festinger explained, as soon as we *commit* ourselves to a particular course of action, the attractive aspects of the unchosen alternatives and the unattractive aspects of our choice are inconsistent with our decision. As the difficulty or importance of the decision increases, the amount of postdecision dissonance increases. Because of our tendency to react to decisions in this manner, we often try to reduce dissonance by *altering our perceptions* of the choices. We do this by improving our evaluation of the chosen alternative and lowering our evaluations of the unchosen alternatives (Frenkl & Doob, 1976). Such after-the-fact, altered perceptions have been found among consumers following product purchases (Gilovich et al., 1995), voters on election day (Regan & Kilduff, 1988), and even bettors at a racetrack (Brownstein et al., 2004). In one of the racetrack studies (Knox & Inkster, 1968), researchers found that bettors who had just placed their wager on a horse were significantly more optimistic about winning than those who were still standing in line. Indeed, one of the bettors who gave his horse a fair chance of winning prior to placing his bet approached the researchers again after leaving the betting window and asked whether he could change his vote to a "good chance." Then he exclaimed, "No, by God, make that an excellent chance!" The lesson here is, when you put your money where your mouth is, your confidence is very likely to follow... at least until the end of the race.

Can you think of instances in your own life in which you convinced yourself that a bad experience was really a good and worthwhile one?

5.3b Cognitive Consistency Is Not a Universal Motive.

In Festinger's theory, he assumed that everyone has an equal desire to engage in cognitively consistent actions. However, cross-cultural research later found that this desire is more typical of individualist cultures than collectivist ones (Hoshino-Browne, 2012; Kokkoris & Kühnen, 2013). Based on these findings, many cross-cultural researchers argued that the need for consistency is based on the premise that the person is an independent entity unaffected by the social context. Although this is the way people in individualist cultures are generally taught to think, people in collectivist cultures are socialized to develop interdependent selves, which are defined in relation to others, and thus tend to be more flexible. This more flexible conception of the self encourages people from collectivist cultures to think in more holistic ways than individualists, making them more comfortable with contradiction and inconsistency (Choi & Nisbett, 2000; Kitayama et al., 2006).

> "Consistency, madam, is the first of Christian duties."
>
> —Charlotte Brontë, British author, 1816–1855

An illustration of the weaker attitude-behavior consistency need can be seen in the Japanese notion of the self. In traditional Japanese culture, there are two important aspects to the self: *omote* ("front") is presented to the public as a socially acceptable aspect of the self, whereas *ura* ("back") is that aspect of the self that is hidden from the public (Bachnik, 1992). The Japanese value both self-aspects and teach their young how to appropriately use them. Thus, when presenting *omote*, not acting according to one's true attitudes is perfectly acceptable and would not cause dissonance. For example, in one study, Japanese and American students read episodes in which hypothetical characters had to choose between honestly expressing their attitudes and not doing so to maintain social appropriateness (Iwao, 1989). As expected, American students more likely favored attitude-consistent choices than their Japanese counterparts. For instance, in one hypothetical situation, a father privately disapproved of his daughter marrying someone of another race. Almost half of the American students (49%) stated that it would be wrong for the father to think to himself that he would never allow the marriage yet to tell the couple that he favored it. On the contrary, less than 7% of the Japanese felt this sort of attitude-discrepant behavior was inappropriate.

> "The only completely consistent people are the dead."
>
> —Aldous Huxley, British novelist, 1894–1963

In summary, then, what many North Americans and other individualists consider to be discrepant and psychologically aversive—namely, believing one thing but saying something else—may not be as troubling to collectivists.

However it is important to note that there are exceptions to this Japanese–American dissonance distinction. Japanese citizens living on Hokkaido, the country's northern island with a frontier tradition and a spirit of independence, exhibit cognitive dissonance similar to that of North Americans and unlike Japanese in other areas (Kitayama et al., 2006; Takemura & Arimoto, 2008).

If you are from an individualist culture, you might be thinking, "It doesn't usually bother me when I act differently from my attitudes. What gives?" Beyond cultural considerations, research indicates that some people tolerate cognitive inconsistencies better than others. Spend a few minutes completing the Preference for Consistency Scale in *Self/Social Connection Exercise 5.1*. Robert Cialdini and his colleagues (1995) have found that people who score high on this scale are highly motivated to keep their behavior consistent with their attitudes, as predicted by cognitive dissonance theory. In contrast, those who score low on this preference scale are much less bothered by inconsistent actions; instead, they appear open and oriented to flexibility in their behavior. Given these diverging motivational patterns, it is not surprising that those with a high preference for consistency are more likely to experience cognitive dissonance than those with a low consistency preference (Newby-Clark et al., 2002).

Self/Social Connection Exercise 5.1

The Preference for Consistency Scale

Instructions

The extent to which people have a preference for consistency is measured by items on the Preference for Consistency Scale (PCS; Cialdini et al., 1995). To take the PCS, read each item below and then indicate how well each statement describes you using the following response formats:

1 = Strongly disagree	6 = Slightly agree
2 = Disagree	7 = Somewhat agree
3 = Somewhat disagree	8 = Agree
4 = Slightly disagree	9 = Strongly agree
5 = Neither agree nor disagree	

1. It is important to me that those who know me can predict what I will do.
2. I want to be described by others as a stable, predictable person.
3. The appearance of consistency is an important part of the image I present to the world.
4. An important requirement for any friend of mine is personal consistency.
5. I typically prefer to do things the same way.
6. I want my close friends to be predictable.
7. It is important to me that others view me as a stable person.
8. I make an effort to appear consistent to others.
9. It doesn't bother me much if my actions are inconsistent.

Directions for Scoring

The last PCS item (9) is reverse-scored; that is, for this item a lower rating actually indicates a higher level of consistency preference. Before summing the items, recode item 9 so that 1 = 9, 2 = 8, 3 = 7, 4 = 6, 6 = 4, 7 = 3, 8 = 2, or 9 = 1. To calculate your preference for consistency score, add up your responses to the nine items.

Interpretation of Scores   When Cialdini and his colleagues developed the PCS in 1995, the mean score for college students was about 48. The higher your score is above this value, the greater is your preference for consistency. The lower your score is below this value, the less of this preference you probably possess.

Adapted from "Preference for Consistency: The Development of a Valid Measure and the Discovery of Surprising Behavioral Implications," by R. B. Cialdini et al., 1995, *Journal of Personality and Social Psychology, 69*(2), pp. 318–328 (Appendix, p. 328). Copyright © 1995 by the American Psychological Association.

When we consider the cognitive consistency motive, it appears that at least two factors can derail expected cognitive dissonance effects when otherwise they should be aroused: A person's cultural upbringing may make attitude-discrepant behavior an appropriate and valued option, and a person's underlying psychological needs may reduce the aversiveness of attitude–discrepant acts.

> "Consistency is the last refuge of the unimaginative."
> —Oscar Wilde, Irish author, 1854–1900

In closing our discussion, it should be noted that cognitive dissonance theory is an excellent example of a "fertile" theory (see Chapter 2, section 2.1b) that continues to generate novel ways of understanding attitudes (Halliwell & Diedrichs, 2014; Pugh et al., 2011). We now know that cognitive dissonance does not always result when we act in a counterattitudinal manner. Whether or not dissonance is aroused depends not only on how central the need for cognitive consistency is in our thinking but also on whether the attitude-behavior discrepancy is important to the self and is substantial (Cooper, 2007).

5.3c   Self-Perception Theory Contends That Behavior Causes Attitudes.

When Deb was an undergraduate student, she initially did not declare a major and, although she was doing well in all of her courses, she didn't have a strong inclination for any particular field of study. Upon returning home for winter break, she found herself talking a lot about what she had been learning in her introductory psychology course (and likely driving her parents crazy with her new psychological analysis of everything). As she contemplated her previous semester behavior—that she had read the extra "suggested readings" from the back of her textbook, stopped in during office hours to ask her psychology professor numerous questions, and had already enrolled in another psychology course—she thought, "Maybe I would like psychology for a major." At that moment, according to Daryl Bem's (1965, 1972) **self-perception theory**, Deb simply formed an attitude by observing her behavior toward the attitude object.

Influenced by Skinner's behaviorist perspective, Bem's self-perception theory posed the first serious challenge to cognitive dissonance theory. Bem argues that we often do not know what our attitudes are and, instead, infer them from our behavior and the situation in which the behavior occurs. Self-perception theory is a radical explanation of the attitude concept because it contends that, instead of attitudes causing behavior, behavior causes attitudes.

The process of inferring attitudes based on observing behavior should sound familiar because it describes the attribution principles introduced in Chapter 4 (see section 4.4). Self-perception theory contends that when we form attitudes, we function like an observer—closely observing our past actions and then attributing them to either external (situational) or internal (attitudinal) sources. Comparable to the *discounting principle* in Kelley's (1967) covariation model of attribution (section 4.4b), Bem argues that we are more likely to make attitude inferences when our behavior is *freely chosen* rather than coerced. In Deb's example, Bem would assert that the reason she did not initially infer an attitude about psychology was because she didn't take the class out of

self-perception theory
The theory that we often infer our internal states, such as our attitudes, by observing our own behavior

interest (an internal attribution) but rather because it fulfilled a university graduation requirement (an external attribution). However, her subsequent behaviors in the class (doing extra readings, asking questions during office hours) were freely chosen; thus her enthusiasm could not be easily attributed to an external source.

Shelly Chaiken and Mark Baldwin (1981) conducted an interesting empirical demonstration of how the self-perception process influences attitudes. First, they separated participants into two groups: those who held strong, consistent, proenvironmental attitudes and those who had weak, inconsistent attitudes on this issue. They then induced participants to endorse either relatively proenvironment or relatively antienvironment behavioral statements on a questionnaire. They were able to secure the desired behavioral endorsements by inserting either the word *frequently* or *occasionally* into the questions. For example, participants who were asked "Do you occasionally carpool?" were more likely to answer "Yes" and perceive themselves as proenvironment. In contrast, those asked "Do you frequently carpool?" were more likely to answer "No" and feel somewhat antienvironment. Figure 5.7 shows that participants who were induced into reporting proenvironmental behaviors later rated their attitude as more proenvironmental than those who were induced into reporting antienvironmental behaviors—but only if their initial environmental attitudes were weak and inconsistent. Among the participants whose prior attitudes were strong and consistently proenvironment, the manipulation of self-reported environmentalist behaviors had no significant impact on their attitudes.

FIGURE 5.7   **Self-Perception of Environmental Attitudes**

In a study of environmental attitudes, Chaiken and Baldwin (1981) found that when people were induced into reporting past personal behavior that was either proenvironment or antienvironment, they came to view themselves in ways consistent with this behavior, but only if their prior environmental attitudes were weak and vaguely defined. What limits does this suggest about the self-perception process in attitude formation?

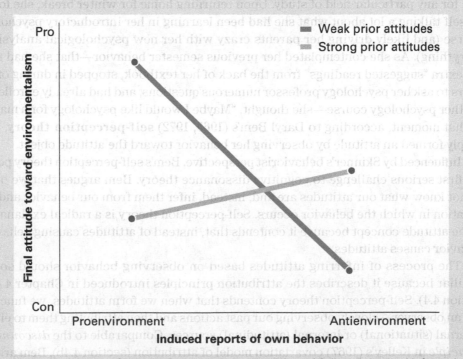

Data source: "Affective-Cognitive Consistency and the Effect of Salient Behavioral Information on the Self-Perception of Attitudes," by S. Chaiken and M. W. Baldwin, 1981, *Journal of Personality and Social Psychology, 41*(1), pp. 1–12.

Based on a number of such studies, it appears that when we behave in ways that are significantly at odds with well-defined attitudes, we are likely to experience cognitive dissonance and change our attitudes to rationalize our behavior. However, consistent with self-perception theory, when we act in ways that are only slightly out of line with our attitudes, we may experience no dissonance and simply change our attitudes by making inferences from our behavior. Research suggests that this self-perception process is most likely to operate when we have little prior experience with an attitude object or our attitudes are vaguely defined (Schnall et al., 2002).

"Our lives teach us who we are."

—Salman Rushdie, British Indian author, [born 1947]

In closing our examination of self-perception theory, allow us to suggest that this theory may also provide an explanation for how implicit attitudes become explicit attitudes. That is, we may have an implicit attitude that is influencing our behavior, prompting us to consistently behave toward a target object in a particular way. This implicit attitude is influencing our actions, but we have not yet formed an explicit attitude toward the target object. Then something happens that causes us to consider what our explicit attitude is toward this target object. We examine our past behavior, infer that we have an attitude that is consistent with our past actions, and articulate to ourselves an explicit attitude that is consistent with our already-existing and long-operating implicit attitude. To date, no research has specifically tested this possible extension of self-perception theory, so it remains a speculative hunch.

How do implicit and explicit attitudes relate to the self-perception process?

5.3d The Theory of Planned Behavior Explains "Thought-Through" Actions.

While both cognitive dissonance theory and self-perception theory predict how our attitudes are shaped by a desire to justify or explain our past actions, the **theory of planned behavior** (Ajzen, 1991, 2001) argues that people rationally think about the consequences of their behavior prior to acting.

According to this theory, the reason attitudes are often not better predictors of behavior is that people contemplate more than just their attitudes prior to deciding whether to initiate an action (Fishbein & Ajzen, 2009). As you can see in Figure 5.8, the theory of planned behavior contends that our behavior is guided by three kinds of considerations: our *attitudes* toward performing the behavior, our perceptions about whether other people will approve of the behavior (*subjective norms*), and our beliefs about how easy or difficult it is to perform the behavior (*perceived behavioral control*). These three factors jointly determine whether we form a behavioral intention, which is a conscious decision to carry out a specific action (Sheeran et al., 1999). The importance that each of these three factors has in determining a person's behavioral intention can vary depending upon the behavior.

Is it possible that we infer that we like someone simply because we happened to spend time with him or her on a few noteworthy occasions? Self-perception theory contends that we infer our attitudes by looking at our past actions, similar to how we infer other people's attitudes.

theory of planned behavior

The theory that people's conscious decisions to engage in specific actions are determined by their attitudes toward the behavior in question, the relevant subjective norms, and their perceived behavioral control

The theory of planned behavior further states that our behavioral intentions are influenced less by general attitudes than by attitudes toward performing the specific behavior in question. Furthermore, attitudes are better predictors of behaviors when the attitude expressed is stable over time and easily accessible from one's memory (Glasman & Albarracin, 2006). Consider again our chapter-opening story of college binge drinking. Students' general attitudes about alcohol consumption are less likely to predict their intentions to engage in binge drinking than are their specific attitudes about binge drinking.

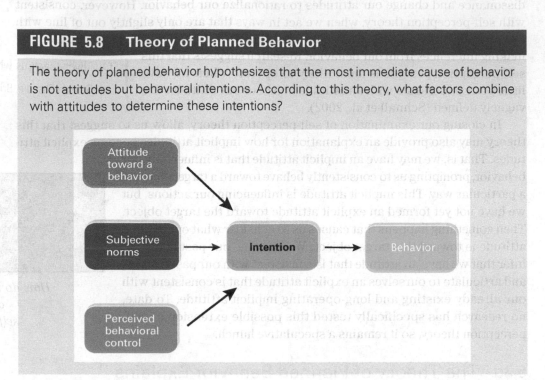

FIGURE 5.8   Theory of Planned Behavior

The theory of planned behavior hypothesizes that the most immediate cause of behavior is not attitudes but behavioral intentions. According to this theory, what factors combine with attitudes to determine these intentions?

What about subjective norms? Subjective norms are shaped by the perceived expectations of significant others and the person's motivation to conform to those expectations. Thus, college students' subjective norms about binge drinking are determined both by the beliefs that significant others have about binge drinking ("My roommates think that pounding down beer proves your toughness." "My parents think binge drinking is immature.") and their motivation to conform to these expectations ("I want to fit in with my roommates." "My parents' views are outdated.").

> "The ancestor of every action is a thought."
>
> —Ralph Waldo Emerson, American philosopher/poet, 1803–1882

In many instances, attitudes and subjective norms are adequate determinants of behavioral intention (Armitage & Conner, 1999; Ross & Jackson, 2013). Yet when people have low perceived behavioral control because they believe they lack ability or resources, then their behavioral intentions will be low regardless of their attitudes or subjective norms (Kaiser et al., 2010). For example, suppose that Lyle desires to quit his 30-year smoking habit (positive attitude toward quitting smoking). In addition, he knows that his family and doctor approve of him quitting and he would like to please them (subjective norm). But over time, after realizing how ingrained this habit is in his everyday activities, Lyle may lose confidence in his ability to become a nonsmoker (low perceived behavioral control). Thus, despite the proper attitude and subjective norm, Lyle is likely to change his intention to quit smoking.

Steve's daughter Lillian, when she was 3 years old, demonstrated another example of perceived control thwarting intention. He had been trying to get her to stop sucking her thumb. One day she said to him, "Dad, do you know…do you know…do you know why I don't like sucking my thumb anymore? Because…because…because I want to get big." Steve was pleased. Their little talks were finally paying off: She understood and wanted to conform to the household's "no thumb-sucking" norm. Later that night, however, Lillian was vigorously sucking her thumb. When Steve reminded her about her previous pronouncement, she first claimed that she was not sucking it but merely giving it a "good cleaning." Then, in the exasperated anger typical of 3-year-olds, she blurted out, "But I *have* to suck my thumb!" Despite Lillian's attitude and the subjective norm both pointing toward the termination of thumb-sucking, at the end of a hard day's play, she just did not feel capable of keeping that thumb out of her mouth.

Quite a few studies have tested the theory of planned behavior, and the general conclusion is that it does a good job of explaining behavior based on rational thinking and planning, such as eating healthier, preparing for a job interview, or practicing safe sex (Ajzen & Sheikh, 2013; Corby et al., 1996; Gissel et al., 2013). The more "mindful" people are when making decisions about their future actions, the more likely they will act according to their intentions (Chatzisarantis & Hagger, 2007). However, by placing intention after attitudes and before behavior, the theory ignores the possibility that attitudes sometimes result in impulsive, *unintentional* behavior. For example, an employee who strongly dislikes his boss may fully intend to hide his loathing because he realizes that expressing such negativity is inconsistent with workplace social norms. Yet when stressed, the harried employee may experience a loss of self-control (see Chapter 3, section 3.1c) and unintentionally tell his boss what he really thinks about him.

Another class of behaviors that the planned behavior model cannot explain is well-established *habits* (de Bruijn et al., 2007). With habits, there is no assessment of attitudes and norms prior to behaving. There is no real planning or conscious intention. Instead, the behavior is performed in a relatively unthinking fashion, with little self-regulation (Ajzen, 2001). Research indicates that habits shape many different kinds of behavior, including donating blood, attending college classes, and voting for a particular political party (Bagozzi, 1981; Echabe et al., 1988). At one time, all of these behaviors were exclusively under conscious, self-regulatory control. However, through repetition, they may have slipped into a rather automatic mode and thus are now less influenced by conscious intentions. Under these circumstances, this relatively *mindless behavior* limits the likelihood that we will act deliberately. Ask anyone who has ever tried to break a bad habit, such as eating fatty foods or tailgating fellow motorists on the highway. They will attest to the power that habitual behavior can have in overriding rational action.

Section Summary

- Cognitive consistency is an important motive in many people's attitudes and behavior.

- Cognitive dissonance theory contends that if people hold inconsistent cognitions, they experience an unpleasant emotion (cognitive dissonance), which they try to reduce.

- Cognitive dissonance is most likely when the attitude is important to the self and the inconsistency is substantial.

- The need for cognitive consistency appears to be less in collectivist cultures.

- According to self-perception theory, we infer our attitudes based on observing our past behavior.

- The theory of planned behavior contends that behavioral intentions are shaped by attitudes, subjective norms, and perceived behavioral control.

- The theory of planned behavior is based on explicit attitudes and cannot explain unintentional or habitual behavior.

5.4   The Nature of Persuasion

Having examined how attitudes are formed and how they influence behavior, let us now turn our attention to **persuasion**, which is the process of consciously attempting to change attitudes through the transmission of some message. Social psychologists' interest in understanding persuasion began in earnest during World War II. The resulting research and theory over the next 20 years are credited with providing a good deal of insight into *when* and *how* persuasion occurs. In the 1970s, the increasing popularity of the social-cognitive perspective resulted in social psychologists focusing their attention on understanding *why* people change their attitudes in response to persuasive messages (Chaiken, 1980; Petty & Cacioppo, 1986). The assumption in this social-cognitive approach is that the thoughts that people generate in response to a message are believed to be the end result of information-processing activity (Chaiken & Trope, 1999). In this section we will examine the insights from both the early persuasion researchers and contemporary social psychologists.

5.4a   Persuasion Can Occur Through Both Effortful and Effortless Thinking.

A number of theories have been developed to explain how people respond to persuasive messages. Generally these theories propose that people either (1) attempt to carefully and intentionally judge the truth of a persuasive message or (2) use simple decision rules to spontaneously and automatically estimate the validity of a persuasive message (Tormala & Petty, 2007). Arguably the most influential theory in the past 35 years has been Richard Petty and John Cacioppo's (1986) **elaboration likelihood model** (ELM), which assumes that people want to be correct in their attitudes. The term *elaboration likelihood* refers to the probability that the target of a persuasive message will elaborate (that is, carefully analyze and attempt to comprehend) the information contained in the message. According to the model, we engage in either high or low elaboration when attending to and processing persuasive messages (Petty et al., 2009).

When motivated and able to think carefully about the content of a message (high elaboration), we are influenced by the strength and quality of the arguments being made; Petty and Cacioppo would say we have taken the **central route to persuasion**. Whether central-route processing leads to attitude change or not is determined by the proportion of thoughts we generate that are consistent with or counter to the persuasive message. If our elaboration of the message yields more thoughts consistent with the message arguments, we are likely to be persuaded, but no attitude change occurs when we generate many counterarguments.

In contrast to this critical thinking, when we are unable or unwilling to analyze message content, we take the **peripheral route to persuasion**. In peripheral-route processing, we pay attention to cues that are irrelevant to the content or quality of the communication (low elaboration), such as the attractiveness of the communicator or the sheer amount of information presented (San Martin et al., 2011). By attending to these peripheral cues, we evaluate a message without extensively thinking about the actual issues under consideration. This means that it is not necessary for a person who takes the peripheral route to comprehend the content of a message: Attitude change can occur without comprehension. Figure 5.9 depicts these two different persuasion routes.

persuasion
The process of consciously attempting to change attitudes through the transmission of some message

elaboration likelihood model
A theory that persuasive messages can cause attitude change in two ways, each differing in the amount of cognitive effort or elaboration it requires

central route to persuasion
Persuasion that occurs when people think carefully about a communication and are influenced by the strength of its arguments

peripheral route to persuasion
Persuasion that occurs when people do not think carefully about a communication and instead are influenced by cues that are irrelevant to the content or quality of the communication

People attempt to carefully judge the truth of a persuasive message. Juries do this every day in a courtroom.

(iStock)

FIGURE 5.9   Two Routes to Persuasion

According to the elaboration likelihood model, when motivated and capable of thinking about a persuasive message, people are likely to carefully scrutinize its content, which is referred to as central-route processing. However, when proper motivation or ability is absent, evaluation of the persuasive message is based on shallow analysis of incidental cues, which is known as peripheral-route processing. Successful persuasion can occur through either of these two routes, but which of the two do you think secures the most enduring attitude change?

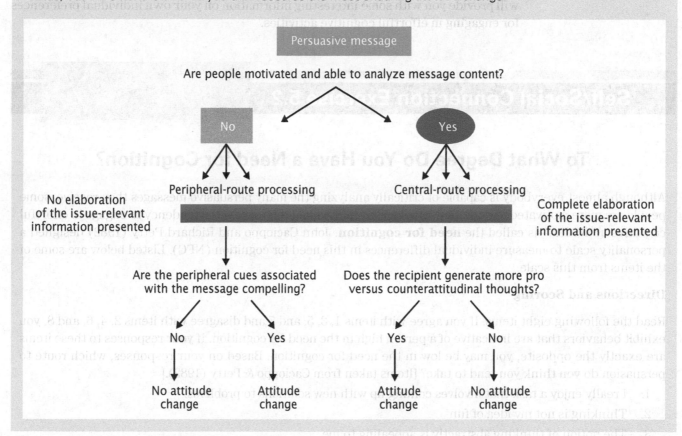

Do these two different types of cognitive processes sound familiar? Think back to our discussion of social cognition in Chapter 4. As flexible social thinkers, we sometimes carefully analyze all relevant factors and behave in a systematic and rational fashion; at other times we rely upon a quick analysis by taking mental shortcuts. This "effortful" versus "effortless" way of thinking is essentially what comprises the two routes to persuasion. When elaboration is high, central-route processing dominates thinking, but when elaboration is low, peripheral-route processing is dominant (Wegener et al., 2004). Under conditions of moderate elaboration, a combination of central- and peripheral-route processing determines whether persuasion occurs.

Although attitude change can occur through either the effortful mode of central processing or the effortless mode of peripheral processing, attitudes formed by means of the effortless route are weaker, less resistant to counterarguments, and less predictive of actual behavior than those formed through the more effortful route (Petty et al., 1995). An analogy might be that if attitudes are like houses, then attitudes formed by the peripheral route are like houses made from straw or sticks. They require little effort to develop and are extremely vulnerable to

> "Profound thoughts arise only in debate, with a possibility of counterargument, only when there is a possibility of expressing not only correct ideas, but also dubious ideas."
>
> —Andrei Sakharov, Russian scientist and social critic, 1921–1989

destruction. In contrast, attitudes formed by the central route are like houses made of bricks. They take a good deal of effort to construct and are strong and durable. As we know from both childhood fairy tales and our own life experiences, well-built houses and highly elaborated attitudes are the best insurance against the huffing and puffing of someone with either a strong set of lungs or a strong set of counterarguments. Before reading further, spend a few minutes with *Self/Social Connection Exercise 5.2*, which will provide you with some interesting information on your own individual preferences for engaging in effortful cognitive activities.

Self/Social Connection Exercise 5.2

To What Degree Do You Have a Need for Cognition?

Although almost everybody is capable of critically analyzing the many persuasive messages they receive, some people are more motivated to do so than others. This individual preference—the tendency to engage in effortful cognitive activities—is called the **need for cognition**. John Cacioppo and Richard Petty (1982) designed a personality scale to measure individual differences in this need for cognition (NFC). Listed below are some of the items from this scale.

Directions and Scoring

Read the following eight items. If you agree with items 1, 3, 5, and 7 and disagree with items 2, 4, 6, and 8, you exhibit behaviors that are indicative of a person high in the need for cognition. If your responses to these items are exactly the opposite, you may be low in the need for cognition. Based on your responses, which route to persuasion do you think you tend to take? [Items taken from Cacioppo & Petty (1982).]

1. I really enjoy a task that involves coming up with new solutions to problems.
2. Thinking is not my idea of fun.
3. The notion of thinking abstractly is appealing to me.
4. I like tasks that require little thought once I've learned them.
5. I usually end up deliberating about issues even when they do not affect me personally.
6. It's enough for me that something gets the job done; I don't care how or why it works.
7. I prefer my life to be filled with puzzles that I must solve.
8. I only think as hard as I have to.

Interpretation   High-NFC persons are much more likely than low-NFC persons to be motivated by cognitive challenges and to actively seek out and persist in difficult cognitive tasks (Fleischhauer et al., 2010; Furnham & Thorne, 2013). High-NFC persons tend to take the central route to persuasion and are more influenced by fact-based messages, while low-NFC individuals are more likely to take the peripheral route and are more influenced by emotion-based persuasive messages (Cacioppo et al., 1996; Lin et al., 2011). As a result, the attitudes of low NFCs are easier to change than those of high NFCs (Cárdaba et al., 2013; Shestowsky et al., 1998).

need for cognition
An individual preference for and tendency to engage in effortful cognitive activities

5.4b Persuader Credibility and Attractiveness Can Affect Persuasion.

An important component in persuasion is the audience's perception of the persuader. Although the qualities of the persuader are peripheral cues to the actual content of the message, as the message source, the persuader is nonetheless vitally important in determining whether the message will be effective in producing attitude change (Jones et al., 2003). This is especially true when the recipient lacks the motivation to think about the message arguments carefully. Two factors that affect persuader effectiveness are credibility and attractiveness (Hovland et al., 1949; McGuire, 1999).

> "Man is but a reed, the weakest in nature, but he is a thinking reed."
>
> —Blaise Pascal, French philosopher, 1623–1662

> "To most people, nothing is more troublesome than the effort of thinking."
>
> —James Bryce, British statesman, 1838–1922

Persuader Credibility

People listening to a persuader pay a good deal of attention to his or her *credibility* or believability (Lee & Cheng, 2010). Persuader credibility is based on perceptions of expertise and trustworthiness. Expert persuaders are those who appear to have extensive knowledge regarding the topic of the persuasive message. Trustworthy persuaders are those who seem to lack hidden motives and instead express honest opinions based on the information they possess. Persuaders who are perceived as both expert and trustworthy have high credibility, but expert credibility is seriously undermined if their opinions are perceived as biased.

> "Propaganda, to be effective, must be believed. To be believed, it must be credible."
>
> —Hubert H. Humphrey, US senator and vice president, 1911–1978

Thus, if you were a college administrator developing an ad campaign to change students' attitudes toward binge drinking, it might be a mistake to use as persuaders governmental scientists who study alcohol abuse (Johnston et al., 2003). Research suggests that teenagers and young adults often perceive antidrinking campaigns from governmental agencies as lacking credibility due to low trustworthiness ("They're adults who don't want us partying and having fun!"). Social psychologist Lloyd Johnston, who tracks drug use trends among this age group, commented that he was "worried that putting that tagline [a governmental affiliation] causes kids to dismiss the message they've just consumed because they're not sure they like who is giving it to them."

Numerous studies have found that a source's low credibility is a *discounting cue* that results in the audience rejecting the message (Lev-Ari & Keysar, 2010; Zhu et al., 2010). For example, Carl Hovland and Walter Weiss (1951) asked American college students to read an article proposing that nuclear-powered submarines were both feasible and safe (at the time, no such submarines had yet been built). Some of those reading the article were told that the author was J. Robert Oppenheimer, the American physicist who supervised the construction of the atomic bomb. Others were told that the source was the Soviet newspaper *Pravda*. The researchers assumed that during the height of the Cold War, the average American would perceive Oppenheimer as a highly credible source (expert and trustworthy) and would consider *Pravda* a low-credibility source. True to expectations, readers who believed that the highly credible Oppenheimer had written the article were more persuaded by its message immediately after reading it than those who believed they were reading a Soviet article.

> "We are not won by arguments that we can analyze but by tone and temper, by the manner which is the man himself."
>
> —Samuel Butler, English author, 1835–1902

If this was all there was to learn about source credibility, we might conclude that persuasion seems pretty straightforward and uncomplicated. Yet 4 weeks after the initial reading of the submarine article, Hovland and Weiss again measured their participants' attitudes toward nuclear-powered submarines and found a surprise. As you can see in Figure 5.10, the highly credible Oppenheimer had lost some of his persuasive power, whereas *Pravda* had actually gained in persuasiveness. Similar studies revealed the same delayed effects: Immediately after the message presentation, highly credible sources are more persuasive than less credible sources; over time, however, the credibility gap weakens. The researchers called the enhanced, delayed effect of low-credibility sources on attitude change the **sleeper effect**.

FIGURE 5.10   The Sleeper Effect

Immediately following the reception of a message, people are more likely to be persuaded by a highly credible source than one of low credibility. However, as Hovland and Weiss (1951) found, over time the message becomes disassociated from its source, resulting in less agreement with the highly credible source and more agreement with the source that had lower credibility. What is a possible explanation for this effect?

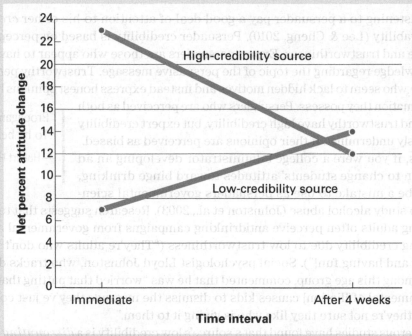

Data source: "The Influence of Source Credibility on Communication Effectiveness," by C. I. Hovland and W. Weiss, 1951, *Public Opinion Quarterly, 15*, pp. 635–650.

What could explain the sleeper effect? Herbert Kelman and Hovland (1953) believed it occurs because people who receive a message from a low-credibility source eventually forget where they heard it and are then influenced by the message content alone. If true, this would also explain why the highly credible Oppenheimer lost some of his persuasive power over time—the message became disassociated from the credible source. To test this hypothesis, the researchers extended the Hovland and Weiss (1951) design by adding a condition in which participants were reminded of the source's identity before their attitudes were reassessed. If the sleeper effect occurred because people forgot that the persuasive message came from a low-credibility source, then reestablishing this link would eliminate the effect. This is exactly what happened. Participants who were not reminded of the source showed the expected sleeper effect, but those who were reminded did not.

A meta-analysis of over 70 different sleeper effect studies found that the magnitude of this effect depends on the strength of the discounting cue (Kumkale & Albarracín,

sleeper effect
The delayed effectiveness of a persuasive message from a low-credibility source

2004). The more effective the discounting cue in suppressing the immediate impact of the persuasive message, the larger the sleeper effect. Not surprisingly, the meta-analysis also found that when the discounting cue is ineffective, there is no delayed increase in persuasion (that is, no sleeper effect). This and one other meta-analysis (Pratkanis et al., 1988) indicate that the sleeper effect most likely occurs under the following conditions:

1. When the message is convincing enough to lead to persuasion by itself

2. When people are sufficiently able and motivated to elaborate on the message arguments prior to receiving the discounting cue

3. When people are given information discounting the credibility of the source following the persuasive message, not before

4. When the impact of the discounting cue (the low-credibility information) decays in memory faster than the persuasive message

What if a highly credible person provides weak arguments? Recent research by Dolores Albarracín and her colleagues (2017) suggests that a sleeper effect can also occur if people focus on the source's credibility rather than the arguments. In their research they found that when a high or low credible speaker gave weak arguments there was no initial attitude change. However, after a delay, research participants who had focused on the speaker's high credibility were more persuaded by the message arguments, demonstrating a sleeper effect. However, the sleeper effect did not occur for participants who were told to focus on the quality of the arguments. This suggests that after a delay, message arguments become more persuasive because of the weight given to the credibility of the speaker.

How might these sleeper effects impact your attitudes in a world where both high and low credible people are constantly trying to persuade you to buy their products, support their policies, or vote them into office?

Observe the content of TV commercials in the morning, in the evening, and during weekend sports shows. When are female and male characters with either traditional or nontraditional gender roles most likely to appear in these commercials? How do these characters enhance the persuasive power of these advertisements?

Persuader Attractiveness

During the 1920s, when feminists were demonstrating against women's inequality, Edward Bernays (the nephew of Sigmund Freud) was a public relations executive for the cigarette industry. In trying to persuade women to smoke cigarettes, Bernays thought that cigarettes could serve as a "torch of freedom" symbol for women if he could photograph attractive and "liberated" women using the product. Bernays arranged to have a group of attractive, cigarette-smoking women marching in Manhattan's 1929 Easter Parade; when photographs of this event appeared in the nation's newspapers, many women took up the "torch of freedom" habit (Greaves, 1996). Since Bernays's time, research has demonstrated that a communicator's attractiveness can be based on several factors, including *likability, similarity to the audience,* and *physical attractiveness.*

Regarding likability, merely saying nice things is often enough to get people to like you and thereby increase your ability to

"To please people is the greatest step toward persuading them."

—Philip Dormer Stanhope, Earl of Chesterfield, 1694–1773

persuade (Eagly & Chaiken, 1993). In a world where much of our interaction and persuasion happens online, researchers have similarly found that adolescents are more likely to "like" social media posts that already have many likes compared to ones with few likes (Sherman et al., 2016). Furthermore, viewing social media posts with numerous likes is correlated with neural activity in brain regions that are associated with social cognition, social memories, and imitation. These findings highlight that likability of the source, whether a person or social media post, is associated with heightened information processing.

We are also attracted to those who are similar to us, and this attraction often results in us being influenced by similar others (Böhm et al., 2010). Communicators can be similar to their audience in a number of ways, including sharing attitudes and values ("Are his politics and morals like mine?"), having similar backgrounds ("Is he from my hometown?"), and having a similar appearance ("Does he look like me?"). Of the different ways in which people can be similar, perceived similarity in attitudes and values appears to be the most important in enhancing persuasion (Simons et al., 1970). This is why politicians try to present themselves as having attitudes and values in step with the majority. This is also why effective campaigns to reduce binge drinking on college campuses use fellow students to deliver the persuasive messages; compared with nonstudents, student communicators are more likely to be perceived by the message recipients as sharing their attitudes, values, and interests (Johnston & White, 2003).

Beautiful people are very attractive to most people and are effective persuaders.

("Natalie Portman and Chris Hemsworth" by Gage Skidmore, available under a CC by SA 2.0 license via Wikimedia.)

Finally, beautiful people are highly attractive to most of us; thus they are effective persuaders (Petty et al., 1997; Vogel et al., 2010). For example in one study by Shelly Chaiken (1979), university undergraduates attempted to persuade fellow students to sign a petition to get the university to stop serving meat during breakfast and lunch. Although less attractive persuaders only secured signatures 32% of the time, the more attractive students convinced 41% of the students they approached to sign the petition. Marketing studies have found that attractive salespersons who explicitly disclose their desire to influence potential customers to buy a product are not only rated as more likeable by those customers than are less attractive salespersons, they also are more successful in inducing stronger intentions to buy the product (Reinhard et al., 2006). Other persuasion studies have found that good looks can even sometimes overcome a poor presentation style (Pallak, 1983).

Why is it that radio lottery advertisers trying to persuade you to spend your money speak at a normal rate of speed, yet when they convey the odds of winning, their speech rate dramatically increases? Are they simply trying to save money by cutting down the length of the commercial, or is there an equally important reason for this shift to fast-paced speech?

When advertisers associate their products with attractive persons, do you think they are trying to induce central-route or peripheral-route processing in their target audience? Have you noticed how many beer commercials feature young, attractive women in skimpy clothing? These women are peripheral cues, consciously placed in commercials to induce positive feelings in male viewers, which then become associated with the beer through classical conditioning (see section 5.2b). This attitude change takes place without much thought—peripheral-route processing. Putting on your hypothetical college administrator hat again, if you were developing an ad campaign to change students' attitudes toward binge drinking, how could you use the powerful peripheral cue of attractiveness to enhance your message?

5.4c   Rapid Speech Discourages Central-Route Processing.

Another quality that affects persuasion is the persuader's speaking pace. Research indicates that people who speak rapidly are generally more persuasive than those who speak more slowly because fast talkers convey the *impression* that they are more credible (Miller et al., 1976). Marketing studies also report the benefit of rapid speech:

People seem to be more favorably disposed toward advertisements—and the products advertised—when the product spokesperson talks at a faster-than-normal rate (LaBarbera & MacLachlan, 1979; Street & Brady, 1982). But is fast talking always beneficial to persuasion?

According to the elaboration likelihood model, fast talking will be *beneficial* to the persuasive communicator only when the audience's initial attitudinal position is *opposite* to that of the communicator (Petty & Wegener, 1998). Because the audience's counter arguing is "short-circuited" by the sheer speed at which the opposing viewpoints are presented, audience members are more likely to be persuaded by the message than if they had more time to scrutinize it. In contrast, the elaboration likelihood model further predicts that fast talking will *hurt* the persuasive power of the message when it is presented to an audience that *favors* the communicator's point of view. Why? Because the arguments are presented so quickly that the audience cannot adequately process them and incorporate them into their existing belief system to further bolster their current attitudes on the issue.

Stephen Smith and David Shaffer (1991) found support for this explanation in a study in which college students listened to persuasive messages arguing for or against raising the legal drinking age. A survey conducted prior to the study revealed that the overwhelming majority of undergraduates on campus opposed such a law. Students heard the persuasive arguments at either a slow, normal, or rapid rate of speech. Consistent with the elaboration likelihood hypothesis, when students listened to arguments counter to their perspective, rapid speech suppressed the tendency to rebut the counterattitudinal message; hence listeners were more susceptible to persuasion. However, when students listened to arguments consistent with their own attitudes toward the drinking-age law, rapid speech inhibited favorable elaboration of the proattitudinal message, thus undermining its persuasive impact. These findings suggest that rapid speech may either promote or inhibit persuasion through its impact on message elaboration.

5.4d Emotions Can Motivate, Enhance, or Hinder Persuasion.

For many years, social scientists made predictions about elections under the assumption that voters made their decisions based on deliberate, rational thought (Kinder, 1998). However, this approach then changed to take into account the role that emotions play in the voting process (Lakoff, 2005). Drew Westen (2007) contends that research findings strongly suggest that when political decisions evoke strong emotional reactions in voters, reason plays virtually no role in the decision-making of the average citizen. Based on his analysis of controversial political issues and how the two major political parties in the United States have crafted their persuasive messages, Westen concludes that the Republican Party has a better understanding than does the Democratic Party of how emotions shape voter decision-making. Put simply, Democrats emphasize the crafting of strong arguments to shift voters' attitudes, while Republicans emphasize strong emotional appeals.

Why do emotions play such a pivotal role in many persuasion attempts? Early research indicated that people who are in a positive mood are more susceptible to persuasion than the average person. For example, Irving Janis and his colleagues (1965) had some people read persuasive messages while they ate a snack and drank soda, while others simply read the messages without the accompanying treats. Greater attitude change occurred among the "munchers" than among the "food-free" group. Similar effects were also found among people listening to pleasant music (Milliman, 1986).

> "There are two levers for moving man—interest and fear."
>
> —Napoleon Bonaparte, French general and emperor, 1769–1821

> "People react to fear, not love—they don't teach that in Sunday school, but it's true."
>
> —Richard M. Nixon, US president, 1913–1994

Why do you think these effects might occur? Many social psychologists believe that emotion has an indirect influence on persuasion and other behavior, rather than playing a direct role (Baumeister et al., 2007a; Briñol et al., 2010). The *feelings-as-information* explanation suggests that positive moods signal to people that everything is fine in their environment and no effortful thought is necessary (Isbell, 2004). As a result, happy people are likely to be influenced by poor arguments because they are unlikely to engage in extensive processing of the presented message (Cesario et al., 2006). What about people in negative moods? Their moods signal that something is wrong and that some action is necessary. Unhappy people adopt a problem-solving mode, and central-route processing is associated with problem-solving.

While the feelings-as-information view contends that happy people are more susceptible to persuasion than unhappy people because they engage in less effortful thinking, there is evidence that people in positive moods sometimes engage in effortful thinking. The *hedonic-contingency* view asserts that happy people will engage in cognitive tasks that allow them to remain happy and will avoid tasks that lower their mood (Wegener & Petty, 1994). Consistent with this view, research indicates that those in positive moods will engage in central-route processing if the message is expected to advocate something pleasant (Wegener et al., 1995). Thus, counter to the feelings-as-information view, it appears that happy people do not always process information less than neutral or sad people. Overall, the research suggests that happy people are generally more susceptible to persuasion than neutral or sad people. However, when a persuasive message does not threaten happy people's moods, they may carefully scrutinize it.

I started using e-cigarettes but kept smoking. Right up until my lung collapsed.

Kristy, age 35, Tennessee

(Source: Tips From Former Smokers ® by Centers for Disease Control and Prevention.)

Fear appeals capture people's attention, but they also often induce anxiety and helpless feelings. What can persuaders do to short-circuit helpless reactions in the target audience?

Fear Appeals

Beyond inducing generally positive or negative moods, would-be persuaders sometimes try to evoke the negative emotion of fear in order to persuade. An antismoking ad tells you how your nicotine habit will shorten life expectancy. An antidrinking ad depicts the negative consequences of drunk driving. An antigambling ad warns against the dangers of compulsive gambling (Munoz et al., 2010).

Fear-based messaging is a very common technique employed to persuade people, but how effective is it? In a meta-analysis of 127 studies, Melanie Tannenbaum and her colleagues (2015) found that fear-based persuasion is moderately (d = .29) effective at influencing attitudes, intentions, and behaviors. Inducing moderate amounts of fear appears to be most effective, although there is no negative backlash in inducing extreme fear. Fear appeals are effective at promoting sustained behavior, such as dieting, but they are even more persuasive for promoting one-time behavior, such as getting vaccinated or voting for a political candidate. The likely reason sustained behavior is a more difficult persuasive target is because repeatedly engaging in an action might require a lifestyle change. The meta-analysis also found that fear campaigns are more effective for audiences that have a larger percentage of women than men, but they are equally effective in collectivist and individualist cultures.

"No passion so effectually robs the mind of all its powers of acting and reasoning as fear."

—Edmund Burke, Irish philosopher, 1729–1797

Existing research indicates that fear appeals that are combined with information that one can do something about the danger are especially effective at promoting behavioral changes (Morrison, 2005; Mulilis et al., 2001; Tannenbaum et al., 2015). That is, pairing fear of a negative outcome (such as getting lung cancer) and simultaneously reassuring people they are personally capable of making changes (such as quitting smoking) can be especially useful in inducing behavioral changes. Does this notion of being personally capable of changing one's own behavior sound familiar? It should, because it bears a striking similarity to the concept of *perceived behavioral control* in the theory of planned behavior (see section 5.3d).

Unfortunately, when feeling highly vulnerable to some threat, we often do not critically analyze the recommended actions offered to avoid the danger (Das et al., 2003; de Hoog et al., 2007). Instead, because we desperately want to believe that the recommended actions will work, we ignore information that might cast doubt on the persuaders' message—therefore placing a great deal of power in the hands of those who are offering solutions (Landau et al., 2004). Many individuals with life-threatening illnesses fall victim to medical and religious charlatans who promise renewed health if their highly questionable remedies are followed. Similarly, many voters fail to critically analyze highly questionable social policies because they are accompanied by fear-based appeals.

> "The people can always be brought to the bidding of the leaders. All you have to do is tell them they are being attacked, and denounce the pacifists for lack of patriotism and for exposing the country to danger. It works the same in every country."
>
> —Nazi leader Hermann Göring (1893–1946) explaining how leaders can use fear to induce people to support a war they otherwise would oppose

Humor Appeals

Would-be persuaders also use the positive emotion of humor to prompt attitude change, which is why about 40% of all advertisements employ humor (Unger, 1996). Public relations consultants also believe that humor is an effective persuader, and they regularly recommend that their clients punch up their persuasive speeches with humorous anecdotes (Weinberger & Campbell, 1991). Even some student-designed ad campaigns to increase alcohol awareness on college campuses have employed humor to change students' attitudes toward drinking (Saltzman, 2002). Are they correct in their beliefs?

Research clearly shows that using humor in persuasive messages does increase people's *attention* to the message more than serious-sounding communication attempts (Duncan & Nelson, 1985; Nabi et al., 2007). People are simply more likely to listen to persuaders who are trying to make them laugh—or at least smile. However, one of the problems with using humor is that it may interfere with the listener's *scrutiny* of the message by directing attention away from the persuasive content (Young, 2008). That is, the jokes catch people's attention and those listening to the jokes are less likely to think deeply about the message arguments. Thus, if a persuader merely wants to get people to notice the message, humor may be useful in this regard. However, with no message elaboration, any attitude change is likely to be extremely vulnerable to a counterpersuasive attack (Haugtvedt & Petty, 1992).

A study conducted by Stephen Smith and his coworkers (1994) found that whether humor promotes or disrupts message processing is determined by the *relevance* of the humor to the message content. When humor is relevant, people appear to be more motivated to take a central route to persuasion and process the message arguments. However when humor is irrelevant to the message content, people are likely to take a peripheral route and base their evaluation of the message merely on cues such as source credibility.

Given our previous discussion of fear and persuasion, it is interesting to note that humor may be effective in persuading certain

In addition to using humor to combat binge drinking on college campuses, many college anti–binge drinking ads also provide information on how much alcohol the typical student on campus consumes. Why might this information be effective in reducing binge drinking? When would reporting such normative information possibly promote—rather than reduce—binge drinking?

individuals to take protective steps when facing potential health threats. In studies of persuasive appeals involving health issues—such as the responsible consumption of alcohol, sunscreen use to avoid skin cancer, and condom use to prevent HIV/AIDS—humorous messages appear to be more effective than nonhumorous messages for men and women high in psychological masculinity (Conway & Dubé, 2002). *Psychological masculinity* consists of an assertive, task-oriented approach to life, reflected in such personality characteristics as being independent, forceful, and dominant. Although men are, on average, higher than women in masculinity, these gender differences are slowly shrinking and are largely due to women's increase in masculine traits (Donnelly & Twenge, 2017; Twenge, 1997).

Recall from Chapter 3 that masculinity is associated with *manly emotion*, in which people exert control over their emotions, just as they try to exert control over other aspects of their lives (Shields, 2002). For individuals who place a high value on controlling their emotions, humor in the context of a fear-inducing message may be very much appreciated because it helps them manage their fear, which then allows them to more effectively process the message.

5.4e Two-Sided Messages Inoculate Audiences Against Opposing Views.

Beyond who is presenting the message and the emotions of the recipient, another factor in determining whether a message will persuade is whether it is "one-sided" or "two-sided." *One-sided messages* are those in which persuaders try to convince others by presenting only their arguments. In contrast, *two-sided messages* involve acknowledging opposing arguments and then refuting them.

In a study conducted during World War II, Hovland and his colleagues (1949) attempted to determine whether one-sided or two-sided messages were more effective audience persuaders. Working in the US Army's Information and Education Division immediately after the surrender of Nazi Germany, their objective was to convince American soldiers that the war was far from over and that the armed conflict against Japan would last at least 2 more years. Some soldiers heard a one-sided message that did not bring up opposing viewpoints, and other soldiers heard a two-sided message that also mentioned and then refuted opposing viewpoints. As illustrated in Figure 5.11, the effectiveness of the appeal depended on who was listening. A one-sided appeal was most effective with those who already believed that the war would be long, while a two-sided appeal worked better with those who initially believed that the war would be over soon.

Later research found that two-sided messages are more effective in persuading not only those who initially disagree but also people who either are well-informed on the topic or are going to be exposed to opposing viewpoints in the future (Crowley & Hoyer, 1994; Lumsdaine & Janis, 1953). In such circumstances, mentioning the opposition's arguments suggests that you are being an objective, fair-minded person, thereby increasing your trustworthiness; your effectiveness at persuasion is therefore also increased (Bohner et al., 2003).

Besides increasing communicator trustworthiness, another important factor is operating in two-sided messages. For those who are soon going to hear the opposition state its case, raising and then refuting its arguments can *inoculate* these people against them, making persuasion more difficult for the opposition. William McGuire developed this inoculation explanation during the 1950s in partial response to Cold War fears about Americans' susceptibility to communist propaganda from the Soviet Union. McGuire reasoned that people become vulnerable to propaganda when they are raised in a society that overprotects them from hearing things that attack culturally shared beliefs. Using a biological analogy, he stated that people who are raised in such a "germ-free" environment would not have developed appropriate mechanisms to adequately defend themselves against attacking viruses (i.e., outside propaganda). However, just as administering a small dose of a dangerous virus will stimulate the body to develop defenses to fight off the disease, McGuire asserted that exposing people to a weakened dose of the attacking material would also stimulate the development of resistance-promoting counterarguments.

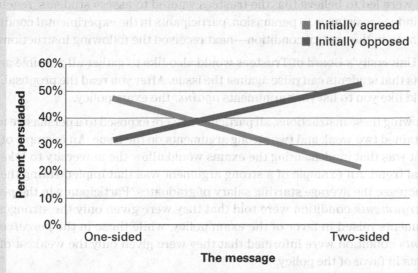

FIGURE 5.11   One-Sided Versus Two-Sided Appeals

Following Germany's defeat in World War II, American soldiers who initially agreed with a message that Japan was strong and that the war in the Pacific would last a long time were more persuaded by a one-sided appeal. In contrast, soldiers who were skeptical of this message were more persuaded by a two-sided appeal.

Source: Data from *Experiments on Mass Communications*, by C. I. Hovland et al., 1949, Princeton, NJ: Princeton University Press.

Research supports the basic elements of inoculation theory. In a meta-analysis of 41 research studies, people's attitudes were found to be more resistant to counterattack after receiving two-sided appeals rather than one-sided appeals, with the Cohen's effect size d = .43 (Banas & Rains, 2010). Furthermore, the meta-analysis found that the inoculation resulted in people having stronger resistance to novel arguments (that weren't presented in the initial two-sided appeal). Inoculation theory and its principles have been effectively applied in many realms, including commercial advertising, political campaigning, and health-intervention programs (Goldberg et al., 2006; McGuire & Papageorgis, 1961). However, as the application of inoculation theory spread, it became clear that the inoculation effect not only protects people from "dangerous" political perspectives, but can also be used to manipulate people's attitudes and beliefs on any topic.

5.4f Resisting Strong Arguments Creates Greater Attitude Certainty.

What happens when people successfully resist persuasion? The typical assumption has been that if persuasion is resisted, people's attitudes remain unchanged. Is this true? Petty and his colleagues (2002) questioned this widespread assumption and suggested instead that when people resist persuasion, they often become more confident in the attitude that was targeted. Successful resistance increases confidence in the attitude because people infer that their resistance was due to the validity of the attitude. The researchers further hypothesize that people will experience the greatest increase in attitude confidence after resisting messages they perceive to be very strong. In contrast, when people successfully defend their attitude against a weak attack, their confidence in the attitude should not increase, because they cannot be certain that the attitude would have survived a strong challenge.

> "It is true that you may fool all the people some of the time; you can even fool some of the people all the time; but you can't fool all of the people all the time."
>
> —Abraham Lincoln, US president, 1809–1865

In a test of these hypotheses, Zakary Tormala and Petty (2002) conducted a study in which college students were presented with a proposal, supposedly from the University's Board of Trustees, to implement a new policy in 2 years that would require graduating seniors to pass a comprehensive exam in their major field of study. As justification for the experiment, students were led to believe that the trustees wanted to assess students' reactions. In order to induce resistance to persuasion, participants in the experimental conditions—but not those in the control condition—next received the following instructions:

> The University's Board of Trustees would also like to gather all possible arguments that students can raise against the issue. After you read the proposal, we would like you to list your arguments *against* the exam policy.

Following these instructions, all participants were exposed to a persuasive message that contained two weak and two strong arguments on the issue. An example of a weak argument was that implementing the exams would allow the university to take part in a national trend. An example of a strong argument was that implementing the exams would increase the average starting salary of graduates. Participants in the *perceived strong arguments* condition were told that they were given only the strongest of all the arguments raised in favor of the exam policy, while those in the *perceived weak arguments* condition were informed that they were given only the weakest of all the arguments in favor of the policy.

After receiving the persuasive message, participants in the two experimental conditions—but not those in the control condition—were told to generate a list of as many counterarguments as they could. All participants then completed measures to assess their attitudes and attitude certainty toward the comprehensive exam proposal. Results found no group differences in attitude toward the exam proposal. However, as expected, the groups did differ in their later attitude confidence. When participants resisted what was described as a strong message, their attitude confidence increased compared with those who thought they received a weak message and those in the no-message control group. Subsequent studies in this same series found that successful resistance to persuasion not only enhances people's confidence in their initial attitude but also renders the attitude more resistant to subsequent attacks—and increases the likelihood that people will later behave in a manner consistent with the attitude (Tormala & Petty, 2002).

These studies demonstrate how counterarguing can produce successful and sustained resistance to persuasion. But what happens if the persuasive arguments are so strong that people cannot generate convincing counterarguments? Derek Rucker and Petty (2004) predicted that, if people try to find fault in a persuasive message and fail, the new attitude resulting from this successful persuasion attempt will be held with more conviction and certainty. In testing this hypothesis, the researchers used the ever-popular scenario of telling students about a new proposal to require graduating seniors to pass a comprehensive exam. However, in this study, students in the two experimental conditions received very strong message arguments that were designed to be difficult to counterargue.

An example of one of these hard-to-refute arguments was:

Universities that implement senior comprehensive exams are given additional funding by a new government program that rewards performance-based education. For students, this means that at least a 5% tuition decrease would accompany the passing of the exam proposal. In addition to an immediate 5% tuition decrease, the government program provides funds to ensure that students' tuition will not be raised for a period of at least 5 years.

Before receiving the message arguments, participants in the experimental conditions were instructed to either (1) focus on their thoughts while the message was presented (*thought condition*) or (2) generate counterarguments to the message (*counterargument condition*). Students in the control condition did not receive any persuasive message. All participants then completed measures to assess their attitudes and attitude certainty toward the comprehensive exam proposal.

The researchers found that students in the two experimental conditions—those who received the persuasive message—had more favorable attitudes toward the comprehensive exam proposal than students in the no-message control group. This suggests that the persuasive message was successful in securing attitude change. More important, these new attitudes were held with greater certainty in the *counterargument condition* than in the *thought condition*. In other words, when students were told to generate counterarguments toward a strong persuasive message, their failure to refute the message caused them to adopt a new attitude that was stronger than the attitudes of students who did not try to find fault with the message. Being impressed with how hard it was to counterargue, the active resisters became more confident in their new attitudes than did people who simply thought about the persuasive message without engaging in active resistance.

Considering these findings from the persuader's point of view, when you are trying to persuade others and are convinced that you have very strong arguments that cannot be refuted, you might consider going against intuition by encouraging your audience to try to find fault in your message. When audience members fail to find fault, they may say to themselves, "I changed my attitude even though I tried to fight the persuasive attempt. I now know that I have few negative thoughts about the message and my new attitude is a good one." In essence, this is a form of self-generated persuasion (Darke & Chaiken, 2005).

Thus far, we have examined the conditions under which we may become impressed with our ability or inability to counterargue a persuasive message. As demonstrated in these studies, being impressed with our resistance can lead to increased confidence in our initial attitude, but being impressed with our failure to resist can lead to increased confidence in our new attitude. But what if we are not so impressed with either our resistance or our lack of resistance?

In such instances, we should have less confidence in our attitudes. Consider first the case in which we are able to counterargue and resist persuasion, but we believe that our resistance was difficult or lacking in some way. Even though we do not change our attitude, we may now be less confident in the attitude—rendering it more susceptible to future persuasion attempts. In the case of failing to resist persuasion, if we believe that our changed attitude occurred because we did not try very hard to resist or that there were many distractions that prevented us from mounting a good defense, we may have less confidence in our new attitude. Figure 5.12 presents a summary of the key ideas developed by Petty and his colleagues (2004) regarding the process of counterarguing and the conditions under which various outcomes are likely. Table 5.2 reviews some of the factors that influence central versus peripheral processing.

FIGURE 5.12   A Model of Attempted Resistance to Persuasion

Petty and his colleagues (2004) outlined how attempts at counterarguing a persuasive message can either succeed or fail. Being impressed or unimpressed with one's ability to resist or not resist a persuasive message will either increase or decrease one's confidence in the new or old attitude.

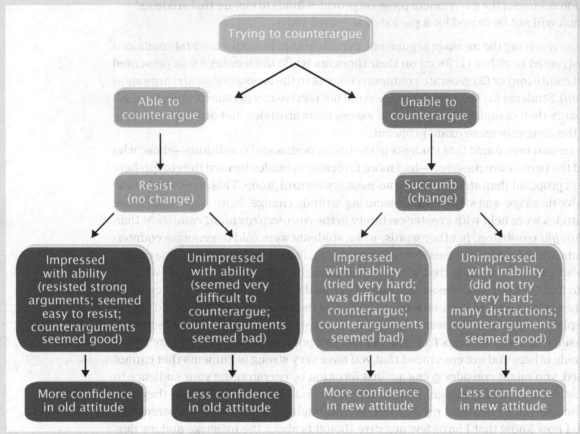

Source: Adapted from "Resisting Persuasion by Counterarguing: An Attitude Strength Perspective," by R. E. Petty et al., 2004, in *Perspectivism in Social Psychology: The Yin and Yang of Scientific Progress*, edited by J. T. Jost, M. R. Banaji, and D. A. Prentice, Washington, DC: American Psychological Association.

TABLE 5.2   Central Versus Peripheral Processing of Persuasive Messages

Route to Persuasion	Most Likely to Occur When	Effect on Attitudes
Central Route The person carefully scrutinizes all the available information in the persuasion environment in an attempt to determine the merits of the presented arguments.	People find the message personally relevant and involving. People are high in need for cognition. People are in a neutral or mildly negative mood. The communicator speaks at a normal rate of speed.	Attitudes tend to be strong, resistant to counterarguments, and predictive of behavior.
Peripheral Route Instead of actively thinking about the attitude object, the person relies on incidental cues and simple rules of thumb, such as the attractiveness of the communicator or the length of the message.	People find the message to be irrelevant and noninvolving. People are low in need for cognition. People are in a positive mood. The communicator speaks rapidly.	Attitudes tend to be weak, susceptible to counterarguments, and not predictive of behavior.

Section Summary

- Persuasion involves conscious attempts to change attitudes through the transmission of some message.

- The elaboration likelihood model contends that people engage in either high or low cognitive elaboration when attending to persuasive messages.
    central-route processing: high elaboration of message content by focusing on information central to message
    peripheral-route processing: low elaboration of message content by focusing on information not central to message

- Highly credible sources are more persuasive, at least initially, than less credible sources.

- Attractive sources are more persuasive than unattractive sources.

- Rapid speech can increase or decrease persuasiveness, depending on the audience's initial position and the message strength.

- Positive moods generally induce more persuasion than neutral or somber moods.

- Fear can persuade, yet it can also immobilize an audience with anxiety.

- Humor increases message attention, but it can interfere with message comprehension.

- Two-sided messages are effective in persuading those who initially disagree, who are well informed, or who are going to be exposed to opposing viewpoints.

- Encouraging people to actively counterargue a message can strengthen or weaken either an existing attitude or a new attitude.

Applications

Are Mass Media Campaigns Effective in Changing Risky Health Behaviors?

Turn on the TV, listen to the radio, or browse social media and you are likely to come across advertisements that are part of a mass media campaign designed to change your health-related behaviors. Perhaps the campaign is promoting healthy behaviors, such as getting a vaccine flu shot, practicing safe sex, exercising, or eating healthy. Other campaigns might be aimed at preventing negative behaviors, such as not texting while driving, binge drinking, smoking e-cigarettes, or bullying. How effective do you think these campaigns are in changing behavior?

Mass media campaigns generally seek to inform the audience about the social and health consequences of the targeted behavior, as well as any legal consequences (e.g. fines for underage drinking, etc.)(Elder et al., 2004). The hope is that the message increases the public's knowledge about the unhealthy behavior, promotes a change in attitudes, and increases behavioral intentions to change undesirable behavior. Ideally, the campaigns will also reshape social norms that promote the unhealthy behaviors. For example, a campaign about drinking and driving seeks to increase a person's knowledge about the risk of accidents and create a negative attitude toward drinking and driving. If enough people develop this new negative attitude toward drinking and driving, then a new social norm can create social pressure against engaging in this risky behavior. With a change in social norms, friends might take the keys away from a person who has been drinking and make plans for "designated drivers" when they plan to drink. Hopefully, these new attitudes and behavioral intentions result in less alcohol-related accidents. See Figure 5.13.

FIGURE 5.13   The Effects of Mass Media Campaigns on Injuries from Alcohol-Related Crashes—a Conceptual Framework

This framework can help you understand how mass media campaigns can reduce drinking and driving.

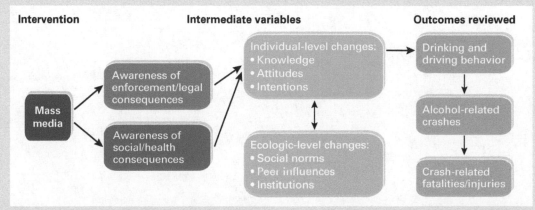

Source: Adapted from "Effectiveness of Mass Media Campaigns for Reducing Drinking and Driving and Alcohol-Involved Crashes: A Systematic Review," by R. W. Elder et al., 2004, *American Journal of Preventive Medicine, 27*(1), pp. 57–65. © 2004 American Journal of Preventive Medicine.

Are these campaigns effective? In a comprehensive review of the effectiveness of health-targeting mass media campaigns, Melanie Wakefield (2010) and her colleagues concluded there is strong evidence that anti-tobacco and road safety (safety belts, decreased drinking and driving) campaigns are effective. For example, car crashes caused by drinking and driving are estimated to have declined by 13% due to mass media campaigns (Elder et al., 2004). Campaigns targeting physical activity, nutrition, HIV infection prevention (condom use), and cervical and breast cancer screenings, were also found to be moderately successful (Wakefield et al., 2010). However, the evidence is weak or inconclusive for campaigns targeting alcohol use, skin cancer prevention, mental health awareness, interpersonal violence prevention, and child maltreatment prevention. For example, mass media campaigns targeting alcohol have been effective at increasing people's knowledge about the health effects of drinking, but they have not been effective at decreasing alcohol consumption (Young et al., 2018). Other research has found that alcohol awareness mass media campaigns were effective in changing implicit alcohol-related attitudes, but not explicit attitudes or intentions to drink alcohol (Glock et al., 2015).

What might make a mass media campaign effective at changing behaviors? Given what you have learned in this chapter, what would you recommend? Not surprisingly, research has identified some characteristics of effective public health campaigns that are consistent with the theories covered in this chapter.

You knew the risks when you decided to drive drunk.

People could get hurt ...

You could get arrested ...

You were wrong when you said it was no big deal.

(*"No Big Deal," by National Highway Traffic Safety Administration NHTSA.gov.)

- *Use of fear and emotion in campaigns.* Mass media campaigns that associate tobacco use with graphic images of health damage appear to be effective in anti-smoking campaigns (Wakefield et al., 2010).

- *Message delivery is target appropriate.* How the message is delivered appears to influence the effectiveness of the message. Furthermore, different audiences are likely to respond to different types of messages. For example, messages that are "heavy-handed" and appear to lecture adolescents about risky behaviors appear to be ineffective (Yeager et al., 2018). Instead, programs where the interventions allow adolescents to develop feelings of autonomy, social status, and respect are more effective because they satisfy adolescent desires for independence.

(*continues*)

(**Applications**, *continued*)

- *Peers are used as role models of desired behavior.* Research suggests that adolescents' behavior is often influenced by social norms and peer expectations (Blakemore, 2018). For example, in a public health study examining bullying behaviors in schools, researchers found conflict decreased by 30% when there was a student-led anti-conflict program (Paluck et al., 2016). As we noted earlier in this chapter, reference groups are important for developing attitudes, and this appears to be especially true during adolescence. This finding is also consistent with the Theory of Planned Behavior, where subjective norms play a role in guiding behavioral intentions.

- *Type of behavior change matters.* Campaigns that seek to prevent a new, undesirable behavior (e.g., persuading people to not start smoking) are more effective than campaigns that attempt to change an old behavior (e.g., stop smoking) or start a new behavior (e.g., exercising) (Jeong & Bae, 2018). In other words, it is more difficult to change people's existing behaviors (such as stop smoking or start exercising) than it is to reinforce current healthy behaviors.

- *Targeted behavior is one-time rather than repeated.* The campaigns that are most successful tend to target a one-time behavior (vaccines, preventive screenings) rather than requiring repeated behaviors (exercise, food choice) (Wakefield et al., 2010).

- *Coordination of mass media campaigns with targeted local programming.* While mass media campaigns can be effective in highlighting an issue, including local programming is crucial in ultimately obtaining the desired results. For example, mass campaigns highlighting the need for cancer screening produce little increases in actual screening unless there is a local community program that makes such screenings easily available (Wakefield et al., 2010). Local programming can help to reduce barriers to behavioral change.

- *Health-related products are distributed in conjunction with media messages.* Providing products that support the mass media message and behavioral implementation increase behavioral change (Robinson et al., 2014). For example, campaigns to increase condom use resulted in increased use by 1.5%, but a campaign plus a local condom distribution program increased use by 4%. Similarly, for smoking cessation, a promotion-only message increased calls to a quit line by 50%, but a message with a cigarette substitute increased calls by 100%. Availability of products might increase behavioral intentions, and the self-efficacy to engage in the healthy behavior.

- *Campaigns are more effective if they provoke conversations around healthy behavior.* Participating in conversations engages the central processing route of persuasion, which can result in greater attitude and behavioral change than does the peripheral route of persuasion (Jeong & Bae, 2018).

We end the chapter with our question of college binge drinking. Given what you have learned, what do you recommend? We encourage you to take your ideas to the administration on your campus. Use your newly acquired knowledge to make your campus a healthier place!

THE BIG PICTURE

Attitudes and persuasion are more than just textbook topics. With the information learned in this chapter, do you now have a better understanding of how your own attitudes guide your behavior and why some persuasion attempts are more effective than others? As attitude holders, we are sometimes active and at other times relatively passive in this process of attitude formation and change. One of the more important issues attitude researchers are now exploring involves the conditions under which explicit versus implicit attitudes predict behavior.

Regarding persuasion, when receiving persuasive messages, we either critically analyze the content or attend to incidental cues surrounding the message. Celebrity product endorsers and physically attractive spokespersons are there as peripheral cues to enhance your receptivity to their messages. Fast-talking and wisecracking salespersons also use persuasion strategies that have ties to chapter material. First, they hope that their humor grabs our attention and increases our liking for them. Second, they count on their rapid speech serving as a peripheral cue of their expertise, while simultaneously rendering us less able to fully comprehend what they actually say. And what about our own persuasion attempts? Do you first try to induce a good mood in those you hope to persuade, banking on their happiness lowering their resistance to what you have to say? Perhaps this is a mistake if your message is complex and in need of an audience ready to expend a great deal of cognitive effort. These examples illustrate the essential *message* of this chapter, which is that we are flexible social thinkers who rely on different cognitive strategies when evaluating information designed to shape and change our attitudes and behavior.

KEY TERMS

WEBSITES

Accessed through https://www.bvtlab.com/sop8

Websites for this chapter focus on attitudes and persuasion, including the use of consistency theories to increase retail sales and an analysis of propaganda.

Theories of Cognitive Consistency
This web page analyzes cognitive consistency theories and explores the question of whether cognitive consistency needs can be used to increase retail sales.

Association for Psychological Science
This web page maintained by the Association for Psychological Science contains articles on social influence.

Propaganda Analysis Home Page
This web page contains an analysis of common propaganda techniques, historical examples, and a bibliography of relevant publications.

Chapter 6

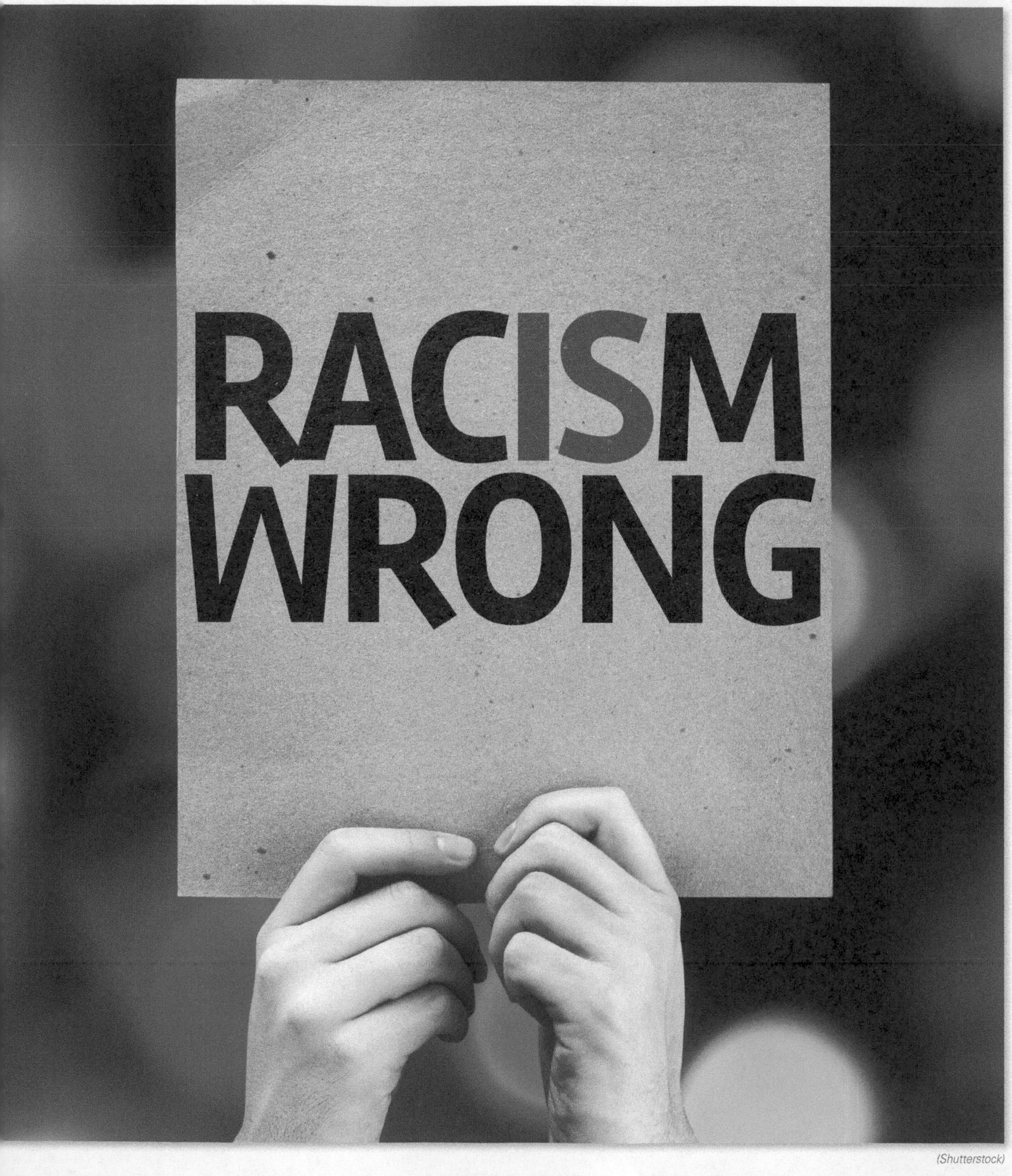

(Shutterstock)

Stereotyping, Prejudice, and Discrimination

FOCUS QUESTIONS

1. What purpose does stereotyping serve as a cognitive process for humans?

2. What is modern racism?

3. Why do social scientists contend that sexism has both a hostile side and a benevolent side?

4. Can prejudice be reduced, or is it so ingrained in our species' evolutionary heritage that it is impossible to reduce?

CHAPTER OUTLINE

Applications: How can our schools be positive institutions of social change?

> **Preview** . . . Over the years, prejudice research has examined both the social conditions that support and weaken intergroup intolerance, and the impact that such intolerance has on those who are its targets. How have social psychologists applied this knowledge to promote diversity acceptance and academic achievement in schools?

The Big Picture

Key Terms

Websites

Introduction

"Give me your tired, your poor,
Your huddled masses yearning to breathe free,
The wretched refuse of your teeming shore.
Send these, the homeless, temptest-tost to me,
I lift my lamp beside the golden door!"

This passage from Emma Lazarus's sonnet, "The New Colossus" (1883), is inscribed on a tablet within the pedestal of the Statue of Liberty that stands on Ellis Island in New York Harbor, greeting immigrants to the United States of America. Despite the welcoming sentiment expressed in this famous poem, immigrants are not always treated fairly when they arrive on this country's shores. For example, during the 1800s and early 20th century, Jews and Italian immigrants were perceived as non-Anglo and nonwhite; as such, they experienced extreme prejudice, discrimination, and even violence. Next to African Americans, Italian Americans were the second most likely ethnic group to be lynched during this time period.

(Courtesy of Bain News Service, George Grantham Bain Collection, Library of Congress, circa 1900)

(Mikeledray / Shutterstock)

Anti-immigrant sentiment is not new to the United States and is fed by the often-false belief that immigrants drain a country's resources. How do such beliefs lead to prejudice and discrimination?

Anti-immigrant bias in this country persists in the 21st century, especially toward people from Latin America and those of Arab descent. In January 2017, President Trump signed a controversial executive order banning refugees from seven predominantly Muslim nations. Similarly, a central Trump campaign pledge was building a wall between the United States and Mexico to stop undocumented immigrants from Central and South America. Survey research indicates that Americans' support for these immigration policies is associated with attitudes that dehumanize Muslim and Mexican immigrants (Kteily & Bruneau, 2017a). Such prejudice can be fueled by a number of factors, including a fear by Americans that these newcomers will take their jobs, threaten their safety, deplete social welfare services, and destroy the American way of life by refusing to adopt mainstream cultural values and practices.

Hostility toward immigrants is not limited to America's shores. In 2014, Switzerland passed a controversial anti-immigration law that set strict quotas on immigration. German Chancellor Angela Merkel declared the death of multiculturalism in her country 3 years earlier, stating that it had been foolhardy to think that Germans and foreign workers could "live happily side-by-side." Similar anti-immigration sentiments are expressed in other European countries, such as Great Britain, France, Austria, Italy, Sweden, Holland, Hungary, and Spain. The factors underlying the anti-immigrant tide in these countries are similar to those in America: fear of job loss, fear of crime, fear of social welfare depletion, and fear of national identity loss.

In all these countries, resentment toward immigrants has been strongly fueled by economic problems and unemployment. Yet Dartmouth business professor Vijay Govindarajan (2010) contends that the reasoning underlying the belief that foreign immigrants take jobs from a country's existing citizens is often both flawed and shortsighted. Govindarajan states that many immigrants have skills and capabilities that are unique and not readily available among most current residents of a country. Further, these talented immigrants regularly create innovation that builds new industries and thereby create more jobs in their host countries. For example, in the United States, Govindarajan notes that the founders or cofounders of the following high-tech companies were all recent immigrants: Google, Sun Microsystems, eBay, Juniper Networks, YouTube, Yahoo!, and Intel. These companies—in which highly skilled immigrants played a lead role—have generated hundreds of thousands of new jobs for Americans. Following the announcement of the 2017 US travel ban, nearly 100 technology firms petitioned the federal

When you think of a recent immigrant to this country what is the most typical image that comes to mind for you? Mexican migrant workers and Chinese high-tech entrepreneurs often elicit very different stereotypes among Americans, but both immigrant groups are targets of prejudice and discrimination.

court to set aside President Trump's ban based on their claim that it would hurt their businesses (Chappell, 2017). Despite evidence that immigrants can strengthen and help to rejuvenate their host countries, hostility toward these people persists around the world; for many citizens, immigrants are "those people" who threaten "us" and "our way of life."

Although government polices often reflect and contribute to anti-immigration attitudes, they can also foster acceptance of those who seek entry into the country. For example, research tracking Canadian public opinion over 18 months found that a pro-immigration shift in Canadian national policy was followed by an increase in positive attitudes about immigrants and refugees (Gaucher et al., 2018). This finding highlights the power of social norms and the central role of leaders in shaping people's attitudes toward immigrants.

In this chapter, we examine the social psychology of intergroup bias and intolerance—including the type of prejudice and discrimination experienced by immigrants around the world—as well as intergroup intolerance based on other social identities. We also analyze the causes of prejudice and the consequences that bias and intolerance have for those who are targeted. Finally, we explore research and theory concerning possible remedies.

The three most important social psychological terms associated with the bias and conflict that occur between members of different social groups are *stereotyping*, *prejudice*, and *discrimination*. These three terms are closely tied yet still distinct. Very few of us view these terms positively and we generally go to great lengths to avoid being accused of stereotyping, being prejudiced, or discriminating against others. Yet what is prejudice? How is prejudice different from discrimination? Is stereotyping sometimes a good thing, or is it always wrong? Can you be prejudiced without knowing it? What causes prejudice, both at the intergroup level and at the interpersonal level? Can you fix a prejudiced mind? These and other important questions will be addressed in this chapter.

6.1 What Are the Components of Intergroup Conflict?

Chapter 5 examined how attitudes and beliefs are related to behavior. On the most basic level, stereotypes involve beliefs about specific groups, prejudice involves attitudes toward those groups, and discrimination involves actions toward those groups.

6.1a Stereotypes Are Beliefs About Social Groups.

As you recall from Chapter 4 (section 4.1a), we naturally and automatically develop social categories based on people's shared characteristics. Once categorized, we begin to perceive people differently. Often the nature of these different perceptions is determined by whether the individuals are ingroup members or outgroup members (Deaux, 1996). An **ingroup** is a group to which we belong and that forms a part of our social identity, while an **outgroup** is any group with which we do not share membership.

The Purpose of Stereotyping

Stereotypes are beliefs about the personalities, abilities, and motives of a social group that don't allow for individual variation. They are a type of *schema*, which is an organized structure of knowledge about a stimulus that is built up from experience and contains causal relations (see Chapter 4, section 4.1b for a review). Stereotyping can involve both deliberate and automatic cognitive processing (Wegener et al., 2006). For example, upon seeing an older adult you might automatically assume that she is frail and forgetful—this is an implicit stereotype. In contrast, if a researcher asked you if you believed "older adults are frail" your answer would reflect an explicit stereotype, or your consciously held beliefs about the group.

Like other types of schemas, stereotypes significantly influence how we process and interpret social information—even when we are not consciously aware that they have been activated from memory (Kiefer & Sekaquaptewa, 2007). Once a stereotype is activated, we tend to see people within that social category as possessing the traits or characteristics associated with the stereotyped group. In the example of the older adult, if the stereotype of weak and forgetful is activated, we might also assume a whole host of other characteristics (such as senile, childlike, and hard of hearing) and modify our behavior toward that individual, perhaps by talking slower, louder, and using simpler sentences that reflect our stereotypes.

In studying stereotyping, social psychologists have pondered what purpose it serves as a cognitive process. The quickness of stereotyped thinking is one of its most apparent qualities: Being *fast*, it gives us a basis for immediate action in uncertain circumstances. In a very real sense, stereotypes are "shortcuts to thinking" that provide us with rich and distinctive information about individuals we do not personally know. Not only do stereotypes provide us with a fast basis for social judgments, but stereotyping also appears to "free up" cognition for other tasks (Macrae et al., 1994). Thus, a second function of stereotyped thinking is that it is *efficient* and allows people to cognitively engage in other necessary activities. Daniel Gilbert (1989) suggests that this resource-preserving effect has an evolutionary basis. That is, expending cognitive resources as cheaply as possible enables perceivers to redirect their energy to more pressing concerns. The speed and efficiency of stereotype-based information apparently motivates people to rely on it over the more time-consuming method of getting to know a person as an individual.

ingroup
A group to which we belong and that forms a part of our social identity

outgroup
Any group with which we do not share membership

stereotypes
Beliefs about the personalities, abilities, and motives of a social group that don't allow for individual variation

"Labels are devices for saving talkative persons the trouble of thinking."

—John Morley, English statesman and author, 1838–1923

Development and Maintenance of Stereotypes

How many times have you heard a woman say, "Well, you know men . . . They're all alike and they all want the same thing!"? Likewise, how often have you heard men describing women in similar terms? How do such "all alike" social beliefs develop and how are they maintained, despite contradictory evidence?

Outgroup Homogeneity Effect   The tendency to perceive outgroup members as being more similar to one another than members of one's ingroup is known as the **outgroup homogeneity effect**, and it is found in children as well as in adults (Guinote et al., 2007). Research has shown that merely assigning people to different social groups can create this effect, but it is stronger when directed toward well-established groups (Boldry et al., 2007) and groups of lower social status (Rubin & Badea, 2012). Furthermore, viewing outgroup members as homogeneous is associated with more negative attitudes towards all members of that group (Brauer & Er-rafiy, 2011). Although we tend to perceive outgroups as being fairly uniform, ingroup members are generally viewed as relatively *distinct* and *complex*. For example, young adults tend to perceive others of their age as having more complex personalities than

Do you think these middle-aged adults are likely to believe that they have more distinct and complex personalities than younger aged adults? If so, what social psychological principal is operating here?

the elderly, whereas older adults hold exactly opposite beliefs (Brewer & Lui, 1984). Brain-imaging studies indicate that this tendency to notice differences among ingroup members while perceiving outgroup members as being more alike is due to the fact that we engage in less thorough neural processing when attending to outgroup members (Ambady & Adams, 2011; Van Bavel & Cunningham, 2012). In other words, we invest less cognitive effort when attending to outgroup members compared to ingroup members, relying more on group-based stereotypes when making social judgments (Amodio, 2011).

Bernadette Park and Charles Judd found that, on college campuses, sorority members, business majors, and engineering students all tended to perceive students in other campus social groups (those in other sororities or those with other majors) as more alike than those in their ingroup (Judd et al., 1991; Park & Rothbart, 1982). Perhaps you have even witnessed some of your own college professors making homogeneous assumptions about certain minority groups by asking minority students in the classroom to represent their group's attitudes and beliefs. Do you think those students—perhaps you were one of those students—might have felt uncomfortable and even stigmatized by being singled out?

Illusory Correlations   Another way in which stereotypes can develop is through the power of an **illusory correlation**, which is the belief that two variables are associated with each other when no actual association exists. At least two factors can produce an illusory correlation. The first is *associative meaning*, in which two variables are associated with each other because of the perceiver's preexisting beliefs. One of the important reasons the activation of stereotypes often results in fast social judgments is that filtering social perceptions through a stereotype causes people to ignore information that is relevant but inconsistent with the stereotype (Dijksterhuis & Knippenberg, 1996). For example, Harriet might believe that Jews are more deceptive in their business dealings than non-Jews. When asked why she holds this belief, Harriet might recall a set of pertinent cases of either business deception or honesty from her own personal experiences or from the experiences of others. In recalling these instances, Harriet selectively

outgroup homogeneity effect
Perception of outgroup members as being more similar to one another than are members of one's ingroup

illusory correlation
The belief that two variables are associated with each other when in fact there is little or no actual association

remembers those few cases that conform to her stereotype of Jews, but she forgets or explains away all those that clash with it. Based on this selective recall of past cases, Harriet concludes that there is an association between Jews and deception, even though the correlation is no greater than it is for non-Jews. Numerous studies have found that people's preexisting attitudes and beliefs can predispose them to perceive associations that are truly illusory (Berndsen et al., 2002). Once the stereotype is activated, the person engages in biased processing of social information by attending to information consistent with the stereotype and ignoring contradictory information.

A second factor contributing to the development of illusory correlations is *shared distinctiveness*, in which two variables are associated because they share some unusual feature (Risen et al., 2007). According to this view, Harriet might have developed an illusory correlation about Jews and dishonesty because both the minority group and the unfavorable trait are "infrequent" or "distinct" variables in the population. These two distinct variables are more likely associated in Harriet's memory simply because of their shared distinctiveness.

In the classic experiment demonstrating this effect, David Hamilton and Robert Gifford (1976) asked participants to read information about people from two different groups, "Group A" and "Group B." Twice as much information was provided about Group A, making Group B the smaller or "minority group" in the study. In addition, twice as much of the information given about both groups involved desirable behaviors rather than undesirable actions. Desirable information included statements such as, "John, a member of Group A, visited a sick friend in the hospital." An example of an undesirable statement was, "Bob, a member of Group B, dropped litter in the subway station." Even though there was no correlation between group membership and the proportion of positive and negative information, participants perceived a correlation.

As Figure 6.1 shows, participants overestimated the frequency with which Group B, the "minority group," behaved undesirably. In this study, the members of the "minority group" (who were described only half as much as the "majority group") and the undesirable actions (which occurred only half as often as the desirable behaviors) were both distinctive. This shared distinctiveness resulted in their illusory correlation, a finding replicated in later studies (Mullen & Johnson, 1995). Together, these studies indicate that although stereotyping may be beneficial because it allows us to redirect our energies to other pressing cognitive activities, the cost appears to be that we run the risk of making faulty social judgments about whomever we stereotype. Such biased information processing often occurs unconsciously (Payne et al., 2004).

subtyping

A cognitive process in which people perceive an individual who doesn't fit their stereotype as being an exception to the rule and they create a separate subcategory of the stereotype for that individual

Subtyping   Consider again cultural stereotypes about older adults: they are often stereotyped as being socially withdrawn and senile. However, everyone has encountered older adults who are socially outgoing and mentally sharp. Why do these individuals rarely change our generally negative stereotypes about the elderly? The simple fact is that, once developed, stereotypes are often maintained through **subtyping**, a cognitive process in which we perceive an individual who doesn't fit our stereotype as being an exception to the rule and we create a separate subcategory of the stereotype for that individual. Doing so allows us to maintain our overall group stereotype (Kunda & Oleson, 1995; Richards & Hewstone, 2001). Research confirms that socially outgoing and mentally sharp older adults are frequently subtyped by young adults as "golden agers" (sociable and capable) who are "exceptions to the rule" of the overall negative elderly

(Shutterstock)

Within our society, there are many different positive and negative stereotypes associated with various groups. For example, older adults are often stereotyped as weak and sickly (a negative stereotype) but wise and venerable (a positive stereotype). Are these positive stereotypes about older adults harmful?

stereotype (Hummert, 2015). Not surprisingly, as people get older and have more experiences with aging, they also show more complexity in their stereotyping of older people and have increasingly more subtypes (such as "activist" and "mildly impaired") about the elderly.

FIGURE 6.1 **Illusory Correlations and the Persistence of Stereotypes**

In Hamilton and Gifford's (1976) study of illusory correlations, participants read sentences in which a person from Group A or Group B was associated with either a desirable or an undesirable behavior. Both groups were described with the same proportion of desirable and undesirable behaviors, but only half of the provided information was about Group B members, making them the "minority group." Participants later overestimated the number of undesirable behaviors in the minority group (Group B), suggesting that people tend to perceive an illusory correlation between variables that stand out because they are unusual or deviant.

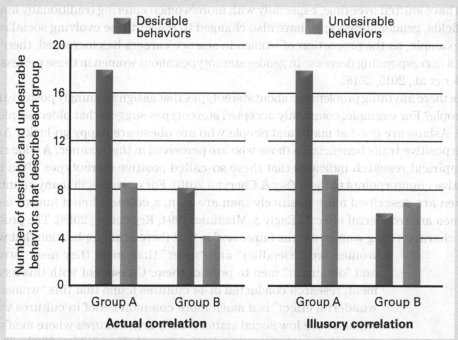

Data source: "Illusory Correlation in Interpersonal Perception: A Cognitive Basis of Stereotypic Judgments," by D. L. Hamilton and R. K. Gifford, 1976, *Journal of Experimental Social Psychology, 12*(4), pp. 392–407.

Stereotype Content: Accurate and Always Harmful?

Although research has traditionally focused on the inaccuracy of stereotypes, Lee Jussim and his coworkers (2015) contend that their review of studies examining stereotype accuracy suggests that it is false to characterize stereotypes as inherently inaccurate. Consider for example gender: men and women are stereotyped as being very different on numerous cognitive skills, personality traits, and social behaviors. On average, women do tend to think and behave in ways reflecting a higher care-focused moral orientation than do men, d = −.28 (Hyde, 2005). In contrast, men are more likely to engage in more physically aggressive behaviors than women (meta effect size d ranges from .33 to .84). Yet, across the hundreds of studies that have compared men and women on a wide variety of traits and behaviors, 78% of these comparisons find effect sizes indicating either no differences or only small differences. Indeed, there is more variation within a gender than there is between women and men. What this means is that our stereotypes about gender are exaggerations of the differences between the two sexes (Ellemers, 2018).

In Chapter 4, (section 4.3b) we reviewed Social Role Theory (Eagly 1987, 1996), which argues that men's and women's different social roles in society have resulted in different perceptions of their behaviors and traits. For example, women are more likely to work in occupations that involve nurturing traits, such as being a teacher, nurse, or day care provider. Likewise, men have historically been more likely to work in occupations involving assertive traits such as being a physician, manager, or police officer. Stereotypes are thought to have some degree of accuracy in describing social groups in society, because they are derived from people's observations of these different social roles (Keoning & Eagly, 2014). Yet people tend to generalize from these observed behaviors and traits to the individual group members' often diverse personalities, which can lead to mistaken perceptions. Thus, stereotyping reflects an overgeneralization and doesn't allow for individual variation. Interestingly, as women and men's occupational roles have shifted over time, especially with more women entering traditionally masculine fields, gender stereotypes have also changed to reflect these evolving social roles. For example, as the proportion of women in science careers has increased, there has been a corresponding decrease in gender stereotypes about women in these professions (Miller et al., 2015, 2018).

Is there anything problematic about stereotypes that assign seemingly positive traits to people? For example, commonly accepted stereotypes suggest that older people are wise, Asians are good at math, and people who are obese are happy-go-lucky. Aren't these positive traits beneficial to those who are perceived in this manner? A wide range of empirical research indicates that these so-called positive stereotypes often have negative counterpoints to them (Siy & Cheryan 2016). For example, in many countries, women are described more positively than are men, a cultural belief known as the "women are wonderful effect" (Eagly & Mladinic, 1994; Krys et al., 2018). The problem with characterizing women as "the fairer sex" is that there is an implication that while women are "friendlier" and "nicer" than men, they need "strong" and "dominant" men to protect them. Consistent with this assessment, research conducted in 44 cultures found that this "women are wonderful effect" is a much more common belief in cultures where women have low social status than it is in cultures where men's and women's social status is relatively equal (Kay & Jost, 2003). This is just one example of how seemingly positive stereotypes can be used to justify societal inequality.

Stereotypes are used more often when we first meet people about whom we know very little. As we get to know a person, we tend to rely less on our stereotypes and more on what we have learned about them as individuals (Jussim et al., 2015). In many ways, stereotypes are like any other heuristic; they are mental shortcuts we use to make quick judgments when we lack cognitive resources or have little motivation to be accurate in our impressions. However, like all heuristics, they can easily lead to inaccurate assessments.

Media commentators in the United States often use the terms "red" and "blue" to refer to perceived cultural differences in America and American politics. Why might the increased use of these terms increase prejudice and conflict between political groups in America?

6.1b Prejudice Is an Attitude and Discrimination Is an Action.

The type of shared social beliefs that some Americans have toward immigrants can create a psychological climate that leads to prejudice and discrimination (Jackson, 2011). Yet what is prejudice, and how is it different from discrimination?

Prejudice is attitudes toward members of specific groups that directly or indirectly suggest they deserve an inferior social status (Glick & Hilt, 2000). Prejudice can be either explicit or implicit. **Explicit prejudice** involves consciously held prejudicial attitudes toward a group, while **implicit prejudice** involves unconsciously held prejudicial attitudes. Explicit prejudice is best assessed by directly asking people about their attitudes toward a certain group of people (Axt, 2018), whereas implicit prejudice is assessed using various techniques, including the Implicit Association Test and brain-imaging technology (see Chapter 2, section 2.2b).

> "The whole world is festering with unhappy souls: The French hate the Germans, the Germans hate the Poles; Italians hate Yugoslavs, South Africans hate the Dutch; And I don't like anybody very much!"
>
> —Sheldon Harnick, American songwriter, born 1924
> from *Merry Little Minuet*[1]

Just as people can have differing explicit and implicit attitudes toward something (see Chapter 5, section 5.1b), they can also have differing explicit and implicit prejudices toward a social group (Devine, 1989; Devine et al., 1991). People with low explicit prejudice but high implicit prejudice toward a specific group may not be aware of their negative bias, but when they do realize that they have this implicit prejudice it may cause them to experience guilt and even shame. For example, you might strongly endorse egalitarian values and think that you do not harbor any anti-immigrant or racist attitudes. However, upon meeting a new immigrant to your city, you may have an automatic negative reaction to the person, reflecting your implicit prejudice. Such sudden awareness of a previously unnoticed prejudice may well motivate you to try to control your implicit prejudice, perhaps by reaffirming your egalitarian beliefs. Individuals who respond to their implicit prejudices in this manner are referred to as having *high internal motivation to control prejudice.* Yet it is also possible that you may not experience any guilt when an implicit bias is activated, and therefore, you are unlikely to be motivated to control or modify your initial reactions. Those who respond to their implicit prejudices in this manner are referred to as having *low internal motivation to control prejudice.*

What is the difference between implicit stereotyping and implicit prejudice?

Implicit prejudice appears to have neurological underpinnings, meaning that it activates specific brain regions associated with threat and fear reactions. In studying implicit racial prejudice, researchers often first use the Implicit Association Test to identify white individuals with high implicit yet low explicit prejudice toward African Americans and then use functional magnetic resonance imaging to scan their brains as they are shown photos of familiar and unfamiliar black and white faces (Amodio & Lieberman, 2009). As depicted in Figure 6.2, these studies find that unfamiliar black faces are much more likely than unfamiliar white faces to activate the *amygdala* in both the right and left cerebral hemispheres and the *anterior cingulate* in the frontal lobes. These brain structures are involved in arousal and emotional learning and play a crucial role in detecting threat and triggering fear (Phelps et al., 2000). No heightened amygdala and cingulate activity occurs when these high implicit/low explicit prejudiced participants view *familiar* black faces. These findings suggest that, despite not consciously reporting any negative racial attitudes toward African Americans, implicitly prejudiced whites perhaps unknowingly experience heightened arousal associated with some level of anxiety and negativity toward blacks. Similar findings have also been obtained from African American students when they viewed photos of white faces (Hart et al., 2000).

prejudice
Attitudes toward members of specific groups that directly or indirectly suggest they deserve an inferior social status

explicit prejudice
Prejudicial attitudes that are consciously held, even if they are not publicly expressed

implicit prejudice
Unconsciously held prejudicial attitudes

---

1 From "Merry Little Minuet," words and music by Sheldon Harnick. Copyright© 1958 by Alley Music Corp. and Bug Music-Trio Music Company. Copyright Renewed; International Copyright Secured. All Rights Reserved. Used by Permission: Reprinted by Permission of Hal Leonard LLC. Copyright©1958 Williamson Music. All Rights Reserved. Used by Permission of Mayerling Productions Ltd., administered by Williamson Music, A Division of Rodgers & Hammerstein: An Imagem Company.

FIGURE 6.2 Measuring Implicit Prejudice Using Brain Scans

When white participants with high scores on an implicit measure of racial prejudice (but low explicit prejudice scores) were shown photos of familiar and unfamiliar black and white faces, the unfamiliar black faces were much more likely than the unfamiliar white faces to activate brain regions associated with arousal and emotional responses and the brain's "alarm" system for threat, pain, and danger (Phelps et al., 2000). What implications does the existence of implicit prejudice have for attempts at reducing intergroup hostility?

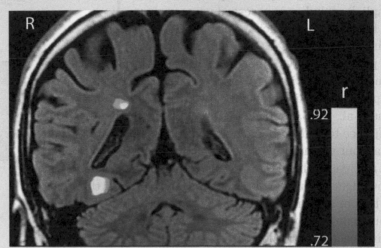

Source: Adapted from "Performance on Indirect Measures of Race Evaluation Predicts Amygdala Activation," by E. A. Phelps et al., 2000, *Journal of Cognitive Neuroscience, 12*(5), pp. 729–738, with permission by the Massachusetts Institute of Technology.

In general, research suggests that implicit prejudice is more stable, enduring, and difficult to change than explicit prejudice (Dasgupta & Greenwald, 2001). Fortunately, some research suggests that, although it is not easy, implicit prejudices can be modified with awareness, motivation, and effort (Forscher et al., 2017). Later in this chapter we will further explore ways in which both stereotypes and prejudices can be modified.

As we well know, attitudes often trigger predictable behavior, and the same is true for the various denigrating attitudes people develop for specific groups. **Discrimination** is a negative and/or patronizing action toward members of specific groups. Disliking, disrespecting, or resenting people because of their group membership are examples of prejudice. Physically attacking them or failing to hire them for jobs because of their group membership are examples of discrimination. A substantial body of research indicates that people who are motivated to express their ethnic prejudices are also more likely to support policies and political candidates that target minority groups and engage in discriminatory behaviors, such as hate crimes and hate speech (Forscher et al., 2015). Yet, as we learned in Chapter 5, behavior does not always follow attitude. Similarly, discrimination is not an inevitable result of prejudice. For example, students with strong antigay attitudes might not act on their prejudice if the college campus climate strongly prohibits such expressions or is supportive of gay rights. In this case, the subjective norm (see Chapter 5, section 5.3d) significantly shapes students' behavior on campus. It is also true that people who are not prejudiced may still engage in *institutional discrimination* by carrying out the discriminatory guidelines of institutions. For instance, due to state immigration laws, police officers in Georgia can demand at traffic stops that people of Hispanic descent show documentation of their citizenship, while not making similar demands of drivers whose facial features fit the European

discrimination
Negative and/or patronizing action toward members of specific groups

American prototype. In enforcing this law, officers with no anti-immigrant biases are still practicing discrimination.

6.1c There Are Three Basic Forms of Prejudice.

Peter Glick and Susan Fiske (2001b) propose that there are three basic forms of prejudice that account for the different ways in which groups are perceived and treated. According to their **Stereotype Content Model**, which form of prejudice is directed toward a particular group is determined by two dimensions: perceptions of the group's warmth and competence. Recall, warmth and competence are also two primary dimensions along which we form impressions of individuals (Chapter 4, section 4.3d).

Warmth refers to the extent to which the target group is perceived as being trustworthy and friendly (Fiske, 2018; Glick & Fiske, 2001). Groups who are seen as cooperative with mainstream society are perceived as high in warmth while groups who are perceived as competing with mainstream society are perceived as low in warmth. Competence refers to the extent to which the target group is perceived as capable and their degree of assertiveness. Groups having high social status are generally viewed as possessing high competence, while groups low in social status are perceived as possessing low competence. The value of the Stereotype Content Model is that it highlights how our stereotypes about groups along these two dimensions can translate into emotional reactions that create different forms of prejudice (Fiske, 2018).

As depicted in Table 6.1, groups perceived as being relatively low in both warmth and competence are likely to become targets of *contemptuous prejudice*, characterized by exclusively negative attitudes, such as disrespect, disgust, resentment, and hostility. Contemptuous prejudice is most people's prototype for prejudice because it is characterized by uniformly negative emotions and attitudes; it most closely fits the traditional definition of prejudice (Cottrell & Neuberg, 2005). The blatant prejudices often expressed toward poor whites, poor blacks, homeless people, obese individuals, welfare recipients, lesbians and gay men, and low-skilled immigrants are examples of contemptuous prejudice.

Stereotype Content Model

A theory that the form of prejudice directed toward a particular group is determined by perceptions of the group's warmth and competence

TABLE 6.1	Stereotype Content Model and 3 Forms of Prejudice	
	High Warmth	**Low Warmth**
High Competence	*No Prejudice*	*Envious Prejudice*
Negative Emotions	None	Envy, fear, resentment, hostility
Positive Emotions	Respect, admiration, affection	Grudging admiration of abilities
Behavior	Defer	Avoid, exclude, segregate, exterminate
Common Targets	Dominant groups perceived as "contributors": middle-class people, white people, Christians, heterosexuals	Jews, Asians, feminists, rich people, female professionals, black professionals
Low Competence	*Paternalistic Prejudice*	*Contemptuous Prejudice*
Negative Emotions	Disrespect, condescension	Disrespect, disgust, resentment, hostility
Positive Emotions	Patronizing affection, pity, liking	None
Behavior	Personal intimacy, but role segregation	Avoid, exclude, segregate, exterminate
Common Targets	The elderly, the disabled, traditional women, adolescents and young adults	Poor people, homeless people, obese persons, welfare recipients, Muslims, lesbians and gay men, illegal immigrants

Adapted from "Sacrificial Lambs Dressed in Wolves' Clothing: Envious Prejudice, Ideology, and the Scapegoating of Jews," by P. Glick, 2002, in *Understanding Genocide: The Social Psychology of the Holocaust*, edited by L. S. Newman & R. Erber, Oxford: Oxford University Press, pp. 113–142.

In contrast to this easily recognized intergroup hostility, the other two forms of prejudice each represent a type of *ambivalent prejudice* because they consist of both negative and positive attitudes. For instance, groups perceived as low in warmth yet high in competence are targeted with *envious prejudice*, in which feelings of resentment and hostility are mixed with fear and envy. These groups are resented for their status. So-called model minorities—such as Jews and Asian Americans—are often targets of envious prejudice (Lin et al., 2005). Similarly, the mixed evaluations of feminists, black professionals, and people in the upper classes of society are often rooted in envious prejudice.

Finally, groups perceived as high in warmth but low in competence are targets of *paternalistic prejudice*. The ambivalent attitudes expressed in this form of prejudice involve patronizing affection and pity mixed with condescension and disrespect. The elderly, the disabled, housewives, women in general, and adolescents and young adults are often the targets of paternalistic prejudice.

Section Summary

- Stereotypes are cognitive schemas about groups and can be explicit or implicitly held.

- Two qualities of stereotyped thinking are that it is fast and efficient, but often faulty.

- The outgroup homogeneity effect is the tendency to perceive people in outgroups as more similar to one another than ingroup members.

- Stereotypes are maintained through illusory correlations and subtyping.

- Prejudice involves attitudes toward members of specific groups that directly or indirectly suggest that they deserve an inferior social status.

- Explicit prejudices are consciously held, while implicit prejudices are unconsciously held.

- Discrimination is a negative and often patronizing action toward members of specific groups.

- The form of prejudice (envious, contemptuous, or paternalistic prejudice) directed toward a group is determined by their perceived warmth and competence.

6.2   Who Are Common Targets of Intolerance?

In all societies, some social groups are valued while other groups are stigmatized. A **stigma** is an attribute that discredits a person or a social group in the eyes of others (Shana & van Laar, 2006; Ullah, 2011). Stigmatized persons are not simply different from others; society also judges their difference to be discrediting. Individual members of society may vary in how they personally respond to a particular stigma, but everyone shares the knowledge that the characteristic in question—the "mark"—is negatively valued; having it "spoils" the person's full humanity (Major & O'Brien, 2005). Being marginalized because of a stigma induces feelings of threat and a loss of social power; the stigma engulfs the person's entire identity (Oswald, 2007). It becomes a central trait for that person (see Chapter 4, section 4.3e), shaping the meaning of all other traits.

stigma
An attribute that serves to discredit a person in the eyes of others

In his classic monograph, *Stigma: Notes on the Management of Spoiled Identity,* Erving Goffman (1963) distinguished the following three different categories of stigma:

1. *Tribal identities*: race, sex, ethnicity, religion, and national origin

2. *Blemishes of individual character:* mental disorders, addictions, homosexuality, and criminality

3. *Abominations of the body:* physical deformities, physical disabilities, diseases, and obesity

The concept of stigma is related to prejudice and discrimination because people who are stigmatized are almost always the targets of intolerance, which can be either subtle or blatant. While anyone can be stereotyped, research indicates that members of stigmatized groups are more frequently stereotyped than members of nonstigmatized groups (Adams et al., 2006). In one such investigation, Jonathan Cook and his colleagues (2011) conducted a 7-day experiential-sampling study in which they measured stigmatized and nonstigmatized individuals' reactions to being stereotyped while they engaged in normal daily activities. Some of the participants were members of stigmatized groups in American society (African Americans, gay men, and lesbians), while other participants were members of the dominant group in the country (heterosexual Caucasian

Do you have an attribute that discredits you in the eyes of others? Members of stigmatized groups face social challenges that nonstigmatized individuals do not encounter.

Americans). As expected, participants who were members of stigmatized groups reported more frequent stereotyping than did nonstigmatized participants. For members of all groups, being stereotyped was associated with feeling more socially anxious and inhibited in "being oneself," as well as feeling low in social power. In essence, rather than feeling in control of the situation, stereotyped people felt like they were controlled by the situation and by the stereotyped role they had been cast into.

Although many societal groups fall into one of the stigma categories, let us examine examples from three different categories that are of particular importance in contemporary society. First we will examine intergroup intolerance associated with race-based and sex-based tribal identity stigmas, then we will analyze intolerance based on perceived blemishes of individual character (homosexuality/bisexuality and mental illness) and perceived abominations of the body (obesity).

6.2a Race-Based Appearance Cues Can Trigger Discrimination

Prejudice and discrimination based on a person's racial background is called **racism**. Blatantly negative stereotypes based on a belief in the racial superiority of one's own group coupled with open opposition to racial equality characterize *old-fashioned racism*. Old-fashioned racism involves contemptuous prejudice and often leads to movement against the despised group, including physical violence, hate crimes, and hate speech.

Although old-fashioned racism is far less common in contemporary American society than a generation ago, racial stereotypes continue to provide fuel for volatile expressions of prejudice and discrimination. Due to socialization about what constitutes different racial categories, a person's skin color and facial characteristics (such as the shape of the eyes, nose, and lips) are physical features that often automatically activate racial stereotypes among people of many different ethnicities in the United States—and in a number of countries around the world (Maddox, 2004). When such race-based stereotype activation occurs, people generally associate more positive personality traits

racism
Prejudice and discrimination based on a person's racial background

The mistaken shooting of Amadou Diallo by New York City police officers is widely considered an example of the sometimes deadly consequences of racial profiling. Was his killing caused by implicit racism?

(AP Photo/Adam Nadell)

with those with lighter skin and Eurocentric facial features than with those with darker skin and Afrocentric features (Blair et al., 2002; Harvey et al., 2017). Consequently, African Americans with more "Afrocentric" facial features (features typically associated with African Americans) are more likely to experience race-based negative stereotypes, prejudice, and discrimination (Hunter, 1998; Telles & Marguia, 1990). For example, Jennifer Eberhardt and her colleagues (2006) found that black defendants in murder cases were more likely to receive the death sentence if they had stereotypically Afrocentric features than those with less Afrocentric features. These findings suggest that physical appearance serves as a cue to activate people's race-based stereotypes, and thereby, influence their social judgments and actions.

The negative effects of automatically stereotyping people with Afrocentric facial features can have real-world, life-and-death consequences. For example, around midnight on February 4, 1999, four white New York City police officers were looking for a rape suspect in the Bronx when they saw 22-year-old Amadou Diallo—a West African immigrant—standing in his apartment building doorway. Stopping their car, they told Diallo to "freeze," but then they saw him reach into his pants pocket. The officers drew their pistols and within 5 seconds had fired a total of 41 shots at the unarmed Diallo, 19 of which found their mark, killing him. The object that Diallo was reaching for was his wallet, which contained his ID. The officers were tried for murder but were acquitted of all charges on the grounds that, although they made a mistake, their actions were justified (Fritsch, 2000). Similar events continue to occur across the United States annually, with court verdicts often in favor of police officers' fatal actions.

Motivated by this high-profile case and the resulting charges of racism and racial profiling by law enforcement officers, Keith Payne (2001) conducted a series of studies to understand how the mere presence of a black face could cause people to misidentify harmless objects as weapons. In his research, Payne showed pictures of guns or tools to white participants and asked them to classify the objects as quickly as possible. Just prior to seeing an object, participants were primed by a brief presentation of either a white or a black face (see Figure 6.3). Results indicated that when a black face immediately preceded a tool, the tool was significantly more likely to be mistaken for a handgun compared with conditions in which the same tool was preceded with a white face. This stereotype difference emerged mainly when participants were required to react quickly, a condition that mimics the time pressure involved in real-world police confrontations like the Diallo shooting.

Subsequent studies have replicated and extended these findings to other ethnic minority groups, such as Muslims/Arabs and Turkish individuals (Essien et al., 2017). If a suspected criminal is an ethnic minority (versus white), people generally require less certainty that he is, in fact, holding a gun before they decide to shoot him (Greenwald et al., 2003; Ito et al., 2006; Essien et al., 2017; Mekawi & Bresin, 2015). This race-based bias has been found in both African American and white participants (Correll et al., 2002).

The rates of false shootings of black targets (versus white targets) is higher in states with permissive gun laws and in ethnically diverse cities where there is a larger proportion of nonwhite people (Mekawi & Bresin, 2015). Further, in different regions of the United States, the disproportionate use of lethal police force against blacks is associated with the average level of racial implicit bias in that region. For example, using data from a website (*Project Implicit*) that collects people's responses to the IAT, Eric Hehman and his coworkers (2018) found that in regions of the United States where people have higher levels of implicit racial prejudice, there were significantly higher incidents of police officers using lethal force against African Americans than in regions with lower levels of implicit racial prejudice. The researchers also found that people's explicit racial prejudice was not associated with excessive force used by police. As you recall from our previous review of implicit prejudice (section 6.1b), when whites with high implicit but low explicit race prejudice see an unfamiliar black face, brain regions that trigger fear and threat responses are activated. Combined with the present results, this research suggests that simply seeing a black man may automatically trigger a fear response in police officers due to racial stereotypes. Further, under conditions that require quick and decisive action, this race-based response may result in police officers misperceiving harmless objects as weapons. This perceptual bias does not appear to be triggered by explicit racial prejudice, but rather, by the racial stereotypes that exist in our culture (Judd et al., 2004).

FIGURE 6.3   Race and the Misperception of Weapons

After being primed by black or white faces, white participants were shown pictures of guns or tools and asked to classify the objects (Payne, 2001). When participants were required to react quickly, they were more likely to misidentify tools as guns after being primed with black faces rather than with white faces. How does this research provide insight into police shootings of unarmed suspects in real-world confrontations?

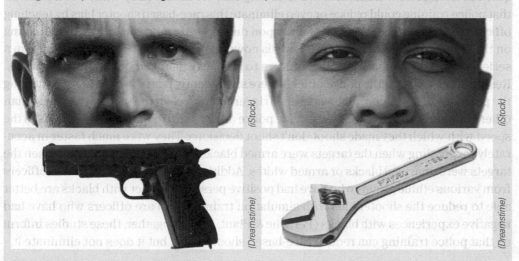

Source: "Prejudice and Perception: The Role of Automatic and Controlled Processes in Misperceiving a Weapon," by B. K. Payne, 2001, *Journal of Personality and Social Psychology, 81*(2), pp. 181–192.

The tendency for racial biases to shape quick decisions—and even to alter what we think we have seen—is due to the fact that negative racial stereotypes are often readily accessible from long-term memory. For example, Vaughn Becker and his coworkers (2010) asked participants to view a white face and a black face—one angry and one neutral—for one-tenth of a second and then briefly distracted them by instructing them to add two numbers that had accompanied the faces (see Figure 6.4). When later asked to describe what they could recall about the faces they had briefly seen, participants' memories reflected racial bias: They were almost twice as likely to falsely recall anger on a black face than to falsely recall anger on a white face.

FIGURE 6.4   Racial Biases Can Shape Our Social Perceptions.

When briefly shown a black face and a white face, one neutral and the other angry, participants more often recalled the black rather than the white face as angry (Becker et al., 2010).

4   -1

(Shutterstock)   *(Shutterstock)*

The findings reviewed here suggest that there are very real, and often deadly, consequences facing ethnic minorities in our society that are not faced by whites. Is it possible that police training could reduce or even eliminate this race-based shooter bias by teaching officers to focus on the presence of a weapon during confrontations rather than fixating on the target's race? Joshua Correll and his coworkers (2007) tested this possibility in a series of studies comparing police officers to similarly matched community members. Results indicated that the police officers were significantly faster in correctly identifying the presence of a weapon, and were less "trigger-happy" when the target was black, than other community members. However, the police officers still manifested racial bias in the speed with which they made shoot/don't shoot decisions: They were much faster in accurately responding when the targets were armed blacks or unarmed whites than when the targets were unarmed blacks or armed whites. Additional research indicates that officers from various ethnic groups who have had positive personal contact with blacks are better able to reduce the shooter bias with simulation training than are officers who have had negative experiences with blacks (Peruche & Plant, 2006). Together, these studies inform us that police training can reduce race-based shooter bias, but it does not eliminate it.

6.2b Modern Racism Is More Subtle than Openly Hostile.

According to a 2018 national poll, 48% of respondents indicated that prejudice against minority groups in the United States is a "very serious problem" (Malloy & Rubenstein, 2018). This reflects an increase from 2016 when 41% of respondents reported that prejudice was a very serious problem. Americans who are more likely to believe that prejudice is a very serious problem are college educated, women, Democrats, and young adults. Comparisons across ethnic groups find that 83% of black and 73% of Hispanic respondents believe that prejudice against minority groups is a very serious problem, but only 39% of white respondents reported the same belief. People who are knowledgeable about the history of racism in the United States are more likely to acknowledge that racism is currently a problem (Bonam et al., 2019). Additional survey studies of African Americans find that more than half report experiencing at least 13 racial hassles per year (Sellers & Shelton, 2003). Most racial hassles involve brief interactions with strangers in which respondents were ignored, overlooked, not given service, treated rudely, or perceived as a threat. Other minorities in the United States report comparable negative experiences (Park et al., 2009). What are some of the underlying causes of this subtler form of racism?

Aversive Racism

At one time in the United States, openly expressed "old-fashioned" racism was prevalent—lynchings, segregated schools, and denial of voting rights were regular occurrences. However, racism today is often much less blatant in its expression. In studying these more contemporary manifestations of racism, most of the research during the past 40 years has examined white Americans' racial attitudes (Pearson et al., 2009). Researchers such as Samuel Gaertner and John Dovidio (2000) and Irwin Katz and R. Glen Hass (1988) assert that the fundamental nature of white Americans' current attitudes toward many racial groups—but especially toward African Americans—is complex and conflicted. They contend that on the one hand, the majority of whites hold to egalitarian values that stress equal treatment of all people and often experience a sense of collective guilt with the realization that their ingroup has harmed and mistreated other social groups in the past. On the other hand, because of exposure to unflattering stereotypes and media images depicting African Americans as lazy, unmotivated, and violent, and due to simple ingroup-outgroup biases, these researchers believe that many whites come to possess negative feelings and beliefs about blacks that directly contradict their egalitarian values. (Dovidio et al., 2017).

The 2014 police-shooting death of unarmed teen Michael Brown in Ferguson, Missouri, was perceived by many people as a chilling example of the extreme danger that young black men face from America's criminal justice system—a danger not shared nearly to the same degree by young white men. How might such social perceptions shape people's racial attitudes?

According to this perspective on contemporary racism, the negative feelings engendered by whites' perceptions of disadvantaged racial groups do not encompass anger or contempt, as in old-fashioned racism; however, they do include uneasiness and even fear. Due to the fact that an egalitarian value system plays an important role in many white Americans' self-concepts, this perspective assumes that they typically do not even acknowledge to themselves—much less to others—that they have these negative feelings (Dovidio et al., 2017). This is why the combination of both positive and negative beliefs and feelings about a particular racial group is called **aversive racism**.

Because aversive racists think of themselves as both egalitarian and nonracist, they do not act in racist ways when it would be clearly identified as such (Dovidio et al. 2017). Instead, their behavior is more subtle, indirect, and expressed only when it could be attributed to something other than racism. For example, in a study of employment decisions, white college students evaluated a job applicant who was either black or white. Furthermore, the applicant was described as either highly qualified, poorly qualified, or had ambiguous qualifications for the position (Dovidio & Gaertner, 2000). Only when the applicant had ambiguous qualifications did the college students show a preference for the white applicant over the black applicant.

Contemporary racism theories suggest that most white Americans are motivated to maintain an unprejudiced self-image and, in part, they are able to do so because they define racism as engaging in overtly racist acts (O'Brien et al., 2010). Holding to this narrow definition, modern-day racism is expressed in ways that can be justified as something other than racism (Crandall & Eshleman, 2003; Vasquez et al., 2019). For example, white Americans who are high in anti-black prejudice are more likely to defend highly negative speech directed towards a black target as simply being an expression of free speech than are white Americans who are low in antiblack prejudice (Roussos &

aversive racism

Attitudes toward members of a racial group that incorporate both egalitarian social values and negative emotions

Dovidio, 2018; White & Crandall, 2017). However, these same Americans with high levels of antiblack prejudice do not similarly defend highly negative speech directed towards their white coworkers or the police. In other words, for high-prejudice people, endorsement of free-speech values appears to be reserved only for defending antiblack speech by fellow whites. Such selective endorsement of free-speech values is just one example of how aversive racism might be expressed, allowing high-prejudice people to support antiblack speech under the guise of something other than racist beliefs. This further highlights that in modern society, racism continues in a subtle, indirect manner and can be more difficult to identify and address.

> "He flattered himself on being a man without any prejudices; and this pretension itself is a very great prejudice."
>
> —Anatole France, French novelist and poet, 1844–1924

> "A gender line . . . helps to keep women not on a pedestal, but in a cage."
>
> —Ruth Bader Ginsburg, US Supreme Court judge, b. 1933

6.2c   Sexism Has Both a Hostile and a Benevolent Component.

Another destructive form of intergroup intolerance is **sexism**, which is any attitude, action, or institutional structure that subordinates a person because of their sex or gender (Swim & Hyers, 2009). Sexism around the globe primarily focuses on the prejudice and discrimination that males direct at females. This is because virtually all societies in the world are *patriarchal*, meaning that the social organization is such that males dominate females (Neely, 2008). While old-fashioned sexism, much like old-fashioned racism reflects overt hostility and male dominance over women, much of modern-day sexism reflects a more subtle and ambivalent attitude towards women.

How have patriarchal beliefs fostered the expression of sexism in society?

(Shutterstock)

Ambivalent Sexism

Peter Glick and Susan Fiske (1996, 2001a, 2001c) contend that modern-day sexism toward women consists of both positive (benevolence) and negative (hostile) attitudes rather than uniform dislike. These two components constitute **ambivalent sexism**. *Hostile sexism* reflects overt hostility and derogatory attitudes towards women and is what most people typically think of as sexism. In contrast, *benevolent sexism* reflects a paternalistic attitude towards women that suggests that women are "warm and wonderful" people who are in need of male protection. While on the surface this attitude seems positive, it also reflects the belief that women are inferior and need to be cared for, much like children. Although these two attitudes of hostility and benevolence seem to be diametrically opposed to one another, research indicates that they, in fact, are *positively* correlated. In other words, individuals who endorse hostile sexist attitudes also tend to endorse benevolent sexist attitudes.

According to Glick and Fiske, whether someone who is ambivalently sexist responds to a woman with hostility or benevolence depends on the "type" of woman she is. Ambivalently sexist individuals are more likely to subtype women, and their behavior is determined by these subtypes (Glick et al., 1997). As you recall from the Stereotype Content Model (section 6.1c), contemptuous prejudice is directed at women who are perceived as having high status and low warmth (feminists and career women). These are women who are perceived by ambivalently sexist individuals as having stepped out of their traditional gender role and are attempting to change the status quo by gaining power over men. Thus, those who are ambivalently sexist direct hostility as a punishment towards these women. Also consistent with the Stereotype Content Model, women who are perceived as having low status and high warmth (housewives, mothers) are the

sexism
Any attitude, action, or institutional structure that subordinates a person because of her or his sex or gender

ambivalent sexism
Sexism directed against women based on both positive and negative attitudes (hostility and benevolence) rather than on uniform dislike

recipients of paternalistic prejudice. Ambivalently sexist individuals express benevolence—in the form of restrictive protection—toward these women as a reward for them "staying in their place." Thus, ambivalently sexist individuals respond differently (with hostility or warmth) to women based on whether they are perceived to be conforming or rebelling against traditional gender roles.

A field experiment tested Glick and Fiske's theory by having female confederates pose as either job applicants or customers at retail stores while wearing or not wearing padding that made them appear pregnant (Hebl et al., 2007). How people responded to the confederates was predicted by whether they conformed to traditional gender roles. Store employees behaved more rudely toward the female job applicants when they looked pregnant versus not pregnant, but employees were friendlier toward the female customers when they looked pregnant versus not pregnant. Further, the "pregnant" confederates encountered greater hostility from both men and women when applying for masculine compared to feminine jobs.

A similar set of experimental studies examined the effect of power-seeking intentions on backlash toward women in political office (Okimoto & Brescoll, 2010). Results indicated that both men and women were less likely to vote for a female politician if they believed she had aspirations for power. No similar negative effects were found for male politicians who sought power. These results suggest that a female politician's career progress may be hindered by the belief that she seeks power, because such desire violates the feminine gender role and, thus, elicits interpersonal penalties. Together, these findings of benevolent responses toward women who conform to traditional gender roles and hostility toward those who seek nontraditional roles demonstrate how sexist beliefs foster and maintain sexual inequality in the workforce. Not surprisingly, women who experience benevolently sexist events, especially paternalistic behaviors, tend to experience increased self-doubt, feelings of incompetence, and worse performance in stereotypical masculine tasks (Gervais & Vescio, 2012; Oswald et al., 2019).

The degree to which ambivalent sexist views are held varies across cultures and is related to cultural differences in gender equality (Glick et al., 2004; Sakalli-Ugurlu & Glick, 2003). As demonstrated in the pregnant-nonpregnant field experiment, although benevolent sexist beliefs lead people to express many positive attitudes about women, they share common assumptions with hostile sexism—namely, that women belong in restricted domestic roles and are the "weaker" sex. Both beliefs serve to justify male social dominance (Feather, 2004). For example, in Turkey, Brazil, and Japan, men and women who endorse hostile and benevolent sexist beliefs toward women justify and also minimize domestic violence against women; they are also more likely to blame women for triggering the violence against them (Russell & Trig, 2004; Yamawaki et al., 2009). Spend a few minutes completing the Ambivalent Sexism Inventory in *Self/Social Connection Exercise 6.1.*

"The prejudice against color, of which we hear so much, is no stronger than that against sex. It is produced by the same cause, and manifested very much in the same way. The Negro's skin and the woman's sex are both prima facie evidence that they were intended to be in subjection to the white Saxon man."

—Elizabeth Cady Stanton, US feminist and abolitionist, 1815–1902

How might some Americans' negative reactions to Hillary Clinton as a politician be explained by ambivalent sexism and the belief that she has a desire for power?

Shouldn't people experience considerable cognitive dissonance if they simultaneously believe that women are inferior, ungrateful, sexual teasers who are also refined, morally superior goddesses? Based on your understanding of cognitive dissonance theory (Chapter 5, section 5.3a), how might ambivalent sexists avoid feeling conflicted about their positive and negative beliefs and attitudes toward women?

"The word 'demand' is a tricky word when used by our gender. When used by men, it's part of their vernacular."

—Robin Wright, b. 1966, American actress and director

Self/Social Connection Exercise 6.1

What Is Your Degree of Ambivalent Sexism Toward Women?

The Ambivalent Sexism Inventory

Instructions

Below is a series of statements concerning men and women and their relationships in contemporary society. Please indicate the degree to which you agree or disagree with each statement using the following scale:

0 = Disagree strongly   3 = Agree slightly

1 = Disagree somewhat   4 = Agree somewhat

2 = Disagree slightly   5 = Agree strongly

1. No matter how accomplished he is, a man is not truly complete as a person unless he has the love of a woman.
2. Many women are actually seeking special favors, such as hiring policies that favor them over men, under the guise of asking for "equality."
3. In a disaster, women ought not necessarily be rescued before men.*
4. Most women interpret innocent remarks as being sexist.
5. Women are too easily offended.
6. People are often truly happy in life without being romantically involved with a member of the other sex.*
7. Feminists are not seeking for women to have more power than men.*
8. Many women have a quality of purity that few men possess.
9. Women should be cherished and protected by men.
10. Most women fail to appreciate fully all that men do for them.
11. Women seek to gain power by getting control over men.
12. Every man ought to have a woman whom he adores.
13. Men are complete without women.*
14. Women exaggerate problems they have at work.
15. Once a woman gets a man to commit to her, she usually tries to put him on a tight leash.
16. When women lose to men in a fair competition, they typically complain about being discriminated against.
17. A good woman should be set on a pedestal by her man.
18. There are actually very few women who get a kick out of teasing men by seeming sexually available and then refusing male advances.*
19. Women, compared with men, tend to have a superior moral sensibility.
20. Men should be willing to sacrifice their own well-being in order to provide financially for the women in their lives.
21. Feminists are making entirely reasonable demands of men.*
22. Women, as compared with men, tend to have a more refined sense of culture and good taste.

Scoring Instructions

Before summing either scale, first reverse the scores for the "*" items:

     0 = 5, 1 = 4, 2 = 3, 3 = 2, 4 = 1, 5 = 0.

Hostile Sexism Scale Score: Add items 2, 4, 5, 7, 10, 11, 14, 15, 16, 18, 21.

The average score for men is about 29, while the average score for women is about 20. Higher scores indicate greater degrees of hostile sexism.

Benevolent Sexism Scale Score: Add items 1, 3, 6, 8, 9, 12, 13, 17, 19, 20, 22.

The average score for men is about 28, while the average score for women is about 24.

Higher scores indicate greater degrees of benevolent sexism.

Total Ambivalent Sexism Inventory Score: Sum the Hostile Sexism Scale score and the Benevolent Sexism Scale score.

The average score for men is about 57, while the average score for women is about 44.

Higher scores indicate greater degrees of ambivalent sexism.

6.2d Intolerance Based on Weight, Sexual Orientation, and Mental Illness Is Often Accepted.

Aversive racism and ambivalent sexism both involve the expression of positive and negative attitudes toward the target group. Yet there are other social groups within society that arouse little positive feelings in those who are biased against them. Instead, these groups are more likely to arouse only feelings of revulsion and contempt. Three examples of such contemptuous prejudice involve weight, sexual orientation, and mental illness.

Antifat Prejudice

Obese people in the United States are subjected to disdain and discrimination in their daily lives (Crandall et al., 2009; Diedrichs & Puhl, 2017). Such prejudice is substantially due to the fact that most people view obesity as a condition that is controllable (Vartanian & Smyth, 2013). Thus, heavy individuals also are viewed as weak willed, lazy, and self-indulgent (Puhl & Brownell, 2006). In this sense, their stigma involves not only an "abomination of the body" but also a "blemish of individual character." Antifat prejudice is more pronounced in individualist cultures like the United States and Australia compared with collectivist cultures like Mexico and India, partly because individualists are more likely than collectivists to hold people accountable for personal outcomes (Crandall et al., 2001).

The prejudice and discrimination faced by obese people permeates both their personal and professional lives, and also negatively affects their physical and mental health (Schafer & Ferraro, 2011). They are less likely to be chosen as friends and romantic partners than normal-weight persons, and they are treated in a less friendly manner by healthcare workers (Harvey & Hill, 2001; Hebl et al., 2003). The stigma of obesity is especially strong for women. One study even found that heavier college women were less likely than normal-weight women to receive financial assistance from their own parents (Crandall, 1995). In the job market, obese individuals are discriminated against at every stage of employment, from being hired to being fired (Agerström & Rooth, 2011; Muennig, 2008).

Obesity is such a strong stigmatizing characteristic in our culture that it even affects how people evaluate individuals who are merely seen with obese persons. Michelle Hebl and Laura Mannix (2003) found that an average-weight male job applicant was rated more negatively when seen with an overweight woman prior to a job interview than when seen with a woman of normal weight. Antifat prejudice is so pervasive in our society that even children evaluate normal-weight peers more negatively when they are seen with an obese child (Penny & Haddock, 2007). This tendency for individuals who are associated with stigmatized people to also face negative evaluations from others is known as **courtesy stigma** (Goffman, 1963). The threat of negative evaluation causes many nonstigmatized people to avoid those who are stigmatized (Swim et al., 1999).

In the United States and Canada, antifat attitudes are stronger among men, whites, and people with traditional gender roles compared with women, blacks, and individuals with nontraditional gender roles (Hebl & Turchin, 2005; Puhl et al., 2008). One explanation for these differences is that the female thinness standard in North American culture is most closely associated with white, heterosexual beauty ideals that are closely aligned with traditional gender roles (see Chapter 9, section 9.3b). Antifat prejudice can exert a substantial toll upon the well-being of overweight individuals, who often internalize these negative attitudes and experience depression, negative body esteem, and general negative self-esteem (Puhl & Heuer, 2010).

("Kira Nerusskaya 2," by David Shankbone, available under a CC by SA 3.0 license via Wikimedia.)

Fat-acceptance movement advocates, such as documentary filmmaker Kira Nerusskaya, contend that TV shows like The Biggest Loser *perpetuate anti-fat prejudice because the objective of the show is to remove contestants from the stigmatized obese outgroup and into the "healthy" weight ingroup.*

A series of studies have found strong implicit antifat prejudice that is resistant to change, even among people with few explicit antifat attitudes—and even among individuals who were once overweight themselves (Schwartz et al., 2006; Wang et al., 2004). For example, Bethany Teachman and her coworkers (2003) found that even after informing people that obesity is mainly due to genetic factors, there was no significant reduction in their implicit fat bias. When these same individuals read stories of discrimination against obese persons designed to evoke empathy, diminished implicit bias was observed only among those who were overweight. This last finding may be important, given that self-blame and internalizing negative social messages are common in obese individuals. Reminding obese persons about antifat discrimination may promote ingroup support and help them develop a positive social identity (Saguy & Ward, 2011).

As previously discussed in Chapter 3, (section 3.2), being categorized as part of a stigmatized group is threatening to the self because self-concept consists not only of your individual attributes but also your identification with social groups. Thus, the problem faced by anyone categorized within a stigmatized group is how to create and maintain a positive sense of self (Major et al., 2012). In many industrialized societies, medical professionals and popular media strongly encourage obese people to improve their social standing—and health—by trying to remove themselves from the stigmatized fat category through dieting, exercise, and other weight-loss strategies, including surgical procedures such as gastric bypass or liposuction (Brochu et al., 2014).

In contrast to these widely promoted individual change strategies that stigmatize obesity, a growing number of obese individuals are focusing on collective change strategies to enhance fat people's feelings of self-worth and social status by both altering expanding cultural standards of what is an acceptable body size and by passing laws to prevent weight discrimination (Lindly et al., 2014; Nario-Redmond et al., 2013). Throughout North America and Europe, fat acceptance movements are increasingly using legal challenges and other political means to promote anti-size-discrimination policies and systemically advance fat acceptance (Fletcher, 2009). However, in the United States, there is little legal protection for individuals experiencing employment discrimination based on weight (Monahan et al., 2014). Furthermore, weight-based prejudice is positively associated with support for punitive public policies directed towards obese individuals (Berg et al., 2016). Thus, overweight individuals continue to experience discrimination in both the workforce and in their personal relationships, with little likelihood of change in the near future.

courtesy stigma

The tendency for individuals who are associated with stigmatized people to also face negative evaluations from others

Sexual Prejudice

Despite rigorous scientific studies finding no evidence of an association between homosexuality and psychopathology, many conservative religious and political organizations persist in stigmatizing lesbians, gay men, bisexuals, and transgender (LGBT) individuals as sexually deviant and mentally disturbed—and therefore less deserving of the same civil rights as heterosexual individuals (Herek & Garnets, 2007; Minton, 2002). This societal reaction is an example of stigma based on "blemishes of individual character," with nonheterosexual and transgender individuals being targets of a type of contemptuous prejudice (refer to section 6.1c) called **sexual prejudice**. Sexual prejudice refers to all negative attitudes based on sexual orientation, whether the target is homosexual, bisexual, or heterosexual (Herek & McLemore, 2013).

Prejudice and discrimination directed towards people because of their sexual orientation is extensive and ongoing. For example, Sabra Katz-Wise and Janet Hyde (2012) found that approximately 55% of lesbian, gay, and bisexual (LGB) individuals experienced verbal harassment, 45% experienced sexual harassment, 28% experienced physical assault, and 44% reported discrimination. Prejudice directed towards people who are bisexual or transgender tends to be even more negative than that directed towards lesbians and gay men (Burke et al., 2017). Unfortunately, physical and verbal bullying is a far too common problem for LGBT students in school (Goodenow et al., 2016). These bullying experiences take a devastating toll on the victims' mental and physical health and on their academic achievement.

Social scientists often explain sexual prejudice as being caused and fueled by **heterosexism**, which is a system of cultural beliefs, values, and customs that exalts heterosexuality and denies, denigrates, and stigmatizes any nonheterosexual form of behavior or identity (Fernald, 1995; Herek, 2004). Calling another person a derogatory name is certainly an example of heterosexism, but this cultural belief system also operates on a subtler level. Like the fish that doesn't realize it's wet, most people are so used to defining heterosexual behaviors as normal and natural that they cease to think of them as being a manifestation of sexuality. For instance, heterosexuals who wouldn't look twice at a man and woman holding hands, hugging, or even kissing in public often react very differently if the couple is of the same sex. Gay couples expressing affection in public are typically criticized for flaunting their sexuality. Even when they are not victims of openly blatant discrimination, gay men, lesbians, bisexuals, and transgendered individuals often experience *interpersonal discrimination*, where they are treated in a less friendly manner and made to feel unwelcome or "invisible" in various social settings (Hebl et al., 2002).

Although many cultures can be characterized as heterosexist, people in those cultures who conform most strongly to socially conservative—and even racist and sexist—value systems are also those who hold extremely negative attitudes toward gay men and lesbians. In contrast to less-prejudiced individuals, people who express antigay attitudes tend to have the following characteristics:

1. Are male rather than female (Ratcliff et al., 2006)

2. Are racially prejudiced, sexist, and authoritarian (Case et al., 2008)

3. Are members of conservative religious organizations (Herek, 1987; Herek & Gonzalez-Rivera, 2006)

4. Hold traditional attitudes toward gender roles (Kite & Whitley, 1996)

> "All of us who are openly gay are living and writing the history of our movement. We are no more—and no less—heroic than the suffragists and abolitionists of the 19th century; and the labor organizers, Freedom Riders, Stonewall demonstrators, and environmentalists of the 20th century. We are ordinary people, living our lives, and trying as civil-rights activist Dorothy Cotton said, to 'fix what ain't right' in our society."
>
> —Senator Tammy Baldwin, US senator, b. 1962

sexual prejudice

Negative attitudes based on sexual orientation, whether the target is homosexual, bisexual, or heterosexual

heterosexism

A system of cultural beliefs, values, and customs that exalts heterosexuality and denies, denigrates, and stigmatizes any nonheterosexual form of behavior or identity

5. Have friends and family who hold similarly negative attitudes (Franklin, 2000; Lehmiller et al., 2010)

6. Have had less personal contact with gay men or lesbians (Sakalli-Ugurlu, 2002; Vonofakou et al., 2007)

Why do heterosexual men have more negative attitudes than heterosexual women? Social scientists contend that this gender difference exists because many cultures emphasize the importance of heterosexuality in the male gender role in particular (Jellison et al., 2004). A defining characteristic of this *heterosexual masculinity* is to reject men who violate the heterosexual norm—namely, gay men. This is also why heterosexual men express more negative attitudes toward gay men than toward lesbians. They perceive a male transgression of the heterosexual norm to be a more serious violation than a female transgression. As we will discuss in Chapter 10 (section 10.3b), the fact that heterosexual male same-sex friendships are often lacking in emotional tenderness may be mainly due to concerns about not straying from the narrowly defined boundaries of heterosexual masculinity. This is especially true for men with strongly antigay attitudes (Devlin & Cowan, 1985).

Highlighting the important role that reference groups play in the formation of attitudes, research finds that people who hold strongly antigay attitudes also have friends who hold similar opinions (see Chapter 5, section 5.1c). Similarly, schools that have gay/straight alliances also have fewer bullying incidents, and LGBT students report feeling safer on campus (Ioverno et al., 2016). In recent years, there has also been a shift in institutional policies regarding support for same-sex marriage, which can foster more positive attitudes toward LGBT individuals. For example, following the United States Supreme Court decision allowing same-sex marriage, there was an increase in the perceived social norms supporting gay marriage (Tankard & Levy Paluck, 2017). This research demonstrates the importance of reference groups, whether it's peers in school or the larger cultural institutions, in changing attitudes towards stigmatized groups.

Although sexual prejudice is typically targeted at sexual minorities, heterosexual individuals are also at risk. Friends, family members, and "allies" who take a public stand against sexual prejudice often experience courtesy stigma. Heterosexual individuals can also become victims of sexual prejudice because of "mistaken identity." That is, due to the fact that sexual orientation is concealable, inferences are often made about people's sexual orientation based on the degree to which they deviate from traditional gender roles or gendered behavior (Majied, 2010; Poteat et al., 2007). For example, when heterosexual men hug other men in public outside the confines of a sporting event, they run the risk of being labeled "gay" and targeted for verbal and physical assault. However, when the social norms are nonprejudicial towards LGBT individuals, then heterosexual individuals' fear of "courtesy stigma" decreases (Cascio & Plant, 2016). This again demonstrates the power of nonprejudicial social norms in not only decreasing stigma for the LGBT community, but for heterosexual individuals as well.

Try the following exercise. Listen to some of your favorite songs with lyrics involving romance. Do you tend to automatically imagine that the person singing the song is expressing his or her love for a person of the other sex? How do these reactions relate to heterosexism? Now, actively imagine that the song is about same-sex love. How do you react to these lyrics and any visual images that come to mind?

Mental Illness Prejudice

All available evidence strongly indicates that people identified as having psychological disorders are often severely stigmatized in the United States and in other Western, African, and Asian cultures (Brohan et al., 2012; Edwards, 2014). In the United States, a national survey found that Americans perceived people with psychological disorders as dangerous and as less capable than the average person of handling their daily affairs

(Pescosolido et al., 1999). Such stigmatization is fostered and strengthened by television shows, movies, and news outlets that regularly portray people with often-unnamed mental illnesses as being dangerous or incompetent (Angermeyer & Matschinger, 1996). Indeed, one recent study found that the more often people watch television, the less accurate their knowledge is about schizophrenia and obsessive-compulsive disorder (Kimmerle & Cress, 2013). This widespread bias against individuals suffering from psychological disorders extends into our judicial system. Studies of court proceedings in both the United States and Canada find that judges often use and allow others to use language in their courtrooms that stigmatizes mental illness and those who suffer from psychological disorders (Black & Downie, 2013).

"It wasn't easy telling my parents that I'm gay. I made my carefully worded announcement at Thanksgiving. I said, 'Mom, would you please pass the gravy to a homosexual.' Then my Aunt Lorraine piped in, 'Bob, you're gay. Are you seeing a psychiatrist?' I said, 'No, I'm seeing a lieutenant in the Navy.'"

—Bob Smith, American comedian, b. 1959

Faced with this social stigma and the fear of being negatively evaluated, people with psychological problems often conceal their symptoms and avoid seeking therapy (Held & Owens, 2013; Wahl, 2012). In many Asian countries, the stigma of mental illness is so severe that it can damage the reputation of the family lineage and thereby significantly reduce the marriage and career prospects of other family members (Ng, 1997). This stigma is also pervasive among Asian Americans in the United States (Moon & Cho, 2012). For example, a mental health survey in Los Angeles (Zhang et al., 1998) found that Asian Americans were less than half as likely as white Americans to mention their mental health problems to a friend or relative (12% versus 25%), and only 4% stated that they would seek help from a psychiatrist or psychotherapist (compared to 26% of white Americans). In addition to preventing people from seeking help for their psychological problems, the stigma surrounding mental illness lowers self-esteem while increasing a sense of social isolation and hopelessness.

(Shutterstock)

The stigma surrounding psychological disorders causes many people to avoid seeking help. What is one of the most common stereotypes about people with mental illness?

Why do many people hold such negative attitudes toward those who are afflicted with a mental illness? David Feldman and Christian Crandall (2007) found that three factors seem to be central in triggering such prejudice. First, people respond more negatively when the mentally ill person is perceived as being responsible or at fault for their disorder. Second, people express more negative attitudes when the mentally ill person is perceived as being dangerous or posing a threat to others. Third, people respond more negatively when they mistakenly believe that mental illness is rare and uncommon.

So what is the truth about one of the most common stereotypes of the mentally ill—namely, that they are more violent than the average person? One study monitored the behavior of more than 1,000 individuals during the year after they had been discharged from psychiatric hospitals (Steadman et al., 1998). Results found no significant difference in the incidence of violence between the former patients and a control group of people living in the same neighborhoods with no history of serious mental health problems. Other research indicates that heightened violence is only slightly more likely among people with severe psychological disorders who are currently experiencing extreme psychological symptoms, such as bizarre delusional thoughts and hallucinated voices (Link et al., 1992). All other individuals with psychological disorders who are not experiencing these severe symptoms are no more likely than the average person to be violent. Thus, the research clearly indicates that the cultural stereotype associating mental illness with violence is grossly exaggerated and largely unfounded. However, until such negative stereotypes surrounding psychological disorders are reduced, the stigma of the mental illness label will remain the most formidable obstacle to future progress in the area of mental health.

6.2e Being Stigmatized Has Negative Consequences for the Targets.

What are the implications of constantly being the target of discrimination, prejudice, and stereotypes? Perhaps you experience regular discrimination because of your ethnicity, gender, sexual orientation, or other socially stigmatized identities. How might such experiences impact your life?

Physical and Mental Health Outcomes

There is a substantial body of research indicating that experiencing prejudice and discrimination is associated with poorer short- and long-term mental and physical health (Schmitt et al., 2014). Among African Americans, for example, experiencing racism has been linked to poorer physical health and heart disease than the general population, especially when African Americans live in communities where whites express higher levels of racism (Leitner et al., 2016; Pascoe & Smart Richman, 2009). The negative impact that prejudice and discrimination has on health is especially strong among groups that have a stigmatizing condition that is concealable—meaning, not automatically visible to others—such as various types of mental illness, sexual orientation or HIV+ status.

Academic Performance

Stereotypes can also negatively impact the performance of stigmatized group members in areas where the negative stereotype is relevant to performance. For example, a common belief about women is that they are not as good at math as men. Is it possible that, when competing against male students in a college math course, female students might experience a nagging possibility that they might confirm this negative stereotype? Similarly, black students might feel that they carry the burden of "representing their race" in academic pursuits. Claude Steele (1997) defined **stereotype threat** as is the apprehension people feel when performing a task in which their group is stereotyped to lack ability (Steele & Aronson, 1995; Steele et al., 2002). People experience this apprehension because they are concerned that if they perform poorly, they will be confirming or perpetuating the negative stereotype (Shapiro & Neuberg, 2007). According to Steele, this apprehension interferes with actual performance in the negatively stereotyped task.

The first evidence for the stereotype threat effect among African American college students came from a series of experiments conducted by Steele and Joshua Aronson (1995). In one of these studies, black and white student volunteers were given a difficult English test. In the *stereotype threat condition*, the test was described as a measure of intellectual ability; in the *nonstereotype threat condition*, it was described as a laboratory problem-solving task that did not measure intelligence. Because cultural stereotypes depict blacks as intellectually inferior to whites, the researchers presumed that describing the test as an intellectual measure would induce stereotype threat among the black students. In contrast, when the task was described as not measuring intelligence, this should make the negative racial stereotype about ability irrelevant to the black students' performance; therefore, it would not arouse stereotype threat. As you can see in Figure 6.5, when the test was presented as a measure of ability, blacks performed worse than whites. However, when the stereotype threat was removed there was no difference between the two groups' performances.

Stereotype threat has also been found to negatively impact women on math tasks (Grand, 2017; Gunderson et al., 2012). For example, Steven Spencer and his colleagues (1999) gave male and female college students a difficult math test, but divided it into two halves and presented it as two distinct tests. Half of the students were told that the first test was one on which men outperformed women, and that the second test was

stereotype threat
The apprehension people feel when performing a task in which their group is stereotyped to lack ability

one on which there were no gender differences. The other students were told the opposite—Test 1 was described as exhibiting no gender differences, but men outperformed women on Test 2. As you can see in Figure 6.6, when told that the test yielded gender differences, women greatly underperformed in relation to men. However, when the test was described as not exhibiting any gender differences, women's underperformance disappeared. Meta-analyses have found this effect to be robust (d = .29) and is stronger for women who are highly identified with math (report math to be an important part of their self-concept) than for women who are not as highly identified with math (Doyle & Voyer, 2016). This suggests that women who care about performing well in math feel a stronger burden not to confirm the negative math stereotype about women, and thus, are more likely to experience stereotype threat.

FIGURE 6.5   African American Intellectual Test Performance and Stereotype Threat

Steele and Aronson (1995) administered a difficult English test to black and white college students. When the test was described as a measure of intellectual ability (stereotype threat condition), blacks performed worse than whites. However, when it was not associated with ability (nonstereotype threat condition), no racial differences were found. How are these findings consistent with the stereotype threat hypothesis?

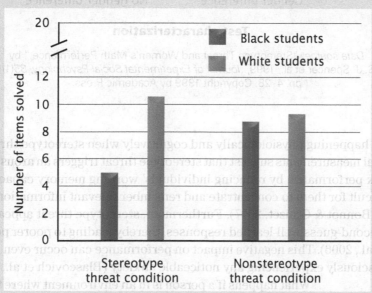

Data source: "Stereotype Threat and the Intellectual Test Performance of African Americans," by C. M. Steele and J. Aronson, 1995, *Journal of Personality and Social Psychology, 69*(5), pp. 797–811. Copyright 1995 by the American Psychological Association.

Stereotype threat is most noticeable and problematic among social groups that have been historically disadvantaged (Nadler & Clark, 2011), but it also occurs among members of dominant groups. For example, compared to girls, boys are negatively stereotyped about their reading proficiency. In a study of school-aged children, boys performed worse than girls on a reading test when the children were told that the test was a measure of their reading ability, but boys performed as well as girls when told that the test was merely a game (Pansu et al., 2016).

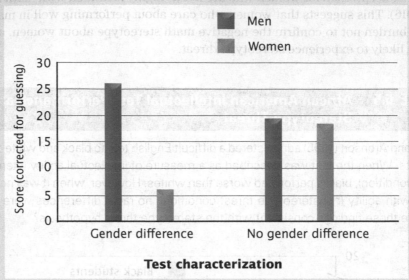

FIGURE 6.6   Stereotype Threat and Women's Math Performance

Spencer and his colleagues (1999) found that when a difficult math test was described as exhibiting gender differences (men outperforming women), women did indeed underperform. However, when the test was described as exhibiting no gender differences, women's underperformance disappeared. How do these results support the stereotype threat hypothesis?

Data source: "Stereotype Threat and Women's Math Performance," by S. J. Spencer et al., 1999, *Journal of Experimental Social Psychology, 35*(1), pp. 4–28. Copyright 1999 by Academic Press.

What is happening physiologically and cognitively when stereotype threat occurs? Physiological measurements suggest that stereotype threat triggers an arousal state that hinders task performance by reducing individuals' working memory capacity, making it more difficult for them to concentrate and remember relevant information (Ben-Zeev et al., 2005; Bonnot & Croizet, 2007). Furthermore, stereotype threat appears to cause people to second-guess well-learned responses, thereby leading to poorer performance (Beilock et al., 2006). This negative impact on performance can occur even without the person consciously experiencing any noticeable anxiety (Blascovich et al., 2001).

What happens if a person is in an environment where they repeatedly experience stereotype threat? One likely consequence is that the person will avoid and *disidentify* with whatever task is associated with the threatening scrutiny (Davies et al., 2005). For example, if the stereotype threat involves intellectual performance, you may change your self-concept so that academic achievement is no longer very important to your self-esteem. This sort of academic disidentification is much more common among African American students than among white American students, and it often begins in the lower elementary grades (Ambady et al., 2001; Osbourne, 1995). Consistent with Steele's notion of stereotype threat, academic disidentification among African American students is most likely to occur when negative racial stereotypes concerning black intellectual inferiority are salient in an academic setting. Stereotype threat and academic disidentification also occur among American Indians, Hispanic Americans, lower-class whites, and female students in male-dominated majors

Can you think of a negative stereotype about whites relative to blacks that might cause white individuals to experience stereotype threat in a particular area of pursuit, thereby motivating them to disidentify with this activity?

(Croizet & Claire, 1998; Inzlicht & Ben-Zeev, 2000). Although such disidentification protects self-esteem and is a coping response to prejudice and discrimination, it also is one of the psychological factors that undermines school achievement (Aronson et al., 2002). In the Applications section at the end of the chapter, we discuss possible ways to reduce the effects of stereotype threat in academic settings.

Section Summary

- There are three different categories of stigma:
  tribal identities,
  blemishes of individual character, and
  abominations of the body.

- Race-based cues automatically activate threat responses and negative stereotypes, which may contribute to shooter bias among law enforcement officers.

- Aversive racism is a combination of both positive and negative beliefs and feelings about a racial group.

- Sexism is best conceptualized as involving *ambivalence*; it is based on both hostility and benevolence.

- Obesity is an example of both a "blemish of individual character" stigma and an "abomination of the body" stigma, and antifat prejudice permeates society.

- Homosexuality is an example of a "blemish of individual character" stigma, and it is related to the cultural ideology of heterosexism.

- Mental illness is another example of a "blemish of individual character" stigma, and the fear of being stigmatized is perhaps the leading reason sufferers avoid seeking help.

- Experiencing prejudice and discrimination results in poorer mental and physical health.

- Stigmatized groups can respond to negative stereotypes by experiencing stereotype threat.

6.3   What Shapes Prejudice and Discrimination?

Beyond the role that negative stereotypes (and other cultural beliefs and values) play in both the causes and effects of prejudice and discrimination, additional powerful motivational and social variables exert a significant influence in the creation of intergroup intolerance (Gerstenfeld, 2002). In this section of the chapter we examine some of these causes, beginning with how group membership creates ingroup bias.

6.3a   Ingroup Members Are Favored Over Outgroup Members.

Have you ever gone to a campus social event and felt that students who were members of different campus groups than your own were evaluating you less positively simply because you were not "one of them"? Have you ever engaged in this sort of biased evaluation of other students yourself? We have already discussed how social categorization sets the stage for perceiving members of other groups as having similar characteristics—and how such stereotyping can lead to intergroup intolerance. However, research by Henri Tajfel and John Turner demonstrates that the simple act of categorizing people as ingroup or outgroup members affects how we evaluate and compare them, independent of stereotyping (Tajfel et al., 1971).

As you recall from Chapter 3 (section 3.2c), besides our personal identity, another important aspect of our self-concept is our social identity, which we derive from the groups to which we belong. Our social identity establishes what and where we are in social terms. Because our social identity forms a central aspect of our own self-definition, our self-esteem is partly determined by the social esteem of our ingroups. According to Tajfel and Turner's **social identity theory**, we seek to enhance our self-esteem by identifying with specific social groups and perceiving these groups as being better than other groups (Tajfel & Turner 1979; Turner 1987). When our ingroups are successful—or even when members of our ingroups achieve some level of personal success—we can bask in their reflected glory. However, when the social esteem of our ingroup is threatened, we often attempt to maintain a positive social identity by engaging in ingroup biasing—perceiving our ingroup as being better than other groups (Vanhoomissen & Overwalle, 2010).

Consistent with social identity theory, research indicates that people habitually engage in **ingroup bias** when evaluating others. That is, when they observe an ingroup member and an outgroup member performing the same task, their evaluations of these two people's performances will be biased in favor of the ingroup member. This ingroup favoritism manifests itself by people selectively remembering the ingroup member's good behavior and the outgroup member's bad behavior, or by selectively forgetting or trivializing the ingroup member's bad behavior and the outgroup member's good behavior (Dovidio & Gaertner, 2010). Such selective information processing causes an overestimation of ingroup performance relative to outgroup performance. Because of this ingroup bias, ingroup members are consistently rewarded more than outgroup members (Crisp et al., 2001; Reynolds et al., 2000).

To test the hypothesis that group membership is sufficient to foster ingroup favoritism, researchers created what they called *minimal groups*, which are groups selected from a larger collection of people using some trivial—or minimal—criteria such as eye color, a random number table, or the flip of a coin (Otten, 2016). The people comprising these newly created groups were strangers to one another and were never given the opportunity to get acquainted. In some studies, participants were then individually taken into a room with the experimenter and asked how much money the other two participants should be paid for a subsequent task. These two people were identified only by code numbers, indicating to the participant that one came from his or her own group and the other was a member of the other group. Based on this information alone, participants proceeded to reward the ingroup person more than the outgroup person (Tajfel et al., 1971).

Ingroup preference tends to be so automatically activated that simply using ingroup pronouns is often sufficient to arouse positive emotions, while using pronouns signifying outgroups can trigger negative emotions. Evidence for this effect comes from a series of studies conducted by Charles Perdue and his coworkers (1990), in which college students saw 108 seemingly randomly paired letter strings on a computer screen. Each pair of letter strings consisted of a nonsense syllable (*xeh, yof, laj*) presented with either an ingroup-designating pronoun (*we, us, ours*), an outgroup-designating pronoun (*they, them, theirs*), or, on the control trials, some other pronoun (*he, she, his, hers*). Students were told to quickly decide which letter string in each pair was a real word (*we-xeh, they-yof*).

social identity theory
A theory suggesting that people seek to enhance their self-esteem by identifying with specific social groups and perceiving these groups as being better than other groups

ingroup bias
The tendency to give more favorable evaluations and great rewards to ingroup members than to outgroup members

Unbeknownst to the students, one nonsense syllable was consistently paired with ingroup pronouns and another with outgroup pronouns. After the trials, students were asked to rate each of the nonsense syllables in terms of its degree of pleasantness–unpleasantness. As you can see from Figure 6.7, students evaluated the nonsense words that had previously been paired with the ingroup pronouns as more pleasant than those paired either with outgroup pronouns or with the control pronouns. These results suggest that merely associating a previously neutral stimulus to words that designate either ingroup or outgroup affiliations is sufficient to create biased emotional responses. As you might guess, ingroup biasing is often subtle and not recognized as being unfair by either the target or the perpetrator.

(Shutterstock)

Have you ever gone to a social event and felt that others were evaluating you less positively simply because you were not part of their ingroup?

FIGURE 6.7   Us and Them: Ingroup Biasing

How pervasive is ingroup biasing? Perdue and colleagues (1990) found that nonsense words that had previously been paired with ingroup pronouns (e.g., *us*) were evaluated as more "pleasant" than nonsense words that had been paired with either outgroup pronouns (e.g., *them*) or control pronouns (e.g., *hers*). This study suggests that the ingroup–outgroup distinction has such emotional meaning to people that it can even shape their evaluation of unfamiliar words.

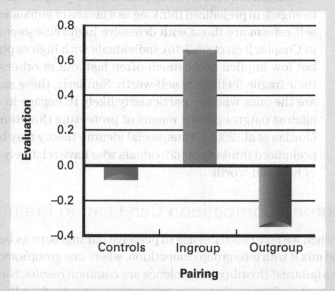

Data source: "Us and Them: Social Categorization and the Process of Intergroup Bias," by C. W. Perdue et al., 1990, *Journal of Personality and Social Psychology, 59*(3), pp. 475–486. Copyright 1990 by the American Psychological Association, Inc.

Not only do people evaluate ingroup members more positively than outgroup members, studies show that they are more likely to be sensitive to ingroup members' emotions and feelings than to those of outgroup members (Chambon et al.,2008). The neurological basis of such emotional sensitivity can literally be seen in the brain scans of people who are watching someone who is sad. If the sad person is a member of their ingroup, observers' neural activity is the same as when they feel sad themselves, yet if the sad person is an outgroup member, observers' neural activity is actually heightened in brain areas associated with positive affect, suggesting they are pleased to see this person suffering (Scheepers & Derks, 2016). This pleasure in witnessing an outgroup member's misfortune is recognized in cultures around the world—the Germans refer to it as *Schadenfreude*, or "harm-joy"—and illustrates how ingroup biasing can trigger petty reactions toward people we perceive as "those others."

Given our tendency to revel in the misfortunes of those who are not members of our own social groups, it isn't surprising that we also tend to spontaneously prefer other ingroup members who are openly biased toward our ingroup—even when doing so violates egalitarian values (Castelli et al., 2008). Overall, this desire to place our ingroup higher than a comparison outgroup results in us more positively evaluating other ingroup members who enable our ingroup to be perceived as better than other groups (Castelli & Carraro, 2010). This is the reason some politicians openly express prejudicial attitudes toward outgroups that their supporters perceive as undesirable; doing so increases the politicians' popularity among their ingroups. Those who exhibit great pride in their ingroups and believe these groups are a central component of their own self-identity are more likely to engage in ingroup biasing than those who do not identify so strongly with their ingroups (Mohr & Fassinger, 2006; Verkuyten et al., 1999). For example, following the terrorist attacks on September 11th, 2001, there was a dramatic increase in prejudice directed toward people of Arab ethnicity or Muslim beliefs. Consistent with social identity theory, those citizens who strongly identified with being "American" were more likely to report prejudicial beliefs than those whose nationality was less central to their self-identity (Oswald, 2005).

How would social identity theory explain the relationship between "pride" and "prejudice"?

Additional research suggests that the people who are most likely to engage in prejudiced thinking as a means of enhancing or protecting self-esteem are those with defensive high self-esteem. As discussed in Chapter 3 (section 3.4b), individuals with high explicit self-esteem but low implicit self-esteem often lash out at others who threaten their fragile feelings of self-worth. Similarly, these same individuals are the ones who are particularly likely to engage in discrimination against outgroups as a means of protecting threatened self-esteem (Jordan et al., 2005). Thus, social identity theory may best explain the prejudiced thinking of individuals who have relatively fragile feelings of high self-worth.

6.3b   Intergroup Competition Can Lead to Prejudice.

What happens when we take this tendency to perceive our ingroups as being better than other groups and mix it with intergroup competition, where one group's successes become the other group's failures? Hostility and violence are common results. Numerous studies and real-world events inform us that when two groups compete for a limited number of scarce resources such as jobs, housing, consumer sales, or even food, tensions dramatically increase and create a breeding ground for prejudice (Duckitt & Mphuthing, 1998; Quillian, 1995).

Realistic Group Conflict Theory

realistic group conflict theory

The theory that intergroup conflict develops from competition for limited resources

Realistic group conflict theory focuses on examining the competitive roots of intergroup intolerance (Levine & Campbell, 1972). It argues that groups become prejudiced toward one another because they are in conflict due to competition for scarce resources.

The group conflict is considered "realistic" because it is based on real competition. Contemptuous prejudice and envious prejudice are often fed by the intergroup competition examined by this theory. According to realistic group conflict theory, some Americans' hostility toward immigrants is escalating because of the perception that many immigrants are taking jobs away from American citizens and draining resources from various social service agencies.

Realistic group conflict theory contends that when groups are in conflict, two important changes occur in each group. The first change involves increased hostility toward the opposing outgroup, and the second change involves an intensification of ingroup loyalty. This pattern of behavior is referred to as **ethnocentrism** (Bizumic & Duckitt, 2012; Sumner, 1906). In an archival study of ethnocentrism, Taya Cohen and her colleagues (2006) analyzed data from 186 preindustrialized societies between 1850 and 1950 and found that as people's loyalty to their local communities increased, they valued outgroup violence more than ingroup violence, engaged in more external than internal warfare, and placed a higher

In October 2018, a gunman shot and killed 11 people during a Jewish service in Pittsburgh, Pennsylvania. How can social psychology theories help us understand these extreme forms of prejudice?

(Source: "Tree of Life Synagogue memorials 10-30-2018 01," Official White House Photo by Andrea Hanks, via Wikimedia.)

value on external warfare. To better understand how ethnocentrism can develop due to conflict, let's examine a classic field study investigating this psychological phenomenon.

The Robbers Cave Study

What happens if you randomly place people into one of two groups and manipulate circumstances to promote intergroup competition? This was the central question surrounding a classic participant observation study designed by Muzafer Sherif and his colleagues (Sherif et al., 1961; Sherif & Sherif, 1956). They conducted the study in the summer of 1954 at a densely forested and hilly 200-acre camp that the researchers had created at Robbers Cave State Park, in Oklahoma. Participants were 20 white, middle-class, well-adjusted, 11- and 12-year-old boys who had never met one another before. In advance, the researchers divided the boys into two groups; each group was assigned a separate cabin out of sight of the other, and thus, neither knew of the other's existence. The camp counselors were actually researchers who unobtrusively observed and recorded day-to-day camp events as the study progressed.

The study had three phases. The first phase was devoted to *creating ingroups*, the second was devoted to *instilling intergroup competition*, and the third phase involved *encouraging intergroup cooperation*. During the first week of ingroup creation, each group separately engaged in cooperative activities, such as hiking, hunting for hidden treasures, making meals, and pitching tents. As the week progressed, each group developed its own leader and unique social identity. One group named itself the "Rattlers," established a tough-guy group norm, and spent a good deal of time cursing and swearing. The other group called itself the "Eagles," and they instituted a group norm forbidding profanity. As the first week drew to a close, each group became aware of the other's existence. How do you think they responded? By making clear and undeniable ingroup-outgroup statements: "*They* better not be in *our* swimming hole!" "*Those* guys are using *our* baseball diamond again!"

During the second phase of the study, Sherif tested his main hypothesis that intergroup competition would cause prejudice. To do this, he created a weeklong tournament between the two groups, consisting of 10 athletic events including things like baseball, football, and tug-of-war. The winner of each event would receive points, and at the end of

ethnocentrism
A pattern of increased hostility toward outgroups accompanied by increased loyalty to one's ingroup

(Images from Intergroup Conflict and Cooperation: The Robbers Cave Experiment, by M. Sherif et al., 1961, Norman, OK: Oklahoma Book Excharge, p. 105. Copyright © 1988 by Wesleyan University Press. Reprinted by permission of Wesleyan University Press; permission conveyed through Copyright Clearance Center, Inc.)

Sherif and his colleagues (1961) created intergroup hostility between two groups of boys (the "Eagles" and the "Rattlers") at a summer camp by having them compete against one another. In the photo on the left shown here, the Eagles grab and burn the Rattlers' group flag after losing a tug-of-war contest. Later (right photo), the Rattlers hang an Eagle's pair of jeans—upon which they had painted, "The Last of the Eagles"—from a pole. Can you recall incidents from your own life where competition with another group resulted in the development of prejudicial attitudes and discriminatory behavior?

the week the group with the most points would receive highly prized medals and impressive four-bladed pocketknives. True to Sherif's expectations, the intergroup conflict transformed these normal, well-adjusted boys into what a naive observer would have thought were "wicked, disturbed, and vicious" youngsters (Sherif, 1966, p. 58).

During this phase, the counselors heard a sharp increase in the number of unflattering names used to refer to outgroup members (for example, "pig" and "cheater"). The boys also rated their own group as being "brave," "tough," and "friendly," while those in the outgroup were "sneaky," "smart alecks," and "stinkers." This ingroup favoritism was also manifested in the boys' friendship preferences. Sherif, playing the role of camp handyman, asked the boys to tell him who their friends were at camp. The sharp division between the two groups was reflected in the fact that 93% of the friendship preferences were of the ingroup variety. If negative attitudes previously existed between ingroup members, they were now redirected against the outgroup, indicating that one by-product of intergroup hostility is an increase in ingroup solidarity.

As the two groups competed in the various games, intergroup hostility quickly escalated from name-calling to acts of physical aggression. For example, at the end of the first tug-of-war contest, the losing Eagles demonstrated their outgroup attitudes by seizing and burning the Rattlers' group flag. Not to be outdone, the Rattlers raided the Eagles' cabin, overturning cots, ripping mosquito netting, and carrying off one of the Eagles' blue jeans as booty. The next day, armed with bats and sticks, the Eagles returned the favor. Then they retreated to their cabin, proceeded to stuff rocks in their socks, and waited for the next wave of Rattler reprisals.

Who ultimately won the valued prizes for which they were competing? The Eagles. Not surprisingly, the Rattlers thought they had been cheated. While the victors were taking a celebratory swim, the Rattlers stole their medals and knives. When the Eagles returned to find their prizes gone, the Rattlers admitted to the deed and told the incensed Eagles they could have them back . . . if they got down on their bellies and crawled for them! These are only a few of the incidents that occurred between the Eagles and the Rattlers. Intergroup hostility became so intense that members of the opposing groups held their noses whenever they passed by one another in camp.

The third phase of the study was designed to reverse the hostility, a task that proved to be much more difficult to accomplish. First, the researchers sought to determine whether simple noncompetitive contact between the groups would ease tensions. They tested this hypothesis during the first two days of phase three by bringing the groups together for some pleasant activity, such as a meal or a movie. The results were not encouraging. Both groups used each interaction merely as an opportunity to increase their mutual animosity for one another. During mealtimes, for example, food was more likely to be thrown at opposing group members than eaten.

The failure of simple contact to reduce hostility did not surprise Sherif and his colleagues. They hypothesized that to reduce intergroup conflict, they needed to introduce what they called a **superordinate goal**, which is a mutually shared goal that can be achieved only through intergroup cooperation. To test this hypothesis, the researchers arranged for a series of problem situations to develop over the course of the next 6 days. Each problem was urgent and involved both groups. The first problem was the "failure" of the camp's water supply. The groups initially responded to this emergency by trying to solve it on their own. However, after converging on the source of the water problem—the camp water tank's plugged faucet—they cooperated in fixing it.

A few days later, the camp truck "broke down"; all the boys had to work together to pull it up a steep hill. Outgroup friendships grew from a measly 7% average at the end of phase one to a rather robust 30% average during this phase. At their final campfire, the two groups decided to put on a joint entertainment program consisting of skits and songs. When departing from camp the following day, the two groups insisted on traveling home on the same bus and the Rattlers used their prize money to buy milkshakes for everyone.

Taken as a whole, the Robbers Cave study is an excellent example of how ethnocentrism can develop when two groups compete for scarce resources. It also demonstrates that having a superordinate goal can lead to peaceful coexistence between previously antagonistic groups. Although this study used children as participants, similar results have also been obtained with adult samples (Jackson, 1993).

Broader Role of Competition and Threats

Although the original theory assumed that prejudice develops due to real, tangible conflict between groups, later work demonstrated that the mere *perception* of conflict is often sufficient to fuel intolerance (Esses et al., 1998). For example, Michael Zárate and his colleagues (2004) found that when American research participants were led to believe that Mexican immigrants had similar skills and attributes as themselves, their sense of job security was threatened, which led to more negative attitudes toward immigrants. These findings suggest that the perceived threat of competing for jobs was sufficient to induce prejudice. Similarly, heterosexual individuals who perceive threats from gay men and lesbians—such as unwanted sexual attention, fear of HIV infection, or courtesy stigma—display more antigay prejudice than do people who do not perceive such threats (Pirlott & Cook, 2018).

Beyond feeling threatened due to perceived safety or resource threats, studies find that some people feel threatened because they perceive that an outgroup is culturally changing their "way of life" by practicing a different religion, celebrating different holidays, or having different values. These types of concerns reflect symbolic threats and can also lead to prejudice (Stephan & Stephan, 2017; Tsukamoto & Fiske, 2018). For example, white Americans are less threatened by immigrants who have lighter skin features (e.g., "look white") because they are perceived as more likely to assimilate to an American culture that is predominantly defined by Anglo-Saxon European standards (Kunst et al., 2018).

superordinate goal
A mutually shared goal that can be achieved only through intergroup cooperation

Of course, not everybody responds to real and perceived threats with fear and intolerance. Research demonstrates that a major factor in short-circuiting prejudicial responses is an individual's personal value system. For example, in a series of experimental studies, Amy Krosch and her colleagues (2017) manipulated conditions so that white participants experienced scarce economic resources. When later given the opportunity to provide financial resources to others, participants who had been previously identified as having a high internal motivation to respond without prejudice (that is, they held egalitarian beliefs) gave more resources to black targets than did participants who had a low internal motivation to respond without prejudice (that is, they held anti-egalitarian beliefs). This finding suggests that people who are motivated by their internalized egalitarian beliefs are less likely to respond to perceived threats with prejudice and discrimination. The takeaway message in all of this research is that prejudice and discrimination toward outgroups can be triggered by real threats, perceived threats, and symbolic threats, but such fear-based intolerance is especially likely among people whose personal values encourage rather than discourage anti-egalitarian behavior.

6.3c   Prejudice Can Serve as a Justification for Oppression.

What if two groups come into contact with one another, but one group is much more powerful than the other? In laboratory experiments, when groups are given different amounts of social power, members of high-power groups discriminate more against outgroups than members of low-power groups (Sachdev & Bourhis, 1987, 1991). Additional research suggests that having social power increases automatic negative evaluations of stigmatized groups and increases the experience of negative affect when encountering stigmatized group members (Guinote et al., 2010). What sort of beliefs might foster and justify these automatically activated negative feelings that often lead to discrimination?

Social Dominance Theory

Social dominance theory proposes that in all societies, groups can be organized in a hierarchy of power with at least one group being dominant over all others (Pratto, 1996). Dominant groups enjoy a lopsided share of the society's assets, such as wealth, prestige, education, and health. In contrast, subordinate groups receive most of the society's liabilities, such as poverty, social stigma, illiteracy, poor health, and high levels of criminal punishment. History teaches us that the negative stereotypes and prejudicial attitudes that dominant groups develop about those they oppress serve to justify their continued oppression (Bergh et al., 2016; Rosenthal & Levy, 2010).

"The Whites told only one side. Told it to please themselves. Told much that is not true. Only his own best deeds, only the worst deeds of the Indians, has the White man told."

—Yellow Wolf, Nez Perce Indian, 1855–1935

Contemptuous prejudice and paternalistic prejudice are the two forms of intolerance expressed by the oppressor group, while the prejudice that subordinate groups express toward those who oppress them is of the envious form.

A good deal of the prejudice that has occurred in the history of the United States has rested on social dominance. The Europeans who founded this country did not arrive on uninhabited shores in the "New World." These settlers used their superior weapons to dominate and conquer the indigenous people of North America. At the same time that Europeans were colonizing North America, they were also capturing and buying Africans and transporting them to the colonies as slaves. They justified this inhuman exploitation by stigmatizing both American Indians and Africans as biologically inferior races who needed civilizing (see Figure 6.8). To this day, people who hold such beliefs about racial groupings display increased support for social hierarchies and racial prejudice (Mandalaywala et al., 2018).

social dominance theory

A theory contending that societal groups can be organized in a power hierarchy in which the dominant groups enjoy a disproportionate share of the society's assets and the subordinate groups receive most of its liabilities

FIGURE 6.8   **An Example of Racist Attitudes in an Old American Textbook**

This American high school geography book published in 1880 categorized "Races of Man" around the globe in a descending order of capacity for civilization. The white American author described the two races that his social group had the most contact with, and whom they had historically treated so harshly, in a particularly condescending manner. African tribes are described as living in a "savage or barbarous state," while the American descendants of native Africans are described as having "been Christianized and civilized" by whites. Similarly, the native races of America, whose land had been taken by the European colonizers, are described as having "always shown but little capacity for civilization" (Swinton, 1880, p. 17). In these characterizations, we see how an oppressor group justifies its exploitation of less powerful groups by denigrating them.

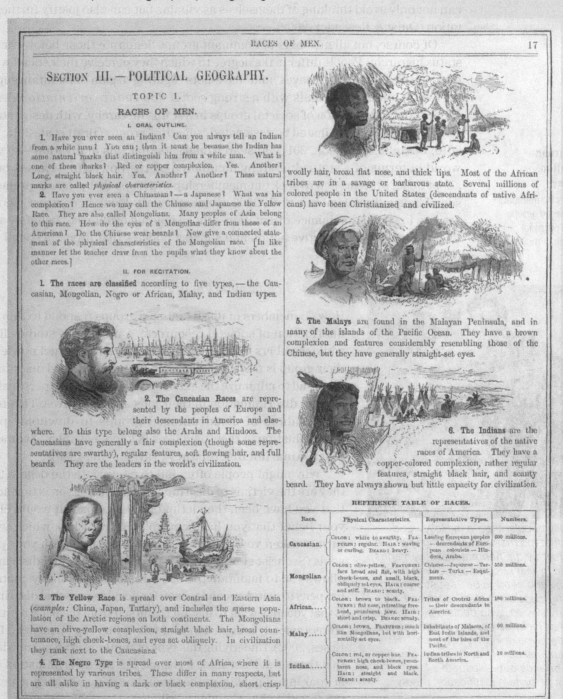

Source: A Complete Course in Geography: Physical, Industrial and Political, by W. Swinton, 1880, New York, NY: Ivison, Blakeman, Taylor, p. 17, via California Digital Library.

Consistent with social dominance theory, research indicates that people develop less egalitarian beliefs toward outgroups as the social status of their own group increases in comparison to the target outgroups (Levin, 2004; Schmitt et al., 2003). A number of experimental studies have also demonstrated that developing prejudicial and stigmatizing attitudes toward the victims of one's own harmful actions is a common response (Georgesen & Harris, 2000; Rodríguez-Bailón et al., 2000). For example, Stephen Worchel and Virginia Mathie Andreoli (1978) found that, when instructed to deliver electric shocks to a man when he responded incorrectly on a learning task, college students were more likely to dehumanize him than were students who were instructed to reward the man for correct answers. By dehumanizing and derogating their own victims, powerful exploiters can not only avoid thinking of themselves as villains but can also justify further exploitation (Quist & Resendez, 2002).

Of course, not all members of dominant groups denigrate those below them in the status hierarchy. People differ in the degree to which they perceive their social world as a competitive jungle, with "haves" and "have-nots" fighting to gain or maintain supremacy over each other. Individuals with a strong *social dominance orientation* desire and support the organization of societal groups in a status hierarchy, with designated "inferior" groups being dominated by designated "superior" groups (Bratt et al., 2016; Bassett, 2010; Costello & Hodson, 2011). Research suggests that this motivation—to view the world in terms of a status hierarchy dominated by the powerful—causes people to adopt belief systems and to seek out membership in groups that promote prejudice and social inequality (Dambrun et al., 2002; Guimond et al., 2003). In contrast, people who are low in social dominance orientation—those holding egalitarian beliefs—are more likely to engage in collective action and support policies that promote social equality (Stewart & Tran, 2018).

personal-group discrimination discrepancy

The tendency for members of disadvantaged groups to downplay personal discrimination in their own lives

System Justification Theory

How do members of disadvantaged groups respond to this unequal distribution of societal resources? A number of studies find that, while members of disadvantaged groups readily acknowledge that their group is frequently targeted for prejudice and discrimination, they tend to minimize the extent to which they have personally experienced discrimination in their jobs and daily lives. This tendency for members of disadvantaged groups to downplay personal discrimination in their own lives is known as the **personal-group discrimination discrepancy** (Taylor et al., 1990).

Why might people often fail to appreciate the degree to which they are the victims of discrimination? One reason is that admitting that you have been the victim of discrimination would challenge your belief that you have control over your life, which would, in turn, weaken your confidence that you can obtain your personal goals (Sechrist et al., 2004). Thus, denying personal discrimination allows you to maintain the belief that you personally control what happens to you. A second reason for denying personal discrimination is that you may want to distance yourself from the negative attributes stereotypically assigned to your fellow ingroup members (Hodson & Esses, 2002). Underlying this type of thinking is an acknowledgment that there is at least some legitimacy to the discrimination directed at your ingroup while at the same time denying that you personally possess the objectionable attributes.

A historically popular theme in Hollywood movies is that the material advantages of the rich are offset by the nonmaterial advantages of the poor. In Mary Poppins, *the well-to-do are unhappy and need to be "set straight" by jolly working-class characters, such as Bert the chimney sweep, who declares, "A sweep is as lucky as lucky can be . . . When you're with a sweep, you're in glad company." How does this cultural belief—that overall benefits in society balance out—illustrate a key component of system justification theory?*

One of the consequences of failing to realize that you have been the victim of discrimination is that such denial increases the likelihood that the existing unfair status hierarchy in society will remain intact. **System justification theory** contends that members of both advantaged and disadvantaged groups often endorse the group status hierarchy in society as being legitimate and fair. Unfortunately, this endorsement of the existing status quo often serves as a stumbling block to disadvantaged individuals' own personal and social advancement (Jost et al., 2007; Osborne & Sibley, 2013).

Societal stereotypes play an important role in system justification because they justify the positive outcomes of dominant groups, the negative outcomes of subordinate groups, and the exploitation of subordinate groups by dominant groups (Howard & Sommers, 2017; Jost et al., 2005). For example, women are often rewarded and encouraged to conform to the feminine gender role by presenting themselves as "nice, but weak" (Rudman, 2005). Women who adopt this benevolently sexist self-presentation style receive positive reinforcement for being warm and nurturing, but they also are perceived as being less competent and powerful (Jackman, 1994). Despite these negative consequences, by focusing on the rewards of this subordinate role, women tend to develop an automatic preference for male over female authority, which perpetuates the existing status quo and short-circuits any collective action to reduce gender inequality (Becker & Wright, 2011).

Similar system justification is observed among the social classes. Throughout literature, film, and popular culture, poor people are often stereotyped as being happier and more honest than rich people, and also as being more likely to be rewarded in the afterlife (Streib et al., 2016). Aaron Kay and John Jost (2003) found that, when people read stories about characters who matched societal stereotypes of rich and poor, they were more likely than those not exposed to such stereotyped characters to later believe that the status hierarchy in society is fair and equitable. Although believing that existing social arrangements are generally desirable may reduce personal distress and lead to greater satisfaction among those at the lower end of the status hierarchy, it also breeds inaction (Kay et al., 2007). If moral outrage is one of the primary motivators of social reform and efforts to help the disadvantaged, then system justification effectively defuses the emotional component that would trigger such social action (Wakslak et al., 2007).

system justification theory

A theory proposing that members of both advantaged and disadvantaged groups often adopt beliefs endorsing the legitimacy and fairness of the unequal group status hierarchy in society

authoritarian personality

A personality type characterized by submissiveness to authority, rigid adherence to conventional values, and prejudice toward outgroups

6.3d Authoritarianism Is Associated with Hostility Toward Outgroups.

One of the early inquiries into prejudice-prone personalities was the work of Theodor Adorno and Else Frenkel-Brunswik—two social scientists who fled Nazi Germany during World War II. Motivated by a desire to explain the psychology underlying the mass genocide of millions of Jews and other "undesirables" by the Nazi regime, Adorno and Frenkel-Brunswik believed that the cause of extreme prejudice could be traced to personality conflicts developed during childhood (Adorno et al., 1950). Operating from a psychoanalytic perspective and using survey, case study, and interview methods, they identified what they called the **authoritarian personality**. Based on their studies, the researchers concluded that authoritarian personalities develop from harsh child-rearing practices that teach children to repress their hostility toward authority, and instead, redirect or displace it onto less powerful targets who cannot retaliate. As adults, these authoritarians are submissive to authority figures and intolerant of those who are weak or different. Although this original theory is acknowledged as an important attempt to understand prejudice in terms

(AP Photo)

The widespread abuse of Iraqi detainees by US occupying forces in Abu Ghraib prison was widely condemned. Which type of person is more likely to excuse such prisoner abuse: an individual with an authoritarian personality, or someone with a high social dominance orientation?

of personality conflict and child-rearing practices, questions about how people actually become authoritarians and criticisms of the research methods employed in the original studies resulted in this approach losing credibility by the late 1960s (Van Hiel et al., 2004).

In the 1980s, interest in the authoritarian personality was revived when Bob Altemeyer (1981, 1988) suggested that its origins have nothing to do with personality conflicts from childhood; instead, he proposed, it is caused by children learning a prejudicial style of thinking from their parents and other important people in their lives. Operating from a social learning perspective, Altemeyer contended that children who are socialized by authoritarians and strict disciplinarians develop similar tendencies because they model and reinforce this intolerant worldview. He further asserted that most of this social learning occurs during adolescence, with the principal modelers being parents and peers. Socialized to view their world as a dangerous and threatening place, and isolated from personal contact with nonconventional people or minorities, adolescents in authoritarian environments learn that it is acceptable and even encouraged to express hostility toward various outgroups.

A number of studies conducted over the past 20 years support Altemeyer's social learning view over the earlier psychoanalytic perspective (Duckitt & Fisher, 2003; Feldman & Stenner, 1997). What appears to motivate the prejudice of the authoritarian personality is a strong desire to identify with, and conform to, the existing social order, coupled with a learned sense of fearfulness and insecurity about the social world and a perception that other groups pose a threat to one's ingroup (Altemeyer, 2004; Jost et al., 2003). Individuals growing up in authoritarian households are most likely to adopt authoritarian attitudes and beliefs when they have strong needs for social order and conformity.

In many different societies, people with authoritarian personalities not only express greater antipathy toward threatening outgroups than the average person but are also more likely to act on their hostility (Lippa & Arad, 1999). Authoritarians also tend to generalize their outgroup prejudices and have lower pro-diversity beliefs (Asbrock & Kauff, 2015). For example, authoritarians are likely to express hostility toward blacks, Jews, feminists, gay men and lesbians, the homeless, and people with AIDS (Crawford et al. 2016; Pek & Leong, 2003). Authoritarians' distaste for threatening outgroups is also reflected in greater support for their government's military actions against other countries during times of international tension. They not only support such actions but are also more likely to excuse atrocities committed by their own military forces during these interventions (Doty et al., 1997; Unger, 2002).

Besides identifying individual variations in authoritarianism, social scientists have also examined how it might vary on a societal level over time. An important catalyst for the manifestation of societal authoritarianism is *perceived social threat* (Doty et al., 1991). That is, when societies undergo economic hardships and social upheaval, mildly authoritarian individuals may become motivated to join social, political, or religious organizations that express dogmatic and rigid social attitudes and preach intolerance of outgroups who are perceived as threats to the social order (Ludeke et al., 2018; McCann, 1999). For example, in a series of archival studies of church membership patterns in the United States, Stuart McCann (1999) found that people were most attracted to intolerant religious teachings and authoritarian churches when the country was experiencing heightened social and economic threat. Similarly, longitudinal studies of South Koreans' social values between 1982 and 1996 found that as economic and military threats diminished, endorsement of authoritarian beliefs also diminished among the young and the educated portions of the population (Lee, 2003).

In 2018, there was much political discussion and controversy around "immigrant caravans" coming from Central America, which greatly increased some Americans' perceived social threat. For example, television and radio commentator Glenn Beck stated, "This is an invasion. There's no other way to describe it." Based on authoritarianism research, what type of social consequences might we see in this country due to this heightened perceived threat?

Section Summary

- People appear to be automatically biased toward ingroup members.

- Social identity theory asserts that prejudice and discrimination can result from people trying to increase or maintain self-esteem.

- Realistic group conflict theory argues that groups become prejudiced toward one another because they are in competition for scarce resources.

- Social dominance theory explains how dominant groups develop stereotypes and prejudicial attitudes to justify their oppression of others.

- System justification theory explains how disadvantaged groups endorse oppressive societal beliefs.

- Research on authoritarianism suggests that some forms of prejudice can be traced to personality and socialization factors.

6.4   Can We Reduce Intergroup Bias and Intolerance?

Having analyzed the psychological and social mechanisms underlying intergroup bias and intolerance, let us now explore the prospects for reducing prejudice and discrimination. First, we examine whether changing people's thinking can reduce prejudice (an *individual-based approach*), and then we outline situational factors necessary to reduce intergroup intolerance (a *group-based approach*). Finally, the chapter ends with a brief look at social psychological attempts to remedy some of the negative consequences of prejudice and discrimination in our educational system.

6.4a   Prejudice and Discrimination Can Be Reduced by Monitoring Stereotyped Thinking.

Given the fact that stereotypes are resistant to change, how can motivated individuals avoid judging others in this manner? For example, imagine that Clayton has grown up being taught that women are intellectually inferior to men. However, during the course of his life, Clayton has been exposed to people who do not fit this gender stereotype. Because of these experiences—and his desire to perceive himself as nonsexist—Clayton may begin to adopt a more egalitarian view of women. Although Clayton no longer accepts the stereotype, he has not eliminated it from his memory. Suppose that upon learning that his new boss is a woman he makes an automatic assumption that she will not be good at her job. Upon realizing that this negative assumption is inconsistent with his newer, egalitarian view of women, Clayton is likely to experience guilt and be motivated to avoid such biased thinking in the future. Yet how might he best accomplish that goal?

In a very real sense, for a person like Clayton, censoring the negative stereotype and guarding against ingroup biasing takes conscious and deliberate attention—like trying to break a bad habit. Patricia Devine and Margo Monteith contend that people can circumvent stereotypical thinking if they make a conscious effort to use more rational, inductive strategies (Devine & Sharp, 2009; Monteith & Mark, 2009). Although the unwanted stereotype will likely be automatically activated as soon as Clayton encounters a woman, the good news is that this stereotype is likely to become weaker with self-awareness and self-regulation. As depicted in Figure 6.9, whenever Clayton encounters a woman, the gender stereotype is involuntarily activated. If he does not consciously monitor his thoughts, he may automatically slip back into acting as though women are the intellectual inferiors of men (a *discrepant response*). Becoming aware of this discrepancy in his actions, Clayton will experience *discrepancy-associated consequences*. These include feelings of guilt and self-criticism that will, in turn, motivate him to heighten his self-awareness and search for situational cues that may have spontaneously triggered this prejudiced response (Hing et al., 2002). Through such attentiveness to prejudice-triggering cues, Clayton will slowly build up self-regulatory mechanisms that should produce more controlled and careful responses on future occasions (Kawakami et al., 2000).

FIGURE 6.9 Reducing Prejudiced Responding Through Self-Regulation

According to Devine and Monteith, when low-prejudiced persons first begin to try to respond in a nonprejudiced manner toward previously denigrated outgroup members, stereotype activation often spontaneously triggers a discrepant (i.e., prejudiced) response, which then triggers a series of discrepancy-associated consequences. This cognitive process is depicted by the arrows running vertically from top to bottom in the left side of the figure. Over time, through careful self-regulation of one's thoughts and attention to one's nonprejudiced standards, low-prejudiced people break the "prejudice habit" and respond as depicted by the horizontal arrows at the top of the figure. According to this model, what would be the first step you would need to take to reduce your own prejudiced responding?

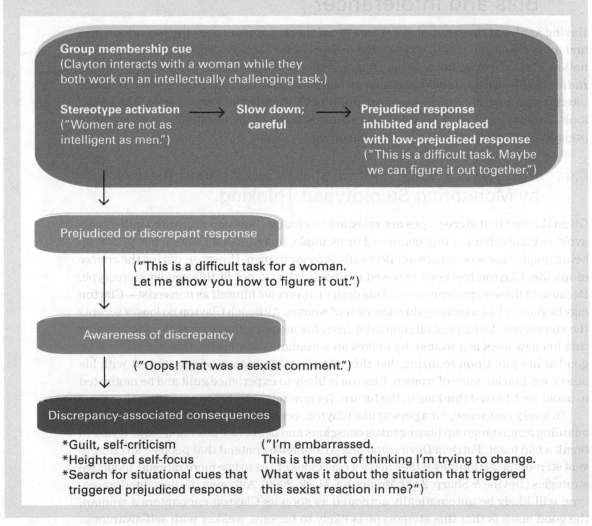

Group membership cue
(Clayton interacts with a woman while they both work on an intellectually challenging task.)

Stereotype activation ⟶ **Slow down;** ⟶ **Prejudiced response**
("Women are not as   **careful**   **inhibited and replaced**
intelligent as men.")   **with low-prejudiced response**
                                             ("This is a difficult task. Maybe
                                             we can figure it out together.")

Prejudiced or discrepant response

("This is a difficult task for a woman.
Let me show you how to figure it out.")

Awareness of discrepancy

("Oops! That was a sexist comment.")

Discrepancy-associated consequences

*Guilt, self-criticism   ("I'm embarrassed.
*Heightened self-focus   This is the sort of thinking I'm trying to change.
*Search for situational cues that   What was it about the situation that triggered
 triggered prejudiced response   this sexist reaction in me?")

According to Devine and Monteith, the two critical factors in reducing prejudice are that people must first be aware of their biases and then also be concerned about their biases. If people engage in self-awareness, they can learn to avoid using stereotypes in their social judgments (Kawakami et al., 2000). This perspective also holds out hope for reducing prejudice even among aversive racists. Recall, aversive racists are convinced they are nonprejudiced, so they believe there is no need to monitor their thoughts for bias. How can their prejudiced thinking be reduced without them engaging in careful self-regulation? The answer is that someone else must make aversive racists aware that there is a discrepancy between their explicit and implicit attitudes. Research by Leanne Son Hing and her coworkers (2002) indicates that when aversive racists are confronted with evidence exposing their hidden biases, they tend to experience guilt and make conscious efforts to behave in a nonprejudiced manner.

The importance of Devine and Monteith's perspective for reducing prejudice and discrimination is that it proposes that we can avoid prejudiced responding (and discrimination) if low-prejudiced standards are central to our self-concept *and* we bring these standards to mind before acting. In other words, although automatic stereotype activation makes nonprejudiced responding difficult, we can inhibit such intolerance through conscious and deliberate self-regulation (Legault et al., 2007).

6.4b People Can Become Agents of Positive Social Change.

Thus far, our discussion has focused on how prejudiced individuals can reduce their own biased thinking and responding, but can we also induce change in our wider social groups? Furthermore, can those who are the targets of prejudice and discrimination become powerful agents of social change themselves? For example, imagine that you are in a class and someone blurts out "That's so gay!" to express a negative opinion of another student's comments. What would you do? Would you confront the person who made the statement? Would your response be different if you were a member of the LGBT community than if you were a heterosexual person?

Confrontation can occur in a variety of ways, ranging from pointing out the inappropriateness of the comment, expressing disagreement, or requesting the perpetrator refrain from expressing their biased beliefs or discriminatory behaviors. A number of studies find that individuals who are the targets of negative stereotyping and prejudice report that they often want to respond by assertively communicating their displeasure to the perpetrator, but that they do not always act on this desire (Swim et al., 1998). One important social benefit of assertively responding is that it provides the opportunity to educate perpetrators by raising their awareness and hopefully reducing their prejudice (Zitek & Hebl, 2007). An additional personal benefit is that an assertive response often reduces negative feelings aroused by the perpetrators' comments (Hyers, 2007).

Despite these benefits, survey studies find that targets of negative stereotyping and prejudice sometimes decide to remain silent (Foster, 1999; Wright et al., 1990). The most common reason for not assertively responding to others' biased thinking is a concern about being judged negatively (Dodd et al., 2001). Assertive confrontations risk confirming stereotypes that your group is "difficult," "aggressive," or "oversensitive" when interacting with outgroup members (Latting, 1993). A related reason for not assertively responding is a desire to avoid conflict. Yet one negative personal consequence of not assertively responding to prejudice is that targets report that they carry negative feelings with them afterward (Hyers, 2007).

"If we accept and acquiesce in the face of discrimination, we accept the responsibility ourselves and allow those responsible to salve their conscience by believing that they have our acceptance and concurrence. . . . We should, therefore, protest openly everything . . . that smacks of discrimination."

—Mary McLeod Bethune, US educator and civil rights activist, 1875–1955

Individuals from the nonstereotyped group can play a significant role as an "ally" in confronting prejudice. Confrontation of prejudice by allies is especially helpful because it is generally not perceived as being self-serving, and therefore, it may be more effective than confrontation by those who were targeted (Czopp & Monteith, 2003). Although many people report that they would confront prejudice when it occurs, the reality is that many people remain silent (Kawakami et al., 2009; LeMarie & Oswald, 2016). However, those who confront prejudice by speaking up or doing something often report positive feelings about their intervention (Dickter & Newton, 2013). Furthermore, confrontation can be effective at initiating the sort of self-awareness and self-regulation that is necessary for prejudiced people to reduce their biased responses (Czopp et al., 2006). For example, Kimberly Chaney and Diana Sanchez (2018) found that people who expressed prejudiced thoughts were much less likely to express such thoughts one week later if others had confronted them following their initial biased statements. Interviews with these individuals revealed that this reduction in prejudice was at least partly due to them feeling guilty about their behavior and running the incident over in their minds. Such results suggest that confrontation can motivate long-term prejudice reduction, thereby nurturing the seeds of social change that might otherwise lie dormant.

6.4c The Contact Hypothesis Identifies Social Conditions That Reduce Intergroup Conflict.

At the time of the original U.S. Supreme Court *Brown v. Board of Education* decision on school desegregation, Gordon Allport (1954) outlined how desegregation might reduce racial prejudice. Later, other social psychologists also contributed to what came to be known as the **contact hypothesis** (Amir, 1969; Hewstone, 1996). The contact hypothesis can be thought of as a blueprint for reducing hostility by manipulating situational variables between groups that have had a history of conflict. According to this perspective, intergroup contact will decrease hostility when specific situational conditions are met (refer to Table 6.2).

contact hypothesis
The theory that under certain conditions, direct contact between antagonistic groups will reduce prejudice

TABLE 6.2 Reducing Prejudice Through Social Contact
According to the contact hypothesis, intergroup prejudice can be reduced if the four conditions listed below are met. Does research indicate that all four conditions are essential for prejudice reduction to occur?
Four Situational Conditions
1. *Equal Social Status*: Members of groups in conflict should interact in settings where everyone has roughly equal status.
2. *Sustained Close Contact*: Interaction between members of different groups should be one-on-one and should be maintained over an extended period of time.
3. *Intergroup Cooperation*: Members of different groups should engage in joint activities to achieve superordinate goals.
4. *Social Norms Favoring Equality*: There must be a clear social perception, largely fostered by group authority figures, that prejudice and discrimination are not condoned.
Fifth Condition in the Reformulated Model
Friendship Potential: Developing friendships with outgroup members precipitates initial reductions in intergroup tensions and fosters emotional ties that are important in reducing prejudice over time.

Equal Social Status

The first necessary condition is that the groups interacting must be roughly *equal in social status*. When this condition is not met and traditional status imbalances are maintained, long-standing stereotypes that are largely based on status discrepancies are generally not revised (Gaertner & Dovidio, 2000). However, research indicates that when equal-status people from different racial and ethnic groups interact, such as soldiers in the U.S. Armed Forces, racial stereotyping and prejudices decline (Pettigrew, 1969).

> "Only equals can be friends."
> —Ethiopian proverb

> "You cannot judge another person until you have walked a mile in his moccasins."
> —North American proverb

Sustained Close Contact

The second condition is that the two groups must have *sustained close contact*. Several public-housing studies conducted in the 1940s and 1950s demonstrated the importance of this condition in reducing prejudice. Reflecting on these social experiments in racial integration, Stuart Cook stated:

> One of the clearest findings of studies on the relation between intergroup contact and attitude change is that, while individuals rather quickly come to accept and even approve of association with members of another social group in situations of the type where they have experienced such association, this approval is not likely to be generalized to other situations unless the individuals have quite close personal relationships with members of the other group. (Cook, 1964, pp. 41–42)

Similarly, survey studies and field experiments in France, Chile, Great Britain, Germany, Finland, and the Netherlands confirm that intergroup friendships significantly reduce both subtle and blatant explicit prejudice, as well as implicit prejudice (e.g., R. Brown et al., 2007; Gonzalez et al., 2010). The sustained close contact necessary to reduce prejudice does not even have to be something that one directly experiences; simply knowing that some of your ingroup members have outgroup friends is often sufficient to reduce prejudice toward that outgroup (Wright et al., 1997).

One likely reason school desegregation has not produced a significant reduction in racial prejudice is that students of different races generally avoid interacting with one another. That is, even though the school building is integrated, students segregate themselves on the bus and playground, and in the cafeteria and classroom. School officials often magnify the problem by separating students based on academic achievement, which results in advantaged white students and disadvantaged minority students having very little classroom contact (Epstein, 1985). One type of school activity that is fairly effective in reducing racial prejudice is team sports. When sports teams have a high percentage of minority athletes, there is a decrease in intergroup intolerance among the participants (Brown et al., 2003).

Which of the two types of personality-influenced prejudice—prejudice based on the authoritarian personality or on social dominance orientation—is most likely to be positively influenced by sustained close contact with members of a group toward which a person holds prejudiced attitudes?

> "And if a house be divided against Itself, that house cannot stand."
> —Mark 3:24–25, The New Testament

Intergroup Cooperation

A third necessary condition in reducing hostility is *intergroup cooperation*. As the Robbers Cave study demonstrated, animosity between the Rattlers and the Eagles subsided when they engaged in a joint activity to achieve mutually shared goals (*superordinate goals*). Similar results have been obtained in a variety of experimental and field settings, including school, work, and the armed forces (Desforges et al., 1997). One possible reason cooperation reduces intergroup bias and hostility is that cooperating

(U.S. Navy photo by Anastasia Puscian, via Wikimedia, Camp Pendleton, 2009)

When individuals from various ethnic groups join the armed services, situational conditions often reduce previously learned ethnic prejudices. In school settings, what type of activity is also likely to have these same situational conditions?

"Let's go hand in hand, not one before another."

—William Shakespeare, English dramatist and poet, 1564–1616

"When Mexico sends its people, they're not sending their best. . . . They're bringing drugs. They're bringing crime. They're rapists. And some, I assume, are good people."

—Donald Trump, 2015 presidential campaign speech

members of different social groups appear to cognitively *recategorize* one another into a new ingroup (Gaertner & Dovidio, 2009).

Social Norms Favoring Equality

The fourth condition for successful conflict reduction is a social environment that contains *social norms favoring equality* (Monteith et al., 1996). Here is where authority figures and group leaders play a pivotal role. If they publicly state support for equality and actively oppose intolerance, others are likely to follow their lead (Bahns & Branscombe, 2011). If they oppose intergroup contact, prejudice reduction is unlikely (Nesdale & Dalton, 2011). Institutional policies and social movements also play a significant role in shaping social norms. For example, surveys of American citizens found that during the "Black Lives Matter" movement both explicit and implicit racial attitudes became more egalitarian among both white and black respondents (Sawyer & Gampa, 2018). In contrast, during the 2016 United States presidential election, Republican candidate Donald Trump routinely expressed negative attitudes and prejudice towards a number of stigmatized groups (Muslims, immigrants, Asian Americans, disabled people, people who are obese). Not surprisingly, perceived tolerance for prejudice was higher following the election of Trump as president than before the election (Crandall et al., 2018). That is, many people perceived that America's social norms had changed to reflect increased prejudice directed towards specific groups targeted by the new leader of the country. These two examples highlight the power that authority figures and social movements can have in altering social norms regarding tolerance of outgroups, for better or for worse.

Are All Four Conditions Necessary?

Recent meta-analyses support the argument that contact, under the conditions outlined by Allport, can result in decreased prejudice with the effect sizes estimated between .25 and .37 (Paluck et al., 2018; Zhou et al., 2018). Contact appears to be especially useful in decreasing prejudice directed towards individuals with mental and physical disabilities and religious outgroups (Paluck et al., 2018; Zhou et al., 2018). In Thomas Pettigrew's and Linda Tropp's (2006) meta-analysis of 713 separate studies, they found that the greatest reductions in prejudice tended to occur when all four conditions in Allport's model were present, yet significant reductions emerged even when some conditions were absent. Thus, counter to Allport's initial thinking, while these four conditions do facilitate prejudice reduction, all four conditions are not necessary for reductions to occur.

"Progress is a nice word, but change is its motivator. And change has its enemies."

—Robert Kennedy, US senator, 1925–1968

Beyond the four conditions outlined in the original theory, Pettigrew (1998) has offered a reformulated version of the contact hypothesis in which he adds a fifth situational factor that facilitates prejudice reduction—namely, *friendship potential*. Pettigrew argued not only that developing friendships with outgroup members is important in precipitating the initial reduction in intergroup tensions, but also that fostering these emotional ties becomes increasingly important in reducing prejudice over time. Subsequent research has found that establishing a positive emotional relationship with even a single outgroup member can reduce both explicit and implicit prejudice toward the outgroup as a whole (Gulker & Monteith, 2013). Further, these cross-group friendships are most effective in reducing prejudice when individuals live in segregated neighborhoods and have had only occasional, or no, previous contact with outgroup members (Baum, 2010; Christ et al., 2010). Other research suggests that even imagined contact with outgroup members can initiate prejudice reduction, which illustrates the importance of simply anticipating positive interactions between groups (Yetkili et al., 2018; Zhou et al., 2018).

Intergroup Anxiety and the Contact Hypothesis

A criticism of the contact hypothesis has been its overemphasis on changing the dominant group's prejudicial attitudes, while ignoring the attitudes of minority group members (Devine et al., 1996). To more effectively promote intergroup harmony, social scientists must also consider (1) the attitudes and beliefs of minority group members, and (2) the beliefs and anxieties of everyone involved in intergroup contact. According to this perspective, during intergroup contact, minority group members may feel anxious because they fear being victimized and negatively evaluated (Shelton et al., 2005). They may also have negative stereotypes about the dominant group members (Trawlater et al., 2009). In turn, dominant group members may be anxious from fear of saying or doing something that might be interpreted as a sign of prejudice (Shelton et al., 2005).

In a meta-analysis of 108 samples, Negin Toosi and her colleagues (2012) found that people report more anxiety during interracial interactions than when interacting with someone of the same race. Compounding this anxiety is the concern of both parties that their interest in contact and interaction will not be reciprocated (Shelton & Richeson, 2005). This **intergroup anxiety** often creates difficulties in such social encounters, even in the absence of any real prejudicial attitudes (Ashburn-Nardo & Smith, 2008; Littleford et al., 2005). Among low-prejudiced individuals, those who have had very limited contact with the outgroup are the ones most likely to experience intergroup anxiety (Blair et al., 2003; Brown et al., 2001). The good news is that when people place themselves in intergroup situations and do so with an open mind, their intergroup anxiety often diminishes (Flynn, 2005; Phills et al., 2011). Intergroup anxiety tends to decrease during long-term interactions rather than during those that are fleeting (Toosi et al., 2012). Yet even imagined contact with members of another group can begin to decrease intergroup anxiety and decrease prejudice (Zhou et al., 2018).

In the final analysis, no single strategy eliminates prejudice and discrimination from the vocabulary of intergroup relations (Walsh, 2011). Because of the manner in which we as a species process information from our social world, and because of the importance we place on our group affiliations, we will always need to be attentive to the way we judge others. Otherwise, stereotyping can easily diminish our ability to see the shared humanity in those who fall outside the favored category of "we."

intergroup anxiety
Anxiety due to anticipating negative consequences when interacting with an outgroup member

"Most of the bigoted remarks I have heard and prejudice I have experienced came from people who were trying to be popular, not despised. They were following what they believed to be acceptable behavior in their group or sub-group, not deviating from it."

—Clarence Page, US author and social commentator, born 1947

Intergroup anxiety can lead to awkward social situations, but such anxiety often disappears through repeated interactions.

Section Summary

- Stereotypical and prejudicial thinking can be reduced through self-regulation, if one is motivated.

- Confrontation is an effective weapon against intolerance.

- The contact hypothesis identifies four conditions to reduce prejudice:
  equal social status
  sustained close contact
  intergroup cooperation
  social norms favoring equality

- A reformulated version of the contact hypothesis adds a fifth condition: friendship potential.

- Intergroup anxiety hinders the development of greater understanding between conflicted social groups.

Applications

How Can Our Schools Be Positive Institutions of Social Change?

The concepts that we have reviewed in this chapter have clear applications to a number of social settings, and one that has received specific attention is schooling. Here we focus on how social psychological research has attempted to address two educational issues (1) how schools can foster intergroup tolerance between students and (2) how schools can counter the negative effects of stereotype threat.

The Jigsaw Classroom

In 1971, Elliot Aronson was asked by the superintendent of the Austin, Texas, schools to devise a plan to reduce interracial tensions in the recently desegregated classrooms. After observing student interaction, Aronson realized that the social dynamics were strikingly similar to those described by Sherif in the Robbers Cave field study (refer back to section 6.3b, The Robbers Cave Study). Using that study and the contact hypothesis as guides, he and his colleagues developed a cooperative learning technique that came to be called the **jigsaw classroom** (Aronson et al., 1978; Aronson & Thibodeau, 1992). The technique was so named because students had to cooperate in "piecing together" their daily lessons, much the way a jigsaw puzzle is assembled. Ten fifth-grade classrooms were introduced to this technique, and three additional classes served as control groups.

jigsaw classroom
A cooperative group-learning technique designed to reduce prejudice and raise self-esteem

In the jigsaw classroom, students were placed in six-person racially and academically mixed learning groups. The day's lesson was divided into six subtopics, and each student was responsible for learning one piece of this lesson and then teaching it to the other group members. With the lesson divided up in this manner, cooperation was essential for success. In contrast to traditional classroom learning, in which students compete against one another, the jigsaw classroom promoted superordinate goals. It also promoted racial harmony. Compared with students in the control classrooms (in which traditional learning techniques were employed), students in the jigsaw groups showed a decrease in prejudice and an increase in liking for one another. This change in students' attitudes toward one another was due to them recategorizing previous outgroup members as new ingroup members— "we" versus "us against them." Their liking for school also improved, as did their level of self-esteem. The cooperative learning also improved minority students' academic test scores, while white students' scores remained the same. Since these studies were first conducted and reported, meta-analysis of results from similar cooperative classroom settings has found that the jigsaw method offers a promising way to improve race relations in desegregated schools by breaking down the "outgroup" barriers that drive a cognitive and emotional wedge between students (Miller & Davidson-Podgorny, 1987).

How did social psychologist Elliot Aronson use the insights of the contact hypothesis in designing jigsaw classrooms to both foster cooperative learning and reduce prejudice?

(Shutterstock)

(*continues*)

(**Applications**, *continued*)

Defusing Stereotype Threat

Beyond reducing intergroup tensions, research on stereotype threat highlights a second serious problem for many of our students, namely, struggling with negative cultural stereotypes regarding their academic potential. Unfortunately, many underrepresented students (such as ethnic minorities and women in math and science fields) fail to perform up to their intellectual potential. For example, African American college students tend to underachieve academically—even when their college equivalency scores are equal to those of white students (Neisser et al., 1996). Based on our previous discussion of stereotype threat, this underachievement may be partly caused by two factors. First, the anxiety and extra cognitive burden associated with stereotype threat may directly impair students' academic achievement (Blascovich et al., 2001). Second, following repeated instances of this anxiety-induced underperformance, many students may disidentify with academic achievement so that it is no longer important to their self-esteem.

To counteract these two negative effects of stereotype threat, social psychologists have been instrumental in developing a new—and still evolving—educational approach, often referred to as "wise" schooling (Walton, 2014). An important component in wise schooling is to provide students with critical feedback concerning their academic progress in a manner that does not induce stereotype threat (Steele, 2010). Thus, instead of offering students stigmatizing remedial help—which often only reinforces doubts they may have about their intelligence and academic ability—wise schooling invites minority students to participate in a racially integrated and intellectually challenging learning program. Often working cooperatively, students receive the message that regardless of their current skill level, they have the ability to reach their academic potential. This message is another important component in wise schooling: Intelligence is not fixed and unchanging, but rather, through hard work, it is expandable (Aronson et al., 2002). Research on wise schooling programs among low-income, minority, and female students indicates that wise schooling fosters greater enjoyment of the academic process, greater sense of belonging at college and identification with college-based careers, and higher grade-point averages—compared with control groups who receive conventional schooling—among stigmatized groups who are most likely to experience stereotype threat (Good et al., 2003; Walton, 2014).

What about school districts that do not have wise schooling programs? Is there anything that educators and parents can do on their own to increase the likelihood that students perform up to their potential? Research suggests some possibilities. For example, regarding math achievement, a number of studies indicate that girls are less susceptible to stereotype threat in math when their parents and teachers not only encourage them in math activities, but also intentionally shelter them from negative gender stereotypes (Oswald & Harvey, 2003). This does not mean that adults should not discuss negative stereotypes with children, but rather, when doing so, adults should provide a cultural context for such discussion that emphasizes children's academic potential. Additional research indicates that girls and young women are much less likely to underperform in math when they are not only taught about women's achievements in masculine-type fields but they also actually witness women succeeding in these fields (Cheryan et al., 2011; McIntyre et al., 2003). Female role models and mentors are important both in challenging negative gender stereotypes and in encouraging college-aged women to pursue careers in science and math (Drury et al., 2011; Herrmann et al., 2016; Shin et al., 2016).

In a very real sense, both wise schooling programs and the individual efforts of informed parents and teachers described above are examples of the self-fulfilling prophecy. Yet, now teachers and parents are not expecting failure from students; they're setting high expectations, and through their conviction, those expectations are much more likely to become reality.

THE BIG PICTURE

John Dovidio (2001) suggests that there have been three "waves" of scholarship in the study of prejudice. The first wave developed after World War II and conceived of prejudice as a form of personal psychopathology. The authoritarian personality is this wave's most identifiable theory. The second wave began in the 1950s and approached prejudice as more of a social problem, much like a social cancer that spread from person to person. A number of theories developed from this social perspective, including realistic group conflict theory, the social contact hypothesis, and social identity theory.

This second wave, which peaked during the early 1990s, did not consider prejudice to be a manifestation of mental illness. Instead, it was conceptualized as an outgrowth of socialization, normal cognitive processes, and the natural desire to receive rewards and raise self-esteem. Now we are in the third wave of research on prejudice. Here, more attention is paid to understanding unconsciously held prejudicial attitudes, as well as how the targets of intergroup intolerance adapt to and cope with stigmatization. Examples of recent work in this third wave include implicit prejudice, stereotype threat, and ambivalent sexism. Together, these three research waves have deepened our understanding of how prejudice develops, spreads, and diminishes, as well as what consequences it has for both its targets and perpetrators.

We are far from being a nonprejudiced species. Our natural inclination to categorize people can set the stage for prejudice. It is also true that competition, ingroup loyalties, and social ideologies fan the flames of this tendency to see people as "them" rather than "us" (Lanning, 2002). However, as has been demonstrated throughout this text, our ability to reflect on our actions, our desire to act in ways consistent with our internalized personal beliefs, and our ability to reshape social reality all mean that prejudice can be reduced. If self-concept is truly a process of identification, what we need to do on an individual level is expand our ingroup identification to include humanity as a whole (Gaertner & Dovidio, 2009). In doing so, we will be able to see ourselves in those who were previously thought of as merely inferior "others." This is by no means an insignificant cognitive shift. As you will discover in Chapter 10, when we include others in our self-concept, our resources become theirs to share and their successes and failures become our own. Therefore, the first step in achieving a community with a low level of prejudice is to monitor our own thinking and actions. The second step is to work collectively to change the perceptions of others. The question to ask yourself is whether you are ready to take that first step.

KEY TERMS

WEBSITES

Accessed through https://www.bvtlab.com/sop8

Websites for this chapter focus on the nature of prejudice, including an analysis of ethnic stereotypes, sexual harassment, antigay prejudice, the history and psychology of hate crimes, and how to break prejudicial habits.

American Psychological Association

The American Psychological Association has web pages that explore a number of issues related to prejudice and discrimination. For example, one web page analyzes whether all of us have some degree of prejudice, as well as the possibility that we can break our prejudicial habits. Another web page explores the history of hate crimes, including their prevalence, perpetrators, and emotional effects.

American Association of University Women

This website for the American Association of University Women has separate pages devoted to sexual harassment (Hostile Hallways: The AAUW Survey on Sexual Harassment in America's Schools) and gender discrimination in education (Gender Gaps: Where Schools Still Fail Our Children).

Sexual Orientation: Science, Education, and Policy

This website features the work of Dr. Gregory Herek, a noted authority on antigay prejudice, and his Northern California Community Research Group. A number of the studies conducted by Herek and this group are cited in the present chapter.

Breaking the Prejudice Habit

This is the website of Awareness Harmony Acceptance Advocates, an organization dedicated to spreading awareness around prejudice and discrimination.

Chapter 7

WOMEN'S WAVE RISE

19 WOMEN'S MARCH ON WASHINGTON

Social Influence

FOCUS QUESTIONS

1. Can situations automatically activate social norms from your memory without your awareness?

2. Americans often admire nonconformists, but what typically happens to people who fail to conform to others' opinions or behaviors?

3. How do people from individualist and collectivist cultures differ in their tendencies to conform?

4. What social factors influence whether we obey or disobey the destructive commands of authority figures?

CHAPTER OUTLINE

Applications: How can the internet influence voting behavior?

> **Preview** . . . The internet saturates many aspects of everyday living. How can the internet be used to shape the voting behavior of citizens?

The Big Picture

Key Terms

Websites

Introduction

In December 2017, *Time* magazine awarded its "Person of the Year" to what it called "The Silence Breakers"—individuals who experienced sexual harassment or sexual assault on the job and, despite great personal risk to their safety and fear of professional retaliation, chose to "break the silence" and talk about their harassment. In announcing the annual award, *Time* reporters stated:

> This reckoning appears to have sprung up overnight. But it has actually been simmering for years, decades, centuries. Women have had it with bosses and co-workers who not only cross boundaries but don't even seem to know that boundaries exist. They've had it with the fear of retaliation, of being blackballed, of being fired from a job they can't afford to lose. They've had it with the code of going along to get along. They've had it with men who use their power to take what they want from women. (Zacharek et al., 2017)

There was no leader of this social movement, but the voice of the Silence Breakers resulted in a flood of victims sharing their own experiences of sexual harassment and abuse in the workplace. Notably, the hashtag #MeToo became the defining symbol of this movement in which victims—mostly women, but also men—shared their experiences with sexual harassment and sexual assault. At first glance, this movement to hold abusers accountable seemed to erupt out of nowhere, but the hashtag #MeToo was first started in 2006 by Tarana Burker, a social activist who was working with sexual harassment survivors. Then, in 2016, almost on a whim, actor Alyssa Milano wrote online, "If you've been sexually harassed or assaulted write 'me too' as a reply to this tweet." Within a day, over 30,000 people had replied using the same #MeToo hashtag. To date, the hashtag has spread to 85 countries and been used in more than 19 million tweets, with those using it documenting their own experiences. The movement gained power, in part, because of the ability of people, worldwide, to unite and provide both informational and social support to one another. As the movement grew, individuals from all sectors of the workforce—politicians, CEOs, journalists, actors, and university professors—were called out for their sexually harassing behaviors and abuses of power. The vast majority of those called out were men, and some lost their jobs and/or had legal action taken against them. Although not all who were accused were held accountable for their actions, it is unlikely that any of them would have been stopped without the Silence Breakers starting the discussion of sexual harassment and sexual assault in the workforce. As the reporters in the *Time* article noted, "Norms evolve, and it's long past time for any culture to view harassment as acceptable" (Zacharek et al., 2017).

(Sundry Photography / Shutterstock)

The "Time Person of the Year" in 2017 was given to the Silence Breakers for their efforts at stopping sexual harassment of women. How does the #MeToo movement represent social influence on both the individual and group levels?

How did these Silence Breakers gain the courage to speak up despite the strong cultural norms that minimize such harassment and violence, often implying that victims should endure it in silence, especially when the perpetrator has high social status and power? How much did it matter that many of the first victims who gained attention and generated public outrage were of high status themselves—famous actresses, musicians, and television news reporters, such as Ashley Judd, Alyssa Milano, Selma Blair, Taylor Swift, and Megyn Kelly? Did their status give them additional power or lend greater credibility to their accusations? To what extent did the Silence Breakers influence other victims into speaking out about their experiences? Can this movement, and other online movements like it, create long-term change for victims and perpetrators of sexual harassment and sexual assault?

7.1   What Is Social Influence?

Social influence involves the exercise of social power by a person or group to change the attitudes or behavior of others in a particular direction (Forsyth, 2013). Our chapter-opening story represents social influence on both the individual and group level. The Silence Breakers influenced other victims to speak out about sexual harassment and assault, and to also challenge social norms and public opinion about the acceptability of sexual harassment in the workplace.

As this movement demonstrates, social influence moves both up and down—and across—the social hierarchy of society. Those who can wield the power of societal institutions typically have much more influence than those outside the power structure. However, at times, lower status individuals can change majority-held attitudes and beliefs. In this chapter, we examine the social psychology of influence in its various forms. Let's begin by identifying and defining the behavioral consequences of social influence.

7.1a   Conformity, Compliance, and Obedience Are Different Types of Social Influence.

Social psychologists typically identify three main behavioral consequences of social influence. The first consequence that we will examine is **conformity**, which involves yielding to perceived group pressure by copying the behavior and beliefs of others. To what degree do you conform to others' social influence? Consider the clothing you wear, the food you eat, the music you prefer, the religion you practice, and so on. How are these areas of your life influenced by the social standards of your friends, family, and larger culture? How about when you yawn after seeing someone else do so? Is this imitative response an example of conformity? What about when you actively defy a particular person's influence, such as when the Silence Breakers publicly criticized their abusers? In such instances, are people acting independently, or are these acts simply instances of conforming to different reference group standards?

Sometimes it's difficult, if not impossible, to distinguish conformity from independence. Even though the former is characterized by yielding to group standards, while **independence** means being free of others' control, they often result in the same behavioral outcomes. We discuss this issue and many others in more detail later in the chapter.

The second behavioral consequence of social influence is **compliance**, which is publicly acting in accord with a direct request. In compliance, people responding to a direct request may privately agree or disagree with the action in which they are engaging, or they may have no opinion about their behavior. Complying with a request toward which you have no personal attitude is not uncommon. Do you really think about what passing the salt to a dinner companion implies about your relationship with this person or your own values? Probably not. You simply comply out of habit.

Now consider, for a moment, a cultural ritual that you have probably engaged in on numerous occasions—namely, singing your country's national anthem. Being asked to stand and sing the national anthem during public ceremonies and before sporting events illustrates compliance. Many Americans stand and sing the "The Star-Spangled Banner" without considering the meaning of their actions. To them, it is a ritual with which they habitually comply before all sporting events, and they do so in a mindless fashion

social influence
The exercise of social power by a person or group to change the attitudes or behavior of others in a particular direction

conformity
Yielding to perceived group pressure by copying the behavior and beliefs of others

independence
Not being subject to control by others

compliance
Publicly acting in accord with a direct request

(Langer, 1989). However, during the 2017 National Football League season, a number of football players began kneeling during the anthem to peacefully protest police brutality directed toward African Americans. Their actions became highly controversial when high-profile politicians condemned them for being unpatriotic. Suddenly, standing or kneeling for the anthem became a decidedly mindful action for most players and fans.

External compliance—acting in accord with a direct request despite privately disagreeing with it—occurs because we are concerned how others might respond if we refuse them (Deutsch & Gerard, 1955; Tyler, 1997). Singing the national anthem or saying the Pledge of Allegiance because of fear of backlash or penalty are the result of external compliance. On the other hand, we often comply with a request because we have a personal allegiance to the values and principles associated with it. Such *internal compliance* (or *internalization*) involves both acting and believing in accord with a request (Kelman, 1958, 2006). Expressing your patriotism by singing the national anthem or saying the Pledge of Allegiance are manifestations of the internalization process.

What happens when you do not respond by complying with others' requests? Well, they may simply shrug their shoulders and forget about it, or they may conclude that you're a jerk and resolve to return your noncompliance at an opportune future date. However, another possible response to noncompliance is to up the ante by trying to secure the third behavioral consequence of social influence—namely, obedience. **Obedience** is the performance of an action in response to a direct order, usually from a person of high status or authority. Because most of us are taught from childhood to respect and obey authority figures (parents, teachers, police officers), obedience to those of higher status is common and is often perceived as a sign of maturity. However, all things being equal, most people prefer being "asked" to do something (compliance) rather than being "ordered" (obedience). Obedient behavior is more likely than compliant behavior to imply a loss of personal freedom, which is a valued commodity by most people—especially in individualist cultures (Moghaddam, 2013). Two months before the start of the 2018 football season, NFL Commissioner Roger Goodell introduced a new policy that ordered all NFL players to either stand during the national anthem or to remain in the locker room until the anthem was played. This demand of obedience was severely criticized by the NFL Players' Union, which contended that it restricted players' free choice to express their opinions. Realizing that this new policy was likely to create even greater social discord, the commissioner backtracked and announced that "no new rules relating to the anthem will be issued or enforced" until the league and players' association reached an agreement regarding protests. Although the NFL's demand of obedience was withdrawn, in 2018 many fewer players protested than in 2017, suggesting that the league's initial attempt to stifle dissent was largely effective. This incident suggests that even when people challenge the orders from authority figures, their subsequent behavior may still fall in line with obedience.

7.1b People with Social Power Are More Likely to Initiate Action.

How powerful are you? We are referring not to your physical strength but to your social strength. Do you exercise power or do you shrink from possessing it? There is a famous saying: "Power corrupts, and absolute power corrupts absolutely." Is there any truth to this assertion?

As previously defined, social influence is the exercise of social power to change people's attitudes or behavior in a particular direction. **Social power** refers to the force available to the influencer in motivating this change (Cook et al., 2006). This power can originate from having access to certain resources (for example, rewards, punishments, information), due to one's social position in society, or from being liked and admired by others (Jetten et al., 2006; Raven, 2001). It is not surprising to find that people like

obedience
The performance of an action in response to a direct order

social power
The force available to the influencer to motivate attitude or behavior change

having social power; they are more likely to identify with social roles that possess power than those that do not (Joshi & Fast, 2013). In most instances, those who are the targets of influence resent the use of social power when they perceive it as coercive and heavy-handed, but they often respond positively to "soft" power usage based on accepted social norms, expertise, and likability (Elias & Mace, 2005).

Why might the difference in social power between a professor and her students contribute to student apathy in the classroom?

(Shutterstock)

The findings from a number of empirical studies support the commonly held belief that possessing social power increases people's tendencies to take action, whereas powerlessness activates a general tendency to inhibit action (Anderson & Berdahl, 2002; Keltner et al., 2003). For example, when research participants are randomly assigned to experimental conditions with high or low social power, those given high power are more likely than those with low power to take action to achieve goals, even when their social power has nothing to do with the task at hand (Galinsky et al., 2003). This suggests that the possession of power in one context can lead to action in an unrelated context.

Why might people with social power be more likely to initiate action compared with those without much power? One reason is that having power makes people less dependent on others; they feel better equipped to act on their own without having to consider how others might impede or obstruct their actions. Because social power allows them to ignore or pay less attention to other people's viewpoints, powerful people tend to act more quickly—and with less deliberation—than those with low power (Magee & Smith, 2013; Smith & Trope, 2006). In essence, possessing power allows people to loosen the grip that social norms and standards typically exert on their behavior (Hays & Goldstein, 2015). With power, people can more easily and quickly exert their influence on the situation—including influencing those individuals in the situation (Gommans et al., 2017).

How might an individual's personality and behavior change as that person gains or loses social power?

The fact that people with social power tend to be less concerned about the social consequences of their actions creates a paradox. The decisions made and the actions taken by those with high social power are much more likely to affect other people's lives than are the decisions and actions of those with little power. Thus, the people who have the biggest influence on others' lives are the very people who often seem to care least about the social consequences of their actions. Do you see a potential danger here for those with less power?

Section Summary

- Social influence is the exercise of social power by a person or group to change the attitudes or behavior of others in a particular direction.

- Conformity, compliance, and obedience represent the three main behavioral consequences of social influence:
  Conformity: yielding to perceived group pressure
  Compliance: publicly acting in accord with a direct request
  Obedience: performing an action in response to a direct order

- Social power increases people's tendencies to take action, perhaps because power gives them more freedom from social constraints.

7.2   Classic and Contemporary Conformity Research

To better understand social influence, let's begin by analyzing three classic conformity studies conducted more than 40 years ago: Muzafer Sherif's work on norm development, Solomon Asch's work on group pressure, and Stanley Schachter's work on how people react to nonconformists. Analysis of each of these classic studies is followed by discussion of additional studies that provide further insight into the psychology of conformity.

7.2a   Sherif Analyzed Conformity to an Ambiguous Reality.

The first widely recognized conformity study was that of Turkish-born Muzafer Sherif, who in 1935 published his research on the development of social norms. Sherif's research was partly spurred by his disagreement with the prevailing individualist view of social psychology that a group was merely a collection of individuals and that no new group qualities arise when individuals form into a collective entity. Sherif countered that a group was more than the sum of its individuals' nongroup thinking, and he set out to test this hypothesis by studying how social norms develop in a group (Sherif, 1936).

In his study, Sherif enlisted college students into what was described as a visual perception experiment. Participants were individually placed in a small, totally darkened laboratory where, 15 feet in front of them, a small dot of light appeared. They were told that, after a short time, the light would move, and their task would be to judge how far it moved. In all cases the light was left on for 2 seconds after the participants indicated the beginning of movement. Each participant made 100 light movement judgments. Although they did not realize it, the experimenter never actually moved the dot of light. What the participants perceived as light movement was really an optical illusion known as the autokinetic effect. The *autokinetic effect* refers to the fact that when someone stares at a stationary point of light in a darkened room where there is no frame of reference, it appears to move in various directions.

In this highly ambiguous situation, each participant's first few guesses were generally quite different from one another. However, after a few more trials, they settled on a consistent range of light movement. Thus, even though this was an optical illusion, participants assigned some order to the visual chaos—zeroing in on a stable estimate as if they were actually mastering this perceptual task. Yet, because the light movement was illusory, there was not much consistency between those making their isolated judgments. One person would settle on a stable range of about 2 inches, while another would make an estimate of 6 inches. During the experiment's second phase, Sherif placed these same individuals together in groups of two and three and asked them to publicly announce their estimates after each trial. What ensued was not a free-for-all bickering of light-movement experts. Instead, all participants tended to gradually change their estimates to be more similar to the others. Moving from their individual standards, they converged on an expected standard established and enforced by the group, known as a **social norm** (Figure 7.1).

This demonstration of the process by which social norms develop is also an illustration of the more general process of social influence. Participants were in a fluid and ambiguous situation, and they looked to the group to help them define reality. They all conformed to an emerging social norm that was different from their individually developed standards. Interestingly, even though the data clearly indicated such social influence occurred, most of Sherif's participants denied that the others had influenced their own judgments.

social norm
An expected standard of behavior and belief established and enforced by a group

FIGURE 7.1   Norm Development

In Sherif's autokinetic experiments, when participants in three-person groups announced their individual judgments of light movement to one another, their initial divergent norms gradually converged over the course of the trials. In other words, in an ambiguous reality, the individuals established an expected standard (a social norm) of light movement. Can you think of instances in your own life where you and others established social norms to guide your own behavior and beliefs?

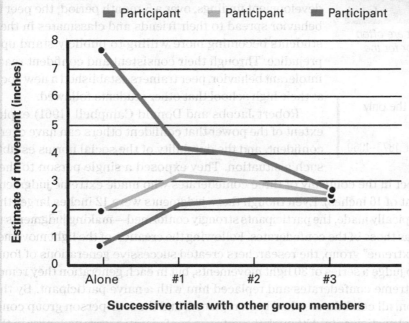

Data source: *The Psychology of Social Norms*, by M. Sherif, 1936, Oxford, England: Harper, pp. 91–93. Copyright 1936 by Harper.

The Power of Confidence in Shaping Norm Development

A third finding of Sherif's study was that when participants were uncertain about how to define reality, they were highly influenced by others who appeared confident. The basis for these findings was formed by placing a participant in the lab with a confederate who had been instructed to make all of his judgments within a predetermined range. As expected, the participant quickly adopted the confederate's range of judgments, and later used this social norm when placed in the autokinetic situation alone. In essence, faced with a confusing situation, people conformed to those who appeared confident in dealing with their surroundings, and they continued to be influenced by these opinions even after the confident individual had left.

In the expression of intergroup attitudes, one person's confident declaration of a social norm often shapes other people's thinking and behavior. A number of studies have found that people express more tolerance of prejudiced speech following a peer's expression of prejudiced views, and less tolerance after a peer condemns such speech (Blanchard et al., 1994; Ford & Ferguson, 2004). Capitalizing on the power that confident individuals have when influencing others, Elizabeth Paluck (2011) designed an

> "No written law has ever been more binding than unwritten custom supported by popular opinion."
>
> —Carrie Chapman Catt, US women's suffrage and peace activist, 1859–1947

> "A stranger must conform to his host's customs."
>
> —Euripides, Greek dramatist, fifth century BC

(Shutterstock)

Why is it that people who act confident are often the ones who set the norms of behavior for the group?

"To do exactly as your neighbors do is the only sensible rule."

— Emily Post, US author, 1873–1960

"Never throw away hastily any old faith, tradition, or convention . . . they are the result of the experience of many generations."

—Sir Oliver Lodge, English physicist, 1851–1940

anti-prejudice intervention program at five different high schools in which "peer trainers" were trained to confront expressions of intergroup prejudice. Suggested actions given to the peer trainers included speaking directly to the perpetrator (either as the incident unfolded or afterward), making their disapproval known to other students, calling an adult to intervene, and offering support to the target of prejudice following the incident.

All these actions conveyed assertiveness and confidence on the part of the peer trainers. Consistent with Sherif's norm development findings, over a 5-month period, the peer trainers' behavior spread to their friends and classmates in the form of students becoming more willing to publicly stand up against prejudice. Through their consistent and confident reactions to intolerant behavior, peer trainers established a new social norm at their high school that other students followed.

Robert Jacobs and Donald Campbell (1961) explored the extent of the power that confident others can have over the less confident, and the durability of the social norms established in such a situation. They exposed a single person to the autokinetic effect in the company of three confederates who made extreme judgments (light movement of 16 inches). Even though these judgments were 12 inches larger than what people typically made, the participants strongly conformed—making judgments nearly as extreme as those of the confederates. Following the creation of the light movement norm in this "extreme" group, the researchers created successive generations of four-person groups to judge a series of 30 light movements, but in each generation they removed one of the extreme confederates and replaced him with a naive participant. By the fourth generation, all confederates had been replaced, and the four-person group consisted of four actual participants. Although the extreme confederates were no longer in the group, their extreme group-derived norm continued to influence the judgment of successive generations of groups for quite some time. Jacobs and Campbell's study demonstrates, experimentally, a regularly occurring social phenomena—the views of past generations largely shape the thinking of current and future generations.

Taken together, these studies indicate that, when faced with uncertainty about how to interpret or judge events, we are influenced by others, especially if they appear confident. Not only are we likely to conform to their view of reality, we are also likely to continue to use their perspective in rendering judgments even in their absence (Nye & Brower, 1996). This conformity forms the bedrock of the socialization process in all societies. First, we learn and practice common ways of conduct that are characteristic for our social group. Through rehearsal, we develop mental representations, or *schemas* (see Chapter 4, section 4.1b), of how to behave according to these social norms. Our social environment—parents, friends, teachers, and popular culture—regularly communicate and enforce beliefs concerning which social norms should be used as guidelines for behavior in different situations. This socialization process helps us develop cognitive scripts for a wide variety of social situations. As discussed in Chapter 4 (section 4.1b), these scripts—which contain perceptions of relevant social norms—guide our behavior and problem-solving in the situation. Without this script learning, coordinated social interaction would be very difficult.

In understanding conformity to social norms—and conformity in general—there is one important social psychological process to keep in mind. When we are uncertain about how to understand an event, we often misperceive what others are thinking.

We think that everyone else is interpreting a situation in a certain way, when in fact they are not. This state of mind is known as **pluralistic ignorance**, and it plays a role in a wide range of social mishaps.

For example, imagine sitting in a large class and getting very confused as you listen to a professor lecture. Your confusion could be due to the complexity of the topic, the poor lecture style of the professor, or some combination of these two factors. After several minutes, the professor pauses and asks if there are any questions. You certainly have questions; yet, before raising your hand, you look around the room. No hands are raised—so you interpret the other students' passive response as a sign that they understand the lecture and have no questions. However, your conclusion is almost certainly incorrect; there are most likely numerous students who are equally as confused as you, yet are similarly under the impression that they are the only ones lost.

Pluralistic ignorance is driven by conformity to social norms—in this instance, conforming to the normative expectation that students will comprehend the professor's lecture and will not question the professor's competence. One outcome of the Silence Breakers is that they broke pluralistic ignorance around workplace sexual harassment. The flood of postings with the hashtag #MeToo let other victims know that they also had similar experiences and the victims were not alone.

7.2b Social Norms Are Often Automatically Activated.

As discussed in Chapter 4 (section 4.1c), *priming* is the process by which recent exposure to certain stimuli or events increases the accessibility of related memories, categories, or schemas. Priming is a good example of automatic thinking because it occurs spontaneously and unconsciously. How is priming related to social norms? Research suggests that, over time and with experience and practice, social norms become associated with specific settings, so that those settings can actually activate normative behaviors automatically. This idea—that situations automatically activate social norms from memory—is consistent with research discussed in Chapters 4 and 6 showing that specific social groups often automatically activate stereotypes from memory (Dijksterhuis & Bargh, 2001). Both stereotype activation and norm activation illustrate how social stimuli can spontaneously trigger well-learned thoughts and responses.

Jonah Berger and his colleagues (2008) tested the hypothesis that specific settings can automatically activate specific social norms by analyzing voter data from an election in the state of Arizona. They found that people were more likely to vote in support of an education funding initiative if their polling location was a school rather than other locations, such

The situation we are in can often automatically—and nonconsciously—activate the relevant social norms for that situation, which then directly shapes our behavior. Approaching a library is likely to cause you to act more subdued and being in a school can cause you to care more about education.

(*Shutterstock*)

as municipal buildings or churches. This was true even after controlling for voters' political views, demographics, and how far they lived from a school. Overall, this study suggests that a school setting can prime voters' existing social norms related to the value of education and thereby increase the likelihood that they will vote in favor of educational initiatives. These results were replicated in a follow-up experiment where Berger and his co-workers randomly assigned participants to first view and rate photographs associated with either school settings (such as images of student lockers and desks) or office buildings (the control condition) and then complete a survey that was described as being part of a second unrelated study in which participants reported their degree of

pluralistic ignorance
The tendency to think that everyone else is interpreting a situation in a certain way, when in fact they are not

support for an education funding initiative. Consistent with the previous voting study, participants expressed greater support for educational funding when they were exposed to images of schools rather than images of offices. It should be added that in a post-study debriefing, the participants did not make a conscious connection between their support for education funding and the images they had earlier viewed.

Other research suggests that the *anticipation* of entering a specific situation automatically heightens the accessibility of the relevant social norms for that situation from memory, which can then have a direct effect on subsequent behavior (Cesario et al., 2006). For example, when preparing to visit the library, the social norm of being quiet while in the library automatically becomes more accessible in your memory, which may result in your behavior becoming more subdued before you even open the library door. Do you see how these findings challenge a basic assumption of the theory of planned behavior (which was discussed in Chapter 5, section 5.3d)? The theory of planned behavior contends that our perception of the social norms in a given situation *indirectly* influences our behavior by shaping our behavioral intentions. These findings suggest that situational norms are able to guide social behavior *directly*. In essence, we have conformed to these situational norms so often that our norm-consistent behavior in the situation becomes a *habit* that occurs without conscious attention or monitoring.

Does this, then, mean that *all* situational norms guide social behavior directly? Of course not. Research by Aarts and Dijksterhuis (2003) suggests that only well-learned situational norms have the ability to directly guide social behavior. If situational norms are not well learned, then they are not readily accessible in memory and norm-consistent behavior is not spontaneously expressed. Further, even when situational norms are well learned, there are many instances in which we consciously consider how to match our behavior to these norms; and there are also many situations in which we consciously consider whether we should flout the relevant norms. However, norm-consistent automatic behavior is fairly common, and the cognitive resources we save by acting on automatic pilot allow us to consciously think about other matters, which can increase our overall social efficiency. For example, don't you enjoy an elegant meal better when you don't have to spend time thinking about which of the five utensils in front of you is the correct one to use when eating the next course?

7.2c   Asch Analyzed Conformity to a Unanimous Majority.

In the spring of 1992, Los Angeles was rocked by its worst race riot in 25 years following a jury trial in which four Los Angeles police officers were acquitted of using excessive force in the beating of Rodney King—a black man. The actual beating was captured on videotape, and most who viewed the tape believed that King was a victim of police brutality. One of the jurors, Virginia Loya, stated shortly after the trial that she initially favored a guilty verdict. Yet when the jury deliberated, the strength of her convictions waned as other jurors argued that King deserved the beating he received. In reflecting on her fellow jurors' thinking, Loya said, "The tape was the big evidence to me. They couldn't see. To me, they were people who were blind and couldn't get their glasses clean. If anything, I wish these people weren't so blind."

Despite her belief that the other jurors were incorrectly assigning blame, Loya conformed to their judgment and changed her vote from guilty to not guilty on all counts but one. Why did she accept what she believed to be an incorrect judgment by the rest of the jurors? To understand her actions, we might be tempted to search for character flaws or an all-too-compliant personality structure. Yet in doing so, we would be overlooking the power of social influence and how group pressure can cause us to go against what our eyes tell us about social reality.

This account of an important jury trial bears a striking resemblance to the experience of participants in a classic study of conformity conducted by Solomon Asch (1951, 1952, 1956) over 50 years ago. In a series of experiments, college students volunteered for what was described as a visual perception experiment. Upon arriving at the lab, they discovered that six other students would also be participating in the study. All six were confederates who were given prior instructions by Asch to behave a certain way. After the assembled students were seated around a table, Asch placed a card on an easel and pointed to a vertical line on the card that he said was the standard line. On this same card were three more vertical lines labeled "a," "b," and "c" (see Figure 7.2). Asch explained that the students' task was to call out the letter corresponding to the line that was the same length as the standard line. Participants made a total of 18 different line judgments and were seated so that five of the six confederates stated their judgments before the actual participant gave an opinion.

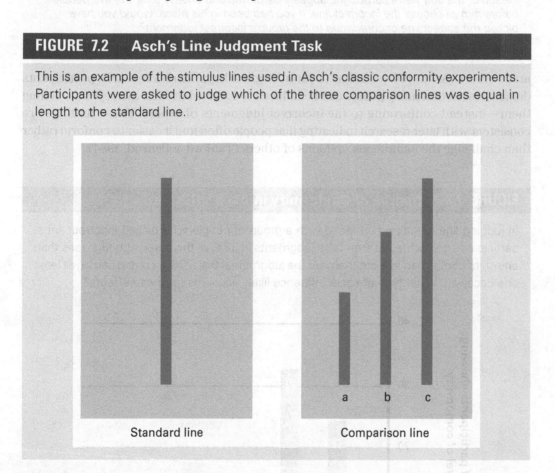

FIGURE 7.2   Asch's Line Judgment Task

This is an example of the stimulus lines used in Asch's classic conformity experiments. Participants were asked to judge which of the three comparison lines was equal in length to the standard line.

Standard line   Comparison line
                        a   b   c

Undoubtedly, all participants in this study must have initially thought that their task would be simple, for it was obvious that "c" was the correct answer. For the first two trials, confederates picked the correct line; but thereafter, on a prearranged basis, they unanimously chose a clearly incorrect line in 12 of the remaining 16 trials. What would the second-to-last student—the only "real" participant—do when faced with this dilemma? Would he conform to the judgment of others, or would he stick with what his eyes told him?

In over one-third (37%) of the critical trials, participants conformed by naming the same incorrect line as the confederates. Further, a majority (76%) conformed to the incorrect judgment in at least one of the critical trials (see Figure 7.3). In contrast, when other participants in a control condition made their judgments privately, less than 1%

(Reproduced with permission from Springer Nature)

In Asch's conformity experiments, individuals in seven-person groups publicly announced their judgments of which comparison line matched the standard line. Person 6, the only naive participant, appears perplexed and uneasy after the five people before him all choose the incorrect line. If you had been in his place, would you have picked the correct line or conformed to the group's incorrect judgment?

made errors (Asch, 1951). Similar to juror Virginia Loya, Asch's research participants demonstrated that many people can be induced to forgo what their own eyes are telling them—instead conforming to the incorrect judgments of others. These findings are consistent with later research indicating that people often find it easier to conform rather than challenge the unanimous opinions of others (Tanford & Penrod, 1984).

FIGURE 7.3   Degree of Conformity in Asch's Research

In judging line length, when faced with a group of people who picked incorrect lines, participants conformed to their false judgments in 33% of the trials. Although less than one-third conformed in more than half the judgmental trials, 76% conformed on at least one occasion. What type of social influence likely accounts for these effects?

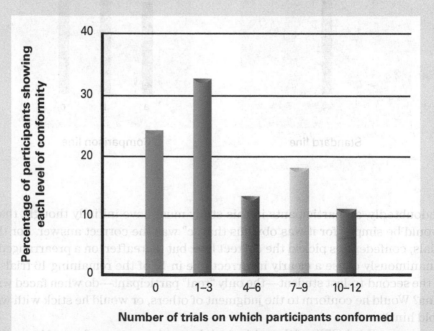

Data source: "Effects of Group Pressure Upon the Modification and Distortion of Judgements," by S. E. Asch, 1951, in *Groups, Leadership and Men,* edited by H. Guetzkow, Pittsburgh, PA: Carnegie Press.

Although the Asch findings demonstrate the strength of social influence even when the group's judgment seems clearly misguided, they do not imply that we are merely slaves to others' judgments. As illustrated in Figure 7.3, 24% of Asch's participants never followed the group on a single trial—and less than one-third conformed on more than half the trials. Likewise, in explaining why she dissented from the majority of the jurors on one count against one of the police officers after conforming to their not guilty judgment on all other counts, juror Loya stated, "They couldn't make me change my mind on guilty for [that officer]. I wasn't going to give in." As heartening as this act of independence may appear, the fact that people are often willing to go along with erroneous group judgments—or are willing to accept the judgments of others when they feel uncertain about how to define their surrounding reality—suggests that there are compelling social forces in play that are deserving of further inquiry.

> "Once conform, once do what other people do because they do it, and a lethargy steals over all the finer nerves and faculties of the soul. She becomes all outer show and inward emptiness; dull, callous, and indifferent."
>
> —Virginia Woolf, British writer, 1882–1941

7.2d Normative and Informational Influence Shape Conformity.

Let's explore the differing dilemmas that participants faced in the Sherif and Asch experiments a bit further. First, Sherif's participants found themselves in an ambiguous reality in which they undoubtedly felt less than confident about their own abilities to judge the movement of this fluctuating point of light. They could stumble along doing the best they could under the circumstances, or they could seek the guidance of others.

Did the participants in the Asch experiments face a similar ambiguous reality? Hardly. In fact, in one form of the experiment, Asch (1952) tested 16 naive participants and instructed a lone confederate to answer incorrectly, like the majority had in the original experiment. How did the naive participants respond when the confederate repeatedly picked the wrong lines? At first they were stunned, but soon they were laughing uproariously at each of his judgments! Clearly, there was no ambiguity here.

The dilemma faced by Asch's original participants was deciding whether to maintain their own judgments and thereby stick out like a sore thumb, or to go along with the group and thus avoid the uncomfortable stares and raised eyebrows of others. In the Asch study, by publicly adopting the opinions of others, participants demonstrated that "fitting in" was of greater concern to them than giving the correct answer. In the Sherif study, however, adopting the opinions of others was the avenue participants followed in their search for the correct answer.

In explaining the different social pressures in these two studies, Morton Deutsch and Henry Gerard (1955) suggested that group pressure derives from two sources: normative and informational influence. **Normative influence** occurs when a person conforms in order to gain rewards or avoid punishment from another person or group. If Asch's participants changed their judgments because they were afraid others might laugh at them or evaluate them negatively, they were responding to normative pressure. However, if instead they modified their answers because they thought the unanimously responding confederates might have a more accurate view of the lines, then they were responding to informational pressure. **Informational influence** occurs when an individual conforms due to the belief that others may have more accurate information. We often look to groups for information, especially if we doubt our own judgment. Because it is unlikely that very many participants in the Asch studies actually believed that the group was correct in its line judgments, we are probably safe in concluding that their conformity was principally due to normative influence rather than informational influence. In the Sherif study, on the other hand, the conformity exhibited was more likely due to informational influence because light movement was extremely ambiguous.

normative influence
Conformity based on a desire to gain rewards or avoid punishments

informational influence
Conformity based on the belief that others may have more accurate information

Although in some cases these two mechanisms of influence operate separately, in many others they function simultaneously (Insko et al., 1985). This is likely what occurred as Virginia Loya deliberated with her fellow jurors in the Rodney King case. Faced with fellow jurors who pressured her to accept defense claims that the videotape did not tell the entire story (normative influence), the strength of her convictions weakened and she may well have begun to more seriously consider their interpretation of events (informational influence).

If you would like to try creating a situation that induces informational influence, check out *Self/Social Connection Exercise 7.1.*

Self/Social Connection Exercise 7.1

What's Up?

We often conform to other people's actions, even in subtle and trivial ways. In the 1960s, Stanley Milgram and his colleagues demonstrated this social psychological process by instructing a group of confederates to gather together on a busy New York City sidewalk and simultaneously gaze up at nothing in the sky. When one confederate looked up at nothing, only 4% of passersby imitated this behavior. When five people stood on the sidewalk looking up at nothing, 18% of passersby imitated their upward gazing. When a group of 15 confederates gazed skyward, 40% of passersby joined in this action—nearly stopping surrounding traffic.

(Shutterstock)

Do you think you could replicate this study yourself? Enlist your friends and classmates in this exercise. Have your confederates stand together in a public setting looking up in the air. Tell them to simply tilt their heads up and look skyward. Do not have them point skyward with their arms. Watch passersby from a short distance. Do they look up?

First try this exercise with only one confederate looking up in the air and then add more skyward-gazing confederates with each trial. Does adding these confederates increase conformity? How long do bystanders look up and how long do they linger in the vicinity? How would you describe their facial expressions? Do they look confused? Do they ask your confederates any questions? Why is this behavior an example of conformity and not compliance or obedience? Is their behavior more related to normative influence or informational influence? Why?

Approach some of the individuals who look up and try to engage them in conversation. Ask why they looked up. Also ask them if they think their behavior is an example of conformity. How do they respond? If they allow you to ask them more questions, ask them whether they think that conformity is a good or a bad thing? How might this type of conformity have survival value for the human species? How do your results compare to Milgram's findings?

"The fish dies because he opens his mouth."

—Spanish proverb

Social norms can be powerful in influencing people's behaviors and can be used in ways to benefit society. For example, research has found that normative influence can be effective for promoting pro-environment behavior, such as conservation of energy and water (Nolan et al., 2008; Richetin et al., 2016; Schultz et al., 2018). In a field study in California, researchers sought to reduce energy consumption by informing residents about their energy consumption compared to similar households in their neighborhood. When high energy-consuming households received weekly written information that they used more energy than their neighbors, they reduced their energy consumption. Furthermore, low energy-consuming households maintained their low energy consumption if they received a message that they used less energy than their neighbors and were also praised (in the form of a smiley face on their feedback) for their energy conservation. Following this study, the company, Opower, implemented a new policy where it provided residents with written reports of their energy use that included neighbors' data for comparison along with praise for low energy consumption. Over the next 10 years, household energy costs decreased by about $1 billion, CO_2 emissions decreased by nearly 13 billion pounds, and 11 billion kilowatt hours were saved, which is enough electricity to power 1 million US homes for a year (Schultz et al., 2018, p. 251).

7.2e Schachter Investigated the Rejection of the Nonconformist.

Thus far we have discussed the forces brought to bear on us so that we will conform to the group's judgment. But what about those of us who do not knuckle under to this influence—who, instead, openly oppose the majority? How does a group typically respond to the nonconformist who never offers anything resembling consensus with their views?

About the same time that Asch was conducting his group conformity research, Stanley Schachter (1951) provided an excellent experimental analysis of the consequences of not conforming to majority opinion. Schachter arranged for groups of 8 to 10 volunteers to form a "case study club" to discuss the case of a juvenile delinquent, Johnny Rocco, and then make a recommendation of what the authorities should do with Johnny. In making their recommendations, participants used a 7-point love–punishment rating scale ranging from 1, "loving" treatment of Johnny, to 7, "punishment" treatment. Unknown to the participants, each group contained three confederates instructed to take a particular position in the discussion of Johnny.

Expecting that the participants would select a position closer to the "loving" end of the scale, Schachter instructed his confederates to take differing positions. The "deviate" argued for position 7 throughout the discussion, acting unswayed by contrary opinions; the "slider" began at position 7 but slid toward the majority position of the group; the "mode" held the group's most agreed upon position throughout the discussion.

How do you think the participants reacted to these three different positions during the discussion? How do you think they dealt with the deviate at the end, when their best efforts at persuasion failed to secure conformity? At first, participants communicated a great deal with the deviate and the slider in an attempt to convince them to change their minds about Johnny. During this same time period, very little attention was paid to the right-thinking mode. Once participants concluded that the deviate was not going to alter his judgment, and once the slider adopted the group's position, communication toward them dropped sharply. These findings suggest that those who hold minority opinions become the focus of influence attempts until they either conform or convince the group that such attempts are fruitless. This direct persuasive communication is a form of normative influence.

At the end of the group discussion, Schachter informed everyone that the group was simply too large for their next discussion and that he wanted them to decide whom to retain in the group. Participants' responses provided the answer to how groups respond to nonconformists—the deviate was excluded from future discussions. A meta-analysis of 23 Schachter-like "deviant" studies found that rejection by the group is most likely when there are only one or two nonconformists rather than a more substantial number (Tata et al., 1996). Additional research suggests that group members are least likely to tolerate dissension when it involves an important group value and when the dissent is expressed in an intergroup context (Matheson et al., 2003). "Airing the group's dirty laundry" is perceived as the ultimate sign of disloyalty to the group and leads to very harsh judgments by the majority. Together, these studies provide compelling evidence that social rejection is the final, and perhaps most powerful, form of normative influence directed toward nonconformists.

Facing the threat of rejection from a group, individuals often inflate the group's importance to them, which increases the group's influence (Knowles & Gardner, 2008). Given this reaction to the threat of rejection, it isn't surprising that in high school and in college, many teenagers and young adults conform to their friends' alcohol and drug use to gain or regain acceptance (Reifman et al., 2006). Nonconformists are generally banished from the group (Williams & Zadro, 2001). *Ostracism* is used as a social control mechanism at all age levels, and it is such a powerful tactic of social influence that it is even effective when used over the internet (Williams, 2007).

> "I could never divide myself from any man upon the difference of an opinion, or be angry with his judgment for not agreeing with me in that from which perhaps within a few days I should dissent myself."
>
> —Sir Thomas Browne, English physician, 1605–1682

Brain-imaging studies indicate that the social pain we experience following rejection is neurologically similar to physical pain, with both originating in the brain's anterior cingulate cortex (Eisenberger, 2011; Onoda, 2010). Why might social and physical pain have similar neural origins? Due to the fact that social bonds promote survival in most species of mammals, it is possible that during the course of human evolution our social attachment "alarm system" came under the control of the same brain area that already controlled the physical pain system. Because pain is the most primitive signal that something is wrong, piggybacking the social attachment system onto the physical pain system would have kept young human children near their caregivers, thus increasing their chances of survival (MacDonald & Leary, 2005).

The greater neural activity in the anterior cingulate caused by social rejection may be associated with another consequence of being excluded by others: impairment in reasoning and logic. Studies suggest that when people believe they are going to be excluded by others, their reasoning and complex thinking skills suffer (Baumeister et al., 2005; Baumeister et al., 2002). Because the anterior cingulate plays a role in both the social attachment alarm system and the process of self-regulation (see Chapter 3, section 3.1b), the threat of social exclusion disrupts self-regulation (Salvy et al., 2011).

Interestingly, excluded people don't actually lose the cognitive ability to self-regulate; instead, they become unwilling to do so. Facing social rejection, excluded people lose their desire to put forth the effort or make the sacrifices that self-regulation often requires. Part of this lack of desire to self-regulate is undoubtedly due to the fact that effective self-regulation requires self-awareness (see Chapter 3, section 3.1c). Yet self-awareness is problematic when facing social rejection because this state heightens the negative emotions induced by rejection (Twenge et al., 2003). People can diminish these negative emotions by avoiding self-awareness, but the cost is diminished self-regulation. Although being ostracized is a powerful experience for individuals in all age groups, research suggests that adolescents and emerging adults may be the age groups most sensitive to such rejection (Pharo et al., 2011).

Although the studies discussed thus far highlight the costs incurred by those who are socially rejected, additional research suggests that one possible benefit of being ostracized is an increased appreciation for religion and communion with a Supreme Being. That is, experiencing social exclusion can motivate some people to develop a greater appreciation for God and a heightened level of religious affiliation (Epley et al., 2008). Further, this increased religious identification often has the effect of reducing loneliness and the stress caused by social rejection (Aydin et al., 2010). In other words, at least for some individuals, developing a close relationship with God can provide a suitable substitute for the social and emotional bonds that are lost due to interpersonal rejection. A challenge for future research is to determine under what conditions ostracized individuals are likely to seek positive alternative relationships—versus spiraling into a state of negativity after being rejected by friends or family members.

Having considered some of the effects of social exclusion on the targets of this social process, let us now consider how ostracism affects the perpetrators. When people use their social power to ostracize someone, it typically comes at a psychological price (Kerr et al., 2008). For example, in a series of studies, Natalie Ciarocco and her coworkers (2001) found that ostracizing someone temporarily depletes the self's resources, making it more difficult to engage in self-regulation on other tasks. In other words, just as being shunned has a negative impact on our ability to think clearly, shunning someone takes substantial cognitive effort, and the stress is likely to make you less effective in other areas of your life. Thus, although ostracism is an effective way to "straighten out" nonconformists, those who use it are also likely to suffer from the strains of silence.

Section Summary

- Sherif's norm development research demonstrated that we look to others when defining social reality and are most influenced by people who appear confident.

- Informational influence is social influence that derives its power from people's desire for accurate information.

- Asch's line judgment experiments demonstrated that we often conform out of concern for "fitting in."

- Normative influence is social influence that derives its power from people's desire to gain rewards or avoid punishments.

- Schachter's "Johnny Rocco" study demonstrated that cohesive groups react to nonconformists by first trying to persuade them, and then rejecting nonconformists if persuasion is unsuccessful.

7.3 What Factors Influence Conformity?

Thus far, we have learned that people sometimes mindlessly conform due to the automatic activation of situational norms. We have also learned that people are likely to conform when they are uncertain about their own ability to make accurate judgments and others are confident, or when they are concerned about being negatively evaluated by others. What social and personal factors foster this uncertainty and concern?

7.3a Situational Factors Impact Conformity.

In attempting to understand the conditions that facilitate conformity, social psychologists have paid particular attention to the social setting. The assumption is that these situational factors exert a social force on individuals that can cause uniform behavior.

Group Size

One situational factor contributing to conformity is the size of the influencing group. When Asch (1955) varied the number of unanimous confederates (from 1 to 15) he found that conformity increased as group size increased, but only up to a certain size (Figure 7.4). Conformity was near its peak level when the number of confederates was between 3 and 4, with no additional increases in conformity with more confederates.

FIGURE 7.4   Group Size and Conformity

In Asch's (1955) conformity research, when the number of unanimous confederates was varied from 1 to 15, conformity approached its maximum level when the number of confederates was between 3 and 4. Why do you think group-size effects leveled off in this manner?

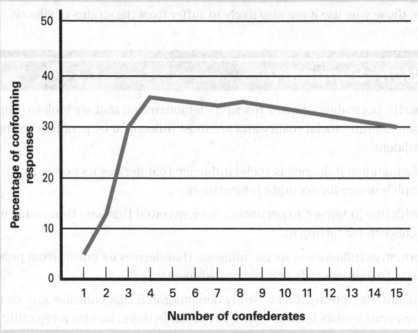

Data Source: "Opinions and Social Pressure," by S. Asch, 1955, Scientific American, 193(5), pp 31–35.

Other research suggests that group size will only be a predictor of conformity levels in certain situations. Jennifer Campbell and Patricia Fairey (1989) found that group size is important when the social reality is clear (judgments are easy), but that the size of the group is relatively unimportant when the social reality is ambiguous (judgments are difficult). When the reality is clear, whether or not you conform depends on the amount of normative influence the group can exert. Larger groups are often implicitly perceived as more competent and as having higher social status than are smaller groups (Cao & Banaji, 2017). Thus, adding more people to the group will increase normative influence and conformity. On the other hand, if the reality is ambiguous, informational influence is more of a factor than normative influence. In this case, one or two people may influence you just as well as three, four, or many more.

Group Cohesiveness and Topic Relevance

A group is termed cohesive when its members are highly attracted to one another. In general, cohesive groups engender more conformity than noncohesive groups (Christensen et al., 2004; Hogg, 1992). For example, in other conditions of Schachter's

(1951) deviant study, he varied the cohesiveness of the group as well as the relevance of the contested discussion topic. When the group was highly cohesive and the topic was also highly relevant, the group exerted its greatest pressure on deviates and was most likely to reject nonconformists. These findings indicate that if groups with a strong sense of togetherness are discussing important topics, they will tend to be intolerant of those who hold differing opinions. The best examples of cohesive groups influencing members come from our own friendship networks. We are much more likely to accept their influence than that of others because of our respect for their opinions, our desire to please them, and our fear of rejection.

Why do friendship networks typically exert greater influence over us than other social relationships?

Social Support

In Asch's study, what sort of effect do you think a single confederate picking the correct line would have on the conformity levels of the participants? Asch (1956) found that when one of the confederates picked the correct line, conformity dropped dramatically—to one-fourth the original levels. Research by Vernon Allen and John Levine (1969) indicates that a social supporter reduces conformity by diminishing the group's normative influence. In one of their studies, participants worked with four confederates on a visual perception task. Three of the confederates had previously been instructed to consistently agree on incorrect judgments. The fourth confederate went along with the other confederates, agreed with the participant, or made a different incorrect judgment. Conformity was reduced not only when the fourth confederate agreed with the participant but also when this confederate merely disagreed with all opinions, including the participants' opinions. In a second experiment (Allen & Levine, 1971), conformity was reduced even when the social supporter wore thick glasses and complained about not being able to see the visual displays!

These findings suggest that almost any dissent from the majority can diminish normative influence and thereby reduce conformity. Although breaking social consensus appears to be the crucial factor here, receiving social support early is more effective than receiving such support after normative pressures have already built up (Morris et al., 1977). Unfortunately, if this support is later removed, normative influence again is exerted. In one of Asch's studies, when the confederate who had previously agreed with the participant switched and began to conform to the majority opinion, the participants' own level of conformity returned to near the levels observed in the original experiments (Asch, 1955). Thus, to promote nonconformity in others, one should voice dissent, and do so early and consistently. Remember this bit of advice, for it will be important when we later discuss how minorities can exert influence not only in resisting majority opinion but also in actually changing it.

7.3b   Personal Factors Influence Conformity.

The consensus is that situational forces are most important in determining whether we conform or not. Yet we are not machines who respond identically to these situational factors. Although specific personality traits related to conformity have been difficult to identify (McGuire, 1968), research does suggest that conforming to group pressure is related to our *values* and *self-concept*.

Self-Awareness

As noted in Chapter 3, whether behavior is more influenced by personal or social standards is at least partially determined by what aspect of the self is salient (private or public). When people are privately self-aware, they tend to act in line with their own personal standards; however, social standards are more influential when people are publicly self-aware (Froming et al., 1982; Kallgren et al., 2000). Thus, being privately self-aware reduces conformity, while being publicly self-aware increases conformity.

Self-Presentation

The irony of yielding to social influence out of concern for how others might evaluate you is that, in many cultures, it is not desirable to be recognized as a conformist. For example, Robert Cialdini and his coworkers (1974) found that American college students generally perceived people as more intelligent if they did not yield to social influence—unless, of course, they were the ones trying to get others to conform! Further research found that calculated assessments of the impressions they are making on those present often underlie people's conformity and independence responses (Collins & Brief, 1995; Santee & Maslach, 1982).

Conformity is most likely to occur when self-presenters are alone with those trying to influence them and when the conformity will be viewed as indicating intelligence or open-mindedness. On the other hand, open defiance of influence attempts is most likely under two conditions (Baumeister, 1982): (1) when others not involved in the influence attempt are present and (2) when the attitude of those exerting the influence makes any subsequent yielding seem like weak-kneed surrender rather than intelligent decision-making. Under such conditions, it would be difficult to conform and still maintain a public image of independence and autonomy.

Imagine that you are conducting an Asch-type conformity experiment. Simultaneously, you want to test whether you can increase nonconformity by inducing public self-presentation concerns in your participants. What variable could you introduce to the standard Asch research design to test the possibility that inducing public self-presentation concerns in your participants would increase nonconformity?

The Desire for Personal Control

Although self-presentation concerns may sometimes explain conformity and nonconformity, on other occasions we may resist social influence simply to feel that we personally control our own actions. Jack Brehm (Brehm, 1966; Brehm & Brehm, 1981) has proposed a theory of **psychological reactance**; it states that people believe they possess specific behavioral freedoms and that they will react against, and resist, attempts to limit this sense of freedom. However, assuring them that "they can do as they wish" can increase social influence by reducing the perceived threats to their freedoms (Carpenter & Pascual, 2016).

Jerry Burger (1987) found evidence indicating that individual differences in desire for personal control may partly explain susceptibility to social influence. In his study, he asked college students to rate the humor in a series of newspaper cartoons using a scale from 1 ("very unfunny") to 100 ("very funny"). In one condition, participants rated the cartoons alone; in another condition, they rated them after hearing two other students' evaluations. These other students, being confederates, had been instructed to rate the cartoons as being relatively funny (averaging 70 on the 100-point scale)—even though Burger had specifically chosen cartoons that had previously been judged to be quite dull (average humor rating of only 25). Prior to rating the cartoons, participants' desire for personal control (DPC) had been measured by a paper-and-pencil questionnaire. Results indicated that DPC did not predict how students

"I wouldn't have turned out the way I was if I didn't have all those old-fashioned values to rebel against."

—Madonna, American rock singer, born 1958

psychological reactance
The tendency to react against and resist attempts to limit one's sense of freedom

rated the cartoons when they were alone (both groups rated them as not very funny), but high DPC participants were less likely to agree with confederates' favorable ratings than were low DPCs. Although the high DPCs certainly were not immune to the confederates' influence, they did appear to be better equipped to resist conformity than those who had a low desire for control.

Due to their desire for personal control, individuals may not conform to social pressures, but this does not mean that they are necessarily acting independently. There are two different types of nonconformity responses. One is *independence*, which was previously defined as not being subject to others' control. The person who dresses in an unusual way because she genuinely likes that style is demonstrating independence; psychological reactance does not play a factor in her behavioral choices. On the other hand, opposition to social influence on all occasions characterizes **anticonformity**; psychological reactance often explains these behavioral choices (Nail et al., 2000). The anticonformist would purposefully dress in an unusual, and perhaps offensive, way in order to demonstrate nonconformity. Thus, the actions of two people may be identical but may be motivated by very different desires. Some people "take the road less traveled" not because they disagree with the group's direction but because, by disagreeing, they can satisfy their need for personal control.

> "The young always have the same problem—how to rebel and conform at the same time. They have now solved this by defying their parents and copying one another."
>
> —Quentin Crisp, British author, 1908–1999

Is an anticonformist really a good example of an independent person? If anticonformity is fueled by psychological reactance, is it another example of how a person can be influenced by others?

7.3c Cultures Differ in Their Conformity Patterns.

Does knowing a person's cultural background give you any insight into how he or she might respond to social influence? The guiding principle of individualism is that individual interests are more important than those of the group. In decided contrast, collectivism asserts that group interests should guide the thinking and behavior of individual members (Ho & Chiu, 1994). Thus, it is not surprising that people from collectivist cultures are more concerned than individualists with maintaining group harmony and gaining the approval of their group (Triandis, 1989). A person from an individualist culture, on the other hand, has a higher need for autonomy from the group and a desire to feel unique. Because of these different orientations, people from collectivist cultures tend to be more conforming to their own group than individualists (Morling & Kitayama, 2008; Wall et al., 2010). This yielding to the group by collectivists is not considered to be a sign of weakness, as it is often perceived to be in our individualist culture; rather, it is believed to indicate self-control, flexibility, and maturity (White & LeVine, 1986). Because people from collectivist cultures are much less likely than those from individualist cultures to view conformity as a sign of weakness, they are also less likely than individualists to engage in psychological reactance when their individual freedom is threatened (Jonas et al., 2009).

Although these cultural differences suggest that conformity is generally more likely in a collectivist culture, this does not mean that collectivists submit to any and all group influence attempts. To understand social influence in such a culture, it is important to distinguish *ingroups* from *outgroups*. As described in Chapter 6, an ingroup is a group to which you belong and which forms a part of your social identity, whereas an outgroup is any group with which you do not share membership. Research suggests that people from collectivist cultures perceive ingroup norms as universally valid and feel obligated to obey ingroup authorities. On the other hand, collectivists tend to distrust outgroup norms and, as a result, are often unwilling to yield to their influence (Triandis, 1972; Wosinska et al., 2001).

anticonformity
Opposition to social influence on all occasions, often caused by psychological reactance

> "I'm not gonna change the way I look or the way I feel to conform to anything. I've always been a freak. So I've been a freak all my life and I have to live with that, you know. I'm one of those people."
>
> —John Lennon, English rock musician, 1940–1980

Most of the nonconformity that occurs in a collectivist culture is to the social norms of outgroups, not ingroups. This difference in the perceived validity of ingroup norms is one of the reasons that collectivist cultures tend to breed more conformity than individualist cultures. Therefore, a person from a collectivist culture—such as traditional Greece—might be very yielding to his family's and his village's influence attempts (his ingroup), yet be staunchly defiant of any pressure exerted by the distant national authorities (a perceived outgroup). When we consider those who belong to an individualist culture, although they too tend to trust ingroup norms more than outgroup norms, they are more likely than collectivists to question ingroup norms as well—especially when those norms run counter to their self-interests or when adherence to these social norms makes them feel average or ordinary (that is, not unique).

> "The man who never submitted to anything will soon submit to a burial mat."
>
> — Nigerian proverb

7.3d   The Minority Can Influence the Majority.

History is filled with stories of lone individuals or small, relatively powerless groups expressing unpopular views and enduring abuse from the majority until their views are eventually adopted. Our chapter-opening story of the Silence Breakers represents a small group of people whose minority opinions were aimed at majority group members. The process by which dissenters produce change within a group is called **minority influence**.

Commenting on what it takes to exert minority influence, 19th century feminist Susan B. Anthony said, "Cautious, careful people always casting about to preserve their reputation and social standing never can bring about a reform. Those who are really in earnest must be willing to be anything or nothing in the world's estimation." Social research bears out Anthony's pronouncement. Those who dissent from the majority, although generally perceived as competent, are often heartily disliked (Bassili & Provencal, 1988). Indeed, during the 1960s, civil rights movement in this country, dissenters such as Medgar Evers, Malcolm X, and Martin Luther King Jr. were so heartily despised by some people that they were murdered to eliminate their nonconforming voices. One consequence of the social isolation experienced by those in the minority is hesitancy in voicing their opinions. This tendency of those who hold a minority opinion to express that opinion less quickly than people who hold the majority opinion is called the **minority slowness effect**. People with a minority opinion are particularly slow in stating their views when they perceive the majority opinion to be widely held (Bassili, 2003), perhaps because taking a minority position is often perceived as a risky option (Erb et al., 2015). As articulated by Ms. Anthony, championing the minority viewpoint is not for the weak of heart.

Martin Luther King Jr. and Malcom X were two powerful influence agents during the 1960s' civil rights movement. Which one of these individuals' actions most closely demonstrated effective minority influence principles?

(Photo by Marion S. Trikosko, 1964, courtesy of U.S. News & World Report Magazine Photograph Collection, Library of Congress)

> "All men should have a drop of treason in their veins, if nations are not to go soft like so many sleepy pears."
>
> —Rebecca West, English novelist, 1892–1983

minority influence

The process by which dissenters produce change within a group

minority slowness effect

The tendency of those who hold a minority opinion to express that opinion less quickly than people who hold the majority opinion

Unlike the majority group, minority groups tend to be viewed negatively by others; therefore, their viewpoints are subject to more critical analysis and need greater time to register with group members (Martin et al., 2003). The good news for minority persuaders is that if their views are eventually adopted by the majority, these new attitudes and beliefs tend to be more resistant to change than those adopted from majority persuaders (Martin et al., 2008). Do you know why? As discussed in Chapter 5, attitudes changed through critical analysis (*central-route processing*) are stronger and more resistant to change than attitudes changed through lazy thinking (*peripheral-route processing*).

French social psychologist Serge Moscovici (1980) contended that the most important factor in determining the effectiveness of minority group influence is the *style of behavior* used in presenting nonconforming views. For minorities to exert influence on majority members, they must consistently and confidently state their dissenting opinions (Moscovici & Mugny 1983). In a demonstration of the importance of consistency in minority group influence, Moscovici and Marisa Zavalloni (1969) asked groups of individuals to judge whether the color of projected blue slides was blue or green. Each group consisted of four participants and two confederates. In the *inconsistent minority condition*, the confederates randomly varied calling the blue slide green and blue, while in the *consistent minority condition* they always claimed that it was green.

> "Whenever you find yourself on the side of the majority, it is time to pause and reflect."
>
> —Mark Twain, American author and satirist, 1835–1910

Figure 7.5 shows that when the confederates were inconsistent in labeling the blue slide "green," their ability to influence the majority's opinion was negligible (1.25%). However, when the confederates were consistent, participants conformed to this minority point of view more than 8% of the time. In addition, after the color trials, those who were exposed to the consistent minority shifted the point on the blue–green color spectrum where they identified a color as green instead of blue; now they called more stimuli "green" and fewer "blue." These findings not only suggest that a consistent minority can affect overt responses in the majority but also that a unified minority can cause majority members to alter their private beliefs as well.

FIGURE 7.5   Conformity to Consistent and Inconsistent Minorities

Moscovici and Zavalloni (1969) found that the degree to which participants labeled a blue slide "green" was partly determined by whether they were tested alone (control condition), with a minority saying "green" inconsistently (inconsistent condition), or with a minority saying "green" consistently (consistent condition). Why is consistency so important for minority group influence?

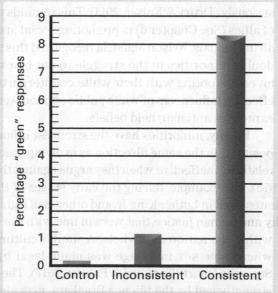

Data source: "The Group as a Polarizer of Attitudes," by S. Moscovici and M. Zavalloni, 1969, *Journal of Personality and Social Psychology, 12*(2), pp. 125–135.

Although this research indicates that those sharing minority opinions must appear confident in consistently stating their views, other research indicates that minorities must walk a fine line in presenting their nonconforming opinions. They cannot appear dogmatic or rigid, for that will reduce their influence (Mugny & Perez, 1991; Nemeth et al., 1974). Therefore, for majority members to consider their perspective in the first place, the minority must come across as consistent and confident, and also flexible. Nelson Mandela, a longtime opponent of the former apartheid government of South Africa, is an excellent example of a minority group leader (a minority in power but not in numbers) whose consistent, unwavering call for black equality was combined with a nondogmatic approach to reform that won over many white South Africans. In 1994, he became the first president of a nonapartheid South Africa.

One other factor that affects the ability of the minority to influence the majority is the *degree of difference* between the minority and the majority. *Single minorities* are individuals who differ from the majority only in terms of their beliefs, while *double minorities* are those who differ from the majority in terms of both beliefs and group membership (Martin, 1988). An example of a single minority is a heterosexual arguing for equal rights for gay people to the heterosexual majority. A gay person advocating such rights is a double minority. Research indicates that single minorities are more likely to exert influence over the majority than are double minorities (Alvaro & Crano, 1997).

For example, in one study (Maass et al., 1982), conservative male participants engaged in a discussion of abortion with either a single minority (male confederate) or

a double minority (female confederate). In these discussions, the minority consistently defended a liberal position rather than the conservative viewpoint of the male participants. Results indicated that the male participants perceived the double minorities (the liberal females) as having a stronger self-interest in the discussion, and were less influenced by them than they were by the single minorities (the liberal males). By perceiving self-interest in the position of a double minority, it appears that people can more easily discount their arguments. Similarly, men who confront sexism often experience fewer social costs than do women who confront sexism; men are viewed more positively, and their confrontations are taken more seriously (Drury & Kaiser, 2014). This reminds us of the importance of allies (See Chapter 6) in promoting social justice and equality for all individuals. Nelson Mandela recognized this tendency to discount double minorities in the struggle to put black South Africans on an equal footing with their white counterparts. Some of the most effective influencers of white public opinion were fellow whites who expressed antiapartheid beliefs.

In 1977, Harvey Milk became the first openly gay politician elected to public office in California. Championing gay rights, Milk was a "double minority" influencer. On November 27, 1978, Milk was assassinated by a fellow politician. He was posthumously awarded the Presidential Medal of Freedom in 2009.

(AP Photo)

Finally, minorities have the strongest influence when they take positions in the same direction as evolving cultural norms; they are relatively ineffective when they argue against these emerging norms (Kiesler & Pallak, 1975). For example, during the early stages of the civil rights movement in the United States, Martin Luther King Jr. and other civil rights activists espoused beliefs about equality and human justice that were in line with the emerging liberalism within the nation as a whole. A similar cultural shift was evident when same-sex marriage was made legal by the United States Supreme Court (Tankard & Paluck, 2017). The #MeToo movement, strengthened by the Silence Breakers, may also reflect a changing social norm regarding sexual harassment and sexual assault. Yet, at the same time that this movement was gaining strength, a counter movement developed to challenge the Silence Breakers and defend alleged perpetrators (sometimes referred

"Every society honors its live conformists and its dead troublemakers."

—Mignon McLaughlin, US author, 1913–1983

to as "#HimToo"). The future will tell us which of these social movements has the most influence in shaping cultural norms.

Overall, minorities are most successful in exerting influence on the majority when arguing for positions that are not too far from the prevailing majority position, and when they show a *consistent behavioral style* that the majority interprets as indicating *certainty* and *confidence*. On the other hand, minority influence will surely fail if the minority group *argues against evolving social norms* and exhibits a *rigid* style of negotiation with *inconsistently held beliefs*.

Even if minority groups follow a consistent avenue of persuasion, this does not mean that those holding majority beliefs will necessarily change. Remember, majority groups can impose sanctions and withdraw rewards from their members if they begin to espouse minority viewpoints; this often is enough to maintain public compliance with majority opinions. Further, people's social identities generally consist of majority-held values and beliefs, and those aspects of the self-concept are resistant to change. However, although overt change toward minority positions may not readily take place, when majority members engage in critical analysis of these positions, it often stimulates *divergent thinking*—a cognitive process in which one considers a problem from varying perspectives (Gruenfeld & Preston, 2000). What appears to initially motivate this enhanced scrutiny of the minority message is simply that it is different and unexpected (Baker & Petty, 1994). The benefit for the minority persuader is that this increased scrutiny often causes people to consider a wider variety of possible explanations or novel solutions to problems (Peterson & Nemeth, 1996).

Interestingly, when majority opinions eventually change due to the impact of the minority viewpoint, people often forget where they first heard their newly adopted views (refer to the *sleeper effect* in Chapter 5, section 5.4b). In other words, the efforts of those who first propose minority positions are often not acknowledged when their influence attempts finally succeed. Such is the thankless job of the dissenter.

"The power of a movement lies in the fact that it can indeed change the habits of people. This change is not the result of force but of dedication, of moral persuasion."

—Steve Biko, South African activist, 1946–1977

Can you use Harold Kelley's attribution theory described in Chapter 4 to explain why minorities are most successful in exerting influence on the majority when they show a consistent behavioral style *that the majority interprets as indicating* certainty *and* confidence?

Section Summary

- Situational forces that influence conformity include:
  - the size of the influencing group
  - the cohesiveness of the influencing group
  - whether there is any social support for contrary positions

- Personal factors that influence conformity include:
  - private and public self-awareness
  - self-presentational concerns
  - desire for personal control

- Collectivists engage in more ingroup conforming than individualists do.

- Minority group influence is most likely when the minority group consistently and confidently states its dissenting views and presents itself as flexible and open-minded.

7.4   Compliance

In trying to "get our way" with others, sometimes we forget the most direct route—simply asking them to do what we desire. However, because compliance involves a direct request, it generally induces more thinking and critical analysis by the target of social influence than conformity. As a compliance seeker, what strategies can you employ to increase the likelihood that others will grant your requests?

7.4a   Manipulating Moods and Invoking Norms Foster Compliance.

When people are roughly equal in social status, establishing the correct atmosphere or mood is especially important to increase compliance. Three factors that help create the proper atmosphere are making people feel good, doing something for them, and giving them reasons to comply. As you will discover, these factors also often reduce the likelihood that people will critically analyze the request.

Positive Mood

In the course of making requests, people soon discover that others are more likely to comply when they are in a good mood—especially when requests are prosocial, such as helping others (Forgas, 1998). One reason for this is that people who are in good moods are simply more likely to be active; thus, they are more likely to engage in a range of behaviors, including granting requests (Batson et al., 1979). A second reason is that pleasant moods activate pleasant thoughts and memories, which likely make people feel more favorable toward those making requests (Carlson et al., 1988). A third reason is that people in a happy mood are often less likely to critically analyze events, including requests; thus, they are more likely to grant them (Bless et al., 1996).

> "Don't open a shop unless you know how to smile."
>
> —Jewish proverb

Because of this general awareness that good moods foster compliance, we often try to "butter someone up" before making a request. As discussed in Chapter 3 this self-presentation strategy of *ingratiation* is designed to get others to view us favorably. Although people may be suspicious of ingratiators' motives after receiving their requests, the preceding flattery is still often effective in securing compliance (Kacmar et al., 1992); however, subtlety is the best strategy. A survey study of managers and chief executive officers at Forbes 500 companies found that managers and directors were more successful in having their requests for board appointments at other firms granted when they employed relatively subtle forms of flattery and opinion conformity—rather than blatant ingratiation (Stern & Westphal, 2010).

Reciprocity

Have strangers ever offered you small gifts—such as flowers, pencils, or flags—and then asked you to donate money to their organization? If so, they were hoping that the token would lower your resistance to their request. This hope rested on a powerful social norm that people in all cultures follow—namely, the **reciprocity norm**. Although this unwritten social norm helps to maintain fairness in social relationships by prescribing that favors or good deeds should be reciprocated, it can also be used to increase compliance (Uehara, 1995).

> "One does not give a gift without motive."
>
> —Malian proverb

reciprocity norm
The expectation that one should return a favor or a good deed

Research clearly demonstrates that giving someone a small gift, or doing him or her a favor, can easily lead to reciprocal compliance—especially if you seek compliance shortly after doing the good turn (Chartrand et al., 1999). For example, Dennis Regan (1971) had a college student work on a task with another student (a confederate) who acted in either a friendly or an unfriendly manner. During a break, the confederate left and returned a few minutes later either with a soft drink for the student participant or with nothing. Shortly afterward, the confederate asked the student to buy $0.25 raffle tickets. Those given the soft drink "gift" bought an average of two tickets, whereas those not given a soft drink bought only one. The effect of reciprocity was so strong that the students returned the favor even when the confederate had previously acted in an unlikable manner.

Everyday experience tells us that reciprocity is commonly used as a strategy in making sales (Howard, 1995). Grocery stores provide free product samples. Insurance agents give away free pens or calendars. Car salespeople give potential customers new key rings worth $0.25—just right to hold the key to that new $35,000 automobile. In offering these "gifts," salespeople are often counting on the salience of the reciprocity norm overriding customers' careful consideration of the consequences of purchasing these products.

However, it is not just professional salespeople who employ such tactics. Those who habitually use reciprocity to secure compliance are called *creditors*, because they try to keep others in their debt so they can cash in when necessary. People who are creditors tend to agree with statements such as, "If someone does me a favor, it's a good idea to repay that person with a greater favor." Creditors know the power of indebtedness, and they work hard to make sure they are on the influential side of the reciprocity equation (Eisenberger et al., 1987). They know all too well the wisdom of the proverb, "Beware of strangers bearing gifts."

Why is it that people who are seeking favors or compliance from you often give you something before making their request? What social norm are they trying to invoke?

(Getty Images)

Giving Reasons

In granting someone's request, we often require a reason for complying. For instance, if you are in line at a grocery store with a small number of food items, and someone with only one item asks to go ahead because his sick grandmother is waiting for her cold medicine, you are likely to grant the request. The explanation given for his request strikes a responsive chord within you—it is "reasonable."

Ellen Langer (1978) and her colleagues found evidence for the power of reason giving in gaining compliance when they had confederates try to cut in line ahead of others at a photocopying machine. In one condition the confederates gave no reason, merely asking, "May I use the photocopying machine to make five copies?" Of those waiting, 60% complied with this "no reason" request. In another condition, when the confederates gave an explanation for their request ("May I use the photocopying machine to make five copies because I'm in a hurry?"), compliance increased to 94%—a significant difference. What Langer was interested in determining at this point was whether the actual content of the reason was important, or whether any reason at all would suffice. To test this, she had her confederates try a third version of the request, where the reason given for cutting in line was really no explanation at all; it was merely a restatement of their desire to make copies ("May I use the photocopying machine to make five copies because I have to make copies?"). Surprisingly, this mere reiteration of the desire to make copies resulted in 94% compliance—identical to when an actual explanation was given ("I'm in a hurry").

Why does merely giving a reason—any reason—result in greater compliance? Giving reasons may be important because of our habitual desire to explain others' actions (refer to Chapter 4). We have learned through experience that there are exceptions to social norms (such as not cutting in line); and when people ask to be granted an exception, it is expected that they will provide a reason. Further, because we believe that others are as concerned about acting appropriately as we are, we tend to assume that when someone gives us a reason for doing something, it must be worthy of an exception. As a result, we may often mindlessly grant a request accompanied by a reason because we assume the requester would not ask if the request were illegitimate. Providing an object that seemingly legitimizes the request can further increase compliance. Nicolas Guéguen and his colleagues (2015) found that asking a stranger for money to buy a stamp resulted in compliance 80% of the time if the requester also held an envelope, compared to 27% of the time without an envelope.

When Steve's daughter Lillian was 2 years old, she had already learned the importance of giving reasons when seeking compliance from her parents. In asking to go outside she would say, "Can I go outside and play? Because I have to go outside and play." Based on Langer's findings, when it comes to securing compliance, Lillian had already developed sufficient social skills to do quite nicely in the adult world.

> "A fair request should be followed by the deed in silence."
>
> —Dante Alighieri, Italian poet, 1265–1321

In summarizing this analysis of factors that affect compliance, additional insight is provided by the *elaboration likelihood model* of persuasion discussed in Chapter 5 (section 5.4). As you recall, according to this model, persuasion can occur through either the thoughtful mode of central-route processing or the lazy mode of peripheral-route processing. Regarding compliance, the research discussed here suggests that positive mood, the salience of the reciprocity norm, and the inclusion of reasons for why one should grant a request are all likely to foster compliance by inducing lazy, peripheral-route processing of the requester's message. In other words, whenever any of these factors are present, the resulting compliance is less likely to be based on thoughtful consideration of the request.

7.4b Two-Step Strategies Are Effective Compliance Traps.

Earlier, we discussed how "creditors" secure compliance by keeping tabs on others' debts to them. Professional creditors—such as insurance agents, car dealers, or door-to-door salespersons—rely on more than just indebtedness to secure compliance to their sales requests. In making sales, they realize that it often takes more than a single plea to win over a potential customer. Social psychologists have studied how two requests, employed in different ways, can result in some very effective compliance techniques. The first request sets the trap, while the second request captures the prey.

Foot-in-the-Door

In Chapter 5, we saw that many people feel pressure to remain consistent in their beliefs. Salespersons, recognizing this need for consistency, often employ a two-step compliance strategy known as the **foot-in-the-door technique**. In this strategy, the person secures compliance with a small request and then follows it up later with a larger, less desirable request. For example, imagine that a young woman knocks on your door and tells you she is gathering signatures on a petition supporting environmental protection. Would you be willing to sign? This question represents the first small request. Being proenvironment, you readily agree. After signing, the woman says she is also seeking money for her organization to better fight for the environment, and would you be willing to make a contribution? This is the second, larger request. Chances are, if you signed the petition you will also contribute some money. Using a very similar scenario, Joseph Schwarzwald and his coworkers (1983) found that they were able to produce a 75% increase in donations over a comparison request

How might the foot-in-the-door compliance strategy be combined with the effects of postdecision dissonance to partly explain how some people initially become involved with, and then committed to, religious or political cults?

foot-in-the-door technique

A two-step compliance technique in which the influencer secures compliance to a small request, and then later follows this with a larger, less desirable request strategy involving no prior petition signing. Similar results have also been obtained in fund-raising efforts on the internet (Guéguen & Jacob, 2001).

Meta-analyses of studies using the foot-in-the-door technique indicate that it is fairly reliable in securing compliance (Beaman et al., 1983; Cialdini & Trost, 1998). However, if people reject the small request, they are even less likely to comply with the larger request than those who were not approached with the small request (Snyder & Cunningham, 1975). Can you guess why? It appears that the foot-in-the-door effect causes a change in self-perception (Burger & Caldwell, 2003). In not granting the small first request, people may decide that they are not the type of person who grants those kinds of requests. Therefore, because of this new self-image, they are more likely to later reject the larger request. The same self-perception process operates for those who do grant the small request. They now perceive themselves as cooperative; therefore, they later comply to the second, larger request in order to be consistent with their cooperative self-image. For this technique to work, the initial request must be large enough to cause people to think about the implications of their behavior, and they must believe they are freely complying (Gorassini & Olson, 1995).

Additional cross-cultural studies indicate that people from individualist cultures are more susceptible to the foot-in-the-door technique than people from collectivist cultures (Petrova et al., 2007). Why? As discussed in Chapter 5, individualists have a higher need to behave consistently than collectivists; this results in higher compliance to the second, larger request in this strategy.

Door-in-the-Face

A second compliance technique that also uses multiple requests is the **door-in-the-face technique**, which is in some sense the reverse of the foot-in-the-door strategy. In this technique, the person seeking compliance starts by asking for a very large favor—one the recipient is almost certain to reject. When the rejection occurs, the request is changed to a much less costly request. Securing this second request was the objective of the influencer from the start. The first rejection is the door in the face, and it is presumed that the second request stands a better chance of being accepted if it is preceded by this rejection (Cialdini & Trost, 1998). Phone solicitors for charities and other nonprofit organizations typically employ this technique by first asking people for a large donation and then reducing their request when the large request is refused. Likewise, teenagers have been known to ask their parents whether they could go on an unsupervised weekend trip with their friends (a fabrication), and then respond to the inevitable refusal by asking whether they could at least join their friends at a local party (their actual goal).

> "He that does not ask will never get a bargain."
>
> —French proverb

A study by Robert Cialdini and his colleagues (1975) illustrates the effectiveness of this compliance strategy. College students were approached by teams of confederates who asked them to volunteer to spend 2 hours a week over the next year as "big brothers" or "big sisters" to juveniles in need of older role models. Not surprisingly, no one agreed to this request, which is exactly what Cialdini expected. Then the confederates followed this rejection with a second request: Would the students be willing to spend 2 hours just once taking the same kids to the zoo? Fifty percent agreed to this request. In a control condition, when this smaller request had been presented without being preceded by the large request, less than 17% of the students agreed to comply.

For the door-in-the-face effect to occur, three conditions must be met. First, the initial request must be very large so that when people refuse they make no negative inferences about themselves (for example, "I'm not a very generous person"). Second, the interval between the first and second requests must be relatively short so that the feeling of obligation is still salient. In contrast, a longer interval (weeks or even months) between the two requests can still be effective for the foot-in-the-door technique. Finally,

door-in-the-face technique

A two-step compliance technique in which, after having a large request refused, the influencer counteroffers with a much smaller request the third condition is that the same person who made the first large request must make the subsequent smaller request. People perceive this second request as a concession by the requester that the first request was too large. Once this perceived concession occurs, due to the reciprocity norm, people feel pressure to reciprocate with a concession of their own—by agreeing to the second request. Of the two sequential compliance techniques discussed thus far, the "face" approach has been shown to be more effective than the "foot" technique (Harari et al., 1980; Rodafinos et al., 2005).

The door-in-the-face strategy is often used by both parties in negotiating contracts for such things as houses, cars, and salaries. Both parties begin with an economic position that is extremely favorable to themselves but very unfavorable to the other side. Following the initial proposal rejections, one or both of them might make concessions that are actually closer to what they really hope to obtain from the other. Often, those who make less reciprocal concessions and who are also less concerned with appearing unreasonable are the ones who secure the best deals (Pendleton & Batson, 1979).

That's Not All

Closely related to the door-in-the-face technique is the **that's-not-all technique**, which involves the influencer making a large request, but then immediately offering a discount or bonus that makes the request more reasonable. Unlike the door-in-the-face technique, however, the person is not given the opportunity to reject the large request before it is reduced or "sweetened." The lowered price tags on store merchandise and the ads for "Buy One, Get One Free" deals are examples of this two-step compliance strategy.

Jerry Burger (1986) demonstrated the effectiveness of this tactic when he conducted a bake sale at Santa Clara University. On the table where the sale was taking place were a number of cupcakes with no indicated price. In one condition, when potential buyers asked how much one cupcake cost, they were given a high price. Then, before they could respond, they were also told that this price included a "bonus" bag of cookies. In a control condition, potential buyers were immediately shown the bag of cookies and then given a total price for the cupcake and cookies together. Results indicated that 73% of those who experienced the that's-not-all tactic bought the sweets, versus only 40% of those who were offered everything up front.

(Shutterstock)

How could you use the that's-not-all technique to increase your cupcake sales?

In a second cupcake study, instead of the request being "sweetened" by a bonus, it was reduced in size. In the that's-not-all condition, people were told that the cupcakes cost $1.25 but that they would be sold to the buyer at $1 because the booth would be closing soon. In the control condition, people were merely told that the cupcakes cost $1. As shown in Figure 7.6, the that's-not-all strategy was again more effective in selling cupcakes; 55% of those in this condition bought cupcakes, versus only 20% in the control condition.

Burger was also interested in determining whether the that's-not-all effect occurred only because the offered items were now a bargain, and so he created a third condition. In this *bargain* condition, the seller stated to the potential buyer that the cupcakes were now priced at $1, although formerly they were $1.25. The bargain condition resulted in only a 25% purchase rate (see Figure 7.6). This finding suggests that the that's-not-all strategy is not just effective because it offers a bargain to the influence target; there also appears to be a psychological potency, created by the influencer personally sweetening the deal, that lowers people's resistance to the request.

that's-not-all technique

A two-step compliance technique in which the influencer makes a large request, then immediately offers a discount or bonus before the initial request is refused

FIGURE 7.6   That's Not All!

The effectiveness of the that's-not-all compliance technique was demonstrated in a campus bake sale. Customers purchased the most cupcakes when the deal was "sweetened" by first stating one price and then lowering it before the customer could respond. When customers were told that the price had already been lowered (bargain), or when they were merely given the low price right away (control), purchases were much less likely.

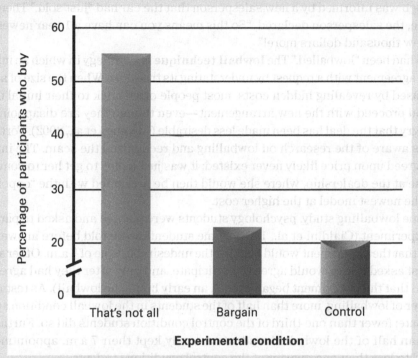

Data source: "Increasing Compliance by Improving the Deal: The That's-Not-All Technique," by J. M. Burger, 1986, *Journal of Personality and Social Psychology 51*(2), pp. 277–283.

How exactly does the that's-not-all technique lower resistance? One possibility is that when the salesperson's request is reduced or sweetened, the customer may perceive this as a concession that the original request was unreasonable. Following the norm of reciprocity, the customer may now feel an increased obligation to reciprocate this act by agreeing to the better price (as in the door-in-the-face effect). Another possible way in which the that's-not-all technique may lower resistance is by altering the customer's "anchor point" against which the purchase decision is made (see Chapter 4's discussion of the *anchoring and adjustment heuristic*, section 4.1d). That is, if customers are contemplating the purchase of a product for which they themselves don't have a fixed price in mind (such as cupcakes at a bake sale), the salesperson's costly first request sets the price standard, or anchor. When the second, cheaper price immediately follows the costly price, it is compared to the anchor point and creates the impression that the product is a bargain.

Although the that's-not-all technique is effective, success appears to depend on targets responding rather mindlessly to the request (Pollock et al., 1998). For example, one study found that compliance occurs only when the initial request is within reason (Burger, 1999). If you first ask people to buy cupcakes for the extremely high price of $3 apiece, lowering your price to $1 is unlikely to induce compliance because the initial request appears ridiculous and places potential customers on guard. Now, instead of engaging in the type of "lazy" thinking discussed in Chapter 4 (*heuristics*) and Chapter 5 (*peripheral-route processing*), the target is motivated to more critically analyze the offer. Under this greater scrutiny, compliance decreases.

Lowballing

A few years ago, Deb was shopping for a new car and while communicating with an online salesperson, she came to an agreement on a price for a previous year's model car that was still brand new. However, upon arriving at the dealership (a mere 30 minutes later), Deb was informed by a new salesperson that the car had "just sold." Then, with a big smile, the salesperson declared, "So this means you can have a 1 year newer car for only a few thousand dollars more!"

Deb had been "lowballed." The **lowball technique** is a strategy in which an influencer secures agreement with a request by understating its true cost. When the size of a request is increased by revealing hidden costs, most people often stick to their initial commitment and proceed with the new arrangement—even though they are disappointed and even angry that the deal has been made less desirable (Guéguen et al., 2002). Fortunately, Deb was aware of the research on lowballing and recognized the scam. The initial car at the agreed upon price likely never existed; it was just a ploy to get her to commit to a purchase at the dealership, where she would then be presented with the "opportunity" to buy the newest model at the higher cost.

In one lowballing study, psychology students were phoned and asked to participate in an experiment (Cialdini et al., 1978). Some students were told before answering the request that the experiment would begin at the undesirable time of 7 a.m. Other students were first asked if they would agree to participate, and only after they had agreed were they told that the experiment began at such an early hour (the lowball). As testament to the power of lowballing, more than half of the students in the lowball condition agreed to participate; fewer than one-third of the control condition students did so. Furthermore, more than half of the lowballed students actually kept their 7 a.m. appointment—as opposed to less than one-quarter of the control condition students.

A meta-analysis of lowball studies found that this tactic is reliable and effective for increasing compliance, especially when the person states their agreement publicly and the second request is only slightly more expensive than the first request (Burger & Caputo, 2015). Why does the lowball procedure work? One important factor is the psychology of commitment. As people become increasingly committed to their course of action, they grow more resistant to changing their minds. This is why car dealers will let you, the prospective buyer, sit in the showroom for a while before telling you that they require more money. During that time, they count on you fantasizing about "your new car" so that later you will pay the extra money to drive it off the lot. People also feel a commitment to honor their agreement with the requestor. Finally, when a person publicly agrees to a request, changing their minds for the second request can cause self-presentation concerns. If you find yourself in a similar situation, we recommend that you review what you have learned here so you stand a better chance of leaving with a deal that's to your liking. In this case, knowledge truly is power—social influence power.

7.4c Intense Social Influence Can Lead to Unusual Compliance.

lowball technique

A two-step compliance strategy in which the influencer secures agreement with a request by understating its true cost

In 2006, following the brutal sexual assault and murder of Teresa Halbach in northern Manitowoc County, Wisconsin, police invited Brendan Dassey, a 16-year-old, intellectually disabled teenager (a neighbor of the victim) to assist them in the investigation against his uncle Steven Avery. Detectives questioned Dassey for hours, implying at least 24 times that they knew how the victim had been murdered (Kassin, 2018; Weintraub & Najdowski,

2018). This is an interrogation technique known as *maximization,* where detectives imply they have more evidence than they actually have. Later, during the interrogation, the detectives expressed sympathy for Dassey, indicating that they understood that he was working under his uncle's direction. One detective is quoted as having stated, "I promise I will not leave you high and dry." This technique is known as *minimization,* and it often leads defendants to believe that confessing to the crime is a away to avoid harsher punishment (Kassin, 2019). Finally, after hours of interrogation, Dassey confessed to the crime with his uncle. Later, he retracted this confession, telling his mother that "they got into my head," but the confession still played a central role in his conviction. In 2016, his conviction was overturned but later upheld by a seven-judge panel. Currently, Dassey is serving a life sentence in prison and he continues to maintain his innocence.

In support of Dassey's petition to have his conviction overturned, the American Psychological Association reviewed social psychological research on how certain techniques, such as the ones employed during Dassey's interrogation, can cause compliance in the form of false confessions. False confessions can occur through external compliance (see section 7.1a), where innocent suspects admit to crimes they know they did not commit in order to avoid further interrogation. Internal compliance can occur when police interrogators' influence techniques result in innocent suspects not only falsely confessing but also actually believing that they are indeed guilty. In some cases, they will even offer rich details that later strengthen jury members' confidence in convicting them (Hasel & Kassin, 2012; Kassin, 2012). Do you think you could fall prey to either one of these influence processes if you were a suspect in a crime you didn't commit?

In one representative investigation of false confessions, Saul Kassin and Katherine Kiechel (1996) tested the following two hypotheses: (1) False evidence can lead people who are in a heightened state of uncertainty to confess to an act they did not commit; (2) These "false confessors" will internalize the confession and create details in memory consistent with this new guilt. In this study, college students who thought they were participating in a reaction time study were randomly assigned to one of four experimental conditions involving either high or low vulnerability and either the presence or absence of a false incriminating witness.

(AP Photo / Morry Gash)

How might informational influence and normative influence cause someone like Brendan Dassey to falsely confess to a crime while being interrogated by the police? Why might Dassey have been particularly vulnerable to such harsh interrogation techniques?

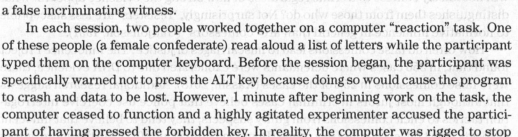

Given what we know about compliance and false confessions, do you think extreme interrogation techniques, such as use of torture, can result in accurate information from detainees?

In each session, two people worked together on a computer "reaction" task. One of these people (a female confederate) read aloud a list of letters while the participant typed them on the computer keyboard. Before the session began, the participant was specifically warned not to press the ALT key because doing so would cause the program to crash and data to be lost. However, 1 minute after beginning work on the task, the computer ceased to function and a highly agitated experimenter accused the participant of having pressed the forbidden key. In reality, the computer was rigged to stop functioning through no fault of the participant.

When first accused, all participants denied responsibility for the computer damage. However, in the false-witness condition, the confederate disputed the participant's denial, testifying that she saw the participant press the forbidden key. In the no-witness condition, the confederate did not challenge the participant's denial, but simply stated that she did not see the key pressed. The participant's vulnerability was manipulated by varying the pace of the task. In the high-vulnerability condition, the confederate—following the beat of a metronome—read the letters at a frenzied pace of 67 letters per minute; in the low-vulnerability condition, the pace was set at a leisurely 43 letters per minute.

The dependent measures involved three forms of social influence. To measure external compliance, the experimenter asked participants to sign a handwritten confession stating that they had hit the ALT key and caused the program to crash. To assess internal compliance, participants' private descriptions of what happened—told to a second confederate waiting outside the lab—were recorded and later coded for whether they unambiguously internalized guilt for what happened. To measure the creation of memories, the experimenter also asked participants to "recall" specific details of how they caused the computer program to crash.

Results indicated no gender differences in susceptibility to influence. Overall, 69% of the participants signed the confession, 28% exhibited internalization, and 9% created false memories to support their false beliefs. As expected, participants in the high-vulnerability condition were most susceptible to all three forms of social influence following the false accusation. In addition, regardless of the vulnerability condition, participants in the false-witness conditions were not only more likely to sign a confession prepared by the experimenter but were also more likely to later admit their guilt to the second confederate. Finally, participants in the low-vulnerability/no-witness condition were the least susceptible to these effects, while those in the high-vulnerability/false-witness condition were the most susceptible. Although the false confessions coerced out of participants in this study are much less dramatic than many of the false confessions squeezed out of suspects in criminal cases, they do demonstrate that people can be induced to erroneously confess to crimes—and to believe in their own guilt—following the presentation of false evidence.

Instead of presenting false evidence, sometimes police interrogators use the bluff tactic: They pretend to have evidence that may or may not implicate the suspect. When researchers used this tactic in the previously described computer-crash experiment, they found that bluffing increases false confessions at a rate comparable to the effect produced by the presentation of false evidence (Perillo & Kassin, 2011). These results suggest that innocent suspects can sometimes be tricked into falsely confessing to a crime even when interrogators employ relatively subtle compliance techniques. These techniques are even more effective when they are used against individuals who are young, have a cognitive or intellectual impairment, or suffer from mental illness (Kassin et al., 2018).

In actual criminal cases, suspects generally make false confessions due to external compliance in exchange for penalty reductions. Here, their perceptions of the strength of the evidence against them—which police interrogators may highly exaggerate—significantly determine whether they will confess (Gudjonsson, 2003). Of course, many suspects will not falsely confess to a crime regardless of how strong the evidence appears. What distinguishes them from those who do? Not surprisingly, "resisters" are less susceptible to normative influence in general than are "confessors" (Gudjonsson, 1991).

How often do false confessions lead to miscarriages of justice? The Innocence Project found that, in 356 cases where defendants were exonerated due to DNA evidence, there were false confessions in 25% of the cases (Kassin, 2018). Additional research suggests that although most jurors in criminal cases believe that police use coercive interrogation tactics to elicit confessions from guilty suspects, they tend to believe that innocent suspects won't falsely confess to a crime (Blandón-Gitlin et al., 2011). Furthermore, jurors fail to discount the confession even when the interrogation methods are coercive and the defendants are young or suffer from mental illness (Kassin, 2015, 2017). When the accused are exonerated from a crime (often through DNA or other evidence), those who falsely confessed are viewed as being of lower intelligence, having mental health issues, and being less deserving of psychological and career counseling and job training; and this is especially true of black exonerees (Howard, 2019; Scherr et al., 2018).

Fortunately, few of you reading this text will ever be falsely accused of murder. However, all of you have been—and will continue to be—falsely accused of less serious transgressions. When facing your accusers, you will stand a better chance of successfully professing your innocence if you keep in mind the lessons learned here.

Section Summary

- Factors that foster compliance include:
  positive mood
  reciprocity norm
  giving reasons

- Compliance techniques that utilize multiple requests include:
  foot-in-the-door
  door-in-the-face
  that's-not-all
  lowballing

- False confessions can occur due to either:
  external compliance
  internal compliance

7.5   Obedience

As you can see from our overview of both conformity processes and compliance strategies, many social influence pressures are relatively hidden and subtly employed. In this respect, obedience differs from other types of influence because it is overt and easily recognized as an exercise of power.

When authority figures order people to obey their commands, you might expect that people's need for personal control would trigger disobedience. If the order involved possibly causing serious harm to others, you might further predict that wide-scale disobedience would occur. But is this really what takes place? What would you do under such circumstances? Let's explore the most discussed social psychological study ever conducted examining this very issue (Blass, 2000).

> "Obedience to the law is demanded as a right, not asked as a favor."
>
> —Theodore Roosevelt, US president, 1858–1919

7.5a   Milgram Discovered That Destructive Obedience Is Common.

Imagine that you have volunteered to participate in an experiment on learning. Upon arriving at the laboratory, you find that a 50-year-old man is also taking part in the study. The experimenter explains that the study will investigate the effects of punishment on the learning of word pairs. The punishment will be electrical shock. One of you will be the "teacher," and the other will be the "learner." A drawing of names determines that you will be the teacher. When the learner discovers that he will be receiving shocks, he tells the experimenter that he has a mild heart condition ("Nothing serious, but since electricity is being used, I thought I should tell you"). The experimenter replies that while the shocks may be painful, they will not cause permanent tissue damage.

(Top) Stanley Milgram and the "shock generator" used in his obedience experiments. (Bottom) In this replication of the obedience experiment, the teacher (participant) had to force the learner's (confederate's) hand onto a shock plate. Less than one-third obeyed the experimenter under these conditions.

(Reprinted with permission by Alexandra Milgram)

The learner is then taken to an adjacent room where he is strapped into a chair and electrodes are attached to his arms. As this is being done, the experimenter explains that your task is to teach the learner a list of word pairs, to then test him on the list, and to administer punishment whenever he makes a mistake. In front of you is a shock generator, which has a row of 30 switches ranging from 15 to 450 volts. You are instructed to start at the lowest intensity level and to increase the shock by one switch (15 volts) for each subsequent learner error. To give you some idea of what the shock feels like, the experimenter gives you a 45-volt shock—and it hurts. You are a bit nervous now, but you do not say anything.

Once the study begins, the learner makes many mistakes, and you respond by flipping the shock switches. Starting at 75 volts, through the intercom system, you hear the learner grunting and moaning in pain whenever you deliver the shocks. At 150 volts he demands to be released, shouting, "Experimenter! That's all! Get me out of here. My heart's starting to bother me now. I refuse to go on!" Now your nervousness becomes nail-biting anxiety. At 180 volts, he shouts that he can no longer stand the pain. At 300 volts, he says that he absolutely refuses to provide any more answers. In response to this, the experimenter instructs you to treat the absence of a response as equivalent to an error and to deliver the appropriate level of shock. Even though the learner no longer gives answers, he continues to scream in agony whenever your finger flips the shock generator switch.

When you surpass the 330-volt switch, the learner not only refuses to answer—he falls silent, not to be heard from again. As you continue to increase the shock intensity, the labels under the switches now read, "Danger—Severe Shock" and you realize you are getting closer to the last switch, the 450-volt switch, which is simply labeled "XXX." When you hesitate, the experimenter first tells you, "Please continue," then "The experiment requires that you continue," then "It is absolutely essential that you go on," and finally, "You have no other choice, you must go on!"

What would you do? Would you disobey the experimenter's commands? When would you stop obeying? Is it possible that you would continue to deliver all the shocks, including the dangerous 450 volts, despite the learner's protests? How many of your friends do you think would obey the experimenter's orders if they were the teachers?

You probably predicted that you and your friends would disobey the experimenter's authority and refuse to continue the learning experiment well before the 450-volt limit. If this is your prediction, you are in good company: Widespread disobedience is exactly what was predicted by college students, middle-class adults, and psychiatrists who were presented with this hypothetical scenario (Milgram, 1963). People in all three groups guessed that they would disobey by about 135 volts, and none thought they would go beyond 300 volts. The psychiatrists, when asked about other people's level of obedience, predicted that less than one-tenth of 1% of participants—1 person out of 1,000—would obey the experimenter completely.

To determine the actual level of obedience, Milgram conducted this study at Yale University using 40 adult males who ranged in age from 20 to 50 years. The drawing

"Far more, and far more hideous, crimes have been committed in the name of obedience than have ever been committed in the name of rebellion."

—C. P. Snow, English chemist and novelist, 1905–1980

was rigged so that the participant always became the teacher. The learner was a confederate and received no actual shocks. Even his screams of protest and pain were prerecorded so that all participants heard exactly the same thing. To Milgram's surprise, 65% of the participants (26 out of 40) obeyed the experimenter completely, despite the learner's convincing cries of agony. In fact, all participants who reached 450 volts obeyed the experimenter's command to continue with the procedure by using the 450-volt switch; the experiment was halted a short time later. Those who disobeyed often did so at the 150-volt level—when the learner demanded his release, claiming that his heart was bothering him.

A simple interpretation of the high obedience levels in this study is that Milgram inadvertently recruited closet sadists who were more than willing to inflict pain on the hapless learner. However soothing this explanation would be to our collective psyches, it does not stand up to the available evidence (Darley, 1995). Milgram's participants were not suffering from any personality disorders that would cause them to enjoy their destructive obedience. In fact, their actions caused them a great deal of stress (Elms, 1995; Elms & Milgram, 1966). Participants were observed sweating, trembling, stuttering, biting their lips, and groaning as they struggled through the experimental procedure.

Some sense of their state of mind can be gleaned from remarks made by one of the fully obedient individuals in Milgram's fifth study, who began his participation calmly but became increasingly tense as the learner protested the shocks being delivered:

150 volts delivered: "You want me to keep going?"

165 volts delivered: "That guy is hollering in there. There's a lot of them here. He's liable to have a heart condition. You want me to go?"

180 volts delivered: "He can't stand it! I'm not going to kill that man in there! You hear him hollering? He's hollering. He can't stand it. What if something happens to him? . . . I'm not going to get that man sick in there. He's hollering in there. You know what I mean? I mean I refuse to take the responsibility. He's getting hurt in there. He's in there hollering. Too many left here. Geez, if he gets them wrong. There's too many of them left. I mean who is going to take responsibility if anything happens to that gentleman?"

[The experimenter accepts responsibility]: "All right."

195 volts delivered: "You see he's hollering. Hear that. Gee, I don't know."

[The experimenter says, "The experiment requires that you go on."]: "I know it does, sir, but I mean—ugh—he don't know what he's in for. He's up to 195 volts."

210 volts delivered.

225 volts delivered.

240 volts delivered: "Aw no. You mean I've got to keep going up with the scale? No sir. I'm not going to kill that man! I'm not going to give him 450 volts!"

[The experimenter says, "The experiment requires that you go on."]: "I know it does, but that man is hollering there, sir . . . ."

Because the findings were so unexpected, Milgram carried out a number of variations of his experiment to better understand the conditions under which obedience and

"In schools all over the world, little boys learn that their country is the greatest in the world, and the highest honor that could befall them would be to defend it heroically someday. The fact that empathy has traditionally been conditioned out of boys facilitates their obedience to leaders who order them to kill strangers."

—Myriam Miedzian, US author

"Obedience, bane of all genius, virtue, freedom, truth, makes slaves of men, and, of the human frame, a mechanized automaton."

—Percy Bysshe Shelley, English poet, 1792–1822

disobedience would be most likely. When college students and women served as participants, the same level of destructive obedience was found (Milgram, 1974). Different researchers also obtained similar results in several other countries, suggesting that these high levels of obedience were not solely an American phenomenon. Australia had a 68% obedience level (Kilham & Mann, 1974), Jordan was at 63% (Shanab & Yahya, 1977), and Germany was the highest at 85% (Mantell, 1971).

> "The doctrine of blind obedience and unqualified submission to any human power, whether civil or ecclesiastical, is the doctrine of despotism."
>
> —Angelina Grimké, US abolitionist and feminist, 1805–1879

Some critics initially suggested that the high obedience was due to the prestige of Yale University; participants' presumed that no one at Yale would allow harm to come to anyone in the study (Baumrind, 1964; Orne, 1962). To test this possibility, Milgram (1965) moved the experimental site to a rundown office building in Bridgeport, Connecticut, with no noticeable affiliation with Yale. Although obedience decreased slightly, the difference was not significant—48% of the participants delivered the maximum shock level. Switching locations from a prestigious to a nonprestigious institution also did not significantly reduce obedience; however, when the experimenter was replaced with an ordinary person (actually a confederate), obedience dropped to 20%. These findings suggest that the social role of "scientist" or "researcher" has sufficient prestige and authority to secure obedience, regardless of the social context (Blass, 1996).

Although an authority figure is much more likely to be obeyed than an ordinary individual, situational factors strengthen or weaken this influence. In a follow-up study, Milgram varied the proximity of the experimenter to the teacher. In one condition, the experimenter sat a few feet from the teacher as he delivered the electrical shocks to the learner. In a second condition, after giving initial instructions, the experimenter left the room and gave his orders by phone. In a third condition, the teacher received his instructions on a tape recorder and never actually met the experimenter. Findings from these three conditions indicated that obedience decreased as the distance from the experimenter increased. In fact, when the experimenter was absent, several participants administered shocks of a lower voltage than the experimenter called for.

In another series of experiments, the proximity of the learner to the teacher was varied (Milgram, 1974). In one condition, the learner and teacher were located in separate rooms without access to intercom systems; thus, the teacher could not hear the learner's cries of protest and pain. The teacher's only knowledge of the victim's reaction was that he pounded on the adjoining wall at 300 volts and subsequently stopped responding to the word pairs. In another condition, the learner and teacher were seated in the same room—only a few feet apart. In a third condition, the learner sat right next to the teacher, resting his hand on a metal plate in order to receive the shock. At 350 volts, the learner refused to put his hand on the plate to receive the shock; the experimenter then ordered the teacher to force the learner's hand onto the shock plate. In all of these studies, results indicated that the closer the teacher was to the learner, the lower the level of obedience.

In addition to testing for proximity and site effects, Milgram also investigated how group pressure might influence obedience. In one study, three teachers (two of them confederates) split up the duties previously assigned to one. The naive participant was always assigned the role of actually delivering the electrical shock, while the confederate-teachers read the word pairs and told the learner if his answers were correct. In one condition, the confederate-teachers simply followed the experimenter's commands and did not express any sympathy for the learner. In another condition, the confederates were openly rebellious—one refused to continue after 150 volts and the other quit at the 210-volt level. The first condition only slightly increased obedience (72%) above the original study's level, but the second condition resulted in complete obedience in only 10% of the participants.

The likely explanation for this sharp drop in obedience is that the open defiance of the confederates broke the social consensus of the situation and reduced the strength of the experimenter's social power. Did the participants in this study recognize the liberating effect that the rebellious confederate-teachers had on their own willingness to disobey the orders of the authority figure? No. Three-fourths of the participants who disobeyed believed that they would have stopped even without the other teachers' examples. Yet the previous studies strongly argue against this belief, suggesting that people seriously underestimate the impact that others have on their own behavior. Figure 7.7 summarizes the findings of some of these studies and identifies factors that foster or inhibit obedience.

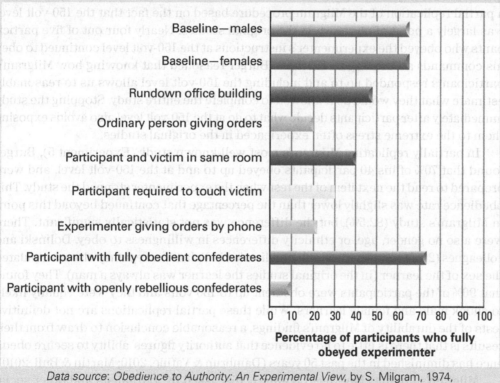

FIGURE 7.7   Some Factors That Influence Obedience and Disobedience to Authority

To determine what factors increase or decrease obedience beyond the baseline 65% level, Milgram varied the location of the experiment, the participant's proximity to the victim and the experimenter, and the presence of obedient or disobedient confederates. As you can see, all of these factors influenced obedience levels.

Baseline—males
Baseline—females
Rundown office building
Ordinary person giving orders
Participant and victim in same room
Participant required to touch victim
Experimenter giving orders by phone
Participant with fully obedient confederates
Participant with openly rebellious confederates

0 10 20 30 40 50 60 70 80 90 100
Percentage of participants who fully obeyed experimenter

Data source: *Obedience to Authority: An Experimental View*, by S. Milgram, 1974, New York, NY: Harper & Row.

7.5b Recent Studies Partially Replicated Milgram's Original Findings.

Four decades after Milgram's research, two separate investigations have reanalyzed his data, revealing additional insights. First, François Rochot and his coworkers (2000) analyzed the audio recordings of one of Milgram's obedience studies to better understand how participants behaved over the course of the experiment. Seeking similar answers,

Dominic Packer (2008) conducted a meta-analysis of data from eight of Milgram's studies involving 320 participants.

Both investigations found that a crucial factor in resisting the destructive commands of authority figures is an early and firm statement of opposition to what is transpiring. As you recall, all participants were initially cooperative toward the experimenter, but that changed at the 150-volt level as the learner began complaining and made his first demand for release. That was the point of no return for many participants regarding obedience (Gilbert, 1989). Rochot's analysis of the audio recordings revealed that those who firmly, verbally opposed the experimenter by 150 volts all ended up defying his authority by disobeying. In contrast, if participants began their verbal challenges after 150 volts, only about half of them ever disobeyed. For disobedient participants, a crucial factor in them disobeying was an early and firm questioning of the experimenter's authority to disregard the rights of the learner. These participants' verbal questioning signaled their refusal to passively accept the experimenter's definition of reality in this emotionally charged and conflicted situation.

When people learn about Milgram's findings, they often speculate whether similar results would be obtained today. Ethical concerns prevent a definitive answer to this question, but Jerry Burger (2009) and Dariusz Doliński and colleagues (2017) conducted a partial replication of the Milgram procedure based on the fact that the 150-volt level was largely a point of no return in the original studies. Nearly four out of five participants who obeyed the experimenter's instructions at the 150-volt level continued to obey his commands all the way to 450 volts. Burger reasoned that knowing how Milgram's participants responded up to and including the 150-volt level allows us to reasonably estimate what they would do if allowed to complete the entire study. Stopping the study immediately after participants decide what to do at the 150-volt level also avoids exposing them to the extreme stress often experienced in the original studies.

In partially replicating Milgram's most well-known study (Experiment 5), Burger found that 70% of his 40 participants obeyed up to and at the 150-volt level, and were prepared to read the next item of the test when the experimenter stopped the study. This obedience rate was slightly lower than the percentage that continued beyond this point in Milgram's study (82.5%), but the difference was not statistically significant. There were also no gender, age, or ethnicity differences in willingness to obey. Doliński and colleagues (2017) completed a similar replication in Poland, except they also manipulated the sex of the learner (in the original studies the learner was always a man). They found that 90% of the participants were obedient up to 150 volts and they were equally likely to shock male and female learners. While these partial replications are not definitive tests of the durability of Milgram's findings, a reasonable conclusion to draw from their results is that there is little to no evidence that authority figures' ability to secure obedience has diminished in the past 50 years (Dambrun & Vatiné, 2010; Martin & Bull, 2010).

Milgram's findings have been regularly discussed by journalists and other social commentators when trying to make sense of the mistreatment of prisoners of war and suspected terrorists by American military personnel in Iraq, Afghanistan, and Cuba (Dutton & Tetreault, 2009). While discussing the meaning of his obedience experiments, Milgram made the following remarks, which are as relevant today as they were in his time:

> The behavior revealed in the experiments reported here is normal human behavior but revealed under conditions that show with particular clarity the danger to human survival inherent in our make-up. And what is it we have seen? Not aggression, for there is no anger, vindictiveness, or hatred in those who shocked the victim. Men do become angry; they do act hatefully and explode in rage against others. But not here. Something far more dangerous is revealed:

the capacity for man to abandon his humanity, indeed, the inevitability that he does so, as he merges his unique personality into larger institutional structures. This is a fatal flaw nature has designed into us, and which in the long run gives our species only a modest chance of survival. (1974, p. 188)

7.5c   Observing Others Defying Authority Greatly Reduces Obedience.

Milgram's commentary on his own obedience research paints a bleak picture of humankind's ability to resist destructive authoritarian pressure. Yet is the abandonment of our humanity as inevitable as he suggests? Perhaps the depth of Milgram's pessimism is partly due to the special circumstances created in his research design. In most of the obedience studies discussed thus far, a lone individual engages in destructive behavior after being placed in a situation in which he or she receives orders from an authority figure. What would happen if antisocial orders were delivered not to a lone individual but to an entire group of people? Would this collective be as malleable as the lone individual?

William Gamson and his colleagues (1982) explored this question when they recruited groups of people to participate in a supposed discussion of community standards. Participants, scheduled in groups of nine, arrived at a local motel for the discussion and were greeted by the "coordinator." This coordinator told them that the proceedings would be videotaped for a large oil company that was being sued by a former manager of one of its local gas stations. This former employee was fired after the company learned that he was living with a woman to whom he was not married. The company justified its actions by stating that its representatives must be beyond moral reproach. Despite this explanation by the coordinator, participants soon learned some additional information that cast a different light on the firing—the manager was fired after appearing on local TV, where he spoke out against higher gas prices.

Shortly after discussion began about whether the manager's lifestyle was morally offensive to those in the community, the coordinator interrupted and told three group members to argue on camera as if they were offended by the manager's lifestyle. A short time later, he again interrupted and told three more members to also act offended. Soon the coordinator had instructed all members to act offended on camera, concerning the manager's lifestyle, and to state that they would not do business at his gas station. Then he told them there was an affidavit to be signed and notarized that gave the oil company the right to introduce the videotapes as evidence in court, editing them as they saw fit.

> "I hold it that a little rebellion now and then is a good thing, and as necessary in the political world as storms in the physical. . . . It is a medicine for the sound health of government."
>
> —Thomas Jefferson, US president, 1743–1826

Why does observing others defying authority often weaken the influence the authority has over those observers?

As originally designed, some discussion groups were to include a confederate member who would take either a more or less active role in mobilizing rebellion against the oil company's actions. However, as the malicious intent of the videotaped discussion began to dawn on the actual group participants, they began to rebel on their own. One participant, when told to act offended before the video camera, expressed his defiance by adopting a mocking, twangy accent and stating, "Next to ma waaf, ma car is my favritt thing, an ah

> "Disobedience when it is not criminally—but morally, religiously, or politically—motivated is always a collective act, and it is justified by the values of the collectivity and the mutual engagements of its members."
>
> —Michael Walzer, social historian, born 1935

ain't sending neither of 'em tuh that gas stoishen." Some groups became so outraged at the company's attempts to use them to discredit the former employee that they threatened to forcibly confiscate the videotapes and expose the company to the local news media. Confronted by one outraged group after another, the researchers were forced to terminate the experiment due to fears that it was causing the participants too much stress.

> "One who breaks an unjust law that conscience tells him is unjust, and who willingly accepts the penalty of imprisonment in order to arouse the consciousness of the community over its injustice, is in reality expressing the highest respect for the law."
>
> — Martin Luther King Jr., US civil rights leader, 1929–1968

Why did this experiment result in such open disobedience when Milgram's research produced such widespread obedience? In both studies, there were agents of authority: the experimenter and the coordinator. In both studies, the original intention of participants was to obey the instructions of these authorities. In both studies, the authorities overstepped the proper moral boundaries and began to demand unjust actions by the participants. The possibility that people generally became less prone to obedience over the 20 years separating these studies is not supported by an analysis of other obedience studies conducted during this time period (Blass, 1999). Instead, the basic difference between these studies is that Milgram's participants were alone, whereas Gamson's were in groups. Because eight or nine of Gamson's group members were naive participants, the possibility of collective action always existed. Milgram's design, on the other hand, has never been tried with more than one naive participant in the teacher role, and so the possibility of collective action here has never been studied.

Although the Milgram design never tested more than one participant at a time, in one of his experiments he did use two confederates who posed as coteachers along with the actual participant. As discussed previously (section 7.5a), when the participant observed others openly defying the destructive commands of the authority figure, he became much more willing to disobey as well. In a very real psychological sense, the rebellious confederates served as models for the participant's own disobedience. Similar findings were also obtained in Asch's conformity studies: Social support allowed others to more easily express their own opinions.

Section Summary

- Obedience research indicates that almost two-thirds of Milgram's participants obeyed the destructive commands of an authority figure.
- Social support helps people follow their own beliefs when confronted by powerful others.
- A recent partial replication of Milgram's original study finds no evidence that obedience levels have diminished in the past 40 years.

7.6   Toward a Unified Understanding of Social Influence

Although different factors are involved in the various forms of social influence discussed in this chapter, the task of social scientists is to discover common principles operating in the exercise of social power. In this section, we examine one theory that attempts to predict when influence attempts are most likely to succeed.

7.6a Social Impact Theory Explains Influence Strength.

As developed by Bibb Latané (1981), **social impact theory** states that the amount of influence others have in a given situation (their social impact) is a function of three factors: their *number*, *strength*, and *immediacy*. This social impact operates like physical impact. For example, the amount of light falling on a surface depends not only on how many lights are turned on but also on the strength or power of the bulbs and how close they are to the surface. Similarly, as illustrated in Figure 7.8 A, a person will be more influenced by others when there are more of them, when they are stronger sources of influence, and when they are physically closer (Pederson et al., 2008).

FIGURE 7.8 **The Psychology of Social Impact: Source and Target Factors**

According to social impact theory, the impact of other people on the target person depends on (A) the number of people present (number of source circles), the strength or importance of these people (size of the source circles), and their immediacy to the target person (nearness of the source circles to the target). Social impact increases as source factors increase. In addition, the total impact of other people on target persons depends on (B) the number of target persons (number of target circles), the strength of these targets (size of target circles), and their immediacy (nearness to one another). Social impact decreases as target factors increase.

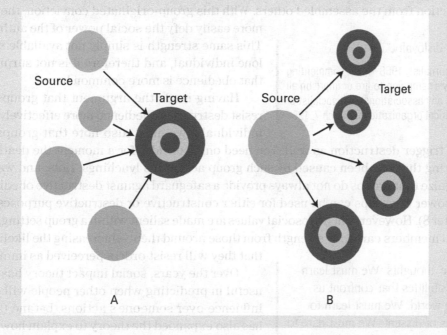

Although social impact theory predicts that people become more influential as their numbers increase, what about the "leveling off" effect found in the Asch (1956) conformity research? In that study, adding more confederates beyond three or four had little impact on conformity. Latané contends that this is due to another principle of social impact theory, which states that as the number of influencing persons increases, their individual impact decreases. Returning to the light bulb analogy, when you turn on a second light in a room that previously had only one bulb illuminating it, the increased impact that the second light has on your sight is quite perceptible. Yet the impact of adding a 15th bulb to a room illuminated by 14 lights is hardly seen at all. Latané claims

social impact theory
The theory that the amount of social influence others have depends on their number, strength, and immediacy

that the same is true with individuals and their social impact on others: The second person has less impact than the first, and the *n*th person has less effect than the (*n*–1)th.

Latané states that the strength of would-be influencers depends on their status, expertise, and power. For example, in most circumstances, a police officer will have greater social impact than a mail carrier. Similarly, in the Milgram studies, the experimenter was more successful in securing obedience than an ordinary person. Finally, the immediacy of others is determined by their closeness to the individual in time or space. In other words, others will have greater social impact on you if they are actually present than if they are watching you on a monitor in another location or watching a videotape of your actions at a later date (Latané et al., 1995). In the obedience studies, people were more likely to obey the experimenter when he was physically present rather than when he gave orders over the phone.

Social impact theory can explain the social influence exerted in the Asch and Milgram studies, but how would it explain the *disobedience* in Gamson's oil company research? As you can see in Figure 7.8 B, social impact theory also predicts that people are more likely to *resist* others' influence attempts when the social impact is dispersed among many strong and closely situated targets. In the oil company study, the social impact of the authority figure was divided among nine participants—rather than being directed at only one—making disobedience easier. Similar disobedience occurred in the Milgram study when participants were in the presence of confederates who actively resisted the authority's orders. These findings indicate that when a group of individuals is confronted with the dictates of an immoral authority, there is always the possibility that the group will collectively redefine social reality and draw individual strength and conviction from the assembled others. With this group-originated conviction, they can more easily defy the social power of the authority. This same strength is simply not available to the lone individual, and therefore it is not surprising that obedience is more common here.

> "We must not confuse dissent with disloyalty."
>
> —Edward R. Murrow, US broadcast journalist, 1908–1965, commenting on Senator Joseph McCarthy's campaign to fire or imprison all governmental employees who ever had any associations with socialist or communist political organizations, March 7, 1954

Having made the argument that groups can resist destructive obedience more effectively than individuals, we must also note that groups can often trigger destruction as well. You need only consider for a moment the death and suffering that has been caused by such group actions as lynchings, riots, and wars to recognize that groups do not always provide a safeguard against destructive obedience. The power of groups can be used for either constructive or destructive purposes (see Chapter 8). However, when prosocial values are made salient within a group setting, individual members can draw strength from those around them—increasing the likelihood that they will resist orders perceived as immoral.

> "We must dare to think 'unthinkable' thoughts. We must learn to explore all the options and possibilities that confront us in a complex and rapidly changing world. We must learn to welcome and not to fear the voices of dissent. We must dare to think about 'unthinkable things' because when things become unthinkable, thinking stops and action becomes mindless."
>
> —Senator J. William Fulbright, 1905–1995, speech in the Senate, March 27, 1964

Over the years, social impact theory has been useful in predicting when other people will exert influence over someone's actions. Latané (2000) has also expanded the theory to explain how ordinary communication between people can create what he calls *dynamic social impact*, in which targets of social influence can, in turn, influence those who are exerting social power. In a series of studies, he and his coworkers found that people who are physically closer and/or in regular direct contact with one another become more similar in their attitudes and beliefs than those separated by greater distances and infrequent contact (Huguet et al., 1998; Latané & L'Herrou, 1996). In essence, the social impact that these individuals regularly exert on one another appears to increase their similarity. Latané believes that this tendency for people to create like-minded *social clusters* when they regularly interact helps explain how regional differences may come to exist within a country, how minority viewpoints can survive within a larger culture, and why minority opinions in a culture tend to increase in size over time and reshape the opinions of the majority (Richardson & Latané, 2001). In all of these instances, through the operation of dynamic social impact, people become organized into social clusters where they collectively reinforce one another's similarly held attitudes, values, and worldviews (Latané, 1997; Latané & Bourgeois, 1996). Latané also speculates that, with the sharp increase of internet use by people around the world, physical proximity will be a relatively unimportant factor in determining the strength of web-based social influence attempts, which is the topic of our *Applications* section.

Section Summary

- Social impact theory contends that the amount of influence people have is a function of three factors:
  - their number
  - their strength
  - their immediacy

- Dynamic social impact can create social clusters of individuals who become more similar to each other as they interact.

Applications

How Can the Internet Influence Voting Behavior?

The internet offers many ways to influence others, such as posting an opinion, request, or appeal on Facebook and discovering how many people respond by hitting the "Like" button; or by writing a blog and discovering how many followers you can attract (Guadagno & Cialdini, 2005).

One area where social media is gaining increasing attention is in the area of political persuasion and voting behaviors. Social media can be used to influence people to engage in socially beneficial behaviors, such as voting. However, the 2016 US presidential election also highlighted the fact that social media can be used as a social influence tool with potentially harmful consequences.

In one internet study examining social influence on voting behavior, James Fowler and his colleagues arranged to have more than 60 million Facebook users see a nonpartisan "Today Is Election Day" message at the top of their news feeds on November 2, 2010, reminding them to vote in the midterm congressional elections (Bond et al., 2012). The message included a clickable "I Voted" button, a link to local polling places, a counter displaying how many Facebook users had already reported voting, and (most important) up to six profile photos of users' own Facebook friends who had clicked on the "I Voted" button. The researchers randomly selected another 600,000 Facebook users to receive the same "Today is Election Day" message, but without the pictures of their Facebook friends; a third randomly selected group of 600,000 individuals received no election-day message at all from Facebook.

Results indicated that those who received information that their friends had voted were significantly more likely than other Facebook users not only to publicly declare they voted (by later clicking the "I Voted" button), but also to seek out information regarding the voting process and actually vote. Furthermore, when Fowler and his colleagues asked some of these same Facebook users to identify their closest friends, they found evidence that close friendships had the most influence on people's voting behavior. In contrast, those

Today Is Election Day   What's this? • close

Find your polling place on the U.S. Politics Page and click the "I Voted" button to tell your friends you voted.

`0 0 4 6 6 4 8 7`
People on Facebook Voted

I Voted

 ⓕ Fran Stevens, Henry Chantel, and 20 other friends have voted.

(Modified Shutterstock)

On US election day 2010, more than 60 million Facebook users received a "Get out the vote" message similar to the one shown here, while other users saw an informational message that was identical in all respects except for the pictures of the user's friends. A control group received no election-day message from Facebook

who received the same voting message without the pictures of their Facebook friends voted at the same rates as those who saw no message at all. In other words, being encouraged to vote had no effect on people's behavior unless they also learned that their friends had voted. The researchers estimated that this 2010 internet experiment influenced approximately 340,000 more people to vote. The takeaway message here is that for political mobilization to work effectively on the internet, it must somehow become associated with friendship networks because such networks are influential and online social network friendships can reach huge numbers of people.

Social media appears to have the ability to not only influence whether you vote, but also who you vote for. In the 2016 US presidential election, there was an unprecedented attempt by Russian agents to influence who US citizens voted for through intentional misinformation campaigns or "fake news" (Allcott & Gentzkow, 2017; Raju et al., 2017). *Fake news* refers to articles designed to appear as news, but they are intentionally and verifiably incorrect. Researchers estimate that the average US adult was exposed to between one and three politically oriented fake

(Getty Images)

According to the U.S. Census Bureau, voter participation is just a little over 50% of the voting-age population for most presidential elections, and less than 40% for most congressional midterm elections. Could the internet be used to increase voting behavior?

news stories on Facebook, and there were 6.6 million Twitter tweets of fake news in the month leading up to the election (Allcott & Gentzkow, 2017; Hindman & Barash, 2018).

Although fake news targeted both Democrats and Republicans, there were about three times as many pro-Trump (the Republican candidate) fake news stories as pro-Clinton (the Democrat candidate) stories. Furthermore, misinformation can spread through a person's social network, which often consists of people who have similar beliefs and views (Törnberg, 2018). Indeed, the fake news stories were shared extensively; however, the pro-Trump stories were shared on Facebook more than the pro-Clinton stories. This highlights the fact that fake news displayed a partisan bias and potentially influenced the election results.

Unfortunately, many of the people who read these fake news stories believed them to be true in the time leading up to the US presidential election (Allcott & Gentzkow, 2017). People are more likely to believe fake news if it is consistent with their preexisting political beliefs than when it challenges those beliefs (Duran et al., 2017). Once we have heard fake news, it can be especially difficult to debunk the misinformation (Chan et al., 2017). Furthermore, research on the sleeper effect (Chapter 5) suggests that information from a non-credible source might not influence people immediately, but it can result in persuasion at a later date because we forget the source and only recall the (misinformed) arguments.

Given that it will be difficult for fake news to be eliminated from social media, it is especially important for readers to learn how to identify such misinformation. Education and a high need for cognition (see Chapter 5, section 5.4a) appear to be important for resisting misinformation influence tactics (Allcott & Gentzkow, 2017; Rapp, 2016). Not surprisingly, people with an analytic thinking style are better able to accurately identify fake news than people with a less analytic thinking style (Pennycook & Rand, 2019).

How could politicians use the findings from this study to increase their likelihood of winning elections?

Considering what social psychology has informed us about attitudes, persuasion, and social influence, we recommend that readers of social media and online news do the following things:

- Determine if the source is credible before even reading the article.

- Critically evaluate the news and provide counterarguments for potentially inaccurate information.

- Refrain from "sharing" social media posts of questionable accuracy so as not to spread fake news through your social network.

- Resist misinformation influence attempts by being the minority voice who speaks out against fake news articles once they are identified.

As students in a social psychology course, you are at an advantage in guarding yourselves against fake news because you are learning about the power of social influence. Furthermore, through your college education, you are developing critical-thinking skills to carefully evaluate the credibility of both the information and the source. Now, more than ever, it seems you need to be on guard when reading information presented in social media and use caution when making decisions based on such information. Our shared future depends on everyone making wise and (accurately) informed decisions.

THE BIG PICTURE

Earlier, when describing the situation confronting participants in Milgram's research, we asked whether you would have fully obeyed the experimenter's commands. This is a question we have asked ourselves over the years. Most people emphatically believe that they would resist the destructive commands and openly rebel. They further believe that those who would obey fully must be more aggressive, cold, and unappealing than the average person (Miller et al., 1973). This harsh judgment is consistent with the belief that those who are susceptible to influence are weak-minded (Douglas et al., 2010). How do we reconcile these beliefs with the actual experimental findings?

To answer this question, let us return to information presented in Chapter 4. There is a widely held assumption—more common in individualist than in collectivist cultures—that people's actions are caused by internal dispositions rather than by external forces. This fundamental attribution error often results in a gross underestimation of the inherent power of the situation to shape behavior (Haney & Zimbardo, 2009; Masters, 2009). The likely source for this belief in the power of the individual to act independently of situational forces resides in the desire of many people to believe that they have control over their own lives. This need to believe that the self is relatively uninfluenced by outside forces fosters a misrepresentation of how the social world actually operates.

Gunter Bierbrauer (1979) attempted to eliminate this misperception by having college students either observe a vivid reenactment of the Milgram experiment or play the role of obedient teachers themselves. Despite being exposed to the power of situational factors in causing high levels of obedience, students still predicted that their friends would be only minimally obedient if they participated in Milgram's study. Even after being confronted by the social psychological facts, these students still essentially believed that only bad people do bad deeds, and good people do only good deeds. The danger in such a view of the social world is that it leaves us wide open to being manipulated by the very social forces we underestimate. Previous chapters have documented how the self and self-beliefs shape our interpretation and response to our social surroundings. In the matter of social influence, it is our misinterpretation of the social world's constitution that helps to explain how we are so often easily manipulated. If our self-beliefs were not so firmly based on our power to remain uninfluenced by the wishes, desires, and dictates of others, we might be better able to recognize when we are in danger of falling prey to such social manipulation.

In closing this chapter on social influence, we would like to introduce you to an excerpt from a humorous poem by Russell Edson (1976), in which a man awakens one morning to find strings coming through his window attached to his hands and feet.

. . . I'm not a marionette, he says, his voice rising with the question, am I? Am I a marionette?

One of the strings loosens and jerks as he scratches his head.

. . . Hmmm, he says, I just wonder if I am a marionette?

And then all the strings pull and jerk and he is jumping out of bed.

Now that he's up he'll just go to the window and see who's doing tricks with him when he's half asleep . . .

He follows the strings up into the sky with his eyes and sees a giant hand sticking through a cloud, holding a crossbar to which the strings are attached . . .

Hmmm, he says, that's funny, I never saw that crossbar before . . . I guess I am a marionette . . .

Based on your own newfound knowledge of the social influence process, you are undoubtedly more aware of the social strings to which you, too, are attached. The "anchor" for these social strings may well be based in an evolutionary past, predisposing you to be naturally receptive to others' influence. However, as Stanley Milgram's quote in the margin reminds us, the difference between you and a marionette (and many other animal species) is that you can reflect on your own actions, and you can analyze the strings that bind you to your social world. Through such analysis, you can become less a puppet of other people's desires and more a coactor in a rich and interlocking web of social intercourse.

"It may be that we are puppets—puppets controlled by the strings of society. But at least we are puppets with perception, with awareness. And perhaps our awareness is the first step to our liberation."

—Stanley Milgram, social psychologist, 1933–1984

KEY TERMS

WEBSITES

Accessed through https://www.bvtlab.com/sop8

Websites for this chapter focus on the social influence process, including ordinary and extraordinary varieties.

Social Influence Website

This website is devoted to the psychological study of social influence, examining everyday and interpersonal influence, mindful versus mindless behavior, and the influence tactics used by cults.

Social Psychology Network

Among other things, this large social psychology database offers links to other websites dealing with social influence, including those that discuss marketing and sales techniques, social influence countermeasures, and relevant research.

"The Milgram Experiment"

Saul McLeod created this website to describe Stanley Milgram's obedience research and to discuss its implications, including the ethical issues raised by this study.

Chapter 8

(Drop of Light / Shutterstock)

Group Behavior

FOCUS QUESTIONS

1. How are people changed through their group membership, and how is the group changed by members' ideas and actions?

2. How do groups sometimes lower the inhibitions of members, causing them to impulsively engage in such antisocial behavior as vandalism, aggression, and rioting?

3. Are group decisions more or less cautious than individual decisions?

4. What is more important in determining the effectiveness of leaders—their personalities or the factors they encounter?

5. How can cooperation be encouraged among group members so that selfish behavior is minimized?

CHAPTER OUTLINE

Introduction

O ver the past couple of decades, the American public has become more politically polarized. For example, in a national poll by the Gallup organization, the number of Democrats who identified themselves as having a "liberal" ideology

"The polarization of Congress; the decline of civility; and the rise of attack politics in the 1980s, the 1990s, and the early years of the new century are a blot on our political system and a disservice to the American people."

—Edward Brooke, former US senator, 1919–2015

increased from about 25% in 1994 to 51% in 2018, while the number of Republicans who identified with a "conservative" ideology increased from 58% to 73% during that same time period (Saad, 2019). Interestingly, this shift toward a more conservative or liberal ideology has not occurred among citizens who do not identify with one of the two main political parties in the country. Because bipartisan political cooperation is often necessary to address a wide range of problems, a country that has political parties with sharply divergent beliefs and values may be unable to find common ground in successfully addressing the challenges they collectively face. For example, while most American citizens recognize that climate change is a real problem, political polarization has impeded actual support for concrete policies to address this issue (Van Boven et al., 2018). A similar political stalemate occurred in 2019 regarding immigration policy, resulting in the longest partial federal government shut down in US history. A further sign of the lack of cooperation between the two main political parties is that the number of bipartisan amendments to legislation that are voted on by the U.S. House of Representatives has decreased dramatically over the last 25 years (Willis, 2019).

The current division between Americans who are members of the two major political parties is so deep that many of them actually perceive the other as a threat to the nation's well-being (Cohn, 2014). Think about your own political beliefs and affiliations and those of your family, friends, and acquaintances. Are they similar or decidedly different? Have your own political beliefs become more extreme or polarized? How does this group polarization occur? How can members of different groups learn to cooperate for the greater good? How can leaders ensure that groups will function properly to make good decisions, especially in the face of conflict or group threats? These are just a few of the questions we will examine in this chapter on group behavior.

8.1   The Nature of Groups

The essential message of social psychology is that humans are social animals. Through the process of natural selection and evolutionary adaptation, we have inherited specialized skills from our ancestors that help us efficiently perform tasks that are essential for survival. Because our ancestors lived together in small groups, it makes evolutionary sense that many of these specialized skills relate to group behavior. In this chapter, we examine how specific social skills operate in a group context. First, let's start with the most basic of questions: What is a group?

There is little agreement about how to precisely define a **group**, but one common definition is that it consists of several interdependent people who have emotional ties

group
Several interdependent people who have emotional ties and interact on a regular basis

and who interact on a regular basis (Kessler & Hollbach, 2005; McGrath et al., 2000). By *interdependence*, we not only mean that members depend on one another to achieve group goals but also that events that affect one member affect others as well.

8.1a Groups Accomplish Instrumental Tasks and Satisfy Socioemotional Needs.

Have you ever wondered why people join groups? Existing evidence suggests that they do so for several reasons, all of which can be traced to the accomplishment of *instrumental* tasks and the satisfaction of *socioemotional* or affiliation needs (Schachter, 1959). Put simply, people often join groups because of a desire to achieve certain task-oriented goals that they cannot attain alone. For example, you will have a much better chance of extinguishing a burning building, or of finding shelter for the homeless, if you pursue these tasks within the supportive network of a group. Similarly, your concern about a societal problem might motivate you to become active with a political party that proposes a solution that is consistent with your values. In addition, becoming a group member provides one with an opportunity to satisfy such affiliative motives as the desire for approval, belonging, prestige, friendship, and even love. These mutual desires for task accomplishment and emotional fulfillment in a group setting are observed across many species and are an integral part of our evolutionary heritage.

> "When spiders unite, they can tie down a lion."
> —Ethiopian proverb

> "Two heads are better than one."
> —North American folk saying

The work of Robert Bales, which began in the late 1940s, suggests that *accomplishing tasks* and *dealing with emotional and social relationships* are indeed the two principal functions of groups (Bales, 1970; Bales & Slater, 1955). Some groups are primarily task-oriented, while others are principally constituted to foster social relationships (Johnson et al., 2006). An example of a *task-oriented* group is a work group—such as a surgical team operating on a patient, postal workers delivering the mail, or elected officials passing laws. Examples of *socioemotional* groups are friendship and family groups, which nurture and emotionally support fellow members, and neighbor groups, which might organize a summer block party.

Although some groups can be identified as more oriented toward one function than the other, almost all groups engage in at least some degree of both task and socioemotional activity. Indeed, Bales contends that this continual oscillation between task and socioemotional activities is what characterizes group processes. As a group engages in task-oriented activities, members' feelings tend to be neglected; this inattention creates group tension in the socioemotional area. However, when the group attempts to reduce this socioemotional tension by paying more attention to members' feelings, task goals become temporarily sidetracked; this, in turn, creates task tension. According to Bales, groups constantly strive to strike a proper balance between task and socioemotional concerns so that they can keep group tension to a minimum.

Socioemotional groups can center around friendships, family members, or neighbors.

8.1b There Are Five Phases to Group Membership.

An important characteristic of group membership is that it is a *temporal* process, meaning that change occurs over time, involving different *phases* (Arrow et al., 2005). Richard Moreland and John Levine's (1988, 2002) **temporal model of group membership** examines not only how people are changed through their membership to a group, but also how the group is changed by members' ideas and actions. Three psychological

temporal model of group membership

A theory of group membership describing the changes that occur over time in members and in the group due to their mutual influence and interdependence processes that propel people into and out of groups are the *ongoing evaluations* the individual and the group make of one another, the *feelings of commitment* that follow these evaluations, and the *role transitions* that result from these changes in commitment (Levine & Moreland, 1998; Van Vugt & Hart, 2004). The two phases of evaluation that occur during the course of group membership involve (1) the degree to which the individual meets the needs of the group, and (2) the degree to which the group meets the needs of the individual.

According to Moreland and Levine, the temporal passage of the individual through the group generally occurs in five phases; each phase is associated with a different social role played by the individual. The movement from one membership phase to the next represents a role transition. In Figure 8.1, the line of the bell-shaped curve represents the personal history of someone passing through all five phases of group membership. As people move up the line, their commitment to the group and the group's commitment to them strengthens, while as they move down the line, this mutual commitment weakens. Commitment is most likely to weaken during times of change within the group (Prislin & Christensen, 2005).

FIGURE 8.1   A Temporal Model of Group Membership

Based on Moreland and Levine's (1982) model of the phases of group membership, in what phase is commitment the greatest?

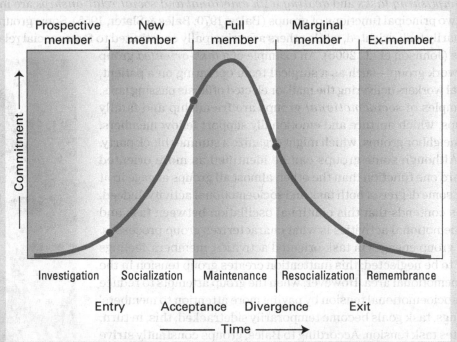

Data source: "Socialization in Small Groups: Temporal Changes in Individual-Group Relations," by R. L. Moreland and J. M. Levine, 1982, in *Advances in Experimental Social Psychology*, edited by J. E. McGrath, pp. 137–192. Copyright Academic Press, 1982.

In the *investigation phase*, the group seeks people who seem likely to attain group goals, and prospective members seek groups that provide the opportunity to satisfy personal needs. Prospective members also have a strong preference for groups they perceive as treating their members equitably and respectfully, and also those that allow members to freely voice their opinions (Poepsel & Schroeder, 2013). If both the individual's and the group's interest levels are sufficiently strong, a prospective member enters the group. Although many groups have low entrance criteria and continually admit new members, other groups establish strict criteria and only periodically allow others to join.

> "I don't care to belong to any club that will have me as a member."
>
> —Groucho Marx, US comedian, 1890–1977

In the *socialization phase*, the group tries to shape the new members' thinking and behavior so that they can and will make the maximum contribution to the group (Moreland & Levine, 2001; Ryan et al., 2004). Groups accomplish this task through formal and informal indoctrination sessions and through "coaches" who model the appropriate thinking and behaviors (Keating et al., 2005). While this socialization process is taking place, new members often try to change the group so that it will accommodate their needs (Swann et al., 2000). But in seeking such accommodations, new members must not overreach; doing so will result in established members forming unfavorable first impressions, which will harm the new members' social status (Pinto et al., 2010). The socialization phase ends when the individual's and the group's commitment levels increase so that the individual becomes a full member of the group.

During the *maintenance phase*, the group attempts to define specialized roles for full members that maximize their contributions to the group's goals (J. Levine et al., 2005). In contrast, the full members often try to define their roles in the group to maximize personal needs. If this influence process is mutually satisfying, commitment is increased on both sides. However, if role negotiation fails the individual will now be viewed as a marginal member, which can lead to conflict and decreased productivity (Dimas et al., 2007).

When relabeled as marginal, group members enter the *resocialization phase*, in which both parties once again try to persuade the other to meet their expectations. Feeling uncertain about their group membership often results in marginal members more strongly identifying with the group and giving preferential treatment to other group members (e.g., ingroup bias) as a way to reestablish their membership (Hohman et al., 2017). If the group or the individual succeeds in convincing the other to accept their role expectations—or if a mutually agreeable compromise can be struck—the marginal member once again becomes a full member. As Figure 8.1 shows, this means that the person moves backward on the curve toward a higher commitment level. If no agreement is reached, however, the individual's and the group's commitment levels fall even further, prompting the individual to exit the group. Leaving a group can be emotionally stressful, especially if the exiting member feels compelled or is forced to leave due to unresolvable differences with the group. In the resulting *remembrance phase*, the group develops a consensus concerning the ex-member's contributions to the group's goals; similarly, the ex-member reminisces about the benefits and costs of being a member of the group.

You may have noticed that Moreland and Levine's depiction of the phases of group membership has an individualist bent to it; they assume that members' personal goals often diverge from group goals. In a collectivist culture, phases of group membership are less affected by tension between the individual and the group (Abrams et al., 1998; Markus & Kitayama, 1994).

8.1c Group Structure Develops Quickly and Changes Slowly.

One characteristic in which groups differ is *structure*: the regular, stable patterns of behavior between members (Wilke, 1996). These group behavior patterns generally develop quickly and change slowly. In analyzing the structure of groups, social psychologists from different theoretical perspectives have identified a number of common elements (Poole et al., 2004). Three of the more important ones are social norms, social roles, and status systems.

Social Norms

As defined in Chapter 7 (section 7.2a), *social norms* are expected standards of behavior and beliefs established and enforced by a group. Some groups have norms for personal appearance (for example, shaved heads for Marine recruits), others have norms for opinions (for example, liberal views in environmental organizations), and most have norms for behavior (for example, profanity is forbidden in school classrooms). Sometimes, these norms are formally conveyed to group members in written guidelines. However, most often these norms are learned through everyday conversations or by observing other members (Miller & Prentice, 1996). As demonstrated by Sherif's classic studies (see Chapter 7, section 7.2), once norms are established, they tend to be stable over time—despite changes in group membership. Social norms certainly increase conformity and reduce deviancy within groups; they can also enhance performance when structured in such a way as to reward effort, efficiency, and quality (Taggar & Ellis, 2007). When a member severely violates group norms, other group members will perceive this behavior as attempting to change the group identity and they will often exclude the person from the group (Ditrich et al., 2017).

Social Roles

As defined in Chapter 4 (section 4.3b), *social roles* are clusters of socially defined expectations that individuals in a given situation are expected to fulfill. In a group, roles often define the division of labor, and well-defined roles improve group dynamics and performance (Barley & Bechky, 1994). In some cases, social roles *evolve* during group interaction, while in other cases, people *import* a role into their new group that they enjoyed playing in previous groups (Rose, 1994). For instance, if you were known as a "good listener" in your high school friendship group, you may import this role into your college friendships. Likewise, others may try to shape their "comedian" friendship role into the "class clown" role at school.

(Shutterstock)

When joining a new group, you may import social roles you played in previous groups. Can you identify roles that you have imported from your high school friendships into your college friendships?

expectation states theory

A theory that the development of group status is based on members' expectations of others' probable contributions to the achievement of group goals, and that these expectations are shaped not only by members' task-relevant characteristics but also by diffuse-status characteristics, such as race, sex, age, and wealth

Status Systems

The third aspect of group structure is its *status system*, which reflects the distribution of power among members (Kaplan & Martin, 1999). Status is a valued commodity in a group. Even in groups that do not have formal status systems—such as friendship cliques—members often differ in their prestige and authority. You can tell who has higher status in a group by paying attention to verbal and nonverbal behavior: Higher-status members maintain greater eye contact; they stand more erect; they are more likely to criticize, command, or interrupt others; and they not only speak more often but are also spoken to more often than those of lower status (Fournier et al., 2002). Although status can be *achieved* by helping a group reach its goals, it is often *ascribed* rather than earned: People are given higher status simply because of who or what they are (Ridgeway, 1991).

How exactly are these status differences created in the first place? According to **expectation states theory**, when group members first meet, they form expectations about each other's probable contributions to the achievement of group goals (Berger & Webster, 2006). These expectations are based not only on members' *task-relevant characteristics* (such as social skills and past experience) but also on *diffuse-status* *characteristics* (such as race, sex, age, and wealth) (Correll & Ridgeway, 2003; Kalkhoff & Thye, 2006). Those members whose characteristics produce higher expectations in fellow members are assigned higher status in the group. Thus, white, middle-aged, wealthy men might be perceived as better potential leaders than young, poor, Hispanic women by other group members. Although these initial status assignments can be later modified based on actual performance, members who are unfairly given an initially low status will have trouble proving their worth to the group (Kalish & Luria, 2016; van Dijk & van Engen, 2013). Because women have lower ascribed status than men in many groups, they report more dissatisfaction with their group status and must work harder to gain influence with other members (Burke et al., 2007; Ridgeway, 2001).

As this brief overview suggests, there are many advantages to having high status in a group. Higher-status individuals have higher self-esteem, are better liked by other group members, and are more satisfied with their group relations than lower-status persons (Lovaglia & Houser, 1996). Further, when high-status individuals make decisions that lead to minor negative consequences for the group, they are more likely than lower-status members to be forgiven. However, when the bad decisions cause major negative group consequences, high-status persons are judged more severely than those with low or medium status (Wiggins et al., 1965). This is one instance where high-status members can be treated very harshly by the group.

In Chapter 6, you learned how ingroup biases can lead to prejudice and discrimination. How might this knowledge help you better understand the process by which group members' diffuse-status characteristics might significantly determine their power in the group?

8.1d Group Success Fosters Social Identification.

As first discussed in Chapter 6 (section 6.1a), an *ingroup* is a group to which we belong and which forms a part of our social identity. Identifying with an ingroup is associated with a variety of positive consequences, including health and well-being (Amiot & Sansfacon, 2011; Greenaway et al., 2015). For example, in a field study of students who were completing a stressful, day-long aptitude test for university admission, the students who reported the lowest levels of stress and whose blood tests revealed they had the lowest cortisol levels (a stress hormone) were those who most strongly identified with the other members of their testing group (Ketturat et al., 2016).

One factor that encourages ingroup identification is being associated with a successful group. When our group achieves success or when individual ingroup members are singled out for praise or awards, we tend to respond with pride and satisfaction, even if we had nothing to do with the achievement. This identification with and embracing of ingroup success is known as *basking in reflected glory* (BIRGing) and it is common in a variety of social arenas (Cialdini et al., 1976; Burger, 2012). Examples are the joy expressed by citizens following their nation's military and political successes, fans' reactions to their sports teams' victories, and the pride ethnic group members have regarding other members' accomplishments. When such successes occur, group members often describe the success as "our victory." This process of reflected glory enhances members' personal self-esteem because their group identity constitutes an integral part of their self-concept (Boen et al., 2002; End et al., 2004).

> "All things being equal, you root for your own sex, your own culture, your own locality. . . . Whoever you root for represents you. And when he or she wins, you win."
>
> —Isaac Asimov, US science fiction writer, 1920–1992

Although we often readily share our group's and individual members' successes, what happens following failure? The common reaction is to make excuses ("Our group was treated unfairly!"), while devaluing the qualities in the successful outgroup that led to our defeat ("I'm glad our group isn't that vicious!"). If we strongly identify with our group, we tend to be more angry than sad following defeat, while the reverse is true if our ingroup identity is not strong (Crisp et al., 2007). For strong ingroup identifiers, defending the ingroup and angrily blasting the competition indirectly defends self-esteem (Hastorf & Cantril, 1954).

What happens when our group is repeatedly outperformed by other groups? To protect self-esteem, we may psychologically distance ourselves from the group, a process called *cutting off reflected failure* (CORFing). Embracing success and psychologically distancing ourselves from failure—exactly the type of identification that William James contended was typical of the self—both play an important role in attracting or repelling new members and in enhancing or diminishing strong ingroup emotional bonds. In the arena of sports competition, where there are clear winners and losers, fair-weather fans often engage in CORFing (Bernache-Assollant et al., 2010). Yet what about sports fans whose teams truly are an integral part of their self-concepts?

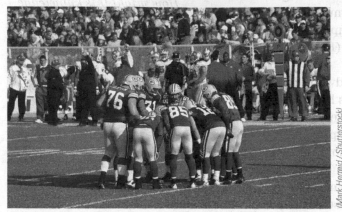

We treat our favorite sports team's successes as if they were our own, and we suffer their defeats as well. What are the two psychological terms for how we often respond to our team's successes and failures?

(Mark Herreid / Shutterstock)

Research by Edward Hirt and his coworkers (1992) suggests that a team's poor performance can significantly lower fans' own self-evaluations. In one of their studies, college students who were avid fans of their school's men's basketball team watched live televised games in which their team either won or lost. Not only were the moods of these zealous fans lower following defeat, but their immediate self-esteem and feelings of competence were also depressed. These and other studies suggest that forming a strong allegiance to a team is a risky venture (Bristow & Sebastian, 2001; Dalakas et al., 2004). Because true fans generally do not CORF, each season they subject themselves to an emotional roller coaster that must be ridden out, regardless of how exhilarating or nauseating the ride. CORFing—or adopting a more successful team—would certainly make life easier for a fan. However, true fans could no sooner change teams than they could change their names; for better or worse, their team affiliation is an important social identity. Because of that fact, to protect their psychological health, some highly identified fans actually bet money against their team in games where they expect them to lose (Agha et al., 2016). Their reasoning is that, while they hope their team wins, the financial gain they receive with a loss helps offset their resulting emotional pain.

"The Packers are like your children. You don't love them because they're good. You love them because they're YOURS."

—Green Bay Packers fan, Steve Gay

8.1e   Groups Differ in Their Social Cohesiveness.

Group success and failure are affected by—and influence—*social cohesiveness*, or "groupiness" (Goncalo et al., 2010; Yoon et al., 2013). As social cohesion increases, people think, feel, and act more like group members and less like isolated individuals (Sani et al., 2005). They are more likely to highly value their social identity with the group and are more willing to sacrifice for the good of the group than those in low cohesive groups (Gomez et al., 2011; Swann et al., 2010). In turn, high cohesiveness allows the group to exert more influence on members, which often leads to greater productivity (Gammage et al., 2001). Beyond group success and failure, additional factors that influence group cohesion are *group size, member similarity and diversity, perceived subversion of the group's identity,* and *gossip.*

"Three stinking cobblers with their wits combined can equal the wisest philosopher."

—Chinese folk saying

Group Size

Although the size of the group in which animals live in a given habitat is partly determined by existing resources and other environmental limitations, comparative studies of various species indicate that the upper limit of group size is set by each species' cognitive abilities. Based on his analysis of humans and various nonhuman primate species (New and Old World monkeys and apes), Robin Dunbar (1993, 2002) concluded that the average size of a species' social group is directly related to what percentage of the species' brain is devoted to higher cognitive functions (the *neocortex* ratio). The group size identified by this relationship refers to the maximum number of individuals with whom an animal can maintain social relationships by personal contact. Subsequent research indicated that this relationship between group size and neocortex size involves the areas of the frontal lobes of the cerebral cortex, which are crucial for social cognition (Stuss et al., 2001). According to Dunbar (2003), animals cannot maintain the cohesion and integrity of groups larger than the size set by the information-processing capacity of their frontal lobes.

FIGURE 8.2   Does Brain Size Limit the Size of Social Groups in Primates?

Plotting the average group size in different primate species against the percentage of the species' brain devoted to higher cognitive functions (the neocortex ratio), yields a positive linear relationship (Dunbar, 1992). That is, as the neocortex size of monkeys' and apes' brains increases relative to other brain areas, the average size of a primate species' social group also increases. This research suggests that the maximum size for modern human groups to function most effectively is about 150 individuals. Do these findings have any implications for the type of social problems found in large metropolitan settings?

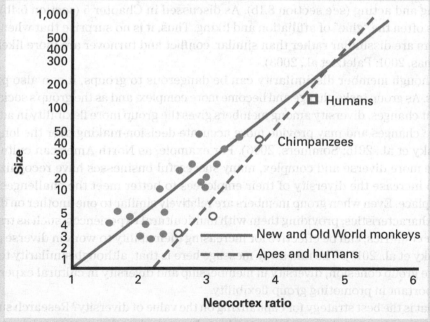

Data source: "Neocortex Size as a Constraint on Group Size in Primates," by R. I. Dunbar, 1992, *Journal of Human Evolution, 20*, pp. 469–493.

What is the upper limit of group size for which human brains are best adapted? As depicted in Figure 8.2, Dunbar's calculations suggest that the relevant group size for modern humans is about 150 individuals—which approximates quite closely the observed sizes of clan-like groupings in contemporary and early human hunter-gatherer cultures. In contrast, the average group size among chimpanzees is about 50 individuals. Given that human brain size has remained unchanged over the past 250,000 years, we can assume that our current brain size is more a product of the evolutionary pressures of hunter-gatherer groups than of the environmental demands we now face in our technologically advanced cultures (Barrett et al., 2003). Dunbar contends that if this assumption is correct, then it is possible that our current brains are not well adapted to the very large social groupings sometimes found in modern societies.

Even in modern societies, most groups contain fewer than four persons (Mullen & Copper, 1994). As a group grows, and as it reaches or exceeds the upper limit of our brain's capacity to process information on the individual members, there is a tendency for member participation to decline, power to become concentrated in the hands of a few, conflicts to increase, and cooperation to decrease (Hill & Dunbar, 2003). Large groups make it harder for members to control what happens to them, and as group size increases, members become more selfish and less group-focused because they perceive the impact of their own behavior on group success or failure as being weaker and less identifiable (see *social loafing*, section 8.2b).

Member Similarity and Diversity

Within groups, members tend to be more similar than different (Jackson et al., 1991). One reason for this similarity characteristic is that membership in many groups involves the performance of specific activities (for example, volunteers for a nonprofit organization or members of a political party engaging in activism); thus, people are attracted to a specific group because they mutually share an interest or values (van Veelen et al., 2016). Another reason for within-group similarity is socialization. That is, in the process of socializing new members, attempts are made to mold them to the group's way of thinking and acting (see section 8.1b). As discussed in Chapter 5 (section 5.4b), similarity is often the "glue" of affiliation and liking. Thus, it is no surprise that when group members are dissimilar rather than similar, conflict and turnover are more likely (Ely & Thomas, 2001; Paletz et al., 2003).

Although member dissimilarity can be dangerous to groups, it can also provide benefits. As group tasks change and become more complex, and as the group's social environment changes, diversity among members gives the group more flexibility in adapting to these changes and may provide more accurate decision-making over the long term (Galinsky et al., 2015; Sommers, 2006). For example, as North American culture has become more diverse and complex, many successful businesses have recognized the need to increase the diversity of their employees to better meet the challenges in the marketplace. Even when group members are relatively similar to one another on diffuse-status characteristics, providing them with multicultural experiences, such as traveling in other countries, can be effective for increasing their ability to work in diverse groups (Galinsky et al., 2015). The takeaway message here is that, although similarity tends to promote group cohesion, diversity in membership and diversity in cultural experiences are important in promoting group flexibility.

What is the best strategy for capitalizing on the value of diversity? Research suggests that creative group problem-solving can be enhanced when diversity is celebrated and embraced rather than minimized (Galinsky et al., 2015). This highlighting of diversity creates a social environment in which members' distinct personal and social qualities are verified and validated by the group. Receiving such feedback from the group promotes satisfaction and commitment among members (Swann et al., 2000). Consistent with the contact hypothesis in Chapter 6 (section 6.4c), group leaders play a pivotal role in establishing a social environment that recognizes the value of each member's unique characteristics. When a group has a great deal of diversity in its membership, productivity is highest when the leader treats members as unique individuals rather than as interchangeable components, because doing so sends a message to all members that diversity is valued (Homan & Greer, 2013).

Perceived Subversion of Group Identity

Members' emotional identification with the group is vitally important to group cohesiveness. However, when members believe that a current or proposed group norm strongly deviates from the group's identity, this cohesiveness and emotional connection is seriously threatened (Ditrich et al., 2017; Sani & Todman, 2002). For example, in 1992, more than 700 male clergy in the Church of England left the group in protest when church leaders decided to ordain women priests. By the year 2000, there were about 1,000 congregations in the Church of England that refused to accept the authority of women priests because they believed it was counter to the group's beliefs and values. In an analysis of this conflict, Fabio Sani and his colleagues found that when church members began believing that their group's identity was being subverted by this new norm of ordaining female priests, their resulting negative emotions undermined group cohesiveness and emotional identification with the Church of England (Sani & Reicher, 2000; Sani & Todman, 2002).

How do savvy leaders try to manage such group discontent? As previously discussed, prospective members are drawn toward groups that allow members to freely voice their opinions. Thus, it is not surprising that additional research by Sani (2005) found that group leaders often try to manage member dissatisfaction during times of group change by providing the opportunity for displeased members to voice dissent. Allowing dissent is often effective in maintaining dissatisfied members' group identification, but only if the dissent is moderate and not radical. When members of a group who hold radical views about change realize that others do not share their opinions, they often disidentify with their group and leave (Becker et al., 2011).

Gossip

Gossip, or evaluative talk between and about others, is a common occurrence in groups. This form of communication often conveys negative information about others and frequently occurs when a group member violates social norms (Foster & Rosnow, 2006; Peters et al., 2017). Gossiping has a bad reputation, but the simple fact is that all of us engage in it. Throughout the world, both women and men equally devote anywhere from one-fifth to two-thirds or more of their daily conversations to gossip (Dunbar, 1996). Although you might think that group cohesiveness is undermined when members gossip about one another, research suggests that this is often not the case. Despite the fact that gossiping can harm the reputation of the target, it often simultaneously strengthens group norms and can facilitate bonding between the group members who are gossiping (Peters et al., 2017). Furthermore, the mere possibility of being the target of gossip can increase members' contributions to the group and their generosity toward others if they believe others will gossip about their prosocial behavior (Beersma & Van Kleef, 2011; Wu et al., 2016).

While some gossip involves talking about the positive actions of others, group members are most interested in discussing other members' negative actions. Why might this be so? In a brain-imaging study that attempted to answer

> "If you haven't got anything nice to say about anybody come sit next to me."
>
> —Alice Roosevelt Longworth, American writer and daughter of President Theodore Roosevelt, 1884–1980

> "Some say our national pastime is baseball. Not me. It's gossip."
>
> —Erma Bombeck, American humorist, 1927–1996

How might gossiping have given our human ancestors an adaptive advantage? Can gossiping be overdone and actually harm the gossiper?

this question, Eric Anderson and his coworkers (2011) first showed participants photos of individuals with neutral facial expressions paired with negative, positive, or neutral gossip about them (see Figure 8.3). An example of negative gossip was "threw a chair at his classmate," an example of positive gossip was "helped an elderly woman with her groceries," and an example of neutral gossip was "passed a man on the street." Next, while their brain activity was being measured, participants were presented with different visual images to their two eyes: one image of a human face and one nonhuman image, such as a house. The human faces presented to the participants were those that were previously associated with negative, neutral, or positive gossip. Because the brain can only process one visual image at a time when competing images are presented to the two different eyes, the brain tends to focus on the image it considers more important. Results indicated that participants' brains were most likely to focus on faces associated with negative gossip.

FIGURE 8.3   Gossiping May Have Survival Value

When participants were shown a neutral face paired with (A) negative gossip, (B) positive gossip, or (C) neutral gossip, their brains were later more likely to fix on the faces associated with negative gossip. How do these findings relate to the negativity effect in impression formation?

A   "got into a fight on the street"   B   "takes care of stray animals"   C   "took a drink of water"

Adapted from "The Visual Impact of Gossip," by E. Anderson et al., 2011, *Science, 322*(6036), pp. 1446–1448.

Based on these findings, Anderson and his coworkers concluded that our brains appear to be hardwired to pay more attention to people if we've been told they are dangerous, dishonest, or unpleasant, similar to how we are also more attentive to angry and fearful facial expressions than we are to positive facial expressions (see Chapter 4, section 4.3a). From this perspective, you could argue that interest in negative gossip is not necessarily a character flaw—it may simply be a basic human trait that exists for good evolutionary reasons. In other words, even when primitive humans lived in small groups, they needed to know who in their group might be a threat to them and who couldn't be trusted. One shortcut in obtaining such important information would have been gossip. Our ancestors who had an interest in gossip gained a competitive advantage over those in their group who did not engage in gossiping. Of course, this does not mean that all gossip is good for a group and that all gossipers are viewed positively. Studies find that self-serving gossip is frowned upon and can actually harm a group because it poses a threat to healthy group functioning and productivity (Kniffin & Wilson, 2005). Further, people who are known to be high-frequency gossipers tend to be viewed negatively, especially if their gossiping emphasizes negative information about others (Farley,

2011). Yet, overall, despite its bad reputation, gossip between group members appears to generally strengthen the cohesiveness of the group.

Section Summary

- A group consists of several interdependent people who have emotional ties and interact on a regular basis.

- There are two main functions of groups:
  - to accomplish instrumental tasks
  - to satisfy socioemotional needs

- There are five phases to group membership, each with an associated social role:
  - investigation phase—prospective member
  - socialization phase—new member
  - maintenance phase—full member
  - resocialization phase—marginal member
  - remembrance phase—ex-member

- Every group has a structure, consisting of:
  - social norms
  - social roles
  - status systems

- We often bask in the reflected glory of our ingroup members' successes.

- Factors that affect group cohesion include the following:
  - group size
  - member similarity and diversity
  - perceived subversion of group identity
  - gossip

8.2   Group Influence on Individual Behavior

If one of the main functions of groups is to perform tasks, what factors influence the ability of people to successfully engage in task activities? In this section, we examine how the presence of others affects a person's work performance. The two types of situations investigated are (1) an individual performing an activity in the presence of an audience (*social facilitation*), and (2) an individual performing an activity as part of a larger group of performers (*social loafing*). We also examine how both being aroused and being hidden in the group can loosen one's behavioral inhibitions.

8.2a   The Presence of Others Can Energize Us.

Have you ever watched a basketball game and wondered how effective fans are at distracting the players who are shooting free throws? Do the opposing team's noisy fans distract the players, harming their ability to make the shot? Or do the fans energize the player and improve performance? Does it matter if the player is someone like your textbook authors (who confess to having questionable athletic talent) or a well-trained athlete?

In 1895, Norman Triplett was pondering a similar question: "How does a person's performance of a task change when other people are present?" The question was prompted by Triplett noticing that a bicycle racer's speed was faster when the biker was paced by other cyclists than when racing alone. Desiring to learn what caused these different race times, he devised the first social scientific experiment by having children quickly wind line on a fishing reel either alone or in the presence of other competing children. As he had predicted, the children wound the line faster when in the presence of other children (Triplett, 1898). Subsequent experiments during the first quarter of the 20th century found that the presence of others enhances the speed with which people perform relatively simple tasks but inhibits task efficiency in more complex activities (Allport, 1920; Travis, 1925). This *social facilitation* effect, as it came to be called, was also found in other animals—such as dogs, rats, birds, fish, and even ants and cockroaches (Chen, 1937; Gates & Allee, 1933). Although researchers extensively documented these divergent effects through the 1930s and 1940s, no one could explain why the presence of others would sometimes enhance and sometimes hinder individual performance. This explanatory conundrum ultimately led to a loss of interest in social facilitation as a research topic.

The Mere-Presence Explanation

In the mid-1960s, Robert Zajonc (1965) renewed the field's interest in social facilitation by proposing a theory to reconcile the contradictory findings. His social facilitation theory involved three basic propositions or steps (see Figure 8.4). First, he argued that all animals (including humans) are genetically predisposed to become physiologically aroused when around *conspecifics* (members of one's own species). This is so, he believed, because animals receive most of their rewards and punishments in life from conspecifics and through the process of evolution have developed an innate arousal response due to their *mere presence*. Second, resurrecting an old behaviorist principle of learning (Hull, 1943), Zajonc stated that this physiological arousal enhances the performance of whatever response tendency is dominant (that is, well-learned) in an animal. Third, and last, he contended that for well-learned tasks, the correct responses are also the dominant responses; but for novel, unlearned tasks, the dominant responses are the incorrect ones. What this means is that the presence of others will enhance correct execution of well-learned tasks at the same time that it will interfere with or inhibit correct performance of novel, unlearned tasks.

In one study supporting this explanation, participants worked on a task either alone, in the presence of confederates who were also working on the task, or in the presence of blindfolded confederates who supposedly were preparing for a perception experiment (Cottrell et al., 1968). Participants working on the task in the company of "seeing" confederates exhibited social facilitation effects when compared with those working alone. Both the evaluation-apprehension and the mere-presence explanations would predict this outcome. However, in the presence of blindfolded confederates, there was no evidence of social facilitation. Participants' dominant responses did not differ from those who were alone. Because the blindfolded confederates were physically present but could not evaluate the performance of participants, these findings support the evaluation-apprehension explanation at the same time that they contradict the mere-presence explanation. Similar effects were found in other studies in which observers were present but not evaluating an individual's performance (Worringham & Messick, 1983). According to the evaluation-apprehension perspective, if people are present but not attending to another person's task performance, their presence is unlikely to produce social facilitation effects. A meta-analysis of past studies also suggests that the people who are most adversely affected by evaluation apprehension when performing tasks in others' presence are those with low self-esteem (Uziel, 2007).

Zajonc argued that when we perform a simple task like hand-clapping, the mere presence of an audience increases our arousal; this elicits the dominant response and we clap more vigorously than when we are alone and not aroused. Now, if we instead calculated difficult math problems in front of others, our increased arousal would inhibit execution of this task because the correct answers are not dominant responses. They would be dominant responses only if we had them memorized. Taken together, these two different effects due to the presence of others—enhancement of correct performance on easy tasks and inhibition of correct performance on difficult tasks—are known as **social facilitation**. The reason the same term is used for both effects is that on both easy and difficult tasks, the performance of the dominant response is *facilitated* in the presence of others. For easy tasks, the correct response is dominant; thus, the person's performance is enhanced. Yet for difficult tasks the correct response is not dominant; hence the decline in performance efficiency.

FIGURE 8.4   Zajonc's Drive Theory of Social Facilitation

According to Zajonc (1965), the presence of other people increases arousal; this, in turn, enhances dominant responses. If the dominant responses are correct, performance will also be enhanced. However, if the dominant responses are incorrect, performance will be inhibited. Can you think of instances from your own life in which the presence of others had these two contrasting effects?

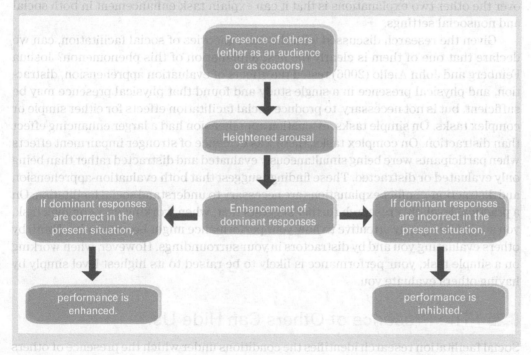

The Evaluation-Apprehension Explanation

Numerous studies either specifically tested Zajonc's theory or more generally examined social facilitation. Two separate meta-analyses of more than 300 experiments involving more than 25,000 participants indicate that social facilitation does indeed exist (Bond & Titus, 1983; Guerin, 1986), but there is considerable debate concerning the nature of this arousal. Some contend that, rather than being due to the mere presence of others, arousal is a result of *evaluation apprehension*—concern over being judged by others (Aiello & Douthitt, 2001; Strauss, 2002).

social facilitation
The enhancement of dominant responses due to the presence of others

The Distraction-Conflict Explanation

As appealing as the evaluation-apprehension explanation is, there are social facilitation effects it cannot explain. Recall that social facilitation has been observed in such animals as ants and cockroaches. Does this mean that insects "worry" about other insects evaluating them? Because this possibility is unlikely, other social scientists contend that heightened arousal is simply caused by a conflict between two tendencies (Baron, 1986). This *distraction-conflict theory* states that when an animal (human or otherwise) is working on a task in the presence of other conspecifics, it experiences conflict regarding whether to attend to its companions or the task at hand. Distraction-conflict theorists contend that it is this conflict, and this conflict alone, that induces heightened arousal.

Because conflict is a well-documented source of arousal, this perspective can explain both human and nonhuman social facilitation effects. In addition to social stimuli (that is, conspecifics) causing conflict—thus, arousal—the distraction-conflict theory hypothesizes that nonsocial objects that distract a performer can also induce conflict. True to this contention, loud noises and flashing lights have been found to produce the same enhancement/impairment effects produced by the presence of others (Pessin, 1933; Wanshaffe, 2002). Research has also found that people perform simple tasks better and complex tasks worse in the presence of a picture of a favorite TV character, but not when in the presence of a nonfavorite TV character (Park & Catrambone, 2007). In this instance, favorite TV characters were apparently more distracting than nonfavorite TV characters. Taken together, the one advantage that the distraction-conflict theory has over the other two explanations is that it can explain task enhancement in both social and nonsocial settings.

Given the research discussed with the three theories of social facilitation, can we declare that one of them is clearly the best explanation of this phenomenon? Joshua Feinberg and John Aiello (2006) tested the effects of evaluation apprehension, distraction, and physical presence in a single study and found that physical presence may be sufficient, but is not necessary, to produce social facilitation effects for either simple or complex tasks. On simple tasks, evaluation apprehension had a larger enhancing effect than distraction. On complex tasks, there was evidence of stronger impairment effects when participants were being simultaneously evaluated and distracted rather than being only evaluated or distracted. These findings suggest that both evaluation-apprehension and distraction-conflict explanations are necessary to understand social facilitation. On a practical level, this research further suggests that, when working on a complex task, you should be equally attentive to how your performance might be undermined both by others evaluating you and by distractors in your surroundings. However, when working on a simple task, your performance is likely to be raised to its highest level simply by having others evaluate you.

8.2b The Presence of Others Can Hide Us.

Social facilitation research identifies the conditions under which the presence of others can motivate individuals to enhance their performance. Usually this enhancement occurs when a person's efforts can be individually evaluated. So what if the performers' efforts are *pooled*, so that individually judging them is difficult or even impossible? Do you know what often happens? If you guessed that individuals do not work as hard under these conditions as when performing alone, you are correct. This group-induced reduction in individual output is known as **social loafing** (Karau & Williams, 1995).

social loafing

Group-induced reduction in individual output when performers' efforts are pooled and cannot, therefore, be individually judged

French agricultural engineer Max Ringelmann (1913) conducted the first empirical study suggesting such an effect in the 1880s. He found that people's efforts at pulling on a rope or pushing a cart were less when they worked in a group than when they performed these tasks alone. Since then, social loafing has been documented in a host of behaviors. For example, Bibb Latané and his associates (1979) had six blindfolded college students sit in a semicircle and wear headphones that blasted sounds of people shouting into their ears. The students' task was to shout as loud as possible while listening to the headphone noise. On some trials, they believed that the five other students were also shouting, while on other trials they believed they were either shouting alone or with only one other person. In actuality, on all these trials only one student was performing. Consistent with what you would expect due to social loafing, when students thought one other person was yelling, they shouted 82% as intensely as when alone, and when they believed everyone was yelling, they shouted 75% as intensely.

Social loafing is not restricted to simple motor tasks like rope pulling or cheering; it also takes place when people perform cognitive tasks (Price et al., 2006). In addition, cross-cultural research indicates that social loafing occurs in both individualist and collectivist societies—although the effect is not as strong in the latter (Gabrenya et al., 1985; Karau & Williams, 1993).

What might explain social loafing? A likely explanation is that when people work in a group, they realize that their individual output will be "lost in the crowd." As a result, they feel less personally responsible for the outcome, and their performance effort declines (Comer, 1995). The cognitive process that group performers go through in feeling less personally responsible for task outcomes is known as the **diffusion of responsibility**; in Chapter 12 (section 12.2c) we will examine how it causes a variation of social loafing—in an emergency, when bystanders fail to aid victims.

Reducing Social Loafing

If social loafing is truly caused by a diffusion of responsibility, then it is also true that social loafing is not an inevitable consequence of people working together in groups. That is, if people's individual efforts can be judged while they work on a group task, they should not lose personal responsibility for their actions, and there should be no social loafing. This is exactly what was found in a variation of the cheering study (Williams et al., 1981). Here, as before, participants shouted alone or in groups. In some conditions, shouters were led to believe that their individual performance was being monitored; in other conditions they believed their output was never identifiable. Results indicated that if participants believed their individual shouting was being monitored, no performance drop off occurred in a group context. This study suggests that when group performers cannot conceal minimal effort from observers, social loafing is unlikely.

The fact that social loafing is greatly reduced when individual effort can be identified and evaluated suggests that evaluation apprehension can curtail minimal effort. However, what if performers in a group are made aware of their own individual efforts—or those of the group—in comparison with a social standard without others being privy to this information? Would this private information still reduce social loafing on their part? There is ample evidence that people tend to overestimate their individual contributions to group efforts (Savitsky et al., 2005). This being so, perhaps receiving private feedback that one is underperforming might be sufficient to reduce social loafing. Research indicates that receiving such feedback does increase individual effort (Harkins & Szymanski, 1989). Thus, providing the potential for *evaluation*—even if it is only private self-evaluation— seems essential in reducing the loss of individual output on a group task.

Although informing group members of the potential for evaluation may generally reduce loafing, how should habitual social loafers be handled? Short of physically rejecting lazy workers from the group, one common technique to increase their output is to socially shun them until they conform to the group productivity norm. Yet is such *ostracism* effective? Singling out group members for deliberate disrespect runs the risk of alienating them, but it could also motivate these targeted members to increase their

diffusion of responsibility

The belief that the presence of other people in a situation makes one less personally responsible for the events that occur in that situation

Imagine that you have been hired to design a training course to teach company employees how to efficiently use a complex computer program. How can you use the findings of social loafing research to design a training course that not only facilitates quick learning, but also encourages high productivity following learning?

work efforts and win back the group's respect (Branscombe et al., 2002; Sleebos et al., 2006). Kipling Williams and Kristin Sommer (1997) found that the effectiveness of this technique was different for female and male loafers.

The women loafers reacted to ostracism by socially acknowledging their feelings of rejection and openly questioning their own attractiveness and abilities. When given a chance to get back into the good graces of the group, the women worked hard to do so. In contrast, the men appeared to cope with ostracism by redirecting their interests toward nontask objects in their surroundings. Also, their concern for impression management caused the men to hide their emotions and to reinterpret the situation: They tended to perceive their separation from the group as being their own personal choice rather than something imposed on them. Because they were engaged in these facesaving coping strategies, the men had a lower need to seek the group's approval; hence, they were more likely to continue loafing.

Williams and Sommer speculate that these gender differences are due to the fact that most societies socialize women to be emotionally expressive and men to be nonexpressive. That is, women's learned response of attending to and expressing their emotions enhances the effectiveness of ostracism as a control technique. For men, however, their learned response of directing their attention away from their emotions to other environmental stimuli dilutes the effectiveness of ostracism. These findings suggest that, although ostracism may be an effective control strategy for social loafing in people who regularly attend to and publicly express their emotions, it may be ineffective for those who are psychologically invested in controlling any such public displays.

Are Group Performance Settings Always Demotivating?

So far, we've assumed that there is something about group settings that lowers people's motivation to perform. Yet research suggests that there are circumstances in which group performance triggers higher motivation than does individual performance. The individuals who are most likely to become highly motivated during group performance are members who have either high or low competence regarding the task at hand (Kerr et al., 2007). Highly competent group members often increase their efforts on collective tasks to compensate for the expected poor performance of other members (Hart et al., 2001; Todd et al., 2006). In sports, these are the superstar athletes who "carry" their lower-performing team members to victory with their superb playing. Such heightened motivation, however, typically occurs only when success at the group task is highly valued. Exhibition games don't motivate highly skilled athletes nearly as much as championship games do.

What about group members who have relatively low skills? In performance settings where group success hinges on the performance of the least competent members, the motivation level of these poor performers tends to be significantly higher than when they are performing solely for themselves (Hertel et al., 2000; Kozlowski & Bell, 2003). In sports, these are the bench athletes who are periodically given the opportunity to compete side-by-side with their more highly skilled teammates. In such settings, these lower-skilled members typically exert great effort in trying to match others' performance levels. Unlike their highly skilled group mates, it appears that the motivation of low-skilled performers is less adversely affected by the value that the group places on task success. Even when success isn't that important to the group, low-skilled group members work hard to do as well as—or better than—their more highly skilled group mates.

8.2c Being Both Energized and Hidden Can Lower Our Inhibitions.

One Halloween night a few years ago, Steve heard a noise outside his house. Looking out the window, he saw a group of teenagers in masks and costumes carrying his pumpkins. Steve quickly went to the front porch and noticed that his lamppost light had been shattered by one of the pumpkins being thrown against it. Although barefoot and dressed in pajamas, he gave chase after these "hooligans." As he sprinted toward them, they took off running. They ran faster than Steve sprinted and he abruptly gave up the chase.

As Steve ended his pursuit they stopped, too, and turned back to check him out. Standing there in the cold and the dark, it suddenly dawned on Steve that he was their "old geezer"—the angry man who chases pranksters on Halloween night. At that moment, memories of his own youthful Halloween escapades came back to haunt him. Just like Steve years ago, these "hooligans" were normally well-behaved adolescents who had been caught up in a one-night, antisocial neighborhood romp. What caused them to act this way? Have you ever been in a similar situation and later wondered why you behaved in a way so contrary to acceptable standards?

Group-Induced Lowering of Inhibitions

Social facilitation research demonstrates that groups can arouse us. Social loafing studies indicate that groups can also diffuse responsibility and lower evaluation apprehension. What happens when groups diffuse responsibility and lower evaluation apprehension at the same time that they arouse us? In such circumstances, our normal inhibitions may diminish, and we may engage in behaviors we normally avoid. This state of mind has come to be called **deindividuation**.

Deindividuation not only helps to explain the vandalism of many Halloween pranksters but also provides insight into other forms of collective antisocial behavior. Philip Zimbardo (1969, 2007) outlined the antecedents and consequences of a deindividuated state, noting that important contributing factors are *arousal*, *anonymity*, and *diffused responsibility*. Zimbardo argued that when people become deindividuated by a combination of these factors, their inhibitions will be lowered and they will be much more likely to impulsively engage in such antisocial behavior as vandalism, aggression, and rioting.

Steven Prentice-Dunn and Ronald Rogers (1980) believe that *accountability cues*, such as anonymity, tell people how far they can go without being held responsible for their actions. These cues loosen restraints against deviant behavior by altering a person's *cost-reward calculations*. For example, during a riot, people often think they won't be caught and punished for engaging in illegal activities, and

(erlucho / Shutterstock)

How does the state of mind known as deindividuation explain why normally law-abiding individuals occasionally behave counter to social norms?

this reassessment of the costs and rewards lowers inhibitions. Although early investigators often assumed that deindividuation occurred only in groups, a number of studies have demonstrated that it can be induced outside of a collective (Chiou, 2006; Festinger et al., 1952).

An example of deindividuation causing antisocial consequences can be seen in America's history of lynching African Americans (Ritchey & Ruback, 2018). Andrew Ritchey and R. Barry Ruback (2018) analyzed newspaper photographs of lynchings

deindividuation

The loss of a sense of individual identity and a loosening of normal inhibitions against engaging in behavior that is inconsistent with internal standards in Georgia from 1882 to 1926. They found that as the number of people in the crowd increased, so did the level of atrocity of the lynching (such violence as beating and burning the victim, or multiple victims). Similarly, in an analysis of newspaper accounts of people witnessing someone threatening suicide by jumping from a building or bridge, Leon Mann (1981) found that when a crowd of onlookers was large or masked by darkness (that is, deindividuated) they often jeered and encouraged the person to jump. Large crowds and darkness facilitated the antisocial actions of onlookers during suicide attempts; in contrast, when people were more easily identifiable—small crowds exposed by daylight—Mann found that they generally did not jeer the would-be jumper.

The perceived anonymity of the internet also causes some people to experience diffused responsibility while interacting in "chat rooms" or accessing pornographic material on various websites. Does this diffused responsibility loosen people's normal inhibitions? In one study investigating internet-induced deindividuation, Christina Demetriou and Andrew Silke (2003) established a website to determine whether people who visited it to gain access to legal material would also try to access illegal and/or pornographic material at the site when they discovered it was available (no such material was actually available). Over a 3-month period, a majority of the more than 800 visitors who entered the site to view the advertised legal materials also tried to access the illegal and/or pornographic material. Like actual groups, it appears that the "virtual" groups created on internet sites have the capacity to induce deindividuation.

Because Halloween festivities tend to deindividuate celebrants, it is not surprising that researchers have used this annual event to investigate this process. In one such study, Ed Diener and his colleagues (1976) set up testing sites in 27 homes throughout Seattle and waited for young trick-or-treaters to come calling. Some children arrived alone, and others came in groups. On some trials, the experimenter asked the children their names and where they lived, and on other trials the children remained anonymous. Then, the experimenter showed the children a bowl of candy and told them to "take *one* of the candies." Then the children were left alone with the candy bowl while hidden observers recorded how much candy the children actually took. The researchers discovered that, compared to those who were alone, children in a group were more than twice as likely to take extra candy. In addition, compared with children who identified themselves, those who remained anonymous were also more than twice as likely to take more than one piece of candy. As you can see in Figure 8.5, the greatest candy stealing occurred when children were in a group and remained anonymous.

Deindividuation and Reduced Self-Awareness

In explaining deindividuation, Diener (1980) argued that the crucial cognitive factor is a lack of self-awareness. Without such self-awareness, the deindividuated do not think of themselves as separate individuals and do not attend to their own inner values and behavioral standards (see Chapter 3 for a discussion of self-awareness effects). To test this hypothesis, Diener and his coworkers conducted a second Halloween study in which, as before, experimenters waited for young trick-or-treaters to arrive to request candy (Beaman et al., 1979). After the children were asked to give their names, they were told to take only one candy each and were then left alone by the candy bowl. On some trials, a mirror was placed behind the bowl so that when the children reached for the candy, they saw their own image in the mirror. On other trials, no mirror was present.

FIGURE 8.5 **Effects of Deindividuation on Stealing Among Halloween Trick-or-Treaters**

When trick-or-treating in a group or when anonymous, children were more likely to take extra Halloween candy. However, when both of these factors were present (group immersion and anonymity), candy stealing rose dramatically. What do these results tell us about the effect that deindividuation has on people's normal inhibitions?

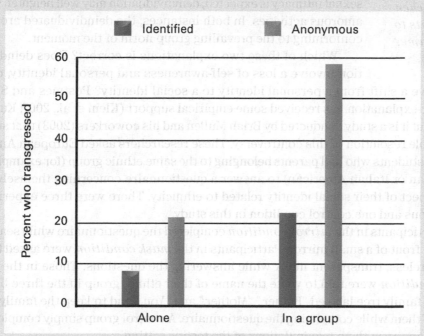

Data source: "Deindividuation: The Absence of Self-Awareness and Self-Regulation in Group Members," by E. Diener, 1980, in *Psychology of Group Influence*, edited by P. B. Paulus, pp. 209–242, Hillsdale, NJ: Lawrence Erlbaum Associates.

As you may recall from Chapter 3, a mirror induces self-awareness—a psychological state in which one is aware of oneself as an object of attention and is also more attentive to behavioral standards. In such a state, one is not deindividuated. Not surprisingly, in the *mirror present* condition, only 12% of the children took extra candy; yet when the mirror was absent, candy stealing increased to 34%. These results—and those of other investigations—suggest that *reduced self-awareness* is a component of deindividuation (Diener & Wallbom, 1976; Prentice-Dunn & Rogers, 1982); the deindividuated lose their sense of personal identity in a group by not engaging in self-awareness. Here—as in other aspects of social behavior discussed throughout the text—people abdicate their personal standards of conduct and fall prey to the influence of the immediate situation when they fail to take themselves as objects of attention.

Can Social Identity Activation Explain Deindividuation?

Throughout the past 40-some years of deindividuation research, the prevailing view has been that it is an expression of antinormative and disinhibited behavior caused by a loss of personal identity. However, Dutch social psychologists Tom Postmes and Russell Spears (1998) propose that what we call antinormative and disinhibited behavior in such situations may actually be a behavioral expression of *conformity* to group norms specific to the situation. Arguing from a social identity perspective (see Chapter 3), Postmes and Spears assert that deindividuating settings do not lead to a loss of personal identity

How could you use your knowledge of deindividuation when designing social environments to reduce crime?

and acting on impulse; instead, deindividuating settings facilitate a transition from a personal to a more social identity. The so-called antinormative behavior is really an expression of whatever group norm is salient in the situation. Thus, if teenagers' Halloween trick-or-treating group norm involves pranks and minor vandalism, taking extra candy and stealing pumpkins may be on the agenda. However, if these same Halloween revelers are attending a costume party where sexual intimacy is expected, deindividuation may well heighten various amorous activities. In both instances, the deindividuated are simply conforming to the prevailing group norm of the moment.

Which of these two explanations is correct? Does deindividuation involve a loss of self-awareness and personal identity, or does it involve a shift from a personal identity to a social identity? Postmes and Spears's counter-explanation has received some empirical support (Klein et al., 2007; Kugihara, 2001), but it is a study conducted by Brian Mullen and his coworkers (2003) that suggests a possible resolution of this controversy. These researchers asked European American college students who had parents belonging to the same ethnic group (for example, Irish American or Italian American) to answer a questionnaire concerning themselves and that aspect of their social identity related to ethnicity. There were three experimental conditions and one control condition in this study.

Participants in the *mirror condition* completed the questionnaire while seated at a table in front of a small mirror. Participants in the *mask condition* were asked to wear a featureless, transparent mask while answering the questions. Those in the *family tree condition* were told to write the name of their ethnic group in the three boxes of a small family tree labeled "Father," "Mother," and "You," and to keep the family tree in front of them while completing the questionnaire. A control group simply completed the questionnaire with no manipulations of the testing setting.

The questionnaire measured participants' current degree of self-awareness and their current degree of identification with their ethnic group. The researchers reasoned that if the conventional view of deindividuation is correct, participants in the mask condition would exhibit a decrease in both self-awareness and ethnic identity awareness (which is a form of social identity awareness). However, if the social identity explanation is correct, Mullen and his colleagues reasoned that the mask condition would cause an increase in ethnic identity awareness.

As expected, the mirror condition caused an increase in self-awareness and a decrease in ethnic identity awareness in participants, and the family tree condition caused a decrease in self-awareness and an increase in ethnic identity awareness. However, more important, the mask condition caused a decrease in both self-awareness and ethnic identity awareness, which is consistent with the conventional view of deindividuation, but inconsistent with the social identity explanation. As such, this study suggests that deindividuation involves different psychological processes from social identity awareness. This does not mean that certain crowd behavior is not sometimes caused by the activation of a common social identity among crowd members. However, it does suggest that deindividuation is a distinct psychological state, separate from social identification. The deindividuated mind-set of being "lost in the crowd" involves a psychological shifting of awareness away from the self; it does not appear to involve a shift from a personal identity to a social identity.

Section Summary

- Social facilitation involves the enhancement of dominant responses due to the presence of others.

- In social facilitation, others affect our performance:
  by their mere presence,
  as evaluators, and
  by distracting us.

- Social loafing occurs when the presence of co-performers reduces individual output because co-performers allow diffusion of task outcome responsibility.

- Group members will work hard on a task when it is highly involving for them, they believe that success depends on their efforts, and their efforts can be judged.

- Deindividuation occurs when people's normal inhibitions are diminished due to a loss of individual identity, triggered by anonymity and reduced self-awareness.

8.3 Decision-making in Groups

Due to the fact that groups sometimes influence people to behave in ways that are antisocial, some social scientists have suggested that this is evidence that people in groups think and behave more irrationally than they would alone. Although this belief in the inferiority of group thinking and action may be partly a function of the individualist bias of these scientists (Markus & Kitayama, 1994), it is not a new view in the social sciences—nor is it unique to North American scholars. Over a century ago, French sociologists Gustave LeBon (1903) and Gabriel Tarde (1903) described people being magnetically drawn toward crowds, where they then develop a "collective mind." Although the research already discussed in this chapter indicates that people in groups can sometimes act in an inferior and impulsive manner (due to social loafing and deindividuation, respectively), you have also learned in previous chapters that individuals acting alone can exhibit similar undesirable actions. Thus group processes— like individual processes—are amply designed to foster both positive and negative outcomes (Luhan et al., 2009). In this chapter section, we examine the decision-making process of groups and the conditions under which group decision-making meets with success and failure.

"I am the people—the mob—the crowd—the mass. Do you know that all the great work of the world is done through me?"

—Carl Sandburg, US poet and historian, 1878–1967

8.3a Group Decision-making Occurs in Stages and Follows Various Rules.

In making decisions, groups typically move through four distinct stages (Forsyth, 1990). As depicted in Figure 8.6, the *orientation stage* involves the group identifying both the task it is trying to accomplish and the strategy it will use to do so. As you will shortly discover, the type of task presented to the group generally determines the strategy it chooses. In the *discussion stage*, the group gathers information, identifies possible solutions, and evaluates them. Members' influence attempts—either normative or informational—are most apparent in this second stage and in the following *decision stage*. In making decisions, the group relies on either implicit or explicit decision rules. Finally, in the *implementation stage*, the group first carries out the decision and then evaluates its effectiveness.

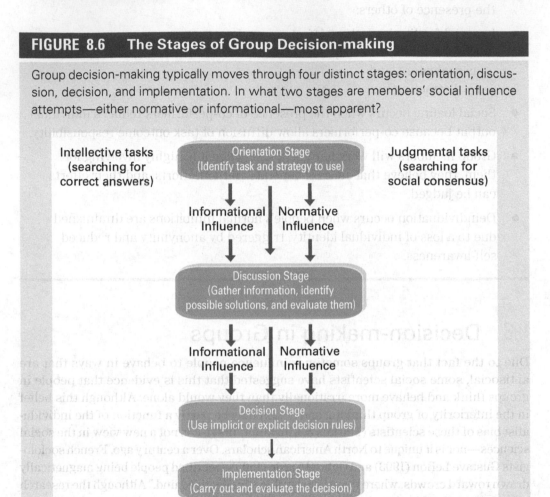

FIGURE 8.6   The Stages of Group Decision-making

Group decision-making typically moves through four distinct stages: orientation, discussion, decision, and implementation. In what two stages are members' social influence attempts—either normative or informational—most apparent?

Intellective tasks
(searching for
correct answers)

Orientation Stage
(Identify task and strategy to use)

Judgmental tasks
(searching for
social consensus)

Informational
Influence

Normative
Influence

Discussion Stage
(Gather information, identify
possible solutions, and evaluate them)

Informational
Influence

Normative
Influence

Decision Stage
(Use implicit or explicit decision rules)

Implementation Stage
(Carry out and evaluate the decision)

Beyond the stages in group decision-making, *how* a group makes a decision depends on what *kind* of decision it is making. Many of the issues on which groups make decisions can be located on a continuum (Laughlin, 1996). At one end of the continuum are *intellective* issues, for which there are demonstrably correct solutions. Here, the group's task is to discover the "true" or "correct" answer. Scientists searching for a cure for AIDS or campers trying to determine how to put together a tent are both examples of groups struggling with an intellective task. In contrast, at the other end of the continuum are *judgmental* issues involving behavioral, ethical, or aesthetic judgments for which there are no demonstrably correct answers. Examples of judgmental tasks are members of an arts council deciding which artists are most worthy of receiving monetary awards, or corporate executives deciding how to market their products. In these types of cases, although the groups' decisions often involve weighing facts, the ultimate decision is principally based on the appeal to social norms and group consensus.

The type of social influence that shapes group decision making often depends on what type of issue a group is addressing (Green, 1998). As you recall from Chapter 7 (section 7.2d), there are two principal types of social influence: informational influence and normative influence. *Informational influence* occurs when a person accepts others' logical arguments and factual information in defining reality; *normative influence* involves accepting others' definition of reality based on the desire to win approval or avoid criticism. Informational influence is most likely to shape the discussion and decision stages when groups work on intellective tasks. The goal is to find and use any information that helps solve the problem. In reaching this goal, group members tend to engage in a thorough search for relevant information, and they are generally eager to share what they find with other members during the discussion stage.

On the other hand, when working on judgmental tasks, normative influence is most likely to be used. Because there is no purely "correct" answer, the decision goal is to persuade other group members to accept your judgment. In reaching this goal, group members are less diligent in trying to uncover information, and some members may even withhold information during discussion if divulging it would weaken their arguments. Because of this different strategy, groups working on judgmental tasks tend to discuss only enough information to reach consensus (Wittenbaum & Stasser, 1996).

Scientists trying to find the cure for AIDS are struggling with intellective tasks.

Informational influence generally dictates decision-making on intellective tasks. But when groups have to make a quick decision, they often do not have the luxury of systematically searching for information during the discussion stage and instead must rely on more superficial or heuristic information processing (Karau & Kelly, 1992). In such instances, regardless of whether the task is judgmental or intellective, members tend to rely on normative influence when reaching a decision (Kelly et al., 1997).

Because group decision-making requires some level of agreement or consensus among members, groups also develop rules that determine when a sufficient level of consensus has been reached. A *group decision rule* is simply the required number of group members that must agree with a position for the group as a whole to adopt it. Common decision rules include the following:

Unanimity rule: All group members must agree on the same position before a decision is finalized.

Majority-wins rule: A group opts for whatever position is held by more than 50% of its members.

Plurality-wins rule: When there is no clear majority, the group opts for the position that has the most support.

Decision rules may be explicit and formal, as is the case when instructions are given to a jury to return a unanimous verdict; or they may be implicit and informal, such as a chairperson's intuitive assessment that the group agrees on a previously disputed topic sufficiently to consider it settled. Compared to groups employing majority or plurality decision rules, groups that use the unanimity rule are not only more thorough in discussing the issues but are also more likely to use compromise in reaching a decision; not surprisingly, this results in greater satisfaction with the final decision (Miller, 1989).

The importance of the group decision rule in shaping the group's final decision has been demonstrated in jury trials (Kaplan & Miller, 1987). The two decision rules employed in the civil jury system in the United States are the unanimity rule and the majority-wins rule. Because the unanimity rule gives every jury member veto power over the group's decision, Yuhsuke Ohtsubo and his coworkers (2004) hypothesized that jury decisions under that rule would be more influenced by extreme member opinions than jury decisions under the majority rule. To test this hypothesis, participants were placed in six-person groups and randomly assigned to either a unanimity-rule or a majority-rule condition. The defendant in the civil case they analyzed was a hospital whose allegedly negligent treatment left a newborn child with incurable disabilities.

Pilot testing indicated that this case would likely produce an initial distribution of juror preferences containing at least one or two opinions that recommended high punitive damages. After reading the case—but before discussing it with fellow jurors—participants were asked to individually indicate their opinions about the appropriate level of punitive damages. Next, each group was given 20 minutes to deliberate the case and make a group decision on the punitive damages.

In the majority-rule condition, participants were told that, to reach a group decision, at least four members had to agree on the level of damages (if any) to be awarded. All groups were successful in reaching a decision within the time frame. Consistent with predictions, the correlation between the group decision and the initial preference of the most extreme group member was significant in the unanimity rule condition ($r = .58$), but not in the majority rule condition ($r = .01$), with the difference between these correlations also significant.

This finding indicates that group decisions took the preferences of extreme members more into account under the unanimity rule than under the majority rule. In other words, when the initial preferences of one or two jury members were for high punitive damages, jury decisions were influenced more by those jurors under the unanimity rule than when juries worked under the majority rule. Because assigning the unanimity rule to civil juries appears to increase the influence of jurors with extreme opinions, some might consider the use of that rule undesirable compared to the use of the majority rule. However, the end-of-chapter Applications section discusses research indicating that there are some real benefits to the greater consideration given minority opinions under the unanimity rule as compared with the majority rule in civil jury trials.

8.3b Group Discussion Enhances Majority Opinions.

Imagine that you are on the board of directors of a computer company that strives to act in a socially responsible manner. Tomorrow the board will be voting on whether to buy a key component for your new line of laptop computers from supplier A, which is a traditional business, or get them for the same price from supplier B, which employs handicapped workers and does wonderful things in its community. At first, the choice seems clear because giving business to supplier B fulfills your company's goal of social responsibility. Upon closer inspection, however, you discover that the traditional supplier has years of experience producing both high-volume and high-quality components while the nontraditional supplier has never produced these components in such huge quantities. In choosing supplier B, you run the risk that your own product could be compromised if the supplier cannot meet your high-volume, high-quality requirements. In making a decision, what would you consider the *lowest* acceptable probabilities (or odds) of supplier B meeting your requirements to be? A 5 in 10 chance? What about 7 in 10, or 9 in 10? Would it surprise you to know that the level of risk you would settle on would likely be different if you made the decision on your own versus as part of the board?

Are Group Decisions More or Less Cautious?

Using hypothetical situations like the preceding one, James Stoner (1961) set out to test the commonly held belief that group decision-making is more cautious than individual decision-making. To accomplish this task, Stoner asked management students to individually respond to 12 hypothetical dilemmas. When done, he brought them together in groups with instructions to discuss each of the problems until they reached a unanimous decision on what odds they would accept as a group. His findings indicated that the final group decisions were actually *riskier* than the initial individual decisions. For a time, this effect was called the *risky shift* (Cartwright, 1971; Pruitt, 1971). However, as more studies were conducted, researchers realized that some group decisions became reliably *more* cautious after discussion—not riskier (Fraser et al., 1971; Knox & Safford, 1976).

How could group discussion produce both greater risk-taking and greater conservativism? In time, researchers understood that what was occurring in these group discussions was not a consistent shift toward risk or caution; rather, it was a tendency for discussion to *enhance* the initial attitudes of people who already agree (Myers & Lamm, 1976). This group-produced enhancement or exaggeration of members' initial attitudes through discussion was called **group polarization**, and its basic nature is outlined in Figure 8.7 (Zhu, 2013). In many respects, group polarization is psychologically similar to what Bibb Latané refers to as *dynamic social impact*, in which people become organized into social clusters where they collectively reinforce one another's similarly held attitudes, values, and world views (see Chapter 7, section 7.6a). Political talk shows and online news coverage with either conservative or liberal leanings are good examples of how the group polarization process pushes listeners and viewers more to the extreme partisan positions described in our chapter-opening story (Turetsky & Riddle, 2018).

group polarization
Group-produced enhancement or exaggeration of members' initial attitudes through discussion

---

FIGURE 8.7   The Process of Group Polarization

In group polarization, group discussion enhances the initial attitudes or views of those who already agree—regardless of whether those views reflect caution or risk. In Scenario A, before discussion, members A, B, C, D, E, and F have varying degrees of support for engaging in a particular course of action, reflecting their willingness to take risks. Member A is most willing to take a risk and member F is least willing. Following discussion, the group's average opinion has shifted to being strongly in favor of the proposed group action (a shift to greater risk). Similarly, in Scenario B, before discussing the issue, members G, H, I, J, K, and L have varying degrees of opposition to the proposed course of action, with member L being most cautious and member G being least cautious. After discussion, the group's average opinion has shifted to being strongly opposed to the group action (a shift to greater caution).

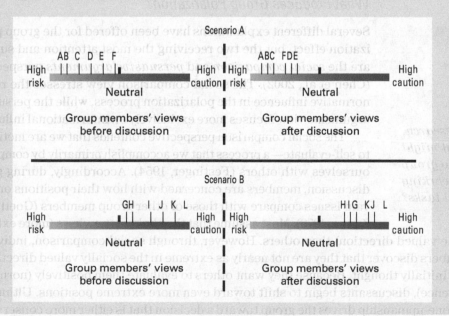

Research indicates that group polarization is more likely to occur on important issues rather than on trivial ones. For example, people reported more extreme political attitudes after engaging in a 15-minute discussion with like-minded individuals about whether Barack Obama or George W. Bush was a better president. Furthermore, they misremembered their pre-discussion attitudes as more extreme than was actually reported in a pre-discussion survey (Keating et al., 2016). Thus, not only do people's attitudes become more polarized, they are also not necessarily aware that their attitudes had shifted during the discussion. Furthermore, current events and social factors can increase political polarization. For example, Bryan McLaughlin (2018) found that when people simply read a news story that highlighted conflict between the political parties, they subsequently identified more strongly with their own political party and expressed more extreme political beliefs than when they did not read such stories. The demonizing of conservatives by liberals—and vice-versa—in contemporary American politics highlighted in our chapter-opening story illustrates one of the consequences of group polarization.

> "When politicians start talking about large groups of their fellow Americans as 'enemies,' it's time for a quiet stir of alertness. Polarizing people is a good way to win an election, and also a good way to wreck a country."
>
> —Molly Ivins, American newspaper columnist and humorist, 1944–2007

Even terrorist groups' actions appear to be shaped by group polarization effects. An analysis of terrorist organizations around the world found that these groups typically become more extreme only gradually over time (McCauley & Segal, 1987). Being relatively isolated from those who hold more moderate views, terrorists become more extreme as they interact with one another. The result is increased violence—something the individual members may never have initially endorsed. In response to the increase in terrorist attacks around the world over the past two decades, social scientists have analyzed the socialization process in terrorist organizations and found that it typically involves isolating recruits from other belief systems, dehumanizing potential targets, and demanding complete obedience (McCauley, 2004; Moghaddam, 2005). To varying degrees, a similar socialization process occurs in many countries' armed service units during times of war. In that process, group polarization contributes to the escalating calls for retribution and violence among the soldiers who are actively engaged in battle (Kunovich & Deitelbaum, 2004).

What Produces Group Polarization?

Based on social influence research, what type of individual might be more susceptible to group polarization effects when working on judgmental tasks?

Several different explanations have been offered for the group polarization effect, but the two receiving the most attention and support are the *social comparison* and *persuasive arguments* perspectives (Chen et al., 2002). The social comparison view stresses the role of normative influence in the polarization process, while the persuasive arguments view focuses more exclusively on informational influence.

The social comparison perspective contends that we are motivated to self-evaluate—a process that we accomplish primarily by comparing ourselves with others (Festinger, 1954). Accordingly, during group discussion, members are concerned with how their positions on relevant issues compare with those of other group members (Goethals & Zanna, 1979). Most assume that they hold better views (more extreme in the valued direction) than others. However, through social comparison, individual members discover that they are not nearly as extreme in the socially valued direction as they initially thought. Because they want others to evaluate them positively (normative influence), discussants begin to shift toward even more extreme positions. Ultimately, this one-upmanship drives the group toward a decision that is either more conservative or riskier than individual members would otherwise have chosen (McGarty et al., 1992).

In contrast to this view, the persuasive arguments position states that group polarization involves *mutual persuasion*. According to this perspective, group discussion is driven not by the desire to be evaluated positively by oneself and others but by the desire to arrive at the correct or true solution. Here, the sheer strength of the arguments offered for certain decision choices is relevant (informational influence). Put simply, when people hear arguments from others, they learn new information. If even a slight majority of group members supports a particular position, most of the arguments presented will favor this view. As more arguments are presented in favor of their own position (rather than against it), and after hearing new supportive arguments that they had not initially considered, members gradually adopt more extreme positions (Brauer et al., 1995).

A host of group polarization studies find that social comparison and persuasive argumentation often occur in combination to produce extreme group decisions (Aloka & Bojuwoye, 2013; Isenberg, 1986). In an attempt to explain how these two forces could both produce group polarization, Martin Kaplan (1987) suggests that they sometimes may operate in different situations. That is, when the issue involves fact-based intellective tasks ("Is the defendant guilty based on the evidence?"), group members will be primarily concerned with the information presented in people's arguments. In such a scenario, the persuasiveness of the arguments is what pushes their position toward extremity. However, when the issue involves value-based judgmental tasks for which there are clearly no objectively right or wrong solutions ("How long a sentence should the guilty defendant serve?"), people are more likely to compare their views with those of others. Here, social comparison is more important in group polarization effects.

8.3c   Consensus Seeking Overrides Critical Analysis in Groupthink.

On March 19, 2003, President George W. Bush ordered the invasion of Iraq with the objective of overthrowing the dictatorial government of Saddam Hussein. The Central Intelligence Agency (CIA) provided evidence indicating that Iraq had weapons of mass destruction and that Hussein's government was planning terrorist attacks with Osama bin Laden's al-Qaeda organization. Citing this evidence, President Bush launched a preemptive military strike, believing that his forces would achieve a quick and decisive victory, the Iraqi people would welcome the invading force, and America would become a beacon of hope for people in the Middle East.

(Courtesy of Lance Corporal Kevin C. Quihuis Jr., United States Marine Corp, via Wikimedia)

Many social commentators used the term groupthink *to characterize the group dynamics of President George W. Bush and his cabinet during their decision to invade Iraq in 2003. To best prevent groupthink, what stage in group decision-making should be principally targeted?*

Nothing could have been further from the truth. Sixteen months following the invasion of Iraq, with American soldiers being killed daily, the U.S. Senate Select Committee on Intelligence issued a highly critical report on the decision-making leading up to the war, charging that CIA analysts withheld information from Congress that did not support a military strike. Individual members of the committee also accused the Bush administration of actively orchestrating this distortion of information so that it could win public support for the war. In assessing the war's effects on the nation's security and prestige, Senate committee member John Rockefeller stated, "Our credibility is diminished. Our standing in the world has never been lower. We have fostered a deep hatred of Americans in the Muslim world, and that will grow. As a direct consequence, our nation is more vulnerable today than ever before."

How could otherwise intelligent and competent people make such poor decisions? After analyzing an equally disastrous 1961 decision by the Kennedy administration to invade Cuba, Irving Janis (1982, 1996) contended that groups are sometimes susceptible to an extreme form of group polarization, which he called **groupthink**. This condition refers to a deterioration of mental efficiency, reality testing, and moral judgment in groups that have an excessive desire to reach consensus. According to Janis, groupthink emerges when maintaining a pleasant social atmosphere becomes more important than making the best decision.

Janis hypothesized that three major factors contribute to groupthink. The first factor is *high group cohesiveness*. Although a high level of cohesiveness among group members would seem to be a very positive group characteristic, it also is associated with increased conformity. That is, when people are strongly attracted to a group and want badly to be accepted by it, they are more likely to allow group members to influence their thinking and actions (t'Hart et al., 1993). Janis believed that when high cohesiveness is combined with the other two factors—namely, a *threatening situational context* and *structural and procedural faults*—groups become more susceptible to groupthink.

Regarding the situational context, Janis contended that groups faced with a threatening or stressful situation may value speed of decision-making over accuracy. In addition, as we will discuss in Chapter 9 (section 9.2b), during times of stress people become more dependent on the reassuring support of others, which should increase the group's influence on individual members. According to Janis, structural and procedural faults that contribute to groupthink are a lack of systematic procedures for making and reviewing decisions; the isolation of the group from others; and a strong, directive leader who lets other members know what his or her inclinations are regarding the group's final decision.

Symptoms of Groupthink

Janis believed that there are three symptoms indicating that a group is suffering from groupthink. They are as follows:

1. *An overestimation of one's ingroup*

   Members develop an illusion of invulnerability and an unquestioned belief in the ingroup's own morality. During the Iraq War decision-making process, the Bush ingroup uncritically accepted the CIA's flawed information on Iraq's alleged weapons of mass destruction and their ties to al-Qaeda. They also falsely assumed that the US military could simultaneously crush armed opposition and win the "hearts and minds" of the Iraqi people (Rodrigues et al., 2005).

2. *Close-mindedness*

   Members rationalize the correctness of their decisions and develop a stereotyped view of their opponents. "It was all about finding a way to do it. That was the tone of it," said Paul O'Neill, Bush's Treasury secretary. "The President saying, 'Go find me a way to do this'" (Mackay, 2004). Because Bush and his advisers were convinced that Iraq had a program to develop weapons of mass destruction, they ignored evidence that disconfirmed their beliefs and instead emphasized information provided by discredited Iraqi defectors. Later, Secretary of State Colin Powell stated that after the September 11th terrorist attacks, Deputy Defense Secretary Paul Wolfowitz "was always of the view that Iraq was a problem that had to be dealt with. . . . And he saw this as one way of using this event" (Smith, 2004).

3. *Increased conformity pressure*

   Members reject those who raise doubts about the group's assumptions and decisions, and they censor their own misgivings in what becomes a "spiral

groupthink
A deterioration of mental efficiency, reality testing, and moral judgment in a group that results from an excessive desire to reach consensus

of silence." With all this conformity pressure, members develop an illusion that everyone is in agreement, which serves to confirm the group's ill-chosen decisions. "Groupthink is more likely to arise when there is a strong premium on loyalty and when there is not a lot of intellectual range or diversity within a decision-making body," says political scientist Stephen Walt. "The Bush administration has been an unusually secretive group of like-minded people where a high premium is placed on loyalty" (Kemper, 2004).

> "That is no use at all. What I want is men who will support me when I am in the wrong."
>
> —Lord Melbourne, British prime minister, 1779–1848, in reply to a politician's pledge: "I will support you as long as you are in the right."

Research on Groupthink

Groupthink tendencies have been identified in various tragedies, political blunders, and national conflicts besides the Iraq War and the invasion of Cuba, such as the decision to launch the space shuttle *Challenger* on its doomed mission in January of 1986 (Moorhead et al., 1991), the long-lasting Northern Ireland conflict (Hergovich & Olbrich, 2003), the 1994 genocide of ethnic Tutsis during the Rwandan Civil War (Dutton, 2007), and the Bush administration's policies endorsing torture at Abu Ghraib prison during the Iraq War (Post & Panis, 2011). However, in the years since the theory's creation, research has called into question some of its proposed causes (Turner et al., 2007).

In a comprehensive test of Janis's theory, Philip Tetlock and his colleagues (1992) conducted a content analysis of the factual accounts of 10 historic decisions that potentially involved groupthink. Consistent with the theory, historic events involving disastrous decisions exhibited significantly more groupthink characteristics than those that led to successful decisions. Some of these groupthink characteristics were suspicion of outsiders, restriction of information exchange, and punishment of group dissenters. Further, as groups became more concerned with maintaining consensus, they exhibited more groupthink symptoms, which in turn caused more defective decision-making. However, contrary to Janis's theory, this study did not find any evidence that group cohesiveness or situational threat were predictors of groupthink symptoms. Later research indicates that cohesiveness can increase the risk of groupthink when it is accompanied by other risk factors, such as high stress or directive leaders who promote their own agenda rather than encouraging alternative viewpoints (Chapman, 2006). These and other findings suggest that groupthink does exist, but it does not appear to function in the exact manner first proposed by Janis (Straus et al., 2011).

Due to the potential harm groupthink processes generate, what can groups do to prevent it? Based on the available evidence, the most important recommendation is to improve decision-making structures and procedures during the group's orientation stage (Groot et al., 2013; Schafer & Crichlow, 1996). Doing so will increase the likelihood that alternative perspectives will be fully weighed and considered during the discussion and decision stages. To facilitate this process, group leaders should encourage criticism and skepticism of all ideas, and once a decision has been reached, the group should return to the discussion stage so that members can express any lingering doubts (Kowert, 2002).

At the individual level, other studies have provided additional insight into the characteristics of group members that make them more or less willing to express unpopular opinions that can short-circuit groupthink. Dominic Packer (2009) found that strongly identified group members are more attentive to group decision-making and are often more willing than those who are weakly identified to express dissenting opinions about a group problem they believe is collectively harmful. As a result, groups with strongly identified members may be less likely to fall prey to groupthink than groups that have less involved members.

There is also evidence that a group with diversity in its membership is less likely to fall prey to groupthink than a group with a more homogenized membership. The key contribution that group diversity appears to provide is an increased resistance to group consensus. In a study of bicultural individuals' actions during group decision-making, Aurelia Mok and Michael Morris (2011) found that bicultural individuals with conflicted cultural identities were more likely to challenge bad group decisions than were bicultural individuals with highly integrated cultural identities. Mok and Morris contend that the conflict between cultural identities that some bicultural individuals experience provides them with a contrarian mind-set that makes it easier for them to play the "devil's advocate" in challenging faulty group decision-making. Combining Packer's findings with those of Mok and Morris, it appears that groups will be more resistant to groupthink to the extent that their membership is strongly identified with the group and has the type of diversity that encourages contrarian thinking.

Section Summary

- Most group decisions involve intellective or judgmental issues:
  Intellective decisions are generally reached through informational influence.
  Judgmental decisions typically rely on normative influence.

- Group decisions are also influenced by formal and informal rules.

- Group polarization occurs when group discussion enhances the initial positions of members.

- Groupthink is an extreme form of group polarization, which refers to a deterioration of mental efficiency, reality testing, and moral judgment resulting from an excess desire to reach consensus.

8.4   Leadership

Members of a group accept influence from others whom they believe have greater ability. In this chapter section, we examine these high-status individuals and the nature of their relationship with those who have lower status.

8.4a   A Leader Is an Influence Agent.

When asked what leadership means to him, former president Bill Clinton answered, "Leadership means bringing people together in pursuit of a common cause, developing a plan to achieve it, and staying with it until the goal is achieved" (Colvin, 2014, p. 66). That definition is in line with the way most social psychologists conceive of a **leader**—namely, the person who exerts the most influence and provides direction and energy to the group (Riggio & Conger, 2007). A leader is the person who initiates action, gives orders, doles out rewards and punishments, settles disputes between fellow members, and pushes and pulls the group toward its goals. Many groups have only one leader; other groups have two or more individuals with equally high levels of influence. Generally, groups tend to have multiple leaders as their tasks become more diverse and complex (Fletcher & Käufer, 2003).

In their position of social influence, leaders are called on to perform two basic types of activities. *Task leadership* consists of accomplishing the goals of the group, and

leader
The person who exerts the most influence and provides direction and energy to the group

socioemotional leadership involves attention to the emotional and interpersonal aspects of group interaction (Bales, 1970; Klonsky, 2013). The necessary qualities for effective task leadership are efficiency, directiveness, and knowledge about the relevant group task. Task leaders tend to have a directive style, giving orders and being rather impersonal in their dealings with group members. In contrast, friendliness, empathy, and an ability to mediate conflicts are important qualities for effective socioemotional leadership. A socioemotional leader's style is more democratic, with greater emphasis on delegating authority and inviting input from others (Fiedler, 1987).

> "No man will make a good leader who wants to do it all himself or to take all the credit for doing it."
>
> —Andrew Carnegie, Scottish American industrialist and philanthropist, 1835–1919

> "Without a shepherd, sheep are not a flock."
>
> —Russian proverb

> "An army of sheep led by a lion would defeat an army of lions led by a sheep."
>
> —Arab proverb

8.4b The Contingency Model Is an Interactionist View of Leadership.

One approach to predicting whether leaders will be effective or not draws inspiration from Kurt Lewin's notion of *interactionism* (see Chapter 1, end of section 1.2a) by contending that leader effectiveness is determined by the interaction of personal and situational factors. Fred Fiedler's (1967, 1993) **contingency model of leadership** contends that people do not become effective leaders because they possess a particular set of personality traits; rather, they become successful leaders because their particular personality matches the circumstances of a particular group. In other words, the traits that make a leader effective are *contingent* on the circumstances the leader encounters. Fiedler's model has four basic components, the first dealing with leadership style and the remaining three encompassing the characteristics of the situation.

Leadership Style

Fiedler argued that there are two basic types of leaders. A *task-oriented leader* is one who gives highest priority to getting the work of the group accomplished and is much less concerned with relations among group members. In contrast, a *relationship-oriented leader* assigns highest priority to group relations, with task accomplishment being of secondary concern. Vince Lombardi, who coached the Green Bay Packers football team in the 1960s, was a task-oriented leader. In describing his focus of concern as a leader, he stated, "Winning isn't everything; it's the *only* thing." Although Lombardi's leadership style was instrumental in the Packers winning five championships in 9 years, his style would be ill-suited for a children's team, where coaches must attend to players' feelings. Instead, this situation requires a relationship-oriented leader who would place priority on fostering positive social relationships first ("Having fun is more important than winning or losing"). Fiedler believed that these contrasting leadership styles were a product of enduring personality traits and, thus, would be difficult or impossible to change.

To identify these two leadership styles, Fiedler developed the *Least Preferred Coworker Scale*, which asks leaders to evaluate the person in the group they like least. Fiedler found that leaders who evaluated their least preferred coworker (LPC) very negatively were primarily motivated to attain successful task performance and only secondarily motivated to seek good interpersonal relations among group members. These low-LPC leaders fit the mold of the task-oriented leader. In contrast, Fiedler found that leaders who evaluated their LPCs positively were primarily motivated to achieve satisfactory interpersonal relationships among the group members and only secondarily motivated to successfully complete group tasks. These high-LPC leaders fit the mold of the relationship-oriented leader. Spend a few minutes completing *Self/Social Connection Exercise 8.1* to gain some insight into your own leadership style.

contingency model of leadership
The theory that leadership effectiveness depends both on whether leaders are task-oriented or relationship-oriented and on the degree to which they have situational control

Self/Social Connection Exercise 8.1

Who Is Your Least Preferred Coworker?

Directions

To learn more about your own leadership style, think of all the individuals with whom you have ever worked—in school organizations, sports teams, jobs, or whatever. Now, think of the one person with whom you worked least well, the person with whom you had the most difficulty completing a task, the person you want to work with least. Describe this individual using the following scale, circling numbers between each of the following opposing adjectives:

Unfriendly	1	2	3	4	5	6	7	8	Friendly
Uncooperative	1	2	3	4	5	6	7	8	Cooperative
Unsupportive	1	2	3	4	5	6	7	8	Supportive
Unpleasant	1	2	3	4	5	6	7	8	Pleasant
Closed	1	2	3	4	5	6	7	8	Open
Depressing	1	2	3	4	5	6	7	8	Cheerful
Disloyal	1	2	3	4	5	6	7	8	Loyal
Gloomy	1	2	3	4	5	6	7	8	Jovial
Negative	1	2	3	4	5	6	7	8	Positive

Scoring

Determine your total score by adding all nine circled numbers. If your score is 36 or above, this indicates you tend to have a relationship-oriented leadership style. If your score is 32 or below, this indicates you tend to have a task-oriented leadership style. If your score is 33 to 35, you may have a mixture of both.

Source: A Theory of Leadership Effectiveness, by F. E. Fiedler, 1967, New York, NY: McGraw-Hill. Used with permission by McGraw-Hill.

Situational Control

According to Fiedler, the favorability of the situation for task-oriented (low-LPC) and relationship-oriented (high-LPC) leaders will depend on the degree to which the situation allows them to exert influence over group members. This *situational control* depends on three factors:

1. *The leader's relations with the group*

   The leader's personal relations with group members can range from very good to very poor. Fiedler believes that leader/member relations is the most important factor determining the leader's influence on followers (Fiedler, 1967).

2. *Task structure*

   How clearly defined are the goals and the tasks of the group? The amount of structure can vary a great deal, from clear to unclear.

3. *The leader's position power*

   This factor includes the power and authority inherent in the leadership position. Does the organization back the leader? Does the leader have the power to reward and punish followers? The leader's position power can vary from strong to weak.

Taking these three situational factors into consideration, a leader has high situational control when leader/member relations are good, there is clear task structure, and the leader has strong position power. In contrast, poor leader/member relations, an unstructured task, and weak position power indicate low situational control.

Predicting Leader Effectiveness

As Figure 8.8 shows, Fiedler hypothesizes that task-oriented (low-LPC) leaders are the most effective in situations in which they have either high or low situational control. In contrast, relationship-oriented (high-LPC) leaders should be associated with better group performance when they have only a moderate degree of control (Ayman et al., 2007).

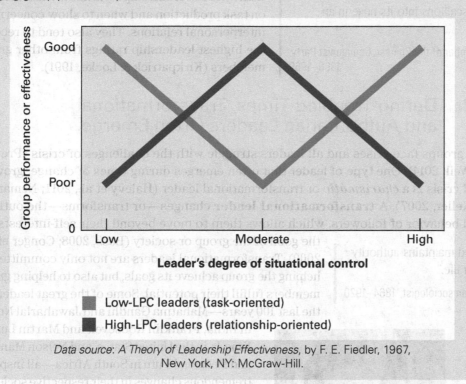

FIGURE 8.8   Predicting Group Effectiveness Based on Leadership Style and Situational Control

Based on your understanding of Fiedler's contingency theory of leadership and your reading of the figure, when are high-LPC (relationship-oriented) leaders most effective in encouraging group productivity? How about low-LPC (task-oriented) leaders?

Data source: A Theory of Leadership Effectiveness, by F. E. Fiedler, 1967, New York, NY: McGraw-Hill.

As Fiedler explains, under difficult conditions of low situational control, groups need considerable guidance to be productive, and thus they benefit from leaders who have this as their primary motivating goal. This challenging situation plays to the strengths of the task-oriented leader. In contrast, a relationship-oriented leader's more democratic style offers too little guidance in these low-control situations. When the situation in the group is very favorable, task-oriented leaders realize that their goal of task accomplishment is likely to be met and relationship-oriented leaders realize that they already enjoy good relations with their followers. With both leaders' primary motivating goals already achieved, they switch to achieving their respective secondary motives. For task-oriented leaders, their subsequent adoption of a more relaxed style increases group productivity, but the more directive style adopted by relationship-oriented leaders harms group performance because members perceive it as needless meddling. The only situation in which relationship-oriented leaders are more effective than task-oriented leaders is when they have only moderate situational control, such as when the task is unclear or the leader has little power. In such circumstances, a considerate, open-minded management approach should be best at rallying group support and fostering creative solutions to problems.

In support of the contingency model, both field and laboratory studies find that no one style of leadership is effective in all situations (Peters et al., 1985; Schriesheim et al., 1994). Effective leadership requires a good fit between the leader's personal style and the demands of the situation. When the fit is not good, group productivity suffers (Ayman, 2004). When a leader's style does not properly fit the situation, this mismatch also causes increased job stress and stress-related illnesses in the leader (Graen & Hui, 2001)—a bad situation for all concerned. One limitation of this theory is that it assumes leaders can have only one style—yet some leaders can adapt their style to meet the needs of the situation (Huczynski & Buchanan, 1996). In such instances, the leader must know when to be the taskmaster and when to be the supportive confidant. Research indicates that individuals with a *flexible* leadership style know when to focus on task production and when to show concern for interpersonal relations. They also tend to receive the highest leadership ratings from other group members (Kirkpatrick & Locke, 1991).

> "There is no such thing as a perfect leader either in the past or present, in China or elsewhere. If there is one, he is only pretending, like a pig inserting scallions into its nose in an effort to look like an elephant."
>
> —Liu Shao-chíi, founding member of the Chinese Communist Party, 1898–1969

8.4c During Troubled Times, Transformational and Authoritarian Leaders Often Emerge.

transformational leader

A leader who changes (transforms) the outlook and behavior of followers so that they move beyond their self-interests for the good of the group or society

All groups face crises and all leaders struggle with the challenges of crisis (Prewitt & Weil, 2014). One type of leader that often emerges during times of change, growth, and crisis is a *charismatic* or transformational leader (Halevy et al., 2011; Nemanich & Keller, 2007). A **transformational leader** changes—or transforms—the outlook and behavior of followers, which allows them to move beyond their self-interests for the good of the group or society (Bass, 2008; Conger et al., 2000). Transformational leaders are not only committed to helping the group achieve its goals, but also to helping group members fulfill their potential. Some of the great leaders of the last 100 years—Mahatma Gandhi and Jawaharlal Nehru in India, Franklin Roosevelt and Martin Luther King Jr. in the United States, and Nelson Mandela and Desmond Tutu in South Africa—all inspired tremendous changes in their respective societies by making supporters believe that anything was possible if they collectively worked toward a common good. The general view of transformational leaders is that they are "natural born" influence agents who are emotionally intelligent, energetic, and passionate, and their leadership style inspires high devotion, motivation, and productivity among group members (Lowe et al., 1996; Sy et al., 2018).

> "The charismatic leader gains and maintains authority solely by proving his strength in life."
>
> —Max Weber, German sociologist, 1864–1920

Two transformational leaders on the world stage were Mahatma Gandhi, leader of the Indian independence movement against British rule, and Ronald Reagan, 39th president of the United States. What other leaders do you think fit this leadership style?

Another type of leader that can emerge during harsh times is an *autocratic* or authoritarian leader (Bass & Bass, 2009; Harms et al.,

2018). An **authoritarian leader** dictates group policies, procedures, and goals and controls all activities without any meaningful participation by others. The mind-set of an authoritarian leader is that group members allowed to work autonomously, without their actions being controlled by the leader, will be unproductive. Such a "take charge/no input" approach can be effective when decisions must come quickly, without time to consult others, such as in the military where officers order soldiers to carry out carefully orchestrated assignments during chaotic and life-threatening situations. Yet despite the advantage that a "take charge/no input" approach can have in certain circumstances, the authoritarian leader's approach also increases the likelihood of groupthink (see section 8.3c), which often results in disastrous consequences, especially in military settings (Kirkland, 1990; Mastroianni et al., 2011).

> "I am a leader by default, only because nature does not allow a vacuum."
>
> —Archbishop Desmond Tutu, Nobel Peace Prize winner and primate of the Anglican Church in South Africa, born 1931

The potential toxicity of the authoritarian leadership style can be seen in its associated personality traits. There is fairly consistent evidence that such leaders are high on neuroticism and low on agreeableness (Kant et al., 2013; Redeker et al., 2014). Given these traits

(Free Wind 2014 / Shutterstock)

(Alexander Khitrov / Shutterstock)

Two current authoritarian leaders are Vladimir Putin, president of Russia, and Kim Jong-un, supreme leader of North Korea. What other current leaders do you think fit this leadership style?

and the fact that authoritarian leaders often show little respect for subordinates' input, it isn't surprising that the feedback they give to others is generally negative, not very constructive, and typically accompanied by overt anger (Bhatti et al., 2012). It also isn't surprising that this leadership style often decreases initiative, productivity, and creative problem-solving in groups, while simultaneously increasing followers' cynicism and prompting members to leave the group due to their dissatisfaction (Jiang et al., 2017; Lewin et al., 1939).

Despite such negative consequences, it is also true that some members derive a sense of security and satisfaction from identifying closely with an authoritarian leader who simply tells them how to think and behave, especially during times of crisis and high uncertainty (Kakkar & Sivanathan, 2017). As discussed in Chapter 6 (section 6.3d), group members who are most susceptible to the influence of authoritarian leaders are those who have been socialized to view their world as a dangerous and threatening place that requires strong, harsh leadership to establish a sense of order.

In an attempt to identify preferences for authoritarian leadership worldwide, Robert House and his colleagues (2004) conducted a cross-cultural study in which they asked respondents to rate the degree to which certain behaviors were reflective of "outstanding" leadership on items such as "is in charge and does not tolerate disagreement or questioning; gives orders" and "inclined to dominate others." Their results indicated that the country with the highest scores for preferred authoritarian leadership was China, while the country with the lowest scores was Germany. Interestingly, three generations ago, in the 1930s, German citizens strongly supported one of the most authoritarian leaders of the 20th century, Adolf Hitler. The fact that German citizens' support for authoritarian leadership changed so drastically over a few generations suggests that cultural norms regarding authoritarian leaders are changeable and responsive to historical events.

In the second decade of the 21st century, a number of social scientists are expressing increasing concerns that an opposite shift in preferences for authoritarian leadership is taking place in a number of democracies around the world, including the United States (Levitsky & Ziblatt, 2019). Nearly 80 years ago, social psychologist Kurt Lewin and his

authoritarian leader
A leader who dictates group policies, procedures, and goals and controls all activities without any meaningful participation by others

colleagues (1939) perceived the very real threat of authoritarian leadership in Nazi Germany and responded by initiating a research program to investigate how best to understand and counteract that threat. A similar program of research may need to be implemented today. It is crucial that, as researchers, educators and students of social psychology, once we identify a problem, we use our knowledge for the betterment of society. As Lewin once argued "research that produces nothing but books will not suffice."

> "I guarantee freedom of speech, but I cannot guarantee freedom after speech."
>
> —Idi Amin, 3rd authoritarian leader of Uganda, 1925–2003

> "Sooner will a camel pass through a needle's eye than a great man be discovered by an election."
>
> —Adolf Hitler, dictator of Nazi Germany, 1889–1945

8.4d   Gender and Culture Can Influence Leadership Style.

Women are assuming larger leadership positions in many countries around the world; at the same time, the general public believes that the sexes differ substantially in their style or approach to leadership. Although there appear to be some gender differences in leadership, research indicates that there are more similarities than differences (Eagly & Johannesen-Schmidt, 2001). In a meta-analysis of more than 150 studies of leadership in which men and women were compared, Alice Eagly and Blair Johnson (1990) found that in organizational settings, female leaders are as task-oriented as their male counterparts. Where they differ from males is in their tendency to adopt a more democratic or participative leadership style. That is, women are more likely than men to invite subordinates to participate in the decision-making process. In contrast, male leaders tend to have an autocratic or directive style, in which orders are given rather than suggestions solicited. A meta-analysis of leadership styles found similar results, including that women are somewhat more likely than men to acknowledge and reward subordinates for good performance (Eagly et al., 2003).

These leader differences, while relatively small, are consistent with findings indicating that women tend to be friendlier and agree more in group discussions than men, and men tend to have higher rates of counterarguments (Johnson et al., 1996). Overall, it appears that male leaders tend to be more purely task-oriented types, while female leaders blend in a bit more of the interpersonal concerns typical of relationship-oriented leaders (Eagly et al., 1995; Helgesen, 1990).

> "You could certainly say that I've never underestimated myself, there's nothing wrong with being ambitious."
>
> —Angela Merkel, German Chancellor, b. 1954

In explaining these small, yet significant, gender differences, various social psychologists suggest that they may exist because women are more socialized to develop stronger empathic and interpersonal skills than men; in contrast, men are more socialized to seek dominance in their social relationships (Foels & Pappas, 2004; Wilson & Liu, 2003). Women's apparent superiority in attending to others' concerns and feelings may allow them to more easily adopt a leadership style employing considerable give-and-take with subordinates, which can facilitate group productivity (Bartone et al., 2002; Peterson, 2003).

One potential impediment to women assuming leadership positions in mixed-sex groups is gender stereotypes. In many cultures around the world, the leader prototype is closely associated with male stereotypes (Eagly & Karau, 2002). This masculinization of the leader role often leads to the perception that women are less qualified for elite leadership positions than men, and it often causes people to react negatively to women acting in a powerful manner (Becker et al., 2002). Indeed, there is evidence that people—including women—react more negatively to women than men who adopt a directive leadership style (Eagly et al., 1992; Garcia-Retamero & López-Zafra, 2006). This is especially so among people who endorse traditional gender beliefs and perceive women leaders as threatening male dominance and power (Brescoll et al., 2018; Hoyt & Burnette, 2013).

Although gender-based stereotypes can make it more difficult for women to become leaders, it appears that these stereotypes are slowly diminishing as more women take on leadership positions (Koenig et al., 2011). There is also evidence suggesting that women who are highly confident in their leadership abilities are not negatively affected by the "women are not natural leaders" stereotype (Hoyt & Blascovich, 2007; Singh & Vinnicombe, 2006). Additional research suggests that female leaders can defuse traditional gender stereotypes that impede their effectiveness by adopting leadership styles combining assertiveness with nonverbal behavior that communicates friendliness and affiliation (Carli et al., 1995). Of course, this research also suggests that women—compared to men—often must monitor more of their behavior to be perceived as an effective leader and their success is often less certain than their male counterparts who do not experience the same challenges (Eagly, 2018). Therefore, while these findings may provide useful guidance for female leaders, they also highlight the fact that in the 21st century men still benefit from gender-based privileges related to leadership roles that likewise hinder women.

Moving from gender to cultural considerations, how might leadership style operate differently in individualist and collectivist cultures? A growing body of research suggests that the ideal leader may be different in these two cultures (Teagarden, 2007). Collectivists' concerns about group needs and interpersonal relations appear to foster a social climate in which nurturing, relationship-oriented leaders are highly desired by group members (Smith et al., 1990; Walumbwa et al., 2007). In contrast, individualists are socialized to work alone, to concentrate on the task, and to emphasize achievement over socializing (Sanchez-Burks et al., 2000). This training appears to make individualists somewhat more responsive to task-oriented leaders.

One possible implication of these findings is that the previously discussed contingency model of leadership—which proposes that task-oriented leaders exhibit greater effectiveness in more varied situations than relationship-oriented leaders—may be better suited to explaining leadership in individualist cultures than in those that are collectivist. What about people living in multicultural societies, like the United States and Canada, who are members of collectivist-oriented ethnic groups within these predominantly individualist societies? If you are a member of one of these ethnic groups, does your collectivist heritage cause you to respond to leaders somewhat differently than the typical individualist? It's possible. Jeffrey Sanchez-Burks and his coworkers (2000) found that Mexican Americans tend to be more responsive to relationship-oriented work groups than are Anglo-Americans. These findings raise the possibility that even within an individualist society like the United States, how we respond to task-oriented versus relationship-oriented leaders may be partly determined by whether our ethnic heritage has individualist or collectivist roots (Ayman & Korabik, 2010).

Section Summary

- A leader is the person who exerts the most influence and provides direction and energy to the group.

- Transformational leaders are those who dramatically change the outlook and behavior of followers. Their attributes include the ability to communicate and implement a vision and engage in charismatic communication.

- In the contingency model of leadership, leader effectiveness is determined by the interaction of the personal factor of leadership style (task-oriented or

(*continues*)

(**Section Summary** *continued*)

relationship-oriented) and three situational factors that provide the leader with situational control:

leader's relations with the group

task structure

leader's position power

- Although female leaders are as task-oriented as male leaders, women tend to have a more democratic leadership style.

- Due to gender stereotypes, men enjoy privileges over women in seeking leadership roles.

- In collectivist cultures, relationship-oriented leaders may be more effective than they are in individualist cultures.

8.5 Group Interests Versus Individual Interests

The idea that followers' responsiveness to certain types of leaders may partly depend on whether they are individualists or collectivists has relevance to the final topic in this chapter. Whenever individuals are involved in group activities, the possibility always exists that they will be faced with a situation in which their own immediate interests diverge from those of the group. How individuals resolve this conflict has been the subject of considerable attention by social psychologists over the years.

8.5a Social Dilemmas Occur When Short-term and Long-term Interests Conflict.

A **social dilemma** is any situation in which the most rewarding short-term choice for an individual will ultimately cause negative consequences for the group as a whole (Bernard et al., 2013; de Kwaadsteniet et al., 2010). A classic example of a social dilemma concerning how two or more people share a limited resource is the "tragedy of the commons" described by ecologist Garret Hardin (1968). Imagine a small town with a communal piece of land—the commons—available to all the townspeople's cattle. For many years, the commons has been able to grow enough grass to support 50 cattle—one for each farmer. Now suppose that one farmer selfishly adds another cow to the commons to increase his milk production. Other farmers, noticing this addition, also add more cattle. Soon the farmers reap the results of their selfishness and competitiveness—the commons dies and all the cattle perish. By pursuing short-term individual gains, the farmers orchestrated a collective disaster. This type of social dilemma is known as a *resource dilemma* (Kortenkamp & Moore, 2006).

We read about numerous examples of resource dilemmas in the newspapers or confront them in our daily lives. The depletion of the South American rain forests brings timber companies short-term profits, but it poses a serious long-term threat to our environment. Even closer to home is the tendency for people to regularly use or benefit from certain public services—such as schools, libraries, parks, roads, public radio, and consumer groups—at the same time that they fail to support tax policies that contribute to their continued existence. If users do not contribute, the services will no longer be available. This willingness to use a public good, coupled with an unwillingness to contribute to it, has been called the *free-rider problem*.

social dilemma

Any situation in which the most rewarding short-term choice for an individual will ultimately cause negative consequences for the group as a whole

In all social dilemmas, people are in a situation of *mixed motives* in which it is to their advantage both to cooperate and to act selfishly. Their short-term interests will be advanced if they act selfishly, but their long-term interests and those of the group will be advanced if they cooperate. Although you might expect that people would cooperate when such cooperation will enhance their long-term interests, this is often not the case. For example, in a study of resource dilemmas, Julian Edney (1979) had college students play a game in which 10 metal nuts were placed into a bowl. They were told that the goal of the game was for each student to gather as many nuts as possible. They were further told that they could remove as many nuts from the bowl as they wished, and every 10 seconds the number of nuts remaining in the bowl would be doubled. Despite the fact that the most rational choice for individual players was to leave the nuts in the bowl for a period of time so that they would multiply in numbers, this was not the typical strategy players adopted. Instead, when the game started, most players simply grabbed as many nuts as they could snatch from the grasp of others. Of Edney's groups, 65% did not even make it past the first 10-second replacement period!

> "I have labored to procure the good of every individual everywhere, so far as this did not conflict with the good of the whole."
>
> —Catherine II, Empress of Russia, 1729–1796

Have you noticed a psychological similarity between resource dilemmas and the phenomenon of social loafing examined earlier? In resource dilemmas, individuals deplete the group resource by taking from it more than their fair share; in social loafing, individuals deplete group productivity (a group resource) by taking some of their own effort out of the collective effort. In both instances, being "lost in the crowd"—or deindividuated—allows members the protection necessary to behave selfishly (Williams et al., 1995). Although there are these similarities, research indicates that—unlike in social loafing—fear and greed are two primary motives driving social dilemma decisions (Bruins et al., 1989; Simpson, 2006). When people notice that others are taking a free ride or depleting collective resources, they abandon a socially responsible strategy and grab what they can.

Social dilemmas are not limited to conflicts involving limited resources. Another type of dilemma, the *prisoner's dilemma*, derives its name from the research paradigm employed by social psychologists to study it. In its original format, the prisoner's dilemma involves a situation in which two men suspected of a crime are arrested by the police and placed into separate interrogation rooms (Luce & Raiffa, 1957). The district attorney is confident that the two committed the crime together, but she does not have sufficient evidence to convict them. She approaches each suspect individually and tells him he has two alternatives: to confess to the crime the police are certain they both committed or not to confess. If neither one confesses, the district attorney states that she will charge them on some minor offense and each will get 1 year in prison. If both confess, they will be prosecuted, but the district attorney will recommend less than the most severe sentence; both will get 8 years in prison. However, if one confesses and the other does not, then the one who confesses will receive a very lenient sentence of only 6 months for testifying against the other; the one who holds out, on the other hand, will get the maximum penalty of 20 years in prison.

The essentials of the prisoner's dilemma are presented in Figure 8.9, representing what will happen to each prisoner in the four possible combinations of confessing and not confessing. Each prisoner knows that the other has the same options and knowledge as himself. Mutual nonconfession would produce a reasonably agreeable outcome for both; it would be their second choice of the four outcomes. However, the outcome most advantageous for one prisoner (getting 6 months) is the outcome that the other prisoner would least prefer (getting 20 years). Both prisoners would select mutual confession as their third choice among the outcomes. What would you do in this situation?

FIGURE 8.9 The Prisoner's Dilemma

In this form of social dilemma, two suspected criminals are interrogated separately and are given a choice: to confess or not to confess. If both cooperate with each other by staying silent, both get off with fairly light sentences (upper left). If both compete with each other by confessing, both receive moderate sentences (lower right). But if one confesses while the other stays silent, the confessor gets a very light sentence and the nonconfessor spends a long time in prison (lower left and upper right).

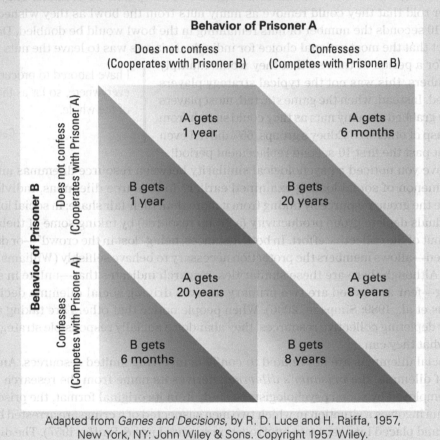

Adapted from *Games and Decisions*, by R. D. Luce and H. Raiffa, 1957, New York, NY: John Wiley & Sons. Copyright 1957 Wiley.

Numerous studies have used variations of the prisoner's dilemma to identify the factors that tip the balance toward cooperation or competition (Liberman et al., 2004). Frequently, the game is played over a series of trials so that players can alter their choices based on how their partner/competitor previously behaved. One variation entails two countries involved in an arms race, with each trial involving decision makers from each country choosing between competing (by building missiles) or cooperating (by building factories) with the other country. Initially in these multiple-trial games, competition typically occurs in the early trials; but then people begin to cooperate as they experience the negative consequences of competition and try to reduce them (Insko et al., 2001; Nowak & Sigmund, 1993). The findings from prisoner's dilemma studies and those involving resource dilemmas suggest that many factors play a role in promoting cooperation versus competition in mixed-motives situations. Let us now turn our attention to those factors.

8.5b Cooperation Is Necessary to Resolve Social Dilemmas

The basic problem in resolving many social dilemmas is that it requires the cooperative efforts of numerous people (Stouten et al., 2006). Yet all too often, people are unwilling to give up their short-term gain strategies until the social dilemma becomes quite serious or they sustain many competitive losses. Resolving social dilemmas is not easy under such conditions, but research reveals several ways to promote cooperation.

Sanctioning Cooperative Behavior

Without a sanctioning system in place to regulate people's short-term interest strategies, cooperative group members are often taken advantage of by their more competitive neighbors (Pfattheicher & Keller, 2013). One way to increase the cooperation of selfish individuals is to threaten them with punishment. Often this is accomplished by establishing an authority that will set up guidelines of conduct that are consistent with the collective welfare of the group. Interestingly, people who tend to be less cooperative and less trusting of others' behavior are more willing to contribute money to establish such an authority (Yamagishi, 1986). A sanctioning system that intermittently punishes noncooperators increases cooperation among those not punished (Loukopoulos et al., 2006). Is punishment the only effective sanctioning system to increase cooperation? A meta-analysis of 187 studies found that offering incentives for cooperation is as effective as doling out punishment in resolving social dilemmas (Balliet et al., 2011).

> "He who acts with a constant view to his own advantage will be much murmured against."
>
> —Confucius, Chinese philosopher, 551–479 BCE

Education

A second way to solve a social dilemma is to educate group members. For example, in one study using a laboratory simulation of a water shortage, participants were told that they could draw water from a hypothetical lake, which would then renew itself by a small amount, much as rain replenishes a real lake (Allison & Messick, 1985). Those who understood the consequences of their actions behaved in a more socially responsible manner. Similarly, other studies have found that after receiving training in cooperation, even habitual competitors tend to become more cooperative and sustain this prosocial behavior over extended periods of time (Sheldon, 1999).

> "We are all members of one another."
>
> —James Baldwin, African American author, 1924–1987

Group Identification

Solutions to social dilemmas also may be achieved by encouraging the adoption of a meaningful group identity (Swann et al., 2010). For example, in resource dilemmas, people are more likely to cooperate if they think of the other users of limited resources as being a part of their ingroup rather than as mere competitors. In support of this hypothesis, research has found that when situational cues prime people's group identity or their interdependent selves, they are more likely to exercise personal restraint in their use of an endangered resource (Brewer & Kramer, 1986; Liu & Li, 2009). Similarly, when participants play the prisoner's dilemma game, they are more likely to cooperate rather than compete when exposed to situational cues that prime their interdependent selves (Wong & Hong, 2005). How might these research findings reduce the "tragedy of the commons" currently afflicting our national political scene described in our chapter-opening story? One recent study suggests that if you can prompt Americans to think about their common national identity—for example, by simply showing them 4th of July events where people are basking in the glow of being "US citizens"—this can reduce political polarization and dislike of members from the other political party (Levendusky, 2017). Of course, resolving politically based social dilemmas requires more than members of two conflicted parties holding hands and singing "Kumbaya." Both scientific research and real-world events inform us that if groups can develop a "sense of community" in their members, they are more likely to be able to call on this group identification when it is crucial that individuals put collective needs ahead of immediate self-interest.

Promoting a Cooperative Orientation

As we have already seen, not everyone automatically places cooperation ahead of competition when confronted with a social dilemma. This is because people differ in their *social value orientation*, which is a person's rules specifying how outcomes or resources should be divided between oneself and others (Van Lange, 1999). Those with a *cooperative orientation* seek to maximize joint gains; those with an *individualistic orientation* try to maximize their own well-being regardless of what happens to others; and those with a *competitive orientation* strive to outdo others by as much as possible. Cooperators see the long-term value of sustained mutual cooperation, and they focus on how the future can be better from the past (Parks et al., 2003). Not surprisingly, it is far easier to solve a social dilemma when you are dealing with cooperators rather than individualists or competitors (Joireman et al., 2001; Zettler et al., 2013).

> "Who see Me in all, And sees all in Me, For him I am not lost, And he is not lost for Me."
>
> —Bhagavad Gita ("The Lord's Song"), a sacred writing of Hinduism

Given the communal social role that women are traditionally expected to fill in society, are they more likely to cooperate in social dilemmas than are men? Following a meta-analysis of 50 years of social dilemma studies, Daniel Balliet and his colleagues (2011) found that although there was no difference in women's and men's overall cooperation (d = –.05), there were small gender differences in certain situations. For example, men's interactions with other men were more cooperative than were female same-sex interactions (d = .16), but women were more cooperative than men in coed interactions (d = –.22). Overall, these findings suggest both women and men have the ability to cooperate during social dilemmas, despite gender-role expectations.

Recognizing that a cooperative value system should be internalized early in life, educational programs have been established to teach children how to think and behave cooperatively rather than competitively in social interaction (Van Lange et al., 1997). In addition to instilling cooperation as an important self-defining value, research indicates that social value orientations become better predictors of behavior when situational cues activate them from memory (Sagiv et al., 2011). Thus, while instilling a cooperative orientation is a crucial first step in promoting cooperative solutions to social dilemmas, priming this positive social value orientation within the actual situation where cooperation is needed is also important.

Promoting Group Discussion

One final way to reduce the free-rider problem is simply to give people the opportunity to discuss the dilemma among themselves (Bicchieri & Lev-On, 2007). Studies indicate that groups allowed to talk about the dilemma cooperate more than 95% of the time (van de Kragt et al., 1986). Why is discussion so effective? The most likely explanation appears to be that group discussion allows members to make explicit promises as to how they will behave, and these promises act as a binding social contract (Kiesler et al., 1996). If individual members hesitate to go along with this commitment to cooperate, group pressure is often sufficient to eventually secure compliance.

Taking these strategies together, we can escape the destructive consequences of social dilemmas by (1) establishing guidelines and sanctions against self-serving behavior, (2) getting people to understand how their actions help or hurt everyone's long-term welfare, (3) encouraging people to develop a group identity, (4) fostering the internalization of social values that encourage cooperation rather than competition, and (5) promoting group discussion that leads to cooperation commitments.

> "It is our task in our time and in our generation to hand down undiminished to those who come after us, as was handed down to us by those who went before, the natural wealth and beauty which is ours."
>
> —John F. Kennedy, 35th US president, 1917–1963

Section Summary

- Social dilemmas occur when people's most rewarding short-term choices ultimately cause negative consequences for the group.

- Several factors help resolve social dilemmas:
    sanctioning cooperative behavior
    education
    group identification
    promoting a cooperative orientation
    promoting group discussion

Applications

How Do Juries Make Decisions?

In Chapter 7, you learned how people can be coerced into confessing to a crime they did not commit. In this section, let's examine how juries weigh the evidence presented by both prosecution and defense attorneys. What goes on behind those closed doors once the jury has gone into seclusion to deliberate? Unfortunately for those interested in better understanding the social psychological dynamics of this process, federal and virtually all state laws forbid eavesdropping on jury deliberations. Interestingly, the catalyst for these laws was the public outrage that ensued when a judge in the 1950s allowed University of Chicago researchers to tape-record the deliberations of five juries (Ferguson, 1955).

Due to the inaccessibility of real juries, social scientists have resorted to alternative means of gaining insight into the inner workings of this kind of group. Some of these are (1) interviewing jurors once a verdict has been reached, (2) analyzing court records, and (3) simulating the jury deliberation process by staging simulated trials using mock juries. What do these studies tell us about the jury as a decision-making group?

The Deliberation Process

As in most groups, juries move through distinct stages in making their decisions (see section 8.3a). During the orientation stage, jurors pick a foreperson, set an agenda, and begin to get to know one another. Next, in the discussion stage, they tackle the task of reviewing the evidence. This review process and the following decision stage can generate considerable tension because jurors often actively disagree with one another. Post-trial interviews with jurors in criminal cases indicate that the deliberation process typically involves remarkably high levels of competent and critical analysis (Bornstein & Greene, 2011; Gastil et al., 2007). As jurors move toward a decision in the third stage, the majority exerts pressure on dissenters to fall in line so that a unanimous verdict can be reached. Once consensus is within reach, the group tries to resolve the remaining differences and conflicts so that a verdict can be rendered. If no such consensus is reached, however, a jury does not have the option open to most other groups—rejecting nonconforming members. Instead, jurors who hold the majority opinion must continue to search for consensus with their minority counterparts. If, after exhaustive and fruitless discussion, the jury proclaims itself hung—and if the judge agrees that further deliberation would be fruitless—a mistrial is declared.

As important as the deliberation process is to our legal system, in most cases the verdict is actually determined before the jurors even begin discussing the case. Harry Kalven and Hans Zeisel (1966) found that in 97% of the court cases they reviewed, the jury's final decision was the same as the one a majority of the jurors favored on the initial vote before deliberation commenced. Similar results have been obtained in other studies (Bornstein & Greene, 2011), suggesting that by the time the first vote is taken, the jury has generally already decided about the defendant's guilt. It appears that the initial majority opinion wins over the entire group due to the greater informational influence and normative influence that majority members have at their disposal. That is, jury discussion is more likely to focus on majority-held opinions rather than opinions shared by the minority, and those sharing the majority opinion exert greater pressure to conform than do those who hold minority positions (Wittenbaum et al., 1999).

Does this mean, then, that group discussion of the facts does not significantly influence individual juror opinions? Maybe not. When jurors on 50 randomly selected felony cases were contacted by researchers and interviewed regarding their jury experience, they revealed that even when first-ballot votes were taken before formal discussion of the evidence, some informal discussion almost always took place among individual jurors (Sandys & Dillehay, 1995). In such cases, it's possible that jurors were indeed influenced by the other jurors' opinions. In only 11% of these trials did the first ballot occur before any discussion or deliberation took place at all. These trials, then, represent individual juror first-ballot verdicts with the least amount of influence from other jurors. Did these individual first-ballot verdicts predict the jury's subsequent final verdicts? Interestingly, they did not. Furthermore, jurors with minority opinions appear to be influenced by majority opinion holders only when presented with a thorough review of the evidence (Salerno & Diamond, 2010). These findings suggest that the deliberation process, and informational influence, may play a more significant role in shaping the verdicts of juries than was previously thought.

Although jurors holding minority viewpoints have little chance of dramatically shifting majority opinion, the research on minority influence described in Chapter 7 suggests that jurors may be persuasive when their positions are not too far away from the prevailing majority position. Support for this hypothesis comes from a mock jury study that Nancy Pennington and Reid Hastie (1990) conducted, in which they found that a minority on a jury was often able to change the majority's minds on the degree of guilt of a defendant. This suggests that if 10 out of 12 jurors believe a defendant is guilty of first-degree murder, even though there is virtually no chance that the dissenting jurors will be able to convince the majority that the defendant is innocent, the 10 might be able to convince the other two to change their verdict to second-degree murder. Based on minority influence research, jurors holding minority positions would be most persuasive when they consistently and confidently state their dissenting views and, at the same time, come across as flexible and open-minded.

The Consequences of Small Juries

In the 1970 case of *Williams v. Florida*, the U.S. Supreme Court heard the appeal of a defendant who was convicted of armed robbery by a six-person jury instead of the traditional 12-person jury. In their arguments, his lawyers contended that a six-person jury was biased against defendants because the possibility of juror dissent was greatly reduced with such a small group. The Supreme Court justices disagreed, ruling that in civil cases and state criminal cases not involving the death penalty, courts could use six-person juries instead of the traditional 12. In making their rulings, the justices stated that there is no reason to believe that smaller juries will arrive at different decisions than the traditional jury. Is this true?

Although research indicates that jury size does not appear to affect rates of convictions or acquittals, a meta-analysis of studies involving 15,000 mock jurors who deliberated in over 2,000 juries with either six or 12 people found that smaller juries spend less time deliberating, recall less of the evidence, and are less likely to represent minority segments of the population (Saks & Marti, 1997). In addition, other studies have found that six-person juries are only half as likely as 12-person juries to become hung (Kerr & MacCoun, 1985). Because trials resulting in hung juries often do so because of legitimate disagreements, it may be that smaller juries weaken a necessary safeguard in our legal system (Davis et al., 1997). One likely reason 12-person juries are more likely to become deadlocked is that with more people in a group, there is a greater likelihood that more than one person will be dissenting from the majority. As Asch's (1956) conformity research suggests (see Chapter 7, Social Support portion of section 7.3a), when someone has a social supporter, he or she is much more likely to resist majority pressure to conform.

The Consequences of Nonunanimous Verdicts

In 1972, the U.S. Supreme Court ruled in a split 5–4 decision that courts could accept verdicts based on less-than-unanimous majorities. The majority of the justices stated that a nonunanimous decision rule (for example, a guilty verdict by a 9 to 3 margin) would not adversely affect the jury; however, four justices disagreed, arguing that it would reduce the intensity of deliberations and negatively affect the potential for minority influence. Was this Supreme Court decision consistent with the findings from scientific studies of juries? Based on your own understanding of group influence, do you think that people on a jury that needs only a 9–3 majority would engage in a different type of deliberation process than juries that require a unanimous decision?

Reid Hastie and his colleagues (1983) studied the deliberations of more than 800 people in 69 different mock jury trials and found that juries with rules requiring less-than-unanimous verdicts behaved very differently from juries requiring unanimous verdicts. Their results indicated that majority-wins-rule juries (10–2 or 8–4 margins) are not only less likely to end up hung than unanimity-rule juries (12–0 margin) but are also likely to render harsher verdicts—and to do so in a relatively short period of time using a bullying persuasive style rather than relying on carefully reasoned arguments. Jurors who participate in these nonunanimous juries also emerge rating themselves as less informed, feeling less confident about their final decision, and perceiving their peers as more close-minded than jurors in the unanimous-rule groups (Nemeth, 1977). These findings clearly suggest that allowing nonunanimous verdicts is very likely to decrease the robustness of the arguments heard in deliberation. This, in turn, may well hinder the minority's ability to persuade the majority.

(continues)

(**Applications**, *continued*)

Today, only two states permit nonunanimous verdicts in criminal trials, but 33 states permit such verdicts in civil cases. Most civil cases today also employ six-member juries. Based on the research conducted since the Supreme Court loosened the restraints on jury size and unanimity, it appears that these changes result in faster and harsher trials by encouraging close-mindedness in jurors. The question we must ask ourselves is whether this is what we want to call "justice under the law."

THE BIG PICTURE

What we hope you understand by this time is that, although you are a unique individual in your own right, you are also a creature of the group. In a psychological sense, you are not fully mature until you have internalized the group into your everyday thinking. As already discussed in Chapter 7, an important aspect of group living is the process of social influence. There is nothing inherently wrong with such influence—in fact, it is the social "stitching" that organizes the fabric of everyday life. Yet, in our individualist culture, the group has often been viewed with distrust and even condescension. It is true that you can sometimes act in an inferior and impulsive manner when in a group (due to social loafing and deindividuation, respectively), but you can also exhibit similar undesirable actions when acting alone. Thus, group processes—like individual processes—are amply designed to foster both positive and negative outcomes.

Whenever you become involved in a group, the possibility always exists that your own personal, self-focused interests will diverge from those of the collective. In such social dilemmas, your short-term interests will be advanced if you act selfishly, but your long-term interests and those of the group will be advanced if you cooperate. Resolving social dilemmas—and maintaining group membership itself—may be harder for individualists than collectivists (Chen et al., 2007). Based on your responses to the "Values Hierarchy" exercise in Chapter 1 (see *Self/Social Connection Exercise 1.1*), do you think it would be difficult or easy for you to work to resolve social dilemmas when they arise in your own groups?

To summarize the content of this chapter, contemporary social science confirms that the group fabric of human nature is strong. Yet, within the fabric of the group, you will find the creative weaving of the many interconnected selves. This unique blending of the self with others is what powers group dynamics. When you interact with group members, you are actively creating and recreating your social reality—yet you are often unaware of the situational forces that shape this reality. Despite the fact that you may think of yourself as being a relatively autonomous creature, your current understanding of group processes should tell you that much of this self-perceived independence is illusory. Regardless of your culture of origin, you are influenced by others—both singly and collectively. One of the most important goals of social psychology as a discipline is to increase knowledge of how the person—as a self—helps to weave the fabric of group life and how the paths of these individual life threads are influenced by one another. The better you understand the complex nature and influence of the group fabric, the better you will be able to weave your own unique, yet group-influenced, patterns.

◼ KEY TERMS

◼ WEBSITES

Accessed through https://www.bvtlab.com/sop8

Websites for this chapter focus on why we form into groups and what needs and functions they serve, as well as the psychology of collective behavior and social institutions.

APA Div. 49: Society of Group Psychology and Group Psychotherapy

This is a website for psychologists interested in group dynamics. Division 49 promotes group psychology and group psychotherapy through research, education, and clinical practice.

Center for Leadership Studies

This website for the Center for Leadership Studies contains the findings of studies on the social psychological dynamics of leaders as instruments of change within a group.

Self-Directed Work Teams

This website analyzes self-directed work teams, discussing research on group work and how to improve teamwork.

Chapter 9

Interpersonal Attraction

FOCUS QUESTIONS

1. How do our dual desires to understand ourselves and receive rewards influence with whom we choose to spend time?
2. How does culture shape our belongingness needs?
3. When it comes to physical appearance, is it true that we tend to believe that "beauty is only skin deep"?
4. Do "birds of a feather flock together," or is it more accurate that "opposites attract"?

CHAPTER OUTLINE

Introduction

"Short men! Short men! What do you think of them? Some people say that short men are deceitful; that they're always sneakin' around causin' trouble; that they are insecure and always out to put other people down because of their insecurity, especially women. . . . Well, today I'm going to talk to short men who have felt insecure about their height at different times in their lives. . . . And we will also talk to a social psychologist who studies the effect of height on a man's self-esteem."

This was Oprah Winfrey's introduction, on her widely popular television talk show, for an episode about short men. The three diminutive men who were Oprah's guests for this episode—all ranging in height from 4'10" to 5'2"—were outgoing, seemingly well-adjusted adults who had been shunned, taunted, and discriminated against throughout their adolescent and adult lives. Steve was the fourth guest, there to provide a scientific perspective on why these men faced obstacles in their daily lives. What was the motivation for the severe judgments these men often received because of their physical appearance?

Issues related to interpersonal attraction, such as a person's physical appearance, have always been popular topics on television talk shows. Why is physical appearance so important to interpersonal attraction?

("Oprah in 2014," by Aphrodite-in-nyc, under a CC 2.0 license via Wikimedia)

At one point Steve mentioned that there is a "male-taller norm" in heterosexual dating relationships, meaning that women prefer to date men who are about 4 inches taller than themselves (Yancey & Emerson, 2014). He further explained that this unwritten social norm is shaped by cultural beliefs concerning proper gender roles. After his comments, Oprah responded, "There's a psychological feeling of protection when the guy is taller. . . . We admit it; it's a terrible thing. But if I date a shorter guy I feel like I'm his mother!" A female audience member agreed and disclosed that, "I like to hug 'up' rather than hug 'down.' Short guys make me feel bigger than I am, and they're like a little boy that I'm dragging along with me."

These comments were sharply challenged by another woman who defended short men by stating, "I can't believe the insensitivity of the women in the audience toward those men! My husband is short and I love him. He is a great man and he has a great personality. I just cannot believe that they would act like these men are second-class citizens because they're short. . . . It doesn't matter how tall you are!"

The comments made by Oprah and her audience members are directly related to the subject matter of this chapter: **interpersonal attraction**, which is the desire to approach other people. You may not know what it feels like to be the target of the type of ridicule that these short men experienced in their lives, but many of us have been shunned or rejected by others because one or more of our personal qualities does not measure up to others' standards of acceptability.

interpersonal attraction
The desire to approach other people

Besides physical appearance, what qualities influence your need to seek out others for interaction? What situational factors shape your desire to approach or avoid others? As a way to help you ponder these questions, try the following exercise. Think about your best friend. How did you first meet? On paper, list up to 10 reasons why you were initially attracted to this person. These reasons could be profound or mundane. Now think about a casual friend. In addition to listing factors that initially attracted you, also identify reasons why you think this relationship hasn't come close to achieving the level of "best friend." Finally, think about someone you dislike. List the factors that shaped the course of this bad relationship. Now compare the three lists. How are they different? How are they similar? Can you develop any hypotheses about the nature of interpersonal attraction based on any patterns you observe?

As we study the "chemistry" of interpersonal attraction, keep these lists handy and remember the obstacles faced by the short men in our chapter-opening story, for we will refer to them on more than one occasion. Following a discussion of two basic reasons why people affiliate, we examine how personal characteristics of the individual, situational factors, and characteristics of others influence the attraction process. Then we analyze how social interaction can be chronically problematic for some people, and end by discussing ways to improve the interpersonal skills of the socially anxious and lonely. Next, in Chapter 10, we will investigate how this interpersonal process can progress—and sometimes deteriorate—in close friendships and romantic relationships.

9.1   Belongingness Needs

Our **need to belong**—which is the need to interact with others and be socially accepted—is a powerful, fundamental, and extremely pervasive motivation (Baumeister & Leary, 1995). Abraham Maslow (1970), one of the founders of humanistic psychology, identified the need to belong as one of five essential human needs in his hierarchy of needs, along with physiological needs, safety needs, self-esteem needs, and self-actualization needs. Indeed, research finds that having supportive social relationships can facilitate personal growth and is positively associated with physical and mental health and well-being (Feeney & Collins, 2014; Lee et al., 2018).

While you may realize that the need to belong is often an important motivator of your thinking and behavior, have you ever wondered why your need to be around other people often changes due to your daily experiences? Have you ever questioned why your need to belong is different from that of some of your friends and acquaintances? In this first chapter section, you can explore how closely your personal musings on affiliating with others match the insights of social scientific theory and research.

9.1a   Two Reasons for Affiliation Are Comparison and Exchange.

Two factors that cause us to seek out others—to affiliate with them—are our desire to gain knowledge about ourselves and the world through *social comparison*, and our desire to secure psychological and material rewards through *social exchange*. These two reasons for affiliation relate to our dependence on others for information (information dependence) and our dependence on others for positive outcomes (outcome dependence). Can you guess which of these two factors is more associated with the "cold" perspective of human nature, and which is more associated with the "hot" perspective?

Social Comparison

According to Leon Festinger's (1954) **social comparison theory**, we possess a strong need to have accurate views—both about our social world and about ourselves. One way to know ourselves and better understand our place in the social environment is to compare ourselves with others (Locke, 2007). The information that such social comparison provides is used to evaluate the self (Wadsworth, 2014). According to Festinger, social comparison is most likely when we are in a state of *uncertainty* concerning a relevant self-aspect. He further hypothesized that we generally prefer to compare ourselves with *similar* others. The more similar people are to us, the more likely we are to use the information gained through social comparison to better understand ourselves and our future actions.

For example, imagine trying to decide whether to take a particular course next semester. You know three people who were previously enrolled in the course: Juan, who is always the top student in every course; Vanessa, who usually receives grades similar to

need to belong
The need to interact with others and be socially accepted

social comparison theory
The theory that we evaluate our thoughts and actions by comparing them with those of others

yours; and Sarah, who is always on academic probation. According to social comparison theory, you should go to Vanessa for information about the course because of her academic similarity to you. Her opinions and her actual final grade will be much more useful in predicting your own performance than information learned from Juan and Sarah.

We use social comparison not only to judge—and improve—ourselves but also to judge our emotions and choose our friends (Buunk et al., 2007; Wood, 1996). Today, our understanding of social comparison processes is more complex than originally formulated by Festinger, but it still conforms to the general principles outlined here. This knowledge-based motive for affiliation largely reflects the "cold" perspective of human nature.

Social Exchange

Although the desire to evaluate ourselves through social comparison is one reason for affiliation, a second theory explaining why we seek others' company focuses more closely on the *interactions* between people. According to **social exchange theory,** people seek out and maintain those relationships in which rewards exceed costs, and they avoid or terminate relationships when costs are greater than rewards (Erdogan & Enders, 2007; van de Rijt & Macy, 2006). The assumption underlying this "hot" perspective on affiliation is that people are basically *hedonists*—they seek to maximize pleasure and minimize pain, and to do so at minimal cost. Operating from this assumption, the theory also states that people will be attracted to those who best reward them.

One of the earliest versions of social exchange theory was presented by George Homans (1958), who stated that all social relationships are like economic bargains in which each party places a value on the goods they exchange with one another. The "goods" exchanged could be either material (for example, money, flowers, food) or nonmaterial (for example, social influence, information, affection). For instance, Kelly may do the grocery shopping, daily food preparation, and weekly yard work; in exchange, Morgan may do the laundry, dinner cleanup, and weekly vacuuming and dusting. Social exchange theory assumes that people keep track of the goods they exchange, and on some level they know whether their rewards are exceeding their costs.

"Almost all of our relationships begin, and most of them continue, as forms of mutual exploitation, a mental or physical barter, to be terminated when one or both parties run out of goods."

—W. H. Auden, English poet, 1907–1973

John Thibaut and Harold Kelley (1959) stated that, when people are deciding whether to remain in a relationship, they will not consider the rewards and costs in isolation. Instead, the level of costs and rewards accruing in the current relationship will be compared with the possible rewards and costs available in alternative relationships. If no alternative relationships are available, or none appear appreciably more rewarding than the current one, the person will make no changes. This is one reason why some people remain in dissatisfying or even harmful relationships—they would rather receive some rewards than run the risk of receiving none at all (Rusbult & Martz, 1995).

These two explanations for why we affiliate—the desire for social comparison and the desire for social exchange—do not exhaust the explanatory powers of current social psychological theories. Instead, they provide an anchoring point for the discussion that follows. With this in mind, let us now explore more specific aspects of interpersonal attraction.

9.1b Our Evolutionary Heritage and Biology Influence Our Belongingness Needs.

social exchange theory
The theory that we seek out and maintain those relationships in which the rewards exceed the costs

When our need to belong is unfulfilled due to social exclusion or rejection, we often react with increased stress, anxiety, anger, jealousy, sadness, and decreased physical health (DeWall et al., 2011a; Gere & MacDonald, 2010). The popularity of rejection-based television shows such as *Big Brother* and *Dancing with the Stars* is substantially based on the importance of belongingness and our fascination with how others handle rejection.

If you are a fan of reality TV shows such as American Idol *or* Dancing with the Stars, *do you think your fascination is at least partly based on the human need to belong and the corresponding fear of being rejected?*

As discussed in Chapter 7 (section 7.2e), human brain-imaging studies indicate that the social pain we experience following rejection is neurologically similar to the affective distress associated with physical pain, with both originating in the brain's anterior cingulate cortex in the frontal lobes (Eisenberger, 2011). Neuroscientists contend that the pain experienced following both social rejection and physical injury is your brain's attempt to send a warning signal that your survival is being threatened (Taylor & Gonzaga, 2007).

Evolutionary psychologists suggest that during the course of primate evolution, the social attachment "alarm" system came under the control of the same brain area involved in pain detection because this promoted the goal of social connectedness. In other words, our tendency to seek out others, to make friends, and to form enduring close relationships seems to be an inherited trait that has helped us survive and reproduce.

The strength of the need to belong is also associated with central nervous system arousability and brain activity related to the experience of positive and negative emotions. *Arousability* is the habitual degree to which stimulation produces arousal of the central nervous system (Stelmack & Geen, 1992). Research inspired by Hans Eysenck's (1990) work on introversion and extroversion suggests that introverts have inherited a nervous system that operates at a higher level of arousal than extroverts. For example, brain-imaging studies suggest that the anterior cingulate cortex—the brain's danger and pain alarm system—is more active among introverts than extroverts (Johnson et al., 1999). Because of this higher arousability, introverts avoid a great deal of social interaction and situational change in order to keep their arousal from reaching uncomfortable levels.

Similar patterns of hypersensitivity to stimuli and overstimulation are also associated with shyness, a personality characteristic related to introversion (Aron et al., 2001). Extroverts have the opposite problem. Because their nervous system normally operates at a relatively low level of arousal, they seek out situations that stimulate them (Depue & Collins, 1999). For instance, while extroverted students prefer studying in relatively noisy settings where they can socialize with others, introverted students prefer studying in quiet, socially isolated settings (Campbell & Hawley, 1982). Socially active extroverts not only choose to perform tasks in noisy settings but actually perform better in such settings (Beauducel et al., 2006; Geen, 1984).

Our affiliation desires are associated with heightened central nervous system activity. Do introverts and extroverts respond differently to such heightened arousal?

Beyond arousability, extroverts appear to experience greater activation of dopamine pathways in the brain associated with reward and positive affect than introverts (Lucas et al., 2000). Further, when introverts and extroverts are shown positive images (for example, puppies, a happy couple, or sunsets), extroverts experience greater activation of brain areas that control emotion, namely the frontal cortex and the amygdala (Canli et al., 2001). This research suggests that introversion and extroversion are associated with distinct patterns of brain activity, and that the experience of positive affect may be a primary feature of extroversion. Overall, it appears that each of us is born with a nervous system that causes us to have varying degrees of tolerance for the stimulation resulting from social interaction, which may influence the emotions we experience in such settings. It is this biological difference that significantly shapes our affiliation desires.

9.1c Socialization Shapes Our Belongingness Needs.

Although we have inborn belongingness needs, our cultural experiences further shape and direct these tendencies. For instance, Geert Hofstede's (1980) study of 22 countries found a positive relationship ($r = .46$) between a culture's degree of individualism and its citizens' belongingness needs; the more individualist cultures had higher needs for belonging. In explaining this finding, Hofstede stated that in individualist cultures, people are generally expected to individually develop their own relationships and to do so in many varied social settings. Because they develop social ties with people in various social groups, their relationships may be numerous, but they are not particularly intimate.

> "I'll do my thing and you do yours. If two people find each other—it's beautiful. If not, it can't be helped."
>
> —An individualist "prayer" by Fritz Perls, psychotherapist, 1893–1970

This affiliative, yet relatively nonintimate approach to social relationships typifies our own culture. Individualist Americans have numerous relationships that are marked by friendliness, fairness, and informality, but relatively few develop into deep and lasting friendships (Miller et al., 2017; Stewart & Bennett, 1991). Whereas many Americans tend to restrict friendship to an area of common interest, collectivist Russians expect to form deep bonds with their friends and to have these intimate friendships extend over many years (Glenn, 1966). As Harry Triandis observed in his analysis of these possible cross-cultural belongingness differences:

> People in individualist cultures often have greater skills in entering and leaving new social groups. They make "friends" easily, but by "friends" they mean nonintimate acquaintances. People in collectivist cultures have fewer skills in making new "friends" but "friend" in their case implies a life-long intimate relationship with many obligations. So the quality of the friendships is different. This difference in quality may complicate our understanding of the construct of collectivism, since people in individualistic cultures are likely to *appear* more sociable, while intimacy is not a readily observable attribute. (Triandis et al., 1988, p. 325)

Although individualists' social relationships tend to be less intimate than those of collectivists, some individualists cultivate more intimacy than others (Chen et al., 2006). In North America, members of many ethnic and religious groups are taught to think of themselves as *interdependent* with close others and as defined by their social relationships (Oved, 1988).

In terms of gender, girls are also more likely than boys to be raised to think, act, and define themselves in ways that emphasize their emotional connectedness to other individuals (Cross & Madson, 1997; Yang & Girgus, 2019). This more socially connected *relational self* can be contrasted with the more solitary *independent* self typically taught

(Shutterstock)

Women tend to remember events, important conversations, and even what casual acquaintances look like more so than men. What does this suggest about women's and men's emotional connectedness to others?

to boys, which conceives of the person as independent and less interested in cultivating emotional relationships (see Chapter 3, section 3.2b).

A number of studies find that people with a relational self-concept are more committed to and involved in their social relationships, self-disclose more personal information to friends, and are more likely to consider the needs of others when making decisions than those who have a more independent self-concept (Gore & Cross, 2006; Mattingly et al., 2011). Susan Cross and her coworkers (2002) have also found that people who primarily define themselves in terms of close personal relationships (high RISCs) have a much richer network of cognitive associations in memory for relationship-oriented terms than people who are less likely to think of themselves in this manner. One consequence of this different way of defining the self is that high relational individuals have better memories for relational events than low relational persons. This might explain why women are more likely than men to remember birthdays, anniversaries, who said what during important conversations with friends or loved ones, and even what casual acquaintances sound and look like (Schmid Mast & Hall, 2006; Ross & Holmberg, 1993). Before reading further, complete *Self/Social Connection Exercise 9.1*, which contains the *Relational-Interdependent Self-Construal (RISC) Scale* developed by Cross and her colleagues (2000).

Self/Social Connection Exercise 9.1

How Important Are Your Close Relationships in Defining You?

The Relational-Interdependent Self-Construal (RISC) Scale

To what degree do you define yourself in terms of your close relationships with others? In other words, to what degree are your friendships and other close relationships an important aspect of your self-concept? The Relational-Interdependent Self-Construal Scale (Cross et al., 2000) measures your relational interdependence.

Instructions

Below is a series of statements concerning men and women and their relationships in contemporary society. Please indicate the extent to which you agree or disagree with each of these statements using the following scale:

Strongly disagree   1   2   3   4   5   6   7   Strongly agree

1. My close relationships are an important reflection of who I am.
2. When I feel very close to someone, it often feels to me like that person is an important part of who I am.
3. I usually feel a strong sense of pride when someone close to me has an important accomplishment.
4. I think one of the most important parts of who I am can be captured by looking at my close friends and understanding who they are.
5. When I think of myself, I often think of my close friends or family also.
6. If a person hurts someone close to me, I feel personally hurt as well.
7. In general, my close relationships are an important part of my self-image.
8. Overall, my close relationships have very little to do with how I feel about myself.*
9. My close relationships are unimportant to my sense of what kind of person I am.*
10. My sense of pride comes from knowing who I have as close friends.
11. When I establish a close friendship with someone, I usually develop a strong sense of identification with that person.

(continues)

(Self/Social Connection Exercise 9.1 *continued*)

Directions for Scoring

Two of the Relational-Interdependent Self-Construal (RISC) Scale items are reverse-scored; that is, for these items, a lower rating actually indicates a higher level of relational interdependence. Before summing the items for a total score, recode those with an asterisk ("*") so that 1 = 7, 2 = 6, 3 = 5, 5 = 3, 6 = 2, and 7 = 1

When Cross and her colleagues (2000) developed the RISC, the mean score for 2,330 female college students was about 57, whereas the average score for 1,819 male college students was about 53—indicating significant differences between women and men. Higher scores indicate greater interest in developing close, committed social relationships.

One important thing to keep in mind in interpreting these findings and your own RISC score is that your sex does not necessarily determine your gender beliefs and expectations (Hyde, 2005). There are many men who score considerably higher on the RISC than the average woman; likewise, there are many women who score considerably lower than the average man. In other words, many men construct a relational self-concept and many women develop an independent self-concept. However, despite this qualifier, there are differences in the way women and men define themselves, with women generally having a greater sense of relational interdependence than men.

Based on this brief overview of possible influences on belongingness needs, we can tentatively conclude that the need to belong is an important defining characteristic of our species; yet individuals differ in the expression of this need. For some, our optimal arousal level is fairly high, and we seek a great deal of social and nonsocial stimulation. For others, our optimal arousal level is relatively low, and we live our lives in a more socially introverted fashion. Within our pursuit of social relationships, we also differ in the degree of emotional connectedness we seek; and our culture substantially shapes this individual difference in seeking interdependence.

Section Summary

- Two basic reasons for interpersonal attraction are social comparison and social exchange:

    In social comparison, we seek out similar others for comparison purposes due to our need to have an accurate self- and world-view.

    In social exchange, we seek out others because of the social rewards exchanged in such interactions, and we maintain the relationships if the rewards exceed the costs.

- Belongingness desires are influenced by the following:

    evolutionary heritage

    biological arousability and other neural activity

    culture and gender

9.2 Characteristics of the Situation and Attraction

Individual differences can foster social contact or withdrawal, but a number of situational factors also can trigger belongingness needs and interpersonal attraction. In the following sections, we consider two of the more important situational factors: proximity and anxiety.

9.2a Close Proximity Fosters Liking.

One of the most powerful factors in determining whether you become friends with other people is their sheer *proximity* to you (Back et al., 2008). Is this one of the reasons why you were initially attracted to your best friend? Chances are, most of your friends live in close proximity to you, or at least did so in the past.

Leon Festinger, Stanley Schachter, and Kurt Back (1950) conducted one of the earlier and better studies of how proximity influences social relationships when they investigated the development of friendships in married graduate student housing at the Massachusetts Institute of Technology. Following World War II, the university had randomly assigned these student families to available apartments in 17 different buildings; therefore, virtually none of the residents knew one another prior to moving in. When residents were asked to name their three closest friends in the housing units, physical proximity was the single most important determinant of friendship choices. Not only did about two-thirds of the listed friends reside in the same building as those who nominated them but about two-thirds also lived on the same floor. Further, 41%

We often grow to like our neighbors. How might the mere exposure effect explain why proximity fosters liking?

(Shutterstock)

of next-door neighbors were chosen, compared with only 22% of those living two doors away and 10% of those at the end of the hall (see Figure 9.1). Similar proximity effects have been found in urban housing projects for the elderly (Nahemow & Lawton, 1975), in freshmen college dormitories (Priest & Sawyer, 1967), in office work environments (Conrath, 1973), and even in classroom settings (Segal, 1974). In the latter study, police academy trainees who were assigned classroom seats based on the alphabetical order of their last names made friends with those who sat adjacent to them.

For you romantics, there is even evidence that proximity can affect intimate relationships. In an early sociological study, James Bossard (1932) plotted the residences of each applicant on 5,000 marriage licenses in Philadelphia and found a clear relation between proximity and love. Couples were more likely to get married the closer they lived to each other. This finding was replicated in later research as well (Ramsoy, 1966).

At least part of the reason close proximity fosters liking is that it often leads to more frequent exposure and increased familiarity (Reis et al., 2011). As discussed in Chapter 5 (section 5.2a), Robert Zajonc's (1968) *mere exposure hypothesis* proposes that repeated exposure to something or someone is sufficient, by itself, to increase attraction. The mere exposure effect also helps in explaining why you can become attracted to someone through the internet's electronic proximity (Bargh & McKenna, 2004). The increased use of electronic mail and internet chat rooms provides people with the opportunity to be "virtually close" to others without ever physically meeting.

FIGURE 9.1	Proximity and Friendship Development

This schematic diagram of an apartment building in the Festinger et al. (1950) study shows the two floors containing five apartments each, connected by two staircases. Within each floor, people were more likely to be nominated as close friends if they lived in the middle apartments on their floors (apartments 3 and 8) rather than in the end apartments. Further, those who lived in the first-floor apartments near the staircases (apartments 1 and 5) were nominated more than those living farther away from the stairs. The reason for this effect was that the residents living near the staircase had less "functional distance" from others in the building; people were more likely to bump into them as they came and went during the day. If you live—or have lived—in an apartment complex, does this pattern of results mirror your own friendship patterns?

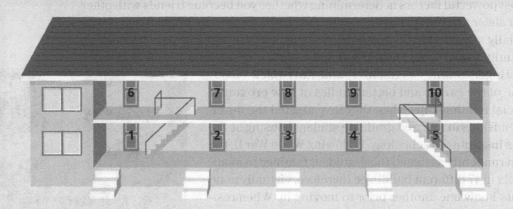

Adapted from: *Social Pressures in Informal Groups: A Study of a Housing Community,*
by L. Festinger et al., 1950, New York, NY: Harper.

Based on the studies discussed in this section, you might think we have stumbled on a solution to the anger and violence in our world; move enemies next door to one another, and soon they will be friends! Before you act on this newfound belief, let's consider one last study. Ebbe Ebbesen and his colleagues (1976) found that residents in a California condominium complex not only established most of their friendships with people who lived in the same housing units but also developed most of their enemies close by as well. Was proximity one of the contributing factors in the development of your own "bad relationship" listed earlier? Ebbesen explains this effect by stating that those who live closer to you are better able to spoil your happiness and peace of mind by having loud parties late at night, throwing trash on your lawn, and just generally getting on your nerves than those living farther away. Thus, although proximity typically leads to liking, the lamb lying down next to the lion is not likely to develop anything that could be called a friendship.

9.2b Our Affiliation Desires Increase with Anxiety.

Although individuals differ in their need to belong, external events can motivate people to seek out others. For example, when Americans first learned about the terrorist attacks on New York City and Washington, DC, on September 11, 2001, most responded with anxiety, grief, and uncertainty, which motivated them to seek the companionship of others who were similarly affected by this tragedy (Mehl & Pennebaker, 2003). How can social psychological research and theory help us understand our need for others during such times of anxiety and crisis? Does misery love company?

Schachter's Anxiety Research

In the late 1950s, Stanley Schachter attempted to answer this question by bringing female college students into the laboratory and creating a stressful event. In his initial study, Schachter (1959) introduced himself to the women as "Dr. Gregor Zilstein" of the Neurology and Psychiatry Department. He told them that they would receive a series of electrical shocks as part of an experiment on their physiological effects. In the "high-anxiety" condition, participants were told that the shocks would be quite painful but would cause no permanent damage. In the "low-anxiety" condition, they were led to believe that the shocks were virtually painless, no worse than a little tickle. In actuality, no shocks were ever delivered—the intent was merely to cause participants to believe that they soon would be receiving these shocks.

After hearing this information, the women were told there would be a 10-minute delay while the equipment was set up. They could spend this time waiting either in a room alone or in a room with another participant in the study. Their stated preference was the dependent variable. As soon as participants stated their preference, they were told the true purpose of the study. As Figure 9.2 shows, 63% of those in the high-anxiety condition chose to wait with others, while only 33% of the women in the low-anxiety condition did so. Thus, it appears that high anxiety caused people to seek out others. Misery does indeed appear to love company.

FIGURE 9.2   Desire to Affiliate Among High- and Low-Anxiety Individuals

Schachter (1959) found that research participants' desire to be with others depended on their level of anxiety and the similarity of their potential "waiting mates." His findings indicated that when anxious or fearful, people desire to affiliate with others who are experiencing similar feelings. Based on these findings, how would you amend the old folk saying "misery loves company" to better reflect how we react to anxious situations?

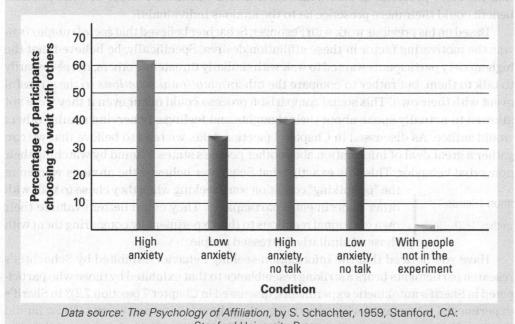

Data source: The Psychology of Affiliation, by S. Schachter, 1959, Stanford, CA: Stanford University Press.

Why did they desire affiliation? Perhaps others serve as a *social distraction* to anxious individuals, temporarily taking their minds off their anxiety. If this were the case, then anyone would be an acceptable "waiting mate" for these anxious individuals. To test this hypothesis, Schachter (1959) conducted a follow-up study identical to the first experiment except for one important variation: Some of the high-anxiety participants were told they could wait either alone or with other students who weren't in the experiment but who were in the building to see their advisers. If anxious people merely want to be around others—regardless of who they are—then these nonanxious students would be acceptable "waiting mates."

Results did not support this reasoning: High-anxiety participants overwhelmingly wanted to wait with others undergoing the same stress, and they were not interested in waiting with students who were not in the experiment (see Figure 9.2). Schachter somewhat facetiously asserted that these findings added a new wrinkle to the old "misery loves company" proverb—misery appears to love only *miserable* company. Put another way, when anxious or fearful, people desire to affiliate with others who are experiencing similar feelings. Why?

As you might have guessed, Schachter (1959) conducted a third experiment to determine whether anxious participants were motivated to seek out similarly anxious others in order to share their thoughts about the impending event, or whether there was something more basic about this affiliation desire. If they sought out others in order to verbally discuss and compare information, then they shouldn't bother seeking out this company if it was made clear that such information exchange wasn't allowed. Schachter created such a scenario by having "Dr. Zilstein" inform certain high-anxiety participants that they could choose to wait with other participants, but they would not be allowed to discuss the upcoming experiment while in their presence. Even with these restrictions on information exchange, high-anxiety participants exhibited a greater desire to wait with others experiencing the same anxiety-producing event than did those in the low-anxiety condition (again, refer to Figure 9.2). Thus, in addition to a specific desire to discuss their anxiety with others who were similarly anxious, these findings suggest that the *mere* presence of others also motivates the affiliative need. Of what possible benefit could their mere presence be to the anxious individuals?

Based on his previous work with Festinger, Schachter believed that *social comparison* was the motivating factor in these affiliation desires. Specifically, he believed that the high-anxiety participants wanted to wait with similarly threatened others, not necessarily to talk to them, but rather to compare the others' *emotional reactions* to the stressful event with their own. This social comparison process could occur even if they were not allowed to actually speak about their thoughts and feelings; observing similar others would suffice. As discussed in Chapter 4 (section 4.3a), we tend to believe that we can gather a great deal of information about other people's states of mind by watching their nonverbal behavior. This was exactly what Schachter believed the anxious women in the "no-talking" condition were seeking when they chose to wait with other experimental participants. They could better evaluate their own emotional reactions to this experiment by comparing them with those of similarly distressed people.

> "Common danger makes common friends."
>
> —Zora Neale Hurston, US author, 1891–1960

Have you noticed that the information-seeking behavior exhibited by Schachter's research participants bears a striking resemblance to that exhibited by those who participated in Sherif's autokinetic experiments, discussed in Chapter 7 (section 7.2)? In Sherif's experiments, when faced with uncertainty about how to interpret events ("How far did the dot of light move?"), people became dependent on others for information. Likewise, in Schachter's research, when people faced an uncertain future ("How worried should I be about the impending, painful electrical shocks?"), they too looked toward those who might help them evaluate their circumstances. Although Sherif's research demonstrated that *information dependence* makes us more susceptible to others' influence, Schachter's work indicates that it also causes us to be drawn toward others in the first place to gather the necessary information to hopefully make sound social judgments. In this regard, Schachter's anxiety research marked the first major extension of social comparison theory. Subsequent research has largely supported Schachter's general conclusion that stress increases the desire to affiliate (Rofé, 1984; Taylor et al., 2003).

Limitations and Wrinkles in the Anxiety-Affiliation Effect

One limitation to this stress-induced affiliation response has to do with people who are faced with an upcoming embarrassing event. When college students were told that they would soon be expected to suck on large nipples and baby pacifiers in the presence of an experimenter (as part of a study related to Freud's "oral stage of psychosexual development"), most preferred to wait alone for this embarrassing event to start (Sarnoff & Zimbardo, 1961). Further, if they did choose to affiliate, they preferred to do so with people who were not going to be in the same embarrassing experiment (Firestone et al., 1973). Under these circumstances, the type of social dependence most likely influencing participants' behavior was not information dependence but outcome dependence. Participants avoided social contact because they did not want anyone to know that they were about to engage in a series of infantile acts. For these individuals, affiliation was expected to increase—not decrease—the negative impact of the stressful situation. They chose to affiliate only when others had no knowledge of their impending embarrassment.

Besides this limitation to the anxiety-affiliation effect, there also is a "wrinkle" involved in this social comparison process. Although Schachter believed that anxious people affiliate with others who are similarly anxious in order to compare emotional states, this is not always so. Sometimes, when anticipating a fearful event, people prefer not to be around those who are also fearful. Instead, they prefer someone who has already experienced the fearful event and who can tell them something about it. In such instances, people are seeking *cognitive clarity*—they are experiencing a desire to obtain information from others regarding the nature and dangerousness of the threat (Shaver & Klinnert, 1982). For example, a field study (Kulik & Mahler, 1989) found that the vast majority of hospital patients about to undergo coronary bypass surgery preferred to room with someone who had already undergone the procedure rather than with someone like them who had not yet had surgery (78% versus 22%). Subsequent research suggests that the cognitive clarity gained from having a postoperative heart patient as a roommate not only does the best job lowering anxiety but also results in faster recovery from surgery (Kulik et al., 1996). These findings and others like them suggest that our desire to affiliate when anxious is not only based on a need to compare our emotional state with others but is also fueled by our need to appraise the stressful situation itself so that we have better cognitive clarity; this cognitive clarity provides us with both psychological and physical benefits (Van der Zee et al., 1998).

Immediately following the New York and Washington, DC, terrorist attacks on 9/11, people around the country were highly anxious and uncertain about what was happening. How do you think information dependence and outcome dependence shaped their thoughts, feelings, and behavior during this time?

Section Summary

- Two situational factors that influence interpersonal attraction are:
  proximity: We form emotional bonds with those who are physically (or virtually) close to us.
  anxiety-inducing events: The desire for social comparison attracts us to similarly anxious others.
- Affiliation provides opportunities for cognitive clarity.
- Dyadic interactions satisfy belongingness needs more than large group gatherings.

9.3 Characteristics of Others and Attraction

Reconsider your list of 10 reasons why you were attracted to your best friend. What did you list as reasons you wanted to form a relationship with that person? Did you consider their appearance? How about their personality? Did they have similar interests and values to your own? Perhaps you considered their opinion of you—did they seem to like you? As outlined in the following sections, each of these factors plays a role in whether we form relationships with others.

9.3a We Are Drawn Toward the Physically Attractive.

In all cultures, people respond favorably to those who are physically attractive. Yet, are beautiful people better than average people in their personalities or mental health?

physical attractiveness stereotype
The belief that physically attractive individuals possess socially desirable personality traits and lead happier lives than less attractive persons

Do you recall the negative comments made about short men in our chapter-opening story? Despite the frequently quoted folk saying that "you can't judge a book by its cover," people tend to believe that they know a good deal about others based on their "external packaging." Unfortunately for short men, in many cultures their physical appeal is much less than that of tall men (Brewer & Riley, 2009). According to evolutionary theorists, this difference in appeal is because taller men are stronger than their shorter male counterparts; thus, they typically achieve greater social power and status in their groups (Pawtowski, 2012). An example of the warm glow that tall men have received over the centuries (compared to the cold shoulder that short men often experience) is the first-century judgment by the Roman historian Tacitus that male height indicated not only physical strength but also moral virtue. In this chapter section, we will review research indicating that physical qualities associated with physical attractiveness provide advantages to those who possess them. Another way to describe this appeal is that we have a very favorable *implicit personality theory* for physical attractiveness (see Chapter 4, section 4.3e). The appeal of physical attractiveness can even be observed in brain-scan studies: When people are shown photos of attractive faces, they have greater activation in brain areas associated with more positive emotions compared to when they are shown photos of unattractive faces (Principe & Langlois, 2011).

What Is Beautiful Is Good

In one of the first studies of the **physical attractiveness stereotype**, Karen Dion, Ellen Berscheid, and Elaine (Walster) Hatfield (1972) asked college students to look at pictures of men and women who were good-looking, average, or homely—and to then evaluate their personalities. Results indicated that students tended to assume that physically attractive persons possessed a host of socially desirable personality traits relative to those who were unattractive.

This beauty-goodness effect has also been documented in Hollywood movies. Steven Smith and his coworkers (1999) asked people to watch the 100 most popular movies between 1940 and 1990 and to evaluate the movies' main characters. Consistent with the physical attractiveness stereotype, beautiful and handsome characters were significantly more likely to be portrayed as virtuous, romantically active, and successful than their less attractive counterparts. A similar beauty-goodness effect has been documented in animated Disney movies, where, for example, the heroic prince and virtuous princess are attractive, but the wicked witch and evil giant are ugly (Bazzini et al., 2010). Over the past 35 years, many researchers have examined this stereotype; and two separate meta-analyses of these studies reveal that physically attractive people are perceived to be more sociable, successful, happy, dominant, sexually warm, mentally healthy, intelligent, and socially skilled than those who are unattractive (Eagly et al., 1991; Feingold 1992b). Additional research indicates that these positive associations between attractiveness and socially desirable traits happen automatically and without conscious awareness (Mello & Garcia-Marques, 2018). The positive glow generated by physical attractiveness is not reserved solely for adults. Attractive infants are perceived as more likable, sociable, competent, and easier to care for than unattractive babies (Casey & Ritter, 1996; Karraker & Stern, 1990). In elementary school, cute children are more popular with their peers than unattractive children (Vaughn & Langlois, 1983).

Although these findings are based solely on samples from individualist cultures, the physical attractiveness stereotype also occurs in collectivist cultures; its impact is typically less influential in shaping life outcomes, however, because interpersonal relationships are based more on kinship or social arrangements than on personal choice (Anderson et al., 2008). Also, the content of the physical attractiveness stereotype is a bit different in collectivist cultures (Chen et al., 1997). For example, Ladd Wheeler and Youngmee Kim (1997) found that, as in individualist cultures, physically attractive Koreans are perceived to be more sexually warm, mentally healthy, intelligent, and socially skilled than unattractive Koreans. However, consistent with the greater emphasis on harmonious relationships in collectivist cultures, physically attractive Koreans are also assumed to have higher integrity and to be more concerned for others than those who are physically unattractive. These findings suggest that although the physical attractiveness stereotype appears to be universal, its actual content is shaped by cultural values.

Can physical attractiveness impact earning potential and career success in adulthood? Field and laboratory studies conducted in both individualist and collectivist cultures indicate that physical attractiveness does have a moderate impact on a variety of job-related outcomes, including hiring, termination, salary, and promotion decisions (Commisso & Finkelstein, 2012; Johnson et al., 2010). For example, in a field study conducted at five different restaurants, Matt Parrett (2015) examined how server physical attractiveness influenced customers' tipping behavior. As they were leaving the restaurant, customers were asked to complete a survey indicating, among other things, their satisfaction with the service, the amount of their bill and tip, and their evaluation of the server's attractiveness. After controlling for service satisfaction, Parrett found that both attractive male and female servers earned significantly higher tips than their unattractive counterparts; over the course of a year, this difference would yield a higher annual wage of $1,261. Interestingly, female customers exhibited a larger "beauty bias" in their tipping than did male customers.

> "Beauty is power."
>
> —Arab proverb

Is the Attractiveness Stereotype Accurate?

Based on our analysis thus far, it is clear that we tend to give beautiful people high marks on many socially desirable personality traits and, as a result, give them high social exchange value. But do the beautiful really have more desirable personalities? Overall, the answer is clearly no. Alan Feingold (1992b) conducted a meta-analysis of more than 90 studies that investigated whether physically attractive and physically unattractive people actually differed in their basic personality traits. His analysis indicated no significant relationships between physical attractiveness and such traits as intelligence, dominance, self-esteem, and mental health. In another study, Sean Talamas and colleagues (2016) found that, while ratings of students' physical attractiveness was not significantly correlated with their actual academic performance, it was strongly correlated with others' *perceptions* of both their intelligence ($r = .81$) and academic performance ($r = .74$), which indicates a strong beauty bias. Thus, even though we think good-looking people are more intelligent, dominant, happy, and mentally healthy than unattractive people, this is not really the case.

Feingold (1992b) did discover, however, that good-looking people do tend to be less socially anxious, more socially skilled, and less lonesome than those who are unattractive; this has been confirmed in other studies (Meier et al., 2010). One likely reason good-looking individuals are more at ease socially is that people generally seek out their company and respond favorably to them. As a result of this history of rewarding social encounters, the physically attractive have an increased sense of personal control when interacting with others (Diener et al., 1995).

Together, these findings suggest that there is a self-fulfilling prophecy involved in the physical attractiveness stereotype. As discussed in Chapter 1 (section 1.1c), the self-fulfilling prophecy is the process by which someone's beliefs about another person can cause that person to behave in a manner that confirms those expectations. The apparent reason physically attractive people tend to be socially poised and confident is that those who interact with them convey the clear impression that they truly are very interesting and sociable individuals.

When people think that the individuals they are interacting with are physically attractive, they tend to act more outgoing and sociable toward them—which, in turn, results in those individuals acting more warm, confident, animated, and attractive (Andersen & Bem, 1981; Snyder et al., 1977). How do these findings relate to one of the basic messages of social psychology? Further, how can you generalize these findings beyond physical attractiveness effects to create a more pleasant and rewarding social world for yourself?

9.3b   There Are Gender-Based Attractiveness Standards.

Thus far, our examination of the research evidence suggests that we are drawn to physically attractive people like bees to honey. Yet what makes a person physically attractive? Is there a universal standard that can be identified and measured?

Cross-cultural studies indicate that men value physical attractiveness in a partner—however defined—more than women do (Fales et al., 2016; Townsend & Wasserman, 1997). Similarly, physical attractiveness is an important quality for gay men, and is a less important feature for lesbians (Fawkner & McMurray, 2002; Harrison & Saeed, 1977). This suggests that men, regardless of their sexual orientation, place greater value on the physical appearance of a potential romantic partner than do either lesbians or heterosexual women. However, this gender difference is much stronger when people are contemplating long-term romantic relationships rather than casual, short-term sexual encounters or when first meeting someone. In initial encounters or when considering a one-night stand, women—like men—tend to place a high value on physical attractiveness (Bryan et al., 2011; Fletcher et al., 2014).

(Shutterstock)

Cross-culturally, the most desirable female waist-to-hip ratio is 0.7. How is this body-type preference explained by evolutionary psychologists?

Although culture does have an impact on who is judged physically appealing (Langlois et al., 2000; Marcus & Miller, 2003), cross-cultural studies have found some interesting, universal gender-based attractiveness standards. For example, men worldwide are generally attracted to women who have a lower waist-to-hip ratio, meaning that the circumference of their waist is smaller than that of their hips (Furnham et al., 2003; Singh, 1993). The most desirable waist-to-hip ratio appears to be 0.7, so that a desirable woman with a waist of 25 inches would have a 35-inch hip size, or a desirable woman with a 35-inch waist would have 50-inch hips (Streeter & McBurney, 2003). Consistent with these findings are brain-scan studies indicating that men show the most activation in brain reward centers when they are shown naked female bodies with waist-to-hip ratios of 0.7 compared to when they are shown thinner or larger female body shapes (Platek & Singh, 2010). Evolutionary psychologists contend that this 0.7 waist-to-hip ratio is universally perceived as attractive because it is a biologically accurate indicator that the woman is young, fertile, and currently not pregnant (Crandall et al., 2001; Furnham et al., 2002).

Beyond body type, there is also evidence that there are universal standards of *facial attractiveness*. For

> "Besides being young, a desirable sex partner—especially a woman—should also be fat."
>
> —Observations of the seminomadic Siriono Indians of Bolivia, 1946

example, a number of studies indicate that we prefer faces in which the right and left sides are well matched, or *symmetrical* (Burriss et al., 2011; Said & Todorov, 2011). What is so appealing about symmetry? Evolutionary psychologists contend that we prefer facial symmetry because symmetry generally indicates physical health and the lack of genetic defects, which are important attributes for a sexual partner to possess (Henderson & Anglin, 2003; Özener & Fink, 2010).

Besides symmetry influencing attractiveness, studies of people's perceptions of young men and women's individual faces and composite faces (computer-generated "averages" of all the individual faces) indicate that what people judge most attractive

> "No woman can be too slim"
>
> —Wallis Simpson, the Duchess of Windsor, 1896–1986

are faces that represent the average face in the population (Baudouina & Tiberghienb, 2004; Langlois et al., 1994). This tendency to define physical attractiveness according to the "average rule" has been found in many cultures (Jones & Hill, 1993; Sorokowski et al., 2011). Why might we perceive averaged faces as attractive? One likely reason is that averaged faces tend to be very symmetrical (Brown et al., 2008). Another reason averaged faces are more attractive to us than unusual faces has to do with the *mere exposure effect* or familiarity: Averaged faces are more attractive because they are more prototypically face-like; thus, they seem more familiar to us (Hoss et al., 2005; Langlois et al., 1994). Consistent with this hypothesis is research indicating that we are also more attracted to average dogs, fish, birds, and wristwatches (Halberstadt & Rhodes, 2003).

Evolutionary psychologists further contend that, besides symmetry and averageness, youthfulness and maturity figure into facial attractiveness judgments (Cunningham et al., 1990; Valenzano et al., 2006). For example, in a survey of over 10,000 participants from 37 cultures around the world, David Buss (1989) found that men express a preference for women who are younger than themselves and women prefer men slightly older. This gender difference has been confirmed in both a large-scale national sample in the

United States (Sprecher et al., 1994) and in a meta-analysis of 40 different attractiveness studies including both North American and non–North American samples (Feingold, 1992a). In analyzing these findings (see Figure 9.3), social scientists conclude that they reflect a *looks-for-status exchange* in mating relationships (Fletcher et al., 2004; Li et al., 2011). Men are attracted to young women because female youth signifies beauty, and women are attracted to older men because male maturity signifies higher social status. Despite these gender differences in the looks-for-status exchange, both women and men in all cultures still rate kindness and intelligence more highly in a potential mate than either physical attractiveness or earning potential (Buss, 1989).

FIGURE 9.3   Gender Differences in Mate Selection Preferences

Sprecher, Sullivan, and Hatfield (1994) asked more than 1,300 English-speaking and Spanish-speaking Americans who were single and under the age of 35 to consider some possible assets and liabilities in a marriage partner and to indicate their willingness to marry someone possessing each of these characteristics. A score of 1 indicated "not at all," while a score of 7 indicated "very willing." All of the gender comparisons listed below are significant. What do these findings tell us about gender differences in heterosexual mate preferences?

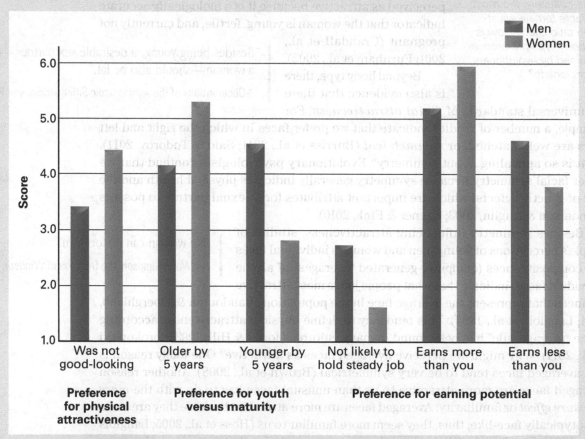

Data source: "Mate Selection Preferences: Gender Differences Examined in a National Sample," by S. Sprecher et al., 1994, *Journal of Personality and Social Psychology, 66*, pp. 1074–1080, American Psychological Association.

In terms of facial features, a number of studies have found that possessing youthful or slightly *immature* facial features (large eyes and thin eyebrows, full lips, small nose and chin) enhances female attractiveness, while possessing *mature* facial characteristics related to social dominance (small eyes, broad forehead, thick eyebrows, thin lips, large jaw) increases the attractiveness of males (Cunningham, 1986; Johnston &

Franklin, 1993). Although additional studies indicate that heterosexual women are also attracted to men with large eyes (an immature feature) and heterosexual men show a preference for women with high cheekbones (a mature feature), male preferences for youthfulness and female preferences for slightly more maturity appear to be the norm (Cunningham et al., 1990; Valenzano et al., 2006).

What are the attributions people make about those with immature facial features? Based on their studies of infant faces, Leslie Zebrowitz and her colleagues contend that immature features signal to people that the observed individual is dependent and helpless—like an infant (Andreoletti et al., 2001; Zebrowitz, 1997). Accompanying these perceptions are attributions that adults with immature features are weaker, less competent, less dominant, and less intelligent than the average adult (Poutvaara et al., 2009). In the workplace, these attributions result in baby-faced applicants being recommended for lower-status jobs than applicants with mature-looking faces (Zebrowitz et al., 1991). Taken as a whole, these findings suggest a double bind that women face in their social lives. When they try to match physical attractiveness standards by using cosmetics to enlarge the appearance of their eyes and lips and make their eyebrows thin, others may perceive them as more beautiful—but also as more weak and helpless.

Do you think this looks-for-status effect is influenced more by biology or by social conditions? The evolutionary perspective contends that what will be valued as desirable and attractive in men and women is that which increases their probability of producing offspring who will carry their genes to the next generation (Kenrick & Trost, 1987). Given the biological fact that women have a shorter time span to reproduce than do men, evolutionary psychologists assume that evolution predisposes men to perceive women who look *young* as being more desirable (that is, more physically attractive) because youth implies high reproductive potential (Alley & Cunningham, 1991). Using this same logic, evolutionary theorists also assume that women will instead favor male traits signifying an ability to provide and protect resources for them and their offspring. Thus, instead of valuing youth in men, women should place more importance on status, ambition, and other signs of *social dominance* (Kenrick & Luce, 2000).

In contrast to this evolutionary explanation, sociocultural theorists maintain that men seek beauty in a woman and women seek power in a man because of the widely different social statuses they have historically held in society (Howard et al., 1987; Zentner & Eagly, 2015). This social-exchange explanation argues that women have historically been excluded from power and are viewed by men as objects of exchange in the social marketplace. Men place a premium on the quality or the beauty of this exchange object, and that is why physical attractiveness is sought in a woman. Because of their historically low status and their restricted ability to socially advance based on their own individual skills, women have been forced to tie their social advancement with the status of their mate. Thus, women seek men who are socially dominant and can be good providers.

Actors Javier Bardem and Jennifer Lawrence were cast as romantic partners in the 2017 film Mother!, despite a 21-year age difference. How do different theories explain this common heterosexual romantic age mismatch?

(Matteo Chinellato / Shutterstock.com)

Which of these perspectives provides the best explanation is currently a hotly debated topic in social psychology. If the sociocultural perspective is correct, the recent social advances made by many women in North American and European countries (higher pay and increased social status) may cause shifts in the attractiveness preferences of both women and men. Women may look for more "beauty" in men, and men may look for more "economic status" in women. In a 41-nation study involving over 12,000 participants, Marcel Zentner and Klaudia Mitura (2012) examined the association between a nation's gender equality and its gender differences in mate preferences. A nation's gender equality was operationally defined by the degree of gender equality in the areas of economics (workforce participation, wage equality), political participation (government representatives), educational attainment (literacy and higher education attainment) and health (life expectancy). The largest gender differences—with men preferring physically attractive partners and women preferring financially resourceful partners—were found in countries that are gender inequitable. Consistent with the sociocultural perspective, gender differences in desired mate characteristics were smaller in the more gender-equitable countries. If future studies continue to provide evidence that mate preferences are indeed changing, this would not necessarily mean that evolutionary forces don't shape perceptions of physical attractiveness. It may simply mean that these inherited tendencies have been overridden by more powerful cultural forces.

9.3c Gender-Based Attractiveness Standards Shape Body Esteem.

Our culture, like many around the world, places a premium on physically attractive women; as a result, women frequently express concerns about being rejected based on their appearance (Park, 2007; Homan et al., 2012). Starting at a very young age—from the Barbie dolls and toy makeup cases with which girls are encouraged to play, to the close attention given to clothing fashion and other bodily adornments—females are taught that their body as an *object* is a significant factor in how others will judge their overall value. The act of treating a person as a mere object of sexual desire is referred to as **sexual objectification**. The pervasiveness of this attention is seen in the messages conveyed across multiple forms of media. In television commercials, magazine advertisements, social media, and music videos, difficult-to-attain standards of female beauty are established, especially relating to weight (Bessenoff & Del Priore, 2007; Karsay et al., 2018).

One consequence of this is that women of all age groups are more aware of and influenced by attractiveness standards than are men, and this heightened focus has a lasting negative impact on their body attitudes, or **body esteem** (Cordero, 2011). Beginning in late childhood and early adolescence, girls not only experience more dissatisfaction with their bodies than boys, they also experience a steady increase in this dissatisfaction over time (Feingold & Mazzella, 1998; Karazsia et al., 2017). By adulthood, negative affect is a pervasive quality of female body esteem, and women are more likely than men to habitually experience what researchers identify as *social physique anxiety*—anxiety about others observing or evaluating their bodies (Szymanski & Henning, 2007). Curiously, women's evaluations of their own bodies tend to be more negative than their perceptions of how others evaluate their bodies—women are their own harshest critics (Dijkstra & Barelds, 2011; Franzoi et al., 2012). The women most likely caught in this hypercritical "beauty trap" are those who are most attentive to cultural beauty standards (Vartanian & Hopkinson, 2010).

Although women generally have more negative body esteem than men, evidence shows that minority women and lesbians feel less pressure than white, heterosexual women to conform to the unrealistic standard of thinness in the larger culture (Franzoi & Chang, 2002; Yean et al., 2013). As a result, they are less concerned about dieting and weight loss—although the differences are not large (Grabe & Hyde, 2006). For example, survey studies find that most women prefer a curvaceous body shape; but more Caucasian American women prefer this ideal to be slender with medium breasts, whereas more African American women prefer this ideal to be curvier with medium breasts and large buttocks (Overstreet et al., 2010).

sexual objectification
The act of treating a person as a mere object of sexual desire

body esteem
A person's attitudes toward his or her body

These somewhat different body shape and size preferences appear to be partly due to the greater value attributed to larger body sizes in minority and lesbian cultures, but they may also be a by-product of a more general tendency for these groups to reject white and heterosexual cultural standards, respectively (Share & Mintz, 2002; Webb et al., 2004). However just because minority heterosexual women appear to have greater body satisfaction than white heterosexual women, this does not mean they are unconcerned about weight issues (Stephens & Few, 2007). In general, they are still more dissatisfied with their bodies—particularly their weight—than are heterosexual minority men (Harris, 1995; Mintz & Kashubeck, 1999). Young-adult lesbians experience similar ambivalent feelings regarding the importance of weight and overall physical appearance (Beren et al., 1997). These findings suggest that although lesbians and minority women may adhere less to the dominant, white heterosexual standard of female thinness, they are not immune to this beauty norm.

In contrast to the way that most women are socialized, men are taught to view their bodies as dynamic instruments of action, and they are judged more positively if they engage in physical activities (Shields et al., 2007). For boys, the ability to perform well in sporting activities is an important contributor to their overall self-esteem (Langlois & Downs, 1980). In adulthood, power and function are important criteria for evaluating the male physical self, and women judge the male body-as-object more positively if it is muscular (Parent & Moradi, 2011). Because greater importance is placed on the body as a functioning unit in the daily experiences of men, they are less likely than women to judge their bodies as a collection of parts (Franzoi, 1995). This more unified view of their own bodies may be one reason male body esteem is more positive than female body esteem (Frederick et al., 2006; Karazsia et al., 2017). One notable exception to this general finding is gay men. Like many heterosexual women, many gay men experience considerable pressure to conform to attractiveness standards that are difficult to attain (Wiseman & Moradi, 2010). This heightened scrutiny of the body as a beauty object undoubtedly accounts for the lower levels of body esteem found in this population (Martins et al., 2007).

> "The pursuit of beauty is much more dangerous nonsense than the pursuit of truth or goodness, because it affords a stronger temptation to the ego."
>
> —Northrop Frye, Canadian literary critic, 1912–1991

Although men generally have more positive body esteem than women, their negative body attitudes are often linked to the large and muscular male body standard, which is the typical way in which men are sexually objectified within our culture (Mulgrew et al., 2013). A survey of American male college students found that over 90% wanted to be more muscular (Frederick et al., 2007). The desire for muscles is not a new phenomenon, but heightened media and cultural attention to this masculine body ideal is playing a role in the increasing trend of male body dissatisfaction (Leit et al., 2001; Oehlhoff et al., 2009). In an attempt to match this hypermuscular male standard, an increasing number of teenage boys and young men are taking anabolic steroids and untested dietary supplements that can cause a variety of health problems (Moradi & Huang, 2008). Before reading further, spend a few minutes completing *Self/Social Connection Exercise 9.2* to gain additional insight into your own body esteem.

Self/Social Connection Exercise 9.2

What Is Your Level of Body Esteem?

The Body Esteem Scale—Revised

Instructions: Below are listed a number of body parts and functions. Please read each item and indicate how you feel about this part or function of your own body, using the following response categories:

1 = Have strong negative feelings

2 = Have moderate negative feelings

3 = Have no feeling one way or the other

4 = Have moderate positive feelings

5 = Have strong positive feelings

1. Body scent	11. Skin condition	21. Appearance of eyes
2. Head hair	12. Biceps	22. Face
3. Hips	13. Weight	23. Physical condition
4. Physical stamina	14. Body build	24. Legs
5. Reflexes	15. Figure/Physique	25. Sex drive
6. Arms	16. Buttocks	26. Appearance of stomach
7. Muscular strength	17. Agility	27. Sex organs
8. Waist	18. Health	28. Physical coordination
9. Energy level	19. Sex activities	
10. Thighs	20. Chest or breasts	

Scoring Instructions and Standards

Over the past four decades, research indicates that body esteem is best understood as multidimensional and gender specific, with three different dimensions emerging for women and men. What this means is that (1) women's and men's body esteem is qualitatively different, and (2) the way that both women and men evaluate their bodies is not "as a whole" but in terms of three distinct, though interrelated dimensions. The BES-R measures three different body esteem dimensions in women and men. To determine your score for each of the subscales for your gender, simply add up your responses for the items corresponding to each body esteem dimension. The subscale items—plus the means and standard deviations—are listed below. How do you suppose your own body esteem has been influenced by your culture's physical attractiveness standards?

Women

Sexual attractiveness: body scent, buttocks, chest or breasts, appearance of eyes, sex drive, sex activities, face, head hair, skin condition ($M = 32.67$, $SD = 5.18$)

Weight concern: waist, thighs, body build, hips, legs, figure or physique, appearance of stomach, weight ($M = 23.31$, $SD = 6.95$)

Physical condition: physical stamina, muscular strength, energy level, physical coordination, health, physical condition ($M = 20.56$, $SD = 4.67$)

Men

Sexual attractiveness: body scent, appearance of eyes, sex drive, sex organs, sex activities, face, head hair, skin condition ($M = 28.79$, $SD = 4.97$)

Upper body strength: muscular strength, biceps, body build, arms, chest or breasts (M = 16.63, SD = 4.46)

Physical condition: physical stamina, reflexes, energy level, physical coordination, agility, figure or physique, appearance of stomach, health, physical condition, weight (M = 35.47, SD = 7.76)

Reprinted by permission from Springer Nature, "Revising the Body Esteem Scale with a US College Student Sample: Evaluation, Validation and Uses for the BES-R," by K. Frost, S. Franzoi, D. Oswald, S. Shields, 2018, *Sex Roles, 78*(1–2), pp. 1–17. Copyright © 2018.

9.3d Social Comparison Influences Attractiveness Judgments.

Sometimes factors other than one's actual appearance influence physical attractiveness judgments. In fact, sometimes it is the attractiveness of others that determines how we ourselves are judged. In general, we tend to be judged more attractive after others have seen an unattractive same-sex person and less attractive when others have just seen someone who is very good-looking (Kenrick et al., 1989; Wedell et al., 1987). Such social comparison effects can also shape how we evaluate ourselves. In research that Jonathan Brown and his colleagues (1992) conducted, female undergraduates evaluated their own physical attractiveness after being exposed to either an attractive or an unattractive man or woman. Results indicated that participants' perceptions of their own beauty were greater after they were exposed to unattractive female targets than after they were exposed to attractive female targets (refer to Figure 9.4). Male targets did not influence the women's self-perceptions. Not surprisingly, this social comparison process has more of an effect on the self-evaluations of those of us who place a high importance on our physical appearance (Patrick et al., 2004). Given the fact that very attractive same-sex persons make most of us feel less attractive by comparison, it is also not surprising that some of us are uncomfortable—and even avoid—interacting with these "perfect 10s." Such avoidance of attractive same-sex persons is most likely among those of us who are relatively insecure about our appearance (Agthe et al., 2014).

> "First man: 'How's your wife?' Second man: 'Compared to what?'"
>
> —Vaudeville joke

Our tendency to compare our physical appearance to others is likely to happen in all areas of our social world (Safronova, 2019). For example, Markia Tiggemann and her colleagues (2018) showed 220 female college students a set of Instagram photos of women who either had the "thin ideal" body or an average-sized body. Women who viewed the "thin ideal" photographs reported more body dissatisfaction than those who saw the average body photographs. Similar results have been found for men (Tamplin et al., 2018).

If you feel less positive about your physical appearance after spending time browsing social media sites, you are in good company. One notable feature of Instagram and other social media sites is that when people post photographs, they often carefully select their best images, edit them, and use filters to further maximize their attractiveness. Thus, the images posted not only are the person's "best" photographs, they are idealized images of the person. It is not surprising then that frequent social media use is associated with body dissatisfaction (Tamplin et al., 2018). However, you can minimize the negative effects of viewing these social media sites if you develop "social media literacy" by understanding the underlying motives people have for posting such idealized images and by further recognizing that these photographs may well have been edited to make these individuals appear to more closely match their culture's beauty standards.

FIGURE 9.4   Self-Ratings of Attractiveness Following Exposure to Attractive and Unattractive Same-Sex and Other-Sex Individuals

When women evaluated their own physical attractiveness after being exposed to either an attractive or unattractive man or woman, their perceptions of their own beauty were greater after they were exposed to unattractive female targets than after they were exposed to attractive female targets. Male targets' attractiveness did not influence the women's self-perceptions. What do these findings tell us about how social comparison influences self-perceptions of attractiveness?

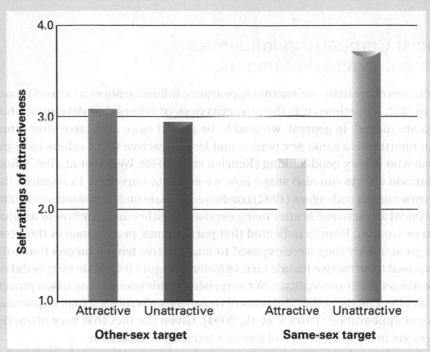

Data source: "When Gulliver Travels: Social Context, Psychological Closeness, and Self-Appraisals," by J.D. Brown et al, 1992, *Journal of Personality and Social Psychology, 62*(5), p. 719.

9.3e   Birds of a Feather Really Do Flock Together.

Recall again the things that first attracted you to your best friend or romantic partner. Did you list any of their hobbies or interests that you both have in common? How similar are the two of you in age; personality; social class standing; level of education; and political, social, or religious beliefs? Would you say this person is more similar to you than different? Also, in new surroundings, what sort of people do you typically seek out?

"To like and dislike the same things, that is indeed true friendship."

—Gaius Crispus, Roman historian and politician, 86–34 BCE

Social psychological research generally indicates that we are attracted to those who are similar to us in particular characteristics, a tendency known as the **matching hypothesis** (Lee et al., 2009; Selfhout et al., 2009). Matching characteristics is a common practice in forming many different types of social relationships. For example, when seeking romantic partners on a popular online dating site, people often seek to match themselves with others based on self-worth, physical attractiveness, and popularity (Taylor et al., 2011). We also tend to have similar personalities to our friends and romantic partners (Youyou et al., 2017). In general, this desire to seek similarity is an important factor in the earliest stages of a relationship and is often what motivates us to initiate the relationship in the first place (Bahns et al., 2017; Selfhout et al., 2009).

matching hypothesis
The proposition that people are attracted to others who are similar to them in particular characteristics

In one of the first tests of the matching hypothesis, Theodore Newcomb (1961) conducted a longitudinal study of friendship development in an all-male boardinghouse. He found that the residents tended to like other residents who were similar to them in age and family background, as well as in social attitudes. In later laboratory studies, Donn Byrne and his colleagues accelerated the getting-acquainted process by having participants complete attitude questionnaires and later "introducing" them to another person by having them read his or her responses to a similar questionnaire (Byrne & Nelson, 1965; Schöneman et al., 1977). As you might have already guessed, the researchers had actually filled out the questionnaire so that the answers were either similar or dissimilar to the participants' own attitudinal responses. As you can see from Figure 9.5, participants expressed much stronger liking when they thought they shared a greater percentage of similar attitudes with the individual. This finding is important because it suggests that the *proportion* of similar attitudes is more important than the actual *number* of similar attitudes. Thus, we should be more attracted to someone who agrees with us on 4 of 6 topics (66% similarity) than someone with whom we share similar opinions on 10 of 25 topics (40% similarity). Additional research indicates that the matching hypothesis is strongest for attitudes that are most important to us (Bahns et al., 2017; Montoya & Horton, 2013). Further, we particularly like others who share our rare attitudes, meaning attitudes not shared by many others (Alves, 2018).

FIGURE 9.5   Similarity and Attraction

Donn Byrne and his colleagues found that the greater the proportion of similar attitudes held by people, the greater their attraction to one another. Does this type of relationship between attitude similarity and attraction help explain why you are attracted to or repelled by certain people in your own life?

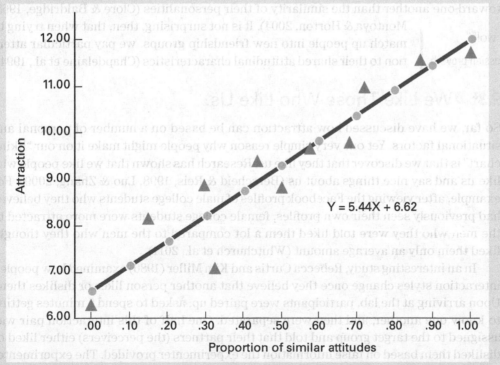

Data source: "The Ubiquitous Relationship: Attitude Similarity and Attraction. A Cross Cultural Study," by D. Byrne et al., 1971, *Human Relations, 24*(3), pp. 201–207.

Why are similar others interpersonally attractive? One reason is our desire for social comparison. As Schachter's anxiety experiments demonstrated, when we are uncertain about how to define social reality, we are drawn to those with whom we can best compare ourselves. Meeting others who share our views on important issues makes us feel better because it reassures us that essential aspects of our self-concept have social validity. According to this social comparison perspective, when others validate our own self-beliefs through agreement, we should develop positive attitudes toward them. In contrast, when others disagree with us, this questioning of our judgment may raise doubts in our own minds about our self-concept and world view. The negative feelings created by such nonagreement should cause us to avoid these people in the future.

Another reason why we may be attracted to similar others is that we like that which is familiar. As we have already discussed (section 9.2), it may have been evolutionarily adaptive to perceive unfamiliar others with caution and distrust because of the dangers inherent in dealing with the unfamiliar (Bornstein, 1989). Due to this biological predisposition, we may perceive similar others as attractive because they *mimic* familiarity. That is, their similarity to us makes them seemingly familiar creatures! Thus, similarity may lead to liking because the similar appear familiar.

The attractive power of similar attitudes has been demonstrated not only in mixed and same-sex dyads but also in various cultures throughout the world (Byrne, 1997; Byrne et al., 1971). Indeed, as we learned from the "Johnny Rocco" study in Chapter 7 (section 7.2e), our desire for attitudinal similarity is sufficiently strong that we will actively eject members from our groups if they refuse to share our attitudes on important issues. In fact, research indicates that the similarity of people's attitudes is more important in determining their attraction toward one another than the similarity of their personalities (Clore & Baldridge, 1968; Montoya & Horton, 2004). It is not surprising, then, that when trying to match up people into new friendship groups, we pay particular attention to their shared attitudinal characteristics (Chapdelaine et al., 1994).

How has the similarity effect influenced your own personal relationships? Consider your best friends and your more casual friends. With whom do you share more similarities? Do these similarities fall into a particular category, such as shared values versus shared preferences?

"Live with wolves, howl like a wolf."

—Russian proverb

9.3f   We Like Those Who Like Us.

So far, we have discussed how attraction can be based on a number of personal and situational factors. Yet one very simple reason why people might make it on our "liking chart" is that we discover that they like us. Research has shown that we like people who like us and say nice things about us (Berscheid & Reis, 1998, Luo & Zhang, 2009). For example, after viewing the Facebook profiles of male college students who they believed had previously seen their own profiles, female college students were more attracted to the men who they were told liked them a lot compared to the men who they thought liked them only an average amount (Whitchurch et al., 2011).

In an interesting study, Rebecca Curtis and Kim Miller (1986) examined how people's interaction styles change once they believe that another person likes or dislikes them. Upon arriving at the lab, participants were paired up, asked to spend 5 minutes getting to know one another, and then were separated. One half of this interaction pair was assigned to the target group and told that their partners (the perceivers) either liked or disliked them based on false information the experimenter provided. The experimenter stressed to the target person that she was interested in determining how the perceivers would act now that they had been given this false information about the targets. In actuality, the perceivers were never given any information at all. The experimenter's real goal was to manipulate the targets' perceptions, not the perceivers'. After this manipulation, the targets were asked to act as naturally as possible when they interacted again with the perceivers during a 10-minute discussion of current events.

These false perceptions about the perceivers not only influenced the targets' behavior but also influenced the perceivers' beliefs about their partner. Those targets who believed the other person liked them disclosed more, had a more pleasant tone of voice and general attitude, and disagreed less with the perceiver than those who thought the perceiver disliked them. How did the perceivers evaluate their partners? They liked better those targets who had been led to believe they were liked compared to those who thought they were disliked. These findings suggest there is a *self-fulfilling prophecy* when it comes to liking, just as there is for the physical attractiveness stereotype. If we think others like us, we tend to act in ways that increase the likelihood that they will, indeed, like us. However, if we think they dislike us, our subsequent interaction style may fulfill the negative prophecy even if it is based on false information.

Section Summary

- We are attracted to beautiful people.
- Regarding the physical attractiveness stereotype, beautiful people are perceived as having better personalities and as leading healthier and happier lives; this stereotype is untrue, except that beautiful people are less socially anxious.
- Cross-cultural studies find some universal beauty standards:
  Men place a higher value on a physically attractive partner than do women.
  Women are judged more attractive if they have immature and dependent-looking facial features.
  Men are judged more attractive if they have mature facial characteristics related to social dominance.
- Greater focus on the female body as a thin beauty object causes lower body esteem.
- Negative body esteem in men is often linked to the large and muscular male body standard.
- We are attracted to those similar to us.
- We are attracted to those who like us.

9.4 When Social Interaction Becomes Problematic

Throughout this chapter we have examined factors that prompt us to seek out others. However, whenever we approach others, we risk rejection. Even if others do accept our social overtures, there is the further possibility that we may commit a social blunder that will cause them to form a negative impression of us. How do we respond to these social "land mines"?

"The only way to have a friend is to be one."

—Ralph Waldo Emerson, US poet, 1803–1882

9.4a Social Anxiety Can Keep Us Isolated from Others.

Social anxiety is the unpleasant emotion we experience due to our concern with interpersonal evaluation and the loss of social status (Weeks et al., 2011). This anxiety is what causes us to occasionally (or frequently) avoid social interaction—even virtual interaction on the internet (Valkenburg & Peter, 2007). When socially anxious, we are less likely to initiate interactions; when in an interaction, we talk less, sometimes stammer and stutter when we do speak, disclose less about ourselves, and occasionally even withdraw from the anxiety-producing situation altogether (Daly et al., 1997; McCroskey, 1997). This tendency to socially withdraw is not an effect characteristic of anxiety, per se. As you have already discovered (see Schachter's Anxiety Research in section 9.2b), when we are anxious due to nonsocial factors, we often affiliate more, not less (Schachter, 1959). Therefore, affiliation avoidance generally occurs only when other people, either real or imagined, are involved in the source of the anxiety.

The Self-Fulfilling Prophecy of Social Anxiety.

When people are thrust unexpectedly into the social spotlight, they often overestimate the extent to which onlookers notice their thoughts, feelings, and emotions—a reaction known as the *illusion of transparency* (Savitsky & Gilovich, 2003). Although almost everyone occasionally thinks that others can "see right through them" more than is actually the case, people whose social anxiety is more trait-like and chronic rather than purely situational are more susceptible to the illusion that others notice their nervousness. In this uncomfortable state of mind, socially anxious individuals come to expect, readily perceive, and intensely react to rejection cues in their surroundings (Gutierrez-Garcia & Calvo, 2014). For example, they are more attentive to faces with negative expressions than they are to those with positive or neutral expressions (Pishyar et al., 2004). It is not surprising, then, to find that individuals with high social anxiety often evaluate their performance in social settings more unfavorably than do others judging them.

This attentional bias in noticing negative social feedback often results in highly anxious persons acting in ways (like avoiding eye contact or appearing nervous and jittery) that fulfill the self-prophecy more in their own minds than in the minds of others (Pozo et al., 1991).

Friends' Effects on Social Anxiety.

When researchers have used experience-sampling methodology to randomly sample participants' feelings and experiences while they go about their daily activities, they have found that social anxiety does not always cause people to avoid affiliation. When participants became socially anxious while conversing with others, they wanted to end the interaction more when

Individuals high in social anxiousness often withdraw from social situations, and such behavior on their part is sometimes interpreted as unfriendliness. How can nonanxious friends help socially anxious individuals overcome their social anxiety?

they were with less familiar and trusted individuals than when they were with close friends (L. Brown et al., 2007; Kashdan & Steger, 2006). These findings suggest that trusted friends can help us effectively deal with social anxiety, yet it is also true that there are times when friends can make matters worse. At least one study suggests that socially anxious adolescents tend to choose friends who are similarly socially anxious, and over time they influence each other into becoming still more socially anxious (Van Zalk et al., 2011). The disheartening insight here is that friends who have socially anxious tendencies can, through their daily interactions, socialize and strengthen each other's social anxiety.

social anxiety
The unpleasant emotion people experience due to their concern with interpersonal evaluation

On the positive side, there is also evidence that friends who do not suffer from debilitating social anxiety can help pull their socially anxious peers out of self-defeating behavior patterns. In a study that examined this possibility, Beth Pontari (2009) had people who were either high or low in social anxiety interact with a stranger, either in the presence of a close friend or alone. Although the presence of friends had no effect on the social performance or anxiety of the participants who were low in social anxiety, a friend's presence was beneficial to the socially anxious participants. They appeared more socially competent and experienced less negative self-focused thoughts when their friend was present than when they were alone with the stranger.

Further analyses revealed that high socially anxious participants seemed to benefit from their friend's subtle prompting during the interaction with the stranger. There was a typical pattern in which socially anxious participants would hesitate for a moment during their introductions and the friend would respond by briefly reminding them of something to share. Pontari contends that these small suggestions helped the socially anxious participants avoid resorting to some of their "safe" self-presentation tactics that signal social awkwardness and nervousness. Instead, the friend's prompts helped the socially anxious participant to engage in more assertive self-presentation strategies. Results also indicated that socially anxious participants appreciated, rather than resented, their friend's presence and support. In return, friends did not seem to mind supporting their anxious comrades and responded positively to their role as social facilitators.

In summary, the findings on friends' effects on social anxiety suggest that while similarly anxious friends can strengthen each other's anxiety around others, the subtle but helpful behavior of nonanxious friends can encourage socially anxious individuals to put aside their protective yet socially awkward self-presentation strategies in favor of more assertive strategies that convey social competence. Over time, and with continued practice and their friends' assistance, these self-presentation strategies will begin to be automatically activated so that socially anxious individuals will not only be less dependent on their friends' presence but also less likely to define themselves as being socially anxious.

> "I turn pale at the outset of a speech and quake in every limb and in all my soul."
>
> —Marcus Tullius Cicero, Roman philosopher and politician, 106–43 BCE

9.4b Loneliness Is the Consequence of Social Isolation.

Although the anticipation of evaluation can make us anxious, how do you think you would react to being cut off from meaningful interaction with others? Because of our need for others, the loss of meaningful social exchange is literally detrimental to our health. Feeling socially isolated significantly increases our risk for depression, obesity, elevated blood pressure, sleep problems, and diminished immunity to various diseases, including heart disease and Alzheimer's disease (Cacioppo & Cacioppo, 2018; Wilson et al., 2007).

Defining and Measuring Loneliness

Loneliness is defined as having a smaller or less satisfying network of social and intimate relationships than we desire (Rokach, 2007). In understanding loneliness, keep in mind that this is a subjective experience, reflecting what we feel and think about our interpersonal life; as such, it is not the same thing as solitude or being alone. We can spend long periods of time alone without feeling lonely, and we can also feel terribly lonely in a crowd. In fact, research has shown that lonely and nonlonely people do not differ in the *quantity* of their social interaction, but rather in the *quality* of such exchanges. Chronically lonely individuals tend not to trust other people, partly explaining why they spend more time with strangers and acquaintances and less time with friends and family compared to those who are not lonely (Jones et al., 1985;

loneliness
Having a smaller or less satisfactory network of social and intimate relationships than one desires

> "To whom can I speak today? I am heavy-laden with trouble through lack of an intimate friend."
>
> —"The Man Who Was Tired of Life," circa 1990 BCE

Rotenburg et al., 2010). As we will explore more fully in Chapter 10, feelings of trust are a critical component of intimate relationships during all stages of life (see section 10.2).

Similar to social anxiety, we can experience loneliness as both a short-lived *state* and a chronic, long-term *trait*. For example, when you first arrived on campus your freshman year, you may have experienced a temporary sense of loneliness until you became integrated into the college community. In contrast, some people suffer from chronic loneliness—regardless of the length of time they spend becoming acclimated to new social settings.

Although almost everyone experiences loneliness, adoption and twin studies indicate that some people are more likely to experience loneliness due to inherited traits (Bartels et al., 2008; Cacioppo et al., 2014). While genetics plays an important role in susceptibility to loneliness, our recovery from it often depends on how we interpret and react to its perceived causes (Anderson et al., 1994). In an examination of the duration of loneliness experienced by first-year college students, Carolyn Cutrona (1982) found that it lasted longer among those who initially blamed themselves for their social isolation. That is, the chronically lonely made significantly more *internal, stable attributions* for their loneliness (for example, "I'm too shy" or "I don't know how to start a new relationship") than did those who overcame their sense of isolation.

Unfortunately, as can be seen in Table 9.1, this sort of self-blaming can discourage people from seeking out others and can perpetuate their dissatisfaction with social relationships. On the other hand, Cutrona found that those who thought of loneliness as being caused by a combination of personal and external factors (for example, "I'm lonely because I don't know anyone here. Things will get better as I meet others") seemed to be more hopeful that they could make things change for the better. True to what would be expected from attribution theory (refer to Chapter 4, section 4.4), these *external, unstable attributions* resulted in relatively short-lived loneliness for most of these students.

TABLE 9.1	Causal Attributions Loneliness	
STABILITY	**LOCUS OF CAUSALITY**	
	Internal	**External**
Stable	"I'm too shy." "I don't know how to start new relationships."	"No one here is looking for new friends."
Unstable	"I'm lonely because I haven't tried hard enough to meet others. I can change that by letting others know I'm fun to be around."	"I'm lonely because I don't know anyone here. Things will get better as I meet others."

Adapted from: "Transition to College: Loneliness and the Process of Social Adjustment," by C. Cutrona, 1982, in *Loneliness: A Sourcebook of Current Theory, Research and Therapy*, edited by L. A. Peplau and D. Perlman, pp. 291–309. Copyright 1982, Wiley.

Age, Gender, Culture, and Loneliness

Beyond those with a genetic predisposition, who suffers the most from loneliness? Loneliness appears to peak at several different points across the lifespan. In a community sample of adults ranging from ages 27 to 101, loneliness was higher for people in their late 20s, mid-50s and late 80s (Lee et al., 2019). In this sample, loneliness was associated with increased depression, anxiety, stress, and cognitive complaints. However, people who reported higher levels of wisdom were less lonely. The researchers suggested that wisdom may facilitate and improve the quality of people's relationships. However, relatively late in life loneliness increases when factors such as poor health and the death of loved ones increase social isolation (Fung et al., 2008).

Numerous studies have identified the young—adolescents and young adults—as the loneliest age groups (Peplau et al., 1982). One reason why adolescents and young adults may be lonelier than older individuals is that young people face many more social transitions, such as annually entering increasingly challenging academic settings, falling in and out of love for the first time, moving to live in new areas, and starting new jobs. While such transitions can provide new opportunities for social growth, they also often cause disruptions in well-established relationships, which can trigger loneliness (Benner, 2011; Luong et al., 2010).

There are clear age differences in loneliness, but gender differences are not as clear-cut. Some studies have found a slight tendency for women to report greater loneliness than men; other studies fail to find any differences at all (Archibald et al., 1995; Brage et al., 1993; Lee et al., 2019). Despite the lack of any firm evidence for gender differences in the *degree* of loneliness, there does appear to be evidence that men and women feel lonely for different reasons. Men tend to feel lonely when deprived of group interaction; women are more likely to feel lonely when they lack one-to-one emotional sharing (Stokes & Levin, 1986). This different pattern of loneliness reflects a difference in the friendship patterns of women and men that we will discuss in Chapter 10 (section 10.3b).

Regarding cultural differences, research suggests that loneliness shares common features across cultures, yet culture also shapes loneliness (van Staden & Coetzee, 2010). For example, a survey of people living in Canada, Turkey, and Argentina conducted by Ami Rokach and Hasan Bacanli (2001) found that the individualist Canadians not only experienced higher levels of loneliness than the collectivist Turks and Argentineans but also that they had different perceptions of what caused their loneliness. Canadians were much more likely to explain their loneliness as being caused by personal inadequacies than the Argentineans and Turks.

Studies have shown that adolescents and young adults are the loneliest age groups.

These cultural differences in loneliness are most likely due to the expectations that individualists and collectivists have about social relationships and the degree of help they receive in establishing social ties. While individualists are socialized to develop loosely knit relationships, and to do so by relying on their own social skills and initiative, collectivists are taught to develop tightly knit relationships within their existing group, and to do so with the assistance and supervision of ingroup members (Tower et al., 1997). In a very real sense, the social world constructed by individualists is more likely to create loneliness in its members than the social world created by collectivists.

Further, when loneliness is experienced, individualists are more likely than collectivists to explain it in terms of internal, stable factors ("I'm lonely because I'm personally inadequate"). As we have just learned, this type of self-blaming creates a mind-set that discourages lonely people from seeking out others. Overall, Rokach and Bacanli's findings suggest that the social world created in an individualist culture is not only more likely to cause loneliness but is also more likely to perpetuate it. The takeaway message here is that the more that you conceive of yourself as being embedded in a network of social relationships—being an interdependent self—the less likely you will feel lonely, even during the latter stages of life when many important social bonds are broken through death (Zhang et al., 2011).

> "I felt so lonesome I most wished I was dead."
>
> —Huck Finn in *The Adventures of Huckleberry Finn*, by Mark Twain

> "I see loneliness ooze damply from people's bodies, trail after them, trickling, widening, running deep, flowing on and on forever."
>
> —Mitsuharu Kaneko, Japanese poet, 1895–1975

Is Loneliness Contagious?

Although it is only natural to think of loneliness as a uniquely individualistic experience, like social anxiety, research suggests that one person's loneliness can influence another person's loneliness. Using data from a large-scale longitudinal study begun in

1948, John Cacioppo and his coworkers (2009) examined the life experiences of more than 5,000 people for 60 years. The researchers found that loneliness occurred in clusters and that as people who experienced loneliness got older, they tended to spread their loneliness among others, often by pushing people away. Instead of engaging with and supporting one another, lonely people gradually became more isolated from others over time. Further, nonlonely individuals who were around lonely individuals tended to become lonelier over time. As Cacioppo and his colleagues describe this process: like the fraying of a sweater, lonely people make others around them feel lonely; and the social fabric that knits people together starts to unravel.

This study also found that the social contagion of loneliness was more likely to spread through women's social networks than through men's. This gender difference may be partly due to the fact that women are more likely than men to express and share their emotions and are more attentive to the emotions of others (Hatfield & Rapson, 1996). There is also a stigma associated with loneliness, particularly among men. As such, women might be more willing than men to engage in intimate self-disclosure about their lonely feelings, which may hasten the spread of loneliness among women compared to men.

How did members of a social network respond to loneliness in their midst? Interestingly, nonlonely people tended to distance themselves from lonely people, avoiding or rejecting them. In explaining this distancing effect by nonlonely people, Cacioppo and his coworkers stated that if loneliness is contagious, social distancing might be an attempt to keep the contagion in check. That is, because loneliness spreads through a network and reduces the social ties among its members, isolating lonely people may be an attempt by the larger group to protect the health and structure of their social network. Knowing that loneliness is associated with a variety of mental and physical diseases that can shorten life, Cacioppo and his colleagues contend that if loneliness does indeed function like a contagious disease, it is important to identify loneliness in a social network as early as possible and prevent it from spreading.

Social Skills Deficits and Loneliness

One important factor that contributes to lonely people being likely targets for social rejection is that they often think and behave in ways that reduce their likelihood of establishing new, rewarding relationships. Studies conducted with college students illustrate some of these self-defeating patterns of behavior. Typically in these investigations, students who are strangers to one another are asked to briefly interact in either pairs or groups, after which they rate themselves and their partners on such interpersonal dimensions as friendliness, honesty, and openness. Compared with nonlonely individuals, lonely college students rate themselves negatively following such laboratory interactions. They perceive themselves as having been less friendly, less honest and open, and less warm (Christensen & Kashy, 1998; Jones et al., 1983). They also expect those who interact with them to perceive them in this negative manner. This expectation of failure in social interaction appears all the more hopeless to the chronically lonely because they believe that improving their social life is beyond their control (Duck et al., 1994).

If chronically lonely people were merely misperceiving their effect on others, you might expect that other people's positive feedback concerning their social competence would break down their misperceptions. The problem, however, is that the chronically lonely tend to lack social skills; as a result, they receive little positive reinforcement from others concerning their interaction style. Indeed, they are generally disliked or ignored by others, who see them as weak, unattractive, and insincere (Rotenberg et al., 1997).

What sort of social skills deficits do chronically lonely persons exhibit in their daily interactions? Self-centeredness is one key deficit. That is, when conversing with others, the chronically lonely spend more time talking about themselves and take less interest in what their partner has to say than do nonlonely people (Jones et al., 1982). Longitudinal research with older and middle-aged adults indicates that the relationship between loneliness and self-centeredness is reciprocal; loneliness increases self-centeredness, which then increases future loneliness (Cacioppo et al., 2017). A second key deficit in chronically lonely people is negativity toward others. Consistent with the interaction style of those with low self-esteem, lonely people tend to perceive others in a negative light (Rotenberg & Kmill, 1992). Not surprisingly, when meeting such a person, new acquaintances often come away with negative impressions (Jones et al., 1983).

Confronted with negative social judgments resulting from their inept social style, lonely individuals often immerse themselves in their occupations, withdraw into wish-fulfilling fantasies, or engage in self-destructive activities such as alcohol and drug abuse. In their leisure activities, lonely people often rely upon the television, computer, and radio as substitutes for interpersonal relationships; and their content often focuses on failed relationships and sadness, which can deepen one's sense of social isolation (Greenwood & Long, 2011). People who do have a romantic partner, but feel otherwise socially isolated and lonely, can become overly dependent on the relationship (Hasan & Clark, 2017). Such dependency is especially pronounced for men, and in Chapter 10 we will examine these and other gender differences related to social support in more detail.

One type of nonsocial activity that appears to raise the spirits of those suffering from loneliness is the consumption of "comfort food." Research suggests that because certain foods are typically initially eaten with intimate family members and friends, the experience of eating those foods is encoded into long-term memory along with the emotion of social comfort. Later, eating this food when feeling lonely and depressed automatically activates the experience of psychological comfort that was initially encoded along with the food (Troisi & Gabriel, 2011). Similar comforting effects can be achieved by literally embracing objects—such as your favorite childhood stuffed animal—that are associated with previous nurturing life experiences (Bartz et al., 2016; Harlow & Harlow, 1962). The take-home lesson here is that a move away from home, a fight with a close friend, and many other instances when you feel socially isolated can all be temporarily remedied by "embracing" a familiar food or object that is associated with previous nurturing relationships.

> "Sitting down to one plate, that loneliest of all positions."
>
> —Caroline Gilman, US author and educator, 1794–1888

Section Summary

- Social anxiety can cause people to avoid interaction, and chronic social anxiety can lead to increasingly unpleasant social exchanges.
    - Socially anxious individuals are attracted to one another and can heighten each other's anxiety.
    - Nonanxious friends can reduce socially anxious individuals' awkwardness by prompting them during social exchanges.
- Loneliness is an unpleasant subjective state in which a person has a smaller or less satisfying network of social and intimate relationships than desired.
    - Adolescents and young adults are the loneliest age groups.
    - As people mature, loneliness decreases until relatively late in life.
    - Loneliness tends to cluster in social networks and spread through them.
    - The chronically lonely often lack social skills.

Applications

How Can Social Skills Training Improve Your Life?

One of the most important obstacles that socially anxious and chronically lonely people must overcome is their lack of social skills (Curran, 1977; Solano & Koester, 1989). This social deficiency is likely one of the more important causes of the low self-esteem of lonely and socially anxious individuals. It can also lead to a feeling of hopelessness and increased social withdrawal (Page, 1991). On the other hand, those who have well-developed social skills find it easy to talk to strangers, are perceived by others as friendly, are not easily angered, possess high self-esteem, and experience less stress in their lives (Segrin, 2019).

What makes a person socially skilled? One of the most important factors determining social skill is the *amount of personal attention given to one's partner* in interaction (Kupke et al., 1979). People who are judged to be socially skilled direct more questions toward their conversational partners and make more positive personal statements about them. On the other hand, the unskilled are more self-focused and less responsive when conversing. These "conversational narcissists" have taken the individualist notion that personal needs are more important than group needs to the point where they ignore the interaction needs of others (Vangelisti et al., 1990). The price for such narcissism is social rejection.

A second factor related to social effectiveness is the *ability to recognize and conform to social norms.* People who have social skills problems often engage in situationally inappropriate behavior. For example, they may make new acquaintances uncomfortable by disclosing very personal details about their lives. Although this sort of self-disclosure is important and valuable in intimate relationships, it is considered inappropriate when interacting with strangers and new acquaintances. Such norm violations generally discourage future encounters.

A third factor associated with social skill is *regulating one's mood prior to commencing social interaction.* Research indicates that people who are socially skilled monitor and impose constraints on their emotions prior to interacting with others (Tamir & Mauss, 2011). In general, when people anticipate interacting with a stranger, they try to regulate their mood in the direction of *neutrality* (Erber et al., 1996). This is done because being perceived by new acquaintances as "cool" and "calm" is a socially desirable goal for most people, and a neutral mood is most consistent with attaining that goal. The only times the socially skilled do not seek mood neutrality is when they know beforehand that the person they are about to meet shares their current mood, or when they are happy and anticipate that the person they are about to meet is depressed. Maintaining a happy mood when meeting a depressed person is likely a self-protective strategy employed by socially skilled people to shield them from their partner's mood.

Finally, a fourth factor in fostering effective social interaction is *realizing that others do not generally notice another's nervousness.* The belief that one's thoughts, feelings, and emotions are more transparent to others than is actually the case is known as the illusion of transparency (see section 9.4a). As a result, people overestimate the degree to which others can detect their private thoughts and feelings. Research indicates that when socially anxious individuals are educated about the illusion of transparency and realize that their nervousness is not as apparent as they think, this knowledge not only reduces their anxiety but also improves their ability to speak in a public setting (Savitsky & Gilovich, 2003).

The rise in popularity of social networking sites and other computer-mediated forms of communicating provide a new way to practice this newfound knowledge of effective social interaction (Okdie & Ewoldsen, 2018). In a survey of almost 800 adolescents, Patti Valkenburg and Jochen Peter (2007) found that socially anxious individuals perceived the internet as a valuable social arena for them to develop friendships—possibly because online communication induced less anxiety and allowed more time to formulate conversational responses. Other research has found that people who are socially anxious experience less anxiety when communicating via text rather than face-to-face (Okdie & Ewoldsen, 2018).

In a study of internet use and shyness, Paul Brunet and Louis Schmidt (2007) asked female college students to engage in a 10-minute, online, free-chat conversation with and without a live webcam. Analysis of these conversations found that shy women disclosed less personal information than non-shy women only when their visual image was being transmitted. When the webcam was not present, the shy women's conversations were no different in quality from those of the non-shy women. Additional research finds that internet sites such as Facebook help shy people to become better acquainted with others and make them feel more comfortable socially (Baker & Oswald, 2010).

Together, these studies suggest that the internet—under the proper conditions—can provide individuals who lack confidence in their social skills with a relatively safe social arena to practice the art of social interaction. Online communications can be especially useful for such individuals during the early stages of initiating and forming new relationships (Waytz & Gray, 2018). In general, online interactions appear most beneficial when they complement— and allow people to build upon—their face-to-face interactions with others (Nowland et al., 2018). In contrast, superficial or passive online social interactions—such as simply reading or "liking" others' posts but not actually interacting with them—can actually increase loneliness. Therefore, it's important to understand that online social interactions should not be a substitute for intimate in-person interactions (Oswald, 2017; Waytz & Gray, 2018).

Besides simply encouraging people to enhance their social skills through practice, considerable research has been devoted to developing **social skills training** programs to promote greater relationship satisfaction (Margie, 2006). The social skills taught in these training sessions cover such areas as initiating conversations, speaking fluently on the telephone, giving and receiving compliments, handling periods of silence, learning nonverbal methods of communication, and actively listening to what others have to say in conversation (Brackett et al., 2007).

social skills training
A behavioral training program designed to improve interpersonal skills through observation, modeling, role-playing, and behavioral rehearsal

Training is usually conducted in groups and, in a typical session, the instructor might show a videotape of a model starting a conversation inappropriately or failing to respond to someone's compliment. The group might then discuss ways in which the model could have acted more appropriately. Following this discussion, another videotape might be shown in which the model performs more effectively. Each person in the training group might then role-play a conversation while others observe and then provide feedback. The session might end with a homework assignment for group members to start a conversation with a stranger during the following week.

The particular social skills emphasized in many training programs appear best suited for *initiating* social relationships. Although this is a necessary starting point, there are other important social skills required for deepening relationships and overcoming interpersonal conflict. In an attempt to better understand effective strategies for teaching such skills to socially impaired individuals, Robin Cappe and Lynn Alden (1986) recruited men and women who were at least moderately socially impaired and exposed them to different types of training programs. One group of recruits was taught the following four skills necessary in developing and strengthening friendships: *active listening, communicating respect, empathic responding,* and *self-disclosing* (remembered by the acronym *ACES*). In addition to learning ACES social skills, some recruits also learned how to relax in anxiety-producing situations. Another group of recruits was not given any social skills training, but merely learned how to relax when feeling anxious. Finally, a control group received no training at all.

Results indicated that those who received a combination of social skills training and relaxation instruction reported significantly greater improvements in their social functioning than those who either received only relaxation training or no instruction at all. In addition, those who were given social skills training were judged by independent observers as more comfortable and skillful in social settings than those in the other groups. A 3-month follow-up found that those who had received social skills training reported significantly more positive social changes in their lives than did the other recruits, varying from minor changes ("I was able to join a club") to major changes ("I was able to date and am now engaged"). A growing body of research indicates that those who participate in such training exercises show improvements in their social skills and an increased level of social satisfaction (Hennessey, 2007). Because of their established effectiveness these training programs are also being used to help people who struggle with social interaction due to autism or other similar disorders (Wolstencroft et al., 2018).

THE BIG PICTURE

In studying social psychology, have you noticed a recurring set of psychological principles that appear to shape people's thoughts and actions? These two psychological cousins are the general desire to be liked and accepted by others and the general desire to have an accurate view of things. They correspond to the "hot" and "cold" perspectives on the nature of human behavior first mentioned in Chapter 1. You can see these two perspectives operating in your attraction to others. According to social exchange theory, you seek out and maintain those relationships that make you feel good about yourself and bring you more rewards than costs. According to social comparison theory, you seek out similar others for accurate comparison so that you can judge and improve yourself.

What you have learned about the psychology of relationships should prove useful in the coming years. As you seek the company of others, remember that a self-fulfilling prophecy is associated with the "desire to be liked" principle. If you approach new social settings thinking that others will like you, you will probably act in ways that fulfill this prophecy. However, if you expect rejection, your subsequent interaction style may fulfill the negative prophecy, even if it is based on false information.

Also keep in mind that although almost everyone experiences loneliness, your recovery often depends on how you interpret and react to its perceived causes. People who make *internal, stable attributions* for their loneliness ("I just don't know how to make new friends") tend to be chronically lonely, while those who make *external, unstable attributions* ("I'm lonely because I don't know anyone here") are generally only temporarily lonely. The advice to be gleaned from this research is that you should be careful what you think you are, for you will likely behave consistent with those self-beliefs. Here, again, is an example of how the self is an active participant in creating its social reality.

KEY TERMS

■ WEBSITES

Accessed through https://www.bvtlab.com/sop8

Websites for this chapter focus on research and theory on interpersonal relationships, as well as an analysis of shyness, social anxiety, and loneliness.

International Association for Relationship Research

This website for the International Association for Relationship Research lists information about interpersonal relationship publications and conferences, as well as links to other relevant sites.

Shyness Institute

This web page is a gathering of network resources for people seeking information and services for shyness and social anxiety.

American Psychological Association

The American Psychological Association website contains a web page that discusses research indicating that the internet increases social isolation among users.

Chapter 10

Intimate Relationships

FOCUS QUESTIONS

1. How do early parent-child relationships shape later adult friendships and romantic relationships?

2. How does culture, gender, and sexual orientation influence the nature of friendships and romantic relationships?

3. What is the difference between passionate and companionate love?

4. What are some factors that strengthen or weaken satisfaction in romantic relationships?

CHAPTER OUTLINE

10.5e Being Playful and Expressing Gratitude Fosters Relationship Satisfaction.

10.5f People Use Different Strategies to Cope with a Troubled Relationship.

10.5g Romantic Breakups Often Cause Emotional Distress.

Applications: What causes jealousy and how can you cope with it?

Preview . . . Jealousy can cause irreparable harm to romantic relationships. What are some of the short-term and long-term strategies that you can use to constructively resolve jealousy?

The Big Picture

Key Terms

Websites

Introduction

One evening many years ago, while Steve was still single and unattached, he attended a modern dance concert near the Indiana University campus in downtown Bloomington. Steve wasn't really much of a modern dance enthusiast, but he was new to the area and thought this might be a good way to meet new people. Okay, more specifically, he thought this might be a good way to meet single women.

When purchasing his ticket, the ticket taker ripped it in two and gave Steve half, instructing him to remember the number on his ticket stub because it would later be used in the performance. The dance company was very avant-garde, and just before beginning the last performance piece, they brought a hat onstage filled with ticket stubs. If your ticket number was called, you were supposed to walk onstage and become part of the performance. Upon hearing this, Steve instinctively sunk lower in his seat. Ever since his sister had tried to teach him to dance during his teenaged years—while laughing uncontrollably—Steve has felt self-conscious on the dance floor (an excellent example of operant conditioning).

(Franzoi)

Steve's future wife, Cheryl Figg, performing for Windfall Dancers around the time of "the Incident."

As luck would have it, Steve's number was called by one of the performers—a tall, attractive woman with long, blonde hair. Maybe this wouldn't be so bad after all, he thought as he walked onstage. But what did she want Steve to do? You guessed it, learn a complicated dance routine in front of the entire audience! As she led him through the steps, his heart began to beat rapidly and his face became flushed, but he concentrated as best he could and was doing okay (meaning he didn't trip over his own feet). Then, halfway through the routine, in the middle of a big leg swing, Steve's brand-new reversible belt buckle popped completely off his belt and shot across the dance floor! The dancer laughed, the audience roared. In response, Steve pulled off his belt and tossed it toward the audience, trying to appear nonplussed by what had happened, but he was mortified. It didn't help that the local public television station was on hand to videotape the performance. Somehow Steve finished the dance routine and sat down.

Although Steve's primary intention for attending this concert was to meet single women, and despite the fact that he ended up dancing with this attractive woman, he quickly bolted from the scene shortly after "The Incident." Bloomington is a relatively small town, so on occasion over the next few months, Steve would see this dancer while going about his daily activities. Whenever this happened, his heart would race and his face would become flushed as he relived "The Incident." What were his feelings toward her? Attraction. Definitely attraction. Eight months later, Steve finally introduced himself when their paths once again crossed, and they began dating. A year and a half later they were married.

Years later, while writing a first draft of the current chapter, Steve thought a bit more about this initial encounter with his future wife: attractive woman + acute embarrassment = romantic feelings. He suddenly realized that this incident was an excellent illustration of the two-factor theory of emotion! But that's getting ahead of the larger story of this chapter: the social psychological dynamics of intimate relationships. So, let's begin our examination of intimacy by first defining this concept. Later, we will return to how Steve's long-ago experience can be psychologically understood, and also how we can all benefit from understanding how intimacy, or its absence, affects our health and welfare (Perlman, 2007).

10.1 What Is Intimacy?

Imagine that you overhear another person make a disparaging remark about someone you love. How would you feel, and how might you respond? Now imagine that the one you care about has succeeded (or failed) on an important task. How would his or her success or failure influence your mood? If you are like most people, you would *share* with that person the emotional highs and lows accompanying these events. **Intimacy** refers to sharing that which is inmost with others (McAdams, 1988). The word itself is derived from the Latin *intimus*, which means "inner" or "inmost." People define intimacy by focusing on aspects of physical and emotional closeness, communication, trust, and commitment (Frost & Gola, 2015). Cross-cultural studies find that having successful intimate relationships is among our most important life goals and aspirations, and it is the only factor that consistently predicts happiness in every country studied (Diener et al., 1999; Reis & Gable, 2003).

10.1a Intimacy Involves Including Another in Your Self-Concept.

As you recall from Chapter 3 (section 3.1a), William James conceived of the "self as object" (or self-concept) as being a process of identification, expanding and contracting to include that which one values. Arthur Aron and Elaine Aron (1986, 1997) employed James's notion of *self-expansion* in their analysis of intimacy. They contend that in intimate relationships, we seek to psychologically expand ourselves by acting as if some or all aspects of our partner are part of our own selves (Aron et al., 2001). The process of self-expansion is associated with greater relationship quality, commitment, and relationship-maintaining behaviors (Mattingly et al., 2019; McIntyre et al., 2015). Figure 10.1 provides a schematic illustration of different levels of intimacy through this self-expansion process.

> "A friend is, as it were, a second self."
>
> —Marcus Tullius Cicero, Roman statesman, 106–43 BCE

This removal of psychological boundaries between people, so that one experiences another as part of him- or herself, is often identified as the most important distinguishing feature of intimacy (Knee et al., 2013; Rempel & Burris, 2006). Yet if intimacy is really an inclusionary experience, can researchers detect it by studying the structure and the process of the self? A number of social psychologists respond affirmatively to this question. They contend that in memory, this inclusion of the other in the self is represented by a direct link between the self and the close other, so that activating either memories of the self or the close other will automatically activate memories of both persons and their associated traits (Mashek et al., 2003). Neurologically, scientists have observed this inclusion of the other in the self in terms of how the brain processes names. This research indicates that recognizing our own names and the names of our loved ones involves similar patterns of brain activity that are different from the neural patterns that occur when we recognize the names of people in general (Gainotti, 2013). The implication of these studies as a whole is that we will think about and respond to intimate others very similarly to the way we think about and respond to ourselves.

intimacy
Sharing that which is inmost with others

> "We are molded and remolded by those who have loved us; and, though the love may pass, we are nevertheless their work, for good or ill."
>
> —François Mauriac, French novelist, 1885–1970

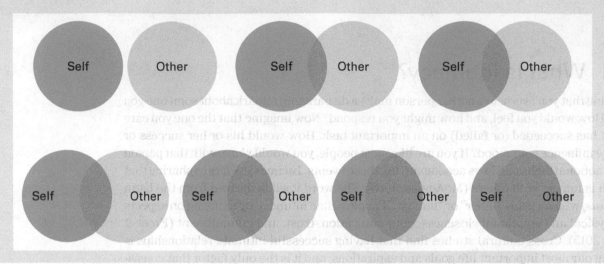

FIGURE 10.1 Inclusion of Other in the Self

This is a schematic illustration of seven different degrees of self-other relatedness, from no inclusion of the other in the self to an immersion of the other in one's self. Which of the pictures best describes different intimate relationships in your own life?

Another way in which intimate relationships reflect the inclusion of the other into the self-concept is in the ease with which we recognize our self-schemas. As discussed in Chapter 4 (section 4.1), *self-schemas* are the personal attributes with which we identify; they are the ingredients of our self-concept. Research comparing the self-schemas of strangers, friends, and married couples has found that as the intimacy bond deepens between two people, they begin to incorporate some of the other's self-schemas into their own self-concepts. As a result of this cognitive blurring of the self-other distinction, people involved in intimate relationships need less time to recognize self-descriptive traits if the traits are also shared with their partner (Aron et al., 1991).

For example, imagine that Ann and Stephanie are involved in an intimate relationship. Ann has self-schemas consisting of such traits as independent, tidy, and industrious. Stephanie sees herself as independent, industrious, and athletic. The speed at which they can individually process and recall self-descriptive traits will be faster for traits they share (independent, industrious) than for those upon which they differ. Even though Ann has a self-schema for "tidy" and Stephanie has a self-schema for "athletic," because the intimate other does not share this trait, it takes them longer to identify it as being self-descriptive. Given that we include our intimate others in our self-concepts, the loss of such relationships has a significant impact on how we conceive of ourselves. For example, after a romantic breakup, individuals' self-concepts typically become both less clear and smaller, with these effects being stronger the more emotionally committed people were to the relationship (Slotter et al., 2010).

(Shutterstock)

What are some ways in which people often demonstrate the inclusion of intimate others in their self-concepts?

10.1b Intimacy Involves Treating Your Loved Ones' Needs as Your Own.

As discussed in Chapter 9 (section 9.1a), most of our everyday relationships operate on the principle of *social exchange* in which we carefully tally our costs and balance those against our rewards to determine whether we should maintain the relationship. However, a number of studies demonstrate that when we are involved in intimate relationships, we often do not think about our rewards and costs as if we were balancing our bank accounts (Clark & Mills, 2012). Instead, these *communal relationships* are organized according to the principle that people should be given what they need, with little concern for what we will receive in return (Medvene et al., 2000).

Thus, in intimate relationships, we treat our loved ones' needs as if they were our own, with little to no tallying of costs. Because these intimate others are important elements in our own self-concept, our needs and their needs are intertwined and often indistinguishable; when our friends, family members, or romantic partners need help we freely lend a hand. Establishing a communal relationship in a budding romance or friendship is so important to many people that the relationship can be destroyed if one partner maintains an exchange orientation by regularly trying to balance costs and rewards. Furthermore, having a communal orientation toward a relationship is positively associated with relationship well-being, as well as overall personal well-being (Le et al., 2018). Table 10.1 summarizes the differences between these two different types of relationships.

> "If I have no love, I am nothing. . . . Love is patient; love is kind and envies no one. Love is never boastful, nor conceited, nor rude; never selfish, not quick to take offence. Love keeps no score of wrongs; does not gloat over other men's sins, but delights in the truth. . . . Love will never come to an end."
>
> —I Corinthians 13

TABLE 10.1	**Exchange Versus Communal Relationships**	
Exchange Relationships (Governed by concern for equity)		**Communal Relationships** (Governed by responsiveness to the other's needs)
1. Person motivated by a desire to have a "fair" relationship		1. Person motivated by a desire to please the other person
2. Person desires to be immediately repaid for favors		2. Person dislikes being immediately repaid for favors
3. Person feels exploited when favors are not returned		3. Person does not feel exploited when favors are not returned
4. Person keeps track of who is contributing what to the relationship		4. Person does not keep track of who is contributing what to the relationship
5. Helping one's partner doesn't elevate one's mood		5. Helping one's partner elevates one's mood

Section Summary

- Intimacy is an inclusion of others in one's self-concept.
- True intimacy is based on a communal relationship rather than an exchange relationship.

10.2 Parent-Child Attachment and Later Adult Relationships

When a national sample of American teenagers and young adults were asked to identify what makes them happy and who their heroes were in life, spending time with family was the top answer for happiness, and nearly half of the respondents listed one or both of their parents as heroes (Noveck & Tompson, 2007). These findings suggest that the majority of young people in America have a healthy emotional attachment to their families. Psychologists define **attachment** as the strong emotional bond that develops between infants and their caregivers; it is considered the cornerstone for all other relationships in a child's life (Beebe & Lachmann, 2014). This bond is not unique to humans but is found in most species of birds and mammals (Graves & Hennessy, 2000; Mason, 1997).

10.2a Attachment Is an Inborn, Adaptive Response.

As with belongingness needs discussed in Chapter 9 (section 9.1b), the emotional bond of attachment is sparked by biological processes and genetic tendencies. Human infants have an inborn attachment response that is observable within minutes of birth, beginning with attempts to suckle their mother's breasts (the *rooting instinct*) and the ability to grasp and hold fast when startled (the *Moro reflex*). Within days, newborns recognize and prefer the face, voice, and smell of their mother to those of unfamiliar people, and they spontaneously imitate their caretakers' facial expressions (Jones, 2007; Maestripieri, 2001).

New mothers are similarly predisposed to bond with their infants. During labor and later when breastfeeding their children, mothers produce *oxytocin*, a hormone that also acts as a neurotransmitter in the brain and has a positive influence on parenting behavior. Both human and animal studies indicate that individuals—both females and males—with higher levels of oxytocin more strongly desire companionship, have higher levels of trust, and take better care of their young than those with lower levels (Carter, 2014; Taylor & Gonzaga, 2007). The positive effects that oxytocin has on intimate emotions and behavior have led some scientists to call it the "love hormone."

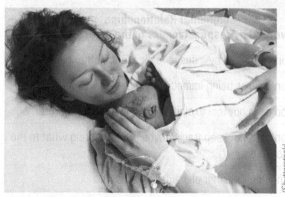

The affection of mothers for their offspring is at least partly based on the hormones present during the birth process and later during nursing. Whether children develop a secure versus an insecure attachment style is significantly determined by the parenting style of the primary caregiver.

British psychiatrist John Bowlby (1969) was one of the first social scientists to systematically study the attachment process. Based on his analysis of human infants and the young of other species, Bowlby proposed that attachment is part of many species' genetic heritage, with its evolutionary function being the protection of immature, highly vulnerable animals. Infants who cling or remain close to their parents are better protected from predators and thus stand a better chance of surviving to adulthood than those who wander away from parental care.

In his evolutionary analysis of attachment, Bowlby proposed a standard pattern of three responses produced by infants of many species when they become separated from their primary caregivers: protest, despair, and detachment. Protest is the first strategy employed following parental separation, and is characterized by infants creating a ruckus. Infants who wail and scream are likely to draw their parents near, thus increasing the likelihood that they will be protected and fed. However, if this protest strategy does not succeed, Bowlby reasoned that the next best survival strategy is for infants to remain quiet (despair), thus reducing the likelihood of attracting the attention of predators. Finally, if left unattended for long periods, infants will develop emotional detachment and begin to behave independently.

One of Bowlby's associates, Mary Ainsworth (1989), took his basic ideas about attachment and studied how human infants develop different attachment styles. Ainsworth reasoned that although our biological heritage may propel us toward caregivers, the basic principles of reinforcement theory suggest that the caregiver's response will influence the strength of this desire to establish such proximity. Subsequent research on parent-child attachment indicated that as infants interact with their parents, they develop either optimistic or pessimistic beliefs about human relationships (Moss et al., 2004). Children

attachment
The strong emotional bond between an infant and a caregiver

with parents who are nurturing and sensitively responsive to their needs develop a secure attachment style characterized by a belief that they are worthy of others' love and that people can be trusted. In marked contrast, children with parents who are inattentive to their needs develop an insecure attachment style characterized by a belief that they are unworthy love objects and that others cannot be relied upon (Huth-Bocks et al., 2004). Not surprisingly, people who are insecurely attached are much less likely than those who are securely attached to experience positive emotions associated with safety and contentment (Gilbert et al., 2008).

From a social cognitive perspective, one way to understand attachment styles is to conceptualize them as consisting of people's cognitive representations of what constitutes love and intimacy (Dykas & Cassidy, 2011). In essence, individuals with different attachment styles have different *prototypes* for intimate relationships (Vicary & Fraley, 2007). As you recall from Chapter 4 (section 4.1a), a prototype is the most representative member of a category. Securely attached individuals quickly recognize the warm and affectionate behavior of others toward them as an overture for intimacy; but those with insecure attachment will be less likely to do so because the behavior does not match their "intimate relationship" prototype. This difficulty in associating signals of intimacy with the cognitive category of "intimate relationships" causes trouble in the social worlds of the insecurely attached (Knee & Canevello, 2006).

Generally speaking, throughout childhood, insecurely attached children exhibit less social competence and lower levels of self-esteem and self-concept complexity than children with secure attachment (Shulman et al., 1994). Insecurely attached children often exhibit contradictory social behavior, sometimes initiating social contact but then unexpectedly spurning others' social advances. This vacillating pattern of approach-avoidance invites social rejection from peers, which then serves to confirm the child's original sense of insecurity and distrust.

10.2b Attachment Styles Influence Romantic Relationships.

Up until the mid-1980s, all research on attachment styles focused on the social relationships of children and adolescents. Then, in 1987, social psychologists Cindy Hazan and Philip Shaver developed self-report measures of secure and insecure attachment styles derived from the work of Ainsworth and other developmental psychologists. Hazan and Shaver were interested in determining whether these attachment styles might affect adult romantic relationships. Inserting their attachment measures into a "love quiz" printed in a local newspaper, they asked respondents questions about their current romantic relationships. The results of this pioneering study found that the percentage of adults who identified with a particular attachment style were similar to the figures obtained in studies of infant-parent attachment (Fraley, 2002). Hazan and Shaver also found that securely attached adults reported more positive relationships with their parents than did adults with insecure attachment styles.

After the publication of this research, many social psychologists began exploring how attachment styles influenced the nature and quality of adult social relationships and found that they were consistent with the findings for children (Mikulincer & Shaver, 2006; Powers et al., 2006). Furthermore, recent conceptualizations of attachment find that both infant and adult attachment styles are best thought of as being determined by two underlying dimensions, anxiety and avoidance, that are experienced in social relationships (Pietromonaco & Beck, 2015; Simons et al., 2014). Anxiety is triggered by low self-esteem. Avoidance is triggered by low interpersonal trust. As depicted in Figure 10.2, this new dimensional approach to attachment—which is still consistent with Ainsworth's original research—yields four attachment styles.

Individuals with a **secure attachment style** experience low anxiety and low avoidance in their social relationships. People with this attachment style have positive self-esteem and believe that people are basically loving and trustworthy. Securely attached adults easily become close to others, expect intimate relationships to endure, and handle relationship conflict constructively by discussing problems and forgiving occasional transgressions (Creasey & Ladd, 2005; Lawler-Row et al., 2011). Securely attached individuals are less likely to engage in behaviors that harm a relationship, such as being sexually unfaithful to a spouse or experiencing relationship jealousy, than are people who have less secure attachment styles (Huelsnitz et al., 2018; V. Russell et al., 2013). In a longitudinal study, childhood secure attachment was found to be positively associated with later academic achievement in adolescence, which appears to occur because individuals with secure attachment are better able to effectively persist at tasks than those with insecure attachments (Dindo et al., 2017).

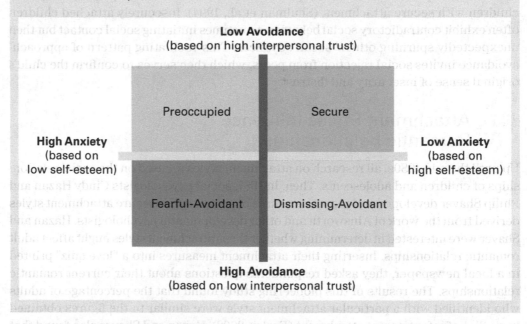

FIGURE 10.2 Four Attachment Styles Based on Perceptions of Self-Worth and Others' Trustworthiness

Attachment style is shaped by two dimensions, anxiety and avoidance, that result in four attachment styles. Which attachment style is associated with the most successful intimate relationships?

Low Avoidance
(based on high interpersonal trust)

| Preoccupied | Secure |

High Anxiety
(based on
low self-esteem)

Low Anxiety
(based on
high self-esteem)

| Fearful-Avoidant | Dismissing-Avoidant |

High Avoidance
(based on low interpersonal trust)

secure attachment style
An expectation about social relationships characterized by trust, a lack of concern with being abandoned, and a feeling of being valued and well-liked

preoccupied attachment style
An expectation about social relationships characterized by trust but combined with a feeling of being unworthy of others' love and a fear of abandonment

dismissing-avoidant attachment style
An expectation about social relationships characterized by low trust and avoidance of intimacy, combined with high self-esteem and compulsive self-reliance

Persons with a **preoccupied attachment style** are low on avoidance but high on anxiety. They have positive expectations that people will be loving and trustworthy, but they have a negative view of themselves as not being worthy of others' love. Thus, they desperately seek out intimate relationships, but they tend to be obsessed and preoccupied with their friends and romantic partners, and they fear that their friendship and love will not be reciprocated. Preoccupied individuals often judge their self-worth in terms of their physical attractiveness, and their orientation toward sexual activity is strongly shaped by their insecurity and strong intimacy needs (D. Davis et al. 2004; Park et al., 2004). They tend to have sex as a way to feel valued by their partners or as a means to induce their partners to love them more (Schachner & Shaver, 2004).

In contrast, people with a **dismissing-avoidant attachment style** have little faith in other people; thus, they avoid intimacy. They find it hard to trust others, have difficulty even recognizing expressions of warmth and empathy from others, and often withdraw from relationships when conflicts arise (Schindler et al., 2010). Due to their positive self-esteem and lack of self-insight, dismissing-avoidant individuals typically experience little interpersonal anxiety (Gjerde et al., 2004). In fact, they are generally confident—even arrogant—but because they do not trust others, they exhibit a compulsive self-reliance. Unlike preoccupied individuals who are motivated to engage in sexual activity to reduce insecurity and foster intense intimacy, dismissives are likely to have sex simply because they enjoy it or because they can then brag about it and increase their status with their social group (Schachner & Shaver, 2004). This pattern of behavior might suggest that dismissive-avoidant individuals have a low need to belong (see Chapter 9, section 9.1b). However, a series of studies indicate that individuals with a dismissive-avoidant style experience higher-than-average levels of positive affect and heightened self-esteem after being accepted by others, while they simultaneously take steps to avoid becoming dependent on others (Beck et al., 2014; MacDonald & Borsook, 2010). This research suggests that dismissive avoidants do indeed desire social inclusion, even though they avoid intimacy, and it provides further evidence that a strong and basic need to belong is present in all humans (Carvallo & Gabriel, 2006).

Finally, similar to dismissives, people with a **fearful-avoidant attachment style** do not trust others; however, unlike dismissives, they also have a low opinion of themselves and therefore experience a great deal of anxiety in interpersonal settings. Fearful-avoidant individuals expect to be rejected by others, and they have a heightened attentiveness and reaction to angry and sad facial expressions (Niedenthal et al., 2003). Like preoccupied individuals, fearful avoidants base their self-worth on their physical level of attractiveness (Park et al., 2004). As you might guess, this attachment style is associated with negative interpersonal experiences and the abuse of alcohol to reduce anxiety in social settings (McNally et al., 2003). Fearful avoidants often have a history of psychological, physical, or sexual abuse (Bartholomew, 1990; Bartholomew et al., 2001). To better understand how social psychologists identify these four different attachment styles in adults using self-report questionnaires, spend a few minutes completing the Relationship Questionnaire in *Self/Social Connection Exercise 10.1*.

fearful-avoidant attachment style
An expectation about social relationships characterized by low trust and avoidance of intimacy, combined with a feeling of being unworthy of others' love and a fear of rejection

Self/Social Connection Exercise 10.1

What Is Your Adult Attachment Style?

The Relationship Questionnaire

Instructions

Following are four general relationship styles that people often report having. Read each description and indicate the degree to which each style describes you using the following 7-point scale.

Disagree strongly   1   2   3   4   5   6   7   Agree strongly

____ A. It is easy for me to become emotionally close to others. I am comfortable depending on them and having them depend on me. I don't worry about being alone or having others not accept me.

____ B. I am uncomfortable getting close to others. I want emotionally close relationships, but I find it difficult to trust others completely or to depend on them. I worry that I will be hurt if I allow myself to become too close to others.

(continues)

(Self/Social Connection Exercise 10.1 *continued*)

_____ C. I want to be completely emotionally intimate with others, but I often find that others are reluctant to get as close as I would like. I am uncomfortable being without close relationships, but I sometimes worry that others don't value me as much as I value them.

_____ D. I am comfortable without close emotional relationships. It is very important to me to feel independent and self-sufficient, and I prefer not to depend on others or have others depend on me.

Scoring

Based on your own evaluations, which of these relationship styles best fits you?

Style A = Secure Style   Style B = Fearful-Avoidant Style

Style C = Preoccupied Style   Style D = Dismissing-Avoidant Style

Source: Adapted from "Attachment Styles Among Young Adults: A Test of a Four-Category Model," by K. Bartholomew and L. M. Horowitz, 1991, *Journal of Personality and Social Psychology, 61*(2), pp. 226–244.

"What is love? Ask him who lives, what is life. Ask him who adores, what is God . . . [Love] is that powerful attraction towards all that we conceive, or fear, or hope beyond ourselves, when we find within our own thoughts the chasm of an insufficient void, and seek to awaken in all things that are, a community with what we experience within ourselves."

—Percy Bysshe Shelley, English poet, 1792–1822

The self-sufficient cowboy who keeps to himself and doesn't engage in idle chitchat is one of the great icons of the American West. Hollywood actors John Wayne, Gary Cooper, and Clint Eastwood personified this extreme form of individualism in many of their film roles. Today, Hollywood uses this same rugged, individualist personality in creating the lead male role in action adventure films (Matt Damon, George Clooney, Will Smith). What attachment style would you say these film characters most often represent? Is this an attachment style we should be emphasizing in our male cultural role models?

Research that has examined the childhood experiences of adults who differ in attachment styles finds that the securely attached report positive family relationships when young, with memories of firm, authoritative parenting, while the insecurely attached rate their childhood family environments as emotionally cold and openly conflicted, with either harsh, authoritarian parenting or lax, disengaged parenting (Millings et al., 2013; Waldinger & Schulz, 2016). Parents with secure attachment, in turn, engage in more nurturing parental behaviors with their children than do parents with insecure attachment styles (Groh & Haydon, 2018; Jones et al., 2015). These findings suggest that securely attached people have learned how to foster intimacy, while adults with one of the three insecure attachment styles have unwittingly learned how to destroy it. The dismissing-avoidant lover tends to starve intimacy by being emotionally distant and aloof, while the preoccupied lover smothers intimacy by being overly possessive, jealous, and emotionally demanding. Finally, fearful-avoidant lovers have perhaps the worst dilemma because they want approval, however not only do they not feel worthy of receiving it but they also do not believe others can be trusted. So they avoid intimacy in relationships, thinking it is safer to fantasize about a relationship instead of actually trying to establish one.

Is it surprising to you that securely attached lovers are the most desired partners by the vast majority of adults, regardless of their own attachment style (Chappell & Davis, 1998)? Does it further surprise you that the two least desirable attachment styles in romantic relationships are the dismissing avoidants and the fearful avoidants (Pietromonaco & Carnelley, 1994)? What about securely attached people makes them so desirable? Given the warmth and openness that securely attached people bring to romantic relationships, plus their willingness to forgive others for transgressions, it is not surprising that securely attached adults are attracted to each other and are the happiest couples (Holmes

(continued)

& Johnson, 2009). For other securely attached people, a secure partner confirms their expectations of love; they each share the same intimate relationship prototype.

Warmth and openness are such desirable qualities in a potential romantic partner that insecurely attached individuals often present themselves as warm and open when communicating with potential romantic partners (Brumbaugh & Fraley, 2010). This engaging interaction style may be successful in attracting a securely attached individual, but what happens as the romantic relationship progresses? When securely attached people become romantically involved with insecure partners, there is prototype mismatch; however, secure types can buffer the negative effects that their partners bring to the relationship, providing the emotional stability necessary to disconfirm negative expectations (Simpson & Overall, 2014; Stanton et al., 2017). Relationship interactions that boost partner self-esteem—such as making a partner feel validated and appreciated—can reduce relationship-related anxiety (Arriaga, et al., 2018). Furthermore, relationship avoidance decreases when the partners' interactions—such as engaging in intimate self-disclosure and other enjoyable activities—promote a greater sense of trust and closeness. Essentially, any interactions that reduce anxiety and/or avoidance in insecurely attached partners can eventually result in them adopting a new prototype for the category "intimate relationship" that conforms to the secure attachment style.

Section Summary

- Attachment evolved to keep the young close to adults where they are better protected from predators.

- Parent-child attachment patterns influence later childhood peer relations and intimate adult relationships.

- Attachment style is shaped by two basic dimensions: relationship anxiety and avoidance.

- Four adult attachment styles:
    Secure attachment style: low anxiety and low avoidance
    Preoccupied attachment style: high anxiety and low avoidance
    Dismissing-avoidant attachment style: low anxiety and high avoidance
    Fearful-avoidant attachment style: high anxiety and high avoidance

- People with a secure attachment style have more successful intimate relationships later in life than those who are insecurely attached.

10.3 Friendship

As we mature, we not only form emotional ties with our family members, we also form friendships outside the home. Although intimacy is expressed in both social arenas, friendships often satisfy different needs than do family relationships. While relationships with relatives are based on largely nonvoluntary forces, relationships based on friendship are primarily voluntary and mutually satisfying. The distinction between friends and family is summed up in the old saying, "you can pick your friends, but not your family."

As we mature, we form friendships outside of the family.

10.3a Self-Disclosure Shapes Friendship Development and Maintenance.

One of the prime avenues for creating close friendships is through **self-disclosure**, which is the revealing of personal information about oneself to other people (Derlega et al., 2011). Disclosing emotional and private information about oneself conveys a sense of trust; thus, this type of *emotional self-disclosure* is most important in developing intimate relationships (Kashdan & Roberts, 2006). Individuals who do not avail themselves of emotional self-disclosure tend to have dysfunctional relationships and experience greater loneliness than those who reveal their important private self-aspects to friends and lovers (Brunell et al., 2007).

Irving Altman and Dalmas Taylor (1973) sought to explain the self-disclosure process in their **social penetration theory**. According to Altman and Taylor, the development of a relationship is associated with communication moving gradually from a discussion of superficial topics to more intimate exchanges. During initial interactions, people are likely to discuss such impersonal topics as the weather, sports events, or popular culture. If this superficial discussion is rewarding, they may broaden and deepen the social exchange by covering a wider range of topics and choosing to divulge more personal and sensitive information. As you can see in Figure 10.3, when discussion topics move from the very narrow and shallow range to a broader and deeper scope, the intimacy level also increases (Gibbs et al., 2006).

"Fondness is a poor substitute for friendship."

—Anna Green Winslow, American diarist, 1759–1780

FIGURE 10.3   The Theory of Social Penetration

According to Altman and Taylor's (1973) theory of social penetration, the amount of information people disclose early in a relationship is rather narrow and shallow; yet as the relationship progresses, self-disclosure becomes broader (covering a wider range of topics) and deeper (revealing more personal information).

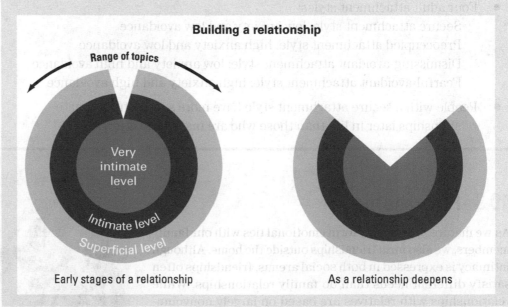

self-disclosure
The revealing of personal information about oneself to other people

social penetration theory
A theory that describes the development of close relationships in terms of increasing self-disclosure

During first meetings, new acquaintances usually follow the norm of *self-disclosure reciprocity*—they match each other's level of self-disclosure, revealing more when the other person does so, and decreasing personal revelations if the other person becomes reticent (Omarzu, 2000). In most first encounters, self-disclosure reciprocity is useful in building a mutually satisfying level of information exchange that benefits relationship development. However, if one person ignores this gradual self-disclosure process and instead reveals a great deal of personal information, there is a good chance the recipient will feel threatened with this premature rush to intimacy and will evaluate the discloser negatively (Lips-Wiersma & Mills, 2002). Once the relationship progresses beyond the "getting acquainted" stage and intimacy barriers have been lowered, this tit-for-tat exchange of personal information is not as important and occurs much less frequently (Altman, 1973). In fact, in an intimate relationship, instead of reciprocating with self-disclosure, a partner may simply offer support and understanding.

What happens to self-disclosure in troubled friendships? In their theory, Altman and Taylor also discuss the dynamics of what they called *depenetration*, which is the disengagement from an intimate relationship. When intimate relationships are in trouble, some people emotionally withdraw by engaging in less breadth and depth in their personal revelations (Baxter, 1987). Other people reduce the number of topics they discuss but increase the depth of their self-disclosure (Tolstedt & Stokes, 1984). The deeply personal feelings and beliefs that are disclosed are usually negative and are designed to accuse and hurt the other person. Thus, just as self-disclosure can build a relationship and provide it with a solid emotional foundation, it can also serve to weaken and tear it down.

Due to the increasing use of social media and online dating apps, there has been a rise in ghosting, *which is the ceasing of all communication and contact with someone without any apparent warning. Is ghosting an extreme form of depenetration?*

(Shutterstock)

Although social penetration theory's description of a gradually increasing self-disclosure fits most developing relationships, other times intimate self-disclosure develops almost immediately (Collins & Miller, 1994). For example, in studies of friends, roommates, and dating partners, some relationships just "click" right from the start rather than gradually becoming close over time (Berg, 1984; Berg & Clark, 1986). This early exchange of highly personal information likely occurs because the respective partners make quick judgments that the other person fits their prototype of the ideal friend or romantic partner. When the partners recognize that this is an intimate relationship, the highly personal self-disclosures begin to flow.

> "Each friend represents a world in us, a world possibly not born until they arrive, and it is only by this meeting that a new world is born."
>
> —Anaïs Nin, US novelist, 1903–1977

Cultural Differences in Self-Disclosure

Despite the importance of self-disclosure in friendship development and maintenance, research indicates that there are cultural differences in self-disclosure tendencies (Adams et al., 2004). North Americans tend to disclose more about themselves in a wider variety of social settings than do people from collectivist cultures such as China, Japan, and the West African nation of Ghana (Chen, 1995; Kito, 2005). These differences do not mean that Americans have more intimate relationships than people from China or Japan (refer to Chapter 9, section 9.1c), but they may be rooted in their respective individualist and collectivist orientations. For example, in Chapter 3 (section 3.2a, *Individualist-Collectivist Comparisons*) we discussed research indicating that many individualist Americans have a need to feel unique or distinct from others (Pratt, 1991; Triandis, 1989). Perhaps the willingness to reveal private self-aspects through self-disclosure provides individualists with the opportunity to identify and share their uniqueness.

> "He who has nothing has no friends."
>
> —Greek proverb

These self-disclosure differences may also be partly due to preferred communication channels within the respective cultures. In many Western societies, social expressiveness tends to be a sign of social competence and is valued as an avenue to intimacy; but in Eastern cultures such as Japan, China, and Korea, oral communication skills are not as highly valued. In fact, being socially *nonexpressive* is often interpreted as an indication of emotional strength and trustworthiness (Kim & Sherman, 2007; Russell & Yik, 1996). Although great value is not placed on social expressiveness in these collectivist cultures, it is considered virtuous to be able to quickly and accurately interpret and respond to others' vaguely expressed feelings and desires before they have to be clearly articulated. In this kind of cultural context, self-disclosing one's desires or fears may be considered inappropriate, because others are expected to "read" them through indirect means.

10.3b Gender Differences Exist in Heterosexual Friendships.

Both men and women value friendship throughout their lives, and both have satisfying and stable relationships (Rose & Asher, 2017). However, research suggests that there are certain gender differences in heterosexual friendship patterns from childhood through adulthood (Johnson et al., 2007; Zarbatany et al., 2007).

Intimacy

Why is it that in North American culture male friendships often are less intimate than female friendships?

(Shutterstock)

One notable gender difference involves the level of emotional expressiveness within same-sex friendships. Women's friendships tend to involve more emotional sharing than men's friendships (Fehr, 2004; Thomas & Daubman, 2001). In trying to explain this difference, researchers initially characterized women's and men's orientation toward friendship as *face-to-face* versus *side-by-side*: Women spend a good deal of time together talking about personal and intimate matters, and men spend the majority of their time together working or playing. Even though these contrasting descriptions of men's and women's friendships have an appealing simplicity, later studies found that they were just that—too simplistic. Research by Steve Duck and Paul Wright (1993) found that both women *and* men meet most often just to talk. They also discovered that although women are indeed more emotionally expressive than men in their friendships, they are just as likely as men to engage in shared activities. Furthermore, men appear to facilitate intimacy in their friendships in ways other than intimate talking. For example, boys are more likely to forgive their friends for transgressions and express less friendship jealousy than do girls in their same-sex friendships (Rose & Asher, 2017). Therefore, just as it is misleading to describe men's friendships as being exclusively side-by-side encounters and women's friendships as being exclusively face-to-face interactions, it may also be that male-male friendships are somewhat more intimate than we currently recognize. To summarize, although our current understanding is that women's friendships are more intimate than men's, it's possible that future research will discover that this gender difference is at least partly accounted for by how we are currently identifying intimate behaviors; friendship intimacy may be expressed somewhat differently by women and men.

Self-Disclosure

In a meta-analysis of 205 studies, Kathryn Dindia and Mike Allen (1992) found that women generally self-disclose more than men, especially in intimate relationships. Their analysis indicates that women self-disclose more than men to their same-sex friends and other-sex romantic partners, but men and women do not differ in their disclosure to male friends. They also found that these gender differences, although not as great as once thought, have shown no evidence of reduction during the past few decades. Additional research confirms these findings; women emphasize self-disclosure and emotional support in their friendships more so than men (Fehr, 2004; Oswald et al., 2004). These gender differences likely stem from different ways that we socialize boys and girls to behave in relationships. Research suggests that males in North American culture are governed by a more rigid set of gender rules than females, especially regarding emotional expression (Bank & Hansford, 2000; Timmers et al., 1998). As a result, out of fear of "losing face," a man is likely to have a more difficult time disclosing vulnerable emotions to others (Felmlee, 1999).

Consistent with this gender socialization explanation, a recent study of adolescents found that girls disclosed more of their problems to their same-sex friends than did boys (Rose et al., 2016). Furthermore, girls responded to their friends' self-disclosure with more statements of agreement, asked more questions, and acknowledged the problem more than did boys. This type of empathic support was positively correlated with both girls' and boys' friendship closeness. Interestingly, boys were more likely than girls to respond to their friends' problems with humor, and this use of humor was associated with friendship closeness for boys, but it wasn't for girls. Why might the use of humor by boys in self-disclosing situations increase friendship closeness? Perhaps because, for boys, the use of humor in responding to another boy's self-disclosure is an act of empathic support, given the constraints of the masculine gender role. In other words, the humorous response allows the discloser to express his problems while still "saving face" by all parties making light of the issue.

Challenging such restrictive gender norms can be beneficial for boys and men. For example, adolescent boys who participated in a school-based program that challenged gender norms subsequently reported improvements in their friendship closeness and overall mental health (Exner-Cortens et al., 2019). Notably, the improvements in friendship closeness were related to the boys' increased levels of intimate disclosure and increased likelihood of seeking emotional support, two behaviors often associated with femininity. These findings are consistent with past research indicating that both men and women who possess personality traits associated with psychological femininity report being more intimate in their same-sex friendships and engage in more communal behaviors to resolve relationship conflict than men and women who exhibit few feminine traits (Keener & Strough, 2017; Williams, 1985).

Before reading further, take a few minutes to complete the self-disclosure questionnaire in *Self/Social Connection Exercise 10.2*. If possible, ask some of your male and female friends to complete it as well so that you can informally test for some of the gender differences we have discussed concerning friendship self-disclosure.

Self/Social Connection Exercise 10.2

Do You Self-Disclose Differently to Your Male and Female Friends?

Instructions

Think of a close male friend and a close female friend. Indicate for the topics listed below the degree to which you have disclosed to each person using the following scale:

Discussed not at all   1   2   3   4   Discussed fully and completely

Male Friend		Female Friend
____	1. My personal habits	____
____	2. Things I have done that I feel guilty about	____
____	3. Things I wouldn't do in public	____
____	4. My deepest feelings	____
____	5. What I like and dislike about myself	____
____	6. What is important to me in life	____
____	7. What makes me the person I am	____
____	8. My worst fears	____
____	9. Things I have done that I am proud of	____
____	10. My close relationships with other people	____
____ **Male friend total score**		**Female friend total score** ____

Scoring

You can determine your overall self-disclosure score for each of your friends by adding up the scores in the column. The higher the score, the greater the self-disclosure to the person. Is there an appreciable difference between these two scores? If there is a difference, does it correspond to what has been found in more systematic investigations of self-disclosure in intimate relationships?

Source: Adapted from "Openers: Individuals Who Elicit Intimate Self-Disclosure," by L. C. Miller et al., 1983, *Journal of Personality and Social Psychology, 44,* pp. 1234–1244.

Physical Touching

Beyond verbal communication, men and women also differ in the degree to which they engage in physical contact with a same-sex friend (Felmlee, 1999). In North American culture, both heterosexual men and women view hugging and other forms of physical intimacy among men as less appropriate than among male-female and female-female pairings (Derlega et al., 2001). Generally, men are encouraged to hug one another only when they are involved in sporting events where expressions of physical intimacy are consistent with the masculine gender role (Mormon & Floyd, 1998). This injunction against male physical intimacy is not the norm in many European, Latin, African, and Middle Eastern cultures (Axtell, 1993; DiBaise & Gunnoe, 2004).

In one study investigating this physical touching taboo in the United States, Val Derlega and his colleagues (1989) asked friends and heterosexual dating partners to act out an imaginary scene where one person was greeting the other at the airport after returning from a trip. The greetings were photographed and later evaluated by judges for the intimacy of physical contact, ranging from no touch at all to combinations of hugging and kissing. As Figure 10.4 shows, dating partners exhibited the highest levels of physical intimacy; all of them engaged in a combination of hugging and kissing. When friendship touching was analyzed, male friends employed significantly less touching than did either female friends or mixed-sex friends. Further investigation of participants' perceptions of physical touch indicated that men were more likely than women to interpret touching as an indication of sexual desire.

FIGURE 10.4   **Gender Differences in Touching During Social Interaction**

How do men and women differ with respect to touching when greeting a friend or dating partner? In North American cultures, physical intimacy is highest among dating partners, second highest among female friends and mixed-sex friends, and lowest among male friends. Have you observed and/or experienced such gender differences in your own life?

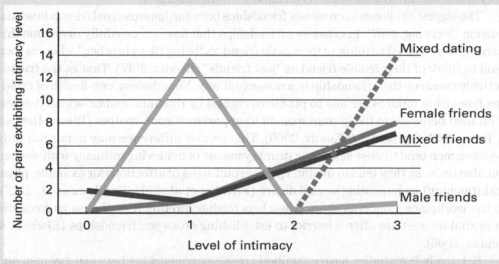

Data source: "Gender Differences in the Initiation and Attribution of Tactile Intimacy," by V. J. Derlega et al., 1989 *Journal of Nonverbal Behavior, 13*(2), pp. 83–96.

Why are male friendships less intimate than female friendships, and why is there this social injunction against men being emotionally and physically expressive? A number of social scientists contend that this avoidance of emotional and physical expressiveness is due to males being socialized to conform to *heterosexual masculinity*, which entails valuing masculine traits related to power and control, while devaluing feminine traits related to the expression of tenderness and vulnerability (Gough, 2002). One important aspect of heterosexual masculinity involves the denigration of male homosexuality because it is perceived to be the antithesis of masculinity (Herek, 2000). For a man to express warmth, nurturance, or caring toward another man is often interpreted as an indication of homosexuality (Derlega et al., 2001). Thus, being masculine requires men to avoid acting in ways that might signal homosexual desires to other men (Theodore & Basow, 2000). As we move through the 21st century, changes in gender roles may eventually lead more men to feel less constrained in their expression of tenderness and affection toward other men.

"The locker room has become a kind of home to me. . . . I relax, my concerns lost among relationships that are warm and real, but never intimate, lost among the constants of an athlete's life. . . . We are at ease in the setting of satin uniforms and shower nozzles."

—Bill Bradley, former professional basketball player and US senator

10.3c Cross-Sex Friendships Are a Valuable Source of Support.

What happens when men and women are friends? Research suggests that in these friendships there is a gravitation to the "intimacy mean." Men tend to be more emotionally open and self-disclosing, while women disclose less and are not as intimate (Monsour, 1997). Generally, heterosexual men believe their female friends provide more emotional support and security than their male friends, but not as much as women with whom they have romantic relationships. Women, on the other hand, do not perceive their cross-sex friendships as being that intimate, and they are likely to turn to female friends for highly personalized interaction (Wright & Scanlon, 1991). Although cross-sex friendships are quite common, as in all friendships, similarity attracts. Heidi Reeder (2003) found that young adults who have a nontraditional gender-role orientation (masculine women and feminine men) have a higher proportion of cross-sex friendships than those with a traditional orientation (feminine women and masculine men). In other words, consistent with the matching hypothesis (Chapter 9, section 9.3e), men and women are more likely to form and maintain friendships with the other sex when they have interests and personality traits that are traditionally associated with the other sex.

The biggest challenge in cross-sex friendships between heterosexual friends is sexual tension (Werking, 1997). In cross-sex friendships that have successfully overcome this barrier, women tend to think of their male friend as "being like a brother," whereas men tend to think of their female friend as "just friends" (Reeder, 2017). That is, the friends actively construe their friendship in a nonsexual way. Nonetheless, one-fourth of cross-sex friendship failures are due to problems caused by romantic and/or sexual desires, with men being more likely than women to experience such desires (Bleske-Rechek & Buss, 2001; Schneider & Kenny, 2000). This gender difference may occur not only because men tend to view sex as the primary means of achieving intimacy with women but also because they tend to misinterpret certain signs of affection (for example, physical touching) as indicating sexual desire (Fletcher et al., 2014; Perilloux et al., 2012). In the workplace, concerns about coworkers misinterpreting friendliness as romantic or sexual interest are often a barrier to establishing cross-sex friendships (Elsesser & Peplau, 2006).

Relatively few studies have examined cross-sex friendships between gay men and heterosexual women (Rumens, 2012). Eric Russell and his colleagues (2018) found that women, but not men, reported more comfort when interacting with a man upon learning he was gay rather than heterosexual. This greater reported comfort for women was due to them not needing to worry about their male friends' sexual intentions. There is also evidence that a further benefit of such friendships is receiving trustworthy mating advice (E. Russell et al., 2013). That is, straight women tend to perceive mating-relevant advice from a gay man as more trustworthy than similar advice offered by a straight man or woman. Similarly, gay men tend to perceive mating advice offered by a straight woman as more trustworthy than advice offered by a lesbian woman or another gay man.

"Friendship is love without wings."

—George Gordon (Lord Byron), English poet, 1788–1824

10.3d Friends-with-Benefits Relationships Pose Unique Challenges and Dangers.

Survey research suggests that half of all college students have engaged in sexual activity with an other-sex friend on at least one occasion, and one-third have engaged in sexual activity on multiple occasions (Afifi & Faulkner, 2000; Johnson et al., 2007; McGinty et al., 2007). Sexual contact is much more common in cross-sex friendships that are relatively new than in those that are of longer duration (Reeder, 2000). When sex occurs, it does not necessarily change the friendship into a romantic relationship, nor does it necessarily end the friendship. If the two parties freely discuss the sexual contact and can agree on what it means to their relationship, the experience is likely to build trust and confidence in the friendship. Often these relationships are seen by participants as "placeholders" until a more serious, romantic relationship comes along (Jonason, 2013).

Not surprisingly, individuals involved in friends-with-benefits relationships consider sex with a trusted friend to be the biggest advantage in these relationships, with men mentioning this as a big advantage somewhat more often than women, who mention emotional involvement somewhat more often than men. The biggest potential disadvantage that women and men both report is fear of potential harm to the friendship or someone getting their feelings hurt as a result of the sexual intimacy (Bisson & Levine, 2009). While hurt feelings are certainly a potential risk in sexual friendships, the more serious danger is sexually transmitted diseases. This is so because the friendship component may lead people to mistakenly believe that their partner is not a risk to their health; thus, they forego using condoms despite the fact that they are engaging in a casual sexual relationship that is not necessarily exclusive (Lehmiller et al., 2014).

(vipflash / Shutterstock)

Friends-with-benefits relationships incorporate sexual activity into a friendship. In the movie with the same title, the two main characters, played by Mila Kunis and Justin Timberlake, struggle with the biggest disadvantage of sexual friendships for the partners. What might that be?

For both women and men, friendship is more important than sex in sexual friendships, and the majority of such relationships continue as friendships after the sexual intimacy ceases (Owen et al., 2013). Individuals who enter such relationships tend to have more positive attitudes toward casual sex, and to have a less romanticized view of love, believing that there are multiple people with whom they could fall in love and also that they can have sex without being in love (Olmstead et al., 2016; Puentes et al., 2008). Regarding expectations for the future, it appears that men and women hope that their sexual friendships will evolve differently. Men are more likely to express satisfaction with their sexual friendships staying the same, while women are more likely to hope that these relationships change into either a conventional romantic relationship or a conventional friendship (Lehmiller et al., 2011).

Friends who want their sexual friendship to blossom into a romantic relationship have the highest emotional commitment to the relationship, followed by those who want their relationship to remain as is, with those who want the relationship to transition into a friendship being the least committed (Vanderdrift et al., 2010). Women's greater interest in having a friends-with-benefits relationship transition into a more conventional intimate relationship—either romance or friendship—may be due to cultural norms that evaluate women more negatively than men for engaging in sex outside of an exclusive relationship and also because sex is potentially more costly for women than men due to the possibility of pregnancy. When such relationships transition into romance, they are no more or less successful or satisfying than conventional romantic relationships (Owen & Fincham, 2012).

10.3e Gender Differences Disappear in Same-Sex Gay and Lesbian Friendships.

Sexual orientation appears to play an important role in shaping the same-sex friendship patterns of men. Survey studies by Peter Nardi and Drury Sherrod (1994) find that the same-sex friendships of gay men are as intimate as those of lesbians. This is partly due to heterosexual men avoiding intimacy in same-sex friendships out of fear of being labeled homosexual. Although many gay men are justifiably wary of expressing affection toward one another in heterosexual surroundings because of fear of ridicule and assault, no such anxiety exists in the gay community. Furthermore, because of stigmatization and prejudice from their families and the larger society, many gay people often turn to friendships for their emotional well-being (Kwon, 2013). As a gay man explained:

> Friends become part of my extended family. A lot of us are estranged from our families because we're gay and our parents don't understand or don't want to understand.... I can't talk to them about my relationships. I don't go to them; I've finally learned my lesson: Family is out. Now I've got a close circle of friends that I can sit and talk to about anything, I learned to do without the family. (quoted in Kurdek & Schmitt, 1987, p. 65)

Just as sexual desires often become salient in heterosexual cross-sex friendships, they are a common issue in gay men's and lesbians' same-sex friendships. In both cases, the sexual orientations of the two people can conceivably lead to sexual activity; thus, they pose problems or challenges to the friendship. Nardi and Sherrod's (1994) survey research suggests that about two-thirds of gay men and about one-half of lesbians have had sexual contact with their same-sex "close" or "best" friend, which is comparable to the sexual contact level found in heterosexual cross-sex friendships. As in these heterosexual friendships, sex among gay men and lesbian same-sex friends is much more likely early in the relationship than later (Nardi, 1992). Although more research is needed to better understand the social psychological dynamics underlying same-sex friendship, clearly it provides gay men and lesbians with a vital source of intimacy—and often a surrogate "family"—in a social environment that can be hostile toward their lifestyle.

Section Summary

- Social penetration theory describes the development of relationships in terms of movement from superficial to more intimate levels of self-disclosure.

- People from individualist cultures may self-disclose more than those from collectivist societies.

- Women self-disclose more than men.

- Same-sex heterosexual female friendships are more emotionally intimate than same-sex heterosexual male friendships.

- The biggest problem in cross-sex friendships is sexual tension.

- In friends-with-benefits relationships, the friendship is more important than sex.

- Same-sex friendships of gay men are as intimate as those of lesbians.

10.4 Romantic Relationships

While relationships of all types play an important function in our lives, establishing and maintaining a satisfying romantic relationship is especially important. In fact, having a satisfying romantic relationship, where one's partner is responsive to our needs, is even predictive of our physical health (Robles et al., 2014; Slatcher & Selcuk, 2017). In the remaining sections of this chapter we examine the

> "I believe myself that romantic love is the source of the most intense delight that life has to offer."
>
> —Bertrand Russell, British philosopher, 1872–1970

psychological nature of romantic love and the factors that foster and inhibit it. However, let's first examine how ideas about romance have changed over time and how they differ across cultures.

10.4a Culture Shapes How We Think About Romantic Love.

Romantic love can be found in all recorded time periods, but it has undergone numerous social transformations (Hatfield & Rapson, 2002). The ancient Greeks considered romantic love a form of madness that "wounds" you, and the Greek god of love (Eros) was armed with a bow and a quiver of arrows. For the Greeks, romantic love was experienced almost exclusively outside of marriage and was more likely homosexual rather than heterosexual in nature (Bullough, 1976).

> "Whoever indulges in love without sense or moderation recklessly endangers his life; such is the nature of love that no one involved with it can keep his head."
>
> —Marie de France, Medieval poet

During the Roman era, homosexual love—considered a "Greek vice"—gave way to heterosexual love. Yet the freeborn Roman male's self-concept as a world conqueror led him to view romance as a game played outside of marriage. Perhaps in keeping with this playful view of love, the Romans were one of the first Western societies to institutionalize divorce (Gathorne-Hardy, 1981). Later, as Christianity became more established within Roman society, sex was perceived as a corrupting influence, tolerated only in marriage. Romantic love was not highly valued. During the Middle Ages (1000–1300), European aristocrats practiced courtly love. Romance was no longer a game, even though it still occurred outside of marriage. Courtly love was considered majestic and spiritual and, in theory, was never consummated (Murstein, 1974). It struck at first sight, conquered all, accepted no substitutes, and was a consuming passion of both agony and ecstasy.

> "Marriage is a noose."
>
> —Miguel de Cervantes Saavedra, Spanish novelist, 1547–1616

Cross-cultural research indicates that associating romantic love with marriage typically occurs when people are free to choose their own partners (Rosenblatt & Cozby, 1972), although for centuries before and after courtly love, marriage was arranged by parents and based almost exclusively on political and prop-erty considerations. Beginning in the 17th and 18th centuries, as these more traditional considerations declined in impor-tance, romantic love began to make some limited headway into marital arrangements. This new association of love and marriage first appeared in England but spread faster in the New World of North America, where social class consider-ations were not so rigidly defined. Although love was now considered possible—and perhaps even desirable—within marriage, early-20th-century marriage educators in America still counseled against basing marital choice on this "romantic impulse" (Burgess, 1926). The irrational nature of romantic love was believed to dangerously undermine what should be a very serious, prudent, and rational decision. However, as marriages became more egalitarian and more focused on mutual satisfaction, romance became even more attractive. With this increased desire for romance within marriage came a greater willingness to end marriages that had lost their romantic spark (Scanzoni, 1979).

Romantic love is usually associated with marriage when people are allowed to choose their partners.

(iStock)

Today, our Western conception of romantic love represents a combination of past ideas. It is generally no longer considered a form of madness, but it is something

> "The minute I heard my first love story I started looking for you, not knowing how blind that was. Lovers don't finally meet somewhere. They're in each other all along."
>
> —Jalal ad-Din Rumi, 13th century Persian poet and Sufi mystic

many of us believe we "fall into" and cannot control. Love leads to happiness, but we can also be hurt in love. Love is possible both within and outside of marriage, and as we explore more fully in the next section, it can be either heterosexual or homosexual in nature.

Heterosexist Views of Romantic Love

Despite the fact that between 2% and 5% of the world's adult population is primarily or exclusively attracted to their own sex, until fairly recently virtually all research on romantic relationships focused on heterosexual dating and marriage. The lack of research on gay men's and lesbians' romantic relationships, coupled with heterosexist beliefs that denigrated homosexuality, allowed cultural stereotypes to shape social perceptions by creating myths about the gay lifestyle (Herek, 1991).

"Love is like a virus. It can happen to anybody at any time."

—Maya Angelou, African American writer, 1928–2014

"Many years ago I chased a woman for almost two years, only to discover that her tastes were exactly like mine: We both were crazy about girls."

—Groucho Marx, American comedian, 1890–1977

One of the main myths is that people who are gay drift from one sexual liaison to another and are unsuccessful in developing enduring, committed romantic relationships (De Cecco, 1988). Yet actual surveys indicate that between 40% and 60% of gay men and between 45% and 80% of lesbians are currently in a steady relationship (Peplau et al., 1997). Following the legalization of same-sex marriage, more gay and lesbian couples are also considering having children together. According to a US poll surveying people who identify as lesbian, gay, bisexual, transgender, or queer (LGBTQ), 77% of the respondents aged 18–35 were already parents, or were considering having children (Harris & Hopping-Winn, 2019). These findings suggest that, with the legalization of gay marriage, many people who identify as LGBTQ are planning on establishing families, whether that is through fostering children, adoption, or assisted reproduction.

As you can see in Figure 10.5, lesbians, gay men, and heterosexual people involved in monogamous romantic relationships all tend to score high on scales that evaluate liking and love for one's partner, and all tend to be equally well-adjusted and satisfied (Kurdek, 2006; Kurdek & Schmitt, 1986). Based on our previous discussion of heterosexual men being less emotionally expressive, it isn't surprising to find that gay men and especially lesbian romantic love tends to be *more* emotionally intimate than heterosexual love (Kurdek, 2003; Schreurs & Buunk, 1994). These findings indicate that, counter to cultural stereotypes, many lesbians and gay men establish lifelong partnerships, and the psychological dynamics in these relationships are more similar to than different from married heterosexual partnerships. Regardless of our sexual orientation, our romantic relationships follow a similar psychological course and are influenced by many of the same personal, situational, and cultural factors.

Individualist Versus Collectivist Views

Is there an inherent conflict between individualist values and the interdependence necessary to maintain romantic love?

In general, people from individualist cultures view love as a positive experience. However, in a cross-cultural study of love, Philip Shaver and his coworkers (1991) found that not all contemporary cultures share this perspective. In fact, people from the collectivist culture of China have a more pessimistic outlook on romantic love than most individualist cultures (Rothbaum & Tsang, 1998). Consistent with ancient traditions, most contemporary Chinese associate romance with sorrow, pain, and unfulfilled affection. What do they think of the Western view of love? They regard it as unrealistically optimistic, a view also shared by people in collectivist Lithuania and Russia

(De Munk et al., 2011). In a very real sense, how we experience love speaks volumes about who we are as individuals and what we are as a culture (Dion & Dion, 1991).

FIGURE 10.5 Expressed Love and Liking in Gay, Lesbian, and Heterosexual Romantic Relationships

In a study of married, heterosexual cohabiting, gay, and lesbian monogamous couples, Kurdek and Schmitt (1986) obtained a liking and a loving score from each partner, ranging from a low of 17 to a high of 117, with higher scores indicating greater liking/loving. Results indicated no differences in expressed love for one's partner between any of the different types of romantic relationships, and the married, gay, and lesbian relationships expressed equally high amounts of liking of their partners. In contrast, heterosexual cohabiting couples had lower liking scores than the other couples.

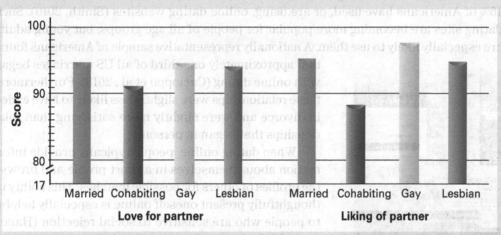

Data source: "Relationship Quality of Partners in Heterosexual Married, Heterosexual Cohabiting, and Gay and Lesbian Relationships," by L. A. Kurdek and J. P. Schmitt, 1986, *Journal of Personality and Social Psychology, 51*(4), pp. 711–720.

A number of studies that have examined the importance of love as a basis for marriage in both individualist and collectivist cultures have found cross-cultural differences in the perceived importance of romantic love (Jackson et al., 2006; Levine et al., 1995). Individualist countries such as the United States, Great Britain, Germany, New Zealand, and Australia place great importance on love in marriage, while collectivist countries such as China, India, Pakistan, Thailand, and the Philippines rate it as much less important. Despite this cultural difference placed on the importance of romantic love as a basis for marriage, people from individualist and collectivist cultures often agree on the traits they seek in a partner. For example, in a survey of Taiwan Chinese and European American college students' ratings of their ideal spouse, Ben Lam and his colleagues (2016) found that in both cultures, "warmth/trustworthiness" was chosen as the most important quality in an ideal spouse, while attractiveness was rated as least important. However, Taiwan Chinese students rated "providing resources" and "family orientation" as more important than did European American students, who judged "openness/independence" more highly than the Taiwan Chinese students. These differing beliefs are thought to be shaped by the fact that collectivist cultures have a tradition of marriages arranged by parents, with family harmony having higher priority than romantic love.

"There is only one happiness in life, to love and be loved."

—George Sand (pen name of Amantine Dupin), French novelist, 1804–1876

Given this cultural difference in who traditionally makes marital decisions, it isn't surprising that collectivists tend to select mates who will best "fit in" to the extended family, while individualists are more likely to select mates who demonstrate independence (Dion & Dion, 2006). This does not mean, however, that love is not a part of a collectivist marriage. Instead it means that, compared with individualist cultures, in collectivist cultures it is more common for people to marry and then fall in love; a common saying in many of these cultures is, "Love comes in the pillow."

10.4b Online Romance Follows Similar Rules to Face-to-Face Romance.

Regardless of your culture or sexual orientation, finding suitable romantic partners is often perceived as a daunting task. An increasing number of people throughout the world are seeking romance through the internet. Indeed, national studies indicate that about 15% of Americans have used, or are using, online dating websites (Smith, 2016). Such dating sites are becoming more popular for people of all age groups, but young adults are especially likely to use them. A nationally representative sample of Americans found that approximately one third of all US marriages began with online dating (Cacioppo et al., 2013). Furthermore, these relationships were slightly less likely to have ended in divorce and were slightly more satisfying than relationships that began in person.

(eharmony.com, match.com, dating.silversingles.com, zoosk.com, tinder.com, okcupid.com)

Marriages and long-term relationships that have started on the internet are on the rise. Why might this be so?

When dating online, people typically provide information about themselves in a short profile and browse the profiles of others for possible matches. This ability to thoughtfully present oneself online is especially helpful to people who are sensitive to social rejection (Hance et al., 2018). Online daters tend to believe that they are more likely to successfully establish a relationship with someone they meet online rather than in person, and indeed, making a positive first impression with their profile is predictive of having a successful first date (Fullwood & Attrill-Smith, 2018; Sharabi & Caughlin, 2017). As in face-to-face encounters, online daters who post physically attractive photos receive more interest than those who post less attractive photos (Whitty & Carr, 2006).

Interviews with young adults who actively use online dating sites indicate that they have the same self-presentation concerns and follow similar rules of social interaction compared to face-to-face meetings. For example, in presenting themselves to possible romantic partners, online daters try to manage initial impressions by creating a profile that is somewhere between their "actual self" and their "ideal self" (Ellison et al., 2006). The risk in this strategy for online daters is that, upon meeting them in person, a date that perceives their online profile as inaccurate is likely to feel deceived, decreasing the likelihood of a second date (Sharabi & Caughlin, 2019).

Although individuals who use online dating websites or apps report that they do provide opportunities for some degree of intimacy, these same individuals also report less intimacy in their face-to-face relationships compared to people who do not use online dating services (Scott et al., 2006). Other research has found that when a person feels they have many possible online dating options, they feel less satisfied and committed to the person with whom they are currently involved (D'Angelo & Toma, 2017). These findings suggest that, when establishing relationships online, one must be careful to engage in behaviors that encourage intimacy (see also Chapter 9, section 9.4b).

10.4c Passionate Love Can Be Triggered by Excitation Transfer.

Beyond the difficulties of finding suitable partners, how do we typically experience romantic intimacy? Research suggests that the two most fundamental types of love are *passionate love* and *companionate love* (Hendrick & Hendrick, 2003; Overbeek et al., 2007). According to Elaine Hatfield (1988), **passionate love** is "a state of intense longing for union with another" (p. 193). It is a type of love that we feel with our bodies—a warm, tingling, body rush, stomach-in-a-knot kind of love. Indeed, neuroscientists have found evidence that passionate love produces changes in brain chemistry, which causes focused attention, concentrated motivation to attain a reward, and a sense of giddiness that is primarily fueled by one of nature's most powerful stimulants: dopamine (Kurup & Kurup, 2003). Spend a few minutes completing the items in *Self/Social Connection Exercise 10.3* to learn more about your own feelings of passionate love.

> "When love is not madness, it is not love."
> —Spanish proverb

> "It's so easy to fall in love."
> —Buddy Holly, US rock 'n' roll singer, 1936–1959

passionate love
A state of intense longing for union with another

Self/Social Connection Exercise 10.3

To What Degree Do You Experience Passionate Love for Someone?

The following items describe how you might feel when experiencing passionate love. In responding to these statements, think of the person with whom you are currently romantically involved or at least attracted to romantically. If you are not currently in love, think of your most recent romantic partner with whom you experienced some degree of passion. If you have never experienced romantic love, think of the person who came closest to sparking passion in you. Using the following 9-point scale, respond to these statements while recalling how you felt when your romantic feelings were the strongest.

Not at all true   1   2   3   4   5   6   7   8   9   Definitely true

1. I would feel deep despair if _____ left me.
2. Sometimes I feel I can't control my thoughts; they are obsessively on _____.
3. I feel happy when I am doing something to make _____ happy.
4. I would rather be with _____ than with anyone else.
5. I'd get jealous if I thought _____ were falling in love with someone else.
6. I yearn to know all about _____.
7. I want _____ physically, emotionally, and mentally.
8. I have an endless appetite for affection from _____.
9. For me, _____ is the perfect romantic partner.
10. I sense my body responding when _____ touches me.
11. _____ always seems to be on my mind.
12. I want _____ to know me, my thoughts, my fears, and my hopes.
13. I eagerly look for signs indicating _____ desire for me.
14. I possess a powerful attraction for _____.
15. I get extremely depressed when things don't go right in my relationship with _____.

(continues)

(Self/Social Connection Exercise 10.3 *continued*)

Scoring

To calculate your passionate love score, add up your responses to the 15 items. Your score can range from 15 to 135, with a higher score indicating greater passionate feelings for your romantic partner. "Very low passion" is in the 12–44 point range, "moderately low passion" is in the 45–74 point range, "moderately high passion" is in the 75–104 point range, and "very high passion" is in the 105–135 point range.

Source: Republished with permission of Taylor and Francis Group LLC Books, from "Passionate Love Scale," by E. Hatfield and S. Sprecher, 2010, in R. R. Milhausen, J. K. Sakaluk, T. D. Fisher, C. M. Davis, & W. L. Yarber (Eds.), *Handbook of Sexuality Related Measures*, pp. 469–472. Permission conveyed through Copyright Clearance Center, Inc.

When neuroscientists conduct brain scans of romantically involved individuals who report high levels of passionate love for their partner, they find that many brain areas become active when these individuals view photos of their beloved (Bartels & Zeki, 2000; Fisher, 2004). Compared with the brain activity produced when they view photos of friends, lovestruck individuals experience increased activity in the *caudate nucleus*, a large, C-shaped region that sits near the center of the brain (see Figure 10.6). This very primitive brain area not only directs bodily movement, it also plays a key role in the brain's "reward and pleasure system." In addition to activation of the caudate nucleus, passionate lovers also experience increased activity in other regions of the reward system, including areas of the septum and a brain region that is activated when people eat chocolate.

FIGURE 10.6 Love Activated in the Brain

When neuroscientists study the brain activity of people experiencing passionate love as they gaze at photos of their loved ones, they find increased activity in the caudate nucleus. This primitive part of the brain processes dopamine and plays a key role in the reward and pleasure system.

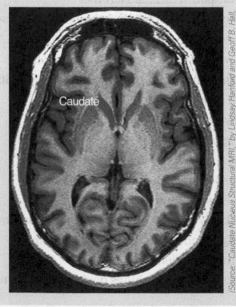

Caudate

(Source: "Caudate Nucleus Structural MRI," by Lindsay Hanford and Geoff B. Hall, available under a CC 1.0 license via Wikimedia.)

Further, when we believe that our passionate love may be reciprocated, regions of the prefrontal cortex responsible for higher-order thinking join in the pursuit, planning tactics, exercising proper restraint, and monitoring our progress toward the goal of romantic bliss. Passionate love is experienced most intensely during the early stages of a romantic relationship. According to Ellen Berscheid and Hatfield (1974), this type of romantic love is produced, or at least enhanced, during early romantic encounters due to a rather interesting transference of arousal from one stimulus to another. As a way to introduce you to this phenomenon, let's revisit the story of how Steve met his wife.

In explaining Steve's initial encounter with his future wife, social psychological research suggests that his acute embarrassment may have actually sparked a romantic attraction toward her. How? As discussed in Chapter 9 (section 9.2b), Stanley Schachter's anxiety-affiliation research indicates that when we are unsure about our own emotional reactions, we often compare them with the reactions of similar others. Schachter (1964) took this insight and expanded on it in his **two-factor theory of emotions**. According to Schachter, our emotions are based on two components: physiological arousal and cognitions about what that arousal means. He proposed that if you are aroused but are not sure what you are feeling, you will look for cues in your surroundings. If everyone is acting happy, their smiles and laughter are likely to shape the emotional label you attach to your own state of arousal. The implication of the two-factor theory is that our emotions are subjective and highly vulnerable to being interpreted based on situational cues. How might this theory explain passionate love?

> "When you are beside me my heart sings; a branch it is, dancing, dancing before the Wind Spirit in the moon of strawberries. When you frown upon me, beloved, my heart grows dark. . . . The shadows of clouds darken, then with your smile comes the sun."
>
> —Anonymous, Ojibway poem

Drawing on Schachter's theory, Berscheid and Hatfield (1974) contended that the spark of passionate love is likely to occur when (1) you meet someone who fits your preconceived beliefs of an appropriate lover, and (2) while in this person's presence, you experience a state of physiological arousal. Returning to Steve's "belt buckle" predicament, what sort of emotional label did he attach to his elevated heart rate and flushed face? Did he simply explain it as being due to the emotion of embarrassment? If he wasn't standing next to someone whom he found attractive, this most certainly would have been the emotional label attached to his arousal. End of story. However, life isn't usually that simple, is it? When arousal occurs in the presence of an appropriate love object, you may well interpret this arousal as romantic and sexual attraction. Dolf Zillmann (1984) has called this psychological process—in which arousal caused by one stimulus is transferred and added to arousal elicited by a second stimulus—**excitation transfer**. In such instances, our increased romantic interest can be traced to the transfer of arousal from one source to the object of our newfound affections.

Capilano Canyon Suspension Bridge, Vancouver, British Columbia: Dutton and Aron (1974) tested the romantic attribution of arousal hypothesis on this bridge, 230 feet above the Capilano River.

("*Capilano Bridge,*" *by Leonard G., available under a CC by SA 1.0 license via Wikimedia*)

Donald Dutton and Arthur Aron (1974) tested this romantic attribution of arousal hypothesis on two bridges at a popular tourist site in North Vancouver, British Columbia. One of the bridges, the Capilano Canyon Suspension Bridge, is 5 feet wide, 450 feet long, and constructed of wooden boards attached to wire cables that span the Capilano River at a height of 230 feet. This bridge is not for those with a fear of heights—it wobbles as you walk on it, and it sways in the wind. Nearby, there is another bridge that does not set your heart aflutter. It is solidly built out of heavy wood and stands only 10 feet above a small, peaceful stream.

two-factor theory of emotions

A theory that emotional experience is based on two factors: physiological arousal and cognitive labeling of the cause of that arousal

excitation transfer

A psychological process in which arousal caused by one stimulus is transferred and added to arousal elicited by a second stimulus

In their experiment, whenever an unaccompanied male began to walk across either bridge, he was approached by either a male or female research assistant and asked to write an imaginative story in response to a picture while standing on the bridge. The assistant also told the man that if he wanted to receive information about the study's results, he could give her (or him) a phone call. Dutton and Aron found that the men who were approached by a woman on the suspension bridge told stories with the highest sexual imagery of all the experimental groups. As you can see in Figure 10.7, these men were also more likely than any of the other groups to call the assistant. Apparently, they had attributed their arousal—which was undoubtedly principally caused by the swaying bridge—to the female assistant.

FIGURE 10.7 Sexual Attraction Under Conditions of High Anxiety

A male or female research assistant asked men to write an imaginative story in response to a picture while standing on either a solid 10-foot-high bridge or a wobbly 230-foot-high bridge. Men who were approached by the female assistant on the wobbly bridge were much more likely to later call her, supposedly to learn more about the study's findings. These men's imaginative stories also contained the highest sexual imagery of all the groups. How do these findings support the misattribution of arousal hypothesis?

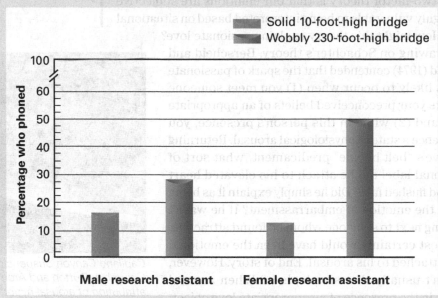

Data source: "Some Evidence For Heightened Sexual Attraction Under Conditions of High Anxiety," by D. G. Dutton and A. P. Aron, 1974, *Journal of Personality and Social Psychology 30*(4), pp. 510–517.

Although this is one interpretation of the results, can you think of another possibility? Perhaps the men who chose to walk across the dangerous-looking suspension bridge were more adventurous, both sexually and physically, than the men who chose the safer bridge. If this were the case, then it was their more adventurous personalities that caused both the bridge choice and the phoning of the female assistant. Dutton and Aron ruled out this possibility by repeating the experiment, but this time using only the suspension bridge. Half of the men were asked to write their stories as they stood on the bridge, while the others were approached after they had completed their walk and had calmed down. As expected, increased sexual imagery and phone calls were associated only with the condition in which men were approached as they crossed the bridge. Excitation transfer, not adventurous personalities, explained the men's actions.

In a meta-analysis of 33 experiments, Craig Foster and his coworkers (1998) confirmed that excitation transfer does influence attractiveness. They also found that while this effect is strongest when the source of arousal is ambiguous, it can even occur when people know the person to whom they are attending does not primarily cause their arousal. In other words, simply being aroused—regardless of its source—facilitates whatever is the most natural response in that situation. If the target person is good-looking and reasonably meets our criteria for a romantic partner, we automatically become more attracted, and the attraction is stronger if the source of arousal is ambiguous. However, if the person is not good-looking or in some other way is an unsuitable romantic partner, we become less attracted.

> "I am your clay. You are my clay.
> In life we share a single quilt.
> In death we will share our coffin."
>
> —Kuan Tao-sheng, Chinese poet and painter, 1262–1319

Finally, one study found that amorous excitation transfer toward a stranger is less likely to occur when we are with our romantic partner. In this study, researchers approached people at amusement parks as they either were waiting to begin or had just finished a roller-coaster ride (Meston & Frohlich, 2003). Participants were shown a photo of a person of the other sex who was of average attractiveness and asked to evaluate the individual on attractiveness and dating desirability. They were also asked to rate the attractiveness of the person sitting next to them on the roller coaster. Consistent with the excitation transfer hypothesis, women and men who were not riding with a romantic partner rated the photo of the other-sex stranger higher in attractiveness and dating desirability immediately after finishing the ride as compared to just prior to taking the ride. For those who were riding with a romantic partner, there were no significant rating differences between persons entering and exiting the ride. These results not only confirm previous findings, but they also raise the possibility that the relatively automatic arousal-attraction effect becomes "deactivated"—or perhaps we are less conscious of its effect—when we are with a current romantic partner.

> "Will he always love me?
> I cannot read his heart.
> This morning my thoughts are as disordered as my black hair."
>
> —Lady Horikawa, 12th-century Harikawa, Japanese poet

Does this research also provide useful information on how you might spark passionate feelings in a desired romantic partner? Perhaps a scary movie, an exciting amusement park ride, or a shared exercise activity would provide the necessary arousal. For your own romantic feelings, the lesson to be learned from all these studies is that when your ticket is pulled out of the hat of romance, it may not matter whether your romantic feelings are initially triggered by excitation transfer or "the real thing." However, you'd better hope that your potential romantic partner's initial reaction toward you is one of attraction rather than repulsion—for excitation transfer may heighten either to equal degrees.

10.4d Companionate Love Is More Stable and Enduring Than Passionate Love.

If you have ever experienced passionate love you have most likely also experienced the hot flames of passion cooling to warm embers. You may well feel very close to your romantic partner, like best buddies, but the passion ebbs and flows. In this state of mind, you may wonder, "Is this what love becomes?" Social psychologists investigating the course of romantic relationships might reply, "Yes, in most cases, this is what becomes of romantic love . . . if you're lucky." Why is this so?

One reason the emotional roller-coaster ride of early love slows over time to a smoother, steadier experience is the fact that passion generally burns itself out. Passionate love is

> "If there is such a thing as a good marriage, it is because it resembles friendship rather than love."
>
> —Michel de Montaigne, French philosopher, 1533–1592

(Franzoli)

As a romantic relationship grows, the emotional highs and lows of passionate love subside. What then predicts relationship satisfaction and longevity is the couple's degree of companionate love.

considered to be a relatively short-lived type of love, more typical of the early stages of a romantic relationship when one's partner's love is less certain (Hatfield et al., 2007). Indeed, passionate love thrives on the thrill and uncertainty of winning over another's affections. As we settle into a romantic relationship, the emotional freshness and uncertainty of passionate love is replaced by a more certain and dependable type of love—if love survives at all (Knobloch, 2007).

In defining this less impassioned, more enduring **companionate love**, Hatfield (1988) states that it is "the affection we feel for those with whom our lives are deeply entwined" (p. 205). Companionate love exists between close friends as well as between lovers. It develops out of a sense of certainty in each other's love and respect, and a feeling of genuine mutual understanding (Acevedo & Aron, 2009). Such unconditional romantic love is not only highly satisfying, it may also benefit physical health. A meta-analysis of 126 published studies over the past 50 years involving 72,000 married individuals found evidence that those whose marriages were characterized by behaviors and attitudes associated with high companionate love were physically healthier than individuals whose marriages lacked those qualities (Robles et al., 2014).

Beyond differences regarding the certainty of a partner's love and respect, another difference between passionate love and companionate love lies in one's beliefs about one's partner. In the early stages of romantic relationships, when passions run high, lovers tend to see their partners through rose-colored glasses (Brehm, 1988). Partners are seen as "perfect," the "ideal man or woman," a "dream come true." As passion fades and couples develop companionate love based on mutual understanding, this idealization of one's beloved often gives way to a more realistic view. Yet, as we will discuss more fully later in the chapter (section 10.5c), although companionate love is a more reality-based love, successful and happy romantic partners are those who tend to see each other's imperfections in the best possible light.

Evolutionary psychologists propose that sex-driven passionate love and commitment-driven companionate love evolved to meet different human needs (Diamond, 2003; Gonzaga & Haselton, 2008). According to this theory, sexual desire is governed by the *sexual mating system*, in which the goal is to sexually reproduce and thereby pass one's genes on to the next generation. In contrast, companionate love is governed by the *attachment system*, in which the goal is to establish and maintain a strong emotional bond between two people. As discussed earlier, attachment is a part of our evolutionary heritage that developed to foster child-rearing and maximize the newborn's survival. Likewise, the attachment bond that develops between two parents in companionate love also ensures the survival of offspring (Fraley et al., 2005). Parents who love each other are more likely to stay together to raise their children, and there is strength in numbers. According to this evolutionary perspective, then, the sexual desire typical of passionate love fuels the sexual mating system, ensuring that a new generation is born into this world. In turn, the sharing and commitment typical of companionate love fuels the attachment system, ensuring that enough members of the new generation will survive childhood.

companionate love
The affection we feel for those with whom our lives are deeply entwined

10.4e Women and Men May Differ in Their Experience of Love.

Although we have described the sexual desire associated with passionate love as preceding the strong emotional bonding associated with companionate love, there is evidence that women and men differ in the degree to which their experience of romantic love adheres to this pattern (Fletcher et al., 2014; Rose & Zand, 2000). Would it surprise you to learn that women appear more likely than men to feel sexually attracted toward others only after feeling romantically attracted to them? Or to pose this question somewhat differently, would it surprise you to learn that, in regard to love, men may be more driven by their passions and women may be more driven by their affections?

> "To be in love is merely to be in a state of perpetual anesthesia—to mistake an ordinary young woman for a goddess."
>
> —H. L. Mencken, US social critic, 1880–1956

When college students were asked what they thought caused sexual desire, both sexes strongly agreed that the causes were often different for women and men (Regan et al., 2000). The most widely endorsed causes of female sexual desire were interpersonal experiences related to companionate love, whereas the most widely endorsed causes of male desire were biological processes and a physical "need" for sex. Thus it appears that women, more so than men, tend to emphasize emotional intimacy as a necessity for sexuality. The same gender difference exists among gay and lesbian adults. Like heterosexual women, lesbians are less likely than gay and heterosexual men to desire or engage in casual sex (Peplau & Fingerhut, 2007; Peplau et al., 2004). This may explain why men are much less "picky" than women in choosing possible romantic partners at speed-dating events (Todd et al., 2007).

In thinking about these gender differences within the contexts of the sexual mating and attachment systems, men appear more focused on the sexual mating aspect of the passionate love process, whereas women are more focused on the attachment aspect that we identify as companionate love. For women more than men, the goal of sex is intimacy, and the best context for pleasurable sex is a committed relationship. For men, this is less true (Peplau, 2003). Of course, this does not mean that women are not interested in casual sex and men do not seek committed romantic relationships. It simply means that gender differences in motivational tendencies regarding sex and intimacy appear to exist. However, these are only tendencies, and many women and men do not fit these general patterns.

But wait a second. Over the years, a number of studies suggest that in some ways heterosexual men have a more romantic view of love than heterosexual women (Hobart, 1958; Spaulding, 1970; Sprecher & Toro-Morn, 2002). That is, men are more likely to believe in love at first sight, in love as the basis for marriage and for overcoming obstacles, and that their romantic partners and their relationships will be perfect (Hendrick et al., 1984). True to these beliefs, other studies indicate that men tend to fall in love faster and fall out of love more slowly than women (Dion & Dion, 1985; Galperin & Haselton, 2010). They also are less likely than women to break up a premarital romance (Fletcher, 2002; Hill et al., 1979).

This does not mean that women are unromantic. Women are typically at least as emotionally involved as their partners once they fall in love. In fact, they are more likely than men to report feeling intense romantic sensations such as euphoria and giddiness for their partner, and to have more vivid memories of past romantic relationships (Dion & Dion, 1973; Harvey et al., 1986). In assessing these findings, it appears that men are more eager to fall in love than women, but once a man and a woman take the plunge, the woman's emotional expressiveness is at least equal to that of her partner's. If this is indeed the way men and women typically approach romance, it begs the question: Why is it that men appear very willing to fall in love, while women initially take a more cautious

"Rank creates its rules: A woman is asked about her husband, a man is asked about his rank."

—From the Palace of Nefertari

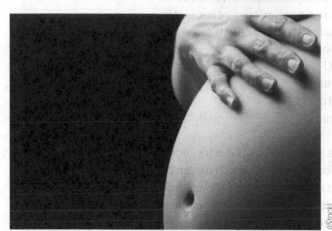

According to evolutionary theorists, how do sex-driven passionate love and commitment-driven companionate love influence women's and men's experiences of romantic love?

approach? Further, how do these differences relate to the already discussed gender differences in the experiences of passionate and companionate love?

In keeping with our previous analysis, evolutionary theorists contend that the different approaches to love that men and women exhibit are principally due to the different investment the two sexes have in the results of sexual bonding, namely, the children that are born (Buss, 1995; Simpson & Gangestad, 2001). To maximize the probability that his genes will live on in future generations, it is to a man's advantage to establish sexual intimacy as quickly as possible in a relationship and to have frequent sexual encounters with many different women. Sparking passionate love is the means to this end. If a man can establish sexual intimacy early in a relationship, he could theoretically court one woman after another and therefore be a big winner in reproductive fitness. For a woman, a more discriminating approach is needed in choosing a mate because she has a limited number of eggs that can be fertilized during her time of reproduction. This biological limitation means that the best strategy for women is to forestall passionate feelings—instead carefully judging potential partners' strengths and weaknesses in order to identify men with the best genes and personality. Thus, according to evolutionary theorists, it is adaptive for men to emphasize passion and fall in love quickly, while the female evolutionary injunction is to move slowly in matters of love and to emphasize commitment.

Although the evolutionary approach provides a plausible explanation for why men fall in love quickly while women are more cautious, how might it explain the fact that men are more reluctant than women to end a romantic relationship? From an evolutionary perspective, it seems to make more sense for men to fall in and out of love quickly because such a strategy of numerous, short romantic relationships will maximize their chances of passing their genes on to future generations. One possible explanation offered by evolutionary theorists is that men have less to lose in a romantic relationship. Because they don't have to worry about a ticking biological clock and the risks of pregnancy, they can waste more time than women in a relationship that is going nowhere.

In contrast to this evolutionary explanation's focus on genetic predispositions, the sociocultural perspective highlights cultural practices and the social distribution of power. According to sociocultural theorists, in most cultures around the world, men and women are traditionally born with different social statuses, with men's *ascribed* status being considerably higher than that of women (Howard et al., 1987). Due to this cultural practice, young men tend to have greater expectations about their social and economic security than young women. Men may therefore feel they can afford to let their emotions and passions rule their mate selection; their status will be determined by them alone, and not by their partner's status. On the other hand, being aware of the sexual inequality in their culture, women might be more likely to believe that their future status will be determined more by their mates' status than their own. Women may therefore believe they cannot afford the luxury of following only their emotions and may adopt a more pragmatic approach to love. This sociocultural explanation is consistent with the data presented in Chapter 9 (section 9.3)

"Marriage, to women as to men, must be a luxury, not a necessity; an incident of life, not all of it. And the only possible way to accomplish this great change is to accord to women equal power in the making, shaping, and controlling of the circumstances of life."

—Susan B. Anthony, US women's rights pioneer, 1820–1906

indicating that men place more importance on physical attractiveness in choosing a partner, while women emphasize social status.

Similarly, the sociocultural perspective further suggests that heterosexual men may fall in love quickly and out of love slowly because men have a greater dependence on romantic relationships for emotional support (Haltzman et al., 2007). Thus, it may be that heterosexual men tend to fall in love more quickly and be less willing to end a romantic relationship because they place all their emotional "eggs" in this romantic basket. In contrast, women are more likely to spread their emotional eggs around, placing a number of them in their same-sex friendships.

Although we have been contrasting the evolutionary and cultural viewpoints, a growing number of social scientists believe that these two perspectives may often complement—rather than compete with—each other (Schaller, 1997). Cultural explanations of why women and men differ in their approach to, and experience of, love emphasize the different social roles and positions of power that the two sexes traditionally hold in society. In other words, they focus on how existing social conditions differentially influence the thinking and decision-making of women and men regarding love. Yet what are the origins of these gender roles and cultural status systems?

Evolutionary explanations focus on how these differences might have initially arisen due to evolutionary selection pressures. Perhaps the ultimate "best" explanation for gender differences in love may describe how selection pressures that operated in our prehuman ancestors shaped certain patterns of social behavior, leaving modern women and men with *certain* capacities to possibly react differently to love. Yet whether women and men actually manifest these inherited capacities is likely determined by current social and environmental forces (Malach, 2001). In other words, culture and social learning may either enhance or override these inherited capacities.

Section Summary

- Cultural and historical views of romance vary.

- Two types of romantic love consistently found in all studies are passionate love and companionate love.

- Passionate love is a relatively short-lived type of romantic love, more typical of the early stages of romance when one's partner's love is less certain.

- Companionate love is a slower developing and more enduring type of romantic love that develops out of a sense of certainty in each other's love and respect.

- Sex-driven passionate love and commitment-driven companionate love may have evolved to meet different human needs.

- Cultural and/or evolutionary forces may explain why women and men often differ in their experience of love.

10.5 Will Love Endure?

More than one million divorces occur each year in the United States, and more than half of all marriages end in divorce (U.S. Bureau of the Census, 1998). Outside of marriage, the mortality rate of romantic relationships is even higher. Although the odds that love will endure are not good, we all know people who have built loving and satisfying relationships lasting many years. In this section we examine some of the factors that contribute to satisfaction and conflict in romance.

10.5a Social Disapproval of One's Partner Harms Relationship Stability.

As we have seen in other chapters, individuals' attitudes and beliefs are significantly shaped by other people's opinions (see Chapter 5, section 5.1c, and Chapter 7, section 7.2d). Given this influence, when partners perceive that their friends and families—and even society at large—disapprove of their romantic relationship, how is its health affected?

For example, research suggests that many Americans—though increasingly not the majority—disapprove of interethnic romantic relationships (Clark et al., 2015; Skinner & Hudac, 2017). Polls also suggest that many Americans express disapproval of same-sex romance and relationships in which one partner is significantly older than the other (Pew Research Center, 2019; Schnabel & Sevell, 2017). When individuals realize that many others perceive that they are in marginalized romantic relationships, what impact does that have?

In a combined internet and conventional survey study, Justin Lehmiller and Christopher Agnew (2006) found that individuals involved in marginalized romantic relationships were well aware of the societal disapproval and expected others to stigmatize them. This perceived disapproval and the expectation of discrimination often had a negative impact on partners' satisfaction with, and commitment to, the relationship. In a 7-month follow-up study, Lehmiller and Agnew (2007) recontacted many of their original participants and discovered that about one-fourth of the couples had broken up. As predicted, individuals who had previously perceived higher levels of disapproval from friends, family, and society at large were more likely to have a failed relationship. Further, this failure was preceded by individuals lowering their commitment to the relationship. While disapproval from others can harm romantic relationships that are marginalized by the larger society, interviews with interracial couples find that if both sets of parents approve of the relationship their support can create a "safe place" that buffers the couple from the harm of societal racism (Bell & Hastings, 2015).

How is the 2015 Supreme Court decision legalizing gay marriage likely to impact both the stability of same-sex romantic relationships and the mental and physical health of gay and lesbian couples in the United States?

Opinion polls indicate that Americans' attitudes toward both same-sex relationships and same-sex marriage have been becoming increasingly supportive over the last 3 decades, with such support increasing further since 2015 when the Supreme Court legalized same-sex marriage throughout the country (Ogolsky et al., 2019; Schnabel & Sevell, 2017). This trend appears to be occurring worldwide; by 2019, 30 countries (mostly in Europe and other parts of the Americas) have legalized same-sex marriage (Tang, 2019). This substantial opinion shift has had a number of positive implications for LGB couples. For example, lesbians who live in accepting communities experience less stress associated with their sexual orientation and, in turn, report stronger romantic relationships (Cao et al., 2017). Furthermore, LGB individuals who live in a community that is more supportive of same-sex marriage experience greater levels of life satisfaction, less stress, and better physical health than those individuals who live in less supportive communities (Hatzenbuehler et al., 2017; Tatum, 2017). Overall, the findings from these studies provide compelling evidence that societal opinions about romantic relationships often negatively affect both the mental and physical health of targeted couples and play an important role in determining whether these relationships survive.

10.5b People Are Happiest with Romantic Equity.

As stated in Chapter 9 (section 9.1a), social exchange theory is based on the assumption that all relationships are like economic bargains in which each party tries to maximize their rewards while minimizing their costs. Although people in intimate relationships often attend to their partners' needs rather than their own, it would be naive to believe that once people fall in love they cease to consider their relationship rewards and costs. Activities such as sharing tasks, self-disclosing, providing or receiving advice, showing or receiving affection, and making sacrifices are *relationship maintenance behaviors*—behaviors couples provide to, and receive from, each other that figure into costs and rewards (Baker et al., 2013; Murray et al., 2015). Yet how are relationship rewards and costs typically tabulated?

In contrast to the selfish outlook proposed by social exchange theory, **equity theory** introduces the notion of fairness, or equity, in how rewards and costs are analyzed in an intimate relationship (Adams, 1965). This theory contends that people don't try to maximize their rewards and minimize their costs but, instead, are most satisfied when the *ratio* between the rewards and costs is similar for both partners. If one partner receives more rewards from the relationship but also makes greater contributions to it, the relationship is still equitable.

For the sake of illustration, consider an imaginary couple, Joyce and Louis, who are married and have a young baby. Joyce has put her career on hold to stay home, and despite the drudgery of household duties, she derives great pleasure in witnessing her child's development. Regarding Louis's perceptions, his career is advancing nicely, but it keeps him from his family for extended periods. Yet overall, he too is pleased with their marriage. Employing some arbitrary numbers to describe these costs and rewards, let's say that Joyce's rewards equal 40, and Louis's amount to 25. Even though Joyce receives more relationship rewards than Louis, the relationship is equitable because her costs are higher: 32 to Louis's 20. As you can see, the basic equation suggests a balanced or equitable relationship:

$$\underset{\text{Joyce's ratio}}{\frac{40}{32}} = \underset{\text{Louis's ratio}}{\frac{25}{20}} = \underset{\text{Relationship ratio}}{\frac{5}{4}}$$

If these two ratios were not equal, equity theory would predict that both partners would become distressed and would try to restore balance. How would this distress manifest itself? The partner who is *overbenefited* should feel guilty about the inequity, while the one who is *underbenefited* should experience anger and depression. Research indicates that inequity does indeed produce these negative emotions in both dating and married couples (Gleason et al., 2003). However, although people who are overbenefited tend to feel guilty, they are generally also very satisfied and contented with the relationship. This is not the case for the underbenefited. Their anger and depression cause a great deal of dissatisfaction with the relationship (Sprecher, 1992). Given the stress that this inequity produces, it is not surprising that inequitable relationships are less likely to endure (Walster et al., 1978).

10.5c Self-Esteem Can Both Facilitate and Undermine Romantic Love.

Beyond perceptions of equity, how is romantic success affected by our feelings of self-worth? A commonly held belief is that self-love is a necessary precondition for loving others. For example, Nathaniel Branden, a writer of popular self-esteem books, specifically states, "If you do not love yourself, you will be unable to love others" (Branden, 1994, pp. 7–8). Is this true?

equity theory
The theory that people are most satisfied in a relationship when the ratio between rewards and costs is similar for both partners

Based on our discussion of attachment styles, this claim appears misleading. There is little evidence that people with high self-esteem are more capable of loving others than those with low self-esteem (Campbell & Baumeister, 2001). Indeed, some studies find that people with low self-esteem have more intense experiences of passionate love than those with high self-esteem (Dion & Dion, 1975; Hendrick & Hendrick, 1986). However, this passion is often fed by insecurity, as is seen in people with a preoccupied attachment style.

Self-esteem may not be related to the capacity to love, but it is related to loving in a way that maintains intimacy over time. Low self-esteem persons appear perfectly capable of experiencing high levels of passionate love, but they have a much more difficult time experiencing the emotional security found in companionate love. As you have already learned, passionate love is often fueled by a sense of uncertainty about winning over another's affections. People with low self-esteem often doubt the strength of their partners' love and tend to constantly seek reassurance (Joiner et al., 1992; Murray et al., 2001). While this emotional neediness can be appealing to romantic partners during the early stages of romance, it often becomes burdensome as the relationship matures.

Low self-esteem and unstable high self-esteem can create problems in a romantic relationship, often due to feelings of inadequacy and/or jealousy.

(Shutterstock)

A series of studies of dating couples conducted by Sandra Murray and her coworkers (2005) found that the insecurity experienced by low self-esteem individuals stems in part from their perception that their romantic partners are "too good for them." Just as low self-esteem people have difficulty generally accepting positive feedback from others as valid, they also have difficulty believing that they deserve other people's love. Instead of feeling secure in their partners' expressions of affection, low self-esteem persons often misinterpret their partners' sometimes negative moods and actions as signals for impending rejection (Bellavia & Murray, 2003). Burdened with these concerns, low self-esteem persons begin finding fault in their partners, which helps them psychologically disengage from the anticipated rejection (Murray et al., 2002). Consistent with the self-fulfilling prophecy discussed in Chapter 1 (section 1.1c), this increased negativity causes their once-admiring partners to feel less satisfied in the relationship, making a breakup much more likely. When the breakup occurs, low self-esteem individuals' feelings of unworthiness are confirmed (Downey et al., 1998).

Although low self-esteem provides hurdles to relationship success, additional research suggests that some forms of high self-esteem can also harm romantic relationships (Schuetz, 1998). For instance, individuals with unstable high self-esteem (see Chapter 3, section 3.4b) tend to respond to relationship problems with jealousy and even violence, especially when their self-esteem is threatened (Baumeister et al., 1996). On the other hand, people identified as *narcissists*—meaning those with grandiose self-concepts, feelings of superiority, and a strong need for power and acclaim—view love as a game and are fickle, selfish, and insensitive lovers (Campbell et al., 2002).

Together, these studies suggest that there is no simple relationship between self-esteem and the durability of romantic relationships. Relationship intimacy can be threatened both by the type of low self-esteem that requires constant emotional reassurance, and by certain types of high self-esteem that induce either hostility when challenged or selfish gamesmanship. In the final analysis, the type of self-esteem that is best suited for enduring romance is that possessed by people with secure attachment styles: self-love that is stable and sufficiently strong to allow for the expression and acceptance of emotional intimacy, while also being capable of handling relationship conflict in a constructive manner (Morrison et al., 1997).

10.5d Romantic Happiness Is Based on Both Positive Illusions and Accurate Judgments.

For many years, most psychologists asserted that lasting satisfaction in romantic relationships depended on people understanding their partners' real strengths and weaknesses (Brickman, 1987; Swann et al., 1994). Although it is hard to argue against the benefits of an occasional good dose of reality, a number of studies suggest that we have a need to perceive our romantic relationships as being better than others' (Gagné & Lydon, 2001; Sanderson & Evans, 2001). Yet how can we satisfy this need if we insist on scrutinizing our partner's flaws? One possible answer to this question is that, if we want happiness in love, we should allow our desire to feel good about our romantic relationships to dominate our desire to critically analyze relationship imperfections (Rusbult et al., 2000; Sedikides et al., 1998). Just as there is a *self-serving bias* that leads people with high self-esteem to see themselves in the best possible light (see Chapter 1, section 1.2a), people in happy romantic relationships tend to attribute their partners' positive behaviors to dispositional causes ("their wonderful personality") and their negative behaviors to situational factors ("a bad day"). This *partner-enhancing bias* not only makes lovers feel better and increases relationship trust, it can also create a self-fulfilling prophecy (Drigotas et al., 1999; Miller et al., 2006).

In a series of studies, Sandra Murray and her colleagues discovered that an important component of a satisfying, stable romantic relationship is the ability to mix positive illusion with sober reality when perceiving one's partner. That is, those who can see virtues in their partners that their partners cannot even see in themselves tend to be happier with the relationship than those who perhaps have a more realistic view (Murray & Holmes, 1999). For instance, in one longitudinal study, dating couples who idealized each other more during the initial stages of their romance reported greater increases in satisfaction and decreases in conflicts and doubts over the course of a year than couples who saw each other in a more realistic light (Murray et al., 1996). In addition, during the year, the targets of these positive illusions actually incorporated these idealized images into their own self-concepts. Similar findings were also obtained with married couples (Murray & Holmes, 1997). These studies suggest that partners who idealize each other often create a self-fulfilling prophecy. By taking a "leap of faith" and seeing imperfect relationships in somewhat idealized ways, people not only satisfy their need to feel that their relationships are better than most other relationships but also create the conditions necessary for their positive illusions to be realized (Murray et al., 2006).

Despite research indicating that positive illusions facilitate the belief that we have found a "perfect match," there are also benefits to accurately reading our partner and the romantic relationship (Thomas et al., 1997). It appears that the key ingredient in differentiating between our accurate judgments and our positive illusions is the degree to which the beliefs focus on us or on our partner (Fletcher & Kerr, 2010). Accuracy is likely to be more important for us when it involves behavior from our partner that provides information

"Things become better when you expect the best instead of the worst."

—Norman Vincent Peale, minister and author, 1898–1993

Earlier in the chapter, you learned that passionate love is associated with perceiving one's partner through rose-colored glasses. This idealization, however, often gives way to a more realistic view with the development of companionate love. Yet, if companionate love is more enduring than passionate love, how can you explain the present findings—that perceiving one's partner in somewhat ideal terms leads to greater romantic happiness than perceiving her or him realistically?

Seeing one's partner through "rose-colored glasses" enhances romantic satisfaction. How can such positive illusions create a self-fulfilling prophecy?

about how we are being perceived by them. Thus, when judging the extent to which our partner forgives us, loves us, or is angry and aggressive toward us, we may be very concerned with making accurate judgments, compared with when we judge the extent to which our partner is attractive, intelligent, creative, or funny. Failing to notice and react appropriately to our partner's actions that relate directly to us is likely to have harmful effects on our relationship. However, evaluating our partner more positively than others evaluate our partner on personal qualities not directly related to us serves to increase our satisfaction with our romantic relationship.

10.5e Being Playful and Expressing Gratitude Fosters Relationship Satisfaction.

During the early stages of romantic relationships, when passionate love likely dominates couples' emotions, a great deal of time is often spent in mutually enjoyable activities. As romantic relationships progress and couples settle into the more mundane daily activities of work, paying bills, doing household chores, and sharing responsibilities, finding time for fun can be challenging (Kohn et al., 2012). As the number of inherently enjoyable activities drops in a romantic relationship, romantic satisfaction also declines (Vanderbleek et al., 2011).

Spending leisure time together by engaging in enjoyable activities is beneficial to relationship satisfaction. How might the two-factor theory of emotion explain this effect?

(Shutterstock)

One way in which relationship satisfaction is often maintained in the face of mundane and even dreary everyday chores is for couples to remain playful with one another (Aune & Wong, 2002). The benefits of playfulness in romantic relationships were demonstrated in an experiment conducted by Arthur Aron and his coworkers (2000). They asked couples who had been married for several years to complete either one of two tasks. One task, which was designed to be both enjoyable and arousing, required the couples to push a ball positioned between their heads across a long mat while they were tied together at the knees with Velcro straps. The other task, which was designed to be rather uninteresting and not arousing, required each member of the couple to individually push a ball to the middle of the mat with a stick (Aron et al., 2000). After completing these tasks, the "Velcro" spouses reported significantly higher marital satisfaction compared to the other spouses. Results further indicated that the "Velcro" spouses' marital satisfaction had increased compared to what they reported before engaging in this amusing joint task. One possible explanation for these findings comes from the two-factor theory of emotion: the couples who mutually engaged in the arousing, playful activity attributed their arousal to their feelings about their partner, which heightened their relationship satisfaction.

Many other forms of playfulness have also been found to heighten relationship satisfaction. For example, using playful nicknames when referring to one another, spending leisure time together dancing, or defusing arguments with playful teasing all have the effect of maintaining couple satisfaction (Gottman, 1993; Keltner et al., 1998; Ricard et al., 2012). Additional research finds that vacation travel provides positive benefits for couples—and families—not only by providing a brief escape from everyday life through sharing new and enjoyable experiences but also by improving communication and a sense of well-being (Durko & Petrick, 2013).

In addition to the positive effects of being playful, another way to foster relationship satisfaction is to express gratitude. For example, Sara Algoe and her colleagues (2017) found that when people in romantic relationships expressed gratitude toward their partners, it induced an increase in the recipients' oxytocin levels, which we previously noted (refer back to section 10.2a) is often referred to as the "love hormone" because of its positive impact on a range of prosocial behaviors, such as trust, generosity, and affection. In this study, recipients of partners' gratitude subsequently reported that they felt more peaceful, amused, and proud, and they perceived their partners as being more understanding, validating, caring, and generally more responsive. Overall, these results and the findings of other studies suggest that expressing gratitude in a romantic relationship—telling your partner that your happiness is due to your partner's role in your life—creates a stronger intimacy bond (Algoe et al., 2016). In essence, expressing gratitude toward your partner is your declaration that they are an important part of your own self-concept, which is the hallmark of intimacy (refer back to section 10.1a).

10.5f People Use Different Strategies to Cope with a Troubled Relationship.

When a relationship becomes troubled, harmful transgressions increase in frequency. People who feel emotionally snubbed respond by behaving badly toward their partner (Murray et al., 2003). In fact, couples headed for a breakup tend to be unable or unwilling to terminate the expression of negative emotions (Halford et al., 1990). For example, in a 4-year longitudinal study of married couples, John Gottman and Robert Levenson (1992) discovered that those relationships that end in divorce tend to involve people who nag and whine a great deal and don't listen very well to their partner's concerns. This defensiveness when discussing romantic conflict is especially true of men.

When troubled couples interact, they often fall into what Gottman (1979) calls a *negative reciprocity cycle*, where positive behaviors tend to be ignored and negative behaviors are reciprocated. Although troubled couples may realize the damage they are inflicting on their relationship with each glare, harsh word, and slammed door, they nevertheless persist in these destructive actions. Happy couples, on the other hand, argue in a more constructive fashion (Blais et al., 1990). When they complain to each other, they also recognize the validity of the other person's feelings and viewpoint (Koren et al., 1980). This tendency to consider one's partner's point of view when arguing (a psychological state known as *perspective taking*) is important in maintaining relationship health (Arriaga & Rusbult, 1998).

The more satisfied and the more invested partners are in a relationship, the more committed they will be to working on solutions when it becomes troubled (Arriaga & Agnew, 2001; Lemay, 2016). Caryl Rusbult and her coworkers have identified four strategies people use in coping with a troubled relationship (Rusbult et al., 1986a, 1987, 2001). Figure 10.8 illustrates the primary qualities of these four strategies. Some people may take a passively constructive approach by exhibiting *loyalty*. They simply wait, hoping that things will improve on their own. Individuals who adopt this strategy are often afraid to "rock the boat," so they say nothing and pray that their loyalty will keep the relationship afloat. Others, especially men, adopt the passively destructive strategy of *neglect*. They "clam up" and ignore their partners or spend less time with them. When together, neglectful persons often treat their partners poorly by constantly criticizing them for things unrelated to the real problem. Those who don't know how to deal with their negative emotions—or who aren't motivated to improve the relationship but also aren't ready to end it—tend to employ this strategy. When people do conclude that the relationship is not worth saving, they *exit*, which is an active, yet destructive, strategy. A much more constructive and active strategy is *voice*. People discuss their problems, seek compromises, consult therapists, and attempt to salvage a relationship they still highly value.

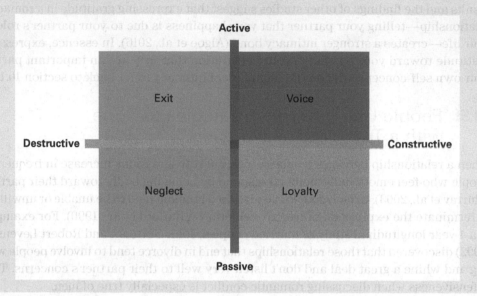

FIGURE 10.8 A Typology of Basic Coping Strategies

In dealing with relationship conflict, people employ different strategies. These strategies differ along the dimensions of active-passive and constructive-destructive. In dealing with dissatisfaction in romantic relationships in your own life, which of these four basic strategies have you used?

Active

Exit | Voice

Destructive — Constructive

Neglect | Loyalty

Passive

Two destructive strategies people employ in dealing with relationship conflict are "exit" and "neglect." What are the two constructive strategies?

There is no one "best" way to resolve conflict. When couples are experiencing relatively severe conflict, an active and constructive approach is likely the most effective course of action (Overall & McNulty, 2017). This might include actively reasoning and negotiating with the partner and generating possible solutions to the conflict. However, in other situations an indirect approach of loyalty might be effective. For example, in order to induce cooperation and promote effective conflict resolution, it might be best to first forgive a partner for his or her transgressions to reduce avoidance, retaliation, and resentment (Fincham et al., 2004). One situation where exiting the relationship is the best course of action is when the partner is being abusive.

Gender, and especially an individual's level of psychological masculinity or femininity, is another determinant of the strategies she or he will choose to employ in dealing with dissatisfaction. In survey studies involving lesbians, gay men, and heterosexual women and men, individuals with many feminine personality traits were much more likely to react constructively to relationship problems (Rusbult et al., 1986b). Either they actively searched for an acceptable resolution, or they remained quietly loyal to the relationship if a solution did not seem possible. In contrast, those who had many masculine traits and few feminine traits tended to respond destructively when trouble developed in their relationships. They passively neglected the problems and allowed things to deteriorate further, or they actively threatened to exit. These patterns were true for both men and women, regardless of sexual orientation. Longitudinal studies of married couples indicate that masculinity's negative impact on relationship satisfaction is due to the influence of the undesirable masculine personality traits

"Love doesn't just sit there, like a stone, it has to be made, like bread; remade all the time, made new."

—Ursula K. Le Guin, US science fiction writer, 1929–2018

in men (but not in women) related to arrogance and aggressiveness—not the more desirable masculine traits related to independence and assertiveness (Bradbury et al., 1995).

Given our previous discussion of attachment styles, it isn't surprising that longitudinal research of romantic couples' conflict resolution strategies also finds that attachment styles figure prominently in what coping strategies people use (Rholes et al., 2014). Those who are more preoccupied and more dismissing-avoidant use less effective conflict resolution strategies than those with a more secure attachment style. Although the research findings indicate that those individuals with strong preoccupied and dismissing-avoidant styles show little improvement in handling relationship conflict over time, individuals with less severe insecure attachment have the ability to alter how they respond to conflict during the course of the relationship, using fewer ineffective and more effective resolution strategies.

Taken together, research on couples' conflict resolution coping strategies informs us that, regardless of gender, those of us who have learned through the course of our upbringing to interact with loved ones with empathy, warmth, trust, compromise, forgiveness, and other constructive interpersonal problem-solving skills are well equipped to navigate the sometimes stormy seas of romantic relationships. The current findings also demonstrate that even when we have not been fortunate enough to develop these constructive social skills, there is still hope. As is the case with all areas of social interaction, all of us have the ability to reflect on and regulate our own behavior so that we can redefine our social reality and live in a more adaptive and healthy manner.

10.5g Romantic Breakups Often Cause Emotional Distress.

Ending a romantic relationship often causes increased emotional insecurity, decreased physical health, and is even a risk factor for early death (Sbarra & Coan, 2017). The two most common emotions following a breakup are sadness and anger, with anger dampening rather quickly and sadness lingering over a longer period of time (Sbarra & Emery, 2005). Not surprisingly, persons who are still in love with their former partner have the most difficulty not getting stuck on sadness (Sbarra, 2006). In both heterosexual dating relationships and marriages, women tend to initiate the breakup more often than men (Hagestad & Smyer, 1982; Rubin et al., 1981). One possible reason for this gender difference is that women appear to be more attentive to and sensitive about relationship problems (Ptacek & Dodge, 1995).

In both heterosexual and same-sex relationships, the partner who initiates the breakup experiences less distress, but this effect is much more apparent for men than women in heterosexual romance (Frazier & Cook, 1993; Helgeson, 1994). Men also tend to suffer more than women when they are romantically rejected. A possible explanation for this effect involves the traditional gender roles taught to men and women. First, because power and control are central aspects of the traditional male gender role (Garfinkel, 1985), men may experience greater self-esteem threat and emotional distress when their partner takes relationship control away from them by ending the romance. Second, because heterosexual men tend to place all their emotional eggs in their romantic baskets, they may suffer more emotional pain when the bottom falls out of the relationship and those eggs are smashed (Barbee et al., 1990).

A similar effect is found regarding the ideologies of individualism and collectivism. In a study of romantic breakups in both the United States and Puerto Rico, Harry Triandis and his colleagues (1988) found that people with a more

When rejected in love, why might heterosexual women suffer less emotionally than heterosexual men?

individualist orientation were the loneliest following a breakup. As discussed in Chapter 9 (section 9.1c), individualists' greater loneliness is most likely due to their less extensive social support network. When romantic relationships fall apart, individualists have fewer people to soothe their emotional pain than collectivists.

In coping with the loss of love, men and women are equally likely to spend considerable time talking to themselves about the relationship ("I'm lucky to have dumped that jerk!" "I've learned a valuable lesson"), distracting themselves by engaging in physical activities, and doing things to improve their looks and sex appeal. However, women are more likely than men to cry, talk things over with their friends, read self-help books, and consult a therapist to better understand their feelings (Orimoto et al., 1993). These results suggest that women, more than men, tend to spend time following a breakup attending to their emotional needs in ways that may promote increased understanding so future relationships can be more satisfying.

Although our analysis thus far has focused on the sadness and distress that people often experience following romantic breakups, aren't there positive outcomes that often occur after leaving a low-quality relationship? Following some breakups, former couples are able to transition into a friendship that is mutually satisfying (Clark et al., 2017). Yet even when breakups end badly, there is always the potential for personal growth (Calhoun et al., 2000; Frazier et al., 2004). For example, one study of college students who had experienced romantic breakups found that they reported an average of five positive changes following the experience, with "positive changes in the self" being reported most frequently (Tashiro & Frazier, 2003). Additional research with college students and divorced couples further supports the hypothesis that a rediscovery of neglected or previously unknown aspects of the self is a commonly reported positive outcome of romantic breakups (Lewandowski & Bizzoco, 2007). Thus, although sadness and anger are common emotions when romantic relationships end, these negative events are often catalysts for personal growth, as well.

Section Summary

- A number of factors determine whether love will endure or fade:
  Social disapproval of a romantic relationship lowers partners' commitment.
  Romantic relationships are happiest when the ratio between the rewards and costs is similar for both partners.
  The positive self-esteem typical of securely attached individuals fosters romantic satisfaction.
  Couples who idealize each other tend to have happier relationships than those who have more accurate views, but accuracy is important when it provides a partner with information on how s/he is being perceived by the other.
  Being playful with and expressing gratitude to one's partner fosters relationship satisfaction.

- In dealing with relationship dissatisfaction, troubled couples often are unable or unwilling to avoid expressing negative emotions toward each other, and they typically employ four distinct coping strategies: loyalty, neglect, voice, and exit.

- Losers in love experience sadness and anger, but breakups also provide the opportunity for personal growth.

Applications

What Causes Jealousy, and How Can You Cope with It?

Besides the many other problems that can besiege an intimate relationship, **jealousy** can also contribute to relationship failure. Jealousy is the negative emotional reaction experienced when a relationship that is important to a person's self-concept is threatened by a real or imagined rival (Harris, 2004). In most cases, the threat is another person, but people can also feel jealous about their partner's time involvement with work, hobbies, and family obligations (Buunk & Bringle, 1987). Some people mistakenly believe that jealousy indicates the depths of a partner's love and, thus, is a healthy sign in romantic relationships. In actuality, research demonstrates that jealousy is a sign of relationship insecurity and it triggers a host of negative feelings and behaviors and tends to lower self-esteem (Buunk & Dijkstra, 2001; Marelich et al., 2003). Given that jealousy is based on relationship insecurity, it isn't surprising that people with a preoccupied attachment style are most susceptible to jealous feelings (Dandurand & Lafontaine, 2014).

jealousy
The negative emotional reaction experienced when a relationship that is important to a person's self-concept is threatened by a real or imagined rival

Are There Gender Differences in Romantic Jealousy?

Jealousy can develop in friendships and family relationships, but romantic jealousy appears to be the strongest and most destructive form (Puente & Cohen, 2003). Both women and men experience jealousy with similar frequency and intensity, but evolutionary psychologists propose that the two sexes are aroused by different triggering events (Buss, 2018; Daly & Wilson, 1996). According to these theorists, due to natural selection pressures, men are genetically predisposed to become upset over a mate's sexual infidelity, while women are predisposed to become upset over a mate's emotional infidelity.

For a man, his mate's sexual philandering increases the risk that the children he supports are not his own ("Mommy's baby, Daddy's maybe"). This is a serious problem because it sharply reduces a man's ability to pass his genes on to the next generation. In contrast, a woman should be concerned with the potential loss of her mate's emotional involvement in the relationship because that could result in him withdrawing his resources for her and her offspring.

Is there empirical support for this theory that jealousy has different evolutionary-based triggers in women and men? Yes and no. Studies that typically support this theory have used a forced-choice hypothetical scenario in which participants are asked to choose whether their partner having sex or forming a deep emotional connection with someone else would be more upsetting to them. In the United States, between 40% and 60% of the men reported they would be more upset by sexual infidelity, whereas around 75% of the women reported that emotional infidelity would be worse. Similar gender differences have also been found in some European and Asian countries; but in China, Korea, Germany, New Zealand, and Holland the percentage of men choosing sexual infidelity as worse drops to as little as 25% to 30% (Brase et al., 2004; Buunk et al., 1996; Geary et al., 1995; Mullen & Martin, 1994). A recent replication with four samples and nearly 2,000 people confirmed the expected gender difference in jealousy, but it was smaller in the new samples compared to the original study, and furthermore, the gender difference was only found among younger people (IJzerman et al., 2014). Taking these studies together, it appears that the evolutionary-based theory of gender differences in jealousy has mixed support (Sabini & Green, 2004; Sagarin, 2005).

(continues)

(**Applications**, *continued*)

In reviewing these findings, some social cognitive theorists have argued that the gender differences that have been found may not reflect inherited sex-based tendencies. Instead, they may simply indicate that women and men draw different conclusions about what infidelity means about their partner's love for them (Harris, 2003a, 2003b). According to this view, men tend to think sexual infidelity is more distressing because they believe that if a woman is having sex with another man, she is probably also in love with him. In other words, sexual infidelity implies emotional infidelity. In contrast, because women tend to believe that men can have sex without being in love, a man's sexual infidelity does not necessarily imply emotional infidelity. So for women, emotional infidelity is much worse than sexual infidelity. This theory of gender differences in jealousy has found support in two American studies and one Dutch study (DeSteno & Salovey, 1996; Dijkstra et al., 2001; Harris & Christenfeld, 1996). However, when Christine Harris (2002, 2003b) studied young adults and older adults who reported having actual experience with a mate's infidelity, no gender differences in jealous responses were found; both women and men reported focusing slightly more on the emotional aspects of their partner's infidelity.

So where are we in our understanding of jealousy in women and men? Regardless of whether gender differences in jealousy are primarily caused by evolutionary-based natural selection pressures or relatively complex cognitive analysis, substantial gender differences probably do not exist (DeSteno et al., 2002; Harris, 2005). Further, instead of natural selection pressures shaping different inborn responses in men and women, it is at least equally likely that natural selection shaped fairly general jealousy mechanisms that evolved outside the mating context as a response to competition between siblings in a family (Harris, 2004). In nonhuman species, sibling rivalry is not uncommon. For example, among black eagles the older sibling in the nest routinely kills the younger one. In humans, infants as young as 6 months express the type of emotional displeasure typically associated with jealousy when their mothers interact with a life-size doll or a similar-aged peer in their presence (Hart et al., 1998). Although more research is needed, it is possible that romantic jealousy has its genetic roots in sibling rivalry and not in the sex-linked human mating system.

Coping with Jealousy

Regardless of the ultimate origins of jealousy in humans, what types of coping strategies—both of the constructive and destructive varieties—could you employ in contending with this destructive emotion? A number of social psychologists suggest that all jealousy-coping strategies boil down to two major goal-oriented behaviors (Bryson, 1991; Marelich & Holt, 2006):

1. Attempts to maintain the relationship
2. Attempts to maintain one's own self-esteem

As can be seen in Table 10.2, if jealous individuals desire to maintain both the relationship and their self-esteem, they will try to negotiate a mutually satisfying solution with their partners. This constructive and active strategy corresponds to Rusbult's notion of relationship voice. However, if jealous individuals desire to maintain their romantic relationships regardless of the loss of self-esteem, they may swallow their pride and put up with the jealousy-inducing behavior. This passive approach corresponds to Rusbult's notion of relationship loyalty. In contrast to these relationship-maintaining strategies, those who are more concerned with self-esteem maintenance often use verbal and physical attacks against their partner or rival. Likewise, jealous people who are not principally attempting to either maintain the relationship or bolster their self-esteem often employ self-destructive behavior.

TABLE 10.2 **Different Ways of Coping with Jealousy**

		Relationship Maintaining Behaviors	
		Yes	**No**
Self-Esteem Maintaining Behaviors	**Yes**	Negotiating a mutually acceptable solution	Verbal/physical attacks against the partner or rival
	No	Clinging to the relationship	Self-destructive behaviors

In commenting on these different coping strategies, Sharon Brehm (1992) brings up a good point: The jealous should think about both the short-term and long-term consequences of their coping responses before acting. For example, verbally or physically attacking your partner may temporarily intimidate him or her into staying in the relationship while it also shores up your own sagging self-esteem; however, in the long run, it will push your partner away and lower your self-worth. Similarly, begging and pleading with your partner to end another romance may succeed in the short run, but it will threaten your self-esteem as it reduces your partner's attraction to you.

A survey of young adults conducted by Peter Salovey and Judith Rodin (1988) found that the strategy of self-reliance was the most effective in reducing jealousy. This strategy involved jealous individuals containing emotional outbursts, maintaining daily routines, and reevaluating the importance of the relationship. Another strategy that reduced depression and anger among the jealous was self-bolstering, which involved thinking positively about oneself and doing nice things for oneself. Similarly, Elaine Hatfield and Richard Rapson (1993) found that encouraging people to make new friends, get a job, or go back to school helped them to think better of themselves, which in turn reduced their jealousy.

The general recommendations coming from all this jealousy work is that the best antidotes to the "green-eyed monster" are to (1) avoid emotional outbursts that are destructive to you and others, and (2) develop a feeling of self-confidence about your ability to act and survive independent of the relationship. In the final analysis, even though intimacy involves an inclusion of the other in our self-concept, our own health—and the health of the relationship—sometimes depends on our ability to maintain a sense of self that is independent of our partners.

THE BIG PICTURE

So what have you learned about intimacy? Do you recognize a connection between the type of attachment style that you developed with your parents and your expectations about friendships and romantic relationships? What about the different types of romantic love? In contrast to the common Hollywood depiction of passion being the cornerstone of romance, research clearly indicates that companionship is what best supports an enduring romantic relationship. Of course, passion is still important—but its primary function is not to preserve your romantic relationship as much as it is to spark the initial attraction. As the relationship progresses and is sustained by your mutual companionship, passion will likely diminish; yet it will probably also sporadically reignite, reminding each of you about your sensual chemistry. Hopefully, this knowledge will inoculate you against habitually entering and leaving relationships in search of the fantasy lover whose passion never fades.

Although "true love" usually does not match the idealized Hollywood version, an important component of a satisfying, stable romantic relationship is the ability to mix positive illusion with sober reality when perceiving your partner. As with your own self-perceptions, overlooking faults and exaggerating virtues in your partner will not only satisfy the need to feel that your relationship is better than most others but can actually create the conditions necessary for your positive illusions to become realized. Here again is an example of how you can shape your social reality and create self-fulfilling prophecies.

Although you have the power to substantially shape the course of your intimate relationships, you can run into problems if you believe that they are invulnerable to outside influences. Despite the folk saying, "No third party can break up a happy relationship," research suggests that friends' and family members' approval or disapproval of your romantic relationships will significantly determine whether they survive or fail (Sprecher & Felmlee, 1992). In addition, although you might believe that "love conquers all," numerous studies indicate that outside influences such as money problems and job stress not only promote hostility in romantic relationships but also make partners less emotionally supportive of each other, all of which contribute to breakups (Lynch et al., 1997).

As you have learned from the attachment studies reviewed in this chapter, the important people in the early years of your life significantly shaped what you expect from intimate relationships and how you behave with those you love. In the coming years, your success in developing and nurturing your intimate relationships will not only determine the quality of your own life, it will also largely shape the next generation's views of intimacy issues.

◼ KEY TERMS

◼ WEBSITES

Accessed through https://www.bvtlab.com/sop8

Websites for this chapter focus on research and theory on adult attachment dynamics and the psychology of personal relationships.

Adult Attachment Lab

This web page for the Adult Attachment Lab, which is directed by Dr. Phillip Shaver at the University of California at Davis, advances understanding of adult attachment dynamics. Here you will find an overview of self-report measures of adult attachment security, as well as recent studies conducted by the lab.

International Association for Relationship Research

This website is devoted to stimulating and supporting scholarship and research on personal relationships.

Relationships and Social Cognition Lab (RASCL) at the University of California, Berkeley

At this website you can learn about the formation, evolution, maintenance, and dissolution of intimate relationships.

Aggression

FOCUS QUESTIONS

1. Do women and men differ in the types of aggression they tend to express?
2. Can you reduce people's aggression by encouraging them to "blow off steam" when angry?
3. Why might laws allowing concealed guns significantly increase gun-related violence?
4. How do myths about rape serve to justify sexual violence against women?

CHAPTER OUTLINE

Applications: **How can cyberbullying be prevented?**

Preview ... Cyberbullying is becoming an increasingly common problem. What is the impact of being the victim of cyberbullying and how can cyberbullying be prevented?

The Big Picture

Key Terms

Websites

Introduction

A 2017 survey by the Pew Research Center found that about 40% of Americans own a gun or live in a household with one. Each year, there are approximately 1.25 million documented cases of violent crimes committed in the United States, with 64% of the country's homicides being gun related, which is the highest rate of any country in the developed world (Uniform Crime Reporting Program, 2018). The United States also has more mass shootings than any other country in the developed world (Fox, 2019).

In response to this high rate of gun-related deaths, the National Rifle Association (NRA) has used its $100 million annual contributions and considerable lobbying power to successfully persuade elected officials in all 50 states to pass laws allowing qualified citizens to carry concealed guns in public, and 31 states allow people to openly carry a handgun without requiring a license or permit (Gifford Law Center, 2017). The reasoning behind these laws spearheaded by the NRA is that if all law-abiding citizens carry firearms, our nation will be safer from gun violence. Or, as NRA Executive Vice President Wayne LaPierre explains, "The only thing that stops a bad guy with a gun is a good guy with a gun." But does arming more people with firearms really provide a remedy for gun violence, or does it simply exacerbate the problem?

Following the December 2012 massacre at Sandy Hook Elementary School in Newtown, Connecticut—in which 20 children and 6 adults were fatally shot by a lone gunman with multiple semiautomatic weapons—a Milwaukee TV news station contacted Steve and asked if he could provide psychological advice to viewers on how to emotionally cope after learning of these tragedies. While the reporter's question was worth asking, Steve's response was that a much more important question that news reporters needed to be asking psychologists—and were not—is whether there is social scientific research that can provide insight into how gun violence can be reduced. Yet, like lawmakers, most local and regional news organizations are intimidated by the NRA and don't ask social scientists such questions.

The all-too-frequent mass shootings in the United States are only a very small percentage of the country's annual gun-related deaths. In this chapter, as we examine the social psychology of aggression, we will investigate not only how aggression—including gun violence—is triggered but also how it can be reduced.

Following the mass shooting deaths of 50 people in New Zealand in 2019, the government announced a national ban on all high-capacity semiautomatic weapons. A similar 1996 gun ban passed in Australia has drastically reduced mass shootings and other gun-related violence in that country. In contrast, politicians in the United States have responded to the country's record-high rate of gun violence by making it easier, not more difficult, for people to obtain deadly firearms.

11.1 What Is Aggression?

Before we try to understand aggression, we first need to define the concept. What is aggression, and how can we distinguish between different types? Also, what is the nature of gender and self-esteem differences in aggressive responding?

11.1a Aggression Is Intentional Harm.

Although there is no universally agreed upon definition of **aggression**, one of the more common ones social psychologists use is that it is any form of behavior that is intended to harm or injure some person, oneself, or an object (Shaver & Mikulincer, 2011). To test whether you can identify aggressive actions based on this definition, read the following vignette and try to identify five acts of aggression.

A thief fires a gun at a man he is trying to rob, but the bullet misses the mark and the man is uninjured. Panicked, the man accidentally knocks down a young girl as he flees the scene, and she badly cuts her knee on the pavement. Later, the girl screams in pain as a doctor puts five stitches in her knee to stop the bleeding. Upon finishing, the doctor asks the girl how badly it hurts. Still crying and now very angry, she grabs his moustache and yanks with all her might and sneers, "That's how much it hurts!" The next day, the thief is arrested and his cellmate verbally berates him for being such an inept burglar. Depressed and angry, the thief smashes his fist into the concrete cell wall, fracturing three fingers. While in the infirmary being treated for his injury, the thief angrily kicks and dents a waste container. In response, the attending medical assistant angrily shouts at the thief that if he does not calm down immediately he will face solitary confinement.

Do you think you can identify aggression when it occurs? The reality is that some forms of aggression are more easily identified than are others.

(Shutterstock)

Can you correctly identify the five aggressive acts in this injury-filled story? What about the thief shooting but missing his intended victim? No harm, no aggression? Even though the bullet missed its mark, this is still an aggressive action because it was the *intention* of the thief to harm the man. In the second action, although the robbery victim's behavior caused injury to the girl, this is not an example of aggression because the man had no intention of hurting the child or anyone else. Neither is the behavior of the doctor treating the girl's wound an aggressive action. Although his actions caused pain and he performed those actions intentionally, the goal was to help the girl recover from her previous injury. Although the man and the doctor did not perform any aggressive actions, the little girl did. In pulling the doctor's moustache, she intentionally tried to seek retribution for the hurt she believed he caused. What about the thief's cellmate? The psychological harm intended in such verbal abuse qualifies this as an aggressive action. The fourth instance of aggression involved the prisoner's self-inflicted injury; intentional actions that cause harm to oneself are considered aggressive, even if they are impulsive. Finally, aggression can be directed against inanimate objects, as was the case when the thief kicked the waste container. The medical assistant's angry response to this outburst is not an example of aggression; rather, it illustrates assertiveness. *Assertiveness* is the ability to express yourself and your rights without violating the rights of others. People sometimes mistakenly label assertiveness as aggression. However unlike aggression, assertiveness is designed not to hurt others.

11.1b Instrumental and Hostile Aggression Have Different Goals.

There is a long history in social psychology distinguishing between two types of aggression, namely, instrumental and hostile. **Instrumental aggression**, which is also referred to as *proactive aggression*, is the intentional use of harmful behavior to achieve some other goal. In the robbery attempt, the thief used aggression as an instrument to achieve

aggression
Any form of behavior that is intended to harm or injure some person, oneself, or an object

instrumental aggression
The intentional use of harmful behavior so that one can achieve some other goal

his real goal, which was obtaining the victim's money. The aggression that occurs in a military context is also often instrumental in nature. Here, the principal goal may be either to defend one's own territory or to confiscate the enemy's land. As a general rule, aggressive acts carried out with the objective of gaining material, psychological, or social benefits all fit our instrumental definition. In addition, aggression carried out to avoid punishment would also be classified as instrumental aggression. Research indicates that observers perceive acts of instrumental aggression differently, depending on their perceptions of the aggressor's motives. People who are perceived to be engaging in instrumental aggression fed by a desire to obtain rewards are evaluated more negatively and are thought to be less moral than those who appear motivated by a desire to avoid punishment (Reeder et al., 2002).

> "You cannot shake hands with a clenched fist."
>
> —Indira Gandhi, India's first woman prime minister, 1917–1984

In contrast to this type of aggression, most of the other aggressive instances in the imaginary vignette were examples of hostile aggression. **Hostile aggression**, which is also referred to as *reactive aggression*, is triggered by anger, and the goal of the intentionally harmful behavior is simply to cause injury or death to the victim (Ostrov et al., 2013). The girl attacking the doctor, the thief smashing his hand against the wall, and the thief then destroying a medicine cabinet were all instances in which the aggressor's principal goal was to cause injury to him- or herself or another person or thing.

In thinking about instrumental and hostile aggression, it is important to keep in mind how they differ. Instrumental aggression is motivated by the anticipation of rewards or the avoidance of punishment. In that sense, it can be thought of as being relatively deliberate and rational. On the other hand, hostile aggression is not really motivated by the anticipation of rewards or the avoidance of punishments—even though these may indeed be ultimate consequences of the aggressive act. Instead, this type of aggression is often impulsive and irrational. There is a goal, but it is simply the desire to cause harm to the victim (Wann et al., 2003). Humor that is sarcastic and disparaging is a form of hostile aggression, and studies find that people who are angry rate hostile humor as funnier than do those who are not angry (Kuiper et al., 2004). Hostile humor is also popular because it is a way to aggress against others without violating social norms (Ford & Ferguson, 2004).

hostile aggression
The intentional use of harmful behavior in which the goal is simply to cause injury or death to the victim

> "The wish to hurt, the momentary intoxication with pain, is the loophole through which the pervert climbs into the minds of ordinary men."
>
> —Jacob Bronowski, British mathematician, 1908–1974

Research suggests that highly aggressive individuals can be distinguished by the degree to which they engage in instrumental and hostile aggression (Berkowitz, 1994). *Instrumental aggressors* tend to use "proactive" force in a cool and collected manner to attain their objectives (Veltri et al., 2014). Many robbers and schoolyard bullies fall into this category, as do individuals diagnosed with antisocial personality disorder, which is also referred to as psychopathy (von Borries et al., 2012; Reidy et al., 2011). In contrast, *hostile aggressors* tend to use "reactive" force in a highly emotional and impulsive manner. Their crimes often entail excessive use of violence due to their tempers getting out of hand. Hostile aggressors are especially likely to perceive danger in their world and to respond to ambiguous stimuli with aggression (Bushman, 1996).

Although the distinction between instrumental and hostile aggression has been useful in helping researchers grasp the complex problem of human violence, some social psychologists have criticized it for being too simplistic (Bushman & Anderson, 2001). The simple fact is that many aggressive actions cannot be neatly placed into only one of the categories. For example, a child may angrily hit another child who has taken her favorite toy, and then she may retrieve the toy

The sarcastic and anger-based humor of Lewis Black illustrates how some people employ hostile aggression in their everyday lives.

(Robert Sholl / Dreamstime)

while the victim cries. The motives underlying this aggression are both the infliction of pain (hostile aggression) and the recovery of the favored toy (instrumental aggression). In such instances, no clear distinctions can be made between hostile and instrumental aggression. In other instances, aggression might start out instrumentally and then turn hostile. For example, a soldier's cool and methodical firing of a weapon at a hidden enemy may turn into impulsive rage when one of his comrades is killed. Despite this problem of multiple motives driving many aggressive actions, an extensive review of existing research suggests that there is a sound scientific basis for retaining the distinction between hostile and instrumental aggression (Vitaro & Brendgen, 2005).

> "A joke's a very serious thing."
>
> —Charles Churchill, British poet and satirist, 1731–1764

11.1c Gender and Personality Moderate the Expression of Aggression.

Research has found considerable evidence that individual differences in aggression are relatively stable, meaning that some people are more prone to aggressive outbursts than others (Farrington, 1994). Attempts to better understand these individual differences have resulted in studies examining gender and personality as variables likely to moderate the expression of aggression.

Why might people who come from a collectivist cultural background be less likely to react negatively to teasing and to perceive it as a form of aggression compared to people who have a strong individualist background?

Gender

A widespread belief in our culture is that men are more aggressive than women. Does research support this cultural belief? The answer is yes and no. Meta-analytic studies indicate that men and women of all ages do differ in one important kind of aggression: physical aggression. That is, men are more likely than women to engage in aggression that produces pain or physical injury (Archer, 2004; Eagly & Steffen, 1986). This gender difference in willingness to cause physical injury is not clearly observable during the first two years of life, but does become apparent thereafter (Nærde et al., 2014). These gender-based differences are more pronounced (1) among children than adults, and (2) for unprovoked aggression than for provoked aggression (Bettencourt & Miller, 1996; Pellegrini & Bartini, 2001). In contrast, men and women are similar to one another in their verbal aggression and in expressing feelings of anger toward members of the other sex, but men are slightly more likely than women to express verbal aggression toward same-sex persons (Archer & Côté, 2005). One additional finding worth mentioning is that sexual orientation appears to moderate the expression of male physical aggression; gay men report significantly lower levels of physical aggression than heterosexual men (Sergeant et al., 2006).

Although gender differences are considerably smaller than what gender stereotypes suggest, women and men do appear to have different social representations of their physical aggression. A number of studies have found that women tend to view their aggression as being stress-induced and precipitated by a loss of self-control that erupts into an antisocial act (Campbell et al., 1996). As such, they perceive their aggression as a negative experience. Men, in contrast, are more likely to perceive their aggression as a means of exerting control over others and reclaiming social power and self-esteem (Bosson et al., 2009). Retaining social power and receiving proper respect is more important for men than it is for women; thus, male aggression is more likely than female aggression to be fueled by perceptions of disrespect (Blincoe & Harris, 2011). Due to their different social perceptions, men often believe that resorting to physical violence is a positive experience. Further, they often mistakenly assume not only that others will approve of

(Shutterstock)

Research suggests that women of all ages engage in more indirect aggression—such as spreading bad or false stories about others or revealing someone's secrets—than men. Why might these gender differences exist?

indirect aggression

A form of aggressive manipulation involving attempts to harm another person without a face-to-face encounter (also known as relational aggression)

them acting aggressively but also that their physical aggression will make them more attractive to women (Vandello et al., 2009). These gender differences in the experience of physical aggression may mean that the more spontaneous and unplanned behaviors typical of hostile aggression are more descriptive of the antisocial actions of women, while the more planned and calculated actions of instrumental aggression are more descriptive of male aggression.

One form of aggression that researchers largely ignored for many years is **indirect aggression**, a form of social manipulation in which the aggressor attempts to harm another person without a face-to-face encounter (Archer & Coyne, 2005). Gossiping, spreading bad or false stories about someone, telling others not to associate with a person, and revealing someone's secrets are all examples of indirect aggression. Field studies by Finnish social psychologists Kaj Björkqvist and Kirsti Lagerspetz (see Figure 11.1) found that among adolescents in Finland, girls were more likely than boys to use indirect aggression (Björkqvist et al., 1992; Lagerspetz et al., 1988). Their research further indicated that while male physical aggression decreased significantly during adolescence, teenage girls continued to exhibit higher levels of indirect aggression at all age levels. Subsequent studies in other countries found similar preferences for indirect aggression among girls and women (Fujihara et al., 1999; Theron et al., 2000). Meta-analyses of the many studies conducted on this topic find that girls and women exhibit more indirect aggression than boys and men (Archer, 2004; Card et al., 2008). One of the insights gained by this research is that, by discovering that aggression is not always direct and physical, we more clearly see the need to reexamine the "peaceful female" stereotype.

FIGURE 11.1   Gender Comparisons in Aggressive Strategies

In a study of the aggressive styles used by adolescents in Finland, Björkqvist and his colleagues (1992) found that verbal aggression (for example, yelling, insulting, name-calling) is the most used by both boys and girls. Boys display more physical aggression (hitting, kicking, shoving), whereas girls utilize more indirect forms of aggression (gossiping, writing nasty notes about another, telling bad or false stories).

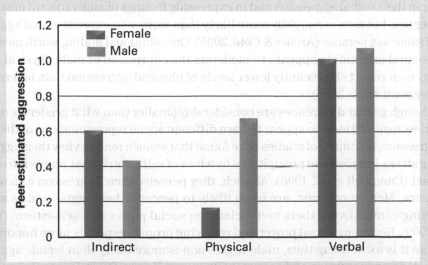

Data source: "Do Girls Manipulate and Boys Fight? Developmental Trends in Regard to Direct and Indirect Aggression," by K. Björkqvist et al., 1992, *Aggressive Behavior, 18*(2), pp. 117–127.

One important question emerging from these studies is: Why might girls and women be more likely to choose indirect rather than direct aggressive means? Björkqvist and Lagerspetz suggest four possible reasons. One explanation is that girls are discouraged more than boys from engaging in direct acts of aggression. Because of this different gender socialization pattern, women may use more indirect aggression simply because it is more socially acceptable (Campbell, 1999).

Another possibility involves the social structure of same-sex peer groups during childhood and adolescence. Girls typically form small, intimate play groups, while boys' groups tend to be bigger and less defined (Maccoby, 1990). Björkqvist and Lagerspetz suggest that indirect aggression may be more effective in the intimate social settings girls usually inhabit because such surroundings create greater opportunities to discover and pass on personal information about others.

A third possibility has to do with the relative physical strengths of the two sexes. Women, typically being smaller than men, may have learned that indirect forms of aggression are more effective and less costly than direct personal attacks. Finally, because research indicates that indirect retaliation to aggression is more common in older than in younger children, Lagerspetz and Björkqvist (1994) suggest that the greater use of indirect means by females during adolescence may reflect their earlier social maturation.

In our examination of gender and aggression, we must always consider the impact that culture has on people's willingness to act in an aggressive manner. Although a good deal of cross-cultural research indicates that women are less physically aggressive than men and less likely to commit homicide (Daly & Wilson, 1988), a number of societies encourage and teach women to be physically aggressive. For example, in her study of aggression among the islanders of Margarita, Venezuela, anthropologist H. B. Kimberley Cook (1992) discovered that aggression was an integral aspect of being a woman in Margarita. As one elderly woman told her:

> Women in Margarita are "*guapa*" (physically strong). When we fight, we punch and tear each other's hair. A long time ago, I had a fight with a woman. I chased her all around the *ranchería*. When I caught her, I grabbed her by the hair and pushed her face into the mud. She was screaming, but I wouldn't let go. I was stronger and I laughed. She didn't talk to me for years afterwards, but later we became friends again. (Cook, 1992, p. 156)

Unlike many women in North America, Margariteño women do not relate their aggression to a loss of self-control. Instead, their antisocial actions are an exercise of control, usually employed against other women in disputes over authority or jealousy concerning a man. When combined with the findings from other cross-cultural aggression studies (Burbank, 1987), Cook's observations illustrate that although women are less lethal and generally less physically aggressive than men, they are by no means the "gentle sex." As a species, we all share the capacity to cause harm to one another.

Personality

Are some people more prone to aggression? Research conducted by Italian social psychologist Gian Vittorio Caprara and his associates (1994, 1996) indicates that three personality traits consistently related to aggression are *irritability* (the tendency to explode at the slightest provocation), *rumination* (the tendency to retain feelings of anger following provocation), and *emotional susceptibility* (the tendency to experience feelings of discomfort and inadequacy). Additional research indicates that adolescents who score low on the personality trait of *agreeableness*—with low scores associated with irritability, ruthlessness, and rudeness—tend to have high levels of both direct and indirect aggression (Gleason et al., 2004). A meta-analysis of 63 studies involving both children and adults found that irritability was positively associated with both provoked and unprovoked aggression, but rumination and emotional susceptibility were associated with greater aggression only after provocation (Bettencourt et al., 2006). Together, these findings suggest that highly aggressive people have a hard time controlling their emotions; they not only have quick tempers but also "stew in their own angry juices" following a confrontation (Denson et al., 2011).

The fact that aggressive-prone individuals tend to experience feelings of inadequacy is relevant to research discussed in Chapter 3 (section 3.4b) suggesting that aggression is one way some people seek to maintain or restore their self-esteem. For many years, it was thought that only low self-esteem individuals were susceptible to these types of aggressive outbursts, but there actually is little evidence to support this claim. For example, depressed people are less aggressive than nondepressed people, and individuals who are shy and self-deprecating are underrepresented among populations of violent criminals (Baumeister & Boden, 1998). A comprehensive review of the research literature suggests that aggression is more commonly a result of threats to highly favorable views of the self and is most likely to occur when a person's high self-esteem is fragile and unstable (Baumeister et al., 1996; Kernis & Goldman, 2006). Apparently, in these instances, aggression is a defensive reaction to avoid having to make any downward revision of self-esteem (Kirkpatrick et al., 2002). This has led some researchers to suggest that there are links between narcissism and aggression, and more specifically that narcissistic personality traits might be underlying mass shootings (Bushman, 2018).

One puzzling aspect of habitual, hot-tempered aggression is that it occurs despite the aggressor often experiencing long-term negative consequences, such as losing friends or being arrested and jailed. Why don't these aggressive-prone individuals learn from their mistakes? A series of studies suggests that a possible reason for these aggressive individuals often not taking long-term consequences into account is that they tend to be habitually impulsive (Joireman et al., 2003). Instead of thinking of future consequences, many aggressive-prone individuals focus on the immediate consequences of their aggressive behavior, which they perceive as beneficial (for example, winning an argument or preserving their self-esteem).

11.1d Intergroup Aggression Is Often More Extreme Than Interpersonal Aggression.

Our analysis in this chapter primarily focuses on interpersonal acts of aggression, but violence also occurs on the group level. Indeed, it has been estimated that approximately 36 million people have died in wars fought over the past 100 years and at least 119 million more have been killed by government genocide, massacres, and other mass killings (Bond, 2004; Rosenberg & Mercy, 1991). In comparing interpersonal versus intergroup acts of aggression, research indicates that group-initiated aggression is often more intense and harmful (Meier & Hinsz, 2004). What are some of the psychological factors that make collective aggression more likely and also more deadly?

"War nourishes war."

—Friedrich Schiller, German writer and philosopher, 1759–1805

As discussed in Chapter 6 (section 6.3b), *realistic group conflict theory* contends that when groups are in conflict, two important changes occur in each group. The first change involves increased hostility toward the opposing outgroup, while the second change involves an intensification of ingroup loyalty (Staub, 2004). This pattern of behavior is referred to as *ethnocentrism.* Both of these changes took place in the United States following the terrorist attacks of September 11, 2001; hatred of Islamic terrorist Osama bin Laden and his followers grew, as did patriotism. Similar changes had already taken place among the terrorists and their supporters long before the attack (Cooper, 2001; Crenshaw, 2000). In fact, the terrorists' hostility was carried to such an extreme that they cognitively placed the United States—the target outgroup—into an extremely negative social category that excluded us from acceptable norms and values (Bar-Tal, 1990; Demoulin et al., 2004). This process of **dehumanization** effectively removes the target outgroup from the perceived world of humanity; thus, ingroup members do not feel inhibited about mistreating and aggressing against them (Leidner et al., 2010; Kteily & Bruneau, 2017b). *They* are not like us, but rather less human and more like an animal.. *They* are trying to destroy our way of life. *They* deserve our aggression. Social neuroscience research indicates that the brain's medial prefrontal cortex—an area important for higher-order cognitive processing and decision-making—is not as active when people are focused on dehumanized targets (Harris & Fiske, 2011).

Groups that are dehumanized tend to have lower social status and less power (Kteily & Bruneau, 2017b). Furthermore, dehumanization often follows incidents of harm or threat to one's ingroup by members of the outgroup (Freyd, 2002; Gerstenfeld, 2002). For example, shortly after the United States' invasion of Iraq, most Americans viewed Iraqi citizens with sympathy and compassion, considering them victims of Saddam Hussein's repressive regime. However, a year later, many Americans' attitudes toward Iraqi citizens had become hostile due to daily reports of US soldiers being killed by Iraqis who opposed the foreign occupation. Likewise, many Iraqi citizens were initially grateful for the removal of their dictator by American troops. Yet when these same troops were perceived to be causing the deaths of many innocent Iraqis, Iraqis' attitudes toward American soldiers became increasingly hostile. Throughout both countries, political leaders, social commentators, and ordinary citizens increasingly defined the opposing country or faction within the country as an "evil" group that must be hunted down and destroyed.

> "As long as your ideology identifies the main source of the world's ills as a definable group, it opens the world up to genocide."
>
> —Steven Pinker, American evolutionary psychologist, born 1954

Another reason collective aggression is more intense and harmful than individual aggression is due to the effects of group polarization. As discussed in Chapter 8 (section 8.3b), *group polarization* refers to group-produced enhancement or exaggeration of members' initial attitudes following discussion. Due to group polarization effects, when planning collective aggression, group members' initial individual attitudes about an outgroup often become more hostile after discussing how they should harm and punish their enemies.

Collective aggression not only has negative consequences for those who are dehumanized; it also hurts the aggressor group. In a cross-national study of 110 countries, Dane Archer and Rosemary Gartner (1984) found a strong tendency for violent crime to increase after major wars, in both defeated and victorious nations. This increase in aggression was found among civilians as well as war veterans, which suggests that there is a generalized behavioral shift across society concerning how to resolve disputes. These results were confirmed in a subsequent study of 186 societies (Ember & Ember, 1994), with additional research indicating that societies with more war tend to have more warlike sports and practice more severe punishments for all kinds of crimes (see Bond, 2004). The likely reason for this behavioral shift is that war legitimizes violence as an acceptable remedy for conflict. The social norms of cultures that go to war indirectly endorse aggression as "the correct way to behave." Based on these findings, Carol and Melvin Ember (1994) offer the following recommendation:

> If we want to reduce the likelihood of interpersonal violence in our society, we may mostly need to reduce the likelihood of war, which would minimize the need to socialize for aggression and possibly reduce the likelihood of all violence. (p. 643)

dehumanization

The process of cognitively placing an outgroup into an extremely negative social category that excludes them from acceptable norms and values, thereby eliminating inhibitions against harming them

Section Summary

- Aggression involves any form of behavior that is intended to harm or injure some person, oneself, or an object.

- Instrumental aggression is the use of harmful behavior to achieve some other goal.

- In hostile aggression, harming another is the goal of the attack.

- Men are more physically aggressive, but women engage in more indirect aggression.

- Personality traits found in aggressive-prone persons include the following:
  irritability
  rumination
  emotional susceptibility
  unstable high self-esteem

- Intergroup aggression is more extreme than interpersonal aggression because it often leads to dehumanization, which eliminates inhibitions against aggression toward outgroup members.

11.2 The Biology of Aggression

Each year about 500,000 people are killed in violent assaults. Does the human race have an inborn tendency for aggression?

Worldwide, about a half-million homicides occur each year, representing a global rate of roughly 6.9 for every 100,000 individuals; more than a third (37%) of those homicides occur in the Americas, 35% in Africa, 23% in Asia, 4.7% in Europe, and 0.2% in Oceania (United Nations Office on Drugs and Crime, 2019). Even when people do not directly participate in aggressive acts themselves, many enjoy watching others do so in action-adventure films or sporting events (Mustonen, 1997). Aggression even manifests itself in the play guns and toy soldiers we produce and purchase for our children's enjoyment. Judging from children's faces as they play with these toys, enjoyment is exactly what these toys often bring them. Based on these observations, is it reasonable to conclude that the human race has an inborn tendency for aggression?

11.2a Evolution Shaped Our Aggressive Behavior Patterns.

A number of social scientists concur with the judgment that we are an innately aggressive species. In fact, for more than 100 years, many biologically oriented scientists have argued that aggression in humans—as well as aggression in other species—can be understood as an adaptive response to the environment (Clutton-Brock & Huchard, 2013). Evolutionary psychologists believe that males of many species, including our own, are more physically aggressive and have a stronger social dominance orientation than females because physical aggression and dominance seeking have been the primary ways males have gained sexual access to females (Buss & Duntley, 2003). That is, by physically intimidating—and sometimes even killing—less aggressive males, the more aggressive males became socially dominant and thus were more likely to sexually reproduce. Over many generations, this difference in the importance of physical aggression and dominance seeking in male and female reproductive success led to genetically based differences in male and female physical aggression.

Unlike males, females' reproductive success did not depend on their level of physical aggression; instead, it relied on their use of indirect aggression. Evolutionary psychologists contend that throughout our species' evolutionary history, the way that women have boosted their social status is through indirect aggression against other women (Stockley & Campbell, 2013). According to this evolutionary-based argument, what increased the likelihood that a woman's offspring would survive and prosper was her ability to attract a man who had high social status within her group—since powerful, physically aggressive men were best equipped to adequately feed and protect their mates and children. In attracting a powerful man, a woman competed against other similarly aged, fertile women, and those women who most effectively used their social networks to not only raise their own status but also damage other women's reputations were most likely to achieve reproductive success. Over many generations, this difference in the importance of indirect aggression and social networking in female and male reproductive success led to genetically based differences in female and male indirect aggression.

The existence of this female intrasexual competition is difficult to study because it is more subtle and indirect (and a lot less violent) than the male variety of aggression. In an attempt to investigate how young women react to a potential female rival, Tracy Vaillancourt and Aanchal Sharma (2011) recruited pairs of female students for what was described as a study about female friendships. As the two participants were sharing their ideas about friendship, another young woman—an attractive female confederate—entered the room asking where to find one of the researchers. In one condition of the experiment, the confederate wore a plain T-shirt and jeans; in another condition, she wore a tight-fitting, low-cut blouse and short skirt. Unknown to the participants, this encounter was being recorded.

How did the two participants react to the confederate? It depended on how she was dressed. When she was dressed casually, the two female participants paid little attention to the confederate and made no negative comments in her presence. However, when the confederate was dressed in the sexually provocative outfit, 85% of the female participants reacted with hostility. These findings are consistent with the hypothesis that women are

In the Vaillancourt and Sharma (2011) experiment, when a female confederate dressed like the woman on the left, she provoked indirect aggression from female research participants. However, when this same confederate dressed like the woman on the right, she attracted little notice at all. How would evolutionary theorists explain these results?

more likely to react with hostility toward women who they perceive to be a high threat to them in attracting eligible men. When the woman was dressed provocatively, participants often stared at her, rolled their eyes, and sometimes showed outright anger. One woman looked her up and down and said, "What the (expletive) is that?" Yet most of the aggression occurred after she left the room. Then participants often laughed about her and questioned her motives. One student suggested that she dressed that way in order to have sex with a professor, while another commented that her breasts "were about to pop out." Additional studies indicate that this sort of indirect aggression is used more by adolescents and young women than by older women, who have less incentive to handicap rivals once they marry (Vaillancourt, 2013). Other studies have shown that the more attractive an adolescent girl or woman is, the more likely she is to become a target for indirect aggression from her female peers (Arnocky et al., 2012).

One important point to keep in mind about evolutionary theory is that it assumes that aggression is not in itself a "bad" or "destructive" behavior; it is a way to secure resources, survive, and successfully reproduce (Tremblay & Nagin, 2005). In that sense, evolutionary psychologists stress the instrumental nature of aggression. By emphasizing genetic survival, evolutionary psychologists contend that aggression should be selective because relatives share many more of the same genes than strangers. In other words, relatives should not be attacked because that would reduce the likelihood that one's gene pool will be passed on to future generations. In general, research supports this hypothesis: Aggression is much more likely to be directed against nonrelatives, and when relatives are attacked, they tend to be "relatives by marriage." For example, stepchildren—who by definition do not have genetic ties to one of their parents—are much more likely to be abused and killed than are other children (Archer, 2013; G. Harris et al., 2007). A similar pattern is found in other animal species (Lore & Schultz, 1993).

"The impulse to mar and to destroy is as ancient and almost nearly as universal as the impulse to create. The one is an easier way than the other of demonstrating power."

—Joseph Wood Krutch, US author and critic, 1893–1970

One problem with solely relying on an evolutionary-based explanation for aggression in humans is that—as Figure 11.2 illustrates—levels of physical aggression vary so widely across cultures. A related problem is that wide differences in aggression occur within cultures over time. For example, 300 years ago Sweden had one of the highest documented rates of interpersonal violence in the Western world; today it has one of the lowest (Lagerspetz, 1985). Genetic changes in human groups over such a short time period (in terms of evolution) are simply not possible. Instead, social and cultural factors are the more likely causes. Of course, this does not mean that evolutionary factors do not influence human aggression. It simply means that evolutionary forces, by themselves, cannot adequately explain human aggression.

11.2b Biological Factors Influence Aggressive Behavior.

Beyond looking into how aggressive tendencies may have been shaped over hundreds of thousands of generations, scientists also study whether individual aggressive tendencies are inherited and whether hormonal fluctuations influence later aggressive responses. Contemporary biologists and evolutionary theorists do not argue that aggressive behavior is determined by some fixed, inborn tendency. Instead, they propose that these biological background variables influence how we respond to situational provocations.

Behavior Genetics

Research in the field of behavior genetics on identical and fraternal twins suggests that our individual aggressiveness is most likely partly due to inheritance (Baker et al., 2007). That is, twins who share exactly the same genetic material (identical twins) tend to have more similar aggressive tendencies than twins who share only 50% of the same genes (fraternal twins). One problem with this research, however, is that parents tend to treat identical twins more similarly than fraternal twins; thus, it is difficult for twin studies to clearly distinguish between genetic and environmental determinants of aggression (McCord, 1994). Despite this difficulty, research indicates that genetic and environmental factors often interact in shaping aggression. For example, a Swedish longitudinal study of more than 1,300 twin pairs found that parents' often harsh punishment of their children's early, genetically influenced aggressive tendencies actually increases their later aggressive behavior (Narusyte et al., 2007). Thus, while it is clear that heritability plays a role in shaping human aggression, its degree of influence is still unknown (Pérusse & Gendreau, 2005).

FIGURE 11.2   Annual Murder Rates Around the Globe

A United Nations study reported that not only does the murder rate vary widely from country to country but also that the murder rates within many countries change substantially from year to year. Do these data suggest that evolutionary-based explanations of aggression are false? How might you explain the data by considering both evolutionary and cultural factors in your analysis?

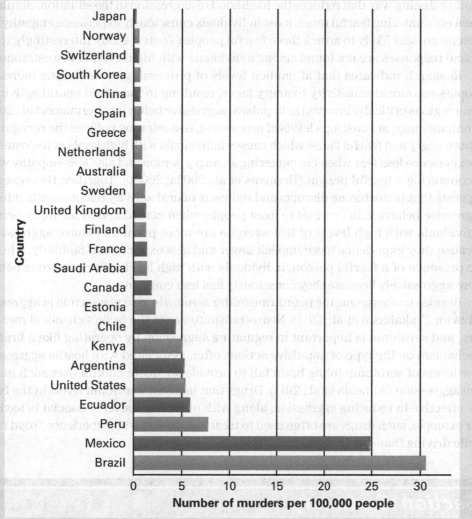

Data source: "Homicide Dataset 2019" (table), by United Nations Office on Drugs and Crime, 2017, UNODC. Copyright 2017 by UNODC. Retrieved from https://dataunodc.un.org/GSH_app

Hormonal Activity

Chemical messengers in the bloodstream, known as hormones, clearly influence human aggression as well—but the exact nature of this relationship is still not clear. The hormone that has been the focus of most research is *testosterone*, the most important male sex hormone (Victoroff et al., 2011). Many experts believe that heightened testosterone levels make aggression more likely, and that aggression—or even nonaggressive competition—causes increases in testosterone levels. Consistent with this thinking, a number of studies have found higher than normal levels of testosterone in individuals of both sexes who exhibit high levels of social dominance, competitiveness, and aggression (Adelson, 2004; Sher, 2014).

Research examining the testosterone-aggression link finds that this hormone appears to affect both conscious and unconscious thinking in ways that provoke anger and inhibit empathy and fear. When encountering angry faces, most people immediately detect a possible threat, consciously experience some degree of fear, and quickly respond in a nonthreatening way that reduces the likelihood of aggression in the situation. Similarly, when encountering fearful faces, most individuals consciously experience empathy and thereby are less likely to attack these fearful people (Toates, 2006). Interestingly, these typical responses are not found among individuals with high levels of testosterone.

Research indicates that at implicit levels of processing, testosterone increases people's emotional sensitivity to angry faces, resulting in increased neural activity in brain regions critically involved in impulsive aggressive behavior (Hermans et al., 2008). Simultaneously, at conscious levels of processing, testosterone reduces the recognition of both angry and fearful faces, which causes individuals with high levels of testosterone to experience less fear when encountering an angry person and also less empathy when encountering a fearful person (Hermans et al., 2006a, 2006b). Together, this research suggests that testosterone disrupts and redirects neural activity that normally inhibits aggressive behavior. In contrast to most people, when confronted by an angry person, individuals with high levels of testosterone are more prone to behave aggressively because they experience more implicit anger and less explicit fear. Similarly, when in the presence of a fearful person, individuals with high levels of testosterone behave more aggressively because they consciously feel less empathy.

Besides testosterone, the neurotransmitter *serotonin* also plays a role in aggressive behavior (Takahashi et al., 2011). Neurotransmitters are the brain's chemical messengers, and serotonin is important in regulating aggression by operating like a braking mechanism on the type of impulsive actions often associated with hostile aggression. Low levels of serotonin in the brain fail to provide adequate control over such impulsive aggression (Almeida et al., 2011). Drugs that increase serotonin levels in the brain are effective in reducing aggression, along with other impulsive, antisocial behaviors. For example, such drugs are often used to treat individuals who experience "road rage" while driving (Sansone & Sansone, 2010).

Section Summary

- Evolutionary theorists contend that aggressive tendencies are selective and based on the principle of genetic survival.

- Biological research suggests that individual differences in aggressiveness are partly due to inheritance and hormonal changes.

11.3 Aggression as a Reaction to Negative Affect

The Japanese are world-famous for their politeness. One notable exception to this courteous behavior is a 200-year-old event that takes place just before midnight on New Year's Eve in Ashikaga, a city 50 miles north of Tokyo. In what outsiders might consider to be a very strange festival, people walk in a procession up a dark mountain road to the Saishoji Temple, screaming curses at those who have frustrated them during the previous 12 months. "You idiot!" "Give me a raise!" "My teacher is stupid!" Although the Japanese would almost never direct these words of blame, hostility, and anger at the real sources of their frustration, participants believe that the screaming is beneficial. Is such behavior really beneficial to people? Does it reduce aggressive tendencies?

11.3a The Frustration-Aggression Hypothesis Asserts That Frustration Triggers Aggression.

If you had asked a group of social psychologists these questions in 1939, they most likely would have replied that releasing pent-up frustrations in this manner is a very good idea. At that time, John Dollard, Neal Miller, Leonard Doob, O. H. Mowrer, and Robert Sears had just published their now classic monograph, *Frustration and Aggression*, which outlined what came to be the most popular theory of aggression in the social sciences—namely, the **frustration-aggression hypothesis**. They defined frustration as any external condition that prevents you from obtaining the pleasures you had expected to enjoy. In other words, if you are prevented from doing something that you want to do, you become frustrated. The original theory had three main propositions. The first proposition was that frustration always elicits the drive to attack others. The second proposition was that every act of aggression could be traced to some previous frustration (this essentially meant that all aggression is of the hostile variety). The third proposition was that engaging in aggression causes **catharsis**, which is the reduction of the aggressive drive following an aggressive act.

Research supports the general proposition that frustration can cause aggression. For example, archival studies have found a negative correlation between economic conditions and lynchings of African Americans in the pre-1930s South (Hepworth & West, 1988; Hovland & Sears, 1940; Tolnay & Beck, 1995). When Southern states experienced economic depression due to a drop in cotton prices, white southerners appeared to vent their frustration by lynching blacks. In other words, African Americans became the scapegoats of displaced white aggression. Other studies have found a correlation between the loss of jobs in communities and an increase in child abuse and other violent behavior (Catalano et al., 1993; Steinberg et al., 1981). In general, frustration is most likely to produce an inclination to aggress when the person believes the hindrance was unfair and intentional (Krieglmeyer et al., 2009).

Although this research established a link between frustration and aggression, additional studies indicate that this link is subject to a rapid rate of decay (Green et al., 1998). If frustration is not acted upon quickly (often in less than an hour), people are unlikely to aggress (Buvinic & Berkowitz, 1976). Furthermore, subsequent research has shown that frustration is simply one among many causes of aggression.

Finally, the claim that aggressive tendencies are reduced following the expression of aggression has been subjected to a great deal of scientific scrutiny. Although the notion of catharsis reflects a common belief that people can purge themselves of powerful emotions by "letting off steam" or "getting it off their chests," what does the research literature tell us? A number of studies indicate that engaging in aggressive behavior can reduce physiological arousal in some people, which is akin to "letting off steam"

frustration-aggression hypothesis
The theory that frustration causes aggression

catharsis
The reduction of the aggressive drive following an aggressive act

(Bresin & Gordon, 2013; Hokanson & Edelman, 1966). But does this mean that such reduction in arousal will lead to less future aggression? Not according to behavioral psychologists and their principles of operant conditioning. Behaviorists would argue that because an aggressive response removes an unpleasant stimulus—namely, heightened arousal—the likelihood of future aggression should increase, not decrease, due to this arousal reduction. Let's more closely examine relevant studies.

In one representative study, Shahbaz Mallick and Boyd McCandless (1966) had third-grade girls and boys work on a block-construction task in pairs. What the young participants did not realize, however, was that the child working with them was a confederate who had been instructed either to allow participants to complete the block-construction task or to act very clumsy and impede completion. Immediately following this frustrating or nonfrustrating experience, participants performed an intervening activity for about 8 minutes. This activity either involved shooting a toy gun at a target or talking with the experimenter. Half of the children who talked with the experimenter were told during the course of the conversation that their partner had been tired and upset, while the rest merely engaged in neutral talk with the experimenter. At the end of this intervening activity, the young confederate was brought into another room, supposedly to work on another block-construction task. Each of the naive participants then was given an opportunity to hinder the confederate's progress by pushing a "hurt"

"I have enjoyed all the pleasures that revenge can give."

—Marie Madeleine de La Fayette, French countess and novelist, 1634–1693

button that would disrupt the confederate's work. Aggression was measured by the number of times the child pushed the button.

As Figure 11.3 shows, frustration generally increased aggression—except when participants were told that fatigue and emotional strain had caused the confederate's clumsiness. This finding is consistent with the previously discussed findings that aggression is much more likely following intentional rather than unintentional frustration. More important for our discussion of catharsis, however, is the fact that children's aggressive play did not result in any reduction in the number of attacks on the frustrator. Put simply, there is no evidence of catharsis in these findings. Engaging in make-believe violence does not purge aggressive drives (Bushman, 2002).

Direct acts of aggression also do not cause catharsis. In fact, a number of experiments indicate that people who are given the opportunity to aggress directly against someone who has frustrated them often become more aggressive—not less so (Buss, 1966; Geen, 1968). Although these results are inconsistent with the notion of catharsis, they are consistent with the theory of operant conditioning, which states that a behavior will increase in future frequency when it has the effect of removing an unpleasant stimulus. Sociologist Murray Straus's research indicates that this sort of escalation of aggression is a common pattern in domestic violence (Straus & Gelles, 1990; Straus et al., 1980). Family conflicts often begin with verbal quarreling, which then escalates to screaming and yelling, and finally to physical aggression (Houry et al., 2004). In contrast,

"No more tears now. I will think about revenge."

—Mary, Queen of Scots, 1542–1587

households that engage in little or no verbal aggression rarely ever experience physical violence (less than 0.5%).

Despite the lack of research support for catharsis, the popular media and many mental health professionals continue to advocate its use. For example, a common belief among many marriage counselors is that "couples who fight [verbally] together, stay together"—as long as they do not engage in vindictive verbal attacks. As Straus points out, however, the research literature indicates that once verbal aggression begins, it is difficult to keep it within manageable bounds. In such instances, advocating the venting of anger through aggressive means may be worse than useless—it may cause a general increase in aggressive behavior. This does not mean you should keep your frustrations and anger bottled up inside yourself.

However, instead of yelling at others—or even punching a pillow when angry—the best strategy is to convey your feelings calmly and clearly, without being intentionally hurtful.

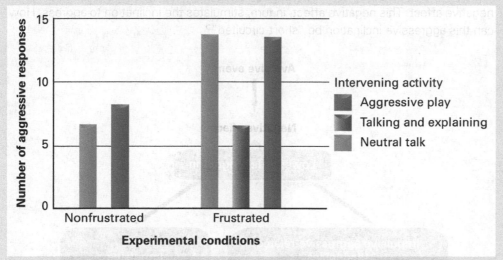

FIGURE 11.3   Does Children's Aggressive Play Have a Cathartic Effect?

In contradiction to the catharsis hypothesis, Mallick and McCandless (1966) found that children who had been frustrated by a "clumsy" child confederate showed no reduction in their aggressive responses after engaging in imaginary aggression. What did reduce aggression in the frustrated children was being told that the confederate's clumsiness had been caused by fatigue and strain (talking and explaining condition). What do these findings suggest about recommendations that aggression can be decreased by having people engage in make-believe violence?

Data source: "A Study of Catharsis of Aggression," by S. K. Mallick and B. R. McCandless, 1966, *Journal of Personality and Social Psychology, 4*(6), pp. 591–596.

11.3b Unpleasant Situations Can Activate Aggressive Thoughts and Associations.

Realizing that the association between frustration and aggression had been overstated, in the late 1960s Leonard Berkowitz (1969, 1989) developed a new theory to explain how hostile aggression is often triggered by circumstances that arouse negative feelings. He asserted that frustration is just one of many factors that can stimulate negative affect. Besides frustration, other aversive factors such as pain, extreme temperatures, and encountering disliked people can also cause negative affect. It is this negative affect, and not frustration itself, that stimulates the inclination to aggress. The stronger the negative affect—whether it is caused by frustration or by some other aversive experience—the greater the aggressive inclination.

Cognitive-Associative Networks

Berkowitz named his theory the **cognitive-neoassociation model** because he believes that when we experience negative affect due to some unpleasant condition, this affect is encoded into memory and becomes cognitively associated with specific types of negative thoughts, emotions, physiological responses, and reflexive behaviors

cognitive-neoassociation model

A theory of impulsive aggression that aversive events produce negative affect, which stimulates the inclination to aggress (see Figure 11.4). Although these cognitive-associative networks are initially weak, the more they are activated, the stronger they become (Ratcliff & McKoon, 1994). When these associations are sufficiently strong, activating any one of them will likely activate the others, a process known as *priming* (see Chapter 4, section 4.1c). Thus, when we recall a past occasion in which we were extremely angry, this memory may prime hostile thoughts, angry feelings, and even anger/aggression-related reflexive actions, such as clenched fists and gritted teeth. One important implication of this theory is that even when our surroundings do not elicit negative affect, simply thinking about aggression can set us on the path to its activation (Dodge, 2011).

FIGURE 11.4   Cognitive-Neoassociation Model of Hostile Aggression

Leonard Berkowitz's theory of impulsive aggression states that aversive events produce negative affect. This negative affect, in turn, stimulates the inclination to aggress. How can this aggressive inclination be "short-circuited"?

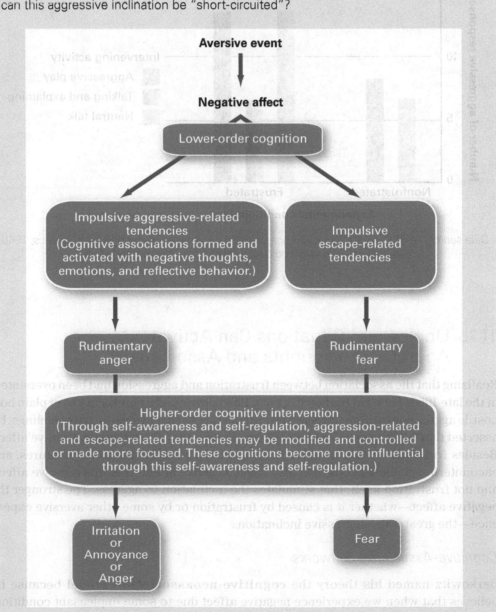

In addition to describing how cognitive-associative networks are formed, the cognitive-neoassociation model further proposes that an aversive event initially activates not one but two different networks at the same time. One network is related to the impulsive aggression-related tendencies already described (the fight response), while the other is related to impulsive escape-related tendencies (the flight response). Whether we react to negative affect with "fight" or "flight" depends on our (1) genetic predispositions, (2) prior conditioning and learning, and (3) attention to aspects of the situation that facilitate or inhibit aggression (Berkowitz, 1993). Because our present objective is to understand how aversive events lead to aggression, we will concentrate on the fight-response side of this model (the left side of Figure 11.4).

One thing to keep in mind is that the cognitive processes discussed thus far are simply *rudimentary emotional reactions* to negative affect; thus, they represent only the potential first stage in aggression. The negative thoughts, emotions, and reflexive actions evoked in the cognitive-associative networks at this stage are primitive, or rudimentary, and have yet to be shaped and developed by the higher-order cognitive processes of the brain's medial prefrontal cortex (Harris & Fiske, 2011). If this more-sophisticated thinking does not come into play, we may simply lash out with anger or aggression, and our targets may not even be those who triggered our anger (Bushman et al., 2005a).

> "No man can think clearly when his fists are clenched."
> —George Jean Nathan, American critic and writer, 1882–1958

> "When anger rises, think of the consequences."
> —Confucius, Chinese philosopher, 551–479 BCE

Although aggression is likely if we reflexively respond to negative affect, a very different outcome often occurs in "stage two" if *higher-order cognitive intervention processes* are activated and we begin self-regulating. The cognitive-neoassociation model contends that if these aggression-related tendencies are subjected to self-regulation, they are often modified and controlled. What causes the aggression-related tendencies in stage one to come under the control of the more complex cognitive processes of stage two? As previously discussed in Chapter 3 (section 3.1c), these cognitive control mechanisms are activated when we become self-aware and attend to what we are thinking, feeling, and doing. Thus, when frustrated, we may try to make sense of—and control—our negative feelings before acting. Research indicates that individuals who are slow to anger when provoked do indeed experience hostile feelings, but they are much more likely than those with hot tempers to spontaneously harness self-regulatory resources and "cool" their anger (Wilkowski & Robinson, 2007). This type of higher-order thinking does not guarantee a nonaggressive response, but it does make it more likely (Kuppens et al., 2004).

The Heat Hypothesis

Beyond providing a better explanation for the association between frustration and aggression, the primary importance of the cognitive-neoassociation model is in its explanation of our impulsive and affect-driven reactions to aggression. The model proposes that events resulting in particularly intense levels of negative affect generate strong activation of aggression-related cognitions and emotions, which produce powerful feelings of anger and inclinations to aggress.

One very common unpleasant situation that has often been associated with such aggressive responses is hot weather. Consistent with the cognitive-neoassociation model, laboratory experiments demonstrate that hot temperatures increase hostile thoughts and feelings (Anderson et al., 1995). Also consistent

How does the heat hypothesis partly account for the increased levels of aggression in urban areas during the summer months of the 1960s?

with the model is the finding of an upward spiral effect, in which the discomfort caused by high temperatures is related to increased levels of aggression (Anderson et al., 1997). For example, archival studies suggest that the urban riots that erupted in many American cities in the 1960s were most likely to occur on hot days and then to diminish in intensity as the weather cooled (Carlsmith & Anderson, 1979). This effect also occurs for such aggressive behaviors as murder, assault, rape, and spousal abuse (Anderson & Anderson, 1984, 1996; Bushman et al., 2005b). Although there is also evidence that extremely high temperatures can actually lower aggression-related crimes due to people being less socially active (Rotton & Cohn, 2000), in general there is a positive relationship between hot weather and hot tempers.

The heat hypothesis also explains why an analysis of more than 57,000 Major League Baseball games finds that pitchers who play in hot weather are much more likely than those who play in cooler weather to retaliate and hit opposing batters after one of their teammates has been hit by a pitch (Larrick et al., 2011). It appears that high temperatures increase retaliation by pitchers because the pitchers are more likely to become angry and make hostile attributions about why their own teammates were hit by a pitch, and also because the high temperatures lower their inhibitions against retaliation.

The fact that hot temperatures appear to increase impulsive, hostile aggression has some disturbing implications for global warming. For example, Solomon Hsiang and his coworkers (2011) examined archival data in tropical countries over the past half century and found that during what are known as El Niño years—when the weather is very hot and dry—there was a dramatic increase in civil conflict. By the middle of the 21st century, we can expect global temperatures to increase by 2 to 8 degrees, which means there will be many more hot days in the summer months (Niemeyer et al., 2005). Craig Anderson (2001) estimates that such temperature increases could increase annual serious and deadly assaults by more than 24,000 incidents in the United States alone. Unless we significantly reduce the concentrations of greenhouse gases produced by human activities, future generations may become all too familiar with the negative effects of the heat hypothesis.

> "There are so many conflicting emotions when your batter gets hit. Because how do you sort it out? How do you know for sure that the pitcher acted intentionally?"
>
> —Tony La Russa, St. Louis Cardinals manager, born 1944

> "Anger blows out the lamp of the mind."
>
> —Robert Ingersoll, American politician, 1833–1899

> "Man only becomes dangerous when he is equipped with weapons."
>
> —Sir Edmund Leach, British social anthropologist, 1910–1989

Aggressive Cues as "Triggers" of Aggression

One question many people rightly ask following mass shootings is whether the aggressors would have acted on their anger if they did not have easy access to firearms. A related question is whether the actual presence of firearms can somehow trigger the resulting aggression. Based on his research, Leonard Berkowitz considers this a distinct possibility, and he refers to this as the *weapons effect*. In addition to anger eliciting aggression, Berkowitz believes that the presence of weapons or other *aggression-associated cues* in the environment can act as triggers for hostile outbursts by making aggressive thoughts more accessible. An aggression-associated cue is anything that is associated with either violence or unpleasantness. The most obvious aggressive cues are weapons, such as guns, knives, and clubs, while less obvious cues are negative attitudes and unpleasant physical characteristics. Numerous

(Shutterstock)

A handgun kept in the home for self-protection is 43 times more likely to kill a friend or family member than an intruder. How is this statistic explained by what Leonard Berkowitz calls the "weapons effect"?

studies indicate that the presence of aggression-associated cues does indeed trigger aggression (Anderson et al., 1998; Lindsay & Anderson, 2000).

In a recent meta-analysis of 78 studies examining the weapons effect, Arlin Benjamin and his coworkers (2018) found modest support for the hypothesis that the mere presence of weapons increases aggressiveness in people who are already angry. This finding may go a long way in explaining the fact that a handgun kept in the home for self-protection is 43 times more likely to kill a friend or family member than an intruder (Hemenway, 2011). When domestic disputes erupt, the presence of firearms may enhance the aggressiveness of the angry parties, resulting in tragic consequences (Anglemyer et al., 2014). People even drive more aggressively when there is a gun in the car (Bushman et al., 2017). As Berkowitz explains, "Guns not only permit violence, they can stimulate it as well. The finger pulls the trigger, but the trigger may also be pulling the finger" (Berkowitz, 1968, p. 22).

An important caveat to Berkowitz's statement is that the weapons effect depends on the meaning people attach to guns and other weapons. For many people, guns are associated in memory with aggression and hostility because they are viewed as instruments designed and used to hurt and kill people. Yet what about people who view guns less as objects of aggression against other people and more as objects to be used for sport? If these people associate guns with having fun outdoors on weekends hunting for wild game, are they unlikely to have aggressive thoughts when in the presence of hunting guns? A series of studies conducted by Bruce Bartholow and his colleagues (2005) indicates that this appears to be the case. They found that although both hunting rifles and assault weapons served as cues for aggression for people with no prior hunting experience, only assault weapons served as an aggressive cue for hunters. Instead of priming negative thoughts and emotions, guns associated with animal hunting tended to activate nonaggressive responses among hunters. These findings suggest that an object serves as a cue to aggression only if it is closely linked with aggression-related concepts in a person's memory.

What are the possible implications of these findings for social debates concerning gun ownership? One implication is that guns used for hunting are less likely than guns used for protection to prime the sort of negative emotions and thoughts that lead to crimes of passion. Consistent with this reasoning, a survey of over 6,000 middle school students found that owning a pistol or handgun in order to gain respect or to frighten others was associated with extremely high levels of antisocial behavior, such as bullying, physical aggression, and delinquency (Cunningham et al., 2000). In contrast, students who owned hunting rifles and shotguns engaged in only slightly greater antisocial behavior than students who did not own guns of any kind.

Returning to Berkowitz's previous statement about the "trigger pulling the finger," it appears that handguns and assault weapons are likely to "itch" more fingers than hunting rifles. So, regarding these overall findings, it appears they directly contradict the recommendation offered by NRA Executive Vice President Wayne LaPierre (refer back to our chapter opener) to give citizens ready access to firearms as a means of reducing gun violence in this country. According to the scientific studies reviewed here—we also recommend the thoughtful review of firearm availability and violent death by Wolfgang Stroebe (2016)—the likely result of following this NRA recommendation would be an increase, not a decrease, in gun violence. Unfortunately, the political reality in our country is that the NRA has more influence than the social scientific community among US lawmakers; thus, the NRA's recommendations will very likely continue to disproportionately shape gun laws in the coming years.

11.3c Alcohol Consumption Increases the Likelihood of Aggression.

Although weapons may trigger aggressive outbursts in those who are already angry, alcohol is involved in about 50% of all violent crimes, including domestic abuse, assault, rape, and homicide (Bachman & Peralta, 2002; Busch & Rosenberg, 2004; Leonard & Quigley, 1999). Experimental studies find that when people drink beverages containing enough alcohol to make them legally intoxicated, they behave more aggressively or respond more strongly to provocation than do people who consume nonalcoholic drinks (Giancola & Zeichner, 1997; MacDonald et al., 2000).

Why does the consumption of alcohol increase aggression? Few researchers contend that alcohol provides a direct biochemical stimulus to aggression. Instead, the general view is that alcohol weakens people's restraints against aggression by adversely affecting more controlled, effortful thinking while simultaneously leaving more automatic, impulsive responses relatively unaffected (Bartholow et al., 2003; Ito et al., 1996). Some researchers believe that this weakening of restraints, or *disinhibition*, is partly caused by an interruption of one's ability to process and respond to the meaning of complex and subtle situational cues (Hull & Bond, 1986; Johnson et al., 2000). In other words, when provoked, people who are drunk are much less attentive than those who are sober to such inhibiting cues as the provocateur's intent and the possible negative consequences

(Shutterstock)

Studies have shown that alcohol is involved in about 50% of all violent crimes.

of violence. For example, in an electric shock competition experiment, Kenneth Leonard (1989) instructed participants to engage in a reaction-time task against an opponent after either consuming alcohol to the point of legal intoxication or receiving no alcohol at all. All the opponents' responses were orchestrated to convey either explicit or subtle aggressive intentions toward participants. Results indicated that alcohol consumption did not influence participants' reactions to their competitors' explicit aggressive or nonaggressive signals, but it did interfere with their understanding of subtle aggressive signals. That is, following an aggressive exchange, intoxicated participants were more likely than those who were sober to misinterpret their competitors' subtly announced intentions of nonaggression as being aggression-as-usual.

Inattention to personal and social standards of nonviolence can also cause disinhibition. As discussed in Chapter 3 (section 3.1b), we are more attentive to personal and social standards of behavior when self-aware. However, alcohol consumption reduces self-awareness (Hull et al., 1986), and this can lead to impulsive, nonnormative actions—such as aggression. Thus, intoxicated people not only have problems attending to external cues that might defuse their inclinations to aggress but also have problems attending to internalized behavioral standards that might also inhibit aggression.

A third way this disinhibition effect may occur is through people's expectations of how alcohol will affect behavior (Bégue et al., 2009). Perhaps you have heard people excuse a drunken individual's verbal aggression by saying, "It's the liquor talking." Such statements imply that it is not the drunken person misbehaving, but rather, it is the alcohol that is to blame. If people learn that normally inappropriate behavior is often excused when performed under the influence of alcohol, they may engage in those behaviors when drinking (Cameron

"O thou invisible spirit wine, if thou hast no name to be known by, let us call thee devil! . . . O God, that men should put an enemy in their mouths to steal away their brains! That we should, with joy, pleasure, revel, and applause, transform into beasts!"

—William Shakespeare, *Othello* (II, iii)

How might alcohol impair judgment and, thus, lead to the aggressive outbursts found in domestic violence cases?

"Drunkenness . . . is the highway to hell."

—Elizabeth Jocelin, English author, 1596–1622

& Stritzke, 2003). From this perspective, alcohol's effect on aggression is due to a *learned disinhibition*. In support of this viewpoint, research indicates that people sometimes become more aggressive, not just when they have consumed alcohol, but also when they think they have consumed it (Lang et al., 1975). There is also evidence that some men who ordinarily disapprove of hitting a woman believe that being in an intoxicated state gives them a socially acceptable excuse to abuse their spouses (Straus & Gelles, 1990).

Undoubtedly, both the chemically induced disinhibiting effects of alcohol and its learned disinhibiting effects offer us possible explanations of why alcohol consumption causes aggression. Alcohol not only reduces self-awareness and disrupts our ability to adequately process situational cues that would normally inhibit our aggressive behavior, but it also provides us with a ready excuse for responding in such an antisocial manner.

Section Summary

- The frustration-aggression hypothesis proposes that blocking a person's goal-directed behavior produces frustration and frustration increases the aggressive drive.

- The cognitive-neoassociation model asserts that:
    1. frustration is just one of many factors that can stimulate negative affect,
    2. negative affect stimulates the inclination to aggress, and
    3. aggressive tendencies are often modified by higher-level thinking.

- Hostile aggression can also be sparked by the following:
    heat aggression-associated cues
    alcohol intoxication

11.4 Learning Aggressive Behavior

Now that we have examined how negative affect can sometimes trigger aggressive outbursts, let us explore how our social environment can shape aggressive behavior. In families where adults use violence, children grow up being much more likely to use it themselves (Guille, 2004; Tjaden & Thoennes, 2000). In communities where aggression is considered a sign of manhood, aggressive behaviors are eagerly and consciously transmitted from generation to generation—especially among men (Rosenberg & Mercy, 1991). How does this learning take place?

11.4a Social Learning Theory Emphasizes the Shaping of Aggressive Behavior.

Albert Bandura, one of the leading proponents of **social learning theory**, contends that people learn when to aggress, how to aggress, and against whom to aggress (Bandura, 1979; Bandura & Walters, 1963). This social learning of appropriate behavior, shaped by operant conditioning principles (see Chapter 5, section 5.2c), occurs through both direct and indirect means.

The Rewards of Aggression

Any behavior that is rewarded, or reinforced, is more likely to occur in the future. Therefore, if people act aggressively and receive rewards, they are more likely to act

social learning theory
A theory that social behavior is primarily learned by observing and imitating the actions of others, and secondarily by being directly rewarded and punished for our own actions

aggressively at some later date. The rewards could be material, such as candy or money, or they could be social, such as praise or increased status and self-esteem (Branscombe & Wann, 1994). When behavior, like aggression, is repeatedly not rewarded—or even punished—this will generally lead to a reduction in the frequency of the behavior. Psychologists call this weakening and eventual termination of behavior *extinction*. Extinction of aggressive actions is exactly what parents are aiming at when they give children "time-outs" following harmful outbursts.

Although withdrawing rewards can lead to the extinction of aggressive behavior, an inconsistent pattern of reward withdrawal can do more harm than good. This is because, like any behavior that people learn and utilize, aggression does not have to be rewarded each time it occurs in order to be maintained. In fact, an important principle of learning is that both people and other animals show greater resistance to the extinction of a behavior when it has been rewarded only intermittently rather than continuously.

In one study demonstrating this principle, young children were rewarded for hitting a doll (Cowan & Walters, 1963). Half were rewarded every time they acted aggressively, but the others were rewarded only periodically. In both instances, the rewards increased the children's aggressive behavior. However, when the experimenters stopped the rewards, the children who had been only periodically reinforced continued to hit the doll longer than those whose aggressiveness had been continuously reinforced. Because in real life people are not always reinforced for their aggressive activities, this study suggests that such periodic reinforcement is ideally suited to the prevention of extinction, not the weakening of aggressive behavior.

Observational Learning

Although learning does occur through direct reinforcement, we most often learn by watching and imitating others without being directly rewarded for doing so. This observational learning is also known as social modeling because the learner imitates the model. Children are most likely to pay attention to and model the behavior of those with whom they have a nurturing relationship and who also have social control over them (Bandura & Huston, 1961; Pettit, 2004). Parents are prime candidates as role models; however, behavior can also be observed and modeled from television, books, and other mass media sources (Basow, 1986).

(© Albert Bandura / Stanford University)

Bandura's Bobo doll studies clearly indicate that children can learn aggressive actions through an adult (Bandura et al., 1961).

In perhaps the most well-known series of observational learning experiments, Bandura and his colleagues (1961) set out to determine whether children would imitate the behavior of an aggressive adult model. In these studies, a child was first brought into a room to work on an art project. In another part of the room, an adult was playing quietly with Tinkertoys. Near these toys were a mallet and a Bobo doll, which is a big, inflatable, clown-like toy that is weighted at the bottom so that when it is pushed or punched down, it will quickly bounce back to an upright position. In the experimental condition, after playing with the Tinkertoys for a minute, the adult stood up, walked over to the Bobo doll, and began to attack it. She punched the doll, kicked it, hit it with the mallet, and even sat on it. As she pummeled the clown doll, she yelled out, "Sock him in the nose!...Kick him!...Knock him down!" In the control condition, the adult simply played quietly and nonaggressively with her toys for 10 minutes. After witnessing either the aggressive or nonaggressive adult model, the child was led into another room filled with many wonderful toys. However, before the child could play with these treasures, the experimenter aroused frustration by saying that these were her best toys and she must "save them for the other children." The child was then led to a third room containing both aggressive and nonaggressive toys, including a Bobo doll.

What did children typically do in this third room? If they had witnessed the nonaggressive adult model, they played calmly. However, if they had been exposed to the aggressive adult, they were likely to beat up the Bobo doll—often shouting the same things at the clown during their attack as the previous adult model. Similar results were obtained when the child had no direct exposure to the adult but merely saw a film of the adult attacking the doll. Other experimental variations demonstrated that children were more likely to imitate same-sex models (boys imitating men and girls imitating women) than those of the opposite sex. Taken as a whole, these studies indicate that observing adult aggression can not only lower children's aggressive inhibitions, but also teach them how to aggress.

As with direct aggression, observational learning experiments demonstrated that children are likely to imitate others' aggressive acts if social models are rewarded for their behavior. For example, Mary Rosekrans and Willard Hartup (1967) had preschool children watch an adult model aggress against a Bobo doll. These aggressive actions were either praised ("Good for you! I guess you really fixed him that time") or scolded ("Now look what you've done; you've ruined it") by another adult. After watching this interaction, the children were allowed to play with the same toys. Another group of children who had not been exposed to the aggressive model also played with the toys. Results indicated that the children who had watched the aggressive model being rewarded were significantly more aggressive in their play behavior than the children in the other two groups (refer to Figure 11.5). This study and others reveal that children do not unthinkingly imitate a model's actions. Rather, they copy the actions of others who have been rewarded rather than punished.

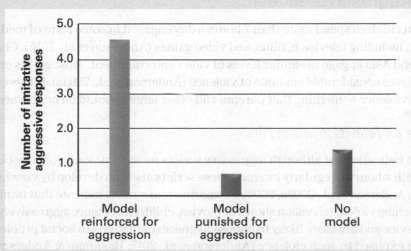

FIGURE 11.5   Modeling Aggression as a Function of Reinforcement and Punishment

A study by Rosekrans and Hartup (1967) showed that children were much more likely to imitate the aggressive behavior of an adult model if the adult had been rewarded rather than punished for said behavior. Can you imagine how these social learning principles might exert their influence on children playing on a grade-school playground?

Data source: "Imitative Influences of Consistent and Inconsistent Response Consequences to a Model on Aggressive Behavior in Children," by M. Rosekrans and W. Hartup, 1967, *Journal of Personality and Social Psychology, 7*(4), pp. 429–434.

Although these findings might leave you with the impression that aggressive models who are punished have little negative impact on children's later behavior, this is not necessarily the case. The research demonstrates that children are less likely to imitate the actions of punished aggressors. Does this mean these children fail to learn the aggressive behavior, or does it mean they simply inhibit the expression of these behaviors? In a study similar to Rosekrans and Hartup's experiment, Bandura (1965) offered all the children in the study a reward if they could imitate the aggressive behavior of the model that they had previously observed. Every single one of the participants could mimic the model's aggressive actions, even those who had seen the punished model. Thus, observing someone being punished for aggression does not prevent the learning of aggression—it simply inhibits its expression in certain circumstances. When children believe aggressive expression will lead to rewards, their inhibitions generally evaporate.

The Formation of Aggressive Scripts

Borrowing a concept from cognitive psychology, Rowell Huesmann (1986b, 1988) proposed that aggression—like other social behavior—is controlled by scripts. As first outlined in Chapter 4 (section 4.1b), a *script* is a preconception about how a series of events is likely to occur, which is developed and stored in memory and used as a guide for behavior and problem-solving. Based on many social learning experiments (for example, Bandura's Bobo doll studies), Huesmann contends that children develop **aggressive scripts** by observing other people's aggressive actions.

For instance, if children learn from their parents or friends that the proper way to respond to insults or other social slights is to physically or verbally assault their antagonists, then when they are later actually insulted by someone, an aggressive script will be recalled from memory. This script not only provides the child with a prediction about what is likely to happen in this situation, but it also prescribes the proper way to act. Huesmann believes that the more exposure children have to aggressive role models, the greater the number of detailed aggressive scripts they will encode into memory. Those with strongly developed aggressive scripts are likely to choose an aggressive solution to social conflict because it will seem to them to be the best and most natural way to respond to such circumstances.

11.4b Media and Video Violence Foster Aggressive Behavior.

American children spend more than 7 hours a day engaged in some form of media entertainment, including television, films, and video games (Anderson et al., 2015). Children in Europe and Asia engage in similar levels of video entertainment. Most of this entertainment involves considerable amounts of violence (Anderson et al., 2003a). Is this exposure to media violence something that parents and other adults should be concerned about?

Violence on Television and in Film

Research indicates that although aggressive scripts most commonly form by observing people with whom we regularly interact, these scripts also can develop by viewing media violence (Anderson et al., 2003a, 2003b). Experimental studies indicate that immediately after watching violent television shows or movies, children act more aggressively in their play behavior and are more likely to choose aggressive solutions to social problems than those not exposed to such violence (Anderson et al., 2015; Bushman & Anderson, 2018). Further, three separate meta-analyses of laboratory and field experiments conducted over the past half century demonstrate that exposure to media violence enhances children's

aggressive scripts
Guides for behavior and problem-solving that are developed and stored in memory and are characterized by aggression

and adolescents' aggression in interactions with strangers, classmates, and friends (Hearold, 1986; Paik & Comstock, 1994; Wood et al., 1991).

Longitudinal studies have also found a link between media violence and aggression. In perhaps the best of these studies, Leonard Eron and Huesmann collected data on 856 people in the state of New York when they were about 8 years old, then again when they were 19, and finally when they were about 30 years of age (Eron & Huesmann, 1984; Huesmann, 1986a). Their results: Early exposure to TV violence was related to later aggression—but only among the males. Boys who preferred to watch violent television shows when they were 8 years of age were significantly more aggressive 10 years later, even after controlling for their initial level of aggressiveness. In addition, as Figure 11.6 illustrates, the 8-year-old boys who had the strongest preference for violent shows were much more likely to have been convicted of a serious crime by the time they reached the age of 30. These findings suggest that the frequent viewing of televised violence contributes to later aggressive behavior beyond what you would expect due to stable aggressive traits (Huesmann et al., 2003).

FIGURE 11.6   Childhood Preference for Violent Television and Later Aggressive Behavior

Eron and Huesmann found that boys who show a high preference for violent television shows at age 8 have been found to exhibit greater aggressive behavior later in life, as indicated by the number of criminal convictions by age 30. Does this mean that TV violence caused their later aggression?

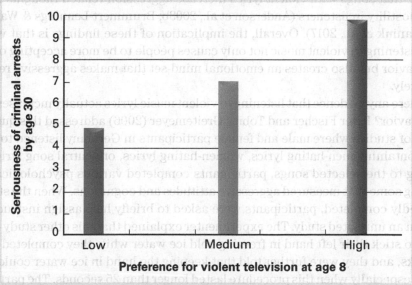

Data source: *Television and the Aggressive Child: A Cross-National Comparison*, by L. R. Huesmann and L. D. Eron, 1986, Hillsdale, NJ: Lawrence Erlbaum Associates. Copyright © 1986 Erlbaum.

Similar findings have been obtained in Europe, except that the European studies found no gender differences in the negative effects of TV violence (Huesmann & Eron, 1986). What appears to influence children's later aggressiveness is their *identification* with aggressive TV characters. Children who watch a lot of TV violence when they are young and who identify with aggressive TV characters are most likely to become highly aggressive in late childhood, adolescence, and even young adulthood (Anderson &

Many studies over the past 50 years provide compelling evidence that media violence contributes to aggressive behavior in viewers. How does viewer identification with aggressive characters impact viewer aggression?

Bushman, 2002). Based on these lab, field, and longitudinal studies, solid evidence indicates that repeated exposure to violence on television can encourage children to develop aggressive scripts that make later antisocial conduct more likely (Huesmann & Miller, 1994; Johnson et al., 2002).

Violence in Music Videos and Lyrics

What about the violence often depicted in music videos and in music lyrics? Music executives and some pop psychologists assert that watching violent music videos and listening to violent music lyrics provide teenagers and young adults the opportunity to harmlessly "vent" their aggressive emotions and thoughts. However, our previous analysis of the catharsis hypothesis refutes this assertion (section 11.3a). Yet is there any scientific evidence that this specific sort of media violence increases aggressive tendencies and behavior?

Several studies have examined how music videos affect adolescents' aggressive thinking and attitudes. In one such study involving young African American men, exposure to violent rap music videos increased endorsement of violent behavior in response to a hypothetical conflict situation (Johnson et al., 1995). Similarly, college students shown rock music videos containing violence subsequently reported a greater acceptance of antisocial behavior compared with students in a control group (Hansen & Hansen, 1990). Regarding the effects of music lyrics, numerous studies have found consistent evidence that songs with violent lyrics increase aggression-related thoughts and feelings of hostility in listeners (Anderson et al., 2003b; Brummert-Lennings & Warburton, 2011; Franiuk et al., 2017). Overall, the implication of these findings is that watching and/or listening to violent music not only causes people to be more accepting of antisocial behavior but also creates an emotional mind-set that makes aggressive responses more likely.

Is there any evidence that listening to violent music lyrics actually increases aggressive behavior? Peter Fischer and Tobias Greitemeyer (2006) addressed this question in a series of studies where male and female participants in Germany listened to popular songs containing men-hating lyrics, women-hating lyrics, or neutral song lyrics. After listening to the selected songs, participants completed various psychological tasks, including some that measured aggressive attitudes and cognitions. When the study was supposedly completed, participants were asked to briefly help assign instructions to people in an unrelated study. The experimenter explained that this other study required people to stick their left hand in freezing cold ice water while they completed intellectual tasks, and they were further told that keeping the hand in ice water could be very painful, especially when this procedure lasted longer than 25 seconds. The participants' task was to decide how long two specific individuals—one female and one male—would hold their hand in the ice water. The assigned times given to the woman and man were the dependent measures of aggression in the study.

Results indicated that male participants who listened to women-hating song lyrics not only reported more aggressive cognitions, but they also later behaved more aggressively to the female target person by assigning her significantly longer times of ice water treatment than did men who listened to neutral or men-hating lyrics. Similarly, women who listened to men-hating song lyrics reported more aggressive cognitions and later assigned significantly longer times of ice water treatment to the male target person than did women who listened to neutral or women-hating lyrics. Overall, these findings provide some evidence that exposure to violent music provokes aggressive thoughts in listeners and increases their aggressive responses toward people who are similar to the targeted victims in the music lyrics.

Violence in Video Games

In addition to the negative effects of watching or listening to violent media, researchers have also been studying whether playing violent video games has similar detrimental effects (Gentile et al., 2004; Krahé & Moller, 2004). Like television viewing and music listening, video game play is an integral part of the lives of many people, especially among adolescents and young adults. A representative national survey indicates that about 97% of American teens play video games, with the average playing time per week being about 13 hours (Lenhart et al., 2008).

In contrast to television and film viewing, video game playing is interactive, meaning that video game players engage in virtual aggression, actively rehearse aggressive scripts, receive rewards for their aggression, and closely identify with the characters they control. Despite denials from the video game industry, a number of meta-analyses of hundreds of video game studies involving tens of thousands of participants find that playing violent video games is modestly associated with aggressive cognitions, aggressive affect, and later aggressive behavior in the real world among both young adults and children (Anderson, 2004; Anderson & Bushman, 2001; Greitemeyer & Mügge, 2014; Furuya-Kanamori & Doi, 2016). In addition, these same meta-analyses reveal that playing violent video games reduces empathy and the willingness to help others. There were no gender differences, and these effects appear to be relatively long lasting.

Beyond the learning of aggressive scripts and the priming of aggressive thoughts and emotions, another negative effect of exposure to media and video violence is emotional blunting or *desensitization*, which means simply becoming indifferent to aggressive outbursts. For example, in a series of experiments conducted by Ronald Drabman and Margaret Thomas (1975), children who had just watched a violent movie were less concerned when they observed other youngsters fighting and were slower to stop the fight than a control group of children who had not seen the movie.

This desensitization to violence was also observed in college students who watched a lot of violent TV programs and among those with a history of high exposure to violent video games. When their physiological responses were monitored, the heavy consumers exhibited the weakest levels of arousal when observing both fictional and realistic aggression (Bartholow et al., 2006). These and other studies suggest that people who watch a lot of media-generated violence or play a lot of violent video games become habituated to violence in other aspects of their lives (Carnagey et al., 2007; Krahé et al., 2011). Because they are less anxious and bothered by aggressive behavior, they may be less inclined to regulate their aggressive urges when angry and more inclined to use the aggressive scripts they have learned as a means to solve social confrontations.

Another way in which media and video violence may increase aggression is through cognitive priming. According to Berkowitz (1984), the aggression-associated cues in television programs and films can cognitively prime a host of aggressive ideas and violent emotions, which in turn may trigger aggressive actions. Brad Bushman and Russell Geen (1990) found support for the priming hypothesis in experiments investigating the effects of media violence on viewers' thoughts and emotional responses. In these studies, college students wrote down the thoughts they had while watching excerpts from such violent movies as *48 Hours* and *The French Connection*. A control group watched a nonviolent scene from the TV series *Dallas*.

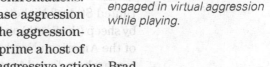

(Christian Bertrand / Shutterstock)

Video game players are often engaged in virtual aggression while playing.

"There is absolutely no evidence, none, that playing a violent video game leads to aggressive behavior."

—Doug Lowenstein, founder of Entertainment Software Association, May 12, 2000

Results indicated that viewers who watched the most aggressive videos had the most aggressive thoughts, experienced the strongest increase in anger-related feelings, and had the greatest physiological arousal. The same effects have been found when people play violent video games (Anderson & Bushman, 2001; Anderson & Dill, 2000). In fact, studies find that when video gamers design and personalize their own in-game characters, they tend to experience even higher levels of arousal than when they play nonpersonalized games. More importantly, this personalization of in-game characters increases gamers' aggressive tendencies (Fischer et al., 2010).

Of course, this does not mean that all or even most children and young adults who regularly view or listen to media violence or play violent video games will begin terrorizing their schools and neighborhoods. However, while exposure to such staged violence is not the primary cause of aggression among the young, it may be the one factor that is easiest to control and reduce.

11.4c Cultures of Honor Encourage Male Violence.

Cross-cultural research suggests that societies with economies based on animal herding have more male violence than farming societies. For example, among the Native American cultures of North America, the herding Navajos were famous for their warring tendencies, while the farming Zunis tended to be nonviolent (Farb, 1978). Within given societies, researchers have also observed this contrast in aggression. In East African cultures, for instance, herders are easily provoked to violence, while farmers go out of their way to get along with their neighbors (Edgerton, 1971). Social psychologists Richard Nisbett and Dov Cohen (1996) believe that the greater violence exhibited by herding people is due to their **culture of honor**, which is a belief system that prepares men to protect their reputation by resorting to violence. In such cultures, honor is a man's most valued personal quality—and a man who claims honor but is not paid honor does not, in fact, have honor. Cultures of honor tend to develop in "lawless" settings, where a weak state cannot enforce laws or contracts, protect individuals from wrongdoing, or punish criminals. Instead, men on their own must be trustworthy, demand respect and fairness, and be prepared to pay back wrongs done to them.

In honor cultures, men learn from childhood that it is important to project a willingness to fight to the death against insults and to vigorously protect their property—specifically, their animals—from theft. Insults have special importance in honor cultures because they are tests of who can do what to whom. Men who will not tolerate disrespect on even small issues send a signal to others that they will not be pushed around on big issues either (IJzerman et al., 2007). Nisbett and Cohen hypothesize that this culture of honor is more necessary in herding than in farming societies because herders' assets (animals) are more vulnerable to theft—and thus, more in need of aggressive protection—than are the assets of farmers (land).

How does this culture of honor theory relate to contemporary violence in the United States? Nisbett and Cohen note that the American South and West were settled by sheep (the South) and cattle (the West) herders, while farmers were the primary settlers of the American North. In an archival analysis of crime statistics in the country, these researchers found that the southern and western states have higher levels of current violence related to honor than the northern states (Cohen, 1996; Cohen & Nisbett, 1994). Honor-related violence involves arguments, brawls, and lovers' triangles where a person's public prestige and honor have been challenged. In addition, the cultures of the South and West are also more likely to approve of violence as indicated by viewership of violent TV programs, subscriptions to violent magazines, hunting license applications, and National Guard enrollments (Baron & Straus, 1989; Lee, 1995). Finally, in a series of experimental studies, Cohen and Nisbett also found that, when insulted, young white men from the

culture of honor
A belief system in which males are socialized to protect their reputations by resorting to violence

South not only became more stressed and angry than young white men from the North but were also more prepared to respond to insults with aggression (Cohen et al., 1996).

What these multi-method studies suggest is that southern and western white men tend to be more physically aggressive than northern white men in certain situations because they have been socialized to live by a code of honor that calls for quick and violent responses to threats to their property or personal integrity. Although the vast majority of these men no longer depend on herding for their livelihood, they still live by the culture of honor of their ancestors; and this code of conduct continues to be legitimated by cultural institutions (Cohen, 1998; Cohen & Vandello, 1998). Fueling such aggression is the belief that aggressive responses to honor-based threats are not only necessary but also socially sanctioned.

In a clever field experiment testing the hypothesis that honor-based violence is more condoned in the South and the West than in the North, Cohen and Nisbett (1997) sent letters to employers in these areas of the country from a fictitious job applicant who admitted that he had served time in prison for a felony. In one condition of this experiment, the applicant stated that he had impulsively killed a man who had an affair with his fiancée and who had then publicly taunted him about it in a bar. In the other experimental condition, the applicant reported that he had stolen a car because he needed money to pay his debts. Consistent with the culture of honor theory, employers from the South and West were significantly more likely than those from the North to respond in an understanding and cooperative manner to the "convicted killer" letter, but there were no regional differences in response to the "auto thief" letter. Additional studies find that white, male college students from the South are significantly more likely than white, male college students from the North to interpret other people's ambiguous advice about how to respond to conflict as sanctioning physical aggression (Vandello et al., 2008).

In December 2014, Jody Lee Hunt of West Virginia murdered his ex-girlfriend, her new boyfriend, a business rival, and his ex-business partner, all of whom Hunt believed had disrespected him in various ways. Before killing himself, Hunt posted on Facebook that he committed the violence against "those who tried to tear me down and take from me." How does this violent outburst by Hunt possibly relate to the culture of honor?

(West Virginia State Police)

Ironically, "honor" cultures tend to have very strong norms of politeness and hospitality. This emphasis on elaborate politeness may have developed as a way to reduce the likelihood that honor-bound men would be insulted during daily interactions. However, the anger suppression resulting from such politeness norms has the unfortunate effect of making it difficult to accurately perceive other people's anger until it has reached the boiling point, triggering aggression on their part.

Interestingly, similar regional differences in violence are not found among young African American males; black southern men are not more violent than black northern men. Thus, this hypothesized culture of honor in the South and West is unique to white males. Having stated this, however, both psychologists and sociologists note that there is a higher incidence of violence among inner-city African American males than among African American males in rural or suburban areas, and this may be partly related to a similar honor code (Cohen et al., 1998; Lee & Ousey, 2011). Thus, just as a culture of honor may exist among southern and western white men, in the street culture of the inner city there may also be a culture of honor that makes violent outbursts more likely. That is, in the inner city—where it is extremely difficult to pull oneself out of poverty by legal means, and where police provide little protection from crime and physical attack—young black males may strive to gain and maintain respect by responding violently to any perceived insults. Of course, within this cultural analysis of violence it is always important to keep in mind that there is a great deal of individual difference in how people respond to such cultural influences (Leung & Cohen, 2011).

Section Summary

- In social learning theory, aggression occurs because it has been rewarded in the past.
- Observational learning can foster the development of aggressive scripts.
- Exposure to media violence promotes antisocial conduct.
- The culture of honor is a belief system that prepares men to protect their reputations by resorting to violence.

11.5 Sexual Aggression

A United Nations study found that approximately 15 million adolescent girls worldwide have been victims of rape or other forced sexual acts, with 9 million of these girls being victimized within the past year (UNICEF, 2017). In the United States it is estimated that approximately 18.3% of women and 1.4% of men will be the victim of a rape in their lifetime (Black et al., 2011). When a broader range of sexually aggressive behaviors, such as unwanted sexual touching and coercion are included, then an alarming 44% of women and 22% of men report experiencing some form of unwanted sexual contact in their lifetime. In 80% of sexual assaults, the assailant is someone who is known to the victim. On American college campuses, one-fourth of college women are victims of rape or attempted rape (Yancey & Hummer, 2003). **Acquaintance rapes** (date rape) accounts for 85% of campus rapes.

More disturbing is the fact that most rapes and other sexual assaults are never reported because the victim is afraid that she or he will be blamed or ostracized for the assault (Magid et al., 2004). In the United States, an estimated 63% of assaults are never reported to a law enforcement agency (Black et al., 2011). In many regions of the world, women who have been raped are disowned by their families or subjected to violence—including honor killings (Esquivel-Santovena et al., 2013).

11.5a Rape Myths Justify Sexual Violence.

One way in which sexual violence against women is justified is through a set of commonly held false beliefs about rape known as **rape myths** (Payne et al., 1999). Rape myths are beliefs that falsely blame the victim for the attack, such as, "If a woman is raped while she is drunk, she is at least somewhat responsible for letting things get out of control." These beliefs often exonerate the attacker's actions by either stating it wasn't his fault ("Men don't usually intend to force sex on a woman, but sometimes they get sexually carried away.") or asserting that he is actually the victim ("Rape accusations are often used as a way of getting back at men."). Rape myths also minimize the violence and harm of the act ("Women tend to exaggerate how much rape affects them.") and can even suggest that the victim found the attack enjoyable ("Many women find forced sex to be very arousing."). Together, endorsing these types of beliefs function to minimize and even justify violence against women. People who endorse rape myths are less likely to empathize with rape victims, are more likely to blame victims for causing the assault, and are less likely to express moral outrage at human suffering in general (Chapleau & Oswald, 2014; Klement et al., 2019; Russell & Hand, 2017). Investigate your own endorsement of rape myths with the *Self/Social Connection Exercise 11.1.*

acquaintance rape
Forced sexual intercourse that occurs either on a date or between people who are acquainted or romantically involved (also known as date rape)

rape myths
False beliefs about rape that justify sexual violence

Self/Social Connection Exercise 11.1

What Are Your Beliefs About Rape and Interpersonal Violence?

Rape Myth Acceptance Scale

Directions

Use the following 7-point scale to indicate your degree of agreement or disagreement for each of the following items:

Strongly Disagree 1   2   3   4   5   6   7 Strongly Agree

1. If a woman is raped while she is drunk, she is at least somewhat responsible for letting things get out of control.
2. Although most women wouldn't admit it, they generally find being physically forced into sex a real "turn on."
3. If a woman is willing to "make out" with a guy, then it's no big deal if he goes a little further and has sex.
4. Many women secretly desire to be raped.
5. If a woman doesn't physically fight back, you can't really say that it was rape.
6. Men from nice middle-class homes almost never rape.
7. Rape accusations are often used as a way of getting back at men.
8. It is usually only women who dress suggestively who are raped.
9. If the rapist doesn't have a weapon, you really can't call it rape.
10. Rape is unlikely to happen in the woman's own familiar neighborhood.
11. Women tend to exaggerate how much rape affects them.
12. A lot of women lead a man on and then they cry rape.
13. A woman who "teases" men deserves anything that might happen.
14. When women are raped, it's often because the way they said "no" was ambiguous.
15. Men don't usually intend to force sex on a woman, but sometimes they get too sexually carried away.
16. A woman who dresses in skimpy clothes should not be surprised if a man tried to force her to have sex.
17. Rape happens when a man's sex drive gets out of control.

Scoring Instructions

To compute your total endorsement of these rape myths, add up your responses for the items. The higher your total score, the greater your belief in rape myths. In Diana Payne and her coworkers' (1999) original sample of 604 American university students (average age of 19 years) the mean total endorsement was 45.9 for men and 35.7 for women. How does your total score compare with Payne's original sample? Are you more or less likely to believe in rape myths than those American university students? Have your friends complete this scale as well. How do your beliefs about rape myths compare with their beliefs?

Total score: _____

Not surprisingly, a number of studies indicate that heterosexual men are much more likely than heterosexual women to believe in rape myths (Bohner et al., 2006; Talbot et al., 2010; Vandiver & Dupalo, 2013). However, women who regularly view or participate in activities involving aggression and/or sexualized content are also more likely to endorse such beliefs. For example, studies suggest that female viewers of mainstream sports media and female video gamers who play the role of hypersexualized female avatars are more likely than others to endorse rape-myth beliefs (Fox et al., 2013; Hust et al., 2013). Furthermore, archival research also suggests that certain segments of the mainstream media perpetuate rape myths in how they sometimes depict and discuss sexual assaults. For example, a longitudinal analysis of text material published in *Playboy* magazine from 1953 to 2003 found that sexual assaults were often ambiguously depicted in this men's magazine, which could implicitly endorse and perpetuate rape myths among subscribers (Kettrey, 2013).

Although most rape myths focus only on women as targets, research suggests that similar myths exist for men who are victims of rape. That is, some people falsely believe that a male victim must have done something to cause the assault or that he would not find a sexual assault distressing, while others even cast doubt that a man can be a sexual assault victim at all (Chapleau et al., 2007). Heterosexual men are most likely to endorse male rape myths, especially when the victim is a gay man; gay men are least likely to endorse such beliefs (Chapleau et al., 2007; Davies & McCartney, 2003).

Not surprisingly, men who believe these rape myths are much more likely to commit sexual assaults than men who do not believe in rape myths. For example, not only do convicted rapists generally hold strong beliefs regarding rape myths (Scully, 1985) but male college students who admit to having engaged in sexual aggression against women hold less negative implicit and explicit attitudes toward rape than other male college students (Nunes et al., 2013; Yapp & Quayle, 2018).

How do these myths about rape form? Like many cultural beliefs, they are likely taught through social learning. For example, there is evidence that exposure to pornography increase ordinary men's rape-myth beliefs. In one such study, Neil Malamuth and James Check (1981) arranged for Canadian college students to attend commercial movies at campus theaters. Half of the students saw two nonviolent romantic movies, *A Man and a Woman* and *Hooper*. The other students saw two sexually aggressive films, *Swept Away* and *The Getaway*; in both films, female characters become sexually aroused by a sexual assault and are romantically attracted to their assailant. Several days later, these same students were asked to complete a class questionnaire about their attitudes toward rape and other forms of aggression against women. None of the students realized that the questionnaire and the movies were connected in any way. Results indicated that exposure to the two films portraying sexual aggression increased male viewers' acceptance of interpersonal aggression against women and tended to increase their acceptance of rape myths (see Figure 11.7). In contrast, women's acceptance of interpersonal aggression against other women and of rape myths decreased after watching these sexually aggressive films. These data, which have been replicated in subsequent studies, indicate that exposure to films that seem to condone sexual violence against women can cause men to become more accepting of such violence (Hald & Malamuth, 2014; Oddone-Paolucci et al., 2000). Another disturbing fact about these findings is that these effects were obtained from exposure to commercially successful, R-rated films that contained commonly used, sexually aggressive elements in their storylines. Hollywood produces such films because there is a profitable market for them; and their target audience is men, who prefer films that mix sex and violence to those that mix sex and tenderness (Emmers-Sommer et al., 2006).

FIGURE 11.7 The Effects of Mass Media Exposure on Acceptance of Violence Against Women

Malamuth and Check (1981) found that men who had watched sexually violent commercial films were more accepting of interpersonal violence against women and were more accepting of the rape myth than men who were not exposed to such violent entertainment. What effect did such exposure have on women viewers?

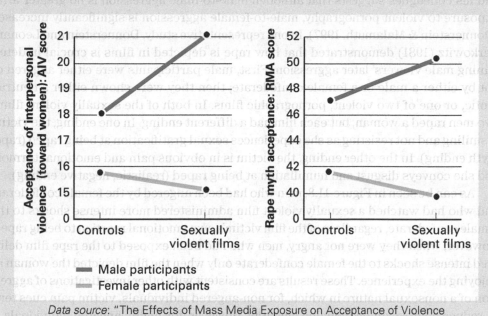

Male participants

Female participants

Data source: "The Effects of Mass Media Exposure on Acceptance of Violence Against Women: A Field Experiment," by N. M. Malamuth and J. V. Check, 1981, *Journal of Research in Personality, 15*(4), pp. 436–446.

Does Pornography Provoke Male Aggression Against Women?

Thus far, we have learned that exposure to sexually violent films can cause men to become more accepting of false beliefs about rape and to have greater tolerance for violence against women. However, does this translate into men actually becoming more aggressive toward women? A large body of research has specifically examined whether pornography contributes to sexual violence against women. Erotica is typically defined as sexually suggestive or arousing material that is nonviolent and respectful of all persons portrayed (Vannier et al., 2014). In contrast, **pornography** is the combination of sexual material with abuse or degradation in a manner that appears to endorse, condone, or encourage such behavior (Brown, 2003). Pornography is problematic not for its sexual content but for its abusive and degrading portrayal of another person, usually a woman. Experimental studies demonstrate that exposure to erotic material generally elicits a pleasant emotional response and increased sexual arousal in both men and women, with no evidence of increased aggression (Davis & Bauserman, 1993; Seto et al., 2001). A different pattern appears to hold for people's responses to pornography, as you will soon discover.

(iStock)

Pornography is objectionable not because of its sexual content but for its abusive and degrading portrayal of another person, usually a woman.

pornography

The combination of sexual material with abuse or degradation in a manner that appears to endorse, condone, or encourage such behavior

In studying the possible link between exposure to pornography and sexual violence, social psychologists have conducted two separate lines of research: (1) lab experiments in which exposure to pornography is manipulated to see how it affects laboratory aggression, and (2) survey and archival research on whether the prevalence of pornography in a particular geographic region is related to sexual assault.

Regarding lab experiments, a series of studies conducted by Edward Donnerstein and his colleagues suggests that although male-to-male aggression is no greater after exposure to violent pornography, male-to-female aggression is significantly increased (Donnerstein & Malamuth, 1997). In one representative study, Donnerstein and Leonard Berkowitz (1981) demonstrated that how rape is depicted in films is crucial in determining male viewers' later aggression. First, male participants were either angered or not by either a male or a female confederate; then they were shown either a neutral, erotic, or one of two violent, pornographic films. In both of the sexually violent films, two men raped a woman, but each film had a different ending. In one ending, the victim is smiling and not resisting as she experiences sexual gratification at being raped (rape-myth ending). In the other ending, the victim is in obvious pain and emotional turmoil, and she conveys disgust and humiliation at being raped (realistic, negative ending).

As can be seen in Figure 11.8, men who had been angered by the female confederate and who had watched a sexually violent film administered more intense shocks to the female confederate, regardless of the film victim's own emotional reaction to being raped. However, when they were not angry, men who had been exposed to the rape film delivered intense shocks to the female confederate only when the film depicted the woman as enjoying the experience. These results are consistent with other investigations of aggression of a nonsexual nature in which, for non-angered individuals, victim pain cues tend to reduce aggression by inducing empathy. However, for highly angered individuals, a victim's pain can actually provoke increased aggression. Why this is the case is a matter of speculation. One possible explanation is that anger raises the threshold for empathy toward the victim's plight (Hartmann, 1969). Another explanation is Berkowitz's notion of aggression-associated cues (see section 11.3b). For men who have been angered, watching a woman become the victim of sexual aggression may not only cause arousal, it may also associate women with aggression. Later, in a situation in which aggression is a behavioral option, the presence of a woman might be a sufficient aggression-eliciting cue for the already aroused male.

To date, a growing body of experimental research in laboratory settings and subsequent meta-analyses have found strong evidence that exposure to pornography between nonconsenting people is linked to increased acceptance of violence against women, rape myths, and aggressive behavior toward female confederates (Malamuth, 2018). This research provides strong cause-and-effect evidence (*internal validity*) of the role that pornography plays in violence against women. Outside experimental laboratories, correlational and longitudinal studies conducted in naturalistic settings have established the *external validity* of the role that pornography plays in violence against women. For example, in a recent meta-analysis of correlational studies, Gert Hald and his coworkers (2010) found a modest correlation ($r = .24$) between viewing violent pornography and attitudes supporting violence against women. More specifically, in a longitudinal study of 1,586 youths, Michele Ybarra and Richard Thompson (2018) found that men who had been exposed to parental spousal abuse while growing up and also had a history of viewing violent pornography were significantly more likely than other men to engage in sexually violent behaviors toward women, such as sexual assault, coercive sex, and sexual harassment. In a systematic review of decades of research, using various methodologies, Neil Malamuth (2018) concluded that "if a man already has strong tendencies to be sexually aggressive toward women, then heavy pornography consumption may 'add fuel to the fire' and increase his aggressive tendencies" (p. 80).

FIGURE 11.8   **How Does the Film Victim's Reaction to Rape Affect Male Viewers' Subsequent Level of Aggression Toward Women?**

Men who had been angered by a female confederate and who had then watched a sexually violent film administered more intense shocks to the female confederate, regardless of the film victim's own emotional reaction to being raped (Donnerstein & Berkowitz, 1981). How were these men's reactions different from men who were not angered by the female confederate, but who also were exposed to one of the two rape films?

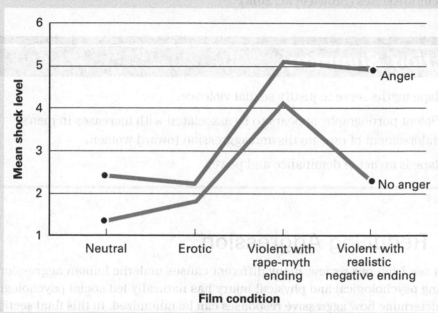

Data source: "Victim Reactions in Aggressive Erotic Films as a Factor in Violence Against Women," 1981, by E. Donnerstein and L. Berkowitz, *Journal of Personality and Social Psychology, 41,* pp. 710–724.

11.5b Rape Is a Display of Power and Dominance.

Rape and other forms of sexual assault are most common in societies characterized by male violence and a social ideology of male dominance (Jewkes & Abrahams, 2002; Muir & Macleod, 2003). Current theories and research on sexual aggression suggest that rape is a display of dominance, power, and hostility toward women (Vandello & Bosson, 2013; Williams et al., 2016). In studies using college and community samples, men who either had a history of sexual aggression or were more accepting of violence against, and dominance over, women were also more likely to be sexually aroused by depictions of rape and to be insensitive to others' feelings (Dean & Malamuth, 1997; Yost & Zurbriggen, 2006). Other research has found that associating sex and power is predictive of men's rape myth acceptance and rape proclivity (Chapleau & Oswald, 2010). Together, this research suggests that the desire to exercise power and the enjoyment of sexual dominance is a more important motive than sexual gratification in sexual assault (Chiroro et al., 2004, Locke & Mahalik, 2005). Social scientists have further suggested that men's displays of power and dominance through the use of sexual aggression toward women is related to their need to conform to rigid masculine gender roles. Such traditional gender beliefs equate manhood with personality traits and behaviors that demonstrate toughness and dominance (Bosson & Vandello, 2011; Vandello & Bosson, 2013). Men who think of themselves in this way must continually prove their manhood through their actions, and some men do so by engaging in sexual aggression and other displays of dominance. For example, studies of convicted rapists have found that they view rape as an aggressive conquest that validates their sense of hypermasculinity (Groth, 1979). Recall our previous discussion of honor cultures (see section 11.4c) where men are socialized to protect their reputation through the use of violence. Not surprisingly, honor cultures also promote male violence against women. In the United States, rates of rape and domestic homicides by white male perpetrators, as well white female teenagers' reports of being the victims of rape and sexual violence, are higher in honor culture states than in non-honor culture states (Brown et al., 2018).

Section Summary

- Rape myths serve to justify sexual violence.

- Violent pornography appears to be associated with increases in men's endorsement of rape myths and aggression toward women.

- Rape is an act of dominance and power.

11.6 Reducing Aggression

As you see from our review, many different causes underlie human aggression. The resulting psychological and physical injury has naturally led social psychologists to try to determine how aggressive responses can be minimized. In this final section, we examine some possible effective strategies.

11.6a Punishment Can Both Decrease and Increase Aggression.

Punishment is the most common treatment societies have employed to control aggression. Following such timeworn prescriptions as "an eye for an eye and a tooth for a tooth," legal systems throughout the world often use aggression to punish violent criminals, sometimes resorting to the ultimate punishment—death. Exercising this extreme form of punishment will certainly "relieve" convicted criminals of their aggressive tendencies, but short of killing aggressors, is punishment a truly effective technique?

"Violence and injury enclose in their net all that do such things, and generally return upon him who began."

—Lucretius Carus, Roman philosopher-poet, c. 99–55 BCE

Three conditions are necessary for punishment to have a chance of being effective (Bower & Hilgard, 1981). First, the punishment must be *prompt*, administered quickly after the aggressive action. Second, it must be *relatively strong*, so that the aggressor duly notes its aversive qualities. Third, it must be *consistently applied* so that the aggressor knows that punishment will likely follow future aggressive actions. Even if these conditions are met, however, reduced aggression is not guaranteed. If potential aggressors are extremely angry, threats of punishment preceding an attack are unlikely to inhibit aggression (Baron, 1973). Here, the strength of the anger supersedes any concerns about the negative consequences of aggression. Likewise, the cognitive-neoassociation model would suggest that punishment following aggression might actually provoke counter-aggression in the aggressor-turned-victim because such punishment might provoke even more intense anger.

In further considering the effectiveness of using punishment to reduce aggression, one should be even more wary of using aggression in doling out punishment. Based on the research inspired by social learning theory, it is entirely possible that employing violent punishment as a treatment for aggression may simply teach and encourage observers to copy these violent actions. That is, the aggressive punisher may serve as an aggressive model. This is exactly the process underlying the continuing cycle of family violence—observing adult aggression appears to encourage rather than discourage aggression in children (Cast et al., 2006; Fosco et al., 2007). Similarly, being spanked as a form of punishment when 3 years old predicts children acting more aggressively when they are 5 years old (Taylor et al., 2010).

Taking these factors into account, even though punishment may reduce aggressive behavior under certain circumstances, it does not teach the aggressor new prosocial forms of behavior. The aggressive behaviors are not being replaced by more productive kinds of actions but are, most likely, being only temporarily suppressed. For this reason, punishment by itself is unlikely to result in long-term changes in behavior.

"Road rage" has unfortunately become an all-too-familiar term we read and hear about to describe violent outbursts by people driving cars. How could you use social psychological knowledge to reduce the likelihood of road rage on city streets and highways?

11.6b Teaching Others How to Behave in a Nonaggressive Manner.

Beyond the double-edged strategy of punishment, social psychologists also recommend three fairly simple techniques for controlling aggression that involve teaching others how to behave in a nonaggressive manner, offering an apology when someone becomes angry, and reducing exposure to violent behavior (Dunn, 2001). Let's briefly examine each of these techniques.

Social Modeling

Just as destructive models can teach people how to act aggressively, social learning theorists contend that nonaggressive models can urge observers to exercise restraint in the face of provocation. In an experiment supporting this claim, research participants who watched a nonaggressive model exhibit restraint in administering shocks to a "victim" in a learning experiment were subsequently less aggressive than those who observed an aggressive model (Baron & Kepner, 1970).

Besides reducing aggression by modeling nonaggressive behavior, aggression can also be controlled by having an authority figure condemn the behavior of aggressive individuals. For example, research demonstrates that if a child watches violence on television in the presence of an adult who condemns the violence, the child is less likely to later imitate this aggression (Hicks, 1968; Horton & Santogrossi, 1978). This bit of knowledge was not lost on Steve and his wife when raising their children. On numerous occasions while watching television with their daughters, the screen would suddenly erupt with violent images so quickly that they did not have time to change the channel. Each time this happened, they condemned the violence. These efforts had an impact. When Steve's daughter, Lillian, was 4 years old, they were watching a Looney Toons cartoon and Elmer Fudd suddenly pulled out a shotgun and blew off Daffy Duck's head. Without missing a beat Lillian said, "Boy, that wasn't very nice was it? People shouldn't be so mean."

Internalizing Anti-Aggression Beliefs

As we have discussed throughout the text, when people internalize certain beliefs and attitudes into their self-concepts, they are more likely to act in ways consistent with those beliefs and attitudes. Recognizing the important role that the self plays in behavior change, social scientists have devised a cognitive strategy to facilitate the internalization of antiviolent beliefs by simply having people think of reasons why aggression is a bad idea. For example, in one study, when children were prompted to generate reasons why it was bad to imitate TV violence, this intervention was effective in later reducing the impact that TV violence had on their attitudes and behavior regarding aggression (Huesmann et al., 1983). Generating these antiviolent beliefs apparently caused the children to incorporate them into their self-concepts and overall world view. The subsequent reduction in aggression through this "belief ownership" was still measurable 2 years after the initial intervention.

Apologies as Aggression Controllers

While this technique may seem too simple to be true, a number of studies indicate that apologies can effectively reduce anger and aggression (Eaton & Struthers, 2006). For example, in an experiment conducted by Kenichi Ohbuchi and his coworkers (1989), Japanese college students were embarrassed by their poor performance while working on a complex experimental task. The reason they did so poorly was that the experimenter's assistant committed a series of errors in presenting the experimental materials to them. When the experimenter learned of each participant's poor performance, he roundly criticized the assistant, who then either apologized for causing the participants to fail or said nothing. After this, participants were asked to rate the assistant on several dimensions and were told that these ratings would be used as a basis for the assistant's grade. A public apology in the experimenter's presence significantly reduced the participants' hostility in these ratings. This study is important because it suggests that merely offering an apology can defuse another's hostile aggression.

There is a gender difference in willingness to apologize, with women being more willing than men to take responsibility for a perceived social transgression (Gonzales et al., 1990). In fact, women tend to become more apologetic when severely reproached for a social transgression, while men respond more defensively to severe reproaches (Hodgins & Liebeskind, 2003). Underlying this greater unwillingness of men to offer apologies is a fear of "losing face" or social status in such confrontations (Hodgins et al., 1996). These gender differences may partly explain why men are more likely than women to be involved in physical altercations.

Reducing Exposure to Violence

An essential ingredient in reducing aggressive responses is to diminish people's exposure to violence. Research indicates that aggressive behavior in children is significantly reduced when they spend less time watching violent television shows and playing violent video games (Rosenkoetter et al., 2004). One such study examined third- and fourth-grade students at two comparable schools over a 6-month period (Robinson et al., 2001). In one of the schools, TV and video game exposure was reduced by one-third by encouraging students and parents to engage in alternative forms of home entertainment, while in the other school no effort was made to reduce exposure. The researchers found that children at the intervention school were subsequently less aggressive on the playground than students at the control school—especially those students who were initially rated as most aggressive by their classmates.

Section Summary

- Punishment can both increase and decrease aggression.
- Nonaggressive responding can occur through the following:
    - social modeling
    - internalizing anti-aggression beliefs
    - offering apologies
    - reducing exposure to violence

Applications

How Can Cyberbullying Be Prevented?

In 2018, 14-year-old actress Millie Bobby Brown became a target of cyberbullying when she received online insults, homophobic slurs, and a #TakeDownMillieBobbyBrown smear campaign. She subsequently shut down her Twitter account.

The internet and social media networking sites provide new ways for initiating, forming, and maintaining relationships. However, the dark side to the internet is that it has also introduced a new form of aggression, notably cyberbullying. *Cyberbullying* is intentional aggression that is repeatedly directed toward another person through electronic methods, such as email, text, blogs, or social media posts (Patchin & Hinduja, 2015; Peterson & Densley, 2017). Cyberbullying can take many different forms including sending threatening, insulting, or abusive messages repeatedly to a person via text, email or instant messaging. Others engage in online abuse such as sharing another's personal information without their consent or impersonating the victim in a negative way. Cyberbullying might include cyber-stalking, spreading rumors, or sexting (sharing nude pictures or videos). These aggressive actions might be done by one person or by a group of people who are targeting the same individual.

Victims of cyberbullying have little ability to defend themselves from attackers. Victims might know their attackers, but the internet also allows people to remain anonymous, making it even more difficult for victims to respond and stop the bullying. Furthermore, once these written materials or photographs have been shared online, victims have little ability to remove those images from the internet or prevent others from downloading the materials to their private computers.

Cyberbullying is occurring at alarming rates throughout the world, with between 10% and 40% of internet users identifying themselves as being cyberbullied at least once (Kowalski et al., 2014). Furthermore, approximately 25% of adolescents report being cyberbullied by a dating partner, with this cyberdating victimization being more common among girls than boys (Peterson & Densley, 2017). Although cyberbullying can happen at any age, it is especially common during the middle-school years (Jenaro et al., 2018). Victims of cyberbullying usually have less physical, social, or relational power than their perpetrator and are also frequently victims of more traditional forms of bullying. It's not surprising, then, that LGBT individuals and ethnic minorities are more likely to experience cyberbullying than are people from other social groups (Jenaro et al., 2018).

"There should be no space in this world for bullying, and I'm not going to tolerate it, and neither should any of you."

—Actress Millie Bobby Brown b. 2004

Also not surprising is that cyberbullying takes a serious toll on victims. They report that these experiences harm their physical and psychological health, including lowering self-esteem and increasing depression, anxiety, loneliness, and suicidal thoughts (Kowalski & Limber, 2013; Zych et al., 2015). Cybervictimization is also associated with behavioral problems such as use of drugs and alcohol. Youths who are cyberbullied also suffer academically.

Who does the bullying and why? Many people who engage in cyberbullying are also bullying others in more traditional ways (Kowalski et al., 2014). People who engage in cyberbullying report higher levels of anxiety, loneliness, depression, and impulsive behavior, while also reporting lower levels of self-esteem, empathy, and self-control than those who do not engage in cyberbullying (Peterson & Densley, 2017). The potential anonymity of the internet can further facilitate impulsivity through deindividuation (See Chapter 8, section 8.2c).

How can cyberbullying be stopped? Given the prevalence of cyberbullying, especially among school-aged youth, many schools and parents are seeking to prevent or at least minimize cyberbullying. Although there are no easy solutions to this problem, here are some steps that you can take to not only minimize your own victimization, but also to create an environment that minimizes cyberbullying for others.

- Decrease the amount of time you spend online or using other electronic forms of communication. Being a bully and being the victim of cyberbullying are both associated with spending more time online (Kowalski et al., 2014).

- Be cautious engaging in risky online behaviors, such as communicating with unknown individuals. Especially for adolescents and young adults, this is associated with increased victimization (Jenaro et al., 2018).

- Being the perpetrator or the victim of cyberbullying is less likely for adolescents who have involved and supportive parents (Kowalski et al., 2014). Intervention programs that include parental training are more successful at reducing cyberbullying than programs that don't include such training (Zych et al., 2015).

- Schools that promote respect, fairness, and kindness among their students and faculty have the lowest cyberbullying rates (Kowalski et al., 2014). Teachers, staff, and school administrators can play an important role in creating social norms against the acceptability of cyberbullying. Furthermore, teachers and staff can be trained to identify cyberbullying when it occurs, act as bystanders who take action against it, and provide support for victims (see Chapter 12, section 12.2a on bystander intervention).

- Because people who engage in cyberbullying tend to have personality profiles marked by low empathy and self-esteem, intervention programs should include components that address these issues (Brewer & Kerslake, 2015).

- Cyberbullying—and especially "revenge pornography" (nonconsensual posting of sexually explicit photos or videos as revenge on a former romantic partner)—is slowly being recognized as a legal issue (Walker & Sleath, 2017). Although creating legislation to prohibit and punish cyberaggression is likely to be a challenging task, doing so is an important step in preventing this form of aggression.

THE BIG PICTURE

Nonviolence is the answer to the crucial political and moral questions of our time; the need for man to overcome oppression and violence without resorting to oppression and violence. Man must evolve for all human conflict a method which rejects revenge, aggression, and retaliation. The foundation of such a method is love.

Rev. Martin Luther King Jr., 1964

I f we could point to one single strategy to effectively control aggression in a wide range of settings, it would simply be the adoption of the nonviolent philosophy practiced by civil rights leader Martin Luther King Jr. Indeed, research suggests that forgiving others' aggressive acts against us can actually enhance our own health by lowering stress and increasing a sense of personal control (Witvliet et al., 2001). Unfortunately, because the widespread adoption of a nonviolent philosophy will not take place anytime soon, we are left with a number of imperfect intervention strategies, each of which has a reasonable chance of reducing aggression when certain conditions are met.

The cognitive-neoassociation model tells us that impulsive aggression is most likely to occur when we are engaged in highly routine activities and thus are not consciously monitoring our thoughts, feelings, or actions. However, if these aggression-related tendencies are subjected to higher-level thinking, we can often modify and control them. What causes these aggression-related tendencies to come under the control of more complex cognitive processes? The answer is self-awareness, one of our great human gifts. Use this "mindfulness" gift to control your aggression (Peters et al., 2015). When you become angry, try to make sense of your negative feelings before reacting. Analyze the implications of your actions and consider alternative, nonaggressive responses. By bringing into play these cognitive control mechanisms, the link between negative affect and aggression can be short-circuited.

In summary, although our present ability to control aggression may seem meager at best, keep in mind that our analysis of aggression reveals that this is a highly complex phenomenon. It not only springs from a number of psychological sources (for example, anger, fear of punishment, desire for rewards), it also appears to be shaped by a variety of environmental factors. The various forms of aggression in society today in some respects resemble a modern-day Hydra. In Greek mythology, the Hydra was a terribly dangerous, nine-headed serpent that was exceedingly difficult to kill. Whenever one head was chopped off, two grew back. Fortunately for the ancient Greeks, the Hydra was finally destroyed by their superhero, Hercules. There are no superheroes in contemporary social psychology, nor in our larger society. But if we ever hope to slay our Hydra, it will entail a Herculean task by all elements of society.

KEY TERMS

WEBSITES

Accessed through https://www.bvtlab.com/sop8

Websites for this chapter focus on research and theory on family violence, acquaintance rape, violence on television, and recommendations on how to control anger before it leads to aggression.

Minnesota Center Against Violence and Abuse

This is the website for the Minnesota Center Against Violence and Abuse, which lists links to education and training resources, papers and reports on aggression, and resource materials for teaching about family violence.

American Psychological Association

The American Psychological Association website has a number of relevant web pages, including one that examines research on the psychological effects of television violence and another on how to control anger before it leads to aggression.

International Society for Research on Aggression

This website is devoted to the scientific study of aggression and violence around the world.

RAINN

RAINN (Rape, Abuse & Incest National Network) is an anti-sexual violence organization that operates the National Sexual Assault Hotline, partners with other organizations to operate the DoD Safe Helpline for the Department of Defense, and offers programs on prevention and help for survivors of sexual violence.

Chapter **12**

Prosocial Behavior: Helping Others

■ FOCUS QUESTIONS

1. Do women and men differ in the types of help they tend to offer?

2. How do bystanders at an emergency short-circuit our tendency to help?

3. What types of people are most likely to receive help when they need it?

4. Why does receiving help sometimes increase people's stress and threaten their mental health?

■ CHAPTER OUTLINE

Introduction

In Chapter 2, you learned how social psychological research is sometimes motivated by the researcher's desire to explain some real-life incident. One of the most powerful and memorable examples of a real-life event spurring social psychological research was the Kitty Genovese murder, which occurred on March 13, 1964, in the New York City borough of Queens. Although you may have previously read or heard about this infamous act of violence, almost all accounts in psychology textbooks have unknowingly misrepresented the facts in this case. Here is the story based on a reanalysis of archived material (Manning et al., 2007; Rasenberger, 2006).

At 3:20 a.m., Kitty Genovese was returning home from work as a bar manager when a man attacked her with a hunting knife near her apartment building. Kitty screamed, "Oh, my God! He stabbed me. Please help me! Please help me!" After her cry rang out in the night, about 3–6 of her neighbors (not 38 onlookers, as is

(Courtesy of Queens, New York Police Department, 1960, via Wikimedia)

On the night of March 31, 1964, Kitty Genovese was repeatedly stabbed outside her apartment building.

often reported) went to their windows to see what was going on. These first eyewitnesses certainly heard Kitty's voice, but they may not have understood her words. One alarmed woman looked out her window, saw Kitty and her assailant "standing close together, not fighting or anything," and decided this was not an emergency. This onlooker went back to bed. A second eyewitness saw the assailant bending over and beating Kitty, who was already on the ground. This onlooker did nothing to intervene. A third eyewitness hollered at the assailant from his seventh-story window, "Hey, get out of there! Let that girl alone!" Probably because of this shouted command, the assailant got into his car and drove away. By then, a large number of neighbors were looking out their apartment windows. They saw Kitty pick herself up off the ground, reach for her purse, look around, and begin walking unsteadily away. She was no longer screaming but seemed to be walking in a slow, "dreamlike" state. A couple of eyewitnesses later told police that Kitty's gait made them think, "she was either drunk, or had been beaten up."

Ten minutes passed in relative silence as Kitty staggered around a corner to a small hallway in a nearby building. She was now out of sight of almost all her neighbors. During that 10-minute time period, there is evidence that a few neighbors phoned the police but may have hung up before providing full details of the assault. Then witnesses saw the assailant return and begin casually walking down the sidewalk, looking side to side. One eyewitness ran from one window of her apartment to the next to keep the attacker in her sight. At the same time, another neighbor reached for the phone to call the police, but his wife told him, "Don't; 30 people have probably called by now." Within seconds, the killer found Kitty in the hallway where he sexually assaulted her and then stabbed her in the throat. Only one person saw part of that second attack. Instead of phoning the police, this man phoned a female neighbor, who immediately contacted the police and then rushed to Kitty's side. The police arrived on the scene within minutes, but Kitty died soon after.

It is now clear that most of the neighbors who were present during this tragic murder were not apathetic bystanders as has been so widely reported for so many years. Yet it is also clear that Kitty Genovese did not receive the timely help that may have saved her life that night. If you had heard Kitty Genovese's cries for help do you think you would have come to her rescue? If, instead, you had seen this victim walking unsteadily but did not see the first attack, do you think you would have understood what was happening? This murder and the events surrounding it—both real and misreported—were instrumental in prompting numerous studies on the social psychology of helping. In this chapter, we address and try to answer five basic questions about helping. First, why do we help? Second, who is most likely to help? Third, when do we help? Fourth, whom do we help? And fifth, are there hidden costs for those who receive help?

12.1 Why Do We Help?

Before tackling these five helping questions, let's begin by defining our topic. **Prosocial behavior** is voluntary behavior that is carried out to benefit another person (Dovidio et al., 2006). This definition excludes beneficial actions that are not performed voluntarily or are not performed with the intention of helping another. Thus, if a store manager forces employees to donate part of their salaries to charity, their actions would not be considered prosocial because they really would have had no *choice* in rendering assistance. Likewise, if a terrified person fleeing from a charging bull accidentally pushes someone out of the path of the animal, this action also would not be prosocial because the pushing was unintentional and was not meant to benefit another. On the other hand, the actions of the female neighbor who called the police and then ran to Kitty Genovese's side perfectly fit our definition because she freely chose those actions and her intention was to benefit another. Volunteering your time at a community food pantry, donating money to a local charity, or mowing the lawn of a sick neighbor would also be examples of prosocial behavior. These behaviors each have unique characteristics, but they all involve intentional actions that benefit others.

> "If you want happiness for an hour, take a nap. If you want happiness for a day, go fishing. If you want happiness for a year, inherit a fortune. If you want happiness for a lifetime, help somebody."
>
> —Chinese Proverb

> "Nothing makes you happier than when you reach out in mercy to someone who is badly hurt."
>
> — Mother Teresa, born Agnes Gonxha Bojaxhiu, Albanian Catholic nun and humanitarian, 1910–1997

12.1a There Are Two Basic Forms of Helping.

Beyond the basic definition, philosophers and a number of social scientists have traditionally described two forms of helpful behavior that are based on very different motives. For example, 19th-century philosopher Auguste Comte (1875) contended that **egoistic helping**—in which the person wants something in return—is based on *egoism*, because the ultimate goal of the helper is to increase his or her own welfare. In contrast, Comte stated that **altruistic helping**, in which the person expects nothing in return, is based on *altruism*, because the ultimate goal is to increase another's welfare.

As we discuss later in the chapter, social scientists disagree on whether any useful distinctions can be made between egoistic and altruistic helping, and some argue that all helping is ultimately egoistic in nature. As already noted, many social scientists believe that people sometimes help solely to benefit another, while at other times they help in order to achieve some personal gain. In addition, it has also been suggested that because of inborn characteristics, people may be predisposed to prosocial behavior. Before reading further, spend a few minutes answering the items in *Self/Social Connection Exercise 12.1.*

prosocial behavior

Voluntary behavior that is carried out to benefit another person

egoistic helping

A form of helping in which the ultimate goal of the helper is to increase his or her own welfare

altruistic helping

A form of helping in which the ultimate goal of the helper is to increase another's welfare without expecting anything in return

Self/Social Connection Exercise 12.1

Is Your Helping Orientation Altruistic, Egoistic, or Unhelpful?

Helping Orientation Questionnaire

Directions

While reading these descriptions of hypothetical situations, imagine yourself in each of them and pick the action that best describes what you would do:

1. You have come across a lost wallet with a large sum of money in it, as well as identification of the owner. You ____
   A. return the wallet without letting the owner know who you are.
   B. return the wallet in hopes of receiving a reward.
   C. keep the wallet and the money.
   D. leave the wallet where you found it.

2. A person in one of your classes is having trouble at home and with school work. You ____
   A. help the person as much as you can.
   B. tell the person not to bother you.
   C. leave the person alone to work out his or her own problems.
   D. agree to tutor the person for a reasonable fee.

3. When it comes to cooperation when you would rather not, you usually ____
   A. cooperate if it is helpful to others.
   B. cooperate if it is helpful to yourself.
   C. refuse to get involved.
   D. avoid situations where you might be asked to cooperate.

4. A neighbor calls you and asks for a ride to a store that is six blocks away. You ____
   A. refuse, thinking you will never need a favor from him (or her).
   B. explain that you are too busy at the moment.
   C. immediately give the ride and wait while the neighbor shops.
   D. consent if the neighbor is a good friend.

5. You are approached by someone asking for a contribution to a well-known charity. You ____
   A. give if there is something received in return.
   B. refuse to contribute.
   C. give whatever amount you can.
   D. pretend you are in a hurry.

6. You are in a waiting room with another person. If you heard a scream in the adjoining room and the other person failed to respond, you would ____
   A. help the screaming person whether the other person helps or not.
   B. help the screaming person only if the other person does too.
   C. wait to see if the screaming continues.
   D. leave the room.

7. When asked to volunteer for a task in which you will receive no pay, you ___

   A. avoid or put off answering.

   B. explain that you don't agree with the objectives to be accomplished and therefore couldn't volunteer.

   C. compromise and help if you will receive some recognition.

   D. volunteer without question.

Scoring

The information below shows which answers on the Helping Orientation Questionnaire indicate altruistic helping, egoistic helping, and unhelpful behavior. It also shows the percentage of people who gave each answer in a survey study. Do your responses indicate that your helping orientation is predominantly altruistic, egoistic, or unhelpful?

Item	Altruistic helping	Egoistic helping	Unhelpful behavior
1.	A (38 percent)	B (47 percent)	C,D (15 percent)
2.	A (86 percent)	D (4 percent)	B,C (10 percent)
3.	A (61 percent)	B (20 percent)	C,D (19 percent)
4.	C (33 percent)	D (56 percent)	A,B (11 percent)
5.	C (70 percent)	A (4 percent)	B,D (26 percent)
6.	A (50 percent)	B (10 percent)	C,D (40 percent)
7.	D (35 percent)	C (27 percent)	A,B (39 percent)

Reproduced with permission from "A Person-Situation Approach to Altruistic Behavior," by D. Romer et al., 1986, *Journal of Personality and Social Psychology, 51*(5), 1001–1012. Copyright © 1986 by the American Psychological Association.

12.1b Helping Is Consistent with Evolutionary Theory.

As discussed in previous chapters, one principle of evolutionary theory is that any social behaviors that enhance reproductive success (the conception, birth, and survival of offspring) will continue to be passed on from one generation to the next. However, to reproduce, an animal must first survive. Often, an animal's survival depends on how well it can compete with other members of its own species for limited resources. This evolutionary fact would seem to dictate that animals should be selfish, looking out first and foremost for themselves. Yet what of the seemingly selfless act of helping?

Evolutionary psychologists have documented countless instances in which animals have put their own lives at risk to protect other members of their own species from danger (Fouts, 1997; Wilson, 1996). For example, a chimpanzee foraging for food with its troop will often emit a warning call to alert the others about a nearby predator. By calling out, this chimp is the one most likely to be caught by the predator. As this example illustrates, helping others can be downright deadly. When you are dead, your reproductive days are over. Thus, from an evolutionary perspective, how could helping be advantageous to reproduction?

Kin Selection

As previously outlined in the Chapter 11 discussion of aggression, evolutionary theorists contend that it is not individual survival that is important; rather, it is *gene* survival that promotes reproductive fitness (Archer, 1991). Because your blood relatives share many of your same genes, by promoting their survival you can also preserve your genes even if you don't survive the helpful act. This principle of **kin selection** states that you will exhibit preferences for helping blood relatives because this will increase the odds that

kin selection

A theory that people will exhibit preferences for helping blood relatives because this will increase the odds that their genes will be transmitted to subsequent generations your genes will be transmitted to subsequent generations (Madsen et al., 2007; Stewart-Williams, 2007).

Although the principle of kin selection explains why we are more likely to help those who are related to us by blood, it does not explain the countless incidents of people helping total strangers. Stranger helping is found not only in humans but in other species as well. For example, female chimpanzees, lions, mule deer, dolphins, and bluebirds have been observed protecting and taking care of nonrelated newborns deserted by or separated from their mothers (Goodall, 1986; Lingle et al., 2007). Given this fact, how can evolutionary theorists explain prosocial behavior that extends beyond one's family?

Reciprocal Helping

Robert Trivers (1971) has described a way in which helping strangers could have arisen through natural selection. This principle, which he called *reciprocal altruism*, involves mutual helping, usually separated in time. However, because "altruism" refers to motives and Trivers was merely referring to behavior, we will use the more accurate term **reciprocal helping** when referring to this mutual helping. According to this principle, people are likely to help strangers if it is understood that the recipient is expected to return the favor at some time in the future. In such a world of reciprocal helping, the cost of aiding another is more than offset by the later returned help (Hames & McCabe, 2007). For reciprocal helping to evolve, the benefit to the recipient must be high and the cost to the helper must be relatively low. In addition, the likelihood of their positions being reversed in the future must also be high, and there must be a way to identify "cheaters"—those who do not reciprocate (Brown & Moore, 2000).

A good example of reciprocal helping is *social grooming*. In many species, one individual cleans the other's fur or feathers; later, the "groomee" returns the favor (Schino et al., 2007). Grooming is a low-cost activity (only time is lost) that returns high benefits to the recipient (removing disease-carrying parasites). Trivers (1983) believes that reciprocal helping is most likely to evolve in a species when certain conditions exist. Three of these conditions are (1) *social group living*, so that individuals have ample opportunity to give and receive help; (2) *mutual dependence*, in which species survival depends on cooperation; and (3) the *lack of rigid dominance hierarchies*, so that reciprocal helping will enhance each animal's power. Reciprocity works best in small groups where one will regularly interact with those whom one helps or for whom one does favors. This is likely why reciprocity is stronger in rural villages than in large cities (Steblay, 1987).

Social grooming among gorillas is an example of reciprocal helping. How does the evolutionary perspective explain such behavior?

("Silverback," by Patrick Cyusa, available under a CC 1.0 license via Wikimedia)

Considerable research supports both kin selection and reciprocal helping among humans and other animals. For example, when threatened by predators, squirrels are much more likely to warn genetically related squirrels and squirrels with which they live than unrelated squirrels or those from other areas (Sherman, 1985). Similarly, across a wide variety of human cultures, relatives receive more help than nonrelatives, especially if the help involves considerable costs—such as being a kidney donor (Borgida et al., 1992). Reciprocal helping is also common in humans. Consistent with evolutionary-based mechanisms to prevent cheating, when people are unable to reciprocate, they tend to experience guilt and shame (Fehr & Gaechter, 2002). However, it is also true that

reciprocal helping

An evolutionary principle stating that people expect that anyone helping another will have that favor returned at some future time; also known as reciprocal altruism people's perceptions of helpers' motives can weaken feelings of obligation to reciprocate. Helpers who appear to render assistance only after weighing their costs and benefits are perceived as less worthy of reciprocal helping than those who appear to help out of empathy for the victim (Ames et al., 2004).

Taken together, this research suggests that there may be mechanisms for the genetic transmission of helpful inclinations from generation to generation. Yet unlike many species where altruistic behavior is closely tied to genetic heritage, human genes influence behavior in a more indirect manner (Kruger, 2003). As we have stated throughout this text, although ancient evolutionary forces may have left us with *capacities* (such as the capacity to behave altruistically), current social and environmental forces encourage or discourage the actual development and use of those capacities.

12.1c Social Norms Define the Rules of Helping Others.

Although prosocial behavior may have a genetic basis, it makes sense that social mechanisms would develop to enforce these evolutionarily adaptive helping strategies (Nesse, 2000). Chapter 7 discussed how general rules of conduct, known as *social norms*, prescribe how people should generally behave. For example, research by Erik Nook and his coworkers (2016) found that people donate more money to a charity if they first observe others giving a generous donation rather than a small donation. These shared expectations are backed up by the proverbial carrot and stick: the threat of group punishment if the norms are not obeyed and the promise of rewards for conforming. Prosocial norms are expectations to behave selflessly in bestowing benefits on others. Three social norms that serve as guidelines for prosocial behavior deal with *reciprocity*, *responsibility*, and *justice*.

The first of these prosocial norms, the *norm of reciprocity*, is based on maintaining fairness in social relationships. As discussed in Chapters 7 (section 7.4a) and 10 (section 10.3a), this norm prescribes that people should be paid back for whatever they give us. Regarding prosocial behavior, this means helping those who help us (Brown & Moore, 2000; Gouldner, 1960). As mentioned in the previous section, this norm also explains the discomfort that people typically experience when they receive help but cannot give something back in return.

In comparison to the reciprocity norm, the other two prosocial norms dictate that people should help due to a greater awareness of what is right. For example, interviews with non-Jewish rescuers of Jews in Nazi-occupied territories during World War II found that the rescuers' willingness to risk their lives to save others was significantly shaped by a sense of social responsibility (Fagin-Jones & Midlarsky, 2007). According to the **norm of social responsibility**, we should help when others are in need and dependent on us. Acting on this norm, adults feel responsible for the health and safety of children, teachers have a sense of duty and obligation to their students, and police and firefighters believe they must help even at the risk of their own lives (Frey et al., 2010). This social responsibility norm requires help givers to render assistance regardless of the recipient's worthiness and without an expectation of being rewarded.

Unfortunately for the needy of the world, even though most people endorse the social responsibility norm, they often do not act in accordance with it. One reason for this nonadherence is that people also often believe in social justice (Darley, 2001). In contrast to the dependent-driven social responsibility norm, the **norm of social justice** stipulates that people should help only when they believe that others *deserve* assistance (Marjanovic et al., 2009). How does one become a "deserving" person? Melvin Lerner (1980, 1997) contends that, at least in North American society, people become entitled to the deserving label by either possessing socially desirable personality characteristics or by engaging in socially desirable behaviors. Thus, according to the social justice

norm of social responsibility
A social norm stating that we should help when others are in need and are dependent on us

norm of social justice
A social norm stating that we should help only when we believe that others deserve our assistance

norm, if "good" people encounter unfortunate circumstances, they deserve our help and we have a duty to render assistance. The norm of social justice appears to be stronger in individualist cultures—where people are held more personally responsible for their actions—than in collectivist cultures (Mullen & Skitka, 2009).

12.1d Political and Social Class Differences Shape Willingness to Help.

During national political campaigns, the Republican Party regularly attempts to dispel public perceptions that their candidates are unsympathetic to the needy by portraying themselves as "compassionate conservatives." Republicans often define *compassionate conservatism* as the belief that conservatism and compassion complement each other, but that the poor and others in need must also accept personal responsibility and strive for self-reliance. In other words, those who seek help need to know that they can't blame "the system" for their own misfortunes. Is there any validity to associating compassion with conservative versus liberal political ideologies?

As previously discussed in Chapter 6 (section 6.2b), American democracy was founded on the sometimes conflicting belief systems of *individualism* (or self-reliance) and *egalitarianism* (equal treatment of groups and sympathy for the disadvantaged). Because conservatives emphasize individualism and liberals emphasize egalitarianism in their respective political ideologies, they often develop different positions regarding the moral obligations society should have toward the disadvantaged (Graham et al., 2009). In essence, willingness to help depends on how conservatives and liberals judge the morality of those in need. For example, in explaining poverty, conservatives tend to make dispositional attributions, blaming poverty on self-indulgence, laziness, or low intelligence; and they respond with anger and neglect. In contrast, liberals tend to make situational attributions, perceiving the poor as victims of social injustice; and they respond with empathy and help giving (Weiner et al., 2011).

Research also finds that conservatives are less willing to help victims of natural disasters than liberals. In a national sample of over 1,000 adults following floods in the Mississippi and Ohio River valleys, Linda Skitka (1999) found that people with a conservative political orientation consistently held flood victims more responsible for their plight and for resolving it than did those with a liberal orientation. Invoking the social justice norm, conservatives were even reluctant to provide public support for immediate humanitarian aid (clean water, food, shelter) to those who had not taken actions to protect themselves against flood risks. Although liberals were significantly more compassionate in their willingness to provide immediate help, like conservatives, they were unenthusiastic about using federal disaster assistance to financially bail out victims. Overall, these studies suggest that, when faced with those who need help in situations not immediately life-threatening, liberals are more likely to adhere to the norm of social responsibility, while conservatives adhere more closely to the norm of social justice. In other words, "compassionate conservatism" is a more discriminating approach to helping others than that practiced by liberals, who have been accused by conservatives of having "bleeding hearts" when it comes to assisting those who are disadvantaged.

Closely related to questions regarding conservative and liberal differences in willingness to help is the question of whether helping might also be associated with socioeconomic status. In the United States, wealth has increasingly become concentrated in the hands of a select few. For example, households in the top 1% of the wealth distribution own 40% of the total wealth in the country (Wolff, 2017). Compared to the wealthy, individuals in the lower social classes have fewer economic resources and educational opportunities, while being exposed to greater everyday violence and hardship (Oakes & Rossi, 2003). Due to these tough life circumstances, lower-class individuals might be expected to focus on their own welfare because helping others drains a larger proportion of their resources compared to the wealthy. An alternative view is that individuals in the lower social classes should help others more because behaving generously is likely to promote trust and cooperation from others, thus ensuring that, in times of hardship, their needs will also be met.

In a series of studies, Paul Piff and his coworkers (2010) analyzed the relationship between Americans' socioeconomic status and their willingness to engage in prosocial actions. Across four studies, the researchers found that—unlike upper-class individuals, who tended to report social values that placed high priority on satisfying their own needs— lower-class individuals expressed more concern for the welfare of others. Further, this difference in social values not only influenced individuals' emotional responses to others' misfortunes, it also influenced their willingness to help. Members of the lower class were more generous, charitable, trusting, and helpful compared with their upper-class counterparts. These findings are consistent with nationwide surveys, which report that lower income Americans give proportionally more of their incomes to charity than do higher income Americans (Greve, 2009; James & Sharpe, 2007). Subsequent research provided additional evidence that people from higher and lower social classes help for different reasons. For example, Michael Kraus and Bennett Callaghan (2016) found that upper-class members are more likely to give money when their donation occurs in public rather than in private. In contrast, lower-class members show the opposite pattern. Similarly, Ashley Whillans and her coworkers (2017) found that upper-class members were more likely to donate when the charity's appeal emphasized personal agency ("You're a life saver") rather than communal agency ("Let's save a life together"), while lower-class members were much more responsive to communal agency appeals. Together, these studies suggest that, while both upper- and lower-class members donate to worthy charities, they appear to do so for different reasons that reflect their different world views. Upper-class members are more motivated to engage in public prosocial behaviors due to individual pride and reputation management, whereas lower-class members are more motivated to privately help based on communal identification and empathy for the suffering and needs of others.

("Media luna roja," by Pasante, 2011, available under a CC by SA 3.0 license via Wikimedia)

Charitable organizations depend on people's generosity to receive the necessary funds to provide disadvantaged individuals with the help they need. Who is more likely to feel empathy for unfortunate others and donate a higher proportion of their income to the needy, the wealthy or the poor?

12.1e Individualists and Collectivists Differ in Their Helping Tendencies.

Research conducted in both individualist and collectivist cultures indicates that the norm of reciprocity is both universal (Gergen et al., 1975) and engaged in by people of all ages; even 3-year-old toddlers display reciprocity by being more willing to share with those who have shared with them (Warneken & Tomasello, 2013). Regarding the norm of social responsibility, a number of cross-cultural studies have found that adult members of collectivist cultures are more likely not only to help others of their ingroup than are members of individualist cultures but also to express greater enjoyment in meeting these social obligations than do individualists (Bontempo et al., 1990). Similar cross-cultural differences have also been obtained when studying children's prosocial actions. For example, children from the collectivist cultures of Kenya, Mexico, and the Philippines were found to be much more helpful than children from the United States (Whiting &

Edwards, 1988). A likely reason for this difference is that collectivists are much more likely than individualists to stress ingroup cooperation and individual sacrifice. In such a context, people may feel greater moral obligation to help than if they grew up in a less group-oriented environment.

> "If a free society cannot help the many who are poor, it cannot save the few who are rich."
>
> —John F. Kennedy, 35th US president, 1917–1963

Joan Miller and her colleagues (1990) found support for this perspective in a study of the moral reasoning of South Asian Indians and Americans. Participants read a series of hypothetical situations in which the main character in the story failed to help someone experiencing either a life-threatening, moderately serious, or minor need. The needy person was either the main character's child, best friend, or a stranger. Results indicated that Indian respondents tended to perceive helping as the main character's social responsibility in all conditions, even when the need was minor. This means they believed that in all situations, giving help should be dictated by social norms and not by the personal norms of the potential helper. In comparison, American respondents believed that the norm of social responsibility should only be dictated in life-threatening cases or when parents were faced with moderately serious needs of their children. In all other instances, Americans believed that the main character's decision to help should be based on his or her own personal norms of help giving and should not be subject to social regulation.

> "Help the weak ones that cry for help, help the prosecuted and the victim . . . they are the comrades that fight and fall."
>
> —Nicola Sacco, Italian-born anarchist, 1891–1927

Overall, it appears that collectivist Indian culture holds to a broader and more stringent view of social responsibility than does individualist American culture (Miller, 1994; Miller et al., 2011). For life-threatening needs of both strangers and loved ones and for moderately serious needs of one's family members, both Indians and Americans are likely to subscribe to the social responsibility norm. However, for needs of friends and strangers that are not life-threatening, Americans are generally less likely than Indians to subscribe to the social responsibility norm.

> "If you don't look out for others, who will look out for you?"
>
> —Whoopi Goldberg, comedian, actress, and social activist for the homeless, born 1955

What about Americans with an ethnic heritage rooted in collectivism? Are they more helpful than Americans with more of an individualist heritage? Ronnie Janoff-Bulman and Hallie Leggatt (2002) tested this hypothesis by having Latino American and Anglo-American college students complete a questionnaire assessing the extent to which they felt obligated to help and wanted to help across a variety of social situations. Results mirrored the cross-cultural findings for people with collectivist versus individualist orientations. Although respondents from both ethnic groups reported a strong sense of obligation to help close friends and family members in need, the more collectivist Latinos expressed a greater desire to engage in these expected behaviors than the more individualist Anglos. In addition, Latino students also felt a stronger sense of social obligation and desire to help more distant family members and friends than did Anglo students. The two ethnic groups did not differ in their motivation to help strangers. Additional research suggests that underlying Latino Americans' greater desire to help more distant family members and friends is a core aspect of traditional Latino American culture, namely *familism*, which refers to a set of norms related to family solidarity and emotional and economic interdependence within an extended family network (Armenta et al., 2011).

So does this mean that people with greater collectivist tendencies are more helpful than those with greater individualist tendencies? Not necessarily. The individualist-collectivist cultural differences discussed thus far apply only to ingroup helping. When ingroup members need help, people from collectivist cultures and collectivist-oriented Americans perceive help giving as both more obligatory ("I must help") and more personally desirable ("I want to help") than people from individualist cultures and

Americans with a more individualist orientation. However, when those needing help are clearly members of an outgroup, research suggests that people with greater collectivist tendencies are often less helpful than people with greater individualist tendencies (Conway et al., 2001; Kemmelmeier et al., 2006). Thus, when it comes to providing help, "compassionate collectivism" does not necessarily extend to those who are seen as "them" rather than "us."

12.1f Gender and Personality Influence Helping Responses.

Do you think your willingness to help is influenced by your personality and gender? Alice Eagly and Maureen Crowley's (1986) meta-analytic review of 172 helping behavior studies indicates that men and women differ in their willingness to engage in certain prosocial actions; men generally help more than women, and they are more likely than women to help strangers. These gender differences are greatest when there is an audience, when there is potential danger involved in helping, and when the person in need is female. Although these differences appear real, they apply most to nonroutine prosocial acts such as offering help to strangers in distress. When other forms of prosocial behavior—such as helping a friend or caring for children—are studied, women generally prove

Women tend to take on the role of caretaker more than men.

to be more helpful than men (Böckler et al., 2016). For example, women are more likely than men to provide social and emotional support to others (Shumaker & Hill, 1991), and they also are more willing to serve as caretakers for children and the elderly (Trudeau & Devlin, 1996). In addition, among children, there are few gender differences in helping, and the few differences that have been found indicate that girls tend to be a bit more helpful than boys (Eisenberg et al., 1996).

Based on these findings, we can draw two conclusions. First, women and men appear to be helpful in different ways. Second, these differences become stronger from childhood to adulthood and are most apparent when gender roles are salient. Consistent with the culturally valued male role of heroic rescuer, men are more likely than women to place themselves in danger when rendering assistance. In contrast, women are more likely than men to provide longer-term help involving empathy and caretaking, qualities consistent with the feminine gender role.

What sorts of cultural role models might influence the "helping habits" of boys and girls? How might greater gender role flexibility influence male and female helping tendencies?

In addition to exploring the role that gender socialization plays in prosocial behavior, researchers have also sought to identify personality traits associated with helping (Decety, 2011). Mera Habashi and her colleagues (2016) found that the personality trait of agreeableness is not only positively associated with prosocial behavior, it is also positively associated with two distinct emotional reactions—empathy and personal distress—that directly impact helping. **Empathy** is the feeling of compassion and tenderness you experience when viewing a victim's plight. This strong emotional reaction to the suffering of others is associated with parasympathetic activity, such as increased heart rate and, respiration (Stellar et al., 2015). The second emotional response is **personal distress**, which is an unpleasant state of arousal in which you become preoccupied with your own anxiety when seeing others in distress. As we will discuss in more detail later in the chapter, experiencing empathy is associated

empathy

A feeling of compassion and tenderness upon viewing a victim's plight

personal distress

An unpleasant state of arousal in which people are preoccupied with their own emotions of anxiety, fear, or helplessness upon viewing a victim's plight with helping in order to address the other person's needs, whereas experiencing personal distress is associated with helping others in order to reduce one's own distress.

There is some research indicating that parents who encourage the expression of emotion in their families tend to have children who experience empathic rather than distress reactions when witnessing others in need of help (Eisenberg et al., 1988). Additional longitudinal research indicates that as children emotionally mature, their feelings of empathy generally increase, while their feelings of personal distress generally decrease (Davis & Franzoi, 1991).

Despite these developmental trends, individual adults differ in the degree to which they habitually experience both empathy and personal distress. Studies of fraternal and identical twins indicate that individual differences in empathy and personal distress may be partly due to genetic factors (Davis et al., 1994; Zahn-Wexler et al., 1992). That is, high empathy and high personal distress people appear to have an inherited sensitivity to emotional experiences that causes them to react more strongly to the observed experiences of others. Before reading further, spend a few minutes answering the items in *Self/Social Connection Exercise 12.2*. Based on your responses, are you high or low on empathic concern and personal distress?

Self/Social Connection Exercise 12.2

What Is Your Degree of Empathic Concern and Personal Distress?

Directions

To discover your level of empathic concern and personal distress, read each item below. Then, using the following response scale, indicate how well each statement describes you.

0 = extremely uncharacteristic (not at all like me)

1 = uncharacteristic (somewhat unlike me)

2 = neither characteristic nor uncharacteristic

3 = characteristic (somewhat like me)

4 = extremely characteristic (very much like me)

Empathic Concern Scale

____ 1. When I see someone being taken advantage of, I feel kind of protective toward him/her.

____ 2. When I see someone being treated unfairly, I sometimes don't feel very much pity for him/her.*

____ 3. I often have tender, concerned feelings for people less fortunate than me.

____ 4. I would describe myself as a pretty soft-hearted person.

____ 5. Sometimes I don't feel very sorry for other people when they are having problems.*

____ 6. Other people's misfortunes do not usually disturb me a great deal.*

____ 7. I am often quite touched by things that I see happen.

Personal Distress Scale

____ 1. When I see someone who badly needs help in an emergency, I go to pieces.

____ 2. I sometimes feel helpless when I am in the middle of a very emotional situation.

____ 3. In emergency situations, I feel apprehensive and ill-at-ease.

_____ 4. I am usually pretty effective in dealing with emergencies.*

_____ 5. Being in a tense emotional situation scares me.

_____ 6. When I see someone get hurt, I tend to remain calm.*

_____ 7. I tend to lose control during emergencies.

Scoring

Several of the items on these two scales are reverse-scored; that is, for these items a lower rating actually indicates a higher level of empathic concern or personal distress. Before summing the items, recode those with an asterisk (*) so that 0 = 4, 1 = 3, 3 = 1, 4 = 0.

Gender Differences in Empathic Concern and Personal Distress

Davis (1980) has found the following gender differences in levels of empathic concern and personal distress:

Empathic concern:

Male mean = 19.04

Female mean = 21.67

Personal distress:

Male mean = 9.46

Female mean = 12.28

Are your scores above or below the mean for your sex?

Research indicates that individuals high in empathy are not only more willing to put themselves in situations in which the experience of sympathy for another is likely but also are generally more willing to help people in trouble than are those low in empathy (Pavey et al., 2012). For example, in an analysis of people's responses to the annual Jerry Lewis muscular dystrophy telethon, Davis (1983) found that people with high empathic concern were more likely to watch the telethon and to contribute their time, effort, and money as a result. In contrast, people high in personal distress showed no such tendency. We can conclude from this research that people who typically feel compassion for unfortunate others tend to be drawn toward situations in which their feelings of sympathy will be aroused. When exposed to others' misfortunes, they don't remain passive bystanders; rather, they tend to take action to try to relieve the suffering. In this regard, the experience of caring for others represents a central self-concept value for those high in empathic concern (Emmons & Diener, 1986). Later in this chapter, we will more closely examine how empathy and personal distress shape bystanders' responses to others' needs.

Before concluding this discussion of empathy and helping, we should mention that there is some evidence that empathy is declining among US college students. Using Mark Davis's empathic concern measure (see *Self/Social Connection Exercise 12.2*), Sara Konrath and her colleagues (2011) conducted a meta-analysis of 72 samples of about 14,000 American college students collected between 1979 and 2009. Their findings indicated that more recent generations of college students are reporting less empathy than earlier generations, and there was no evidence that this decline in empathy was greater for either women or men, nor related to any changes in economic prosperity over the three decades. The data also indicated that the sharpest drop in empathy occurred after the year 2000, or fairly recently. Compared to college students in the late 1970s and early 1980s, college students today are less likely to agree with statements such as "I often have tender, concerned feelings for people less fortunate than me" and "I would describe myself as a pretty soft-hearted person."

So why might empathy be declining among college students? We can only speculate at this point, but these findings are consistent with previously discussed research (see Chapter 1, *The Social World of American Young Adults* in section 1.2c) suggesting that during the past three decades Americans have developed a heightened self-focus and the value placed on individuality has increased (Twenge et al., 2013). From a theoretical standpoint, increasing focus on the self should lead to diminished attention to—and empathy for—others. Surveys do show that this current young generation is less charitable and less likely to volunteer to help others than previous generations (Philanthropic Giving Index, 2008). Critics of the current generation of young adults have referred to them derisively as "Generation Me" or the "Look At Me" generation. It is possible that young adults' widespread use of Facebook, Twitter, and other social media—which reduces face-to-face contacts between people—contributes to this diminished empathic tendency. Future research will provide more conclusive evidence on whether this current speculation is indeed accurate.

12.1g Learning to Be a Helper Involves Both Observation and Direct Reinforcement.

Many people subscribe to the same helping norms, but they differ in their tendencies to act consistently with these norms. The internalization of prosocial values begins in the preschool years, and parents and other adults play a significant role in this developmental process (Grusec et al., 2002). Just as Chapter 11 outlined how aggression can be learned through modeling and direct reinforcement, we now examine how prosocial behavior is similarly learned.

Observational Learning of Prosocial Behavior

Parenting plays an important role in fostering and inhibiting children's prosocial behavior (Knafo & Plomin, 2006). According to social learning theorists, observational learning or modeling can influence the development of helping in at least two ways (Rosenkoetter, 1999). First, it can initially teach children how to engage in helpful actions. Second, it can show children what is likely to happen when they actually engage in helpful (or selfish) behavior. In this learning process, what models *say* and what they *do* have different impacts on shaping observers' prosocial behaviors.

For example, in one study, sixth-grade girls played a game to win chips that could be traded for candy and toys (Midlarsky et al., 1973). Prior to actually playing, each of the girls watched a woman play the game. In the *charitable* condition, the adult put some of the chips she won into a jar labeled "money for poor children" and then urged the girls to think about the poor children who would "love to receive the prizes these chips can buy." In the *selfish* condition, the adult model also urged the child to donate chips to the poor children, but she did so after putting all her chips into a jar labeled "my money." Results indicated a clear effect of prosocial modeling. Girls who had observed the charitable model donated more chips to the poor than those who had seen the selfish model. This study suggests that when an adult declares, "Do as I say, not as I do," children are more likely to model the adult's actions rather than their words.

Modeling prosocial behavior is not confined to children. In one study conducted in a natural setting, motorists who simply saw someone helping a woman change a flat tire were more likely to later stop and assist a second woman who was in a similar predicament (Bryan & Test, 1967). Additional research suggests that the adults who may be most likely to be positively influenced by observing others' helpful actions are those who define themselves as highly moral or helpful individuals. In a set of studies, Karl Aquino and his colleagues (2011) found that people whose moral identities are highly self-defining were more likely than others to not only feel more intense positive emotions after witnessing acts of uncommon goodness but also to profess a greater desire to become a better person by being more helpful to others.

What are some of the social psychological factors that increase our likelihood of helping after witnessing others' helpful actions?

The Lasting Consequences of Modeling

A number of studies have revealed the critically important role that prosocial parental modeling plays in the lives of extra-ordinary helpers. For example, a study of civil rights activists in the late 1950s and 1960s found that previous parental modeling of prosocial behavior distinguished those who made many personal sacrifices from those who participated in only one or two freedom rides or marches. The fully committed activists had parents who had been excellent prosocial models when the activists were children, while the parents of the partially committed tended to be inconsistent models, often preaching prosocial action but not actually practicing it (Rosenhan, 1970). Combined with other studies, these findings indicate that adults' modeling of altruism can have a powerful effect on the altruistic tendencies of children that can last well into adulthood (Fogelman, 1996; Oliner & Oliner, 1988). Over time, helping others not only becomes one of the defining features of these individuals' self-concepts but also contributes to heightened self-esteem (Hitlin, 2007).

Based on this knowledge, social scientists believe they can make a clear recommendation to parents on how to raise children who will help those in need. Put simply, parents who try to instill prosocial values only by preaching and not by modeling altruism will likely raise children who are only weakly altruistic. Parents who not only preach altruism, but also let their prosocial actions serve as guidelines for their children's behavior, are much more likely to foster altruism in the next generation. In a very real sense, to be effective altruistic teachers, one must not only "talk the talk" but also "walk the walk."

Rewarding Prosocial Behavior

Although observing the prosocial actions of others can shape children's and adults' own helping, the consequences of their actions will often determine whether they continue to engage in prosocial behavior. Social rewards, such as praise and gratitude, are generally more effective reinforcers than material rewards, such as money (Grusec, 1991).

For example, imagine yourself walking along the main street in your hometown and being approached by a woman who asks how to get to a local department store. After giving her directions you continue along your way. Shortly, you pass by another woman who accidentally drops a small bag and continues walking, unaware that she has lost this possession. Would you return the bag to her? Do you think your decision to help the second woman would be influenced by how the first woman responded to your attempt to help her?

This was the question that researchers asked in a naturalistic study conducted on the streets of Dayton, Ohio, using just this scenario (Moss & Page, 1972). In the *reward* condition, the woman asking for directions rewarded her helper by saying, "Thank you very much, I really appreciate this." In contrast, in the *punishment* condition the woman responded to help by saying, "I can't understand what you're saying; never mind, I'll ask someone else." Researchers found that when the first woman rewarded people, 90% of them helped the second woman. However, when punished by the first woman, only 40% helped in the later situation.

This study suggests that people's future decisions to help are often influenced by the degree to which current helpful efforts are met by praise or rebuke. Additional research suggests that when helpers are thanked for their efforts, they experience stronger feelings of self-efficacy and social worth, which motivates them to help others in the future (Grant & Gino, 2010). The takeaway message here is that even small expressions of gratitude can motivate prosocial behaviors by leading helpers to feel socially valued (Ma et al., 2017). Therefore, saying thank you is not only the polite and correct thing to do when you receive help from someone, it is also an effective strategy to strengthen the person's tendency to provide you (and others) with help in the future.

Prosocial Video Games and Helping

In Chapter 11 we reviewed the findings from many studies indicating that playing violent video games increases aggressive cognitions, aggressive affect, and later aggressive behavior in the real world among both young adults and children. These same studies also found that playing violent video games reduces empathy and the willingness to help others. Given what we know about the learning of social behavior, if violent video games can increase aggressiveness, is it likely that prosocial video games will have the opposite effect?

That was the question posed by Tobias Greitemeyer and Silvia Osswald (2010) in a series of experiments in which they placed research participants in positions to assist or not assist others shortly after they played a prosocial video game. In one experiment, the researchers randomly assigned participants, ranging in age from 19 to 43, to one of three video game conditions. The prosocial game was Lemmings, in which the game's goal was to help a group of animals (lemmings) past a number of dangerous obstacles to a designated safe location. In contrast, the aggressive game was Lamers, which involved using an arsenal of weapons to destroy as many creatures, called lamers, as possible before they reached their intended destination. The neutral game was Tetris, which is a puzzle game with a number of random shapes the player manipulates to complete a solid row of blocks. After participants in each experimental condition had played their video game for 8 minutes, the female researcher came into the room, acted as if she was reaching for a questionnaire, and spilled a cup of pencils. She then waited five seconds to see if the participant would help. Results indicated that most participants who played the prosocial video game helped; and as a group, they were significantly more likely to help pick up the pencils than those who played the neutral or aggressive game.

In a second experiment, Osswald and Greitemeyer wanted to determine whether participants playing prosocial video games would be more likely than other gamers to intervene when there was possible physical danger involved. Participants were randomly assigned to either play a prosocial video game or the Tetris video game, and they were monitored by a female researcher who remained in the room. After 10 minutes, a male confederate entered the room posing as the female researcher's boyfriend. The "boyfriend" approached the female researcher and yelled, "Ah, there you are! I was looking for you in the whole building! Why do you ignore me like that? Why do you do that to me? Now you have to talk to me!" He then kicked a trashcan and pulled the female researcher's arm to force her to leave the room with him. The female researcher resisted, saying to the boyfriend, "Shush, be quiet please. I have to work in

Research indicates that when people play prosocial video games—such as Zoo Vet, in which gamers take care of zoo animals and help them when they are ill or injured—they are more likely to help others in need in their actual lives.

(Courtesy of Legacy Interactive, Inc.)

here, I cannot talk to you. You are disturbing the experiment. Please do not be so loud." What did the participants do? Intervening was operationally defined as either saying something to the female researcher (for example, "Do you need help?") or saying something to the boyfriend (for example, "I think you need to leave."). Results indicated that participants playing the prosocial video game were significantly more likely to intervene than those playing the neutral video game (56% versus 22%).

Similar results have been obtained in other countries with participants of varying ages (Boduszek et al., 2019; Gentile et al., 2009). Further, a meta-analysis of 98 studies involving about 37,000 participants found that playing video games that encourage prosocial activities within the game increases the likelihood that those playing will behave more prosocially in their everyday lives (Greitemeyer & Mügge, 2014). In essence, just as violent video games prime attitudes and memories that make anger and aggressive behavior more likely, prosocial video games activate attitudes and memories that increase people's willingness to help.

12.1h Being Helpful Can Benefit Personal Well-Being.

The fact that helping others fosters stronger feelings of self-efficacy and social worth suggests that helping might actually be good for our health. Research informs us that donating money to charity activates brain areas associated with pleasure and rewards, and that our motives for happiness, helpfulness, and even popularity are interrelated (Grayman-Simpson & Mattis, 2013; Harbaugh et al., 2007). Happy people are more likely to help others and have satisfying friendships than less happy people (Aknin et al., 2012). Additional studies indicate that not only do happy people have the personal resources to do good for others, but also engaging in helpful behavior—at all ages—increases a sense of well-being (Kahana et al., 2013; Weinstein & Ryan, 2010). Being kind and helpful not only fosters a sense of well-being, but the resulting positive emotions can also enhance both psychological and physical resilience, which has a positive impact on longevity (Post, 2005). For example, Sonya Lyubomirsky (2007) studied five women over a 3-year period who had multiple sclerosis and were volunteering as peer supporters for other people suffering from this same disorder. Lyubomirsky found that, during the course of the 3-year period, these five volunteers experienced positive changes in their health that were significantly larger than the benefits shown by the patients they were supporting.

There is also evidence that encouraging people to engage in helpful behavior can directly impact their personal well-being. In a longitudinal field experiment conducted in 19 elementary classrooms in Vancouver, Kristin Layous and her coworkers (2012) instructed 9- to 11-year-olds to perform three acts of kindness per week over the course of 4 weeks. They also instructed a control group of similar children to simply visit three places during this same time period. Results indicated that students who performed kind acts experienced significantly greater increases in peer acceptance than students who simply visited places. Finally, in a recent meta-analysis of 27 studies, the association between helping others and personal well-being was found to be a small-to medium-effect size, and it occurs regardless of age and gender (Curry et al., 2018). Overall, this research suggests that doing good for others benefits givers, earning them not only improved well-being, but also popularity, which is associated with greater happiness.

Helping others can benefit your own well-being. Why might this be so?

Section Summary

- In kin selection, we exhibit preferences for helping blood relatives because this increases the odds that our genes will be transmitted to subsequent generations.

- In reciprocal helping, aiding strangers can be adaptive because any helpful act or favor is expected to be returned.

- Following are relevant social norms that promote helping:
  Reciprocity norm: Help those who help you.
  Social responsibility norm: Help those in need or those dependent on you.
  Social justice norm: Help those who deserve assistance.

- Liberals tend to follow the social responsibility norm while conservatives tend to follow the social justice norm.

- Lower-class individuals express more concern for, and are more willing to help, unfortunate others than upper-class individuals.

- Collectivist cultures hold to a broader and more stringent view of social responsibility than individualist cultures.

- Women and men appear to be helpful in different ways:
  Men are more likely to help in dangerous situations.
  Women are more likely to provide long-term help.
  These gender differences increase from childhood to adulthood and when gender roles are salient.

- Individual differences in empathy and personal distress have opposite effects on helping responses.

- Prosocial behavior that is rewarded will become stronger.

- Parents who model prosocial behavior raise children who become helpful adults.

- Playing prosocial video games increases the willingness to help.

- People who regularly help others often experience a heightened sense of psychological and physical resilience.

12.2 When Do We Help?

As already mentioned, the chapter-opening story is a more accurate retelling of the Kitty Genovese murder than what has been commonly told over the past 40-some years in psychology textbooks. Rachel Manning and her colleagues (2007) contend that the original story of the 38 unresponsive witnesses became a kind of modern parable of group apathy. Although a good portion of the original story is now discredited, the social psychological insights that indirectly resulted from the widespread media coverage are still relevant—and largely valid—today. Let us now examine some of these classic studies and the theories that emerged from this research.

12.2a Bystander Intervention Involves a Series of Decisions.

The supposed apathy of Kitty Genovese's neighbors was the topic of news stories, commentaries, religious sermons, and dinner conversations for some time after the murder. Two people who discussed the murder at length were social psychologists John Darley and Bibb Latané. Years later, Darley recalled the content of their discussion:

> Latané and I, shocked as anybody else, met over dinner a few days after this terrible incident had occurred and began to analyze this process in social psychological terms. . . . First, social psychologists ask not how are people different or why are the people who failed to respond monsters, but how are all people the same and how might anybody in that situation be influenced not to respond? Second, we asked: What influences reach the person from the group? We argued for a several-step model in which a person first had to define the situation. Emergencies don't come wearing signs saying "I am an emergency." In defining an event as an emergency, one looks at other people to see their reactions to the situation and interpret the meaning that lies behind their actions. Third, when multiple people are present, the responsibility to intervene does not focus clearly on any one person. . . . You feel a diffusion of responsibility in that situation and you're less likely to take responsibility. We argued that these two processes, definition and diffusion, working together, might well account for a good deal of what happened. (Evans, 1980, pp. 216–217)

According to the **bystander intervention model**, which eventually emerged as a result of this dinner discussion, the presence of other bystanders during an emergency inhibits helping. This model further contends that being helpful during an emergency involves not just one decision but, rather, a series of five decisions. As you can see from Figure 12.1, at each point in this five-step process, one decision results in no help being given, while the other decision takes the bystander one step closer to intervention.

The first thing that you, as a potential helper, must do is *notice that something unusual is happening*. Unfortunately, in many social settings, countless sights and sounds flood our senses. Because it is impossible to attend to all these stimuli, and because we may be preoccupied with something else, a cry for help could conceivably go completely unnoticed. This *stimulus overload effect* is more likely to occur in densely populated urban environments than in rural settings (Milgram, 1970). Indeed, it is one of the likely reasons why there is a negative correlation between population density and helping (Levine, 2003; Steblay, 1987). That is, throughout the world, people who live in more crowded cities are less likely to help strangers in need of assistance than those who live in less densely populated urban centers (Levine et al., 1994; Yousif & Korte, 1995). Another reason it is sometimes difficult to notice things out of the ordinary is that what is unusual in one setting may be a normal occurrence in another. For example, in some neighborhoods, a person lying unconscious on the sidewalk may be extremely unusual and cause passersby to take notice. Yet, in other neighborhoods, this same person may be one of many street people who live and sleep outdoors much of the year—an all too common sight that passersby generally would take little, if any, notice of.

bystander intervention model

A theory that whether bystanders intervene in an emergency is a function of a five-step decision-making process

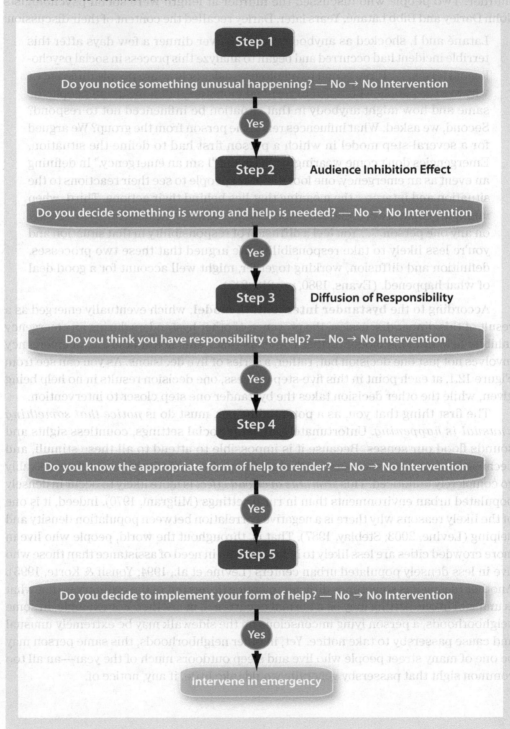

FIGURE 12.1   The Model of Bystander Intervention: A Five-Step Decision Process

As outlined by Latané and Darley (1970), the decision to help someone involves a five-step process. At any step, a bystander's decision could lead to either further analysis of the situation or to nonintervention.

Step 1

Do you notice something unusual happening? — No → No Intervention

Yes

Step 2   **Audience Inhibition Effect**

Do you decide something is wrong and help is needed? — No → No Intervention

Yes

Step 3   **Diffusion of Responsibility**

Do you think you have responsibility to help? — No → No Intervention

Yes

Step 4

Do you know the appropriate form of help to render? — No → No Intervention

Yes

Step 5

Do you decide to implement your form of help? — No → No Intervention

Yes

Intervene in emergency

As a bystander to an emergency, if you do indeed notice that something unusual is happening, you move to the second step in the decision-making process: *deciding whether something is wrong and help is needed.* Returning to the previous example, if you pass by an unconscious man on the sidewalk you may ask yourself, "Did he suffer a heart attack or is he merely sleeping?" This is an extremely important decision, because if you decide he is merely sleeping you will continue on your way. But what if you are mistaken? Consider again the Kitty Genovese murder. After hearing Kitty's scream, one woman in the apartment building jumped out of bed and ran to her window because it was unusual to hear screams at this time of night (the first decision step). However, when she looked out her window and saw Kitty and her assailant "standing close together, not fighting or anything," she decided this was not an emergency (the second decision step). Only later did she learn that she was actually watching the commencement of a sexual assault and murder. Incorrectly defining the situation led to her nonintervention.

Some emergency situations are not as clearly defined as others. How does the presence of other people affect bystanders' decision-making when an emergency unfolds?

When you define the situation as an emergency, the bystander intervention model states that the third decision you must make is *determining the extent to which you have a responsibility to help.* According to Latané and Darley, one factor that may play a role in your decision to help or not is whether an appropriate authority figure is nearby. For instance, imagine sitting in your car at a busy intersection and noticing that in the car ahead of you, two people are arguing heatedly. Suddenly, one of these quarrelers begins hitting the other with a club. This is definitely unusual and it is clearly an emergency. The pertinent question now is: Do you have responsibility to come to the victim's aid? Further, imagine that to your immediate right is a police car with two officers sitting inside. If you decide that it is their responsibility to render assistance, you will likely assume the role of an unresponsive bystander.

Let's continue this hypothetical emergency situation, but now imagine that there is no police car in sight. Faced with the reality of a clear emergency, you still may not help if you convince yourself that all the other motorists watching this incident could help just as well as you. The presence of these other potential helpers, like the presence of authority figures, may cause you to feel less personally responsible for intervening. This is how some—but clearly not all—bystanders in the Kitty Genovese case responded.

If you assume responsibility for helping, a fourth decision you must make is *the appropriate form of assistance to render.* In the heat of the moment, however, what if you are not sure what to do? You may become paralyzed with uncertainty about exactly how to render assistance. Unable to decide, you may not offer any help at all. Children are particularly likely not to have the appropriate skills or confidence to make a decision at this stage in the helping process.

Finally, if you notice something unusual, interpret it as an emergency, assume responsibility, and decide how best to help, you still must decide whether to *implement your course of prosocial action.* If you have decided to run to the car where the person is being beaten and intervene, you must now act on this intention. However, due to fear of injury or concern about testifying at a future trial, you may decide not to implement your previous decision and remain a passive bystander. In the Kitty Genovese case, the only person who directly intervened was the woman who came to her aid, although others did indirectly intervene by either shouting at the assailant or phoning the police.

As you can see from the outline of this model, Latané and Darley believe that the decision to intervene in a possible emergency involves a rather complex set of decisions. As a bystander, if you make an incorrect choice at any point in this process, you will not intervene. Two social psychological processes that often operate in emergency situations are the *audience inhibition effect* and the *diffusion of responsibility*. The inhibition effect can short-circuit helping at Step 2 in the bystander intervention model, and diffusion of responsibility occurs in Step 3.

12.2b Outcome and Information Dependence Produce the Audience Inhibition Effect.

Many emergency situations are not clearly defined as such, but rather, have some degree of ambiguity. You may realize that something unusual is happening (Step 1 in the model), but you are not sure that it's an emergency (Step 2). In one study designed to investigate bystander uncertainty, Latané and Darley (1968) recruited male college students for a study on the problems of urban life. When a research participant arrived at the laboratory, he was ushered into a room, given a questionnaire, and then left alone to complete it. Soon, what looked like white smoke (but wasn't) began to enter the room through a small wall vent. Within 6 minutes, the smoke was so thick it was difficult to see. The dependent variable was whether or not the participant would leave the room to report the problem before the 6 minutes had elapsed. What do you think happened?

When working alone, most participants usually hesitated a moment upon first seeing the smoke, but then walked over to the vent to investigate. In 75% of the trials, the participant finally left the room to report the emergency. In a second experimental condition, groups of three naive participants were seated in the room when smoke began to pour from the vent. In all trials, participants looked to one another to help them decide if there was an emergency, but in only 38% of these three-person groups did even a single person report the incident before the 6-minute mark. Although 55% of the participants in the *alone* condition reported the smoke within the first 2 minutes, only 12% of the three-person groups did so. Finally, in a third condition, two confederates—acting like research participants—joined the one real participant in the room. As it began to fill with smoke, the confederates acted unconcerned. If the real participant asked them any questions, they replied, "I dunno" and continued working on the questionnaire. In the presence of these unconcerned confederates, only 10% of the participants reported the smoke. The other 90% coughed, rubbed their eyes, and opened the window, but they did not leave the room. These findings, summarized in Figure 12.2, indicate that when others are present, people are less likely to define a potentially dangerous situation as an emergency, and they also respond more slowly to the possible emergency. This **audience inhibition effect**, which is driven by *pluralistic ignorance* (see Chapter 7, section 7.2a), is particularly likely when other people are acting calmly.

In another investigation of the inhibition effect, Latané and Judith Rodin (1969) set up a situation in which some other person, besides the research participant, was in possible danger. First, a female researcher set participants to work on a questionnaire and then left through a collapsible curtained doorway to work in an adjoining office. From their room, participants could hear her shuffling papers and opening and closing drawers. After 4 minutes, the researcher turned on a tape recorder that broadcast the sound of her climbing on a chair to reach a stack of papers on a bookcase. Participants then heard the researcher's scream, quickly followed by a loud crash. "Oh, my God, my foot. . . . I . . . I . . . can't move . . . it," she moaned. "Oh . . . my ankle. . . . I . . . can't get this . . . thing . . . off me." After about 2 minutes of moaning, the woman could be heard dragging herself out of her office.

audience inhibition effect
People are inhibited from helping for fear that other bystanders will evaluate them negatively if they intervene and the situation is not an emergency

FIGURE 12.2 The Audience Inhibition Effect

When a room began filling with white smoke, people were much less likely to report the incident—and did so more slowly—when they were with others rather than alone (Latané & Darley, 1968). What two types of social dependence are interacting here to create the audience inhibition effect?

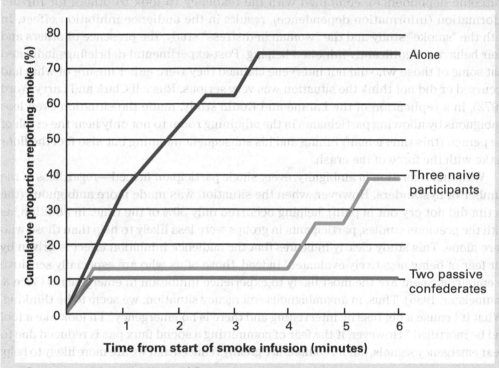

Data source: "Group Inhibition of Bystander Intervention In Emergencies," by B. Latané and J. M. Darley, 1968, *Journal of Personality and Social Psychology, 10*(3), pp. 215–221.

Of the participants who were alone in the room, 70% tried to help by opening the curtain or running out the other door to find help. Consistent with the audience inhibition effect, when two strangers were sitting in the room, only 40% of the time did either of them help. When the two people sitting in the room were friends, at least one of them helped in 70% of the trials. Even though this is the same percentage of helping as in the alone condition, it still indicates an inhibition effect because two people were present. If these two friends did not inhibit each other's response, then helping should have occurred in 91% of the trials (70%$_{friend\ 1}$ + (70% × remaining 30%$_{friend\ 2}$) = 91%). Finally, in the last condition, a naive participant sat in the room with a confederate who acted unconcerned and nonchalant about the ruckus behind the curtain. Again, consistent with the inhibition effect, in this setting the participant tried to help only 7% of the time.

To better understand why the inhibition effect occurs, let's return to two concepts previously discussed in Chapter 9 (section 9.1a), namely, *information dependence* and *outcome dependence*. As discussed in that chapter, when we are not clear about how to define a particular situation, we are likely to become dependent on others for a definition of social reality. Thus, when a group of people witnesses a possible emergency, each person bases his or her interpretation of the event partly or exclusively on the reactions of others (information dependence). The problem with this information seeking in an emergency is that, in our culture, we have learned that it is not socially acceptable to "lose your cool." If we become agitated and excitable during a crisis, we run the risk of being negatively evaluated by others (outcome dependence). Due to this concern, we will often pretend to be calm while witnessing an emergency. Acting cool and calm, we then observe others' behavior for clues for how to define what we all are witnessing. However, because everyone else is also assuming a calm exterior, what we observe is a group of calm bystanders who, by their nonplussed demeanor, are defining the situation as a nonemergency.

In ambiguous emergency situations, then, the fear of being negatively evaluated (outcome dependence), combined with the tendency to look to others for further information (information dependence), results in the audience inhibition effect. In both the "smoke" study and the "woman in distress" study, the presence of others and their behavior significantly inhibited helping. Post-experimental debriefings indicated that some of those who did not intervene claimed they were either unsure of what had occurred or did not think the situation was very serious. Russell Clark and Larry Word (1972), in a replication of the Latané and Rodin study, made the situation even less ambiguous by allowing participants in the adjoining room to not only hear the crash of the person (this time a man) falling and his subsequent moaning but also feel the floor shake with the force of the crash.

With this reduction in ambiguity, every single participant helped—regardless of the number of bystanders. However, when the situation was made more ambiguous (the victim did not cry out in pain), helping occurred only 30% of the time. In addition, as with the previous studies, participants in groups were less likely to help than those who were alone. This study clearly indicates that the audience inhibition effect is driven by our fear of being negatively evaluated. Indeed, those of us who are especially sensitive to embarrassment are the most likely to experience inhibition in emergencies (Tice & Baumeister, 1985). Thus, in an ambiguous emergency situation, we seem to be thinking, "What if I cause a big fuss by intervening and there is no emergency? I'll look like a fool and be mortified." However, if the fear of committing a social faux pas is reduced due to clear emergency signals, our inhibitions are greatly reduced and we are more likely to help.

12.2c Diffusion of Responsibility Increases with the Number of Bystanders.

Fear of embarrassment is one reason we do not intervene in some emergencies, but what about those situations in which someone clearly needs help and no one raises a finger to come to the victim's aid? Surely some other social psychological factor is operating. For example, at least some of the neighbors of Kitty Genovese, sitting in their own separate apartments, correctly guessed what was happening before the second fatal attack occurred. However, they knew—or assumed—that others were also watching this drama unfold below them. Darley and Latané believed that this realization that others could also help diffused these neighbors' own feelings of individual responsibility (Step 3 in the model). They called this response to others' presence the *diffusion of responsibility*—the belief that the presence of other people in a situation makes one less personally responsible for events that occur in that situation (see Chapter 8, section 8.2b).

In an attempt to simulate the social psychological factors that they believed were present in the Genovese case, Darley and Latané (1968) designed an

Why are potential helpers more likely to diffuse responsibility for helping as the number of bystanders to an emergency increases?

(Shutterstock)

experiment in which they placed people in separate areas from which they then heard a victim cry for help. In this study, New York University students thought they were participating in a discussion about the kinds of personal problems undergraduates typically face in a large urban environment. They were also told that, to avoid embarrassment, they would each be placed in a separate booth and would talk to one another through an intercom system. To further ensure they wouldn't be inhibited, the experimenter said he would not eavesdrop on their conversation. The way the intercom system worked was that only one person could speak at a time, and the others had to merely listen.

The study included three different conditions. Some participants were told the discussion would be with just one other student, while others were told they were either part of a three-person or a six-person group. In reality, all the other discussion participants were merely tape recordings. Discussion began with the first speaker stating that he was an epileptic who was prone to seizures when studying hard or when taking exams. When everyone else had spoken, the first speaker began to talk again, but now he was speaking in a loud and increasingly incoherent voice:

> I-er-um-I think I-I need-er-if-if could-er-er-somebody er-er-er-er-er-er-er give me a little-er-give me a little help here because-er-I-er-I'm-er-er-h-h-having a-a-a real problem-er-right now and I-er-if somebody could help me out it would-it would-er-er s-s-sure be-sure be good . . . because-er-there-er-er-a cause I-er-I-uh-I've got a-a one of the-er-seizure-er-things coming on and-and-and I could really-er-use some help so if somebody would-er-give me a little h-help-uh-er-er-er-er-er c-could somebody-er-er-help-er-uh-uh-uh (choking sounds). . . . I'm gonna die-er-er-I'm . . . gonna die-er-help-er-er-seizure-er-[chokes, then quiet]. (Darley & Latané, 1968, p. 379)

How did participants respond to this concocted, yet convincing, emergency? It depended on the number of bystanders they thought were also aware of the epileptic's seizure. When participants thought they were the only ones listening to the emergency unfold, 85% of them left their booths to help before the victim's pleas for help were cut off. When they thought they were one of five bystanders, only 31% reacted in a similar prosocial manner. When participants thought there was one other bystander aware of the emergency, helping was intermediate, with 62% helping. Not only was helping less likely as the number of bystanders increased, but the *speed* of rendering assistance was significantly slower as well. As you can see from Figure 12.3, when participants thought there were four other bystanders, it took them three times longer to take any action (if they helped at all) than it did in the alone condition.

> "Where are they who claim kindred with the unfortunate?"
>
> —Caroline Lamb, English novelist, 1785–1828

More than 50 subsequent laboratory and naturalistic studies have confirmed this diffusion of responsibility effect (Latané & Nida, 1981). On average, when participants believed they were the only bystander to an emergency, 75% of them helped, compared with only 53% of those who were in the presence of others. Diffusion of responsibility also occurs when people need help on the internet (Barron & Yechiam, 2002; Blair et al., 2005). For example, in one study, more than 4,800 people were monitored in 400 different internet chat groups over a month's time to determine the amount of time it took a bystander to render assistance to someone who asked for help (Markey, 2000). Results indicated that it took longer for people to receive help as the number of people present in a computer-mediated chat group increased. However, this diffusion of responsibility was virtually eliminated and help was received more quickly when help was asked for by specifying a bystander's name.

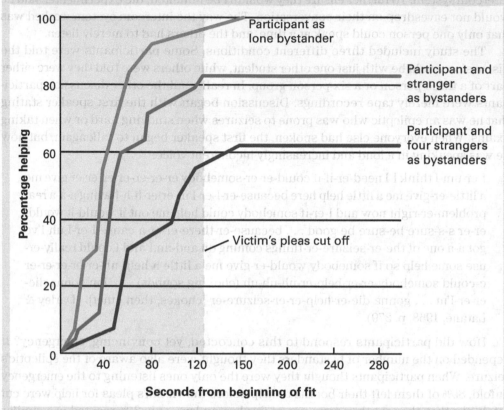

FIGURE 12.3 The Diffusion of Responsibility Effect

When participants heard over an intercom system someone having a seizure, how did the number of perceived bystanders influence their speed and willingness to help the victim (Darley & Latané, 1968)?

Data source: "Bystander Intervention In Emergencies: Diffusion of Responsibility," by John M. Darley and Bibb Latané, 1968, *Journal of Personality and Social Psychology, 8*(4), pp. 377–383.

Do you think you would find these same bystander effects among people whose jobs regularly deal with helping others? How might you test whether the situational context or the salience of their "helping" social roles would influence their tendency to intervene?

A meta-analysis of more than 100 studies, involving over 7,700 participants from the 1960s to 2010, strongly supported the finding that bystanders inhibit helping responses and that this effect becomes stronger with an increasing number of bystanders (Fischer et al., 2011). This meta-analysis also indicated that the audience inhibition effect is less pronounced in dangerous situations than in nondangerous situations. Why might this be so? One likely possibility is that in dangerous situations, bystanders are more likely than in nondangerous situations to label what they are witnessing as a clear-cut emergency because dangerous situations more closely fit the emergency prototype. In other words, the uncertainty and fear of embarrassment that drives the audience inhibition effect is greatly reduced when there is danger present. Does all this research mean that when a crowd of bystanders becomes very large no one will help? Of course not. While it is true that bystanders inhibit individuals from helping, it is also true that if the group size gets sufficiently large, the mathematical odds become better that at least someone will defy the social forces and intervene, however delayed that help might be (Stalder, 2008).

Despite clear evidence that the presence of others influences people's decision to help, in post-experimental interviews, participants in all of Latané and Darley's experiments tended to deny that others' assumed presence had any effect on their actions (or inactions). As discussed in Chapter 7, underestimating the effect that others have on your behavior makes it more likely that you will fall prey to their influence. After all, how can you guard against falling into the nonhelpful mode when you don't recognize how the simple presence of others can change your feelings of personal responsibility?

Besides bystanders influencing helping responses in the traditional ways described thus far, Stephen Garcia and his colleagues (2002) wondered whether the presence of actual people is necessary to induce the bystander effect. Is it possible that simply imagining others is sufficient to induce a similar mental state of diffused responsibility, regardless of whether those others are available to respond? Research on *priming* suggests that merely activating knowledge structures from memory can influence people's social perceptions and behavior (see Chapter 4, section 4.1c). Garcia hypothesized that merely activating the construct of *group* in the minds of people would result in diffusion of responsibility.

To test this hypothesis, he and his colleagues approached students who were sitting alone at a campus student center and asked them to complete a questionnaire. For participants in the *group condition*, the questionnaire included a group prime, which read as follows: "Imagine you won a dinner for yourself and 10 of your friends at your favorite restaurant." For participants in the *one-person condition*, the inserted statement was similar but focused on only one friend: "Imagine you won a dinner for yourself and a friend at your favorite restaurant." Next, all participants answered the filler question: "What time of day would you most likely make your reservation?" The choices were 5 p.m., 6 p.m., 7 p.m., 8 p.m., 9 p.m., or 10 p.m. In the *neutral control condition*, participants read only the filler question, which was slightly modified to "What time of day would you make a dinner reservation?" For all participants, helping behavior was measured by their willingness to volunteer to help out with an experiment. Thus, on the last page of the questionnaire all participants read the following: "In addition to this survey, we are conducting a brief experiment in another room. How much time are you willing to spend on this other experiment?"

As hypothesized, participants who were prompted to imagine a group of 10 people offered less assistance (helping) than did participants in either the one-person condition or the neutral control condition. Even though participants in the group condition imagined their friends, these imagined friends were not in the immediate vicinity to offer helping behavior. Hence, these results suggest that others need not be physically present for diffusion of responsibility to occur; merely imagining a group can lead to feeling lower levels of responsibility for helping others.

12.2d Bystander Intervention Is Shaped by Arousal and Cost-Reward Assessments.

Latané and Darley's bystander intervention model is best at explaining why people in a group of bystanders often don't interpret an event as an emergency, as well as why they often don't help even when it's clearly defined. Although this model provides a number of important pieces to the bystander puzzle, its focus is on the social problem of *nonintervention*. Yet why do we often decide to actually intervene in an emergency?

Jane Piliavin and her colleagues (1981) attempted to answer this question by developing a theory of bystander intervention that extends and complements Latané and Darley's model. These researchers added to the decision-making equation a consideration of bystanders' emotional arousal during an emergency and their assessment of the costs of helping and not helping. Essentially, their work focuses on the second half of Latané and Darley's model—namely, deciding on personal responsibility (Step 3), deciding what to do (Step 4), and implementing action (Step 5).

This **arousal:cost-reward model** of helping contends that witnessing an emergency is emotionally arousing and is generally experienced as an uncomfortable tension that we, as bystanders, seek to decrease (Gaertner & Dovidio, 1977). This tension can be reduced in several different ways. We could intervene and thereby decrease our arousal, but we could also reduce arousal by either ignoring danger signs or benignly interpreting them as nothing to worry about. In addition to these avenues of action, we could reduce arousal by simply fleeing the scene. Which behavior we choose will be a function of our analysis of the costs and rewards for helping and for not helping. What are the costs to the bystander for helping? This could involve a host of expenditures—including loss of time, energy, resources, health (even life), as well as the risk of social disapproval and embarrassment if the help is not needed or is ineffective. Counterbalancing the costs of helping are the costs of not helping. These might include serious harm to the ignored victim and subsequent public scorn of the nonhelpful bystander. Realizing that one did not render assistance could also lead bystanders to engage in self-blame and experience loss of self-esteem.

According to Piliavin and her colleagues, if the costs of helping are low and the costs of not helping are high, bystanders will likely intervene (refer to Figure 12.4). In contrast, if these costs are reversed (high helping costs and low not-helping costs), bystanders are unlikely to render assistance. If both types of costs are low, intervention will depend on the perceived social norms in the situation. The most difficult situation for bystanders is one in which the costs for helping and for not helping are both high. Here, the arousal:cost-reward model suggests two likely courses of action. One is for bystanders to intervene indirectly by calling the police, an ambulance, or some other professional helping source. Another course of action is for bystanders to redefine the situation in a way that results in them not helping. Here, they could decide there really is no emergency after all, or that someone else will help, or that the victim deserves to suffer. For instance, imagine that you are walking down the street when you hear a child screaming in pain. Directing your gaze toward the screams, you see a lone young girl who has slammed a car door on her hand. In this situation, you will likely directly intervene because (1) the costs of not helping are high—the girl may seriously injure her hand if it is not removed from the door's grip soon, and you will experience terrible guilt if you don't help; and (2) the costs of helping are low—opening the car door will require little effort or loss of time, and helping will not put you in any danger.

Now, imagine that the child is not screaming in pain because her hand is caught in a door, but rather because an adult is beating her with a stick. Now what will you do? Here, the costs of both not helping and helping are high—the girl may be seriously hurt, and you will experience guilt if you don't stop the beating; but the adult could seriously injure you if you intervene. Faced with these high costs, you may help indirectly by calling the police or by yelling from a safe distance for the adult to stop. Sadly, you might also convince yourself that the child must deserve the beating she is getting and continue on your way.

(Shutterstock)

According to the arousal:cost-reward model, what factors do we likely consider when trying to decide whether to help homeless people we encounter on city streets?

arousal:cost-reward model
A theory that helping or not helping is a function of emotional arousal and analysis of the costs and rewards of helping

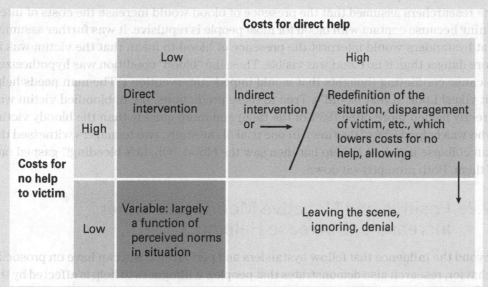

FIGURE 12.4 **The Influence of Costs and Rewards on Direct Helping**

According to Piliavin and Piliavin (1972), the type of response a moderately aroused observer will have to someone's need for help will be influenced by his or her assessment of the combination of personal costs for direct help and costs for no help to the victim. According to this model, when are bystanders most and least likely to help?

Source: Adapted from "The Effect of Blood on Reactions to a Victim," by J. A. Piliavin and I. M. Piliavin, *Journal of Personality and Social Psychology, 23*, pp. 253–261. Copyright © 1972, American Psychological Association.

Now, imagine that the child is screaming in pain because an adult is spanking her bottom with moderate force. In this situation, both the costs of not helping and helping are probably low. Not intervening will probably not cause serious physical injury to the child, and intervening may only result in the adult telling you to mind your own business. If your perception of cultural norms is that spanking children is an unacceptable response to misbehavior, you may try to stop the punishment. Otherwise, you are unlikely to intervene.

Finally, imagine the same scene as in the previous paragraph, but now let's add that you are rushing to an important job interview. If you try to stop the spanking, you run the very real risk of arriving late. Here, your costs for helping are high and the costs for not helping are low. Weighing these factors, you are likely to continue on your way, perhaps muttering about the misguided actions of the adult but justifying your nonintervention to yourself ("If I didn't have this appointment, I'd give that adult a piece of my mind!").

A number of studies support the arousal:cost-reward model's hypothesis that people often weigh the costs of helping and not helping prior to rendering assistance (Dovidio et al., 1991; Fritzsche et al., 2000). For example, Lance Shotland and Margaret Straw (1976) staged a realistic fight between a man and a woman on an elevator. In one condition, 65% of the time bystanders intervened when the woman shouted, "Get away from me! I don't know you!" However, in another condition bystanders helped only 19% of the time when the woman shouted, "Get away from me! I don't know why I ever married you!" These differences in helping were apparently due to perceived costs. People who watched videotapes of the fights perceived the woman as being in greater danger when with the stranger than when with the husband. They also believed that the combatants would be more likely to turn on them if they tried to intervene in the "domestic" fight rather than the "stranger" fight. Thus, the "stranger" condition was perceived to involve higher costs for not helping and lower costs for helping than the "husband" condition.

Another study investigating the costs for helping and the costs for not helping was conducted on the Philadelphia subway system when a male confederate carrying a cane collapsed (Piliavin & Piliavin, 1972). In one condition, the victim had a thin trickle of fake blood slip from his mouth as he fell, while in a second condition he did not. The researchers assumed that the presence of blood would increase the costs of intervening because contact with blood for most people is repulsive. It was further assumed that bystanders would interpret the presence of blood to mean that the victim was in more danger than if no blood was visible. Thus, the "blood" condition was hypothesized to cause conflicting thoughts that would impede intervention ("The man needs help, but yikes! Look at that blood!"). True to these predictions, the unbloodied victim was directly helped more often (95% of the time) and more quickly than the bloody victim (who was helped 65% of the time). In one trial of the study, two teenagers witnessed the man collapse and rose to help but then saw the blood. "Oh, he's bleeding!" gasped one of them. Both promptly sat down.

12.2e Positive and Negative Moods Can Either Increase or Decrease Helping.

Beyond the influence that fellow bystanders and perceived costs can have on prosocial behavior, research also demonstrates that people's willingness to help is affected by the mood they happen to be in when assistance is needed.

Good Moods and Generosity

Imagine this scene. Ralph bounds out of his psychology class feeling on top of the world because he has achieved one of the highest scores on his midterm exam. As he happily walks back to his apartment, he notices a woman carrying a tall stack of papers. Suddenly, the stack slips from her grasp and begins flying in all directions across campus. Without hesitation, Ralph springs into action and helps retrieve the errant papers.

Would Ralph have been so willing to help if he were in a less positive mood? Perhaps not. Consistent with our previous discussion (see section 12.1h) about how people who are dispositionally happy are more likely to help others in need, research also indicates that good moods lead to more prosocial behavior. For example, in one study, Alice Isen (1970) administered a series of tests to college students and teachers, later telling them they had either performed very well or very poorly. Still others were told nothing at all about their performance. In addition to these three experimental conditions, a control group was not administered any tests at all. The participants who had "succeeded" at the tests were later more likely to help a woman struggling with an armful of books than any of the other participants. This *good mood effect* following success has been replicated in other studies (Klein, 2003), and additional research indicates that people are more likely to help others on sunny days than on cloudy ones (Cunningham, 1979), after finding money or being offered a tasty treat (Isen & Levin, 1972), and even after listening to uplifting music or a comedian delivering a funny routine (North et al., 2004; Wilson, 1981).

Other people's nonverbal behavior can also induce the good mood effect. In one field experiment, Nicolas Guéguen and Marie-Agnes De Gail (2003) had a confederate smile or not smile at a passerby a few seconds before another confederate dropped computer diskettes on the ground. Results indicated that the passersby were more likely to help pick up the diskettes if they had just received a smile. This finding is consistent with the more general finding that help seekers are much more successful in receiving aid if they smile while making their requests (Guéguen & Fischer-Lokou, 2004).

Why do positive moods lead to greater helping? Several possibilities have been offered. One is that when we are in a positive mood, we are more likely to perceive other people as "nice," "honest," and "decent," and thus deserving of our help (Isen, 1987). Another possibility is that we help others to enhance or prolong our good mood (Wegener & Petty, 1994). A third reason might be that, when happy, we are less likely to be absorbed in our own thoughts ("stewing in our own juices"); thus, we are more attentive to others' needs (McMillen et al., 1977). A fourth possibility is that good moods increase the likelihood that we think about the rewarding nature of social activities in general. With the rewarding properties of helping being salient, our helping becomes more likely. This enhanced attentiveness to the rewarding properties of helping may explain why good moods increase helpfulness only when the helpful task is expected to be pleasant. If helping is expected to entail unpleasant and aversive experiences, happy people are no more helpful than others (Isen & Simmonds, 1978; Rosenhan et al., 1981).

Bad Moods and Seeking Relief

What about negative moods and helping? Rewind your thoughts to Ralph and his psychology midterm. Imagine now that Ralph's exam grade was not an "A" but rather an "F." Now, instead of bounding out of class, he trudges. Given his present somber mood, will he still dart around campus retrieving wayward sheets of paper? Surprisingly, he might. Isen and her coworkers (1973) found that people who believed they had failed at an experimental task were more likely to help another person than those who did not experience failure. Although this response certainly seems to contradict the good mood effect just described, one possible link between the two is the rewarding properties of helping. Because helping others often makes us feel good about ourselves, when feeling bad we may help as a way of *escaping* our mood—just as we help to maintain a good mood.

Feeling guilty can also increase helping (Basil et al., 2008). Michael Cunningham and his colleagues (1980) conducted a field study in which a young man approached individuals on the street and asked them to use his camera to take his picture for a class project. The problem for the would-be helpers was that the camera had been rigged to malfunction. When the helpers realized the camera was not working, the young man examined it closely and asked the helpers if they touched any of the dials. He then informed them that it would have to be repaired. The researchers assumed that such an encounter would induce a certain degree of guilt in these individuals. As they continued on their way, these now guilty people passed a young woman who suddenly dropped a file folder containing some papers. How do you think they responded to this needy situation? Of those who were led to believe that they had broken the young man's camera, 80% helped the female stranger pick up her papers. Only 40% of the passersby who had no broken-camera experience paused to help. Another field study found that Roman Catholics were more likely to donate money to a charity just prior to confessing their sins to a priest—when their guilt level should have been high—rather than immediately after being absolved of those sins (Harris et al., 1975).

Although these studies demonstrate that negative moods can lead to prosocial behavior, other studies suggest that when we experience extremely negative moods, such as grief or depression, we may be so focused on our own emotional state that we simply don't notice others' needs and concerns (Carlson & Miller, 1987). Still other studies suggest that even when experiencing less severe negative moods, we are less likely to help than those who are in good moods (Isen, 1984). Robert Cialdini and Douglas Kenrick (1976) attempted to explain why this is the case by proposing that when we are in a bad mood, our decision to help is often based on a simple, self-serving question: Will helping make me feel better? This **negative state relief model** asserts that when we are in a bad

negative state relief model

A theory suggesting that, for those in a bad mood, helping others may be a way to lift their own spirits if the perceived benefits for helping are high and the costs are low mood, if the perceived benefits for helping are high and the costs are low, the expected *reward value* for helping will be high; thus, we will likely help to lift our own spirits. However, if the perceived benefits and costs are reversed so that the reward value is low, we are unlikely to help. Essentially, this model predicts that bad moods are more likely to lead to helping than neutral moods when helping is easy and highly rewarding.

The negative state relief model has generated considerable scientific debate over whether it accurately depicts foul mood effects, and even its proponents have pointed out the limits of its application (Glomb et al., 2011). First, research indicates that increased helping due to bad moods is much more common among adults than children (Kenrick et al., 1979). One probable explanation for this age difference is that children are less likely to have learned the self-rewarding properties of helping—that it can pull one out of a bad mood. A second limitation is that the model specifies that only mildly negative feelings such as sadness, guilt, and temporary depression will increase helping. More intense negative emotions, such as hostile anger and resentment, result in decreased helping. Finally, because the helping exhibited by adults in a bad mood is of a self-serving nature, if sad or guilty people get their spirits raised from some other source (such as being complimented or hearing a funny joke), they will no longer have a need to help others (Cunningham et al., 1980). Figure 12.5 summarizes the effects that both bad and good moods have on helping.

FIGURE 12.5   The Varied Effects of Mood on Helping

Depending on the circumstances, positive and negative moods can either increase or decrease helping.

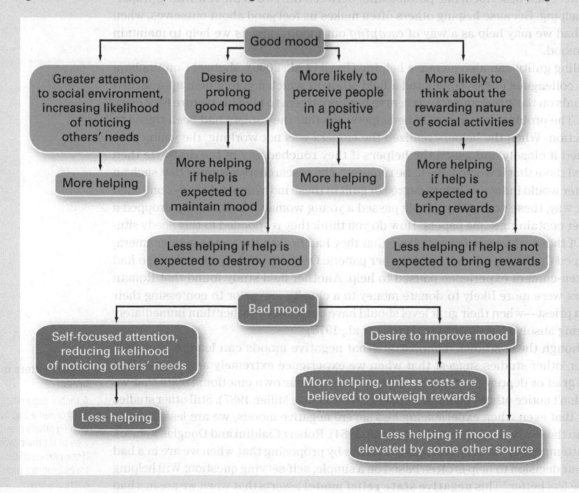

12.2f The Empathy-Altruism Hypothesis Contends That Empathy Produces Altruistic Motivation.

The three previously discussed explanations of the conditions under which people are most likely to help others—the arousal:cost-reward model, good mood effect, and negative state relief model—all assume there is an egoistic motive underlying prosocial behavior. All three explanations contend that helpful bystanders are ultimately trying to improve their own well-being by helping. Yet is egoism all that underlies prosocial action?

Although he does not deny that helping is often motivated by a desire to fulfill egoistic needs, Daniel Batson (1991, 2011) contends that sometimes our prosocial actions are truly *altruistic*, motivated solely by the desire to increase the welfare of another. In Batson's **empathy-altruism hypothesis**, he proposes that we typically experience either personal distress or empathy upon witnessing someone else's suffering (refer back to section 12.1f). Batson contends that these two contrasting emotional reactions to a victim's plight—one focused on our own well-being (personal distress) and the other focused on the victim's (empathy)—result in very different motivations.

Regarding the negative arousal state of personal distress, the greater our personal distress as a bystander, the more we will be motivated to have it reduced. Batson believes that Piliavin's arousal:cost-reward model does a good job of explaining how we respond to personal distress. Because reduction of this unpleasant arousal state is the primary motivation underlying personal distress, we will likely flee the stress-producing situation if at all possible. However, if we cannot easily escape, we will likely lend assistance in order to reduce our own unpleasant arousal. Described in this manner, one can clearly see that helping caused by personal distress is egoistic in nature.

Like personal distress, empathy for someone who is suffering will likely be an unpleasant emotion. However, unlike personal distress, empathy will not be satisfied by flight. Instead, Batson's empathy-altruism hypothesis contends that when we experience empathy, the stronger the feelings of compassion for the victim, the greater our motivation to help. Thus, when we feel great empathy, we are motivated more by our desire to improve the victim's welfare than attend to our own.

Support for the empathy-altruism hypothesis has been found in a number of studies in which bystanders' empathy or personal distress has been manipulated. In one of these studies, Batson and his coworkers (1981) had pairs of female college students participate in a task seemingly investigating how people work under aversive conditions. One participant was the "worker" who received electric shocks at random intervals during two trial periods; the other student observed the worker on a closed-circuit television as she performed the task. In actuality, the worker was a confederate. When the first aversive work trial began, the worker's facial expressions and body movements indicated that she found the shocks to be extremely uncomfortable. At the end of this trial, the worker explained that she had been traumatized by electric shocks in an accident as a child, and now even mild shocks were often very painful. Responding to this "dilemma," the researcher asked the observer—who was naturally disturbed by this story—whether she would be willing to help the woman by trading places with her on the last trial. Batson and his colleagues predicted two factors would determine how participants responded to this dilemma: (1) whether or not they felt personal distress or empathy, and (2) whether or not they could flee this aversive situation.

Regarding the first factor, the experimenters assumed that everyone would experience arousal when witnessing the victim's plight, and that they would naturally attribute this arousal both to sympathy for the victim (empathy) and to personal discomfort (personal distress). To more clearly direct participants' interpretation of their arousal, the experimenters gave them a fictional drug, "Millentana" (a cornstarch placebo), as part of another

empathy-altruism hypothesis

A theory proposing that experiencing empathy for someone in need produces an altruistic motive for helping study just prior to observing their partner being shocked. All participants were told that Millentana had a side effect.

In the *empathy* condition, Batson and his coworkers wanted the participants to misattribute any feelings of personal distress to the drug and not to the victim's plight. To achieve this result, they said that the drug "produces a clear feeling of uneasiness and discomfort, a feeling similar to what you might experience while reading a particularly distressing novel." Due to this misattribution of personal distress to Millentana, the researchers assumed that participants in the empathy condition would perceive their emotional response to the victim to be primarily empathy.

In contrast, those in the *personal distress condition* were told that the drug "produces a clear feeling of warmth and sensitivity, a feeling similar to that you might experience while reading a particularly touching novel." Following a similar logic, the experimenters assumed that these people would misattribute feelings of empathy to Millentana and perceive their emotional response to the victim to be primarily personal distress. Participants' subsequent self-reports indicated that the experimenters were successful in manipulating the women's emotional responses in the desired directions.

Regarding the second factor, ease of escape was manipulated by the instructions participants had previously received concerning their role as observer. In the *easy-escape* condition, they were told they would observe only the first trial, while in the *difficult-escape* condition, participants were told they would observe both trials.

How do you think these different factors affected willingness to help the victim? Results found that regardless of whether escape was difficult or easy, empathic observers tended to help by deciding to trade places with the confederate. On the other hand, the personally distressed observers chose to flee when fleeing was easy; they helped only if that was the only way to relieve their own discomfort. These findings are perfectly consistent with the empathy-altruism hypothesis.

In a replication of this experiment, instead of manipulating empathy and personal-distress arousal by giving people a placebo drug, Batson and his coworkers (1983) asked participants to describe their emotions after watching the confederate suffer. Based on these responses, participants were categorized as being either personally distressed or empathic. As in the previous experiment, the empathic observers chose to help regardless of how easy or difficult it was to escape. Likewise, those who experienced personal distress tended to flee if they could, and helped only if fleeing was not an option. Overall, the pattern that emerged in five separate studies is that, regardless of ease or difficulty of escape, empathic individuals provided help about 75% of the time. Likewise, those who experienced personal distress and could not escape easily tended to help at approximately the same level, about 79%. In contrast, when escape was easy for the personally distressed, their level of helping dropped dramatically—to about 30%.

Based on these and other findings that are consistent with the empathy-altruism hypothesis (Sibicky et al., 1995), can we conclude that people who help due to empathy are motivated by true altruism? Certainly, Batson and most social scientists think there is compelling scientific evidence for this view (Batson, 2011; Fetchenhauer et al., 2007). Yet while empathy may indeed induce altruistic helping, additional research suggests that an important factor in actually triggering empathic feelings toward those in need is whether we highly value their welfare in the first place (Batson et al., 2007; Stürmer et al., 2006). When the welfare of those in need is highly valued, we often experience empathy and are more likely to respond with altruistic helping (M. H. Davis et al., 2004). However, if we perceive victims' welfare as being of relatively low value, we are unlikely

How could you design a donation pitch to members of a local community center to help starving people in a foreign country, knowing that some message receivers will react with empathy, while others will react with personal distress?

to empathize with their plight (Stürmer et al., 2005). Consistent with evolutionary theory, this link between helping and empathic concern is much more pronounced in the context of kinship relationships than among strangers (Maner & Gailliot, 2007).

Given the importance of empathy as a motivator for helping, it is noteworthy that there is new evidence that the ability to experience empathy is at least partly determined by the ability to accurately read people's faces for emotions signaling danger and distress. In a series of studies, Marsh and Ambady (2007) found that participants who were exposed to fear facial expressions experienced more empathy and a greater willingness to help than participants who were exposed to neutral facial expressions. They further found that the participants who showed the greatest prosocial responding were those who recognized facial expressions of fear most accurately. Overall, these findings are consistent with the survival value hypothesis discussed in Chapter 4 (section 4.3a). Marsh and Ambady contend that the facial expression of fear serves as a *distress cue* to bystanders, triggering increased perceptual attention and empathic arousal. These findings are also consistent with one of the main insights from Darley and Latané's bystander intervention model: People are most likely to behave prosocially when they accurately interpret situational cues signaling that something is wrong and help is needed.

Because the experience of empathy often induces a helping response, is it possible that we are sometimes wary of feeling empathy out of concern for the costs of helping? This *empathy-avoidance hypothesis* assumes that we have an implicit knowledge of the empathy-helping relationship, and this knowledge sometimes causes us to actively avoid feeling empathy when we believe the cost of helping will be high. This collapse of compassion is most often motivated by self-interest, and research suggests that it accounts for many instances of nonintervention. For example, in a series of experiments, when people believed that helping a homeless man would entail considerable time and effort, they actively avoided situations in which their empathy for this man would be aroused (Shaw et al., 1994). Because helping large numbers of people is more costly than helping single individuals, empathy avoidance is especially likely when the number of people in need of help increases (Daryl & Keith, 2011). In essence, people often "turn off" their empathy in the face of mass suffering or when they otherwise conclude that helping will entail heavy costs (Slovic, 2007). These findings suggest that even normally softhearted people can steel themselves to the suffering of others if they avoid an empathic connection. Consider this the next time you pass a homeless person on the street or learn of a disaster affecting large numbers of people. Are you actively avoiding an empathic response because the perceived costs of helping are too great?

> "One death is a tragedy; one million is a statistic."
>
> —Joseph Stalin, Soviet Union premier, 1878–1953

Section Summary

- The model of bystander intervention focuses on the influence that bystanders have on prosocial behavior.
    - Audience inhibition effect: Bystanders inhibit people from defining dangerous situations as emergencies.
    - Diffusion of responsibility: Bystanders make people feel less personally responsible for helping.
- The arousal:cost-reward model focuses attention on the perceived costs of prosocial behavior.

(continues)

(Section Summary *continued*)

- Greater helping often follows good moods, but we may sometimes try to eliminate negative moods by helping others.

- The empathy-altruism hypothesis contends that
  bystanders who experience empathy will help to provide comfort for victims and
  bystanders who experience personal distress will help victims only to reduce their own negative arousal state.

- Because empathy motivates helping, people sometimes actively avoid experiencing empathy when the cost of helping is high.

12.3 Whom Do We Help?

Thus far we have examined the *why*, *when*, and *who* of helping. Now it is time to ask the question, *whom* do we help? Are some people more likely to receive help than others?

12.3a We Tend to Help Similar Others.

As we discovered in Chapter 6 (see section 6.3), our natural inclination to place people into "us" and "them" categories often sets the stage for treating them differently. Therefore, it isn't surprising that if we perceive a needy person as similar to us, we are more likely to lend assistance (Stürmer et al., 2005). For example, gay men were more willing than heterosexuals to volunteer at an AIDS service organization, and their willingness to help was strongest when their social identity as "gay men" was most salient (Simon et al., 2000).

Even in natural disasters, we are more likely to donate funds to help victims if we perceive that they are similar rather than dissimilar to us.

("Helicopter Flies Over Sendai," courtesy of the U.S. Navy, via Wikimedia)

In general, studies indicate that we are most willing to help ingroup members who need assistance. As already discussed (see section 12.1e), this preference for providing ingroup help over outgroup help is more pronounced among people with a collectivist orientation than among those with greater individualist tendencies.

We often rely on physical cues in guessing people's ingroup-outgroup status. One salient physical cue often used in categorizing needy people into ingroups and outgroups is the clothes they wear. In a series of studies conducted at Lancaster University in England, individual students on campus observed a young man falling while jogging down a grassy hill; the jogger then proceeded to hold onto his ankle while shouting out in pain (M. Levine et al., 2005). The injured man was either wearing a Lancaster team soccer shirt, a rival Liverpool soccer shirt, or an unbranded, nonsoccer sport shirt. Consistent with the similarity hypothesis, when onlookers had been previously primed to think of themselves as Lancaster soccer fans, the injured man was more likely to be helped while wearing the ingroup shirt than while wearing the outgroup or nonbranded shirts. However, when onlookers had been previously primed to think of themselves simply as soccer fans, they were as likely to help the injured man while he was wearing a Liverpool soccer shirt as while he was wearing a Lancaster shirt; they offered less help to the non–soccer related victim. Together, these findings indicate that not only are we more likely to help people who are similar to us but also perceptions of dissimilarity can be submerged by inducing or encouraging potential helpers to expand their ingroup social categorization.

Given the cultural prejudice that still exists concerning sexual orientation issues, it is not surprising to find an antigay bias among heterosexual adults in their willingness to offer help to those in need. In one study examining this effect, Jason Ellis and Pauline Fox (2001) used an adaptation of the *wrong-number technique* in measuring helping behavior. In this research technique, a confederate places a telephone call to a randomly chosen phone number and informs the respondent that he or she has misdialed while calling from a cell phone. The confederate then asks the respondent to call the confederate's romantic partner and convey an important message, as the confederate's cell phone battery is running out. The phone number given to the respondent is that of the experimenters, who record whether or not the call is made and the gender of the caller.

We tend to help similar others. For example, gay men are more willing than heterosexuals to volunteer at an AIDS service organization, especially when their gay social identity has been primed.

In this field experiment, the two independent variables were the gender of the caller (male or female) and the sexual orientation of the caller. The caller's sexual orientation was indirectly identified during the phone call. In the lesbian condition, the female caller, who identified herself as Jane, stated that she was trying to reach her partner, Karen. In the gay condition, the male caller, who identified himself as Barry, stated that he was trying to reach his partner, John. In the two heterosexual conditions, the female caller mentioned her partner Barry and the male caller mentioned his partner Karen. The dependent variable was whether or not the participant placed the call within 5 minutes of the request for help.

As expected, when the caller was self-identified as gay or lesbian, respondents were much less likely to help than when the caller was self-identified as heterosexual (31% versus 50%). Consistent with the greater prejudice expressed by heterosexual men toward gay men compared to lesbians, male respondents were significantly less likely to give help to gay men than to lesbians (14% versus 48%). In contrast, female respondents did not significantly differ in their helping toward gay men and lesbians. These results suggest that although lesbians and gay men are discriminated against in helping, such discrimination does not appear to be equally applied to both groups by heterosexual men. This finding is consistent with previous research indicating that heterosexual men feel more negatively toward gay men than toward lesbians (Kite & Whitley, 1996).

Unlike sexual orientation issues, the influence that a victim's race has on helping behavior is far more complex. In a meta-analysis of 31 studies published from 1987 to 2002 that examined discrimination against black people in helping situations, Donald Saucier and his coworkers (2005) did not find evidence of blanket discrimination. However, consistent with the prediction of aversive racism (see Chapter 6, section 6.2b), black people were least likely to be helped when white bystanders could rationalize decisions not to help using reasons that had nothing to do with race. Specifically, when helping required lengthier, riskier, more difficult, and more effortful actions by potential helpers, white people were less likely to help black victims compared to white victims. These findings suggest that potential helpers perceive higher costs for helping when the person who needs help is of a different race. This meta-analysis also found that when white bystanders were farther away from victims, victim race predicted whether help was offered: Black victims were offered help less often than white victims. Finally, the researchers found evidence that discrimination against black people was more likely for higher-level emergencies requiring quick helping decisions compared to lower-level emergencies allowing for more decision time. In other words, race discrimination in helping is most likely to occur when the ability to control prejudicial responding is inhibited by having to make fast decisions.

A recent series of studies conducted by Sasha Kimel and her colleagues (2016) found evidence that, when it comes to providing help to members of another ethnic group for which our own group has a history of conflict, whether we help or not is significantly influenced by whether we are made aware of similarities versus differences between our group and the other group. In this research, Kimel focused on Jews and Palestinians, because these two groups not only share a close genetic heritage, they also have a long history of conflict. In one study, the researchers randomly assigned Jewish American and Palestinian American participants to read a news article that described Jews and Palestinians as either genetically similar or genetically different. Participants who read the "genetic similarity" article reported less antipathy and behaved less aggressively toward a Jewish or a Palestinian outgroup member during a subsequent task. Similarly, in an online survey, US Jewish community members expressed more support for Israeli–Palestinian peace efforts when they read a "genetic similarity" article than when they read a "genetic difference" article. Finally, a field study conducted in Israel found that Jewish Israeli participants who read about genetic similarities between the two groups reported increased support and hope for political compromise and decreased support for collective punishment and political exclusion compared to those who read about genetic differences. Together, these findings suggest that when we are reminded about our similar human heritage rather than our superficial differences, we are more likely to extend helping hands to others who we might otherwise define as "other" (Nai et al., 2018).

12.3b We Help Deserving Others, but We Also Blame Victims.

just-world belief
A belief that the world is a fair and equitable place, where people get what they deserve in life

As discussed earlier in the chapter (section 12.1c), whether people receive help in times of need will partly depend on others' inferences about the causes of their troubles. Following the principles of attribution theory discussed in Chapter 4 (see section 4.4a), we are more likely to help someone if we attribute the cause of their problems to external or uncontrollable factors rather than internal ones. For example, college students state that they would be more willing to lend an acquaintance money or give their lecture notes if the need arose due to an uncontrollable cause, such as illness, rather than an internal, controllable cause, such as laziness (Weiner, 1980). Similarly, people's willingness to help the poor and other disadvantaged people is substantially shaped by what they believe caused these unfortunate events in the first place (Dionne, 1991). Put simply, if we believe people could not have prevented their predicament, we are more likely to help.

The reason we are more likely to help deserving others is due to the *norm of social justice* discussed earlier in the chapter. However, the problem in making inferences about the cause of a victim's troubles—and thereby deciding if she or he deserves our help—is that most of us believe in a just world (Callan et al., 2006). The **just-world belief** is a belief that the world is a fair and equitable place, where people get what they deserve (Lerner, 1997; Lucas et al., 2009). According to Melvin Lerner (1980), this social belief system is a defensive reaction to the sometimes cruel twists of fate encountered in life; it is comforting because most of us conceive ourselves to be good and decent people. By believing

(Shutterstock)

Do you believe that the world is a fair and equitable place, with people getting what they deserve? If so, how does assigning blame to accident victims reinforce your just-world beliefs?

in a just world, we have the illusion that we have more control over our lives than we actually do (Lipkus et al., 1996).

Although just-world believers often psychologically benefit from their positive illusions about how the world operates, this social belief can lead to some unfortunate social judgments, as illustrated by people's tendency to blame rape victims for their sexual assaults (Bell et al., 1994; Hayes et al., 2013). Strong believers in a just world tend to make *defensive attributions* when explaining the plight of victims. In other words, they are prone to blame people for their misfortunes. Research demonstrates that this tendency to blame victims is strongest when people feel personally threatened by an apparent injustice (Hafer, 2000). Thus, accident victims are more likely blamed for their fate if they are similar to us on some relevant characteristic, or if their injuries are severe rather than mild (Burger, 1981). By disparaging the victim, we reassure ourselves that the world is not only just, but also that we are not likely to fall victim to similar circumstances ("Because I'm really not like *them*").

Although many people believe in a just world, individual differences exist in the extent to which this belief is held. Because those with a strong just-world belief are more likely to be unsympathetic to victims, it's not surprising to find that they generally are also less likely to help those in need. Does this mean that people who are strong believers in a just world are always unhelpful bystanders? No. When a victim's suffering can be easily and promptly corrected, strong believers in a just world are much more likely to help than when the problems are of a widespread and enduring nature (Bierhoff et al., 1991). The likely reason for this effect is that helping someone who needs just a little bit of assistance to get back on track confirms the just-world believer's perception that the truly deserving will not be unfairly punished. Thus, firm believers in a just world are much more likely to be one-time contributors to little Billy's heart operation fund than they are to be continuing contributors to a fund in search of a cure for AIDS or a program to promote affordable housing for the poor.

Section Summary

- We are most likely to help similar others.

- We are also most likely to help deserving others.

- One unfortunate consequence of believing in a just world is that we tend to blame people for their misfortunes.

12.4 Are There Hidden Costs for Help Recipients?

Throughout the chapter we have examined some of the factors that inhibit bystanders from providing assistance to others—but what if help is given? How do recipients typically respond? And what might prevent a person in need from asking for help?

12.4a Being Unable to Reciprocate Help Can Create Stress.

People recognize that receiving help is a mixed blessing. Those who receive help often respond with feelings of relief and gratitude, but they also often feel embarrassed, indebted, and even inferior (Nadler, 1991). The contradictory feelings that often flow from

(Shutterstock)

Why does receiving help sometimes cause people to suffer a loss of self-esteem? Would allowing them to reciprocate the help in some manner bolster their feelings of self-worth?

prosocial actions help to explain why victims are sometimes less-than-gracious recipients of a helping hand. The potential that help giving has for producing resentment and hostility is aptly recognized in an Indian proverb that states, "Why do you hate me? I never even helped you."

In attempting to explain why receiving help may at times evoke unpleasant emotions, social psychologists have turned their attention to the fact that in exchange relationships (refer to Chapter 10, section 10.1b), people are especially attentive to *reciprocity*—a mutual exchange of resources. *Equity theory* (Chapter 10, section 10.5b) contends that people seek to maintain equity in their social relationships by keeping the exchange ratio of resources balanced, and they feel distressed when inequity exists (Hatfield et al., 1978). When people receive help, they commonly experience a feeling of inequity because, by definition, they realize they have a more favorable ratio of rewards to contributions than does the helper. Under such circumstances, recipients of help are motivated to restore actual equity by trying to return the favor (Greenberg & Frisch, 1972). But what happens if they cannot reciprocate?

Research indicates that recipients not only find nonreciprocal helping distressful but also are less likely to ask for assistance in the first place if they don't think they can repay the person in some way (Riley & Eckenrode, 1986). If they aren't in a position to refuse the help, they might sometimes deal with their inability to restore equity by resenting the helper (Gross & Latané, 1974). In essence, help givers may be resented if they don't allow recipients to restore equity in some way and thereby allow those who have been helped to live up to the reciprocity norm.

> "It is natural to avoid those to whom we have been too much obliged."
>
> —Héloise, French abbess, c. 1090–1164

12.4b Receiving Help Can Threaten Self-Esteem.

The notion that receiving help may produce inequity and feelings of distress in a relationship suggests that it may also pose a threat to the recipient's self-esteem. For instance, in our individualist culture we place a high premium on self-reliance, and this value is often a key defining feature of our self-concept. Receiving help from someone puts us into a dependent role that is contrary to this individualistic value. According to Jeffrey Fisher and Arie Nadler's **threat-to-self-esteem model**, if receiving help contains such negative self-messages, we are likely to feel threatened and respond negatively (Nadler & Fisher, 1986). More specifically, this model states that when receiving help, we can perceive it as either *self-supporting* or *self-threatening*. Aid will be supportive to the extent that it (1) conveys caring for the recipient and (2) provides real benefits (Dakof & Taylor, 1990). It will be threatening to the extent that it (1) implies an inferiority-superiority relationship between recipient and helper and (2) conflicts with important cultural values of self-reliance and independence (Dunkel-Schetter et al., 1992).

> "A charitable deed must be done as a duty which man owes to man, so that it conveys no idea of the superiority of the giver or the inferiority of the receiver."
>
> —The Koran 2:262, sacred scripture of Islam

threat-to-self-esteem model

A theory stating that if receiving help contains negative self-messages, recipients are likely to feel threatened and respond negatively

Revisiting our previous discussion of help giving between conflicted groups, Nadler and Samer Halabi (2006) tested the threat-to-self-esteem model among Arab Israelis, an ethnic group within Israel that has lower social status than the more mainstream Jewish Israelis. The researchers predicted that Arab Israelis would be especially likely to react negatively to help from Jewish Israelis when they perceived such help as threatening to their desire for equality by implying that they are dependent on the higher-status

Jewish Israelis. They also predicted that Arab Israelis who strongly identified with other Arab Israelis would be much more likely to reject such help because they would experience a stronger self-esteem threat than those who self-identified less with their ethnic group. In a series of both lab and field experiments, the researchers' hypotheses were supported: Arab Israelis were much more likely to not seek and also to reject help from Jewish Israelis, and to evaluate the would-be helpers more negatively, when the help was perceived to imply dependency. This negative reaction was especially likely among high ingroup identifiers, probably because they are more likely than low ingroup identifiers to have an "us versus them" mindset regarding their ethnic group and Jewish Israelis. Therefore, just as an "us versus them" mindset can prevent people from helping outgroup members, it can also prevent them from accepting help from those in the outgroup due to self-esteem threat.

Characteristics of the helper and the recipient's own level of self-esteem will also determine whether aid is seen as supportive or threatening. Being helped by a friend, sibling, or a *similar* person is more likely to prompt social comparison, which in turn may call into question the recipient's level of competence (Searcy & Eisenberg, 1992). This is especially true when the helpful task involves something important to the recipient's self-concept. For example, if you are an aspiring psychologist who does not understand the subtleties of a particularly complex theory, asking a fellow student would probably be more threatening to your self-esteem than asking your psychology professor. Why? The threat-to-self-esteem model would hypothesize that asking a fellow student for help would be more likely to reflect negatively on your own level of competence in this area than seeking help from the professor—a person who is clearly dissimilar to you in psychological training and knowledge (Nadler et al., 1983).

In one experiment testing this hypothesis, Nadler (1987) asked Israeli high school students to solve a series of anagrams when working alongside a same-sex partner. While describing the anagrams task the researchers told half of the students that their performance would provide accurate information on their intelligence and creativity. The rest were told that the task had no association with any important intellectual qualities. All the students were also told that during the task, they could ask their partner for help if they wished. Just before they began the anagrams, they were shown an attitude questionnaire their partner had supposedly completed a few minutes earlier. Half of these questionnaires were constructed to be similar to the participants' own attitude questionnaire responses, while the others were dissimilar in content. The question of interest was under what conditions the students would be most likely to avoid help seeking.

"The gods help them that help themselves."

—Aesop, Greek folk hero and teller of fables, 6th century BCE

Consistent with the threat-to-self-esteem model, students were less likely to seek help from their partners when they believed they were similar to them, especially when the task was defined as requiring skills important to self-esteem—namely, intelligence and creativity. This reluctance to ask for help from similar others was greatest among adolescents high in self-esteem, who supposedly had the most self-regard to lose on these important personal qualities. One positive consequence of this self-esteem threat is that people who feel threatened in this manner become motivated to develop the necessary skills so that in the future, they will not have to seek help.

Most men consider asking for help to be a sign of weakness. This is even portrayed by macho movie characters.

(lev radin / Shutterstock)

Section Summary

- The threat-to-self-esteem model hypothesizes that if receiving help poses a threat to self-esteem, the recipient may respond negatively, disparaging the help and the helper.
- Help recipients may resent help givers if they are not given the opportunity to return the favor in some way.

Applications

Can Social Psychological Knowledge Enhance Prosocial Behavior?

Shortly after 6 p.m. on September 5, 1993, a nude man was seen running through Cornell University's campus. Suddenly, he stopped at the College Avenue Bridge and began climbing over the railing so that he could jump into the deep gorge below. But before he could commit suicide, some students grabbed and held him to the ground until police arrived. Although hundreds of people saw him run past and head toward the bridge, only a handful chose to intervene. These Good Samaritans later admitted that they might not have helped if not for the quick thinking of Cornell undergraduate Gretchen Goldfarb.

"Something just clicked," Goldfarb said, in explaining how she realized that this was an emergency and not simply a prank. What was it that "clicked" in her mind? Social psychological knowledge. A few days earlier, she had learned in her psychology class about Darley and Latané's bystander intervention research, which demonstrated that people often do not help in emergencies unless someone first takes action. Armed with this knowledge, she admonished fellow bystanders to grab the man. In that moment, her application of social psychological knowledge played a pivotal role in saving a life.

Learning About the Barriers to Helping

It is very likely that during the course of your life you will find yourself in an emergency situation like the one Gretchen Goldfarb experienced. Perhaps the most disturbing set of findings discussed in this chapter is the tendency of bystanders to fail to act when someone needs help. Because emergencies are often not clearly defined as such, and because of the potential for embarrassment if one intervenes and there is no actual emergency, the presence of others inhibits prosocial responding. However, as Goldfarb's story demonstrates, social psychological knowledge truly can release you from such inhibition.

In an empirical demonstration of the empowering effects of such knowledge, Arthur Beaman and his coworkers (1978) randomly assigned students to listen to either a lecture on Latané and Darley's bystander intervention research or a topic irrelevant to helping. Two weeks later, while participating in a seemingly unrelated study, these same students each walked past a person lying on the ground. A confederate accompanied each student and acted unconcerned at this possible emergency. How did the students react? Only 25% of those not previously exposed to the bystander intervention lecture stopped to offer assistance. This low prosocial response rate is consistent with Latané and Darley's own findings. Undoubtedly, these students took their cue from their unconcerned companion and defined the situation as a nonemergency. In contrast, students who had previously learned about the paralyzing effects of fellow bystanders on the intervention process acted very differently: 43% stopped to help the person. These findings suggest that simply knowing about the social barriers to helping can free one from their antisocial effects.

Jane Piliavin, codeveloper of the arousal:cost-reward model, believes that in addition to this knowledge-created awareness of the social dynamics of emergency situations, we must also understand that in our individualistic society we have been socialized to leave people alone and to mind our own business. Such an upbringing can effectively inhibit intervention:

In our society, we are trained from an early age to see the problems of other people as "none of our business," to close our feelings off from others' experiences. We have only recently "discovered" child abuse, spouse abuse, incest, and other family "traditions" because of the sanctity of the home and

(*continues*)

(**Applications**, *continued*)

respect for others' privacy. This tendency saves all of us a great deal of emotional distress, but it contributes to the bureaucratization of helping in our society and, we believe, to the increasing alienation and self-absorption of which we all are currently being accused. We may need more training as busybodies; respect for privacy prevents empathic arousal, and directs one's attention to the costs of intervention, specifically the cost of being thought "intrusive." (Piliavin et al., 1981, p. 254)

Piliavin and her colleagues state that in classes in which they have discussed the social psychological research and theories of helping, students repeatedly report an increased attentiveness and responsiveness to emergencies.

Current research supports the value of teaching bystander intervention to adolescents and college students for emergency situations that are likely to occur in their lives. As noted in Chapter 11 (section 11.5), sexual aggression on college campuses is a very prevalent problem. Numerous studies find that sexual assault awareness programs are most effective when they train adolescents and young adults to notice the warning signs of an assault and to take personal responsibility for intervening (Kettrey & Marx, 2019). Bystander intervention training is also effective in addressing alcohol-related emergencies on college campuses (Anthenien et al., 2017). In a very real and important sense, making people aware of the social dynamics of emergencies and the inhibiting effects of socialization may be an important key to unlocking people's prosocial tendencies.

THE BIG PICTURE

In this chapter, we addressed five basic questions about helping: Why do we help? Who is most likely to help? When do we help? Whom do we help? And, are there hidden costs for those who receive help? Now, let's turn the tables a bit: What if you are the one who needs help? How can you use your social psychological knowledge to increase the likelihood that others will assist you?

The bystander intervention model provides valuable insights in this regard, for it tells you that deciding to intervene in a possible emergency involves a rather complex set of decisions. If bystanders make an incorrect decision at any point in this process, they will not help you. Faced with these facts, as the victim, you must attack and neutralize the psychological factors that cause nonintervention. Essentially, you need to capitalize on the self's ability to construct social reality. You can do so by actively and forcefully altering people's social perceptions so that they adopt helping social roles.

The first psychological hurdle is the audience inhibition effect, in which the fear of being negatively evaluated, combined with the tendency to look to others for further information, leads bystanders to identify emergencies as nonemergencies. As the victim, you can eliminate this inhibition by clearly letting everyone know that this is an emergency and you need help.

After clearing this hurdle, you must next attack the diffusion of responsibility, which is bystanders' tendency to believe they are less personally responsible for helping when others are present. Here, you should implore specific people to help you, because it's hard to deny assistance when singled out of the crowd.

Finally, because some people may want to help but are unsure what to do, you can overcome this last hurdle by specifically giving them instructions ("You! Call an ambulance!" "You! Gather my belongings and bring them to me!"). Using your most authoritative voice will further increase obedience. And obedience is exactly what you are seeking here. In all likelihood, you probably won't need to direct everyone who is assisting you. Once you get the ball rolling, others are likely to spring into action on their own. However, the more quickly you consciously transform the social dynamics to facilitate helping, the better off you will be. Gretchen Goldfarb can attest to this social fact.

◼ KEY TERMS

◼ WEBSITES

Accessed through https://www.bvtlab.com/sop8

Websites for this chapter focus on research and theory on helping, including how to raise children to be more altruistic and personal life stories of people who help others.

American Psychological Association

The American Psychological Association has a web page that offers suggestions on how to raise children to be more altruistic and supports the suggestion with relevant theories.

Giraffe Project Heroes Program

This website highlights the personal life stories of people who stick their necks out for the common good.

The Altruistic Behavior Institute

This website is devoted to the institute founded in 1982 by Dr. Samuel Oliner and Dr. Pearl Oliner, who recognized the need for more research into the areas of altruism and prosocial behavior.

The University of Illinois at Chicago Bystander Intervention Web Page

This is an education and training page about bystander intervention on the sexual misconduct site for the University of Illinois at Chicago.

The National Sexual Violence Resource Center

This website contains resources and publications for survivors, friends and family, and advocates and educators.

KEY TERMS

altruistic helping	497	kin selection	489
cost-benefit model	512	negative state relief model	515
audience inhibition effect	508	norm of social justice	491
bystander intervention model	508	norm of social responsibility	491
egoistic helping	497	personal distress	495
empathy	495	prosocial behavior	487
empathy-altruism hypothesis	517	reciprocal helping	490
just-world belief	522	threat-to-self-esteem model	524

WEBSITES

Accessed through http://wayne.bedab.com/sop3

Websites for this chapter focus on research and theory on helping, including how to raise children to be more altruistic and personal life stories of people who help others.

American Psychological Association

The American Psychological Association has a web page that offers suggestions on how to raise children to be more altruistic and supports the suggestion with relevant theories.

Giraffe Project Heroes Program

This website highlights the personal life stories of people who stick their necks out for the common good.

The Altruistic Behavior Institute

This website is devoted to the institute founded in 1982 by Dr. Samuel Oliner and Dr. Pearl Oliner, who recognized the need for more research into the area of altruism and prosocial behavior.

The University of Illinois at Chicago Bystander Intervention Web Page

This is an education and training page about bystander intervention on the sexual misconduct site for the University of Illinois at Chicago.

The National Sexual Violence Resource Center

This website contains resources and publications for survivors, friends and family, and advocates and educators.

Appendix

Possible Answers for the Critical Thinking Exercises

A Note from the Authors

This appendix contains possible answers to the critical thinking sidebars in Chapters 1–12. In reading and comparing them with your own responses, analyze each answer's strengths and weaknesses. If you would like to help us improve our responses for the next edition, please email your suggestions (or questions) to Steve at Stephen.Franzoi@marquette.edu or to Debra at Debra.Oswald@marquette.edu. For those critical thinking sidebar questions that asked you to provide personal recollections from your own experiences, we have understandably not provided a possible answer.

Chapter 1   Introducing Social Psychology

Question: *Do you think that a judge's beliefs about the guilt or innocence of a defendant in a criminal trial could create a self-fulfilling prophecy among the jury, even if the judge does not voice her opinions?*

Possible Answer: Actually, several studies have investigated this very question. What they have found is that although judges may not directly convey to the jury their beliefs about the defendant's guilt or innocence, their nonverbal behavior and instructions to the jury prior to them beginning deliberations can influence jurors' decisions (Halverson et al., 1997). For example, scowling or smiling in the general direction of a defendant by a judge can signal to jurors some important information about the judge's beliefs, and this information can steer the evaluative direction of subsequent deliberations. It has been estimated that the effect of such subtle influence is sufficient to potentially increase the rate of guilty findings by 14% for a jury instructed by a judge who believes a defendant to be guilty (Rosenthal, 2003).

Chapter 2   Conducting Research in Social Psychology

Question: *Prior to conducting research, what precautions do you think social psychologists should take to ensure that the people who participate in their research will not be harmed? Should social psychologists be allowed to study people without their consent?*

Possible Answer: Just as you can never guarantee that someone won't be hurt taking a walk around the block, so too you cannot guarantee that participants in a social scientific study will never be harmed. However, what you can do is examine all aspects of your study so that all reasonable precautions are taken to minimize participant risk. Whenever the choice is between securing the welfare of the study or the welfare of the participant, you must always place the participant's welfare first. This means that some studies will simply not be conducted.

In most cases, social scientists should study people only with their "informed consent," meaning that they are provided with enough information about the research to be able to make a conscious choice to participate or not. In some cases, however, it may be necessary to study people without their informed consent. For instance, when researchers study helping behavior, they may stage a fake emergency in a public setting—for example, a person collapsing on the street—and then observe the responses of bystanders. In such a natural setting, you cannot ask people for permission to include them in the study beforehand.

Question: *If you were a member of your college's institutional review board and a research proposal similar to the Milgram obedience study was submitted for approval, what questions would you ask to determine its risk/benefit ratio? Based on your assessment, would you approve the study?*

Possible Answer: Using the risk/benefit ratio, you would weigh the potential risks to the participants against the study's potential benefits to society, with greater weight given to the participants' welfare. While assessing a Milgram-type study proposal, you might ask whether there was any other way the researchers could conduct the study to minimize participant stress. In essence, because of the deception being used, full informed consent could not be obtained. As such, you might ask the researchers whether they were going to let the participants know up front that they could not reveal all the details of the purpose and procedures to be used in the study. You might also ask the researchers how they would respond to a participant who asked them to stop the study. Would they stop the study after the first request? Because of the deception and the destructive obedience that is being studied, you would probably also ask the researchers to specifically detail their debriefing procedures, because these would need to be as sensitive and detailed as possible. You might also require follow-up interviews with participants to determine whether there were any delayed stress responses and further require that free counseling opportunities with a mental health professional be made available to participants if they wanted to discuss their research experience.

Would you approve a Milgram-type study? You might decide to do so only if it were seeking to shed light on an aspect of obedience that had not already been investigated. Given the fact that there already have been a number of Milgram obedience replications, you might find it difficult to justify approving another replication of the original study given the possible harm to participants. However, in considering your own answer to this question, keep in mind the following thought: the decision not to grant a request to conduct research on a particular topic also has ethical implications. If you do not allow certain research to be conducted because the behavior in question is socially undesirable or destructive when it naturally occurs in the "real world," the social sciences are likely to have crucial gaps in their knowledge base, and these gaps may prevent scientists from developing useful intervention strategies to lessen people's future suffering. What will be potentially lost by not allowing this study to go forward? These are just a few of the tough questions that you would grapple with as a member of an institutional review board.

Question: *Imagine that you are the leader of a team of researchers studying social psychological topics at a university. Under your tutelage, students are learning about the research process while working on your team. Besides instructing them on the proper scientific methods, statistical procedures, and ethical standards to adopt when conducting research, what advice would you give them concerning how they should approach scientific problems in their work?*

Possible Answer: In 1973, social psychologist William McGuire wrote an important article on how social psychologists should approach scientific problems. This article, "The Yin and Yang of Progress in Social Psychology," suggested that researchers adopt an Eastern philosophical approach to problem-solving that defies conventional notions of logic by simultaneously entertaining contradictory and opposing explanations of reality. McGuire called this approach to "doing" social psychology *perspectivism*, and it requires that scientists engage in oppositional thinking when developing theories and hypotheses. When a scientist develops a hypothesis from a theory, she must also consider how other theories might also account for this hypothesis, and she must also develop an opposing hypothesis that is also derived from multiple theories. This approach to thinking about scientific problems frees the scientist's mind from being bound by the logic of only one explanation of events. Social psychologist Mahzarin Banaji (2004), a former graduate student of

McGuire's, asserts that the student members of a research team with this perspectivist philosophy would feel safe and even elated when research findings run counter to their hypotheses. Instead of feeling that they somehow "failed" the leader of their research team, these students would view these findings as providing them with an opportunity to entertain alternative explanations that are closer to providing an accurate accounting of the social behavior under study. To learn more about perspectivism, check out the book *Perspectivism in Social Psychology*, edited by John T. Jost, Mahzarin R. Banaji, and Deborah A. Prentice and published in 2004 by the American Psychological Association.

Question: *What are some similarities and some differences between "random assignment" and "random selection"?*

Possible Answer: One similarity is that both of these research procedures are meant to serve as a safeguard against researchers unconsciously allowing their opinions and preferences to influence subject participation. Further, as their names imply, both random selection and random assignment involve the reliance upon a chance selection procedure. The difference is that while random selection has to do with giving everyone in the population being studied an equal chance of being included in the study, random assignment involves giving everyone who is already in the study an equal chance of being exposed to every level of the study's treatment conditions. Random assignment is associated with experimental designs in which there are different treatment conditions, whereas random selection is more often associated with survey research (although it is sometimes used in experiments).

Chapter 3   The Self

Question: *According to the strength model of self-regulation, when would a parent or a spouse be most likely to engage in domestic violence due to losing control of their emotions?*

Possible Answer: According to this theory, each act of self-regulation depletes the limited energy available for this purpose. Thus, immediately after exercising self-regulation in one activity, people will find it harder to regulate their behavior in an unrelated activity. From this perspective, domestic violence is most likely to occur when self-regulatory resources have been recently depleted. Thus, when abusers have just finished controlling or regulating their behavior—for example, working hard to prepare a meal when they would rather be relaxing, or holding their temper in check when talking to their employer on the phone—they are more susceptible to not being able to control their aggressive tendencies toward family members.

Question: *If you were to tell someone to "just be yourself," what would that mean to them depending on whether they were from an individualist or a collectivist culture?*

Possible Answer: When Chie Kanagawa and her colleagues (2001) asked that question of US and Japanese college students, they received decidedly different responses. For the Americans, the statement implied a self consisting of personal attributes that were not influenced by the situation they happened to be in at the time. Further, these attributes reflected the Americans' unique qualities, and these qualities were mostly positive. In contrast, for the Japanese, the statement implied a self that was defined by the relationships inherent in the situation. Here, "being yourself" meant constructing a self-presentation that was fairly self-critical and would help one fit into the situation. This research suggests that, for individualists, being yourself assumes a relatively fixed and stable self-concept made up of generally positive personal attributes. For collectivists, being yourself assumes a self that changes according to the situation to better fit in with the group.

Question: *If your ethnic heritage is relevant to who you think you are, you are experiencing which stage in Phinney's model? Is this model an accurate portrayal of your own ethnic identity development?*

Possible Answer: This answer will be unique to your personal experiences.

Question: *Do you think that people raised in collectivist cultures might sometimes have different self-presentation concerns than those raised in individualist cultures?*

Possible Answer: As discussed in Chapter 3 (section 3.2a), people in collectivist cultures tend to have a more interdependent view of themselves than those in individualist cultures. As a result, collectivists may often be more concerned than individualists about presenting the appropriate public self to their group. In Asian collectivist cultures, "saving face" or avoiding public embarrassment is more important than in individualist cultures. For example, in Japan, there are "convenience agencies" (*benriya*) that supply customers with rented "friends" who become additional guests at their weddings, mourners at family funerals, or romantic partners at important parties. Such extreme measures to manage others' impressions also occur in individualist cultures, but they may be more common in a social environment in which interdependent selves are more salient.

Question: *Consider the different self-presentation strategies you used today. Under what circumstances, and with whom, did you employ them? Which ones achieved the desired effect? Was there one strategy that you frequently employed? If you didn't use any, why was this the case?*

Possible Answer: This answer will be unique to your personal experiences.

Question: *People with low implicit self-esteem don't like themselves, but typically they are not consciously aware of this negative self-regard. If you were a therapist, how might you use classical conditioning techniques to unconsciously increase a person's low implicit self-esteem?*

Possible Answer: Classical conditioning is a type of learning first identified by Russian physiologist Ivan Pavlov, in which a neutral stimulus acquires the capacity to elicit a response after being repeatedly paired with another stimulus that naturally elicits that response. In this nonconscious learning, the two stimuli are repeatedly paired until the presence of one evokes the expectation of the other. In a study, Jodene Baccus and her coworkers (2004) used classical conditioning techniques to increase implicit self-esteem. How did they accomplish this task? Sitting at a computer, research participants were told that a word would appear randomly in some area of the computer screen and their task was to click on the word with the mouse as quickly as possible. They were also told that doing so would cause an image to be displayed briefly (for 400 milliseconds) in that same area. Whenever a word appeared on the screen that the participants had previously noted as self-descriptive, it was paired with an image of a smiling face. The participants completed 240 trials, with 80 of those trials involving self-relevant words. Results indicated that those participants who were repeatedly exposed to pairings of self-relevant words with smiling faces showed enhanced implicit self-esteem compared with participants in a control condition. Although more research is needed to further understand this learning process, the finding in this study suggests that feelings of low self-esteem are not set in stone in childhood but might be raised at a later time using basic learning principles.

Chapter 4   Social Cognition and Person Perception

Question: *If the representativeness heuristic is stereotyping operating in reverse, does that mean that stereotyping is also a heuristic?*

Possible Answer: Yes, stereotyping is definitely a heuristic. Like other heuristics, stereotyping provides a "shortcut in thinking" by supplying us with rich and distinctive—but not necessarily accurate—information about individuals we do not personally know. Stereotypes provide us with a fast basis for social judgments, and they also "free up" cognition for other tasks. Stereotyping is discussed more fully in Chapter 6.

Question: *During the Kavanaugh confirmation hearings Donald Trump Jr. stated that he was more concerned about his son being falsely accused of sexual assault than of his daughters being assaulted. Similar sentiments were expressed by other high-profile men, including President Trump. Statistically, women have a 20% chance of being sexually assaulted (National Sexual Violence Resource Center, 2014). In contrast, it's been estimated that men have somewhere between a 0.6% and a 3.2% chance of being falsely accused of committing a sexual assault (Lisak et al., 2010). What cognitive heuristic might be contributing to this heightened concern about men's false accusations? Why do you think people were relying on this heuristic?*

Possible Answer: In expressing this fear for young men, Donald Trump Jr. was relying upon the *availability heuristic*, which is the tendency to judge the frequency or probability of an event in terms of how easy it is to think of examples of that event. Trump was basing his judgment on the fresh memory of the Kavanaugh accusation, yet his expressed fear wasn't in line with actual facts. According to Department of Justice data, rape and sexual assault are the least likely violent crime to be reported to police, with a rate of 32% of the total number of assaults. Data also indicate that false sexual assault accusations are estimated to occur in only 2%–10% of all reported sexual assaults. If you multiply 32% by 2% and 10%, respectively, you find that the likelihood of a man being falsely accused of sexual assault is actually extremely low, somewhere between 0.6% and 3.2% (Lisak et al., 2010). The Centers for Disease Control and Prevention data also indicate that 1 in 3 women and 1 in 6 men in the US experience some form of sexual violence involving physical contact, so these statistics suggest that Trump's sons are more than five times as likely to be victims of sexual assault than are they likely to be falsely accused of sexual assault. People often rely upon the availability heuristic rather than on actual facts the more the events they readily pull from memory conform to their pre-existing views of the world.

Question: *Why might a neuroscientist argue that the hindsight bias is triggered by some of the same neurological activity that creates the story lines of dreams?*

Possible Answer: Social psychologists explain the hindsight bias as an attempt to make sense out of a surprising outcome—in essence, inserting missing causal connections so that our story of the event makes sense given the outcome. The part of our brains that does this cognitive work is the left hemisphere of the central cortex, or what neuroscientist Mike Gazzaniga (2000) describes as the brain's "interpreter." The left hemisphere always strives to assign some rational meaning to behavior, even when there is none. According to the activation-synthesis theory of dreaming, a dream is the left hemisphere's attempt to interpret the random neural activity initiated in the midbrain during sleep (Hobson & McCarley, 1977; Hobson et al., 1998). Thus, the neurological activity that triggers the hindsight bias may involve some of the same neural activity that triggers dreams, with the right hemisphere helping construct most of the dream's visual features.

Question: *How might an evolutionary theorist explain the gender differences in decoding nonverbal communication? That is, from an evolutionary perspective, why would it be more beneficial for females than males to have good nonverbal skills?*

Possible Answer: According to the evolutionary perspective, human beings—along with all other species on the planet—have evolved in ways that maximize the chances of their genes being passed on to their offspring so that these gene traits survive from generation to generation. Because only women could bear and breastfeed infants, evolutionary theorists contend that they evolved to take on the more nurturing and empathic role of domestic caretaker. To be a good nurturer of infants who cannot yet convey their desires through spoken language, being attentive to nonverbal signals of sickness or distress would be very beneficial. Thus, women who were nonverbally skilled would be most likely to have offspring who survived through this vulnerable age period. Over thousands of generations, a sex difference may have emerged based on this natural selection pressure on women.

Chapter 5   Attitudes and Persuasion

Question: *Is there any wisdom in parents admonishing their children to straighten their posture and avoid slouching? How might the manner in which parents try to correct slouching destroy these possible benefits?*

Possible Answer: Yes there is, because studies suggest that upright postures cannot only cause you to feel happier, but they can also cause you to have a more favorable attitude toward things in general. Yet these subtle effects could easily be destroyed by parents forcing their children to engage in this behavior. In such instances, the child's feeling that her or his parents are trying to control her or his behavior may well be sufficient to create the exact opposite mood. Thus, to capitalize on these positive posture effects, parents should steer clear of orders and threats.

Question: *Can you think of instances in your own life in which you convinced yourself that a bad experience was really a good and worthwhile one?*

Possible Answer: This answer will be unique to your personal experiences.

Question: *How do implicit and explicit attitudes relate to the self-perception process?*

Possible Answer: Bem's self-perception theory proposes that we often do not know our attitudes but simply infer them from our behavior. However, implicit attitude research demonstrates how implicit attitudes can unknowingly shape behavior. One possibility is that self-perception theory actually explains how implicit attitudes sometimes become explicit attitudes. Of course, this explanation is a reinterpretation of Bem's original theory of self-perception. In Step 1, an implicit attitude prompts a person to behave a certain way; and then in Step 2, self-reflection prompts the person to form an explicit attitude that is consistent with the already-existing implicit attitude.

Question: *Observe the content of TV commercials in the morning, in the evening, and during weekend sports shows. When are female and male characters with either traditional or nontraditional gender roles most likely to appear in these commercials? How do these characters enhance the persuasive power of these advertisements?*

Possible Answer: Even with the more balanced portrayal of the two sexes in TV commercials today, they are still constructed in ways that reinforce the image of gender most familiar to and comfortable for their target audience at a particular time of the day. R. Stephen Craig (1992) found that daytime ads, which are typically aimed at the female homemaker, focus on images of the traditional American household, with the wife taking care of the domestic family needs and the husband holding a position of authority at home and at the office. In contrast, weekend commercials targeted at the male sports viewer frequently exclude women and children altogether. These ads—dominated by alcohol and automotive products—stress traditional stereotypes of masculinity, such as the importance of being strong, daring, rugged, independent, and competitive. When women do appear in weekend commercials, they are generally portrayed in either subservient roles to men (for example, secretary or flight attendant) or as sexual objects. The traditional gender stereotyping in daytime and weekend commercials stands in sharp contrast to those shown during the evening and geared toward dual-career couples and single working women. Here, women are more likely to be portrayed in positions of authority and in settings away from home than they are in daytime ads. Men, in contrast, are more likely to be portrayed as a parent or spouse and more in settings at home than they are on weekend TV. Thus, Craig's analysis suggests that how men and women are portrayed in North American TV ads today depends on who is watching. Evening commercials represent a more sophisticated and balanced portrayal of gender roles, but daytime and weekend ads reflect more traditional orientations.

Question: *Why is it that radio lottery advertisers trying to persuade you to spend your money speak at a normal rate of speed, yet when they convey the odds of winning, their speech rate dramatically increases? Are they simply trying to save money by cutting down the length of the commercial, or is there an equally important reason for this shift to fast-paced speech?*

Possible Answer: Although research indicates that fast talkers are generally more persuasive than slow talkers due to listeners' impressions that they are more credible, this is not why fast talking is used when announcing the odds of winning. Instead, a message that is presented very quickly is difficult to process and critically analyze, which is exactly what the advertisers are counting on. They don't want listeners to elaborate on the message that their chances of winning the lottery are about equal to the likelihood that they will be struck by lightning while sitting in their living rooms!

Question: *In addition to using humor to combat binge drinking on college campuses, many college anti-binge drinking ads also provide information on how much alcohol the typical student on campus consumes. Why might this information be effective in reducing binge drinking? When would reporting such normative information possibly promote—rather than reduce—binge drinking?*

Possible Answer: Providing information to fellow students on how much alcohol the typical student consumes may be effective in reducing binge drinking if the campus drinking average is fairly low. Social norms campaigns that inform students that most students don't drink excessively can effectively reduce binge drinking. However, these same social norms campaigns may actually promote binge drinking on campuses where student drinking is very high. Thus, this persuasive approach should be used cautiously, because it can backfire.

Chapter 6   Stereotyping, Prejudice, and Discrimination

Question: *Media commentators in the United States often use the terms "red" and "blue" to refer to perceived cultural differences in America and American politics. Why might the increased use of these terms increase prejudice and conflict between political groups in America?*

Possible Answer: The reason the increased use of the "red" and "blue" terms is likely to increase the conflict between political groups in America is that these categories create a cognitive "us versus them" dichotomy (Seyle & Newman, 2006). Research on minimal groups suggests that simply placing people into a social category different from your own is often sufficient to create an ingroup bias. The Robbers Cave study (section 6.3b) suggests that when two groups perceive that they are competing for scarce resources, it provides fertile psychological ground for the development of prejudice and discrimination. The "red" versus "blue" designations place people into two distinct political factions and fuel the perception that one faction's success is the other faction's failure. This is likely to trigger hostile feelings and increased ethnocentrism.

Question: *What is the difference between implicit stereotyping and implicit prejudice?*

Possible Answer: While implicit stereotyping and implicit prejudice are similar psychological constructs, keep in mind that implicit stereotyping involves the automatic association of a social group with traits and reflects your cognitive schema for that group. In contrast, implicit prejudice is the automatic evaluation of a social group. Research indicates that these two constructs are predictive of different behaviors (Amodio & Devine, 2006). For example, implicit stereotyping of African Americans is associated with further engaging in evaluating an African American student in a stereotypical manner. However, implicit racial prejudice is associated with behaviors, such as socially distancing oneself from a potential interaction partner who is African American.

Question: *Shouldn't people experience considerable cognitive dissonance if they simultaneously believe that women are inferior, ungrateful, sexual teasers who are also refined, morally superior goddesses? Based on your understanding of cognitive dissonance theory (Chapter 5, section 5.3), how might ambivalent sexists avoid feeling conflicted about their positive and negative beliefs and attitudes toward women?*

Possible answer: In two separate studies investigating this apparent internal contradiction, Glick and his colleagues (1997) asked men and women to spontaneously list the different categories they use to classify women. Men who scored high and low on the Ambivalent Sexism Inventory (ASI) generated many of the same subcategories, but ambivalent sexists evaluated their traditional and nontraditional female subcategories in a much more polarized fashion than did the nonsexists. Ambivalent sexist men's negative feelings (fear, envy, competitiveness, intimidation) toward career women were predicted by their degree of hostile sexism, not by their degree of benevolent sexism. Similarly, these men's positive feelings (warmth, respect, trust, happiness) toward homemakers were predicted by their degree of benevolent sexism, not by their degree of hostile sexism. These findings suggest that, among ambivalent sexist men, specific categories of women activate either hostility or benevolence, but not both. Apparently, reserving negative attitudes for nontraditional women (the "bad" women) and positive attitudes for those who are traditional (the "good" women) allows sexist men to simultaneously hold contradictory views of women in general.

Question: *Try the following exercise. Listen to some of your favorite songs with lyrics involving romance. Do you tend to automatically imagine that the person singing the song is expressing his or her love for a person of the other sex? How do these reactions relate to heterosexism? Now, actively imagine that the song is about same-sex love. How do you react to these lyrics and any visual images that come to mind?*

Possible Answer: Whether or not you automatically imagine the lyrics of romantic songs are about heterosexual love tells us little, if anything, about your level of heterosexism. Instead, regardless of your sexual orientation, such imagining simply illustrates how our culture is dominated by heterosexual assumptions about romantic relationships. Yet, it's likely that how you react to imagining homosexual romance in these same lyrics does provides some indication of your level of heterosexism. Given the fact that heterosexual romantic love is our cultural norm, if you regularly imagine that popular songs involve same-sex love, this probably takes more cognitive effort, or at least it may have in the past.

Question: *Can you think of a negative stereotype about white people relative to black people that might cause white individuals to experience stereotype threat in a particular area of pursuit, thereby motivating them to disidentify with this activity?*

Possible Answer: A common negative stereotype about white people is that they do not have the physical skills to compete against black people in most sports. This was the primary theme in the 1992 basketball movie *White Men Can't Jump*. When competing against black basketball players, white players may become aware of this negative stereotype, experience stereotype threat, and underperform.

In an experimental demonstration of this effect, Jeff Stone and his colleagues (1999) described a golf task to white and black college students as either diagnostic of "natural athletic ability" or "sports intelligence." White students performed worse than a control group when the task was thought to be associated with natural ability, while black students performed worse than a control group when the task was framed as measuring intelligence. In a second experiment involving only white students, the researchers found that when the golf task was described as measuring natural athletic ability, those who performed worst were students who had previously stated that their self-esteem was significantly associated with success in athletic endeavors.

One likely consequence of regularly experiencing stereotype threat in athletic competition is that white people may disidentify with sports achievement and choose to identify with other endeavors, such as academic achievement. In other words, they change their self-concept so that sports achievement is no longer very important to their self-esteem. Of course, this disidentification process does not have the negative impact on white people's future career prospects as does black people's disidentification with academic achievement. Why? The answer is that athletic performance, unlike academic performance, is seldom associated with career success in adulthood.

Question: *How would social identity theory explain the relationship between "pride" and "prejudice"?*

Possible Answer: There is a positive correlation between pride and prejudice. To indirectly increase or protect our own self-esteem, we try to bask in the reflected glory of our own group's esteem. To increase this group esteem, we may disparage and discriminate against other groups whose successes might reflect negatively on our own group's accomplishments. This intergroup process is psychologically identical to what we do in our interpersonal relationships when our friends are competing against other people for material and social rewards. In judging the competition, we tend to highlight our friends' good points and their competitors' bad points, while downplaying or forgetting our friends' bad points and their competitors' good points. In both cases, the result is that we actively construct a negative bias against other groups and individuals whose successes might indirectly threaten our own self-esteem.

Question: In 2018, there was much political discussion and controversy around "immigrant caravans" coming from Central America, which greatly increased some Americans' perceived social threat. For example, television and radio commentator Glenn Beck stated, "This is an invasion. There's no other way to describe it." Based on authoritarianism research, what type of social consequences might we see in this country due to this heightened perceived threat?

Possible answer: Authoritarian research suggests that people with authoritarian tendencies may become more dogmatic and rigid in their social attitudes following such events. Thus, what we might expect from these people is a call for immigration laws to be strengthened and increased support for policies that make immigration to the United States more difficult. People with authoritarian traits will probably be more likely to support things such as funding to build a wall between the United States and Mexico, policies that separate immigrant children from parents, sending troops to monitor the border, and policies that make it more difficult for immigrants to seek asylum in the United States.

Authoritarian personalities will also generalize their outgroup prejudices toward groups within American culture that they perceive as "not real Americans." Due to their submission to established legitimate authority figures, authoritarians are likely to criticize anyone who does not support the government's military or civil actions. When immigrants are harmed because of the policies from the United States, such as children being abused while in orphanages after having been separated from their parents or dying from lack of health care while in United States custody, people with authoritarian tendencies are more likely to excuse the actions.

Question: *Which of the two types of personality-influenced prejudice—prejudice based on the authoritarian personality or on social dominance orientation—is most likely to be positively influenced by sustained close contact with members of a group toward which a person holds prejudiced attitudes?*

Possible Answer: Numerous studies find that intergroup contact is among the most effective ways to improve intergroup attitudes, but is it more effective for one type of personality-influenced prejudice than another? Because the authoritarian personality is based on the belief that outgroups are threatening and dangerous while the social dominance orientation is based on the desire to dominate other groups, Frank Asbrock and his coworkers (2012) hypothesized that intergroup contact would be particularly effective for people high in right-wing authoritarianism, but not those high in social dominance orientation, because these ideological attitudes are driven by different underlying motivational goals. Their longitudinal and cross-sectional research supports this hypothesis.

Chapter 7 Social Influence

Question: *How might an individual's personality and behavior change as that person gains or loses social power?*

Possible Answer: If social power increases people's tendencies to take action, then as people gain power they should exhibit a decreased sensitivity to threats (Croizet & Claire, 1998). Their increased power should cause them to develop a more decisive behavioral style, marked by increased confidence. Their personalities may become more extroverted, and they may engage in a wider range of behaviors. They may now approach social situations looking more toward acquiring rewards rather than avoiding losses. What about those who lose power? If powerlessness activates a general tendency to inhibit action, then as people lose power they should show an increased sensitivity to threats. Their behavioral style should become indecisive, marked by decreased confidence. Likewise, their personalities may become more introverted, they may engage in a narrower range of behaviors, and they may approach situations looking to avoid losses rather than acquire rewards.

Question: *Imagine that you are conducting an Asch-type conformity experiment. Simultaneously, you want to test whether you can increase nonconformity by inducing public self-presentation concerns in your participants. What variable could you introduce to the standard Asch research design to test the possibility that inducing public self-presentation concerns in your participants would increase nonconformity?*

Possible Answer: Because nonconformity may increase when others not involved in the influence attempt are present, you could have an experimental condition in which nonparticipants observe the line judgment tasks. If public self-presentation concerns significantly influence conformity, then this condition should result in greater nonconformity than in the standard Asch condition. This effect should occur when the line judgments are clear and easy, but probably won't occur when judgments are ambiguous and difficult. Instead, because the presence of an audience also induces public self-awareness—which leads to greater conformity to social standards—it's possible that ambiguous and difficult judgmental tasks will lead to greater conformity than in the standard Asch condition.

Question: *Can you use Harold Kelley's attribution theory, described in Chapter 4, to explain why minorities are most successful in exerting influence on the majority when they show a consistent behavioral style that the majority interprets as indicating certainty and confidence?*

Possible Answer: According to Serge Moscovici and Charlan Nemeth (1974), we tend to infer that the behavior of others is due to internal causes when (1) consensus is low (few others are behaving this way), (2) consistency is high (these people have behaved the same way over time), and (3) distinctiveness is low (they act this way in other situations). These conditions describe the behavior of strongly committed minorities. Not only are few others taking the belief position of the minority, but the minority consistently maintains this position over time and voices it in many varied situations. The logical conclusion that majority group members draw from all this information is that the voicing of such beliefs can only be due to deep and abiding personal convictions—convictions that perhaps should be seriously considered and scrutinized.

Question: *How might the foot-in-the-door compliance strategy be combined with the effects of post-decision dissonance to partly explain how some people initially become involved with, and then committed to, religious or political cults?*

Possible Answer: In the foot-in-the-door strategy, a person who complies with a small request is more likely to later comply with a larger, less desirable request from the same person. Converts to cults are initially drawn to them by agreeing to read the cult's literature or agreeing to attend one meeting. Cult members use compliance with these small requests to secure even greater degrees of compliance later on. Of course, a cult member also tends to act very warm and accepting toward possible recruits, thus making it more likely that they will want to seek greater ties to this group.

When the recruits do commit themselves to the cult, postdecision dissonance may exert its influence. Now, the attractive aspects of not joining and the unattractive aspects of joining are inconsistent with the decision to join the cult. Because new recruits view this as an important life decision, they will likely experience quite a bit of postdecision dissonance. According to cognitive dissonance theory, the new members will try to reduce the dissonance by focusing only on the positive aspects of the cult, while simultaneously focusing only on the negative aspects of their previous life. Other cult members, both new and old, will eagerly reinforce this sort of thinking—often because they, too, need to justify their own decision to join; thus, the new members' allegiance to the cult is immensely strengthened.

Question: *Given what we know about compliance and false confessions, do you think extreme interrogation techniques, such as use of torture, can result in accurate information from detainees?*

Possible Answer: Based on social psychological studies that have examined harsh interrogation techniques, it is clear that such techniques can cause compliance in the form of false confessions, meaning that they are just as likely to lead to inaccurate information as to accurate information. Innocent suspects who admit to crimes they know they did not commit in order to avoid further torture are very likely to do so due to external compliance rather than internal compliance.

Question: *How could politicians use the findings from this study to increase their likelihood of winning elections?*

Possible Answer: In an internet-based "get out the vote" effort, politicians could reach out to their known supporters on Facebook and invited them to ask their 10 closest friends to join them in clicking on a "We'll vote for (candidate's name)" button. When these close friends click on that button, their photos would automatically be posted next to their other close friends on their Facebook timeline, connected to that button. Such an effort should increase voter turnout among the politicians' support base.

Chapter 8   Group Behavior

Question: *In Chapter 6, you learned how ingroup biases can lead to prejudice and discrimination. How might this knowledge help you better understand the process by which group members' diffuse-status characteristics might significantly determine their power in the group?*

Possible Answer: When observing an ingroup member and an outgroup member performing the same task, performance evaluations will tend to be biased in favor of the ingroup member. This ingroup bias may manifest itself by people selectively remembering ingroup members' good behavior and outgroup members' bad behavior or by selectively forgetting or trivializing ingroup members' bad behavior and outgroup members' good behavior. In a group, the ingroup biasing that will usually have the biggest consequences for how much power and status members individually attain is the biasing exhibited by those members who hold "gatekeeping" roles. Gatekeepers are usually high-status members who give other members access to similar high-status positions. Gatekeepers will tend to single out those members in the group whom they perceive to be "one of them." Often this means they will prefer members who are similar to them on such diffuse-status characteristics as race, sex, age, and wealth.

Question: *Imagine that you have been hired to design a training course to teach company employees how to efficiently use a complex computer program. How can you use the findings of social loafing research to design a training course that not only facilitates quick learning, but also encourages high productivity following learning?*

Possible Answer: Research indicates that people can learn complex tasks more quickly when they believe their individual efforts are not being evaluated, such as when they are performing as part of a larger group. This type of situation also often leads to social loafing on well-learned tasks. In both situations, group performance allows task outcome responsibility to be diffused among fellow co-performers. To facilitate employees learning a complex computer program, you could design the training so that their individual efforts are not evaluated, which could be accomplished by training employees in a group setting. Group co-performance should reduce their evaluation apprehension—and presumably their arousal—and allow them to more carefully concentrate on the task at hand.

Once employees have mastered the computer program, you could then either monitor their individual performance to reduce social loafing or—if you didn't want to be so Orwellian—simply allow them to monitor their own performance by providing them with individual performance feedback. Both strategies have been found to be effective in reducing social loafing.

Question: *How could you use your knowledge of deindividuation when designing social environments to reduce crime?*

Possible Answer: If it is true that anonymity serves as an accountability cue causing people to believe they will not be held accountable for their actions, then environments should be designed to reduce feelings of anonymity. Large mirrors, bright lighting, and even the presence of surveillance cameras (even if they are nonfunctional) will make it much less likely that people will feel anonymous. Large mirrors and surveillance cameras will also induce public self-awareness, making it more likely that people will be attentive to social standards.

Question: *Based on social influence research, what type of individual might be more susceptible to group polarization effects when working on judgmental tasks?*

Possible Answer: When the task is judgmental, people who are more concerned with how others will evaluate them will be more influenced by others' opinions. If they sense that the "socially acceptable" judgment is in a particular direction, they are likely to leapfrog over others to arrive at the most group-praiseworthy position. It's also possible that people with a high need for individuation—a desire to feel unique—may try to grab the most extreme position in the socially acceptable direction to "stand out from the crowd."

Chapter 9   Interpersonal Attraction

Question: *Immediately following the New York and Washington terrorist attacks on 9/11, people around the country were highly anxious and uncertain about what was happening. How do you think information dependence and outcome dependence shaped their thoughts, feelings, and behavior during this time?*

Possible Answer: Information dependence caused confused and anxious people to seek out one another so they could gain an understanding of what was taking place. With this information, they could properly define and then respond to the unfolding events. Such information was most critical to individuals in the buildings attacked by the terrorists, because their lives depended on their correctly defining the situation as an emergency. Outcome dependence involves being dependent on others for rewards. While watching the horrendous events on television in the company of others, people may have monitored the expression of certain emotions (public displays of crying or prejudicial comments about Arab Americans) out of concern over how others might react. Steve knows one person who watched news reports at work all day with coworkers despite not wanting to do so. Her explanation about why she did not walk away was that she was concerned that her colleagues would think of her as heartless if she left.

Question: *When people think that the individuals they are interacting with are physically attractive, they tend to act more outgoing and sociable toward them—which, in turn, results in those individuals acting more warm, confident, animated, and attractive (Anderson & Bem, 1981; Snyder et al., 1977). How do these findings relate to one of the basic messages of social psychology? Further, how can you generalize these findings beyond physical attractiveness effects to create a more pleasant and rewarding social world for yourself?*

Possible answer: One of the basic messages of social psychology is that we actively create and recreate our social reality. The better you understand the psychological dynamics of this social constructive process, the better equipped you will be to shape your reality in the manner you desire. In a larger sense, the research points out that if you treat other people as if they are attractive and a joy to be around, they not only will appreciate and seek out your company, but also—if they weren't before—they will now more likely become people who really are attractive and a joy to be around! This topic also relates to the "we like those who like us" discussion in section 9.3f.

Question: *How has the similarity effect influenced your own personal relationships? Consider your best friends and your more casual friends. With whom do you share more similarities? Do these similarities fall into a particular category, such as shared values versus shared preferences?*

Possible Answer: This answer will be unique to your personal experiences.

Chapter 10   Intimate Relationships

Question: *The self-sufficient cowboy who keeps to himself and doesn't engage in idle chitchat is one of the great icons of the American West. Hollywood actors John Wayne, Gary Cooper, and Clint Eastwood personified this extreme form of individualism in many of their film roles. Today, Hollywood uses this same rugged, individualist personality in creating the lead male role in action adventure films (Matt Damon, George Clooney, Will Smith). What attachment style would you say these film characters most often represent? Is this an attachment style we should be emphasizing in our male cultural role models?*

Possible Answer: Securely attached adults easily become close to others, expect intimate relationships to endure, perceive others as generally trustworthy, and handle relationship conflict constructively. This type of an adult would be a positive role model as a Hollywood movie figure. Unfortunately, this is definitely not how male cowboy/action film characters are typically portrayed. Thus, you already know that these characters are not the best role models for children and adults regarding intimate relationships. Yet it gets even worse. These male film characters represent the absolute worst attachment style for intimacy— namely, an avoidant one. Avoidant adults are uncomfortable with intimacy, have a hard time trusting others, and often express hostility during relationship conflicts. That last difficulty would probably explain all the dead bodies they leave in their wake. These cowboy/action characters sometimes tug at the audience's heartstrings by disclosing that "true love" is very hard to find and hold onto. Usually, there is a woman in their past who emotionally scarred them by either dying or rejecting them. Adults who watch these movies with children would be well advised to point out to children afterward why Mr. Cowboy/Action Figure has such a hard time finding true love, and why imitation is not recommended.

Question: *Is there an inherent conflict between individualist values and the interdependence necessary to maintain romantic love?*

Possible Answer: Because individualists are raised to be autonomous and independent, perhaps they would have greater difficulty than collectivists maintaining an intimate relationship that is defined by partners depending on each other. The curious irony is that although individualists are more likely to marry due to romantic love, the way they've been socialized may make it less likely that their marriages will survive and their love will be nurtured. This is especially true for individualist males, who are most likely to be the ones socialized to be independent and relatively emotionally distant from others. However, because women are more likely socialized to be interdependent in their relations with other people, they may be best equipped to foster relationship success.

Question: *Earlier in the chapter, you learned that passionate love is associated with perceiving one's partner through rose-colored glasses. This idealization, however, often gives way to a more realistic view with the development of companionate love. Yet, if companionate love is more enduring than passionate love, how can you explain the present findings—that perceiving one's partner in somewhat ideal terms leads to greater romantic happiness than perceiving her or him realistically?*

Possible Answer: The giddy, roller-coaster emotional ride associated with passionate love doesn't usually endure in a romantic relationship; rather, it gives way to a more emotionally balanced form of romantic love—namely, companionate love. Passionate love can still exert its influence, but companionate love is the most influential. Yet, even with these romantic facts generally recognized, one manifestation of the importance of passion in an intimate relationship is revealed in the findings we are presently discussing. Put simply, those romantic relationships that have this "partner idealization" tendency appear to be the extra-special romantic relationships, the ones that are perhaps closest to the enduring and happy relationships depicted in Hollywood movies (not necessarily including all the heavy breathing). They also would fall into the category that Sternberg calls "consummate love" and that Lee calls "agape" (altruistic love).

Chapter II   Aggression

Question: *Why might people who come from a collectivist cultural background be less likely to react negatively to teasing and to perceive it as a form of aggression compared to people who have a strong individualist background?*

Possible Answer: People with a strong individualist cultural background think and act in ways that maximize personal desire and positive self-regard, while people with a collectivist cultural background think and act in ways that maximize group goals and group cohesion. Due to these different motives, collectivists should be more likely than individualists to accept criticism from others and value self-critical emotions such as embarrassment. Consistent with this thinking, Belinda Campos and her colleagues (2007) found that Asian American children were more likely than European American children to attribute positive intentions to those who teased them.

Question: *How might alcohol impair judgment and, thus, lead to the aggressive outbursts found in domestic violence cases?*

Possible Answer: When people are intoxicated with alcohol, they are less likely to engage in self-awareness. Because self-awareness is necessary for self-regulation, and because self-regulation is part of the higher-level thinking necessary to control aggressive impulses, intoxication will make aggressive outbursts more likely.

Question: *"Road rage" has unfortunately become an all-too-familiar term we read and hear about to describe violent outbursts by people driving cars. How could you use social psychological knowledge to reduce the likelihood of road rage on city streets and highways?*

Possible Answer: You could employ use of social learning theory to remind adults that they are role models for children and that how they behave while driving will be observed and learned by younger passengers and drivers. This strategy might engage higher-order cognitive processes in angry drivers—as proposed by Berkowitz's cognitive-neoassociationist model—so that their anger doesn't precipitate aggression.

Chapter 12   Prosocial Behavior: Helping Others

Question: *What sorts of cultural role models might influence the "helping habits" of boys and girls? How might greater gender role flexibility influence male and female helping tendencies?*

Possible Answer: Social modeling studies suggest that children are most likely to imitate the behavior of people with whom they strongly identify, and for most children, this means same-sex adults. Thus, to foster good helping habits in children, existing cultural role models for boys and girls could be enlisted to convey this message to children in public service announcements.

In Hollywood movies, most leading-male actors play the traditional masculine role of helping people in dangerous situations, while being rather unwilling or ineffective in providing more mundane, long-term help, such as caring for children and the elderly. The underlying message in many of these movies is that this kind of assistance is unmanly and less important. Yet, in everyday living, this form of help is needed far more frequently than dangerous helping.

In contrast, most leading-female actors play characters with less gender-stereotyped roles. As such, they are often depicted as being willing to intervene in both dangerous situations and in those requiring nurturance and long-term care of needy others. This greater flexibility in helping responses reflects the greater gender flexibility available to women in contemporary culture. For instance, girls are generally allowed to engage in more nontraditional gender behavior than boys. As a result, you might expect that girls will learn to help in a wider variety of situations than boys.

Question: *Do you think you would find these same bystander effects among people whose jobs regularly deal with helping others? How might you test whether the situational context or the salience of their "helping" social roles would influence their tendency to intervene?*

Possible Answer: You probably would not find the same degree of bystander effects among nurses, doctors, and police officers because their experience and skill at handling emergencies would make it less likely that they would (1) worry about overreacting in possible emergency situations and (2) assume that other bystanders have as much responsibility to help as they do. It's likely that their tendency to diffuse responsibility would be further reduced if their "helping" social roles were currently salient to them because they would be even more aware of the social norms regarding helping for their occupations. It's also likely that doctors' and nurses' willingness to help will be greater in those situations for which their occupations best prepare them—namely, emergencies requiring medical attention. However, because police officers are trained to intervene in both physically dangerous and medical emergencies, it's likely that there would be few differences in their willingness to respond. You might test these hypotheses in an experiment by having doctors, nurses, and police officers participate in a typical bystander intervention study, but (1) vary the degree to which their occupations are socially salient and (2) vary the type of emergency (medical or physical endangerment) that they witness.

Question: *How could you design a donation pitch to members of a local community center to help starving people in a foreign country, knowing that some message receivers will react with empathy, while others will react with personal distress?*

Possible Answer: First, you want to convey an emotionally arousing message concerning how desperately these people need the audience's help. For those individuals who experience empathy, you can simply ask for their donations. However, for those who experience personal distress, you have to deal with the fact that they will try to escape the situation to reduce their distress. Thus, you need to make it difficult for them to escape the distress without donating money. You might set up your talk so that it precedes a dinner or event that everyone in attendance generally enjoys. Then, inform the audience that the enjoyable event will commence as soon as the donations reach a specified amount. This scenario is admittedly heavy-handed, but it should induce those who are experiencing personal distress to help in order to facilitate their own escape from this unpleasantly arousing situation.

Glossary

A

acquaintance rape 470
Forced sexual intercourse that occurs either on a date or between people who are acquainted or romantically involved (also known as date rape)

ambivalent sexism 216
Sexism directed against women based on both positive and negative attitudes (hostility and benevolence) rather than on uniform dislike

actor-observer effect 140
The tendency for people to attribute their own behavior to external causes but that of others to internal factors

aggression 441
Any form of behavior that is intended to harm or injure some person, oneself, or an object

aggressive scripts 464
Guides for behavior and problem-solving that are developed and stored in memory and are characterized by aggression

altruistic helping 487
A form of helping in which the ultimate goal of the helper is to increase another's welfare without expecting anything in return

anchoring and adjustment heuristic 115
A tendency to be biased toward the starting value or anchor in making quantitative judgments

anticonformity 273
Opposition to social influence on all occasions, often caused by psychological reactance

archival research 50
A descriptive scientific method in which already-existing records are examined

applied research 39
Research designed to increase the understanding of—and solutions to—real-world problems by using current social psychological knowledge

arousal:cost-reward model 512
A theory that helping or not helping is a function of emotional arousal and analysis of the costs and rewards of helping

attachment 395
The strong emotional bond between an infant and a caregiver

attitude 151
A positive or negative evaluation of an object

attribution 133
The process by which people use information to make inferences about the causes of behavior or events

audience inhibition effect 506
People are inhibited from helping for fear that other bystanders will evaluate them negatively if they intervene and the situation is not an emergency

authoritarian leader 339
A leader who dictates group policies, procedures, and goals and controls all activities without any meaningful participation by others

authoritarian personality 237
A personality type characterized by submissiveness to authority, rigid adherence to conventional values, and prejudice toward outgroups

availability heuristic 114
The tendency to judge the frequency or probability of an event in terms of how easy it is to think of examples of that event

aversive racism 215
Attitudes toward members of a racial group that incorporate both egalitarian social values and negative emotions

B

basic research 39
Research designed to increase knowledge about social behavior

body esteem 372
A person's attitudes toward his or her body

bystander intervention model 503
A theory that whether bystanders intervene in an emergency is a function of a five-step decision-making process

547

C

catharsis 453
The reduction of the aggressive drive following an aggressive act

central route to persuasion 176
Persuasion that occurs when people think carefully about a communication and are influenced by the strength of its arguments

central traits 131
Traits that exert a disproportionate influence on people's overall impressions, causing them to assume the presence of other traits

cerebral cortex 28
The wrinkled-looking outer layer of the brain that coordinates and integrates all other brain areas into a fully functioning unit; the brain's "thinking" center, much larger in humans than in other animals

classical conditioning 157
Learning through association, when a neutral stimulus (conditioned stimulus) is paired with a stimulus (unconditioned stimulus) that naturally produces an emotional response

cognitive consistency 162
The tendency to seek consistency in one's cognitions

cognitive dissonance 163
A feeling of discomfort caused by performing an action that is inconsistent with one's attitudes

cognitive-neoassociation model 455
A theory of impulsive aggression that aversive events produce negative affect, which stimulates the inclination to aggress

collectivism 22
A philosophy of life stressing the priority of group needs over individual needs, a preference for tightly knit social relationships, and a willingness to submit to the influence of one's group

companionate love 420
The affection we feel for those with whom our lives are deeply entwined

compliance 255
Publicly acting in accord with a direct request

confederate 43
A trained member of the research team who follows a script designed to give participants a particular impression about what is going on

confirmation bias 132
The tendency to seek information that supports our beliefs while ignoring disconfirming information

conformity 255
Yielding to perceived group pressure by copying the behavior and beliefs of others

contact hypothesis 242
The theory that under certain conditions, direct contact between antagonistic groups will reduce prejudice

contingency model of leadership 335
The theory that leadership effectiveness depends both on whether leaders are task-oriented or relationship-oriented and on the degree to which they have situational control

correlational research 51
Research designed to examine the nature of the relationship between two or more naturally occurring variables

correlation coefficient 53
A statistical measure of the direction and strength of the linear relationship between two variables, which can range from −1.00 to +1.00

counterfactual thinking 119
The tendency to evaluate events by imagining alternative versions or outcomes to what actually happened

courtesy stigma 220
The tendency for individuals who are associated with stigmatized people to also face negative evaluations from others

covariation model 134
An attribution theory that describes how we make judgments about people's actions by observing them over time (consistency information), across situations (distinctiveness information), and in comparison to others' actions (consensus information)

cultural frame switching 84
The process by which biculturalists switch between different culturally appropriate behaviors depending on the context

culture 20
The total lifestyle of a people, including all the ideas, symbols, preferences, and material objects that they share

culture of honor 468

A belief system in which males are socialized to protect their reputations by resorting to violence

D

debriefing 44

A procedure at the conclusion of a research session in which participants are given full information about the nature and hypotheses of the study

deception 43

A methodological technique in which the researcher misinforms participants about the true nature of what they are experiencing in a study

dehumanization 447

The process of cognitively placing an outgroup into an extremely negative social category that excludes them from acceptable norms and values, thereby eliminating inhibitions against harming them

deindividuation 321

The loss of a sense of individual identity and a loosening of normal inhibitions against engaging in behavior that is inconsistent with internal standards

dependent variable 55

The experimental variable that is measured because it is believed to depend on the manipulated changes in the independent variable

diffusion of responsibility 319

The belief that the presence of other people in a situation makes one less personally responsible for the events that occur in that situation

discrimination 208

Negative and/or patronizing action toward members of specific groups

dismissing-avoidant attachment style 398

An expectation about social relationships characterized by low trust and avoidance of intimacy, combined with high self-esteem and compulsive self-reliance

door-in-the-face technique 281

A two-step compliance technique in which, after having a large request refused, the influencer counteroffers with a much smaller request

dual attitudes 153

The simultaneous possession of contradictory implicit and explicit attitudes toward the same object

dual-process models of attribution 140

Theories of attribution that propose that people initially engage in a relatively automatic and simple attributional assessment but then later consciously correct this attribution with more deliberate and effortful thinking

dual-process theories 19

Theories of social cognition that describe two basic ways of thinking about social stimuli: one involving automatic, effortless thinking and the other involving more deliberate, effortful thinking

E

effect size 46

A quantitative measure of the magnitude of the difference between two groups.

egoistic helping 487

A form of helping in which the ultimate goal of the helper is to increase his or her own welfare

elaboration likelihood model 176

A theory that persuasive messages can cause attitude change in two ways, each differing in the amount of cognitive effort or elaboration it requires

empathy 495

A feeling of compassion and tenderness upon viewing a victim's plight

empathy-altruism hypothesis 517

A theory proposing that experiencing empathy for someone in need produces an altruistic motive for helping

equity theory 425

The theory that people are most satisfied in a relationship when the ratio between rewards and costs is similar for both partners

ethnic identity 86

An individual's sense of personal identification with a particular ethnic group

ethnocentrism 231

A pattern of increased hostility toward outgroups accompanied by increased loyalty to one's ingroup

evolution 25

The genetic changes that occur in a species over generations due to natural selection

evolutionary psychology 25

An approach to psychology based on the principle of natural selection

excitation transfer 417

A psychological process in which arousal caused by one stimulus is transferred and added to arousal elicited by a second stimulus

expectation states theory 308

A theory that the development of group status is based on members' expectations of others' probable contributions to the achievement of group goals, and that these expectations are shaped not only by members' task-relevant characteristics but also by diffuse-status characteristics, such as race, sex, age, and wealth

experimental method 55

Research designed to test cause-effect relationships between variables

explicit attitude 152

A consciously held attitude

explicit cognition 19

Deliberate judgments or decisions of which we are consciously aware

explicit prejudice 207

Prejudicial attitudes that are consciously held, even if they are not publicly expressed

explicit self-esteem 96

A person's conscious and deliberate evaluation of his or her self-concept

external attribution 134

An attribution that locates the cause of an event in factors external to the person, such as luck, other people, or the situation

external validity 56

The extent to which a study's findings can be generalized to people beyond those in the study itself

F

facial feedback effect 160

The tendency of facial expressions to trigger corresponding emotions

fearful-avoidant attachment style 399

An expectation about social relationships characterized by low trust and avoidance of intimacy, combined with a feeling of being unworthy of others' love and a fear of rejection

foot-in-the-door technique 280

A two-step compliance technique in which the influencer secures compliance to a small request, and then later follows this with a larger, less desirable request

frontal lobe 28

The region of the cerebral cortex situated just behind the forehead that is involved in the coordination of movement and higher mental processes, such as planning, social skills, and abstract thinking; the area of the brain that is the originator of self-processes

frustration-aggression hypothesis 453

The theory that frustration causes aggression

fundamental attribution error 136

The tendency to overestimate the impact of dispositional causes and underestimate the impact of situational causes on other people's behavior

G

gender 27

The meanings that societies and individuals attach to being female and male

gender identity 85

The identification of oneself as a male or a female

gender schema 109

A cognitive structure for processing information based on perceived female or male qualities

genes 25

The biochemical units of inheritance for all living organisms

group 304

Several interdependent people who have emotional ties and interact on a regular basis

group polarization 320

Group-produced enhancement or exaggeration of members' initial attitudes through discussion

groupthink 332

A deterioration of mental efficiency, reality testing, and moral judgment in a group that results from an excessive desire to reach consensus

H

heterosexism 221

A system of cultural beliefs, values, and customs that exalts heterosexuality and denies, denigrates, and stigmatizes any nonheterosexual form of behavior or identity

heuristics 113

Time-saving mental shortcuts that reduce complex judgments to simple rules

hindsight bias 118

The tendency, once an event has occurred, to overestimate our ability to have foreseen the outcome

hostile aggression 442

The intentional use of harmful behavior in which the goal is simply to cause injury or death to the victim

hypothesis 41

An educated guess or prediction about the nature of things based upon a theory

I

illusory correlation 203

The belief that two variables are associated with each other when in fact there is little or no actual association

Implicit Association Test (IAT) 51

A technique for measuring implicit attitudes and beliefs based on the idea that people will give faster responses to presented concepts that are more strongly associated in memory

implicit attitude 152

An attitude that is activated automatically from memory, often without the person's awareness that she or he possesses it

implicit cognition 19

Judgments or decisions that are under the control of automatically activated evaluations occurring without our awareness

implicit personality theories 131

A type of schema people use to organize and make sense of which personality traits and behaviors go together

implicit prejudice 207

Unconsciously held prejudicial attitudes

implicit self-esteem 96

A person's unintentional, and perhaps unconscious, evaluation of his or her self-concept

independence 255

Not being subject to control by others

independent self 81

A way of conceiving of the self in terms of unique, personal attributes, as a being that is separate and autonomous from the group

independent variable 55

The experimental variable that the researcher manipulates

indirect aggression 444

A form of aggressive manipulation involving attempts to harm another person without a face-to-face encounter (also known as relational aggression)

individualism 21

A philosophy of life stressing the priority of individual needs over group needs, a preference for loosely knit social relationships, and a desire to be relatively autonomous of others' influence

informational influence 265

Conformity based on the belief that others may have more accurate information

informed consent 43

A procedure by which people freely choose to participate in a study only after they are told about the activities they will perform

ingroup 202

A group to which we belong and that forms a part of our social identity

ingroup bias 228

The tendency to give more favorable evaluations and great rewards to ingroup members than to outgroup members

institutional review boards (IRBs) 43

A panel of scientists and nonscientists who ensure the protection and welfare of research participants by formally reviewing researchers' methodologies and procedures prior to data collection

instrumental aggression 441

The intentional use of harmful behavior so that one can achieve some other goal

interaction effect 56

An experimental result that occurs when two independent variables in combination have a different effect on the dependent variable than when either is alone

interactionism 18

An important perspective in social psychology that emphasizes the combined effects of both the person and the situation on human behavior

interdependent self 81

A way of conceiving of the self in terms of social roles, as a being that is embedded in and dependent on the group

intergroup anxiety 245

Anxiety due to anticipating negative consequences when interacting with an outgroup member

internal attribution 134

An attribution that locates the cause of an event in factors internal to the person, such as personality traits, moods, attitudes, abilities, or effort

internal validity 56

The extent to which cause-and-effect conclusions can validly be made in a study

interpersonal attraction 354

The desire to approach other people

intimacy 393

Sharing that which is inmost with others

J

jealousy 433

The negative emotional reaction experienced when a relationship that is important to a person's self-concept is threatened by a real or imagined rival

jigsaw classroom 247

A cooperative group-learning technique designed to reduce prejudice and raise self-esteem

just-world belief 522

A belief that the world is a fair and equitable place, where people get what they deserve in life

K

kin selection 489

A theory that people will exhibit preferences for helping blood relatives because this will increase the odds that their genes will be transmitted to subsequent generations

L

leader 334

The person who exerts the most influence and provides direction and energy to the group

loneliness 381

Having a smaller or less satisfactory network of social and intimate relationships than one desires

lowball technique 284

A two-step compliance strategy in which the influencer secures agreement with a request by understating its true cost

M

matching hypothesis 376

The proposition that people are attracted to others who are similar to them in particular characteristics

mere exposure effect 155

The tendency to develop more positive feelings toward objects and individuals the more we are exposed to them

meta-analysis 60

The use of statistical techniques to summarize results from similar studies on a specific topic to estimate the reliability and overall size of the effect

minority influence 274

The process by which dissenters produce change within a group

minority slowness effect 274

The tendency of those who hold a minority opinion to express that opinion less quickly than people who hold the majority opinion

N

naturalistic observation 48

A descriptive scientific method that investigates behavior in its natural environment

natural selection 25

The process by which organisms with inherited traits best suited to the environment reproduce more successfully than less well-adapted organisms over a number of generations, which leads to evolutionary changes

need for cognition 178

An individual preference for and tendency to engage in effortful cognitive activities

need to belong 355

The need to interact with others and be socially accepted

negative state relief model 515

A theory suggesting that, for those in a bad mood, helping others may be a way to lift their own spirits if the perceived benefits for helping are high and the costs are low

nonconscious mimicry 125

The tendency to adopt the behaviors, postures, or mannerisms of interaction partners without conscious awareness or intention

nonverbal communication 121

Communicating feelings and intentions without words

normative influence 265

Conformity based on a desire to gain rewards or avoid punishments

norm of social justice 491

A social norm stating that we should help only when we believe that others deserve our assistance

norm of social responsibility 491

A social norm stating that we should help when others are in need and are dependent on us

O

obedience 256

The performance of an action in response to a direct order

observational research 47

A scientific method involving systematic qualitative and/or quantitative descriptions of behavior

observer bias 49

Occurs when preconceived ideas held by the researcher affect the nature of the observations made

operant conditioning 159

A type of learning in which behavior is strengthened if followed by reinforcement and weakened if followed by punishment

operational definition 42

A very clear description of how a variable in a study has been measured

optimistic explanatory style 142

A habitual tendency to attribute negative events to external, unstable, and specific causes, and positive events to internal, stable, and global causes

outgroup 202

Any group with which we do not share membership

outgroup homogeneity effect 203

Perception of outgroup members as being more similar to one another than are members of one's ingroup

P

participant observation 48

A descriptive scientific method where a group is studied from within by a researcher who records behavior as it occurs in its usual natural environment

passionate love 415

A state of intense longing for union with another

peripheral route to persuasion 176

Persuasion that occurs when people do not think carefully about a communication and instead are influenced by cues that are irrelevant to the content or quality of the communication

personal distress 495

An unpleasant state of arousal in which people are preoccupied with their own emotions of anxiety, fear, or helplessness upon viewing a victim's plight

personal-group discrimination discrepancy 236
The tendency for members of disadvantaged groups to downplay personal discrimination in their own lives

person perception 121
The process by which we try to detect other people's temporary states and enduring dispositions (also called social perception)

persuasion 176
The process of consciously attempting to change attitudes through the transmission of some message

pessimistic explanatory style 142
A habitual tendency to attribute negative events to internal, stable, and global causes, and positive events to external, unstable, and specific causes

physical attractiveness stereotype 366
The belief that physically attractive individuals possess socially desirable personality traits and lead happier lives than less attractive persons

pluralistic ignorance 261
The tendency to think that everyone else is interpreting a situation in a certain way, when in fact they are not

population 44
All the members of an identifiable group from which a sample is drawn

pornography 473
The combination of sexual material with abuse or degradation in a manner that appears to endorse, condone, or encourage such behavior

positive psychology 30
An approach to psychology that studies ways to enrich human experience and maximize human functioning

prejudice 207
Attitudes toward members of specific groups that directly or indirectly suggest they deserve an inferior social status

preoccupied attachment style 398
An expectation about social relationships characterized by trust but combined with a feeling of being unworthy of others' love and a fear of abandonment

priming 111
The process by which recent exposure to certain stimuli or events increases the accessibility of certain memories, categories, or schemas

prosocial behavior 487
Voluntary behavior that is carried out to benefit another person

prototype 108
The most representative member of a category

psychological reactance 272
The tendency to react against and resist attempts to limit one's sense of freedom

R

racism 211
Prejudice and discrimination based on a person's racial background

random assignment 57
Placement of research participants into experimental conditions in a manner that guarantees that all have an equal chance of being exposed to each level of the independent variable

random selection 52
A procedure for selecting a sample of people to study in which everyone in the population has an equal chance of being chosen

rape myths 470
False beliefs about rape that justify sexual violence

realistic group conflict theory 230
The theory that intergroup conflict develops from competition for limited resources

reciprocal helping 490
An evolutionary principle stating that people expect that anyone helping another will have that favor returned at some future time; also known as reciprocal altruism

reciprocity norm 278
The expectation that one should return a favor or a good deed

reference group 153
A group to which people orient themselves, using its standards to judge themselves and the world

replication 59
Repeating a study's scientific procedures using different participants in an attempt to duplicate the findings

representativeness heuristic 113
The tendency to judge the category membership of things based on how closely they match the "typical" or "average" member of that category

S

sample 44
A group of people who are selected to participate in a research study

schema 109
An organized structure of knowledge about a stimulus that is built up from experience and that contains causal relations; a theory about how the social world operates

scientific method 39
A set of procedures used to gather, analyze, and interpret information in a way that reduces error and leads to dependable generalizations

script 109
A schema that describes how a series of events is likely to occur in a well-known situation and which is used as a guide for behavior and problem-solving

secure attachment style 397
An expectation about social relationships characterized by trust, a lack of concern with being abandoned, and a feeling of being valued and well-liked

self 16, 69
A symbol-using social being who can reflect on his or her own behavior

self-awareness 70
A psychological state in which one takes oneself as an object of attention

self-concept 69
The sum total of a person's thoughts and feelings that define the self as an object

self-consciousness 72
The habitual tendency to engage in self-awareness

self-disclosure 402
The revealing of personal information about oneself to other people

self-esteem 69
A person's evaluation of his or her self-concept

self-fulfilling prophecy 6
The process by which someone's expectations about a person or group lead to the fulfillment of those expectations

self-handicapping 93
Undertaking actions that sabotage one's performance and enhance the opportunity to excuse the anticipated failure

self-perception theory 171
The theory that we often infer our internal states, such as our attitudes, by observing our own behavior

self-regulation 77
The ways in which people control and direct their own actions

self-serving bias 17
The tendency to take credit for positive outcomes but deny responsibility for negative outcomes in our lives

sex 27
The biological status of being female or male

sexism 216
Any attitude, action, or institutional structure that subordinates a person because of her or his sex or gender

sexual objectification 372
The act of treating a person as a mere object of sexual desire

sexual prejudice 221
Negative attitudes based on sexual orientation, whether the target is homosexual, bisexual, or heterosexual

sleeper effect 180
The delayed effectiveness of a persuasive message from a low-credibility source

social anxiety 380
The unpleasant emotion people experience due to their concern with interpersonal evaluation

social categorization 108
The process of forming categories of people based on their common attributes

social cognition 18, 107
The ways in which we interpret, analyze, remember, and use information about our social world

social comparison theory 355
The theory that we evaluate our thoughts and actions by comparing them with those of others

social desirability bias 51
A type of response bias in surveys in which people respond to a question by trying to portray themselves in a favorable light rather than responding in an accurate and truthful manner

social dilemma 342

Any situation in which the most rewarding short-term choice for an individual will ultimately cause negative consequences for the group as a whole

social dominance theory 234

A theory contending that societal groups can be organized in a power hierarchy in which the dominant groups enjoy a disproportionate share of the society's assets and the subordinate groups receive most of its liabilities

social exchange theory 356

The theory that we seek out and maintain those relationships in which the rewards exceed the costs

social facilitation 317

The enhancement of dominant responses due to the presence of others

social identities 86

Aspects of a person's self-concept based on his or her group memberships

social identity theory 228

A theory suggesting that people seek to enhance their self-esteem by identifying with specific social groups and perceiving these groups as being better than other groups

social impact theory 295

The theory that the amount of social influence others have depends on their number, strength, and immediacy

social influence 255

The exercise of social power by a person or group to change the attitudes or behavior of others in a particular direction

social learning theory 461

A theory that social behavior is primarily learned by observing and imitating the actions of others, and secondarily by being directly rewarded and punished for our own actions

social loafing 318

Group-induced reduction in individual output when performers' efforts are pooled and cannot, therefore, be individually judged

social neuroscience 28

The study of the relationship between neural processes of the brain and social processes

social norm 258

An expected standard of behavior and belief established and enforced by a group

social penetration theory 402

A theory that describes the development of close relationships in terms of increasing self-disclosure

social power 256

The force available to the influencer to motivate attitude or behavior change

social psychology 4

The scientific discipline that attempts to understand and explain how the thoughts, feelings, and behavior of individuals are influenced by the actual, imagined, or implied presence of others

social role 126

A cluster of socially defined expectations that individuals in a given situation are expected to fulfill

social role theory 126

The theory that virtually all of the documented behavioral differences between males and females can be accounted for in terms of cultural stereotypes about gender and the resulting social roles that are taught to the young

social skills training 387

A behavioral training program designed to improve interpersonal skills through observation, modeling, role-playing, and behavioral rehearsal

stereotypes 202

Beliefs about the personalities, abilities, and motives of a social group that don't allow for individual variation

Stereotype Content Model 209

A theory that the form of prejudice directed toward a particular group is determined by perceptions of the group's warmth and competence

stereotype threat 224

The apprehension people feel when performing a task in which their group is stereotyped to lack ability

stigma 210

An attribute that serves to discredit a person in the eyes of others

strategic self-presentation 88

Conscious and deliberate efforts to shape other people's impressions in order to gain power, influence, sympathy, or approval

subliminal conditioning 158
Classical conditioning that occurs in the absence of conscious awareness of the stimuli involved

subtyping 204
A cognitive process in which people perceive an individual who doesn't fit their stereotype as being an exception to the rule and they create a separate subcategory of the stereotype for that individual

superordinate goal 233
A mutually shared goal that can be achieved only through intergroup cooperation

surveys 51
Structured sets of questions or statements given to a group of people to measure their attitudes, beliefs, values, or behavioral tendencies

system justification theory 237
A theory proposing that members of both advantaged and disadvantaged groups often adopt beliefs endorsing the legitimacy and fairness of the unequal group status hierarchy in society

T

temporal model of group membership 305
A theory of group membership describing the changes that occur over time in members and in the group due to their mutual influence and interdependence

that's-not-all technique 282
A two-step compliance technique in which the influencer makes a large request, then immediately offers a discount or bonus before the initial request is refused

theory 41
An organized system of ideas that seeks to explain why two or more events are related

theory of planned behavior 173
The theory that people's conscious decisions to engage in specific actions are determined by their attitudes toward the behavior in question, the relevant subjective norms, and their perceived behavioral control

threat-to-self-esteem model 524
A theory stating that if receiving help contains negative self-messages, recipients are likely to feel threatened and respond negatively

transformational leader 338
A leader who changes (transforms) the outlook and behavior of followers so that they move beyond their self-interests for the good of the group or society

two-factor theory of emotions 417
A theory that emotional experience is based on two factors: physiological arousal and cognitive labeling of the cause of that arousal

V

variables 42
Factors in scientific research that can be measured and that are capable of changing (varying)

References

A

Aarts, H., & Dijksterhuis, A. (2003). The silence of the library: Environment, situational norm, and social behavior. *Journal of Personality and Social Psychology, 84*(1), 18–28.

Abrams, D., Ando, K., & Hinkle, S. (1998). Psychological attachment to the group: Cross-cultural differences in organizational identification and subjective norms as predictors of workers' turnover intentions. *Personality and Social Psychology Bulletin, 24*(10), 1027–1039.

Abramson, L. Y., Bardone-Cone, A. M., Vohs, K. D., Joiner, T. E. Jr., & Heatherton, T. F. (2006). Cognitive vulnerability to bulimia. In L. B. Alloy & J. H. Riskind (Eds.), *Cognitive vulnerability to emotional disorders* (pp. 329–364). Mahwah, NJ: Lawrence Erlbaum Associates.

Abramson, L. Y., Seligman, M. E. P., & Teasdale, J. (1978). Learned helplessness in humans: Critique and reformulation. *Journal of Abnormal Psychology, 87*(1), 49–74.

Acevedo, B. P., & Aron, A. (2009). Does a long-term relationship kill romantic love? *Review of General Psychology, 13*(1), 59–65.

Adame, B. J. (2016). Training in the mitigation of anchoring bias: A test of the consider-the-opposite strategy. *Learning and Motivation, 53*, 36–48.

Adams, G., Anderson, S. L., & Adonu, J. K. (2004). The cultural grounding of closeness and intimacy. In D. J. Mashek & A. P. Aron (Eds.), *Handbook of closeness and intimacy* (pp. 321–339). Mahwah, NJ: Lawrence Erlbaum Associates.

Adams, G., Tormala, T. T., & O'Brien, L. T. (2006). The effect of self-affirmation on perception of racism. *Journal of Experimental Social Psychology, 42*(5), 616–626.

Adams, J. S. (1965). Inequity in social exchange. In L. Berkowitz (Ed.), *Advances in experimental social psychology* (Vol. 2, pp. 267–299). New York, NY: Academic Press.

Adelson, R. (2004). Hormones, stress and aggression: A vicious cycle. *Monitor on Psychology, 35*(10), 18–19.

Adorno, T. W., Frenkel-Brunswik, E., Levinson, D., & Sanford, R. N. (1950). *The authoritarian personality.* New York, NY: Harper.

Afifi, W. A., & Faulkner, S. L. (2000). On being "just friends": The frequency and impact of sexual activity in cross-sex friendships. *Journal of Social and Personal Relationships, 17*(2), 205–222.

Agerström, J., & Rooth, D. (2011). The role of automatic obesity stereotypes in real hiring discrimination. *Journal of Applied Psychology, 96*(4), 790–805.

Agha, N., & Tyler, B. D. (2017). An investigation of highly identified fans who bet against their favorite teams. *Sport Management Review, 20*(3), 296–308.

Agthe, M., Sporrle, M., Frey, D., & Maner, J. K. (2014). Looking up versus looking down: Attractiveness-based organizational biases are moderated by social comparison direction. *Journal of Applied Social Psychology, 44*(1), 40–45.

Aiello, J. R., & Douthitt, E. A. (2001). Social facilitation from Triplett to electronic performance monitoring. *Group Dynamics: Theory, Research, and Practice, 5*(3), 163–180.

Ainsworth, M. S. (1989). Attachments beyond infancy. *American Psychologist, 44*(4), 709–716.

Ajzen, I. (1991). The theory of planned behavior. *Organizational Behavior and Human Decision Processes, 50*(2), 179–204.

Ajzen, I. (2001). Nature and operation of attitudes. *Annual Review of Psychology, 52*, 27–58.

Ajzen, I., & Sheikh, S. (2013). Action versus inaction: Anticipated affect in the theory of planned behavior. *Journal of Applied Social Psychology, 43*(1), 155–162.

Aknin, L. B., Dunn, E. W., & Norton, M. I. (2012) Happiness runs in a circular motion: Evidence for a positive feedback loop between prosocial spending and happiness. *Journal of Happiness Studies, 13*(2), 347–355.

Albarracín, D., Kumkale, G. T., & Del Vento, P. P. (2017). How people can become persuaded by weak messages presented by credible communicators: Not all sleeper effects are created equal. *Journal of Experimental Social Psychology, 68*, 171–180.

Algoe, S. B., Kurtz, L. E., & Grewen, K. (2017). Oxytocin and social bonds: The role of oxytocin in perceptions of romantic partners' bonding behavior. *Psychological Science, 28*(12), 1763–1772.

Algoe, S. B., Kurtz, L. E., & Hilaire, N. M. (2016). Putting the "you" in "thank you": Examining other-praising behavior as the active relational ingredient in expressed gratitude. *Social Psychological and Personality Science, 7*(7), 658–666.

Allcott, H., & Gentzkow, M. (2017). Social media and fake news in the 2016 election. *Journal of Economic Perspectives, 31*(2), 211–236.

Allen, V. L., & Levine, J. M. (1969). Consensus and conformity. *Journal of Experimental Social Psychology, 5*(4), 389–399.

Allen, V. L., & Levine, J. M. (1971). Social support and conformity: The role of independent assessment of reality. *Journal of Experimental Social Psychology, 7*(1), 48–58.

Alley, T. R., & Cunningham, M. R. (1991). Averaged faces are attractive, but very attractive faces are not average. *Psychological Science, 2*(2), 123–125.

Allison, S. T., & Messick, D. M. (1985). Effects of experience on performance in a replenishable resource trap. *Journal of Personality and Social Psychology, 49*(4), 943–948.

Allman, J. M., & Hasenstaub, A. (1999). Brains, maturation times, and parenting. *Neurobiology of Aging, 20*(4), 447–454.

Allport, F. H. (1920). The influence of the group upon association and thought. *Journal of Experimental Psychology, 3*(3), 159–182.

Allport, F. H. (1924). *Social psychology.* Boston, MA: Houghton Mifflin.

Allport, G. W. (1935). Attitudes. In C. Murchison (Ed.), *Handbook of Social Psychology* (pp. 798–844). Worcester, MA: Clark University Press.

Allport, G. W. (1943). The ego in contemporary psychology. *Psychological Review, 50*(5), 451–478.

Allport, G. W. (1954). *The nature of prejudice.* Cambridge, MA: Addison-Wesley.

Allport, G. W. (1985). The historical background of social psychology. In G. Lindzey & E. Aronson (Eds.), *The Handbook of Social Psychology* (Vol. I, 3rd ed., pp. 1–46). New York, NY: Random House.

Almeida, M., Lee, R., & Coccaro, E. F. (2011). Cortisol responses to ipsapirone challenge correlate with aggression, while basal cortisol levels correlate with impulsivity, in personality disorder and healthy volunteer subjects. *Journal of Psychiatric Research, 44*(14), 874–880.

Aloka, P. J. O., & Bojuwoye, O. (2013). Group polarization effects on decisions by selected Kenyan secondary school disciplinary panels. *Journal of Psychology in Africa, 23*(2), 275–282.

Altemeyer, B. (1981). *Right-wing authoritarianism.* Winnipeg, Canada: University of Manitoba Press.

Altemeyer, B. (1988). *Enemies of freedom: Understanding right-wing authoritarianism.* San Francisco, CA: Jossey-Bass.

Altemeyer, B. (2004). Highly dominating, highly authoritarian personalities. *Journal of Social Psychology, 144*(4), 421–447.

Altman, I. (1973). Reciprocity of interpersonal exchange. *Journal of Theory of Social Behavior, 3*(2), 249–261.

Altman, I., & Taylor, D. A. (1973). *Social penetration theory: The development of interpersonal relationships.* New York, NY: Holt, Rinehart, and Winston.

Álvarez, R. (2001). The social problem as an enterprise: Values as a defining factor. *Social Problems, 48*(1), 3–10.

Alvaro, E. M., & Crano, W. D. (1997). Indirect minority influence: Evidence for leniency in source evaluation and counterargumentation. *Journal of Personality and Social Psychology, 72*(5), 949–964.

Alves, H. (2018). Sharing rare attitudes attracts. *Personality and Social Psychology Bulletin, 44*(8), 1270–1283.

Alwin, D. F., Cohen, R. L., & Newcomb, T. M. (1991). *Political attitudes over the life span: The Bennington women after fifty years.* Madison, WI: University of Wisconsin Press.

Ambady, N., & Adams, R. B., Jr. (2011). Us versus them: The social neuroscience of perceiving out-groups. In A. Todorov, S. T. Fiske, & D. A. Prentice (Eds.). *Social neuroscience: Toward understanding the underpinnings of the social mind* (pp. 135–143). New York, NY: Oxford University Press.

Ambady, N., Shih, M., Kim, A., & Pittinsky, T. L. (2001). Stereotype susceptibility in children: Effects of identity activation on quantitative performance. *Psychological Science, 12*(5), 385–390.

Ames, D. R. (2004). Inside the mind reader's tool kit: Projection and stereotyping in mental state inference. *Journal of Personality and Social Psychology, 87*(3), 340–353.

Ames, D. R., Flynn, F. J., & Weber, E. U. (2004). It's the thought that counts: On perceiving how helpers decide to lend a hand. *Personality and Social Psychology Bulletin, 30*(4), 461–474.

Amiot, C. E., & Sansfacon, S. (2011). Motivations to identify with social groups: A look at their positive and negative consequences. *Group Dynamics: Theory, Research, and Practice, 15*(2), 105–127.

Amir, Y. (1969). Contact hypothesis in ethnic relations. *Psychological Bulletin, 71*(5), 319–342.

Amodio, D. M. (2011). Self-regulation in intergroup relations: A social neuroscience framework. In A. Todorov, S. T. Fiske, & D. A. Prentice (Eds.). *Social neuroscience: Toward understanding the underpinnings of the social mind* (pp. 101–122). New York, NY: Oxford University Press.

Amodio, D. M., & Devine, P. G. (2006). Stereotyping and evaluation in implicit race bias: Evidence for independent constructs and unique effects on behavior. *Journal of Personality and Social Psychology, 91*(4), 652–661.

Amodio, D. M., & Lieberman, M. D. (2009). Pictures in our heads: Contributions of fMRI to the study of prejudice and stereotyping. In T. D. Nelson (Ed.). *Handbook of prejudice, stereotyping, and discrimination* (pp. 347–365). New York, NY: Psychology Press.

Amodio, D. M., Shah, J. Y., Sigelman, J., Brazy, P. C., & Harmon-Jones, E. (2004). Implicit regulatory focus associated with asymmetrical frontal cortical activity. *Journal of Experimental Social Psychology, 40*(2), 225–232.

Andersen, S. M., & Bem, S. L. (1981). Sex typing and androgyny in dyadic interaction: Individual differences in responsiveness to physical attractiveness. *Journal of Personality and Social Psychology, 41*(1), 74–86.

Andersen, S. M., & Glassman, N. S. (1996). Responding to significant others when they are not there: Effects on interpersonal inference, motivation, and affect. In R. M. Sorrentino & E. T. Higgins (Eds.), *Handbook of motivation and cognition* (pp. 262–321). New York, NY: Guilford.

Anderson, C., & Berdahl, J. L. (2002). The experience of power: Examining the effects of power on approach and inhibition tendencies. *Journal of Personality and Social Psychology, 83*(6), 1362–1377.

Anderson, C. A. (2001). Heat and violence. *Current Directions in Psychological Science, 10*(1), 33–38.

Anderson, C. A. (2004). An update on the effects of playing violent video games. *Journal of Adolescence, 27*(1), 113–122.

Anderson, C. A., & Anderson, D. C. (1984). Ambient temperature and violent crime: Tests of the linear and curvilinear hypotheses. *Journal of Personality and Social Psychology, 46*(1), 91–97.

Anderson, C. A., & Anderson, K. B. (1996). Violent crime rate studies in philosophical context: A destructive testing approach to heat and Southern culture of violence effects. *Journal of Personality and Social Psychology, 70*(4), 740–756.

Anderson, C. A., Benjamin, A. J., & Bartholow, B. D. (1998). Does the gun pull the trigger? Automatic priming effects of weapon pictures and weapon names. *Psychological Science, 9*(4), 308–314.

Anderson, C. A., Berkowitz, L., Donnerstein, E., Huesmann, L. R., Johnson, J. D., Linz, D.,. . .Wartella, E. (2003a). The influence of media violence on youth. *Psychological Science in the Public Interest, 4*(3), 81–110.

Anderson, C. A., & Bushman, B. J. (2001). Effects of violent video games on aggressive behavior, aggressive cognition, aggressive affect, physiological arousal, and prosocial behavior: A meta-analytic review of the scientific literature. *Psychological Science, 12*(5), 353–359.

Anderson, C. A., & Bushman, B. J. (2002). Media violence and the American public revisited. *American Psychologist, 57*(6–7), 448–450.

Anderson, C. A., & Bushman, B. J. (2018). Media violence and the general aggression model. *Journal of Social Issues, 74*(2), 386–413.

Anderson, C. A., Bushman, B. J., Donnerstein, E., Hummer, T. A., & Warburton, W. (2015). SPSSI research summary on media violence. *Analyses of Social Issues and Public Policy, 15*(1), 4–19.

Anderson, C. A., Bushman, B. J., & Groom, R. W. (1997). Hot years and serious and deadly assault: Empirical tests of the heat hypothesis. *Journal of Personality and Social Psychology, 73*(6), 1213–1223.

Anderson, C. A., Carnagey, N. L., & Eubanks, J. (2003b). Exposure to violent media: The effects of songs with violent lyrics on aggressive thoughts and feelings. *Journal of Personality and Social Psychology, 84*(5), 960–971.

Anderson, C. A., Deuser, W. E., & DeNeve, K. M. (1995). Hot temperatures, hostile affect, hostile cognition, and arousal: Tests of a general model of affective aggression. *Personality and Social Psychology Bulletin, 21*(5), 434–448.

Anderson, C. A., & Dill, K. E. (2000). Video games and aggressive thoughts, feelings, and behavior in the laboratory and in life. *Journal of Personality and Social Psychology, 78*(4), 772–790.

Anderson, C. A., Miller, R. S., Riger, A. L., Dill, J. C., & Sedikides, C. (1994). Behavioral and characterological attributional styles as predictors of depression and loneliness: Review, refinement, and test. *Journal of Personality and Social Psychology, 66*(3), 549–558.

Anderson, C., Brion, S., Moore, D. A., & Kennedy, J. A. (2012). A status-enhancement account of overconfidence. *Journal of Personality and Social Psychology, 103*(4), 718–735.

Anderson, D. E., DePaulo, B. M., Anfield, M. E., Tickle, J. J., & Green, E. (1999). Beliefs about cues to deception: Mindless stereotypes or untapped wisdom? *Journal of Nonverbal Behavior, 23*(1), 67–88.

Anderson, E., Siegel, E. H., Bliss-Moreau, E., & Barrett, L. F. (2011). The visual impact of gossip, *Science, 332*(6036), 1446–1448.

Anderson, S. L., Adams, G., & Plaut, V. C. (2008). The cultural grounding of personal relationships: The importance of attractiveness in everyday life. *Journal of Personality and Social Psychology, 95*(2), 352–368.

Andreoletti, C., Zebrowitz, L. A., & Lachman, M. E. (2001). Physical appearance and control beliefs in young, middle-aged, and older adults. *Personality and Social Psychology Bulletin, 27*(8), 969–981.

Angermeyer, M. C., & Matschinger, H. (1996). The effect of violent attacks by schizophrenic persons on the attitude of the public towards the mentally ill. *Social Science & Medicine, 43*(12), 1721–1728.

Anglemyer, A., Horvath, T., & Rutherford, G. (2014). The accessibility of firearms and risk for suicide and homicide victimization among household members: A systematic review and meta-analysis. *Annals of Internal Medicine, 160*(2), 101–110.

Anseel, F., & Duyck, W. (2008). Unconscious applicants: A systematic test of the name-letter effect. *Psychological Science, 19*(10), 1059–1061.

Anthenien, A., Rosa, J., & Neighbors, C. (2017). Training first-year college students to intervene in alcohol-related emergencies: Addressing bystander beliefs and perceived consequences of intervening. *Journal of Alcohol and Drug Education, 61*(3), 17–36.

Anzures, G., Quinn, P. C., Pascalis, O., Slater, A. M., Lee, K. (2010). Categorization, categorical perception, and asymmetry in infants' representation of face race. *Developmental Science, 13*(4), 553–564.

Apps, M. A., & Tsakiris, M. (2013). The free-energy self: A predictive coding account of self-recognition. *Neuroscience and Biobehavioral Reviews, 41*, 85–97.

Aquino, K., McFerran, B., & Laven, M. (2011). Moral identity and the experience of moral elevation in response to acts of uncommon goodness. *Journal of Personality and Social Psychology, 100*(4), 703–718.

Aquino, K., & Reed, A. (2002). The self-importance of moral identity. *Journal of Personality and Social Psychology, 83*(6), 1423–1440.

Archer, D., & Gartner, R. (1984). *Violence & crime in cross-national perspective*. New Haven, CT: Yale University Press.

Archer, J. (1991). Human sociobiology: Basic concepts and limitations. *Journal of Social Issues, 47*(3), 11–26.

Archer, J. (2004). Sex differences in aggression in real-world settings: A meta-analytic review. *Review of General Psychology, 8*(4), 291–322.

Archer, J. (2013). Can evolutionary principles explain patterns of family violence? *Psychological Bulletin, 139*(2), 403–440.

Archer, J., & Côté, S. (2005). Sex differences in aggressive behavior: A developmental and evolutionary perspective. In R. E. Tremblay, W. W. Hartup, & J. Archer (Eds.), *Developmental origins of aggression* (pp. 425–443). New York, NY: Guilford Press.

Archer, J., & Coyne, S. M. (2005). An integrated review of indirect, relational, and social aggression. *Personality and Social Psychology Review, 9*(3), 212–230.

Archibald, F. S., Bartholomew, K., & Marx, R. (1995). Loneliness in early adolescence: A test of the cognitive discrepancy model of loneliness. *Personality and Social Psychology Bulletin, 21*(3), 296–301.

Arendt, F. (2010). Cultivation effects of a newspaper on reality estimates and explicit and implicit attitudes. *Journal of Media Psychology: Theories, Methods and Applications, 22*(4), 147–159.

Arkes, H. R. (2013). The consequences of the hindsight bias in medical decision making. *Current Directions in Psychological Science, 22*(5), 356–360.

Armenta, B. E., Knight, G. P., Carlo, G., & Jacobson, R. P. (2011). The relation between ethnic group attachment and prosocial tendencies: The mediating role of cultural values. *European Journal of Social Psychology, 41*(1), 107–115.

Armitage, C. J., & Conner, M. (1999). The theory of planned behaviour: Assessment of predictive validity and "perceived control." *British Journal of Social Psychology, 38*(1), 35–54.

Arnocky, S., Sunderani, S., Miller, J. L., & Vaillancourt, T. (2012). Jealousy mediates the relationship between attractiveness comparison and females' indirect aggression. *Personal Relationships, 19*(2), 290–303.

Aron, A., & Aron, E. N. (1986). *Love as the expansion of self: Understanding attraction and satisfaction.* New York, NY: Hemisphere.

Aron, A., & Aron, E. N. (1997). Self-expansion motivation and including other in the self. In S. Duck (Ed.), *Handbook of personal relationships: Theory, research and interventions* (2nd ed., pp. 251–270). Hoboken, NJ: John Wiley & Sons.

Aron, A., Aron, E. N., & Norman, C. (2001). Self-expansion model of motivation and cognition in close relationships and beyond. In G. J. Fletcher & M. S. Clark (Eds.), *Blackwell handbook of social psychology: Interpersonal processes* (pp. 478–502). Malden, MA: Blackwell.

Aron, A., Aron, E. N., Tudor, M., & Nelson, G. (1991). Close relationships as including other in the self. *Journal of Personality and Social Psychology, 60*(2), 241–253.

Aron, A., Norman, C. C., Aron, E. N., McKenna, C., & Heyman, R. E. (2000). Couples' shared participation in novel and arousing activities and experienced relationship quality. *Journal of Personality and Social Psychology, 78*(2), 273–284.

Aronson, E., & Mills, J. (1959). The effect of severity of initiation on liking for a group. *Journal of Abnormal and Social Psychology, 59*(2), 177–181.

Aronson, E., Stephan, C., Sikes, J., Blaney, N., & Snapp, M. (1978). *The jigsaw classroom.* Beverly Hills, CA: Sage.

Aronson, E., & Thibodeau, R. (1992). The jigsaw classroom: A cooperative strategy for reducing prejudice. In J. Lynch, C. Modgil, & S. Modgil (Eds.), *Cultural diversity in the schools.* London, England: Falmer Press.

Aronson, J., Fried, C. B., & Good, C. (2002). Reducing the effects of stereotype threat on African American college students by shaping theories of intelligence. *Journal of Experimental Social Psychology, 38*(2), 113–125.

Arriaga, X. B., & Agnew, C. R. (2001). Being committed: Affective, cognitive, and conative components of relationship commitment. *Personality and Social Psychology Bulletin, 27*(9), 1190–1203.

Arriaga, X. B., Kumashiro, M., Simpson, J. A., & Overall, N. C. (2018). Revising working models across time: Relationship situations that enhance attachment security. *Personality and Social Psychology Review, 22*(1), 71–96.

Arriaga, X. B., & Rusbult, C. E. (1998). Standing in my partner's shoes: Partner perspective taking and reactions to accommodative dilemmas. *Personality and Social Psychology Bulletin, 24*(9), 927–948.

Arrow, H., Henry, K. B., Poole, M. S., Wheelan, S., & Moreland, R. (2005). Traces, trajectories, and timing: The temporal perspective on groups. In M. S. Poole, S. Marshall, & A. B. Hollingshead (Eds.), *Theories of small groups: Interdisciplinary perspectives* (pp. 313–367). Thousand Oaks, CA: Sage.

Asbrock, F., & Kauff, M. (2015). Authoritarian disbeliefs in diversity. *The Journal of Social Psychology, 155*(6), 553–558.

Asch, S. E. (1946). Forming impressions of personality. *Journal of Abnormal and Social Psychology, 41*(3), 258–290.

Asch, S. E. (1951). Effects of group pressure upon the modification and distortion of judgments. In H. Guetzkow (Ed.), *Groups, leadership, and men: Research in human relations* (pp. 177–190). Pittsburgh, PA: Carnegie Press.

Asch, S. E. (1952). *Social psychology.* Englewood Cliffs, NJ: Prentice-Hall.

Asch, S. E. (1955). Opinions and social pressure. *Scientific American, 193*(5), 31–35.

Asch, S. E. (1956). Studies of independence and conformity: A minority of one against a unanimous majority. *Psychological Monographs: General and Applied, 70*(9), 1–70.

Asendorpf, J. B., Conner, M., De Fruyt, F., De Houwer, J., Denissen, J. J., Fiedler, K.,. . .Wicherts, J. M.. (2013). Recommendations for increasing replicability in psychology. *European Journal of Personality, 27*(2), 108–119.

Ash, M. G. (1992). Cultural contexts and scientific change in psychology: Kurt Lewin in Iowa. *American Psychologist, 47*(2), 198–207.

Ashburn-Nardo, L., & Smith, J. S. (2008). Black college students' extropunitive and intropunitive responses to prejudice: Implications for concrete attitudes toward school in a predominantly white institution. *Journal of Black Psychology, 34*(4), 479–493.

Ashton-James, C. E., & Levordashka, A. (2013). When the wolf wears sheep's clothing: Individual differences in the desire to be liked influence nonconscious behavioral mimicry. *Social Psychological and Personality Science, 4*(6), 643–648.

Aune, K. S., & Wong, N. C. (2002). Antecedents and consequences of adult play in romantic relationships. *Personal Relationships, 9*(3), 279–286.

Axsom, D. (1989). Cognitive dissonance and behavior change in psychotherapy. *Journal of Experimental Social Psychology, 25*(3), 234–252.

Axt, J. R. (2018). The best way to measure explicit racial attitudes is to ask about them. *Social Psychological and Personality Science, 9*(8), 896–906.

Axtell, R. E. (1993). *Gestures: The Do's and Taboos of Body Language Around the World* (3rd ed.). New York, NY: John Wiley & Sons.

Aydin, N., Fischer, P., & Frey, D. (2010). Turning to God in the face of ostracism: Effects of social exclusion on religiousness. *Personality and Social Psychology Bulletin, 36*(6), 742–753.

Ayman, R. (2004). Situational and contingency approaches to leadership. In J. Antonakis, A. T. Cianciolo, & R. J. Sternberg (Eds.), *The nature of leadership* (pp. 148–170). Thousand Oaks, CA: Sage.

Ayman, R., Chemers, M. M., & Fiedler, F. (1995). The contingency model of leadership effectiveness: Its levels of analysis. *The Leadership Quarterly, 6*(2), 147–167.

Ayman, R., & Korabik, K. (2010). Leadership: Why gender and culture matter. *American Psychologist, 65*(3), 157–170.

B

Bachman, R., & Peralta, R. (2002). The relationship between drinking and violence in an adolescent population: Does gender matter? *Deviant Behavior: An Interdisciplinary Journal, 23,* 1–19.

Bachnik, J. M. (1992). The two "faces" of self and society in Japan. *Ethos, 20*(1), 3–32.

Back, M. D., Schmukle, S. C., & Egloff, B. (2008). Becoming friends by chance. *Psychological Science, 19*(5), 439–440.

Back, M. D., Stopfer, J. M., Vazire, S., Gaddis, S., Schmukle, S. C., Egloff, B. & Gosling, S. D. (2010). Facebook profiles reflect actual personality, not self-idealization. *Psychological Science, 21*(3), 372–374.

Bagozzi, R. P. (1981). Attitudes, intentions, and behavior: A test of some key hypotheses. *Journal of Personality and Social Psychology, 41*(4), 607–627.

Bahns, A. J., & Branscombe, N. R. (2011). Effects of legitimizing discrimination against homosexuals on gay bashing. *European Journal of Social Psychology, 41*(3), 388–396.

Bahns, A. J., Crandall, C., Gillath, O., & Preacher, K. J. (2017). Similarity in relationships as niche construction: Choice, stability, and influence within dyads in a free choice environment. *Journal of Personality and Social Psychology, 11*(2), 329–355.

Bailey, D. F., & Bradbury-Bailey, M. (2010). Promoting the self-esteem of adolescent African American males. In M. H. Guindon (Ed.). *Self-esteem across the lifespan* (pp. 159–172). New York, NY: Routledge.

Baker, L. A., Jacobson, K. C., Raine, A., Lozano, D. I., & Bezdjian, S. (2007). Genetic and environmental bases of childhood antisocial behavior: A multi-informant twin study. *Journal of Abnormal Psychology, 116*(2), 219–235.

Baker, L. R., McNulty, J. K., Overall, N. C., Lambert, N. M., & Fincham, F. D. (2013). How do relationship maintenance behaviors affect individual well-being? A contextual perspective. *Social Psychology and Personality Science, 4*(3), 282–289.

Baker, L. R., & Oswald, D. L. (2010). Shyness and online social networking services. *Journal of Social and Personal Relationships, 27*(7), 873–889.

Baker, S. M., & Petty, R. E. (1994). Majority and minority influence: Source-position imbalance as a determinant of message scrutiny. *Journal of Personality and Social Psychology, 67*(1), 5–19.

Bales, R. F. (1970). *Personality and interpersonal behavior.* Fort Worth, TX: Holt, Rinehart & Winston.

Bales, R. F., & Slater, P. E. (1955). Role differentiation. In T. Parsons & R. F. Bales (Eds.), *Family, socialization, and interaction processes* (pp. 259–306). Glencoe, IL: Free Press.

Balliet, D., Li, N. P., Macfarlan, S. J., & Van Vugt, M. (2011). Sex differences in cooperation: A meta-analytic review of social dilemmas. *Psychological Bulletin, 137*(6), 881–909.

Balliet, D., Mulder, L. B., Van Lange, P. A. (2011). Reward, punishment, and cooperation: A meta-analysis. *Psychological Bulletin, 137*(4), 594–615.

Banaji, M. R., Bazerman, M. H., & Chugh, D. (2003, December). How (un)ethical are you? *Harvard Business Review,* 3–10.

Banaji, M. R., & Heiphetz, L. (2010). Attitudes. In S. T. Fiske, D. T. Gilbert, & G. Lindzey (Eds.). *Handbook of social psychology, Vol. 1* (5th ed.) (pp. 353–393). Hoboken, NJ: John Wiley & Sons.

Banas, J. A., & Rains, S. A. (2010). A meta-analysis of research on inoculation theory. *Communication Monographs, 77*(3), 281–311.

Bandura, A. (1965). Influences of models' reinforcement contingencies on the acquisition of initiative responses. *Journal of Personality and Social Psychology, 1*(6), 589–595.

Bandura, A. (1979). The social learning perspective: Mechanism of aggression. In H. Toch (Ed.), *Psychology of crime and criminal justice* (pp. 198–236). New York, NY: Holt, Rinehart.

Bandura, A. (1986). *Social foundations of thought and action: A social-cognitive theory.* Englewood Cliffs, NJ: Prentice-Hall.

Bandura, A. (2005). Toward a psychology of human agency. *Perspectives on Psychological Science, 1*(2), 164–180.

Bandura, A., & Huston, A. C. (1961). Identification as a process of incidental learning. *Journal of Abnormal and Social Psychology, 63*(2), 311–318.

Bandura, A., Ross, D., & Ross, S. A. (1961). Transmission of aggression through imitation of aggressive models. *Journal of Abnormal and Social Psychology, 63*(3), 575–582.

Bandura, A., & Walters, R. H. (1963). *Social learning and personality development.* New York, NY: Holt, Rinehart.

Bank, B. J., & Hansford, S. L. (2000). Gender and friendship: Why are men's best same-sex friendships less intimate and supportive? *Personal Relationships, 7*(1), 63–78.

Bar, M., Neta, M., & Linz, H. (2006). Very first impressions. *Emotion, 6*(2), 269–278.

Barbee, A. P., Gulley, M. R., & Cunningham, M. R. (1990). Support seeking in personal relationships. *Journal of Social and Personal Relationships, 7*(4), 531–540.

Bargh, J. A., & Chartrand, T. L. (1999). The unbearable automaticity of being. *American Psychologist, 54*(7), 462–479.

Bargh, J. A., & McKenna, K. Y. (2004). The Internet and social life. *Annual Review of Psychology, 55*(1), 573–590.

Barkan, R., Ayal, S., Gino, F., & Ariely, D. (2012). The pot calling the kettle black: Distancing response to ethical dissonance. *Journal of Experimental Psychology: General, 141*(4), 757–773.

Barley, S. R., & Bechky, B. A. (1994). In the backrooms of science: The work of technicians in science labs. *Work and Occupations, 21*(1), 85–126.

Baron, L., & Straus, M. A. (1989). *Four theories of rape in American society: A state-level analysis.* New Haven, CT: Yale University Press.

Baron, R. A. (1973). Threatened retaliation from the victim as an inhibitor of physical aggression. *Journal of Research in Personality, 7*(2), 103–115.

Baron, R. A., & Kepner, C. R. (1970). Model's behavior and attraction toward the model as determinants of adult aggressive behavior. *Journal of Personality and Social Psychology, 14*(4), 335–344.

Baron, R. S. (1986). Distraction-conflict theory: Progress and problems. In L. Berkowitz (Ed.), *Advances in experimental social psychology* (Vol. 19, pp. 1–40). New York, NY: Academic Press.

Barrett, L., Henzi, P., & Dunbar, R. (2003). Primate cognition: From "what now?" to "what if?" *Trends in Cognitive Sciences, 7*(11), 494–497.

Barron, G., & Yechiam, E. (2002). Private e-mail requests and the diffusion of responsibility. *Computers in Human Behavior, 18*(5), 507–520.

Bar-Tal, D. (1990). Causes and consequences of delegitimization: Models of conflict and ethnocentrism. *Journal of Social Issues, 46*(1), 65–81.

Bartels, A., & Zeki, S. (2000). The neural basis of romantic love. *Neuroreport, 11*(17), 3829–2834.

Bartels, M., Cacioppo, J. T., Hudziak, J. J., & Boomsma, D. I. (2008). Genetic and environmental contributions to stability in loneliness throughout childhood. *American Journal of Medical Genetics Part B (Neuropsychiatric Genetics), 147*(3), 385–391.

Bartholomew, K. (1990). Avoidance of intimacy: An attachment perspective. *Journal of Social and Personal Relationships, 7*(2), 147–178.

Bartholomew, K., & Horowitz, L. M. (1991). Attachment styles among young adults: A test of a four-category model. *Journal of Personality and Social Psychology, 61*(2), 226–244.

Bartholomew, K., Kwong, M. J., & Hart, S. D. (2001). Attachment. In W. J. Livesley (Ed.). *Handbook of personality disorders: Theory, research, and treatment* (pp. 196–230). New York, NY: Guilford.

Bartholow, B. D., Anderson, C. A., Carnagey, N. L., & Benjamin, A. J., Jr. (2005). Interactive effects of life experience and situational cues on aggression: The weapons priming effect in hunters and nonhunters. *Journal of Experimental Social Psychology, 41*(1), 48–60.

Bartholow, B. D., Bushman, B. J., & Sestir, M. A. (2006). Chronic violent video game exposure and desensitization to violence: Behavioral and event-related brain potential data. *Journal of Experimental Social Psychology, 42*(4), 532–539.

Bartholow, B. D., Pearson, M. A., Gratton, G., & Fabiani, M. (2003). Effects of alcohol on person perception: A social cognitive neuro-science approach. *Journal of Personality and Social Psychology, 85*(4), 627–638.

Barton, J., Stephens, J., & Haslett, T. (2009). Action research: Its foundations in open systems thinking and relationship to the scientific method. *Systemic Practice and Action Research, 22*, 475–488.

Bartone, P. T., Snook, S. A., & Tremble, T. R., Jr. (2002). Cognitive and personality predictors of leader performance in West Point cadets. *Military Psychology, 14*(4), 321–338.

Bartz, J. A., Tchalova, K., Fenerci, C. (2016). Reminders of social connection can attenuate anthropomorphism: A replication and extension of Epley, Akalis, Waytz, and Cacioppo (2008). *Psychological Science, 27*(12), 1644–1650.

Basil, D. Z., Ridgway, N. M., & Basil, M. D. (2008). Guilt and giving: A process model of empathy and efficacy. *Psychology & Marketing, 25*(1), 1–23.

Basow, S. A. (1986). *Gender stereotypes: Traditions and alternatives* (2nd ed.). Monterey, CA: Brooks/Cole.

Bass, B. M. (2008). *The Bass handbook of leadership: Theory, research, and managerial applications.* New York, NY: Free Press.

Bass, B. M., & Bass, R. (2009). *The Bass handbook of leadership: Theory, research, and managerial applications* (4th ed.). New York, NY: Free Press.

Bassett, J. F. (2010). The effects of mortality salience and social dominance orientation on attitudes toward illegal immigrants. *Social Psychology, 41*(1), 52–55.

Bassett, J. F., Cate, K. L., & Dabbs, J. M., Jr. (2002). Individual differences in self-presentation style: Driving an automobile and meeting a stranger. *Self and Identity, 1*(3), 281–288.

Bassili, J. N. (2003). The minority slowness effect: Subtle inhibitions in the expression of views not shared by others. *Journal of Personality and Social Psychology, 84*(2), 261–276.

Bassili, J. N., & Provencal, A. (1988). Perceiving minorities: A factor-analytic approach. *Personality and Social Psychology Bulletin, 14*(1), 5–15.

Batson, C. D. (1991). *The altruism question: Toward a social-psychological answer.* Hillsdale, NJ: Lawrence Erlbaum Associates.

Batson, C. D. (2011). *Altruism in humans.* New York, NY: Oxford University Press.

Batson, C. D., Coke, J. S., Chard, F., Smith, D., & Taliaferro, A. (1979). Generality of the "glow of goodwill": Effects of mood on helping and information acquisition. *Social Psychology Quarterly, 42*(2), 176–179.

Batson, C. D., Duncan, B. D., Ackerman, P., Buckley, T., & Birch, K. (1981). Is empathic emotion a source of altruistic motivation? *Journal of Personality and Social Psychology, 40*(2), 290–302.

Batson, C. D., Eklund, J. H., Chermok, V. L., Hoyt, J. L., & Ortiz, B. G. (2007). An additional antecedent of empathic concern: Valuing the welfare of the person in need. *Journal of Personality and Social Psychology, 93*(1), 65–74.

Batson, C. D., O'Quinn, K., Fultz, J., Vanderplas, N., & Isen, A. M. (1983). Influence of self-reported distress and empathy on egoistic versus altruistic motivation to help. *Journal of Personality and Social Psychology, 45*(3), 706–718.

Baudouina, J. Y., & Tiberghienb, G. (2004). Symmetry, averageness, and feature size in the facial attractiveness of women. *Acta Psychologica, 117*(3), 313–332.

Baum, N. (2010). After a terror attack: Israeli-Arab professionals' feelings and experiences. *Journal of Social and Personal Relationships, 27*(5), 685–704.

Baumeister, R. F. (1982). A self-presentational view of social phenomena. *Psychological Bulletin, 91*(1), 3–26.

Baumeister, R. F., & Alquist, J. L. (2009). Is there a downside to good self-control? *Self and Identity, 8*(2–3), 115–130.

Baumeister, R. F., & Boden, J. M. (1998). Aggression and the self: High self-esteem, low self-control, and ego threat. In R. Geen & E. Donnerstein (Eds.), *Human aggression: Theories, research, and implications for social policy* (pp. 111–137). San Diego, CA: Academic Press.

Baumeister, R. F., DeWall, C. N., Ciarocco, N. J., & Twenge, J. M. (2005). Social exclusion impairs self-regulation. *Journal of Personality and Social Psychology, 88*(4), 589–604.

Baumeister, R. F., & Heatherton, T. F. (1996). Self-regulation failure: An overview. *Psychological Inquiry, 7*(1), 1–15.

Baumeister, R. F., Heatherton, T. F., & Tice, D. M. (1994). *Losing control: How and why people fail at self-regulation.* San Diego, CA: Academic Press.

Baumeister, R. F., & Jones, E. E. (1978). When self-presentation is constrained by the target's knowledge: Consistency and compensation. *Journal of Personality and Social Psychology, 36*(6), 608–618.

Baumeister, R. F., & Leary, M. R. (1995). The need to belong: Desire for interpersonal attachments as a fundamental human motivation. *Psychological Bulletin, 117*(3), 497–529.

Baumeister, R. F., Smart, L., & Boden, J. M. (1996). Relation of threatened egotism to violence and aggression: The dark side of high self-esteem. *Psychological Review, 103*(1), 5–33.

Baumeister, R. F., Twenge, J. M., & Nuss, C. K. (2002). Effects of social exclusion on cognitive processes: Anticipated aloneness reduces intelligent thought. *Journal of Personality and Social Psychology, 83*(4), 817–827.

Baumeister, R. F., & Vohs, K. D. (2016). Misguided effort with elusive implications. *Perspectives on Psychological Science, 11*(4), 574–575.

Baumeister, R. F., Vohs, K. D., DeWall, C. N., & Zhang, L. (2007a). How emotion shapes behavior: Feedback, anticipation, and reflection, rather than direct causation. *Personality and Social Psychology Review, 11*(2), 167–203.

Baumeister, R. F., Vohs, K. D., & Funder, D. C. (2007b). Psychology as the science of self-reports and finger movements: Or whatever happened to actual behavior? *Perspectives on Psychological Science, 2*(4), 396–403.

Baumrind, D. (1964). Some thoughts on ethics of research: After reading Milgram's "Behavioral Study of Obedience." *American Psychologist, 19*(6), 421–423.

Baxter, L. A. (1987). Self-disclosure and relationship disengagement. In V. Derlega & J. H. Berg (Eds.), *Self-disclosure: Theory, research, and therapy* (pp. 155–174). New York, NY: Plenum Press.

Bazzini, D., Curtin, L., Joslin, S., Regan, S., & Martz, D. (2010). Do animated Disney characters portray and promote the beauty-goodness stereotype? *Journal of Applied Social Psychology, 40*(10), 2687–2709.

Beaman, A. L., Barnes, P. J., Klentz, B., & McQuirk, B. (1978). Increasing helping rates through information dissemination: Teaching pays. *Personality and Social Psychology Bulletin, 9*(3), 181–196.

Beaman, A. L., Cole, M., Preston, M., Klentz, B., & Steblay, N. M. (1983). Fifteen years of the foot-in-the-door research: A meta-analysis. *Personality and Social Psychology Bulletin, 9*(2), 181–186.

Beaman, A. L., Klentz, B., Diener, E., & Svanum, S. (1979). Self-awareness and transgression in children: Two field studies. *Journal of Personality and Social Psychology, 37*(10), 1835–1846.

Beauducel, A., Brocke, B., & Leue, A. (2006). Energetical bases of extraversion: Effort, arousal, EEG, and performance. *International Journal of Psychophysiology, 62*(2), 212–223.

Beck, L. A., Pietromonaco, P. R., DeVito, C. C., Powers, S. I., & Boyle, A. M. (2014). Conturence between spouses' perceptions and observers' ratings of responsiveness: The role of attachment avoidance. *Personality and Social Psychology Bulletin, 40*(2), 164–174.

Becker, D. V., Neel, R., & Anderson, U. S. (2010). Illusory conjunctions of angry facial expressions follow intergroup biases. *Psychological Science, 21*(7), 938–940.

Becker, J., Ayman, R., & Korabik, K. (2002). Discrepancies in self/subordinates' perceptions of leadership behavior: Leader's gender, organizational context and leader's self-monitoring. *Group and Organization Management, 27*(2), 226–244.

Becker, J. C., Tausch, N., Spears, R., & Christ, O. (2011). Committed Dis(s)idents: Participation in radical collective action fosters disidentification with the broader in-group but enhances political identification. *Personality and Social Psychology Bulletin, 37*(8), 1104–1116.

Becker, J. C., & Wright, S. C. (2011). Yet another dark side of chivalry: Benevolent sexism undermines and hostile sexism motivates collective action for social change. *Journal of Personality and Social Psychology, 101*(1), 62–77.

Beebe, B., & Lachmann, F. M. (2014). *The origins of attachment: Infant research and adult treatment.* New York, NY: Routledge.

Beersma, B., & Van Kleef, G. A. (2011). How the grapevine keeps you in line: Gossip increases contributions to the group. *Social Psychological and Personality Science, 2*(6), 642–649.

Bègue, L., Subra, B., Arvers, P., Muller, D., Bricout, V., & Zorman, M. (2009). A message in a bottle: Extrapharmacological effects of alcohol on aggression. *Journal of Experimental Social Psychology, 45*, 137–142.

Beilock, S. L., Jellison, W. A., Rydell, R. J., McConnell, A. R., & Carr, T. H. (2006). On the causal mechanisms of stereotype threat: Can skills that don't rely heavily on working memory still be threatened? *Personality and Social Psychology Bulletin, 32*(8), 1059–1071.

Bell, G. C., & Hastings, S. O. (2015). Exploring parental approval and disapproval for black and white interracial couples. *Journal of Social Issues, 71*(4), 755–771.

Bell, S. T., Kuriloff, P. J., & Lottes, I. (1994). Understanding attributions of blame in stranger-rape and date-rape situations: An examination of gender, race, identification, and students' social perception of rape victims. *Journal of Applied Social Psychology, 24*(19), 1719–1734.

Bellavia, G., & Murray, S. L. (2003). Did I do that? Self-esteem-related differences in reactions to romantic partners' moods. *Personal Relationships, 10*, 77–95.

Bem, D. J. (1965). An experimental analysis of self-persuasion. *Journal of Experimental Social Psychology, 1*(3), 199–218.

Bem, D. J. (1972). Self-perception theory. In L. Berkowitz (Ed.), *Advances in experimental social psychology* (Vol. 6, pp. 1–62). New York, NY: Academic Press.

Benet-Martínez, V., Lee, F., & Leu, J. (2006). Biculturalism and cognitive complexity: Expertise in cultural representations. *Journal of Cross-Cultural Psychology, 37*(4), 1–23.

Benjamin, A. J., Jr., Kepes, S., & Bushman, B. J. (2018). Effects of weapons on aggressive thoughts, angry feelings, hostile appraisals, and aggressive behavior: A meta-analytic review of the weapons effect literature. *Personality and Social Psychology Review, 22*(4), 347–377.

Benner, A. D. (2011). Latino adolescents' loneliness, academic performance, and the buffering nature of friendships. *Journal of Youth and Adolescence, 40*(5), 556–567.

Bennett, K. K., & Elliott, M. (2005). Pessimistic explanatory style and cardiac health: What is the relation and the mechanism that links them? *Basic and Applied Social Psychology, 27*(3), 239–248.

Ben-Zeev, T., Fein, S., & Inzlicht, M. (2005). Arousal and stereotype threat. *Journal of Experimental Social Psychology, 41*(2), 174–181.

Beren, S. E., Hayden, H. A., Wilfley, D. E., & Striegel-Moore, R. H. (1997). Body dissatisfaction among lesbian college students: The conflict of straddling mainstream and lesbian cultures. *Psychology of Women Quarterly, 21*(3), 431–445.

Berg, J. H. (1984). The development of friendships between roommates. *Journal of Personality and Social Psychology, 46*(2), 346–356.

Berg, J. H., & Clark, M. S. (1986). Differences in social exchange between intimate and other relationships: Gradually evolving or quickly apparent? In V. J. Derlega & B. A. Winstead (Eds.), *Friendship and social interaction* (pp. 101–128). New York, NY: Springer-Verlag.

Berg, M. B., Lin, L., Hollar, S. M., Walker, S. N., & Erickson, L. E. (2016). The relationship between weight-based prejudice and attitudes towards obesity-reducing public policies. *Analyses of Social Issues and Public Policy, 16*(1), 125–142.

Berger, J., Meredith, M., & Wheeler, C. (2008). Contextual priming: Where people vote affects how they vote. *PNAS, 105*(26), 8846–8849.

Berger, J., & Webster, M., Jr. (2006). Expectations, status, and behavior. In P. J. Burke (Ed.), *Contemporary social psychological theories* (pp. 268–300). Stanford, CA: Stanford University Press.

Bergh, R., Akrami, N., Sidanius, J., & Sibley, C. G. (2016). Is group membership necessary for understanding generalized prejudice? A re-evaluation of why prejudices are interrelated. *Journal of Personality and Social Psychology, 111*(3), 367–395.

Berkowitz, L. (1968). Impulse, aggression, and the gun. *Psychology Today, 2*, 19–22.

Berkowitz, L. (1969). The frustration-aggression hypothesis revisited. In L. Berkowitz (Ed.), *Roots of aggression* (pp. 1–28). New York, NY: Atherton Press.

Berkowitz, L. (1984). Some effects of thoughts on anti- and prosocial influences of media events: A cognitive-neoassociation analysis. *Psychological Bulletin, 95*(3), 410–427.

Berkowitz, L. (1989). Frustration-aggression hypothesis: Examination and reformulation. *Psychological Bulletin, 106*(1), 59–73.

Berkowitz, L. (1993). *Aggression: Its causes, consequences, and control*. New York, NY: McGraw-Hill.

Berkowitz, L. (1994). On the escalation of aggression. In M. Potegal & J. F. Knutson (Eds.), *The dynamics of aggression: Biological and social processes in dyads and groups* (pp. 33–41). Hillsdale, NJ: Lawrence Erlbaum Associates.

Bernache-Assollant, I., Laurin, R., Bouchet, P., Bodet, G., & Lacassagne, M. F. (2010). Refining the relationship between ingroup identification and identity management strategies in the sport context: The moderating role of gender and the mediating role of negative mood. *Group Processes & Intergroup Relations, 13*(5), 639–652.

Bernard, M., Dreber, A., Strimling, P., & Eriksson, K. (2013). The subgroup problem: When can binding voting on extractions from a common pool resource overcome the tragedy of the commons? *Journal of Economic Behavior & Organization, 91*, 122–130.

Berndsen, M., Spears, R., Pligt, J., & McGarty, C. (2002). Illusory correlation and stereotype formation: Making sense of group differences and cognitive biases. In C. McGarty, V. Y. Yzerbyt, & R. Spears (Eds.). *Stereotypes as explanations: The formation of meaningful beliefs about social groups* (pp. 90–110). New York, NY: Cambridge University Press.

Bernstein, D. M., Erdfelder, E., Meltzoff, A. N., Peria, W., & Loftus, G. R. (2011). Hindsight bias from 3 to 95 years of age. *Journal of Experimental Psychology: Learning, Memory and Cognition, 37*(2), 378–391.

Berscheid, E., & Hatfield, E. (1972). A little bit about love. In T. Huston (Ed.), *Foundations of interpersonal attraction* (pp. 355–381). New York, NY: Academic Press.

Berscheid, E., & Reis, H. T. (1998). Attraction and close relationships. In D. Gilbert, S. Fiske, & G. Lindzey (Eds.), *The handbook of social psychology* (4th ed., Vol 2, pp. 193–281). New York, NY: Oxford University Press.

Bessenoff, G. R., & Del Priore, R. E. (2007). Women, weight, and age: Social comparison to magazine images across the lifespan. *Sex Roles, 56*(3–4), 215–222.

Bettencourt, B. A., & Miller, N. (1996). Gender differences in aggression as a function of provocation: A meta-analysis. *Psychological Bulletin, 119*(3), 422–447.

Bettencourt, B. A., Talley, A., Benjamin, A. J., & Valentine, J. (2006). Personality and aggressive behavior under provoking and neutral conditions: A meta-analytic review. *Psychological Bulletin, 132*(5), 751–777.

Bhatti, N., Maitlo, G. M., Shaikh, N., Hashmi, M. A., & Shaikh, F. M. (2012). The impact of autocratic and democratic leadership style on job satisfaction. *International Business Research, 5*(2), 192.

Bicchieri, C., & Lev-On, A. (2007). Computer-mediated communication and cooperation in social dilemmas: An experimental analysis. *Politics, Philosophy & Economics, 6*(2), 139–168.

Bierbrauer, G. (1979). Why did he do it? Attribution of obedience and the phenomenon of dispositional bias. *European Journal of Social Psychology, 9*(1), 67–84.

Bierhoff, H. W., Klein, R., & Kramp, P. (1991). Evidence for the altruistic personality from data on accident research. *Journal of Personality, 59*(2), 263–280.

Bisson, M. A., & Levine, T. R. (2009). Negotiating a friends with benefits relationship. *Archives of Sexual Behavior, 38*(1), 66–73.

Bizumic, B., & Duckitt, J. (2012). What is and is not ethnocentrism? A conceptual analysis and political implications. *Political Psychology, 33*(6), 887–909.

Björkqvist, K., Lagerspetz, K. M. J., & Kaukiainen, A. (1992). Do girls manipulate and boys fight? Developmental trends regarding direct and indirect aggression. *Aggressive Behavior, 18*(2), 117–127.

Black, M., & Downie, J. (2013). Watch your language: A review of the use of stigmatizing language by Canadian judges. In D. A. Sisti, A. L. Caplan, & H. Rimon-Greenspan (Eds.), *Applied ethics in mental health care: An interdisciplinary reader* (pp. 267–282). Cambridge, MA: MIT Press.

Black, M. C., Basile, K. C., Breiding, M. J., Smith, S. G., Walters, M. I., Merrick, M. T.,. . .Stevens, M. R. (2011). *The national intimate partner and sexual violence survey (NISVS): 2010 summary report*. Atlanta, GA: National Center for Injury Prevention and Control, Centers for Disease Control and Prevention.

Blair, C. A., Thompson, L. F., & Wuensch, K. L. (2005). Electronic helping behavior: The virtual presence of others makes a difference. *Basic and Applied Social Psychology, 27*(2), 171–178.

Blair, I. V., Judd, C. M., Sadler, M. S., & Jenkins, C. (2002). The role of Afrocentric features in person perception: Judging by features and categories. *Journal of Personality and Social Psychology, 83*(1), 5–25.

Blair, I. V., Park, B., & Bachelor, J. (2003). Understanding intergroup anxiety: Are some people more anxious than others? *Group Processes and Intergroup Relations, 6*(2), 151–169.

Blair, J. P., Levine, T. R. & Shaw, A. S. (2010). Content in context improves deception detection accuracy. *Human Communication Research, 30*(3), 423–442.

Blais, M. R., Sabourin, S., Boucher, C., & Vallerand, R. J. (1990). Toward a motivational model of couple happiness. *Journal of Personality and Social Psychology, 59*(5), 1021–1031.

Blakemore, S. -J. (2018). Avoiding social risk in adolescence. *Current Directions in Psychological Science, 27*(2), 116–122.

Blanchard, F., Crandall, C., Brigham, J., & Vaughn, L. (1994). Condemning and condoning racism: A social context approach to interracial settings. *The Journal of Applied Psychology, 79*(6), 993–997.

Blandón-Gitlin, I., Sperry, K., & Leo, R. (2011). Jurors believe interrogation tactics are not likely to elicit false confessions: Will expert witness testimony inform them otherwise? *Psychology, Crime & Law, 17*(3), 239–260.

Blascovich, J., Spencer, S. J., Quinn, D., & Steele, C. (2001). African Americans and high blood pressure: The role of stereotype threat. *Psychological Science, 12*(3), 225–229.

Blass, T. (1996). Attribution of responsibility and trust in the Milgram obedience experiment. *Journal of Applied Social Psychology, 26*(17), 1529–1535.

Blass, T. (1999). The Milgram paradigm after 35 years: Some things we now know about obedience to authority. *Journal of Applied Social Psychology, 29*(5), 955–978.

Blass, T. (Ed.). (2000). *Obedience to authority: Current perspectives on the Milgram paradigm*. Mahwah, NJ: Lawrence Erlbaum Associates.

Bleske-Rechek, A. L., & Buss, D. M. (2001). Opposite-sex friendship: Sex differences and similarities in initiation selection and dissolution. *Personality and Social Psychology Bulletin, 27*(10), 1310–1323.

Bless, H., Clore, G. L., Schwarz, N., Golisano, V., Rabe, C., & Wölk, M. (1996). Mood and the use of scripts: Does a happy mood really lead to mindlessness? *Journal of Personality and Social Psychology, 71*(4), 665–679.

Blincoe, S., & Harris, M. J. (2011). Status and inclusion, anger and sadness: Gendered responses to disrespect. *European Journal of Social Psychology, 41*(4), 508–517.

Böckler, A., Tusche, A., & Singer, T. (2016). The structure of human prosociality: Differentiating altruistically motivated, norm motivated, strategically motivated, and self-reported prosocial behavior. *Social Psychological and Personality Science, 7*(6), 530–541.

Boduszek, D., Debowska, A., Jones, A. D., Ma, M., Smith, D., Willmott, D.,. . .Kirkman, G. (2019). Prosocial video game as an intimate partner violence prevention tool among youth: A randomised controlled trial. *Computers in Human Behavior, 93*, 260–266.

Boen, F., Vanbeselaere, N., Pandelaere, M., Dewitte, S., Duriez, B., Snauwaert, B.,. . .Van Avermaet, E. (2002). Politics and basking in reflected-glory: A field study in Flanders. *Basic and Applied Social Psychology, 24*(3), 205–214.

Böhm, R., Funke, F., & Harth, N. S. (2010). Same-race and same-gender voting preferences and the role of perceived realistic threat in the democratic primaries and caucuses 2008. *Analyses of Social Issues and Public Policy, 10*(1), 248–261.

Bohner, G., Einwiller, S., Erb, H. -P., & Siebler, F. (2003). When small means comfortable: Relations between product attributes in two-sided advertising. *Journal of Consumer Psychology, 13*(4), 454–463.

Bohner, G., Siebler, F., & Schmelcher, J. (2006). Social norms and the likelihood of raping: Perceived rape myth acceptance of others affects men's rape proclivity. *Personality and Social Psychology Bulletin, 32*(3), 286–297.

Boldry, J. G., Gaertner, L., & Quinn, J. (2007). Measuring the measures: A meta-analytic investigation of the measures of outgroup homogeneity. *Group Processes & Intergroup Relations, 10*(2), 157–178.

Bonam, C. M., Das, V. N., Coleman, B. R., & Salter, P. (2019). Ignoring history, denying racism: Mounting evidence for the Marley hypothesis and epistemologies of ignorance. *Social Psychological and Personality Science, 10*(2), 257–265.

Bond, C. F., Jr., & DePaulo, B. M. (2006). Accuracy of deception judgments. *Personality and Social Psychology Review, 10*(3), 214–234.

Bond, C. F., Jr., & Titus, L. J. (1983). Social facilitation: A meta-analysis of 241 studies. *Psychological Bulletin, 94*(2), 265–292.

Bond, M. H. (2004). Culture and aggression—From context to coercion. *Personality and Social Psychology Review, 8*(1), 62–78.

Bond, R. M., Fariss, C. J., Jones, J. J., Kramer, A. D., Marlow, C., Settle, J. E., & Fowler, J. H. (2012). A 61-million-person experiment in social influence and political mobilization. *Nature, 489*, 295–298.

Bonnot, V., & Croizet, J. -C. (2007). Stereotype internalization and women's math performance: The role of interference in working memory. *Journal of Experimental Social Psychology, 43*(6), 857–866.

Bontempo, R., Lobel, S., & Triandis, H. (1990). Compliance and value internalization in Brazil and the U.S. *Journal of Cross-Cultural Psychology, 21*(2), 201–213.

Borgida, E., Conner, C., & Manteufel, L. (1992). Understanding living kidney donation: A behavioral decision-making perspective. In S. Spacapan & S. Oskamp (Eds.), *Helping and being helped* (pp. 183–212). Thousand Oaks, CA: Sage.

Bornstein, B. H., & Greene, E. (2011). Jury decision making: Implications for and from psychology. *Current Directions in Psychological Science, 20*(1), 63–67.

Bornstein, R. F. (1989). Exposure and affect: Overview and meta-analysis of research, 1968–1987. *Psychological Bulletin, 106*(2), 265–289.

Bossard, J. (1932). Residential propinquity as a factor in marriage selection. *American Journal of Sociology, 38*(2), 219–224.

Bosson, J. K., & Vandello, J. A. (2011). Precarious manhood and its links to action and aggression. *Current Directions in Psychological Science, 20*(2), 82–86.

Bosson, J. K., Vandello, J. A., Burnaford, R. M., Weaver, J. R., & Wasti, S. A. (2009). Precarious manhood and displays of physical aggression. *Personality and Social Psychology Bulletin, 35*(5), 623–634.

Boven, L. V., White, K., Kamida, A., & Gilovich, T. (2003). Intuitions about situational correction in self and others. *Journal of Personality and Social Psychology, 85*(2), 249–258.

Bower, G. H., & Hilgard, E. R. (1981). *Theories of learning* (5th ed.). Englewood Cliffs, NJ: Prentice Hall.

Bowlby, J. (1969). *Attachment and loss. (Vol. I. Attachment).* New York, NY: John Wiley & Sons.

Boysen, S. T., & Himes, G. T. (1999). Current issues and emerging theories in animal cognition. *Annual Review of Psychology, 50*, 683–705.

Brackett, M. A., Alster, B., Wolfe, C. J., Katulak, N. A., & Fale, E. (2007). Creating an emotionally intelligent school district: A skills-based approach. In R. Bar-On, J. G. Maree, & M. J. Elias (Eds.). *Educating people to be emotionally intelligent* (pp. 123–137). Westport, CT: Praeger.

Bradbury, T. N., Campbell, S. M., & Fincham, F. D. (1995). Longitudinal and behavioral analysis of masculinity and femininity in marriage. *Journal of Personality and Social Psychology, 68*(2), 328–341.

Brage, D., Meredith, W., & Woodward, J. (1993). Correlates of loneliness among midwestern adolescents. *Adolescence, 28*(111), 685–693.

Branden, N. (1994). *The six pillars of self-esteem.* New York, NY: Bantam Books.

Brandstätter, V., Lengfelder, A., & Gollwitzer, P. M. (2001). Implementation intentions and efficient action initiation. *Journal of Personality and Social Psychology, 81*(5), 946–960.

Brannon, T. N., Markus, H. R., & Taylor, V. J. (2015). "Two souls, two thoughts," two self-schemas: Double consciousness can have positive academic consequences for African Americans. *Journal of Personality and Social Psychology, 108*(4), 586–609.

Branscombe, N. R., Spears, R., Ellemers, N., & Doosje, B. (2002). Intragroup and intergroup evaluations on group behavior. *Personality and Social Psychology Bulletin, 28*(6), 744–753.

Branscombe, N. R., & Wann, D. L. (1994). Collective self-esteem consequences of outgroup derogation when a valued social identity is on trial. *European Journal of Social Psychology, 24*(6), 641–651.

Brase, G. L., Caprar, D., & Voracek, M. (2004). Sex differences in responses to relationship threats in England and Romania. *Journal of Social and Personal Relationships, 21*(6), 763–778.

Bratt, C., Sidanius, J., Sheehy-Skeffington, J. (2016). Shaping the development of prejudice: Latent growth modeling of the influence of social dominance orientation on outgroup affect in youth. *Personality and Social Psychology Bulletin, 42*(12), 1617–1634.

Brauer, M., & Er-rafiy, A. (2011). Increasing perceived variability reduces prejudice and discrimination. *Journal of Experimental Social Psychology, 47*(5), 871–881.

Brauer, M., Judd, C. M., & Gliner, M. D. (1995). The effects of repeated expressions on attitude polarization during group discussions. *Journal of Personality and Social Psychology, 68*(6), 1014–1029.

Breckler, S. J. (1984). Empirical validation of affect, behavior, and cognition as distinct components of attitude. *Journal of Personality and Social Psychology, 47*(6), 1191–1205.

Brehm, J. W. (1966). *A theory of psychological reactance.* New York, NY: Academic Press.

Brehm, S. S. (1988). Passionate love. In R. J. Sternberg & M. L. Barnes (Eds.), *The psychology of love* (pp. 232–263). New Haven, CT: Yale University Press.

Brehm, S. S. (1992). *Intimate relationships.* New York, NY: McGraw-Hill.

Brehm, S. S., & Brehm, J. W. (1981). *Psychological reactance: A theory of freedom and control.* New York, NY: Academic Press.

Brendl, C. M., Chattopadhyay, A., Pelham, B. W., & Carvallo, M. (2005). Name letter branding: Valence transfers when product specific needs are active. *Journal of Consumer Research, 32*(3), 405–415.

Brescoll, V. L., Okimoto, T. G., & Vial, A. C. (2018). You've come a long way . . . maybe: How moral emotions trigger backlash against women leaders. *Journal of Social Issues, 74*(1), 144–164.

Bresin, K., & Gordon, K. H. (2013). Aggression as affect regulation: Extending catharsis theory to evaluate aggression and experiential anger in the laboratory and daily life. *Journal of Social and Clinical Psychology, 32*(4), 400–423.

Brewer, G., & Kerslake, J. (2015). Cyberbullying, self-esteem, empathy and loneliness. *Computers in Human Behavior, 48*, 255–260.

Brewer, G., & Riley, C. (2009). Height, relationship satisfaction, jealousy, and mate retention. *Evolutionary Psychology, 7*(3), 477–489.

Brewer, M. B., & Kramer, R. K. (1986). Choice behavior in social dilemmas: Effects of social identity, group size, and decision framing. *Journal of Personality and Social Psychology, 50*(3), 543–549.

Brewer, M. B., & Lui, L. (1984). Categorization of the elderly by the elderly: Effects of perceiver's category membership. *Personality and Social Psychology Bulletin, 10*(4), 585–595.

Brickman, P. (1987). *Commitment, conflict, and caring.* Englewood Cliffs, NJ: Prentice-Hall.

Briñol, P., Gandarillas, B., Horcajo, J., & Becerra, A. (2010). Emotion and meta-cognition: Implications for attitude change. *Revista de Psicología Social, 25*(2), 157–183.

Briñol, P., Petty, R. E., & Wagner, B. (2009). Body posture effects on self-evaluation: A self-validation approach. *European Journal of Social Psychology, 39*(6), 1053–1064.

Bristow, D. N., & Sebastian, R. J. (2001). Holy cow! Wait til next year! A closer look at the brand loyalty of Chicago Cubs baseball fans. *Journal of Consumer Marketing, 18*(3), 256–275.

Brochu, P. M., Pearl, R. L., Puhl, R. M., & Brownell, K. D. (2014). Do media portrayals of obesity influence support for weight-related medical policy? *Health Psychology, 33*(2), 197–200.

Broda, M., Yun, J., Schneider, B., Yeager, D. S., Walton, G. M., & Diemer, M. (2018). Reducing inequality in academic success for incoming college students: A randomized trial of growth mindset and belonging interventions. *Journal of Research on Educational Effectiveness, 11*(3), 317–338.

Brody, L. R. (1999). *Gender, emotion, and the family.* Cambridge, MA: Harvard University Press.

Brody, L. R., & Hall, J. A. (1993). Gender and emotion. In M. Lewis, & J. M. Haviland (Eds.), *Handbook of emotions* (pp. 447–460). New York, NY: Guilford Press.

Brohan, E., Henderson, C., Wheat, K., Malcolm, E., Clement, S., Barley, E. A.,...Thornicroft, G. (2012). Systematic review of beliefs, behaviours and influencing factors associated with disclosure of a mental health problem in the workplace. *BMC Psychiatry, 12*, 11.

Broussard, K. A., & Harton, H. C. (2018). Tattoo or taboo? Tattoo stigma and negative attitudes toward tattooed individuals. *The Journal of Social Psychology, 158*(5), 521–540.

Brown, D. (2003). Pornography and erotica. In J. Bryant & D. Roskos-Ewoldsen (Eds.), *Communication and emotion: Essays in honor of Dolf Zillmann. LEA's communication series* (pp. 221–253). Mahwah, NJ: Lawrence Erlbaum Associates.

Brown, J. D., Novick, N. J., Lord, K. A., & Richards, J. M. (1992). When Gulliver travels: Social context, psychological closeness, and self-appraisals. *Journal of Personality and Social Psychology, 62*(5), 717–727.

Brown, K. T., Brown, T. N., Jackson, J. S., Sellers, R. M., & Manuel, W. J. (2003). Teammates on and off the field? White student athletes. *Journal of Applied Social Psychology, 33*(7), 1379–1403.

Brown, L. H., Silvia, P. J., Myin-Germeys, I., & Kwapil, T. R. (2007). When the need to belong goes wrong: The expression of social anhedonia and social anxiety in daily life. *Psychological Science, 18*(9), 778–782.

Brown, R., Eller, A., Leeds, S., & Stace, K. (2007). Intergroup contact and intergroup attitudes: A longitudinal study. *European Journal of Social Psychology, 37*(4), 692–703.

Brown, R., Maras, P., Masser, B., Vivian, J., & Hewstone, M. (2001). Life on the ocean wave: Testing some intergroup hypotheses in a naturalistic setting. *Group Processes and Intergroup Relations, 4*(2), 81–97.

Brown, R. P., Baughman, K., & Carvallo, M. (2018). Culture, masculine honor, and violence toward women. *Personality and Social Psychology Bulletin, 44*(4), 538–549.

Brown, W. M., & Moore, C. (2000). Is prospective altruist-detection an evolved solution to the adaptive problem of subtle cheating in cooperative ventures? Supportive evidence using the Wason selection task. *Evolution and Human Behavior, 21*(1), 25–37.

Brown, W. M., Price, M. E., Kang, J., Pound, N., Zhao, Y., & Yu, H. (2008). Fluctuating asymmetry and preferences for sex-typical bodily characteristics. *Proceedings of the National Academy of Sciences USA, 105*(35), 12938–12943.

Brownstein, A. L., Read, S. J., & Simon, D. (2004). Bias at the racetrack: Effects of individual expertise and task importance on predecision reevaluation of alternatives. *Personality and Social Psychology Bulletin, 30*(7), 891–904.

Bruins, J. J., Liebrand, W. P., & Wilke, H. A. (1989). About the saliency of fear and greed in social dilemmas. *European Journal of Social Psychology, 19*(2), 155–162.

Brumbaugh, C. C., Fraley, R. C. (2010). Adult attachment and dating strategies: How do insecure people attract mates? *Personal Relationships, 17*(4), 599–614.

Brummert-Lennings, H. I., & Warburton, W. A. (2011). The effect of auditory versus violent media exposure on aggressive behavior: The role of song lyrics, video clips and musical tone. *Journal of Experimental Social Psychology, 47*(4), 794–799.

Brunell, A. B., Pilkington, C. J., & Webster, G. D. (2007). Perceptions of risk in intimacy in dating couples: Conversation and relationship quality. *Journal of Social & Clinical Psychology, 26*(1), 92–119.

Bruner, J. S., & Taguiri, R. (1954). Person perception. In G. Lindzey (Ed.), *Handbook of social psychology* (Vol. 2, pp. 634–654). Reading, MA: Addison-Wesley.

Brunet, P. M., & Schmidt, L. A. (2007). Is shyness context specific? Relation between shyness and online self-disclosure with and without a live webcam in young adults. *Journal of Research in Personality, 41*(4), 938–945.

Bryan, A. D., Webster, G. D., & Manaffiey, A. L. (2011). The big, the rich and the powerful: Physical, financial, and social dimensions of dominance in mating and attraction. *Personality and Social Psychology Bulletin, 37*(3), 363–382.

Bryan, C. J., Dweck, C. S., Ross, L., Kay, A. C., & Mislavsky, N. O. (2009). Political mindset: Effects of schema priming on liberal-conservative political positions. *Journal of Experimental Social Psychology, 45*(4), 890–895.

Bryan, J. H., & Test, N. A. (1967). Models and helping: Naturalistic studies in aiding behavior. *Journal of Personality and Social Psychology, 6*(4), 400–407.

Bryant, F. B., & Guilbault, R. L. (2002). "I knew it all along" eventually: The development of hindsight in reaction to the Clinton impeachment verdict. *Basic and Applied Social Psychology, 24*(1), 27–41.

Bryson, J. B. (1991). Modes of response to jealousy-evoking situations. In P. Salovey (Ed.), *The psychology of jealousy and envy* (pp. 178–207). New York, NY: Guilford Press.

Buhrmester, M. D., Kwang, T., & Gosling, S. D. (2011). Amazon's Mechanical Turk: A new source of inexpensive, yet high-quality, data? *Perspectives on Psychological Science, 6*(1), 3–5.

Buhrmester, M. D., Talaifar, S., & Gosling, S. D. (2018). An evaluation of Amazon's mechanical Turk, its rapid rise, and its effective use. *Perspectives on Psychological Science, 13*(2), 149–154.

Bullough, V. L. (1976). *Sexual variance in society and history.* Chicago, IL: University of Chicago Press.

Burbank, V. K. (1987). Female aggression in cross-cultural perspective. *Behavior Science Research, 21*(1–4), 70–100.

Burger, J. M. (1981). Motivational biases in the attribution of responsibility for an accident: A meta-analysis of the defensive-attribution hypothesis. *Psychological Bulletin, 90*(3), 496–512.

Burger, J. M. (1986). Increasing compliance by improving the deal: The that's-not-all technique. *Journal of Personality and Social Psychology, 51*(2), 277–283.

Burger, J. M. (1987). Desire for control and conformity to a perceived norm. *Journal of Personality and Social Psychology, 53*(2), 355–360.

Burger, J. M. (1999). The foot-in-the-door compliance procedure: A multiple-process analysis and review. *Personality and Social Psychology Bulletin, 3*(4), 303–325.

Burger, J. M. (2009). Replicating Milgram: Would people still obey today? *American Psychologist, 64*(1), 1–11.

Burger, J. M. (2012). Basking in reflected glory and compliance with requests from people like us. In D. T. Kenrick, N. Goldstein, & S. L. Braver (Eds.), *Six degrees of social influence: Science, application, and the psychology of Robert Cialdini* (pp. 59–67). New York, NY: Oxford University Press.

Burger, J. M., & Caldwell, D. F. (2003). The effects of monetary incentives and labeling on the foot-in-the-door effect: Evidence for a self-perception process. *Basic and Applied Social Psychology, 25*(3), 235–241.

Burger, J. M., & Caputo, D. (2015). The low-ball compliance procedure: A meta-analysis. *Social Influence, 10*(4), 214–220.

Burgess, E. W. (1926). The romantic impulse and family disorganization. *Survey, 57,* 290–294.

Burke, P. J., Stets, J. E., & Cerven, C. (2007). Gender, legitimation, and identity verification in groups. *Social Psychology Quarterly, 70*(1), 27–42.

Burke, S. E., Dovidio, J. F., LaFrance, M., Przedworski, J. M., Perry, S. P., Phelan, S. M.,. . .van Ryn, M. (2017). Beyond generalized sexual prejudice: Need for closure predicts negative attitudes toward bisexual people relative to gay/ lesbian people. *Journal of Experimental Social Psychology, 71,* 145–150.

Burriss, R. P., Roberts, S. C., Welling, L. L., Puts, D. A., & Little, A. C. (2011). Heterosexual romantic couples mate assortatively for facial symmetry, but not masculinity. *Personality and Social Psychology Bulletin, 37*(5), 601–013.

Burt, M. (1980). Cultural myths and supports for rape. *Journal of Personality and Social Psychology, 38,* 217–230.

Busch, A. L., & Rosenberg, M. S. (2004). Comparing women and men arrested for domestic violence: A preliminary report. *Journal of Family Violence, 19*(1), 49–57.

Bushman, B. J. (1996). Individual differences in the extent and development of aggressive cognitive-associative networks. *Personality and Social Psychology Bulletin, 22*(8), 811–819.

Bushman, B. J. (2002). Does venting anger feed or extinguish the flame? Catharsis, rumination, distraction, anger, and aggressive responding. *Personality and Social Psychology Bulletin, 28*(6), 724–731.

Bushman, B. J. (2018). Narcissism, fame seeking, and mass shootings. *American Behavioral Scientist, 62*(2), 229–241.

Bushman, B. J., & Anderson, C. A. (2001). Is it time to pull the plug on the hostile versus instrumental aggression dichotomy? *Psychological Review, 108*(1), 273–279.

Bushman, B. J., & Baumeister, R. F. (2002). Does self-love or self-hate lead to violence? *Journal of Research in Personality, 36*(6), 543–545.

Bushman, B. J., Bonacci, A. M., Pedersen, W. C., Vasquez, E. A., & Miller, N. (2005a). Chewing on it can chew you up: Effects of rumination on triggered displaced aggression. *Journal of Personality and Social Psychology, 88*(6), 969–983.

Bushman, B. J., & Geen, R. G. (1990). Role of cognitive-emotional mediators and individual differences in the effects of media violence on aggression. *Journal of Personality and Social Psychology, 58*(1), 156–163.

Bushman, B. J., Kerwin, T., Whitlock, T., & Weisenberger, J M. (2017). The weapons effect on wheels: Motorists drive more aggressively when there is a gun in the vehicle. *Journal of Experimental Social Psychology, 73,* 82–85.

Bushman, B. J., Wang, M. C., & Anderson, C. A. (2005b). Is the curve relating temperature to aggression linear or curvilinear? Assaults and temperature in Minneapolis reexamined. *Journal of Personality and Social Psychology, 89*(1), 62–66.

Buss, A. H. (1966). Instrumentality of aggression, feedback, and frustration as determinants of physical aggression. *Journal of Personality and Social Psychology, 3*(2), 153–162.

Buss, A. H. (1980). *Self-consciousness and social anxiety.* San Francisco, CA: W. H. Freeman.

Buss, D. M. (1989). Sex differences in human mate preferences: Evolutionary hypotheses tested in 37 cultures. *Behavioral and Brain Sciences, 12*(1), 1–49.

Buss, D. M. (1995). Evolutionary psychology: A new paradigm for psychological science. *Psychological Inquiry, 6*(1), 1–30.

Buss, D. M. (2018). Sexual and emotional infidelity: Evolved gender differences in jealousy prove robust and replicable. *Perspectives on Psychological Science, 13*(2), 155–160.

Buss, D. M., & Duntley, J. D. (2003). Homicide: An evolutionary psychological perspective and implications for public policy. In R. W. Bloom & N. Dess (Eds.), *Evolutionary psychology and violence: A primer for policymakers and public policy advocates* (pp. 115–128). Westport, CT: Praeger.

Buunk, A. P., Groothof, H. A. K., & Siero, F. W. (2007). Social comparison and satisfaction with one's social life. *Journal of Social and Personal Relationships, 24*(2), 197–205.

Buunk, B. J., Angleitner, A., Oubaid, V., & Buss, D. M. (1996). Sex differences in jealousy in evolutionary and cultural perspective: Tests from the Netherlands, Germany, and the United States. *Psychological Science, 7*(6), 359–363.

Buunk, B. J., & Bringle, R. G. (1987). Jealousy in love relationships. In D. Perlman & S. Duck (Eds.), *Intimate relationships: Development, dynamics, and deterioration* (pp. 123–147). Thousand Oaks, CA: Sage.

Buunk, B. P., & Dijkstra, P. (2001). Evidence from a homosexual sample for a sex-specific rival-oriented mechanism: Jealousy as a function of a rival's physical attractiveness and dominance. *Personal Relationships, 8*(4), 391–406.

Buunk, B. J., & van der Laan, V. (2002). Do women need female role models? Subjective social status and the effects of same-sex and opposite-sex comparisons. *Revue Internationale de Psychologie Sociale, 15*(3–4), 129–155.

Buvinic, M. L., & Berkowitz, L. (1976). Delayed effects of practiced versus unpracticed responses after observation of movie violence. *Journal of Experimental Social Psychology, 12*(3), 283–293.

Byrne, D. (1997). An overview (and underview) of research and theory within the attraction paradigm. *Journal of Social and Personal Relationships, 14*(3), 417–431.

Byrne, D., Gouaux, C., Griffitt, W., Lamberth, J., Murakawa, N., Prasad, M. B., & Ramirez, M. III. (1971). The ubiquitous relationship: Attitude similarity and attraction. A cross-cultural study. *Human Relations, 24*(3), 201–207.

Byrne, D., & Nelson, D. (1965). Attraction as a linear function of proportion of positive reinforcements. *Journal of Personality and Social Psychology, 1*(6), 659–663.

C

Cacioppo, J. T., & Cacioppo, S. (2013). Social neuroscience. *Perspectives on Psychological Science, 8*(6), 667–669.

Cacioppo, J. T., & Cacioppo, S. (2018). The growing problem of loneliness. *The Lancet, 391*(10119), 426.

Cacioppo, J. T., Cacioppo, S., & Boomsma, D. I. (2014). Evolutionary mechanisms for loneliness. *Cognition and Emotion, 28*(1), 3–21.

Cacioppo, J. T., Cacioppo, S., Gonzaga, G. C., Ogburn, E. L., & VanderWeele, T. J. (2013). Marital satisfaction and break-ups differ across on-line and off-line meeting venues. *PNAS, 110*(25), 10135–10140.

Cacioppo, J. T., Chen, H. Y., & Cacioppo, S. (2017). Reciprocal influences between loneliness and self-centeredness: A cross-lagged panel analysis in a population-based sample of African American, Hispanic, and Caucasian adults. *Personality and Social Psychology Bulletin, 43*(8), 1125–1135.

Cacioppo, J. T., Fowler, J. H., & Christakis, N. A. (2009). Alone in the crowd: The structure and spread of loneliness in a large social network. *Journal of Personality and Social Psychology, 97*(6), 977–991.

Cacioppo, J. T., Lorig, T. S., Nusbaum, H. C., & Bernston, G. G. (2004). Social neuroscience: Bridging social and biological systems. In C. Sansone, C. C. Morf, & A. T. Panter (Eds.), *The SAGE handbook of methods in social psychology* (pp. 383–404). Thousand Oaks, CA: Sage.

Cacioppo, J. T., & Petty, R. E. (1982). The need for cognition. *Journal of Personality and Social Psychology, 42*(1), 116–131.

Cacioppo, J. T., Petty, R. E., Feinstein, J. A., & Jarvis, W. B. (1996). Dispositional differences in cognitive motivation: The life and times of individuals varying in need for cognition. *Psychological Bulletin, 119*(2), 197–253.

Calhoun, L. G., Cann, A., Tedeschi, R. G., & McMillan, J. (2000). A correlational test of the relationship between posttraumatic growth, religion, and cognitive processing. *Journal of Traumatic Stress, 13*(3), 521–527.

Callan, M. J., Ellard, J. H., & Nicol, J. E. (2006). The belief in a just world and immanent justice reasoning in adults. *Personality and Social Psychology Bulletin, 32*(12), 1645–1658.

Calzada, E. J., Tamis-LeMonda, C. S., & Yoshikawa, H. (2013). Familismo in Mexican and Dominican families from low-income, urban communities. *Journal of Family Issues, 34*(12), 1696–1724.

Cameron, C. A., & Stritzke, W. G. (2003). Alcohol and acquaintance rape in Australia: Testing the presupposition model of attributions about responsibility and blame. *Journal of Applied Social Psychology, 33*(5), 983–1008.

Cameron, J. J., & Granger, S. (2019). Does self-esteem have an interpersonal imprint beyond self-reports? A meta-analysis of self-esteem and objective interpersonal indicators. *Personality and Social Psychology Review, 23*(1), 73–102.

Campbell, A. (1999). Staying alive: Evolution, culture, and women's intrasexual aggression. *Behavioral and Brain Sciences, 22*(2), 203–252.

Campbell, A., Muncer, S., Guy, A., & Banim, M. (1996). Social representations of aggression: Crossing the sex barrier. *European Journal of Social Psychology, 26*(1), 135–147.

Campbell, J. B., & Hawley, C. W. (1982). Study habits and Eysenck's theory of extraversion-introversion. *Journal of Research in Personality, 16*(2), 139–146.

Campbell, J. D., & Fairey, P. J. (1989). Informational and normative routes to conformity: The effect of faction size as a function of norm extremity and attention to the stimulus. *Journal of Personality and Social Psychology, 57*(3), 457–468.

Campbell, W. K., & Baumeister, R. F. (2001). Is loving the self necessary for loving another? An examination of identity and intimacy? In M. Clark & G. Fletcher (Eds.), *The Blackwell handbook of social psychology: Vol. 2. Interpersonal processes* (pp. 437–456). London, England: Blackwell.

Campbell, W. K., Bonacci, A. M., Shelton, J., Exline, J. J., & Bushman, B. J. (2004). Psychological entitlement: Interpersonal consequences and validation of a new self-report measure. *Journal of Personality Assessment, 83*(1), 29–45.

Campbell, W. K., Foster, C. A., & Finkel, E. J. (2002). Does self-love lead to love for others? A story of narcissistic game playing. *Journal of Personality and Social Psychology, 83*(2), 340–354.

Campbell, W. K., & Sedikides, C. (1999). Self-threat magnifies the self-serving bias: A meta-analytic integration. *Review of General Psychology, 3*(1), 23–43.

Canli, T., Zhao, Z., Desmond, J. E., Kang, E., Gross, J., & Gabrieli, J. D. E. (2001). An fMRI study of personality influences on brain reactivity to emotional stimuli. *Behavioral Neuroscience, 115*(1), 33–42.

Cao, H., Zhou, N., Fine, M., Liang, Y., Li, J., & Mills-Koonce, W. R. (2017). Sexual minority stress and same-sex relationship well-being: A meta-analysis of research prior to the U.S. nationwide legalization of same-sex marriage. *Journal of Marriage and Family, 79*(5), 1258–1277.

Cao, J., & Banaji, M. R. (2017). Social inferences from group size. *Journal of Experimental Social Psychology, 70*, 204–211.

Caporael, L. R. (2001). Parts and whole: The evolutionary importance of groups. In C. Sedikides & M. B. Brewer (Eds.), *Individual self, relational self, collective self* (pp. 241–258). New York, NY: Psychology Press.

Cappe, R. F., & Alden, L. E. (1986). A comparison of treatment strategies for clients functionally impaired by extreme shyness and social avoidance. *Journal of Consulting and Clinical Psychology, 54*(6), 796–801.

Caprara, G. V., Barbaranelli, C., & Zimbardo, P. G. (1996). Understanding the complexity of human aggression: Affective, cognitive, and social dimensions of individual differences in propensity toward aggression. *European Journal of Personality, 10*(2), 133–155.

Caprara, G. V., Perugini, M., & Barbaranelli, C. (1994). Studies of individual differences in aggression. In M. Potegal & J. F. Knutson (Eds.), *The dynamics of aggression: Biological and social processes in dyads and groups* (pp. 123–153). Hillsdale, NJ: Lawrence Erlbaum Associates.

Card, N. A., & Casper, D. M. (2013). Meta-analysis and quantitative research synthesis. In T. D. Little (Ed.). *The Oxford handbook of quantitative methods: Vol 2. Statistical analysis* (pp. 701–717). New York, NY: Oxford University Press.

Card, N. A., Stucky, B. D., Sawalani, G. M., & Little, T. D. (2008). Direct and indirect aggression during childhood and adolescence: A meta-analytic review of gender differences, intercorrelations, and relations to maladjustment. *Child Development, 79*(5), 1185–1229.

Cárdaba, M. A., Briñol, P., Horcajo, J., & Petty, R. E. (2013). The effect of need for cognition on the stability of prejudiced attitudes toward South American immigrants. *Psicothema, 25*(1), 73–78.

Carey, K. B, Borsari, B., Carey, M. P., & Maisto, S. A. (2006). Patterns and importance of self-other differences in college drinking norms. *Psychology of Addictive Behaviors, 20*(4), 385–393.

Carli, L. L. (1999). Cognitive reconstruction, hindsight, and reactions to victims and perpetrators. *Personality and Social Psychology Bulletin, 25*(8), 966–979.

Carli, L. L., Alawa, L., Lee, Y., Zhao, B., & Kim, E. (2016). Stereotypes about gender and science: Women ≠ Scientists. *Psychology of Women Quarterly, 40*(2), 244–260.

Carli, L. L., LaFleur, S. J., & Loeber, C. C. (1995). Nonverbal behavior, gender, and influence. *Journal of Personality and Social Psychology, 68*(6), 1030–1041.

Carlsmith, J. M., & Anderson, C. A. (1979). Ambient temperature and the occurrence of collective violence: A new analysis. *Journal of Personality and Social Psychology, 37*(3), 337–344.

Carlson, M., Charlin, V., & Miller, N. (1988). Positive mood and helping behavior: A test of six hypotheses. *Journal of Personality and Social Psychology, 55*(2), 211–299.

Carlson, M., & Miller, N. (1987). Explanation of the relation between negative mood and helping. *Psychological Bulletin, 102*(1), 91–108.

Carnagey, N. L., Anderson, C. A., & Bushman, B. J. (2007). The effect of video game violence on physiological desensitization to real-life violence. *Journal of Experimental Social Psychology, 43*(3), 489–496.

Carpenter, C. J., & Pascual, A. (2016). Testing the reactance vs. the reciprocity of politeness explanations for the effectiveness of the "but you are free" compliance-gaining techniques. *Social Influence, 11*(2), 101–110.

Carter, C. S. (2014). Oxytocin pathways and the evolution of human behavior. *Annual Review of Psychology, 65*, 17–39.

Carter, E. C., Kofler, L. M., Forster, D. E., & McCullough, M. E. (2015). A series of meta-analytic tests of the depletion effect: Self-control does not seem to rely on a limited resource. *Journal of Experimental Psychology: General, 144*(4), 796–815.

Carter, P. L. (2003). "Black" cultural capital, status positioning, and schooling conflicts for low-income African American youth. *Social Problems, 50*(1), 136–155.

Cartwright, D. (1971). Risk taking by individuals and groups: An assessment of research employing choice dilemmas. *Journal of Personality and Social Psychology, 20*(3), 245–261.

Caruso, E. M., Epley, N., & Bazerman, M. H. (2004). *Leader of the packed: The costs and benefits of perspective taking in group endeavors.* Unpublished manuscript, Harvard University.

Carvallo, M., & Gabriel, S. (2006). No man is an island: The need to belong and dismissing avoidant attachment style. *Personality and Social Psychology Bulletin, 32*(5), 697–709.

Cascio, J. L., & Plant, A. (2016). Judged by the company you keep? Exposure to nonprejudiced norms reduces concerns about being misidentified as gay/lesbian. *Personality and Social Psychology Bulletin, 42*(9), 1164–1176.

Case, K. A., Fishbein, H. D., Ritchey, P. N. (2008). Personality, prejudice and discrimination against women and homosexuals. *Current Research in Social Psychology, 14*, article ID 2.

Casey, B. J., Somerville, L. H., Gotlib, I. H., Ayduk, O., Franklin, N. T., Askren, M. K.,. . .Shoda, Y. (2011). Behavioral and neural correlates of delay of gratification 40 years later. *Proceedings of the National Academy of Sciences, 108*(36), 14998–15003.

Casey, R. J., & Ritter, J. M. (1996). How infant appearance informs: Child care providers' responses to babies varying in appearance of age and attractiveness. *Journal of Applied Developmental Psychology, 17*(4), 495–518.

Cast, A. D., Schweingruber, D., & Berns, N. (2006). Childhood physical punishment and problem solving in marriage. *Journal of Interpersonal Violence, 21*(2), 244–261.

Castelli, L., & Carraro, L. (2010). Striving for difference: On the spontaneous preference for ingroup members who maximize ingroup positive distinctiveness. *European Journal of Social Psychology, 40*(6), 881–890.

Castelli, L., Tomelleri, S., & Zogmaister, C. (2008). Implicit ingroup metafavoritism: Subtle preference for ingroup members displaying ingroup bias. *Personality and Social Psychology Bulletin, 34*(6), 807–818.

Castro, V. S. (2003). *Acculturation and psychological adaptation.* Westport, CT: Greenwood Press.

Catalano, R., Dooley, D., Novaco, R. W., Wilson, G., & Hough, R. (1993). Using ECA survey data to examine the effect of job layoffs on violent behavior. *Hospital and Community Psychiatry, 44*(9), 874–879.

Cesario, J., Plaks, J. E., & Higgins, E. T. (2006). Automatic social behavior as motivated preparation to interact. *Journal of Personality and Social Psychology, 90*(6), 893–910.

Chaiken, S. (1979). Communicator physical attractiveness and persuasion. *Journal of Personality and Social Psychology, 37*(8), 1387–1397.

Chaiken, S. (1980). Heuristic versus systematic information processing and the use of source versus message cues in persuasion. *Journal of Personality and Social Psychology, 39*(5), 752–766.

Chaiken, S., & Baldwin, M. W. (1981). Affective-cognitive consistency and the effect of salient behavioral information on the self-perception of attitudes. *Journal of Personality and Social Psychology, 41*(1), 1–12.

Chaiken, S., & Trope, Y. (Eds.) (1999). *Dual-process theories in social psychology.* New York, NY: Guilford Press.

Chambon, M., Droit-Volet, S., & Niedenthal, P. M. (2008). The effect of embodying the elderly on time perception. *Journal of Experimental Social Psychology, 44*(3), 672–678.

Chan, M.-p. S., Jones, C. R., Jamieson, K. H., & Albarracin, D. (2017). Debunking: A meta-analysis of the psychological efficacy of messages countering misinformation. *Psychological Science, 28*(11), 1531–1546.

Chaney, K. E., & Sanchez, D. T. (2018). The endurance of interpersonal confrontations as a prejudice reduction strategy. *Personality and Social Psychology Bulletin, 44*(3), 418–429.

Chang, L., Hau, K. -T., & Guo, A. M. (2001). The effect of self-consciousness on the expression of gender views. *Journal of Applied Social Psychology, 31*(2), 340–351.

Chapdelaine, A., Kenny, D. A., & LaFontana, K. M. (1994). Matchmaker, matchmaker, can you make me a match? Predicting liking between two unacquainted persons. *Journal of Personality and Social Psychology, 67*(1), 83–91.

Chapleau, K. M., & Oswald, D. L. (2010). Power-sex association: Two paths to sexual aggression. *Journal of Sex Research, 47,* 66–78.

Chapleau, K. M., & Oswald, D. L. (2014). A system justification view of sexual violence: Legitimizing gender inequality and reduced moral outrage are connected to greater rape myth acceptance. *Journal of Trauma & Dissociation, 15*(2), 204–218.

Chapleau, K. M., Oswald, D. L., & Russell, B. L. (2007). How ambivalent sexism toward women and men supports rape myth acceptance. *Sex Roles, 57*(1–2), 131–136.

Chapman, J. (2006). Anxiety and defective decision making: An elaboration of the groupthink model. *Management Decision, 44*(10), 1391–1404.

Chappell, B. (2017, February 6). Nearly 100 tech firms ask federal court to block Trump's travel ban. *National Public Radio.* Retrieved from https://www.npr.org/sections/thetwo-way/2017/02/06/513703440/nearly-100-tech-firms-ask-federal-court-to-block-trumps-travel-ban

Chappell, K. D., & Davis, K. E., (1998). Attachment, partner choice, and perception of romantic partners: An experimental test of the attachment-security hypothesis. *Personal Relationships, 5*(3), 327–342.

Chartrand, T. L., & Bargh, J. A. (1999). The chameleon effect: The perception-behavior link and social interaction. *Journal of Personality and Social Psychology, 76*(6), 893–910.

Chartrand, T. L., & Lakin, J. L. (2013). The antecedents and consequences of human behavioral mimicry. *Annual Review of Psychology, 64,* 285–308.

Chartrand, T. L., Maddux, W. W. & Lakin, J. L. (2005). Beyond the perception-behavior link: The ubiquitous utility and motivational moderators of nonconscious mimicry. In R. R. Hassin, J. S. Uleman, & J. A. Bargh (Eds.). (2005). *The new unconscious* (pp. 334–361). New York, NY: Oxford University Press.

Chartrand, T., Pinckert, S., & Burger, J. M. (1999). When manipulation backfires: The effects of time delay and requester on the foot-in-the-door technique. *Journal of Applied Social Psychology, 29*(1), 211–221.

Chatzisarantis, N. L., & Hagger, M. S. (2007). Mindfulness and the intention-behavior relationship within the theory of planned behavior. *Personality and Social Psychology Bulletin, 33*(5), 663–676.

Chen, C. -K., Gustafson, D. H., & Lee, Y. -D. (2002). The effect of a quantitative decision aid—Analytic Hierarchy Process—on group polarization. *Group Decision and Negotiation, 11*(4), 329–344.

Chen, F. F., & Jing, Y. (2012). The impact of individualistic and collectivistic orientation on the judgment of self-presentation. *European Journal of Social Psychology, 42*(4), 470–481.

Chen, G. (1995). Differences in self-disclosure patterns among Americans versus Chinese. *Journal of Cross-Cultural Psychology, 26*(1), 84–91.

Chen, H. -J., Yates, B. T., & McGinnies, E. (1988). Effects of involvement on observers' estimates of consensus, distinctiveness, and consistency. *Personality and Social Psychology Bulletin, 14*(3), 468–478.

Chen, N. Y., Shaffer, D. R., & Wu, C. (1997). On physical attractiveness stereotyping in Taiwan: A revised sociocultural perspective. *Journal of Social Psychology, 137*(1), 117–124.

Chen, S., Boucher, H. C., & Tapias, M. P. (2006). The relational self revealed: Integrative conceptualization and implications for interpersonal life. *Psychological Bulletin, 132*(2), 151–179.

Chen, S. C. (1937). Social modification of the activity of ants in nest-building. *Physiological Zoology, 10*(4), 420–436.

Chen, X. P., Wasti, S. A., & Triandis, H. C. (2007). When does group norm or group identity predict cooperation in a public goods dilemma? The moderating effects of idiocentrism and allocentrism. *International Journal of Intercultural Relations, 31*(2), 259–276.

Chen, Y., Wang, Q., & Xie, J. (2011). Online social interactions: A natural experiment on word of mouth versus observational learning. *Journal of Marketing Research, 48*(2), 238–254.

Cheryan, S., Siy, J. O., Vichayapai, M., Drury, B. J., & Kim, S. (2011). Do female and male role models who embody STEM stereotypes hinder women's anticipated success in STEM? *Social Psychological and Personality Science, 2*(6), 656–664.

Cheung, B. Y., Chudek, M., & Heine, S. J. (2011). Evidence for a sensitive period for acculturation: Younger immigrants report acculturating at a faster rate. *Psychological Science, 22*(2), 147–152.

Cheung, H. K., Hebl, M., King, E. B., Markell, H., Moreno, C., & Nittrouer, C. (2017). Back to the future: Methodologies that capture real people in the real world. *Social Psychological and Personality Science, 8*(5), 564–572.

Chiou, W. B. (2006). Adolescents' sexual self-disclosure on the Internet: Deindividuation and impression management. *Adolescence, 41*(163), 547–561.

Chiroro, P., Bohner, G., Viki, G. T., & Jarvis, C. I. (2004). Rape myth acceptance and rape proclivity: Expected dominance versus expected arousal as mediators in acquaintance-rape situations. *Journal of Interpersonal Violence, 19*(4), 427–442.

Chiu, C. –y. & Hong, Y. –y. (2005). Cultural competence: Dynamic processes. In A. Elliot & C. S. Dweck (eds.), *Handbook of competence and motivation* (pp. 489–505). New York, NY: Guilford Press.

Chiu, C. Morris, M. W., Hong, Y., & Menon, T. (2000). Motivated cultural cognition: The impact of implicit cultural theories on disposition attribution varies as a function of need for closure. *Journal of Personality and Social Psychology, 78*(2), 247–259.

Choi, I., & Nisbett, R. E. (2000). Cultural psychology of surprise: Holistic theories and recognition of contradiction. *Journal of Personality and Social Psychology, 79*(6), 890–905.

Choi, I., Nisbett, R. E., & Norenzayan, A. (1999). Causal attribution across cultures: Variation and universality. *Psychological Bulletin, 125*(1), 47–63.

Christ, O., Hewstone, M., Tausch, N., Wagner, U., Voci, A., Hughes, J., & Cairns, E. (2010). Direct contact as a moderator of extended contact effects: Cross-sectional and longitudinal impact on outgroup attitudes, behavioral intentions, and attitude certainty. *Personality and Social Psychology Bulletin, 36*(12), 1662–1674.

Christensen, L. (1988). Deception in psychological research: When is its use justified? *Personality and Social Psychology Bulletin, 14*, 664–675.

Christensen, P. N., & Kashy, D. A. (1998). Perceptions of and by lonely people in initial social interaction. *Personality and Social Psychology Bulletin, 24*(3), 322–329.

Christensen, P. N., Rothberger, H., Wood, W., & Matz, D. C. (2004). Social norms and identity relevance: A motivational approach to normative behavior. *Personality and Social Psychology Bulletin, 30*(10), 1295–1309.

Christopher, A. N., Morgan, R. D., Marek, P., Keller, M., & Drummond, K. (2005). Materialism and self-presentational styles. *Personality and Individual Differences, 38*(1), 137–149.

Chua, H. F., Leu, J., & Nisbett, R. E. (2005). Culture and diverging views of social events. *Personality and Social Psychology Bulletin, 31*(7), 925–934.

Cialdini, R. B., Borden, R. J., Thorne, A., Walker, M. R., Freeman, S., & Sloan, L. R. (1976). Basking in reflected glory: Three (football) field studies. *Journal of Personality and Social Psychology, 34*(3), 366–375.

Cialdini, R. B., Braver, S. L., & Lewis, S. K. (1974). Attributional bias and the easily persuaded other. *Journal of Personality and Social Psychology, 30*(5), 631–637.

Cialdini, R. B., Cacioppo, J. T., Bassett, R., & Miller, J. A. (1978). Low-ball procedure for producing compliance: Commitment then cost. *Journal of Personality and Social Psychology, 36*(5), 463–476.

Cialdini, R. B., & Kenrick, D. T. (1976). Altruism as hedonism: A social development perspective on the relationship of negative mood state and helping. *Journal of Personality and Social Psychology, 34*(5), 907–914.

Cialdini, R. B., & Trost, M. R. (1998). Social influence: Social norms, conformity, and compliance. In D. T. Gilbert, S. T. Fiske, & G. Lindzey (Eds.), *The handbook of social psychology* (4th ed., Vol. 2, pp. 151–192). New York, NY: McGraw-Hill.

Cialdini, R. B., Trost, M., & Newsom, J. (1995). Preference for consistency: The development of a valid measure and the discovery of surprising behavioral implications. *Journal of Personality and Social Psychology, 69*(2), 318–328.

Cialdini, R. B., Vincent, J. E., Lewis, S. K., Catalan, J., Wheeler, D., & Darby, B. L. (1975). Reciprocal concessions procedure for inducing compliance: The door-in-the-face technique. *Journal of Personality and Social Psychology, 31*(2), 206–215.

Ciarocco, N. J., Sommer, K. L., & Baumeister, R. F. (2001). Ostracism and ego depletion: The strains of silence. *Personality and Social Psychology Bulletin, 27*(9), 1156–1163.

Clark, E. M., Fernandez, P., Harris, A. L., Hasan, M., & Votaw, K. B. (2017). The aftermath: Friendship after romantic relationship termination. In M. Hojjat & A. Moyer (Eds.), *The psychology of friendship* (pp. 177–194). New York, NY: Oxford University Press.

Clark, E. M., Harris, A. L., Hasan, M., Votaw, K. B., & Fernandez, P. (2015). Concluding thoughts: Interethnic marriage through the lens of interdependence theory. *Journal of Social Issues, 71*(4), 821–833.

Clark, K. B., & Clark, M. K. (1939). The development of self and the emergence of racial identifications in Negro preschool children. *Journal of Social Psychology, 10*, 591–599.

Clark, M. S., & Mills, J. (2012). A theory of communal (and exchange) relationships. In P. M. Van Lange, A. W. Kruglanski, & E. Higgins (Eds.)., *Handbook of theories of social psychology* (Vol. 2, pp. 232–250). Thousand Oaks, CA: Sage.

Clark, R. D., III, & Word, L. E. (1972). Why don't bystanders help? Because of ambiguity? *Journal of Personality and Social Psychology, 24*(3), 392–400.

Clore, G. L., & Baldridge, B. (1968). Interpersonal attraction: The role of agreement and topic interest. *Journal of Personality and Social Psychology, 9*(4), 340–346.

Clutton-Brock, T. H., & Huchard, E. (2013). Review article: Social competition and selection in males and females. *Philosophical Transactions of the Royal Society, 368*(1631).

Clyman, J. A., & Pachankis, J. E. (2014). The relationship between objectively coded explanatory style and mental health in the stigma-related narratives of young gay men. *Psychology of Men & Masculinity, 15*(1), 110–115.

Cohen, D. (1996). Law, social policy, and violence: The impact of regional cultures. *Journal of Personality and Social Psychology, 70*(5), 961–978.

Cohen, D. (1998). Culture, social organization, and patterns of violence. *Journal of Personality and Social Psychology, 75*(2), 408–419.

Cohen, D., Hoshino-Browne, E., & Leung, A. K. (2007). Culture and the structure of personal experience: Insider and outsider phenomenologies of the self and social world. In M. P. Zanna (Ed.), *Advances in experimental social psychology* (Vol. 39, pp. 1–67). San Diego, CA: Elsevier Academic Press.

Cohen, D., & Nisbett, R. E. (1994). Self-protection and the culture of honor: Explaining southern violence. *Personality and Social Psychology Bulletin, 20*(5), 551–567.

Cohen, D., & Nisbett, R. E. (1997). Field experiments examining the culture of honor: The role of institutions in perpetuating norms about violence. *Personality and Social Psychology Bulletin, 23*(11), 1188–1199.

Cohen, D., Nisbett, R. E., Bowdle, B., & Schwarz, N. (1996). Insult, aggression, and the southern culture of honor: An "experimental ethnography." *Journal of Personality and Social Psychology, 70*(5), 945–960.

Cohen, D., & Vandello, J. A. (1998). Meanings of violence. *Journal of Legal Studies, 27*(52), 501–518.

Cohen, D., Vandello, J. A., & Rantilla, A. K. (1998). The sacred and the social: Cultures of honor and violence. In P. Gilbert & B. Andrews (Eds.), *Shame: Interpersonal behavior, psychopathology, and culture* (pp. 261–282). Oxford, England: Oxford University Press.

Cohen, R. L., & Alwin, D. F. (1993). Bennington women of the 1930s: Political attitudes over the life course. In K. D. Hulberet, & D. T. Schuster (Eds.), *Women's lives through time: Educated American women of the twentieth century* (pp. 117–139). San Francisco, CA: Jossey-Bass.

Cohen, T. R., Montoya, R. M., & Insko, C. A. (2006). Group morality and intergroup relations: Cross-cultural and experimental evidence. *Personality and Social Psychology Bulletin, 32*(11), 1559–1572.

Cohn, N. (2014, June 12). Polarization is dividing American society, not just politics. *The New York Times*. Retrieved from https://www.nytimes.com/2014/06/12/upshot/polarization-is-dividing-american-society-not-just-politics.html

Collins, B. E., & Brief, D. E. (1995). Using person-perception vignette methodologies to uncover the symbolic meanings of teacher behaviors in the Milgram paradigm. *Journal of Social Issues, 51*(3), 89–106.

Collins, N. L., & Miller, L. C. (1994). Self-disclosure and liking: A meta-analytic review. *Psychological Bulletin, 116*(3), 457–475.

Colvin, G. (2014, April 7). Bill Clinton on leadership. *Fortune*, 66. Retrieved from https://fortune.com/2014/03/20/bill-clinton-on-leadership/

Comer, D. R. (1995). A model of social loafing in real work groups. *Human Relations, 48*(6), 647–667.

Commisso, M., & Finkelstein, L. (2012). Physical attractiveness bias in employee termination. *Journal of Applied Social Psychology, 42*(12), 2968–2987.

Comte, I. A. (1875). *Systems of positive polity* (Vol. 1). London, England: Longmans, Green. (First published 1851.)

Conger, A. J., Dygdon, J. A., & Rollock, D. (2012). Conditioned emotional responses in racial prejudice. *Ethnic and Racial Studies, 35*(2), 298–319.

Conger, J. A., Kanungo, R. N., & Menon, S. T. (2000). Charismatic leadership and follower effects. *Journal of Organizational Behavior, 21*(7), 747–767.

Conrath, D. W. (1973). Communication patterns, organizational structure, and man: Some relationships. *Human Factors, 15*(5), 459–470.

Conway, L. G., III, Houck, S. C., & Gornick, L. J. (2014). Regional differences in individualism and why they matter. In P. J. Rentfrow (Ed.), *Geographical psychology: Exploring the interaction of environment and behavior* (pp. 31–50). Washington, DC: American Psychological Association.

Conway, L. G., III, Ryder, A. G., Tweed, R. G., & Sokol, B. W. (2001). Intranational cultural variation: Exploring further implications of collectivism within the United States. *Journal of Cross-Cultural Psychology, 32*(6), 681–697.

Conway, M., & Dubé, L. (2002). Humor in persuasion on threatening topics: Effectiveness is a function of audience sex role orientation. *Personality & Social Psychology Bulletin, 28*(7), 863–873.

Cook, H. B. K. (1992). Matrifocality and female aggression in Margariteño society. In K. Björkqvist & P. Niemelä (Eds.), *Of mice and women: Aspects of female aggression* (pp. 149–162). San Diego, CA: Harcourt Brace Jovanovich.

Cook, J. E., Arrow, H., & Malle, B. F. (2011). The effect of feeling stereotyped on social power and inhibition. *Personality and Social Psychology Bulletin, 37*(2), 165–180.

Cook, K. S., Cheshire, C., & Gerbasi, A. (2006). Power, dependence, and social exchange. In P. Burke (Ed.), *Contemporary social psychological theories* (pp. 194–215). Stanford, CA: Stanford University Press.

Cook, S. W. (1964). Desegregation: A psychological analysis. In W. W. Charters, Jr., & N. L. Gage (Eds.), *Readings in the social psychology of education*. Boston, MA: Allyn & Bacon.

Cooley, C. H. (1902). *Human nature and the social order*. New York, NY: Charles Scribner's Sons.

Cooper, H. H. (2001). Terrorism: The problem of definition revisited. *American Behavioral Scientist, 44*(6), 881–893.

Cooper, J. (2007). *Cognitive dissonance: Fifty years of a classic theory*. Thousand Oaks, CA: Sage.

Cooper, J., Mirabile, R., & Scher, S. J. (2005). Actions and attitudes: The theory of cognitive dissonance. In T. C. Brock & M. C. Green (Eds.). *Persuasion: Psychological insights and perspectives* (2nd ed., pp. 63–79). Thousand Oaks, CA: Sage.

Corby, N. H., Jamner, M. S., & Wolitski, R. J. (1996). Using the theory of planned behavior to predict intention to use condoms among male and female injecting drug users. *Journal of Applied Social Psychology, 26*(1), 52–75.

Cordero, E. D. (2011). Self-esteem, social support, collectivism, and the thin-ideal in Latina undergraduates. *Body Image, 8*(1), 82–85.

Correll, J., Park, B., Judd, C. M., & Wittenbrink, B. (2002). The police officer's dilemma: Using ethnicity to disambiguate potentially threatening individuals. *Journal of Personality and Social Psychology, 83*(6), 1314–1329.

Correll, J., Park, B., Judd, C. M., Wittenbrink, B., Sadler, M. S., & Keesee, T. (2007). Across the thin blue line: Police officers and racial bias in the decision to shoot. *Journal of Personality and Social Psychology, 92*(6), 1006–1023.

Correll, S. J., & Ridgeway, C. L. (2003). Expectation states theory. In J. Delamater (Ed.), *Handbook of social psychology and social research* (pp. 29–51). New York, NY: Kluwer Academic/Plenum.

Costello, K., & Hodson, G. (2011). Social dominance-based threat reactions to immigrants in need of assistance. *European Journal of Social Psychology, 41*(2), 220–231.

Cottrell, C. A., & Neuberg, S. L. (2005). Different emotional reactions to different groups: A sociofunctional threat-based approach to "prejudice." *Journal of Personality and Social Psychology, 88*(5), 770–789.

Cottrell, N. B., Wack, D. L., Sekerak, G. J., & Rittle, R. H. (1968). Social facilitation of dominant responses by the presence of an audience and the mere presence of others. *Journal of Personality and Social Psychology, 9*(3), 245–250.

Cowan, P. A., & Walters, R. H. (1963). Studies of reinforcement of aggression: I. Effects of scheduling. *Child Development, 34*(3), 543–551.

Crandall, C. S. (1995). Do parents discriminate against their heavyweight daughters? *Personality and Social Psychology Bulletin, 21*(7), 724–735.

Crandall, C. S., D'Anello, S., Sakalli, N., Lazarus, E., Wieczorkowska, G., & Feather, N. T. (2001). An attribution-value model of prejudice: Anti-fat attitudes in six nations. *Personality and Social Psychology Bulletin, 27*(1), 30–37.

Crandall, C. S., & Eshleman, A. (2003). A justification-suppression model of the expression and experience of prejudice. *Psychological Bulletin, 129*(3), 414–446.

Crandall, C. S., Merman, A., & Hebl, M. (2009). Anti-fat prejudice. In T. D. Nelson (Ed.), *Handbook of prejudice, stereotyping, and discrimination* (pp. 469–487). New York, NY: Psychology Press.

Crandall, C. S., Miller, J. M., White, M. H., II. (2018). Changing norms following the 2016 U.S. presidential election: The Trump effect on prejudice. *Social Psychological and Personality Science, 9*(2), 186–192.

Crandall, C. S., & Sherman, J. W. (2016). On the scientific superiority of conceptual replications for scientific progress. *Journal of Experimental Social Psychology, 66*, 93–99.

Crawford, J. T., Brandt, M. J., Inbar, Y., & Malllinas, S. R. (2016). Right-wing authoritarianism predicts prejudice equally toward "gay men and lesbians" and "homosexuals." *Journal of Personality and Social Psychology, 111*(2), e31–e45.

Crawford, L. A., & Novak, K. B. (2013). The effects of public self-consciousness and embarrassability on college student drinking: Evidence in support of a protective self-presentational model. *The Journal of Social Psychology, 153*(1), 109–122.

Creasey, G., & Ladd, A. (2005). Generalized and specific attachment representations: Unique and interactive roles in predicting conflict behaviors in close relationships. *Personality and Social Psychology Bulletin, 31*(8), 1026–1038.

Crenshaw, M. (2000). The psychology of terrorism: An agenda for the 21st century. *Political Psychology, 21*(2), 405–420.

Crisp, R. J., Heuston, S., Farr, M. J., & Turner, R. N. (2007). Seeing red or feeling blue: differentiated emotions and ingroup identification in soccer fans. *Group Processes, Intergroup Relations, 10*(1), 9–26.

Crisp, R. J., Hewstone, M., & Rubin, M. (2001). Does multiple categorization reduce intergroup bias? *Personality and Social Psychology Bulletin, 27*(1), 76–89.

Crocker, J., & Canevello, A. (2012). Self and identity: Dynamics of persons and their situations. In K. Deaux & M. Snyder (Eds.), *The Oxford handbook of personality and social psychology* (pp. 263–286). New York, NY: Oxford University Press.

Crocker J., Luhtanen, R. K., Blaine, B., & Broadnax, S. (1994). Collective self-esteem and psychological well-being among White, Black, and Asian college students. *Psychology Bulletin, 20*(5), 503–513.

Crocker, J., & Park, L. E. (2004). The costly pursuit of self-esteem. *Psychological Bulletin, 130*(3), 392–414.

Croizet, J. -C., & Claire, T. (1998). Extending the concept of stereotype threat to social class: The intellectual underperformance of students from low socioeconomic backgrounds. *Personality and Social Psychology Bulletin, 24*(6), 588–594.

Cross, S. E., Bacon, P. L., & Morris, M. L. (2000). The relational-interdependent self-construal and relationships. *Journal of Personality and Social Psychology, 78*(4), 791–808.

Cross, S. E., & Gore, J. (2002). Cultural models of the self. In M. R. Leary & J. P. Tangney (Eds.), *Handbook of self and identity* (pp. 536–564). New York, NY: Guilford Press.

Cross, S. E., & Gore, J. S. (2004). The relational self-construal and the construction of closeness. In A. Aron & D. Mashek (Eds.), *The handbook of closeness and intimacy* (pp. 229–245). Mahwah, NJ : Lawrence Erlbaum Associates.

Cross, S. E., Hardin, E. E., & Gercek-Swing, B. (2011). The what, how, why, and where of self-construal. *Personality and Social Psychology Review, 15*(2), 142–179.

Cross, S. E., & Madson, L. (1997). Models of the self: Self-construals and gender. *Psychological Bulletin, 122*(1), 5–37.

Cross, S. E., & Morris, M. L. (2003). Getting to know you: The relational self-construal, relational cognition, and well-being. *Personality and Social Psychology Bulletin, 29*(4), 512–523.

Cross, S. E., Morris, M. L., & Gore, J. S. (2002). Thinking about oneself and others: The relational-interdependent self-construal and social cognition. *Journal of Personality and Social Psychology, 82*(3), 399–418.

Cross, W. E. (1991). *Shades of black: Diversity in African-American identity*. Philadelphia, PA: Temple University Press.

Crowley, A. E., & Hoyer, W. D. (1994). An integrative framework for understanding two-sided persuasion. *Journal of Consumer Research, 20*(4), 561–574.

Csikszentmihalyi, M. (1997). *Creativity: Flow and the psychology of discovery and invention*. New York, NY: Harper Perennial.

Culos-Reed, S. N., Brawley, L. R., Martin, K. A., & Leary, M. R. (2002). Self-presentation concerns and health behaviors among cosmetic surgery patients. *Journal of Applied Social Psychology, 32*(3), 560–569.

Cunningham, M. R. (1979). Weather, mood, and helping behavior: Quasi-experiments with the sunshine Samaritan. *Journal of Personality and Social Psychology, 37*(11), 1947–1956.

Cunningham, M. R. (1986). Measuring the physical in physical attractiveness: Quasi-experiments on the sociobiology of female facial beauty. *Journal of Personality and Social Psychology, 50*(5), 925–935.

Cunningham, M. R., Barbee, A. P., & Pike, C. L. (1990). What do women want? Facialmetric assessment of multiple motives in the perception of male physical attractiveness. *Journal of Personality and Social Psychology, 59*(1), 61–72.

Cunningham, M. R., Steinberg, J., & Grev, R. (1980). Wanting to and having to help: Separate motivation for positive mood and guilt-induced helping. *Journal of Personality and Social Psychology, 38*(2), 181–192.

Cunningham, P. B., Henggeler, S. W., Limber, S. P., Melton, G. B., & Nation, M. A. (2000). Patterns and correlates of gun ownership among nonmetropolitan and rural middle school students. *Journal of Clinical Child Psychology, 29*(3), 432–442.

Curran, J. P. (1977). Skills training as an approach to the treatment of heterosexual-social anxiety: A review. *Psychological Bulletin, 84*(1), 140–157.

Curry, O. S., Rowland, L. A., Van Lissa, C. J., Zlotowitz, S., McAlaney, J., & Whitehouse, H. (2018). Happy to help? A systematic review and meta-analysis of the effects of performing acts of kindness on the well-being of the actor. *Journal of Experimental Social Psychology, 76,* 320–329.

Curtis, R. C., & Miller, K. (1986). Believing another likes or dislikes you: Behaviors making the beliefs come true. *Journal of Personality and Social Psychology, 51*(2), 284–290.

Custers, R., & Aarts, H. (2007). Goal-discrepant situations prime goal-directed actions if goals are temporarily or chronically accessible. *Personality and Social Psychology Review, 33*(5), 623–633.

Cutrona, C. (1982). Transition to college: Loneliness and the process of social adjustment. In L. A. Peplau & D. Perlman (Eds.), *Loneliness: A sourcebook of current theory, research and therapy* (pp. 291–309). New York, NY: Wiley Interscience.

Czopp, A. M., & Monteith, M. J. (2003). Confronting prejudice (literally): Reactions to confrontations of racial and gender bias. *Personality and Social Psychology Bulletin, 29*(4), 532–544.

Czopp, A. M., Monteith, M. J., & Mark, A. Y. (2006). Standing up for a change: Reducing bias through interpersonal confrontation. *Journal of Personality and Social Psychology, 90*(5), 784–803.

D

Dakof, G. A., & Taylor, S. E. (1990). Victims' perceptions of social support: What is helpful from whom? *Journal of Personality and Social Psychology, 58*(1), 80–89.

Dalakas, V., Madrigal, R., & Anderson, K. L. (2004). "We are number one!" The phenomenon of basking-in-reflected-glory and its implications for sports marketing. In L. R. Kahle, & C. Riley (Eds.), *Sports marketing and the psychology of marketing communication* (pp. 67–79). Mahwah, NJ: Lawrence Erlbaum Associates.

Dal Cin, S., Gibson, B., Zanna, M. P., Shumate, R. & Fong, G. T. (2007). Smoking in movies, implicit associations of smoking with the self, and intentions to smoke. *Psychological Science, 18*(7), 559–563.

Dalton, M. A., Sargent, J. D., Dalton, M. A., Sargent, J. D., Beach, M. L., Titus-Ernstoff, L.,. . .Heatherton, T. F. (2003). Effect of viewing smoking in movies on adolescent smoking initiation: A cohort study. *The Lancet, 362*(9380), 281–285.

Daly, J. A., Caughlin, J. P., & Stafford, L. (1997). Correlates and consequences of social-communicative anxiety. In J. A. Daly, J. C. McCroskey, J. Ayres, T. Hopf, & D. M. Ayres (Eds.), *Avoiding communication: Shyness, reticence, and communication apprehension* (2nd ed., pp. 21–71). Creskill, NJ: Hampton Press.

Daly, M., & Wilson, M. (1988). *Homicide.* New York, NY: Aldine De Gruyer.

Daly, M., & Wilson, M. I. (1996). Violence against stepchildren. *Current Directions in Psychological Science, 5*(3), 77–81.

Damasio, A. R., & Anderson, S. W. (2003). The frontal lobes. In K. M. Heilman and E. Valenstein (Eds.), *Clinical neuropsychology,* (4th ed., pp. 404–446). New York, NY: Oxford University Press.

Dambrun, M., Guimond, S., & Duarte, S. (2002). The impact of hierarchy-enhancing vs. attenuating academic major on stereotyping: The mediating role of perceived social norm. *Current Research in Social Psychology, 7*(8), 114–136.

Dambrun, M., & Vatiné, E. (2010). Reopening the study of extreme social behaviors: Obedience to authority within an immersive video environment. *European Journal of Social Psychology, 40*(5), 760–773.

Dandurand, C., & Lafontaine, M. F. (2014). Jealousy and couple satisfaction: A romantic attachment perspective. *Marriage & Family Review, 50*(2), 154–173.

D'Angelo, J. D., & Toma, C. L. (2017). There are plenty of fish in the sea: The effects of choice overload and reversibility on online daters' satisfaction with selected partners. *Media Psychology, 20*(1), 1–27.

Darke, P. R., & Chaiken, S. (2005). The pursuit of self-interest: Self-interest bias in attitude judgment and persuasion. *Journal of Personality and Social Psychology, 89*(6), 864–883.

Darley, J. M. (1995). Constructive and destructive obedience: A taxonomy of principal-agent relationships. *Journal of Social Issues, 51*(3), 125–154.

Darley, J. M. (2001). Citizens' sense of justice and the legal system. *Current Directions in Psychological Science, 10*(1), 10–13.

Darley, J. M., & Latané, B. (1968). Bystander intervention in emergencies: Diffusion of responsibility. *Journal of Personality and Social Psychology, 8*(4), 377–383.

Darwin, C. (1859). *On the origin of species by natural selection.* London, England: John Murray.

Darwin, C. (1871). *The descent of man.* London, England: John Murray.

Darwin, C. (1872). *Expression of emotion in man and animals.* London, England: John Murray.

Daryl, C. C., & Keith, P. B. (2011). Escaping affect: How motivated emotion regulation creates insensitivity to mass suffering. *Journal of Personality and Social Psychology, 100*(1), 1–15.

Das, E. H., de Wit, J. B., & Stroebe, W. (2003). Fear appeals motivate acceptance of action recommendations: Evidence for a positive bias in the processing of persuasive messages. *Personality and Social Psychology Bulletin, 29*(5), 650–664.

Dasgupta, N., & Greenwald, A. G. (2001). On the malleability of automatic attitudes: Combating automatic prejudice with images of admired and disliked individuals. *Journal of Personality and Social Psychology, 81*(5), 800–814.

David, E. J., Okazaki, S., & Giroux, D. (2014). A set of guiding principles to advance multicultural psychology and its major concepts. In F. T. Leong, L. Comas-Diaz, G. C. Nagayama Hall, V. C. McLoyd, & J. E. Trimble (Eds.), *APA handbook of multicultural psychology, Vol. 1: Theory and research* (pp. 85–104). Washington, DC: American Psychological Association.

Davies, M. F. (1994). Private self-consciousness and the perceived accuracy of true and false personality feedback. *Personality and Individual Differences, 17*(5), 697–701.

Davies, M., & McCartney, S. (2003). Effects of gender and sexuality on judgements of victim blame and rape myth acceptance in a depicted male rape. *Journal of Community and Applied Social Psychology, 13*(5), 391–398.

Davies, P. G., Spencer, S. J., & Steele, C. M. (2005). Clearing the air: Identity safety moderates the effects of stereotype threat on women's leadership aspirations. *Journal of Personality and Social Psychology, 88*(2), 276–287.

Davis, C. G., Lehman, D. R., Silver, R. C., Wortman, C. B., & Ellard, J. H. (1996). Self-blame following a traumatic life event: The role of perceived avoidability. *Personality and Social Psychology Bulletin, 22*(6), 557–567.

Davis, C. G., Lehman, D. R., Wortman, C. B., Silver, R. C., & Thompson, S. C. (1995). The undoing of traumatic life events. *Personality and Social Psychology Bulletin, 21*(2), 109–124.

Davis, C. M., & Bauserman, R. (1993). Exposure to sexually explicit materials: An attitude change perspective. In J. Bancroft (Ed.), *Annual Review of Sex Research* (Vol. 4, pp. 121–209). Mt. Vernon, IA: Society for the Scientific Study of Sex.

Davis, D., Shaver, P. R., & Vernon, M. L. (2004). Attachment style and subjective motivations for sex. *Personality and Social Psychology Bulletin, 30*(8), 1076–1090.

Davis, J. H., Au, T., Hulbert, L., Chen, X. -p., & Zarnoth, P. (1997). Effects of group size and procedural influence on consensual judgments of quantity: The example of damage awards and mock civil juries. *Journal of Personality and Social Psychology, 73*(4), 703–718.

Davis, M. H. (1980). A multidimensional approach to individual differences in empathy. *Psychological Documents, 10*, 85.

Davis, M. H. (1983). Empathic concern and the muscular dystrophy telethon: Empathy as a multidimensional construct. *Personality and Social Psychology Bulletin, 9*(2), 223–229.

Davis, M. H. (1996). Interpersonal reactivity index. In M. H. Davis, *Empathy: A social psychological approach* (table 3.1), Boulder, CO: Westview Press.

Davis, M. H., & Franzoi, S. L. (1991). Stability and change in adolescent self-consciousness and empathy. *Journal of Research in Personality, 25*(1), 70–87.

Davis, M. H., Luce, C., & Kraus, S. J. (1994). The heritability of characteristics associated with dispositional empathy. *Journal of Personality, 62*(3), 369–391.

Davis, M. H., Soderlund, T., Cole, J., Gadol, E., Kute, M., Myers, M., & Weihing, J. (2004). Cognitions associated with attempts to empathize: How do we imagine the perspective of another? *Personality and Social Psychology Bulletin, 30*(12), 1625–1635.

Davis, T. L. (1995). Gender differences in masking negative emotions: Ability or motivation? *Developmental Psychology, 31*(4), 660–667.

Dawson, E., Gilovich, T., & Regan, D. T. (2002). Motivated reasoning and performance on the Wason Selection Task. *Personality and Social Psychology Bulletin, 28*(10), 1379–1387.

Dean, K. E., & Malamuth, N. M. (1997). Characteristics of men who aggress sexually and of men who imagine aggressing: Risk and moderating variables. *Journal of Personality and Social Psychology, 72*(2), 449–455.

Deaux, K. (1996). Social identification. In E. T. Higgins & A. W. Kruglanski (Eds.), *Social psychology: Handbook of basic principles* (pp. 777–798). New York, NY: Guilford Press.

de Bruijn, G. J., Kremers, S. P., De Vet, E., De Nooijer, J., Van Mechelen, W., & Brug, J. (2007). Does habit strength moderate the intention-behaviour relationship in the theory of planned behaviour? The case of fruit consumption. *Psychology & Health, 22*(8), 899–916.

De Cecco, J. P. (Ed.). (1988). *Gay relationships*. Binghamton, NY: The Haworth Press.

Decety, J. (2011). Promises and challenges of the neurobiological approach to empathy. *Emotion Review, 3*(1), 115–116.

Dechêne, A., Stahl, C., Hansen J., & Wänke, M. (2009). Mix me a list: Context moderates the truth effect and the mere-exposure effect. *Journal of Experimental Social Psychology, 45*(5), 1117–1122.

DeHart, T., Pena, R., & Tennen, H. (2013). The development of explicit and implicit self-esteem and their role in psychological adjustment. In V. Zeigler-Hill (Ed.), *Current issues in social psychology: Self-esteem* (pp. 99–123). New York, NY: Psychology Press.

de Hoog, N., Stroebe, W., & de Wit, J. B. (2007). The impact of vulnerability to and severity of a health risk on processing and acceptance of fear-arousing communications: A meta-analysis. *Review of General Psychology, 11*(3), 258–285.

de Kwaadsteniet, E. W., van Dijk, E., Wit, A., & De Cremer, D. (2010). Anger and retribution after collective overuse: The role of blaming and environmental uncertainty in social dilemmas. *Personality and Social Psychology Bulletin, 36*(1), 59–70.

Demetriou, C., & Silke, A. (2003). A criminological Internet "sting": Experimental evidence of illegal and deviant visits to a website trap. *British Journal of Criminology, 43*(1), 213–222.

de Miguel, M., Sanchez, I. L., & Luis M. (2011). Origins and development of American psychosocial research applied during Second World War. *Revista de Historia de la Psicologia, 32*(2–3), 69–84.

Demoulin, S., Rodriguez, R. T., Rodriguez, A. P., Vaes, J., Paladino, M. P., Gaunt, R.,...Leyens, J.-P. (2004). Emotional prejudice can lead to infra-humanization. In W. Stroebe & M. Hewstone (Eds.), *European Review of Social Psychology* (Vol. 15, pp. 259–296). Chichester, England: Wiley.

De Munck, V. C., Korotayev, A., de Munck, J., & Khaltourina, D. (2011). Cross-cultural analysis of models of romantic love among U.S. residents, Russians, and Lithuanians. *Cross-Cultural Research, 45*(2), 128–154.

Denny, D., & Pittman, C. (2007). Gender identity: From dualism to diversity. In M. S. Tepper & A. F. Owens (Eds.), *Sexual Health, Vol 1: Psychological Foundations* (pp. 205–229). Westport, CT: Praeger.

Denson, T. F., Pedersen, W. C., Friese, M., Hahm, A., & Roberts, L. (2011). Understanding impulsive aggression: Angry rumination and reduced self-control capacity are mechanisms underlying the provocation-aggression relationship. *Personality and Social Psychology Bulletin, 37*(6), 850–862.

DePaulo, B. M., Lindsay, J. J., Malone, B. E., Muhlenbruck, L., Charlton, K., & Cooper, H. (2003). Cues to deception. *Psychological Bulletin, 129*(1), 74–118.

DePaulo, B. M., & Morris, W. L. (2004). Discerning lies from truths: Behavioural cues to deception and the indirect pathway of intuition. In P. -A. Granhag & L. Strömwall (Eds.), *The detection of deception in forensic contexts* (pp. 15–40). New York, NY: Cambridge University Press.

Depue, R. A., & Collins, P. F. (1999). Neurobiology of the structure of personality: Dopamine, facilitation of incentive motivation, and extraversion. *Behavioral and Brain Sciences, 22*(3), 491–569.

de Ridder, D. T., Lensvelt-Mulders, G., Finkenauer, C., Stok, F. M., & Baumeister, R. F. (2012). Taking stock of self-control: A meta-analysis of how trait self-control relates to a wide range of behaviors. *Personality and Social Psychology Review, 16*(1), 76–99.

Derlega, V. J., Anderson, S., Winstead, B. A., & Greene, K. (2011). Positive disclosure among college students: What do they talk about, to whom, and why? *The Journal of Positive Psychology, 6*(2), 119–130.

Derlega, V. J., Catanzaro, D., & Lewis, R. J. (2001). Perceptions about tactile intimacy in same-sex and opposite-sex pairs based on research participants' sexual orientation. *Psychology of Men and Masculinity, 2*(2), 124–132.

Derlega, V. J., Lewis, R. J., Harrison, S., Winstead, B. A., & Costanza, R. (1989). Gender differences in the initiation and attribution of tactile intimacy. *Journal of Nonverbal Behavior, 13*(2), 83–96.

Desforges, D. M., Lord, C. G., Pugh, M. A., Sia, T. L., Scarberry, N. C., & Ratcliff, C. D. (1997). Role of group representativeness in the generalization part of the contact hypothesis. *Journal of Applied Social Psychology, 19*, 183–204.

Deska, J. C., Lloyd, E. P., & Hugenberg, K. (2018). Facing humanness: Facial width-to-height ratio predicts ascriptions of humanity. *Journal of Personality and Social Psychology, 114*(1), 75–94.

DeSteno, D., Bartlett, M. Y., Braverman, J., & Salovey, P. (2002). Sex differences in jealousy: Evolutionary mechanism or artifact of measurement? *Journal of Personality and Social Psychology, 83*(5), 1103–1116.

DeSteno, D. A., & Salovey, P. (1996). Evolutionary origins of sex difference in jealousy? Questioning the fitness of the model. *Psychological Science, 7*(6), 367–372.

de Tocqueville, A. (1969). *Democracy in America* (13th ed., J. P. Mayer, Ed., & G. Lawrence, Trans.). New York, NY: Doubleday. (Original work published 1862)

Deutsch, M., & Gerard, H. B. (1955). A study of normative and informational social influence upon individual judgment. *Journal of Abnormal and Social Psychology, 51*(3), 629–636.

Deutsch, R., Gawronski, B., & Strack, F. (2006). At the boundaries of automaticity: Negation as reflective operation. *Journal of Personality and Social Psychology, 91*(3), 385–405.

Devine, P. G. (1989). Stereotypes and prejudice: Their automatic and controlled components. *Journal of Personality and Social Psychology, 56*(1), 5–18.

Devine, P. G., Evett, S. R., & Vasquez-Suson, K. A. (1996). Exploring the interpersonal dynamics of intergroup contact. In R. M. Sorrentino & E. T. Higgins (Eds.), *Handbook of motivation and cognition: The interpersonal context* (Vol. 3, pp. 423–464). New York, NY: Guilford Press.

Devine, P. G., Monteith, M. J., Zuwerink, J. R., & Elliot, A. J. (1991). Prejudice with and without compunction. *Journal of Personality and Social Psychology, 60*(6), 817–830.

Devine, P. G., & Sharp, L. B. (2009). Automaticity and control in stereotyping and prejudice. In T. D. Nelson (Ed.), *Handbook of prejudice, stereotyping, and discrimination* (pp. 61–88). New York, NY: Psychology Press.

Devlin, P. K., & Cowan, G. A. (1985). Homophobia, perceived fathering, and male intimate relationships. *Journal of Personality Assessment, 49*(5), 467–473.

de Waal, F. (2002). *The ape and the sushi master: Cultural reflections of a primatologist.* New York, NY: Basic Books.

DeWall, C. N., Deckman, T., Pond, R. S., Jr., & Bonser, I. (2011a). Belongingness as a core personality trait: How social exclusion influences social functioning and personality expression. *Journal of Personality, 79*(6), 979–1012.

DeWall, C. N., Maner, J. K., & Rouby, D. A. (2009). Social exclusion and early-stage interpersonal perception: Selective attention to signs of acceptance. *Journal of Personality and Social Psychology, 96*(4), 729–741.

DeWall, C. N., Pond, R. S., Jr., Campbell, W. K., & Twenge, J. M. (2011b). Tuning in to psychological change: Linguistic markers of psychological traits and emotions over time in popular U.S. song lyrics. *Psychology of Aesthetics, Creativity, and the Arts, 5*(3), 200–207.

Diamond, L. M. (2003). What does sexual orientation orient? A biobehavioral model distinguishing romantic love and sexual desire. *Psychological Review, 110*(1), 173–192.

DiBaise, R., & Gunnoe, J. (2004). Gender and culture differences in touching behavior. *Journal of Social Psychology, 144*(1), 49–62.

Dickens, L., & DeSteno, D. (2014). Pride attenuates nonconscious mimicry. *Emotion, 14*(1), 7–11.

Dickter, C. L., & Newton, V. A. (2013). To confront or not to confront: Non-targets' evaluations of and responses to racist comments. *Journal of Applied Social Psychology, 43*(52), E262–E275.

Di Conza, A., Gnisci, A., Perugini, M., & Senese, V. P. (2010). Implicit and explicit attitudes and voting behavior. 2004 European election in Italy and 2005 general election in England. *Psicologia Sociale, 2*, 301–329.

Diedrichs, P. C., & Puhl, R. (2017). Weight bias: Prejudice and discrimination toward overweight and obese people. In C. G. Sibley & F. K. Barlow (Eds.), *The Cambridge handbook of the psychology of prejudice* (pp. 392–412). Cambridge, England: Cambridge University Press.

Diehl, K., Zauberman, G., & Barasch, A. (2016). How taking photos increases enjoyment of experiences. *Journal of Personality and Social Psychology, 111*(2), 119–140.

Diekmann, K. A., Tenbrunsel, A. E., & Galinsky, A. D. (2003). From self-prediction to self-defeat: Behavioral forecasting, self-fulfilling prophecies, and the effect of competitive expectations. *Journal of Personality and Social Psychology, 85*(4), 672–683.

Diener, E. (1980). Deindividuation: The absence of self-awareness and self-regulation in group members. In P. B. Paulus (Ed.), *Psychology of group influence* (pp. 209–242). Hillsdale, NJ: Lawrence Erlbaum Associates.

Diener, E., Fraser, S. C., Beaman, A. L., & Kelem, R. T. (1976). Effects of deindividuation variables on stealing among Halloween trick-or-treaters. *Journal of Personality and Social Psychology, 33*(2), 178–183.

Diener, E., Suh, E. M., Lucas, R. E., & Smith, H. L. (1999). Subjective well-being: Three decades of progress. *Psychological Bulletin, 125*(2), 276–302.

Diener, E., & Wallbom, M. (1976). Effects of self-awareness on antinormative behavior. *Journal of Research in Personality, 10*(1), 107–111.

Diener, E., Wolsie, B., & Fujita, F. (1995). Physical attractiveness and subjective well-being. *Journal of Personality and Social Psychology, 69*(1), 120–129.

Dijksterhuis, A. (2010). Automaticity and the unconscious. In S. T. Fiske, D. T. Gilbert, & G. Lindzey (Eds.), *Handbook of social psychology* (5th ed., Vol. 1, pp. 228–267). Hoboken, NJ: John Wiley & Sons.

Dijksterhuis, A., & Bargh, J. A. (2001). The perception-behavior expressway: The automatic effects of social perception on social behavior. In M. P. Zanna (Ed.), *Advances in experimental social psychology* (Vol. 33, pp. 1–40). San Diego, CA: Academic Press.

Dijkstra, P., & Barelds, D. P. H. (2011). Women's meta-perceptions of attractiveness and their relations to body image. *Body Image, 8*(1), 74–77.

Dijkstra, P., Groothof, H. A. K., Poel, G. A., Laverman, T. T. G., Schrier, M., & Buunk, B. P. (2001). Sex differences in the events that elicit jealousy among homosexuals. *Personal Relationships, 8*(1), 41–54.

Dillon, K. P., & Jones, E. B. (2019). How "real" is reality television? Marginalized group representativeness in competitive reality television programming. *Psychology of Popular Media Culture, 8*(3), 319–328.

Dimas, I. C. D., Lourenco, P. R., & Miguez, J. (2007). (Re) thinking intragroup conflict: performance and group development. *Psicologia: Revista da Associacao Portuguesa Psicologia, 21*, 183–205.

Dimberg, U., & Söderkvist, S. (2011). The voluntary facial action technique: A method to test the facial feedback hypothesis. *Journal of Nonverbal Behavior, 35*(1), 17–33.

Dindia, K., & Allen, M. (1992). Sex differences in self-disclosure: A meta-analysis. *Psychological Bulletin, 112*(1), 106–124.

Dindo, L., Brock, R. L., Aksan, N., Gamez, W., Kochanska, G., & Clark, L. A. (2017). Attachment and effortful control in toddlerhood predict academic achievement over a decade later. *Psychological Science, 28*(12), 1786–1795.

Dion, K. K., Berscheid, E., & [Walster] Hatfield, E. (1972). What is beautiful is good. *Journal of Personality and Social Psychology, 24*(3), 285–290.

Dion, K. K., & Dion, K. (1975). Self-esteem and romantic love. *Journal of Personality, 43*(1), 39–57.

Dion, K. K., & Dion, K. L. (1985). Personality, gender, and the phenomenology of romantic love. In P. R. Shaver (Ed.), *Self, situations and behavior: Review of personality and social psychology* (Vol. 6, pp. 209–239). Beverly Hills, CA: Sage.

Dion, K. K., & Dion, K. L. (1991). Psychological individualism and romantic love. *Journal of Social Behavior and Personality, 6*(1), 17–33.

Dion, K. K., & Dion, K. L. (2006). Individualism, collectivism, and the psychology of love. In R. J. Sternberg & K. Weis (Eds.), *The new psychology of love* (pp. 298–312). New Haven, CT: Yale University Press.

Dion, K. L., & Dion, K. K. (1973). Correlates of romantic love. *Journal of Consulting and Clinical Psychology, 41*(1), 51–56.

Dionne, E. J., Jr. (1991). *Why Americans hate politics*. New York, NY: Simon & Schuster.

Ditrich, L., Scholl, A., & Sassenberg, K. (2017). Time to go! Leaving the group in response to norm-deviations. *Journal of Experimental Social Psychology, 73*, 259–267.

Ditto, P. H., Scepansky, J. A., Munro, G. D., Apanovich, A. M., & Lockhart, L. K. (1998). Motivated sensitivity to preference-inconsistent information. *Journal of Personality and Social Psychology, 75*(1), 53–69.

Dodd, E., Giuliano, T., Boutell, J., & Moran, B. (2001). Respected or rejected: Perceptions of women who confront sexist remarks. *Sex Roles, 45*(7–8), 567–577.

Dodge, K. A. (2011). Social information processing patterns as mediators of the interaction between genetic factors and life experiences in the development of aggressive behavior. In P. R. Shaver & M. Mikulincer (Eds.), *Human aggression and violence: Causes, manifestations, and consequences* (pp. 165–185). Washington, DC: American Psychological Association.

Doebel, S., & Munakata, Y. (2018). Group influences on engaging self-control: Children delay gratification and value it more when their in-group delays and their out-group doesn't. *Psychological Science, 29*(5), 738–748.

Doliński, D. (2018). Is psychology still a science of behavior? *Social Psychological Bulletin, 13*(2), e25025.

Doliński, D., Grzyb, T., Folwarczny, M., Grzybala, P., Krzyszycha, K., Martynowska, K., & Trojanowski, J. (2017). Would you deliver an electric shock in 2015? Obedience in the experimental paradigm developed by Stanley Milgram in the 50 years following the original studies. *Social Psychological and Personality Science, 8*(8), 927–933.

Donnelly, K., & Twenge, J. M. (2017). Masculine and feminine traits on the Bem Sex-Role Inventory, 1993–2012: A cross-temporal meta-analysis. *Sex Roles, 76*(9–10), 556–565.

Donnerstein, E., & Berkowitz, L. (1981). Victim reactions in aggressive erotic films as a factor in violence against women. *Journal of Personality and Social Psychology, 41*(4), 710–724.

Donnerstein, E., & Malamuth, N. (1997). Pornography: Its consequences on the observer. In L. B. Schlesinger, & E. Revitch (Eds.), *Sexual dynamics of anti-social behavior* (2nd ed., pp. 30–49). Springfield, IL: Charles C. Thomas.

Dordick, G. A. (1997). *Something left to lose: Personal relations and survival among New York's homeless.* Philadelphia, PA: Temple University Press.

Doty, R. M., Peterson, B. E., & Winter, D. G. (1991). Threat and authoritarianism in the United States, 1978–1987. *Journal of Personality and Social Psychology, 61*(4), 629–640.

Doty, R. M., Winter, D. G., Peterson, B. E., & Kemmelmeier, M. (1997). Authoritarianism and American students' attitudes about the Gulf War, 1990–1996. *Personality and Social Psychology Bulletin, 23*(11), 1133–1143.

Douglas, K. M., Sutton, R. M., & Stathi, S. (2010). Why I am less persuaded than you: People's intuitive understanding of the psychology of persuasion. *Social Influence, 5*(2), 133–148.

Dovidio, J. F. (2001). On the nature of contemporary prejudice: The third wave. *Journal of Social Issues, 57*(4), 829–849.

Dovidio, J. F., & Gaertner, S. L. (2000). Aversive racism and selection decisions: 1989 and 1999. *Psychological Science, 11*(4), 315–319.

Dovidio, J. F., & Gaertner, S. L. (2010). Intergroup bias. In S. T. Fiske, D. T. Gilbert, & G. Lindzey (Eds.), *Handbook of social psychology* (5th ed., Vol. 2, pp. 1084–1121). Hoboken, NJ: John Wiley & Sons.

Dovidio, J. F., Gaertner, S. L., & Pearson, A. R. (2017). Aversive racism and contemporary bias. In C. G. Sibley & F. K. Barlow (Eds.), *The Cambridge handbook of the psychology of prejudice* (pp. 267–294). New York, NY: Cambridge University Press.

Dovidio, J. F., Piliavin, J. A., & Clark, R. D., III (1991). The arousal: cost reward model and the process of intervention: A review of the evidence. In M. S. Clark (Ed.), *Review of personality and social psychology: Vol. 12. Prosocial behavior* (pp. 86–118). Newbury Park, CA: Sage.

Dovidio, J. F., Piliavin, J. A., Schroeder, D. A., & Penner, L. (2006). *The social psychology of prosocial behavior.* Mahwah, NJ: Lawrence Erlbaum Associates.

Downey, G., Freitas, A. L., Michaelis, B., & Khouri, H. (1998). The self-fulfilling prophecy in close relationships: Rejection sensitivity and rejection by romantic partners. *Journal of Personality and Social Psychology, 75*(2), 545–560.

Doyle, R. A., & Voyer, D. (2016). Stereotype manipulation effects on math and spatial test performance: A meta-analysis. *Learning and Individual Differences, 47*, 103–116.

Drabman, R. S., & Thomas, M. H. (1975). Does TV violence breed indifference? *Journal of Communications, 25*(4), 86-89.

Draelants, H., & Darchy Koechlin, B. (2011). Flaunting one's academic pedigree? Self-presentation of students from elite French schools. *British Journal of Sociology of Education, 32*(1), 17–34.

Drigotas, S. M., Rusbult, C. E., Wieselquist, J., & Whitton, S. W. (1999). Close partner as sculptor of the ideal self: Behavioral affirmation and the Michelangelo phenomenon. *Journal of Personality and Social Psychology, 77*(2), 293–323.

Drury, B. J., & Kaiser, C. R. (2014). Allies against sexism: The role of men in confronting sexism. *Journal of Social Issues, 70*(4), 637–652.

Drury, B. J., Siy, J. O., & Cheryan, S. (2011). When do female role models benefit women? The importance of differentiating recruitment from retention in STEM. *Psychological Inquiry, 22*(4), 265–269.

Duck, S., Pond, K., & Leatham, G. (1994). Loneliness and the evaluation of relational events. *Journal of Social and Personal Relationships, 11*(2), 253–276.

Duck, S., & Wright, P. H. (1993). Reexamining gender differences in same-gender friendships: A close look at two kinds of data. *Sex Roles, 28*(11–12), 709–727.

Duckitt, J., & Fisher, K. (2003). The impact of social threat on worldview and ideological attitudes. *Political Psychology, 24*(1), 199–222.

Duckitt, J., & Mphuthing, T. (1998). Group identification and intergroup attitudes: A longitudinal analysis in South Africa. *Journal of Personality and Social Psychology, 74*(1), 80–85.

Duckworth, A. L., Tsukayama, E., & Kirby, T. A. (2013). Is it really self-control? Examining the predictive power of the delay of gratification task. *Personality and Social Psychology Bulletin, 39*(7), 843–855.

Dufner, M., Gebauer, J. E., Sedikides, C., & Denissen, J. J. (2019). Self-enhancement and psychological adjustment: A meta-analytic review. *Personality and Social Psychology Review, 23*(1), 48–72.

Dunbar, R. I. (2002). Brains on two legs: Group size and the evolution of intelligence. In F. B. de Waal (Ed.), *Tree of origin: What primate behavior can tell us about human social evolution* (pp. 173–191). Cambridge, MA: Harvard University Press.

Dunbar, R. I. (1993). Coevolution of neocortical size, group size and language in humans. *Behavioral and Brain Sciences, 16*(4), 681–735.

Dunbar, R. I. (2003). Evolution of the social brain. *Science, 302*(5648), 1160–1161.

Dunbar, R. I. (1996). *Grooming, gossip, and the evolution of language.* Cambridge, MA: Harvard University Press.

Duncan, C. P., & Nelson, J. E. (1985). Effects of humor in a radio advertising experiment. *Journal of Advertising, 14*(2), 33–64.

Dunkel-Schetter, C., Blasband, D. E., Feinstein, L. G., & Herbert, T. B. (1992). Elements of supportive interactions: When are attempts to help effective? In S. Spacapan & S. Oskamp (Eds.), *Helping and being helped: Naturalistic studies* (pp. 83–114). Thousand Oaks, CA: Sage.

Dunn, E. W., Biesanz, J. C., Human, L. J., & Finn, S. (2007). Misunderstanding the affective consequences of everyday social interactions: The hidden benefits of putting one's best face forward. *Journal of Personality and Social Psychology, 92*(6), 990–1005.

Dunn, J. (2001). The development of children's conflict and prosocial behaviour: Lessons from research on social understanding and gender. In J. Hill & B. Maughan (Eds.), *Conduct disorders in childhood and adolescence: Cambridge child and adolescent psychiatry* (pp. 49–66). New York, NY: Cambridge University Press.

Dunning, D. (1999). A newer look: Motivated social cognition and the schematic representation of social concepts. *Psychological Inquiry, 10*(1), 1–11.

Duran, N. D., Nicholson, S. P., & Dale, R. (2017). The hidden appeal and aversion to political conspiracies as revealed in the response dynamics of partisans. *Journal of Experimental Social Psychology, 73*, 268–278.

Durko, A. M., & Petrick, J. F. (2013). Family and relationship benefits of travel experiences: A literature review. *Journal of Travel Research, 52*(6), 720–730.

Dutton, D. G. (2007). *The psychology of genocide, massacres, and extreme violence: Why "normal" people come to commit atrocities.* Westport, CT: Praeger Security International.

Dutton, D. G., & Aron, A. P. (1974). Some evidence for heightened sexual attraction under conditions of high anxiety. *Journal of Personality and Social Psychology, 30*(4), 510–517.

Dutton, D. G., & Tetreault, C. (2009). Who will act badly in toxic situations? *Journal of Aggression, Conflict, and Peace Research, 1*(1), 45–57.

Duval, S., & Wicklund, R. A. (1972). *A theory of objective self-awareness.* New York, NY: Academic Press.

Dweck, C. S., Chiu, C. -y., & Hong, Y. -y. (1995). Implicit theories and their role in judgments and reactions: A word from two perspectives. *Psychological Inquiry, 6*(4), 267–285.

Dykas, M. J., & Cassidy, J. (2011). Attachment and the processing of social information across the life span: Theory and evidence. *Psychological Bulletin, 137*(1), 19–46.

E

Eagly, A. H. (1987). *Sex differences in social behavior: A social-role interpretation.* Hillsdale, NJ: Lawrence Erlbaum & Associates.

Eagly, A. H. (1996). Differences between women and men: Their magnitude, practical importance, and political meaning. *American Psychologist, 51*(2), 158–159.

Eagly, A. H. (2018). Some leaders come from nowhere: Their success is uneven. *Journal of Social Issues, 74*(1), 184–196.

Eagly, A. H., Ashmore, R. D., Makhijani, M. G., & Longo, L. C. (1991). What is beautiful is good, but...: A meta-analytic review of research on the physical attractiveness stereotype. *Psychological Bulletin, 110*(1), 107–128.

Eagly, A. H., & Chaiken, S. (1993). *The psychology of attitudes.* Fort Worth, TX: Harcourt Brace Jovanovich.

Eagly, A. H., & Crowley, M. (1986). Gender and helping behavior: A meta-analytic review of the social psychological literature. *Psychological Bulletin, 100*(3), 283–308.

Eagly, A. H., & Johannesen-Schmidt, M. C. (2001). The leadership styles of women and men. *Journal of Social Issues, 57*(4), 781–797.

Eagly, A. H., Johannesen-Schmidt, M. C., & van Engen, M. L. (2003). Transformational, transactional, and laissez-faire leadership styles: A meta-analysis comparing women and men. *Psychological Bulletin, 129*(4), 569–591.

Eagly, A. H., & Johnson, B. T. (1990). Gender and leadership style: A meta-analysis. *Psychological Bulletin, 108*(2), 233–256.

Eagly, A. H., & Karau, S. J. (2002). Role congruity theory of prejudice toward female leaders. *Psychological Review, 109*(3), 573–598.

Eagly, A. H., Karau, S. J., & Makhijani, M. G. (1995). Gender and the effectiveness of leaders: A meta-analysis. *Psychological Bulletin, 117*(1), 125–145.

Eagly, A. H., Makhijani, M. G., & Klonsky, B. G. (1992). Gender and the evaluation of leaders: A meta-analysis. *Psychological Bulletin, 111*(1), 3–22.

Eagly, A. H., & Mladinic, A. (1994). Are people prejudiced against woman? Some answers from research on attitudes, gender stereotypes, and judgments of competence. *European Review of Social Psychology, 5*(1), 1–35.

Eagly, A. H., & Steffen, V. J. (1986). Gender and aggressive behavior: A meta-analytic review of the social psychological literature. *Psychological Bulletin, 100*(3), 309–330.

Eaton, J., & Struthers, C. W. (2006). The reduction of aggression in varied interpersonal contexts through repentance and forgiveness. *Aggressive Behavior, 32*(3), 195–206.

Ebbesen, E. B., Kjos, G. L., & Konecni, V. J. (1976). Spatial ecology: Its effects on the choice of friends and enemies. *Journal of Experimental Social Psychology, 12*(6), 505–518.

Eberhardt, J. L., Davies, P. G., Purdie-Vaughns, V. J., & Johnson, S. L. (2006). Looking deathworthy: Perceived stereotypicality of black defendants predicts capital-sentencing outcomes. *Psychological Science, 17*(5), 383–386.

Echabe, A. E., Rovira, D. P., & Garate, J. F. (1988). Testing Ajzen and Fishbein's attitudes model: The prediction of voting. *European Journal of Social Psychology, 18*(2), 181–189.

Edgerton, R. B. (1971). *The individual in cultural adaptation.* Berkeley, CA: University of California Press.

Edlund J. E., Nichols, A. L., Okdie, B. M., Guadagno, R. E., Eno, C. A., Heider , J. D.,. . .Wilcox, K. T. (2014). The Prevalence and Prevention of Crosstalk: A Multi-Institutional Study. *The Journal of Social Psychology, 154*(3), 181–185.

Edney, J. J. (1979). The nuts game: A concise commons dilemma analog. *Environmental Psychology and Nonverbal Behavior, 3*(4), 252–254.

Edson, R. (1976). *The intuitive journey and other works.* New York, NY: Harper & Row.

Edwards, J. (2014). Ghana's mental health patients confined to prayer camps. *The Lancet, 383*(9911), 15–16.

Edwards, K., & Smith, E. E. (1996). A disconfirmation bias in the evaluation of arguments. *Journal of Personality and Social Psychology, 71*(1), 5–24.

Eisenberg, N., Martin, C. L., & Fabes, R. A. (1996). Gender development and gender effects. In D. C. Berliner & R. C. Calfee (Eds.), *Handbook of educational psychology* (pp. 358–396). New York, NY: Prentice-Hall.

Eisenberg, N., Schaller, M., Fabes, R. A., Bustamante, D., Mathy, R. M., Shell, R., & Rhodes, K. (1988). Differentiation of personal distress and sympathy in children and adults. *Developmental Psychology, 24*(6), 766–775.

Eisenberger, N. I. (2011). Social pain: Experiential, neurocognitive, and genetic correlates. In A. Todorov, S. T. Fiske, & D. A. Prentice (Eds.), *Social neuroscience: Toward understanding the underpinnings of the social mind* (pp. 229–248). New York, NY: Oxford University Press.

Eisenberger, R., Cotterell, N., & Marvel, J. (1987). Reciprocation ideology. *Journal of Personality and Social Psychology, 53*(4), 743–750.

Ekman, P. (1994). Strong evidence for universals in facial expressions: A reply to Russell's mistaken critique. *Psychological Bulletin, 115*(2), 268–287.

Ekman, P., Friesen, W. V., & O'Sullivan, M. (1988). Smiles when lying. *Journal of Personality and Social Psychology, 54*(3), 414–420.

Ekman, P., & O'Sullivan, M. (1991). Who can catch a liar? *American Psychologist, 46*(9), 913–920.

Elder, R. W., Shults, R. A., Sleet, D. A., Nichols, J. L., Thompson, R. S., Rajab, W., & Task Force on Community Preventative Services. (2004). Effectiveness of mass media campaigns for reducing drinking and driving and alcohol-involved crashes: A systematic review. *American Journal of Preventative Medicine, 27*(1), 57–65.

Elfenbein, H. A., & Ambady, N. (2002). On the universality and cultural specificity of emotion recognition: A meta-analysis. *Psychological Bulletin, 128*(2), 203–235.

Elias, S. M., & Mace, B. L. (2005). Social power in the classroom: Student attributions for compliance. *Journal of Applied Social Psychology, 35*(8), 1738–1754.

Ellemers, N. (2018). Gender stereotypes. *Annual Review of Psychology, 69*, 275–298.

Ellemers, N., Rijswijk, W. V., Roefs, M., & Simons, C. (1997). Bias in intergroup perceptions: Balancing group identity with social reality. *Personality and Social Psychology Bulletin, 23*(2), 186–198.

Ellemers, N., Spears, R., & Doosje, B. (2002). Self and social identity. *Annual Review of Psychology, 53*, 161–186.

Ellis, A. P., West, B. J., Ryan, A. M., & DeShon, R. P. (2002). The use of impression management tactics in structured interviews: A function of question type? *Journal of Applied Psychology, 87*(6), 1200–1208.

Ellis, J., & Fox, P. (2001). The effect of self-identified sexual orientation on helping behavior in a British sample: Are lesbians and gay men treated differently? *Journal of Applied Social Psychology, 31*(6), 1238–1247.

Ellison, N., Heino, R., & Gibbs, J. (2006). Managing impressions online: Self-presentation processes in the online dating environment. *Journal of Computer-Mediated Communication, 11*(2), 415–441.

Elms, A. C. (1975). The crisis of confidence in social psychology. *American Psychologist, 30*(10), 967–976.

Elms, A. C. (1994). Keeping deception honest: Justifying conditions for social scientific research stratagems. In E. Erwin, S. Gendin, & L. Kleiman (Eds.), *Ethical issues in scientific research: An anthology* (pp. 121–140). New York, NY: Garland.

Elms, A. C. (1995). Obedience in retrospect. *Journal of Social Issues, 51*(3), 21–31.

Elms, A. C., & Milgram, S. (1966). Personality characteristics associated with obedience and defiance toward authoritative command. *Journal of Experimental Research in Personality, 1*(4), 282–289.

Elsesser, K., & Peplau, L. A. (2006). The glass partition: Obstacles to cross-sex friendships at work. *Human Relations, 59*(8), 1077–1100.

Ely, R. J., & Thomas, D. A. (2001). Cultural diversity at work: The effects of diversity perspectives on work group processes and outcomes. *Administrative Science Quarterly, 46*(2), 229–273.

Ember, C. R., & Ember, M. (1994). War, socialization, and interpersonal violence: A cross-cultural study. *Journal of Conflict Resolution, 38*(4), 620–646.

Emmers-Sommer, T. M., Pauley, P., Hanzal, A., & Triplett, L. (2006). Love suspense, sex, and violence: Men's and women's film predilections, exposure to sexually violent media, and their relationship to rape myth acceptance. *Sex Roles, 55*(5–6), 311–320.

Emmons, R. A., & Diener, E. (1986). A goal-affect analysis of everyday situational choices. *Journal of Research in Personality, 20*(3), 309–326.

End, C. M., Kretschmar, J. M., & Dietz-Uhler, B. (2004). College students' perceptions of sports fandom as a social status determinant. *International Sports Journal, 8*(1), 114–123.

Epley, N., Akalis, S., Waytz, A, & Cacioppo, J. T. (2008). Creating social connection through inferential reproduction: Loneliness and perceived agency in gadgets, gods, and greyhounds. *Psychological Science, 19*(2), 114–120.

Epley, N., & Gilovich, T. (2001). Putting adjustment back in the anchoring and adjustment heuristic: Differential processing of self-generated and experimenter-provided anchors. *Psychological Science, 12*(5), 391–396.

Epley, N., & Huff, C. (1998). Suspicion, affective response, and educational benefit as a result of deception in psychology research. *Personality and Social Psychology Bulletin, 24*(7), 759–768.

Epstein, J. L. (1985). After the bus arrives: Resegregation in desegregation schools. *Journal of Social Issues, 41*(3), 23–43.

Erb, H. -P., Hilton, D. J., Bohner, G., & Roffey, L. (2015). The minority decision—a risky choice. *Journal of Experimental Social Psychology, 57*, 43–50.

Erber, R., Wegner, D. M., & Therriault, N. (1996). On being cool and collected: Mood regulation in anticipation of social interaction. *Journal of Personality and Social Psychology, 70*(4), 757–766.

Erdogan, B., & Enders, J. (2007). Support from the top: Supervisors' perceived organizational support as a moderator of leader-member exchange to satisfaction and performance relationships. *Journal of Applied Psychology, 92*(2), 321–330.

Eron, L. D., & Huesmann, L. R. (1984). The control of aggressive behavior by changes in attitudes, values, and the conditions of learning. In R. J. Blanchard & D. C. Blanchard (Eds.), *Advances in the study of aggression* (Vol. 1, pp. 139–171). New York, NY: Academic Press.

Esquivel-Santovena, E. E., Lambert, T. L., & Hamel, J. (2013). Partner abuse worldwide. *Partner Abuse, 4*(1), 6–75.

Esses, V. M., Jackson, L. M., & Armstrong, T. L. (1998). Intergroup competition and attitudes toward immigrants and immigration: An instrumental model of group conflict. *Journal of Social Issues, 54*(4), 699–724.

Essien, I., Stelter, M., Kalbe, F., Koehler, A., Mangels, J., & Meliß, S. (2017). The shooter bias: Replicating the classic effect and introducing a novel paradigm. *Journal of Experimental Social Psychology, 70,* 41–47.

Evans, A. D., Xu, F., & Lee, K. (2011). When all signs point to you: Lies told in the face of evidence. *Developmental Psychology, 47*(1), 39–49.

Evans, D. R., Boggero, I. A., & Segerstrom, S. C. (2016). The nature of self-regulatory fatigue and "ego depletion": Lessons from physical fatigue. *Personality and Social Psychology Review, 20*(4), 291–310.

Evans, R. I. (1980). *The making of social psychology: Discussions with creative contributors.* New York, NY: Gardner Press.

Exner-Cortens, D., Hurlock, D., Wright, A., Carter, R. & Krause, P. (2019). Preliminary evaluation of a gender-transformative healthy relationships program for adolescent boys. *Psychology of Men & Masculinities.* Advance online publication. doi:10.1037/men0000204

Eysenck, H. J. (1990). Biological dimensions of personality. In L. A. Pervin (Ed.), *Handbook of personality theory and research* (pp. 244–276). New York, NY: Guilford Press.

F

Fagin-Jones, S., & Midlarsky, E. (2007). Courageous altruism: Personal and situational correlates of rescue during the Holocaust. *The Journal of Positive Psychology, 2*(2), 136–147.

Fales, M. R., Frederick, D. A., Garcia, J. R., Gildersleeve, K. A., Haselton, M. G., & Fisher, H. E. (2016). Mating markets and bargaining hands: Mate preferences for attractiveness and resources in two national U.S. studies. *Personality and Individual Differences, 88,* 78–87.

Falk, C. F., Heine, S. J., Yuki, M., & Takemura, K. (2009). Why do Westerners self-enhance more than East Asians? *European Journal of Personality, 23*(3), 183–203.

Farb, P. (1978). *Man's rise to civilization: The cultural ascent of the Indians of North America.* New York, NY: Penguin.

Farley, S. D. (2011). Is gossip power? The inverse relationships between gossip, power, and likability. *European Journal of Social Psychology, 41*(5), 574–579.

Farley, S. D. (2014). Nonverbal reactions to an attractive stranger: The role of mimicry in communicating preferred social distance. *Journal of Nonverbal Behavior, 38*(2), 195–208.

Farr, R. M. (1996). *The roots of modern social psychology.* Cambridge, MA: Blackwell.

Farrington, D. P. (1994). Childhood, adolescent, and adult features of violent males. In L. R. Huesmann (Ed.), *Aggressive behavior: Current perspectives* (pp. 215–240). New York, NY: Plenum Press.

Fausto-Sterling, A. (2000). The five sexes, revisited: The varieties of sex will test the medical values and social norms. *The Sciences, 40*(4), 18–23.

Fawkner, H. J., & McMurray, N. (2002). Body image in men: Self-reported thoughts, feelings, and behaviors in response to media images. *International Journal of Men's Health, 1*(2), 137–162.

Fazio, R. H. (2007). Attitudes as object-evaluation associations of varying strength. *Social Cognition, 25,* 603–637.

Feather, N. T. (2004). Value correlates of ambivalent attitudes toward gender relations. *Personality and Social Psychology Bulletin, 30*(1), 3–12.

Feeney, B. C., & Collins, N. L. (2014). A new look at social support: A theoretical perspective on thriving through relationships. *Personality and Social Psychology Review, 19*(2), 113–147.

Fehr, B. (2004). Intimacy expectations in same-sex friendships: A prototype interaction-pattern model. *Journal of Personality and Social Psychology, 86*(2), 265–284.

Fehr, E., & Gaechter, S. (2002). Altruistic punishment in humans. *Nature, 415,* 137–140.

Feinberg, J. M., & Aiello, J. R. (2006). Social facilitation: A test of competing theories. *Journal of Applied Social Psychology, 36*(5), 1087–1109.

Feingold, A. (1992a). Gender differences in mate selection preferences: A test of the parental investment model. *Psychological Bulletin, 112*(1), 125–139.

Feingold, A. (1992b). Good-looking people are not what we think. *Psychological Bulletin, 111*(2), 304–341.

Feingold, A., & Mazzella, R. (1998). Gender differences in body image are increasing. *Psychological Science, 9*(3), 190–195.

Feldman, D. B., & Crandall, C. S. (2007). Dimensions of mental illness stigma: What about mental illness causes social rejection? *Journal of Social and Clinical Psychology, 26*(2), 137–154.

Feldman, G., Lian, H., Kosinski, M., & Stillwell, D. (2017). Frankly, we do give a damn: The relationship between profanity and honesty. *Social Psychological and Personality Science, 8*(7), 816–826.

Feldman, S., & Stenner, K. (1997). Perceived threat and authoritarianism. *Political Psychology, 18*(4), 741–770.

Felmlee, D. H. (1999). Social norms in same- and cross-gender friendships. *Social Psychology Quarterly, 62*(1), 53–67.

Fenigstein, A., Scheier, M. F., & Buss, A. H. (1975). Public and private self-consciousness: Assessment and theory. *Journal of Consulting and Clinical Psychology, 43*(4), 522–527.

Ferguson, G. (1955). Legal research on trial. *Judicature, 39,* 78–82.

Ferguson, M. J. (2007). On the automatic evaluation of end-states. *Journal of Personality and Social Psychology, 92*(4), 596–611.

Fernald, J. L. (1995). Interpersonal heterosexism. In B. Lott, & D. Maluso (Eds.), *The social psychology of interpersonal discrimination* (pp. 80–117). New York, NY: Guilford Press.

Ferrari, J. R., & Tice, D. M. (2000). Procrastination as a self-handicap for men and women: A task-avoidance strategy in a laboratory setting. *Journal of Research in Personality, 34*(1), 73–83.

Festinger, L. (1954). A theory of social comparison processes. *Human Relations, 7*(2), 117–140.

Festinger, L. (1957). *A theory of cognitive dissonance.* Stanford, CA: Stanford University Press.

Festinger, L., & Carlsmith, J. M. (1959). Cognitive consequences of forced compliance. *Journal of Abnormal and Social Psychology, 58*(2), 382–389.

Festinger, L., Pepitone, A., & Newcomb, T. (1952). Some consequences of deindividuation in a group. *Journal of Abnormal and Social Psychology, 47*(2), 382–389.

Festinger, L., Reicken, H. W., & Schachter, S. (1956). *When prophecy fails.* Minneapolis, MN: University of Minnesota Press.

Festinger, L., Schachter, S., & Back, K. (1950). *Social pressures in informal groups: A study of a housing community.* New York, NY: Harper and Brothers.

Fetchenhauer, D., Flache, A., Buunk, A. P., & Lindenberg, S. (Eds.) (2007). *Solidarity and prosocial behavior: An integration of sociological and psychological perspectives.* New York, NY: Springer.

Fiedler, F. E. (1967). *A theory of leadership effectiveness.* New York, NY: McGraw-Hill.

Fiedler, F. E. (1987). When to lead, when to stand back. *Psychology Today, 21*(9), 26–27.

Fiedler, F. E. (1993). The leadership situation and the black box in contingency theories. In M. M. Chemers & R. Ayman (Eds.), *Leadership theory and research: Perspectives and directions* (pp. 1–28). San Diego, CA: Academic Press.

Figueredo, A. J., Landau, M. J., & Sefcek, J. A. (2004). Apes and angels: Adaptionism versus panglossianism. *Behavioral and Brain Sciences, 27*(3), 334–335.

Fincham, F. D., Beach, S. R., & Davila, J. (2004). Forgiveness and conflict resolution in marriage. *Journal of Family Psychology, 18*(1), 72–81.

Fine, G. A., & Elsbach, K. D. (2000). Ethnography and experiment in social psychological theory building: Tactics for integrating qualitative field data with quantitative lab data. *Journal of Experimental Social Psychology, 36*(1), 51–76.

Firestone, I. J., Kaplan, K. J., & Russell, J. C. (1973). Anxiety, fear, and affiliation with similar-state versus dissimilar-state others: Misery sometimes loves nonmiserable company. *Journal of Personality and Social Psychology, 26*(3), 409–414.

Fischer, A., & LaFrance, M. (2015). What drives the smile and the tear: Why women are more emotionally expressive than men. *Emotion Review, 7*(1), 22–29.

Fischer, P. & Greitemeyer, T. (2006). Music and aggression: The impact of sexual-aggressive song lyrics on aggression-related thoughts, emotions, and behavior toward the same and the opposite sex. *Personality and Social Psychology Bulletin, 32*(9), 1165–1176.

Fischer, P., Kastenmuller, A., & Greitemeyer, T. (2010). Media violence and the self: The impact of personalized gaming characters in aggressive video games on aggressive behavior. *Journal of Experimental Social Psychology, 46*(1), 192–195.

Fischer, P., Krueger, J. I., Greitemeyer, T., Vogrincic, C., Kastenmuller, A., Frey, D.,. . .Kainbacher, M. (2011). The bystander-effect: A meta-analytic review on bystander intervention in dangerous and non-dangerous emergencies. *Psychological Bulletin, 137*(4), 517–537.

Fishbein, M., & Ajzen, I. (2009). *Predicting and changing behavior: The reasoned action approach.* New York, NY: Taylor & Francis.

Fisher, H. E. (2004). *Why we love: The nature and chemistry of romantic love.* New York, NY: Henry Holt.

Fiske, A. P., & Haslam, N. (1996). Social cognition is thinking about relationships. *Current Directions in Psychological Science, 5,* 143–148.

Fiske, S. T. (2004). Developing a program of research. In C. Sansone, C. C. Morf, & A. T. Panter (Eds.), *The SAGE handbook of methods in social psychology* (pp. 70–90). Thousand Oaks, CA: Sage.

Fiske, S. T. (2016). How to publish rigorous experiments in the 21st century. *Journal of Experimental Social Psychology, 66,* 145–147.

Fiske, S. T. (2018). Stereotype content: Warmth and competence endure. *Current Directions in Psychological Science, 27*(2), 67–73.

Fiske, S. T., & Cox, M. G. (1979). Person concepts: The effect of target familiarity and descriptive purpose on the process of describing others. *Journal of Personality, 47*(1), 136–161.

Fiske, S. T., & Molm, L. D. (2010). Bridging inequality from both sides now. *Social Psychology Quarterly, 73*(4), 341–346.

Fleischhauer, M., Enge, S., Brocke, B., Ullrich, J., Strobel, A., & Strobel, A. (2010). Same or different? Clarifying the relationship of need for cognition to personality and intelligence. *Personality and Social Psychology Bulletin, 36*(1), 82–96.

Fletcher, D. (2009, July 31). The fat-acceptance movement. *Time Magazine.* Retrieved from http://content.time.com/time/nation/article/0,8599,1913858,00.html

Fletcher, G. J. (2002). *The new science of intimate relationships.* Malden, MA: Blackwell.

Fletcher, G. J., & Kerr, P. S. (2010). Through the eyes of love: Reality and illusion in intimate relationships. *Psychological Bulletin, 136*(4), 627–658.

Fletcher, G. J., Tither, J. M., O'Loughlin, C., Friesen, M., & Overall, N. (2004). Warm and homely or cold and beautiful? Sex differences in trading off traits in mate selection. *Personality and Social Psychology Bulletin, 30*(6), 659–672.

Fletcher, J. K., & Käufer, K. (2003). Shared leadership: Paradox and possibility. In C. L. Pearce & J. A. Conger (Eds.), *Shared leadership. Reframing the hows and whys of leadership* (pp. 21–47). Thousand Oaks, CA: Sage.

Fletcher, J. O., Kerr, P. S., Li, N. P., & Valentine, K. A. (2014). Predicting romantic interest and decisions in the very early stages of mate selection: Standards, accuracy, and sex differences. *Personality and Social Psychology Bulletin, 40*(4), 540–550.

Flynn, F. J. (2005). Having an open mind: The impact of openness to experience on interracial attitudes and impression formation. *Journal of Personality and Social Psychology, 88*(5), 816–826.

Foels, R., & Pappas, C. J. (2004). Learning and unlearning the myths we are taught: Gender and social dominance orientation. *Sex Roles, 50*(11–12), 743–757.

Fogelman, E. (1996). Victims, perpetrators, bystanders, and rescuers in the face of genocide and its aftermath. In C. B. Strozier & M. Flynn (Eds.), *Genocide, war, and human survival* (pp. 87–97). Lanham, MD: Rowman & Littlefield.

Ford, T. E., & Ferguson, M. A. (2004). Social consequences of disparagement humor: A prejudice norm theory. *Personality and Social Psychology Review, 8*(1), 79–94.

Forgas, J. P. (1998). Asking nicely? The effects of mood on responding to more or less polite requests. *Personality and Social Psychology Bulletin, 24*(2), 173–185.

Forgeard, M. J., & Seligman, M. E. P. (2012). Seeing the glass half full: A review of the causes and consequences of optimism. *Pratiques Psychologiques, 18*(2), 107–120.

Forrest, J. A., & Feldman, R. S. (2000). Detecting deception and judge's involvement: Lower task involvement leads to better lie detection. *Personality and Social Psychology Bulletin, 26*(1), 118–125.

Forscher, P. S., Cox, W. T., Graetz, N., & Devine, P. G. (2015). The motivation to express prejudice. *Journal of Personality and Social Psychology, 109*(5), 791–812.

Forscher, P. S., Mitamura, C., Dix, E. L., Cox, W. T., & Devine, P. G. (2017). Breaking the prejudice habit: Mechanisms, timecourse, and longevity. *Journal of Experimental Social Psychology, 72*, 133–146.

Förster, J., & Strack, F. (1996). Influence of overt head movements on memory for valenced words: A case of conceptual-motor compatibility. *Journal of Personality and Social Psychology, 71*(3), 421–430.

Forsyth, D. R. (1990). *Group dynamics* (2nd ed.). Pacific Grove, CA: Brooks/Cole.

Forsyth, D. R. (2013). Social influence and group behavior. In H. Tennen, J. Suls, & I. B. Weiner (Eds.). *Handbook of psychology: Personality and social psychology* (Vol. 5, 2nd ed., pp. 305–328). Hoboken, NJ: John Wiley & Sons.

Fosco, G. M., DeBoard, R. L., & Grych, J. H. (2007). Making sense of family violence: Implications of children's appraisals of interparental aggression for their short- and long-term functioning. *European Psychologist, 12*(1), 6–16.

Foster, C. A., Witcher, B. S., Campbell, W. K., & Green, J. D. (1998). Arousal and attraction: Evidence for automatic and controlled processes. *Journal of Personality and Social Psychology, 74*(1), 86–101.

Foster, E. K., & Rosnow, R. L. (2006). Gossip and network relationships. In D. C. Kirkpatrick, S. W. Duck, & M. K. Foley (Eds.), *Relating difficulty: The processes of constructing and managing difficult interaction* (pp. 161–180). Mahwah, NJ: Lawrence Erlbaum Associates.

Foster, M. D. (1999). Acting out against gender discrimination: The effects of different social identities. *Sex Roles, 40*(3–4), 167–186.

Fournier, M. A., Moskowitz, D. S., & Zuroff, D. C. (2002). Social rank strategies in hierarchical relationships. *Journal of Personality and Social Psychology, 83*(2), 425–433.

Fouts, R. (1997). *Next of kin: What chimpanzees have taught me about who we are.* New York, NY: William Morrow.

Fox, J., Bailenson, J. N., & Tricase, L. (2013). The embodiment of sexualized virtual selves: The Proteus effect and experiences of self-objectification via avatars. *Computers in Human Behavior, 29*(3), 930–938.

Fox, K. (2019, August 6). How US gun culture compares with the world. *CNN.* Retrieved from https://www.cnn.com/2017/10/03/americas/us-gun-statistics/index.html

Fraley, R. C. (2002). Attachment stability from infancy to adulthood: Meta-analysis and dynamic modeling of developmental mechanisms. *Personality and Social Psychology Review, 6*(2), 123–151.

Fraley, R. C., Brumbaugh, C. C., & Marks, M. J. (2005). The evolution and function of adult attachment: A comparative and phylogenetic analysis. *Journal of Personality and Social Psychology, 89*(5), 731–746.

Franiuk, R., Coleman, J., & Apa, B. (2017). The influence of non-misogynous and mixed portrayals of intimate partner violence in music on beliefs about intimate partner violence. *Violence Against Women, 23*(2), 243–257.

Frank, M. G., Ekman, P., & Friesen, W. V. (1993). Behavioral markers and recognizability of the smile of enjoyment. *Journal of Personality and Social Psychology, 64*(1), 83–93.

Franklin, K. (2000). Antigay behaviors among young adults: Prevalence, patterns and motivators in a noncriminal population. *Journal of Interpersonal Violence, 15*(4), 339–362.

Franzoi, S. L. (1995). The body-as-object versus the body-as-process: Gender differences and gender considerations. *Sex Roles, 33*(5–6), 417–437.

Franzoi, S. L. (2007). History of social psychology. In R. F. Baumeister & K. D. Vohs (Eds.), *Encyclopedia of Social Psychology* (pp. 431–439). Thousand Oaks, CA: Sage.

Franzoi, S. L., & Chang, Z. (2002). The body esteem of Hmong and Caucasian young adults. *Psychology of Women Quarterly, 26*(1), 89–91.

Franzoi, S. L., Vasquez, K., Sparapani, E., Frost, K., Martin, J., & Aebly, M. (2012). Exploring body comparison tendencies: Women are self-critical whereas men are self-hopeful. *Psychology of Women Quarterly, 36*(1), 99–109.

Fraser, C., Gouge, C., & Billig, M. (1971). Risky shifts, cautious shifts, and group polarization. *European Journal of Social Psychology, 1*(1), 7–30.

Frazier, P. A., & Cook, S. W. (1993). Correlates of distress following heterosexual relationship dissolution. *Journal of Social and Personal Relationships, 10*(1), 55–67.

Frazier, P. A., Steward, J., & Mortensen, H. (2004). Perceived control and adjustment to trauma: A comparison across events. *Journal of Social and Clinical Psychology, 23*(3), 303–324.

Frederick, D. A., Buchanan, G. M., Sadehgi-Azar, L., Peplau, L. A., Haselton, M.G., Berezovskaya, A., & Lipinski, R. E. (2007). Desiring the muscular ideal: Men's body satisfaction in the United States, Ukraine, and Ghana. *Psychology of Men & Masculinity, 8*(2), 103–117.

Frederick, D. A., Peplau, L. A., & Lever, J. (2006). The swimsuit issue: Correlates of body image in a sample of 52,677 heterosexual adults. *Body Image, 3*(4), 413–419.

Freeman, J. B., & Ambady, N. (2011). A dynamic interactive theory of person construal. *Psychological Review, 118*(2), 247–279.

Frenkl, O. J., & Doob, A. N. (1976). Post-decision dissonance at the polling booth. *Canadian Journal of Behavioral Science, 8*(4), 347–350.

Frey, B. S., Savage, D. A., & Torgler, B. (2010). Noblesse oblige? Determinants of survival in a life-and-death situation. *Journal of Economic Behavior & Organization, 74*(1–2), 1–11.

Freyd, J. J. (2002). In the wake of terrorist attack, hatred may mask fear. *Analyses of Social Issues and Public Policy, 2*(1), 5–8.

Friedkin, N. E. (2010). The attitude-behavior linkage in behavioral cascades. *Social Psychology Quarterly, 73*(2), 96–213.

Frimer, J. A., Skitka, L. J., & Motyl, M. (2017). Liberals and conservatives are similarly motivated to avoid exposure to another's opinions. *Journal of Experimental Social Psychology, 72*, 1–12.

Fritsch, J. (2000, February 26). The Diallo verdict: The overview; 4 officers in Diallo shooting are acquitted of all charges. *The New York Times*, A1. Retrieved from https://www.nytimes.com/2000/02/26/nyregion/diallo-verdict-overview-4-officers-diallo-shooting-are-acquitted-all-charges.html

Fritzsche, B. A., Finkelstein, M. A., & Penner, L. A. (2000). To help or not to help: Capturing individuals' decision policies. *Social Behavior and Personality, 28*(6), 561–578.

Froming, W. J., Corley, E. B., & Rinker, L. (1990). The influence of public self-consciousness and the audience's characteristics on withdrawal from embarrassing situations. *Journal of Personality, 58*(4), 603–622.

Froming, W. J., Nasby, W., & McManus, J. (1998). Prosocial self-schemas, self-awareness, and children's prosocial behavior. *Journal of Personality and Social Psychology, 75*(3), 766–777.

Froming, W. J., Walker, G. R., & Lopyan, K. J. (1982). Public and private self-awareness: When personal attitudes conflict with societal expectations. *Journal of Experimental Social Psychology, 18*(5), 476–487.

Frost, D. M., & Gola, K. A. (2015). Meanings of intimacy: A comparison of members of heterosexual and same-sex couples. *Analyses of Social Issues and Public Policy, 15*(1), 382–400.

Frost, K. A., Franzoi, S. L., Oswald, D. L., & Shields, S. A. (2018). Revising the Body Esteem Scale with a U.S. college student sample: Evaluation, validation, and uses for the BES-R. *Sex Roles, 78*(1–2), 1–17.

Fujihara, T., Kohyama, T., Andreu, J. M., & Ramirez, J. M. (1999). Justification of interpersonal aggression in Japanese, American and Spanish students. *Aggressive Behavior, 25*(3), 185–195.

Fullwood, C., & Attrill-Smith, A. (2018). Up-dating: Ratings of perceived dating success are better online than offline. *Cyberpsychology, Behavior, and Social Networking, 21*(1), 11–15.

Fung, H. H., Stoeber, F. S., Yeung, D. Y., & Lang, F. R. (2008). Cultural specificity of socioemotional selectivity: Age differences in social network composition among Germans and Hong Kong Chinese. *Journal of Gerontology: Psychological Sciences, 63*(3), 156–164.

Furnham, A., McClelland, A., & Omer, L. (2003). A cross-cultural comparison of ratings of perceived fecundity and sexual attractiveness as a function of body weight and waist-to-hip ratio. *Psychology Health and Medicine, 8*(2), 219–230.

Furnham, A., Moutafi, J., & Baguma, P. (2002). A cross-cultural study on the role of weight and waist-to-hip ratio on female attractiveness. *Personality and Individual Differences, 32*(4), 729–745.

Furnham, A., & Thorne, J. D. (2013). Need for cognition: Its dimensionality and personality and intelligence correlates. *Journal of Individual Differences, 34*(4), 230–240.

Furuya-Kanamori, L., & Doi, S. A. (2016). Angry birds, angry children, and angry meta-analysts: A reanalysis. *Perspectives on Psychological Science, 11*(3), 408–414.

G

Gabrenya, W. K., Jr., Wang, Y. E., & Latané, B. (1985). Social loafing on an optimizing task: Cross-cultural differences among Chinese and Americans. *Journal of Cross-Cultural Psychology, 16*(2), 223–242.

Gabrieli, J. D. (1999). The architecture of human memory. In J. K. Foster & M. Jelicic (Eds.), *Memory: Systems, process, or function?* (pp. 205–231). Oxford, England: Oxford University Press.

Gaertner, S. L., & Dovidio, J. F. (1977). The subtlety of white racism, arousal, and helping behavior. *Journal of Personality and Social Psychology, 35*, 691–707.

Gaertner, S. L., & Dovidio, J. F. (2000). *Reducing intergroup bias: The common ingroup identity model.* Philadelphia, PA: Psychology Press.

Gaertner, S. L., & Dovidio, J. F. (2009). A common ingroup identity: A categorization-based approach for reducing intergroup bias. In T. D. Nelson (Ed.), *Handbook of prejudice, stereotyping, and discrimination* (pp. 489–505). New York, NY: Psychology Press.

Gagné, F. M., & Lydon, J. E. (2001). Mindset and relationship illusions: The moderating effects of domain specificity and relationship commitment. *Personality and Social Psychology Bulletin, 27*(9), 1144–1155.

Gaines, S. O., Jr. (1995). Relationships between members of cultural minorities. In J. T. Wood & S. Duck (Eds.), *Under-studied relationships: Off the beaten track* (pp. 51–88). Thousand Oaks, CA: Sage.

Gainotti, G. (2013). Laterality effects in normal subjects' recognition of familiar faces, voices and names. Perceptual and representational components. *Neuropsychologia, 51*(7), 1151–1160.

Galinsky, A. D., Gruenfeld, D. H., & Magee, J. C. (2003). From power to action. *Journal of Personality and Social Psychology, 85*(3), 453–466.

Galinsky, A. D., Todd, A. R., Homan, A. C., Phillips, K. W., Apfelbaum, E. P., Sasaki, S. J.,. . .Maddux, W. W. (2015). Maximizing the gains and minimizing the pains of diversity: A policy perspective. *Perspectives on Psychological Science, 10*(6), 742–748.

Gallese, V., Eagle, M. N., & Migone, P. (2007). Intentional attunement: Mirror neurons and the neural underpinnings of interpersonal relations. *Journal of the American Psychoanalytic Association, 55*(1), 131–176.

Galperin, A., & Haselton, M. (2010). Predictors of how often and when people fall in love. *Evolutionary Psychology, 8*(1), 5–28.

Gammage, K. L., Carron, A. V., & Estabrooks, P. A. (2001). Team cohesion and individual productivity: The influence of the norm for productivity and the identifiability of individual effort. *Small Group Research, 32*(1), 3–18.

Gamson, W. A., Fireman, B., & Rytina, S. (1982). *Encounters with unjust authority.* Homewood, IL: Dorsey Press.

Gan, M., Heller, D., & Chen, S. (2018). The power in being yourself: Feeling authentic enhances the sense of power. *Personality and Social Psychology Bulletin, 44*(10), 1460–1472.

Gangestad, S. W. (2012). Evolutionary perspectives. In K. Deaux & M. Snyder (Eds.), *The Oxford handbook of personality and social psychology* (pp. 151–181). New York, NY: Oxford University Press.

Garcia, S. M., Weaver, K., Moskowitz, G. B., & Darley, J. M. (2002). Crowded minds: The implicit bystander effect. *Journal of Personality and Social Psychology, 83*(4), 843–853.

Garcia-Retamero, R., & López-Zafra, E. (2006). Prejudice against women in male-congenial environments: Perceptions of gender role congruity in leadership. *Sex Roles, 55*(1–2), 51–61.

Gardner, W. L., Gabriel, S., & Lee, A. Y. (1999). "I" value freedom, but "we" value relationships: Self-construal priming mirrors cultural differences in judgment. *Psychological Science, 10*(4), 321–326.

Garfinkel, P. (1985). *In a man's world*. New York, NY: New American Library.

Gastil, J., Burkhalter, S., & Black, L. W. (2007). Do juries deliberate? A study of deliberation, individual difference, and group member satisfaction at a municipal courthouse. *Small Group Research, 38*(3), 337–359.

Gates, M. F., & Allee, W. C. (1933). Conditioned behavior of isolated and grouped cockroaches on a simple maze. *Journal of Comparative Psychology, 15*(2), 331–358.

Gathorne-Hardy, J. (1981). *Marriage, love, sex and divorce*. New York, NY: Summit Books.

Gaucher, D., Friesen, J. P., Neufeld, K. H., & Esses, V. M. (2018). Changes in the positivity of migrant stereotype content: How system-sanctioned pro-migrant ideology can affect public opinions of migrants. *Social Psychological and Personality Science, 9*(2), 223–233.

Gazzaniga, M. S. (Ed.). (2000). *The new cognitive neuroscience*. Cambridge, MA: MIT Press.

Geary, D. C., Rumsey, M., Bow-Thomas, C. C., & Hoard, M. K. (1995). Sexual jealousy as a facultative trait: Evidence from the pattern of sex differences in adults from China and the United States. *Ethology and Sociobiology, 16*(5), 355–383.

Geary, J., & DePaulo, B. M. (2007). Can People Accurately Detect Lies? No. In J. A. Nier (Ed.), *Taking sides: Clashing views in social psychology* (2nd ed., pp. 156–162). New York, NY: McGraw-Hill.

Geen, R. G. (1968). Effects of frustration, attack, and prior training on aggressiveness upon aggressive behavior. *Journal of Personality and Social Psychology, 9*(4), 316–321.

Geen, R. G. (1996). Preferred stimulation levels in introverts and extraverts: Effects on arousal and performance. *Journal of Personality and Social Psychology, 46*(6), 1303–1312.

Geniole, S. N., Denson, T. F., Dixson, B. J., Carré, J. M., & McCormick, C. M. (2015). Evidence from meta-analyses of the facial width-to-height ratio as an evolved cue of threat. *PLoS One, 10*(7).

Gentile, D. A., Anderson, C. A., Yukawa, S., Ihori, N., Saleem, M., Kam, L., . . .Sakamoto, A. (2009). The effects of prosocial video games on prosocial behaviors: International evidence from correlational, longitudinal, and experimental studies. *Personality and Social Psychology Bulletin, 35*(6), 752–763.

Gentile, D. A., Lynch, P. J., Linder, J. R., & Walsh, D. A. (2004). The effects of violent video game habits on adolescent hostility: Aggressive behaviors and school performance. *Journal of Adolescence, 27*(1), 5–22.

Georgesen, J. C., & Harris, M. J. (2000). The balance of power: Interpersonal consequences of differential power and expectancies. *Personality and Social Psychology Bulletin, 26*(10), 1239–1257.

Gerard, H. B., & Mathewson, G. C. (1966). The effects of severity of initiation on liking for a group: A replication. *Journal of Experimental Social Psychology, 2*(3), 278–287.

Gere, J., & MacDonald, G. (2010). An update of the empirical case for the need to belong. *The Journal of Individual Psychology, 66*(1), 93–115.

Gergen, K. J. (2012). The social dimension of social psychology: A historical analysis. In A. W. Kruglanski & W. Stroebe (Eds.), *Handbook of the history of social psychology* (pp. 137–158). New York, NY: Psychology Press.

Gergen, K. J., Ellsworth, P., Maslach, C., & Seipel, M. (1975). Obligation, donor resources, and reactions to aid in 3 cultures. *Journal of Personality and Social Psychology, 31*(3), 390–400.

Gerlach, A. L., Wilhelm, F. H., & Roth, W. T. (2003). Embarrassment and social phobia: The role of parasympathetic activation. *Journal of Anxiety Disorders, 17*(2), 197–210.

Gerstenfeld, P. B. (2002). A time to hate: Situational antecedents of intergroup bias. *Analyses of Social Issues and Public Policy, 2*(1), 61–67.

Gervais, S. J., & Vescio, T. K. (2012). The effect of patronizing behavior and control on men and women's performance in stereotypically masculine domains. *Sex Roles, 66*(7–8), 479–491.

Giancola, P. R., & Zeichner, A. (1997). The biphasic effects of alcohol on human physical aggression. *Journal of Abnormal Psychology, 106*(4), 598–607.

Gibbs, J. L., Ellison, N. B., & Heino, R. D. (2006). Self-presentation in online personals: The role of anticipated future interaction, self-disclosure, and perceived success in internet dating. *Communication Research, 33*(2), 152–177.

Gibson, B., & Maurer, J. (2000). Cigarette smoking in the movies: The influence of product placement on attitudes toward smoking and smokers. *Journal of Applied Social Psychology, 30*(7), 1457–1473.

Giffords Law Center. (2017, November). Open carry. *Giffords Law Center to Prevent Gun Violence*. Retrieved from https://lawcenter.giffords.org/gun-laws/policy-areas/guns-in-public/open-carry/

Gilbert, D. T. (1989). Thinking lightly about others: Automatic components of the social inference process. In J. Uleman & J. Bargh (Eds.), *Unintended thought* (pp. 189–211). New York, NY: Guilford Press.

Gilbert, D. T. (1998). Ordinary personalogy. In D. T. Gilbert, S. T. Fiske, & G. Lindzey (Eds.), *The handbook of social psychology* (4th ed., Vol. 2, pp. 89–150). New York, NY: McGraw-Hill.

Gilbert, P., McEwan, K., Mitra, R., Franks, L., Richter, A., & Rockliff, H. (2008). Feeling safe and content: A specific affect regulation system? Relationship to depression, anxiety, stress and self-criticism. *Journal of Positive Psychology, 3*(3), 182–191.

Gilovich, T., Medvec, V. H., & Chen, S. (1995). Commission, omission, and dissonance reduction: Coping with regret in the "Monty Hall" problem. *Personality and Social Psychology Bulletin, 21*(2), 182–190.

Gissel, A. L., Thompson, L. F., & Pond, S. B. III. (2013). A theory-driven investigation of prospective applicants' intentions to submit video résumés. *Journal of Applied Social Psychology, 43*(12), 2449–2461.

Gjerde, P. F., Onishi, M., & Carlson, K. S. (2004). Personality characteristics associated with romantic attachment: A comparison of interview and self-report methodologies. *Personality and Social Psychology Bulletin, 30*(11), 1402–1415.

Glasman, L. R., & Albarracin, D. (2006). Forming attitudes that predict future behavior: A meta-analysis of the attitude-behavior relation. *Psychological Bulletin, 132*(5), 778–822.

Gleason, K. A., Jensen-Campbell, L. A., & Richardson, D. S. (2004). Agreeableness as a predictor of aggression in adolescence. *Aggressive Behavior, 30*(1), 43–61.

Gleason, M. E., Iida, M., Bolger, N., & Shrout, P. E. (2003). Daily supportive equity in close relationships. *Personality and Social Psychology Bulletin, 29*(8), 1036–1045.

Glenn, E. S. (1966). *Mind, culture and politics.* Cited in Stewart, E. C., & Bennett, M. J. (1991). *American cultural patterns: A cross-cultural perspective* (p. 102). Yarmouth, ME: Intercultural Press.

Glick, P., Lameiras, M., Fiske, S. T., Eckes, T., Masser, B., Volpato, C.,. . .Wells, R. (2004). Bad but bold: Ambivalent attitudes toward men predict gender inequality in 16 nations. *Journal of Personality and Social Psychology, 86*(5), 713–728.

Glick, P., Diebold, J., Bailey-Werner, B., & Zhu, L. (1997). The two faces of Adam: Ambivalent sexism and polarized attitudes toward women. *Personality and Social Psychology Bulletin, 23*(12), 1323–1334.

Glick, P., & Fiske, S. T. (1996). The ambivalent sexism inventory: Differentiating hostile and benevolent sexism. *Journal of Personality and Social Psychology, 70*(3), 491–512.

Glick, P., & Fiske, S. T. (2001a). Ambivalent sexism. In M. P. Zanna (Ed.), *Advances in experimental social psychology* (pp. 115–188). San Francisco, CA: Academic Press.

Glick, P., & Fiske, S. T. (2001b). Ambivalent stereotypes as legitimizing ideologies: Differentiating paternalistic and resentful prejudice. In J. T. Jost & B. Major (Eds.), *The psychology of legitimacy: Emerging perspectives on ideology, justice, and intergroup relations* (pp. 278–306). New York, NY: Cambridge University Press.

Glick, P., & Fiske, S. T. (2001c). An ambivalent alliance: Hostile and benevolent sexism as complementary justifications for gender inequality. *American Psychologist, 56*(2), 109–118.

Glick, P., & Hilt, L. (2000). Combative children to ambivalent adults: The development of gender prejudice. In T. Eckes & M. Trautner (Eds.), *The developmental social psychology of gender* (pp. 243–272). Hillsdale, NJ: Lawrence Erlbaum Associates.

Glock, S., Klapproth, F., & Müller, B. C. (2015). Promoting responsible drinking? A mass media campaign affects implicit but not explicit alcohol-related cognitions and attitudes. *British Journal of Health Psychology, 20*(3), 482–497.

Glomb, T. M., Bhave, D. P., Miner, A. G., & Wall, M. (2011). Doing good, feeling good: Examining the role of organizational citizenship behaviors in changing mood. *Personnel Psychology, 64*(1), 191–223.

Godfrey, D. K., Jones, E. E., & Lord, C. G. (1986). Self-promotion is not ingratiating. *Journal of Personality and Social Psychology, 50*(1), 106–115.

Goethals, G. R., & Zanna, M. P. (1979). The role of social comparison in choice shifts. *Journal of Personality and Social Psychology, 37*(9), 1469–1476.

Goffman, E. (1959). *The presentation of self in everyday life.* Garden City, NY: Doubleday.

Goffman, E. (1963). *Stigma: Notes on the management of spoiled identity.* Englewood Cliffs, NJ: Prentice-Hall.

Goldberg, C. (2003, May 1). Some fear loss of privacy as science pries into brain. *Boston Globe,* A1. Retrieved from http://www.cognitiveliberty.org/ccle1/neuro/brain_privacy.htm

Goldberg, I., Harel, M., & Malach, R. (2006). When the brain loses its self: Prefrontal inactivation during sensorimotor processing. *Neuron, 50*(2), 329–339.

Gomez, A., Brooks, M. L., Buhrmester, M. C., Vazquez, A., Jetten, J., & Swann, W. B. Jr. (2011). On the nature of identity fusion: Insights into the construct and a new measure. *Journal of Personality and Social Psychology, 100*(5), 918–933.

Gommans, R., Sandstrom, M. J., Stevens, G. W., ter Bogt, T. F., & Cillessen, A. H. (2017). Popularity, likeability, and peer conformity: Four field experiments. *Journal of Experimental Social Psychology, 73,* 279–289.

Goncalo, J. A., Polman, E., & Maslach, C. (2010). Can confidence come too soon? Collective efficacy, conflict and group performance over time. *Organizational Behavior and Human Decision Processes, 113*(1), 13–24.

Gonzaga, G. C., & Haselton, M. G. (2008). The evolution of love and long-term bonds. In J. P. Forgas & J. Fitness (Eds.), *Social relationships: Cognitive, affective, and motivational processes* (pp. 39–54). Hove, England: Psychology Press.

Gonzales, M. H., Pederson, J. H., Manning, D. J., & Wetter, D. W. (1990). Pardon my gaffe: Effects of sex, status, and consequence severity on accounts. *Journal of Personality and Social Psychology, 58*(4), 610–621.

Gonzalez, R., Sirlopu, D., & Kessler, T. (2010). Prejudice among Peruvians and Chileans as a function of identity, intergroup contact, acculturation preferences, and intergroup emotions. *Journal of Social Issues, 66*(4), 803–824.

Good, C., Aronson, J., & Inzlicht, M. (2003). Improving adolescents' standardized test performance: An intervention to reduce the effects of stereotype threat. *Journal of Applied Developmental Psychology, 24*(6), 645–662.

Goodall, J. (1986). *The chimpanzees of Gombe.* Cambridge, MA: Harvard University Press.

Goodenow, C., Watson, R. J., Adjei, J., Homma, Y., & Saewyc, E. (2016). Sexual orientation trends and disparities in school bullying and violence-related experiences, 1999–2013. *Psychology of Sexual Orientation and Gender Diversity, 3*(4), 386–396.

Goodwin, G. P. (2015). Moral character in person perception. *Current Directions in Psychological Science, 24*(1), 38–44.

Gorassini, D. R., & Olson, J. M. (1995). Does self-perception change explain the foot-in-the-door effect? *Journal of Personality and Social Psychology, 69*(1), 91–105.

Gordon, R. A. (1996). Impact of ingratiation on judgments and evaluations: A meta-analytic investigation. *Journal of Personality and Social Psychology, 71*(1), 54–70.

Gore, J. S., & Cross, S. E. (2006). Pursuing goals for us: Relationally autonomous reasons in long-term goal pursuit. *Journal of Personality and Social Psychology, 90*(5), 848–861.

Göregenli, M. (1997). Individualist-collectivist tendencies in a Turkish sample. *Journal of Cross-Cultural Psychology, 28*(6), 787–794.

Gosnell, C. L., Britt, T. W., & Mckibben, E. S. (2011). Self-presentation in everyday life: Effort, closeness, and satisfaction. *Self and Identity, 10*(1), 18–31.

Gottman, J. M. (1979). *Marital interaction.* New York, NY: Academic Press.

Gottman, J. M. (1993). *Why marriages succeed or fail.* New York, NY: Simon & Schuster.

Gottman, J. M., & Levenson, R. W. (1992). Marital processes predictive of later dissolution: Behavior, physiology, and health. *Journal of Personality and Social Psychology, 63*(2), 221–233.

Gough, B. (2002). "I've always tolerated it but . . .": Heterosexual masculinity and the discursive reproduction of homophobia. In A. Coyle & C. Kitzinger, Celia (Eds.), *Lesbian and gay psychology: New perspectives* (pp. 219–238). Malden, MA: Blackwell.

Goukens, C., Dewitte, S., & Warlop, L. (2009). Me, myself, and my choices: The influence of private self-awareness on choice. *Journal of Marketing Research, 46*(5), 682–692.

Gouldner, A. W. (1960). The norm of reciprocity: A preliminary statement. *American Sociological Review, 25*(2), 161–178.

Govindarajan, V. (2010, March 26). Why open immigration is good for America. *Harvard Business Review.* Retrieved from https://hbr.org/2010/03/why-open-immigration-is-good-f

Grabe, S., & Hyde, J. S. (2006). Ethnicity and body dissatisfaction among women in the United States: A meta-analysis. *Psychological Bulletin, 132*(4), 622–640.

Graen, G. B., & Hui, C. (2001). Approaches to leadership: Toward a complete contingency model of face-to-face leadership. In M. Erez & U. Kleinbeck (Eds.), *Work motivation in the context of a globalizing economy* (pp. 211–225). Mahwah, NJ: Lawrence Erlbaum Associates.

Graham, J., Haidt, J., & Nosek, B. A. (2009). Liberals and conservatives rely on different set of moral foundations. *Journal of Personality and Social Psychology, 96*(5), 1029–1046.

Grand, J. A. (2017). Brain drain? An examination of stereotype threat effects during training on knowledge acquisition and organizational effectiveness. *Journal of Applied Psychology, 102*(2), 115–150.

Grant, A., & Gino, F. (2010). A little thanks goes a long way: Explaining why gratitude expressions motivate prosocial behavior. *Journal of Personality and Social Psychology, 98*(6), 946–955.

Graves, F. C., & Hennessy, M. B. (2000). Comparison of the effects of the mother and an unfamiliar adult female on cortisol and behavioral responses of pre- and postweaning guinea pigs. *Developmental Psychobiology, 36*(2), 91–100.

Grayman-Simpson, N., & Mattis, J. S. (2013). Doing good and feeling good among African Americans: Subjective religiosity, helping, and satisfaction. *Journal of Black Psychology, 39*(4), 411–427.

Greaves, L. (1996). *Smoke screen: Women's smoking and social control.* Halifax, Canada: Fernwood.

Green, C. W. (1998). Normative influence on the acceptance of information technology: Measurement and effects. *Small Group Research, 29*(1), 85–123.

Green, D. P., Glaser, J., & Rich, A. (1998). From lynching to gay bashing: The elusive connection between economic conditions and hate crime. *Journal of Personality and Social Psychology, 75*(1), 82–92.

Green, J. D., & Sedikides, C. (1999). Affect and self-focused attention revisited: The role of affect orientation. *Personality and Social Psychology Bulletin, 25*(1), 104–119.

Greenaway, K. H., Haslam, S. A., Cruwys, T., Branscombe, N. R., Ysseldyk, R., & Heldreth, C. (2015). From "we" to "me": Group identification enhances perceived personal control with consequences for health and well-being. *Journal of Personality and Social Psychology, 109*(1), 53–74.

Greenberg, M. S., & Frisch, D. M. (1972). Effects of intentionality on willingness to reciprocate a favor. *Journal of Experimental Social Psychology, 8*(2), 99–111.

Greenwald, A. G. (1980). The totalitarian ego: Fabrication and revision of personal history. *American Psychologist, 35*(7), 603–618.

Greenwald, A. G., McGhee, D. E., & Schwartz, J. L. (1998). Measuring individual differences in implicit cognition: The implicit association test. *Journal of Personality and Social Psychology, 74*(6), 1464–1480.

Greenwald, A. G., Oakes, M. A., & Hoffman, H. G. (2003). Targets of discrimination: Effects of race on responses to weapons holders. *Journal of Experimental Social Psychology, 39*(4), 399–405.

Greenwald, A. G., & Ronis, D. L. (1978). Twenty years of cognitive dissonance: Case study of the evolution of a theory. *Psychological Review, 85*(1), 53–57.

Greenwood, D. N., & Long, C. R. (2011). Attachment, belongingness needs, and relationship status predict imagined intimacy with media figures. *Communication Research, 38*(2), 278–297.

Greitemeyer, T., & Mügge, D. O. (2014). Video games do affect social outcomes: A meta-analytic review of the effects of violent and prosocial video game play. *Personality and Social Psychology Bulletin, 40*(5), 578–589.

Greitemeyer, T., & Osswald, S. (2010) Effects of prosocial video games on prosocial behavior. *Journal of Personality and Social Psychology, 98*(2), 211–221

Greve, F. (2009, May 23). America's poor are its most generous donors. *The Seattle Times*. Retrieved from https://www.seattletimes.com/nation-world/americas-poor-are-its-most-generous-donors/

Griffith, R. L. Chmielowski, T., & Yoshita, Y. (2007). Do applicants fake? An examination of the frequency of applicant faking behavior. *Personnel Review, 36*(3), 341–355.

Groh, A. M., & Haydon, K. C. (2018). Mothers' neural and behavioral responses to their infants' distress cues: The role of secure base script knowledge. *Psychological Science, 29*(2), 242–253.

Groot, E., Endedijk, M., Jaarsma, D., van Beukelen, P., & Simons, R. -J. (2013). Development of critically reflective dialogues in communities of health professionals. *Advances in Health Sciences Education, 18*(4), 627–643.

Gross, A. E., & Latané, J. G. (1974). Receiving help, reciprocation, and interpersonal attraction. *Journal of Applied Social Psychology, 4*(3), 210–223.

Grossmann, I., & Na, J. (2014). Research in culture and psychology: Past lessons and future challenges. *Wiley Interdisciplinary Reviews: Cognitive Science, 5*(1), 1–14.

Groth, A. N. (1979). *Men who rape: The psychology of the offender.* New York, NY: Plenum Press.

Grubb, A., & Turner, E. (2012). Attribution of blame in rape cases: A review of the impact of rape myth acceptance, gender role conformity and substance use on victim blaming. *Aggression and Violent Behavior, 17*(5), 443–452.

Gruenfeld, D. H., & Preston, J. (2000). Upending the status quo: Cognitive complexity in U.S. Supreme Court justices who overturn legal precedent. *Personality and Social Psychology Bulletin, 26*(8), 1013–1022.

Grusec, J. E. (1991). The socialization of empathy. In M. S. Clark (Ed.), *Review of personality and social psychology: Vol. 12: Prosocial behavior* (pp. 9–33). Thousand Oaks, CA: Sage.

Grusec, J. E., Davidov, M., & Lundell, L. (2002). Prosocial and helping behavior. In P. K. Smith, & C. H. Hart (Eds.), *Blackwell handbook of childhood social development. Blackwell handbooks of developmental psychology* (pp. 457–474). Malden, MA: Blackwell.

Guadagno, R. E., & Cialdini, R. B. (2005). Online persuasion and compliance: Social influence on the Internet and beyond. In Y. Amichai-Hamburger (Ed.), *The social net: The social psychology of the Internet* (pp. 91–113). New York, NY: Oxford University Press.

Gudjonsson, G. H. (1991). Suggestibility and compliance among alleged false confessors and resisters in criminal trials. *Medicine, Science, and the Law, 31*(2), 147–151.

Gudjonsson, G. H. (2003). *The psychology of interrogations and confessions: A handbook.* New York, NY: John Wiley & Sons.

Guéguen, N., & De Gail, M.-A. (2003). The effect of smiling on helping behavior: Smiling and good samaritan behavior. *Communication Reports, 16*(2), 133–140.

Guéguen, N., & Fischer-Lokou, J. (2004). Hitchhikers' smiles and receipt of help. *Psychological Reports, 94*(3), 756–760.

Guéguen, N., & Jacob, C. (2001). Fund-raising on the Web: The effect of an electronic foot-in-the-door on donation. *Cyberpsychology and Behavior, 4*(6), 705–709.

Guéguen, N., Pascual, A., & Dagot, L. (2002). Low-ball and compliance to a request: An application in a field setting. *Psychological Reports, 91*(1), 81–84.

Guéguen, N., Pascual, A., Silone, F., & David, M. (2015). When legitimizing a request increases compliance: The legitimizing object technique. *The Journal of Social Psychology, 155*(6), 541–544.

Guerin, B. (1986). Mere presence effects in humans: A review. *Journal of Personality and Social Psychology, 22*(1), 38–77.

Guilbault, R. L., Bryant, F. B., Howard Brockway, J., & Posavac, E. J. (2004). A meta-analysis of research on hindsight bias. *Basic and Applied Social Psychology, 26*(2–3), 103–117.

Guille, L. (2004). Men who batter and their children: An integrated review. *Aggression and Violent Behavior, 9*(2), 129–163.

Guimond, S., Dambrun, M., Michinov, M., & Duarte, S. (2003). Does social dominance generate prejudice? Integrating individual and contextual determinants of intergroup cognitions. *Journal of Personality and Social Psychology, 84*(4), 697–721.

Guinote, A., Mauro, C., Pereira, M. H., & Monteiro, M. B. (2007). Children's perceptions of group variability as a function of status. *International Journal of Behavioral Development, 31*(2), 97–104.

Guinote, A., Willis, G. B., & Martellotta, C. (2010). Social power increases implicit prejudice. *Journal of Experimental Social Psychology, 46*(2), 299–307.

Gulker, J. E., & Monteith, M. J. (2013). Intergroup boundaries and attitudes: The power of a single potent link. *Personality and Social Psychology Bulletin, 39*(7), 943–955.

Gunderson, E. A., Ramirez, G., Levine, S. C., & Beilock, S. L. (2012). The role of parents and teachers in the development of gender-related math attitudes. *Sex Roles, 66*(3–4), 153–166.

Gurung, R. A., Brickner, M., Leet, M., & Punke, E. (2018a). Dressing "in code": Clothing rules, propriety, and perceptions. *The Journal of Social Psychology, 158*(5), 553–557.

Gurung, R. A., Punke, E., Brickner, M., & Badalamenti, V. (2018b). Power and provocativeness: The effects of subtle changes in clothing on perceptions of working women. *The Journal of Social Psychology, 158*(2), 252–255.

Gutierrez-Garcia, A., & Calvo, M. G. (2014). Social anxiety and interpretation of ambiguous smiles. *Anxiety, Stress & Coping: An International Journal, 27*(1), 74–89.

H

Habashi, M. M., Graziano, W. G., & Hoover, A. E. (2016). Searching for the prosocial personality: A big five approach to linking personality and prosocial behavior. *Personality and Social Psychology Bulletin, 42*(9), 1177–1192.

Hafer, C. L. (2000). Investment in long-term goals and commitment to just means drive the need to believe in a just world. *Personality and Social Psychology Bulletin, 26*(9), 1059–1073.

Hagestad, G. O., & Smyer, M. A. (1982). Dissolving long-term relationships: Patterns of divorcing in middle age. In S. Duck (Ed.), *Personal relationships, 4: Dissolving relationships* (pp. 155–188). New York, NY: Academic Press.

Hagger, M. S., Chatzisarantis, N. L., Alberts, H., Anggono, C. O., Batailler, C., Birt, A. R.,. . . .Zwienenberg, M. (2016). A multilab preregistered replication of the ego-depletion effect. *Perspectives on Psychological Science, 11*(4), 546–573.

Hagger, M. S., Koch, S., Chatzisarantis, N. L., & Orbell, S. (2017). The common sense model of self-regulation: Meta-analysis and test of a process model. *Psychological Bulletin, 143*(11), 1117–1154.

Hagger, M. S., Wood, C., Stiff, C., & Chatzisarantis, N. L. (2010). Ego depletion and the strength model of self-control: A meta-analysis. *Psychological Bulletin, 136*(4), 495–525.

Hahn, A., Judd, C. M., Hirsh, H. K., & Blair, I. V. (2014). Awareness of implicit attitudes. *Journal of Experimental Psychology: General, 143*(3), 1369–1392. doi:10.1037/a0035028.

Haidt, J., & Kesebir, S. (2010). Morality. In S. T. Fiske, D T. Gilbert, & G. Lindzey (Eds.), *Handbook of social psychology* (5th ed., Vol. 1, pp. 797–832). Hoboken, NJ: John Wiley & Sons.

Haimovitz, K., & Dweck, C. S. (2016). Parents' views of failure predict children's fixed and growth intelligence mind-sets. *Psychological Science, 27*(6), 859–869.

Halberstadt, J., & Rhodes, G. (2003). It's not just average faces that are attractive: Computer-manipulated averageness makes birds, fish, and automobiles attractive. *Psychonomic Bulletin and Review, 10*(1), 149–156.

Hald, G. M., & Malamuth, N. N. (2014). Experimental effects of exposure to pornography: The moderating effect of personality and mediating effect of sexual arousal. *Archives of Sexual Behavior, 44*(1), 99–109.

Hald, G. M., Malamuth, N. M., & Yuen, C. (2010). Pornography and attitudes supporting violence against women: Revisiting the relationship in nonexperimental studies. *Aggressive Behavior, 36*(1), 14–20.

Halevy, N., Berson, Y., & Galinsky, A. D. (2011). The mainstream is not electable: When vision triumphs over representativeness in leader emergence and effectiveness. *Personality and Social Psychology Bulletin, 37*(7), 893–904.

Halford, W. K., Hahlweg, K., & Dunne, M. (1990). The cross-cultural consistency of marital communication associated with marital distress. *Journal of Marriage and the Family, 52*(2), 487–500.

Hall, J. A. (1978). Gender effects in decoding nonverbal cues. *Psychological Bulletin, 85*(4), 845–875.

Hall, J. A. (1984). *Nonverbal sex differences: Communication accuracy and expressive style.* Baltimore, MD: Johns Hopkins University Press.

Halliwell, E., & Diedrichs, P. C. (2014). Testing a dissonance body image intervention among young girls. *Health Psychology, 33*(2), 201–204.

Halpern, D. F. (2017). Whither psychology. *Perspectives on Psychological Science, 12*(4), 665–668.

Haltzman, S., Holstein, N., & Moss, S. B. (2007). Men, marriage, and divorce. In J. E. Grant & M. N. Potenza (Eds.), *Textbook of men's mental health* (pp. 283–305). Washington, DC: American Psychiatric.

Hamamura, T. (2012). Are cultures becoming individualistic? A cross-temporal comparison of individualism-collectivism in the United States and Japan. *Personality and Social Psychology Review, 16*(1), 3–24.

Hames, R., & McCabe, C. (2007). Meal sharing among the Ye'Kwana. *Human Nature, 18*(1), 1–21.

Hamilton, D. L., & Gifford, R. K. (1976). Illusory correlation in interpersonal perception: A cognitive basis of stereotypic judgments. *Journal of Experimental Social Psychology, 12*(4), 392–407.

Hammond, K. R. (2004). The wrong standard: Science, not politics, needed. *Behavioral and Brain Sciences, 27*(3), 341.

Han, S. (2013). Understanding the self: A cultural neuroscience perspective. In S. Barnow & N. Balkir (Eds.), *Cultural variations in psychopathology: From research to practice* (pp. 27–42). Cambridge, MA: Hogrefe.

Han, S., & Northoff, G. (2009). Understanding the self: A cultural neuroscience perspective. *Progress in Brain Research, 178*, 203–212.

Hance, M. A., Blackhart, G., & Dew, M. (2018). Free to be me: The relationship between the true self, rejection sensitivity, and use of online dating sites. *The Journal of Social Psychology, 158*(4), 421–429.

Haney, C., & Zimbardo, P. G. (2009). Persistent dispositionalism in interactionist clothing: Fundamental attribution error in explaining prison abuse. *Personality and Social Psychology Bulletin, 35*(6), 807–814.

Hansen, C. H., & Hansen, R. D. (1988). Finding the face in the crowd: An anger superiority effect. *Journal of Personality and Social Psychology, 54*(6), 917–924.

Hansen, C. H., & Hansen, R. D. (1990). Rock music videos and antisocial behavior. *Basic and Applied Social Psychology, 11*(4), 357–369.

Hansen, J., & Wanke, M. (2009). Liking what's familiar: The importance of unconscious familiarity in the mere-exposure effect. *Social Cognition, 27*(2), 161–182.

Hantke, M. (2013). How to prepare an IRB application. In L. W. Roberts (Ed.), *The academic medicine handbook: A guide to achievement and fulfillment for academic faculty* (pp. 251–256). New York, NY: Springer.

Harari, G. M., Lane, N. D., Wang, R., Crosier, B. S., Campbell, A. T., & Gosling, S. D. (2016). Using smartphones to collect behavioral data in psychological science: Opportunities, practical considerations, and challenges. *Perspectives on Psychological Science, 11*(6), 838–854.

Harari, H., Mohr, D., & Hosey, K. (1980). Faculty helpfulness to students: A comparison of compliance techniques. *Personality and Social Psychology Bulletin, 6*(3), 373–377.

Harbaugh, W. T., Mayr, U., & Burghart, D. R. (2007). Neural responses to taxation and voluntary giving reveal motives for charitable donations. *Science, 316*(5831), 1622–1625.

Harbus, A. (2002). The medieval concept of the self in Anglo-Saxon England. *Self and Identity, 1*(1), 77–97.

Hardin, G. (1968). The tragedy of the commons. *Science, 162*(3859), 1243–1248.

Harkins, S. G., & Symanski, K. (1989). Social loafing and group evaluation. *Journal of Personality and Social Psychology, 56*(6), 934–941.

Harlow, H. F., & Harlow, M. K. (1962). Social deprivation in monkeys. *Scientific American, 207,* 136–146.

Harms, P. D., Wood, D., Landay, K., Lester, P. B., Lester, G. V. (2018). Autocratic leaders and authoritarian followers revisited: A review and agenda for the future. *The Leadership Quarterly, 29*(1), 105–122.

Harris, C. R. (2002). Sexual and romantic jealousy in heterosexual and homosexual adults. *Psychological Science, 13*(1), 7–12.

Harris, C. R. (2003a). A review of sex differences in sexual jealousy, including self-report data, psychophysiological responses, interpersonal violence, and morbid jealousy. *Personality and Social Psychology Review, 7*(2), 102–128.

Harris, C. R. (2003b). Factors associated with jealousy over real and imagined infidelity: An examination of the social-cognitive and evolutionary psychology perspectives. *Psychology of Women Quarterly, 27*(4), 319–329.

Harris, C. R. (2004). The evolution of jealousy. *American Scientist, 92,* 62–71.

Harris, C. R. (2005). Male and female jealousy, still more similar than different: Reply to Sagarin (2005). *Personality and Social Psychology Review, 9*(1), 76–86.

Harris, C. R., & Christenfeld, N. (1996). Gender, jealousy, and reason. *Psychological Science, 7*(6), 364–366.

Harris, E., & Hopping-Winn, A. (2019, February 6). LGBTQ Family Building Survey: Executive Summary. *Family Equality.* Retrieved from https://www.familyequality.org/resources/lgbtq-family-building-survey/

Harris, G. T., Hilton, N. Z., Rice, M. E., & Eke, A. W. (2007). Children killed by genetic parents versus stepparents. *Evolution and Human Behavior, 28*(2), 85–95.

Harris, K. J., Kacmar, K. M., Zivnuska, S., & Shaw, J. D. (2007). The impact of political skill on impression management effectiveness. *Journal of Applied Psychology, 92*(1), 278–285.

Harris, L. T, & Fiske, S. T. (2011). Perceiving humanity or not: A social neuroscience approach to dehumanized perception. In A. Todorov, S. T. Fiske, & D. A. Prentice (Eds.), *Social neuroscience: Toward understanding the underpinnings of the social mind* (pp. 123–134). New York, NY: Oxford University Press.

Harris, M. (1999). *Theories of culture in postmodern times.* Walnut Creek, CA: Alta Mira Press.

Harris, M. B., Benson, S. M., & Hall, C. L. (1975). The effects of confession on altruism. *Journal of Social Psychology, 96*(2), 187–192.

Harris, M. J., Milich, R., Corbitt, E. M., Hoover, D. W., & Brady, M. (1992). Self-fulfilling effects of stigmatizing information on children's social interactions. *Journal of Personality and Social Psychology, 63*(1), 41–50.

Harris, S. M. (1995). Family, self, and sociocultural contributions to body-image attitudes of African-American women. *Psychology of Women Quarterly, 19*(1), 129–145.

Harrison, A., & Saeed, L. (1977). Let's make a deal: An analysis of revelations and stipulations in lonely hearts advertisements. *Journal of Personality and Social Psychology, 35*(4), 257–264.

Hart, A. J., Whalen, P. J., Shin, L. M., McInerney, S. C., Fischer, H., & Rauch, S. L. (2000). Differential response in the human amygdala to racial outgroup vs. ingroup face stimuli. *Neuroreport, 11*(11), 2351–2355.

Hart, J. W., Bridgett, D. J., & Karau, S. J. (2001). Coworker ability and effort as determinants of individual effort on a collective task. *Group Dynamics: Theory, Research, and Practice, 5*(3), 181–190.

Hart, S., Field, T., del Valle, C., & Letourneau, M. (1998). Infants protest their mothers' attending to an infant-size doll. *Social Development, 7*(1), 54–61.

Hart, W., Albarracín, D., Eagly, A. H., Brechan, I., Lindberg, M. J., & Merrill, L. (2009). Feeling validated versus being correct: A meta-analysis of selective exposure to information. *Psychological Bulletin, 135*(4), 555–588.

Hartley, W. S. (1970). *Manual for the twenty statements problem.* Kansas City, MO: Department of Research, Greater Kansas City Mental Health Foundation.

Hartmann, D. P. (1969). Influence of symbolically modeled instrumental aggression and pain cues on aggressive behavior. *Journal of Personality and Social Psychology, 11*(3), 280–288.

Hartung, F. M., & Renner, B. (2011). Social curiosity and interpersonal perception: A judge X trait interaction. *Personality and Social Psychology Bulletin, 37*(6), 796–814.

Hartwig, M., & Bond, C. F. (2011). Why do lie-catchers fail? A lens model meta-analysis of human lie judgments. *Psychological Bulletin, 137*(4), 643–659.

Harvey, E. L., & Hill, A. J. (2001). Health professionals' views of overweight people and smokers. *International Journal of Obesity, 25*(8), 1253–1261.

Harvey, J. H., Flanary, R., & Morgan, M. (1986). Vivid memories of vivid loves gone by. *Journal of Social and Personal Relationships, 3*(3), 359–373.

Harvey, R. D., Tennial, R. E., & Banks, K. H. (2017). The development and validation of a colorism scale. *Journal of Black Psychology, 43*(7), 740–764.

Hasan, M., & Clark, E. M. (2017). I get so lonely, baby: The effects of loneliness and social isolation on romantic dependency. *The Journal of Social Psychology, 157*(4), 429–444.

Hasel, L. E., & Kassin, S. M. (2012). False confessions. In B. L. Cutler (Ed), *Conviction of the innocent: Lessons from psychological research* (pp. 53–77). Washington, DC: American Psychological Association.

Haselton, M. G., & Nettle, D. (2006). The paranoid optimist: An integrative evolutionary model of cognitive biases. *Personality and Social Psychology Review, 10*(1), 47–66.

Hashimoto, H. (2011). Interdependence as a self-sustaining set of beliefs. *The Japanese Journal of Experimental Social Psychology, 50*(2), 182–193.

Hastie, R., Penrod, S., & Pennington, N. (1983). *Inside the jury.* Cambridge, MA: Harvard University Press.

Hastorf, A., & Cantril, H. (1954). They saw a game: A case study. *Journal of Abnormal and Social Psychology, 49*(1), 129–134.

Hatfield, E. (1988). Passionate and companionate love. In R. J. Sternberg & M. L. Barnes (Eds.), *The psychology of love* (pp. 191–217). New Haven, CT: Yale University Press.

Hatfield, E., & Rapson, R. L. (1993). *Love, sex, and intimacy: Their psychology, biology, and history.* New York, NY: HarperCollins.

Hatfield, E., & Rapson, R. L. (1996). *Love and sex: Crosscultural perspectives.* Boston, MA: Allyn & Bacon.

Hatfield, E., & Rapson, R. L. (2002). Passionate love and sexual desire: Cultural and historical perspectives. In A. L. Vangelisti, H. T. Reis, & M. A. Fitzpatrick (Eds.), *Stability and change in relationships. Advances in personal relationships* (pp. 306–324). New York, NY: Cambridge University Press.

Hatfield, E., Rapson, R. L., & Martel, L. D. (2007). Passionate love and sexual desire. In S. Kitayama, Shinobu & D. Cohen (Eds.), *Handbook of cultural psychology* (pp. 760–779). New York, NY: Guilford Press.

Hatfield, E., & Sprecher, S. (2010). Passionate love scale. In R. R. Milhausen, J. K. Sakaluk, T. D. Fisher, C. M. Davis, & W. L. Yarber (Eds.), *Handbook of sexuality-related measures* (pp. 469–472).

Hatfield, E., Walster, G. W., & Piliavin, J. (1978). Equity theory and helping relationships. In L. Wispé (Ed.), *Altruism, sympathy and helping* (pp. 115–139). New York, NY: Academic Press.

Hatzenbuehler, M. L., Flores, A. R., & Gates, G. J. (2017). Social attitudes regarding same-sex marriage and LGBT health disparities: Results from a national probability sample. *Journal of Social Issues, 73*(3), 508–528.

Hauch, V., Blandón-Gitlin, I., Masip, J. M., & Sporer, S. L. (2015). Are computers effective lie detectors? A meta-analysis of linguistic cues to deception. *Personality and Social Psychology Review, 19*(4), 307–342.

Haugtvedt, C. P., & Petty, R. E. (1992). Personality and persuasion: Need for cognition moderates the persistence and resistance of attitude changes. *Journal of Personality and Social Psychology, 63*(2), 308–319.

Hawkins, S. A., & Hastie, R. (1990). Hindsight: Biased judgments of past events after the outcomes are known. *Psychological Bulletin, 107*(3), 311–327.

Hayashi, M. (2006). Spindle neurons in the anterior cingulate cortex of humans and great apes. In T. Matsuzawa, M. Tomonaga, & M. Tanaka (Eds.), *Cognitive development in chimpanzees* (pp. 64–74). Tokyo, Japan: Springer.

Hayes, R. M., Lorenz, K., & Bell, K. A. (2013). Victim blaming others: Rape myth acceptance and the just world belief. *Feminist Criminology, 8*(3), 202–220.

Hays, N. A., & Goldstein, N. J. (2015). Power and legitimacy influence conformity. *Journal of Experimental Social Psychology, 60,* 17–26.

Hazan, C., & Shaver, P. (1987). Romantic love conceptualized as an attachment process. *Journal of Personality and Social Psychology, 52*(3), 511–524.

Hearold, S. (1986). A synthesis of 1043 effects of television on social behavior. In G. Comstock (Ed.), *Public communication and behavior* (Vol. 1, pp. 66–133). New York, NY: Academic Press.

Heatherton, T. F. (2011). Building a social brain. In A. Todorov, S. T. Fiske, & D. A. Prentice (Eds.), *Social neuroscience: Toward understanding the underpinnings of the social mind* (pp. 274–283). New York, NY: Oxford University Press.

Heatherton, T. F., & Baumeister, R. F. (1991). Binge eating as escape from self-awareness. *Psychological Bulletin, 110*(1), 86–108.

Hebl, M. R., Foster, J. B., Mannix, L. M., & Dovidio, J. F. (2002). Formal and interpersonal discrimination: A field study of bias toward homosexual applicants. *Personality and Social Psychology Bulletin, 28*(6), 815–825.

Hebl, M. R., King, E. B., Glick, P., Singletary, S. L., & Kazama, S. (2007). Hostile and benevolent reactions toward pregnant women: Complementary interpersonal punishments and rewards that maintain traditional roles. *Journal of Applied Psychology, 92*(6), 1499–1511.

Hebl, M. R., & Mannix, L. M. (2003). The weight of obesity in evaluating others: A mere proximity effect. *Personality & Social Psychology Bulletin, 29*(1), 28–38.

Hebl, M. R., & Turchin, J. M. (2005). The stigma of obesity: What about men? *Basic and Applied Social Psychology, 27*(3), 267–275.

Hebl, M. R., Xu, J., & Mason, M. F. (2003). Weighing the care: Patients' perceptions of physician care as a function of gender and weight. *International Journal of Obesity, 27*(2), 269–275.

Hecht, M. A., & LaFrance, M. (1998). License or obligation to smile: The effect of power and sex on amount and type of smiling. *Personality and Social Psychology Bulletin, 24*(12), 1332–1342.

Heffner, K. L., Ginsburg, G. P., & Hartley, T. R. (2002). Appraisals and impression management opportunities: Person and situation influences on cardiovascular reactivity. *International Journal of Psychophysiology, 44*(2), 165–175.

Hehman, E., Flake, J. K., & Calanchini, J. (2018). Disproportionate use of lethal force in policing is associated with regional racial biases of residents. *Social Psychological and Personality Science, 9*(4), 393–401.

Heider, F. (1946). Attitudes and cognitive organization. *Journal of Psychology, 21*(1), 107–112.

Heider, F. (1958). *The psychology of interpersonal relations.* New York, NY: John Wiley & Sons.

Heiervang, E., & Goodman, R. (2011). Advantages and limitations of web-based surveys: Evidence from a child mental health survey. *Social Psychiatry and Psychiatric Epidemiology, 46*(1), 69–76.

Heine, S. J., & Hamamura, T. (2007). In search of East Asian self-enhancement. *Personality and Social Psychology Review, 11*(1), 4–27.

Heine, S. J., & Lehman, D. R. (1999). Culture, self-discrepancies, and self-satisfaction. *Personality and Social Psychology Bulletin, 25*(8), 915–925.

Heine, S. J., & Raineri, A. (2009). Self-improving motivations and collectivism: The case of Chileans. *Journal of Cross-Cultural Psychology, 40*(1), 158–163.

Heine, S. J., Takemoto, T., Moskalenko, S., Lasaleta, J., & Henrich, J. (2008). Mirrors in the head: Cultural variation in objective self-awareness. *Personality and Social Psychology Bulletin, 34*(7), 879–887.

Heintzelman, S. J., Christopher, J., Trent, J., & King, L. A. (2013). Counterfactual thinking about one's birth enhances well-being judgments. *The Journal of Positive Psychology, 8*(1), 44–49.

Held, P., & Owens, G. P. (2013). Stigmas and attitudes toward seeking mental health treatment in a sample of veterans and active duty service members. *Traumatology, 19*(2), 136–143.

Helgesen, S. (1990). *The female advantage: Women's ways of leadership.* New York, NY: Doubleday.

Helgeson, V. S. (1994). Long-distance romantic relationships: Sex differences in adjustment and breakup. *Personality and Social Psychology Bulletin, 20*(3), 254–265.

Hemenway, D. (2011). Risks and benefits of a gun in the home. *American Journal of Lifestyle Medicine, 5*(6), 502–511.

Henderson, J. J., & Anglin, J. M. (2003). Facial attractiveness predicts longevity. *Evolution and Human Behavior, 24*(5), 351–356.

Hendrick, C., & Hendrick, S. (1986). A theory and method of love. *Journal of Personality and Social Psychology, 50*(2), 392–402.

Hendrick, C., & Hendrick, S. S. (2003). Romantic love: Measuring cupid's arrow. In S. J. Lopez & C. R. Snyder (Eds.), *Positive psychological assessment: A handbook of models and measures* (pp. 235–249). Washington, DC: American Psychological Association.

Hendrick, C., Hendrick, S., Foote, F. H., & Slapion-Foote, M. J. (1984). Do men and women love differently? *Journal of Social and Personal Relationships, 1*(2), 177–195.

Hennessey, B. A. (2007). Promoting social competence in school-aged children: The effects of the Open Circle Program. *Journal of School Psychology, 45*(3), 349–360.

Hepworth, J. T., & West, S. G. (1988). Lynchings and the economy: A time-series reanalysis of Hovland and Sears (1940). *Journal of Personality and Social Psychology, 55*(2), 239–247.

Herek, G. M. (1987). Religious orientation and prejudice: A comparison of racial and sexual attitudes. *Personality and Social Psychology Bulletin, 13*(1), 34–44.

Herek, G. M. (1991). Myths about sexual orientation: A lawyer's guide to social science research. *Law and Sexuality: A Review of Lesbian and Gay Legal Issues, 1*, 133–172.

Herek, G. M. (2000). The psychology of sexual prejudice. *Current Directions in Psychological Science, 9*(1), 19–22.

Herek, G. M. (2004). Beyond "homophobia": Thinking about sexual prejudice and stigma in the twenty-first century. *Sexuality Research and Social Policy, 1*(2), 6–24.

Herek, G. M., & Garnets, L. D. (2007). Sexual orientation and mental health. *Annual Review of Clinical Psychology, 3*, 353–375.

Herek, G. M., & Gonzalez-Rivera, M. (2006). Attitudes toward homosexuality among U.S. residents of Mexican descent. *Journal of Sex Research, 43*(2), 122–135.

Herek, G. M., & McLemore, K. A. (2013). Sexual prejudice. *Annual Review of Psychology, 64*, 309–333.

Hergovich, A., & Olbrich, A. (2003). The impact of the Northern Ireland conflict on social identity, groupthink and integrative complexity in Great Britain. *Review of Psychology, 10*(2), 95–106.

Hermans, E. J., Putnam, P., Baas, J., Koppeschaar, H. P., & van Honk, J. (2006a). A single administration of testosterone reduces fear-potentiated startle in humans. *Biological Psychiatry, 59*(9), 872–874.

Hermans, E. J., Putnam, P., & van Honk, J. (2006b). Testosterone administration reduces empathetic behavior: A facial mimicry study. *Psychoneuroendocrinology, 31*(7), 859–866.

Hermans, E. J., Ramsey, N. F., & van Honk, J. (2008). Exogenous testosterone potentiates the neural circuitry of reactive aggression in humans. *Biological Psychiatry, 63*(3), 263–270.

Herrmann, S. D., Adelman, R. M., Bodford, J. E., Graudejus, O., Okun, M. A., & Kwan, V. S. (2016). The effects of a female role model on academic performance and persistence of women in STEM courses. *Basic and Applied Social Psychology, 38*(5), 258–268.

Hershfield, H. E., Brown, C. E., & Kray, L. J. (2013). Any second could be *the* second: How thinking about what might have been affects the emergence of meaning and commitment across the adult life span. In J. A. Hicks & C. Routledge (Eds.), *The experience of meaning in life: Classical perspectives, emerging themes, and controversies* (pp. 151–162). New York, NY: Springer.

Hershfield, H. E., Mogilner, C., & Barnea, U. (2016). People who choose time over money are happier. *Social Psychological and Personality Science, 7*(7), 697–706.

Hertel, G., Kerr, N. L., & Messé, L. A. (2000). Motivation gains in groups: Paradigmatic and theoretical advances on the Köhler effect. *Journal of Personality and Social Psychology, 79*(4), 580–601.

Hertwig, R., & Hoffrage, U. (Eds.). (2013). *Simple heuristics in a social world.* New York, NY: Oxford University Press.

Hewstone, M. (1996). Contact and categorization: Social psychological interventions to change intergroup relations. In C. N. Macrae, C. Stangor, & M. Hewstone (Eds.), *Stereotypes and stereotyping* (pp. 323–368). New York, NY: Guilford Press.

Heyman, G. D., Hsu, A. S., Fu, G., & Lee, K. (2013). Instrumental lying by parents in the US and China. *International Journal of Psychology, 48*(6), 1176–1184.

Hicks, D. (1968). Short- and long-term retention of affectively varied modeled behavior. *Psychonomic Science, 11*(10), 369–370.

Higgins, E. T. (1996). The "self digest": Self-knowledge serving self-regulatory functions. *Journal of Personality and Social Psychology, 71*(6), 1062–1083.

Higgins, E. T. (2000). Social cognition: Learning about what matters in the social world. *European Journal of Social Psychology, 30*(1), 3–39.

Higgins, E. T. (2004). Making a theory useful: Lessons handed down. *Personality and Social Psychology Review, 8*(2), 138–145.

Hill, C. T., Rubin, Z., & Peplau, L. A. (1979). Breakups before marriage: The end of 103 affairs. In G. Levinger & O. C. Moles (Eds.), *Divorce and separation* (pp. 64–82). New York, NY: Basic Books.

Hill, R. A., & Dunbar, R. I. (2003). Social network size in humans. *Human Nature, 14*(1), 53–72.

Hindman, M., & Barash, V. (2018). *Disinformation, 'fake news' and influence campaigns on Twitter.* Miami, FL: Knight Foundation.

Hine, C. (2013). *The internet: Understanding qualitative research.* New York, NY: Oxford University Press.

Hing, L. S., Li, W., & Zanna, M. P. (2002). Inducing hypocrisy to reduce prejudicial responses among aversive racists. *Journal of Experimental Social Psychology, 38*(1), 71–78.

Hirata, S., Fuwa, K., & Myowa, M. (2017). Chimpanzees recognize their own delayed self-image. *Royalty Society Open Science, 4*(8), 1–9.

Hirt, E. R. (1990). Do I see only what I expect? Evidence for an expectancy-guided retrieval model. *Journal of Personality and Social Psychology, 58*(6), 937–951.

Hirt, E. R., Zillmann, D., Erickson, G. A., & Kennedy, C. (1992). Costs and benefits of allegiance: Changes in fans' self-ascribed competencies after team victory versus defeat. *Journal of Personality and Social Psychology, 63*(5), 724–738.

Hitlin, S. (2007). Doing good, feeling good: Values and the self's moral center. *Journal of Positive Psychology, 2*(4), 249–259.

Ho, D. Y. -F., & Chiu, C. -Y. (1994). Component ideas of individualism, collectivism, and social organization: An application in the study of Chinese culture. In U. Kim, H. C. Triandis, C. Kâğitçibaşi, S. -C. Choi, & G. Yoon (Eds.), *Individualism and collectivism: Theory, method, and applications* (pp. 137–156). Thousand Oaks, CA: Sage.

Hobart, C. W. (1958). The incidence of romanticism during courtship. *Social Forces, 36*(4), 364–367.

Hodgins, H. S., & Liebeskind, E. (2003). Apology versus defense: Antecedents and consequences. *Journal of Experimental Social Psychology, 39*(4), 297–316.

Hodgins, H. S., Liebeskind, E., & Schwartz, W. (1996). Getting out of hot water: Facework in social predicaments. *Journal of Personality and Social Psychology, 71*(2), 300–314.

Hodson, G., & Esses, V. M. (2002). Distancing oneself from negative attributes and the personal/group discrimination discrepancy. *Journal of Experimental Social Psychology, 38*(5), 500–507.

Hof, P. R., & Van der Gucht, E. (2007). The structure of the cerebral cortex of the humpback whale, Megaptera novaeangliae (Cetacea, Mysticeti, Balaenopteridae). *The Anatomical Record, 290*(1), 1–31.

Hoffman, L. E. (1992). American psychologists and wartime research on Germany, 1941–1945. *American Psychologist, 47*(2), 264–273.

Hofstede, G. (1980). *Culture's consequences: International differences in work related values.* Beverly Hills, CA: Sage.

Hogg, M. A. (1992). *The social psychology of group cohesiveness: From attraction to social identity.* London, England: Harvester-Wheatsheaf.

Hogg, M. A., & Abrams, D. (1998). *Social identifications: A social psychology of intergroup relations and group processes.* London, England: Routledge.

Hohman, Z. P., Gaffney, A. M., & Hogg, M. A. (2017). Who am I if I am not like my group? Self-uncertainty and feeling peripheral in a group. *Journal of Experimental Social Psychology, 72,* 125–132.

Hokanson, J. E., & Edelman, R. (1966). Effects of three social responses on vascular processes. *Journal of Personality and Social Psychology, 3*(4), 442–447.

Holmes, B. M., & Johnson, K. R. (2009). Adult attachment and romantic partner preference: A review. *Journal of Social and Personal Relationships, 26*(6–7), 833–852.

Holtgraves, T. (2004). Social desirability and self-reports: Testing models of socially desirable responding. *Personality and Social Psychology Bulletin, 30*(2), 161–172.

Homan, A. C., & Greer, L. L. (2013). Considering diversity: The positive effects of considerate leadership in diverse teams. *Group Processes & Intergroup Relations, 16*(1), 105–125.

Homan, K., McHugh, E., Wells, D., Watson, C., & King, C. (2012). The effect of viewing ultra-fit images on college women's body dissatisfaction. *Body Image, 9*(1), 50–56.

Homans, G. C. (1958). Social behavior as exchange. *American Journal of Sociology, 63,* 597–606.

Honeycutt, J. M. (2003). *Imagined interactions: Daydreaming about communication.* Cresskill, NJ: Hampton Press.

Hong, Y. -Y., Benet-Martínez, V., Chiu, C. -Y., & Morris, M. W. (2003). Boundaries of cultural influence: Construct activation as a mechanism for cultural differences in social perception. *Journal of Cross-Cultural Psychology, 34*(4), 453–464.

Hong, Y. -Y., Coleman, J., Chan, G., Wong, R. Y., Chiu, C. -Y., Hansen, I. G.,. . .Fu, H. -y. (2004). Predicting intergroup bias: The interactive effects of implicit theory and social identity. *Personality and Social Psychology Bulletin, 30*(8), 1035–1047.

Hong, Y. -Y., Ip, G., Chiu, C. -Y., Morris, M., & Menon, T. (2001). Cultural identity and dynamic construction of the self: Collective duties and individual rights in Chinese and American cultures. *Social Cognition, 19*(3), 251–268.

Hong, Y. -Y., Morris, M. W., Chiu, C. -Y., & Benet-Martínez, V. (2000). Multicultural minds: A dynamic constructivist approach to culture and cognition. *American Psychologist, 55*(7), 709–720.

Hoorens, V., & Nuttin, J. M. (1993). Overevaluation of own attributes: Mere ownership or subjective frequency? *Social Cognition, 11*(2), 177–200.

Hornsey, M. J., & Jetten, J. (2004). The individual within the group: Balancing the need to belong with the need to be different. *Personality and Social Psychology Review, 8*(3), 248–264.

Horton, R. W., & Santogrossi, D. A. (1978). The effect of adult commentary on reducing the influence of televised violence. *Personality and Social Psychology Bulletin, 4*(2), 337–340.

Hoshino-Browne, E. (2012). Cultural variations in motivation for cognitive consistency: Influences of self-systems on cognitive dissonance. *Social and Personality Psychology Compass, 6*(2), 126–141.

Hoss, R. A., Ramsey, J. L., Griffin, A. M., & Langlois, J. H. (2005). The role of facial attractiveness and facial masculinity/femininity in sex classification of faces. *Perception, 34*(12), 1459–1474.

Houry, D., Feldhaus, K., Peery, B., Abbott, J., Lowenstein, S. R., Al-Bataa-De-Montero, S., & Levine, S. (2004). A positive domestic violence screen predicts future domestic violence. *Journal of Interpersonal Violence, 19*(9), 955–966.

House, R., Hanges, P., Javidan, M., Dorfman, P., & Gupta, V. (2004). *Culture, leadership, and organizations: The GLOBE study of 62 societies.* Thousand Oaks, CA: Sage.

Hovland, C. I., Lumsdaine, A. A., & Sheffield, F. D. (1949). *Experiments on mass communication (studies in social psychology in World War II).* Princeton, NJ: Princeton University Press.

Hovland, C. I., & Sears, R. R. (1940). Minor studies in aggression: VI. Correlation of lynchings with economic indices. *Journal of Personality, 9*(2), 301–310.

Hovland, C. I., & Weiss, W. (1951). The influence of source credibility on communication effectiveness. *Public Opinion Quarterly, 15*, 635–650.

Howard, D. J. (1995). "Chaining" the use of influence strategies for producing compliance behavior. *Journal of Social Behavior and Personality, 10*(1), 169–185.

Howard, J. A., Blumstein, P., & Schwartz, P. (1987). Social evolutionary theories? Some observations on preferences in human mate selection. *Journal of Personality and Social Psychology, 53*(1), 194–200.

Howard, S. (2019). Exonerees in black and white: The influence of race on perceptions of those who falsely confessed to a crime. *Psychology, Crime & Law, 25*(9), 911–924.

Howard, S., & Sommers, S. R. (2017). White religious iconography increases anti-Black attitudes. *Psychology of Religion and Spirituality* (in-press).

Hoyle, R. H. (2005). Design and analysis of experimental research on groups. In S. A. Wheelan (Ed.), *Handbook of group research and practice* (pp. 223–239). Thousand Oaks, CA: Sage.

Hoyt, C. L., & Blascovich, J. (2007). Leadership efficacy and women leaders' responses to stereotype activation. *Group Processes and Intergroup Relations, 10*(4), 595–616.

Hoyt, C. L., & Burnette, J. L. (2013). Gender bias in leader evaluations: Merging implicit theories and role congruity perspectives. *Personality and Social Psychology Bulletin, 39*(10), 1306–1319.

Hsiang, S. M., Meng, K. C., & Cane, M. A. (2011). Civil conflicts are associated with the global climate. *Nature, 476*(7361), 438–441.

Huczynski, A., & Buchanan, D. (1996). Can leaders change their styles? In J. Billsberry (Ed.), *The effective manager: Perspectives and illustrations* (pp. 42–46). Thousand Oaks, CA: Sage.

Huelsnitz, C. O., Farrell, A. K., Simpson, J. A., Griskevicius, V., & Szepsenwol, O. (2018). Attachment and jealousy: Understanding the dynamic experience of jealousy using the response escalation paradigm. *Personality and Social Psychology Bulletin, 44*(12), 1664–1680.

Huesmann, L. R. (1986a). The effects of film and television violence among children. In S. J. Katz & P. Vesin (Eds.), *Children and the media* (pp. 101–128). Paris, France: Centre International de l'Enfance.

Huesmann, L. R. (1986b). Psychological processes promoting the relation between exposure to media violence and aggressive behavior by the viewer. *Journal of Social Issues, 42*(3), 125–140.

Huesmann, L. R. (1988). An information processing model for the development of aggression. *Aggressive Behavior, 14*(1), 125–139.

Huesmann, L. R., & Eron, L. D. (Eds.). (1986). *Television and the aggressive child: A cross-national comparison.* Hillsdale, NJ: Lawrence Erlbaum Associates.

Huesmann, L. R., Eron, L. D., Klein, R., Brice, P., & Fischer, P. (1983). Mitigating the imitation of aggressive behaviors by changing children's attitudes about media violence. *Journal of Personality and Social Psychology, 44*(5), 899–910.

Huesmann, L. R., & Miller, L. S. (1994). Long-term effects of repeated exposure to media violence in childhood. In L. R. Huesmann (Ed.), *Aggressive behavior: Current perspectives* (pp. 153–186). New York, NY: Plenum Press.

Huesmann, L. R., Moise-Titus, J., Podolski, C. L., Eron, L. D. (2003). Longitudinal relations between children's exposure to TV violence and their aggressive and violent behavior in young adulthood: 1977–1992. *Developmental Psychology, 39*(2), 201–221.

Huguet, P., Latané, B., & Bourgeois, M. (1998). The emergence of a social representation of human rights via interpersonal communication: Empirical evidence for the convergence of two theories. *European Journal of Social Psychology, 28*(5), 831–846.

Hull, C. L. (1943). *Principles of behavior: An introduction to behavior theory.* New York, NY: Appleton-Century-Crofts.

Hull, J. G. (1981). A self-awareness model of the causes and effects of alcohol consumption. *Journal of Abnormal Psychology, 90*(6), 586–600.

Hull, J. G., & Bond, C. F., Jr. (1986). Social and behavioral consequences of alcohol consumption and expectancy: A meta-analysis. *Psychological Bulletin, 99*(3), 347–360.

Hull, J. G., & Young, R. D. (1983). Self-consciousness, self-esteem, and success-failure as determinants of alcohol consumption in male social drinkers. *Journal of Personality and Social Psychology, 44*(6), 1097–1109.

Hull, J. G., Young, R. D., & Jouriles, E. (1986). Applications of the self-awareness model of alcohol consumption: Predicting patterns of use and abuse. *Journal of Personality and Social Psychology, 51*(4), 790–796.

Hummert, M. L. (2015). Experimental research on age stereotypes: Insights for subjective aging. *Annual Review of Gerontology and Geriatrics, 35*(1), 79–97.

Hunter, M. L. (1998). Colorstruck: Skin color stratification in the lives of African American women. *Sociological Inquiry, 68*(4), 517–535.

Huskinson, T. L., & Haddock, G. (2004). Individual differences in attitude structure: Variance in the chronic reliance on affective and cognitive information. *Journal of Experimental Social Psychology, 40*(1), 82–90.

Hust, S. J., Lei, M., Ren, C., Chang, H., McNab, A. L., Marett, E. G., & Willoughby, J. F. (2013). The effects of sports media exposure on college students' rape myth beliefs and intentions to intervene in a sexual assault. *Mass Communication & Society, 16*(6), 762–786.

Huth-Bocks, A. C., Levendosky, A. A., Bogat, G. A., & von Eye, A. (2004). The impact of maternal characteristics and contextual variables on infant-mother attachment. *Child Development, 75*(2), 480–496.

Huynh, Q. -L., Devos, T., & Smalarz, L. (2011). Perpetual foreigner in one's own land: Potential implications for identity and psychological adjustment. *Journal of Social and Clinical Psychology, 30*(2), 133–162.

Hyde, J. S. (2005). The gender similarities hypothesis. *American Psychologist, 60*(6), 581–592.

Hyers, L. L. (2007). Resisting prejudice every day: Exploring women's assertive responses to anti-Black racism, anti-Semitism, heterosexism, and sexism. *Sex Roles, 56*(1–2), 1–12.

I

Iacoboni, M. (2007). Face to face: The neural basis of social mirroring and empathy. *Psychiatric Annals, 37*(4), 236–241.

Ichheiser, G. (1934). Über zurechnungstäuschungen. [About misattributions]. *Monatsschrift für Kriminalpsycholgie und Strafrechtsreform, 25,* 129–142.

Ichheiser, G. (1943). Misinterpretations of personality in everyday life and the psychologist's frame of reference. *Character and Personality, 12,* 145–160.

IJerzman, H., Blanken, I., Brandt, M. J., Oerlemans, J. M., Van den Hoogenhof, M. M., Franken, S. J., & Oerlemans, M. W. (2014). Sex differences in distress from infidelity in early adulthood and in later life: A replication and meta-analysis of Shackelford et al. (2004). *Social Psychology, 45*(3), 202–208.

IJzerman, H., van Dijk, W., & Gallucci, M. (2007). A bumpy train ride: A field experiment on insult, honor, and emotional reactions. *Emotion, 7*(4), 869–875.

Imada, T., & Yussen, S. R. (2012). Reproduction of cultural values: A cross-cultural examination of stories people create and transmit. *Personality and Social Psychology Bulletin, 38*(1), 114–128.

Inglehart, R., & Oyserman, D. (2004). Individualism, autonomy, and self-expression: The human development syndrome. *International Studies in Sociology and Social Anthropology, 93,* 74–96.

Ingram, R. E. (1990). Self-focused attention in clinical disorders: Review and a conceptual model. *Psychological Bulletin, 107*(2), 156–176.

Inman, M. L., McDonald, N., & Ruch, A. (2004). Boasting and firsthand and secondhand impressions: A new explanation for the positive teller-listener extremity effect. *Basic and Applied Social Psychology, 26*(1), 59–75.

Inman, M. L., Reichl, A. J., & Baron, R. S. (1993). Do we tell less than we know or hear less than we are told? Exploring the teller-listener extremity effect. *Journal of Experimental Social Psychology, 29*(6), 528–550.

Insko, C. A., Schopler, H. J., Gaertner, G., Wildschutt, T., Kozar, R., Pinter, B.,. . .Montoya, M. R. (2001). Interindividual-intergroup discontinuity reduction through the anticipation of future interaction. *Journal of Personality and Social Psychology, 80*(1), 95–111.

Insko, C. A., Smith, R. H., Alicke, M. D., Wade, J., & Taylor, S. (1985). Conformity and group size: The concern with being right and the concern with being liked. *Personality and Social Psychology Bulletin, 11*(1), 41–50.

Inzlicht, M., & Ben-Zeev, T. (2000). A threatening intellectual environment: Why females are susceptible to experiencing problem-solving deficits in the presence of males. *Psychological Science, 11*(5), 365–371.

Ioverno, S., Belser, A.B., Baiocco, R., Grossman, A. H., & Russell, S. T. (2016). The protective role of gay-straight alliances for lesbian, gay, bisexual, and questioning students: A prospective analysis. *Psychology of Sexual Orientation and Gender Diversity, 3*(4), 397–406.

Isbell, L. M. (2004). Not all happy people are lazy or stupid: Evidence of systematic processing in happy moods. *Journal of Experimental Social Psychology, 40*(3), 341–349.

Isen, A. M. (1970). Success, failure, attention, and reactions to others: The warm glow of success. *Journal of Personality and Social Psychology, 15*(4), 294–301.

Isen, A. M. (1984). Toward understanding the role of affect in cognition. In S. R. Wyer & T. K. Srull (Eds.), *Handbook of social cognition* (Vol. 3, pp. 179–236). New York, NY: Academic Press.

Isen, A. M. (1987). Positive affect, cognitive processes, and social behavior. In L. Berkowitz (Ed.), *Advances in experimental social psychology* (Vol. 20, pp. 203–253). New York, NY: Academic Press.

Isen, A. M., Horn, N., & Rosenhan, D. L. (1973). Effects of success and failure on children's generosity. *Journal of Personality and Social Psychology, 27*(2), 239–247.

Isen, A. M., & Levin, P. A. (1972). Effect of feeling good on helping: Cookies and kindness. *Journal of Personality and Social Psychology, 21*(3), 384–388.

Isen, A. M., & Simmonds, S. F. (1978). The effect of feeling good on a helping task that is incompatible with good mood. *Social Psychology Quarterly, 41*(4), 346–349.

Isenberg, D. (1986). Group polarization: A critical review and meta-analysis. *Journal of Personality and Social Psychology, 50*(6), 1141–1151.

Ishii-Kuntz, M. (1989). Collectivism or individualism? Changing patterns of Japanese attitudes. *Social Science Review, 73*(4), 174–179.

Ito, T. A., Miller, N., & Pollock, V. E. (1996). Alcohol and aggression: A meta-analysis on the moderating effects of inhibitory cues, triggering effects, and self-focused attention. *Psychological Bulletin, 120*(1), 60–82.

Ito, T. A., Urland, G. R., Willadsen-Jensen, E., & Correll, J. (2006). The social neuroscience of stereotyping and prejudice: Using event-related brain potentials to study social perception. In J. T. Cacioppo, P. S. Visser, & C. L. Pickett (Eds.), *Social Neuroscience: People thinking about thinking people* (pp. 189–212). Cambridge, MA: MIT Press.

Iwao, S. (1989). Social psychology's models of social behavior: Is it not time for West to meet East? Unpublished manuscript. Keio University, Institute for Communications Research, Tokyo, Japan.

Izard, C. E. (1994). Innate and universal facial expressions: Evidence from developmental and cross-cultural research. *Psychological Bulletin, 115*(2), 288–299.

J

Jackman, M. R. (1994). *The velvet glove: Paternalism and conflict in gender class and race relations.* Berkeley, CA: University of California Press.

Jackson, J. C., Bilkey, D., Jong, J., Rossignac-Milon, M., & Halberstadt, J. (2017). Strangers in a stadium: Studying group dynamics with in vivo behavioral tracking. *Social Psychological and Personality Science, 8*(5), 509–518.

Jackson, J. W. (1993). Realistic group conflict theory: A review and evaluation of the theoretical and empirical literature. *Psychological Record, 43*(3), 395–413.

Jackson, L. M. (2011). *The psychology of prejudice: From attitudes to social action.* Washington, DC: American Psychological Association.

Jackson, L. M., Esses, V. M., & Burris, C. T. (2001). Contemporary sexism and discrimination: The importance of respect for men and women. *Personality and Social Psychology Bulletin, 27*(1), 48–61.

Jackson, R., Chen, H., Gao, X. (2006). Stories we love by: Conceptions of love among couples from People's Republic of China and the United States. *Journal of Cross-Cultural Psychology, 37*(4), 446–464.

Jackson, S. E., Brett, J. F., Sessa, V. I., Cooper, D. M., Julin, J. A., & Peyronnin, K. (1991). Some differences make a difference: Individual dissimilarity and group heterogeneity as correlates of recruitment, promotions, and turnover. *Journal of Applied Psychology, 76*(5), 675–689.

Jacobs, R. C., & Campbell, D. T. (1961). The perpetuation of an arbitrary tradition through several generations of a laboratory microculture. *The Journal of Abnormal and Social Psychology, 62*(3), 649–658.

James, R. N., III, & Sharpe, D. L. (2007). The nature and causes of the U-shaped charitable giving profile. *Nonprofit and Voluntary Sector Quarterly, 36*(2), 218–238.

James, W. (1890). *The principles of psychology* (2 vols.). New York, NY: Henry Holt.

Janis, I. L. (1982). *Groupthink* (2nd ed.). Boston, MA: Houghton Mifflin.

Janis, I. L. (1996). Groupthink. In J. Billsberry (Ed.), *The effective manager: Perspectives and illustrations* (pp. 166–178). Thousand Oaks, CA: Sage.

Janis, I. L., Kaye, D., & Kirschner, P. (1965). Facilitating effects of "eating while reading" on responsiveness to persuasive communications. *Journal of Personality and Social Psychology, 1*(2), 17–27.

Janoff-Bulman, R., & Leggatt, H. K. (2002). Culture and social obligation: When "shoulds" are perceived as "wants." *Journal of Research in Personality, 36*(3), 260–270.

Jebb, A. T., Tay, L., Diener, E., & Oishi, S. (2018). Happiness, income satiation and turning points around the world. *Nature Human Behavior, 2*(1), 33–38.

Jeffrey, L. R., Miller, D., & Linn, M. (2001). Middle school bullying as a context for the development of passive observers to the victimization of others. *Journal of Emotional Abuse, 2*(2–3), 143–156.

Jellison, W. A., McConnell, A. R., & Gabriel, S. (2004). Implicit and explicit measures of sexual orientation attitudes: Ingroup preferences and related behaviors and beliefs among gay and straight men. *Personality and Social Psychology Bulletin, 30*(5), 629–642.

Jenaro, C., Flores, N., & Frías, C. P. (2018). Systematic review of empirical studies on cyberbullying in adults: What we know and what we should investigate. *Aggression and Violent Behavior, 38*, 113–122.

Jeong, M., & Bae, R. E. (2018). The effect of campaign-generated interpersonal communication on campaign-targeted health outcomes: A meta-analysis. *Health Communication, 33*(8), 988–1003.

Jetten, J., Hornsey, M. J., & Adarves-Yorno, I. (2006). When group members admit to being conformist: The role of relative intragroup status in conformity self-reports. *Personality and Social Psychology Bulletin, 32*(2), 162–173.

Jetter, M., & Walker, J. K. (2017). Anchoring in financial decision-making: Evidence from *Jeopardy! Journal of Economic Behavior & Organization, 141*, 164–176.

Jewkes, R., & Abrahams, N. (2002). The epidemiology of rape and sexual coercion in South Africa: An overview. *Social Science and Medicine, 55*(7), 1231–1244.

Jia, L., Lee, L. N., & Tong, E. M. (2015). Gratitude facilitates behavioral mimicry. *Emotion, 15*(2), 134–138.

Jiang, H., Chen, Y., Sun, P., & Yang, J. (2017). The relationship between authoritarian leadership and employees' deviant workplace behaviors: The mediating effects of psychological contract violation and organizational cynicism. *Frontiers in Psychology, 8*(732).

Johnson, A. L., Crawford, M. T., Sherman, S. J., Rutchick, A. M., Hamilton, D. L., Ferreira, M. B., & Petrocelli, J. V. (2006). A functional perspective on group memberships: Differential need fulfillment in a group typology. *Journal of Experimental Social Psychology, 42*(6), 707–719.

Johnson, C., Clay-Warner, J., & Funk, S. J. (1996). Effects of authority structures and gender on interaction in same-sex task groups. *Social Psychology Quarterly, 59*(3), 221–236.

Johnson, D. L., Wiebe, J. S., Gold, S. M., Andreasen, N. C., Hichwa, R. D., Watkins, G. L., & Boles Ponto, L. L. (1999). Cerebral blood flow and personality: A positron emission tomography study. *American Journal of Psychiatry, 156*(2), 252–257.

Johnson, H. D., Brady, E., McNair, R., Congdon, D., Niznik, J., & Anderson, S. (2007). Identity as a moderator of gender differences in the emotional closeness of emerging adults' same- and cross-sex friendships. *Adolescence, 42*(165), 1–23.

Johnson, J. D., Jackson, L. A., & Gatto, L. (1995). Violent attitudes and deferred academic aspirations: Deleterious effects of exposure to rap music. *Basic and Applied Social Psychology, 16*(1–2), 27–41.

Johnson, J. D., Noel, N. E., & Sutter-Hernandez, J. (2000). Alcohol and male acceptance of sexual aggression: The role of perceptual ambiguity. *Journal of Applied Social Psychology, 30*(6), 1186–1200.

Johnson, J. G., Cohen, P., Smailes, E. M., Kasen, S., & Brook, J. S. (2002). Television viewing and aggressive behavior during adolescence and adulthood. *Science, 295*(5564), 2468–2471.

Johnson, S. K., Podratz, K. E., Dipboye, R. L., & Gibbons, E. (2010). Physical attractiveness biases in ratings of employment suitability: Tracking down the "beauty is beastly" effect. *The Journal of Social Psychology, 150*(3), 301–318.

Johnston, K. L., & White, K. M. (2003). Binge-drinking: A test of the role of group norms in the theory of planned behaviour. *Psychology and Health, 18*(1), 63–77.

Johnston, L. D., O'Malley, P. M., & Bachman, J. G. (2003). *Monitoring the Future national survey results on drug use, 1975–2002. Volume II: College students and adults ages 19–40* (NIH Publication No. 03–5376). Bethesda, MD: National Institute on Drug Abuse.

Johnston, V. S., & Franklin, M. (1993). Is beauty in the eye of the beholder? *Ethology and Sociobiology, 14*(3), 183–199.

Joiner, T. E., Alfano, M. S., & Metalsky, G. I. (1992). When depression breeds contempt: Reassurance seeking, self-esteem and rejection of depressed college students and their roommates. *Journal of Abnormal Psychology, 101*(1), 165–173.

Joireman, J., Anderson, J., & Strathman, H. (2003). The aggression paradox: Understanding links among aggression, sensation seeking, and the consideration of future consequences. *Journal of Personality and Social Psychology, 84*(6), 1287–1302.

Joireman, J. A., Lasane, T. P., Bennett, J., Richards, D., & Solaimani, S. (2001). Integrating social value orientation and the consideration of future consequences within the extended form activation model of proenvironmental behavior. *British Journal of Social Psychology, 40*(1), 133–145.

Jonas, E., Graupmann, V., Kayser, D. N., Zanna, M., Traut-Mattausch, E., & Frey, D. (2009). Culture, self, and the emergence of reactance: Is there a "universal" freedom? *Journal of Experimental Social Psychology, 45*(5), 1068–1080.

Jonason, P. K. (2013). Four functions for four relationships: Consensus definitions of university students. *Archives of Sexual Behavior, 42*(8), 1407–1414.

Jones, D., & Hill, K. (1993). Criteria of facial attractiveness in five populations. *Human Nature, 4*(3), 271–296.

Jones, E. E. (1990). *Interpersonal perception.* New York, NY: W. H. Freeman.

Jones, E. E., & Davis, K. E. (1965). A theory of correspondent inferences: From acts to dispositions. In L. Berkowitz (Ed.), *Advances in experimental social psychology* (Vol. 2, pp. 219–266). New York, NY: Academic Press.

Jones, E. E., & Nisbett, R. E. (1972). The actor and the observer: Divergent perceptions of the causes of behavior. In E. E. Jones, D. E. Kanouse, H. H. Kelley, R. E. Nisbett, S. Valins, & B. Weiner (Eds.), *Attribution: Perceiving the causes of behavior* (pp. 79–94). Hillsdale, NJ: Lawrence Erlbaum Associates.

Jones, E. E., & Pittman, T. S. (1982). Toward a general theory of strategic self-presentation. In J. Suls (Ed.), *Psychological perspectives on the self* (pp. 231–262). Hillsdale, NJ: Lawrence Erlbaum Associates.

Jones, J. D., Cassidy, J., & Shaver, P. R. (2015). Parents' self-reported attachment styles: A review of links with parenting behaviors, emotions, and cognitions. *Personality and Social Psychology Review, 19*(1), 44–76.

Jones, L. W., Sinclair, R. C., & Courneya, K. A. (2003). The effects of source credibility and message framing on exercise intentions, behaviors and attitudes: An integration of the elaboration likelihood model and prospect theory. *Journal of Applied Social Psychology, 33*(1), 179–196.

Jones, S. S. (2007). Imitation in infancy: The development of mimicry. *Psychological Science, 18*(7), 593–599.

Jones, W. H., Carpenter, B. N., & Quintana, D. (1985). Personality and interpersonal predictors of loneliness in two cultures. *Journal of Personality and Social Psychology, 48*(6), 1503–1511.

Jones, W. H., Hobbs, S. A., & Hockenbury, D. (1982). Loneliness and social skills deficits. *Journal of Personality and Social Psychology, 42*(4), 682–689.

Jones, W. H., Sansone, C., & Helm, B. (1983). Loneliness and interpersonal judgments. *Personality and Social Psychology Bulletin, 9*(3), 437–441.

Jordan, C. H., Spencer, S. J., & Zanna, M. P. (2003). "I love me . . . I love me not": Implicit self-esteem, explicit self-esteem, and defensiveness. In S. J. Spencer, S. Fein, M. P. Zanna, & J. M. Olson (Eds.), *Motivated social perception: The Ontario symposium* (Vol. 9, pp. 117–145). Mahwah, NJ: Lawrence Erlbaum Associates.

Jordan, C. H., Spencer, S. J., & Zanna, M. P. (2005). Types of high self-esteem and prejudice: How implicit self-esteem relates to ethnic discrimination among high explicit self-esteem individuals. *Personality and Social Psychology Bulletin, 31*(5), 693–702.

Joseph, N., & Hunter, C. D. (2011) Ethnic-racial socialization messages in the identity development of second-generation Haitians. *Journal of Adolescent Research, 26*(3), 344–380.

Joshi, P. D., & Fast, N. J. (2013). I am my (high-power) role: Power and role identification. *Personality and Social Psychology Bulletin, 39*(7), 898–910.

Jost, J. T., Glaser, J., Kruglanski, A., & Sulloway, F. (2003). Political conservatism as motivated social cognition. *Psychological Bulletin, 129*(3), 339–375.

Jost, J. T., Kivetz, Y., Rubini, M., Guermandi, G., & Mosso, C. (2005). System-justifying functions of complementary regional and ethnic stereotypes: Cross-national evidence. *Social Justice Research, 18*(3), 305–333.

Jost, J. T., Pietrzak, J., Liviatan, I., Mandisodza, A., & Napier, J. (2007). System justification as conscious and nonconscious goal pursuit. In J. Shah & W. Gardner (Eds.), *Handbook of motivation science* (pp. 591–605). New York, NY: Guilford Press.

Judd, C. M., Blair, I. V., & Chapleau, K. M. (2004). Automatic stereotypes vs. automatic prejudice: Sorting out the possibilities in the Payne (2001) weapon paradigm. *Journal of Experimental Social Psychology, 40*(1), 75–81.

Judd, C. M., James-Hawkins, L., Yzerbyt, V., & Kashima, Y. (2005). Fundamental dimensions of social judgment: Understanding the relations between judgments of competence and warmth. *Journal of Personality and Social Psychology, 89*(6), 899–913.

Judd, C. M., Ryan, C. S., & Park, B. (1991). Accuracy in the judgment of in-group and out-group variability. *Journal of Personality and Social Psychology, 61*(3), 366–379.

Jussim, L., Crawford, J. T., & Rubinstein, R. S. (2015). Stereotype (in)accuracy in perceptions of groups and individuals. *Current Directions in Psychological Science, 24*(6), 490–497.

Jussim, L., Robustelli, S. L., & Cain, T. R. (2009). Teacher expectations and self-fulfilling prophecies. In K. R. Wenzel & A. Wigfield (Eds.), *Handbook of motivation at school* (pp. 349–380). New York, NY: Routledge/Taylor & Francis Group.

K

Kacmar, K. M., Delery, J. E., & Ferris, G. R. (1992). Differential effectiveness of applicant impression management tactics on employment interview decisions. *Journal of Applied Social Psychology, 22*(16), 1250–1272.

Kâğitçibaşi, C. (1994). A critical appraisal of individualism and collectivism: Toward a new formulation. In U. Kim, H. C. Triandis, C. Kâğitçibaşi, S. -C. Choi, & G. Yoon (Eds.), *Individualism and collectivism: Theory, method, and applications* (pp. 52–65). Thousand Oaks, CA: Sage.

Kahana, E., Bhatta, T., Lovegreen, L. D., Kahana, B., & Midlarsky, E. (2013). Altruism, helping, and volunteering: Pathways to well-being in late life. *Journal of Aging and Health, 25*(1), 159–187.

Kahneman, D., & Tversky, A. (1973). On the psychology of prediction. *Psychological Review, 80*(4), 237–251.

Kaiser, F. G., Byrka, K., & Hartig, T. (2010). Reviving Campbell's paradigm for attitude research. *Personality and Social Psychology Review, 14*(4), 351–367.

Kakkar, H., & Sivanathan, N. (2017). When the appeal of a dominant leader is greater than a prestige leader. *PNAS, 114*(26), 6734–6739.

Kalish, Y., & Luria, G. (2016). Leadership emergence over time in short-lived groups: Integrating expectations states theory with temporal person-perception and self-serving bias. *Journal of Applied Psychology, 101*(10), 1474–1486.

Kalkhoff, W., & Thye, S. R. (2006). Expectation states theory and research: New observations from meta-analysis. *Sociological Methods & Research, 35*(2), 219–249.

Kallgren, C. A., Reno, R. R., & Cialdini, R. B. (2000). A focus theory of normative conduct: When norms do and do not affect behavior. *Personality and Social Psychology Bulletin, 26*(8), 1002–1012.

Kalven, H., Jr., & Zeisel, H. (1966). *The American jury.* Boston, MA: Little, Brown.

Kämpf, M. S., Liebermann, H., Kerschreiter, R., Krause, S., Nestler, S., & Schmukle, S. C. (2018). Disentangling the sources of mimicry: Social relations analyses of the link between mimicry and liking. *Psychological Science, 29*(1), 131–138.

Kanagawa, C., Cross, S. E., & Markus, H. R. (2001). "Who am I?" The cultural psychology of the conceptual self. *Personality and Social Psychology Bulletin, 27*(1), 90–103.

Kanazawa, S. (1992). Outcome or expectancy? Antecedent of spontaneous causal attribution. *Personality and Social Psychology Bulletin, 18*(6), 659–668.

Kanny, D., Naimi, T. S., Liu, Y., Lu, H., & Brewer, R. D. (2018). Annual total binge drinks consumed by U.S. adults, 2015. *American Journal of Preventive Medicine, 54*(4), 486–496.

Kant, L., Skogstad, A., Torsheim, T., & Einarsen, S. (2013). Beware the angry leader: Trait anger and trait anxiety as predictors of petty tyranny. *The Leadership Quarterly, 24*(1), 106–124.

Kaplan, M. F. (1987). The influencing process in group decision making. In C. Hendrick (Ed.), *Review of personality and social psychology: Group processes* (Vol. 8, pp. 189–212). Thousand Oaks, CA: Sage.

Kaplan, M. F., & Martin, A. M. (1999). Effects of differential status of group members on process and outcome of deliberation. *Group Processes and Intergroup Relations, 2*(4), 347–364.

Kaplan, M. F., & Miller, C. E. (1987). Group decision making and normative versus informational influence: Effects of type of issue and assigned decision rule. *Journal of Personality and Social Psychology, 53*(2), 306–313.

Karasawa, K. (1995). An attributional analysis of reactions to negative emotions. *Personality and Social Psychology Bulletin, 21*(5), 456–467.

Karau, S. J., & Kelly, J. R. (1992). The effects of time scarcity and time abundance on group performance quality and interaction process. *Journal of Experimental Social Psychology, 28*(6), 542–571.

Karau, S. J., & Williams, K. D. (1993). Social loafing: A meta-analytic review and theoretical integration. *Journal of Personality and Social Psychology, 65*(4), 681–706.

Karau, S. J., & Williams, K. D. (1995). Social loafing, research findings, implications, and future directions. *Current Directions in Psychological Science, 4*(5), 134–140.

Karazsia, B. T., Murnen, S. K., & Tylka, T. L. (2017). Is body dissatisfaction changing across time? A cross-temporal meta-analysis. *Psychological Bulletin, 143*(3), 293–320.

Karraker, K. H., & Stern, M. (1990). Infant physical attractiveness and facial expression: Effects on adult perceptions. *Basic and Applied Social Psychology, 11*(4), 371–385.

Karsay, K., Matthes, J., Buchsteiner, L., & Grosser, V. (2019). Increasingly sexy? Sexuality and sexual objectification in popular music videos, 1995–2016. *Psychology of Popular Media Culture, 8*(4), 346–357.

Kashdan, T. B., & Roberts, J. E. (2006). Affective outcomes in superficial and intimate interactions: Roles of social anxiety and curiosity. *Journal of Research in Personality, 40*(2), 140–167.

Kashdan, T. B., & Steger, M. F. (2006). Expanding the topography of social anxiety: An experience-sampling assessment of positive emotions, positive events, and emotion suppression. *Psychological Science, 17*(2), 120–128.

Kashima, Y. (2009). Culture comparison and culture priming: A critical analysis. In R. S. Wyer, C. -y. Chiu, & Y. -y. Hong (Eds.), *Understanding culture: Theory, research, and application* (pp. 53–77). New York, NY: Psychology Press.

Kashima, Y., & Foddy, M. (2002). Time and self: The historical construction of the self. In Y. Kashima, M. Foddy, & M. Platow (Eds.), *Self and identity: Personal, social and symbolic* (pp. 181–206). Mahwah, NJ: Lawrence Erlbaum Associates.

Kashima, Y., Yamaguchi, S., Kim, U., Choi, S. C., Gelfand, M. J., & Yuki, M. (1995). Culture, gender, and self: A perspective from individualism-collectivism research. *Journal of Personality and Social Psychology, 69*(5), 925–937.

Kashy, D. A., & DePaulo, B. M. (1996). Who lies? *Journal of Personality and Social Psychology, 70*(5), 1037–1051.

Kassin, S. M., & Kiechel, K. L. (1996). The social psychology of false confessions: Compliance, internalization, and confabulation. *Psychological Science, 7*(3), 125–128.

Kassin, S. M. (2012). Why confessions trump innocence. *American Psychologist, 67*(6), 431–445.

Kassin, S. M. (2015). The social psychology of false confessions. *Social Issues and Policy Review, 9*(1), 25–51.

Kassin, S. M. (2017). False confessions: How can psychology so basic be so counterintuitive? *American Psychologist, 72*(9), 951–964.

Kassin, S. M. (2018, June 12). Why SCOTUS should examine the case of "making a murderer's" Brendan Dassey. *American Psychological Association*. Retrieved from https://www.apa.org/news/press/op-eds/scotus-brendan-dassey

Katz, I., & Hass, R. G. (1988). Racial ambivalence and American value conflict: Correlational and priming studies of dual cognitive structures. *Journal of Personality and Social Psychology, 55*(6), 893–905.

Katz-Wise, S. L., & Hyde, J. S. (2012). Victimization experiences of lesbian, gay, and bisexual individuals: A meta-analysis. *The Journal of Sex Research, 49*(2–3), 142–167.

Kawakami, K., Dovidio, J. F., Moll, J., Hermsen, S., & Russin, A. (2000). Just say no (to stereotyping): Effects of training in the negation of stereotypic associations on stereotype activation. *Journal of Personality and Social Psychology, 78*(5), 871–888.

Kawakami, K., Dunn, E., Karmali, F., & Dovidio, J. F. (2009). Mispredicting affective and behavioral responses to racism. *Science, 323*(5911), 276–278.

Kawakami, N., & Yoshida, F. (2010). Effects of subliminal mere exposure to group members on intergroup evaluation: Category evaluation measured in the Implicit Association Test. *Japanese Journal of Psychology, 81*(4), 364–372.

Kay, A. C., & Jost, J. T. (2003). Complementary justice: Effects of "poor but happy" and "poor but honest" stereotype exemplars on system justification and implicit activation of the justice motive. *Journal of Personality and Social Psychology, 85*(5), 823–837.

Kay, A. C., Jost, J. T., Mandisodza, A. N., Sherman, S. J., Petrocelli, J. V., & Johnson, A. L. (2007). Panglossian ideology in the service of system justification: How complementary stereotypes help us to rationalize inequality. In M. Zanna (Ed.), *Advances in Experimental Social Psychology*, (Vol. 39, pp. 305–358). San Diego, CA: Academic Press.

Keating, C. F. (2006). Why and how the silent self speaks volumes: Functional approaches to nonverbal impression management. In V. Manusov & M. L. Patterson (Eds.), *The Sage handbook of nonverbal communication* (pp. 321–339). Thousand Oaks, CA: Sage.

Keating, C. F., Pomerantz, J., Pommer, S. D., Ritt, S. J. H., Miller, L. M., & McCormick, J. (2005). Going to college and unpacking hazing: A functional approach to decrypting initiation practices among undergraduates. *Group Dynamics: Theory, Research, and Practice, 9*(2), 104–126.

Keating, J., Van Boven, L., & Judd, C. M. (2016). Partisan underestimation of the polarizing influence of group discussion. *Journal of Experimental Social Psychology, 65*, 52–58.

Keener, E., & Strough, J. (2017). Having and doing gender: Young adults' expression of gender when resolving conflicts with friends and romantic partners. *Sex Roles, 76*(9–10), 615–626.

Kelley, H. H. (1950). The warm-cold variable in first impressions of persons. *Journal of Personality, 18*, 431–439.

Kelley, H. H. (1967). Attribution theory in social psychology. *Nebraska symposium on motivation, 15*, 192–238.

Kelly, J. R., Jackson, J. W., & Hutson-Comeaux, S. L. (1997). The effects of time pressure and task differences on influence modes and accuracy in decision-making groups. *Personality and Social Psychology, 23*(1), 10–22.

Kelman, H. C. (1958). Compliance, identification and internalization: Three processes of attitude change. *Journal of Conflict Resolution, 2*(1), 51–60.

Kelman, H. C. (2006). Interests, relationships, identities: Three central issues for individuals and groups in negotiating their social environment. *Annual Review of Psychology, 57*, 1–26.

Kelman, H. C., & Hovland, C. I. (1953). "Reinstatement" of the communicator in delayed measurement of opinion change. *Journal of Abnormal and Social Psychology, 48*(3), 327–335.

Keltner, D., Gruenfeld, D. H., & Anderson, C. (2003). Power, approach, and inhibition. *Psychological Review, 110*(2), 265–284.

Keltner, D., & Lerner, J. S. (2010). Emotion. In S. T. Fiske, D. T. Gilbert, & G. Lindzey (Eds.), *Handbook of social psychology* (5th ed., Vol. 1, pp. 317–352). Hoboken, NJ: John Wiley & Sons.

Keltner, D., Young, R. C., Heerey, E. A., Oemig, C., & Monarch, N. D. (1998). Teasing in hierarchial and intimate relations. *Journal of Personality and Social Psychology, 75*(5), 1231–1247.

Kemmelmeier, M. (2001). Private self-consciousness as a moderator of the relationship between value orientations and attitudes. *Journal of Social Psychology, 141*(1), 61–74.

Kemmelmeier, M., Jambor, E. E., & Letner, J. (2006). Individualism and good works: Cultural variation in giving and volunteering across the United States. *Journal of Cross-Cultural Psychology, 37*(3), 327–344.

Kemper, V. (2004, July 10). Groupthink viewed as culprit in move to war. *Los Angeles Times*. Retrieved from https://www.latimes.com/archives/la-xpm-2004-jul-10-na-groupthink10-story.html

Kenrick, D. T., Baumann, D. J., & Cialdini, R. B. (1979). A step in the socialization of altruism as hedonism: Effects of negative mood on children's generosity under public and private conditions. *Journal of Personality and Social Psychology, 37*(5), 747–755.

Kenrick, D. T., Gutierres, S. E., & Goldberg, L. L. (1989). Influence of popular erotica on judgments of strangers and mates. *Journal of Experimental Social Psychology, 25*(2), 159–167.

Kenrick, D. T., & Luce, C. L. (2000). An evolutionary life-history model of gender differences and similarities. In T. Eckes & H. M. Trautner (Eds.), *The developmental social psychology of gender* (pp. 35–63). Mahwah, NJ: Lawrence Erlbaum Associates.

Kenrick, D. T., & Trost, M. R. (1987). A biosocial theory of heterosexual relationships. In K. Kelly (Ed.), *Families, males, and sexuality* (pp. 59–100). Albany, NY: State University of New York Press.

Keonig, A. M., & Eagly, A. H. (2014). Evidence for the social role theory of stereotype content: Observations of groups' roles shape stereotypes. *Journal of Personality and Social Psychology, 107*(3), 371–392.

Kernis, M. H. (2003). Toward a conceptualization of optimal self-esteem. *Psychological Inquiry, 14*(1), 1–26.

Kernis, M. H, & Goldman, B. M. (2006). Assessing stability of self-esteem and contingent self-esteem. In M. H. Kernis (Ed.), *Self-esteem issues and answers: A sourcebook of current perspective* (pp. 77–85). New York, NY: Psychology Press.

Kernis, M. H., & Lakey, C. E. (2010). Fragile versus secure high self-esteem: Implications for defensiveness and insecurity. In R. M. Arkin, K. C. Oleson, & P. J. Carroll (Eds.). *Handbook of the uncertain self* (pp. 360–378). New York, NY: Psychology Press.

Kernis, M. H., Paradise, A. W., Whitaker, D. J., Wheatman, S. R., & Goldman, B. N. (2000). Master of one's psychological domain? Not likely if one's self-esteem is unstable. *Personality and Social Psychology Bulletin, 26*(10), 1297–1305.

Kerr, N. L., & MacCoun, R. J. (1985). The effects of jury size and polling method on the process and product of jury deliberation. *Journal of Personality and Social Psychology, 48*(2), 349–363.

Kerr, N. L., Messé, L. A., Seok, D., Sambolec, E. J., Lount, Jr., R. B., & Park, E. S. (2007). Psychological mechanisms underlying the Köhler motivation gain. *Personality and Social Psychology Bulletin, 33*(6), 828–841.

Kerr, N. L., Seok, D. -H., Poulsen, J. R., Harris, D. W., & Messé, L. A. (2008). Social ostracism and group motivation gain. *European Journal of Social Psychology, 38*(4), 736–746.

Kessler, K., & Hollbach, S. (2005). Group-based emotions as determinants of ingroup identification. *Journal of Experimental Social Psychology, 41*(6), 677–685.

Kettrey, H. H. (2013). Reading *Playboy* for the articles: The graying of rape myths in black-and-white text, 1953 to 2003. *Violence Against Women, 19*(8), 968–994.

Kettrey, H. H, & Marx, R. A. (2019). The effects of bystander programs on the prevention of sexual assault across the college years: A systematic review and meta-analysis. *Journal of Youth and Adolescence, 48*(2), 212–227.

Ketturat, C., Frisch, J. U., Ullrich, J., Häusser, J. A., van Dick, R., & Mojzisch, A. (2016). Disaggregating within- and between-person effects of social identification on subjective and endocrinological stress reactions in a real-life stress situation. *Personality and Social Psychology Bulletin, 42*(2), 147 160.

Kiefer, A. K., & Sekaquaptewa, D. (2007). Implicit stereotypes, gender identification, and math-related outcomes. *Psychological Science, 18*(1), 13–18.

Kiesler, C. A., & Pallak, M. S. (1975). Minority influence: The effect of majority reactionaries and defectors, and minority and majority compromisers, upon majority opinion and attraction. *European Journal of Social Psychology, 5*(2), 237–256.

Kiesler, S., Sproull, L., & Waters, K. (1996). A prisoner's dilemma experiment on cooperation with people and human-like computers. *Journal of Personality and Social Psychology, 70*(1), 47–65.

Kilham, W., & Mann, L. (1974). Level of destructive obedience as a function of transmitter and executant roles in the Milgram obedience paradigm. *Journal of Personality and Social Psychology, 29*(5), 696–702.

Kim, H., & Markus, H. R. (1999). Deviance of uniqueness, harmony or conformity? A cultural analysis. *Journal of Personality and Social Psychology, 77*(4), 785–800.

Kim, H. S., & Sherman, D. K. (2007). "Express yourself": Culture and the effect of self-expression on choice. *Journal of Personality and Social Psychology, 92*(1), 1–11.

Kim, U., & Choi, S. -H. (1994). Individualism, collectivism, and child development: A Korean perspective. In P. M. Greenfield & R. R. Cocking (Eds.), *Cross-cultural roots of minority child development* (pp. 227–257). Hillsdale, NJ: Lawrence Erlbaum Associates.

Kimel, S. Y., Huesmann, R., Kunst, J. R., & Halperin, E. (2016). Living in a genetic world: How learning about interethnic genetic similarities and differences affects peace and conflict. *Personality and Social Psychology Bulletin, 42*(5), 688–700.

Kimmerle, J., & Cress, U. (2013). The effects of TV and film exposure on knowledge about and attitudes toward mental disorders. *Journal of Community Psychology, 41*(8), 931–943.

Kinder, D. R. (1998). Opinion and action in the realm of politics. In D. T. Gilbert, S. T. Fiske, & G. Lindzey (Eds.), *The handbook of social psychology* (4th ed., Vol. 2, pp. 778–867). New York, NY: McGraw-Hill.

Kirkland, F. (1990). Combat leadership styles: Empowerment versus authoritarian. *Parameters, 20*, 61–72.

Kirkpatrick, L. A., Waugh, C. E., Valencia, A., & Webster, G. D. (2002). The functional domain specificity of self-esteem and the differential prediction of aggression. *Journal of Personality and Social Psychology, 82*(5), 756–767.

Kirkpatrick, S. A., & Locke, E. A. (1991). Leadership: Do traits matter? *Academy of Management Executives, 5*(2), 48–60.

Kirkpatrick, S. A., & Locke, E. A. (1996). Direct and indirect effects of three core charismatic leadership components on performance and attitudes. *Journal of Applied Psychology, 81*, 36–51.

Kitayama, S. (2007, May 25). Voluntary settlement and the spirit of independence: Some more evidence from Japan's "northern frontier." Paper presented at the American Psychological Science 19th Annual Convention, Washington, DC.

Kitayama, S., Ishii, K., Imada, T., Takemura, K., & Ramaswamy, J. (2006). Voluntary settlement and the spirit of independence: Evidence from Japan's "northern frontier." *Journal of Personality and Social Psychology, 91*(3), 369–384.

Kitayama, S., Park, H., Sevincer, A. T., Karasawa, M., & Uskul, A. K. (2009). A cultural task analysis of implicit independence: Comparing North America, Western Europe, and East Asia. *Journal of Personality and Social Psychology, 97*(2), 236–255.

Kite, M. E., & Whitley, B. E., Jr. (1996). Sex differences in attitudes toward homosexual persons, behaviors, and civil rights: A meta-analysis. *Personality and Social Psychology Bulletin, 22*(4), 336–353.

Kito, M. (2005). Self-disclosure in romantic relationships and friendships among American and Japanese college students. *Journal of Social Psychology, 145*(2), 127–140.

Klement, K. R., Sagarin, B. J., & Skownronski, J. J. (2019). Accusers lie and other myths: Rape myth acceptance predicts judgments made about accusers and accused perpetrators in a rape case. *Sex Roles, 81*(1–2), 16–33.

Klein, O., Spears, R., & Reicher, S. (2007). Social identity performance: Extending the strategic side of SIDE. *Personality and Social Psychology Review, 11*(1), 28–45.

Klein, W. M. (2003). Effects of objective feedback and "single other" or "average other" social comparison feedback on performance judgments and helping behavior. *Personality and Social Psychology Bulletin, 29*(3), 418–429.

Kliemann, D., Rosenblau, G., Bolte, S., Heekeren, H. R., & Dziobek, I. (2013). Face puzzle: Two new video-based tasks for measuring explicit and implicit aspects of facial emotion recognition. *Frontiers in Psychology, 4*, 376.

Klonsky, B. (2013). Leadership styles and leader effectiveness. In M. A. Paludi (Ed.), *Psychology for business success.* (Vol. 1, pp. 1–19). Santa Barbara, CA: Praeger.

Knafo, A., & Plomin, R. (2006). Parental discipline and affection and children's prosocial behavior: Genetic and environmental links. *Journal of Personality and Social Psychology, 90*(1), 147–164.

Knapp, M. L., Stafford, L., & Daly, J. A. (1986). Regrettable messages: Things people wish they hadn't said. *Journal of Communication, 36*(4), 40–58.

Knee, C. R., & Canevello, A. (2006). Implicit theories of relationships and coping in romantic relationships. In K. D. Vohs & E. J. Finkel (Eds.), *Self and relationships: Connecting intrapersonal and interpersonal processes* (pp. 160–176). New York, NY: Guilford Press.

Knee, C. R., Hadden, B. W., Porter, B., & Rodriguez, L. M. (2013). Self-determination theory and romantic relationship processes. *Personality and Social Psychology Review, 17*(4), 307–324.

Kniffin, K. M., & Wilson, D. S. (2005). Utilities of gossip across organizational levels: Multilevel selection, free-riders, and teams. *Human Nature, 16*(3), 278–292.

Knobloch, L.K. (2007). Perceptions of turmoil within courtship: Associations with intimacy, relational uncertainty, and interference from partners. *Journal of Social and Personal Relationships, 24*(3), 363–384.

Knowles, M. L., & Gardner, W. L. (2008). Benefits of membership: The activation and amplification of group identities in response to social rejection. *Personality and Social Psychology Bulletin, 34*(9), 1200–1213.

Knox, R. E., & Inkster, J. A. (1968). Postdecision dissonance at posttime. *Journal of Personality and Social Psychology, 8*(4), 319–323.

Knox, R. E., & Safford, R. K. (1976). Group caution at the race track. *Journal of Experimental Social Psychology, 12*(3), 317–324.

Koenig, A. M., Eagly, A. H., Mitchell, A. A., & Ristikari, T. (2011). Are leader stereotypes masculine? A meta-analysis of three research paradigms. *Psychological Bulletin, 137*(4), 616–642.

Koffka, K. (1935). *Principles of gestalt psychology.* London, England: Routledge.

Köhler, W. (1929). *Gestalt psychology.* Oxford, England: Liveright.

Kohn, J. L., Rholes, W. S., Simpson, J. A., Martin, A. M. III., Tran, S., & Wilson, C. L. (2012). Changes in marital satisfaction across the transition to parenthood: The role of adult attachment orientations. *Personality and Social Psychology Bulletin, 38*(11), 1506–1522.

Kokkoris, M. D., & Kühnen, U. (2013). Choice and dissonance in a European cultural context: The case of Western and Eastern Europeans. *International Journal of Psychology, 48*(6), 1260–1266.

Konrath, S. H., O'Brien, E. H., & Hsing, C. (2011). Changes in a dispositional empathy in American college students over time: A meta-analysis. *Personality and Social Psychology Review, 15*(2), 180–198.

Koren, P., Carlton, K., & Shaw, D. (1980). Marital conflict: Relations among behaviors, outcomes, and distress. *Journal of Consulting and Clinical Psychology, 48*(4), 460–468.

Kortenkamp, K. V., & Moore, C. F. (2006). Time, uncertainty, and individual differences in decisions to cooperate in resource dilemmas. *Personality and Social Psychology Bulletin, 32*(5), 603–615.

Kowalski, R. M., Giumetti, G. W., Schroeder, A. N., & Lattanner, M. R. (2014). Bullying in the digital age: A critical review and meta-analysis of cyberbullying research among youth. *Psychological Bulletin, 140*(4), 1073–1137.

Kowalski, R. M., & Limber, S. P. (2013). Psychological, physical, and academic correlates of cyberbullying and traditional bullying. *Journal of Adolescent Health, 53*(Suppl 1), S13–S20.

Kowert, P. A. (2002). *Groupthink or deadlock: When do leaders learn from their advisors?* Albany, NY: State University of New York Press.

Kozlowski, S. W., & Bell, B. S. (2003). Work groups and teams in organizations. In W. C. Borman, D. R. Ilgen, & R. J. Klimoski (Eds.), *Comprehensive handbook of psychology: Industrial and organizational psychology* (Vol. 12, pp. 333–375). New York, NY: John Wiley & Sons.

Krahé, B., & Moller, I. (2004). Playing violent electronic games, hostile attributional style, and aggression-related norms in German adolescents. *Journal of Adolescence, 27*(1), 53–69.

Krahé, B., Möller, I., Heusmann, L. R., Kirwil, L., Felber, J., & Berger, A. (2011). Desensitization to media violence: Links with habitual media violence exposure, aggressive cognitions, and aggressive behavior. *Journal of Personality and Social Psychology, 100*(4), 630–646.

Kraus, M. W., & Callaghan, B. (2016). Social class and prosocial behavior: The moderating role of public versus private contexts. *Social Psychological and Personality Science, 7*(8), 769–777.

Krieglmeyer, R., Wittstadt, D., & Strack, F. (2009). How attribution influences aggression: Answers to an old question by using an implicit measure of anger. *Journal of Experimental Social Psychology, 45*(2), 379–385.

Krosch, A. R., Tyler, T. R., & Amodio, D. M. (2017). Race and recession: Effects of economic scarcity on racial discrimination. *Journal of Personality and Social Psychology, 113*(6), 892–909.

Krosnick, J. A. (1999). Survey research. *Annual Review of Psychology, 50,* 537–567.

Krosnick, J. A., Betz, A. L., Jussim, L. J., & Lynn, A. R. (1992). Subliminal conditioning of attitudes. *Personality and Social Psychology Bulletin, 18*(2), 152–162.

Kruger, D. J. (2003). Evolution and altruism: Combining psychological mediators with naturally selected tendencies. *Evolution and Human Behavior, 24*(2), 118–125.

Kruger, J., & Dunning, D. (1999). Unskilled and unaware of it: How difficulties in recognizing one's own incompetence lead to inflated self-assessments. *Journal of Personality and Social Psychology, 77*(6), 1121–1134.

Kruglanski, A. W., & Orehek, E. (2007). Partitioning the domain of social inference: Dual mode and systems models and their alternatives. *Annual Review of Psychology, 58,* 291–316.

Krull, D. S., & Dill, J. C. (1996). On thinking first and responding fast: Flexibility in social inference processes. *Personality and Social Psychology Bulletin, 22*(9), 949–959.

Krys, K., Capaldi, C. A., van Tilburg, W., Lipp, O. V., Bond, M. H., Vauclair, C.-M.,. . .Ahmed, R. A. (2018). Catching up with wonderful women: The women-are-wonderful effect is smaller in more gender egalitarian societies. *International Journal of Psychology, 53*(51), 21–26.

Kteily, N. S., & Bruneau, E. (2017a). Backlash: The politics and real-world consequences of minority group dehumanization. *Personality and Social Psychology Bulletin, 43*(1), 87–104.

Kteily, N. S., & Bruneau, E. (2017b). Darker demons of our nature: The need to (re)focus attention on blatant forms of dehumanization. *Current Directions in Psychological Science, 26*(6), 487–494.

Kugihara, N. (2001). Effects of aggressive behaviour and group size on collective escape in an emergency: A test between a social identity model and deindividuation theory. *British Journal of Social Psychology, 40*(4), 575–598.

Kuhn, M. H., & McPartland, T. S. (1954). An empirical investigation of self-attitudes. *American Sociological Review, 19*(1), 68–76.

Kühnen, U., Hannover, B., & Schubert, B. (2001). The semantic-procedural interface model of the self: The role of self-knowledge for context-dependent versus context-independent modes of thinking. *Journal of Personality and Social Psychology, 80*(3), 397–409.

Kühnen, U., & Oyserman, D. (2002). Thinking about the self influences thinking in general: Cognitive consequences of salient self-concept. *Journal of Experimental Social Psychology, 38,* 492–499.

Kuiper, N., Grimshaw, M., Leite, C., & Kirsh, G. (2004). Humor is not always the best medicine: Specific components of sense of humor and psychological well-being. *Humor: International Journal of Humor Research, 17*(1–2), 135–168. doi:10.1515/humr.2004.002

Kulik, J. A., & Mahler, H. I. (1989). Stress and affiliation in a hospital setting: Preoperative roommate preferences. *Personality and Social Psychology Bulletin, 15*(2), 183–193.

Kulik, J. A., Mahler, H. I. M., & Moore, P. J. (1996). Social comparison and affiliation under threat: Effects on recovery from major surgery. *Journal of Personality and Social Psychology, 71*(5), 967–979.

Kumkale, G. T., & Albarracín, D. (2004). The sleeper effect in persuasion: A meta-analytic review. *Psychological Bulletin, 130*(1), 143–172.

Kunda, Z. (1999). *Social cognition: Making sense of people.* Cambridge, MA: MIT Press.

Kunda, Z., & Oleson, K. C. (1995). Maintaining stereotypes in the face of disconfirmation: Constructing grounds for subtyping deviants. *Journal of Personality and Social Psychology, 68*(4), 565–579.

Kunovich, R. M., & Deitelbaum, C. (2004). Ethnic conflict, group polarization, and gender attitudes in Croatia. *Journal of Marriage and Family, 66*(5), 1089–1107.

Kunst, J. R., Dovidio, J. F., & Dotsch, R. (2018). White look-alikes: Mainstream culture adoption makes immigrants "look" phenotypically white. *Personality and Social Psychology Bulletin, 44*(2), 265–282.

Kupke, T., Hobbs, S. A., & Cheney, T. H. (1979). Selection of heterosocial skills: I. Criterion-related validity. *Behavior Therapy, 10*(3), 327–335.

Kuppens, P., Van Mechelen, I., & Meulders, M. (2004). Every cloud has a silver lining: Interpersonal and individual differences determinants of anger-related behaviors. *Personality and Social Psychology Bulletin, 30*(12), 1550–1564.

Kurdek, L. A. (2003). Differences between gay and lesbian cohabiting couples. *Journal of Social and Personal Relationships, 20*(4), 411–436.

Kurdek, L. A. (2006). Differences between partners from heterosexual, gay, and lesbian cohabiting couples. *Journal of Marriage and Family, 68*(2), 509–528.

Kurdek, L. A., & Schmitt, J. P. (1986). Relationship quality of partners in heterosexual married, heterosexual cohabiting, and gay and lesbian relationships. *Journal of Personality and Social Psychology, 51*(4), 711–720.

Kurdek, L. A., & Schmitt, J. P. (1987). Perceived emotional support from families and friends in members of homosexual, married, and heterosexual cohabiting couples. *Journal of Homosexuality, 14*(3–4), 57–68.

Kurup, R. K., & Kurup, P. A. (2003). Hypothalamic digoxin, hemispheric dominance, and neurobiology of love and affection. *International Journal of Neuroscience, 113*(5), 721–729.

Kuster, F., Orth, U., & Meier, L. L. (2012). Rumination mediates the prospective effect of low self-esteem on depression: A five-wave longitudinal study. *Personality and Social Psychology Bulletin, 38*(6), 747–759.

Kwon, P. (2013). Resilience in lesbian, gay, and bisexual individuals. *Personality and Social Psychology Review, 17*(4), 371–383.

L

LaBarbera, P., & MacLachlan, J. (1979). Time-compressed speech in radio advertising. *Journal of Marketing, 43*(1), 30–36.

LaFrance, M., Hecht, M. A., & Paluck, E. L. (2003). The contingent smile: A meta-analysis of sex differences in smiling. *Psychological Bulletin, 129*(2), 305–334.

Lagerspetz, K. (1985). Are wars caused by aggression? In F. L. Denmark (Ed.), *Social/ecological psychology and the psychology of women*. New York, NY: Elsevier (North-Holland).

Lagerspetz, K. M., & Björkqvist, K. (1994). Indirect aggression in boys and girls. In L. R. Huesmann (Ed.), *Aggressive behavior: Current perspectives* (pp. 131–150). New York, NY: Plenum Press.

Lagerspetz, K. M., Björkqvist, K., & Peltonen, T. (1988). Is indirect aggression typical of females? Gender differences in aggressiveness in 11- to 12-year-old children. *Aggressive Behavior, 14*(6), 403–414.

Lakoff, R. T. (2005). Talking terrorism: A dictionary of the loaded language of political violence (book review). *Language in Society, 34*(4), 638–641.

Lam, B. C., Cross, S. E., Wu, T.-F., Yeh, K.-H., Wang, Y.-C., Su, J. C. (2016). What do you want in a marriage? Examining marriage ideals in Taiwan and the United States. *Personality and Social Psychology Bulletin, 42*(6), 703–722.

Landau, M. J., Solomon, S., Greenberg, J., Cohen, F., Pyszczyhski, T., Arndt, J.,. . .Cook, A. (2004). Deliver us from evil: The effects of mortality salience and reminders of 9/11 on support for President George W. Bush. *Personality and Social Psychology Bulletin 30*(9), 1136–1150.

Lang, A. R., Goeckner, D. J., Adesso, V. J., & Marlatt, G. A. (1975). Effects of alcohol on aggression in male social drinkers. *Journal of Abnormal Psychology, 84*(5), 508–518.

Langer, E. J. (1978). Rethinking the role of thought in social interaction. In J. H. Harvey, W. J. Ickes, & R. F. Kidd (Eds.), *New directions in attribution research* (Vol. 2, pp. 35–58). Hillsdale, NJ: Lawrence Erlbaum Associates.

Langer, E. J. (1989). Minding matters: The consequences of mindlessness-mindfulness. In L. Berkowitz (Ed.), *Advances in experimental social psychology* (Vol. 22, 137–173). San Diego, CA: Academic Press.

Langfur, S. (2013). The You-I event: On the genesis of self-awareness. *Phenomenology and the Cognitive Sciences, 12*(4), 769–790.

Langlois, J. H., & Downs, A. C. (1980). Mothers, fathers, and peers as socialization agents of sex-typed behaviors in young children. *Child Development, 51*(4), 1237–1247.

Langlois, J. H., Kalakanis, L., Rubenstein, A. J., Larson, A., Hallam, M., & Smoot, M. (2000). Maxims or myths of beauty? A meta-analytic and theoretical review. *Psychological Bulletin, 126*(3), 390–423.

Langlois, J. H., Roggman, L. A., & Musselman, L. (1994). What is average and what is not average about attractive faces? *Psychological Science, 5*(4), 214–220.

Lanning, K. (2002). Reflections on September 11: Lessons from four psychological perspectives. *Analysis of Social Issues and Public Policy, 2*, 27–34.

Lanzetta, J. T., Cartwright-Smith, J., & Eleck, R. E. (1976). Effects of nonverbal dissimulation on emotional experience and autonomic arousal. *Journal of Personality and Social Psychology, 33*(3), 354–370.

Larrick, R. P., Timmerman, T. A., Carton, A. M., & Abrevaya, J. (2011). Temper, temperature, and temptation: Heat-related retaliation in baseball. *Psychological Science, 22*(4), 423–428.

Lassiter, G. D., Geers, A. L., Handley, I. M., Weiland, P. E., & Munhall, P. J. (2002). Videotaped interrogations and confessions: A simple change in camera perspective alters verdicts in simulated trials. *Journal of Applied Psychology, 87*(5), 867–874.

Latané, B. (1981). The psychology of social impact. *American Psychologist, 36*(4), 343–356.

Latané, B. (1997). Dynamic social impact: The social consequences of human interaction. In C. McGarty & S. A. Haslam (Eds.), *The message of social psychology: Perspectives on mind in society* (pp. 200–220). Cambridge, MA: Blackwell.

Latané, B. (2000). Pressures to uniformity and the evolution of cultural norms: Modeling dynamic social impact. In D. R. Ilgen & C. L. Hulin (Eds.), *Computational modeling of behavior in organizations: The third scientific discipline* (pp. 189–220). Washington, DC: American Psychological Association.

Latané, B., & Bourgeois, M. J. (1996). Experimental evidence for dynamic social impact: The emergence of subcultures in electronic groups. *Journal of Communication, 46*(4), 35–47.

Latané, B., & Darley, J. M. (1968). Group inhibition of bystander intervention in emergencies. *Journal of Personality and Social Psychology, 10*(3), 215–221.

Latané, B., & Darley, J. M. (1970). *The unresponsive bystander: Why doesn't he help?* Englewood Cliffs, NJ: Prentice-Hall.

Latané, B., & L'Herrou, T. (1996). Spatial clustering in the conformity game: Dynamic social impact in electronic groups. *Journal of Personality and Social Psychology, 70*(6), 1218–1230.

Latané, B., Liu, J. H., Nowak, A., Bonevento, M., & Zheng, L. (1995). Distance matters: Physical space and social impact. *Personality and Social Psychology Bulletin, 21*(8), 795–805.

Latané, B., & Nida, S. (1981). Ten years of research on group size and helping. *Psychological Bulletin, 89*(2), 308–324.

Latané, B., & Rodin, J. (1969). A lady in distress: Inhibiting effects of friends and strangers on bystander intervention. *Journal of Experimental Social Psychology, 5*(2), 189–202.

Latané, B., Williams, K., & Harkins, S. (1979). Many hands make light the work: The causes and consequences of social loafing. *Journal of Personality and Social Psychology, 37*(6), 822–832.

Latting, J. K. (1993). Soliciting individual change in an interpersonal setting: The case of racially or sexually offensive language. *Journal of Applied Behavioral Science, 29*(4), 464–484.

Laughlin, P. R. (1996). Group decision making and collective induction. In E. Witte & J. Davis (Eds.), *Understanding group behavior: Vol. 1. Small group processes and interpersonal relations* (pp. 61–80). Hillsdale, NJ: Lawrence Erlbaum Associates.

Lawler-Row, K. A., Hyatt-Edwards, L, Wuensch, K. L., & Karremans, J. C. (2011). Forgiveness and health: The role of attachment. *Personal Relationships, 18*(2), 170–183.

Laws, V. L., & Rivera, L. M. (2012). The role of self-image concerns in discrepancies between implicit and explicit self-esteem. *Personality and Social Psychology Bulletin, 38*(11), 1453–1466.

Layous, K., & Lyubomirsky, S. (2014). The how, why, what, when, and who of happiness: Mechanisms underlying the success of positive interventions. In J. Gruber & J. T. Moscowitz (Eds.), *Positive emotion: Integrating the light sides and dark sides* (pp. 473–495). New York, NY: Oxford University Press.

Layous, K., Nelson, S. K., Oberle, E., Schonert-Reichl. K. A., & Lyubomirsky, S. (2012). Kindness counts: Prompting prosocial behavior in preadolescents boosts peer acceptance and well-being. *PLoS ONE, 7*(12), e51380.

Lazarus, E. (1883, November 2). The new colossus. First published in *The New York Times* (1903).

Lazarus, R. S. (1984). On the primacy of cognition. *American Psychologist, 39*(2), 124–129.

Le, B. M., Impett, E. A., Lemay, E. P., Jr., Muise, A., & Tskhay, K. O. (2018). Communal motivation and well-being in interpersonal relationships: An integrative review and meta-analysis. *Psychological Bulletin, 144*(1), 1–25.

Leary, M. R. (1996). *Self-presentation: Impression management and interpersonal behavior.* Madison, WI: Brown & Benchmark.

Leary, M. R. (2005). Sociometer theory and the pursuit of relational value: Getting to the root of self-esteem. *European Review of Social Psychology, 16*, 75–111.

Leary, M. R., Tambor, E. S., Terdal, S. K., & Downs, D. L. (1995). Self-esteem as an interpersonal monitor: The sociometer hypothesis. *Journal of Personality and Social Psychology, 68*(3), 518–530.

LeBon, G. (1903). *Psychologie des foules [The psychology of the crowd].* Paris, France: Alcan.

Lee, A. R. (2003). Stability and change in Korean values. *Social Indicators Research, 62*(1–3), 93–117.

Lee, D. S., Ybarra, O., Gonzalez, R., & Ellsworth, P. (2018). I-through-we: How supportive social relationships facilitate personal growth. *Personality and Social Psychology Bulletin, 44*(1), 37–48.

Lee, E. E., Depp, C., Palmer, B. W., Glorioso, D., Daly, R., Liu, J.,. . .Jeste, D. V. (2019). High prevalence and adverse health effects of loneliness in community-dwelling adults across the lifespan: Role of wisdom as a protective factor. *International Psychogeriatrics, 18*, 1–16.

Lee, K., Ashton, M. C., Pozzebon, J. A., Visser, B. A., Bourdage, J. S., Ogunfowora, B. (2009). Similarity and assumed similarity in personality reports of well-acquainted persons. *Journal of Personality and Social Psychology, 96*(2), 460–472.

Lee, M. R., & Ousey, G. C. (2011). Reconsidering the culture and violence connection: Strategies of action in the rural south. *Journal of Interpersonal Violence, 26*(5), 899–929.

Lee, R. S. (1995). Regional subcultures as revealed by magazine circulation patterns. *Cross-Cultural Research, 29*, 91–120.

Lee, S. T., & Cheng, I. H. (2010). Assessing the TARES as an ethical model for antismoking ads. *Journal of Health Communication, 15*(1), 55–75.

Lee, T. M., Liu, H. L., Tan, L. H., Chan, C. C., Mahankali, S., Feng, C. M.,. . .Gao, J. H. (2002). Lie detection by functional magnetic resonance imaging. *Human Brain Mapping, 15*(3), 157–164.

Legault, L., Green-Demers, I., Grant, P., & Chung, J. (2007). On the self-regulation of implicit and explicit prejudice: A self-determination theory perspective. *Personality and Social Psychology Bulletin, 33*(5), 732–749.

Lehmiller, J. J., & Agnew, C. R. (2006). Marginalized relationships: The impact of social disapproval on romantic relationship commitment. *Personality and Social Psychology Bulletin, 32*(1), 40–51.

Lehmiller, J. J., & Agnew, C. R. (2007). Perceived marginalization and the prediction of romantic relationship stability. *Journal of Marriage and Family, 69*(4), 1036–1049.

Lehmiller, J. J., Law, A. T., & Tormala, T. T. (2010). The effect of self-affirmation on sexual prejudice. *Journal of Experimental Social Psychology, 46*(2), 276–285.

Lehmiller, J. J., VanderDrift, L. E., & Kelly, J. R. (2011). Sex differences in approaching friends with benefits relationships. *Journal of Sex Research, 48*(2–3), 275–284.

Lehmiller, J. J., VanderDrift, L. E., & Kelly, J. R. (2014). Sexual communication, satisfaction, and condom use behavior in friends with benefits and romantic partners. *Journal of Sex Research, 51*(1), 74–85.

Leidner, B., Castano, E., Zaiser, E., & Giner-Sorolla, R. (2010). Ingroup glorification, moral disengagement, and justice in the context of collective violence. *Personality and Social Psychology Bulletin, 36*(8), 1115–1129.

Leit, R. A., Pope, H. G., & Gray, J. J. (2001). Cultural expectations of muscularity in men: The evolution of *Playgirl* centerfolds. *International Journal of Eating Disorders, 29*(1), 90–93.

Leitner, J. B., Hehman, E., Ayduk, O., & Mendoza-Denton, R. (2016). Blacks' death rate due to circulatory diseases is positively related to whites' explicit racial bias: A nationwide investigation using project implicit. *Psychological Science, 27*(10), 1299–1311.

LeMarie, K. L., & Oswald, D. L. (2016). How gender affects heterosexual allies' intentions of confronting sexual prejudice. *Psychology of Sexual Orientation and Gender Diversity, 3*(4), 453–464.

Lemay, E. P., Jr. (2016). The forecast model of relationship commitment. *Journal of Personality and Social Psychology, 111*(1), 34–52.

Lenhart, A., Kahne, J., Middaugh, E., Macgill, A. R., Evans, C., & Vitak, J. (2008). *Teens, video games, and civics.* (Report No. 202-415-4500). Washington, DC: Pew Internet and American Life Project. Retrieved from https://www.pewresearch.org/internet/2008/09/16/teens-video-games-and-civics/

Leonard, K. (1989). The impact of explicit aggressive and implicit nonaggressive cues on aggression in intoxicated and sober males. *Personality and Social Psychology Bulletin, 15*(3), 390–400.

Leonard, K. E., & Quigley, B. M. (1999). Drinking and marital aggression in newlyweds: An event-based analysis of drinking and the occurrence of husband marital aggression. *Journal of Studies on Alcohol, 60*(4), 537–545.

Lerner, M. J. (1980). *The belief in a just world: A fundamental delusion.* New York, NY: Plenum Press.

Lerner, M. J. (1997). What does the belief in a just world protect us from: The dread of death or the fear of undeserved suffering? *Psychological Inquiry, 8*(1), 29–32.

Leung, A. K., & Cohen, D. (2011). Within and between-culture variation: Individual differences and the cultural logistics of honor, face and dignity cultures. *Journal of Personality and Social Psychology, 100*(3), 507–526.

Lev-Ari, S., & Keysar, B. (2010). Why don't we believe non-native speakers? The influence of accent on credibility. *Journal of Experimental Social Psychology, 46*(6), 867–1158.

Levelt Committee, Noort Committee, & Drenth Committee. (2012, November 28). *Flawed science: The fraudulent research practices of social psychologist Diederik Stapel.* Tilburg, The Netherlands: Tilburg University, University of Amsterdam, and University of Groningen.

Levendusky, M. S. (2017). Americans, not partisans: Can priming American national identity reduce affective polarization? *The Journal of Politics, 80*(1).

Levin, S. (2004). Perceived group status differences and the effects of gender, ethnicity, and religion on social dominance orientation. *Political Psychology, 25*(1), 31–48.

Levine, J. M., & Moreland, R. L. (1998). Small groups. In D. Gilbert, S. T. Fiske, & G. Lindzey (Eds.), *Handbook of social psychology* (4th ed., pp. 415–469). New York, NY: McGraw-Hill.

Levine, J. M., Moreland, R. L., & Hausmann, L. R. M. (2005). Managing group composition: Inclusive and exclusive role transitions. In D. Abrams, M. A. Hogg, & J. M. Marques (Eds.), *The social psychology of inclusion and exclusion* (pp. 137–160). New York, NY: Psychology Press.

Levine, M., Prosser, A., Evans, D., & Reicher, S. (2005). Identity and emergency intervention: How social group membership and inclusiveness of group boundaries shape helping behavior. *Personality and Social Psychology Bulletin, 31*(4), 443–453.

Levine, R., Sata, S., Hashimoto, T., & Verma, J. (1995). Love and marriage in eleven cultures. *Journal of Cross-Cultural Psychology, 26*(5), 554–571.

Levine, R. A., & Campbell, D. T. (1972). *Ethnocentrism: Theories of conflict, ethnic attitudes, and group behavior.* New York, NY: John Wiley & Sons.

Levine, R. V. (2003). The kindness of strangers. *American Scientist, 91*, 226–233.

Levine, R. V., Martinez, T. S., Brase, G., & Sorenson, K. (1994). Helping in 36 U.S. cities. *Journal of Personality and Social Psychology, 67*(1), 69–82.

Levine, R. V., & Norenzayan, A. (1999). The pace of life in 31 countries. *Journal of Cross-Cultural Psychology, 30*(2), 178–205.

Levine, T. R., Shaw, A., & Shulman, H. C. (2010). Increasing deception detection accuracy with strategic questioning. *Human Communication Research, 36*(2), 216–231.

Levitsky, S., & Ziblatt, D. (2019). *How democracies die.* New York, NY: Broadway Books.

Levy, B. R. (1996). Improving memory in old age through implicit self-stereotyping. *Journal of Personality and Social Psychology, 71*(6), 1092–1107.

Levy, B. R., Pilver, C., Chung, P. H., & Slade, M. D. (2014). Subliminal strengthening: Improving older individuals' physical function over time with an implicit-age-stereotype intervention. *Psychological Science, 25*(12), 2127–2135.

Levy, S. R., Stroessner, S. J., & Dweck, C. S. (1998). Stereotype formation and endorsement: The role of implicit theories. *Journal of Personality and Social Psychology, 74*(6), 1421–1436.

Lewandowski, G. G., Jr., Aron, A., Bassis, S., & Kunak, J. (2006). Losing a self-expanding relationship: Implications for the self-concept. *Personal Relationships, 13*(3), 317–331.

Lewandowski, G. W., & Bizzoco, N. M. (2007). Addition through subtraction: Growth following the dissolution of a low quality relationship. *The Journal of Positive Psychology, 2*(1), 40–54.

Lewin, K. (1951). Problems of research in social psychology. In D. Cartwright (Ed.), *Field theory in social science* (pp. 155–169). New York, NY: Harper & Row.

Lewis, M. (2011). The origins and uses of self-awarenesss or the mental representation of me. *Consciousness and Cognition: An International Journal, 20*(1), 120–129.

Lewis, M., & Brooks, J. (1978). Self-knowledge in emotional development. In M. Lewis & L. Rosenblum (Eds.), *The development of affect* (pp. 205–226). New York, NY: Plenum Press.

Li, N. P., Valentine, K. A., & Patel, L. (2011). Mate preferences in the US and Singapore: A cross-cultural test of the mate preference priority model. *Personality and Individual Differences, 50*(2), 291–294.

Liberman, V., Samuels, S. M., & Ross, L. (2004). The name of the game: Predictive power of reputations versus structural labels in determining prisoner's dilemma game moves. *Personality and Social Psychology Bulletin, 30*(9), 1175–1185.

Lieberman, M. D., Jarcho, J. M., Obayashi, J. (2005). Attributional inference across cultures: Similar automatic attributions and different controlled corrections. *Personality and Social Psychology Bulletin, 31*(7), 889–901.

Lieder, F., Griffiths, T. L., & Hsu, M. (2018). Overrepresentation of extreme events in decision making reflects rational use of cognitive resources. *Psychological Review, 125*(1), 1–32.

Lin, C. -L., Lee, S. -H., & Horng, D. -J. (2011). The effects of online reviews on purchasing intention: The moderating role of need for cognition. *Social Behavior and Personality, 39*(1), 71–82.

Lin, M. H., Kwan, V. S., Cheung, A., & Fiske, S. T. (2005). Stereotype content model explains prejudice for an envied outgroup: Scale of anti-Asian American stereotypes. *Personality and Social Psychology Bulletin, 31*(1), 34–47.

Lindberg, M. J., Markman, K. D., & Choi, H. (2013). "It was meant to be": Retrospective meaning construction through mental simulation. In K. D. Markman, T. Proulx, & M J. Lindberg (Eds.), *The psychology of meaning* (pp. 339–355). Washington, DC: American Psychological Association.

Linder, D. E., Cooper, J., & Jones, E. E. (1967). Decision freedom as a determinant of the role of incentive magnitude in attitude change. *Journal of Personality and Social Psychology, 6*(3), 245–254.

Lindly, O. J., Nario-Redmond, M. R., & Noelc, J. G. (2014). Creatively re-defining fat: Identification predicts strategic responses to stigma, ingroup attitudes and well-being. *Fat Studies, 3*(2), 179–195.

Lindsay, D. S. (2017). Sharing data and materials in *Psychological Science*. *Psychological Science, 28*(6), 699–702.

Lindsay, J. J., & Anderson, C. A. (2000). From antecedent conditions to violent actions: A general affective aggression model. *Personality and Social Psychology Bulletin, 26*(5), 533–547.

Lingle, S., Rendall, D., Wilson, W. F., DeYoung, R. W., & Pellis, S. M. (2007). Altruism and recognition in the antipredator defence of deer: 2. Why mule deer help nonoffspring fawns. *Animal Behaviour, 73*(5), 907–916.

Link, B. G., Andrews, H., & Cullen, F. T. (1992). The violent and illegal behavior of mental patients reconsidered. *American Sociological Review, 57*(3), 275–292.

Lipkus, I. M., Dalbert, C., & Siegler, I. C. (1996). The importance of distinguishing the belief in a just world for self versus for others: Implications for psychological well-being. *Personality and Social Psychology Bulletin, 22*(7), 666–677.

Lippa, R. A. (2005). Sex and gender. In V. J. Derlega, B. A. Winstead, & W. H. Jones (Eds.), *Personality: Contemporary theory and research* (3rd ed., pp. 332–365). Belmont, CA: Thomson/Wadsworth.

Lippa, R., & Arad, S. (1999). Gender, personality, and prejudice: The display of authoritarianism and social dominance in interviews with college men and women. *Journal of Research in Personality, 33*(4), 463–493.

Lips-Wiersma, M., & Mills, C. (2002). Coming out of the closet: Negotiating spiritual expression in the workplace. *Journal of Managerial Psychology, 17*(3), 183–202.

Lisak, D., Gardinier, L., Nicksa, S. C., & Cote, A. M. (2010). False allegations of sexual assault: An analysis of ten years of reported cases. *Violence Against Women, 16*(12), 1318–1334.

Littleford, L. N., Wright, M. O., & Sayoc-Parial, M. (2005). White students' intergroup anxiety during same-race and interracial interactions: A multimethod approach. *Basic and Applied Social Psychology, 27*(1), 85–94.

Liu, B., & Sundar, S. S. (2018). Microworkers as research participants: Does underpaying Turkers lead to cognitive dissonance? *Computers in Human Behavior, 88*, 61–69.

Liu, C. J., & Li, S. (2009). Contextualized self: When the self runs into social dilemmas. *International Journal of Psychology, 44*(6), 451–458.

Locke, B.D., & Mahalik, J. R. (2005). Examining masculinity norms, problem drinking, and athletic involvement as predictors of sexual aggression in college men. *Journal of Counseling Psychology, 52*(3), 279–283.

Locke, K. D. (2007). Personalized and generalized comparisons: Causes and consequences of variations in the foci of social comparisons. *Personality and Social Psychology Bulletin, 33*(2), 213–225.

Lore, R. K., & Schultz, L. A. (1993). Control of human aggression: A comparative perspective. *American Psychologist, 48*(1), 16–25.

Loukopoulos, P., Eek, D., Garling, T., & Fujii, S. (2006). Palatable punishment in real-world social dilemmas? Punishing others to increase cooperation among the unpunished. *Journal of Applied Social Psychology, 36*(5), 1274–1290.

Lovaglia, J. J., & Houser, J. A. (1996). Emotional reactions and status in groups. *American Sociological Review, 61*(5), 867–883.

Lowe, K. B., Kroeck, K. G., & Sivasubramaniam, N. (1996). Effectiveness correlates of transformational and transactional leadership: A meta-analytic review of the mlq literature. *The Leadership Quarterly, 7*(3), 385–425.

Lucas, R. E., Diener, E., Grob, A., Suh, E., & Shao, L. (2000). Cross-cultural evidence for the fundamental features of extraversion. *Journal of Personality and Social Psychology, 79*(3), 452–468.

Lucas, T., Alexander, S., Firestone, I., & Lebreton, J. M (2009). Belief in a just world, social influence and illness attributions: Evidence of a just world boomerang effect. *Journal of Health Psychology, 14*(2), 258–266.

Luce, R. D., & Raiffa, H. (1957). *Games and decisions.* New York, NY: John Wiley & Sons.

Ludeke, S. G., Klitgaard, C. N., & Vitriol, J. (2018). Comprehensively-measured authoritarianism *does* predict vote choice: The importance of authoritarianism's facets, ideological sorting, and the particular candidate. *Personality and Individual Differences, 123*, 209–216.

Luhan, W. J., Kocher, M. G., & Sutter, M. (2009). Group polarization in the team dictator game reconsidered. *Experimental Economics, 12*(1), 26–41.

Lumsdaine, A., & Janis, I. (1953). Resistance to "counterpropaganda" produced by one-sided and two-sided "propaganda" presentations. *Public Opinion Quarterly, 17*(3), 311–318.

Luo, S., & Zhang, G. (2009). What leads to romantic attraction: Similarity, reciprocity, security, or beauty? Evidence from a speed-dating study. *Journal of Personality, 77*(4), 933–964.

Luong, G., Charles, S. T., & Fingerman, K. L. (2010). Better with age: Social relationships across adulthood. *Journal of Social and Personal Relationships, 28*(1), 9–23.

Luttrell, A., Petty, R. E., Briñol, P., & Wagner, B. C. (2016). Making it moral: Merely labeling an attitude as moral increases its strength. *Journal of Experimental Social Psychology, 65*, 82–93.

Lynch, J. W., Kaplan, G. A., & Shema, S. J. (1997). Cumulative impact of sustained economic hardship on physical, cognitive, psychological, and social functioning. *New England Journal of Medicine, 337*(26), 1889–1895.

Lyubomirsky, S. (2007). *The how of happiness: A new approach to getting the life you want.* New York, NY: Penguin Group.

Lyubomirsky, S., Caldwell, N. D., & Nolen-Hoeksema, S. (1998). Effects of ruminative and distracting responses to depressed mood on retrieval of autobiographical memories. *Journal of Personality and Social Psychology, 75*(1), 166–177.

M

Ma, L. K., Tunney, R. J., & Ferguson, E. (2017). Does gratitude enhance prosociality? A meta-analytic review. *Psychological Bulletin, 143*(6), 601–635.

Ma, V., & Schoeneman, T. J. (1997). Individualism versus collectivism: A comparison of Kenyan and American self-concepts. *Basic and Applied Social Psychology, 19*(2), 261–273.

Maass, A., Clark, R. D., III, & Haberkorn, G. (1982). The effects of differential ascribed category membership and norms on minority influence. *European Journal of Social Psychology, 12*(1), 89–104.

Maccoby, E. E. (1990). Gender and relationships: A developmental account. *American Psychologist, 45*(4), 513–520.

Maccoby, E. E. (1998). *The two sexes: Growing up apart, coming together.* Stanford, CA: Stanford University Press.

MacDonald, G., & Borsook, T. K. (2010). Attachment avoidance and feelings of connection in social interaction. *Journal of Experimental Social Psychology, 46*(6), 1122–1125.

MacDonald, G., & Leary, M. R. (2005). Why does social exclusion hurt? The relationship between social and physical pain. *Psychological Bulletin, 131*(2), 202–223.

MacDonald, G., Zanna, M. P., & Holmes, J. G. (2000). An experimental test of the role of alcohol in relationship conflict. *Journal of Experimental Social Psychology, 36*(2), 182–193.

Mackay, N. (2004, January 11). Former Bush aide: U.S. plotted Iraq invasion long before 9/11. *Sunday Herald.* Retrieved from http://www.twf.org/News/Y2004/0111-Before911.html

Macrae, C. N., Milne, A. B., & Bodenhausen, G. V. (1994). Stereotypes as energy saving devices: A peek inside the cognitive toolbox. *Journal of Personality and Social Psychology, 66*(1), 37–47.

Macrae, C. N., & Quadflieg, S. (2010). Perceiving people. In S. T. Fiske, D. T. Gilbert, & G. Lindzey (Eds.), *Handbook of social psychology* (5th ed., Vol. 1, pp. 428–463). Hoboken, NJ: John Wiley & Sons.

Maddison, R., & Prapavessis, H. (2007). Self-handicapping in sport: A self-presentation strategy. In S. Jowette, & D. Lavallee (Eds.), *Social psychology in sport* (pp. 209–220). Champaign, IL: Human Kinetics.

Maddox, K. B. (2004). Perspectives on racial phenotypicality bias. *Personality and Social Psychology Bulletin, 8*(4), 383–401.

Madon, S., Guyll, M., Scherr, K. C., Willard, J., Spoth, R., & Vogel, D. L. (2013). The role of the self-fulfilling prophecy in young adolescents' responsiveness to a substance use prevention program. *Journal of Applied Social Psychology, 43*(9), 1784–1798.

Madsen, E. A., Tunney, R. J., Fieldman, G., Plotkin, H. C., Dunbar, R. I., Richardson, J-M., & McFarland, D. (2007). Kinship and altruism: A cross-cultural experimental study. *British Journal of Psychology, 98*(2), 339–359.

Maestripieri, D. (2001). Biological bases of maternal attachment. *Current Directions in Psychological Science, 10*(3), 79–82.

Magee, J. C., & Smith, P. K. (2013). The social distance theory of power. *Personality and Social Psychology Review, 17*(2), 158–186.

Magid, D. J., Houry, D., Koepsell, T. D., Ziller, A., Soules, M. R., & Jenny, C. (2004). The epidemiology of female rape victims who seek immediate medical care: Temporal trends in the incidence of sexual assault and acquaintance rape. *Journal of Interpersonal Violence, 19*(1), 3–12.

Maio, G. R., Olson, J. M., & Cheung, I. (2013). Attitudes in social behavior. In H. Tennen, J. Suls, & I. B. Weiner (Eds.), *Handbook of psychology, Vol. 5: Personality and social psychology* (2nd ed., pp. 275–304). Hoboken, NJ: John Wiley & Sons.

Majied, K. F. (2010). The impact of sexual orientation and gender expression bias on African American students. *The Journal of Negro Education, 79*(2), 151–165.

Major, B., Eliezer, D., & Rieck, H. (2012). The psychological weight of weight stigma. *Social Psychological and Personality Science, 3*(6), 651–658.

Major, B., Kaiser, C. R., O'Brien, L. T., & McCoy, S. K. (2007). Perceived discrimination as worldview threat or worldview confirmation: Implications for self-esteem. *Journal of Personality and Social Psychology, 92*(6), 1068–1086.

Major, B., & O'Brien, L. T. (2005). The social psychology of stigma. *Annual Review of Psychology, 56*, 393–421.

Malach, P. A. (2001). The role of gender and culture in romantic attraction. *European Psychologist, 6*(2), 96–102.

Malamuth, N. M. (2018). "Adding fuel to the fire"? Does exposure to non-consenting adult or to child pornography increase risk of sexual aggression? *Aggression and Violent Behavior, 41*, 74–89.

Malamuth, N. M., & Check, J. V. (1981). The effects of mass media exposure on acceptance of violence against women: A field experiment. *Journal of Research in Personality, 15*(4), 436–446.

Malle, B. F. (2006). The actor-observer asymmetry in attribution: A (surprising) meta-analysis. *Psychological Bulletin, 132*(6), 895–919.

Mallick, S. K., & McCandless, B. R. (1966). A study of catharsis of aggression. *Journal of Personality and Social Psychology, 4*(6), 591–596.

Malloy, T., & Rubenstein, P. S. (2018, January 24). Dems, Trump share blame for 'unnecessary' shutdown, Quinnipiac University national poll finds; voters are dissatisfied, angry with government. *Quinnipiac University Poll.* Retrieved from https://poll.qu.edu/images/polling/us/us01242018_ufks28.pdf/

Manago, A. M., Graham, M. B., Greenfield, P. M., & Salimkhan, G. (2008). Self-presentation and gender on MySpace. *Journal of Applied Developmental Psychology, 29*(6), 446–458.

Mandalaywala, T. M., Amodio, D. M., & Rhodes, M. (2018). Essentialism promotes racial prejudice by increasing endorsement of social hierarchies. *Social Psychological and Personality Science, 9*(4), 461–469.

Mandel, D. R. (2003). Counterfactuals, emotions, and context. *Cognition and Emotion, 17*(1), 139–159.

Mandela, N. (1994). *Long walk to freedom: The autobiography of Nelson Mandela.* Boston, MA: Little, Brown.

Maner, J. K. (2016). Into the wild: Field research can increase both replicability and real-world impact. *Journal of Experimental Social Psychology, 66*, 100–106.

Maner, J. K., & Gailliot, M. T. (2007). Altruism and egoism: Prosocial motivations for helping depend on relationship context. *European Journal of Social Psychology, 37*(2), 347–358.

Mann, L. (1981). The baiting crowd in episodes of threatened suicide. *Journal of Personality and Social Psychology, 41*(4), 703–709.

Mann, S., Ewens, S., Shaw, D., Vrij, A., Leal, S., & Hillman, J. (2013). Lying eyes: Why liars seek deliberate eye contact. *Psychiatry, Psychology and Law, 20*(3), 452–461.

Manning, R., Levine, M., & Collins, A. (2007). The Kitty Genovese murder and the social psychology of helping: The parable of the 38 witnesses. *American Psychology, 62*(6), 555–562.

Mantell, D. M. (1971). The potential for violence in Germany. *Journal of Social Issues, 27*(4), 101–112.

Marcus, D. K., & Miller, R. S. (2003). Sex differences in judgments of physical attractiveness: A social relations analysis. *Personality and Social Psychology Bulletin, 29*(3), 325–335.

Marcus, D. K., Wilson, J. R., & Miller, R. S. (1996). Are perceptions of emotion in the eye of the beholder? A social relations analysis of judgments of embarrassment. *Personality and Social Psychology Bulletin, 22*(12), 1220–1228.

Marelich, W. D., Gaines, S. O., Jr. & Branzet M. R. (2003). Commitment, insecurity and arousability: Testing a transactional model of jealousy. *Representative Research in Social Psychology, 27,* 23–31.

Marelich, W. D., & Holt, T. (2006). Salvaging the self and romantic jealousy response. In A. P. Prescott (Ed.), *The concept of self in psychology* (pp. 167–181). Hauppauge, NY: Nova Science.

Margie, O. (2006). Training in communication skills: Research, theory and practice. In O. Margie (Ed), *The handbook of communication skills* (3rd ed., pp. 553–565). New York, NY: Routledge.

Marjanovic, Z., Greenglass, E. R., Struthers, C. W., & Faye, C. (2009). Helping following natural disasters: A social-motivational analysis. *Journal of Applied Social Psychology, 39,* 2604–2625.

Markey, P. M. (2000). Bystander intervention in computer-mediated communication. *Computers in Human Behavior, 16*(2), 183–188.

Markman, A. B. (1999). *Knowledge representation.* Mahwah, NJ: Lawrence Erlbaum Associates.

Markus, H. R., & Kitayama, S. (1991). Culture and the self: Implications for cognition, emotion, and motivation. *Psychological Review, 98*(2), 224–253.

Markus, H. R., & Kitayama, S. (1994). A collective fear of the collective: Implications for selves and theories of selves. *Personality and Social Psychology Bulletin, 20*(5), 568–579.

Marsh, A. A., & Ambady, N. (2007). The influence of the fear facial expression on prosocial responding. *Cognition & Emotion, 21*(2), 225–247.

Martin, C. J. H., & Bull, P. (2010). The situational argument: Do midwives agree or acquiesce with senior staff? *Journal of Reproductive and Infant Psychology, 28*(2), 180–190.

Martin, J. L., Groth, G., Buckner, L., Gale, M. M., & Kramer, M. E. (2013). Perceived drinking norms among Black college students: The race of reference group members. *Addictive Behaviors, 38*(10), 2586–2588.

Martin, R. (1988). Ingroup and outgroup minorities: Differential impact upon public and private responses. *European Journal of Social Psychology, 18*(1), 39–52.

Martin, R., Hewstone, M., & Martin, P. Y. (2003). Resistance to persuasive messages as a function of majority and minority source status. *Journal of Experimental Social Psychology, 39*(6), 585–593.

Martin, R., Hewstone, M., & Martin, P. Y. (2008). Majority versus minority influence: the role of message processing in determining resistance to counter-persuasion. *European Journal of Social Psychology, 38*(1), 16–34.

Martins, Y., Tiggemann, M., & Kirkbride, A. (2007). Those Speedos become them: The role of self-objectification in gay and heterosexual men's body image. *Personality and Social Psychology Bulletin, 33*(5), 634–647.

Marwell, G., Aiken, M. T., & Demerath, N. J., III. (1987). The persistence of political attitudes among 1960s civil rights activists. *Public Opinion Quarterly, 51*(3), 359–375.

Marzoli, D., Custodero, M., Pagliara, A., & Tommasi, L. (2013). Sun-induced frowning fosters aggressive feelings. *Cognition and Emotion, 27*(8), 1513–1521.

Mashek, D. J., Aron, A., & Boncimino, M. (2003). Confusion of self with close others. *Personality and Social Psychology Bulletin, 29*(3), 382–392.

Maslow, A. H. (1970). *Motivation and personality* (2nd ed.). New York, NY: Harper & Row.

Mason, W. A. (1997). Discovering behavior. *American Psychologist, 52*(7), 713–720.

Mast, M. S., & Hall, J. A. (2004). When is dominance related to smiling? Assigned dominance, dominance preference, trait dominance, and gender as moderators. *Sex Roles, 50*(5–6), 387–399.

Masters, K. S. (2009). Milgram, stress research, and the Institutional Review Board. *American Psychologist, 64*(7), 621–622.

Mastroianni, G. R., Kimmelman, S., Doty, J., & Thomas, J. J. (2011). Obedience and personal responsibility. In P. Sweeney, M. Matthews, & P. B. Lester (Eds.), *Leading in dangerous contexts* (pp. 97–120). Annapolis, MD: Naval Institute Press.

Matheson, K., Cole, B., & Majka, K. (2003). Dissidence from within: Examining the effects of intergroup context on group members' reactions to attitudinal opposition. *Journal of Experimental Social Psychology, 39*(2), 161–169.

Mathie, N. L., & Wakeling, H. C. (2011). Assessing socially desirable responding and its impact on self-report measures among sexual offenders. *Psychology, Crime & Law, 17*(3), 215–237.

Mattingly, B. A., McIntyre, K. P., Knee, R., & Loving, T. J. (2019). Implicit theories of relationships and self-expansion: Implications for relationship functioning. *Journal of Social and Personal Relationships, 36*(6), 1579–1599.

Mattingly, B. A., Oswald, D. L., & Clark, E. M. (2011). An examination of relational-interdependent self-construal, communal strength, and pro-relationship behaviors in friendships. *Personality and Individual Differences, 50*(8), 1243–1248.

McAdams, D. P. (1988). Personal needs and personal relationships. In S. Duck (Ed.), *Handbook of personal relationships: Theory, research, and interventions* (pp. 7–22). New York, NY: John Wiley & Sons.

McCall, M., & Nattrass, K. (2001). Carding for the purchase of alcohol: I'm tougher than other clerks are! *Journal of Applied Social Psychology, 31*(10), 2184–2194.

McCann, S. J. (1999). Threatening times and fluctuations in American church memberships. *Personality and Social Psychology Bulletin, 25*(3), 325–336.

McCauley, C. R. (2004). Psychological issues in understanding terrorism and the response to terrorism. In C. E. Stout (Ed.), *Psychology of terrorism: Coping with the continuing threat, condensed edition* (pp. 33–65). Westport, CT: Praeger/Greenwood.

McCauley, C. R., & Segal, M. E. (1987). Social psychology of terrorist groups. In C. Hendrick (Ed.), *Group processes and intergroup relations: Review of personality and social psychology* (Vol. 9, pp. 231–256). Thousand Oaks, CA: Sage.

McCord, J. (1994). Aggression in two generations. In L. R. Huesmann (Ed.), *Aggressive behavior: Current perspectives* (pp. 241–251). New York, NY: Plenum Press.

McCroskey, J. C. (1997). Willingness to communicate, communication apprehension, and self-perceived communication competence: Conceptualizations and perspectives. In J. A. Daly, J. C. McCroskey, J. Ayres, T. Hopf, & D. M. Ayres (Eds.), *Avoiding communication: Shyness, reticence, and communication apprehension* (2nd ed., pp. 75–108). Creskill, NJ: Hampton Press.

McDuff, D., Girard, J. M., & Kaliouby, R. e. (2017). Large-scale observational evidence of cross-cultural differences in facial behavior. *Journal of Nonverbal Behavior, 41*(1), 1–19.

McDuff, D., Kodra, E., Kaliouby, R. e., & LaFrance, M. (2017). A large-scale analysis of sex differences in facial expressions. *PLoS One, 12*(4), e0173942.

McGarty, C. (2004). Forming stereotypes of entitative groups. In V. Yzerbyt, C. M. Judd, & O. Corneille (Eds.), *The psychology of group perception: Perceived variability, entitativity, and essentialism* (pp. 161–178). New York, NY: Psychology Press.

McGarty, C., Turner, J. C., Hogg, M. A., David, B., & Wetherell, M. S. (1992). Group polarization as conformity to the prototypical group member. *British Journal of Social Psychology, 31*(1), 1–19.

McGinty, K., Knox, D., & Zusman, M. E. (2007). Friends with benefits: Women want "friends," men want "benefits." *College Student Journal, 41*(4), 1128–1131.

McGowan, S. (2002). Mental representations in stressful situations: The calming and distressing effects of significant others. *Journal of Experimental Social Psychology, 38*(2), 152–161.

McGrath, J. E., Arrow, H., & Berdahl, J. L. (2000). The study of groups: Past, present, and future. *Personality and Social Psychology Review, 4*(1), 95–105.

McGrath, R. E. (2011). *Quantitative models in psychology.* Washington, DC: American Psychological Association.

McGraw, A. P., Mellers, B. A., & Tetlock, P. E. (2005). Expectations and emotions of Olympic athletes. *Journal of Experimental Social Psychology, 41*(4), 438–446.

McGuire, J. F., Small, B. J., Lewin, A. B., Murphy, T. K., De Nadai, A. S., Phares, V., . . .Storch, E. A. (2013). Dysregulation in pediatric obsessive compulsive disorder. *Psychiatry Research, 209*(3), 589–595.

McGuire, W. J. (1968). Personality and susceptibility to social influence. In E. F. Borgatta & W. W. Lambert (Eds.), *Handbook of personality theory and research* (pp. 1130–1187). Chicago: Rand McNally.

McGuire, W. J. (1999). *Constructing social psychology: Creative and critical processes.* Cambridge, England: Cambridge University Press.

McGuire, W. J., & Papageorgis, D. (1961). The relative efficacy of various types of prior belief-defense in producing immunity against persuasion. *Journal of Abnormal and Social Psychology, 62*(2), 327–337.

McIntyre, K. P., Mattingly, B. A., & Lewandowski, G. W., Jr. (2015). When "we" changes "me": The two-dimensional model of relational self-change and relationship outcomes. *Journal of Social and Personal Relationships, 32*(7), 857–878,

McIntyre, R. B., Paulson, R. M., Lord, C. G. (2003). Alleviating women's mathematics stereotype threat through salience of group achievements. *Journal of Experimental Social Psychology, 39*(1), 83–90.

McLaughlin, B. (2018). Commitment to the team: Perceived conflict and political polarization. *Journal of Media Psychology: Theories, Methods, and Applications, 30*(1), 41–51.

McMillen, D. L., Sander, D. V., & Solomon, G. S. (1977). Self-esteem, attentiveness, and helping behavior. *Personality and Social Psychology Bulletin, 3*(2), 257–261.

McMullen, M. N., & Markman, K. D. (2000). Downward counterfactuals and motivation: The wake-up call and the Pangloss effect. *Personality and Social Psychology Bulletin, 26*(5), 575–584.

McNally, A. M., Palfai, T. P., Levine, R. V., & Moore, B. M. (2003). Attachment dimensions and drinking-related problems among young adults: The mediational role of coping motives. *Addictive Behaviors, 28*(6), 1115–1127.

Mead, G. H. (1925). The genesis of the self and social control. *International Journal of Ethics, 35*(3), 251–277.

Mead, G. H. (1934*). Mind, self, and society.* Chicago, IL: University of Chicago Press.

Medvene, L. J., Teal, C. R., & Slavich, S. (2000). Including the other in self: Implications for judgments of equity and satisfaction in close relationships. *Journal of Social and Clinical Psychology, 19*(3), 396–419.

Meevissen, Y. M., Peters, M. L., & Alberts, H. J. (2011). Become more optimistic by imagining a best possible self: Effects of a two week intervention. *Journal of Behavior Therapy and Experimental Psychiatry, 42*(3), 371–378.

Mehl, M. R., & Conner, T. S. (Eds.). (2012). *Handbook of research methods for studying daily life.* New York, NY: Guilford Press.

Mehl, M. R., & Pennebaker, J. W. (2003). The social dynamics of a cultural upheaval: Social interactions surrounding September 11, 2001. *Psychological Science, 14*(6), 579–585.

Meier, B. P., & Hinsz, V. B. (2004). A comparison of human aggression committed by groups and individuals: An interindividual-intergroup discontinuity. *Journal of Experimental Social Psychology, 40*(4), 551–559.

Meier, B. P., Robinson, M. D., Carter, M. S., & Hinsz, V. B. (2010). Are sociable people more beautiful? A zero-acquaintance analysis of agreeableness, extraversion, and attractiveness. *Journal of Research in Personality, 44*(2), 293–296.

Meisner, B. A. (2012). A meta-analyis of positive and negative age stereotype priming effects on behavior among older adults. *The Journals of Gerontology, Series B, 67*(1), 13–17.

Mekawi, Y., & Bresin, K. (2015). Is the evidence from racial bias shooting task studies a smoking gun? Results from a meta-analysis. *Journal of Experimental Social Psychology, 61,* 120–130.

Mello, J., & Garcia-Marques, T. (2018). The attractiveness-positivity link: Let's contextualize it. *The Journal of Social Psychology, 158*(5), 639–645.

Meltzoff, A. N., & Moore, M. K. (1989). Imitation in newborn infants: Exploring the range of gestures imitated and the underlying mechanisms. *Developmental Psychology, 25*(6), 954–962.

Merton, R. (1948). The self-fulfilling prophecy. *The Antioch Review, 8*(2), 193–210.

Mesagno, C., Marchant, D., & Morris, T. (2009). Alleviating choking: The sounds of distraction. *Journal of Applied Sport Psychology, 21*(2), 131–147.

Mesquita, B., & Frijda, N. (1992). Cultural variations in emotions: A review. *Psychological Bulletin, 112*(2), 179–204.

Meston, C. M., & Frohlich, P. F. (2003). Love at first fright: Partner salience moderates roller-coaster-induced excitation transfer. *Archives of Sexual Behavior, 32*(6), 537–544.

Michel, M., Corneille, O., & Rossion, B. (2009). Holistic face encoding is modulated by perceived face race: Evidence form perceptual adaptation. *Visual Cognition, 18*(3), 434–455.

Midlarsky, E., Bryan, J. H., & Brickman, P. (1973). Aversive approval: Interactive effects of modeling and reinforcement on altruistic behavior. *Child Development, 44*(2), 321–328.

Mikulincer, M., & Shaver P. R. (2006). *Attachment in adulthood structure, dynamics, and change.* New York, NY: Guilford Press.

Milgram, S. (1963). Behavioral study of obedience. *Journal of Abnormal and Social Psychology, 67*(4), 371–378.

Milgram, S. (1965). Some conditions of obedience and disobedience to authority. *Human Relations, 18*(1), 57–76.

Milgram, S. (1970). The experience of living in cities. *Science, 167*(3924), 1461–1468.

Milgram, S. (1974). *Obedience to authority: An experimental view.* New York, NY: Harper & Row.

Miller, A. G., Gillen, B., Schenker, C., & Radlove, S. (1973). Perception of obedience to authority. *Proceedings of the 81st Annual Convention of the American Psychological Association, 8,* 127–128.

Miller, C. E. (1989). The social psychological effects of group decision rules. In P. B. Paulus (Ed.), *Psychology of group influence* (2nd ed., pp. 327–355). Hillsdale, NJ: Lawrence Erlbaum Associates.

Miller, D. I., Eagly, A. H., & Linn, M. C. (2015). Women's representation in science predicts national gender-science stereotypes: Evidence from 66 nations. *Journal of Educational Psychology, 107*(3), 631–644.

Miller, D. I., Nolla, K. M., Eagly, A. H., & Uttal, D. H. (2018). The development of children's gender-science stereotypes: A meta-analysis of 5 decades of U.S. draw-a-scientist studies. *Child Development, 89*(6), 1943–1955.

Miller, D. T., & Prentice, D. A. (1996). The construction of social norms and standards. In E. T. Higgins & A. W. Kruglanski (Eds.), *Social psychology: Handbook of basic principles* (pp. 799–829). New York, NY: Guilford Press.

Miller, J. G. (1984). Culture and the development of everyday social explanation. *Journal of Personality and Social Psychology, 46*(5), 961–978.

Miller, J. G. (1988). Bridging the content-structure dichotomy: Culture and the self. In M. H. Bond (Ed.), *The cross-cultural challenge to social psychology* (pp. 266–281). Thousand Oaks, CA: Sage.

Miller, J. G. (1994). Cultural diversity in the morality of caring: Individually oriented versus duty-based interpersonal moral codes. *Cross-Cultural Research, 28*(1), 3–39.

Miller, J. G., Akiyama, H., & Kapadia, S. (2017). Cultural variation in communal versus exchange norms: Implications for social support. *Journal of Personality and Social Psychology, 113*(1), 81–94.

Miller, J. G., Bersoff, D. M., & Harwood, R. L. (1990). Perceptions of social responsibilities in India and in the United States: Moral imperatives or personal decisions? *Journal of Personality and Social Psychology, 58*(1), 33–47.

Miller, J. G., Das, R., & Chakravarthy, S. (2011). Culture and the role of choice in agency. *Journal of Personality and Social Psychology, 101*(1), 45–61.

Miller, L. C., Berg, J. H., & Archer, R. L. (1983). Openers: Individuals who elicit intimate self-disclosure. *Journal of Personality and Social Psychology, 44,* 1234–1244.

Miller, L. C., Cooke, L. L., Tsang, J., & Morgan, F. (1992). Should I brag? Nature and impact of positive and boastful disclosures for women and men. *Human Communication Research, 18*(3), 364–399.

Miller, N., & Davidson-Podgorny, G. (1987). Theoretical models of intergroup relations and the use of cooperative teams as an intervention for desegregated settings. In C. Hendrick (Ed.), *Review of personality and social psychology: Group processes and intergroup relations* (Vol. 9, pp. 41–67). Thousand Oaks, CA: Sage.

Miller, N., Maruyama, G., Beaber, R. J., & Valone, K. (1976). Speed of speech and persuasion. *Journal of Personality and Social Psychology, 34*(4), 615–624.

Miller, P. J., Niehuis, S., & Huston, T. L. (2006). Positive illusions in marital relationships: A 13-year longitudinal. study. *Personality and Social Psychology Bulletin, 32*(12), 1579–1594.

Miller, R. S. (1995). Embarrassment and social behavior. In J. P. Tangney & K. W. Fischer (Eds.), *Self-conscious emotions: The psychology of shame, guilt, embarrassment, and pride* (pp. 322–339). New York, NY: Guilford Press.

Miller, R. S., & Schlenker, B. R. (1985). Egotism in group members: Public and private attributions of responsibility for group performance. *Social Psychology Quarterly, 48*(1), 85–89.

Milliman, R. E. (1986). The influence of background music on the behavior of restaurant patrons. *Journal of Consumer Research, 13*(2), 286–289.

Millings, A., Walsh, J., Hepper, E., & O'Brien, M. (2013). Good partner, good parent: Responsiveness mediates the link between romantic attachment and parenting style. *Personality and Social Psychology Bulletin, 39*(2), 170–180.

Mills, J. (1958). Changes in moral attitudes following temptation. *Journal of Personality, 26,* 517–531.

Minton, H. L. (2002). *Departing from deviance: A history of homosexual rights and emancipatory science in America.* Chicago, IL: University of Chicago Press.

Mintz, L. B., & Kashubeck, S. (1999). Body image and disordered eating among Asian American and Caucasian college students: An examination of race and gender differences. *Psychology of Women Quarterly, 23*(4), 781–796.

Mischel, W., Ebbesen, E. B., & Zeiss, A. R. (1972). Cognitive and attentional mechanisms in delay of gratification. *Journal of Personality and Social Psychology, 21*(2), 204–218.

Miyamoto, Y., & Kitayama, S. (2002). Cultural variation in correspondence bias: The critical role of attitude diagnosticity of socially constrained behavior. *Journal of Personality and Social Psychology, 83*(5), 1239–1248.

Moghaddam, F. M. (2005). The staircase to terrorism: A psychological exploration. *American Psychologist, 60*(2), 161–169.

Moghaddam, F. M. (2013). Conformity, obedience, and behavior regulation. In F. M. Moghaddam (Ed.), *The psychology of dictatorship* (pp. 123–139). Washington, DC: American Psychological Association.

Mohr, J. J., & Fassinger, R. E. (2006). Sexual orientation identity and romantic relationship quality in same-sex couples. *Personality and Social Psychology Bulletin, 32*(8), 1085–1099.

Mok, A., & Morris, M. W. (2011). An upside to bicultural identity conflict: Resisting groupthink in cultural ingroups. *Journal of Experimental Social Psychology, 46*(6), 1114–1117.

Mok, A., & Morris, M. W. (2012). Managing two cultural identities: The malleability of bicultural identity integration as a function of induced global or local processing. *Personality and Social Psychology Bulletin, 38*(2), 233–246.

Monahan, C., Goldman, T., & Oswald, D. (2014). Establishing a physical impairment of weight under the ADA/ADAA: Problems of bias in the legal system. *Journal of Labor & Employment Law, 29*(3), 537–562.

Monsour, M. (1997). Communication and cross-sex friendship across the lifecycle: A review of the literature. *Communication Yearbook, 20,* 375–414.

Monteith, M. J., & Mark, A. (2009). The self-regulation of prejudice. In T. D. Nelson (Ed.), *Handbook of prejudice, stereotyping, and discrimination* (pp. 507–524). New York: Psychology Press.

Monteith, M. J., Deneen, N. E., & Tooman, G. D. (1996). The effect of social norm activation on the expression of opinions concerning gay men and blacks. *Basic and Applied Social Psychology, 18*(3), 267–288.

Montepare, J. M., & Zebrowitz-McArthur, L. (1988). Impressions of people created by age-related qualities of their gaits. *Journal of Personality and Social Psychology, 55*(4), 547–556.

Montoya, R. M., & Horton, R. S. (2004). On the importance of cognitive evaluation as a determinant of interpersonal attraction. *Journal of Personality and Social Psychology, 86*(5), 696–712.

Montoya, R. M., & Horton, R. S. (2013). A meta-analytic investigation of the processes underlying the similarity-attraction effect. *Journal of Social and Personal Relationships, 30*(1), 64–94.

Montoya, R. M., Horton, R. S., Vevea, J. L., Citkowicz, M., & Lauber, E. A. (2017). A re-examination of the mere exposure effect: The influence of repeated exposure on recognition, familiarity, and liking. *Psychological Bulletin, 143*(5), 459–498.

Moon, A., & Cho, I. (2012). Psychology of Asian American older adults: Status, challenges, and strengths. In E. C. Chang, & C. A. Downey (Eds.), *Handbook of race and development in mental health* (pp. 189–206). New York, NY: Springer Science + Business Media.

Moore, D. A., & Small, D. A. (2007). Error and bias in comparative judgment: On being both better and worse than we think we are. *Journal of Personality and Social Psychology, 92*(6), 972–989.

Moorhead, G., Ference, R., & Neck, C. P. (1991). Group decision fiascoes continue: Space shuttle *Challenger* and a revised groupthink framework. *Human Relations, 44*(6), 539–550.

Moors, A., & De Houwer, J. (2006). Automaticity: A theoretical and conceptual analysis. *Psychological Bulletin, 132*(2), 297–326.

Moradi, B., & Huang, Y. P. (2008). Objectification theory and psychology of women: A decade of advances and future directions. *Psychology of Women Quarterly, 32*(4), 377–398.

Morawski, J. G., & Bayer, B. M. (2013). Social psychology. In D. K. Freedheim & I. B. Weiner (Eds.), *Handbook of psychology, Vol. 1: History of psychology* (2nd ed., pp. 248–278). Hoboken, NJ: John Wiley & Sons.

Moreland, R. L., & Levine, J. M. (1982). Socialization in small groups: Temporal changes in individual group relations. In L. Berkowitz (Ed.), *Advances in experimental social psychology* (Vol. 15, pp. 137–192). New York, NY: Academic Press.

Moreland, R. L., & Levine, J. M. (1988). Group dynamics over time: Development and socialization in small groups. In J. E. McGrath (Ed.), *The social psychology of time: New perspectives* (pp. 151–181). Newbury Park, CA: Sage.

Moreland, R. L., & Levine, J. M. (2001). Socialization in organizations and work groups. In M. E. Turner (Ed.), *Applied social research. Groups at work: Theory and research* (pp. 69–112). Mahwah, NJ: Lawrence Erlbaum Associates.

Moreland, R. L., & Levine, J. M. (2002). Socialization and trust in work groups. *Group Processes and Intergroup Relations, 5*(3), 185–201.

Morell, V. (2013). *Animal wise: The thoughts and emotions of our fellow creatures.* Collingwood, Australia: Black.

Morling, B., & Kitayama, S. (2008). Culture and motivation. In J. Y. Shah & W. L. Gardner (Eds.), *Handbook of motivation science* (pp. 417–433). New York, NY: Guilford Press.

Mormon, M. T., & Floyd, K. (1998). "I love you, man": Overt expressions of affection in male-male interaction. *Sex Roles, 38*(9–10), 871–881.

Morris, W. L., Sternglanz, W., Ansfield, M. E., Anderson, E., Snyder, J. L., & DePaulo, B. M. (2016). A longitudinal study of the development of emotional deception detection within new same-sex friendships. *Personality and Social Psychology Bulletin, 42*(2), 204–218.

Morris, W. N., Miller, R. S., & Spangenberg, S. (1977). The effects of dissenter position and task difficulty on conformity and response to conflict. *Journal of Personality, 45*(2), 251–266.

Morrison, K. (2005). Motivating women and men to take protective action against rape: Examining direct and indirect persuasive fear appeals. *Health Communication, 18*(3), 237–256.

Morrison, T. L., Urquiza, A. J., & Goodlin-Jones, B. L. (1997). Attachment, perceptions of interaction, and relationship adjustment. *Journal of Social and Personal Relationships, 14*(5), 627–642.

Moscovici, S. (1980). Toward a theory of conversion behavior. In L. Berkowitz (Ed.), *Advances in experimental social psychology* (Vol. 13, pp. 209–239). New York, NY: Academic Press.

Moscovici, S., & Mugny, G. (1983). Minority influence. In P. B. Paulus (Ed.), *Basic group processes* (pp. 41–64). New York, NY: Springer-Verlag.

Moscovici, S., & Nemeth, C. (1974). Social influence II: Minority influence. In C. Nemeth (Ed.), *Social psychology: Classic and contemporary integrations* (pp. 217–249). Chicago, IL: Rand McNally.

Moscovici, S., & Zavalloni, M. (1969). The group as a polarizer of attitudes. *Journal of Personality and Social Psychology, 12*(2), 125–135.

Moskalenko, S., & Heine, S. J. (2003). Watching your troubles away: Television viewing as a stimulus for subjective self-awareness. *Personality and Social Psychology Bulletin, 29*(1), 76–85.

Moss, E., Bureau, J. F., Cyr, C., Mongeau, C., & St. Laurent, D. (2004). Correlates of attachment at age 3: Construct validity of the preschool attachment classification system. *Developmental Psychology, 40*(3), 323–334.

Moss, M. K., & Page, R. A. (1972). Reinforcement and helping behavior. *Journal of Applied Social Psychology, 2*(4), 360–371.

Motyl, M., Demos, A. P., Carsel, T. S., Hanson, B. E., Melton, Z. J., Mueller, A. B.,. . .Skitka, L. J. (2017). The state of social and personality science: Rotten to the core, not so bad, getting better, or getting worse? *Journal of Personality and Social Psychology, 113*(1), 34–58.

Moyer, A. (2013). The psychology of human research participation. In G. J. Feist & M. E. Gorman (Eds.), *Handbook of the psychology of science* (pp. 419–436). New York, NY: Springer.

Muennig, P. (2008). The body politic: The relationship between stigma and obesity-associated disease. *BMC Public Health, 8,* 128–38.

Mugny, G., & Perez, J. A. (1991). *The social psychology of minority influence.* Cambridge, England: Cambridge University Press.

Muir, G., & Macleod, M. D. (2003). The demographic and spatial patterns of recorded rape in a large UK metropolitan area. *Psychology, Crime & Law, 9*(4), 345–355.

Mulgrew, K. E., Johnson, L. M., Lane, B. R., & Katsikitis, M. (2013). The effect of aesthetic versus process images on men's body satisfaction. *Psychology of Men and Masculinity, 15*(4), 452–459.

Mulilis, J. -P., Duval, T. S., & Rombach, D. (2001). Personal responsibility for tornado preparedness: Commitment or choice? *Journal of Applied Social Psychology, 31*(8), 1659–1688.

Mullen, B., & Copper, C. (1994). The relation between group cohesiveness and performance: An integration. *Psychological Bulletin, 115*(2), 210–227.

Mullen, B., & Johnson, C. (1995). Cognitive representation in ethnophaulisms and illusory correlation in stereotyping. *Personality and Social Psychology Bulletin, 21*(5), 420–433.

Mullen, B., Migdal, M. J., & Rozell, D. (2003). Self-awareness, deindividuation, and social identity: Unraveling theoretical paradoxes by filling empirical lacunae. *Personality and Social Psychology Bulletin, 29*(9), 1071–1081.

Mullen, E., & Skitka, L. J. (2009). Comparing Americans' and Ukranians' allocations of public assistance: The role of affective reactions in helping behavior. *Journal of Cross-Cultural Psychology, 40*(2), 301–318.

Mullen, P. E., & Martin, J. (1994). Jealousy: A community study. *British Journal of Psychiatry, 164,* 35–43.

Müller, P. A., & Stahlberg, D. (2007). The role of surprise in hindsight bias: A metacognitive model of reduced and reversed hindsight bias. *Social Cognition, 25*(1), 165–184.

Munoz, Y., Chebat, J. C., & Suissa, J. A. (2010). Using fear appeals in warning labels to promote responsible gambling among VLT players: The key role of Depth of Information Processing. *Journal of Gambling Studies, 26*(4), 593–609.

Muraven, M., Tice, D. M., & Baumeister, R. F. (1998). Self-control as limited resource: Regulatory depletion patterns. *Journal of Personality and Social Psychology, 74*(3), 774–789.

Murphy, S. C. (2017). A hands-on guide to conducting psychological research on Twitter. *Social Psychological and Personality Science, 8*(4), 396–412.

Murphy, S. T. (2001). Feeling without thinking: Affective primacy and the nonconscious processing of emotion. In J. A. Bargh & D. K. Apsley (Eds.), *Unraveling the complexities of social life: A festschrift in honor of Robert B. Zajonc* (pp. 39–53). Washington, DC: American Psychological Association.

Murray, S. L., Bellavia, G., Rose, P., & Griffin, D. W. (2003). Once hurt, twice hurtful: How perceived regard regulates daily marital interactions. *Journal of Personality and Social Psychology, 84*(1), 126–147.

Murray, S. L., & Holmes, J. G. (1997). A leap of faith? Positive illusions in romantic relationships. *Personality and Social Psychology Bulletin, 23*(6), 586–604.

Murray, S. L., & Holmes, J. G. (1999). The (mental) ties that bind: Cognitive structures that predict relationship resilience. *Journal of Personality and Social Psychology, 77*(6), 1228–1244.

Murray, S. L., Holmes, J. G., & Collins, N. L. (2006). Optimizing assurance: The risk regulation system in relationships. *Psychological Bulletin, 132*(5), 641–666.

Murray, S. L., Holmes, J. G., & Griffin, D. W. (1996). The benefits of positive illusions: Idealization and the construction of satisfaction in close relationships. *Journal of Personality and Social Psychology, 70*(1), 79–98.

Murray, S. L., Holmes, J. G., Griffin, D. W., Bellavia, G., & Rose, P. (2001). The mismeasure of love: How self-doubt contaminates relationship beliefs. *Personality and Social Psychology Bulletin, 27*(4), 423–436.

Murray, S. L., Holmes, J. G., Griffin, D. W., & Derrick, J. L. (2015). The equilibrium model of relationship maintenance. *Journal of Personality and Social Psychology, 108*(1), 93–113.

Murray, S. L., Rose, P., Bellavia, G., Holmes, & Kusche, A. (2002). When rejection stings: How self-esteem constrains relationship-enhancement processes. *Journal of Personality and Social Psychology, 83*(3), 556–573.

Murray, S. L., Rose, P., Holmes, J. G., Derrick, J., Podchaski, E. J., Bellavia, G., & Griffin, D. W. (2005). Putting the partner within reach: A dyadic perspective on felt security in close relationships. *Journal of Personality and Social Psychology, 88*(2), 327–347.

Murstein, B. I. (1974). *Love, sex, and marriage through the ages.* New York, NY: Springer.

Mussweiler, T., & Strack, F. (2000). The use of category and exemplar knowledge in the solution of anchoring tasks. *Journal of Personality and Social Psychology, 78*(6), 1038–1052.

Mustonen, A. (1997). Nature of screen violence and its relation to program popularity. *Aggressive Behavior, 23*(4), 281–292.

Myers, D. G., & Diener, E. (2018). The scientific pursuit of happiness. *Perspectives on Psychological Science, 13*(2), 218–225.

Myers, D. G., & Lamm, H. (1976). The group polarization phenomenon. *Psychological Bulletin, 83*(4), 602–627.

N

Nabi, R. L., Moyer-Gusé, E., & Byrne, S. (2007). All joking aside: A serious investigation into the persuasive effect of funny social issue messages. *Communication Monographs, 74*(1), 29–54.

Nadler, A. (1987). Determinants of help seeking behaviour: The effects of helper's similarity, task centrality and recipient's self-esteem. *European Journal of Social Psychology, 17*(1), 57–67.

Nadler, A. (1991). Help-seeking behavior: Psychological costs and instrumental benefits. In M. S. Clark (Ed.), *Prosocial behavior: Review of personality and social psychology* (Vol. 12, pp. 290–311). Thousand Oaks, CA: Sage.

Nadler, A., & Fisher, J. D. (1986). The role of threat to self-esteem and perceived control in recipient reactions to help: Theory development and empirical validation. In L. Berkowitz (Ed.), *Advances in Experimental Social Psychology* (Vol. 19, pp. 81–122). New York, NY: Academic Press.

Nadler, A., Fisher, J. D., & Ben-Itzhak, S. (1983). With a little help from my friend: Effects of single or multiple act aid as a function of donor and task characteristics. *Journal of Personality and Social Psychology, 44*(2), 310–321.

Nadler, A., & Halabi, S. (2006). Intergroup helping as status relations: Effects of status stability, identification, and type of help on receptivity to high-status group's help. *Journal of Personality and Social Psychology, 91*(1), 97–110.

Nadler, J. T., & Clark, M. H. (2011). Stereotype threat: A meta-analysis comparing African Americans to Hispanic Americans. *Journal of Applied Social Psychology, 41*(4), 872–890.

Nærde, A., Ogden, T., Janson, H., & Zachrisson, H. D. (2014). Normative development of physical aggression from 8 to 26 months. *Developmental Psychology, 50*(6), 1710–1720.

Nagy, T. F. (2011). *Essential ethics for psychologists: A primer for understanding and mastering core issues.* Washington, DC: American Psychological Association.

Nahemow, L., & Lawton, M. P. (1975). Similarity and propinquity in friendship formation. *Journal of Personality and Social Psychology, 32*(2), 205–213.

Nai, J., Narayanan, J., Hernandez, I., & Savani, K. (2018). People in more racially diverse neighborhoods are more prosocial. *Journal of Personality and Social Psychology, 114*(4), 497–515.

Nail, P. R., MacDonald, G., & Levy, D. A. (2000). Proposal of a four-dimensional model of social response. *Psychological Bulletin, 126*(3), 106–116.

Nardi, P. M. (1992). Sex, friendship, and gender roles among gay men. In P. M. Nardi (Ed.), *Men's friendships* (pp. 173–185). Thousand Oaks, CA: Sage.

Nardi, P. M., & Sherrod, D. (1994). Friendship in the lives of gay men and lesbians. *Journal of Social and Personal Relationships, 11*(2), 185–199.

Nario-Redmond, M. R., Noel, J. G., & Fern, E. (2013). Redefining disability, re-imagining the self: Disability identification predicts self-esteem and strategic responses to stigma. *Self and Identity, 12*(5), 468–488.

Narusyte, J., Andershed, A. K., Neiderhiser, J. M., & Lichtenstein, P. (2007). Aggression as a mediator of genetic contributions to the association between negative parent-child relationships and adolescent antisocial behavior. *European Child & Adolescent Psychiatry, 16*(2), 128–137.

National Sexual Violence Resource Center. (2014, December 18). Statistics about sexual violence. *National Sexual Violence Resource Center.* Retrieved from http://www.nsvrc.org/sites/default/files/publications_nsvrc_factsheet_media-packet_statistics-about-sexual-violence_0.pdf

Naumann, L. P., Vazire, S., Rentfrow, P. J., Gosling, S. D. (2009). Personality judgments based on physical appearance. *Personality and Social Psychology Bulletin, 35*(12), 1661–1671.

Nauts, S., Langner, O., Huijsmans, I., Vonk, R., & Wigboldus, D. H. (2014). Forming impressions of personality: A replication and review of Asch's (1946) evidence for a primacy-of-warmth effect in impression formation. *Social Psychology, 45*(3), 153–163.

Neely, C. L. (2008). Indian feminisms: Law, patriarchies, and violence in India and body evidence: Intimate violence against South Asian women in America (book reviews). *Violence Against Women, 14*(4), 496–501.

Neighbors, C., Larimer, M. E., Geisner, I. M., & Knee, C. R. (2004). Feeling controlled and drinking motives among college students: Contingent self-esteem as a mediator. *Self and Identity, 3*(3), 207–224.

Neisser, U., Boodoo, G., Bouchard, T. J., Jr., Boykin, A. W., Brody, N., Ceci, S. J.,. . .Urbina, S. (1996). Intelligence: Knowns and unknowns. *American Psychologist, 51*(2), 77–101.

Nelson, K. (1986). *Event knowledge: Structure and function in development.* Mahwah, NJ: Lawrence Erlbaum Associates.

Nemanich, L. A., & Keller, R. T. (2007). Transformational leadership in an acquisition: A field study of employees. *The Leadership Quarterly, 18*(1), 49–68.

Nemeth, C. (1977). Interactions between jurors as a function of majority vs. unanimity decision rules. *Journal of Applied Social Psychology, 7*(1), 38–56.

Nemeth, C. J., Swedlund, M., & Kanki, B. (1974). Patterning of the minority's responses and their influence on the majority. *European Journal of Social Psychology, 4*(1), 53–64.

Nesdale, D., & Dalton, D. (2011) Children's social groups and intergroup prejudice: Assessing the influence and inhibition of social group norms. *British Journal of Developmental Psychology, 29*(4), 895–909.

Nesse, R. M. (2000). How selfish genes shape moral passions. *Journal of Consciousness Studies, 7*(1–2), 227–231.

Neumann, R., Hess, M., Schulz, S. M. & Alpers, G. W. (2005). Automatic behavioural responses to valence: Evidence that facial action is facilitated by evaluative processing. *Cognition and Emotion, 19*(4), 499–513.

Newby-Clark, I. R., McGregor, I., & Zanna, M. P. (2002). Thinking and caring about cognitive inconsistency: When and for whom does attitudinal ambivalence feel uncomfortable? *Journal of Personality and Social Psychology, 82*(2), 157–166.

Newcomb, T. M. (1943). *Personality and social change: Attitude formation in a student community.* New York, NY: Dryden Press.

Newcomb, T. M. (1961). *The acquaintance process.* New York, NY: Holt, Rinehart & Winston.

Newcomb, T. M., Koenig, K. E., Flacks, R., & Warwick, D. P. (1967). *Persistence and change: Bennington College and its students after twenty-five years.* New York, NY: John Wiley & Sons.

Newman, L. S. (2001). A cornerstone for the science of interpersonal behavior? Person perception and person memory, past, present, and future. In G. B. Moskowitz (Ed.), *Cognitive social psychology: The Princeton symposium on the legacy and future of social cognition* (pp. 191–207). Mahwah, NJ: Lawrence Erlbaum Associates.

Newman, M. L., Pennebaker, J. W., Berry, D. S., & Richards, J. M. (2003). Lying words: Predicting deception from linguistic styles. *Personality and Social Psychology Bulletin, 29*(5), 665–675.

Nezlek, J. B., & Leary, M. R. (2002). Individual differences in self-presentational motives in daily social interaction. *Personality and Social Psychology Bulletin, 28*(2), 211–223.

Nezlek, J. B., Schütz, A., & Sellin, I. (2007). Self-presentational success in daily social interaction. *Self and Identity, 6*(4), 361–379.

Ng, C. H. (1997). The stigma of mental illness in Asian cultures. *Australian and New Zealand Journal of Psychiatry, 31*(3), 382–390.

NIAAA. (2019, August 15). Fall semester—a time for parents to discuss the risks of college drinking. *NIH: National Institute on Alcohol Abuse and Alcoholism.* Retrieved from https://www.niaaa. nih.gov/publications/brochures-and-fact-sheets/ time-for-parents-discuss-risks-college-drinking

Niedenthal, P. M., Brauer, M., Robin, L., & Innes-Ker, A. (2003). Adult attachment and the perception of facial expression of emotion. *Journal of Personality and Social Psychology, 82*(3), 419–433.

Niemeyer, S., Petts, J., & Hobson, K. (2005). Rapid climate change and society: Assessing responses and thresholds. *Risk Analysis, 25*(6), 1443–1456.

Nisbett, R. E., & Cohen, D. (1996). *Culture of honor: The psychology of violence in the South.* Boulder, CO: Westview Press.

Nix, G., Watson, C., Pyszcznski, T., & Greenberg, J. (1995). Reducing depressive affect through external focus of attention. *Journal of Social and Clinical Psychology, 14*(1), 36–52.

Noah, T., Schul, Y., & Mayo, R. (2018). When both the original study and its failed replication are correct: Feeling observed eliminates the facial-feedback effect. *Journal of Personality and Social Psychology, 114*(5), 657–664.

Nolan, J. M., Schultz, P. W., Cialdini, R. B., Goldstein, N. J., & Griskevicius, V. (2008). Normative social influence is underdetected. *Personality and Social Psychology Bulletin, 34*(7), 913–923.

Nolen-Hoeksma, S., Girgus, J. S., & Seligman, M. E. P. (1992). Predictors and consequences of childhood depressive symptoms: Five year longitudinal study. *Journal of Abnormal Psychology, 101*(3), 405–422.

Nook, E. C., Ong, D. C., Morelli, S. A., Mitchell, J. P., & Zaki, J. (2016). Prosocial conformity: Prosocial norms generalize across behavior and empathy. *Personality and Social Psychology Bulletin, 42*(8), 1045–1062.

Norenzayan, A., Choi, I., & Nisbett, R. E. (2002). Cultural similarities and differences in social inference: Evidence from behavioral predictions and lay theories of behavior. *Personality and Social Psychology Bulletin, 28*(1), 109–120.

Norenzayan, A., & Nisbett, R. E. (2000). Culture and causal cognition. *Current Directions in Psychological Science, 9*(4), 132–135.

North, A. C., Tarrant, M., & Hargreaves, D. J. (2004). The effects of music on helping behavior: A field study. *Environment and Behavior, 36*(2), 266–275.

Noveck, J., & Tompson, T. (2007, August 20). Young people name family as key happiness factor. *Journal Sentinel,* p. 1B. Retrieved from http://freerepublic.com/ focus/f-news/1884090/posts

Nowak, M., & Sigmund, K. (1993). A strategy of win-stay, lose-shift that outperforms tit-for-tat in the Prisoner's Dilemma game. *Nature, 364,* 56–58.

Nowland, R., Necka, E. A., & Cacioppo, J. T. (2018). Loneliness and social internet use: Pathways to reconnection in a digital world? *Perspectives on Psychological Science, 13*(1), 70–87.

Nunes, K. L., Hermann, C. A., & Ratcliffe, K. (2013). Implicit and explicit attitudes toward rape are associated with sexual aggression. *Journal of Interpersonal Violence, 28*(13), 2657–2675.

Nuttin, J. M. (1985). Narcissism beyond Gestalt and awareness: The name letter effect. *European Journal of Social Psychology, 15*(3), 353–361.

Nye, J. L., & Brower, A. M. (Eds.). (1996). *What's social about social cognition? Research on socially shared cognition in small groups.* Thousand Oaks, CA: Sage.

O

Oakes, J. M., & Rossi, R. H. (2003). The measurement of SES in health research: Current practice and steps toward a new approach. *Social Science and Medicine, 56*(4), 769–784.

O'Brien, L. T., Crandall, C. S., Horstman-Reser, A., Warner, R., Alsbrooks, A., & Blodorn, A. (2010). But I'm no bigot: How prejudiced white Americans maintain unprejudiced self-images. *Journal of Applied Social Psychology, 40*(4), 917–946.

Oda, R. (2001). Lemur vocal communication and the origin of human language. In T. Matsuzawa (Ed.), *Primate origins of human cognition and behavior* (pp. 115–134). New York, NY: Springer-Verlag.

Oddone-Paolucci, E., Genuis, M., & Violato, C. (2000). A meta-analysis of the published research on the effects of pornography. In C. Violato & E. Oddone-Paolucci (Eds.), *The changing family and child development* (pp. 48–59). Aldershot, England: Ashgate.

Oehlhof, M. E., Musher-Eizenman, D. R., Neufeld, J. M., & Hauser, J. C. (2009). Self-objectification and ideal body shape for men and women. *Body Image, 6*(4), 308–310.

Ogolsky, B. G., Monk, J. K., Rice, T. M., & Oswald, R. F. (2019). Personal well-being across the transition to marriage equality: A longitudinal analysis. *Journal of Family Psychology, 33*(4), 422–432.

Ohbuchi, K., Kamdea, M., & Agarie, N. (1989). Apology as aggression control: Its role in mediating appraisal of and response to harm. *Journal of Personality and Social Psychology, 56*(2), 219–227.

Öhman, A., Lundqvist, D., & Esteves, F. (2001). The face in the crowd revisited: A threat advantage with schematic stimuli. *Journal of Personality and Social Psychology, 80*(3), 381–396.

Ohtsubo, Y., Miller, C. E., Hayashi, N., & Masuchi, A. (2004). Effects of group decision rules on decisions involving continuous alternatives: The unanimity rule and extreme decisions in mock civil juries. *Journal of Experimental Social Psychology, 40*(3), 320–331.

Oishi, S., Lun, J., & Sherman, G. D. (2007). Residential mobility, self-concept, and positive affect in social interactions. *Journal of Personality and Social Psychology, 93*(1), 131–141.

Okdie, B. M., & Ewoldsen, D. R. (2018). To boldly go where no relationship has gone before: Commentary on interpersonal relationships in the digital age. *The Journal of Social Psychology, 158*(4), 508–513.

Okimoto, T. G., & Brescoll, V. L. (2010). The price of power: Power seeking and backlash against female politicians. *Personality and Social Psychology Bulletin, 36*(7), 923–935.

Oliner, S. P., & Oliner, P. M. (1988). *The altruistic personality: Rescuers of Jews in Nazi Europe.* New York, NY: Free Press.

Olmstead, S. B., Pasley, K., & Fincham, F. D. (2016). College men's involvement in friends with benefits relationships. *College Student Journal, 50*(3), 398–403.

Olson, K. R., Lambert, A. J., & Zacks, J. M. (2004). Graded structure and the speed of category verification: On the moderating effects of anticipatory control for social vs. non-social categories. *Journal of Experimental Social Psychology, 40*(2), 239–246.

Omarzu, J. (2000). A disclosure decision model: Determining how and when individuals will self-disclose. *Personality and Social Psychology Review, 4*(2), 174–185.

Onoda, K. (2010). Why mind feels pain: Current status of studies on ostracism from social neuroscience. *Japanese Journal of Physiological Psychology and Psychophysiology, 28*(1), 29–44.

Open Science Collaboration. (2015). Estimating the reproducibility of psychological science. *Science, 349*(6251).

Orimoto, L., Hatfield, E., Yamakawa, R., & Denney, C. (1993). Gender differences in emotional reactions and coping strategies following a break-up. Reported in E. Hatfield & R. Rapson, *Love, sex, and intimacy: Their psychology, biology, and history* (pp. 369–370). Needham Heights, MA: Allyn & Bacon.

Orne, M. T. (1962). On the social psychology of the psychological experiment: With particular reference to demand characteristics and their implications. *American Psychologist, 17*(11), 776–783.

Orpen, C. (1996). The effects of ingratiation and self promotion tactics on employee career success. *Social Behavior and Personality, 24*(3), 213–214.

Orth, U. & Robins, R. W. (2013). Understanding the link between low self-esteem and depression. *Current Directions in Psychological Science, 22*(6), 455–460.

Orth, U., Robins, R. W., & Widaman, K. F. (2012). Life-span development of self-esteem and its effects on important life outcomes. *Journal of Personality and Social Psychology, 102*(6), 1271–1288.

Osborne, D., & Sibley, C. G. (2013). Through rose-colored glasses: System-justifying beliefs dampen the effects of relative deprivation on well-being and political mobilization. *Personality and Social Psychology Bulletin, 39*(8), 991–1004.

Osborne, R. E. (2002). "I may be homeless, but I'm not helpless": The costs and benefits of identifying with homelessness. *Self and Identity, 1*(1), 43–52.

Osbourne, J. W. (1995). Academics, self-esteem, and race: A look at the underlying assumptions of the disidentification hypothesis. *Personality and Social Psychology Bulletin, 21*(5), 449–455.

Ost, J., Costall, A., & Bull, R. (2001). False confessions and false memories: A model for understanding retractors' experiences. *Journal of Forensic Psychiatry, 12*(3), 549–579.

Ostrov, J. M., Murrary-Close, D., Godleski, S. A., & Hart, E. J. (2013). Prospective associations between forms and functions of aggression and social and affective processes during early childhood. *Journal of Experimental Child Psychology, 116*(1), 19–36.

Oswald, D. L. (2005). Understanding anti-Arab reactions post-9/11: The role of threats, social categories, and personal ideologies. *Journal of Applied Social Psychology, 35*(9), 1775–1799.

Oswald, D. L. (2007). "Don't ask, don't tell": The influence of stigma concealing and perceived threat on perceiver's reactions to a gay target. *Journal of Applied Social Psychology, 37*(5), 928–947.

Oswald, D. L. (2017). Maintaining long-lasting friendships. In M. Hojjat & A. Moyer (Eds.), *The psychology of friendship* (pp. 267–282). New York, NY: Oxford University Press.

Oswald, D. L., Baalbaki, M., & Kirkman, M. (2019). Experiences with benevolent sexism: Scale development and associations with women's well-being. *Sex Roles, 80*(5–6), 362–380.

Oswald, D. L., Clark, E. M., & Kelly, C. M. (2004). Friendship maintenance behaviors: An analysis of individual and dyad behaviors. *Journal of Social and Clinical Psychology, 23*(3), 413–441.

Oswald, D. L., & Harvey, R. D. (2003). A Q-methodological study of women's subjective perspectives on mathematics. *Sex Roles, 49*(3–4), 133–142.

Otten, S. (2016). The minimal group paradigm and its maximal impact in research on social categorization. *Current Opinion in Psychology, 11*, 85–89.

Oved, Y. (1988). *Two hundred years of American communes.* New Brunswick, NJ: Transaction Press.

Over, H., & Cook, R. (2018). Where do spontaneous first impressions of faces come from? *Cognition, 170*, 190–200.

Overall, N. C., & McNulty, J. K. (2017). What type of communication during conflict is beneficial for intimate relationships? *Current Opinion in Psychology, 13*, 1–5.

Overbeek, G., Ha, T., Scholte, R., de Kemp, R., & Engels, R. C. (2007). Intimacy, passion, and commitment in romantic relationships: Validation of a "triangular love scale" for adolescents. *Journal of Adolescence, 30*(3), 523–528.

Overstreet, N. M., Quinn, D. M., & Agocha, V. B. (2010). Beyond thinness: The influence of a curvaceous body ideal on body dissatisfaction in Black and White women. *Sex Roles, 63*(1–2), 91–103.

Owe, E., Vignoles, V. L., Becker, M., Brown, R., Smith, P. B., Lee, S. W.,. . .Jalal, B. (2013). Contextualism as an important facet of individualism-collectivism: Personhood beliefs across 37 national groups. *Journal of Cross-Cultural Psychology, 44*(1), 24–45.

Owen, J., & Fincham, F. D. (2012). Friends with benefits relationships as a start to exclusive romantic relationships. *Journal of Social and Personal Relationships, 29*(7), 982–996.

Owen, J., Fincham, F. D., & Manthos, M. (2013). Friendship after a friends with benefits relationship: Deception, psychological functioning, and social connectedness. *Archives of Sexual Behavior, 42*(8), 1443–1449.

Oyserman, D., Coon, H. M., & Kemmelmeier, M. (2002). Rethinking individualism and collectivism: Evaluation of theoretical assumptions and meta-analysis. *Psychological Bulletin, 128*(1), 3–72.

Özener, B., & Fink, B. (2010). Facial symmetry in young girls and boys from a slum and a control area of Ankara Turkey. *Evolution and Human Behavior, 31*(6), 436–441.

P

Packer, D. J. (2008). Identifying systematic disobedience in Milgram's obedience experiments: A meta-analytic review. *Association for Psychological Science, 3*(4), 301–304.

Packer, D. J. (2009). Avoiding groupthink: Whereas weakly identified members remain silent, strongly identified members dissent about collective problems. *Psychological Science, 20*(5), 546–548.

Page, R. M. (1991). Loneliness as a risk factor in adolescent hopelessness. *Journal of Research in Personality, 25*(2), 189–195.

Paik, H., & Comstock, G. (1994). The effects of television violence on anti-social behavior: A meta-analysis. *Communication Research, 21*(4), 516–546.

Paletz, S. B., Peng, K., Erez, M., & Maslach, C. (2003). Ethnic composition and its differential impact on group processes in diverse teams. *Small Group Research, 35*(2), 128–157.

Pallak, S. R. (1983). Salience of a communicator's physical attractiveness and persuasion: A heuristic versus systematic processing interpretation. *Social Cognition, 2*(2), 158–170.

Palmer, C., & Thompson, K. (2010). Everyday risks and professional dilemmas: Fieldwork with alcohol-based (sporting) subcultures: Corrigendum. *Qualitative Research, 10*(4), 112.

Paluck, E. L. (2011). Peer pressure against prejudice: A high school field experiment examining social network change. *Journal of Experimental Social Psychology, 47*(2), 350–358.

Paluck, E. L., Green, S. A., & Green, D. P. (2018). The contact hypothesis re-evaluated. *Behavioural Public Policy*, 1–30.

Paluck, E. L., Shepherd, H., & Aronow, P. M. (2016). Changing climates of conflict: A social network experiment in 56 schools. *PNAS, 113*(3), 566–571.

Palus, S. (2015, December 8). Diederik Stapel now has 58 retractions. *Retraction Watch*. Retrieved from https://retractionwatch.com/2015/12/08/diederik-stapel-now-has-58-retractions/

Pansu, P., Régner, I., Max, S., Colé, P., Nezlek, J. B., & Huguet, P. (2016). A burden for the boys: Evidence of stereotype threat in boys' reading performance. *Journal of Experimental Social Psychology, 65*, 26–30.

Parent, M. C., & Moradi, B. (2011). His biceps become him: A test of objectification theory's application to drive for muscularity and propensity for steroid use in college men. *Journal of Counseling Psychology, 58*(2), 246–256.

Park, B. (1986). A method for studying the development of impressions of real people. *Journal of Personality and Social Psychology, 51*(5), 907–917.

Park, B., & Rothbart, M. (1982). Perception of out-group homogeneity and levels of social categorization: Memory for the subordinate attributes of ingroup and outgroup members. *Journal of Personality and Social Psychology, 42*(6), 1051–1068.

Park, J., Malachi, E., Sternin, O., & Tevet, R. (2009). Subtle bias against Muslim job applicants in personnel decisions. *Journal of Applied Social Psychology, 39*(9), 2174–2190.

Park, L. E. (2007). Appearance-based rejection sensitivity: Implications for mental and physical health, affect, and motivation. *Personality and Social Psychology Bulletin 33*(4), 490–504.

Park, L. E., Crocker, J., & Mickelson, K. D. (2004). Attachment styles and contingencies of self-worth. *Personality and Social Psychology Bulletin, 30*(10), 1243–1254.

Park, L. E., Streamer, L., Huang, L., & Galinsky, A. D. (2013). Stand tall, but don't put your feet up: Universal and culturally specific effects of expansive postures on power. *Journal of Experimental Social Psychology, 49*(6), 965–971.

Park, S., & Catrambone, R. (2007). Social facilitation effects of virtual humans. *Human Factors, 49*(6), 1054–1060.

Parks, C. D., Sanna, L. J., & Posey, D. C. (2003). Retrospection in social dilemmas: How thinking about the past affects future cooperation. *Journal of Personality and Social Psychology, 84*(5), 988–996.

Parnell, R. J., & Buchanan-Smith, H. M. (2001). Animal behaviour—an unusual social display by gorillas. *Nature, 412*(6844), 294.

Parrett, M. (2015). Beauty and the feast: Examining the effect of beauty on earnings using restaurant tipping data. *Journal of Economic Psychology, 49*, 34–46.

Pascoe, E. A., & Smart Richman, L. (2009). Perceived discrimination and health: A meta-analytic review. *Psychological Bulletin, 135*(4), 531–554.

Patchin, J. W., & Hinduja, S. (2015). Measuring cyberbullying: Implications for research. *Aggression and Violent Behavior, 23*, 69–74.

Patrick, H., Neighbors, C., & Knee, C. R. (2004). Appearance-related social comparisons: The role of contingent self-esteem and self-perceptions of attractiveness. *Personality and Social Psychology Bulletin, 30*(4), 501–514.

Patterson, M. L. (2008). Back to social behavior: Mining the mundane. *Basic and Applied Social Psychology, 30*(2), 93–101.

Patterson, M. L., Giles, H., & Teske, M. (2011). The decline of behavioral research? Examining language and communication journals. *Journal of Language and Social Psychology 30*(3), 326–340.

Pattyn, S., Rosseel, Y., & Van Hiel, A. (2013). Finding our way in the social world: Exploring the dimensions underlying social classification. *Social Psychology, 44*(5), 329–348.

Paunesku, D., Walton, G. M., Romero, C., Smith, E. N., Yeager, D. S., & Dweck, C. S. (2015). Mind-set interventions are a scalable treatment for academic underachievement. *Psychological Science, 26*(6), 784–793.

Pavey, L., Greitemeyer, T., & Sparks, P. (2012). "I help because I want to, not because you tell me to": Empathy increases autonomously motivated helping. *Personality and Social Psychology Bulletin, 38*(5), 681–689.

Pawtowski, B. (2012). Body height. In T. F. Cash (Ed.), *Encyclopedia of body image and human appearance* (Vol. 1, pp. 82–88). San Diego, CA: Elsevier Academic Press.

Payne, B. K. (2001). Prejudice and perception: The role of automatic and controlled processes in misperceiving a weapon. *Journal of Personality and Social Psychology, 81*(2), 181–192.

Payne, B. K., Jacoby, L. L., & Lambert, A. J. (2004). Memory monitoring and the control of stereotype distortion. *Journal of Experimental Social Psychology, 40*(1), 52–64.

Payne, D. L., Lonsway, K. A., & Fitzgerald, L. F. (1999). Rape myth acceptance: Exploration of its structure and its measurement using the Illinois Rape Myth Acceptance Scale. *Journal of Research in Personality, 33*(1), 27–68.

Pearson, A. R., Dovidio, J. F., & Gaertner, S. L. (2009). The nature of contemporary prejudice: Insights from aversive racism. *Social and Personality Compass, 3*(3), 314–338.

Peck, T. C., Seinfeld, S., Aglioti, S. M., & Slater, M. (2013). Putting yourself in the skin of a black avatar reduces implicit racial bias. *Consciousness and Cognition, 22*(3), 779–787.

Peer, E., Brandimarte, L., Samat, S., Acquisti, A. (2017). Beyond the Turk: Alternative platforms for crowdsourcing behavioral research. *Journal of Experimental Social Psychology, 70*, 153–163.

Pedersen, W., & von Soest, T. (2013). Socialization to binge drinking: A population-based, longitudinal study with emphasis on parental influences. *Drug and Alcohol Dependence, 133*(2), 587–592.

Pederson, E. R., LaBrie, J. W., & Lac, A. (2008). Assessment of perceived and actual norm in varying contexts: Exploring Social Impact Theory among college students. *Addictive Behaviors, 33*(4), 525–564.

Pek, J. C., & Leong, F. T. (2003). Sex-related self-concepts, cognitive styles and cultural values of traditionality-modernity as predictors of general and domain-specific sexism. *Asian Journal of Social Psychology, 6*(1), 31–49.

Pelham, B. W., Carvallo, A., & Jones, J. T. (2005). Implicit egotism. *Current Directions in Psychological Science, 14*(2), 106–110.

Pelham, B. W., Mirenberg, M. C., & Jones, J. T. (2002). Why Susie sells seashells by the seashore: Implicit egotism and major life decisions. *Journal of Personality and Social Psychology, 82*(4), 469–487.

Pellegrini, A. D., & Bartini, M. (2001). Dominance in early adolescent boys: Affiliative and aggressive dimensions and possible functions. *Merrill-Palmer Quarterly, 47*(1), 142–163.

Pendleton, M. G., & Batson, C. D. (1979). Self-presentation and the door-in-the-face technique for inducing compliance. *Personality and Social Psychology Bulletin, 5*(1), 77–81.

Pennington, N., & Hastie, R. (1990). Practical implications of psychological research on juror and jury decision making. *Personality and Social Psychology Bulletin, 16*(1), 90–105.

Penny, H., & Haddock, G. (2007). Anti-fat prejudice among children: The "mere proximity" effect in 5–10 year olds. *Journal of Experimental Social Psychology, 43*(4), 678–683.

Pennycook, G., & Rand, D. G. (2019). Lazy, not biased: Susceptibility to partisan fake news is better explained by lack of reasoning than by motivated reasoning. *Cognition, 188*, 39–50.

Peplau, L. A. (2003). Human sexuality: How do men and women differ? *Current Directions in Psychological Science, 12*(2), 37–40.

Peplau, L. A., Bikson, T. K., Rook, K. S., & Goodchilds, J. D. (1982). Being old and living alone. In L. A. Peplau & D. Perlman (Eds.), *Loneliness: A sourcebook of current theory, research and therapy* (pp. 327–347). New York, NY: John Wiley & Sons.

Peplau, L. A., Cochran, S. D., & Mays, V. M. (1997). A national survey of the intimate relationships of African American lesbians and gay men: A look at commitment, satisfaction, sexual behavior and HIV disease. In B. Greene & G. Herek (Eds.), *Psychological perspectives on lesbian and gay issues: Ethnic and cultural diversity among lesbians and gay men* (pp. 11–38). Thousand Oaks, CA: Sage.

Peplau, L. A., & Fingerhut, A. W. (2007). The close relationships of lesbians and gay men. *Annual Review of Psychology, 58,* 405–424.

Peplau, L. A., Fingerhut, A., & Beals, K. (2004). Sexuality in the relationships of lesbians and gay men. In J. Harvey, A. Wenzel, & S. Sprecher (Eds.), *Handbook of sexuality in close relationships* (pp. 349–369). Mahwah, NJ: Lawrence Erlbaum Associates.

Perdue, C. W., Dovidio, J. F., Gurtman, M. B., & Tyler, R. B. (1990). Us and them: Social categorization and the process of intergroup bias. *Journal of Personality and Social Psychology, 59*(3), 475–486.

Perillo, J. T., & Kassin, S. M. (2011). Inside interrogation: The lie, the bluff, and false confessions. *Law and Human Behavior, 35*(4), 327–337.

Perilloux, C., Easton, J. A., & Buss, D. M. (2012). The misperception of sexual interest. *Psychological Science, 23*(2), 146–151.

Perlman, D. (2007). The best of times, the worst of times: The place of close relationships in psychology and our daily lives. *Canadian Psychology, 48*(1), 7–18.

Peruche, B. M., & Plant, E. A. (2006). The correlates of law enforcement officers' automatic and controlled race-based responses to criminal suspects. *Basic and Applied Social Psychology, 28*(2), 193–199.

Pérusse, D., & Gendreau, P. L. (2005). Genetics and the development of aggression. In R. E. Tremblay, W. W. Hartup, & J. Archer (Eds.), *Developmental origins of aggression* (pp. 223–241). New York, NY: Guilford Press.

Pescosolido, B. A., Monahan, J., Link, B. G., Stueve, A., & Kikuzawa, S. (1999). The public's view of the competence, dangerousness, and need for legal coercion of persons with mental health problems. *American Journal of Public Health, 89*(9), 1339–1345.

Pessin, J. (1933). The comparative effects of social and mechanical stimulation on memorizing. *American Journal of Psychology, 45,* 263–270.

Peters, K., Jetten, J., Radova, D., & Austin, K. (2017). Gossiping about deviance: Evidence that deviance spurs the gossip that builds bonds. *Psychological Science, 28*(11), 1610–1619.

Peters, L. H., Hartke, D. D., & Pohlmann, J. T. (1985). Fiedler's contingency theory of leadership: An application of the meta-analytic procedures of Schmidt and Hunter. *Psychological Bulletin, 97*(2), 274–285.

Peters, J. R., Smart, L. M., Eisenlohr-Moul, T. A., Geiger, P. J., Smith, G. T., & Baer, R. A. (2015). Anger rumination as a mediator of the relationship between mindfulness and aggression: The utility of a multidimensional mindfulness model. *Journal of Clinical Psychology, 71*(9), 871–884.

Peterson, B. E. (2003). Authoritarianism and methodological innovation. *Analyses of Social Issues and Public Policy, 3*(1), 185–187.

Peterson, C., Park, N., & Seligman, M. E. P. (2013). Orientations to happiness and life satisfaction: The full life versus the empty life. In A. Delle Fave (Ed.), *The exploration of happiness: Present and future perspectives* (pp. 161–173). New York, NY: Springer.

Peterson, C., & Seligman, M. E. P. (1987). Explanatory style and illness. *Journal of Personality, 55*(2), 237–265.

Peterson, C., Seligman, M. E. P., & Vaillant, G. E. (1988). Pessimistic explanatory style is a risk factor for physical illness: A thirty-five-year longitudinal study. *Journal of Personality and Social Psychology, 55*(1), 23–27.

Peterson, C., Semmel, A., von Baeyer, C., Abramson, L. Y., Metalsky, G. I., & Seligman, M. E. P. (1982). The attributional style questionnaire. *Cognitive Therapy and Research, 6*(3), 287–299.

Peterson, J., & Densley, J. (2017). Cyber violence: What do we know and where do we go from here? *Aggression and Violent Behavior, 34,* 193–200.

Peterson, R. S., & Nemeth, C. J. (1996). Focus versus flexibility: Majority and minority influence can both improve performance. *Personality and Social Psychology Bulletin, 22*(1), 14–23.

Petrocelli, J. V., Percy, E. J., Sherman, S. J., & Tormala, Z. L. (2011). Counterfactual potency. *Journal of Personality and Social Psychology, 100*(1), 30–46.

Petrova, P. K., Cialdini, R. B., & Sills, S. J. (2007). Consistency-based compliance across cultures. *Journal of Experimental Social Psychology, 43*(1), 104–111.

Pettigrew, T. F. (1969). Racially separate or together? *Journal of Social Issues, 25*(1), 43–69.

Pettigrew, T. F. (1998). Intergroup contact theory. *Annual Review of Psychology, 49,* 65–85.

Pettigrew, T. F. (2010). The ultimate Lewinian. In M. H. Gonzales, C. Tavris, & J. Aronson (Eds.), *The scientist and the humanist: A festschrift in honor of Elliot Aronson* (pp. 21–29). New York, NY: Psychology Press.

Pettigrew, T. F. (2018). The emergence of contextual social psychology. *Personality and Social Psychology Bulletin, 44*(7), 963–971.

Pettigrew, T. F., & Cherry, F. (2012). The intertwined histories of personality and social psychology. In K. Deaux & M. Snyder (Eds.), *The Oxford handbook of personality and social psychology* (pp. 13–32). New York, NY: Oxford University Press.

Pettigrew, T. F., & Tropp, L. R. (2006). A meta-analytic test of intergroup contact theory. *Journal of Personality and Social Psychology, 90*(5), 751–783.

Pettijohn, T. F., II, & Walzer, A. S. (2008). Reducing racism, sexism, and homophobia in college students by completing a psychology of prejudice course. *College Student Journal, 42*(2), 459–468.

Pettit, G. S. (2004). Violent children in developmental perspective: Risk and protective factors and the mechanisms through which they (may) operate. *Current Directions in Psychological Science, 13*(5), 194–197.

Petty, R. E. (2004). Multi-process models in social psychology provide a more balanced view of social thought and action. *Behavioral and Brain Sciences, 27*(3), 353–354. http://dx.doi.org/10.1017/S0140525X0448008X

Petty, R. E., Barden, J., & Wheeler, S. C. (2009). The Elaboration Likelihood Model of persuasion: Developing health promotions for sustained behavioral change. In R. J. DiClemente, R. A. Crosby, & M. C. Kegler (Eds.), *Emerging theories in health promotion practice and research* (2nd ed., pp. 185–214). San Francisco, CA: Jossey-Bass.

Petty, R. E., Briñol, P., & Tormala, Z. L. (2002). Thought confidence as a determinant for persuasion: The self-validation hypothesis. *Journal of Personality and Social Psychology, 82*(5), 722–741.

Petty, R. E., & Cacioppo, J. T. (1986). *Communication and persuasion: Central and peripheral routes to attitude change.* New York, NY: Springer-Verlag.

Petty, R. E., DeStono, D., & Rucker, D. D. (2001). The role of affect in attitude change. In J. P. Forgas (Ed.), *Handbook of affect and social cognition* (pp. 212–233). Mahwah, NJ: Lawrence Erlbaum Associates.

Petty, R. E., Haugtvedt, C. P., & Smith, S. M. (1995). Elaboration as a determinant of attitude strength: Creating attitudes that are persistent, resistant, and predictive of behavior. In R. E. Petty & J. A. Krosnick (Eds.), *Attitude strength: Antecedents and consequences* (pp. 93–130). Hillsdale, NJ: Lawrence Erlbaum Associates.

Petty, R. E., Tormala, Z. L., & Rucker, D. D. (2004). Resisting persuasion by counterarguing: An attitude strength perspective. In J. T. Jost, M. R. Banaji, & D. A. Prentice (Eds.), *Perspectivism in social psychology: The yin and yang of scientific progress* (pp. 37–51). Washington, DC: American Psychological Association.

Petty, R. E., & Wegener, D. T. (1998). Attitude change: Multiple roles for persuasion variables. In D. Gilbert, S. Fiske, & G. Lindzey (Eds.), *The handbook of social psychology* (4th ed., pp. 323–390). New York, NY: McGraw-Hill.

Petty, R. E., Wegener, D. T., & Fabrigar, L. R. (1997). Attitudes and attitude change. *Annual Review of Psychology, 48,* 609–647.

Pew Research Center. (2007, January 9). *How young people view their lives, futures, and politics: A portrait of "Generation Next."* Washington, DC: Pew Research Center for the People & the Press.

Pew Research Center. (2019, May 14). Attitudes on same-sex marriage: Public opinion on same-sex marriage. *Pew Research Center.* Retrieved from https://www.pewforum.org/fact-sheet/changing-attitudes-on-gay-marriage/

Pezzo, M. V. (2003). Surprise, defence, or making sense: What removes hindsight bias? *Memory, 11*(4–5), 421–441.

Pfattheicher, S., & Keller, J. (2013). Vigilant self-regulation and costly punishment in public goods situations. *European Journal of Personality, 27*(4), 346–354.

Pfeffer, J., Fong, C. T., Cialdini, R. B., & Portnoy, R. R. (2006). Overcoming the self-promotion dilemma: Interpersonal attraction and extra help as a consequence of who sings one's praises. *Personality and Social Psychology Bulletin, 32*(10), 1362–1374.

Pharo, H., Gross, J., Richardson, R. & Hayne, H. (2011). Age-related changes in the effect of ostracism. *Social Influence, 6*(1), 22–38.

Phelps, E. A., O'Connor, K. J., Cunningham, W. A., Funayama, E. S., Gatenby, J. C., Gore, J. C., & Banaji, M. R. (2000). Performance on indirect measures of race evaluation predicts amygdala activation. *Journal of Cognitive Neuroscience, 12*(5), 729–738.

Philanthropic Giving Index. (2008, December). *Briefing on the economy and charitable giving.* Bloomington, IA: The Center on Philanthropy at Indiana University.

Phills, C. E., Kawakami, K., Tabi, E., Nadolny, D., & Inzlicht, M. (2011). Mind the gap: Increasing associations between the self and blacks with approach behaviors. *Journal of Personality and Social Psychology, 100*(2), 197–210.

Phinney, J. S. (1991). Ethnic identity and self-esteem: A review and integration. *Hispanic Journal of Behavioral Sciences, 13*(2), 193–208.

Phinney, J. S., Cantu, C. L., & Kurtz, D. A. (1997). Ethnic and American identity and self-esteem. *Journal of Youth and Adolescence, 26*(2), 165–185.

Phinney, J. S., & Kohatsu, E. (1997). Ethnic and racial identity and mental health. In J. Schulenberg, J. L. Maggs, & K. Hurrelmann (Eds.), *Health risks and developmental transitions during adolescence* (pp. 420–443). New York, NY: Cambridge University Press.

Pietromonaco, P. R., & Beck, L. A. (2015). Attachment processes in adult romantic relationships. In M. Mikulincer, P. R. Shaver, J. A. Simpson & J. Dovidio (Eds.), *APA handbook of personaliy and social psychology: Vol 3. Interpersonal relations* (pp. 33–64). Washington, DC: American Psychological Association.

Pietromonaco, P. R., & Carnelley, K. B. (1994). Gender and working models of attachment: Consequences for perception of self and romantic relationships. *Personal Relationships, 1*(1), 3–26.

Piff, P. K., Kraus, M. W., Cote, S., Cheng, B. H., & Keltner, D. (2010). Having less, giving more: The influence of social class on prosocial behavior. *Journal of Personality and Social Psychology, 99*(5), 771–784.

Piliavin, J. A., Dovidio, J. F., Gaertner, S. L., & Clark, R. D., III. (1981). *Emergency intervention.* New York, NY: Academic Press.

Piliavin, J. A., & Piliavin, I. M. (1972). The effect of blood on reactions to a victim. *Journal of Personality and Social Psychology, 23*(3), 353–361.

Pinto, I. R., Marques, J. M., Levine, J. M., & Abrams, D. (2010). Membership status and subjective group dynamics: Who triggers the black sheep effect? *Journal of Personality and Social Psychology, 99*(1), 107–119.

Pirlott, A. G., & Cook, C. L. (2018). Prejudices and discrimination as goal activated and threat driven: The affordance management approach applied to sexual prejudice. *Psychological Review, 125*(6), 1002–1027.

Pishyar, R., Harris, L. M., & Menzies, R. G. (2004). Attentional bias for words and faces in social anxiety. *Anxiety, Stress, and Coping, 17*(1), 23–36.

Platek, S. M., & Singh, D. (2010). Optimal waist-to-hip ratios in women activate neural reward centers in men. *PLoS ONE, 5*(2), e9042. doi:10.1371/journal.pone.0009042

Poepsel, D. L., & Schroeder, D. A. (2013). Joining groups: How resources are to be divided matters. *Group Dynamics: Theory, Research, and Practice, 17*(3), 180–193.

Pohl, R. F., Bender, M., & Lachman, G. (2002). Hindsight bias around the world. *Experimental Psychology, 49*(4), 270–282.

Pollock, C. L., Smith, S. D., Knowles, E. S., & Bruce, H. J. (1998). Mindfulness limits compliance with the that's-not-all technique. *Personality and Social Psychology, 24*(11), 1153–1157.

Pomerantz, E. M., Ruble, D. N., & Bolger, N. (2004). Supplementing the snapshots with video footage: Taking a developmental approach to understanding social psychological phenomena. In C. Sansone, C. C. Morf, & A. T. Panter (Eds.), *The SAGE handbook of methods in social psychology* (pp. 405–425). Thousand Oaks, CA: Sage.

Pontari, B. A. (2009). Appearing socially competent: The effects of a friend's presence on the socially anxious. *Personality and Social Psychology Bulletin, 35*(3), 283–294.

Poole, M. S., Hollingshead, A. B., McGrath, J. E., & Moreland, R. L. (2004). Interdisciplinary perspectives on small groups. *Small Group Research, 35*(1), 3–16.

Pope, K. S. (2013). Fulfilling informed consent responsibilities. In G. P. Koocher, J. C. Norcross, & B. A. Greene (Eds.), *Psychologists' desk reference* (3rd ed., pp. 658–660). New York: Oxford University Press.

Post, J. M., Panis, L. K. (2011). Crime of obedience: "Groupthink" at Abu Ghraib. *International Journal of Group Psychotherapy. 61*(1), 49–66.

Post, S.G. (2005). Altruism, happiness, and health: It's good to be good. *International Journal of Behavioral Medicine, 12*(2), 66–77.

Postmes, T., & Spears, R. (1998). Deindividuation and antinormative behavior: A meta-analysis. *Psychological Bulletin, 123*(3), 238–259.

Poteat, V. P., Espelage, D. L., & Green, H. D., Jr. (2007). The socialization of dominance: Peer group contextual effects on homophobic and dominance attitudes. *Journal of Personality and Social Psychology, 92*(6), 1040–1050.

Pouliasi, K., & Verkuyten, M. (2007). Networks of meaning and the bicultural mind: A structural equation modeling approach. *Journal of Experimental Social Psychology, 43*(6), 955–963.

Poutvaara, P., Jordahl, H., & Berggren, N. (2009). Faces of politicians: Babyfacedness predicts inferred competence but not electoral success. *Journal of Experimental Social Psychology, 45*(5), 1132–1135.

Powers, S. I., Pietromonaco, P. R., Gunlicks, M., & Sayer, A. (2006). Dating couples' attachment styles and patterns of cortisol reactivity and recovery in response to a relationship conflict. *Journal of Personality and Social Psychology, 90*(4), 613–628.

Powers, T. A., & Zuroff, D. C. (1988). Interpersonal consequences of overt self-criticism: Comparison with neutral and self-enhancing presentations of self. *Journal of Personality and Social Psychology, 54*(6), 1054–1062.

Pozo, C., Carver, C. S., Wellens, A. R., & Scheier, M. F. (1991). Social anxiety and social perception: Construing others' reactions to the self. *Personality and Social Psychology Bulletin, 17*(4), 355–362.

Pratkanis, A. R., Greenwald, A. G., Leippe, M. R., & Baumgardner, M. H. (1988). In search of reliable persuasion effects: III. The sleeper effect is dead. Long live the sleeper effect. *Journal of Personality and Social Psychology, 54*(2), 203–218.

Pratt, D. D. (1991). Conceptions of self within China and the United States: Contrasting foundations for adult education. *International Journal of Intercultural Relations, 15*(3), 285–310.

Pratto, F. (1996). Sexual politics: The gender gap in the bedroom, the cupboard, and the cabinet. In D. M. Buss & N. M. Malamuth (Eds.), *Sex, power, and conflict: Evolutionary and feminist perspectives* (pp. 179–230). New York, NY: Oxford University Press.

Prentice-Dunn, S., & Rogers. R. W. (1980). Effects of deindividuating situational cues and aggressive models on subjective deindividuation and aggression. *Journal of Personality and Social Psychology, 39*(1), 104–113.

Prentice-Dunn, S., & Rogers, R. W. (1982). Effects of public and private self-awareness on deindividuation and aggression. *Journal of Personality and Social Psychology, 43*(3), 503–513.

Prewitt, J. E., & Weil, R. (2014). Organizational opportunities endemic in crisis leadership. *Journal of Management Policy & Practice, 15*(2), 72–87.

Price, K. H., Harrison, D. A., & Gavin, J. H. (2006). Withholding inputs in team contexts: Member composition, interaction processes, evaluation structure, and social loafing. *Journal of Applied Psychology, 91*(6), 1375–1384.

Priest, R. F., & Sawyer, J. (1967). Proximity and peership: Bases of balance in interpersonal attraction. *American Journal of Sociology, 72*(6), 633–649.

Principe, C. P., & Langlois, J. H. (2011). Faces differing in attractiveness elicit corresponding affective responses. *Cognition and Emotion, 25*(1), 140–148.

Prislin, R., & Christensen, P. N. (2005). The effects of social change within a group on membership preferences: To leave or not to leave? *Personality and Social Psychology Bulletin, 31*(5), 595–609.

Pronin, E., & Ross, L. (2006). Temporal differences in trait self-ascription: When the self is seen as an other. *Journal of Personality and Social Psychology, 90*(2), 197–209.

Proulx, T. (2013). Beyond mortality and the self: Meaning makes a comeback. In K. D. Markman, T. Proulx, & M. J. Lindberg (Eds.), *The psychology of meaning* (pp. 71–87). Washington, DC: American Psychological Association.

Pruitt, D. G. (1971). Choice shifts in group discussion: An introductory review. *Journal of Personality and Social Psychology, 20*(3), 339–360.

Ptacek, J. T., & Dodge, K. L. (1995). Coping strategies and relationship satisfaction in couples. *Personality and Social Psychology Bulletin, 21*(1), 76–84.

Puente, S., & Cohen, D. (2003). Jealousy and the meaning (or nonmeaning) of violence. *Personality and Social Psychology Bulletin, 29*(4), 449–460.

Puentes, J., Knox, D., & Zusman, M. E. (2008). Participants in "friends with benefits" relationships. *College Student Journal, 42*(1), 176–180.

Pugh, S. D., Groth, M., & Hennig-Thurau, T. (2011). Willing and able to fake emotions: A closer examination of the link between emotional dissonance and employee well-being. *Journal of Applied Psychology, 96*(2), 377–390.

Puhl, R. M., & Brownell, K. D. (2006). Confronting and coping with weight stigma: An investigation of overweight and obese adults. *Obesity, 14*(10), 1802–1815.

Puhl, R. M., & Heuer, C. A. (2010). Obesity stigma: Important considerations for public health. *American Journal of Public Health, 100*(6), 1019–1028.

Puhl, R. M., Moss-Racusin, C. A., Schwartz, M. B., & Brownell, K. D. (2008). Weight stigmatization and bias reduction: Perspectives of overweight and obese adults. *Health Education Research, 23*(2), 347–358.

Pyszczynski, T., & Greenberg, J. (1992). *Hanging on and letting go: Understanding the onset, progression, and remission of depression.* New York, NY: Springer-Verlag.

Q

Quillian, L. (1995). Prejudice as a response to perceived group threat: Population composition and anti-immigrant and racial prejudice in Europe. *American Sociological Review, 60*(4), 586–611.

Quist, R. M., & Resendez, M. G. (2002). Social dominance threat: Examining social dominance theory's explanation of prejudice as legitimizing myths. *Basic and Applied Social Psychology, 24*(4), 287–293.

R

Raju, M., Byers, D., & Bash, D. (2017, October 4). Exclusive: Russian-linked Facebook ads targeted Michigan and Wisconsin. *CNN.* Retrieved from https://www.cnn.com/2017/10/03/politics/russian-facebook-ads-michigan-wisconsin/index.html

Ramsoy, N. R. (1966). Assortive mating and the structure of cities. *American Journal of Sociology, 31*(6), 773–786.

Rapp, D. N. (2016). The consequences of reading inaccurate information. *Current Directions in Psychological Science, 25*(4), 281–285.

Rasenberger, J. (2006, October). "Nightmare on Austin Street." *American Heritage Magazine, 57*(5), 65–67.

Ratcliff, J. J., Lassiter, G. D., Markman, K. D., & Snyder, C. J. (2006). Gender differences in attitudes toward gay men and lesbians: The role of motivation to respond without prejudice. *Personality and Social Psychology Bulletin, 32*(10), 1325–1338.

Ratcliff, R., & McKoon, G. (1994). Retrieving information from memory: Spreading-activation theories versus compound-cue theories. *Psychological Review, 101*(1), 177–184.

Rattan, S. N. (2011). Self, culture, and anxious experiences. *Journal of Adult Development, 18*(1), 28–36.

Raven, B. H. (2001). Power/interaction and interpersonal influence: Experimental investigations and case studies. In A. Lee-Chai & J. Bargh (Eds.), *The use and abuse of power: Multiple perspectives on the causes of corruption* (pp. 217–240). New York, NY: Psychology Press.

Redding, R. E. (2001). Sociopolitical diversity in psychology: The case for pluralism. *American Psychologist, 56*(3), 205–215.

Redeker, M., de Vries, R., Rouckhut, D., Vermeren, D., & de Fruyt, F. (2014). Integrating leadership: The leadership circumplex. *European Journal of Work and Organizational Psychology, 23*(3), 435–455.

Reeder, G. D., Kumar, S., Hesson-McInnis, M. S., & Trafimow, D. (2002). Inferences about the morality of an aggressor: The role of perceived motive. *Journal of Personality and Social Psychology, 83*(4), 789–803.

Reeder, H. M. (2000). "I like you . . . as a friend": The role of attraction in cross-sex friendship. *Journal of Social and Personal Relationships, 17*(3), 329–348.

Reeder, H. M. (2003). The effect of gender role orientation on same- and cross-sex friendship formation. *Sex Roles, 49*(3–4), 143–152.

Reeder, H. M. (2017). "He's like a brother": The social construction of satisfying cross-sex friendship roles. *Sexuality & Culture, 21*(1), 142–162.

Regan, D. T. (1971). Effects of a favor and liking on compliance. *Journal of Experimental Social Psychology, 7*(6), 627–639.

Regan, D. T., & Kilduff, M. (1988). Optimism about elections: Dissonance reduction at the ballot box. *Political Psychology, 9*(1), 101–107.

Regan, P. C., Levin, L., Sprecher, S., Christopher, F. S., & Cate, R. (2000). Partner preferences: What characteristics do men and women desire in their short-term sexual and long-term romantic partners? *Journal of Psychology & Human Sexuality, 12*(3), 1–21.

Reidy, D. E., Shelley-Tremblay, J. F., & Lilienfeld, S. O. (2011). Psychopathy, reactive aggression, and precarious proclamations: A review of behavioral, cognitive, and biological research. *Aggression and Violent Behavior, 16*(6), 512–524.

Reifman, A., Watson, W. K., & McCourt, A. (2006). Social networks and college drinking: Probing processes of social influence and selection. *Personality and Social Psychology Bulletin, 32*(6), 820–832.

Reinhard, M. -A., Messner, M., & Sporer, S. L. (2006). Explicit persuasive intent and its impact on success at persuasion—the determining roles of attractiveness and likeableness. *Journal of Consumer Psychology, 16*(3), 249–259.

Reinhard, M. A., Scharmach, M., & Stahlberg, D. (2013). Too exhausted to see the truth: Ego depletion and the ability to detect deception. *British Journal of Social Psychology, 52*(4), 618–630.

Reis, H. T., & Gable, S. L. (2003). Toward a positive psychology of relationships. In C. L. Keyes & J. Haidt (Eds.), *Flourishing: Positive psychology and the life well-lived* (pp. 129–159). Washington, DC: American Psychological Association.

Reis, H. T., & Gosling, S. D. (2010). Social psychological methods outside the laboratory. In S. T. Fiske, D. T. Gilbert, & G. Lindzey (Eds.), *Handbook of social psychology* (5th ed., Vol. 1, pp. 82–114). Hoboken, NJ: John Wiley & Sons.

Reis, H. T., Maniaci, M. R., Caprariello, P. A., Eastwick, P. W., & Finkel, E. J. (2011). Familiarity does indeed promote attraction in live interaction. *Journal of Personality and Social Psychology, 101*(3), 557–570.

Rempel, J. K., & Burris, C. T. (2006). Push-you-pull-you: The boundaried self in close relationships. *Personality and Social Psychology Bulletin, 32*(2), 256–269.

Rendell, L., Fogarty, L., Hoppitt, W. J., Morgan, T. J., Webster, M. M., & Laland, K. N. (2011). Cognitive culture: Theoretical and empirical insights into social learning strategies. *Trends in Cognitive Sciences, 15*(2), 68–76.

Reynolds, K. J., Turner, J. C., & Haslam, S. A. (2000). When are we better than them and they worse than us? A closer look at social discrimination in positive and negative domains. *Journal of Personality and Social Psychology, 78*(1), 64–80.

Rholes, W. S., Kohn, J. L., & Simpson, J. A. (2014). A longitudinal study of conflict in new parents: The role of attachment. *Personal Relationships, 21*(1), 1–21.

Ricard, N. C., Beaudry, S. G., & Pelletier, L. G. (2012). Lovers with happy feet: The interdependence of relationship and activity factors for individuals dancing with a romantic partner. *Journal of Applied Social Psychology, 42*(4), 939–963.

Richards, Z., & Hewstone, M. (2001). Subtyping and subgrouping: Processes for the prevention and promotion of stereotype change. *Personality and Social Psychology Review, 5*(1), 52–73.

Richardson, D. S., & Latané, B. (2001). Dynamic social impact theory predicts regional variation in, and the development of social representations of, aggression. In J. M. Ramirez & D. S. Richardson (Eds.), *Cross-cultural approaches to research on aggression and reconciliation* (pp. 9–21). Hauppauge, NY: Nova Science.

Richetin, J., Perugini, M., Mondini, D., & Hurling, R. (2016). Conserving water while washing hands: The immediate and durable impacts of descriptive norms. *Environment and Behavior, 48*(2), 343–364.

Richter, A., & Ridout, N. (2011). Self-esteem moderates affective reactions to briefly presented emotional faces. *Journal of Research in Personality, 45*(3), 328–331.

Ridgeway, C. L. (1991). The social construction of status value: Gender and other nominal characteristics. *Social Forces, 70*(2), 367–386.

Ridgeway, C. L. (2001). Gender, status, and leadership. *Journal of Social Issues, 57*(4), 637–655.

Riggio, R. E., & Conger, J. A. (2007). Getting it right: The practice of leadership. In J. A. Conger & R. E. Riggio (Eds.), *The practice of leadership: Developing the next generation of leaders* (pp. 331–344). San Francisco, CA: Jossey-Bass.

Riley, D., & Eckenrode, J. (1986). Social ties: Subgroup differences in costs and benefits. *Journal of Personality and Social Psychology, 51*(4), 770–778.

Rilling, J. K. (2011). The social brain in interactive games. In A. Todorov, S. T. Fiske, & D. A. Prentice (Eds.), *Social neuroscience: Toward understanding the underpinnings of the social mind* (pp. 217–228). New York, NY: Oxford University Press.

Ringelmann, M. (1913). Research on animate sources of power: The work of man. *Annales de l'Institut National Agronomique, 2*(12)I, 2–40.

Risen, J. L., Gilovich, T., & Dunning, D. (2007). One-shot illusory correlations and stereotype formation. *Personality and Social Psychology Bulletin, 33*(11), 1492–1502.

Ritchey, A. J., & Ruback, B. (2018). Predicting lynching atrocity: The situational norms of lynchings in Georgia. *Personality and Social Psychology Bulletin, 44*(5), 619–637.

Roberts, B. W., & Helson, R. (1997). Changes in culture, changes in personality: The influence of individualism in a longitudinal study of women. *Journal of Personality and Social Psychology, 72*(3), 641–651.

Roberts, W. R. (1954). *Aristotle.* New York: Modern Library.

Robins, R. W., & Beer, J. S. (2001). Positive illusions about the self: Short-term benefits and long-term costs. *Journal of Personality and Social Psychology, 80*(2), 340–352.

Robinson, M. N., Tansil, K. A., Elder, R. W., Soler, R. E., Labre, M. P., Mercer, S. L.,. . .Community Preventive Services Task Force. (2014). Mass media health communication campaigns combined with health-related product distribution: A community guide systematic review. *American Journal of Preventative Medicine, 47*(3), 360–371.

Robinson, T. N., Wilde, M. L., Navracruz, L. C., Haydel, K. F., & Varady, A. (2001). Effects of reducing children's television and video game use on aggressive behavior: A randomized controlled trial. *Archives of Pediatric & Adolescent Medicine, 155*(1), 17–23.

Robles, T. F., Slatcher, R. B., Trombello, J. M., & McGinn, M. M. (2014). Marital quality and health: A meta-analytic review. *Psychological Bulletin, 140*(1), 140–187.

Rochot, F., Maggioni, O., & Modigliani, A. (2000). The dynamics of obeying and opposing authority: A mathematical model. In T. Blass (Ed.), *Obedience to authority: Current perspectives on the Milgram paradigm* (pp. 161–192). Mahwah, NJ: Lawrence Erlbaum Associates.

Rocklage, M. D., & Fazio, R. H. (2018). Attitude accessibility as a function of emotionality. *Personality and Social Psychology Bulletin, 44*(4), 508–520.

Rodafinos, A., Vucevic, A., & Sideridis, G. D. (2005). The effectiveness of compliance techniques: Foot in the door versus door in the face. *Journal of Social Psychology, 145*(2), 237–239.

Rodrigues, A., Assmar, E. M. L, & Jablonski, B. (2005). Social psychology and the invasion of Iraq. *Revista de Psicología Social, 20*(3), 387–398.

Rodríguez-Bailón, R., Moya, M., & Yzerbyt, V. (2000). Why do superiors attend to negative stereotypic information about their subordinates? Effects of power legitimacy on social perception. *European Journal of Social Psychology, 30*(5), 651–671.

Roese, N. J. (1997). Counterfactual thinking. *Psychological Bulletin, 121*(1), 133–148.

Roese, N. J., Smallman, R., & Epstude, K. (2017). Do episodic counterfactual thoughts focus on controllable action? The role of self-initiation. *Journal of Experimental Social Psychology, 73*, 14–23.

Roese, N. J., Hur, T., & Pennington, G. L. (1999). Counterfactual thinking and regulatory focus: Implications for action versus inaction and sufficiency versus necessity. *Journal of Personality and Social Psychology, 77*(6), 1109–1120.

Roese, N. J., & Vohs, K. D. (2012). Hindsight bias. *Perspectives on Psychological Science, 7*(5), 411–426.

Rofé, Y. (1984). Stress and illness: A utility theory. *Psychological Review, 91*(2), 235–250.

Rogers, C. R. (1947). Some observations on the organization of personality. *American Psychologist, 2*(9), 358–368.

Rogoff, B., Paradise, R., Arauz, R. M., Correa-Chávez, M., & Angelillo, C. (2003). Firsthand learning through intent participation. *Annual Review of Psychology, 54*(1), 175–203.

Rokach, A. (2007). The effect of age and culture on the causes of loneliness. *Social Behavior and Personality, 35*(2), 169–186.

Rokach, A., & Bacanli, H. (2001). Perceived causes of loneliness: A cross-cultural comparison. *Social Behavior and Personality, 29*, 169–182.

Romer, D., Lizzadro, T., & Gruder, C. L. (1986). A person-situation approach to altruistic behavior. *Journal of Personality and Social Psychology, 51*(5), 1001–1012.

Rose, A. J., & Asher, S. R. (2017). The social tasks of friendship: Do boys and girls excel in different tasks? *Child Development Perspectives, 11*(1), 3–8.

Rose, A. J., Rhiannon, S. L., Glick, G. C., & Schwartz-Mette, R. A. (2016). Girls' and boys' problem talk: Implications for emotional closeness in friendships. *Developmental psychology, 52*(4), 629–639.

Rose, J. (1994). Communication challenges and role functions of performing groups. *Small Group Research, 25*(3), 411–432.

Rose, S., & Zand, D. (2000). Lesbian dating and courtship from young adulthood to midlife. *Journal of Gay and Lesbian Social Services, 11*(2–3), 77–104.

Rosekrans, M., & Hartup, W. (1967). Imitative influences of consistent and inconsistent response consequences to a model on aggressive behavior in children. *Journal of Personality and Social Psychology, 7*(4), 429–434.

Rosenberg, M. (1965). *Society and the adolescent child.* Princeton, NJ: Princeton University Press.

Rosenberg, M. L., & Mercy, J. A. (1991). Assaultive violence. In M. L. Rosenberg & M. A. Fenley (Eds.), *Violence in America: A public health approach* (pp. 14–50). New York, NY: Oxford University Press.

Rosenblatt, P. C., & Cozby, P. C. (1972). Courtship patterns associated with freedom of choice of spouse. *Journal of Marriage and the Family, 34*(4), 689–695.

Rosenhan, D. L. (1970). The natural socialization of altruistic autonomy. In J. Macaulay & L. Berkowitz (Eds.), *Altruism and helping behavior* (pp. 251–268). New York, NY: Academic Press.

Rosenhan, D. L., Salovey, P., & Hargis, K. (1981). The joys of helping: Focus of attention mediates the impact of positive affect on altruism. *Journal of Personality and Social Psychology, 40*(5), 899–905.

Rosenkoetter, L. I. (1999). The television situation comedy and children's prosocial behavior. *Journal of Applied Social Psychology, 29*(5), 979–993.

Rosenkoetter, L. I., Rosenkoetter, S. E., Ozretich, R. A., & Acock, A. C. (2004). Mitigating the harmful effects of violent television. *Journal of Applied Developmental Psychology, 25*(1), 25–47.

Rosenthal. L., & Levy, S. R. (2010). Understanding women's risk for HIV infection using social dominance theory and the four bases of gendered power. *Psychology of Women Quarterly, 34*(1), 21–35.

Rosenthal, R. (2003). Covert communication in laboratories, classrooms, and the truly real world. *Current Directions in Psychological Science, 12*(5), 151–154.

Rosenthal, R., & Jacobson, L. (1968). *Pygmalion in the classroom: Teacher expectation and pupils' intellectual development.* New York, NY: Holt, Rinehart and Winston.

Ross, A., & Jackson, M. (2013). Investigating the theory of planned behaviour's application to binge drinking among university students. *Journal of Substance Use, 18*(3), 184–195.

Ross, L. (1977). The intuitive psychologist and his shortcomings: Distortions in the attribution process. In L. Berkowitz (Ed.), *Advances in experimental social psychology* (Vol. 10, pp. 174–221). New York, NY: Academic Press.

Ross, L., Amabile, T. M., & Steinmetz, J. L. (1977). Social roles, social control, and biases in social perception processes. *Journal of Personality and Social Psychology, 35*(7), 485–494.

Ross, L., Lepper, M., & Ward, A. (2010). History of social psychology: Insights, challenges, and contributions to theory and application. In S. T. Fiske, D. T. Gilbert, & G. Lindzey (Eds.), *Handbook of social psychology* (5th ed., Vol. 1, pp. 3–50). Hoboken, NJ: John Wiley & Sons.

Ross, M. A., & Holmberg, D. (1993). Are wives' memories for events in relationships more vivid than their husbands' memories? *Journal of Social and Personal Relationships, 9*(4), 585–604.

Rossano, M. J. (2003). *Evolutionary psychology: The science of human behavior and evolution.* Hoboken, NJ: John Wiley & Sons.

Rotenberg, K. J., & Kmill, J. (1992). Perception of lonely and nonlonely persons as a function of individual differences in loneliness. *Journal of Social and Personal Relationships, 9*(2), 325–330.

Rotenberg, K. J., Bartley, J. L., & Toivonen, D. M. (1997). Children's stigmatization of chronic loneliness in peers. *Journal of Social Behavior and Personality, 12*, 577–584.

Rotenburg, K. J., Addis, N., Betts, L. R., Corrigan, A., Fox, C., Hobson, Z.,. . .Boulton, M. J. (2010). The relation between trust beliefs and loneliness during early childhood, middle childhood and adulthood. *Personality and Social Psychology Bulletin, 36*(8), 1086–1100.

Rothbaum, F., & Tsang, B. Y. -P. (1998). Lovesongs in the United States and China: On the nature of romantic love. *Journal of Cross-Cultural Psychology, 29*(2), 306–319.

Rotton, J., & Cohn, E. G. (2000). Violence is a curvilinear function of temperature in Dallas: A replication. *Journal of Personality and Social Psychology, 78*(6), 1074–1081.

Roussos, G., & Dovidio, J. F. (2018). Hate speech is in the eye of the beholder: The influence of racial attitudes and freedom of speech beliefs on perceptions of racially motivated threats of violence. *Social Psychological and Personality Science, 9*(2), 176–185.

Rozell, E. J., & Gundersen, D. E. (2003). The effects of leadership impression management on group perceptions of cohesion, consensus, and communication. *Small Group Research, 34*(2), 197–222.

Rubin, M., & Badea, C. (2012). They're all the same!...But for several different reasons: A review of the multicausal nature of perceived group variability. *Current Directions in Psychological Science, 21*(6), 367–372.

Rubin, Z., Peplau, L. A., & Hill, C. T. (1981). Loving and leaving: Sex differences in romantic attachments. *Sex Roles, 7*(8), 821–835.

Rucker, D. D., & Petty, R. E. (2004). When resistance is futile: Consequences of failed counterarguing for attitude certainty. *Journal of Personality and Social Psychology, 86*(2), 219–235.

Rudasill, K. M. (2011). Self and social regulation: Social interaction and the development of social understanding and executive functions (book review). *Developmental Neuropsychology, 36*(3), 403–404.

Rudman, L. A. (2005). Rejection of women? Beyond prejudice as antipathy. In J. F. Dovidio, P. Glick, & L. Rudman (Eds.), *On the nature of prejudice: Fifty years after Allport* (pp. 106–120). Malden, MA: Blackwell.

Rudman, L. A., & Glick, P. (2008). *The social psychology of gender: How power and intimacy shape gender relations.* New York, NY: Guilford Press.

Rumens, N. (2012). Queering cross-sex friendships: An analysis of gay and bisexual men's workplace friendships with heterosexual women. *Human Relations, 65*(8), 955–978.

Rusbult, C. E., Johnson, D. J., & Morrow, G. D. (1986a). Impact of couple patterns of problem solving on distress and nondistress in dating relationships. *Journal of Personality and Social Psychology, 50*(4), 744–753.

Rusbult, C. E., & Martz, J. M. (1995). Remaining in an abusive relationship: An investment model analysis of nonvoluntary dependence. *Personality and Social Psychology Bulletin, 21*(6), 558–571.

Rusbult, C. E., Morrow, G. D., & Johnson, D. J. (1987). Self-esteem and problem-solving behaviour in close relationships. *British Journal of Social Psychology, 26*(4), 293–303.

Rusbult, C. E., Olsen, N., Davis, J. L., & Hannon, P. A. (2001). Commitment and relationship maintenance mechanisms. In J. Harvey & A. Wenzel (Eds.), *Close romantic relationships: Maintenance and enhancement* (pp. 87–113). Mahwah, NJ: Lawrence Erlbaum Associates.

Rusbult, C. E., Van Lange, P. A., Wildschut, T., Yovetich, N. A., & Verette, J. (2000). Perceived superiority in close relationships: Why it exists and persists. *Journal of Personality and Social Psychology, 79*(4), 521–545.

Rusbult, C. E., Zembrodt, I., & Iwaniszek, J. (1986b). The impact of gender and sex-role orientation on responses to dissatisfaction in close relationships. *Sex Roles, 15*(1–2), 1–20.

Russell, B. L., & Trigg, K. Y. (2004). Tolerance of sexual harassment: An examination of gender differences, ambivalent sexism, social dominance, and gender roles. *Sex Roles, 50*(7–8), 565–573.

Russell, E. M., DelPriore, D. J., Butterfield, M. E., & Hill, S. E. (2013). Friends with benefits, but without the sex: Straight women and gay men exchange trustworthy mating advice. *Evolutionary Psychology, 11*(1), 132–147.

Russell, E. M., Ickes, W., & Ta, V. P. (2018). Women interact more comfortably and intimately with gay men—but not straight men—after learning their sexual orientation. *Psychological Science, 29*(2), 288–303.

Russell, J. A., & Yik, S. M. (1996). Emotion among the Chinese. In M. H. Bond (Ed.), *The handbook of Chinese psychology* (pp. 166–188). Hong Kong, China: Oxford University Press.

Russell, K. J., & Hand, C. J. (2017). Rape myth acceptance, victim blame attribution and just world beliefs: A rapid evidence assessment. *Aggression and Violent Behavior, 37,* 153–160.

Russell, V. M., Baker, L. R., & McNulty, J. K. (2013). Attachment insecurity and infidelity in marriage: Do studies of dating relationships really inform us about marriage? *Journal of Family Psychology, 27*(2), 242–251.

Rutherford, A, Unger, R., & Cherry, F. (2011). Reclaiming SPSSI's sociological past: Marie Jahoda and the immersion tradition in social psychology. *Journal of Social Issues, 67*(1), 42–58.

Rutland, A., Cameron, L., Jugert, P., Nigbur, D., Brown, R., Watters, C.,. . .Le Touze, D. (2012). Group identity and peer relations: A longitudinal study of group identity, perceived peer acceptance, and friendships amongst ethnic minority English children. *British Journal of Developmental Psychology, 30,* 283–302.

Ryan, C. S., Robinson, D. R., & Hausmann, R. M. (2004). Group socialization, uncertainty reduction and the development of new members' perceptions of group variability. In V. Yzerbyt, C. M. Judd, & O'Corneille (Eds.), *The psychology of group perception: Perceived variability, entitativity, and essentialism* (pp. 275–292). Philadelphia, PA: Psychology Press.

Ryckman, R. M., Robbins, M. A., Thornton, B., Kaczor, L. M., Gayton, S. L., & Anderson, C. V. (1991). Public self-consciousness and physique stereotyping. *Personality and Social Psychology Bulletin, 17*(4), 400–405.

S

Saad, L. (2019, January 8). U.S. still leans conservative, but liberals keep recent gains. *Gallup.* Retrieved from https://news.gallup.com/poll/245813/leans-conservative-liberals-keep-recent-gains.aspx

Sabini, J., Garvey, B., & Hall, A. L. (2001). Shame and embarrassment revisited. *Personality and Social Psychology Bulletin, 27*(1), 104–117.

Sabini, J., & Green, M. C. (2004). Emotional responses to sexual and emotional infidelity: Constants and differences across genders, samples, and methods. *Personality and Social Psychology Bulletin, 30*(11), 1375–1388.

Sachdev, I., & Bourhis, R. Y. (1987). Status differentials and intergroup behaviour. *European Journal of Social Psychology, 17*(3), 277–293.

Sachdev, I., & Bourhis, R. Y. (1991). Power and status differentials in minority and majority group relations. *European Journal of Social Psychology, 21*(1), 1–24.

Safronova, V., (2019, February 13). Turns out everyone has a good side. *The New York Times.* Retrieved from https://www.nytimes.com/2019/02/13/style/what-is-mariahs-good-side.html

Sagarin, B. J. (2005). Reconsidering evolved sex differences in jealousy: Comment on Harris (2003). *Personality and Social Psychology Review, 9*(1), 62–75.

Sagiv, L., Sverdlik, N., & Schwarz, N. (2011). To compete or to cooperate? Values' impact on perception and action in social dilemma games. *European Journal of Social Psychology, 41*(1), 64–77.

Saguy, A. C., & Ward, A. (2011). Coming out as fat: Rethinking stigma. *Social Psychology Quarterly, 74*(1), 53–75.

Said, C. P., & Todorov, A. (2011). A statistical model of facial attractiveness. *Psychological Science, 22*(9), 1183–1190.

Sakalli-Ugurlu, N. (2002). The relationship between sexism and attitudes toward homosexuality in a sample of Turkish college students. *Journal of Homosexuality, 42*(3), 53–64.

Sakalli-Ugurlu, N., & Glick, P. (2003). Ambivalent sexism and attitudes toward women who engage in premarital sex in Turkey. *Journal of Sex Research, 40*(3), 296–302.

Saks, M. J., & Marti, M. W. (1997). A meta-analysis of the effects of jury size. *Law and Human Behavior, 21*(5), 451–467.

Salerno, J. M., & Diamond, S. S. (2010). The promise of a cognitive perspective on jury deliberation. *Psychonomic Bulletin & Review, 17*(2), 174–179.

Salovey, P., & Rodin, J. (1988). Coping with envy and jealousy. *Journal of Social and Clinical Psychology, 7*(1), 15–33.

Saltzman, S. (2002, November 27). Ad majors raise alcohol awareness. *SMU Daily Campus*. Retrieved from https://www.smudailycampus.com/news/ad-majors-raise-alcohol-awareness

Salvy, S. J., Bowker, J. C., Nitecki, L. A., Kluczynski, M. A., Germeroth, L. J., & Roemmich, J. N. (2011). Impact of simulated ostracism on overweight and normal-weight youths' motivation to eat and food intake. *Appetite, 56*(1), 39–45.

Sanchez-Burks, J., Nisbett, R. E., & Ybarra, O. (2000). Cultural styles, relational schemas, and prejudice against outgroups. *Journal of Personality and Social Psychology, 79*(2), 174–189.

Sanders Thompson, V. L. (1991). Perceptions of race and race relations which affect African-American identification. *Journal of Applied Social Psychology, 21*(18), 1502–1516.

Sanderson, C. A., & Evans, S. M. (2001). Seeing one's partner through intimacy-colored glasses: An examination of the processes underlying the intimacy goals–relationship satisfaction link. *Personality and Social Psychology Bulletin, 27*(4), 463–473.

Sandys, M., & Dillehay, R. C. (1995). First-ballot votes, predeliberation dispositions, and final verdicts in jury trials. *Law and Human Behavior, 19*(2), 175–195.

Sani, F. (2005). When subgroups secede: Extending and refining the social psychological model of schism in groups. *Personality and Social Psychology Bulletin, 31*(8), 1074–1086.

Sani, F., & Reicher, S. (2000). Contested identities and schisms in groups: Opposing the ordination of women as priests in the Church of England. *British Journal of Social Psychology, 39*(1), 95–112.

Sani, F., & Todman, J. (2002). Should we stay or should we go? A social psychological model of schisms in groups. *Personality and Social Psychology Bulletin, 28*(12), 1647–1655.

Sani, F., Todman, J., & Lunn, J. (2005). The fundamentality of group principles and perceived group entitativity. *Journal of Experimental Social Psychology, 41*(6), 567–573.

San Martin, S., Camarero, C., & San José, R. (2011). Does involvement matter in online shopping satisfaction and trust? *Psychology & Marketing, 28*(2), 145–167.

Sanna, L. J., Chang, E. C., & Meier, S. (2001). Counterfactual thinking and self-motives. *Personality and Social Psychology Bulletin, 27*(8), 1023–1034.

Sansone, C., Morf, C. C., & Panter, A. T. (2004). The research process: Of big pictures, little details, and the social psychological road in between. In C. Sansone, C. C. Morf, & A. T. Panter (Eds.), *The SAGE handbook of methods in social psychology* (pp. 3–16). Thousand Oaks, CA: Sage.

Sansone, R. A., & Sansone, L. A. (2010). Road rage: What's driving it? *Psychiatry, 7*(7), 14–18.

Santee, R. T., & Maslach, C. (1982). To agree or not to agree: Personal dissent amid social pressure to conform. *Journal of Personality and Social Psychology, 42*(4), 690–700.

Santos, H. C., Varnum, M., & Grossmann, I. (2017). Global increases in individualism. *Psychological Science, 28*(9), 1228–1239.

Sarnoff, I., & Zimbardo, P. G. (1961). Anxiety, fear, and social affiliation. *Journal of Abnormal and Social Psychology, 62,* 356–363.

Saucier, D. A., Miller, C. T., & Doucet, N. (2005). Differences in helping Whites and Blacks: A meta-analysis. *Personality and Social Psychology Review, 9*(1), 2–16.

Savin, H. B. (1973). Professors and psychological researchers: Conflicting values in conflicting roles. *Cognition, 2*(1), 147–149.

Savitsky, K., Epley, N., & Gilovich, T. (2001). Do others judge us as harshly as we think? Overestimating the impact of our failures, shortcomings, and mishaps. *Journal of Personality and Social Psychology, 81*(1), 44–56.

Savitsky, K., & Gilovich, T. (2003). The illusion of transparency and the alleviation of speech anxiety. *Journal of Experimental Social Psychology, 39*(6), 618–625.

Savitsky, K., Van Boven, L., Epley, N., & Wight, W. M. (2005). The unpacking effect in allocations of responsibility for group tasks. *Journal of Experimental Social Psychology, 41*(5), 447–457.

Sawyer, J., & Gampa, A. (2018). Implicit and explicit racial attitudes changed during Black Lives Matter. *Personality and Social Psychology Bulletin, 44*(7), 1039–1059.

Sbarra, D. A. (2006). Predicting the onset of emotional recovery following nonmarital relationship dissolution: Survival analyses of sadness and anger. *Personality and Social Psychology Bulletin, 32*(3), 298–312.

Sbarra, D. A., & Coan, J. A. Divorce and health: Good data in need of a better theory. *Current Opinion in Psychology, 13,* 91–95.

Sbarra, D. A., & Emery, R. E. (2005). The emotional sequelae of nonmarital relationship dissolution: Analysis of change and intraindividual variability over time. *Personal Relationships, 12*(2), 213–232.

Scalas, L. F., Marsh, H. W., Nagengast, B., & Morin, A. J. (2013). Latent-variable approaches to the Jamesian model of importance-weighted averages. *Personality and Social Psychology Bulletin, 39*(1), 100–114.

Scanzoni, J. (1979). Social exchange and behavioral interdependence. In R. L. Burgess & T. L. Huston (Eds.), *Social exchange in developing relationships* (pp. 61–98). New York, NY: Academic Press.

Schachner, D. A., & Shaver, P. R. (2004). Attachment dimensions and sexual motives. *Personal Relationships, 11*(2), 179–195.

Schachter, S. (1951). Deviation, rejection and communication. *The Journal of Abnormal and Social Psychology, 46*(2), 190–207.

Schachter, S. (1959). *The psychology of affiliation.* Stanford, CA: Stanford University Press.

Schachter, S. (1964). The interaction of cognitive and physiological determinants of emotional state. In L. Berkowitz (Ed.), *Advances in experimental social psychology* (Vol. 1, pp. 49–80). New York, NY: Academic Press.

Schack, C. M. (2010). Identity construction on Facebook—A qualitative study of young people's use of the social online network Facebook. *Psyke & Logos, 31*, 174–192.

Schafer, M., & Crichlow, S. (1996). Antecedents of groupthink: A quantitative study. *Journal of Conflict Resolution, 40*(3), 415–435.

Schafer, M. H., & Ferraro, K. F. (2011). The stigma of obesity: Does perceived weight discrimination affect identity and physical health? *Social Psychology Quarterly, 74*(1), 76–97.

Schaller, M. (1997). Beyond "competing," beyond "compatible." *American Psychologist, 52*(12), 1379–1380.

Schaufeli, W. B. (1988). Perceiving the causes of unemployment: An evaluation of the Causal Dimensions Scale in a real-life situation. *Journal of Personality and Social Psychology, 54*(2), 347–356.

Scheepers, D., & Derks, B. (2016). Revisiting social identity theory from a neuroscience perspective. *Current Opinion in Psychology, 11*, 74–78.

Scheier, M. F. (1980). Effects of public and private self-consciousness on the public expression of personal beliefs. *Journal of Personality and Social Psychology, 39*(3), 514–521.

Scheier, M. F., & Carver, C. S. (1977). Self-focused attention and the experience of emotion: Attraction, repulsion, elation, and depression. *Journal of Personality and Social Psychology, 35*(9), 625–636.

Scheier, M. F., & Carver, C. S. (1980). Private and public self-attention, resistance to change, and dissonance reduction. *Journal of Personality and Social Psychology, 39*(3), 390–405.

Scher, S. J., & Rauscher, F. (Eds.). (2003). *Evolutionary psychology: Alternative approaches.* New York, NY: Kluwer Press.

Scherr, K. C., Normile, C. J., & Putney, H. (2018). Perpetually stigmatized: False confessions prompt underlying mechanisms that motivate negative perceptions of exonerees. *Psychology, Public Policy, and Law, 24*(3), 341–352.

Schindler, I., Fagundes, C. P., & Murdock, K. W. (2010). Predictors of romantic relationship formation: Attachment style, prior relationships, and dating goals. *Personal Relationships, 17*(1), 97–105.

Schino, G., di Sorrentino, E. P., & Tiddi, B. (2007). Grooming and coalitions in Japanese macaques (Macaca fuscata): Partner choice and the time frame reciprocation. *Journal of Comparative Psychology, 121*(2), 181–188.

Schlegel, R. J., Hicks, J. A., King, L. A., & Arndt, J. (2011). Feeling like you know who you are: Perceived true self-knowledge and meaning in life. *Personality and Social Psychology Bulletin, 37*(6), 745–756.

Schlenker, B. R., & Wowra, S. A. (2003). Carryover effects of feeling socially transparent or impenetrable on strategic self-presentation. *Journal of Personality and Social Psychology, 85*(5), 871–880.

Schliemann, A. D., Carraher, D. W., & Ceci, S. (1997). Everyday cognition. In J. W. Berry, P. R. Dasen, & T. S. Saraswathi (Eds.), *Handbook of cross-cultural psychology: Vol. 2. Basic processes and human development* (pp. 177–216). Boston, MA: Allyn & Bacon.

Schmid Mast, M., & Hall, J. A. (2006). Women's advantage at remembering others' appearance: A systematic look at the why and when of a gender difference. *Personality and Social Psychology Bulletin, 32*(3), 353–364.

Schmitt, D. P., & Allik, J. (2005). Simultaneous administration of the Rosenberg Self-Esteem Scale in 53 nations: Exploring the universal and culture-specific features of global self-esteem. *Journal of Personality and Social Psychology, 89*(4), 623–642.

Schmitt, M. T., Branscombe, N. R., & Kappen, D. M. (2003). Attitudes toward group-based inequality: Social dominance or social identity? *British Journal of Social Psychology, 42*(2), 161–186.

Schmitt, M. T., Branscombe, N. R., Postmes, T., & Garcia, A. (2014). The consequences of perceived discrimination for psychological well-being: A meta-analytic review. *Psychological Bulletin, 140*(4), 921–948.

Schnabel, L., & Sevell, E. (2017). Should Mary and Jane be legal? Americans' attitudes toward marijuana and same-sex marriage legalization, 1988–2014. *Public Opinion Quarterly, 81*(1), 157–172.

Schnall, S., Abrahamson, A., & Laird, J. D. (2002). Premenstrual syndrome and misattribution: A self-perception, individual differences perspective. *Basic and Applied Social Psychology, 24*(3), 215–228.

Schneider, C. S., & Kenny, D. A. (2000). Cross-sex friends who were once romantic partners: Are they platonic friends now? *Journal of Social and Personal Relationships, 17*(3), 451–466.

Schoenmakers, T., Wiers, R. W., Jones, B. T., Bruce, G., & Jansen, A. T. (2007). Attentional re-training decreases attentional bias in heavy drinkers without generalization. *Addiction, 102*(3), 399–405.

Schöneman, P. H., Byrne, D., & Bell, P. A. (1977). Statistical aspects of a model for interpersonal attraction. *Bulletin of the Psychonomic Society, 9*(4), 243–246.

Schreurs, K. M. G., & Buunk, B. P. (1994). Intimacy, autonomy, and relationship satisfaction in Dutch lesbian couples and heterosexual couples. *Journal of Psychology and Human Sexuality, 7*(4), 41–57.

Schriesheim, C. A., Tepper, B. J., & Tetrault, L. A. (1994). Least preferred coworker score, situational control, and leadership effectiveness: A meta-analysis of contingency model performance predictions. *Journal of Applied Psychology, 79*(4), 561–573.

Schuetz, A. (1998). Self-esteem and interpersonal strategies. In J. P. Forgas, K. D. Williams, & L. Wheeler (Eds.), *The social mind: Cognitive and motivational aspects of interpersonal behavior* (pp. 157–176). New York, NY: Cambridge University Press.

Schultz, P. W., Nolan, J. M., Cialdini, R. B., Goldstein, N. J., & Griskevicius, V. (2018). The constructive, destructive, and reconstructive power of social norms: Reprise. *Perspectives on Psychological Science, 13*(2), 249–254.

Schuman, H. (2002). Sense and nonsense about surveys. *Contexts, 1*(2), 40–47.

Schwartz, M. B., Vartanian, L. R., Nosek, B. A., & Brownell, K. D. (2006). The influence of one's own body weight on implicit and explicit anti-fat bias. *Obesity, 14*(3), 440–447.

Schwartz, S. H. (2003). Mapping and interpreting cultural differences around the world. In H. Vinken, J. Soeters, & P. Ester (Eds.), *Comparing cultures: Dimensions of culture in a comparative perspective* (pp. 43–73). Leiden, The Netherlands: Brill.

Schwarz, N., Bless, H., Strack, F., Klumpp, G., Rittenauer-Schatka, & Simons, A. (1991). Ease of retrieval as information: Another look at the availability heuristic. *Journal of Personality and Social Psychology, 61*(2), 195–202.

Schwarzwald, J., Bizman, A., & Raz, M. (1983). The foot-in-the-door paradigm: Effects of second request size on donation probability and donor generosity. *Personality and Social Psychology Bulletin, 9*(3), 443–450.

Scott, V. M., Mottarella, K. E., & Lavooy, M. J. (2006). Does virtual intimacy exist? A brief exploration into reported levels of intimacy in online relationships. *Cyberpsychology & Behavior, 9*(6), 759–761.

Scully, D. (1985). The role of violent pornography in justifying rape. Paper prepared for the Attorney General's Commission on Pornography Hearings, Houston, TX.

Searcy, E., & Eisenberg, N. (1992). Defensiveness in response to aid from a sibling. *Journal of Personality and Social Psychology, 62*(3), 422–433.

Sechrist, G. B., Swim, J. K., & Stangor, C. (2004). When do the stigmatized make attributions to discrimination occurring to the self and others? The roles of self-presentation and need for control. *Journal of Personality and Social Psychology, 87*(1), 111–122.

Sedikides, C., Campbell, W. K., Reeder, G. D., & Elliot, A. J. (1998). The self-serving bias in relational context. *Journal of Personality and Social Psychology, 74*(2), 378–386.

Segal, M. W. (1974). Alphabet and attraction: An unobtrusive measure of the effect of propinquity in a field setting. *Journal of Personality and Social Psychology, 30*(5), 654–657.

Segerstrom, S. C., & Nes, L. S. (2007). Heart rate variability reflects self-regulatory strength, effort, and fatigue. *Psychological Science, 18*(3), 275–281.

Segerstrom, S. C., Taylor, S. E., Kemeny, M. E., & Fahey, J. L. (1998). Optimism is associated with mood, coping, and immune change in response to stress. *Journal of Personality and Social Psychology, 74*(6), 1646–1655.

Segrin, C. (2019). Indirect effects of social skills on health through stress and loneliness. *Health Communication, 34*(1), 118–124.

Seiter, J. S. (2007). Ingratiation and gratuity: The effect of complimenting customers on tipping behavior in restaurants. *Journal of Applied Social Psychology, 37*(3), 478–485.

Selfhout, M., Denissen, J., Branje, S., & Meeus, W. (2009). In the eye of the beholder: Perceived, actual, and peer-related similarity in personality, communication, and friendship intensity during the acquaintanceship process. *Journal of Personality and Social Psychology, 96*(6), 1152–1165.

Seligman, M. E. P. (1991). *Learned optimism.* New York, NY: Alfred A. Knopf.

Seligman, M. E. P. (2011). *Flourish: A visionary new understanding of happiness and well-being.* New York, NY: Free Press.

Sellers, R. M., & Shelton, J. N. (2003). The role of racial identity in perceived racial discrimination. *Journal of Personality and Social Psychology, 84*(5), 1079–1092.

Sergeant, M. J., Dickins, T. E., Davies, M. N., & Griffiths, M. D. (2006). Aggression, empathy and sexual orientation in males. *Personallity and Individual Differences, 40*(3), 475–486.

Seto, M. C., Marc, A., & Bararee, H. E. (2001). The role of pornography in the etiology of sexual aggression. *Aggression and Violent Behavior, 6*(1), 35–53.

Sezer, O., Gino, F., & Norton, M. I. (2018). Humblebragging: A distinct—and ineffective—self-presentation strategy. *Journal of Personality and Social Psychology, 114*(1), 52–74.

Shaffer, L. S. (2005). From mirror self-recognition to the looking-glass self: Exploring the justification hypothesis. *Journal of Clinical Psychology, 61*(1), 47–65.

Shana, L., & van Laar, C. (Eds.). (2006). *Stigma and group inequality: Social psychological perspectives.* Mahwah, NJ: Lawrence Erlbaum Associates.

Shanab, M. E., & Yahya, K. A. (1977). A behavioral study of obedience in children. *Journal of Personality and Social Psychology, 35*(7), 530–536.

Shapiro, J. R., & Neuberg, S. L. (2007). From stereotype threat to stereotype threats: Implications of a multi-threat framework for causes, moderators, mediators, consequences, and interventions. *Personality and Social Psychology Review, 11*(2), 107–130.

Sharabi, L. L., & Caughlin, J. P. (2017). What predicts first date success? A longitudinal study of modality switching in online dating. *Personal Relationships, 24*(2), 370–391.

Sharabi, L. L., & Caughlin, J. P. (2019). Deception in online dating: Significance and implications for the first offline date. *New Media & Society, 21*(1), 229–247.

Share, T. L., & Mintz, L. B. (2002). Differences between lesbians and heterosexual women in disordered eating and related attitudes. *Journal of Homosexuality, 42*(4), 89–106.

Shaver, P., & Klinnert, M. (1982). Schachter's theories of affiliation and emotion: Implications of developmental research. In L. Wheeler (Ed.), *Review of personality and social psychology* (Vol. 3, pp. 37–72). Beverly Hills, CA: Sage.

Shaver, P. R., & Mikulincer, M. (Eds.). (2011). *Human aggression and violence: Causes, manifestations, and consequences.* Washington, DC: American Psychological Association.

Shaver, P. R., Wu, S., & Schwartz, J. C. (1991). Cross-cultural similarities and differences in emotion and its representation: A prototype approach. In M. S. Clark (Ed.), *Review of personality and social psychology* (Vol. 13, pp. 175–212). Thousand Oaks, CA: Sage.

Shaw, J. (2003). Automatic for the people: How representations of significant others implicitly affect goal pursuit. *Journal of Personality and Social Psychology, 84*(4), 661–681.

Shaw, L. L., Batson, C. D., & Todd, R. M. (1994). Empathy avoidance: Forestalling feeling for another in order to escape the motivational consequences. *Journal of Personality and Social Psychology, 67*(5), 879–887.

Sheeran, P. (2002). Intention-behavior relations: A conceptual and empirical review. *European Review of Social Psychology, 12*(1), 1–36

Sheeran, P., Orbell, S., & Trafimow, D. (1999). Does the temporal stability of behavioral intentions moderate intention-behavior and past behavior–future behavior relations? *Personality and Social Psychology Bulletin, 25*(6), 721–730.

Sheldon, K. M. (1999). Learning the lessons of tit-for-tat: Even competitors can get the message. *Journal of Personality and Social Psychology, 77*(6), 1245–1253.

Shelton, J. N., & Richeson, J. A. (2005). Intergroup contact and pluralistic ignorance. *Journal of Personality and Social Psychology, 88*(1), 91–107.

Shelton, J. N., Richeson, J. A., & Salvatore, J. (2005). Expecting to be the target of prejudice: Implications for interethnic interactions. *Personality and Social Psychology Bulletin, 31*(9), 1189–1202.

Sher, L. (2014). Testosterone and homicidal behavior. *Australian and New Zealand Journal of Psychiatry, 48*(3), 290.

Sherif, M. (1936). *The psychology of social norms.* Oxford, England: Harper.

Sherif, M. (1966). *In common predicament: Social psychology of intergroup conflict and cooperation.* Boston, MA: Houghton Mifflin.

Sherif, M., Harvey, O. J., White, B. J., Hood, W. R., & Sherif, C. (1961). *Intergroup conflict and cooperation: The Robbers' Cave experiment.* Norman, OK: Oklahoma Book Exchange.

Sherif, M., & Sherif, C. W. (1956). *An outline of social psychology.* New York, NY: Harper & Brothers.

Sherman, L. E., Payton, A. A., Hernandez, L. M., Greenfield, P. M., & Dapretto, M. (2016). The power of the *like* in adolescence: Effects of peer influence on neural and behavioral responses to social media. *Psychologial Science, 27*(7), 1027–1035.

Sherman, P. W. (1985). Alarm calls of Belding's ground squirrels to aerial predators: Nepotism or self-preservation? *Behavioral Ecology and Sociobiology, 17*(4), 313–323.

Shestowsky, D., Wegener, D. T., & Fabrigar, L. R. (1998). Need for cognition and interpersonal influence: Individual differences in impact on dyadic decisions. *Journal of Personality and Social Psychology, 74*(5), 1317–1328.

Shields, C. A., Brawley, L. R., & Ginis, K. A. (2007). Interactive effects of exercise status and observer gender on the impressions formed of men. *Sex Roles, 56*(3–4), 231–237.

Shields, S. A. (2002). *Speaking from the heart: Gender and the social meaning of emotion.* New York, NY: Cambridge University Press.

Shields, S. A. (2007). Passionate men, emotional women: Psychology constructs gender difference in the late 19th century. *History of Psychology, 10*(2), 92–110.

Shimizu, Y., Lee, H., & Uleman, J. S. (2017). Culture as automatic processes for making meaning: Spontaneous trait inferences. *Journal of Experimental Social Psychology, 69*, 79–85.

Shin, J. E., Levy, S. R., & London, B. (2016). Effects of role model exposure on STEM and non-STEM student engagement. *Journal of Applied Social Psychology, 46*(7), 410–427.

Shoda, Y., Mischel, W., & Peake, P. K. (1990). Predicting adolescent cognitive and self-regulatory competencies from preschool delay of gratification: Identifying diagnostic conditions. *Developmental Psychology, 26*(6), 978–986.

Shotland, R. L., & Straw, M. K. (1976). Bystander response to an assault: When a man attacks a woman. *Journal of Personality and Social Psychology, 34*(5), 990–999.

Shu, L. L., Gino, F., & Bazerman, M. H. (2011). Dishonest deed, clear conscience: When cheating leads to moral disengagement and motivated forgetting. *Personality and Social Psychology Bulletin, 37*(3), 330–349.

Shulman, S., Elicker, J., & Sroufe, A. (1994). Stages of friendship growth in preadolescence as related to attachment history. *Journal of Social and Personal Relationships, 11*(3), 341–361.

Shumaker, S. A., & Hill, D. R. (1991). Gender differences in social support and physical health. *Health Psychology, 10*(2), 102–111.

Shutts, K., Banaji, M. R., & Spelke, E. S. (2010). Social categories guide young children's preferences for novel objects. *Developmental Science, 13*(4), 599–610.

Sibicky, M. E., Schroeder, D. A., & Dovidio, J. F. (1995). Empathy and helping: Considering the consequences of intervention. *Basic and Applied Social Psychology, 16*(4), 435–453.

Sieck, W. R., Smith, J. L., Grome, A., & Rababy, D. A. (2011). Expert cultural sensemaking in the management of Middle Eastern crowds. In K. L. Mosier & U. M. Fischer (Eds.), *Informed by knowledge: Expert performance in complex situations* (pp. 103–119). New York, NY: Psychology Press.

Silvia, P. J., & O'Brien, M. E. (2004). Self-awareness and constructive functioning: Revisiting "the human dilemma". *Journal of Social and Clinical Psychology, 23*, 475–489.

Simon, B., Stürmer, S., & Steffens, K. (2000). Helping individuals or group members? The role of individual and collective identification in AIDS volunteerism. *Personality and Social Psychology Bulletin, 26*(4), 497–506.

Simons, H. W., Berkowitz, N. N., & Moyer, R. J. (1970). Similarity, credibility, and attitude change: A review and a theory. *Psychological Bulletin, 73*(1), 1–16.

Simons, L. G., Simons, R. L., Landor, A. M., Bryant, C. M., & Beach, S. R. (2014). Factors linking childhood experiences to adult romantic relationships among African Americans. *Journal of Family Psychology, 28*(3), 368–379.

Simonsohn, U. (2011a). Spurious also? Name-similarity-effects (implicit egotism) in employment decisions. *Psychological Science, 22*(8), 1087–1089.

Simonsohn, U. (2011b). Spurious? Name similarity effects (implicit egotism) in marriage, job, and moving decisions. *Journal of Personality and Social Psychology, 101*(1), 1–24.

Simonton, D. K. (1998). Historiometric methods in social psychology. *European Review of Social Psychology, 9*(1), 267–293.

Simpson, B. (2006). Social identity and cooperation in social dilemmas. *Rationality and Society, 18*(4), 443–470.

Simpson, J. A., & Gangestad, S. W. (2001). Evolution and relationships: A call for integration. *Personal Relationships, 8*(4), 341–355.

Simpson, J. A., & Overall, N. C. (2014). Partner buffering of attachment insecurity. *Current Directions in Psychological Science, 23*(1), 54–59.

Singelis, T. M., Triandis, H. C., Bhawuk, D. S., & Gelfand, M. (1995). Horizontal and vertical dimensions of individualism and collectivism: A theoretical and measurement refinement. *Cross-Cultural Research, 29*(3), 240–275.

Singh, D. (1993). Adaptive significance of female physical attractiveness: Role of waist-to-hip ratio. *Journal of Personality and Social Psychology, 65*(2), 293–307.

Singh, R., & Teoh, J. B. (2000). Impression formation from intellectual and social traits: Evidence for behavioral adaptation and cognitive processing. *British Journal of Social Psychology, 39*(4), 537–554.

Singh, V., & Vinnicombe, S. (2006). Opening the boardroom doors to women directors. In D. McTavish & K. Miller (Eds.), *Women in leadership and management* (pp. 127–147). Northampton, MA: Edward Elgar.

Sisk, V. F., Burgoyne, A. P., Jingze Sun, J. L., & Butler, B. N. (2018). To what extent and under what circumstances are growth mind-sets important to academic achievement? Two meta-analyses. *Psychological Science, 29*(4), 549–571.

Sivunen, A., & Hakonen, M. (2011). Review of virtual environment studies on social and group phenomena. *Small Group Research, 42*(4), 405–457.

Siy, J. O., & Cheryan, S. (2016). Prejudice masquerading as praise: The negative echo of positive stereotypes. *Personality and Social Psychology Bulletin, 42*(7), 941–954.

Skinner, A. L., & Hudac, C. M. (2017). "Yuck, you disgust me!" Affective bias against interracial couples. *Journal of Experimental Social Psychology, 68*, 68–77.

Skinner, B. F. (1938). *The behavior of organisms.* Oxford, England: Appleton-Century-Crofts.

Skitka, L. J. (1999). Ideological and attributional boundaries on public compassion: Reactions to individuals and communities affected by a natural disaster. *Personality and Social Psychology Bulletin, 25*(7), 793–808.

Skitka, L. J. (2006). Patriotism or nationalism? Understanding post-September 11, 2001 flag display behavior. *Journal of Applied Social Psychology, 35*(10), 1995–2011.

Slatcher, R. B., & Selcuk, E. (2017). A social psychological perspective on the links between close relationships and health. *Current Directions in Psychological Science, 26*(1), 16–21.

Sleebos, E., Ellemers, N., & de Gilder, D. (2006). The carrot and the stick: Affective commitment and acceptance anxiety for discretionary group efforts by respected and disrespected group members. *Personality and Social Psychology Bulletin, 32*(2), 244–255.

Slotter, E. B., Gardner, W. L., & Finkel, E. J. (2010). Who am I without you? The influence of romantic breakup on the self-concept. *Personality and Social Psychology Bulletin, 36*(2), 147–160.

Slovic, P. (2007). "If I look at the mass I will never act": Psychic numbing and genocide. *Judgment and Decision Making, 2*(2), 79–95.

Smallman, R. (2013). It's what's inside that counts: The role of counterfactual content in intention formation. *Journal of Experimental Social Psychology, 49*(5), 842–851.

Smith, A. (2016, February 11). 15% of American adults have used online dating sites or mobile dating apps. *Pew Research Center.* Retrieved from https://www.pewresearch.org/internet/2016/02/11/15-percent-of-american-adults-have-used-online-dating-sites-or-mobile-dating-apps/

Smith, A. E., Jussim, L., & Eccles, J. (1999). Do self-fulfilling prophecies accumulate, dissipate, or remain stable over time? *Journal of Personality and Social Psychology, 77*(3), 548–565.

Smith, G. T., Hohlstein, L. A., & Atlas, J. G. (1989, August). Race differences in eating disordered behavior and eating-related experiences. Paper presented at the 97th annual convention of the American Psychological Association, New Orleans, LA.

Smith, M. B. (2002). Self and identity in historical/sociocultural context: "Perspectives on selfhood" revisited. In Y. Kashima, M. Foddy, & M. Platow (Eds.), *Self and identity: Personal, social and symbolic* (pp. 229–243). Mahwah, NJ: Lawrence Erlbaum Associates.

Smith, P. B., Peterson, M. F., Bond, M., & Misumi, J. (1990). Leadership style and leader behaviour in individualistic and collectivist cultures. In S. Iwawaki, Y. Kashima, & K. Leung (Eds.), *Innovations in cross-cultural psychology* (pp. 76–85). Amsterdam, The Netherlands: Swets & Zeitlinger.

Smith, P. K., & Trope, Y. (2006). You focus on the forest when you're in charge of the trees: Power priming and abstract information processing. *Journal of Personality and Social Psychology, 90*(4), 578–596.

Smith, R. J. (2004, July 23). Operational relationship with Al Qaeda discounted. *Washington Post* (p. A01). Retrieved from https://www.washingtonpost.com/archive/politics/2004/07/23/operational-relationship-with-al-qaeda-discounted/3595215f-4ef1-4349-a0f7-ed552cbca820/

Smith, S. M., Haugtvedt, C. P., & Petty, R. E. (1994). Humor can either enhance or disrupt message processing: The moderating role of humor relevance. Unpublished manuscript.

Smith, S. M., McIntosh, W. D., & Bazzani, D. G. (1999). Are the beautiful good in Hollywood? An investigation of the beauty-and-goodness stereotype on film. *Basic and Applied Social Psychology, 21*(1), 69–80.

Smith, S. M., & Shaffer, D. R. (1991). Celerity and cajolery: Rapid speech may promote or inhibit persuasion through its impact on message elaboration. *Personality and Social Psychology Bulletin, 17*(6), 663–669.

Smith-Lovin, L., & Winkielman, P. (2010). The social psychologies of emotion: A bridge that is not too far. *Social Psychology Quarterly, 73*(4), 327–332.

Snyder, M., & Cunningham, M. R. (1975). To comply or not to comply: Testing the self-perception explanation of the foot-in-the-door phenomenon. *Journal of Personality and Social Psychology, 31*(1), 64–67.

Snyder, M., & Swann, W. B. (1978). Hypothesis-testing processes in social interaction. *Journal of Personality and Social Psychology, 36*(11), 1202–1212.

Snyder, M., Tanke, E. D., & Berscheid, E. (1977). Social perception and interpersonal behavior: On the self-fulfilling nature of social stereotypes. *Journal of Personality and Social Psychology, 35*(9), 656–666.

Solano, C. H., & Koester, N. H. (1989). Loneliness and communication problems: Subjective anxiety or objective skills? *Personality and Social Psychology Bulletin, 15*(1), 126–133.

Sommers, S. R. (2006). On racial diversity and group decision making: Identifying multiple effects of racial composition on jury deliberations. *Journal of Personality and Social Psychology, 90*(4), 597–612.

Son Hing, L. S., Li, W., & Zanna, M. P. (2002). Inducing hypocrisy to reduce prejudicial responses among aversive racists. *Journal of Experimental Social Psychology, 38*(1), 71–78.

Sorhagen, N. S. (2013). Early teacher expectations disproportionately affect poor children's high school performance. *Journal of Educational Psychology, 105*(2), 465–477.

Sorokowski, P., Szmajke, A., Sorokowska, A., Cunen, M. B., Fabrykant, M., Zarafshani, K.,. . .Fang, Tzu. (2011). Attractivenss of leg length: Report from 27 nations. *Journal of Cross-cultural Psychology, 42*(1), 131–139.

Sorrentino, R. M. (2003). Motivated perception and the warm look: Current perspectives and future directions. In S. J. Spencer, S. Fein, M. P. Zanna, & J. M. Olson (Eds.), *Motivated social perception: The Ontario symposium* (Vol. 9, pp. 299–316). Mahwah, NJ: Lawrence Erlbaum Associates.

Spaulding, C. (1970). The romantic love complex in American culture. *Sociology and Social Research, 55*(1), 82–100.

Spencer, S. J., Steele, C. M., & Quinn, D. M. (1999). Stereotype threat and women's math performance. *Journal of Experimental Social Psychology, 35*(1), 4–28.

Spencer-Rodgers, J., Peng, K., Wang, L., & Hou, Y. (2004). Dialectical self-esteem and East-West differences in psychological well-being. *Personality and Social Psychological Bulletin, 30*(11), 1416–1432.

Sperry, K., & Siegel, J. T. (2013). Victim responsibility, credibility, and verdict in a simulated rape case: Application of Weiner's attribution model. *Legal and Criminological Psychology, 18*(1), 16–29.

Spies, M., & Sevincer, A. T. (2018). Women outperform men in distinguishing between authentic and nonauthentic smiles. *The Journal of Social Psychology, 158*(5), 574–579.

Sprecher, S. (1992). How men and women expect to feel and behave in response to inequity in close relationships. *Social Psychology Quarterly, 55*(1), 57–69.

Sprecher, S., & Felmlee, D. (1992). The influence of parents and friends on the quality and stability of romantic relationships: A three wave longitudinal investigation. *Journal of Marriage and the Family, 54*(4), 888–900.

Sprecher, S., Sullivan, Q., & Hatfield, E. (1994). Mate selection preferences: Gender differences examined in a national sample. *Journal of Personality and Social Psychology, 66*(6), 1074–1080.

Sprecher, S., & Toro-Morn, M. (2002). A study of men and women from different sides of earth to determine if men are from Mars and women are from Venus in their beliefs about love and romantic relationships. *Sex Roles, 46*(5–6), 131–147.

Sripada, C., Kessler, D., & Jonides, J. (2014). Methylphenidate blocks effort-induced depletion of regulatory control in healthy volunteers. *Psychological Science, 25*(6), 1227–1234.

Staats, A. W., & Staats, C. K. (1958). Attitudes established by classical conditioning. *Journal of Abnormal and Social Psychology, 57*(1), 37–40.

Stalder, D. R. (2008). Revisiting the issue of safety in numbers: The likelihood of receiving help from a group. *Social Influence, 3*, 24–33.

Stangor, C., & McMillan, D. (1992). Memory for expectancy-congruent and expectancy-incongruent information: A review of the social and social developmental literatures. *Psychological Bulletin, 111*(1), 42–61.

Stanley, D., Phelps, E., & Banaji, M. (2008). The neural basis of implicit attitudes. *Current Directions in Psychological Science, 17*(2), 164–170.

Stanton, S. C., Campbell, L., & Pink, J. C. (2017). Benefits of positive relationship experiences for avoidantly attached individuals. *Journal of Personality and Social Psychology, 113*(4), 568–588.

Staub, E. (2004). Understanding and responding to group violence: Genocide, mass killing, and terrorism. In F. M. Moghaddam & A. J. Marsella (Eds.), *Understanding terrorism: Psychosocial roots, consequences, and interventions* (pp. 151–168). Washington, DC: American Psychological Association.

Steadman, H. J., Mulvey, E. P., Monahan, J., Robbins, P. C., Appelbaum, P. S., Grisso, T.,. . .Silver, E. (1998). Violence by people discharged from acute psychiatric inpatient facilities and by others in the same neighborhoods. *Archives of General Psychiatry, 55*(5), 393–401.

Steblay, N. M. (1987). Helping behavior in rural and urban environments: A meta-analysis. *Psychological Bulletin, 102*(3), 346–356.

Steele, C. M. (1997). A threat in the air: How stereotypes shape intellectual identity and performance. *American Psychologist, 52*(6), 613–629.

Steele, C. M. (2010). *Whistling Vivaldi: And other clues to how stereotypes affect us.* New York, NY: W. W. Norton.

Steele, C. M., & Aronson, J. (1995). Stereotype threat and the intellectual test performance of African-Americans. *Journal of Personality and Social Psychology, 69*(5), 797–811.

Steele, C. M., & Josephs, R. A. (1990). Alcohol myopia: Its prized and dangerous effects. *American Psychologist, 45*(8), 921–933.

Steele, C. M., Spencer, S. J., & Aronson, J. (2002). Contending with group image: The psychology of stereotype and social identity threat. In M. P. Zanna (Ed.), *Advances in experimental social psychology* (Vol. 34, pp. 379–440). San Diego, CA: Academic Press.

Steffens, N. K., Goclowska, M. A., Cruwys, T., & Galinsky, A. D. (2016). How multiple social identities are related to creativity. *Personality and Social Psychology Bulletin, 42*(2), 188–203.

Steinberg, L. D., Catalano, R., & Dooley, D. (1981). Economic antecedents of child abuse and neglect. *Child Development, 52*(3), 975–985.

Stellar, J. E., Cohen, A., Oveis, C., & Keltner, D. (2015). Affective and physiological responses to the suffering of others: Compassion and vagal activity. *Journal of Personality and Social Psychology, 108*(4), 572–585.

Stelmack, R. M., & Geen, R. G. (1992). The psychophysiology of extraversion. In A. Gale & M. W. Eysenck (Eds.), *Handbook of individual differences: Biological perspectives* (pp. 227–254). New York, NY: John Wiley & Sons.

Stephan, W. G., & Stephan, C. W. (2017). Intergroup threats. In C. G. Sibley & F. K. Barlow (Eds.), *The Cambridge handbook of the psychology of prejudice* (pp. 131–148). Cambridge, England: Cambridge University Press.

Stephens, D. P., & Few, A. L. (2007). The effects of images of African American women in hip hop on early adolescents' attitudes toward physical attractiveness and interpersonal relationships. *Sex Roles, 56*(3–4), 251–264.

Stepper, S., & Strack, F. (1993). Proprioceptive determinants of emotional and nonemotional feelings. *Journal of Personality and Social Psychology, 64*(2), 211–220.

Stern, C., & Rule, N. O. (2018). Physical androgyny and categorization difficulty shape political conservatives' attitudes toward transgender people. *Social Psychology and Personality Science, 9*(1), 24–31.

Stern, I., & Westphal, J. D. (2010). Stealthy footsteps to the boardroom: Executives' backgrounds, sophisticated interpersonal influence behavior, and board appointments. *Administrative Science Quarterly, 55*(2), 278–319.

Stevens, C. K., & Kristof, A. L. (1995). Making the right impression: A field study of applicant impression management during job interviews. *Journal of Applied Psychology, 80*(5), 587–606.

Stewart, A. L., & Tran, J. (2018). Protesting racial hierarchy: Testing a social dominance theory model of collective action among white Americans. *Journal of Social Issues, 74*(2), 299–316.

Stewart, E. C., & Bennett, M. J. (1991). *American cultural patterns: A cross-cultural perspective.* Yarmouth, ME: Intercultural Press.

Stewart-Williams, S. (2007). Altruism among kin vs. nonkin: Effects of cost of help and reciprocal exchange. *Evolution and Human Behavior, 28*(3), 193–198.

Stinson, D. A., Logel, C., Holmes, J. G., Wood, J. V., Forest, A. L., Gaucher, D.,. . .& Kath, J. (2010). The regulatory function of self-esteem: Testing the epistemic and acceptance signaling systems. *Journal of Personality and Social Psychology, 99*(6), 993–1013.

Stockley, P., & Campbell, A. (2013). Introduction: Female competition and aggression: interdisciplinary perspectives. *Philosophical Transactions of the Royal Society, 368*(1631).

Stokes, J., & Levin, I. (1986). Gender differences in predicting loneliness from social network characteristics. *Journal of Personality and Social Psychology, 51*(5), 1069–1074.

Stone, J., Wiegand, A. W., Cooper, J., & Aronson, E. (1997). When exemplification fails: Hypocrisy and the motive for self-integrity. *Journal of Personality and Social Psychology, 72*(1), 54–65.

Stoner, J. A. (1961). *A comparison of individual and group decisions involving risk* (Masters thesis, Massachusetts Institute of Technology). Retrieved from https://dspace.mit.edu/handle/1721.1/11330

Stouten, J., De Cremer, D., & van Dijk, E. (2006). Violating equality in social dilemmas: Emotional and retributive reactions as a function of trust, attribution, and honesty. *Personality and Social Psychology Bulletin, 32*(7), 894–906.

Strack, F. (2016). Reflection on the smiling registered replication report. *Perspectives on Psychological Science, 11*(6), 929–930.

Strack, F., & Deutsch, R. (2012). A theory of impulse and reflection. In P. A. Van Lange, A. W. Kruglanski, & E. T. Higgins (Eds.), *Handbook of theories of social psychology* (Vol. 1, pp. 97–117). Thousand Oaks, CA: Sage.

Strack, F., Martin, L. L., & Stepper, S. (1988). Inhibiting and facilitating conditions of the human smile: A nonobtrusive test of the facial feedback hypothesis. *Journal of Personality and Social Psychology, 54*(5), 768–777.

Stratham, A., & Rhoades, K. (2001). Gender and self-esteem: Narrative and efficacy in the negotiation of structural factors. In T. J. Owens, S. Stryker, & N. Goodman (Eds.), *Extending self-esteem theory and research: Sociological and psychological currents* (pp. 255–284). Cambridge, England: Cambridge University Press.

Straus, M. A., & Gelles, R. J. (1990). *Physical violence in American families: Risk factors and adaptations to violence in 8,145 families.* New Brunswick, NJ: Transaction.

Straus, M. A., Gelles, R. J., & Steinmetz, S. K. (1980). *Behind closed doors: Violence in the American family.* Garden City, NY: Anchor Press/Doubleday.

Straus, S. G., Parker, A. M., & Bruce, J. B. (2011). The group matters: A review of processes and outcomes in intelligence analysis. *Group Dynamics: Theory, Research, and Practice, 15*(2), 128–146.

Strauss, B. (2002). Social facilitation in motor tasks: A review of research and theory. *Psychology of Sport and Exercise, 3*(3), 237–256.

Street, R. L., Jr., & Brady, R. M. (1982). Speech rate acceptance ranges as a function of evaluative domain, listener speech rate, and communication context. *Communication Monographs, 49*(4), 290–308.

Streeter, S. A., & McBurney, D. H. (2003). Waist-to-hip ratio and attractiveness: New evidence and a critique of a "critical test." *Evolution and Human Behavior, 24*(2), 88–98.

Streib, J., Ayala, M., & Wixted, C. (2016). Benign inequality: Frames of poverty and social class inequality in children's movies. *Journal of Poverty, 21*(1), 1–19.

Stroebe, W. (2016). Firearm availability and violent death: The need for a culture change in attitudes towards guns. *Analyses of Social Issues and Public Policy, 16*(1), 7–35.

Stroebe, W., Postmes, T., & Spears, R. (2012). Scientific misconduct and the myth of self-correction in science. *Perspectives on Psychological Science, 7*(6), 670–688.

Stürmer, S., Snyder, M., Kropp, A., & Siem, B. (2006). Empathy-motivated helping: The moderating role of group membership. *Personality and Social Psychology Bulletin, 32*(7), 943–956.

Stürmer, S., Snyder, M., & Omoto, A. S. M. (2005). Prosocial emotions and helping: The moderating role of group membership. *Journal of Personality and Social Psychology, 88*(3), 532–546.

Stuss, D. T., Gallup, G. G., & Alexander, M. P. (2001). The frontal lobes are necessary for "theory of mind." *Brain, 124*(2), 279–286.

Suardi, A., Sotgiu, I., Costa, T., Cauda, F., & Rusconi, M. (2016). The neural correlates of happiness: A review of PET and fMRI studies using autobiographical recall methods. *Cognitive, Affective, & Behavioral Neuroscience, 16*(3), 383–392.

Sui, J., Zhu, Y., & Chiu, C.-y. (2007). Bicultural mind, self-construal, and self- and mother-reference effects: Consequences of cultural priming on recognition memory. *Journal of Experimental Social Psychology, 43*(5), 818–824.

Sumner, W. G. (1906). *Folkways: A study of the sociological importance of usages, manners, customs, mores, and morals.* New York, NY: Ginn.

Sunstein, C. R., & Zeckhauser, R. (2011). Overreaction to fearsome risks. *Environmental and Resource Economics, 48*(3), 435–449.

Sussman, N. M. (2000). The dynamic nature of cultural identity throughout cultural transitions: Why home is not so sweet. *Personality and Social Psychology Review, 4*(4), 355–373.

Swann, W. B., Jr., & Bosson, J. K. (2010). Self and identity. In S. T. Fiske, D. T. Gilbert, & G. Lindzey (Eds.), *Handbook of social psychology* (5th ed., Vol. 1, pp. 589–628). Hoboken, NJ: John Wiley & Sons.

Swann, W. B., Jr., De La Ronde, C., & Hixon, J. G. (1994). Authenticity and positive strivings in marriage and courtship. *Journal of Personality and Social Psychology, 66*(5), 857–869.

Swann, W. B. Jr., Gomez, A., Huici, C., Morales, J. F., & Hixon, J. G. (2010) Identity fusion and self-sacrifice: Arousal as a catalyst of pro-group fighting, dying and helping behavior. *Journal of Personality and Social Psychology, 99*(5), 82–841.

Swann, W. B., Jr., Milton, L. P., & Polzer, J. T. (2000). Should we create a niche or fall in line? Identity negotiation and small group effectiveness. *Journal of Personality and Social Psychology, 79*(2), 238–250.

Swim, J. K., Cohen, L. L., & Hyers, L. L. (1998). Experiencing everyday prejudice and discrimination. In J. K. Swim & C. Stangor (Eds.), *Prejudice: The targets' perspective* (pp. 37–60). San Diego, CA: Academic Press.

Swim, J. K., Ferguson, M. J., & Hyers, L. L. (1999). Avoiding stigma by distancing: Subtle prejudice against lesbians in the form of social distancing. *Basic and Applied Social Psychology, 21*(1), 61–68.

Swim, J. K, & Hyers, L. L. (2009). Sexism. In T. D. Nelson (Ed.), *Handbook of prejudice, stereotyping, and discrimination* (pp. 407–430). New York, NY: Psychology Press.

Swinton, W. (1880). *A complete course in geography: Physical, industrial, and political.* New York, NY: Ivison, Blakeman, Taylor.

Sy, T., Horton, C., & Riggio, R. (2018). Charismatic leadership: Eliciting and channeling follower emotions. *The Leadership Quarterly, 29*(1), 58–69.

Szymanski, D. M., & Henning, S. L. (2007). The role of self-objectification in women's depression: A test of objectification theory. *Sex Roles, 56*(1–2), 45–53.

T

Taggar, S., & Ellis, R. (2007). The role of leaders in shaping formal team norms. *The Leadership Quarterly, 18*(2), 105–120.

Tajfel, H., Billig, M. G., Bundy, R. P., & Flament, C. (1971). Social categorization and intergroup behavior. *European Journal of Social Psychology, 1*(2), 149–178.

Tajfel, H., & Turner, J. (1979). An integrative theory of intergroup conflict. In W. G. Austin & S. Worchel (Eds.), *The social psychology of intergroup relations* (pp. 33–47). Monterey, CA: Brooks/Cole.

Takahashi, A., Quadros, I. M., de Almeida, R. M. M., & Miczek, K. A. (2011). Brain serotonin receptors and transporters: Initiation vs. termination of escalated aggression. *Psychopharmacology, 213*(2–3), 83–212.

Takemura, K., & Arimoto, H. (2008). Independent self in Japan's "North Frontier": An experiment of cognitive dissonance in Hokkaido. *The Japanese Journal of Experimental Social Psychology, 48*(1), 40–49.

Talamas, S. N., Mavor, K. I., & Perrett, D. I. (2016). Blinded by beauty: Attractiveness bias and accurate perceptions of academic performance. *PLoS One, 11*(2), e0148284.

Talbot, K. K., Neill, K. S., & Rankin, L. L. (2010). Rape-accepting attitudes of university undergraduate students. *Journal of Forensic Nursing, 6*(4), 170–179.

Tamir, M., & Mauss, I. B. (2011). Social cognitive factors in emotion regulation: Implications for well-being. In I. Nyklíček, A. Vingerhoets, & M. Zeelenberg (Eds.), *Emotion regulation and well-being* (pp. 31–47). New York, NY: Springer.

Tamplin, N. C., McLean, S. A., & Paxton, S. J. (2018). Social media literacy protects against the negative impact of exposure to appearance ideal social media images in young adult women but not men. *Body Image, 26*, 29–37.

Tanford, S., & Penrod, S. (1984). Social influence model: A formal integration of research on majority and minority influence. *Psychological Bulletin, 95*(2), 189–225.

Tang, E. (2019, June 26). Here are the 30 countries where same-sex marriage is officially legal. *Good Morning America.* Retrieved from https://www.goodmorningamerica.com/culture/story/27-countries-sex-marriage-officially-legal-56041136

Tankard, M. E., & Paluck, E. L. (2017). The effect of a supreme court decision regarding gay marriage on social norms and personal attitudes. *Psychological Science, 28*(9), 1334–1344.

Tannenbaum, M. B., Hepler, J., Zimmerman, R. S., Saul, L., Jacobs, S., Wilson, K., & Albarracín, D. (2015). Appealing to fear: A meta-analysis of fear appeal effectiveness and theories. *Psychological Bulletin, 141*(6), 1178–1204.

Tarde, G. (1903). *The laws of imitation.* (E. C. Parson, Trans.). New York, NY: Henry Holt. (Original work published in 1890).

Tashiro, T., & Frazier, P. (2003). "I'll never be in a relationship like that again": Personal growth following romantic relationship breakups. *Personal Relationships, 10*(1), 113–128.

Tata, J., Anthony, T., Lin, H., Newman, B., Tang, S., Millson, M., & Sivakumar, K. (1996). Proportionate group size and rejection of the deviate: A meta-analytic integration. *Journal of Social Behavior and Personality, 11,* 739–752.

Tatum, A. K. (2017). The interaction of same-sex marriage access with sexual minority identity on mental health and subjective wellbeing. *Journal of Homosexuality, 64*(5), 638–653.

Taylor, C. A., Manganello, J. A., Lee, S. J., & Rice, J. C. (2010). Mothers' spanking of 3-year-old children and subsequent risk of children's aggressive behavior. *Pediatrics, 125*(5), 1057–1065.

Taylor, D. M., Wright, S. C., Moghaddam, F. M., & Lalonde, R. N. (1990). The personal/group discrimination discrepancy: Perceiving my group, but not myself, to be a target for discrimination. *Personality and Social Psychology Bulletin, 16*(2), 254–262.

Taylor, L. S., Fiore, A. T., Mendelsohn, G. A., & Cheshire, C. (2011). "Out of my league": A real-world test of the matching hypothesis. *Personality and Social Psychology Bulletin, 37*(7), 942–954.

Taylor, S. E., & Brown, J. D. (1988). Illusion and well-being: A social psychological perspective on mental health. *Psychological Bulletin, 103*(2), 193–210.

Taylor, S. E., & Fiske, S. T. (1975). Point of view and perceptions of causality. *Journal of Personality and Social Psychology, 32*(3), 439–445.

Taylor, S. E., & Gonzaga, G. C. (2007). Affiliative responses to stress: A social neuroscience model. In E. Harmon-Jones & P. Winkielman (Eds.), *Social neuroscience: Integrating biological and psychological explanations of social behavior* (pp. 454–473). New York, NY: Guilford Press.

Taylor, S. E., Lerner, J. S., Herman, D. K., Sage, R. M., & McDowell, N. K. (2003). Portrait of the self-enhancer: Well adjusted and well liked or maladjusted and friendless? *Journal of Personality and Social Psychology, 84*(1), 165–176.

Teachman, B. A., Gapinski, K. D., Brownell, K. D., Rawlins, M., & Jeyaram, S. (2003). Demonstrations of implicit anti-fat bias: The impact of providing causal information and evoking empathy. *Health Psychology, 22*(1), 68–78.

Teagarden, M. B. (2007). Best practices in cross-cultural leadership. In J. A. Conger & R. E. Riggio (Eds.), *The practice of leadership: Developing the next generation of leaders* (pp. 300–330). San Francisco, CA: Jossey-Bass.

Telles, E. E., & Marguia, E. (1990). Phenotype discrimination and income differences among Mexican Americans. *Social Science Quarterly, 71*(4), 682–696.

Tetlock, P. E., Peterson, R. S., McGuire, C., Chang, S. -j., & Feld, P. (1992). Assessing political group dynamics: A test of the groupthink model. *Journal of Personality and Social Psychology, 63*(3), 403–425.

t'Hart, P., Rosenthal, U., & Kouzmin, A. (1993). Crisis decision making: The centralization thesis revisited. *Administration and Society, 25*(1), 12–45.

Theodore, P. S., & Basow, S. A. (2000). Heterosexual masculinity and homophobia: A reaction to the self? *Journal of Homosexuality, 40*(2), 31–48.

Theron, W. H., Matthee, D. D., Steel, H. R., & Ramirez, J. M. (2000). Direct and indirect aggression in women: A comparison between South African and Spanish university students. In J. M. Ramirez & D. S. Richardson (Eds.), *Cross-cultural approaches to research on aggression and reconciliation* (pp. 99–109). Huntington, NY: Nova Science.

Thibaut, J. W., & Kelley, H. H. (1959). *The social psychology of groups.* New York, NY: John Wiley & Sons.

Thomaes, S., & Bushman, B. J. (2011). Mirror, mirror, on the wall, who's the most aggressive of them all? Narcissism, self-esteem, and aggression. In P. R. Shaver & M. Mikulincer (Eds.), *Human aggression and violence: Causes, manifestations, and consequences* (pp. 203–219). Washington, DC: American Psychological Association.

Thomas, G. , Fletcher, G. J., & Lange, C. (1997). One-line empathic accuracy in marital interaction. *Journal of Personality and Social Psychology, 72*(4), 839–850.

Thomas, J. J., & Daubman, K. A. (2001). The relationship between friendship quality and self-esteem in adolescent girls and boys. *Sex Roles, 45*(1–2), 53–65.

Thompson, D. K. (2011). Functional magnetic resonance imaging: Critical analysis of techniques and interpretation. *Journal of the International Neuropsychological Society, 17*(2), 376–379.

Thorndike, E. L. (1911). *Animal intelligence: Experimental studies.* New York, NY: Macmillan.

Thornton, K. C. (2003). When the source of embarrassment is a close other. *Individual Differences Research, 1*(3), 189–200.

Tice, D. M. (1991). Esteem protection or enhancement? Self-handicapping motives and attributions differ by trait self-esteem. *Journal of Personality and Social Psychology, 60*(5), 711–725.

Tice, D. M., & Baumeister, R. F. (1985). Masculinity inhibits helping in emergencies: Personality does predict the bystander effect. *Journal of Personality and Social Psychology, 49*(2), 420–428.

Tice, D. M., Baumeister, R. F., Shmueli, D., & Muraven, M. (2007). Restoring the self: Positive affect helps improve self-regulation following ego depletion. *Journal of Experimental Social Psychology, 43*(3), 379–384.

Tice, D. M., Bratslavsky, E., & Baumeister, R. F. (2001). Emotional distress regulation takes precedence over impulse control: If you feel bad, do it! *Journal of Personality and Social Psychology, 80*(1), 53–67.

Tickle, J. J., Hull, J. G., Sargent, J. D., Dalton, M. A., & Heatherton, T. F. (2006). A structural equation model of social influences and exposure to media smoking on adolescent smoking. *Basic and Applied Social Psychology, 28*(2), 117–129.

Tiggemann, M., Hayden, S., Brown, Z., & Veldhuis, J. (2018). The effect of Instagram "likes" on women's social comparison and body dissatisfaction. *Body Image, 26,* 90–97.

Timmers, M., Fischer, A. H., & Manstead, A. S. (1998). Gender differences in motives for regulating emotions. *Personality and Social Psychology Bulletin, 24*(9), 974–985.

Tjaden, P., & Thoennes, N. (2000). *Extent, nature, and consequences of intimate partner violence.* Washington, DC: U.S. Department of Justice.

Toates, F. (2006). A model of the hierarchy of behaviour, cognition, and consciousness. *Consciousness and Cognition: An International Journal, 15*(1), 75–118.

Todd, A. R., Seok, D., Kerr, N. L., & Messé, L. A. (2006). Social compensation: Fact or social comparison artifact? *Group Processes and Intergroup Relations, 9*(3), 431–442.

Todd, P., Penke, L., Fasolo, B., & Lenton, A. P. (2007). Different cognitive processes underlie human mate choices and mate preferences. *Proceedings of the National Academy of Sciences, 104*(38), 15011–15016.

Tolnay, S. E., & Beck, E. M. (1995). *A festival of violence: An analysis of Southern lynchings, 1882–1930*. Urbana, IL: University of Illinois Press.

Tolstedt, B. E., & Stokes, J. P. (1984). Self-disclosure, intimacy, and the depenetration process. *Journal of Personality and Social Psychology, 46*(1), 84–90.

Toma, C. L., & Hancock, J. T. (2013). Self-affirmation underlies Facebook use. *Personality and Social Psychology Bulletin, 39*(3), 321–331.

Tomasello, M. (2011). Human culture in evolutionary perspective. In M. J. Gelfand, C. -y. Chiu, & Y. -y. Hong. (Eds.), *Advances in culture and psychology* (Vol. 1, pp. 5–51). New York, NY: Oxford University Press.

Toosi, N. R., Babbitt, L. G., Ambady, N., & Sommers, S. R. (2012). Dyadic interracial interactions: A meta-analysis. *Psychological Bulletin, 138*(1), 1–27.

Tormala, Z. L., & Petty, R. E. (2002). What doesn't kill me makes me stronger: The effects of resisting persuasion on attitude certainty. *Journal of Personality and Social Psychology, 83*(6), 1298–1313.

Tormala, Z. L., & Petty, R. E. (2007). Contextual contrast and perceived knowledge: Exploring the implications for persuasion. *Journal of Experimental Social Psychology, 43*(1), 17–30.

Törnberg, P. (2018). Echo chambers and viral misinformation: Modeling fake news as complex contagion. *PLoS One, 13*(9), e0203958.

Tower, R. K., Kelly, C., & Richards, A. (1997). Individualism, collectivism and reward allocation: A cross-cultural study in Russia and Britain. *British Journal of Social Psychology, 36*(3), 331–345.

Townsend, J. M., & Wasserman, T. (1997). The perception of sexual attractiveness: Sex differences in variability. *Archives of Sexual Behavior, 26*(3), 243–268.

Trafimow, D., Triandis, H. C., & Goto, S. G. (1991). Some tests of the distinction between the private self and the collective self. *Journal of Personality and Social Psychology, 60*(5), 649–655.

Trapnell, P. D., & Campbell, J. D. (1999). Private self-consciousness and the five-factor model of personality: Distinguishing rumination from reflection. *Journal of Personality and Social Psychology, 76*(2), 284–304.

Travis, L. E. (1925). The effect of a small audience upon eye-hand coordination. *Journal of Abnormal and Social Psychology, 20*(2), 142–146.

Trawalter, S., Richeson, J. A., & Shelton, J. N. (2009). Predicting behavior during interracial interactions: A stress and coping approach. *Personality and Social Psychology Review, 13*(4), 243–268.

Treadway, D. C., Ferris, G. R., Duke, A. B., Adams, G. L., & Thatcher, J. B. (2007). The moderating role of subordinate political skill on supervisors' impressions of subordinate ingratiation and ratings of subordinate interpersonal facilitation. *Journal of Applied Psychology, 92*(3), 848–855.

Tremblay, R. E., & Nagin, D. S. (2005). The developmental origins of physical aggression in humans. In R. E. Tremblay, W. W. Hartup, & J. Archer (Eds.), *Developmental origins of aggression* (pp. 83–106). New York, NY: Guilford Press.

Triandis, H. C. (1972). *The analysis of subjective culture*. Oxford, England: Wiley-Interscience.

Triandis, H. C. (1989). The self and social behavior in differing cultural contexts. *Psychological Review, 96*(3), 506–520.

Triandis, H. C., Botempo, R., Villareal, M. J., Asai, M., & Lucca, N. (1988). Individualism and collectivism: Cross-cultural perspectives on self-ingroup relationships. *Journal of Personality and Social Psychology, 54*(2), 323–338.

Triplett, N. (1897). The dynamogenic factors in pacemaking and competition. *American Journal of Psychology, 9*(4), 507–533.

Triplett, N. (1898). The dynamogenic factors in pacemaking and competition. *American Journal of Psychology, 9*(4), 507–533.

Trivers, R. L. (1971). The evolution of reciprocal altruism. *Quarterly Review of Biology, 46*(1), 35–57.

Trivers, R. L. (1983). The evolution of cooperation. In D. L. Bridgeman (Ed.), *The nature of prosocial development* (pp. 43–61). New York, NY: Academic Press.

Troisi, J. D., & Gabriel, S. (2011). Chicken soup really is good for the soul: "Comfort food" fulfills the need to belong. *Psychological Science, 22*(6), 747–753.

Trudeau, K. J., & Devlin, S. (1996). College students and community service: Who, with whom, and why? *Journal of Applied Social Psychology, 26*(21), 1867–1888.

Tsukamoto, S., & Fiske, S. T. (2018). Perceived threat to national values in evaluating stereotyped immigrants. *The Journal of Social Psychology, 158*(2), 157–172.

Turetsky, K. M., & Riddle, T. A. (2018). Porous chambers, echoes of valence and stereotypes: A network analysis of online news coverage interconnectedness following a nationally polarizing race-related event. *Social Psychological and Personality Science, 9*(2), 163–175.

Turner, F. J. (1920). *The frontier in American history*. New York, NY: Henry Holt.

Turner, J. C. (1987). *Rediscovering the social group: A self-categorization theory*. Oxford, England: Basil Blackwell.

Turner, M. E., Pratkanis, A. R., & Struckman, C. K. (2007). Groupthink as social identity maintenance. In A. R. Pratkanis (Ed.), *The science of social influence: Advances and future progress* (pp. 223–246). New York, NY: Psychology Press.

Tversky, A., & Kahneman, D. (1973). Availability: A heuristic for judging frequency and probability. *Cognitive Psychology, 5*(2), 207–232.

Tversky, A., & Kahneman, D. (1974). Judgment under uncertainty: Heuristics and biases. *Science, 185*(4157), 1124–1131.

Twenge, J. M. (1997). Changes in masculine and feminine traits over time: A meta-analysis. *Sex Roles, 36*(5–6), 305–325.

Twenge, J. M., & Campbell, W. K. (2001). Age and birth cohort differences in self-esteem: A cross-temporal meta-analysis. *Personality and Social Psychology Review, 5*(4), 321–344.

Twenge, J. M., & Campbell, W. K. (2008). Increases in positive self-views among high school students: Birth cohort changes in anticipated performance, self-satisfaction, self-liking, and self-competence. *Psychological Science, 19*(11), 1082–1086.

Twenge, J. M., Campbell, W. K., & Gentile, B. (2013). Changes in pronoun use in American books and the rise of individualism, 1960–2008. *Journal of Cross-Cultural Psychology, 44*(3), 406–415.

Twenge, J. M., Carter, N. T., & Campbell, W. K. (2015). Time period, generational, and age differences in tolerance for controversial beliefs and lifestyles in the United States, 1972–2012. *Social Forces, 94*(1), 379–399.

Twenge, J. M., Catanese, K. R., & Baumeister, R. F. (2003). Social exclusion and the deconstructed state: Time perception, meaninglessness, lethargy, lack of emotion, and self-awareness. *Journal of Personality and Social Psychology, 85*(3), 409–423.

Twenge, J. M., Dawson, L., & Campbell, W. K. (2016). Still standing out: Children's names in the United States during the Great Recession and correlations with economic indicators. *Journal of Applied Social Psychology, 46*(11), 663–670.

Tykocinski, O. E. (2001). I never had a chance: Using hindsight tactics to mitigate disappointments. *Personality and Social Psychology Bulletin, 27*(3), 376–382.

Tyler, J. M. (2012). Triggering self-presentation efforts outside of people's conscious awareness. *Personality and Social Psychology Bulletin, 38*(5), 619–627.

Tyler, J. M., Feldman, R. S., & Reichert, A. (2006). The price of deceptive behavior: Disliking and lying to people who lie to us. *Journal of Experimental Social Psychology, 42*(1), 69–77.

Tyler, T. R. (1997). The psychology of legitimacy: A relational perspective on voluntary deference to authorities. *Personality and Social Psychology Review, 1*(4), 323–345.

U

U.S. Bureau of the Census. (1998). *Statistical abstract of the United States* (118th ed.). Washington, DC: U.S. Government Printing Office.

Uehara, E. S. (1995). Reciprocity reconsidered: Gouldner's "moral norm of reciprocity" and social support. *Journal of Social and Personal Relationships, 12*(4), 483–502.

Uleman, J. S. (1999). Spontaneous versus intentional inferences in impression formation. In S. Chaiken & Y. Trope (Eds.), *Dual-process theories in social psychology* (pp. 141–160). New York, NY: Guilford Press.

Ullah, A. A. (2011). HIV/AIDS-Related stigma and discrimination: A study of health care providers in Bangladesh. *Journal of International Association of Physicians in AIDS Care, 10*(2), 97–104.

Unger, L. S. (1996). The potential for using humor in global advertising. *Humor: International Journal of Humor Research, 9*(2), 143–168.

Unger, R. K. (2002). Them and us: Hidden ideologies—Differences in degree or kind? *Analyses of Social Issues and Public Policy, 2*(1), 43–52.

Unger, R. K. (2011). SPSSI leaders: Collective biography and the dilemma of value-laden action and value-neutral research. *Journal of Social Issues, 67*(1), 73–91.

UNICEF. (2017). *A familiar face: Violence in the lives of children and adolescents.* New York, NY: United Nations Children Fund.

Uniform Crime Reporting (UCR) Program. (2018, September 10). *Federal Bureau of Investigation.* Retrieved from https://www.fbi.gov/services/cjis/ucr

United Nations Office on Drugs and Crime. (2017). Homicide dataset 2019 (table). *UNODC.* Retrieved from https://dataunodc.un.org/GSH_app

United Nations Office on Drugs and Crime. (2019). *Global study on homicide: Trends, context, data.* Vienna, Austria: UNODC.

United States Census Bureau. (2018, July 1). QuickFacts: Cincinnati city, Ohio. *United States Census Bureau.* Retrieved from https://www.census.gov/quickfacts/cincinnaticityohio

Uskul, A. K., Oyserman, D., Schwarz, N., Lee, S. W., & Xu, A. J. (2013). How successful you have been in life depends on the response scale used: The role of cultural mindsets in pragmatic inferences drawn from question format. *Social Cognition, 31*(2), 222–236.

Uziel, L. (2007). Individual differences in the social facilitation effect: A review and meta-analysis. *Journal of Research in Personality, 41*(3), 579–601.

Uziel, L. (2018). The intricacies of the pursuit of higher self-control. *Current Directions in Psychological Science, 27*(2), 79–84.

V

Vadillo, M. A., Gold, N., & Osman, M. (2016). The bitter truth about sugar and willpower: The limited evidential value of the glucose model of ego depletion. *Psychological Science, 27*(9), 1207–1214.

Vaillancourt, T. (2013). Do human females use indirect aggression as an intrasexual competition strategy? *Philosophical Transactions of the Royal Society, 368*(1631) doi:10.1098/rstb.2013.0080

Vaillancourt, T. & Sharma, A. (2011). Intolerance of sexy peers: Intrasexual competition among women. *Aggressive Behavior, 37*(6), 569–577.

Valenzano, D. R., Mennucci, A., Tartarelli, G., & Cellerino, A. (2006). Shape analysis of female facial attractiveness. *Vision Research, 46*(8–9), 1282–1291.

Valkenburg, P. M., & Peter, J. (2007). Preadolescents' and adolescents' online communication and their closeness to friends. *Developmental Psychology, 43*(2), 267 277.

van Baaren, R. B., Fockenberg, D. A., Holland, R. W., Janssen, L., & van Knippenberg, A. (2006). The moody chameleon: The effect of mood on non-conscious mimicry. *Social Cognition, 24*(4), 426–437.

van Baaren, R. B., Holland, R. W., Kawakami, K., & van Knippenberg, A. (2004). Mimicry and prosocial behavior. *Psychological Science, 15*(1), 71–74.

van Baaren, R. B., Maddux, W. W., Chartrand, T. L., de Bouter, C., & van Knippenberg, A. (2003). It takes two to mimic: Behavioral consequences of self-construals. *Journal of Personality and Social Psychology, 84*(5), 1093–1102.

Van Bavel, J. J., & Cunningham, W. A. (2012). A social identity approach to person memory: Group membership, collective identification, and social role shape attention and memory. *Personality and Social Psychology Bulletin, 38*(12), 1566–1578.

Van Boven, L., Ehret, P. J., & Sherman, D. K. (2018). Psychological barriers to bipartisan public support for climate policy. *Perspectives on Psychological Science, 13*(4), 492–507.

van de Kragt, A. J. C., Dawes, R. M., Orbell, J. M., Braver, S. R., & Wilson, L. A. (1986). Doing well and doing good as ways of resolving social dilemmas. In H. A. Wilke, D. M. Messick, & C. G. Rutte (Eds.), *Experimental social dilemmas* (pp. 177–204). Frankfurt, Germany: Verlag Peter Lang.

Vandello, J. A., & Bosson, J. K. (2013). Hard won and easily lost: A review and synthesis of theory and research on precarious manhood. *Psychology of Men and Masculinity, 14*(2), 101–113.

Vandello, J. A., Cohen, D., & Ransom, S. (2008). U.S. southern and northern differences in perceptions of norms about aggression: Mechanisms for the perpetuation of a culture of honor. *Journal of Cross-Cultural Psychology, 39*(2), 162–177.

Vandello, J. A., Ransom, S., Hettinger, V. E., & Askew, K. (2009). Men's misperceptions about the acceptability and attractiveness of aggression. *Journal of Experimental Social Psychology, 45*(6), *1209–*1219.

van de Rijt, A., & Macy, M. W. (2006). Power and dependence in intimate exchange. *Social Forces, 84*(3), 1455–1470.

van den Bos, W., van Dijk, E., Westenberg, M., Rombouts, S. A., & Crone, E. A. (2011). Changing brains, changing perspectives: The neurocognitive development of reciprocity. *Psychological Science, 22*(1), 60–70.

Vanderbleek, L., Robinson, E. H., Casado-Kehoe, M., & Young, M. E. (2011). The relationship between play and couple satisfaction and stability. *The Family Journal, 19*(2), 132–139.

Vanderdrift, L. E., Lehmiller, J. J., & Kelly, J. R. (2010). Commitment in friends with benefits relationships: Implications for relational and safe-sex outcomes. *Personal Relationships, 19*(1), 1–13.

Van der Zee, K., Oldersma, F., Buunk, B. P., & Bos, D. (1998). Social comparison preferences among cancer patients as related to neuroticism and social comparison orientation. *Journal of Personality and Social Psychology, 75*(3), 801–810.

van Dijk, H., & van Engen, M. L. (2013). A status perspective on the consequences of work group diversity. *Journal of Occupational and Organizational Psychology, 86*(2), 223–241.

Vandiver, D. M., & Dupalo, J. R. (2013). Factors that affect college students' perceptions of rape: What is the role of gender and other situational factors? *International Journal of Offender Therapy and Comparative Criminology, 57*(5), 592–612.

Vanhaudenhuyse, A., Demertzi, A., Schabus, M., Noirhomme, Q., Bredart, S., Boly, M., . . .Laureys, S. (2011). Two distinct neuronal networks mediate the awareness of environment and of self. *Journal of Cognitive Neuroscience, 23*(3), 570–578.

Van Hiel, A., Pandelaere, M., & Duriez, B. (2004). The impact of need for closure on conservative beliefs and racism: Differential mediation by authoritarian submission and authoritarian dominance. *Personality and Social Psychology Bulletin, 30*(7), 824–837.

Van Hiel, A., Vanneste, S., & De Cremer, D. (2008). Why did they claim too much? The role of causal attributions in explaining level of cooperation in commons and anticommons dilemmas. *Journal of Applied Social Psychology, 38*(1), 173–197.

Vanhoomissen, T., & Van Overwalle, F. (2010). Me or not me as source of ingroup favoritism and outgroup derogation: A connectionist perspective. *Social Cognition, 28*(1), 84–110.

Van Lange, P. A. M. (1999). The pursuit of joint outcomes and equality in outcomes: An integrative model of social value orientation. *Journal of Personality and Social Psychology, 77*(2), 337–349.

Van Lange, P. A., Otten, W., De Bruin, E. M., & Joireman, J. A. (1997). Development of prosocial, individualistic, and competitive orientations: Theory and preliminary evidence. *Journal of Personality and Social Psychology, 73*(4), 733–746.

Van Overwalle, R., Drenth, T., & Marsman, G. (1999). Spontaneous trait inferences: Are they linked to the actor or to the action? *Personality and Social Psychology Bulletin, 25*(4), 450–462.

van Staden, W., & Coetzee, K. (2010). Conceptual relations between loneliness and culture. *Current Opinion in Psychiatry, 23*(6), 524–529.

van Veelen, R., Eisenbeiss, K. K., & Otten, S. (2016). Newcomers to social categories: Longitudinal predictors and consequences of ingroup identification. *Personality and Social Psychology Bulletin, 42*(6), 811–825.

Van Vugt, M., & Hart, C. M. (2004). Social identity as social glue: The origins of group loyalty. *Journal of Experimental Social Psychology, 86*(4), 585–598.

Van Zalk, N., Van Zalk, M., Kerr, M., & Stattin, H. (2011). Social anxiety as a basis for friendship selection and socialization in adolescents' social networks. *Journal of Personality, 79*(3), 499–526.

Vangelisti, A. L., Knapp, M. L., & Daly, J. A. (1990). Conversational narcissism. *Communication Monographs, 57*(4), 251–274.

Vannier, S. A., Currie, A. B., & O'Sullivan, L. F. (2014). Schoolgirls and soccer moms: A content analysis of free "teen" and "MILF" online pornography. *Journal of Sex Research, 51*(3), 253–264.

Varma, A., Toh, S. M., & Pichler, S. (2006). Ingratiation in job applications: Impact on selection decisions. *Journal of Managerial Psychology, 21*(3), 200–210.

Vartanian, L. R., & Hopkinson, M. M. (2010). Social connectedness, conformity, and internalization of societal standards of attractiveness. *Body Image, 7*(1), 86–89.

Vartanian, L. R., & Smyth, J. M. (2013). Primum non nocere: Obesity stigma and public health. *Journal of Bioethical Inquiry, 10*(1), 49–57.

Vasquez, K., Oswald, D. L., & Hammer, A. (2019). Being dishonest about our prejudices: Moral dissonance and self-justification. *Ethics & Behavior, 29*(5), 382–404.

Vaughn, B. E., & Langlois, J. H. (1983). Physical attractiveness as a correlate of peer status and social competence in preschool children. *Developmental Psychology, 19*(4), 561–567.

Veltkamp, M., Custers, R., & Aarts, H. (2011). Motivating consumer behavior by subliminal conditioning in the absence of basic needs: Striking even while the iron is cold. *Journal of Consumer Psychology, 21*(1), 49–56.

Veltri, C. O., Sellbom, M., Graham, J. R., Ben-Porath, Y. S., Forbey, J. D., & White, R. S. (2014). Distinguishing personality psychopathology five (PSY-5) characteristics associated with violent and nonviolent juvenile delinquency. *Journal of Personality Assessment, 96*(2), 158–165.

Verkuyten, M., Drabbles, M., & van den Nieuwenhuijzen, K. (1999). Self-categorization and emotional reactions to ethnic minorities. *European Journal of Social Psychology, 29*(5–6), 605–619.

Verkuyten, M., & Yildiz, A. A. (2007). National (dis) identification and ethnic and religious identity: A study among Turkish-Dutch Muslims. *Personality and Social Psychology Bulletin, 33*(10), 1448–1462.

Vicary, A. M., & Fraley, R. C. (2007). Choose your own adventure: Attachment dynamics in a simulated relationship. *Personality and Social Psychology Bulletin, 33*(9), 1279–1291.

Victoroff, J., Quota, S., Adelman, J. R., Celinska, B., Stern, N., Wilcox, R., & Sapolsky, R. M. (2011). Support for religio-political aggression among teenaged boys in Gaza: Part II: Neuroendocrinological findings. *Aggressive Behavior, 37*(2), 121–132.

Vince, G. (2006, April 19). Watching the brain "switch off" self-awareness. *NewScientist*. Retrieved from https://www.newscientist.com/article/dn9019-watching-the-brain-switch-off-self-awareness/

Vincent, L. C., Emich, K. J., & Goncalo, J. A. (2013). Stretching the moral gray zone: Positive affect, moral disengagement, and dishonesty. *Psychological Science, 24*(4), 595–599.

Vitaro, F., & Brendgen, M. (2005). Proactive and reactive aggression: A developmental perspective. In R. E. Tremblay, W. W. Hartup, & J. Archer (Eds.), *Developmental origins of aggression* (pp. 178–201). New York, NY: Guilford Press.

Vogel, T., Kutzner, F., Fiedler, K., & Freytag, P. (2010). Exploiting attractiveness in persuasion: Senders' implicit theories about receivers' processing motivation. *Personality and Social Psychology Bulletin, 36*(6), 830–842

von Borries, A. K., Volman, I., de Bruijn, E. R., Bulten, B. H., Verkes, R. J., & Roelofs, K. (2012). Psychopaths lack the automatic avoidance of social threat: Relation to instrumental aggression. *Psychiatry Research, 200*(2–3), 761–766.

Vonofakou, C., Hewstone, M., & Voci, A. (2007). Contact with out-group friends as a predictor of meta-attitudinal strength and accessibility of attitudes toward gay men. *Journal of Personality and Social Psychology, 92*(5), 804–820.

Vrij, A. (2000). *Detecting lies and deceit: The psychology of lying and the implications for professional practice.* Chichester, England: John Wiley & Sons.

W

Wadsworth, T. (2014). Sex and the pursuit of happiness: How other people's sex lives are related to our sense of well-being. *Social Indicators Research, 116*(1), 115–135.

Wagenmakers, E. -J., Beek, T., Dijkhoff, L., Gronau, Q. F., Acosta, A., Adams, R. B., Jr.,. . .Zwaan, R. A. (2016). Registered replication report: Strack, Martin, & Stepper (1988). *Perspectives on Psychological Science, 11*(6), 917–928.

Wahl, O. F. (2012). Stigma as a barrier to recovery from mental illness. *Trends in Cognitive Sciences, 16*(1), 9–10.

Wakefield, M. A., Loken, B., & Hornik, R. C. (2010). Use of mass media campaigns to change health behaviour. *Lancet, 376*(9748), 1261–1271.

Wakslak, C. J., Jost, J. T., Tyler, T. R., & Chen, E. (2007). Moral outrage mediates the dampening effect of system justification on support for redistributive social policies. *Psychological Science, 18*(3), 267–274.

Waldinger, R. J., & Schulz, M. S. (2016). The long reach of nurturing family environments: Links with midlife emotion-regulatory styles and late-life security in intimate relationships. *Psychological Science, 27*(11), 1443–1450.

Walker, K., & Sleath, E. (2017). A systematic review of the current knowledge regarding revenge pornography and non-consensual sharing of sexually explicit media. *Aggression and Violent Behavior, 36*, 9–24.

Wall, J. A., Jr., Beriker, N., & Wu, S. (2010). Turkish community mediation. *Journal of Applied Social Psychology, 40*(8), 2019–2042.

Walsh, R. (2011). Helping or hurting: Are adolescent intervention programs minimizing racial inequality? *Education and Urban Society, 43*(3), 370–395.

Walster, E., Walster, G. W., & Traupmann, J. (1978). Equity and premarital sex. *Journal of Personality, 36*(1), 82–92.

Walton, G. M. (2014). The new science of wise psychological interventions. *Current Directions in Psychological Science, 23*(1), 73–82.

Walumbwa, F. O., Lawler, J. J., & Avolio, B. J. (2007). Leadership, individual differences, and work-related attitudes: A cross-culture investigation. *Applied Psychology: An International Review, 56*(2), 212–230.

Wang, Q. (2006). Culture and the development of self-knowledge. *Current Directions in Psychological Science, 15*(4), 182–187.

Wang, S. S., Brownell, K. D., & Wadden, T. A. (2004). The influence of the stigma of obesity on overweight individuals. *International Journal of Obesity, 28*(10), 1333–1337.

Wann, D. L., Haynes, G., McLean, B., & Pullen, P. (2003). Sport team identification and willingness to consider anonymous acts of hostile aggression. *Aggressive Behavior, 29*(5), 406–413.

Wanshaffe, K. R. (2002). Social facilitation in young toddlers. *Psychological Reports, 90*(1), 349–350.

Ward, A., Lyubomirsky, S., Sousa, L., & Nolen-Hoeksema, S. (2003). Can't quite commit: Rumination and uncertainty. *Personality and Social Psychology Bulletin, 29*(1), 96–107.

Warneken, F., & Tomasello, M. (2013). The emergence of contingent reciprocity in young children. *Journal of Experimental Child Psychology, 116*(2), 338–350.

Watts, T. W., Duncan, G. J., & Quan, H. (2018). Revisiting the marshmallow test: A conceptual replication investigating links between early delay of gratification and later outcomes. *Psychological Science, 29*(7), 1159–1177.

Waytz, A., & Gray, K. (2018). Does online technology make us more or less sociable? A preliminary review and call for research. *Perspectives on Psychological Science, 13*(4), 473–491.

Weary, G., Vaughhn, L. A., Stewart, B. D., & Edwards, J. A. (2006). Adjusting for the correspondence bias: Effects of causal uncertainty, cognitive busyness, and causal strength of situational information. *Journal of Experimental Social Psychology, 42*(1), 87–94.,

Webb, T. T., Looby, E. J., & Fults-McMurtery, R. (2004). African American men's perceptions of body figure attractiveness: An acculturation study. *Journal of Black Studies, 34*(3), 370–385.

Webb, T. L., & Sheeran, P. (2003). Can implementation intentions help to overcome ego-depletion? *Journal of Experimental Social Psychology, 39*(3), 279–286.

Weber, E. U., Böckenholt, U., Hilton, D. J., & Wallace, B. (1993). Determinants of diagnostic hypothesis generation: Effects of information, base rates, and experience. *Journal of Experimental Psychology: Learning, Memory, and Cognition, 19*(5), 1151–1164.

Wechsler, H., Lee, J. E., Kuo, M., Seibring, M., Nelson, T. F., & Lee, H. (2002). Trends in college binge drinking during a period of increased prevention efforts: Findings from 4 Harvard School of Public Health college alcohol study surveys, 1993–2001. *Journal of American College Health, 50*(5), 203–217.

Wedell, D. H., Parducci, A., & Geiselman, R. E. (1987). A formal analysis of ratings of physical attractiveness: Successive contrast and simultaneous association. *Journal of Experimental Social Psychology, 23*(3), 230–249.

Weeks, J. W., Heimberg, R. G., & Heuer, R. (2011). Exploring the role of behavior submissiveness in social anxiety. *Journal of Social and clinical Psychology, 30*(3), 217–249.

Wegener, D. T., Clark, J. K., & Petty, R. E. (2006). Not all stereotyping is created equal: Differential consequences of thoughtful versus nonthoughtful stereotyping. *Journal of Personality and Social Psychology, 90*(1), 42–59.

Wegener, D. T., & Petty, R. E. (1994). Mood management across affective states: The hedonic contingency hypothesis. *Journal of Personality and Social Psychology, 66*(6), 1034–1048.

Wegener, D. T., Petty, R. E., Smoak, N. D., & Fabrigar, L. R. (2004). Multiple routes to resisting attitude change. In E. S. Knowles & J. A. Linn (Eds.), *Resistance and persuasion* (pp. 13–38). Mahwah NJ: Lawrence Erlbaum Associates.

Wegener, D. T., Petty, R. E., & Smith, S. M. (1995). Positive mood can increase or decrease message scrutiny: The hedonic contingency view of mood and message processing. *Journal of Personality and Social Psychology, 69*(1), 5–15.

Wegner, D. M. (1994). Ironic processes of mental control. *Psychological Review, 101*(1), 34–52.

Weinberger, M. G., & Campbell, L. (1991). The use and impact of humor in radio advertising. *Journal of Advertising Research, 30*(6), 44–52.

Weiner, B. (1980). A cognitive (attribution)-emotion-action model of motivated behavior: An analysis of judgments of help-giving. *Journal of Personality and Social Psychology, 39*(2), 186–200.

Weiner, B., Osborne, D., & Rudolph, U. (2011). An attributional analysis of reactions to poverty: The political ideology of the giver and the perceived morality of the receiver. *Personality and Social Psychology Review, 15*(2), 199–213.

Weinstein, N., & Ryan, R. M. (2010). When helping helps: Autonomous motivation for prosocial behavior and its influence on well-being for the helper and recipient. *Journal of Personality and Social Psychology, 98*(2), 222–244.

Weintraub, J. N., & Najdowski, C. J. (2018). Supreme court fails to use science in key decision. *Monitor on Psychology, 49*(9), 31.

Weiss, B., & Feldman, R. S. (2006). Looking good and lying to do it: Deception as an impression management strategy in job interviews. *Journal of Applied Social Psychology, 36*(4), 1070–1086.

Wells, G. L., & Petty, R. E. (1980). The effects of overt head movements on persuasion: Compatibility and incompatibility of responses. *Basic and Applied Social Psychology, 1*(3), 219–230.

Welzel, C., Inglehart, R., & Klingemann, H. -D. (2003). The theory of human development: A cross-cultural analysis. *European Journal of Political Research, 42*(3), 341–379.

Werking, K. (1997). *We're just good friends.* New York, NY: Guilford.

West, J. O. (1988). *Mexican-American folklore.* Little Rock, AK: August House.

Westen, D. (2007). *The political brain: The role of emotion in deciding the fate of the nation.* New York, NY: Public Affairs.

Wheeler, L., & Kim, Y. (1997). What is beautiful is culturally good: The physical attractiveness stereotype has different content in collectivist cultures. *Personality and Social Psychology Bulletin, 23*(8), 795–800.

Wheeler, S. C., Morrison, K. R., DeMarree, K. G., & Petty, R. E. (2008). Does self-consciousness increase or decrease priming effects? It depends. *Journal of Experimental Social Psychology, 44*(3), 882–889.

Whillans, A. V., Caruso, E. M., & Dunn, E. W. (2017). Both selfishness and selflessness start with the self: How wealth shapes responses to charitable appeals. *Journal of Experimental Social Psychology, 70*, 242–250.

Whitchurch, E. R., Wilson, T. D., & Gilbert, D. T. (2011). "He loves me, he loves me not . . . .": Uncertainty can increase romantic attraction. *Psychological Science, 22*(2), 172–175.

White, M. H., II, & Crandall, C. S. (2017). Freedom of racist speech: Ego and expressive threats. *Journal of Personality and Social Psychology, 113*(3), 413–429.

White, M. I., & LeVine, R. A. (1986). What is an *Ii ko* (good child)? In H. Stevenson, H. Azuma, & K. Hakuta (Eds.), *Child development and education in Japan* (pp. 55–62). New York, NY: W. H. Freeman.

Whiteside, U., Chen, E., Neighbors, C., Hunter, D., Lo, T., & Larimer, M. (2007). Difficulties regulating emotions: Do binge eaters have fewer strategies to modulate and tolerate negative affect? *Eating Behaviors, 8*(2), 162–169.

Whiting, B. B., & Edwards, C. P. (1988). *Children of different worlds: The foundation of social behavior.* Cambridge, MA: Harvard University Press.

Whitty, M. T., & Carr, A. N. (2006). *Cyberspace romance: The psychology of online relationships.* New York, NY: Palgrave Macmillan.

Widom, C. S. (1989). Does violence beget violence? A critical examination of the literature. *Psychological Bulletin, 106*(1), 3–28.

Wigboldus, D. H., Dijksterhuis, A., & van Knippenberg, A. (2003). When stereotypes get in the way: Stereotypes obstruct stereotype-inconsistent trait inferences. *Journal of Personality and Social Psychology, 84*(3), 470–484.

Wiggins, J. A., Dill, F., & Schwartz, R. D. (1965). On "status-liability." *Sociometry, 28*(2), 197–209.

Wilke, H. A. (1996). Status congruence in small groups. In E. Witte & J. H. Davis (Eds.), *Understanding group behavior: Vol. 2. Small group processes and interpersonal relations* (pp. 67–91). Hillsdale, NJ: Lawrence Erlbaum and Associates.

Wilkowski, B. M., & Robinson, M. D. (2007). Keeping one's cool: Trait anger, hostile, thoughts, and the recruitment of limited capacity control. *Personality and Social Psychology Bulletin, 33*(9), 1201–1213.

Williams, D. G. (1985). Gender, masculinity-femininity, and emotional intimacy in same-sex friendship. *Sex Roles, 12*(5–6), 587–600.

Williams, E. F., Gilovich, T., & Dunning, D. (2012). Being all that you can be: The weighting of potential in assessments of self and others. *Personality and Social Psychology Bulletin, 38*(2), 143–154.

Williams, K. D. (2007). Ostracism. *Annual Review of Psychology, 58*, 425–452.

Williams, K. D., Harkins, S., & Latané, B. (1981). Identifiability as a deterrent to social loafing: Two cheering experiments. *Journal of Personality and Social Psychology, 40*(2), 303–311.

Williams, K. D., Jackson, J. M., & Karau, S. J. (1995). Collective hedonism: A social loafing analysis of social dilemmas. In D. A. Schroeder (Ed.), *Social dilemmas: Perspectives on individuals and groups* (pp. 116–141). Westport, CT: Praeger.

Williams, K. D., & Sommer, K. L. (1997). Social ostracism by coworkers: Does rejection lead to loafing or compensation? *Personality and Social Psychology Bulletin, 23*(7), 693–706.

Williams, K. D., & Zadro, L. (2001). Ostracism: On being ignored, excluded, and rejected. In M. R. Leary (Ed.), *Interpersonal rejection* (pp. 21–53). New York, NY: Oxford University Press.

Williams, M. J., Gruenfeld, D. H., & Guillory, L. E. (2016). Sexual aggression when power is new: Effects of acute high power on chronically low-power individuals. *Journal of Personality and Social Psychology, 112*(2), 201–223.

Williams-Jones, B., Potvin, M.-J., Mathieu, G., & Smith, E. (2013). Barriers to research on research ethics review and conflict of interest. *IRB: Ethics & Human Research, 35*, 14–19.

Willis, D. (2019, January 2). As Pelosi takes over, an attempt to revive the 'lost art' of legislating. *The New York Times.* Retrieved from https://www.nytimes.com/2019/01/02/upshot/will-pelosi-open-the-floor-to-bipartisan-ideas.html?smid=fb-nytimes&smtyp=cur&fbclid=IwAR2_PB54XQQM2XnKwrGLy_4Yy5CwWvVlP31QJCcNGiPlG26GDxL2jM2v0ZE

Wilson, D. W. (1981). Is helping a laughing matter? *Psychology, 18*(1), 6–9.

Wilson, E. O. (1996). *In search of nature.* Washington, DC: Island Press.

Wilson, M. S., & Liu, J. H. (2003). Social dominance orientation and gender: The moderating role of gender identity. *British Journal of Social Psychology, 42*(2), 187–198.

Wilson, R. S., Krueger, K. R., Arnold, S. E., Schneider, J. A., Kelly, J. F., Barnes, L. L.,...Bennett, D. A. (2007). Loneliness and risk of Alzheimer disease. *Archives of General Psychiatry, 64*(2), 234–240.

Wilson, T. D., Aronson, E., & Carlsmith, K. (2010). The art of laboratory experimentation. In S. T. Fiske, D. T. Gilbert, & G. Lindzey (Eds.), *Handbook of social psychology* (5th ed., Vol. 1, pp. 51–81). Hoboken, NJ: John Wiley & Sons.

Wilson, T. D., Lindsey, S., & Schooler, T. Y. (2000). A model of dual attitudes. *Psychological Review, 107*(1), 101–126.

Windschitl, P. D., & Wells, G. L. (1997). Behavioral consensus information affects people's inferences about population traits. *Personality and Social Psychology Bulletin, 23*(2), 148–156.

Wiseman, M. C., & Moradi, B. (2010). Body image and eating disorder symptoms in sexual minority men: A test and extension of the objectification theory. *Journal of Counseling Psychology, 57*(2), 154–166.

Wittenbaum, G. M., & Stasser, G. (1996). Management of information in small groups. In J. L. Nye & A. M. Brower (Eds.), *What's social about social cognition? Research on socially shared cognition in small groups* (pp. 3–28). Thousand Oaks, CA: Sage.

Wittenbaum, G. M., Hubbell, A. P., & Zuckerman, C. (1999). Mutual enhancement: Toward an understanding of the collective preference for shared information. *Journal of Personality and Social Psychology, 77*(5), 967–978.

Witvliet, C. V., Ludwig, T. E., & Vander Laan, K. L. (2001). Granting forgiveness or harboring grudges: Implications for emotion, physiology, and health. *Psychological Science, 12*(2), 117–123.

Wolf, L. E. (2010). The research ethics committee is not the enemy: Oversight of community-based participatory research. *Journal of Empirical Research on Human Research Ethics, 5*(4), 77–86.

Wolff, E. N. (2017). Household wealth trends in the United States, 1962 to 2016: Has middle class wealth recovered? (Working paper 24085). *The National Bureau of Economic Research.* Retrieved from https://www.nber.org/papers/w24085

Woll, S. (2002). *Everyday thinking: Memory, reasoning, and judgment in the real world.* Mahwah, NJ: Lawrence Erlbaum Associates.

Wolstencroft, J., Robinson, L., Srinivasan, R., Kerry, E., Mandy, W., & Skuse, D. (2018). A systematic review of group social skills interventions, and meta-analysis outcomes, for children with high functioning ASD. *Journal of Autism and Developmental Disorders, 48*(7), 2293–2307.

Wong, R. Y. M., & Hong, Y. Y. (2005). Dynamic influences on cooperation in the prisoner's dilemma. *Psychological Science, 16*(6), 429–434.

Wood, D., Harms, D. P., Lowman, G. H., & DeSimone, J. A. (2017). Response speed and response consistency as mutually validating indicators of data quality in online samples. *Social Psychological and Personality Science, 8*(4), 454–464.

Wood, J. V. (1996). What is social comparison and how should we study it? *Personality and Social Psychology Bulletin, 22*(5), 520–537.

Wood, J. V., Heimpel, S. A., Newby-Clark, I. R., & Ross, M. (2005). Snatching defeat from the jaws of victory: Self-esteem differences in the experience and anticipation of success. *Journal of Personality and Social Psychology, 89*(5), 764–780.

Wood, W., & Eagly, A. H. (2010). Gender. In S. T. Fiske, D. T. Gilbert, & G. Lindzey (Eds.), *Handbook of social psychology* (5th ed., Vol. 1, pp. 629–667). Hoboken, NJ: John Wiley & Sons.

Wood, W., Wong, F. Y., & Chachere, J. G. (1991). Effects of media violence on viewers' aggression in unconstrained social interaction. *Psychological Bulletin, 109*(3), 371–383.

Worchel, S., & Andreoli, V. M. (1978). Facilitation of social interaction through deindividuation of the target. *Journal of Personality and Social Psychology, 36*(5), 549–556.

Worringham, C. F., & Messick, D. M. (1983). Social facilitation of running: An unobtrusive study. *Journal of Social Psychology, 121*(1), 23–29.

Wosinska, W., Cialdini, R. B., Barrett, D. W., & Reykowski, J. (Eds.). (2001). *Applied social research: The practice of social influence in multiple cultures.* Mahwah, NJ: Lawrence Erlbaum Associates.

Wosinska, W., Dabul, A. J., Whetstone-Dion, R., & Cialdini, R. B. (1996). Self-presentational responses to success in the organization: The costs and benefits of modesty. *Basic and Applied Social Psychology, 18*(2), 229–242.

Wright, P. H., & Scanlon, M. B. (1991). Gender role orientations and friendship: Some attenuation, but gender differences abound. *Sex Roles, 24*(9–10), 551–566.

Wright, S. C., Aron, A., McLaughlin-Volpe, T., & Ropp, S. A. (1997). The extended contact effect: Knowledge of cross-group friendships and prejudice. *Journal of Personality and Social Psychology, 73*(1), 73–90.

Wright, S. C., Taylor, D. M., & Moghaddam, F. M. (1990). Responding to membership in a disadvantaged group: From acceptance to collective protest. *Journal of Personality and Social Psychology, 58*(6), 994–1003.

Wu, J., Balliet, D., & Van Lange, P. A. (2016). Reputation, gossip, and human cooperation. *Social and Personality Psychology Compass, 10*(6), 350–364.

Wu, S., & Keysar, B. (2007). The effect of culture on perspective taking. *Psychological Science, 18*(7), 600–606.

Y

Yamagishi, T. (1986). The provision of a sanctioning system as a public good. *Journal of Personality and Social Psychology, 51*(1), 110–116.

Yamagishi, T., Tanida, S., Mashima, R., Shimona, E., & Kanazawa, S. (2003). You can judge a book by its cover: Evidence that cheaters may look different from cooperators. *Evolution and Human Behavior, 24*(4), 290–301.

Yamawaki, N., Ostenson, J., & Brown, C. R. (2009). The functions of gender role traditionality, ambivalent sexism, injury and frequency of assault on domestic violence perception: A study between Japanese and American college students. *Violence Against Women, 15*(9), 1126–1142.

Yancey, G., & Emerson, M. O. (2014). Does Height Matter? An Examination of Height Preferences in Romantic Coupling. *Journal of Family Issues, 37*(1), 53–73.

Yancey, M. P., & Hummer, R. A. (2003). Fraternities and rape on campus. In M. Silberman (Ed.), *Violence and society: A reader* (pp. 215–222). Upper Saddle River, NJ: Prentice-Hall.

Yang, K., & Girgus, J. S. (2019). Are women more likely than men are to care excessively about maintaining positive social relationships? A meta-analytic review of the gender difference in sociotropy. *Sex Roles, 81*(3–4), 157–172.

Yap, A. J., Wazlawek, A. S., Lucas, B. J., Cuddy, A. J., & Carney, D. R. (2013). The ergonomics of dishonesty: The effect of incidental posture on stealing, cheating, and traffic violations. *Psychological Science, 24*(11), 2281–2289.

Yapp, E., & Quayle, E. (2018). A systematic review of the association between rape myth acceptance and male-on-female sexual violence. *Aggression and Violent Behavior, 41*, 1–19.

Ybarra, M. L., & Thompson, R. E. (2018). Predicting the emergence of sexual violence in adolescence. *Prevention Science, 19*(4), 403–415.

Yeager, D. S., Dahl, R. E., & Dweck, C. S. (2018). Why interventions to influence adolescent behavior often fail but could succeed. *Perspectives on Psychological Science, 13*(1), 101–122.

Yeager, D. S., Johnson, R., Spitzer, B. J., Trzesniewski, K. H., Powers, J., & Dweck, C. S. (2014). The far-reaching effects of believing people can change: Implicit theories of personality shape stress, health, and achievement during adolescence. *Journal of Personality and Social Psychology, 106*(6), 867–884.

Yean, C., Benau, E. M., Dakanalis, A., Hormes, J. M., Perone, J., & Timko, C. A. (2013). The relationship of sex and sexual orientation to self-esteem, body shape satisfaction, and eating disorder symptomatology. *Frontiers in Psychology, 4*, 887.

Yetkili, O., Abrams, D., Travaglino, G. A., & Giner-Sorolla, R. (2018). Imagined contact with atypical outgroup members that are anti-normative within their group can reduce prejudice. *Journal of Experimental Social Psychology, 26*, 208–219.

Yip, T. (2005). Sources of situational variation in ethnic identity and psychological well-being: A palm pilot study of Chinese American students. *Personality and Social Psychology Bulletin, 31*(12), 1603–1616.

Yoo, H. C., Steger, M. F., & Lee, R. M. (2010). Validation of the subtle and blatant racism scale for Asian American college students. *Cultural Diversity and Ethnic Minority Psychology, 16*(3), 323–334.

Yoon, J., Thye, S. R., & Lawler, E. J. (2013). Exchange and cohesion in dyads and triads: A test of Simmel's hypothesis. *Social Science Research, 42*(6), 1457–1466.

Yoon, J. M., & Tennie, C. (2010). Contagious yawning: A reflection of empathy, mimicry, or contagion? *Animal Behaviour, 79*(5), e1–e3.

Yost, M. R., & Zurbriggen, E. L. (2006). Gender differences in the enactment of sociosexuality: An examination of implicit social motives, sexual fantasies, coercive sexual attitudes, and aggressive sexual behavior. *Journal of Sex Research, 43*(2), 163–173.

Youyou, W., Stillwell, D., Schwartz, H. A., & Kosinski, M. (2017). Birds of a feather do flock together: Behavior-based personality-assessment method reveals personality similarity among couples and friends. *Psychological Science, 28*(3), 276–284.

Young, B., Lewis, S., Katikireddi, S. V., Bauld, L., Stead, M., Angus, K.,. . .Langley, T. (2018). Effectiveness of mass media campaigns to reduce alcohol consumption and harm: A systematic review. *Alcohol and Alcoholism, 53*(3), 302–316.

Young, D. G. (2008). The privileged role of the late-night joke: Exploring humor's role in disrupting argument scrutiny. *Media Psychology, 11*(1), 119–142.

Yousif, Y., & Korte, C. (1995). Urbanization, culture, and helpfulness: Cross-cultural studies in England and the Sudan. *Journal of Cross-Cultural Psychology, 26*(5), 474–489.

Yu, D. L., & Seligman, M. E. P. (2002). Preventing depressive symptoms in Chinese children. *Prevention & Treatment, 5*(1), Article ID 9.

Yzerbyt, V. Y., Rocher, S., & Schadron, G. (1996). Stereotypes as explanations: A subjective essentialistic view of group perception. In R. Spears, P. J. Oakes, N. Ellemers, & S. A. Haslam (Eds.), *The social psychology of stereotyping and group life* (pp. 20–50). Cambridge: Blackwell.

Z

Zacharek, S., Dockterman, E., & Edwards, H. S. (2017). Person of the year 2017: The silence breakers. *Time.* Retrieved from https://time.com/time-person-of-the-year-2017-silence-breakers/

Zahn-Wexler, C., Robinson, J., & Emde, R. N. (1992). The development of empathy in twins. *Developmental Psychology, 28*(6), 1038–1047.

Zajonc, R. B. (1965). Social facilitation. *Science, 149*(3681), 269–274.

Zajonc, R. B. (1968). Attitudinal effects of mere exposure. *Journal of Personality and Social Psychology, 9*(2, Part 2), 1–27.

Zajonc, R. B. (1984). On the primacy of affect. *American Psychologist, 39*(2), 117–123.

Zárate, M. A., Garcia, B., Garza, A. A., & Hitlan, R. T. (2004). Cultural threat and perceived realistic group conflict as dual predictors of prejudice. *Journal of Experimental Social Psychology, 40*(1), 99–105.

Zarbatany, L., Conley, R., & Pepper, S. (2007). Personality and gender differences in friendship needs and experiences in preadolescence and young adulthood. *International Journal of Behavioral Development, 28*(4), 299–310.

Zebrowitz, L. A. (1997). *Reading faces: Window to the soul?* Boulder, CO: Westview.

Zebrowitz, L. A. (2017). First impressions from faces. *Current Directions in Psychological Science, 26*(3), 237–242.

Zebrowitz, L. A., & Montepare, J. M. (1992). Impressions of babyfaced individuals across the life span. *Developmental Psychology, 28*(6), 1143–1152.

Zebrowitz, L. A., Tenenbaum, D. R., & Goldstein, L. H. (1991). The impact of job applicants' facial maturity, sex, and academic achievement on hiring recommendations. *Journal of Applied Social Psychology, 21*(7), 525–548.

Zebrowitz, L. A., Voinescu, L., & Collins, M. A. (1996). "Wide-eyed" and "crooked-faced": Determinants of perceived and real honesty across the life span. *Personality and Social Psychology Bulletin, 22*(12), 1258–1269.

Zentner, M., & Eagly, A. H. (2015). A sociocultural framework for understanding partner preferences of women and men: Integration of concepts and evidence. *European Review of Social Psychology, 26*(1), 328–373.

Zentner, M., & Mitura, K. (2012). Stepping out of the caveman's shadow: Nations' gender gap predicts degree of sex differentiation in mate preferences. *Psychological Science, 23*(10), 1176–1185.

Zettler, I., Hilbig, B. E., & Heydasch, T. (2013). Two sides of one coin: Honesty-humility and situational factors mutually shape social dilemma decision making. *Journal of Research in Personality, 47*(4), 286–295.

Zhang, A. Y., Snowden, L. R., & Sue, S. (1998). Differences between Asian- and White-Americans' help-seeking and utilization patterns in the Los Angeles area. *Journal of Community Psychology, 26*(4), 317–326.

Zhang, X., Yeung, D. Y., Fung, H. H., & Lang, F. R. (2011). Changes in peripheral social partners and loneliness over time: The moderating role of interdependence. *Psychology and Aging, 26*(4), 823–829.

Zhou, S., Page-Gould, E., Aron, A., Moyer, A., & Hewstone, M. (2018). The extended contact hypothesis: A meta-analysis on 20 years of research. *Personality and Social Psychology Review, 23*(2), 132–160.

Zhu, D., Xie, X., & Gan, Y. (2010). Information source and valence: How information credibility influences earthquake risk perception. *Journal of Environmental Psychology, 31*(2), 129–136.

Zhu, D. H. (2013). Group polarization on corporate boards: Theory and evidence on board decisions about acquisition premiums. *Strategic Management Journal, 34*(7), 800–822.

Zhu, Y., Zhang, L., Fan, J., & Han, S. (2007). Neural basis of cultural influence on self-representation. *Neuroimage, 34*(3), 1310–1316.

Zillmann, D. (1984). *Connections between sex and aggression.* Hillsdale, NJ: Lawrence Erlbaum Associates.

Zimbardo, P. (1969). The human choice: Individuation, reason, and order versus deindividuation, impulse, and chaos. In W. J. Arnold & D. Levine (Eds.), *Nebraska Symposium on Motivation, 17*, 237–307.

Zimbardo, P. (2007). *The Lucifer effect: Understanding how good people turn evil.* New York, NY: Random House.

Zimbardo, P. G. (producer). (1972). *The Stanford prison experiment.* Slide/tape presentation.

Zimmerman, F., & Sieverding, M. (2011). Young adults' images of abstaining and drinking: Prototype dimensions, correlates and assessment methods. *Journal of Health Psychology, 16*(3), 410–420.

Zitek, E. M., & Hebl, M. R. (2007). The role of social norm clarity in the influenced expression of prejudice over time. *Journal of Experimental Social Psychology, 43*(6), 867–876.

Zmyj, N., Prinz, W., & Daum, M. M. (2013). The relation between mirror self-image reactions and imitation in 14- and 18-month-old infants. *Infant Behavior & Development, 36*(4), 809–816.

Zuckerman, M., DePaulo, B. M., & Rosenthal, R. (1981). Verbal and nonverbal communication of deception. In L. Berkowitz (Ed.), *Advances in experimental social psychology* (Vol. 14, pp. 1–59). New York, NY: Academic Press.

Zuckerman, M., & O'Loughlin, R. E. (2006). Self-enhancement by social comparison: A prospective analysis. *Personality and Social Psychology Bulletin, 32*(6), 751–760.

Zunick, P. V., Teeny, J. D., & Fazio, R. H. (2017). Are some attitudes more self-defining than others? Assessing self-related attitude functions and their consequences. *Personality and Social Psychology Bulletin, 43*(8), 1136–1149.

Zurcher, L. A. (1977). *The mutable self.* Beverly Hills, CA: Sage.

Zych, I., Ortega-Ruiz, R., & Del Rey, R. (2015). Systematic review of theoretical studies on bullying and cyberbullying: Facts, knowledge, prevention, and intervention. *Aggression and Violent Behavior, 23*, 1–21.

Name Index

Subject Index